W9-CGZ-128

Spring Recipes

Second Edition

Gary Mak
Josh Long
Daniel Rubio

Apress®

Spring Recipes, Second Edition

Copyright © 2010 by Gary Mak, Josh Long, and Daniel Rubio

All rights reserved. No part of this work may be reproduced or transmitted in any form or by any means, electronic or mechanical, including photocopying, recording, or by any information storage or retrieval system, without the prior written permission of the copyright owner and the publisher.

ISBN-13 (pbk): 978-1-4302-2499-0

ISBN-13 (electronic): 978-1-4302-2500-3

Trademarked names, logos, and images may appear in this book. Rather than use a trademark symbol with every occurrence of a trademarked name, logo, or image we use the names, logos, and images only in an editorial fashion and to the benefit of the trademark owner, with no intention of infringement of the trademark.

The use in this publication of trade names, trademarks, service marks, and similar terms, even if they are not identified as such, is not to be taken as an expression of opinion as to whether or not they are subject to proprietary rights.

President and Publisher: Paul Manning
Lead Editor: Tom Welsh
Technical Reviewer: Manuel Jordan, Mario Gray and Greg Turnquist
Editorial Board: Clay Andres, Steve Anglin, Mark Beckner, Ewan Buckingham, Gary Cornell,
    Jonathan Gennick, Jonathan Hassell, Michelle Lowman, Matthew Moodie, Duncan Parkes,
    Jeffrey Pepper, Frank Pohlmann, Douglas Pundick, Ben Renow-Clarke, Dominic Shakeshaft,
    Matt Wade, Tom Welsh
Coordinating Editor: Laurin Becker
Copy Editor: Mary Ann Fugate, Heather Lang
Production Support: Patrick Cunningham
Indexer: BIM Indexing & Proofreading Services
Artist: April Milne
Cover Designer: Anna Ishchenko

Distributed to the book trade worldwide by Springer Science+Business Media, LLC., 233 Spring Street, 6th Floor, New York, NY 10013. Phone 1-800-SPRINGER, fax (201) 348-4505, e-mail orders-ny@springer-sbm.com, or visit www.springeronline.com.

For information on translations, please e-mail rights@apress.com, or visit www.apress.com.

Apress and friends of ED books may be purchased in bulk for academic, corporate, or promotional use. eBook versions and licenses are also available for most titles. For more information, reference our Special Bulk Sales–eBook Licensing web page at www.apress.com/info/bulksales.

The information in this book is distributed on an "as is" basis, without warranty. Although every precaution has been taken in the preparation of this work, neither the author(s) nor Apress shall have any liability to any person or entity with respect to any loss or damage caused or alleged to be caused directly or indirectly by the information contained in this work.

The source code for this book is available to readers at www.apress.com. You will need to answer questions pertaining to this book in order to successfully download the code.

To my parents, Clark Long and Kathleen MacDonald

–Josh Long

To my family

–Daniel Rubio

Contents at a Glance

Contents

About the Authors

Gary Mak, founder and chief consultant of Meta-Archit Software Technology Limited, has been a technical architect and application developer on the enterprise Java platform for over seven years. He is the author of the Apress books *Spring Recipes: A Problem-Solution Approach* and *Pro SpringSource dm Server*. In his career, Gary has developed a number of Java-based software projects, most of which are application frameworks, system infrastructures, and software tools. He enjoys designing and implementing the complex parts of software projects. Gary has a master's degree in computer science and his research interests include object-oriented technology, aspect-oriented technology, design patterns, software reuse, and domain-driven development.

Gary specializes in building enterprise applications on technologies such as Spring, Hibernate, JPA, JSF, Portlet, AJAX, and OSGi. He has been using the Spring framework in his projects for five years, since Spring version 1.0. Gary has been an instructor of courses on enterprise Java, Spring, Hibernate, Web Services, and agile development. He has written a series of Spring and Hibernate tutorials as course materials, parts of which are open to the public, and they're gaining popularity in the Java community. In his spare time, he enjoys playing tennis and watching tennis competitions.

Josh Long, Spring Developer Advocate for SpringSource, is an engineer (wearing an architect's hat) with more than a decade of experience and a vocal contributor to the community. He is a contributor and committer to open source projects, including the Spring Integration project. He is a member of the JCP, as well as an editor for the popular technology portal InfoQ.com. Josh is a frequent speaker at conferences, both nationally and internationally, on a number of topics ranging from business process management and web frameworks to enterprise application integration and architecture patterns. His interests include scalability, BPM, grid processing, mobile computing, and so-called "smart" systems.

In his function as the Spring Developer Advocate for SpringSource, he focuses on growing and enriching the community around the Spring platform.

Josh lives in sunny southern California with his wife Richelle. He maintains a blog at www.joshlong.com and can be reached via e-mail at josh@joshlong.com.

Daniel Rubio is a consultant with over ten years of experience in enterprise and web technologies. Throughout his career, he's relied on Java, Python, CORBA, and .NET technologies to deliver cost effective solutions to the financial and manufacturing industries. More recently, he has focused on convention-over-configuration web frameworks—Spring, Grails, Roo, and Django—concentrating on their performance and scalability in enterprise settings.

Additionally, he writes articles on emerging technologies for various content networks in this same space, which include Oracle Technology Network, DZone, and his own blog at www.WebForefront.com.

About the Technical Reviewers

■ **Manuel Jordan Elera** is a freelance Java developer. He has designed and developed personal systems for his customers using powerful frameworks based in Java, such as Spring and Hibernate, among others. Manuel is now an autodidact developer and enjoys learning new frameworks to get better results on his projects.

Manuel has a degree in systems engineering with public congratulations, and he is a professor at Universidad Católica de Santa María and Universidad Alas Peruanas in Perú. In his little free time, he likes reading the bible and composing music with his guitar. Manuel is a senior member in the Spring Community Forums known as dr_pompeii.

You can contact him through his blog at http://manueljordan. wordpress.com/.

■ **Mario Gray** is an engineer with more than a decade of experience in systems integration, systems administration, game programming, and highly available enterprise architectures. He is ever vigilant for force-multiplying technologies to better enable businesses. He has developed countless systems, including CRMs, message plants, and highly available web applications using leading open source, enterprise Java frameworks and tools. Mario has a record of successfully leveraging open source frameworks to better serve businesses.

He lives in the city of Chandler, Arizona with his wife Fumiko and his daughter Makani. Enjoying outdoor recreational sports, exercise, and family activities are his main habits outside of his career. He maintains a blog at www.sudoinit5.com and can be reached at mario@sudioinit5.com.

■ **Greg Turnquist** is a test-bitten script junkie always seeking the right tool for the job. He has been a professional software developer since 1997 and has worked on a diverse number of systems, including mission-critical, 24 × 7 × 365 systems. In 2006, he created the Spring Python project, taking the concepts of Spring to the platform of Python. In 2010 he joined the SpringSource team. He is the author of Spring Python 1.1 and is a SpringOne speaker. He graduated with a master's degree from Auburn University and lives in the United States with his family.

Acknowledgments

I'm not going to lie to you. The Acknowledgments section of the book is a scary proposition for me. The notion that I (or anyone) could quantify, or prioritize, the contributions (direct and indirect) by which this book was made possible is fantasy. I'll do my best, but it's entirely possible I'll forget somebody, and for that, I apologize beforehand.

I thank my wife Richelle for her eternal patience, indulgence, wisdom, support, and love. I thank my parents—my mother and father and their spouses, as well as my in-laws—for their influences, their grace, their support, and their love.

I thank my coauthors Gary Mak and Daniel Rubio, who helped make this the most exciting book I've ever read, let alone worked on!

I thank the amazing editors: Steve Anglin, Laurin Becker, Tom Welsh, Manuel Jordan, Mario Gray, and Greg Turnquist. They ensured the highest standards in quality at every step of the way of the process and with the utmost professionalism. I thank Greg Turnquist, in particular, for his help on this book. He provided critical feedback during the process. He's a SpringSource engineer and the lead of the Spring Python project, which delivers a Pythonic port of the Spring framework for use with Python. He's got a book coming out, Manning's *Spring Python in Action*, which should prove a very, very interesting read.

I thank Mark Fisher, the lead of the Spring Integration project. I like the Spring Integration project because it, like the core framework, solves a very complex problem domain with elegance. Impossible problems become difficult; difficult problems become trivial. I owe him a debt of gratitude for the framework and for his indulgence, enthusiasm, and support for my contributions to the project. I also thank him for his kindness.

I am an editor for InfoQ.com. This book represents a year of utterly unpredictable schedules, hectic deadlines, and hard work. The team at InfoQ.com has been more than gracious about my erratic schedule. I thank Floyd Marinescu, Charles Humble, and Ryan Slobojan, and InfoQ.com, for raising the bar on technical journalism and for the endless support and inspiration.

Finally, I'd like to thank my colleagues at Shopzilla. At the time of this writing, I am in a state of transition, leaving Shopzilla to join SpringSource. Shopzilla is easily the most fantastic company I've had the privilege of working for. It is full of amazing people. I learned something everyday and enjoyed a camaraderie I've never felt in a company before. The engineering culture is strong, and an inspired engineer couldn't ask for a better place to work. The results are amazing. While I was there, I was fortunate enough to work with many amazing people, which makes narrowing down the following list particularly difficult. I thank Tim Morrow, Rodney Barlow, Andy Chan, Rob Roland, Paul Snively, Phil Dixon, and Jody Mulkey for their guidance, friendship, and support.

–Josh Long

First off, I thank my coauthors. Gary Mark created this book's first edition, providing it with rock-solid content, making it one of the best selling books in the Spring and Java category. And Josh Long spearheaded the *Spring Enterprise Recipes* book, which is now tightly integrated and upgraded with this newly minted second edition of *Spring Recipes.*

Next, thanks to everyone at Apress. Steve Anglin, Matt Moodie, and Tom Welsh were there through every step of this book's life cycle, from structuring its table of contents to reading every page. Laurin Becker served as project manager and kept all the pieces together, making sure everyone turned in work on time. And of course, every other person at Apress who had a role in this book and with whom I didn't have the opportunity to interact directly, including the copy editor, proofreader, and cover designer, among others.

On the technical front and for helping me keep the content accurate, special thanks go Manuel Jordan, who served as the book's technical reviewer, as well as Mario Gray, who also took part in the technical review process.

In addition, the content of the book would also not be possible were it not for the many articles, documentation, and blog posts I read from many people that shape Spring and Grails; these include Arjen Poutsma, Juergen Hoeller, Alef Arendsen, and Graeme Rocher. And of course, I thanks the many other active people in these areas who have surely influenced my thought process and who I, unfortunately, can't give credit by name due to space constraints.

And finally, I thank my family and friends. Since I had already bewildered them with writing projects, their long blank stares after I tried to explain this book's purpose in layman's terms were a testament to their patience. Yet, even through these stares, they managed to ask some serious questions that kept me upbeat. So to everyone who simply asked, thank you; I consider you much a part of this effort for providing face-to-face morale support.

—Daniel Rubio

Introduction

The Spring framework is growing. It has always been about choice. Java EE focused on a few technologies, largely to the detriment of alternative, better solutions. When the Spring framework debuted, few would have agreed that Java EE represented the best-in-breed architectures of the day. Spring debuted to great fanfare, because it sought to simplify Java EE. Each release since marks the introduction of new features designed to both simplify and enable solutions.

With version 2.0 and later, the Spring framework started targeting multiple platforms. The framework provided services on top of existing platforms, as always, but was decoupled from the underlying platform wherever possible. Java EE is a still a major reference point, but it's not the only target. OSGi (a promising technology for modular architectures) has been a big part of the SpringSource strategy here. Additionally, the Spring framework runs on Google App Engine. With the introduction of annotation-centric frameworks and XML schemas, SpringSource has built frameworks that effectively model the domain of a specific problem, in effect creating domain-specific languages (DSLs). Frameworks built on top of the Spring framework have emerged supporting application integration, batch processing, Flex and Flash integration, GWT, OSGi, and much more.

When it came time to update the seminal *Spring Recipes*, we quickly discovered that it's been a long time since there was, effectively, only one core Spring framework. The SpringSource portfolio, such as it is, describes several frameworks, each of which is dramatically more capable than the alternatives with which it competes in other products. This book will serve you well on your journey through the various frameworks. If you don't need these technologies, you don't need to use them or add them to your project. If you do, it's nice to know they're available for you.

Who This Book Is For

This book is for Java developers who want to simplify their architecture and solve problems outside the scope of the Java EE platform. If you are already developing using Spring in your projects, the more advanced chapters present discussions of newer technologies that you might not know about already. If you are new to the framework, this book will get you started in no time.

This book assumes that you have some familiarity with Java and an IDE of some sort. While it is possible, and indeed useful, to use Java exclusively with client applications, Java's largest community lives in the enterprise space and that, too, is where you'll see most of these technologies deliver the most benefit. Thus, some familiarity with basic enterprise programming concepts like the Servlet API is assumed.

How This Book Is Structured

Chapter 1, "Introduction to Spring," gives a general overview of the Spring framework: how to set it up, what it is, and how it's used.

Chapter 2, "Advanced Spring IoC Container," reviews concepts that, while not as widely used as those discussed in Chapter 1, are still key to fully exploiting the container.

Chapter 3, "Spring AOP and AspectJ Support," discusses Spring's support for aspect-oriented programming using AspectJ. This technology underlies many of the other services provided by the Spring framework.

Chapter 4, "Scripting in Spring," discusses using scripting languages like Groovy, BeanShell, and JRuby with the Spring framework.

Chapter 5, "Spring Security," provides an overview of the Spring Security project, formerly Acegi, to help you better secure your application.

Chapter 6, "Integrating Spring with Other Web Frameworks," introduces the core web-tier support that Spring provides. This provides a base for all technologies that Spring provides in the web tier.

Chapter 7, "Spring Web Flow," provides an introduction of Spring Web Flow, which lets you build UI-flows on the web tier.

Chapter 8, "Spring @MVC," covers web-based application development using the Spring Web MVC framework.

Chapter 9, "Spring REST," provides an introduction to Spring's support for RESTful web services.

Chapter 10, "Spring and Flex," discusses using Spring BlazeDS to integrate your rich Internet application (RIA) with Spring beans. Additionally, this chapter gives an introduction to Spring ActionScript, to let users writing Flash applications in ActionScript enjoy the same container services and conveniences as Java Spring developers do.

Chapter 11, "Grails," discusses the Grails framework, with which can increase your productivity by using best-of-breed pieces and gluing them together with Groovy code.

Chapter 12, "Spring Roo," covers Spring Roo, the pivotal new framework from SpringSource designed to provide a force-multiplying framework for Java developers.

Chapter 13, "Spring Testing," discusses unit testing with the Spring framework.

Chapter 14, "Spring Portlet MVC Framework," covers using the Spring MVC Portlet framework to build applications and leverage the strengths of the Portlet container.

Chapter 15, "Data Access," discusses using Spring to talk to data stores using APIs like JDBC, Hibernate, and JPA.

Chapter 16, "Transaction Management in Spring," introduces the concepts behind Spring's robust transaction management facilities.

Chapter 17, "EJB, Spring Remoting, and Web Services," introduces you to the various facilities for RPC, including the Spring Web Services project.

Chapter 18, "Spring in the Enterprise," discusses many utilities provided by the Spring platform like JMX support, scheduling, and e-mail support.

Chapter 19, "Messaging," discusses using Spring with message-oriented middleware through JMS and the simplifying Spring abstractions.

Chapter 20, "Spring Integration," discusses using the Spring Integration framework to integration disparate services and data.

Chapter 21, "Spring Batch," introduces the Spring Batch framework, which provides a way to model solutions traditionally considered the domain of mainframes.

Chapter 22, "Distributed Spring," talks about various ways of taking scaling Spring using distributed state and grid processing.

Chapter 23, "Spring and jBPM," introduces you to business process management concepts and how to integrate one popular framework, JBoss' jBPM, with the Spring framework.

Chapter 24, "OSGi and Spring," walks you through the robust support for OSGi provided by the Spring framework.

Conventions

Sometimes, when we want you to pay particular attention to a part within a code example, we will make the font bold. Please note that the bold doesn't necessarily reflect a code change from the previous version.

In cases when a code line is too long to fit the page's width, we will break it with a code continuation character. Please note that when you try to type the code, you have to concatenate the line by yourself without any spaces.

Prerequisites

Because the Java programming language is platform independent, you are free to choose any supported operating system. However, some of the examples in this book use platform-specific paths. Translate them as necessary to your operating system's format before typing the examples.

To make the most of this book, install JDK version 1.5 or higher. You should have a Java IDE installed to make development easier. For this book, the sample code is Maven based. If you're running Eclipse and Install the m2Ecliplse plug-in, you can open the same code in Eclipse and the CLASSPATH and dependencies will be filled in the by the Maven metadata.

If you're using Eclipse, you might prefer SpringSource's SpringSource Tool Suite (STS), as it comes preloaded with the plug-ins you'll need to be productive with the Spring framework in Eclipse. If you use NetBeans or IntelliJ IDEA, there are no special configuration requirements: they already support Maven out of the box.

This book uses Maven because the Spring framework, starting with version 3.0.3, no longer ships with all the dependencies needed to use the framework. The recommended approach is to simply use a tool like Maven (or Ant and Ivy) to handle dependency management. If you are unfamiliar with Maven, you might skip ahead briefly to Chapter 12 ("Spring Roo"), where we work through setting up the Spring Roo environment, including Apache Maven.

Downloading the code

The source code for this book is available from the Apress web site (`www.apress.com`) in the Source Code / Download section. The source code is organized by chapters, each of which includes one or more independent examples.

Contacting the Authors

We always welcome your questions and feedback regarding the contents of this book. You can contact Josh Long at josh@joshlong.com (or via his web site, `www.joshlong.com`). You can reach Gary Mak by e-mail at springrecipes@metaarchit.com (or via his web site, `www.metarchit.com`). You can reach Daniel Rubio via his web site at `www.webforefront.com`.

CHAPTER 1

Introduction to Spring

In this chapter, you will be given a crash course introduction (or refresher!) to Spring, the core container, as well as some of the globally available facilities provided by the container. You will also become acquainted with the Spring XML configuration format as well as the annotation-driven support.

This chapter will give you the knowledge you need to deal with the concepts introduced in the rest of the book. You will learn basic component configuration in the Spring IoC container. At the heart of the Spring framework, the IoC container is designed to be highly adaptive and configurable. It provides a set of facilities to make your component configuration as simple as possible. You can easily configure your components to run in the Spring IoC container.

In Spring, components are also called "beans." Note that this is a different concept from the JavaBeans specification defined by Sun. The beans declared in the Spring IoC container are not necessarily required to be JavaBeans. They can be any POJOs (Plain Old Java Objects). The term *POJO* means an ordinary Java object without any specific requirements, such as to implement a specific interface or to extend a specific base class. This term is used to distinguish lightweight Java components from heavyweight components in other complex component models (e.g., EJB components prior to version 3.1 of the EJB specification).

Upon finishing this chapter, you will be able to build a complete Java application using the Spring IoC container. Additionally, if you review your old Java applications, you may find that you can significantly simplify and improve them by using the Spring IoC container.

1-1. Instantiating the Spring IoC Container

Problem

You have to instantiate the Spring IoC container for it to create bean instances by reading their configurations. Then, you can get the bean instances from the IoC container to use.

Solution

Spring provides two types of IoC container implementation. The basic one is called *bean factory*. The more advanced one is called *application context*, which is a compatible extension to the bean factory. Note that the bean configuration files for these two types of IoC containers are identical.

The application context provides more advanced features than the bean factory while keeping the basic features compatible. So we strongly recommend using the application context for every application unless the resources of this application are restricted, such as when running in an applet or a mobile device.

The interfaces for the bean factory and the application context are `BeanFactory` and `ApplicationContext`, respectively. The interface `ApplicationContext` is a subinterface of `BeanFactory` for maintaining compatibility.

■ **Note** In order to compile and run the Spring code presented in this chapter and all subsequent chapters, you'll need to have the dependencies for the Spring framework on your classpath. The recommended way to do this is using a build management solution like Apache Maven or Apache Ant and Ivy. If you are using Maven, add the dependencies listed below to your Maven project. Here, as elsewhere, we use the notation *${spring.version}* to refer to the version. Replace this with the version that is most relevant to you. This book was written and compiled against the version ***3.0.2.RELEASE***.

```
<dependency>
  <groupId>org.springframework</groupId>
  <artifactId>spring-aop</artifactId>
  <version>${spring.version}</version>
</dependency>

<dependency>
  <groupId>org.springframework</groupId>
  <artifactId>spring-web</artifactId>
  <version>${spring.version}</version>
</dependency>

<dependency>
  <groupId>org.springframework</groupId>
  <artifactId>spring-context-support</artifactId>
  <version>${spring.version}</version>
</dependency>
```

```
<dependency>
  <groupId>org.springframework</groupId>
  <artifactId>spring-beans</artifactId>
  <version>${spring.version}</version>
</dependency>

<dependency>
  <groupId>org.springframework</groupId>
  <artifactId>spring-context</artifactId>
  <version>${spring.version}</version>
</dependency>

<dependency>
  <groupId>org.springframework</groupId>
  <artifactId>spring-core</artifactId>
  <version>${spring.version}</version>
</dependency>
```

How It Works

Instantiating an Application Context

`ApplicationContext` is an interface only. You have to instantiate an implementation of it. The `ClassPathXmlApplicationContext` implementation builds an application context by loading an XML configuration file from the classpath. You can also specify multiple configuration files for it.

```
ApplicationContext context = new ClassPathXmlApplicationContext("beans.xml");
```

Besides `ClassPathXmlApplicationContext`, several other `ApplicationContext` implementations are provided by Spring. `FileSystemXmlApplicationContext` is used to load XML configuration files from the file system or from URLs, while `XmlWebApplicationContext` and `XmlPortletApplicationContext` can be used in web and portal applications only.

Getting Beans from the IoC Container

To get a declared bean from a bean factory or an application context, you just make a call to the `getBean()` method and pass in the unique bean name. The return type of the `getBean()` method is `java.lang.Object`, so you have to cast it to its actual type before using it.

```
SequenceGenerator generator =
    (SequenceGenerator) context.getBean("sequenceGenerator");
```

Up to this step, you are free to use the bean just like any object you created using a constructor. The complete source code for running the sequence generator application is given in the following Main class:

```
package com.apress.springrecipes.sequence;

import org.springframework.context.ApplicationContext;
import org.springframework.context.support.ClassPathXmlApplicationContext;

public class Main {

    public static void main(String[] args) {
        ApplicationContext context =
            new ClassPathXmlApplicationContext("beans.xml");

        SequenceGenerator generator =
            (SequenceGenerator) context.getBean("sequenceGenerator");

        System.out.println(generator.getSequence());
        System.out.println(generator.getSequence());
    }
}
```

If everything is fine, you should see the following sequence numbers output, along with some logging messages that you might not be interested in:

30100000A

30100001A

1-2. Configuring Beans in the Spring IoC Container

Problem

Spring offers a powerful IoC container to manage the beans that make up an application. To utilize the container services, you have to configure your beans to run in the Spring IoC container.

Solution

You can configure your beans in the Spring IoC container through XML files, properties files, annotations, or even APIs.

Spring allows you to configure your beans in one or more bean configuration files. For a simple application, you can just centralize your beans in a single configuration file. But for a large application with a lot of beans, you should separate them in multiple configuration files according to their functionalities (e.g., controllers, DAO, and JMS). One useful division is by the architectural layer that a given context services.

How It Works

Suppose that you are going to develop an application for generating sequence numbers. In this application, there may be many series of sequence numbers to generate for different purposes. Each one of them will have its own prefix, suffix, and initial value. So you have to create and maintain multiple generator instances in your application.

Creating the Bean Class

In accordance with the requirements, you create the SequenceGenerator class that has three properties prefix, suffix, and initial—that can be injected via setter methods or a constructor. The private field counter is for storing the current numeric value of this generator. Each time you call the getSequence() method on a generator instance, you will get the last sequence number with the prefix and suffix joined. You declare this method as synchronized to make it thread-safe.

```
package com.apress.springrecipes.sequence;

public class SequenceGenerator {

    private String prefix;
    private String suffix;
    private int initial;
    private int counter;

    public SequenceGenerator() {}

    public SequenceGenerator(String prefix, String suffix, int initial) {
        this.prefix = prefix;
        this.suffix = suffix;
        this.initial = initial;
    }

    public void setPrefix(String prefix) {
        this.prefix = prefix;
    }

    public void setSuffix(String suffix) {
        this.suffix = suffix;
    }

    public void setInitial(int initial) {
        this.initial = initial;
    }
```

```
    public synchronized String getSequence() {
        StringBuffer buffer = new StringBuffer();
        buffer.append(prefix);
        buffer.append(initial + counter++);
        buffer.append(suffix);
        return buffer.toString();
    }
}
```

As you see, this SequenceGenerator class can be configured by getters/setters or by the constructor. When configuring them with the container, this is called constructor injection and setter injection.

Creating the Bean Configuration File

To declare beans in the Spring IoC container via XML, you first have to create an XML bean configuration file with an appropriate name, such as beans.xml. You can put this file in the root of the classpath for easier testing within an IDE.

The Spring configuration XML allows you to use custom tags from different schemas (tx, jndi, jee, and so on) to make the bean configuration simpler and clearer. Here's an example of the simplest XML configuration possible.

```
<beans xmlns="http://www.springframework.org/schema/beans"
    xmlns:xsi="http://www.w3.org/2001/XMLSchema-instance"
    xsi:schemaLocation="http://www.springframework.org/schema/beans
        http://www.springframework.org/schema/beans/spring-beans-3.0.xsd">
    ...
</beans>
```

Declaring Beans in the Bean Configuration File

Each bean should provide a unique name or id and a fully qualified class name for the Spring IoC container to instantiate it. For each bean property of simple type (e.g., String and other primitive types), you can specify a <value> element for it. Spring will attempt to convert your value into the declaring type of this property. To configure a property via setter injection, you use the <property> element and specify the property name in its name attribute. A <property> requires that the bean contain a corresponding setter method.

```
<bean name="sequenceGenerator"
    class="com.apress.springrecipes.sequence.SequenceGenerator">
    <property name="prefix">
        <value>30</value>
    </property>
    <property name="suffix">
        <value>A</value>
    </property>
    <property name="initial">
        <value>100000</value>
    </property>
</bean>
```

You can also configure bean properties via constructor injection by declaring them in the <constructor-arg> elements. There's not a name attribute in <constructor-arg>, because constructor arguments are position-based.

```
<bean name="sequenceGenerator"
    class="com.apress.springrecipes.sequence.SequenceGenerator">
    <constructor-arg>
        <value>30</value>
    </constructor-arg>
    <constructor-arg>
        <value>A</value>
    </constructor-arg>
    <constructor-arg>
        <value>100000</value>
    </constructor-arg>
</bean>
```

In the Spring IoC container, each bean's name should be unique, although duplicate names are allowed for overriding bean declaration if more than one context is loaded. A bean's name can be defined by the name attribute of the <bean> element. Actually, there's a preferred way of identifying a bean: through the standard XML id attribute, whose purpose is to identify an element within an XML document. In this way, if your text editor is XML-aware, it can help to validate each bean's uniqueness at design time.

```
<bean id="sequenceGenerator"
    class="com.apress.springrecipes.sequence.SequenceGenerator">
    ...
</bean>
```

However, XML has restrictions on the characters that can appear in the XML id attribute. But usually, you won't use those special characters in a bean name. Moreover, Spring allows you to specify multiple names, separated by commas, for a bean in the name attribute. But you can't do so in the id attribute because commas are not allowed there.

In fact, neither the bean name nor the bean ID is required for a bean. A bean that has no name defined is called an *anonymous bean*. You will usually create beans like this that serve only to interact with the Spring container itself, that you are sure you will only inject by type later on, or that you will nest, inline, in the declaration of an outer bean.

Defining Bean Properties by Shortcut

Spring supports a shortcut for specifying the value of a simple type property. You can present a value attribute in the <property> element instead of enclosing a <value> element inside.

```
<bean id="sequenceGenerator"
    class="com.apress.springrecipes.sequence.SequenceGenerator">
    <property name="prefix" value="30" />
    <property name="suffix" value="A" />
    <property name="initial" value="100000" />
</bean>
```

This shortcut also works for constructor arguments.

```
<bean name="sequenceGenerator"
      class="com.apress.springrecipes.sequence.SequenceGenerator">
    <constructor-arg value="30" />
    <constructor-arg value="A" />
    <constructor-arg value="100000" />
</bean>
```

Since Spring 2.0 another convenient shortcut to define properties was added. It consists of using the p schema to define bean properties as attributes of the <bean> element. This can shorten the lines of XML configuration.

```
<beans xmlns="http://www.springframework.org/schema/beans"
    xmlns:xsi="http://www.w3.org/2001/XMLSchema-instance"
    xmlns:p="http://www.springframework.org/schema/p"
    xsi:schemaLocation="http://www.springframework.org/schema/beans
        http://www.springframework.org/schema/beans/spring-beans-3.0.xsd">

    <bean id="sequenceGenerator"
        class="com.apress.springrecipes.sequence.SequenceGenerator"
        p:prefix="30" p:suffix="A" p:initial="100000" />
</beans>
```

Configuring Collections for Your Beans

List, Set, and Map are the core interfaces representing the three main types of collections in the Java SDK, part of a framework called the Java Collections framework. For each collection type, Java provides several implementations with different functions and characteristics from which you can choose. In Spring, these types of collections can be easily configured with a group of built-in XML tags, such as <list>, <set>, and <map>.

Suppose you are going to allow more than one suffix for your sequence generator. The suffixes will be appended to the sequence numbers with hyphens as the separators. You may consider accepting suffixes of arbitrary data types and converting them into strings when appending to the sequence numbers.

Lists, Arrays, and Sets

First, let's use a java.util.List collection to contain your suffixes. A *list* is an ordered and indexed collection whose elements can be accessed either by index or with a for-each loop.

```
package com.apress.springrecipes.sequence;
...
public class SequenceGenerator {
    ...
    private List<Object> suffixes;
```

```
    public void setSuffixes(List<Object> suffixes) {
        this.suffixes = suffixes;
    }

    public synchronized String getSequence() {
        StringBuffer buffer = new StringBuffer();
        ...
        for (Object suffix : suffixes) {
            buffer.append("-");
            buffer.append(suffix);
        }
        return buffer.toString();
    }
}
```

To define a property of the interface `java.util.List` in the bean configuration, you specify a `<list>` tag that contains the elements. The elements allowed inside the `<list>` tag can be a simple constant value specified by `<value>`, a bean reference by `<ref>`, an inner bean definition by `<bean>`, an ID reference definition by `<idref>`, or a null element by `<null>`. You can even embed other collections in a collection.

```
<bean id="sequenceGenerator"
    class="com.apress.springrecipes.sequence.SequenceGenerator">

    <property name="initial" value="100000" />
    <property name="suffixes">
        <list>
            <value>A</value>
            <bean class="java.net.URL">
                <constructor-arg value="http" />
                <constructor-arg value="www.apress.com" />
                <constructor-arg value="/" />
            </bean>
            <null />
        </list>
    </property>
</bean>
```

Conceptually, an *array* is very similar to a list in that it's also an ordered and indexed collection that can be accessed by index. The main difference is that the length of an array is fixed and cannot be extended dynamically. In the Java Collections framework, an array and a list can be converted to each other through the `Arrays.asList()` and `List.toArray()` methods. For your sequence generator, you can use an `Object[]` array to contain the suffixes and access them either by index or with a for-each loop.

```
package com.apress.springrecipes.sequence;
...
public class SequenceGenerator {
    ...
    private Object[] suffixes;
```

```
    public void setSuffixes(Object[] suffixes) {
        this.suffixes = suffixes;
    }
    ...
}
```

The definition of an array in the bean configuration file is identical to a list denoted by the `<list>` tag.

Another common collection type is a *set*. Both the `java.util.List` interface and the `java.util.Set` interface extend the same interface: `java.util.Collection`. A set differs from a list in that it is neither ordered nor indexed, and it can store unique objects only. That means no duplicate element can be contained in a set. When the same element is added to a set for the second time, it will replace the old one. The equality of elements is determined by the `equals()` method.

```
package com.apress.springrecipes.sequence;
...
public class SequenceGenerator {
    ...
    private Set<Object> suffixes;

    public void setSuffixes(Set<Object> suffixes) {
        this.suffixes = suffixes;
    }
    ...
}
```

To define a property of `java.util.Set` type, use the `<set>` tag to define the elements in the same way as a list.

```
<bean id="sequenceGenerator"
    class="com.apress.springrecipes.sequence.SequenceGenerator">
    ...
    <property name="suffixes">
        <set>
            <value>A</value>
            <bean class="java.net.URL">
                <constructor-arg value="http" />
                <constructor-arg value="www.apress.com" />
                <constructor-arg value="/" />
            </bean>
            <null />
        </set>
    </property>
</bean>
```

Although there's no order concept in the original set semantics, Spring preserves the order of your elements by using `java.util.LinkedHashSet`, an implementation of the `java.util.Set` interface that does preserve element order.

Maps and Properties

A *map* interface is a table that stores its entries in key/value pairs. You can get a particular value from a map by its key, and also iterate the map entries with a for-each loop. Both the keys and values of a map can be of arbitrary type. Equality between keys is also determined by the equals() method. For example, you can modify your sequence generator to accept a java.util.Map collection that contains suffixes with keys.

```java
package com.apress.springrecipes.sequence;
...
public class SequenceGenerator {
    ...
    private Map<Object, Object> suffixes;

    public void setSuffixes(Map<Object, Object> suffixes) {
        this.suffixes = suffixes;
    }

    public synchronized String getSequence() {
        StringBuffer buffer = new StringBuffer();
        ...
        for (Map.Entry entry : suffixes.entrySet()) {
            buffer.append("-");
            buffer.append(entry.getKey());
            buffer.append("@");
            buffer.append(entry.getValue());
        }
        return buffer.toString();
    }
}
```

In Spring, a map is defined by the <map> tag, with multiple <entry> tags as children. Each entry contains a key and a value. The key must be defined inside the <key> tag. There is no restriction on the type of the key and value, so you are free to specify a <value>, <ref>, <bean>, <idref>, or <null> element for them. Spring will also preserve the order of the map entries by using java.util.LinkedHashMap.

```xml
<bean id="sequenceGenerator"
    class="com.apress.springrecipes.sequence.SequenceGenerator">
    ...
    <property name="suffixes">
        <map>
            <entry>
                <key>
                    <value>type</value>
                </key>
                <value>A</value>
            </entry>
            <entry>
                <key>
                    <value>url</value>
                </key>
```

```
                <bean class="java.net.URL">
                    <constructor-arg value="http" />
                    <constructor-arg value="www.apress.com" />
                    <constructor-arg value="/" />
                </bean>
            </entry>
        </map>
    </property>
</bean>
```

There are shortcuts to defining map keys and values as attributes of the <entry> tag. If they are simple constant values, you can define them by key and value. If they are bean references, you can define them by key-ref and value-ref.

```
<bean id="sequenceGenerator"
    class="com.apress.springrecipes.sequence.SequenceGenerator">
    ...
    <property name="suffixes">
        <map>
            <entry key="type" value="A" />
            <entry key="url">
                <bean class="java.net.URL">
                    <constructor-arg value="http" />
                    <constructor-arg value="www.apress.com" />
                    <constructor-arg value="/" />
                </bean>
            </entry>
        </map>
    </property>
</bean>
```

In all the collection classes seen thus far, you used values to set the properties. Sometimes, the desired goal is to configure a null value using a Map instance. Spring's XML configuration schema includes explicit support for this. Here is a map with null values for the value of an entry:

```
<property name="nulledMapValue">
        <map>
            <entry>
                <key> <value>null</value> </key>
            </entry>
        </map>
    </property>
```

A java.util.Properties collection is very similar to a map. It also implements the java.util.Map interface and stores entries in key/value pairs. The only difference is that the keys and values of a Properties collection are always strings.

```
package com.apress.springrecipes.sequence;
...
public class SequenceGenerator {
    ...
    private Properties suffixes;

    public void setSuffixes(Properties suffixes) {
        this.suffixes = suffixes;
    }
    ...
}
```

To define a `java.util.Properties` collection in Spring, use the `<props>` tag with multiple `<prop>` tags as children. Each `<prop>` tag must have a key attribute defined and the corresponding value enclosed.

```
<bean id="sequenceGenerator"
    class="com.apress.springrecipes.sequence.SequenceGenerator">
    ...
    <property name="suffixes">
        <props>
            <prop key="type">A</prop>
            <prop key="url">http://www.apress.com/</prop>
            <prop key="null">null</prop>
        </props>
    </property>
</bean>
```

Merging the Collection of the Parent Bean

If you define your beans with inheritance, a child bean's collection can be merged with that of its parent by setting the `merge` attribute to `true`. For a `<list>` collection, the child elements will be appended after the parent's to preserve the order. So, the following sequence generator will have four suffixes: A, B, A, and C.

```
<beans ...>
    <bean id="baseSequenceGenerator"
        class="com.apress.springrecipes.sequence.SequenceGenerator">
        <property name="prefixGenerator" ref="datePrefixGenerator" />
        <property name="initial" value="100000" />
        <property name="suffixes">
            <list>
                <value>A</value>
                <value>B</value>
            </list>
        </property>
    </bean>
```

```xml
    <bean id="sequenceGenerator" parent="baseSequenceGenerator">
        <property name="suffixes">
            <list merge="true">
                <value>A</value>
                <value>C</value>
            </list>
        </property>
    </bean>
    ...
</beans>
```

For a `<set>` or `<map>` collection, the child elements will overwrite the parent's if they have the same value. So, the following sequence generator will have three suffixes: A, B, and C.

```xml
<beans ...>
    <bean id="baseSequenceGenerator"
        class="com.apress.springrecipes.sequence.SequenceGenerator">
        <property name="prefixGenerator" ref="datePrefixGenerator" />
        <property name="initial" value="100000" />
        <property name="suffixes">
            <set>
                <value>A</value>
                <value>B</value>
            </set>
        </property>
    </bean>

    <bean id="sequenceGenerator" parent="baseSequenceGenerator">
        <property name="suffixes">
            <set merge="true">
                <value>A</value>
                <value>C</value>
            </set>
        </property>
    </bean>
    ...
</beans>
```

1-3. Creating Beans by Invoking a Constructor

Problem

You would like to create a bean in the Spring IoC container by invoking its constructor, which is the most common and direct way of creating beans. It is equivalent to using the new operator to create objects in Java.

Solution

Normally, when you specify the `class` attribute for a bean, you are asking the Spring IoC container to create the bean instance by invoking its constructor.

How It Works

Suppose you are going to develop a shop application to sell products online. First of all, you create the `Product` class, which has several properties, such as the product name and price. As there are many types of products in your shop, you make the `Product` class abstract for different product subclasses to extend.

```
package com.apress.springrecipes.shop;

public abstract class Product {

    private String name;
    private double price;

    public Product() {}

    public Product(String name, double price) {
        this.name = name;
        this.price = price;
    }

    // Getters and Setters
    ...

    public String toString() {
        return name + " " + price;
    }
}
```

Then you create two product subclasses, `Battery` and `Disc`. Each of them has its own properties.

```
package com.apress.springrecipes.shop;

public class Battery extends Product {

    private boolean rechargeable;

    public Battery() {
        super();
    }

    public Battery(String name, double price) {
        super(name, price);
    }
```

```
    // Getters and Setters
    ...
}

package com.apress.springrecipes.shop;

public class Disc extends Product {

    private int capacity;

    public Disc() {
        super();
    }

    public Disc(String name, double price) {
        super(name, price);
    }

    // Getters and Setters
    ...
}
```

To define some products in the Spring IoC container, you create the following bean configuration file:

```xml
<beans xmlns="http://www.springframework.org/schema/beans"
    xmlns:xsi="http://www.w3.org/2001/XMLSchema-instance"
    xsi:schemaLocation="http://www.springframework.org/schema/beans
        http://www.springframework.org/schema/beans/spring-beans-3.0.xsd">

    <bean id="aaa" class="com.apress.springrecipes.shop.Battery">
        <property name="name" value="AAA" />
        <property name="price" value="2.5" />
        <property name="rechargeable" value="true" />
    </bean>

    <bean id="cdrw" class="com.apress.springrecipes.shop.Disc">
        <property name="name" value="CD-RW" />
        <property name="price" value="1.5" />
        <property name="capacity" value="700" />
    </bean>
</beans>
```

If there's no <constructor-arg> element specified, the default constructor with no argument will be invoked. Then for each <property> element, Spring will inject the value through the setter method. The preceding bean configuration is equivalent to the following code snippet:

```
Product aaa = new Battery();
aaa.setName("AAA");
aaa.setPrice(2.5);
aaa.setRechargeable(true);

Product cdrw = new Disc();
cdrw.setName("CD-RW");
cdrw.setPrice(1.5);
cdrw.setCapacity(700);
```

Otherwise, if there are one or more <constructor-arg> elements specified, Spring will invoke the most appropriate constructor that matches your arguments.

```
<beans ...>
    <bean id="aaa" class="com.apress.springrecipes.shop.Battery">
        <constructor-arg value="AAA" />
        <constructor-arg value="2.5" />
        <property name="rechargeable" value="true" />
    </bean>

    <bean id="cdrw" class="com.apress.springrecipes.shop.Disc">
        <constructor-arg value="CD-RW" />
        <constructor-arg value="1.5" />
        <property name="capacity" value="700" />
    </bean>
</beans>
```

As there is no constructor ambiguity for the Product class and subclasses, the preceding bean configuration is equivalent to the following code snippet:

```
Product aaa = new Battery("AAA", 2.5);
aaa.setRechargeable(true);

Product cdrw = new Disc("CD-RW", 1.5);
cdrw.setCapacity(700);
```

You can write the following Main class to test your products by retrieving them from the Spring IoC container:

```
package com.apress.springrecipes.shop;

import org.springframework.context.ApplicationContext;
import org.springframework.context.support.ClassPathXmlApplicationContext;

public class Main {

    public static void main(String[] args) throws Exception {
        ApplicationContext context =
            new ClassPathXmlApplicationContext("beans.xml");
```

```
        Product aaa = (Product) context.getBean("aaa");
        Product cdrw = (Product) context.getBean("cdrw");
        System.out.println(aaa);
        System.out.println(cdrw);
    }
}
```

1-4. Resolving Constructor Ambiguity

Problem

When you specify one or more constructor arguments for a bean, Spring will attempt to find an appropriate constructor in the bean class and pass in your arguments for bean instantiation. However, if your arguments can be applied to more than one constructor, it may cause ambiguity in constructor matching. In this case, Spring may not be able to invoke your expected constructor.

Solution

You can specify the attributes `type` and `index` for the `<constructor-arg>` element to assist Spring in finding your expected constructor.

How It Works

Now let's add a new constructor to the `SequenceGenerator` class with `prefix` and `suffix` as arguments.

```
package com.apress.springrecipes.sequence;

public class SequenceGenerator {
    ...
    public SequenceGenerator(String prefix, String suffix) {
        this.prefix = prefix;
        this.suffix = suffix;
    }
}
```

In its bean declaration, you can specify one or more constructor arguments through the `<constructor-arg>` elements. Spring will attempt to find an appropriate constructor for that class and pass in your arguments for bean instantiation. Recall that there's not a `name` attribute in `<constructor-arg>`, as constructor arguments are position-based.

```
<bean id="sequenceGenerator"
    class="com.apress.springrecipes.sequence.SequenceGenerator">
    <constructor-arg value="30" />
    <constructor-arg value="A" />
    <property name="initial" value="100000" />
</bean>
```

It's easy for Spring to find a constructor for these two arguments, as there is only one constructor that requires two arguments. Suppose you have to add another constructor to SequenceGenerator with prefix and initial as arguments.

```
package com.apress.springrecipes.sequence;

public class SequenceGenerator {
    ...
    public SequenceGenerator(String prefix, String suffix) {
        this.prefix = prefix;
        this.suffix = suffix;
    }

    public SequenceGenerator(String prefix, int initial) {
        this.prefix = prefix;
        this.initial = initial;
    }
}
```

To invoke this constructor, you make the following bean declaration to pass a prefix and an initial value. The remaining suffix is injected through the setter method.

```
<bean id="sequenceGenerator"
    class="com.apress.springrecipes.sequence.SequenceGenerator">
    <constructor-arg value="30" />
    <constructor-arg value="100000" />
    <property name="suffix" value="A" />
</bean>
```

However, if you run the application now, you will get the following result:

300A

301A

The cause of this unexpected result is that the first constructor, with prefix and suffix as arguments, has been invoked, but not the second. This is because Spring resolved both of your arguments as String type by default and considered that the first constructor was most suitable, as no type conversion was required. To specify the expected type of your arguments, you have to set it in the type attribute in <constructor-arg>.

```
<bean id="sequenceGenerator"
    class="com.apress.springrecipes.sequence.SequenceGenerator">
    <constructor-arg type="java.lang.String" value="30" />
    <constructor-arg type="int" value="100000" />
    <property name="suffix" value="A" />
</bean>
```

Now add one more constructor to SequenceGenerator with initial and suffix as arguments, and modify your bean declaration for it accordingly.

```
package com.apress.springrecipes.sequence;

public class SequenceGenerator {
    ...
    public SequenceGenerator(String prefix, String suffix) {
        this.prefix = prefix;
        this.suffix = suffix;
    }

    public SequenceGenerator(String prefix, int initial) {
        this.prefix = prefix;
        this.initial = initial;
    }

    public SequenceGenerator(int initial, String suffix) {
        this.initial = initial;
        this.suffix = suffix;
    }
}
```

```
<bean id="sequenceGenerator"
    class="com.apress.springrecipes.sequence.SequenceGenerator">
    <constructor-arg type="int" value="100000" />
    <constructor-arg type="java.lang.String" value="A" />
    <property name="prefix" value="30" />
</bean>
```

If you run the application again, you may get the right result or the following unexpected result:

```
30100000null

30100001null
```

The reason for this uncertainty is that Spring internally scores each constructor for compatibility with your arguments. But during the scoring process, the order in which your arguments appear in the XML is not considered. This means that from the view of Spring, the second and the third constructors will get the same score. Which one to pick depends on which one is matched first. According to the Java Reflection API, or more accurately the Class.getDeclaredConstructors() method, the constructors returned will be in an arbitrary order that may differ from the declaration order. All these factors, acting together, cause ambiguity in constructor matching.

To avoid this problem, you have to indicate the indexes of your arguments explicitly through the index attribute of <constructor-arg>. With both the type and index attributes set, Spring will be able to find the expected constructor for a bean accurately.

```
<bean id="sequenceGenerator"
    class="com.apress.springrecipes.sequence.SequenceGenerator">
    <constructor-arg type="int" index="0" value="100000" />
    <constructor-arg type="java.lang.String" index="1" value="A" />
    <property name="prefix" value="30" />
</bean>
```

However, if you are quite sure that your constructors won't cause ambiguity, you can skip the `type` and `index` attributes.

1-5. Specifying Bean References

Problem

The beans that make up your application often need to collaborate with each other to complete the application's functions. For beans to access each other, you have to specify bean references in the bean configuration file.

Solution

In the bean configuration file, you can specify a bean reference for a bean property or a constructor argument by the `<ref>` element. It's as easy as specifying a simple value by the `<value>` element. You can also enclose a bean declaration in a property or a constructor argument directly as an inner bean.

How It Works

Accepting a string value as the prefix of your sequence generator is not flexible enough to adapt to future requirements. It would be better if the prefix generation could be customized with some kind of programming logic. You can create the `PrefixGenerator` interface to define the prefix generation operation.

```
package com.apress.springrecipes.sequence;

public interface PrefixGenerator {

    public String getPrefix();
}
```

One prefix generation strategy is to use a particular pattern to format the current system date. Let's create the `DatePrefixGenerator` class that implements the `PrefixGenerator` interface.

```
package com.apress.springrecipes.sequence;
...
public class DatePrefixGenerator implements PrefixGenerator {
```

```
    private DateFormat formatter;

    public void setPattern(String pattern) {
        this.formatter = new SimpleDateFormat(pattern);
    }

    public String getPrefix() {
        return formatter.format(new Date());
    }
}
```

The pattern of this generator will be injected through the setter method setPattern() and then used to create a java.text.DateFormat object to format the date. As the pattern string will not be used any more once the DateFormat object is created, it's not necessary to store it in a private field.

Now you can declare a bean of type DatePrefixGenerator with an arbitrary pattern string for date formatting.

```
<bean id="datePrefixGenerator"
    class="com.apress.springrecipes.sequence.DatePrefixGenerator">
    <property name="pattern" value="yyyyMMdd" />
</bean>
```

Specifying Bean References for Setter Methods

To apply this prefix generator approach, the SequenceGenerator class should accept an object of type PrefixGenerator instead of a simple prefix string. You may choose setter injection to accept this prefix generator. You have to delete the prefix property, and its setter methods and constructors that cause compile errors.

```
package com.apress.springrecipes.sequence;

public class SequenceGenerator {
    ...
    private PrefixGenerator prefixGenerator;

    public void setPrefixGenerator(PrefixGenerator prefixGenerator) {
        this.prefixGenerator = prefixGenerator;
    }

    public synchronized String getSequence() {
        StringBuffer buffer = new StringBuffer();
        buffer.append(prefixGenerator.getPrefix());
        buffer.append(initial + counter++);
        buffer.append(suffix);
        return buffer.toString();
    }
}
```

Then a SequenceGenerator bean can refer to the datePrefixGenerator bean as its prefixGenerator property by enclosing a <ref> element inside.

```
<bean id="sequenceGenerator"
    class="com.apress.springrecipes.sequence.SequenceGenerator">
    <property name="initial" value="100000" />
    <property name="suffix" value="A" />
    <property name="prefixGenerator">
        <ref bean="datePrefixGenerator" />
    </property>
</bean>
```

The bean name in the `<ref>` element's bean attribute can be a reference to any bean in the IoC container, even if it's not defined in the same XML configuration file. If you are referring to a bean in the same XML file, you should use the `local` attribute, as it is an XML ID reference. Your XML editor can help to validate whether a bean with that ID exists in the same XML file (i.e., the reference integrity).

```
<bean id="sequenceGenerator"
    class="com.apress.springrecipes.sequence.SequenceGenerator">
    ...
    <property name="prefixGenerator">
        <ref local="datePrefixGenerator" />
    </property>
</bean>
```

There is also a convenient shortcut to specify a bean reference in the `ref` attribute of the `<property>` element.

```
<bean id="sequenceGenerator"
    class="com.apress.springrecipes.sequence.SequenceGenerator">
    ...
    <property name="prefixGenerator" ref="datePrefixGenerator" />
</bean>
```

But in this way, your XML editor will not be able to validate the reference integrity. Actually, it has the same effect as specifying the `<ref>` element's bean attribute.

Spring 2.x provides another convenient shortcut for you to specify bean references. It's by using the p schema to specify bean references as attributes of the `<bean>` element. This can shorten the lines of XML configuration.

```
<beans xmlns="http://www.springframework.org/schema/beans"
    xmlns:xsi="http://www.w3.org/2001/XMLSchema-instance"
    xmlns:p="http://www.springframework.org/schema/p"
    xsi:schemaLocation="http://www.springframework.org/schema/beans
        http://www.springframework.org/schema/beans/spring-beans-3.0.xsd">

    <bean id="sequenceGenerator"
        class="com.apress.springrecipes.sequence.SequenceGenerator"
        p:suffix="A" p:initial="1000000"
        p:prefixGenerator-ref="datePrefixGenerator" />
</beans>
```

To distinguish a bean reference from a simple property value, you have to add the `-ref` suffix to the property name.

Specifying Bean References for Constructor Arguments

Bean references can also be applied to constructor injection. For example, you can add a constructor that accepts a `PrefixGenerator` object as an argument.

```
package com.apress.springrecipes.sequence;

public class SequenceGenerator {
    ...
    private PrefixGenerator prefixGenerator;

    public SequenceGenerator(PrefixGenerator prefixGenerator) {
        this.prefixGenerator = prefixGenerator;
    }
}
```

In the `<constructor-arg>` element, you can enclose a bean reference by `<ref>` just like in the `<property>` element.

```
<bean id="sequenceGenerator"
    class="com.apress.springrecipes.sequence.SequenceGenerator">
    <constructor-arg>
        <ref local="datePrefixGenerator" />
    </constructor-arg>
    <property name="initial" value="100000" />
    <property name="suffix" value="A" />
</bean>
```

The shortcut for specifying a bean reference also works for `<constructor-arg>`.

```
<bean id="sequenceGenerator"
    class="com.apress.springrecipes.sequence.SequenceGenerator">
    <constructor-arg ref="datePrefixGenerator" />
    ...
</bean>
```

Declaring Inner Beans

Whenever a bean instance is used for one particular property only, it can be declared as an inner bean. An inner bean declaration is enclosed in `<property>` or `<constructor-arg>` directly, without any `id` or `name` attribute set. In this way, the bean will be anonymous so that you can't use it anywhere else. In fact, even if you define an `id` or a `name` attribute for an inner bean, it will be ignored.

```
<bean id="sequenceGenerator"
    class="com.apress.springrecipes.sequence.SequenceGenerator">
    <property name="initial" value="100000" />
    <property name="suffix" value="A" />
```

```
    <property name="prefixGenerator">
        <bean class="com.apress.springrecipes.sequence.DatePrefixGenerator">
            <property name="pattern" value="yyyyMMdd" />
        </bean>
    </property>
</bean>
```

An inner bean can also be declared in a constructor argument.

```
<bean id="sequenceGenerator"
    class="com.apress.springrecipes.sequence.SequenceGenerator">
    <constructor-arg>
        <bean class="com.apress.springrecipes.sequence.DatePrefixGenerator">
            <property name="pattern" value="yyyyMMdd" />
        </bean>
    </constructor-arg>
    <property name="initial" value="100000" />
    <property name="suffix" value="A" />
</bean>
```

1-6. Specifying the Data Type for Collection Elements

Problem

By default, Spring treats every element in a collection as a string. You have to specify the data type for
your collection elements if you are not going to use them as strings.

Solution

You can either specify the data type for each collection element by the **type** attribute of the **<value>** tag,
or specify the data type for all elements by the **value-type** attribute of the collection tag. If you are using
Java 1.5 or higher, you can define a type-safe collection so that Spring will read your collection's type
information.

How It Works

Now suppose you are going to accept a list of integer numbers as the suffixes of your sequence
generator. Each number will be formatted into four digits by an instance of **java.text.DecimalFormat**.

```
package com.apress.springrecipes.sequence;
...
public class SequenceGenerator {
    ...
    private List<Object> suffixes;
```

```java
    public void setSuffixes(List<Object> suffixes) {
        this.suffixes = suffixes;
    }

    public synchronized String getSequence() {
        StringBuffer buffer = new StringBuffer();
        ...
        DecimalFormat formatter = new DecimalFormat("0000");
        for (Object suffix : suffixes) {
            buffer.append("-");
            buffer.append(formatter.format((Integer) suffix));
        }
        return buffer.toString();
    }
}
```

Then define several suffixes for your sequence generator in the bean configuration file as usual.

```xml
<bean id="sequenceGenerator"
    class="com.apress.springrecipes.sequence.SequenceGenerator">
    <property name="prefixGenerator" ref="datePrefixGenerator" />
    <property name="initial" value="100000" />
    <property name="suffixes">
        <list>
            <value>5</value>
            <value>10</value>
            <value>20</value>
        </list>
    </property>
</bean>
```

However, when you run this application, you will encounter a `ClassCastException`, indicating that the suffixes cannot be cast into integers because their type is `String`. Spring treats every element in a collection as a string by default. You have to set the `type` attribute of the `<value>` tag to specify the element type.

```xml
<bean id="sequenceGenerator"
    class="com.apress.springrecipes.sequence.SequenceGenerator">
    ...
    <property name="suffixes">
        <list>
            <value type="int">5</value>
            <value type="int">10</value>
            <value type="int">20</value>
        </list>
    </property>
</bean>
```

Or you may set the `value-type` attribute of the collection tag to specify the type for all elements in this collection.

```
<bean id="sequenceGenerator"
    class="com.apress.springrecipes.sequence.SequenceGenerator">
    ...
    <property name="suffixes">
        <list value-type="int">
            <value>5</value>
            <value>10</value>
            <value>20</value>
        </list>
    </property>
</bean>
```

In Java 1.5 or higher, you can define your `suffixes` list with a type-safe collection that stores integers.

```
package com.apress.springrecipes.sequence;
...
public class SequenceGenerator {
    ...
    private List<Integer> suffixes;

    public void setSuffixes(List<Integer> suffixes) {
        this.suffixes = suffixes;
    }

    public synchronized String getSequence() {
        StringBuffer buffer = new StringBuffer();
        ...
        DecimalFormat formatter = new DecimalFormat("0000");
        for (int suffix : suffixes) {
            buffer.append("-");
            buffer.append(formatter.format(suffix));
        }
        return buffer.toString();
    }
}
```

Once you have defined your collections in a type-safe way, Spring will be able to read the collection's type information through reflection. In this way, you no longer need to specify the **value-type** attribute of <list>.

```
<bean id="sequenceGenerator"
    class="com.apress.springrecipes.sequence.SequenceGenerator">
    ...
    <property name="suffixes">
        <list>
            <value>5</value>
            <value>10</value>
            <value>20</value>
        </list>
    </property>
</bean>
```

27

1-7. Creating Beans Using Spring's FactoryBean

Problem

You would like to create a bean in the Spring IoC container using Spring's factory bean. A *factory bean* is a bean that serves as a factory for creating other beans within the IoC container. Conceptually, a factory bean is very similar to a factory method, but it is a Spring-specific bean that can be identified by the Spring IoC container during bean construction.

Solution

The basic requirement of a factory bean is to implement the `FactoryBean` interface. For your convenience, Spring provides an abstract template class, `AbstractFactoryBean`, for you to extend. Factory beans are mostly used to implement framework facilities. Here are some examples:

- When looking up an object (such as a data source) from JNDI, you can use `JndiObjectFactoryBean`.

- When using classic Spring AOP to create a proxy for a bean, you can use `ProxyFactoryBean`.

- When creating a Hibernate session factory in the IoC container, you can use `LocalSessionFactoryBean`.

However, as a framework user, you seldom have to write custom factory beans, because they are framework-specific and cannot be used outside the scope of the Spring IoC container. Actually, you are always able to implement an equivalent factory method for a factory bean.

How It Works

Although you'll seldom have to write custom factory beans, you may find it helpful to understand their internal mechanisms through an example. For example, you can write a factory bean for creating a product with a discount applied to the price. It accepts a `product` property and a `discount` property to apply the discount to the product and return it as a new bean.

```
package com.apress.springrecipes.shop;

import org.springframework.beans.factory.config.AbstractFactoryBean;

public class DiscountFactoryBean extends AbstractFactoryBean {

    private Product product;
    private double discount;

    public void setProduct(Product product) {
        this.product = product;
    }
```

```java
    public void setDiscount(double discount) {
        this.discount = discount;
    }

    public Class getObjectType() {
        return product.getClass();
    }

    protected Object createInstance() throws Exception {
        product.setPrice(product.getPrice() * (1 - discount));
        return product;
    }
}
```

By extending the `AbstractFactoryBean` class, your factory bean can simply override the `createInstance()` method to create the target bean instance. In addition, you have to return the target bean's type in the `getObjectType()` method for the auto-wiring feature to work properly.

Next, you can declare your product instances with `DiscountFactoryBean`. Each time you request a bean that implements the `FactoryBean` interface, the Spring IoC container will use this factory bean to create the target bean and return it to you. If you are sure that you want to get the factory bean instance itself, you can use the bean name preceded by &.

```xml
<beans ...>
    <bean id="aaa"
        class="com.apress.springrecipes.shop.DiscountFactoryBean">
        <property name="product">
            <bean class="com.apress.springrecipes.shop.Battery">
                <constructor-arg value="AAA" />
                <constructor-arg value="2.5" />
            </bean>
        </property>
        <property name="discount" value="0.2" />
    </bean>

    <bean id="cdrw"
        class="com.apress.springrecipes.shop.DiscountFactoryBean">
        <property name="product">
            <bean class="com.apress.springrecipes.shop.Disc">
                <constructor-arg value="CD-RW" />
                <constructor-arg value="1.5" />
            </bean>
        </property>
        <property name="discount" value="0.1" />
    </bean>
</beans>
```

The preceding factory bean configuration works in a similar way to the following code snippet:

```
DiscountFactoryBean aaa = new DiscountFactoryBean();
aaa.setProduct(new Battery("AAA", 2.5));
aaa.setDiscount(0.2);
Product aaa = (Product) aaa.createInstance();

DiscountFactoryBean cdrw = new DiscountFactoryBean();
cdrw.setProduct(new Disc("CD-RW", 1.5));
cdrw.setDiscount(0.1);
Product cdrw = (Product) cdrw.createInstance();
```

1-8. Defining Collections Using Factory Beans and the Utility Schema

Problem

When using the basic collection tags to define collections, you can't specify the concrete class of a collection, such as LinkedList, TreeSet, or TreeMap. Moreover, you cannot share a collection among different beans by defining it as a stand-alone bean for other beans to refer to.

Solution

Spring provides a couple of options to overcome the shortcomings of the basic collection tags. One option is to use corresponding collection factory beans like ListFactoryBean, SetFactoryBean, and MapFactoryBean. A *factory bean* is a special kind of Spring bean that is used for creating another bean. The second option is to use collection tags such as <util:list>, <util:set>, and <util:map> in the util schema introduced in Spring 2.x.

How It Works

Specifying the Concrete Class for Collections

You can use a collection factory bean to define a collection and specify its target class. For example, you can specify the targetSetClass property for SetFactoryBean. Then Spring will instantiate the specified class for this collection.

```
<bean id="sequenceGenerator"
    class="com.apress.springrecipes.sequence.SequenceGenerator">
    <property name="prefixGenerator" ref="datePrefixGenerator" />
    <property name="initial" value="100000" />
    <property name="suffixes">
        <bean class="org.springframework.beans.factory.config.SetFactoryBean">
            <property name="targetSetClass">
                <value>java.util.TreeSet</value>
            </property>
```

```
                <property name="sourceSet">
                    <set>
                        <value>5</value>
                        <value>10</value>
                        <value>20</value>
                    </set>
                </property>
            </bean>
        </property>
    </bean>
```

Or you can use a collection tag in the `util` schema to define a collection and set its target class (e.g., by the `set-class` attribute of `<util:set>`). But you must remember to add the `util` schema definition to your `<beans>` root element.

```
<beans xmlns="http://www.springframework.org/schema/beans"
    xmlns:xsi="http://www.w3.org/2001/XMLSchema-instance"
    xmlns:util="http://www.springframework.org/schema/util"
    xsi:schemaLocation="http://www.springframework.org/schema/beans
        http://www.springframework.org/schema/beans/spring-beans-3.0.xsd
        http://www.springframework.org/schema/util
        http://www.springframework.org/schema/util/spring-util-3.0.xsd">

    <bean id="sequenceGenerator"
        class="com.apress.springrecipes.sequence.SequenceGenerator">
        ...
        <property name="suffixes">
            <util:set set-class="java.util.TreeSet">
                <value>5</value>
                <value>10</value>
                <value>20</value>
            </util:set>
        </property>
    </bean>
    ...
</beans>
```

Defining Stand-Alone Collections

Another advantage of collection factory beans is that you can define a collection as a stand-alone bean for other beans to refer to. For example, you can define a stand-alone set by using `SetFactoryBean`.

```
<beans ...>
    <bean id="sequenceGenerator"
        class="com.apress.springrecipes.sequence.SequenceGenerator">
        ...
        <property name="suffixes">
            <ref local="suffixes" />
        </property>
    </bean>
```

```
    <bean id="suffixes"
        class="org.springframework.beans.factory.config.SetFactoryBean">
        <property name="sourceSet">
            <set>
                <value>5</value>
                <value>10</value>
                <value>20</value>
            </set>
        </property>
    </bean>
    ...
</beans>
```

Or you can define a stand-alone set by using the `<util:set>` tag in the `util` schema.

```
<beans ...>
    <bean id="sequenceGenerator"
        class="com.apress.springrecipes.sequence.SequenceGenerator">
        ...
        <property name="suffixes">
            <ref local="suffixes" />
        </property>
    </bean>

    <util:set id="suffixes">
        <value>5</value>
        <value>10</value>
        <value>20</value>
    </util:set>
    ...
</beans>
```

1-9. Checking Properties with Dependency Checking

Problem

In a production-scale application, there may be hundreds or thousands of beans declared in the IoC container, and the dependencies between them are often very complicated. One of the shortcomings of setter injection is that you cannot make sure a property will be injected. It's very hard for you to check if all required properties have been set.

Solution

Spring's dependency checking feature can help you to check if all properties of certain types have been set on a bean. You simply have to specify the dependency checking mode in the dependency-check attribute of `<bean>`. Note that the dependency checking feature can only check if the properties have been set, but can't check if their value is not null. Table 1-1 lists all the dependency checking modes supported by Spring.

Table 1-1. *Dependency Checking Modes Supported by Spring*

Mode	Description
none*	No dependency checking will be performed. Any properties can be left unset.
simple	If any properties of the simple types (the primitive and collection types) have not been set, an UnsatisfiedDependencyException will be thrown.
objects	If any properties of the object types (other than the simple types) have not been set, an UnsatisfiedDependencyException will be thrown.
all	If any properties of any type have not been set, an UnsatisfiedDependencyException will be thrown.

* The default mode is none, but this can be changed by setting the default-dependency-check attribute of the <beans> root element. This default mode will be overridden by a bean's own mode if specified. You must set this attribute with great care as it will alter the default dependency checking mode for all the beans in the IoC container.

How It Works

Checking Properties of the Simple Types

Suppose the suffix property was not set for the sequence generator. Then the generator would generate sequence numbers whose suffix was the string null. This kind of issue is often very hard to debug, especially in a complicated bean. Fortunately, Spring is able to check if all properties of certain types have been set. To ask Spring to check properties of the simple types (i.e., the primitive and collection types), set the dependency-check attribute of <bean> to simple.

```
<bean id="sequenceGenerator"
    class="com.apress.springrecipes.sequence.SequenceGenerator"
    dependency-check="simple">
    <property name="initial" value="100000" />
    <property name="prefixGenerator" ref="datePrefixGenerator" />
</bean>
```

If any properties of such types have not been set, an UnsatisfiedDependencyException will be thrown, indicating the unset property.

```
Exception in thread "main"
org.springframework.beans.factory.UnsatisfiedDependencyException: Error creating
bean with name 'sequenceGenerator' defined in class path resource [beans.xml]:
Unsatisfied dependency expressed through bean property 'suffix': Set this property
value or disable dependency checking for this bean.
```

Checking Properties of the Object Types

If the prefix generator is not set, then the evil `NullPointerException` will be thrown when prefix generation is requested. To enable dependency checking for bean properties of object types, (i.e., other than simple types), change the `dependency-check` attribute to `objects`.

```
<bean id="sequenceGenerator"
    class="com.apress.springrecipes.sequence.SequenceGenerator"
    dependency-check="objects">
    <property name="initial" value="100000" />
    <property name="suffix" value="A" />
</bean>
```

Then when you run the application, Spring will notify you that the `prefixGenerator` property has not been set.

```
Exception in thread "main"

org.springframework.beans.factory.UnsatisfiedDependencyException: Error creating

bean with name 'sequenceGenerator' defined in class path resource [beans.xml]:

Unsatisfied dependency expressed through bean property 'prefixGenerator': Set this

property value or disable dependency checking for this bean.
```

Checking Properties of All Types

If you would like to check all bean properties whatever the type is, you can change the `dependency-check` attribute to `all`.

```
<bean id="sequenceGenerator"
    class="com.apress.springrecipes.sequence.SequenceGenerator"
    dependency-check="all">
    <property name="initial" value="100000" />
</bean>
```

Dependency Checking and Constructor Injection

Spring's dependency checking feature will check only if a property has been injected via the setter method. So, even if you have injected the prefix generator via a constructor, an UnsatisfiedDependencyException will still be thrown.

```
<bean id="sequenceGenerator"
    class="com.apress.springrecipes.sequence.SequenceGenerator"
    dependency-check="all">
    <constructor-arg ref="datePrefixGenerator" />
    <property name="initial" value="100000" />
    <property name="suffix" value="A" />
</bean>
```

1-10. Checking Properties with the @Required Annotation

Problem

Spring's dependency checking feature can check only for all properties of certain types. It's not flexible enough to check for particular properties only. In most cases, you would like to check if particular properties have been set, but not all properties of certain types.

Solution

RequiredAnnotationBeanPostProcessor is a Spring bean post processor that checks if all the bean properties with the @Required annotation have been set. A *bean post processor* is a special kind of Spring bean that is able to perform additional tasks on each bean before its initialization. To enable this bean post processor for property checking, you must register it in the Spring IoC container. Note that this processor can check only if the properties have been set, but can't check if their value is not null.

How It Works

Suppose that both the prefixGenerator and suffix properties are required for a sequence generator. You can annotate their setter methods with @Required.

```
package com.apress.springrecipes.sequence;

import org.springframework.beans.factory.annotation.Required;
```

```
public class SequenceGenerator {

    private PrefixGenerator prefixGenerator;
    private String suffix;
    ...
    @Required
    public void setPrefixGenerator(PrefixGenerator prefixGenerator) {
        this.prefixGenerator = prefixGenerator;
    }

    @Required
    public void setSuffix(String suffix) {
        this.suffix = suffix;
    }
    ...
}
```

To ask Spring to check if these properties have been set on all sequence generator instances, you have to register a RequiredAnnotationBeanPostProcessor instance in the IoC container. If you are using a bean factory, you have to register this bean post processor through the API. Otherwise, you can just declare an instance of this bean post processor in your application context.

```
<bean class="org.springframework.beans.factory.annotation.↵
    RequiredAnnotationBeanPostProcessor" />
```

If you are using Spring 2.5 or later, you can simply include the <context:annotation-config> element in your bean configuration file, and a RequiredAnnotationBeanPostProcessor instance will automatically get registered.

```
<beans xmlns="http://www.springframework.org/schema/beans"
    xmlns:xsi="http://www.w3.org/2001/XMLSchema-instance"
    xmlns:context="http://www.springframework.org/schema/context"
    xsi:schemaLocation="http://www.springframework.org/schema/beans
        http://www.springframework.org/schema/beans/spring-beans-3.0.xsd
        http://www.springframework.org/schema/context
        http://www.springframework.org/schema/context/spring-context-3.0.xsd">

    <context:annotation-config />
    ...
</beans>
```

If any properties with @Required have not been set, a BeanInitializationException will be thrown by this bean post processor.

```
Exception in thread "main" org.springframework.beans.factory.BeanCreationException: Error
creating bean with name 'sequenceGenerator' defined in class path resource [beans.xml]:
Initialization of bean failed; nested exception is org.springframework.beans.factory.
BeanInitializationException: Property 'prefixGenerator' is required for bean
'sequenceGenerator'
```

In addition to the @Required annotation, RequiredAnnotationBeanPostProcessor can also check the properties with your custom annotation. For example, you can create the following annotation type:

```
package com.apress.springrecipes.sequence;
...
@Retention(RetentionPolicy.RUNTIME)
@Target(ElementType.METHOD)
public @interface Mandatory {
}
```

And then you can apply this annotation to the setter methods of the required properties.

```
package com.apress.springrecipes.sequence;

public class SequenceGenerator {

    private PrefixGenerator prefixGenerator;
    private String suffix;
    ...
    @Mandatory
    public void setPrefixGenerator(PrefixGenerator prefixGenerator) {
        this.prefixGenerator = prefixGenerator;
    }

    @Mandatory
    public void setSuffix(String suffix) {
        this.suffix = suffix;
    }
    ...
}
```

To check for the properties with this annotation type, you have to specify it in the requiredAnnotationType property of RequiredAnnotationBeanPostProcessor.

```
<bean class="org.springframework.beans.factory.annotation.↵
    RequiredAnnotationBeanPostProcessor">
    <property name="requiredAnnotationType">
        <value>com.apress.springrecipes.sequence.Mandatory</value>
    </property>
</bean>
```

1-11. Auto-Wiring Beans with XML Configuration

Problem

When a bean requires access to another bean, you can wire it by specifying the reference explicitly. However, if your container can wire your beans automatically, it can save you the trouble of configuring the wirings manually.

Solution

The Spring IoC container can help you to wire your beans automatically. You only have to specify the auto-wiring mode in the `autowire` attribute of `<bean>`. Table 1-2 lists the auto-wiring modes supported by Spring.

Table 1-2. Auto-Wiring Modes Supported by Spring

Mode	Description
no*	No auto-wiring will be performed. You must wire the dependencies explicitly.
byName	For each bean property, wire a bean with the same name as the property.
byType	For each bean property, wire a bean whose type is compatible with that of the property. If more than one bean is found, an `UnsatisfiedDependencyException` will be thrown.
Constructor	For each argument of each constructor, first find a bean whose type is compatible with the argument's. Then, pick the constructor with the most matching arguments. In case of any ambiguity, an `UnsatisfiedDependencyException` will be thrown.
autodetect	If a default constructor with no argument is found, the dependencies will be auto-wired by type. Otherwise, they will be auto-wired by constructor.

* The default mode is no, but this can be changed by setting the `default-autowire` attribute of the `<beans>` root element. This default mode will be overridden by a bean's own mode if specified.

Although the auto-wiring feature is very powerful, the cost is that it will reduce the readability of your bean configurations. Because auto-wiring is performed by Spring at runtime, you cannot derive how your beans are wired from the bean configuration file. In practice, we recommend applying auto-wiring only in applications whose component dependencies are not complicated.

How It Works

Auto-Wiring by Type

You can set the `autowire` attribute of the `sequenceGenerator` bean to `byType` and leave the `prefixGenerator` property unset. Then, Spring will attempt to wire a bean whose type is compatible with `PrefixGenerator`. In this case, the `datePrefixGenerator` bean will be wired automatically.

```
<beans ...>
    <bean id="sequenceGenerator"
        class="com.apress.springrecipes.sequence.SequenceGenerator"
        autowire="byType">
        <property name="initial" value="100000" />
        <property name="suffix" value="A" />
    </bean>

    <bean id="datePrefixGenerator"
        class="com.apress.springrecipes.sequence.DatePrefixGenerator">
        <property name="pattern" value="yyyyMMdd" />
    </bean>
</beans>
```

The main problem of auto-wiring by type is that sometimes there will be more than one bean in the IoC container compatible with the target type. In this case, Spring will not be able to decide which bean is most suitable for the property, and hence cannot perform auto-wiring. For example, if you have another prefix generator generating the current year as the prefix, auto-wiring by type will be broken immediately.

```
<beans ...>
    <bean id="sequenceGenerator"
        class="com.apress.springrecipes.sequence.SequenceGenerator"
        autowire="byType">
        <property name="initial" value="100000" />
        <property name="suffix" value="A" />
    </bean>

    <bean id="datePrefixGenerator"
        class="com.apress.springrecipes.sequence.DatePrefixGenerator">
        <property name="pattern" value="yyyyMMdd" />
    </bean>

    <bean id="yearPrefixGenerator"
        class="com.apress.springrecipes.sequence.DatePrefixGenerator">
        <property name="pattern" value="yyyy" />
    </bean>
</beans>
```

Spring will throw an `UnsatisfiedDependencyException` if more than one bean is found for auto-wiring.

```
Exception in thread "main"
org.springframework.beans.factory.UnsatisfiedDependencyException: Error creating
bean with name 'sequenceGenerator' defined in class path resource [beans.xml]:
Unsatisfied dependency expressed through bean property 'prefixGenerator': No unique
bean of type [com.apress.springrecipes.sequence.PrefixGenerator]
is defined: expected single matching bean but found 2: [datePrefixGenerator,
yearPrefixGenerator]
```

Auto-Wiring by Name

Another mode of auto-wiring is byName, which can sometimes resolve the problems of auto-wiring by type. It works very similarly to byType, but in this case, Spring will attempt to wire a bean whose class name is the same as the property name, rather than with the compatible type. As the bean name is unique within a container, auto-wiring by name will not cause ambiguity.

```
<beans ...>
    <bean id="sequenceGenerator"
        class="com.apress.springrecipes.sequence.SequenceGenerator"
        autowire="byName">
        <property name="initial" value="100000" />
        <property name="suffix" value="A" />
    </bean>

    <bean id="prefixGenerator"
        class="com.apress.springrecipes.sequence.DatePrefixGenerator">
        <property name="pattern" value="yyyyMMdd" />
    </bean>
</beans>
```

However, auto-wiring by name will not work in all cases. Sometimes, it's not possible for you to make the name of the target bean the same as your property. In practice, you often need to specify ambiguous dependencies explicitly while keeping others auto-wired. That means you employ a mixture of explicit wiring and auto-wiring.

Auto-Wiring by Constructor

The auto-wiring mode constructor works like byType, but it's rather more complicated. For a bean with a single constructor, Spring will attempt to wire a bean with a compatible type for each constructor argument. But for a bean with multiple constructors, the process is more complicated. Spring will first attempt to find a bean with a compatible type for each argument of each constructor. Then, it will pick the constructor with the most matching arguments.

Suppose that SequenceGenerator has one default constructor and one constructor with an argument PrefixGenerator.

```
package com.apress.springenterpriserecipes.sequence;

public class SequenceGenerator {

    public SequenceGenerator() {}

    public SequenceGenerator(PrefixGenerator prefixGenerator) {
        this.prefixGenerator = prefixGenerator;
    }
    ...
}
```

In this case, the second constructor will be matched and picked because Spring can find a bean whose type is compatible with PrefixGenerator.

```
<beans ...>
    <bean id="sequenceGenerator"
        class="com.apress.springrecipes.sequence.SequenceGenerator"
        autowire="constructor">
        <property name="initial" value="100000" />
        <property name="suffix" value="A" />
    </bean>

    <bean id="datePrefixGenerator"
        class="com.apress.springrecipes.sequence.DatePrefixGenerator">
        <property name="pattern" value="yyyyMMdd" />
    </bean>
</beans>
```

However, multiple constructors in a class may cause ambiguity in constructor argument matching. The situation may be further complicated if you ask Spring to determine a constructor for you. So, if you use this auto-wiring mode, take great care to avoid ambiguity.

Auto-Wiring by Auto-Detection

The auto-wiring mode autodetect asks Spring to decide the auto-wiring mode between byType and constructor. If at least a default constructor with no argument is found for that bean, byType will be chosen. Otherwise, constructor will be chosen. Because the SequenceGenerator class has a default constructor defined, byType will be chosen. That means the prefix generator will be injected via the setter method.

```
<beans ...>
    <bean id="sequenceGenerator"
        class="com.apress.springrecipes.sequence.SequenceGenerator"
        autowire="autodetect">
        <property name="initial" value="100000" />
        <property name="suffix" value="A" />
    </bean>

    <bean id="datePrefixGenerator"
        class="com.apress.springrecipes.sequence.DatePrefixGenerator">
        <property name="pattern" value="yyyyMMdd" />
    </bean>
</beans>
```

Auto-Wiring and Dependency Checking

As you have seen, if Spring finds more than one candidate bean for auto-wiring, it will throw an `UnsatisfiedDependencyException`. On the other hand, if the auto-wiring mode is set to `byName` or `byType`, and Spring cannot find a matching bean to wire, it will leave the property unset, which may cause a `NullPointerException` or a value that has not been initialized. However, if you want to be notified when auto-wiring cannot wire your beans, you should set the `dependency-check` attribute to `objects` or `all`.

In that case, an `UnsatisfiedDependencyException` will be thrown whenever auto-wiring doesn't work. `objects` tells Spring to raise an error when a collaborating bean can't be found in the same bean factory. `all` tells the container to raise an error when any simple property types (a `String` or a primitive) expressed as dependencies on a bean haven't been set, in addition to the functionality of `objects`.

```
<bean id="sequenceGenerator"
    class="com.apress.springrecipes.sequence.SequenceGenerator"
    autowire="byName" dependency-check="objects">
    <property name="initial" value="100000" />
    <property name="suffix" value="A" />
</bean>
```

1-12. Auto-Wiring Beans with @Autowired and @Resource

Problem

Auto-wiring by setting the `autowire` attribute in the bean configuration file will wire all properties of a bean. It's not flexible enough to wire particular properties only. Moreover, you can auto-wire beans only by either type or name. If neither strategy satisfies your requirements, you must wire your beans explicitly.

Solution

Since Spring 2.5, several enhancements have been made to the auto-wiring feature. You can auto-wire a particular property by annotating a setter method, a constructor, a field, or even an arbitrary method with the @Autowired annotation or the @Resource annotation defined in JSR-250: Common Annotations for the Java Platform. That means you have one more option besides setting the autowire attribute to satisfy your requirements. However, this annotation-based option requires you to be using Java 1.5 or higher.

How It Works

To ask Spring to auto-wire the bean properties with @Autowired or @Resource, you have to register an AutowiredAnnotationBeanPostProcessor instance in the IoC container. If you are using a bean factory, you have to register this bean post processor through the API. Otherwise, you can just declare an instance of it in your application context.

```
<bean class="org.springframework.beans.factory.annotation.↵
    AutowiredAnnotationBeanPostProcessor" />
```

Or you can simply include the <context:annotation-config> element in your bean configuration file, and an AutowiredAnnotationBeanPostProcessor instance will automatically get registered.

```
<beans xmlns="http://www.springframework.org/schema/beans"
    xmlns:xsi="http://www.w3.org/2001/XMLSchema-instance"
    xmlns:context="http://www.springframework.org/schema/context"
    xsi:schemaLocation="http://www.springframework.org/schema/beans
        http://www.springframework.org/schema/beans/spring-beans-3.0.xsd
        http://www.springframework.org/schema/context
        http://www.springframework.org/schema/context/spring-context-3.0.xsd">

    <context:annotation-config />
    ...
</beans>
```

Auto-Wiring a Single Bean of Compatible Type

The @Autowired annotation can be applied to a particular property for Spring to auto-wire it. As an example, you can annotate the setter method of the prefixGenerator property with @Autowired. Then, Spring will attempt to wire a bean whose type is compatible with PrefixGenerator.

```
package com.apress.springrecipes.sequence;

import org.springframework.beans.factory.annotation.Autowired;

public class SequenceGenerator {
    ...
    @Autowired
    public void setPrefixGenerator(PrefixGenerator prefixGenerator) {
        this.prefixGenerator = prefixGenerator;
    }
}
```

If you have a bean whose type is compatible with `PrefixGenerator` defined in the IoC container, it will be set to the `prefixGenerator` property automatically.

```
<beans ...>
    ...
    <bean id="sequenceGenerator"
        class="com.apress.springrecipes.sequence.SequenceGenerator">
        <property name="initial" value="100000" />
        <property name="suffix" value="A" />
    </bean>

    <bean id="datePrefixGenerator"
        class="com.apress.springrecipes.sequence.DatePrefixGenerator">
        <property name="pattern" value="yyyyMMdd" />
    </bean>
</beans>
```

By default, all the properties with `@Autowired` are required. When Spring can't find a matching bean to wire, it will throw an exception. If you want a certain property to be optional, set the `required` attribute of `@Autowired` to `false`. Then, when Spring can't find a matching bean, it will leave this property unset.

```
package com.apress.springrecipes.sequence;

import org.springframework.beans.factory.annotation.Autowired;

public class SequenceGenerator {
    ...
    @Autowired(required = false)
    public void setPrefixGenerator(PrefixGenerator prefixGenerator) {
        this.prefixGenerator = prefixGenerator;
    }
}
```

In addition to the setter method, the `@Autowired` annotation can also be applied to a constructor, and Spring will attempt to find a bean with the compatible type for each of the constructor arguments.

```
package com.apress.springrecipes.sequence;

import org.springframework.beans.factory.annotation.Autowired;

public class SequenceGenerator {
    ...
    @Autowired
    public SequenceGenerator(PrefixGenerator prefixGenerator) {
        this.prefixGenerator = prefixGenerator;
    }
}
```

The `@Autowired` annotation can also be applied to a field, even if it is not declared as `public`. In this way, you can omit the need of declaring a setter method or a constructor for this field. Spring will inject the matched bean into this field via reflection. However, annotating a nonpublic field with `@Autowired` will reduce code testability, because the code will be difficult to unit test (there's no way black-box testing can manipulate that state, such as with mock objects).

```
package com.apress.springrecipes.sequence;

import org.springframework.beans.factory.annotation.Autowired;

public class SequenceGenerator {

    @Autowired
    private PrefixGenerator prefixGenerator;
    ...
}
```

You may even apply the `@Autowired` annotation to a method with an arbitrary name and an arbitrary number of arguments, and, in that case, Spring will attempt to wire a bean with the compatible type for each of the method arguments.

```
package com.apress.springrecipes.sequence;

import org.springframework.beans.factory.annotation.Autowired;

public class SequenceGenerator {
    ...
    @Autowired
    public void inject(PrefixGenerator prefixGenerator) {
        this.prefixGenerator = prefixGenerator;
    }
}
```

Auto-Wiring All Beans of Compatible Type

The `@Autowired` annotation can also be applied to a property of array type to have Spring auto-wire all the matching beans. For example, you can annotate a `PrefixGenerator[]` property with `@Autowired`. Then, Spring will auto-wire all the beans whose type is compatible with `PrefixGenerator` at one time.

```
package com.apress.springrecipes.sequence;

import org.springframework.beans.factory.annotation.Autowired;

public class SequenceGenerator {

    @Autowired
    private PrefixGenerator[] prefixGenerators;
    ...
}
```

If you have multiple beans whose type is compatible with the `PrefixGenerator` defined in the IoC container, they will be added to the `prefixGenerators` array automatically.

```
<beans ...>
    ...
    <bean id="datePrefixGenerator"
        class="com.apress.springrecipes.sequence.DatePrefixGenerator">
        <property name="pattern" value="yyyyMMdd" />
    </bean>

    <bean id="yearPrefixGenerator"
        class="com.apress.springrecipes.sequence.DatePrefixGenerator">
        <property name="pattern" value="yyyy" />
    </bean>
</beans>
```

In a similar way, you can apply the @Autowired annotation to a type-safe collection. Spring can read the type information of this collection and auto-wire all the beans whose type is compatible.

```
package com.apress.springrecipes.sequence;

import org.springframework.beans.factory.annotation.Autowired;

public class SequenceGenerator {

    @Autowired
    private List<PrefixGenerator> prefixGenerators;
    ...
}
```

If Spring notices that the @Autowired annotation is applied to a type-safe java.util.Map with strings as the keys, it will add all the beans of the compatible type, with the bean names as the keys, to this map.

```
package com.apress.springrecipes.sequence;

import org.springframework.beans.factory.annotation.Autowired;

public class SequenceGenerator {

    @Autowired
    private Map<String, PrefixGenerator> prefixGenerators;
    ...
}
```

Auto-Wiring by Type with Qualifiers

By default, auto-wiring by type will not work when there is more than one bean with the compatible type in the IoC container. However, Spring allows you to specify a candidate bean by providing its name in the @Qualifier annotation.

```
package com.apress.springrecipes.sequence;

import org.springframework.beans.factory.annotation.Autowired;
import org.springframework.beans.factory.annotation.Qualifier;

public class SequenceGenerator {

    @Autowired
    @Qualifier("datePrefixGenerator")
    private PrefixGenerator prefixGenerator;
    ...
}
```

Once you've done so, Spring will attempt to find a bean with that name in the IoC container and wire it into the property.

```
<bean id="datePrefixGenerator"
class="com.apress.springrecipes.sequence.DatePrefixGenerator">
    <property name="pattern" value="yyyyMMdd" />
</bean>
```

The @Qualifier annotation can also be applied to a method argument for auto-wiring.

```
package com.apress.springrecipes.sequence;

import org.springframework.beans.factory.annotation.Autowired;
import org.springframework.beans.factory.annotation.Qualifier;

public class SequenceGenerator {
    ...
    @Autowired
    public void inject(
            @Qualifier("datePrefixGenerator") PrefixGenerator prefixGenerator) {
        this.prefixGenerator = prefixGenerator;
    }
}
```

You can create a custom qualifier annotation type for the auto-wiring purpose. This annotation type must be annotated with @Qualifier itself. This is useful if you want a specific type of bean and configuration injected wherever an annotation decorates a field or setter method.

```
package com.apress.springrecipes.sequence;
import java.lang.annotation.Target;
import java.lang.annotation.Retention;
import java.lang.annotation.ElementType;
import java.lang.annotation.RetentionPolicy;import
org.springframework.beans.factory.annotation.Qualifier;

@Retention(RetentionPolicy.RUNTIME)
@Target({ElementType.FIELD, ElementType.PARAMETER })
@Qualifier
```

```
public @interface Generator {

    String value();
}
```

Then, you can apply this annotation to an @Autowired bean property. It will ask Spring to auto-wire the bean with this qualifier annotation and the specified value.

```
package com.apress.springrecipes.sequence;

import org.springframework.beans.factory.annotation.Autowired;

public class SequenceGenerator {

    @Autowired
    @Generator("prefix")
    private PrefixGenerator prefixGenerator;
    ...
}
```

You have to provide this qualifier to the target bean that you want to be auto-wired into the preceding property. The qualifier is added by the <qualifier> element with the type attribute. The qualifier value is specified in the value attribute. The value attribute is mapped to the String value() attribute of the annotation.

```
<bean id="datePrefixGenerator"
    class="com.apress.springrecipes.sequence.DatePrefixGenerator">
    <qualifier type="Generator" value="prefix" />
    <property name="pattern" value="yyyyMMdd" />
</bean>
```

Auto-Wiring by Name

If you want to auto-wire bean properties by name, you can annotate a setter method, a constructor, or a field with the JSR-250 @Resource annotation. By default, Spring will attempt to find a bean with the same name as this property. But you can specify the bean name explicitly in its name attribute.

▓ **Note** To use the JSR-250 annotations, you have to include the JSR 250 dependency. If you are using Maven, add:

```
<dependency>
  <groupId>javax.annotation</groupId>
  <artifactId>jsr250-api</artifactId>
  <version>1.0</version>
</dependency>
```

```
package com.apress.springrecipes.sequence;

import javax.annotation.Resource;

public class SequenceGenerator {

    @Resource(name = "datePrefixGenerator")
    private PrefixGenerator prefixGenerator;
    ...
}
```

1-13. Inheriting Bean Configuration

Problem

When configuring beans in the Spring IoC container, you may have more than one bean sharing some common configurations, such as bean properties and attributes in the <bean> element. You often have to repeat these configurations for multiple beans.

Solution

Spring allows you to extract the common bean configurations to form a *parent bean*. The beans that inherit from this parent bean are called *child beans*. The child beans will inherit the bean configurations, including bean properties and attributes in the <bean> element, from the parent bean to avoid duplicate configurations. The child beans can also override the inherited configurations when necessary.

The parent bean can act as a configuration template and also as a bean instance at the same time. However, if you want the parent bean to act only as a template that cannot be retrieved, you must set the abstract attribute to true, asking Spring not to instantiate this bean.

You must note that not all attributes defined in the parent <bean> element will be inherited. For example, the autowire and dependency-check attributes will not be inherited from the parent. To find out more about which attributes will be inherited from the parent and which won't, please refer to the Spring documentation about bean inheritance.

How It Works

Suppose you need to add a new sequence generator instance whose initial value and suffix are the same as the existing ones.

```
<beans ...>
    <bean id="sequenceGenerator"
        class="com.apress.springrecipes.sequence.SequenceGenerator">
        <property name="initial" value="100000" />
        <property name="suffix" value="A" />
        <property name="prefixGenerator" ref="datePrefixGenerator" />
    </bean>

    <bean id="sequenceGenerator1"
        class="com.apress.springrecipes.sequence.SequenceGenerator">
        <property name="initial" value="100000" />
        <property name="suffix" value="A" />
        <property name="prefixGenerator" ref="datePrefixGenerator" />
    </bean>

    <bean id="datePrefixGenerator"
        class="com.apress.springrecipes.sequence.DatePrefixGenerator">
        <property name="pattern" value="yyyyMMdd" />
    </bean>
</beans>
```

To avoid duplicating the same properties, you can declare a base sequence generator bean with those properties set. Then the two sequence generators can inherit this base generator so that they also have those properties set automatically. You needn't specify the `class` attributes of the child beans if they are the same as the parent's.

```
<beans ...>
    <bean id="baseSequenceGenerator"
        class="com.apress.springrecipes.sequence.SequenceGenerator">
        <property name="initial" value="100000" />
        <property name="suffix" value="A" />
        <property name="prefixGenerator" ref="datePrefixGenerator" />
    </bean>

    <bean id="sequenceGenerator" parent="baseSequenceGenerator" />

    <bean id="sequenceGenerator1" parent="baseSequenceGenerator" />
    ...
</beans>
```

The inherited properties can be overridden by the child beans. For example, you can add a child sequence generator with a different initial value.

```
<beans ...>
    <bean id="baseSequenceGenerator"
        class="com.apress.springrecipes.sequence.SequenceGenerator">
        <property name="initial" value="100000" />
```

```
        <property name="suffix" value="A" />
        <property name="prefixGenerator" ref="datePrefixGenerator" />
    </bean>

    <bean id="sequenceGenerator2" parent="baseSequenceGenerator">
        <property name="initial" value="200000" />
    </bean>
    ...
</beans>
```

The base sequence generator bean can now be retrieved as a bean instance to use. If you want it to act as a template only, you have to set the abstract attribute to true. Then Spring will not instantiate this bean.

```
<bean id="baseSequenceGenerator" abstract="true"
    class="com.apress.springrecipes.sequence.SequenceGenerator">
    ...
</bean>
```

You can also omit the class of the parent bean and let the child beans specify their own, especially when the parent bean and child beans are not in the same class hierarchy, but share some properties of the same name. In this case, the parent bean's abstract attribute must be set to true, as the parent bean can't be instantiated. For example, let's add another ReverseGenerator class that has an initial property also.

```
package com.apress.springrecipes.sequence;

public class ReverseGenerator {

    private int initial;

    public void setInitial(int initial) {
        this.initial = initial;
    }
}
```

Now SequenceGenerator and ReverseGenerator don't extend the same base class—that is, they're not in the same class hierarchy, but they have a property of the same name: initial. To extract this common initial property, you need a baseGenerator parent bean with no class attribute defined.

```
<beans ...>
    <bean id="baseGenerator" abstract="true">
        <property name="initial" value="100000" />
    </bean>

    <bean id="baseSequenceGenerator" abstract="true" parent="baseGenerator"
        class="com.apress.springrecipes.sequence.SequenceGenerator">
        <property name="suffix" value="A" />
        <property name="prefixGenerator" ref="datePrefixGenerator" />
    </bean>

    <bean id="reverseGenerator" parent="baseGenerator"
        class="com.apress.springrecipes.sequence.ReverseGenerator" />

    <bean id="sequenceGenerator" parent="baseSequenceGenerator" />

    <bean id="sequenceGenerator1" parent="baseSequenceGenerator" />

    <bean id="sequenceGenerator2" parent="baseSequenceGenerator"/>

    ...
</beans>
```

Figure 1-1 shows the object diagram for this generator bean hierarchy.

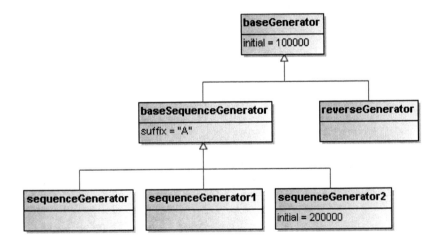

Figure 1-1. *Object diagram for the generator bean hierarchy*

1-14. Scanning Components from the Classpath

Problem

In order for the Spring IoC container to manage your components, you declare them one by one in the bean configuration file. However, it can save you a lot of work if Spring can automatically detect your components without manual configuration.

Solution

Spring provides a powerful feature called *component scanning*. It can automatically scan, detect, and instantiate your components with particular stereotype annotations from the classpath. The basic annotation denoting a Spring-managed component is @Component. Other more particular stereotypes include @Repository, @Service, and @Controller. They denote components in the persistence, service, and presentation layers, respectively.

How It Works

Suppose you are asked to develop your sequence generator application using database sequences and store the prefix and suffix of each sequence in a table. First, you create the domain class Sequence containing the id, prefix, and suffix properties.

```
package com.apress.springrecipes.sequence;

public class Sequence {

    private String id;
    private String prefix;
    private String suffix;

    // Constructors, Getters, and Setters
    ...
}
```

Then, you create an interface for the Data Access Object (DAO), which is responsible for accessing data from the database. The getSequence() method loads a Sequence object from the table by its ID, while the getNextValue() method retrieves the next value of a particular database sequence.

```
package com.apress.springrecipes.sequence;

public interface SequenceDao {

    public Sequence getSequence(String sequenceId);
    public int getNextValue(String sequenceId);
}
```

In a production application, you should implement this DAO interface using a data-access technology such as JDBC or object/relational mapping. But for testing purposes, let's use maps to store the sequence instances and values.

```
package com.apress.springrecipes.sequence;
...
public class SequenceDaoImpl implements SequenceDao {

    private Map<String, Sequence> sequences;
    private Map<String, Integer> values;

    public SequenceDaoImpl() {
        sequences = new HashMap<String, Sequence>();
        sequences.put("IT", new Sequence("IT", "30", "A"));
        values = new HashMap<String, Integer>();
        values.put("IT", 100000);
    }

    public Sequence getSequence(String sequenceId) {
        return sequences.get(sequenceId);
    }

    public synchronized int getNextValue(String sequenceId) {
        int value = values.get(sequenceId);
        values.put(sequenceId, value + 1);
        return value;
    }
}
```

You also need a service object, acting as a façade, to provide the sequence generation service. Internally, this service object will interact with the DAO to handle the sequence generation requests. So it requires a reference to the DAO.

```
package com.apress.springrecipes.sequence;

public class SequenceService {

    private SequenceDao sequenceDao;

    public void setSequenceDao(SequenceDao sequenceDao) {
        this.sequenceDao = sequenceDao;
    }

    public String generate(String sequenceId) {
        Sequence sequence = sequenceDao.getSequence(sequenceId);
        int value = sequenceDao.getNextValue(sequenceId);
        return sequence.getPrefix() + value + sequence.getSuffix();
    }
}
```

Finally, you have to configure these components in the bean configuration file to make the sequence generator application work. You can auto-wire your components to reduce the amount of configurations.

```
<beans ...>
    <bean id="sequenceService"
        class="com.apress.springrecipes.sequence.SequenceService"
        autowire="byType" />

    <bean id="sequenceDao"
        class="com.apress.springrecipes.sequence.SequenceDaoImpl" />
</beans>
```

Then, you can test the preceding components with the following Main class:

```
package com.apress.springrecipes.sequence;

import org.springframework.context.ApplicationContext;
import org.springframework.context.support.ClassPathXmlApplicationContext;

public class Main {

    public static void main(String[] args) {
        ApplicationContext context =
            new ClassPathXmlApplicationContext("beans.xml");

        SequenceService sequenceService =
            (SequenceService) context.getBean("sequenceService");

        System.out.println(sequenceService.generate("IT"));
        System.out.println(sequenceService.generate("IT"));
    }
}
```

Scanning Components Automatically

The component scanning feature provided by Spring since version 2.5 can automatically scan, detect, and instantiate your components from the classpath. By default, Spring can detect all components with a stereotype annotation. The basic annotation type that denotes a Spring-managed component is @Component. You can apply it to your SequenceDaoImpl class.

```
package com.apress.springrecipes.sequence;

import org.springframework.stereotype.Component;
import java.util.Map;

@Component
public class SequenceDaoImpl implements SequenceDao {
    ...
}
```

Also, you apply this stereotype annotation to the SequenceService class for Spring to detect it. In addition, you apply the @Autowired annotation to the DAO field for Spring to auto-wire it by type. Note that because you're using the annotation on a field, you don't need a setter method here.

```
package com.apress.springrecipes.sequence;

import org.springframework.beans.factory.annotation.Autowired;
import org.springframework.stereotype.Component;

@Component
public class SequenceService {

    @Autowired
    private SequenceDao sequenceDao;
    ...
}
```

With the stereotype annotations applied to your component classes, you can ask Spring to scan them by declaring a single XML element: <context:component-scan>. In this element, you need to specify the package for scanning your components. Then the specified package and all its subpackages will be scanned. You can use commas to separate multiple packages for scanning.

The previous stereotype is enough to be able to use the bean. Spring will give the bean a name created by lowercasing the first character of the class and using the rest of the camel-cased name for the bean name. Thus, the following works (assuming that you've instantiated an application context containing the <context:component-scan> element).

```
SequenceService sequenceService = (SequenceService) context.getBean("sequenceService");
```

Note that this element will also register an AutowiredAnnotationBeanPostProcessor instance that can auto-wire properties with the @Autowired annotation.

```
<beans xmlns="http://www.springframework.org/schema/beans"
    xmlns:xsi="http://www.w3.org/2001/XMLSchema-instance"
    xmlns:context="http://www.springframework.org/schema/context"
    xsi:schemaLocation="http://www.springframework.org/schema/beans
        http://www.springframework.org/schema/beans/spring-beans-3.0.xsd
        http://www.springframework.org/schema/context
        http://www.springframework.org/schema/context/spring-context-3.0.xsd">

    <context:component-scan base-package="com.apress.springrecipes.sequence" />
</beans>
```

The @Component annotation is the basic stereotype for denoting components of general purposes. Actually, there are other specific stereotypes denoting components in different layers. First, the @Repository stereotype denotes a DAO component in the persistence layer.

```
package com.apress.springrecipes.sequence;

import org.springframework.stereotype.Repository;

@Repository
public class SequenceDaoImpl implements SequenceDao {
    ...
}
```

Then, the @Service stereotype denotes a service component in the service layer.

```
package com.apress.springrecipes.sequence;

import org.springframework.beans.factory.annotation.Autowired;
import org.springframework.stereotype.Service;

@Service
public class SequenceService {

    @Autowired
    private SequenceDao sequenceDao;
    ...
}
```

There's another component stereotype, @Controller, denoting a controller component in the presentation layer. It will be introduced in Chapter 8, "Spring @MVC."

Filtering Components to Scan

By default, Spring will detect all classes annotated with @Component, @Repository, @Service, @Controller, or your custom annotation type that is itself annotated with @Component. You can customize the scan by applying one or more include/exclude filters.

Spring supports four types of filter expressions. The annotation and assignable types are for you to specify an annotation type and a class/interface for filtering. The regex and aspectj types allow you to specify a regular expression and an AspectJ pointcut expression for matching the classes. You can also disable the default filters with the use-default-filters attribute.

For example, the following component scan includes all classes whose name contains the word Dao or Service, and excludes the classes with the @Controller annotation:

```
<beans ...>
    <context:component-scan base-package="com.apress.springrecipes.sequence">
        <context:include-filter type="regex"
            expression="com\.apress\.springrecipes\.sequence\..*Dao.*" />
        <context:include-filter type="regex"
            expression="com\.apress\.springrecipes\.sequence\..*Service.*" />
```

```
            <context:exclude-filter type="annotation"
                expression="org.springframework.stereotype.Controller" />
    </context:component-scan>
</beans>
```

Because you have applied `include` filters to detect all classes whose name contains the word `Dao` or `Service`, the `SequenceDaoImpl` and `SequenceService` components can be auto-detected even without a stereotype annotation.

Naming Detected Components

By default, Spring will name the detected components by lowercasing the first character of the nonqualified class name. For example, the `SequenceService` class will be named as `sequenceService`. You can define the name for a component explicitly by specifying it in the stereotype annotation's value.

```
package com.apress.springrecipes.sequence;
...
import org.springframework.stereotype.Service;

@Service("sequenceService")
public class SequenceService {
    ...
}

package com.apress.springrecipes.sequence;

import org.springframework.stereotype.Repository;

@Repository("sequenceDao")
public class SequenceDaoImpl implements SequenceDao {
    ...
}
```

You can develop your own naming strategy by implementing the `BeanNameGenerator` interface and specifying it in the `name-generator` attribute of the `<context:component-scan>` element.

Summary

In this chapter, you have learned the basic bean configuration in the Spring IoC container. Spring supports several types of bean configuration. Among them, XML is simplest and most mature. Spring provides two types of IoC container implementation. The basic one is the bean factory, while the advanced one is the application context. If possible, you should use the application context unless resources are restricted. Spring supports both setter injection and constructor injection for defining bean properties, which can be simple values, collections, or bean references.

Dependency checking and auto-wiring are two valuable container features provided by Spring. Dependency checking helps to check if all required properties are set, while auto-wiring can wire your beans automatically either by type, name, or annotation. The old style of configuring these two features is by XML attributes, while the new style is by annotations and bean post processors, which allow greater flexibility.

Spring provides support for bean inheritance by extracting the common bean configurations to form a parent bean. The parent bean can act as a configuration template, a bean instance, or both at the same time.

As collections are essential programming elements of Java, Spring provides various collection tags for you to configure collections in the bean configuration file easily. You can use the collection factory beans or the collection tags in the utility schema to specify more details for a collection, and also define collections as stand-alone beans to share between multiple beans.

Finally, Spring can auto-detect your components from the classpath. By default, it can detect all components with particular stereotype annotations. But you can further include or exclude your components with filters. Component scanning is a powerful feature that can reduce the amount of configurations.

■ ■ ■

CHAPTER 2

Advanced Spring IoC Container

In this chapter, you will learn the advanced features and internal mechanisms of the Spring IoC container, which can help you to increase your efficiency when developing Spring applications. Although these features may not be used very often, they are indispensable to a comprehensive and powerful container. They are also the foundation of other modules of the Spring framework.

The Spring IoC container itself is designed to be easily customizable and extensible. It allows you to customize the default container behaviors through configuration and extend the container's features by registering your container plug-ins that conform to the container specification.

After finishing this chapter, you will be familiar with most features of the Spring IoC container. This will give you a useful basis for learning about different topics of Spring in the subsequent chapters.

2-1. Creating Beans by Invoking a Static Factory Method

Problem

You would like to create a bean in the Spring IoC container by invoking a *static factory method*, whose purpose is to encapsulate the object-creation process in a static method. The client who requests an object can simply make a call to this method without knowing about the creation detail.

Solution

Spring supports creating a bean by invoking a static factory method, which should be specified in the `factory-method` attribute.

How It Works

For example, you can write the following `createProduct()` static factory method to create a product from a predefined product ID. According to the product ID, this method will decide which concrete product class to instantiate. If there is no product matching this ID, it will throw an `IllegalArgumentException`.

```
package com.apress.springrecipes.shop;

public class ProductCreator {

    public static Product createProduct(String productId) {
        if ("aaa".equals(productId)) {
            return new Battery("AAA", 2.5);
        } else if ("cdrw".equals(productId)) {
            return new Disc("CD-RW", 1.5);
        }
        throw new IllegalArgumentException("Unknown product");
    }
}
```

To declare a bean created by a static factory method, you specify the class hosting the factory method in the class attribute and the factory method's name in the factory-method attribute. Finally, you pass the method arguments by using the <constructor-arg> elements.

```
<beans ...>
    <bean id="aaa" class="com.apress.springrecipes.shop.ProductCreator"
        factory-method="createProduct">
        <constructor-arg value="aaa" />
    </bean>

    <bean id="cdrw" class="com.apress.springrecipes.shop.ProductCreator"
        factory-method="createProduct">
        <constructor-arg value="cdrw" />
    </bean>
</beans>
```

In case of any exception thrown by the factory method, Spring will wrap it with a BeanCreationException. The equivalent code snippet for the preceding bean configuration is shown following:

```
Product aaa = ProductCreator.createProduct("aaa");
Product cdrw = ProductCreator.createProduct("cdrw");
```

2-2. Creating Beans by Invoking an Instance Factory Method

Problem

You would like to create a bean in the Spring IoC container by invoking an *instance factory method*, whose purpose is to encapsulate the object-creation process in a method of another object instance. The client who requests an object can simply make a call to this method without knowing about the creation detail.

Solution

Spring supports creating a bean by invoking an instance factory method. The bean instance should be specified in the factory-bean attribute, while the factory method should be specified in the factory-method attribute.

How It Works

For example, you can write the following ProductCreator class by using a configurable map to store the predefined products. The createProduct() instance factory method finds a product by looking up the supplied productId in the map. If there is no product matching this ID, it will throw an IllegalArgumentException.

```
package com.apress.springrecipes.shop;
...
public class ProductCreator {

    private Map<String, Product> products;

    public void setProducts(Map<String, Product> products) {
        this.products = products;
    }

    public Product createProduct(String productId) {
        Product product = products.get(productId);
        if (product != null) {
            return product;
        }
        throw new IllegalArgumentException("Unknown product");
    }
}
```

To create products from this ProductCreator class, you first have to declare an instance of it in the IoC container and configure its product map. You may declare the products in the map as inner beans. To declare a bean created by an instance factory method, you specify the bean hosting the factory method in the factory-bean attribute, and the factory method's name in the factory-method attribute. Finally, you pass the method arguments by using the <constructor-arg> elements.

```
<beans ...>
    <bean id="productCreator"
        class="com.apress.springrecipes.shop.ProductCreator">
        <property name="products">
            <map>
                <entry key="aaa">
                    <bean class="com.apress.springrecipes.shop.Battery">
                        <property name="name" value="AAA" />
                        <property name="price" value="2.5" />
                    </bean>
                </entry>
                <entry key="cdrw">
```

```xml
                    <bean class="com.apress.springrecipes.shop.Disc">
                        <property name="name" value="CD-RW" />
                        <property name="price" value="1.5" />
                    </bean>
                </entry>
            </map>
        </property>
    </bean>

    <bean id="aaa" factory-bean="productCreator"
        factory-method="createProduct">
        <constructor-arg value="aaa" />
    </bean>

    <bean id="cdrw" factory-bean="productCreator"
        factory-method="createProduct">
        <constructor-arg value="cdrw" />
    </bean>
</beans>
```

If any exception is thrown by the factory method, Spring will wrap it with a BeanCreationException. The equivalent code snippet for the preceding bean configuration is shown following:

```java
ProductCreator productCreator = new ProductCreator();
productCreator.setProducts(...);

Product aaa = productCreator.createProduct("aaa");
Product cdrw = productCreator.createProduct("cdrw");
```

2-3. Declaring Beans from Static Fields

Problem

You would like to declare a bean in the Spring IoC container from a static field. In Java, constant values are often declared as static fields.

Solution

To declare a bean from a static field, you can make use of either the built-in factory bean FieldRetrievingFactoryBean, or the <util:contant> tag in Spring 2.x.

How It Works

First, let's define two product constants in the Product class.

```
package com.apress.springrecipes.shop;

public abstract class Product {

    public static final Product AAA = new Battery("AAA", 2.5);
    public static final Product CDRW = new Disc("CD-RW", 1.5);
    ...
}
```

To declare a bean from a static field, you can make use of the built-in factory bean
FieldRetrievingFactoryBean and specify the fully qualified field name in the staticField property.

```
<beans ...>
    <bean id="aaa" class="org.springframework.beans.factory.config.↵
        FieldRetrievingFactoryBean">
        <property name="staticField">
            <value>com.apress.springrecipes.shop.Product.AAA</value>
        </property>
    </bean>

    <bean id="cdrw" class="org.springframework.beans.factory.config.↵
        FieldRetrievingFactoryBean">
        <property name="staticField">
            <value>com.apress.springrecipes.shop.Product.CDRW</value>
        </property>
    </bean>
</beans>
```

The preceding bean configuration is equivalent to the following code snippet:

```
Product aaa = com.apress.springrecipes.shop.Product.AAA;
Product cdrw = com.apress.springrecipes.shop.Product.CDRW;
```

As an alternative to specifying the field name in the staticField property explicitly, you can set it as
the bean name of FieldRetrievingFactoryBean. The downside is that your bean name may get rather
long and verbose.

```
<beans ...>
    <bean id="com.apress.springrecipes.shop.Product.AAA"
        class="org.springframework.beans.factory.config.↵
            FieldRetrievingFactoryBean" />

    <bean id="com.apress.springrecipes.shop.Product.CDRW"
        class="org.springframework.beans.factory.config.↵
            FieldRetrievingFactoryBean" />
</beans>
```

Spring 2 and later allow you to declare a bean from a static field by using the <util:constant> tag.
Compared to using FieldRetrievingFactoryBean, it is a simpler way of declaring beans from static fields.
But before this tag can work, you must add the util schema definition to your <beans> root element.

```
<beans xmlns="http://www.springframework.org/schema/beans"
    xmlns:xsi="http://www.w3.org/2001/XMLSchema-instance"
    xmlns:util="http://www.springframework.org/schema/util"
    xsi:schemaLocation="http://www.springframework.org/schema/beans
        http://www.springframework.org/schema/beans/spring-beans-3.0.xsd
        http://www.springframework.org/schema/util
        http://www.springframework.org/schema/util/spring-util-3.0.xsd">

    <util:constant id="aaa"
        static-field="com.apress.springrecipes.shop.Product.AAA" />

    <util:constant id="cdrw"
        static-field="com.apress.springrecipes.shop.Product.CDRW" />
</beans>
```

2-4. Declaring Beans from Object Properties

Problem

You would like to declare a bean in the Spring IoC container from an object property or a nested property (i.e., a property path).

Solution

To declare a bean from an object property or a property path, you can make use of either the built-in factory bean PropertyPathFactoryBean or the <util:property-path> tag in Spring 2.x.

How It Works

As an example, let's create a ProductRanking class with a bestSeller property whose type is Product.

```
package com.apress.springrecipes.shop;

public class ProductRanking {

    private Product bestSeller;

    public Product getBestSeller() {
        return bestSeller;
    }

    public void setBestSeller(Product bestSeller) {
        this.bestSeller = bestSeller;
    }
}
```

In the following bean declaration, the bestSeller property is declared by an inner bean. By definition, you cannot retrieve an inner bean by its name. However, you can retrieve it as a property of the productRanking bean. The factory bean PropertyPathFactoryBean can be used to declare a bean from an object property or a property path.

```
<beans ...>
    <bean id="productRanking"
        class="com.apress.springrecipes.shop.ProductRanking">
        <property name="bestSeller">
            <bean class="com.apress.springrecipes.shop.Disc">
                <property name="name" value="CD-RW" />
                <property name="price" value="1.5" />
            </bean>
        </property>
    </bean>

    <bean id="bestSeller"
        class="org.springframework.beans.factory.config.PropertyPathFactoryBean">
        <property name="targetObject" ref="productRanking" />
        <property name="propertyPath" value="bestSeller" />
    </bean>
</beans>
```

Note that the propertyPath property of PropertyPathFactoryBean can accept not only a single property name but also a property path with dots as the separators. The preceding bean configuration is equivalent to the following code snippet:

```
Product bestSeller = productRanking.getBestSeller();
```

In addition to specifying the targetObject and propertyPath properties explicitly, you can combine them as the bean name of PropertyPathFactoryBean. The downside is that your bean name may get rather long and verbose.

```
<bean id="productRanking.bestSeller"
    class="org.springframework.beans.factory.config.PropertyPathFactoryBean" />
```

Spring 2.x allows you to declare a bean from an object property or a property path by using the <util:property-path> tag. Compared to using PropertyPathFactoryBean, it is a simpler way of declaring beans from properties. But before this tag can work, you must add the util schema definition to your <beans> root element.

```
<beans xmlns="http://www.springframework.org/schema/beans"
    xmlns:xsi="http://www.w3.org/2001/XMLSchema-instance"
    xmlns:util="http://www.springframework.org/schema/util"
    xsi:schemaLocation="http://www.springframework.org/schema/beans
        http://www.springframework.org/schema/beans/spring-beans-3.0.xsd
        http://www.springframework.org/schema/util
        http://www.springframework.org/schema/util/spring-util-3.0.xsd">
    ...
    <util:property-path id="bestSeller" path="productRanking.bestSeller" />
</beans>
```

You can test this property path by retrieving it from the IoC container and printing it to the console.

```
package com.apress.springrecipes.shop;
...
public class Main {

    public static void main(String[] args) throws Exception {
        ...
        Product bestSeller = (Product) context.getBean("bestSeller");
        System.out.println(bestSeller);
    }
}
```

2-5. Using the Spring Expression Language

Problem

You want to dynamically evaluate some condition or property and use it as the value configured in the IoC container. Or perhaps you need to defer evaluation of something not at design time but at runtime, as might be the case in a custom scope. Or you just need a way to add a strong expression language to your own application.

Solution

Use Spring 3.0's Spring Expression Language (SpEL), which provides functionality similar to the Unified EL from JSF and JSP, or Object Graph Navigation Language (OGNL). SpEL provides easy-to-use infrastructure that can be leveraged outside of the Spring container. Within the container, it can be used to make configuration much easier in a lot of cases.

How It Works

Today, there are many different types of expression languages in the enterprise space. If you use WebWork/Struts 2 or Tapestry 4, you've no doubt used the OGNL. If you've used JSP or JSF in recent years, you've used one or both of the expression languages that are available in those environments. If you've used JBoss Seam, you've used the expression language made available there, which is a superset of the standard expression language shipped with JSF (Unified EL).

The expression language draws its heritage from many places. Certainly, it is a superset of what's available via the Unified EL. Spring.NET has had a similar expression language for awhile, and the feedback has been very favorable. The need to evaluate certain expressions at arbitrary points in a life cycle, such as during a scoped beans initialization, contributed to some of the qualities of this expression language.

Some of these expression languages are very powerful, bordering on being scripting languages in their own right. The SpEL is no different. It's available almost everywhere you can imagine needing it from annotations to XML configuration. The SpringSource Tool Suite also provides robust support for the expression language in the way of auto-completion and lookup.

Features of the Language Syntax

The expression language supports a long list of features. Table 2-1 briefly runs through the various constructs and demonstrates their usage.

Table 2-1. *Expression Language Features*

Type	Use	Example

Literal expression	The simplest thing you can do in the expression language, essentially the same as if you were writing Java code. The language supports `String` literals as well as all sorts of numbers.	`2342`
		
		`'Hello Spring Enterprise Recipes'`

Boolean and relational operator	The expression language provides the ability to evaluate conditionals using standard idioms from Java.	`T(java.lang.Math).random()`↵ `> .5`
Standard expression	You can iterate and return the properties on beans in the same way you might with Unified EL, separating each dereferenced property with a period and using JavaBean-style naming conventions. In the example to the right, the expression would be equivalent to `getCat().getMate().getName()`.	`cat.mate.name`

Class expression	`T()` tells the expression language to act on the type of the class, not an instance. In the examples on the right, the first would yield the `Class` instance for `java.lang.Math`—equivalent to calling `java.lang.Math.class`. The second example calls a static method on a given type. Thus, `T(java.lang.Math).random()` is equivalent to calling `java.lang.Math.random()`.	`T(java.lang.Math)`
		
		`T(java.lang.Math).random()`

Accessing arrays, lists, maps	You can index lists, arrays, and maps using brackets and the key—which for arrays or lists is the index number, and for maps is an object. In the examples, you see a `java.util.List` with four chars being indexed at index 1, which returns `'b'`. The second example demonstrates accessing a map by the index `'OR'`, yielding the value associated with that key.	`T(java.util.Arrays).asList(` ↵
		`'a','b','c','d')[1]`
		
		`T(SpelExamplesDemo)`↵
		`.MapOfStatesAndCapitals['OR']`

Method invocation	Methods may be invoked in instances just as you would in Java. This is a marked improvement over the basic JSF or JSP expression languages.	`'Hello, World'.toLowerCase()`

Continued

Type	Use	Example

Relational operators	You can compare or equate values, and the returned value will be a Boolean.	`23 == person.age`
		
		`'fala' < 'fido'`

Calling constructor	You can create objects and invoke their constructors. Here, you create simple `String` and `Cat` objects.	`new String('Hello Spring↵ Enterprise Recipes, again!')`
		
		`new Cat('Felix')`

Ternary operator	Ternary expressions work as you'd expect, yielding the value in the true case.	`T(java.lang.Math).random() >↵ .5 ? 'She loves me' : 'She↵ loves me not'`

Variable	The SpEL lets you set and evaluate variables. The variables can be installed by the context of the expression parser, and there are some implicit variables, such as #this, which always refer to the root object of the context.	`#this.firstName`
		
		`#customer.email`

Collection projection	A very powerful feature inside of SpEL is the capability to perform very sophisticated manipulations of maps and collections. Here, you create a projection for the list cats. In this example, the returned value is a collection of as many elements being iterated that has the value for the name property on each cat in the collection. In this case, cats is a collection of `Cat` objects. The returned value is a collection of `String` objects.	`cats.![name]`
Collection selection	Selection lets you dynamically filter objects from a collection or map by evaluating a predicate on each item in the collection and keeping only those elements for which the predicate is true. In this case, you evaluate the `java.util.Map.Entry.value` property for each `Entry` in the `Map` and if the value (in this case a `String`), lowercased, starts with "s", then it is kept. Everything else is discarded.	`mapOfStatesAndCapitals.?↵ [value.toLowerCase().↵ startsWith('s')]`
Templated expression	You can use the expression language to evaluate expressions inside of string expressions. The result is returned. In this case, the result is dynamically created by evaluating the ternary expression and including `'good'` or `'bad'` based on the result.	`Your fortune is ${T(java↵ .lang.Math).random()> .5 ?↵ 'good' : 'bad'}`

Uses of the Language in Your Configurations

The expression language is available via XML or annotations. The expressions are evaluated at creation time for the bean, not at the initialization of the context. This has the effect that beans created in a custom scope are not configured until the bean is in the appropriate scope. You can use them in the same way via XML or annotations.

The first example is the injection of a named expression language variable, systemProperties, which is just a special variable for the java.util.Properties instance that's available from System.getProperties(). The next example shows the injection of a system property itself directly into a String variable:

```
@Value("#{ systemProperties }")
private Properties systemProperties;

@Value("#{ systemProperties['user.region'] }")
private String userRegion;
```

You can also inject the result of computations or method invocations. Here, you're injecting the value of a computation directly into a variable:

```
@Value("#{ T(java.lang.Math).random() * 100.0 }")
private double randomNumber;
```

The next examples assume that another bean is configured in the context with the name emailUtilities. The bean, in turn, has JavaBean-style properties that are injected into the following fields:

```
@Value("#{ emailUtilities.email }")
private String email;

@Value("#{ emailUtilities.password }")
private String password;

@Value("#{ emailUtilities.host}")
private String host;
```

You can also use the expression language to inject references to other named beans in the same context:

```
@Value("#{ emailUtilities }")
private EmailUtilities emailUtilities ;
```

In this case, because there's only one bean in the context with the interface EmailUtilities, you could also do this:

```
@Autowired
private EmailUtilities emailUtilities ;
```

Although there are other mechanisms for discriminating against beans of the same interface, the expression language becomes very handy here, because it lets you simply discriminate by bean id.

You can use the expression language in your XML configurations in exactly the same way as with the annotation support. Even the prefix #{ and the suffix } are the same.

```
<bean class="com.apress.springrecipes.spring3. spel.EmailNotificationEngine"
 p:randomNumber="#{  T(java.lang.Math).random() * 100.0 }"
 …
/>
```

Using the Spring Expression Language Parser

The SpEL is used primarily inside the XML configuration and annotation support provided with the Spring framework, but you're free to use the expression language. The centerpiece of the functionality is provided by the expression parser, `org.springframework.expression.spel.antlr.`
`SpelAntlrExpressionParser`, which you can instantiate directly:

```
ExpressionParser parser = new SpelAntlrExpressionParser();
```

Conceivably, you could build an implementation that complies with the ExpressionParser interface and builds your own integration using this API. This interface is central for evaluating expressions written using the SpEL. The simplest evaluation might look like this:

```
Expression exp = parser.parseExpression("'ceci n''est pas une String'" );
String val = exp.getValue(String.class);
```

Here, you evaluate the String literal (notice that you're escaping the single quote with another single quote, not with a backslash) and return the result. The call to getValue() is generic, based on the type of the parameter, so you don't need to cast.

A common scenario is evaluation of expressions against an object. The properties and methods of the object no longer require an instance or class and can be manipulated independently. The SpEL parser refers to it as the *root object*. Let's take an object named SocialNetworkingSiteContext, for example, which, in turn, has other attributes you want to traverse to iterate over the members of the site:

```
SocialNetworkingSiteContext socialNetworkingSiteContext = ↩
    new SocialNetworkingSiteContext();
// … ensure it's properly initialized ...
Expression firstNameExpression = parser.parseExpression("loggedInUser.firstName");
StandardEvaluationContext ctx = new StandardEvaluationContext();
ctx.setRootObject(socialNetworkingSiteContext);
String valueOfLoggedInUserFirstName = firstNameExpression.getValue(ctx, String.class );
```

Because you set the socialNetworkingSiteContext as the root, you could enumerate any child property without qualifying the reference.

Suppose that, instead of specifying a root object, you want to specify a named variable and be able to access it from within your expression. The SpEL parser lets you provide it with variables against which expressions can be evaluated. In the following example, you provide it with a socialNetworkingSiteContext variable. Inside the expression, the variable is prefixed with a "#":

```
StandardEvaluationContext ctx1 = new StandardEvaluationContext ();
SocialNetworkingSiteContext socialNetworkingSiteContext =
        new SocialNetworkingSiteContext();
Friend myFriend = new Friend() ;
myFriend.setFirstName("Manuel");
socialNetworkingSiteContext.setLoggedInUser(myFriend);
ctx1.setVariable("socialNetworkingSiteContext",socialNetworkingSiteContext );
Expression loggedInUserFirstNameExpression =
parser.parseExpression("#socialNetworkingSiteContext.loggedInUser.firstName");
String loggedInUserFirstName = loggedInUserFirstNameExpression.getValue↵
    (ctx1, String.class);
```

Similarly, you can provide the expression language named functions that are available without any qualification inside an expression:

```
StandardEvaluationContext ctx1 = new StandardEvaluationContext();
ctx1.registerFunction("empty", StringUtils.class.getDeclaredMethod(
"isEmpty", new Class[] { String.class }));
Expression functionEval =  parser.parseExpression(
" #empty(null) ? 'empty' : 'not empty' ");
String result = functionEval.getValue(ctx1, String.class );
```

You can use the expression language parser infrastructure to template Strings. The returned value is a String, although within the String, you can have the parser substitute the result of evaluated expressions. This could be useful in any number of scenarios, for example, in simple message preparation. You simply create an instance of org.springframework.expression.ParserContext. This class dictates to the parser which token is a prefix (the prefix token is "${") and which is a suffix (the suffix token is "}"). The following example yields "The millisecond is 1246953975093".

```
ParserContext pc = new ParserContext() {
   public String getExpressionPrefix() {
           return "${";
   }
   public String getExpressionSuffix() {
            return "}";
   }
   public boolean isTemplate() {
           return true;
   }
};

String templatedExample = parser.parseExpression(
    "The millisecond is ${  T(System).currentTimeMillis()  }.", pc).getValue(String.class);
```

2-6. Setting Bean Scopes

Problem

When you declare a bean in the configuration file, you are actually defining a template for bean creation, not an actual bean instance. When a bean is requested by the getBean() method or a reference from other beans, Spring will decide which bean instance should be returned according to the bean scope. Sometimes, you have to set an appropriate scope for a bean other than the default scope.

Solution

In Spring 2.x or later, a bean's scope is set in the scope attribute of the <bean> element. By default, Spring creates exactly one instance for each bean declared in the IoC container, and this instance will be shared in the scope of the entire IoC container. This unique bean instance will be returned for all subsequent getBean() calls and bean references. This scope is called singleton, which is the default scope of all beans. Table 2-2 lists all valid bean scopes in Spring.

Table 2-2. Valid Bean Scopes in Spring

Scope	Description
Singleton	Creates a single bean instance per Spring IoC container
Prototype	Creates a new bean instance each time when requested
Request	Creates a single bean instance per HTTP request; only valid in the context of a web application
Session	Creates a single bean instance per HTTP session; only valid in the context of a web application
GlobalSession	Creates a single bean instance per global HTTP session; only valid in the context of a portal application

In Spring 1.x, singleton and prototype are the only two valid bean scopes, and they are specified by the singleton attribute (i.e., singleton="true" or singleton="false"), not the scope attribute.

How It Works

To demonstrate the concept of bean scope, let's consider a shopping cart example in your shop application. First, you create the ShoppingCart class as follows:

```
package com.apress.springrecipes.shop;
...
public class ShoppingCart {

    private List<Product> items = new ArrayList<Product>();

    public void addItem(Product item) {
        items.add(item);
    }

    public List<Product> getItems() {
        return items;
    }
}
```

Then you declare some product beans and a shopping cart bean in the IoC container as usual:

```
<beans ...>
    <bean id="aaa" class="com.apress.springrecipes.shop.Battery">
        <property name="name" value="AAA" />
        <property name="price" value="2.5" />
    </bean>

    <bean id="cdrw" class="com.apress.springrecipes.shop.Disc">
        <property name="name" value="CD-RW" />
        <property name="price" value="1.5" />
    </bean>

    <bean id="dvdrw" class="com.apress.springrecipes.shop.Disc">
        <property name="name" value="DVD-RW" />
        <property name="price" value="3.0" />
    </bean>

    <bean id="shoppingCart" class="com.apress.springrecipes.shop.ShoppingCart" />
</beans>
```

In the following Main class, you can test your shopping cart by adding some products to it. Suppose that there are two customers navigating in your shop at the same time. The first one gets a shopping cart by the getBean() method and adds two products to it. Then, the second customer also gets a shopping cart by the getBean() method and adds another product to it.

```
package com.apress.springrecipes.shop;

import org.springframework.context.ApplicationContext;
import org.springframework.context.support.ClassPathXmlApplicationContext;

public class Main {
```

```
public static void main(String[] args) {
    ApplicationContext context =
        new ClassPathXmlApplicationContext("beans.xml");

    Product aaa = (Product) context.getBean("aaa");
    Product cdrw = (Product) context.getBean("cdrw");
    Product dvdrw = (Product) context.getBean("dvdrw");

    ShoppingCart cart1 = (ShoppingCart) context.getBean("shoppingCart");
    cart1.addItem(aaa);
    cart1.addItem(cdrw);
    System.out.println("Shopping cart 1 contains " + cart1.getItems());

    ShoppingCart cart2 = (ShoppingCart) context.getBean("shoppingCart");
    cart2.addItem(dvdrw);
    System.out.println("Shopping cart 2 contains " + cart2.getItems());
    }
}
```

As a result of the preceding bean declaration, you can see that the two customers get the same shopping cart instance.

```
Shopping cart 1 contains [AAA 2.5, CD-RW 1.5]

Shopping cart 2 contains [AAA 2.5, CD-RW 1.5, DVD-RW 3.0]
```

This is because Spring's default bean scope is singleton, which means Spring creates exactly one shopping cart instance per IoC container.

```
<bean id="shoppingCart"
    class="com.apress.springrecipes.shop.ShoppingCart"
    scope="singleton" />
```

In your shop application, you expect each customer to get a different shopping cart instance when the getBean() method is called. To ensure this behavior, you should change the scope of the shoppingCart bean to prototype. Then Spring will create a new bean instance for each getBean() method call and reference from the other bean.

```
<bean id="shoppingCart"
    class="com.apress.springrecipes.shop.ShoppingCart"
    scope="prototype" />
```

Now if you run the Main class again, you can see that the two customers get a different shopping cart instance.

```
Shopping cart 1 contains [AAA 2.5, CD-RW 1.5]

Shopping cart 2 contains [DVD-RW 3.0]
```

2-7. Customizing Bean Initialization and Destruction

Problem

Many real-world components have to perform certain types of initialization tasks before they are ready to be used. Such tasks include opening a file, opening a network/database connection, allocating memory, and so on. Also, they have to perform the corresponding destruction tasks at the end of their life cycle. So, you have a need to customize bean initialization and destruction in the Spring IoC container.

Solution

In addition to bean registration, the Spring IoC container is also responsible for managing the life cycle of your beans, and it allows you to perform custom tasks at particular points of their life cycle. Your tasks should be encapsulated in callback methods for the Spring IoC container to call at a suitable time.

The following list shows the steps through which the Spring IoC container manages the life cycle of a bean. This list will be expanded as more features of the IoC container are introduced.

1. Create the bean instance either by a constructor or by a factory method.

2. Set the values and bean references to the bean properties.

3. Call the initialization callback methods.

4. The bean is ready to be used.

5. When the container is shut down, call the destruction callback methods.

There are three ways that Spring can recognize your initialization and destruction callback methods. First, your bean can implement the `InitializingBean` and `DisposableBean` life cycle interfaces and implement the `afterPropertiesSet()` and `destroy()` methods for initialization and destruction. Second, you can set the `init-method` and `destroy-method` attributes in the bean declaration and specify the callback method names. In Spring 2.5 or later, you can also annotate the initialization and destruction callback methods with the life cycle annotations `@PostConstruct` and `@PreDestroy`, which are defined in JSR-250, Common Annotations for the Java Platform. Then you can register a `CommonAnnotationBeanPostProcessor` instance in the IoC container to call these callback methods.

How It Works

To understand how the Spring IoC container manages the life cycle of your beans, let's consider an example involving the checkout function. The following `Cashier` class can be used to check out the products in a shopping cart. It records the time and the amount of each checkout in a text file.

```
package com.apress.springrecipes.shop;
```

```
...
public class Cashier {

    private String name;
    private String path;
    private BufferedWriter writer;

    public void setName(String name) {
        this.name = name;
    }

    public void setPath(String path) {
        this.path = path;
    }

    public void openFile() throws IOException {
        File logFile = new File(path, name + ".txt");
        writer = new BufferedWriter(new OutputStreamWriter(
                new FileOutputStream(logFile, true)));
    }

    public void checkout(ShoppingCart cart) throws IOException {
        double total = 0;
        for (Product product : cart.getItems()) {
            total += product.getPrice();
        }
        writer.write(new Date() + "\t" + total + "\r\n");
        writer.flush();
    }

    public void closeFile() throws IOException {
        writer.close();
    }
}
```

In the Cashier class, the openFile() method opens the text file with the cashier name as the file name in the specified system path. Each time you call the checkout() method, a checkout record will be appended to the text file. Finally, the closeFile() method closes the file to release its system resources.

Then, you declare a cashier bean with the name cashier1 in the IoC container. This cashier's checkout records will be recorded in the file c:/cashier/cashier1.txt. You should create this directory in advance or specify another existing directory.

```
<beans ...>
    ...
    <bean id="cashier1" class="com.apress.springrecipes.shop.Cashier">
        <property name="name" value="cashier1" />
        <property name="path" value="c:/cashier" />
    </bean>
</beans>
```

However, in the Main class, if you try to check out a shopping cart with this cashier, it will result in a NullPointerException. The reason for this exception is that no one has called the openFile() method for initialization beforehand.

```
package com.apress.springrecipes.shop;

import org.springframework.context.ApplicationContext;
import org.springframework.context.support.FileSystemXmlApplicationContext;

public class Main {

    public static void main(String[] args) throws Exception {
        ApplicationContext context =
            new FileSystemXmlApplicationContext("beans.xml");
        Cashier cashier1 = (Cashier) context.getBean("cashier1");
        cashier1.checkout(cart1);
    }
}
```

Where should you make a call to the openFile() method for initialization? In Java, the initialization tasks should be performed in the constructor. But would it work here if you call the openFile() method in the default constructor of the Cashier class? No, because the openFile() method requires both the name and path properties to be set before it can determine which file to open.

```
package com.apress.springrecipes.shop;
...
public class Cashier {
    ...
    public void openFile() throws IOException {
        File logFile = new File(path, name + ".txt");
        writer = new BufferedWriter(new OutputStreamWriter(
                new FileOutputStream(logFile, true)));
    }
}
```

When the default constructor is invoked, these properties have not been set yet. So you may add a constructor that accepts the two properties as arguments, and call the openFile() method at the end of this constructor. However, sometimes you may not be allowed to do so, or you might prefer to inject your properties via setter injection. Actually, the best time to call the openFile() method is after all properties have been set by the Spring IoC container.

Implementing the InitializingBean and DisposableBean Interfaces

Spring allows your bean to perform initialization and destruction tasks in the callback methods afterPropertiesSet() and destroy() by implementing the InitializingBean and DisposableBean interfaces. During bean construction, Spring will notice that your bean implements these interfaces and call the callback methods at a suitable time.

```
package com.apress.springrecipes.shop;
...
import org.springframework.beans.factory.DisposableBean;
import org.springframework.beans.factory.InitializingBean;

public class Cashier implements InitializingBean, DisposableBean {
    ...
    public void afterPropertiesSet() throws Exception {
        openFile();
    }

    public void destroy() throws Exception {
        closeFile();
    }
}
```

Now if you run your Main class again, you will see that a checkout record is appended to the text file c:/cashier/cashier1.txt. However, implementing such proprietary interfaces will make your beans Spring-specific and thus unable to be reused outside the Spring IoC container.

Setting the init-method and destroy-method Attributes

A better approach of specifying the initialization and destruction callback methods is by setting the init-method and destroy-method attributes in your bean declaration.

```
<bean id="cashier1" class="com.apress.springrecipes.shop.Cashier"
    init-method="openFile" destroy-method="closeFile">
    <property name="name" value="cashier1" />
    <property name="path" value="c:/cashier" />
</bean>
```

With these two attributes set in the bean declaration, your Cashier class no longer needs to implement the InitializingBean and DisposableBean interfaces. You can also delete the afterPropertiesSet() and destroy() methods as well.

Annotating the @PostConstruct and @PreDestroy Annotations

In Spring 2.5 or later, you can annotate the initialization and destruction callback methods with the JSR-250 life cycle annotations @PostConstruct and @PreDestroy.

■ **Note** To use the JSR-250 annotations, you have to include the JSR 250 dependency. If you are using Maven, add:

```xml
<dependency>
  <groupId>javax.annotation</groupId>
  <artifactId>jsr250-api</artifactId>
  <version>1.0</version>
</dependency>
```

```java
package com.apress.springrecipes.shop;
...
import javax.annotation.PostConstruct;
import javax.annotation.PreDestroy;

public class Cashier {
    ...
    @PostConstruct
    public void openFile() throws IOException {
        File logFile = new File(path, name + ".txt");
        writer = new BufferedWriter(new OutputStreamWriter(
                new FileOutputStream(logFile, true)));
    }

    @PreDestroy
    public void closeFile() throws IOException {
        writer.close();
    }
}
```

Next, you register a CommonAnnotationBeanPostProcessor instance in the IoC container to call the initialization and destruction callback methods with the life cycle annotations. In this way, you no longer need to specify the init-method and destroy-method attributes for your bean.

```xml
<beans ...>
    ...
    <bean class="org.springframework.context.annotation.↵
        CommonAnnotationBeanPostProcessor" />

    <bean id="cashier1" class="com.apress.springrecipes.shop.Cashier">
        <property name="name" value="cashier1" />
        <property name="path" value="c:/cashier" />
    </bean>
</beans>
```

Or you can simply include the <context:annotation-config> element in your bean configuration file, and a CommonAnnotationBeanPostProcessor instance will automatically get registered. But before this tag can work, you must add the context schema definition to your <beans> root element.

```
<beans xmlns="http://www.springframework.org/schema/beans"
    xmlns:xsi="http://www.w3.org/2001/XMLSchema-instance"
    xmlns:context="http://www.springframework.org/schema/context"
    xsi:schemaLocation="http://www.springframework.org/schema/beans
        http://www.springframework.org/schema/beans/spring-beans-3.0.xsd
        http://www.springframework.org/schema/context
        http://www.springframework.org/schema/context/spring-context-3.0.xsd">

    <context:annotation-config />
    ...
</beans>
```

2-8. Reducing XML Configuration with Java Config

Problem

You enjoy the power of the DI container but want to override some of the configuration, or you simply want to move more configuration out of the XML format and into Java where you can better benefit from refactoring and type safety.

Solution

You can use Java Config, a project which has been in incubation since early 2005 long before Google Guice hit the scene—and has recently been folded into the core framework.

How It Works

The Java Config support is powerful and represents a radically different way of doing things compared with the other configuration options, via XML or annotations. It is important to remember that the Java Config support can be used in tandem with the existing approaches. The simplest way to bootstrap Java configuration is with a plain vanilla XML configuration file. From there, Spring will take care of the rest.

```
ClassPathXmlApplicationContext classPathXmlApplicationContext =
    new ClassPathXmlApplicationContext("myApplicationContext.xml");
```

The configuration for that file looks the same as you'd expect:

```
...
 <context:annotation-config />
 <context:component-scan base-package="com.my.base.package" />
...
```

This will let Spring find any classes marked with @Configuration. @Configuration is metaannotated with @Component, which makes it eligible for annotation support. This means that it will honor injection using @Autowired, for example. Once your class is annotated with @Configuration, Spring will look for bean definitions in the class. (*Bean definitions* are Java methods annotated with @Bean.) Any definition is contributed to the ApplicationContext and takes its beanName from the method used to configure it. Alternatively, you can explicitly specify the bean name in the @Bean annotation. A configuration with one bean definition might look like this:

```
import org.springframework.context.annotation.Bean;
import org.springframework.context.annotation.Configuration;

@Configuration
public class PersonConfiguration {
        @Bean
        public Person josh() {
                    Person josh = new Person();
                    josh.setName("Josh");
                    return josh ;
        }
}
```

This is equivalent to an XML application context with the following definition:

```
<bean id="josh" class="com.apress.springrecipes.↵
spring3.javaconfig.Person" p:name="Josh" />
```

You can access the bean from your Spring application context just as you would normally:

```
ApplicationContext context =  … ;
Person person = context.getBean("josh", Person.class);
```

If you want to specify the id of the bean, you can do so by using the @Bean definitions id attribute:

```
        @Bean(name="theArtistFormerlyKnownAsJosh")
        public Person josh() {
        //  …
        }
```

You can access this bean as follows:

```
ApplicationContext context =  … ;
Person person = context.getBean("theArtistFormerlyKnownAsJosh", Person.class);
```

Now, I know what you're thinking: how is *that* an improvement? It's five times more lines of code! But you mustn't dismiss the inherent readability of the Java example. Also, if the example compiles, you can be reasonably sure that your configuration was correct. The XML example doesn't afford you any of those benefits.

If you want to specify life cycle methods, you have choices. Life cycle methods in Spring were formerly implemented as callbacks against known interfaces, like InitializingBean and DisposableBean, which gets a callback after dependencies have been injected (public void afterPropertiesSet() throws Exception), and before the bean is destroyed and removed from the context (public void destroy()

throws Exception), respectively. You may also configure the initialization and destruction methods manually in the XML configuration, using the init-method and destroy-method attributes of the bean xml element. Since Spring 2.5, you can also use JSR-250 annotations to designate methods as an initialization (@PostConstruct) and destruction method (@PreDestroy). In Java Config, you have options!

You can specify the life cycle methods using the @Bean annotation, or you can simply call the method yourself! The first option, using the initMethod and destroyMethod attributes, is straightforward:

```
@Bean( initMethod = "startLife", destroyMethod = "die")
public Person companyLawyer() {
        Person companyLawyer = new Person();
        companyLawyer.setName("Alan Crane");
        return companyLawyer;
}
```

However, you can readily handle initialization on your own, too:

```
@Bean
public Person companyLawyer() {
    Person companyLawyer = new Person();
    companyLawyer.startLife() ;
    companyLawyer.setName("Alan Crane");
    return companyLawyer;
}
```

Referencing other beans is as simple and very similar:

```
@Configuration
public class PetConfiguration {
        @Bean
        public Cat cat(){
           return new Cat();
        }

        @Bean
        public Person master(){
         Person person = new Person() ;
         person.setPet( cat() );
         return person;
        }
// …
}
```

It just doesn't get any easier than that: if you need a reference to another bean, simply obtain the reference to the other bean just as you would in any other Java application. Spring will ensure that the bean is instantiated only once and that scope rules are applied if relevant.

The full gamut of configuration options for beans defined in XML is available to beans defined via Java Config.

The @Lazy, @Primary, and @DependsOn annotations work exactly like their XML counterparts. @Lazy defers construction of the bean until it's required to satisfy a dependency or it's explicitly accessed from the application context. @DependsOn specifies that the creation of a bean must come after the creation of some other bean, whose existence might be crucial to the correct creation of the bean. @Primary specifies that the bean on whose definition the annotation is placed is the one that should be returned when there are multiple beans of the same interface. Naturally, if you access beans by name from the container, this makes less sense.

The annotations sit above the bean configuration method to which it applies, like the other annotations. Here's an example:

```
@Bean @Lazy
public NetworkFileProcessor fileProcessor(){ … }
```

Often, you'll want to partition your bean configuration into multiple configuration classes, which leaves things more maintainable and modular. Pursuant to that, Spring lets you import other beans. In XML, you do this using the import element (<import resource="someOtherElement.xml" />). In JavaConfig, similar functionality is available through the @Import annotation, which you place at the class level.

```
@Configuration
@Import(BusinessConfiguration.class)
public class FamilyConfiguration {
// ...
}
```

This has the effect of bringing into scope the beans defined in the BusinessConfiguration. From there, you can get access to the beans simply by using @Autowired or @Value if you want. If you inject the ApplicationContext using @Autowired, you can use it to obtain access to a bean. Here, the container imports the beans defined from the AttorneyConfiguration configuration class and then lets you inject them by name using the @Value annotation. Had there been only one instance of that type, you could have used @Autowired.

```
package com.apress.springrecipes.spring3.javaconfig;

import static java.lang.System.*;

import java.util.Arrays;

import org.springframework.beans.factory.annotation.Value;
import org.springframework.context.annotation.Bean;
import org.springframework.context.annotation.Configuration;
import org.springframework.context.annotation.Import;
import org.springframework.context.support.ClassPathXmlApplicationContext;

@Configuration
@Import(AttorneyConfiguration.class)
public class LawFirmConfiguration {

        @Value("#{denny}")
        private Attorney denny;

        @Value("#{alan}")
        private Attorney alan;
```

```
@Value("#{shirley}")
private Attorney shirley;

@Bean
public LawFirm bostonLegal() {
        LawFirm lawFirm = new LawFirm();
        lawFirm.setLawyers(Arrays.asList(denny, alan, shirley));
        lawFirm.setLocation("Boston");
        return lawFirm;
    }
}
```

This functionality is often overkill for defining simple beans. For example, if you want to simply let Spring instantiate the bean, and you don't have anything to contribute to that process, you can either write an @Bean method, or you can fall back and configure it in XML. Which you do is up to you, as a matter of taste. If it were an object specific to my application, I'd handle it in the Java configuration, but I would leave Spring's many FactoryBean implementations inside the XML where they could be made quick work of and where I could benefit from some of the schemas.

2-9. Making Beans Aware of the Container

Problem

A well-designed component should not have direct dependencies on its container. However, sometimes it's necessary for your beans to be aware of the container's resources.

Solution

Your beans can be aware of the Spring IoC container's resources by implementing certain "aware" interfaces, as shown in Table 2-3. Spring will inject the corresponding resources to your beans via the setter methods defined in these interfaces.

Table 2-3. *Common Aware Interfaces in Spring*

Aware Interface	Target Resource
BeanNameAware	The bean name of its instances configured in the IoC container
BeanFactoryAware	The current bean factory, through which you can invoke the container's services
ApplicationContextAware*	The current application context, through which you can invoke the container's services
MessageSourceAware	A message source, through which you can resolve text messages
ApplicationEventPublisherAware	An application event publisher, through which you can publish application events
ResourceLoaderAware	A resource loader, through which you can load external resources

* In fact, the `ApplicationContext` interface extends the `MessageSource`, `ApplicationEventPublisher`, and `ResourceLoader` interfaces, so you only need to be aware of the application context to access all these services. However, the best practice is to choose an aware interface with minimum scope that can satisfy your requirement.

The setter methods in the aware interfaces will be called by Spring after the bean properties have been set, but before the initialization callback methods are called, as illustrated in the following list:

1. Create the bean instance either by a constructor or by a factory method.

2. Set the values and bean references to the bean properties.

3. Call the setter methods defined in the aware interfaces.

4. Call the initialization callback methods.

5. The bean is ready to be used.

6. When the container is shut down, call the destruction callback methods.

Keep in mind that once your beans implement the aware interfaces, they are bound to Spring and may not work properly outside the Spring IoC container. You must consider carefully whether it's necessary to implement such proprietary interfaces.

How It Works

For example, you can make your cashier bean aware of its bean name in the IoC container by implementing the BeanNameAware interface. When this bean name is injected, you can save it as the cashier name. This can save you the trouble of setting another name property for the cashier.

```
package com.apress.springrecipes.shop;
...
import org.springframework.beans.factory.BeanNameAware;

public class Cashier implements BeanNameAware {
    ...
    public void setBeanName(String beanName) {
        this.name = beanName;
    }
}
```

You can simplify your cashier bean declaration by using the bean name as the cashier name. In this way, you can erase the configuration of the name property and perhaps the setName() method as well.

```
<bean id="cashier1" class="com.apress.springrecipes.shop.Cashier">
    <property name="path" value="c:/cashier" />
</bean>
```

■ **Note** Do you remember that you can specify the field name and the property path as the bean names of FieldRetrievingFactoryBean and PropertyPathFactoryBean directly? In fact, both factory beans implement the BeanNameAware interface.

2-10. Loading External Resources

Problem

Sometimes, your application may need to read external resources (e.g., text files, XML files, properties file, or image files) from different locations (e.g., a file system, classpath, or URL). Usually, you have to deal with different APIs for loading resources from different locations.

Solution

Spring's resource loader provides a unified getResource() method for you to retrieve an external resource by a resource path. You can specify different prefixes for this path to load resources from different locations. To load a resource from a file system, you use the file prefix. To load a resource from the classpath, you use the classpath prefix. You may also specify a URL in this resource path.

Resource is a general interface in Spring for representing an external resource. Spring provides several implementations for the Resource interface. The resource loader's getResource() method will decide which Resource implementation to instantiate according to the resource path.

How It Works

Suppose you want to display a banner at the startup of your shop application. The banner is made up of the following characters and stored in a text file called banner.txt. This file can be put in the current path of your application.

```
*************************
*  Welcome to My Shop!  *
*************************
```

Next, you have to write the BannerLoader class to load the banner and output it to the console. Because it requires access to a resource loader for loading the resource, it has to implement either the ApplicationContextAware interface or the ResourceLoaderAware interface.

```
package com.apress.springrecipes.shop;
...
import org.springframework.context.ResourceLoaderAware;
import org.springframework.core.io.Resource;
import org.springframework.core.io.ResourceLoader;

public class BannerLoader implements ResourceLoaderAware {

    private ResourceLoader resourceLoader;

    public void setResourceLoader(ResourceLoader resourceLoader) {
        this.resourceLoader = resourceLoader;
    }

    public void showBanner() throws IOException {
        Resource banner = resourceLoader.getResource("file:banner.txt");
        InputStream in = banner.getInputStream();

        BufferedReader reader = new BufferedReader(new InputStreamReader(in));
        while (true) {
            String line = reader.readLine();
            if (line == null)
                break;
            System.out.println(line);
        }
        reader.close();
    }
}
```

By calling the getResource() method from the application context, you can retrieve an external resource specified by a resource path. Because your banner file is located in the file system, the resource path should start with the file prefix. You can call the getInputStream() method to retrieve the input stream for this resource. Then, you read the file contents line by line with BufferedReader and output them to the console.

Finally, you declare a BannerLoader instance in the bean configuration file to display the banner. Because you want to show the banner at startup, you specify the showBanner() method as the initialization method.

```
<bean id="bannerLoader"
    class="com.apress.springrecipes.shop.BannerLoader"
    init-method="showBanner" />
```

Resource Prefixes

The previous resource path specifies a resource in the relative path of the file system. You can specify an absolute path as well.

```
file:c:/shop/banner.txt
```

When your resource is located in the classpath, you have to use the classpath prefix. If there's no path information presented, it will be loaded from the root of the classpath.

```
classpath:banner.txt
```

If the resource is located in a particular package, you can specify the absolute path from the classpath root.

```
classpath:com/apress/springrecipes/shop/banner.txt
```

Besides a file system path or the classpath, a resource can also be loaded by specifying a URL.

```
http://springrecipes.apress.com/shop/banner.txt
```

If there's no prefix presented in the resource path, the resource will be loaded from a location according to the application context. For FileSystemXmlApplicationContext, the resource will be loaded from the file system. For ClassPathXmlApplicationContext, it will be loaded from the classpath.

Injecting Resources

In addition to calling the getResource() method to load a resource explicitly, you can inject it by using a setter method:

```
package com.apress.springrecipes.shop;
...
import org.springframework.core.io.Resource;

public class BannerLoader {

    private Resource banner;

    public void setBanner(Resource banner) {
        this.banner = banner;
    }
}
```

```
    public void showBanner() throws IOException {
        InputStream in = banner.getInputStream();
        ...
    }
}
```

In the bean configuration, you can simply specify the resource path for this Resource property. Spring will use the preregistered property editor ResourceEditor to convert it into a Resource object before injecting it into your bean.

```
<bean id="bannerLoader"
    class="com.apress.springrecipes.shop.BannerLoader"
    init-method="showBanner">
    <property name="banner">
        <value>classpath:com/apress/springrecipes/shop/banner.txt</value>
    </property>
</bean>
```

2-11. Creating Bean Post Processors

Problem

You would like to register your own plug-ins in the Spring IoC container to process the bean instances during construction.

Solution

A *bean post processor* allows additional bean processing before and after the initialization callback method. The main characteristic of a bean post processor is that it will process all the bean instances in the IoC container one by one, not just a single bean instance. Typically, bean post processors are used for checking the validity of bean properties or altering bean properties according to particular criteria.

The basic requirement of a bean post processor is to implement the BeanPostProcessor interface. You can process every bean before and after the initialization callback method by implementing the postProcessBeforeInitialization() and postProcessAfterInitialization() methods. Then Spring will pass each bean instance to these two methods before and after calling the initialization callback method, as illustrated in the following list:

1. Create the bean instance either by a constructor or by a factory method.

2. Set the values and bean references to the bean properties.

3. Call the setter methods defined in the aware interfaces.

4. Pass the bean instance to the postProcessBeforeInitialization() method of each bean post processor.

5. Call the initialization callback methods.

6. Pass the bean instance to the postProcessAfterInitialization() method of each bean post processor.

7. The bean is ready to be used.

8. When the container is shut down, call the destruction callback methods.

When using a bean factory as your IoC container, bean post processors can only be registered programmatically, or more accurately, via the addBeanPostProcessor() method. However, if you are using an application context, the registration will be as simple as declaring an instance of the processor in the bean configuration file, and then it will get registered automatically.

How It Works

Suppose you would like to ensure that the logging path of Cashier exists before the logging file is open. This is to avoid FileNotFoundException. As this is a common requirement for all components that require storage in the file system, you had better implement it in a general and reusable manner. A bean post processor is an ideal choice to implement such a feature in Spring.

First of all, for the bean post processor to distinguish which beans should be checked, you create a marker interface, StorageConfig, for your target beans to implement. Moreover, for your bean post processor to check for path existence, it must be able to access the path property. This can be done by adding the getPath() method to this interface.

```
package com.apress.springrecipes.shop;

public interface StorageConfig {

    public String getPath();
}
```

Next, you should make the Cashier class implement this marker interface. Your bean post processor will only check the beans that implement this interface.

```
package com.apress.springrecipes.shop;
...
public class Cashier implements BeanNameAware, StorageConfig {
    ...
    public String getPath() {
        return path;
    }
}
```

Now, you are ready to write a bean post processor for path checking. As the best time to perform path checking is before the file is opened in the initialization method, you implement the postProcessBeforeInitialization() method to perform the checking.

```
package com.apress.springrecipes.shop;
...
import org.springframework.beans.BeansException;
import org.springframework.beans.factory.config.BeanPostProcessor;
```

```
public class PathCheckingBeanPostProcessor implements BeanPostProcessor {

    public Object postProcessBeforeInitialization(Object bean, String beanName)
            throws BeansException {
        if (bean instanceof StorageConfig) {
            String path = ((StorageConfig) bean).getPath();
            File file = new File(path);
            if (!file.exists()) {
                file.mkdirs();
            }
        }
        return bean;
    }

    public Object postProcessAfterInitialization(Object bean, String beanName)
            throws BeansException {
        return bean;
    }
}
```

During bean construction, the Spring IoC container will pass all the bean instances to your bean post processor one by one, so you must filter the beans by checking the marker interface StoreConfig. If a bean implements this interface, you can access its path property by the getPath() method and check for its existence in the file system. If that path doesn't exist, just create it with the File.mkdirs() method.

Both the postProcessBeforeInitialization() and postProcessAfterInitialization() methods must return an instance for the bean being processed. That means you may even replace the original bean instance with a brand-new instance in your bean post processor. Remember that you must return the original bean instance even though you do nothing in the method.

To register a bean post processor in an application context, just declare an instance of it in the bean configuration file. The application context will be able to detect which bean implements the BeanPostProcessor interface and register it to process all other bean instances in the container.

```
<beans ...>
    ...
    <bean class="com.apress.springrecipes.shop.PathCheckingBeanPostProcessor" />

    <bean id="cashier1" class="com.apress.springrecipes.shop.Cashier"
        init-method="openFile" destroy-method="closeFile">
        ...
    </bean>
</beans>
```

Note that if you specify the initialization callback method in the init-method attribute, or if you implement the InitializingBean interface, your PathCheckingBeanPostProcessor will work fine because it will process the cashier bean before the initialization method is called.

However, if the cashier bean relies on the JSR-250 annotations @PostConstruct and @PreDestroy, and also a CommonAnnotationBeanPostProcessor instance to call the initialization method, your PathCheckingBeanPostProcessor will not work properly. This is because your bean post processor has a lower priority than CommonAnnotationBeanPostProcessor by default. As a result, the initialization method will be called before your path checking.

```
<beans ...>
    ...
    <bean class="org.springframework.context.annotation.↵
        CommonAnnotationBeanPostProcessor" />

    <bean class="com.apress.springrecipes.shop.PathCheckingBeanPostProcessor" />

    <bean id="cashier1" class="com.apress.springrecipes.shop.Cashier">
        ...
    </bean>
</beans>
```

To define the processing order of bean post processors, you can have them implement the Ordered or PriorityOrdered interface and return their order in the getOrder() method. The lower value returned by this method represents higher priority, and the order value returned by the PriorityOrdered interface will always precede that returned by the Ordered interface.

As CommonAnnotationBeanPostProcessor implements the PriorityOrdered interface, your PathCheckingBeanPostProcessor must also implement this interface to have a chance to precede it.

```
package com.apress.springrecipes.shop;
...
import org.springframework.beans.factory.config.BeanPostProcessor;
import org.springframework.core.PriorityOrdered;

public class PathCheckingBeanPostProcessor implements BeanPostProcessor,
        PriorityOrdered {

    private int order;

    public int getOrder() {
        return order;
    }

    public void setOrder(int order) {
        this.order = order;
    }
    ...
}
```

Now, in the bean configuration file, you should assign a lower order value to your PathCheckingBeanPostProcessor for it to check and create the path of the cashier bean before its initialization method is called by CommonAnnotationBeanPostProcessor. As the default order of CommonAnnotationBeanPostProcessor is Ordered.LOWEST_PRECEDENCE, you can simply assign a zero order value to your PathCheckingBeanPostProcessor.

```
<beans ...>
    ...
    <bean class="org.springframework.context.annotation.↵
        CommonAnnotationBeanPostProcessor" />
```

```
<bean class="com.apress.springrecipes.shop.PathCheckingBeanPostProcessor">
    <property name="order" value="0" />
</bean>

<bean id="cashier1" class="com.apress.springrecipes.shop.Cashier">
    <property name="path" value="c:/cashier" />
</bean>
</beans>
```

As zero is the default order value of your `PathCheckingBeanPostProcessor`, you can simply omit this setting. Moreover, you can continue to use `<context:annotation-config>` to get `CommonAnnotationBeanPostProcessor` registered automatically.

```
<beans ...>
    ...
    <context:annotation-config />

    <bean class="com.apress.springrecipes.shop.PathCheckingBeanPostProcessor" />
</beans>
```

2-12. Externalizing Bean Configurations

Problem

When configuring beans in the configuration file, you must remember that it's not a good practice to mix deployment details, such as the file path, server address, username, and password, with your bean configurations. Usually, the bean configurations are written by application developers while the deployment details are matters for the deployers or system administrators.

Solution

Spring comes with a bean factory post processor called `PropertyPlaceholderConfigurer` for you to externalize part of the bean configurations into a properties file. You can use variables of the form `${var}` in your bean configuration file and `PropertyPlaceholderConfigurer` will load the properties from a properties file and use them to replace the variables.

A *bean factory post processor* differs from a bean post processor in that its target is the IoC container—either the bean factory or the application context—not the bean instances. It will take effect on the IoC container after it loads the bean configurations but before any of the bean instances are created. The typical usage of a bean factory post processor is to alter the bean configurations before the beans are instantiated. Spring comes with several bean factory post processors for you to use. In practice, you seldom need to write your own bean factory post processors.

How It Works

Previously, you specified the logging path for a cashier in the bean configuration file. It is not a good practice to mix such deployment details with your bean configurations. A better approach is to extract the deployment details into a properties file, such as config.properties, in the root of the classpath. Then, define the logging path in this file.

```
cashier.path=c:/cashier
```

Now, you can use variables of the form ${var} in your bean configuration file. To load the external properties from a properties file and use them to replace the variables, you have to register the bean factory post processor PropertyPlaceholderConfigurer in your application context. You can specify either one properties file in the location property or multiple properties files in the locations property.

```
<beans ...>
    ...
    <bean class="org.springframework.beans.factory.config.↵
        PropertyPlaceholderConfigurer">
        <property name="location">
            <value>config.properties</value>
        </property>
    </bean>

    <bean id="cashier1" class="com.apress.springrecipes.shop.Cashier">
        <property name="path" value="${cashier.path}" />
    </bean>
</beans>
```

Implemented as a bean factory post processor, PropertyPlaceholderConfigurer will replace the variables in your bean configuration file with the external properties before your beans get instantiated.

In Spring 2.5 or later, the registration of PropertyPlaceholderConfigurer can be simply through the <context:property-placeholder> element.

```
<beans xmlns="http://www.springframework.org/schema/beans"
    xmlns:xsi="http://www.w3.org/2001/XMLSchema-instance"
    xmlns:context="http://www.springframework.org/schema/context"
    xsi:schemaLocation="http://www.springframework.org/schema/beans
        http://www.springframework.org/schema/beans/spring-beans-3.0.xsd
        http://www.springframework.org/schema/context
        http://www.springframework.org/schema/context/spring-context-3.0.xsd">

    <context:property-placeholder location="config.properties" />
    ...
</beans>
```

2-13. Resolving Text Messages

Problem

For an application to support internationalization (I18N for short, as there are 18 characters between the first character, "i," and the last character, "n"), it requires the capability of resolving text messages for different locales.

Solution

Spring's application context is able to resolve text messages for a target locale by their keys. Typically, the messages for one locale should be stored in one separate properties file. This properties file is called a *resource bundle*.

MessageSource is an interface that defines several methods for resolving messages. The ApplicationContext interface extends this interface so that all application contexts are able to resolve text messages. An application context delegates the message resolution to a bean with the exact name messageSource. ResourceBundleMessageSource is the most common MessageSource implementation that resolves messages from resource bundles for different locales.

How It Works

As an example, you can create the following resource bundle, messages_en_US.properties, for the English language in the United States. Resource bundles will be loaded from the root of the classpath.

```
alert.checkout=A shopping cart has been checked out.
```

To resolve messages from resource bundles, you use ResourceBundleMessageSource as your MessageSource implementation. This bean's name must be set to messageSource for the application context to detect it. You have to specify the base name of the resource bundles for ResourceBundleMessageSource.

```
<beans ...>
    ...
    <bean id="messageSource"
        class="org.springframework.context.support.ResourceBundleMessageSource">
        <property name="basename">
            <value>messages</value>
        </property>
    </bean>
</beans>
```

For this MessageSource definition, if you look up a text message for the United States locale, whose preferred language is English, the resource bundle messages_en_US.properties, which matches both the language and country, will be considered first. If there's no such resource bundle or the message can't be found, the one messages_en.properties that matches the language only will be considered. If this resource bundle still can't be found, the default messages.properties for all locales will be chosen finally. For more information on resource bundle loading, you can refer to the Javadoc of the java.util.ResourceBundle class.

Now, you can ask the application context to resolve a message by the getMessage() method. The first argument is the key corresponding to the message, and the third is the target locale.

```
package com.apress.springrecipes.shop;

import org.springframework.context.ApplicationContext;
import org.springframework.context.support.FileSystemXmlApplicationContext;
```

```
public class Main {

    public static void main(String[] args) throws Exception {
        ApplicationContext context =
            new FileSystemXmlApplicationContext("beans.xml");
        ...
        String alert = context.getMessage("alert.checkout", null, Locale.US);
        System.out.println(alert);
    }
}
```

The second argument of the getMessage() method is an array of message parameters. In the text message, you can define multiple parameters by index:

```
alert.checkout=A shopping cart costing {0} dollars has been checked out at {1}.
```

You have to pass in an object array to fill in the message parameters. The elements in this array will be converted into strings before filling in the parameters.

```
package com.apress.springrecipes.shop;
...
public class Main {

    public static void main(String[] args) throws Exception {
        ...
        String alert = context.getMessage("alert.checkout",
                new Object[] { 4, new Date() }, Locale.US);
        System.out.println(alert);
    }
}
```

In the Main class, you can resolve text messages because you can access the application context directly. But for a bean to resolve text messages, it has to implement either the ApplicationContextAware interface or the MessageSourceAware interface. Now, you can delete the message resolution from the Main class.

```
package com.apress.springrecipes.shop;
...
import org.springframework.context.MessageSource;
import org.springframework.context.MessageSourceAware;

public class Cashier implements BeanNameAware, MessageSourceAware,
        StorageConfig {
    ...
    private MessageSource messageSource;

    public void setMessageSource(MessageSource messageSource) {
        this.messageSource = messageSource;
    }
```

```
public void checkout(ShoppingCart cart) throws IOException {
    ...
    String alert = messageSource.getMessage("alert.checkout",
            new Object[] { total, new Date() }, Locale.US);
    System.out.println(alert);
    }
}
```

2-14. Communicating with Application Events

Problem

In the typical communication model between components, the sender has to locate the receiver to call a method on it. In this case, the sender component must be aware of the receiver component. This kind of communication is direct and simple, but the sender and receiver components are tightly coupled.

When using an IoC container, your components can communicate by interface rather than by implementation. This communication model can help reduce coupling. However, it is only efficient when a sender component has to communicate with one receiver. When a sender needs to communicate with multiple receivers, it has to call the receivers one by one.

Solution

Spring's application context supports event-based communication between its beans. In the event-based communication model, the sender component just publishes an event without knowing who the receiver will be. Actually, there may be more than one receiver component. Also, the receiver needn't know who is publishing the event. It can listen to multiple events from different senders at the same time. In this way, the sender and receiver components are loosely coupled.

In Spring, all event classes must extend the ApplicationEvent class. In that case, any bean can publish an event by calling an application event publisher's publishEvent() method. For a bean to listen to certain events, it must implement the ApplicationListener interface and handle the events in the onApplicationEvent() method. Actually, Spring will notify a listener of all events, so you must filter the events by yourself. If you use exploit generics, however, Spring will deliver only messages that match the generic type parameter.

How It Works

Defining Events

The first step of enabling event-based communication is to define the event. Suppose you would like your cashier bean to publish a CheckoutEvent after the shopping cart has been checked out. This event includes two properties: the payment amount and the checkout time. In Spring, all events must extend the abstract class ApplicationEvent and pass the event source as a constructor argument.

```
package com.apress.springrecipes.shop;
...
import org.springframework.context.ApplicationEvent;

public class CheckoutEvent extends ApplicationEvent {

    private double amount;
    private Date time;

    public CheckoutEvent(Object source, double amount, Date time) {
        super(source);
        this.amount = amount;
        this.time = time;
    }

    public double getAmount() {
        return amount;
    }

    public Date getTime() {
        return time;
    }
}
```

Publishing Events

To publish an event, you just create an event instance and make a call to the publishEvent() method of an application event publisher, which can be accessed by implementing the ApplicationEventPublisherAware interface.

```
package com.apress.springrecipes.shop;
...
import org.springframework.context.ApplicationEventPublisher;
import org.springframework.context.ApplicationEventPublisherAware;

public class Cashier implements BeanNameAware, MessageSourceAware,
        ApplicationEventPublisherAware, StorageConfig {
    ...
    private ApplicationEventPublisher applicationEventPublisher;

    public void setApplicationEventPublisher(
            ApplicationEventPublisher applicationEventPublisher) {
        this.applicationEventPublisher = applicationEventPublisher;
    }
```

```
    public void checkout(ShoppingCart cart) throws IOException {
        ...
        CheckoutEvent event = new CheckoutEvent(this, total, new Date());
        applicationEventPublisher.publishEvent(event);
    }
}
```

Listening to Events

Any bean defined in the application context that implements the ApplicationListener interface will be notified of all events. So in the onApplicationEvent() method, you have to filter the events that your listener wants to handle. In the following listener, suppose you would like to send an e-mail to notify the customer about the checkout. Here, we use an instanceof check to filter on the nongeneric ApplicationEvent parameter.

```
package com.apress.springrecipes.shop;
...
import org.springframework.context.ApplicationEvent;
import org.springframework.context.ApplicationListener;

public class CheckoutListener implements ApplicationListener {

    public void onApplicationEvent(ApplicationEvent event) {
        if (event instanceof CheckoutEvent) {
            double amount = ((CheckoutEvent) event).getAmount();
            Date time = ((CheckoutEvent) event).getTime();

            // Do anything you like with the checkout amount and time
            System.out.println("Checkout event [" + amount + ", " + time + "]");
        }
    }
}
```

Rewritten to take advantage of the generics functionality, it's a bit briefer:

```
package com.apress.springrecipes.shop;
...
import org.springframework.context.ApplicationEvent;
import org.springframework.context.ApplicationListener;

public class CheckoutListener implements ApplicationListener<CheckoutEvent> {

    public void onApplicationEvent(CheckoutEvent event) {
            double amount = ((CheckoutEvent) event).getAmount();
            Date time = ((CheckoutEvent) event).getTime();

            // Do anything you like with the checkout amount and time
            System.out.println("Checkout event [" + amount + ", " + time + "]");
    }
}
```

Next, you have to register this listener in the application context to listen for all events. The registration is as simple as declaring a bean instance of this listener. The application context will recognize the beans that implement the ApplicationListener interface and notify them of each event.

```
<beans ...>
    ...
    <bean class="com.apress.springrecipes.shop.CheckoutListener" />
</beans>
```

Finally, notice that the application context itself will also publish container events such as ContextClosedEvent, ContextRefreshedEvent, and RequestHandledEvent. If any of your beans want to be notified of these events, they can implement the ApplicationListener interface.

2-15. Registering Property Editors in Spring

Problem

A property editor is a feature of the JavaBeans API for converting property values to and from text values. Each property editor is designed for a certain type of property only. You may wish to employ property editors to simplify your bean configurations.

Solution

The Spring IoC container supports using property editors to help with bean configurations. For example, with a property editor for the java.net.URL type, you can specify a URL string for a property of the URL type. Spring will automatically convert the URL string into a URL object and inject it into your property. Spring comes with several property editors for converting bean properties of common types.

Typically, you should register a property editor in the Spring IoC container before it can be used. The CustomEditorConfigurer is implemented as a bean factory post processor for you to register your custom property editors before any of the beans get instantiated.

How It Works

As an example, suppose you would like your product ranking to be based on sales for a particular period. For this change, you add the fromDate and toDate properties to your ProductRanking class.

```
package com.apress.springrecipes.shop;
...
public class ProductRanking {

    private Product bestSeller;
    private Date fromDate;
    private Date toDate;
```

```
    // Getters and Setters
    ...
}
```

To specify the value for a java.util.Date property in a Java program, you can convert it from a date string of particular pattern with the help of the DateFormat.parse() method.

```
DateFormat dateFormat = new SimpleDateFormat("yyyy-MM-dd");
productRanking.setFromDate(dateFormat.parse("2007-09-01"));
productRanking.setToDate(dateFormat.parse("2007-09-30"));
```

To write the equivalent bean configuration in Spring, you first declare a dateFormat bean with the pattern configured. As the parse() method is called for converting the date strings into date objects, you can consider it as an instance factory method to create the date beans.

```
<beans ...>
    ...
    <bean id="dateFormat" class="java.text.SimpleDateFormat">
        <constructor-arg value="yyyy-MM-dd" />
    </bean>

    <bean id="productRanking"
        class="com.apress.springrecipes.shop.ProductRanking">
        <property name="bestSeller">
            <bean class="com.apress.springrecipes.shop.Disc">
                <property name="name" value="CD-RW" />
                <property name="price" value="1.5" />
            </bean>
        </property>
        <property name="fromDate">
            <bean factory-bean="dateFormat" factory-method="parse">
                <constructor-arg value="2007-09-01" />
            </bean>
        </property>
        <property name="toDate">
            <bean factory-bean="dateFormat" factory-method="parse">
                <constructor-arg value="2007-09-30" />
            </bean>
        </property>
    </bean>
</beans>
```

As you can see, the preceding configuration is too complicated for setting date properties. Actually, the Spring IoC container is able to convert the text values for your properties by using property editors. The CustomDateEditor class that comes with Spring is for converting date strings into java.util.Date properties. First, you have to declare an instance of it in the bean configuration file.

```
<beans ...>
    ...
    <bean id="dateEditor"
        class="org.springframework.beans.propertyeditors.CustomDateEditor">
        <constructor-arg>
            <bean class="java.text.SimpleDateFormat">
                <constructor-arg value="yyyy-MM-dd" />
            </bean>
        </constructor-arg>
        <constructor-arg value="true" />
    </bean>
</beans>
```

This editor requires a `DateFormat` object as the first constructor argument. The second argument indicates whether this editor allows empty values.

Next, you have to register this property editor in a `CustomEditorConfigurer` instance so that Spring can convert properties whose type is `java.util.Date`. Now, you can specify a date value in text format for any `java.util.Date` properties:

```
<beans ...>
    ...
    <bean class="org.springframework.beans.factory.config.CustomEditorConfigurer">
        <property name="customEditors">
            <map>
                <entry key="java.util.Date">
                    <ref local="dateEditor" />
                </entry>
            </map>
        </property>
    </bean>

    <bean id="productRanking"
        class="com.apress.springrecipes.shop.ProductRanking">
        <property name="bestSeller">
            <bean class="com.apress.springrecipes.shop.Disc">
                <property name="name" value="CD-RW" />
                <property name="price" value="1.5" />
            </bean>
        </property>
        <property name="fromDate" value="2007-09-01" />
        <property name="toDate" value="2007-09-30" />
    </bean>
</beans>
```

You can test whether your `CustomDateEditor` configuration works with the following `Main` class:

```
package com.apress.springrecipes.shop;

import org.springframework.context.ApplicationContext;
import org.springframework.context.support.ClassPathXmlApplicationContext;

public class Main {

    public static void main(String[] args) throws Exception {
        ApplicationContext context =
            new ClassPathXmlApplicationContext("beans.xml");
        ...
        ProductRanking productRanking =
            (ProductRanking) context.getBean("productRanking");
        System.out.println(
                "Product ranking from " + productRanking.getFromDate() +
                " to " + productRanking.getToDate());
    }
}
```

In addition to `CustomDateEditor`, Spring comes with several property editors for converting common data types, such as `CustomNumberEditor`, `ClassEditor`, `FileEditor`, `LocaleEditor`, `StringArrayPropertyEditor`, and `URLEditor`. Among them, `ClassEditor`, `FileEditor`, `LocaleEditor`, and `URLEditor` are preregistered by Spring, so you don't need to register them again. For more information on using these editors, you can consult the Javadoc of these classes in the `org.springframework.beans.propertyeditors` package.

2-16. Creating Custom Property Editors

Problem

In addition to registering the built-in property editors, you may want to write your own custom property editors for converting your custom data types.

Solution

You can write custom property editors by implementing the `java.beans.PropertyEditor` interface or extending the convenient support class `java.beans.PropertyEditorSupport`.

How It Works

For example, let's write a property editor for the `Product` class. You can design the string representation of a product as three parts, which are the concrete class name, the product name, and the price. Each part is separated by a comma. Then, you can write the following `ProductEditor` class for converting them:

```
package com.apress.springrecipes.shop;

import java.beans.PropertyEditorSupport;

public class ProductEditor extends PropertyEditorSupport {

    public String getAsText() {
        Product product = (Product) getValue();
        return product.getClass().getName() + "," + product.getName() + ","
                + product.getPrice();
    }

    public void setAsText(String text) throws IllegalArgumentException {
        String[] parts = text.split(",");
        try {
            Product product = (Product) Class.forName(parts[0]).newInstance();
            product.setName(parts[1]);
            product.setPrice(Double.parseDouble(parts[2]));
            setValue(product);
        } catch (Exception e) {
            throw new IllegalArgumentException(e);
        }
    }
}
```

The getAsText() method converts a property into a string value, while the setAsText() method converts a string back into a property. The property value is retrieved and set by calling the getValue() and setValue() methods.

Next, you have to register your custom editor in a CustomEditorConfigurer instance before it can be used. Registration is the same as for the built-in editors. Now, you can specify a product in text format for any property whose type is Product.

```
<beans ...>
    ...
    <bean class="org.springframework.beans.factory.config.CustomEditorConfigurer">
        <property name="customEditors">
            <map>
                ...
                <entry key="com.apress.springrecipes.shop.Product">
                    <bean class="com.apress.springrecipes.shop.ProductEditor" />
                </entry>
            </map>
        </property>
    </bean>
```

```
<bean id="productRanking"
    class="com.apress.springrecipes.shop.ProductRanking">
    <property name="bestSeller">
        <value>com.apress.springrecipes.shop.Disc,CD-RW,1.5</value>
    </property>
    ...
</bean>
</beans>
```

In fact, the JavaBeans API will automatically search a property editor for a class. For a property editor to be searched correctly, it must be located in the same package as the target class, and the name must be the target class name with Editor as its suffix. If your property editor is provided in this convention, such as in the preceding ProductEditor, there's no need to register it again in the Spring IoC container.

2-17. Concurrency with TaskExecutors

Problem

Options for building threaded, concurrent programs are myriad, but there's no standard approach. What's more, building such programs tends to involve creating lots of utility classes to support common use cases.

Solution

Use Spring's TaskExecutor abstraction. This abstraction provides numerous implementations for many environments, including basic Java SE Executor implementations, The CommonJ WorkManager implementations, and custom implementations. In Spring 3.0, all the implementations are unified and can be cast to Java SE's Executor interface, too.

How It Works

Threading is a difficult issue, and several difficult use cases remain unapproachable without a sizable amount of effort; others are at least very tedious to implement using standard threading in the Java SE environment. Concurrency is an important aspect of architectures when implementing server-side components and enjoys no standardization in the Java EE space. In fact, it's quite the contrary: some parts of the Java EE specifications forbid the explicit creation and manipulation of threads!

Java SE

In the Java SE landscape, myriad options have been introduced over the years. First, there's the standard java.lang.Thread support present since day one and Java Development Kit (JDK) 1.0. Java 1.3 saw the introduction of java.util.TimerTask to support doing some sort of work periodically. Java 5 debuted the java.util.concurrent package as well as a reworked hierarchy for building thread pools, oriented around the java.util.concurrent.Executor.

The application programming interface (API) for Executor is simple:

```
package java.util.concurrent;
public interface Executor {
    void execute(Runnable command);
}
```

ExecutorService, a subinterface, provides more functionality for managing threads and providing support for raising events to the threads, such as shutdown(). There are several implementations that have shipped with the JDK since Java SE 5.0. Many of them are available via static factory methods on the java.util.concurrent.Executors class, in much the same way that utility methods for manipulating java.util.Collection instances are offered on the java.util.Collections class. What follows are examples. ExecutorService also provides a submit() method, which returns a Future<T>. An instance of Future<T> can be used to track the progress of a thread that's executing—usually asynchronously. You can call Future.isDone() or Future.isCancelled() to determine whether the job is finished or cancelled, respectively. When you use the ExecutorService and submit() a Runnable, whose run method has no return type, calling get() on the returned Future will return null, or the value you specified on submission:

```
Runnable task = new Runnable(){
  public void run(){
    try{
        Thread.sleep( 1000 * 60 ) ;
        System.out.println("Done sleeping for a minute, returning! " );
    } catch (Exception ex) { /* … */ }
  }
};
ExecutorService executorService  = Executors.newCachedThreadPool() ;
if(executorService.submit(task, Boolean.TRUE).get().equals( Boolean.TRUE ))
    System.out.println( "Job has finished!");
```

With that in hand, you can explore some the characteristics of the various implementations. For example, you'll use the following Runnable instance:

```
package com.apress.springrecipes.spring3.executors;

import java.util.Date;
import org.apache.commons.lang.exception.ExceptionUtils;

public class DemonstrationRunnable implements Runnable {
  public void run() {
        try {
          Thread.sleep(1000);
        } catch (InterruptedException e) {
          System.out.println(
                ExceptionUtils.getFullStackTrace(e));
        }
        System.out.println(Thread.currentThread().getName());
        System.out.printf("Hello at %s \n", new Date());
  }
}
```

The class is designed only to mark the passage of time. You'll use the same instance when you explore Java SE Executors and Spring's TaskExecutor support:

```
package com.apress.springrecipes.spring3.executors;
import java.util.Date;
import java.util.concurrent.ExecutorService;
import java.util.concurrent.Executors;
import java.util.concurrent.ScheduledExecutorService;
import java.util.concurrent.TimeUnit;

public class ExecutorsDemo {

    public static void main(String[] args) throws Throwable {
        Runnable task = new DemonstrationRunnable();

        // will create a pool of threads and attempt to
        // reuse previously created ones if possible
        ExecutorService cachedThreadPoolExecutorService = Executors
            .newCachedThreadPool();
        if (cachedThreadPoolExecutorService.submit(task).get() == null)
            System.out.printf("The cachedThreadPoolExecutorService "
                    + "has succeeded at %s \n", new Date());

        // limits how many new threads are created, queueing the rest
        ExecutorService fixedThreadPool = Executors.newFixedThreadPool(100);
        if (fixedThreadPool.submit(task).get() == null)
            System.out.printf("The fixedThreadPool has " +
                    "succeeded at %s \n",
                    new Date());

        // doesn't use more than one thread at a time
        ExecutorService singleThreadExecutorService = Executors
            .newSingleThreadExecutor();
        if (singleThreadExecutorService.submit(task).get() == null)
            System.out.printf("The singleThreadExecutorService "
                    + "has succeeded at %s \n", new Date());

        // support sending a job with a known result
        ExecutorService es = Executors.newCachedThreadPool();
        if (es.submit(task, Boolean.TRUE).get().equals(Boolean.TRUE))
            System.out.println("Job has finished!");

        // mimic TimerTask
        ScheduledExecutorService scheduledThreadExecutorService = Executors
            .newScheduledThreadPool(10);
        if (scheduledThreadExecutorService.schedule(
            task, 30, TimeUnit.SECONDS).get() == null)
            System.out.printf("The scheduledThreadExecutorService "
                    + "has succeeded at %s \n", new Date());
```

```
        // this doesn't stop until it encounters
        // an exception or its cancel()ed
        scheduledThreadExecutorService.scheduleAtFixedRate(task, 0, 5,
            TimeUnit.SECONDS);

    }
}
```

If you use the version of the `submit()` method on the `ExecutorService` that accepts a `Callable<T>`, then `submit()` return whatever was returned from the `Callable` main method `call()`. The interface for `Callable` is as follows:

```
package java.util.concurrent;

public interface Callable<V> {
    V call() throws Exception;
}
```

Java EE

In the Java EE landscape, different approaches for solving these sorts of problems have been created, often missing the point. Java EE has offered no threading issue help for a long time.

There are other solutions for these sorts of problems. Quartz (a job scheduling framework) filled the gap by providing a solution that provided scheduling and concurrency. JCA 1.5 (or the J2EE Connector Architecture; the JCA acronym is most used when referring to this technology, even though it was supposed to be the acronym for the Java Cryptography Architecture) is a specification that supports concurrency in that it provides a primitive type of gateway for integration functionality. Components can be notified about incoming messages and respond concurrently. JCA 1.5 provides primitive, limited enterprise service bus—similar to integration features, without nearly as much of the finesse of something like SpringSource's Spring Integration framework. That said, if you had to tie a legacy application written in C to a Java EE application server and let it optionally participate in container services, and wanted to do it in a *reasonably* portable way before 2006, it worked well.

The requirement for concurrency wasn't lost on application server vendors, though. In 2003, IBM and BEA jointly created the Timer and WorkManager APIs. The APIs eventually became JSR-237, which was subsequently withdrawn and merged with JSR-236 with the focus being on how to implement concurrency in a managed (usually Java EE) environment. JSR-236 is still not final. The Service Data Object (SDO) Specification, JSR-235, also had a similar solution in the works, although it is not final. Both SDO and the WorkManager API were targeted for Java EE 1.4, although they've both progressed independently since. The Timer and WorkManager APIs, also known as the CommonJ WorkManager API, enjoys support on both WebLogic (9.0 or later) and WebSphere (6.0 or later), although they're not necessarily portable. Finally, open source implementations of the CommonJ API have sprung up in recent years.

Confused yet?

The issue is that there's no portable, standard, simple way of controlling threads and providing concurrency for components in a managed environment (or a nonmanaged environment!). Even if the discussion is framed in terms of Java SE–specific solutions, you have an overwhelming plethora of choices to make.

Spring's Solution

In Spring 2.0, a unifying solution was introduced in the `org.springframework.core.task.TaskExecutor` interface. The TaskExecutor abstraction served all requirements pretty well. Because Spring supported Java 1.4, TaskExecutor didn't implement the `java.util.concurrent.Executor` interface, introduced in Java 1.5, although its interface was compatible. And any class implementing TaskExecutor could also implement the Executor interface because it defines the exact same method signature. This interface exists even in Spring 3.0 for backward compatibility with JDK 1.4 in Spring 2.x. This meant that people stuck on older JDKs could build applications with this sophisticated functionality without JDK 5. In Spring 3.0, with Java 5 the baseline, the TaskExecutor interface now extends Executor, which means that all the support provided by Spring now works with the core JDK support, too.

The TaskExecutor interface is used quite a bit internally in the Spring framework. For example, the Quartz integration (which has threading, of course) and the message-driven POJO container support make use of TaskExecutor:

```
// the Spring abstraction
package org.springframework.core.task;

import java.util.concurrent.Executor;

public interface TaskExecutor extends Executor {
  void execute(Runnable task);
}
```

In some places, the various solutions mirror the functionality provided by the core JDK options. In others, they're quite unique and provide integrations with other frameworks such as with a CommonJ WorkManager. These integrations usually take the form of a class that can exist in the target framework but that you can manipulate just like any other TaskExecutor abstraction. Although there is support for adapting an existing Java SE Executor or ExecutorService as a TaskExecutor, this isn't so important in Spring 3.0 because the base class for TaskExecutor is Executor, anyway. In this way, the TaskExecutor in Spring bridges the gap between various solutions on Java EE and Java SE.

Let's see some of the simple support for the TaskExecutor first, using the same Runnable defined previously. The client for the code is a simple Spring bean, into which you've injected various instances of TaskExecutor with the sole aim of submitting the Runnable:

```
package com.apress.springrecipes.spring3.executors;


import org.springframework.beans.factory.annotation.Autowired;
import org.springframework.context.support.ClassPathXmlApplicationContext;
import org.springframework.core.task.SimpleAsyncTaskExecutor;
import org.springframework.core.task.SyncTaskExecutor;
import org.springframework.core.task.support.TaskExecutorAdapter;
import org.springframework.scheduling.concurrent.ThreadPoolTaskExecutor;
import org.springframework.scheduling.timer.TimerTaskExecutor;
```

```java
public class SpringExecutorsDemo {
        public static void main(String[] args) {
            ClassPathXmlApplicationContext ctx =
              new ClassPathXmlApplicationContext("context2.xml");
            SpringExecutorsDemo demo = ctx.getBean(
                "springExecutorsDemo", SpringExecutorsDemo.class);
            demo.submitJobs();
        }

        @Autowired
        private SimpleAsyncTaskExecutor asyncTaskExecutor;

        @Autowired
        private SyncTaskExecutor syncTaskExecutor;

        @Autowired
        private TaskExecutorAdapter taskExecutorAdapter;

        /*  No need, since the scheduling is already configured,
            in the application context
         @Resource(name = "timerTaskExecutorWithScheduledTimerTasks")
        private TimerTaskExecutor timerTaskExecutorWithScheduledTimerTasks;
        */

        @Resource(name = "timerTaskExecutorWithoutScheduledTimerTasks")
        private TimerTaskExecutor timerTaskExecutorWithoutScheduledTimerTasks;

        @Autowired
        private ThreadPoolTaskExecutor threadPoolTaskExecutor;

        @Autowired
        private DemonstrationRunnable task;

        public void submitJobs() {
                syncTaskExecutor.execute(task);
                taskExecutorAdapter.submit(task);
                asyncTaskExecutor.submit(task);

                timerTaskExecutorWithoutScheduledTimerTasks.submit(task);

                /* will do 100 at a time,
                        then queue the rest, ie,
                        should take round 5 seconds total
                    */
                for (int i = 0; i < 500; i++)
                  threadPoolTaskExecutor.submit(task);
        }
}
```

The application context demonstrates the creation of these various TaskExecutor implementations. Most are so simple that you could create them manually. Only in one case (the timerTaskExecutor) do you delegate to a factory bean:

```xml
<?xml version="1.0" encoding="UTF-8"?>
<beans
 xmlns="http://www.springframework.org/schema/beans"
 xmlns:p="http://www.springframework.org/schema/p"
 xmlns:xsi="http://www.w3.org/2001/XMLSchema-instance"
 xmlns:util="http://www.springframework.org/schema/util"
 xmlns:context="http://www.springframework.org/schema/context"
 xsi:schemaLocation="
  http://www.springframework.org/schema/context
  http://www.springframework.org/schema/context/spring-context-3.0.xsd
  http://www.springframework.org/schema/beans
  http://www.springframework.org/schema/beans/spring-beans-3.0.xsd
  http://www.springframework.org/schema/util
  http://www.springframework.org/schema/util/spring-util-3.0.xsd">

<context:annotation-config />

<!-- sample Runnable -->
<bean
 id="task"  class="com.apress.springrecipes.spring3.↵
                    executors.DemonstrationRunnable" />

<!-- TaskExecutors -->
<bean
 class="org.springframework.core.task.support.TaskExecutorAdapter">
 <constructor-arg>
  <bean
   class="java.util.concurrent.Executors"
   factory-method="newCachedThreadPool" />
 </constructor-arg>
</bean>

<bean
 class="org.springframework.core.task.SimpleAsyncTaskExecutor"
 p:daemon="false" />

<bean
 class="org.springframework.core.task.SyncTaskExecutor" />

<bean
 id="timerTaskExecutorWithScheduledTimerTasks"
 class="org.springframework.scheduling.timer.TimerTaskExecutor">
 <property
  name="timer">
  <bean
   class="org.springframework.scheduling.timer.TimerFactoryBean">
   <property
    name="scheduledTimerTasks">
    <list>
     <bean
      class="org.springframework.scheduling.timer.ScheduledTimerTask"
```

```
                p:delay="10"
                p:fixedRate="true"
                p:period="10000"
                p:runnable-ref="task" />
            </list>
          </property>
        </bean>
      </property>

    </bean>

    <bean
     id="timerTaskExecutorWithoutScheduledTimerTasks"
     class="org.springframework.scheduling.timer.TimerTaskExecutor"
     p:delay="10000" />

    <bean
     class="org.springframework.scheduling.concurrent.ThreadPoolTaskExecutor"
     p:corePoolSize="50"
     p:daemon="false"
     p:waitForTasksToCompleteOnShutdown="true"
     p:maxPoolSize="100"
     p:allowCoreThreadTimeOut="true" />

    <!-- client bean -->
    <bean
     id="springExecutorsDemo"
     class="com.apress.springrecipes.spring3.↩
           executors.SpringExecutorsDemo" />
</beans>
```

The previous code shows different implementations of the TaskExecutor interface. The first bean,
the TaskExecutorAdapter instance, is a simple wrapper around a java.util.concurrence.Executors
instance so that you can deal with in terms of the Spring TaskExecutor interface. This is only slightly
useful because you could conceptually deal in terms of the Executor interface now because Spring 3.0
updates the TaskExecutor interface to extend Executor. You use Spring here to configure an instance of
an Executor and pass it in as the constructor argument.

SimpleAsyncTaskExecutor provides a new Thread for each job submitted. It does no thread pooling
or reuse. Each job submitted runs asynchronously in a thread.

SyncTaskExecutor is the simplest of the implementations of TaskExecutor. Submission of a job is
synchronous and tantamount to launching a Thread, running it, and then use join() to connect it
immediately. It's effectively the same as manually invoking the run() method in the calling thread,
skipping threading all together.

TimerTaskExecutor uses a java.util.Timer instance and manages jobs (java.util.concurrent.Callable<T> or java.lang.Runnable instances) for you by running them on the Timer. You can specify a delay when creating the TimerTaskExecutor, after which all submitted jobs will start running. Internally, the TimerTaskExecutor converts Callable<T> instances or Runnable instances that are submitted into TimerTasks, which it then schedules on the Timer. If you schedule multiple jobs, they will be run serialized on the same thread with the same Timer. If you don't specify a Timer explicitly, a default one will be created. If you want to explicitly register TimerTasks on the Timer, use the org.springframework.scheduling.timer.TimerFactoryBean's scheduledTimerTasks property. The TimerTaskExecutor doesn't surface methods for more advanced scheduling like the Timer class does. If you want to schedule at fixed intervals, at a certain Date (point in time) or for a certain period, you need to manipulate the TimerTask itself. You can do this with the org.springframework.scheduling.timer.ScheduledTimerTask class, which provides a readily configured TimerTask that the TimerFactoryBean will schedule appropriately.

To submit jobs just as you have with other TaskExecutors, after a delay simply configure a TimerFactoryBean and then submit as usual:

```
<bean id="timerTaskExecutorWithoutScheduledTimerTasks"
class="org.springframework.scheduling.timer.TimerTaskExecutor" p:delay="10000" />
```

More complex scheduling, such as fixed interval execution, requires that you set the TimerTask explicitly. Here, it does little good to actually submit jobs manually. For more advanced functionality, you'll want to use something like Quartz, which can support cron expressions.

```
<bean
  id="timerTaskExecutorWithScheduledTimerTasks"
  class="org.springframework.scheduling.timer.TimerTaskExecutor">
  <property
   name="timer">
   <bean
    class="org.springframework.scheduling.timer.TimerFactoryBean">
    <property
     name="scheduledTimerTasks">
     <list>
      <bean
       class="org.springframework.scheduling.timer.ScheduledTimerTask"
       p:delay="10"
       p:fixedRate="true"
       p:period="10000"
       p:runnable-ref="task" />
     </list>
    </property>
   </bean>
  </property>
</bean>
```

The last example is ThreadPoolTaskExecutor, which is a full on thread pool implementation building on java.util.concurrent.ThreadPoolExecutor.

If you want to build applications using the CommonJ WorkManager/TimerManager support available in IBM WebSphere 6.0 and BEA WebLogic 9.0, you can use `org.springframework.scheduling.commonj.WorkManagerTaskExecutor`. This class delegates to a reference to the CommonJ Work Manager available inside of WebSphere or WebLogic. Usually, you'll provide it with a JNDI reference to the appropriate resource. This works well enough (such as with Geronimo), but extra effort is required with JBoss or GlassFish. Spring provides classes that delegate to the JCA support provided on those servers: for GlassFish, use `org.springframework.jca.work.glassfish.GlassFishWorkManagerTaskExecutor`; for JBoss, use `org.springframework.jca.work.jboss.JBossWorkManagerTaskExecutor`.

The `TaskExecutor` support provides a powerful way to access scheduling services on your application server via a unified interface. If you're looking for more robust (albeit much more heavyweight) support that can be deployed on any server (even Tomcat and Jetty!), you might consider Spring's Quartz support.

Summary

In this chapter, you have learned various ways of creating a bean, which include invoking a constructor, invoking a static/instance factory method, using a factory bean, and retrieving it from a static field/object property. The Spring IoC container makes it easy to create beans in these ways. In Spring, you can specify the bean scope to control which bean instance should be returned when requested. The default bean scope is `singleton`—Spring creates a single and shared bean instance per Spring IoC container. Another common scope is `prototype`—Spring creates a new bean instance each time when requested.

You can customize the initialization and destruction of your beans by specifying the corresponding callback methods. In addition, your beans can implement certain aware interfaces to be made aware of the container's configurations and infrastructures. The Spring IoC container will call these methods at particular points of a bean's life cycle.

Spring supports registering bean post processors in the IoC container to perform additional bean processing before and after the initialization callback methods. Bean post processors can process all the beans in the IoC container. Typically, bean post processors are used for checking the validity of bean properties or altering the bean properties according to particular criteria.

You have also learned about certain advanced IoC container features, such as externalizing bean configuration into properties files, resolving text messages from resource bundles, publishing and listening to application events, using property editors to convert property values from text values, and loading external resources. You will find these features very useful when developing applications with Spring. Finally, you learned about more exotic features available to you for managing concurrency with Spring's Executor implementations.

■■■

CHAPTER 3

Spring AOP and AspectJ Support

In this chapter, you will learn Spring AOP usage and some advanced AOP topics, such as advice precedence and introduction. AOP has been a cornerstone of the Spring framework since its inception. Though support for AOP between versions 1.x and 2.x of the Spring framework presented significant changes, support for AOP in version 3.x remains the same as in version 2.x. Moreover, you will learn how to use the AspectJ framework in Spring applications.

Starting from Spring version 2.x, you can write your aspects as POJOs with either AspectJ annotations or XML-based configurations in the bean configuration file. As these two types of configurations have the same effect indeed, most of this chapter will focus on AspectJ annotations while describing XML-based configurations for comparison's sake.

The core implementation technology for using Spring AOP remains the same throughout all versions: dynamic proxy. This means Spring AOP is backward compatible, so you can continue to use classic Spring advices, pointcuts, and auto-proxy creators in all Spring AOP versions.

As AspectJ has grown into a complete and popular AOP framework, Spring supports the use of POJO aspects written with AspectJ annotations in its AOP framework. Since AspectJ annotations are supported by more and more AOP frameworks, your AspectJ-style aspects are more likely to be reused in other AOP frameworks that support AspectJ.

Keep in mind that although you can apply AspectJ aspects in Spring AOP, this is not the same as using the AspectJ framework. In fact, there are some limitations on the use of AspectJ aspects in Spring AOP, as Spring only allows aspects to apply to beans declared in the IoC container. If you want to apply aspects outside this scope, you have to use the AspectJ framework, which will be introduced at the end of this chapter.

Upon finishing this chapter, you will be able to write POJO aspects to use in the Spring AOP framework. You should also be able to make use of the AspectJ framework in your Spring applications.

3-1. Enabling AspectJ Annotation Support in Spring

Problem

Spring supports the use of POJO aspects written with AspectJ annotations in its AOP framework. But first, you have to enable AspectJ annotation support in the Spring IoC container.

Solution

To enable AspectJ annotation support in the Spring IoC container, you only have to define an empty XML element <aop:aspectj-autoproxy> in your bean configuration file. Then, Spring will automatically create proxies for any of your beans that are matched by your AspectJ aspects.

For cases in which interfaces are not available or not used in an application's design, it's possible to create proxies by relying on CGLIB. To enable CGLIB, you need to set the attribute proxy-target-class=true in <aop:aspectj-autoproxy>.

How It Works

The following calculator interfaces will serve as the foundations for illustrating the enablement of AspectJ in Spring:

```
package com.apress.springrecipes.calculator;

public interface ArithmeticCalculator {

    public double add(double a, double b);
    public double sub(double a, double b);
    public double mul(double a, double b);
    public double div(double a, double b);
}
```

```
package com.apress.springrecipes.calculator;

public interface UnitCalculator {

    public double kilogramToPound(double kilogram);
    public double kilometerToMile(double kilometer);
}
```

Next, you provide an implementation for each interface with println statements to let you know when the methods are executed.

```
package com.apress.springrecipes.calculator;

public class ArithmeticCalculatorImpl implements ArithmeticCalculator {

    public double add(double a, double b) {
        double result = a + b;
        System.out.println(a + " + " + b + " = " + result);
        return result;
    }

    public double sub(double a, double b) {
        double result = a - b;
        System.out.println(a + " - " + b + " = " + result);
        return result;
    }
```

```java
    public double mul(double a, double b) {
        double result = a * b;
        System.out.println(a + " * " + b + " = " + result);
        return result;
    }

    public double div(double a, double b) {
        if (b == 0) {
            throw new IllegalArgumentException("Division by zero");
        }
        double result = a / b;
        System.out.println(a + " / " + b + " = " + result);
        return result;
    }
}

package com.apress.springrecipes.calculator;

public class UnitCalculatorImpl implements UnitCalculator {

    public double kilogramToPound(double kilogram) {
        double pound = kilogram * 2.2;
        System.out.println(kilogram + " kilogram = " + pound + " pound");
        return pound;
    }

    public double kilometerToMile(double kilometer) {
        double mile = kilometer * 0.62;
        System.out.println(kilometer + " kilometer = " + mile + " mile");
        return mile;
    }
}
```

To enable AspectJ annotation support for this application, you just define an empty XML element, <aop:aspectj-autoproxy>, in your bean configuration file. Moreover, you must add the aop schema definition to your <beans> root element. When the Spring IoC container notices the <aop:aspectj-autoproxy> element in your bean configuration file, it will automatically create proxies for your beans that are matched by your AspectJ aspects.

■ **Note** To use AspectJ annotations in your Spring application, you have to include the appropriate dependencies in your classpath. If you are using Maven, add the following declarations to your Maven project's pom.xml:

<dependency>
  <groupId>org.springframework</groupId>
  <artifactId>spring-aop</artifactId>
  <version>${spring.version}</version>
</dependency>

```
<beans xmlns="http://www.springframework.org/schema/beans"
    xmlns:xsi="http://www.w3.org/2001/XMLSchema-instance"
    xmlns:aop="http://www.springframework.org/schema/aop"
    xsi:schemaLocation="http://www.springframework.org/schema/beans
        http://www.springframework.org/schema/beans/spring-beans-3.0.xsd
        http://www.springframework.org/schema/aop
        http://www.springframework.org/schema/aop/spring-aop-3.0.xsd">

    <aop:aspectj-autoproxy />

    <bean id="arithmeticCalculator"
        class="com.apress.springrecipes.calculator.ArithmeticCalculatorImpl" />

    <bean id="unitCalculator"
        class="com.apress.springrecipes.calculator.UnitCalculatorImpl" />
</beans>
```

3-2. Declaring Aspects with AspectJ Annotations

Problem

Since merging with AspectWerkz in version 5, AspectJ supports its aspects to be written as POJOs annotated with a set of AspectJ annotations. Aspects of this kind are also supported by the Spring AOP framework. But they must be registered in the Spring IoC container to take effect.

Solution

You register AspectJ aspects in Spring simply by declaring them as bean instances in the IoC container. With AspectJ enabled in the Spring IoC container, it will create proxies for your beans that are matched by your AspectJ aspects.

Written with AspectJ annotations, an aspect is simply a Java class with the @Aspect annotation. An *advice* is a simple Java method with one of the advice annotations. AspectJ supports five types of advice annotations: @Before, @After, @AfterReturning, @AfterThrowing, and @Around.

How It Works

Before Advices

To create a *before* advice to handle crosscutting concerns before particular program execution points, you use the @Before annotation and include the pointcut expression as the annotation value.

```
package com.apress.springrecipes.calculator;

import org.apache.commons.logging.Log;
import org.apache.commons.logging.LogFactory;
import org.aspectj.lang.annotation.Aspect;
import org.aspectj.lang.annotation.Before;

@Aspect
public class CalculatorLoggingAspect {

    private Log log = LogFactory.getLog(this.getClass());

    @Before("execution(* ArithmeticCalculator.add(..))")
    public void logBefore() {
        log.info("The method add() begins");
    }
}
```

■ **Note** In order for log messages to be generated, the proper configuration for the Log4J system is needed. A basic Log4J configuration file—defined by default in a file named log4j.properties—would contain the following lines:

```
log4j.rootLogger=DEBUG, A1
log4j.appender.A1=org.apache.log4j.ConsoleAppender
log4j.appender.A1.layout=org.apache.log4j.PatternLayout
```

This pointcut expression matches the add() method execution of the ArithmeticCalculator interface. The preceding wildcard in this expression matches any modifier (public, protected, and private) and any return type. The two dots in the argument list match any number of arguments.

To register this aspect, you just declare a bean instance of it in the IoC container. The aspect bean may even be anonymous if there's no reference from other beans.

```
<beans ...>
    ...
    <bean class="com.apress.springrecipes.calculator.CalculatorLoggingAspect" />
</beans>
```

You can test your aspect with the following Main class:

```
package com.apress.springrecipes.calculator;

import org.springframework.context.ApplicationContext;
import org.springframework.context.support.ClassPathXmlApplicationContext;

public class Main {

    public static void main(String[] args) {
        ApplicationContext context =
            new ClassPathXmlApplicationContext("beans.xml");

        ArithmeticCalculator arithmeticCalculator =
            (ArithmeticCalculator) context.getBean("arithmeticCalculator");
        arithmeticCalculator.add(1, 2);
        arithmeticCalculator.sub(4, 3);
        arithmeticCalculator.mul(2, 3);
        arithmeticCalculator.div(4, 2);

        UnitCalculator unitCalculator =
            (UnitCalculator) context.getBean("unitCalculator");
        unitCalculator.kilogramToPound(10);
        unitCalculator.kilometerToMile(5);
    }
}
```

The execution points matched by a pointcut are called *join points*. In this term, a *pointcut* is an expression to match a set of join points, while an *advice* is the action to take at a particular join point.

For your advice to access the detail of the current join point, you can declare an argument of type JoinPoint in your advice method. Then, you can get access to join point details such as the method name and argument values. Now, you can expand your pointcut to match all methods by changing the class name and method name to wildcards.

```
package com.apress.springrecipes.calculator;
...
import java.util.Arrays;

import org.aspectj.lang.JoinPoint;
import org.aspectj.lang.annotation.Aspect;
import org.aspectj.lang.annotation.Before;

@Aspect
public class CalculatorLoggingAspect {
    ...
    @Before("execution(* *.*(..))")
```

```
    public void logBefore(JoinPoint joinPoint) {
        log.info("The method " + joinPoint.getSignature().getName()
                + "() begins with " + Arrays.toString(joinPoint.getArgs()));
    }
}
```

After Advices

An *after* advice is executed after a join point finishes, whenever it returns a result or throws an exception abnormally. The following after advice logs the calculator method ending. An aspect may include one or more advices.

```
package com.apress.springrecipes.calculator;
...
import org.aspectj.lang.JoinPoint;
import org.aspectj.lang.annotation.After;
import org.aspectj.lang.annotation.Aspect;

@Aspect
public class CalculatorLoggingAspect {
    ...
    @After("execution(* *.*(..))")
    public void logAfter(JoinPoint joinPoint) {
        log.info("The method " + joinPoint.getSignature().getName()
                + "() ends");
    }
}
```

After Returning Advices

An after advice is executed regardless of whether a join point returns normally or throws an exception. If you would like to perform logging only when a join point returns, you should replace the after advice with an *after returning* advice.

```
package com.apress.springrecipes.calculator;
...
import org.aspectj.lang.JoinPoint;
import org.aspectj.lang.annotation.AfterReturning;
import org.aspectj.lang.annotation.Aspect;

@Aspect
public class CalculatorLoggingAspect {
    ...
    @AfterReturning("execution(* *.*(..))")
    public void logAfterReturning(JoinPoint joinPoint) {
        log.info("The method " + joinPoint.getSignature().getName()
                + "() ends");
    }
}
```

In an after returning advice, you can get access to the return value of a join point by adding a returning attribute to the @AfterReturning annotation. The value of this attribute should be the argument name of this advice method for the return value to pass in. Then, you have to add an argument to the advice method signature with this name. At runtime, Spring AOP will pass in the return value through this argument. Also note that the original pointcut expression needs to be presented in the pointcut attribute instead.

```
package com.apress.springrecipes.calculator;
...
import org.aspectj.lang.JoinPoint;
import org.aspectj.lang.annotation.AfterReturning;
import org.aspectj.lang.annotation.Aspect;

@Aspect
public class CalculatorLoggingAspect {
    ...
    @AfterReturning(
        pointcut = "execution(* *.*(..))",
        returning = "result")
    public void logAfterReturning(JoinPoint joinPoint, Object result) {
        log.info("The method " + joinPoint.getSignature().getName()
                + "() ends with " + result);
    }
}
```

After Throwing Advices

An *after throwing* advice is executed only when an exception is thrown by a join point.

```
package com.apress.springrecipes.calculator;
...
import org.aspectj.lang.JoinPoint;
import org.aspectj.lang.annotation.AfterThrowing;
import org.aspectj.lang.annotation.Aspect;

@Aspect
public class CalculatorLoggingAspect {
    ...
    @AfterThrowing("execution(* *.*(..))")
    public void logAfterThrowing(JoinPoint joinPoint) {
        log.error("An exception has been thrown in "
                + joinPoint.getSignature().getName() + "()");
    }
}
```

Similarly, the exception thrown by the join point can be accessed by adding a throwing attribute to the @AfterThrowing annotation. The type Throwable is the superclass of all errors and exceptions in the Java language. So, the following advice will catch any of the errors and exceptions thrown by the join points:

```
package com.apress.springrecipes.calculator;
...
import org.aspectj.lang.JoinPoint;
import org.aspectj.lang.annotation.AfterThrowing;
import org.aspectj.lang.annotation.Aspect;

@Aspect
public class CalculatorLoggingAspect {
    ...
    @AfterThrowing(
        pointcut = "execution(* *.*(..))",
        throwing = "e")
    public void logAfterThrowing(JoinPoint joinPoint, Throwable e) {
        log.error("An exception " + e + " has been thrown in "
                + joinPoint.getSignature().getName() + "()");
    }
}
```

However, if you are interested in one particular type of exception only, you can declare it as the argument type of the exception. Then your advice will be executed only when exceptions of compatible type (i.e., this type and its subtypes) are thrown.

```
package com.apress.springrecipes.calculator;
...
import java.util.Arrays;

import org.aspectj.lang.JoinPoint;
import org.aspectj.lang.annotation.AfterThrowing;
import org.aspectj.lang.annotation.Aspect;

@Aspect
public class CalculatorLoggingAspect {
    ...
    @AfterThrowing(
        pointcut = "execution(* *.*(..))",
        throwing = "e")
    public void logAfterThrowing(JoinPoint joinPoint,
            IllegalArgumentException e) {
        log.error("Illegal argument " + Arrays.toString(joinPoint.getArgs())
                + " in " + joinPoint.getSignature().getName() + "()");
    }
}
```

Around Advices

The last type of advice is an *around* advice. It is the most powerful of all the advice types. It gains full control of a join point, so you can combine all the actions of the preceding advices into one single advice. You can even control when, and whether, to proceed with the original join point execution.

The following around advice is the combination of the before, after returning, and after throwing advices you created before. Note that for an around advice, the argument type of the join point must be

ProceedingJoinPoint. It's a subinterface of JoinPoint that allows you to control when to proceed with the original join point.

```java
package com.apress.springrecipes.calculator;
...
import java.util.Arrays;

import org.aspectj.lang.ProceedingJoinPoint;
import org.aspectj.lang.annotation.Around;
import org.aspectj.lang.annotation.Aspect;

@Aspect
public class CalculatorLoggingAspect {
    ...
    @Around("execution(* *.*(..))")
    public Object logAround(ProceedingJoinPoint joinPoint) throws Throwable {
        log.info("The method " + joinPoint.getSignature().getName()
                + "() begins with " + Arrays.toString(joinPoint.getArgs()));
        try {
            Object result = joinPoint.proceed();
            log.info("The method " + joinPoint.getSignature().getName()
                    + "() ends with " + result);
            return result;
        } catch (IllegalArgumentException e) {
            log.error("Illegal argument "
                    + Arrays.toString(joinPoint.getArgs()) + " in "
                    + joinPoint.getSignature().getName() + "()");
            throw e;
        }
    }
}
```

The around advice type is very powerful and flexible in that you can even alter the original argument values and change the final return value. You must use this type of advice with great care, as the call to proceed with the original join point may easily be forgotten.

■ **Tip** A common rule for choosing an advice type is to use the least powerful one that can satisfy your requirements.

3-3. Accessing the Join Point Information

Problem

In AOP, an advice is applied to different program execution points, which are called join points. For an advice to take the correct action, it often requires detailed information about join points.

Solution

An advice can access the current join point information by declaring an argument of type org.aspectj.lang.JoinPoint in the advice method signature.

How It Works

For example, you can access the join point information through the following advice. The information includes the join point kind (only method-execution in Spring AOP), the method signature (declaring type and method name), and the argument values, as well as the target object and proxy object.

```
package com.apress.springrecipes.calculator;
...
import java.util.Arrays;

import org.aspectj.lang.JoinPoint;
import org.aspectj.lang.annotation.Aspect;
import org.aspectj.lang.annotation.Before;

@Aspect
public class CalculatorLoggingAspect {
    ...
    @Before("execution(* *.*(..))")
    public void logJoinPoint(JoinPoint joinPoint) {
        log.info("Join point kind : "
                + joinPoint.getKind());
        log.info("Signature declaring type : "
                + joinPoint.getSignature().getDeclaringTypeName());
        log.info("Signature name : "
                + joinPoint.getSignature().getName());
        log.info("Arguments : "
                + Arrays.toString(joinPoint.getArgs()));
        log.info("Target class : "
                + joinPoint.getTarget().getClass().getName());
        log.info("This class : "
                + joinPoint.getThis().getClass().getName());
    }
}
```

The original bean that was wrapped by a proxy is called the *target* object, while the proxy object is called the *this* object. They can be accessed by the join point's getTarget() and getThis() methods. From the following outputs, you can see that the classes of these two objects are not the same:

```
Join point kind : method-execution
Signature declaring type : com.apress.springrecipes.calculator.ArithmeticCalculator
Signature name : add
Arguments : [1.0, 2.0]
Target class : com.apress.springrecipes.calculator.ArithmeticCalculatorImpl
This class : $Proxy6
```

3-4. Specifying Aspect Precedence

Problem

When there's more than one aspect applied to the same join point, the precedence of the aspects is undefined unless you have explicitly specified it.

Solution

The precedence of aspects can be specified either by implementing the Ordered interface or by using the @Order annotation.

How It Works

Suppose you have written another aspect to validate the calculator arguments. There's only one before advice in this aspect.

```
package com.apress.springrecipes.calculator;

import org.aspectj.lang.JoinPoint;
import org.aspectj.lang.annotation.Aspect;
import org.aspectj.lang.annotation.Before;

@Aspect
public class CalculatorValidationAspect {

    @Before("execution(* *.*(double, double))")
    public void validateBefore(JoinPoint joinPoint) {
        for (Object arg : joinPoint.getArgs()) {
            validate((Double) arg);
        }
    }
}
```

```
    private void validate(double a) {
        if (a < 0) {
            throw new IllegalArgumentException("Positive numbers only");
        }
    }
}
```

To register this aspect in Spring, you simply declare a bean instance of this aspect in the bean configuration file.

```
<beans ...>
    ...
    <bean class="com.apress.springrecipes.calculator.CalculatorLoggingAspect" />

    <bean class="com.apress.springrecipes.calculator.↵
        CalculatorValidationAspect" />
</beans>
```

However, the precedence of the aspects will be undefined now. Be cautious that the precedence does not depend on the order of bean declaration. So, to specify the precedence, you have to make both of the aspects implement the Ordered interface. The lower value returned by the getOrder() method represents higher priority. So, if you prefer the validation aspect to be applied first, it should return a value lower than the logging aspect.

```
package com.apress.springrecipes.calculator;
...
import org.springframework.core.Ordered;

@Aspect
public class CalculatorValidationAspect implements Ordered {
    ...
    public int getOrder() {
        return 0;
    }
}
```

```
package com.apress.springrecipes.calculator;
...
import org.springframework.core.Ordered;

@Aspect
public class CalculatorLoggingAspect implements Ordered {
    ...
    public int getOrder() {
        return 1;
    }
}
```

Another way to specify precedence is through the @Order annotation. The order number should be presented in the annotation value.

```
package com.apress.springrecipes.calculator;
...
import org.springframework.core.annotation.Order;

@Aspect
@Order(0)
public class CalculatorValidationAspect {
    ...
}
```

```
package com.apress.springrecipes.calculator;
...
import org.springframework.core.annotation.Order;

@Aspect
@Order(1)
public class CalculatorLoggingAspect {
    ...
}
```

3-5. Reusing Pointcut Definitions

Problem

When writing AspectJ aspects, you can directly embed a pointcut expression in an advice annotation. However, the same pointcut expression may be repeated in multiple advices.

Solution

Like many other AOP implementations, AspectJ also allows you to define a pointcut independently to be reused in multiple advices.

How It Works

In an AspectJ aspect, a pointcut can be declared as a simple method with the @Pointcut annotation. The method body of a pointcut is usually empty, as it is unreasonable to mix a pointcut definition with application logic. The access modifier of a pointcut method controls the visibility of this pointcut as well. Other advices can refer to this pointcut by the method name.

```
package com.apress.springrecipes.calculator;
...
import org.aspectj.lang.annotation.Pointcut;

@Aspect
public class CalculatorLoggingAspect {

    ...
    @Pointcut("execution(* *.*(..))")
    private void loggingOperation() {}

    @Before("loggingOperation()")
    public void logBefore(JoinPoint joinPoint) {
        ...
    }

    @AfterReturning(
        pointcut = "loggingOperation()",
        returning = "result")
    public void logAfterReturning(JoinPoint joinPoint, Object result) {
        ...
    }

    @AfterThrowing(
        pointcut = "loggingOperation()",
        throwing = "e")
    public void logAfterThrowing(JoinPoint joinPoint, IllegalArgumentException e) {
        ...
    }

    @Around("loggingOperation()")
    public Object logAround(ProceedingJoinPoint joinPoint) throws Throwable {
        ...
    }
}
```

Usually, if your pointcuts are shared between multiple aspects, it is better to centralize them in a common class. In this case, they must be declared as public.

```
package com.apress.springrecipes.calculator;

import org.aspectj.lang.annotation.Aspect;
import org.aspectj.lang.annotation.Pointcut;

@Aspect
public class CalculatorPointcuts {

    @Pointcut("execution(* *.*(..))")
    public void loggingOperation() {}
}
```

When you refer to this pointcut, you have to include the class name as well. If the class is not located in the same package as the aspect, you have to include the package name also.

```
package com.apress.springrecipes.calculator;
...
@Aspect
public class CalculatorLoggingAspect {
    ...
    @Before("CalculatorPointcuts.loggingOperation()")
    public void logBefore(JoinPoint joinPoint) {
        ...
    }

    @AfterReturning(
        pointcut = "CalculatorPointcuts.loggingOperation()",
        returning = "result")
    public void logAfterReturning(JoinPoint joinPoint, Object result) {
        ...
    }

    @AfterThrowing(
        pointcut = "CalculatorPointcuts.loggingOperation()",
        throwing = "e")
    public void logAfterThrowing(JoinPoint joinPoint, IllegalArgumentException e) {
        ...
    }

    @Around("CalculatorPointcuts.loggingOperation()")
    public Object logAround(ProceedingJoinPoint joinPoint) throws Throwable {
        ...
    }
}
```

3-6. Writing AspectJ Pointcut Expressions

Problem

Crosscutting concerns may happen at different program execution points, which are called join points. Because of the variety of join points, you need a powerful expression language that can help in matching them.

Solution

The AspectJ pointcut language is a powerful expression language that can match various kinds of join points. However, Spring AOP supports only method execution join points for beans declared in its IoC container. For this reason, only those pointcut expressions supported by Spring AOP will be introduced here. For a full description of the AspectJ pointcut language, please refer to the AspectJ programming guide available on AspectJ's web site (http://www.eclipse.org/aspectj/).

Spring AOP makes use of the AspectJ pointcut language for its pointcut definition. Actually, Spring AOP interprets the pointcut expressions at runtime by using a library provided by AspectJ.

When writing AspectJ pointcut expressions for Spring AOP, you must keep in mind that Spring AOP only supports method execution join points for the beans in its IoC container. If you use a pointcut expression out of this scope, an IllegalArgumentException will be thrown.

How It Works

Method Signature Patterns

The most typical pointcut expressions are used to match a number of methods by their signatures. For example, the following pointcut expression matches all of the methods declared in the ArithmeticCalculator interface. The preceding wildcard matches methods with any modifier (public, protected, and private) and any return type. The two dots in the argument list match any number of arguments.

```
execution(* com.apress.springrecipes.calculator.ArithmeticCalculator.*(..))
```

You can omit the package name if the target class or interface is located in the same package as this aspect.

```
execution(* ArithmeticCalculator.*(..))
```

The following pointcut expression matches all the public methods declared in the ArithmeticCalculator interface:

```
execution(public * ArithmeticCalculator.*(..))
```

You can also restrict the method return type. For example, the following pointcut matches the methods that return a double number:

```
execution(public double ArithmeticCalculator.*(..))
```

The argument list of the methods can also be restricted. For example, the following pointcut matches the methods whose first argument is of primitive double type. The two dots then match any number of followed arguments.

```
execution(public double ArithmeticCalculator.*(double, ..))
```

Or, you can specify all the argument types in the method signature for the pointcut to match.

```
execution(public double ArithmeticCalculator.*(double, double))
```

Although the AspectJ pointcut language is powerful in matching various join points, sometimes, you may not be able to find any common characteristics (e.g., modifiers, return types, method name patterns, or arguments) for the methods you would like to match. In such cases, you can consider providing a custom annotation for them. For instance, you can define the following marker annotation. This annotation can be applied to both method level and type level.

```java
package com.apress.springrecipes.calculator;

import java.lang.annotation.Documented;
import java.lang.annotation.ElementType;
import java.lang.annotation.Retention;
import java.lang.annotation.RetentionPolicy;
import java.lang.annotation.Target;

@Target( { ElementType.METHOD, ElementType.TYPE })
@Retention(RetentionPolicy.RUNTIME)
@Documented
public @interface LoggingRequired {
}
```

Next, you can annotate all methods that require logging with this annotation. Note that the annotations must be added to the implementation class but not the interface, as they will not be inherited.

```java
package com.apress.springrecipes.calculator;

public class ArithmeticCalculatorImpl implements ArithmeticCalculator {

    @LoggingRequired
    public double add(double a, double b) {
        ...
    }

    @LoggingRequired
    public double sub(double a, double b) {
        ...
    }

    @LoggingRequired
    public double mul(double a, double b) {
        ...
    }
```

```
@LoggingRequired
public double div(double a, double b) {
    ...
}
}
```

Now, you are able to write a pointcut expression to match all methods with this @LoggingRequired annotation.

```
@annotation(com.apress.springrecipes.calculator.LoggingRequired)
```

Type Signature Patterns

Another kind of pointcut expressions matches all join points within certain types. When applied to Spring AOP, the scope of these pointcuts will be narrowed to matching all method executions within the types. For example, the following pointcut matches all the method execution join points within the com.apress.springrecipes.calculator package:

```
within(com.apress.springrecipes.calculator.*)
```

To match the join points within a package and its subpackage, you have to add one more dot before the wildcard.

```
within(com.apress.springrecipes.calculator..*)
```

The following pointcut expression matches the method execution join points within a particular class:

```
within(com.apress.springrecipes.calculator.ArithmeticCalculatorImpl)
```

Again, if the target class is located in the same package as this aspect, the package name can be omitted.

```
within(ArithmeticCalculatorImpl)
```

You can match the method execution join points within all classes that implement the ArithmeticCalculator interface by adding a plus symbol.

```
within(ArithmeticCalculator+)
```

Your custom annotation @LoggingRequired can be applied to the class level instead of the method level.

```
package com.apress.springrecipes.calculator;

@LoggingRequired
public class ArithmeticCalculatorImpl implements ArithmeticCalculator {
    ...
}
```

Then, you can match the join points within the classes that have been annotated with @LoggingRequired.

```
@within(com.apress.springrecipes.calculator.LoggingRequired)
```

Bean Name Patterns

Starting from Spring 2.5, there is a pointcut type that is used to match bean names. For example, the following pointcut expression matches beans whose name ends with Calculator:

```
bean(*Calculator)
```

■ **Caution** This pointcut type is supported only in XML-based Spring AOP configurations, not in AspectJ annotations.

Combining Pointcut Expressions

In AspectJ, pointcut expressions can be combined with the operators && (and), || (or), and ! (not). For example, the following pointcut matches the join points within classes that implement either the ArithmeticCalculator or UnitCalculator interface:

```
within(ArithmeticCalculator+) || within(UnitCalculator+)
```

The operands of these operators can be any pointcut expressions or references to other pointcuts.

```
package com.apress.springrecipes.calculator;

import org.aspectj.lang.annotation.Aspect;
import org.aspectj.lang.annotation.Pointcut;

@Aspect
public class CalculatorPointcuts {

    @Pointcut("within(ArithmeticCalculator+)")
    public void arithmeticOperation() {}

    @Pointcut("within(UnitCalculator+)")
    public void unitOperation() {}

    @Pointcut("arithmeticOperation() || unitOperation()")
    public void loggingOperation() {}
}
```

Declaring Pointcut Parameters

One way to access join point information is by reflection (i.e., via an argument of type
org.aspectj.lang.JoinPoint in the advice method). Besides, you can access join point information in a
declarative way by using some kinds of special pointcut expressions. For example, the expressions
target() and args() capture the target object and argument values of the current join point and expose
them as pointcut parameters. These parameters will be passed to your advice method via arguments of
the same name.

```
package com.apress.springrecipes.calculator;
...
import org.aspectj.lang.annotation.Aspect;
import org.aspectj.lang.annotation.Before;

@Aspect
public class CalculatorLoggingAspect {
    ...
    @Before("execution(* *.*(..)) && target(target) && args(a,b)")
    public void logParameter(Object target, double a, double b) {
        log.info("Target class : " + target.getClass().getName());
        log.info("Arguments : " + a + ", " + b);
    }
}
```

When declaring an independent pointcut that exposes parameters, you have to include them in the
argument list of the pointcut method as well.

```
package com.apress.springrecipes.calculator;

import org.aspectj.lang.annotation.Aspect;
import org.aspectj.lang.annotation.Pointcut;

@Aspect
public class CalculatorPointcuts {
    ...
    @Pointcut("execution(* *.*(..)) && target(target) && args(a,b)")
    public void parameterPointcut(Object target, double a, double b) {}
}
```

Any advice that refers to this parameterized pointcut can access the pointcut parameters via
method arguments of the same name.

```
package com.apress.springrecipes.calculator;
...
import org.aspectj.lang.annotation.Aspect;
import org.aspectj.lang.annotation.Before;

@Aspect
public class CalculatorLoggingAspect {
    ...
    @Before("CalculatorPointcuts.parameterPointcut(target, a, b)")
```

```
    public void logParameter(Object target, double a, double b) {
        log.info("Target class : " + target.getClass().getName());
        log.info("Arguments : " + a + ", " + b);
    }
}
```

3-7. Introducing Behaviors to Your Beans

Problem

Sometimes, you may have a group of classes that share a common behavior. In OOP, they must extend the same base class or implement the same interface. This issue is actually a crosscutting concern that can be modularized with AOP.

In addition, the single inheritance mechanism of Java only allows a class to extend one base class at most. So, you cannot inherit behaviors from multiple implementation classes at the same time.

Solution

Introduction is a special type of advice in AOP. It allows your objects to implement an interface dynamically by providing an implementation class for that interface. It seems as if your objects had extended the implementation class at runtime.

Moreover, you are able to introduce multiple interfaces with multiple implementation classes to your objects at the same time. This can achieve the same effect as multiple inheritance.

How It Works

Suppose you have two interfaces, MaxCalculator and MinCalculator, to define the max() and min() operations.

```
package com.apress.springrecipes.calculator;

public interface MaxCalculator {

    public double max(double a, double b);
}
```

```
package com.apress.springrecipes.calculator;

public interface MinCalculator {

    public double min(double a, double b);
}
```

Then you have an implementation for each interface with println statements to let you know when the methods are executed.

```
package com.apress.springrecipes.calculator;

public class MaxCalculatorImpl implements MaxCalculator {

    public double max(double a, double b) {
        double result = (a >= b) ? a : b;
        System.out.println("max(" + a + ", " + b + ") = " + result);
        return result;
    }
}

package com.apress.springrecipes.calculator;

public class MinCalculatorImpl implements MinCalculator {

    public double min(double a, double b) {
        double result = (a <= b) ? a : b;
        System.out.println("min(" + a + ", " + b + ") = " + result);
        return result;
    }
}
```

Now, suppose you would like ArithmeticCalculatorImpl to perform the max() and min() calculation also. As the Java language supports single inheritance only, it is not possible for the ArithmeticCalculatorImpl class to extend both the MaxCalculatorImpl and MinCalculatorImpl classes at the same time. The only possible way is to extend either class (e.g., MaxCalculatorImpl) and implement another interface (e.g., MinCalculator), either by copying the implementation code or delegating the handling to the actual implementation class. In either case, you have to repeat the method declarations.

With introduction, you can make ArithmeticCalculatorImpl dynamically implement both the MaxCalculator and MinCalculator interfaces by using the implementation classes MaxCalculatorImpl and MinCalculatorImpl. It has the same effect as multiple inheritance from MaxCalculatorImpl and MinCalculatorImpl. The brilliant idea behind introduction is that you needn't modify the ArithmeticCalculatorImpl class to introduce new methods. That means you can introduce methods to your existing classes even without source code available.

■ **Tip** You may wonder how an introduction can do that in Spring AOP. The answer is a *dynamic proxy*. As you may recall, you can specify a group of interfaces for a dynamic proxy to implement. Introduction works by adding an interface (e.g., MaxCalculator) to the dynamic proxy. When the methods declared in this interface are called on the proxy object, the proxy will delegate the calls to the backend implementation class (e.g., MaxCalculatorImpl).

Introductions, like advices, must be declared within an aspect. You may create a new aspect or reuse an existing aspect for this purpose. In this aspect, you can declare an introduction by annotating an arbitrary field with the @DeclareParents annotation.

```
package com.apress.springrecipes.calculator;
```

139

```
import org.aspectj.lang.annotation.Aspect;
import org.aspectj.lang.annotation.DeclareParents;

@Aspect
public class CalculatorIntroduction {

    @DeclareParents(
        value = "com.apress.springrecipes.calculator.ArithmeticCalculatorImpl",
        defaultImpl = MaxCalculatorImpl.class)
    public MaxCalculator maxCalculator;

    @DeclareParents(
        value = "com.apress.springrecipes.calculator.ArithmeticCalculatorImpl",
        defaultImpl = MinCalculatorImpl.class)
    public MinCalculator minCalculator;
}
```

The value attribute of the @DeclareParents annotation type indicates which classes are the targets for this introduction. The interface to introduce is determined by the type of the annotated field. Finally, the implementation class used for this new interface is specified in the defaultImpl attribute.

Through these two introductions, you can dynamically introduce a couple of interfaces to the ArithmeticCalculatorImpl class. Actually, you can specify an AspectJ type-matching expression in the value attribute of the @DeclareParents annotation to introduce an interface to multiple classes. For the last step, don't forget to declare an instance of this aspect in the application context.

```
<beans ...>
    ...
    <bean class="com.apress.springrecipes.calculator.CalculatorIntroduction" />
</beans>
```

As you have introduced both the MaxCalculator and MinCalculator interfaces to your arithmetic calculator, you can cast it to the corresponding interface to perform the max() and min() calculations.

```
package com.apress.springrecipes.calculator;

public class Main {

    public static void main(String[] args) {
        ...
        ArithmeticCalculator arithmeticCalculator =
            (ArithmeticCalculator) context.getBean("arithmeticCalculator");
        ...
        MaxCalculator maxCalculator = (MaxCalculator) arithmeticCalculator;
        maxCalculator.max(1, 2);

        MinCalculator minCalculator = (MinCalculator) arithmeticCalculator;
        minCalculator.min(1, 2);
    }
}
```

3-8. Introducing States to Your Beans

Problem

Sometimes, you may want to add new states to a group of existing objects to keep track of their usage, such as the calling count, the last modified date, and so on. It should not be a problem if all the objects have the same base class. However, it's difficult for you to add such states to different classes if they are not in the same class hierarchy.

Solution

You can introduce a new interface to your objects with an implementation class that holds the state field. Then, you can write another advice to change the state according to a particular condition.

How It Works

Suppose you would like to keep track of the calling count of each calculator object. Since there is no field for storing the counter value in the original calculator classes, you need to introduce one with Spring AOP. First, let's create an interface for the operations of a counter.

```
package com.apress.springrecipes.calculator;

public interface Counter {

    public void increase();
    public int getCount();
}
```

Next, just write a simple implementation class for this interface. This class has a count field for storing the counter value.

```
package com.apress.springrecipes.calculator;

public class CounterImpl implements Counter {

    private int count;

    public void increase() {
        count++;
    }

    public int getCount() {
        return count;
    }
}
```

To introduce the Counter interface to all your calculator objects with CounterImpl as the implementation, you can write the following introduction with a type-matching expression that matches all the calculator implementations:

```
package com.apress.springrecipes.calculator;
...
import org.aspectj.lang.annotation.Aspect;
import org.aspectj.lang.annotation.DeclareParents;

@Aspect
public class CalculatorIntroduction {
    ...
    @DeclareParents(
        value = "com.apress.springrecipes.calculator.*CalculatorImpl",
        defaultImpl = CounterImpl.class)
    public Counter counter;
}
```

This introduction introduces CounterImpl to each of your calculator objects. However, it's still not enough to keep track of the calling count. You have to increase the counter value each time a calculator method is called. You can write an after advice for this purpose. Note that you must get the *this* object but not the *target* object, as only the proxy object implements the Counter interface.

```
package com.apress.springrecipes.calculator;
...
import org.aspectj.lang.annotation.After;
import org.aspectj.lang.annotation.Aspect;

@Aspect
public class CalculatorIntroduction {
    ...
    @After("execution(* com.apress.springrecipes.calculator.*Calculator.*(..))"
            + " && this(counter)")
    public void increaseCount(Counter counter) {
        counter.increase();
    }
}
```

In the Main class, you can output the counter value for each of the calculator objects by casting them into the Counter type.

```
package com.apress.springrecipes.calculator;

public class Main {

    public static void main(String[] args) {
        ...
        ArithmeticCalculator arithmeticCalculator =
            (ArithmeticCalculator) context.getBean("arithmeticCalculator");
        ...
```

```
        UnitCalculator unitCalculator =
            (UnitCalculator) context.getBean("unitCalculator");
        ...

        Counter arithmeticCounter = (Counter) arithmeticCalculator;
        System.out.println(arithmeticCounter.getCount());

        Counter unitCounter = (Counter) unitCalculator;
        System.out.println(unitCounter.getCount());
    }
}
```

3-9. Declaring Aspects with XML-Based Configurations

Problem

Declaring aspects with AspectJ annotations is fine for most cases. However, if your JVM version is 1.4 or below (and hence doesn't support annotations), or you don't want your application to have a dependency on AspectJ, you shouldn't use AspectJ annotations to declare your aspects.

Solution

In addition to declaring aspects with AspectJ annotations, Spring supports declaring aspects in the bean configuration file. This type of declaration is done by using the XML elements in the aop schema.

In normal cases, annotation-based declaration is preferable to XML-based declaration. By using AspectJ annotations, your aspects will be compatible with AspectJ, whereas XML-based configurations are specific to Spring. As AspectJ is supported by more and more AOP frameworks, aspects written in annotation style will have a better chance of being reused.

How It Works

To enable AspectJ annotation support in Spring, you have already defined an empty XML element, `<aop:aspectj-autoproxy>`, in your bean configuration file. When declaring aspects with XML, this element is not necessary and should be deleted so that Spring AOP will ignore the AspectJ annotations. However, the aop schema definition must be retained in your `<beans>` root element because all the XML elements for AOP configuration are defined in this schema.

```
<beans xmlns="http://www.springframework.org/schema/beans"
    xmlns:xsi="http://www.w3.org/2001/XMLSchema-instance"
    xmlns:aop="http://www.springframework.org/schema/aop"
    xsi:schemaLocation="http://www.springframework.org/schema/beans
        http://www.springframework.org/schema/beans/spring-beans-3.0.xsd
        http://www.springframework.org/schema/aop
        http://www.springframework.org/schema/aop/spring-aop-3.0.xsd">

    <!--
```

```
    <aop:aspectj-autoproxy />
    -->
    ...
</beans>
```

Declaring Aspects

In the bean configuration file, all the Spring AOP configurations must be defined inside the <aop:config> element. For each aspect, you create an <aop:aspect> element to refer to a backing bean instance for the concrete aspect implementation. So, your aspect beans must have an identifier for the <aop:aspect> elements to refer to.

```
<beans ...>
    <aop:config>
        <aop:aspect id="loggingAspect" ref="calculatorLoggingAspect">
        </aop:aspect>

        <aop:aspect id="validationAspect" ref="calculatorValidationAspect">
        </aop:aspect>

        <aop:aspect id="introduction" ref="calculatorIntroduction">
        </aop:aspect>
    </aop:config>

    <bean id="calculatorLoggingAspect"
        class="com.apress.springrecipes.calculator.CalculatorLoggingAspect" />

    <bean id="calculatorValidationAspect"
        class="com.apress.springrecipes.calculator.CalculatorValidationAspect" />

    <bean id="calculatorIntroduction"
        class="com.apress.springrecipes.calculator.CalculatorIntroduction" />
    ...
</beans>
```

Declaring Pointcuts

A pointcut may be defined either under the <aop:aspect> element or directly under the <aop:config> element. In the former case, the pointcut will be visible to the declaring aspect only. In the latter case, it will be a global pointcut definition, which is visible to all the aspects.

You must remember that unlike AspectJ annotations, XML-based AOP configurations don't allow you to refer to other pointcuts by name within a pointcut expression. That means you must copy the referred pointcut expression and embed it directly.

```
<aop:config>
    <aop:pointcut id="loggingOperation" expression=
        "within(com.apress.springrecipes.calculator.ArithmeticCalculator+) || ↵
        within(com.apress.springrecipes.calculator.UnitCalculator+)" />

    <aop:pointcut id="validationOperation" expression=
        "within(com.apress.springrecipes.calculator.ArithmeticCalculator+) || ↵
        within(com.apress.springrecipes.calculator.UnitCalculator+)" />
    ...
</aop:config>
```

When using AspectJ annotations, you can join two pointcut expressions with the operator &&. However, the character & stands for "entity reference" in XML, so the pointcut operator && isn't valid in an XML document. You have to use the keyword and instead.

Declaring Advices

In the aop schema, there is a particular XML element corresponding to each type of advice. An advice element requires either a pointcut-ref attribute to refer to a pointcut or a pointcut attribute to embed a pointcut expression directly. The method attribute specifies the name of the advice method in the aspect class.

```
<aop:config>
    ...
    <aop:aspect id="loggingAspect" ref="calculatorLoggingAspect">
        <aop:before pointcut-ref="loggingOperation"
            method="logBefore" />

        <aop:after-returning pointcut-ref="loggingOperation"
            returning="result" method="logAfterReturning" />

        <aop:after-throwing pointcut-ref="loggingOperation"
            throwing="e" method="logAfterThrowing" />

        <aop:around pointcut-ref="loggingOperation"
            method="logAround" />
    </aop:aspect>

    <aop:aspect id="validationAspect" ref="calculatorValidationAspect">
        <aop:before pointcut-ref="validationOperation"
            method="validateBefore" />
    </aop:aspect>
</aop:config>
```

Declaring Introductions

Finally, an introduction can be declared inside an aspect using the <aop:declare-parents> element.

```
<aop:config>
    ...
    <aop:aspect id="introduction" ref="calculatorIntroduction">
        <aop:declare-parents
            types-matching=
                "com.apress.springrecipes.calculator.ArithmeticCalculatorImpl"
            implement-interface=
                "com.apress.springrecipes.calculator.MaxCalculator"
            default-impl=
                "com.apress.springrecipes.calculator.MaxCalculatorImpl" />

        <aop:declare-parents
            types-matching=
                "com.apress.springrecipes.calculator.ArithmeticCalculatorImpl"
            implement-interface=
                "com.apress.springrecipes.calculator.MinCalculator"
            default-impl=
                "com.apress.springrecipes.calculator.MinCalculatorImpl" />

        <aop:declare-parents
            types-matching=
                "com.apress.springrecipes.calculator.*CalculatorImpl"
            implement-interface=
                "com.apress.springrecipes.calculator.Counter"
            default-impl=
                "com.apress.springrecipes.calculator.CounterImpl" />

        <aop:after pointcut=
            "execution(* com.apress.springrecipes.calculator.*Calculator.*(..)) ↵
            and this(counter)"
            method="increaseCount" />
    </aop:aspect>
</aop:config>
```

3-10. Load-Time Weaving AspectJ Aspects in Spring

Problem

The Spring AOP framework supports only limited types of AspectJ pointcuts and allows aspects to apply to beans declared in the IoC container. If you want to use additional pointcut types or apply your aspects to objects created outside the Spring IoC container, you have to use the AspectJ framework in your Spring application.

Solution

Weaving is the process of applying aspects to your target objects. With Spring AOP, weaving happens at runtime through dynamic proxies. In contrast, the AspectJ framework supports both compile-time and load-time weaving.

AspectJ *compile-time* weaving is done through a special AspectJ compiler called ajc. It can weave aspects into your Java source files and output woven binary class files. It can also weave aspects into your compiled class files or JAR files. This process is known as post-compile-time weaving. You can perform compile-time and post-compile-time weaving for your classes before declaring them in the Spring IoC container. Spring is not involved in the weaving process at all. For more information on compile-time and post-compile-time weaving, please refer to the AspectJ documentation.

AspectJ *load-time* weaving (also known as LTW) happens when the target classes are loaded into JVM by a class loader. For a class to be woven, a special class loader is required to enhance the bytecode of the target class. Both AspectJ and Spring provide load-time weavers to add load-time weaving capability to the class loader. You need only simple configurations to enable these load-time weavers.

How It Works

To understand the AspectJ load-time weaving process in a Spring application, let's consider a calculator for complex numbers. First, you create the Complex class to represent complex numbers. You define the toString() method for this class to convert a complex number into the string representation (a + bi).

```
package com.apress.springrecipes.calculator;

public class Complex {

    private int real;
    private int imaginary;

    public Complex(int real, int imaginary) {
        this.real = real;
        this.imaginary = imaginary;
    }

    // Getters and Setters
    ...

    public String toString() {
        return "(" + real + " + " + imaginary + "i)";
    }
}
```

Next, you define an interface for the operations on complex numbers. For simplicity's sake, only add() and sub() are supported.

```
package com.apress.springrecipes.calculator;

public interface ComplexCalculator {

    public Complex add(Complex a, Complex b);
    public Complex sub(Complex a, Complex b);
}
```

The implementation code for this interface is as follows. Each time, you return a new complex object as the result.

```
package com.apress.springrecipes.calculator;

public class ComplexCalculatorImpl implements ComplexCalculator {

    public Complex add(Complex a, Complex b) {
        Complex result = new Complex(a.getReal() + b.getReal(),
                a.getImaginary() + b.getImaginary());
        System.out.println(a + " + " + b + " = " + result);
        return result;
    }

    public Complex sub(Complex a, Complex b) {
        Complex result = new Complex(a.getReal() - b.getReal(),
                a.getImaginary() - b.getImaginary());
        System.out.println(a + " - " + b + " = " + result);
        return result;
    }
}
```

Before this calculator can be used, it must be declared as a bean in the Spring IoC container.

```
<bean id="complexCalculator"
    class="com.apress.springrecipes.calculator.ComplexCalculatorImpl" />
```

Now, you can test this complex number calculator with the following code in the Main class:

```
package com.apress.springrecipes.calculator;
...
public class Main {

    public static void main(String[] args) {
        ...
        ComplexCalculator complexCalculator =
            (ComplexCalculator) context.getBean("complexCalculator");
        complexCalculator.add(new Complex(1, 2), new Complex(2, 3));
        complexCalculator.sub(new Complex(5, 8), new Complex(2, 3));
    }
}
```

So far, the complex calculator is working fine. However, you may want to improve the performance of the calculator by caching complex number objects. As caching is a well-known crosscutting concern, you can modularize it with an aspect.

```
package com.apress.springrecipes.calculator;

import java.util.Collections;
import java.util.HashMap;
import java.util.Map;
```

```
import org.aspectj.lang.ProceedingJoinPoint;
import org.aspectj.lang.annotation.Around;
import org.aspectj.lang.annotation.Aspect;

@Aspect
public class ComplexCachingAspect {

    private Map<String, Complex> cache;

    public ComplexCachingAspect() {
        cache = Collections.synchronizedMap(new HashMap<String, Complex>());
    }

    @Around("call(public Complex.new(int, int)) && args(a,b)")
    public Object cacheAround(ProceedingJoinPoint joinPoint, int a, int b)
            throws Throwable {
        String key = a + "," + b;
        Complex complex = cache.get(key);
        if (complex == null) {
            System.out.println("Cache MISS for (" + key + ")");
            complex = (Complex) joinPoint.proceed();
            cache.put(key, complex);
        }
        else {
            System.out.println("Cache HIT for (" + key + ")");
        }
        return complex;
    }
}
```

In this aspect, you cache the complex objects in a map with their real and imaginary values as keys. For this map to be thread-safe, you should wrap it with a synchronized map. Then, the most suitable time to look up the cache is when a complex object is created by invoking the constructor. You use the AspectJ pointcut expression call to capture the join points of calling the Complex(int, int) constructor. This pointcut is not supported by Spring AOP, so you haven't seen it in this chapter before.

Next, you need an around advice to alter the return value. If a complex object of the same value is found in the cache, you return it to the caller directly. Otherwise, you proceed with the original constructor invocation to create a new complex object. Before you return it to the caller, you cache it in the map for subsequent usages.

Because this type of pointcut is not supported by Spring AOP, you have to use the AspectJ framework to apply this aspect. The configuration of the AspectJ framework is done through a file named aop.xml in the META-INF directory in the classpath root.

```
<!DOCTYPE aspectj PUBLIC "-//AspectJ//DTD//EN"
    "http://www.eclipse.org/aspectj/dtd/aspectj.dtd">

<aspectj>
    <weaver>
        <include within="com.apress.springrecipes.calculator.*" />
    </weaver>
```

```
    <aspects>
        <aspect
            name="com.apress.springrecipes.calculator.ComplexCachingAspect" />
    </aspects>
</aspectj>
```

In this AspectJ configuration file, you have to specify the aspects and which classes you want your aspects to weave in. Here, you specify weaving ComplexCachingAspect into all the classes in the com.apress.springrecipes.calculator package.

Load-Time Weaving by the AspectJ Weaver

AspectJ provides a load-time weaving agent to enable load-time weaving. You need only to add a VM argument to the command that runs your application. Then your classes will get woven when they are loaded into the JVM.

```
java -javaagent:c://lib/aspectjweaver.jarcom.apress.springrecipes.calculator.Main
```

■ **Note** to use the AspectJ weaver, you need to include the **aspectjweaver.jar** in the invocation. If you simply intended to load the jar on your classpath, you could add the dependency to your Maven project using the following declaration:

```
<dependency>
    <groupId>org.aspectj</groupId>
    <artifactId>aspectjweaver</artifactId>
    <version>1.6.8</version>
</dependency>
```

However, since you need to include it on the invocation, you download the dependency manually.

If you run your application with the preceding argument, you will get the following output and cache status. The AspectJ agent advises all calls to the Complex(int, int) constructor.

```
Cache MISS for (1,2)

Cache MISS for (2,3)

Cache MISS for (3,5)

(1 + 2i) + (2 + 3i) = (3 + 5i)

Cache MISS for (5,8)

Cache HIT for (2,3)

Cache HIT for (3,5)

(5 + 8i) - (2 + 3i) = (3 + 5i)
```

Load-Time Weaving by Spring Load-Time Weaver

Spring has several load-time weavers for different runtime environments. To turn on a suitable load-time weaver for your Spring application, you need only to declare the empty XML element `<context:load-time-weaver>`. This element is defined in the context schema.

```
<beans xmlns="http://www.springframework.org/schema/beans"
    xmlns:xsi="http://www.w3.org/2001/XMLSchema-instance"
    xmlns:aop="http://www.springframework.org/schema/aop"
    xmlns:context="http://www.springframework.org/schema/context"
    xsi:schemaLocation="http://www.springframework.org/schema/beans
        http://www.springframework.org/schema/beans/spring-beans-3.0.xsd
        http://www.springframework.org/schema/aop
        http://www.springframework.org/schema/aop/spring-aop-3.0.xsd
        http://www.springframework.org/schema/context
        http://www.springframework.org/schema/context/spring-context-3.0.xsd">

    <context:load-time-weaver />
    ...
</beans>
```

Spring will be able to detect the most suitable load-time weaver for your runtime environment. Some Java EE application servers have class loaders that support the Spring load-time weaver mechanism, so there's no need to specify a Java agent in their startup commands.

However, for a simple Java application, you still require a weaving agent provided by Spring to enable load-time weaving. You have to specify the Spring agent in the VM argument of the startup command.

```
java -javaagent:c:/lib/spring-instrument.jarcom.apress.springrecipes.calculator.Main
```

■ **Note** to use the AspectJ weaver, you need to include the **spring-instrument.jar** in the invocation. If you simply intended to load the jar on your classpath, you could add the dependency to your Maven project using the following declaration:

<dependency>
  <groupId>org.springframework</groupId>
  <artifactId>spring-instrument</artifactId>
  <version>${spring.version}</version>
</dependency>

However, since you need to include it on the invocation, you should download the dependency manually.

However, if you run your application, you will get the following output and cache status. This is because the Spring agent advises only the Complex(int, int) constructor calls made by beans declared in the Spring IoC container. As the complex operands are created in the Main class, the Spring agent will not advise their constructor calls.

```
Cache MISS for (3,5)

(1 + 2i) + (2 + 3i) = (3 + 5i)

Cache HIT for (3,5)

(5 + 8i) - (2 + 3i) = (3 + 5i)
```

3-11. Configuring AspectJ Aspects in Spring

Problem

Spring AOP aspects are declared in the bean configuration file so that you can easily configure them. However, aspects to be used in the AspectJ framework are instantiated by the AspectJ framework itself. You have to retrieve the aspect instances from the AspectJ framework to configure them.

Solution

Each AspectJ aspect provides a static factory method called aspectOf(), which allows you to access the current aspect instance. In the Spring IoC container, you can declare a bean created by a factory method by specifying the factory-method attribute.

How It Works

For instance, you can allow the cache map of ComplexCachingAspect to be configured via a setter method and delete its instantiation from the constructor.

```
package com.apress.springrecipes.calculator;
...
import java.util.Collections;
import java.util.Map;

import org.aspectj.lang.annotation.Aspect;

@Aspect
public class ComplexCachingAspect {

    private Map<String, Complex> cache;

    public void setCache(Map<String, Complex> cache) {
        this.cache = Collections.synchronizedMap(cache);
    }
    ...
}
```

To configure this property in the Spring IoC container, you can declare a bean created by the factory method aspectOf().

```
<bean class="com.apress.springrecipes.calculator.ComplexCachingAspect"
    factory-method="aspectOf">
    <property name="cache">
        <map>
            <entry key="2,3">
                <bean class="com.apress.springrecipes.calculator.Complex">
                    <constructor-arg value="2" />
                    <constructor-arg value="3" />
                </bean>
            </entry>
```

```
            <entry key="3,5">
                <bean class="com.apress.springrecipes.calculator.Complex">
                    <constructor-arg value="3" />
                    <constructor-arg value="5" />
                </bean>
            </entry>
        </map>
    </property>
</bean>
```

■ **Tip** You may wonder why your ComplexCachingAspect has a static factory method aspectOf() that you have not declared. This method is woven by AspectJ at load time to allow you to access the current aspect instance. So, if you are using Spring IDE, it may give you a warning because it cannot find this method in your class.

3-12. Injecting Spring Beans into Domain Objects

Problem

Beans declared in the Spring IoC container can wire themselves to one another through Spring's dependency injection capability. However, objects created outside the Spring IoC container cannot wire themselves to Spring beans via configuration. You have to perform the wiring manually with programming code.

Solution

Objects created outside the Spring IoC container are usually domain objects. They are often created using the new operator or from the results of database queries.

To inject a Spring bean into domain objects created outside Spring, you need the help of AOP. Actually, the injection of Spring beans is also a kind of crosscutting concern. As the domain objects are not created by Spring, you cannot use Spring AOP for injection. Spring supplies an AspectJ aspect specialized for this purpose. You can enable this aspect in the AspectJ framework.

How It Works

Suppose you have a global formatter to format complex numbers. This formatter accepts a pattern for formatting.

```
package com.apress.springrecipes.calculator;

public class ComplexFormatter {

    private String pattern;

    public void setPattern(String pattern) {
        this.pattern = pattern;
    }

    public String format(Complex complex) {
        return pattern.replaceAll("a", Integer.toString(complex.getReal()))
                .replaceAll("b", Integer.toString(complex.getImaginary()));
    }
}
```

Next, you configure this formatter in the Spring IoC container and specify a pattern for it.

```
<bean id="complexFormatter"
    class="com.apress.springrecipes.calculator.ComplexFormatter">
    <property name="pattern" value="(a + bi)" />
</bean>
```

In the Complex class, you want to use this formatter in the toString() method to convert a complex number into string. It exposes a setter method for the ComplexFormatter.

```
package com.apress.springrecipes.calculator;

public class Complex {

    private int real;
    private int imaginary;
    ...
    private ComplexFormatter formatter;

    public void setFormatter(ComplexFormatter formatter) {
        this.formatter = formatter;
    }

    public String toString() {
        return formatter.format(this);
    }
}
```

However, as complex objects were not created within the Spring IoC container, they cannot be configured for dependency injection. You have to write code to inject a ComplexFormatter instance into each complex object.

The good news is that Spring includes AnnotationBeanConfigurerAspect in its aspect library for configuring the dependencies of any objects, even if they were not created by the Spring IoC container. First of all, you have to annotate your object type with the @Configurable annotation to declare that this type of object is configurable.

```
package com.apress.springrecipes.calculator;

import org.springframework.beans.factory.annotation.Configurable;

@Configurable
public class Complex {
    ...
}
```

Spring defines a convenient XML element, <context:spring-configured>, for you to enable the mentioned aspect.

```
<beans ...>
    ...
    <context:load-time-weaver />

    <context:spring-configured />

    <bean class="com.apress.springrecipes.calculator.Complex"
        scope="prototype">
        <property name="formatter" ref="complexFormatter" />
    </bean>
</beans>
```

When a class with the @Configurable annotation is instantiated, the aspect will look for a prototype-scoped bean definition whose type is the same as this class. Then, it will configure the new instances according to this bean definition. If there are properties declared in the bean definition, the new instances will also have the same properties set by the aspect.

Finally, the aspect needs to be enabled by the AspectJ framework to take effect. You can weave it into your classes at load time with the Spring agent.

```
java -javaagent:c:/lib/spring-instrument.jarcom.apress.springrecipes.calculator.Main
```

Another way of linking up a configurable class with a bean definition is by the bean ID. You can present a bean ID as the @Configurable annotation value.

```
package com.apress.springrecipes.calculator;

import org.springframework.beans.factory.annotation.Configurable;

@Configurable("complex")
public class Complex {
    ...
}
```

Next, you must add the id attribute to the corresponding bean definition to link with a configurable class.

```
<bean id="complex" class="com.apress.springrecipes.calculator.Complex"
    scope="prototype">
    <property name="formatter" ref="complexFormatter" />
</bean>
```

Similar to normal Spring beans, configurable beans can also support auto-wiring and dependency checking.

```
package com.apress.springrecipes.calculator;

import org.springframework.beans.factory.annotation.Autowire;
import org.springframework.beans.factory.annotation.Configurable;

@Configurable(
    value = "complex",
    autowire = Autowire.BY_TYPE,
    dependencyCheck = true)
public class Complex {
    ...
}
```

Note that the dependencyCheck attribute is of Boolean type but not enumeration type. When it's set to true, it has the same effect as dependency-check="objects"—that is, to check for nonprimitive and noncollection types. With auto-wiring enabled, you no longer need to set the formatter property explicitly.

```
<bean id="complex" class="com.apress.springrecipes.calculator.Complex"
    scope="prototype" />
```

Starting from Spring 2.5, you no longer need to configure auto-wiring and dependency checking at the class level for @Configurable. Instead, you can annotate the formatter's setter method with the @Autowired annotation.

```
package com.apress.springrecipes.calculator;

import org.springframework.beans.factory.annotation.Autowired;
import org.springframework.beans.factory.annotation.Configurable;

@Configurable("complex")
public class Complex {
    ...
    private ComplexFormatter formatter;

    @Autowired
    public void setFormatter(ComplexFormatter formatter) {
        this.formatter = formatter;
    }
}
```

After that, enable the `<context:annotation-config>` element in the bean configuration file to process the methods with these annotations.

```
<beans ...>
    <context:annotation-config />
    ...
</beans>
```

Summary

In this chapter, you have learned how to write aspects with either AspectJ annotations or XML-based configurations in the bean configuration file and how they are registered in the Spring IoC container. Spring AOP supports five types of advices: before, after, after returning, after throwing, and around.

You have also learned various types of pointcuts to match join points by method signature, type signature, and bean name. However, Spring AOP supports method execution join points only for beans declared in its IoC container. If you use a pointcut expression out of this scope, an exception will be thrown.

Introduction is a special type of AOP advice. It allows your objects to implement an interface dynamically by providing an implementation class. It can achieve the same effect as multiple inheritance. Introductions are often used to add behaviors and states to a group of existing objects.

If you want to use pointcut types that are not supported by Spring AOP or apply your aspects to objects created outside the Spring IoC container, you have to use the AspectJ framework in your Spring application. Aspects can be woven into your classes by a load-time weaver. Spring also supplies several useful AspectJ aspects in its aspect library. One of them injects Spring beans into domain objects created outside of Spring.

CHAPTER 4

■■■

Scripting in Spring

In this chapter, you will learn how to use scripting languages in Spring applications. Spring supports three different scripting languages: JRuby, Groovy, and BeanShell. They are the most popular scripting languages in the Java community, and most Java developers find these languages easy to learn.

JRuby (`http://jruby.codehaus.org/`) is an open source Java-based implementation of the popular Ruby programming language (`http://www.ruby-lang.org/`). JRuby supports two-way access between Java and Ruby, which means that you can call a Ruby script directly from a Java program and also access Java classes in a Ruby script.

Groovy (`http://groovy.codehaus.org/`) is a dynamic language for the Java platform that integrates the features of other excellent programming languages. It can be compiled directly into Java bytecode or used as a dynamic scripting language. The syntax of Groovy is very similar to Java, so Java developers can learn Groovy quickly. Moreover, you can access all Java classes and libraries in Groovy.

BeanShell (`http://www.beanshell.org/`) is a lightweight Java scripting language that can dynamically execute Java code fragments while supporting scripting features like those of other scripting languages. With BeanShell, you can simply script a dynamic module of your Java application without having to learn a new language.

After finishing this chapter, you will be able to script parts of your Spring application using these scripting languages.

19-1. Implementing Beans with Scripting Languages

Problem

Sometimes, your application may have certain modules that require frequent and dynamic changes. If implementing these modules with Java, you have to recompile, repackage, and redeploy your application each time after the change. You may not be allowed to perform these actions at any time you want or need, especially for a 24/7 application.

Solution

You can consider implementing any modules that require frequent and dynamic changes with scripting languages. The advantage of scripting languages is that they don't need to be recompiled after changes, so you can simply deploy the new script for the change to take effect.

Spring allows you to implement a bean with one of its supported scripting languages. You can configure a scripted bean in the IoC container just like a normal bean implemented with Java.

How It Works

Suppose you are going to develop an application that requires interest calculation. First of all, you define the following InterestCalculator interface:

```
package com.apress.springrecipes.interest;

public interface InterestCalculator {

    public void setRate(double rate);
    public double calculate(double amount, double year);
}
```

Implementing this interface is not difficult at all. However, as there are many interest calculation strategies, users may need to change the implementation very frequently and dynamically. You don't want to recompile, repackage, and redeploy your application every time this happens. So, you consider implementing this interface with one of the supported scripting languages in Spring.

In Spring's bean configuration file, you have to include the lang schema definition in the <beans> root element to make use of the scripting language support.

```
<beans xmlns="http://www.springframework.org/schema/beans"
    xmlns:xsi="http://www.w3.org/2001/XMLSchema-instance"
    xmlns:lang="http://www.springframework.org/schema/lang"
    xsi:schemaLocation="http://www.springframework.org/schema/beans
        http://www.springframework.org/schema/beans/spring-beans-3.0.xsd
        http://www.springframework.org/schema/lang
        http://www.springframework.org/schema/lang/spring-lang-3.0.xsd">
    ...
</beans>
```

Spring 2.5 supports three scripting languages: JRuby, Groovy, and BeanShell. Next, you will implement the InterestCalculator interface with these languages one by one. For simplicity's sake, let's consider the following simple interest formula for interest calculation:

```
Interest = Amount x Rate x Year
```

Scripting Beans with JRuby

First, let's implement the InterestCalculator interface with JRuby by creating the JRuby script, SimpleInterestCalculator.rb, in the com.apress.springrecipes.interest package of your classpath.

```ruby
class SimpleInterestCalculator

    def setRate(rate)
        @rate = rate
    end

    def calculate(amount, year)
        amount * year * @rate
    end
end

SimpleInterestCalculator.new
```

The preceding JRuby script declares a `SimpleInterestCalculator` class with a setter method for the `rate` property and a `calculate()` method. In Ruby, an instance variable begins with the @ sign. Note that, in the last line, you return a new instance of your target JRuby class. Failure to return this instance may result in Spring performing a lookup for an appropriate Ruby class to instantiate. As there can be multiple classes defined in a single JRuby script file, Spring will throw an exception if it cannot find an appropriate one that implements the methods declared in the interface.

In the bean configuration file, you can declare a bean implemented with JRuby by using the `<lang:jruby>` element and specifying the script's location in the `script-source` attribute. You can specify any resource path with a resource prefix supported by Spring, such as `file` or `classpath`.

■ **Note** To use JRuby in your Spring application, you have to include the appropriate dependencies on your classpath. If you are using Maven, then add the following definition to your Maven project:

```xml
<dependency>
  <groupId>org.jruby</groupId>
  <artifactId>jruby</artifactId>
  <version>1.0</version>
</dependency>
```

```xml
<lang:jruby id="interestCalculator"
    script-source="classpath:com/apress/springrecipes/interest/↵
        SimpleInterestCalculator.rb"
    script-interfaces="com.apress.springrecipes.interest.InterestCalculator">
    <lang:property name="rate" value="0.05" />
</lang:jruby>
```

You also have to specify one or more interfaces in the `script-interfaces` attribute for a JRuby bean. It's up to Spring to create a dynamic proxy for this bean and convert the Java method calls into JRuby method calls. Finally, you can specify the property values for a scripting bean in the `<lang:property>` elements.

Now, you can get the `interestCalculator` bean from the IoC container to use and inject it into other bean properties as well. The following `Main` class will help you verify whether your scripted bean works properly:

```
package com.apress.springrecipes.interest;

import org.springframework.context.ApplicationContext;
import org.springframework.context.support.ClassPathXmlApplicationContext;

public class Main {

    public static void main(String[] args) throws Exception {
        ApplicationContext context =
            new ClassPathXmlApplicationContext("beans.xml");

        InterestCalculator calculator =
            (InterestCalculator) context.getBean("interestCalculator");
        System.out.println(calculator.calculate(100000, 1));
    }
}
```

Scripting Beans with Groovy

Next, let's implement the `InterestCalculator` interface with Groovy by creating the Groovy script, `SimpleInterestCalculator.groovy`, in the `com.apress.springrecipes.interest` package of your classpath.

```
import com.apress.springrecipes.interest.InterestCalculator;

class SimpleInterestCalculator implements InterestCalculator {

    double rate

    double calculate(double amount, double year) {
        return amount * year * rate
    }
}
```

The preceding Groovy script declares a `SimpleInterestCalculator` class that implements the `InterestCalculator` interface. In Groovy, you can simply declare a property with no access modifier, and then it will generate a private field with a public getter and setter automatically.

In the bean configuration file, you can declare a bean implemented with Groovy by using the `<lang:groovy>` element and specifying the script's location in the `script-source` attribute. You can specify the property values for a scripting bean in the `<lang:property>` elements.

■ **Note** To use Groovy in your Spring application, you need to add the dependency to the classpath. If you are using Maven, add the following dependency to your Maven project:

```
<dependency>
  <groupId>org.jruby</groupId>
  <artifactId>jruby</artifactId>
  <version>1.0</version>
</dependency>
```

```
<lang:groovy id="interestCalculator"
    script-source="classpath:com/apress/springrecipes/interest/SimpleInterestCalculator.groovy">
    <lang:property name="rate" value="0.05" />
</lang:groovy>
```

Notice that it's unnecessary to specify the `script-interfaces` attribute for a Groovy bean, as the Groovy class has declared which interfaces it implements.

Scripting Beans with BeanShell

Last, let's implement the `InterestCalculator` interface with BeanShell by creating the BeanShell script, `SimpleInterestCalculator.bsh`, in the `com.apress.springrecipes.interest` package of your classpath.

```
double rate;

void setRate(double aRate) {
    rate = aRate;
}

double calculate(double amount, double year) {
    return amount * year * rate;
}
```

In BeanShell, you cannot declare classes explicitly, but you can declare variables and methods. So, you implement your `InterestCalculator` interface by providing all the methods required by this interface.

In the bean configuration file, you can declare a bean implemented with BeanShell by using the `<lang:bsh>` element and specifying the script's location in the `script-source` attribute. You can specify the property values for a scripting bean in the `<lang:property>` elements.

■ **Note** To use BeanShell Spring application, you need to add the dependency to the classpath. If you are using Maven, add the following dependency to your Maven project:

<dependency>
  <groupId>org.beanshell</groupId>
  <artifactId>bsh</artifactId>
  <version>2.0b4</version>
</dependency>

```
<lang:bsh id="interestCalculator"
    script-source="classpath:com/apress/springrecipes/interest/SimpleInterestCalculator.bsh"
    script-interfaces="com.apress.springrecipes.interest.InterestCalculator">
    <lang:property name="rate" value="0.05" />
</lang:bsh>
```

You also have to specify one or more interfaces in the `script-interfaces` attribute for a bean implemented with BeanShell. It's up to Spring to create a dynamic proxy for this bean and convert the Java method calls into BeanShell calls.

19-2. Injecting Spring Beans into Scripts

Problem

Sometimes, your scripts may need the help of certain Java objects to complete their tasks. In Spring, you have to allow your scripts to access beans declared in the IoC container.

Solution

You can inject beans declared in the Spring IoC container into scripts in the same way as properties of simple data types.

How It Works

Suppose you would like the interest rate to be calculated dynamically. First, you define the following interface to allow implementations to return the annual, monthly, and daily interest rates:

```
package com.apress.springrecipes.interest;

public interface RateCalculator {

    public double getAnnualRate();
    public double getMonthlyRate();
    public double getDailyRate();
}
```

For this example, you simply implement this interface by calculating these rates from a fixed annual interest rate, which can be injected through a setter method.

```
package com.apress.springrecipes.interest;

public class FixedRateCalculator implements RateCalculator {

    private double rate;

    public void setRate(double rate) {
        this.rate = rate;
    }

    public double getAnnualRate() {
        return rate;
    }

    public double getMonthlyRate() {
        return rate / 12;
    }

    public double getDailyRate() {
        return rate / 365;
    }
}
```

Then declare this rate calculator in the IoC container by supplying an annual interest rate.

```
<bean id="rateCalculator"
    class="com.apress.springrecipes.interest.FixedRateCalculator">
    <property name="rate" value="0.05" />
</bean>
```

Last, your interest calculator should use a RateCalculator object rather than a fixed rate value.

```
package com.apress.springrecipes.interest;

public interface InterestCalculator {

    public void setRateCalculator(RateCalculator rateCalculator);
    public double calculate(double amount, double year);
}
```

Injecting Spring Beans into JRuby

In the JRuby script, you can store the injected `RateCalculator` object in an instance variable and use it for rate calculation.

```
class SimpleInterestCalculator

    def setRateCalculator(rateCalculator)
        @rateCalculator = rateCalculator
    end

    def calculate(amount, year)
        amount * year * @rateCalculator.getAnnualRate
    end
end

SimpleInterestCalculator.new
```

In the bean declaration, you can inject another bean into a scripted bean's property by specifying the bean name in the `ref` attribute.

```
<lang:jruby id="interestCalculator"
    script-source="classpath:com/apress/springrecipes/interest/↵
        SimpleInterestCalculator.rb"
    script-interfaces="com.apress.springrecipes.interest.InterestCalculator">
    <lang:property name="rateCalculator" ref="rateCalculator" />
</lang:jruby>
```

Injecting Spring Beans into Groovy

In the Groovy script, you just declare a property of type `RateCalculator`, and it will generate a public getter and setter automatically.

```
import com.apress.springrecipes.interest.InterestCalculator;
import com.apress.springrecipes.interest.RateCalculator;

class SimpleInterestCalculator implements InterestCalculator {

    RateCalculator rateCalculator

    double calculate(double amount, double year) {
        return amount * year * rateCalculator.getAnnualRate()
    }
}
```

Again, you can inject another bean into a scripted bean's property by specifying the bean name in the `ref` attribute.

```
<lang:groovy id="interestCalculator"
    script-source="classpath:com/apress/springrecipes/interest/SimpleInterestCalculator.groovy">
    <lang:property name="rateCalculator" ref="rateCalculator" />
</lang:groovy>
```

Injecting Spring Beans into BeanShell

In the BeanShell script, you need a global variable of type RateCalculator and a setter method for it.

```
import com.apress.springrecipes.interest.RateCalculator;

RateCalculator rateCalculator;

void setRateCalculator(RateCalculator aRateCalculator) {
    rateCalculator = aRateCalculator;
}

double calculate(double amount, double year) {
    return amount * year * rateCalculator.getAnnualRate();
}
```

Also, you can inject another bean into a scripted bean's property by specifying the bean name in the ref attribute.

```
<lang:bsh id="interestCalculator"
    script-source="classpath:com/apress/springrecipes/interest/↵
        SimpleInterestCalculator.bsh"
    script-interfaces="com.apress.springrecipes.interest.InterestCalculator">
    <lang:property name="rateCalculator" ref="rateCalculator" />
</lang:bsh>
```

19-3. Refreshing Beans from Scripts

Problem

As the modules implemented with scripting languages may have to be changed frequently and dynamically, you would like the Spring IoC container to be able to detect and refresh changes automatically from the script sources.

Solution

Spring is able to refresh a scripted bean definition from its source once you have specified the checking interval in the refresh-check-delay attribute. When a method is called on that bean, Spring will check the script source if the specified checking interval has elapsed. Then, Spring will refresh the bean definition from the script source if it has been changed.

How It Works

By default, the `refresh-check-delay` attribute is negative, so the refresh checking feature is disabled. You can assign the milliseconds for refresh checking in this attribute to enable this feature. For example, you can specify 5 seconds for the refresh checking interval of your JRuby bean.

```
<lang:jruby id="interestCalculator"
    script-source="classpath:com/apress/springrecipes/interest/↵
        SimpleInterestCalculator.rb"
    script-interfaces="com.apress.springrecipes.interest.InterestCalculator"
    refresh-check-delay="5000">
    ...
</lang:jruby>
```

Of course, the `refresh-check-delay` attribute also works for a bean implemented with Groovy or BeanShell.

```
<lang:groovy id="interestCalculator"
    script-source="classpath:com/apress/springrecipes/interest/↵
        SimpleInterestCalculator.groovy"
    refresh-check-delay="5000">
    ...
</lang:groovy>

<lang:bsh id="interestCalculator"
    script-source="classpath:com/apress/springrecipes/interest/↵
        SimpleInterestCalculator.bsh"
    script-interfaces="com.apress.springrecipes.interest.InterestCalculator"
    refresh-check-delay="5000">
    ...
</lang:bsh>
```

19-4. Defining Script Sources Inline

Problem

You would like to define the script sources, which are not likely to be changed often, in the bean configuration file directly, rather than in external script source files.

Solution

You can define an inline script source in the `<lang:inline-script>` element of a scripted bean to replace a reference to an external script source file by the `script-source` attribute. Note that the refresh checking feature is not applicable for an inline script source, because the Spring IoC container only loads the bean configuration once, at startup.

How It Works

For example, you can define the JRuby script inline using the `<lang:inline-script>` element. To prevent the characters in your script from conflicting with the reserved XML characters, you should surround your script source with the `<![CDATA[...]]>` tag. You no longer have to specify the reference to the external script source file in the `script-source` attribute.

```
<lang:jruby id="interestCalculator"
    script-interfaces="com.apress.springrecipes.interest.InterestCalculator">
    <lang:inline-script>
    <![CDATA[
    class SimpleInterestCalculator

        def setRateCalculator(rateCalculator)
            @rateCalculator = rateCalculator
        end

        def calculate(amount, year)
            amount * year * @rateCalculator.getAnnualRate
        end
    end

    SimpleInterestCalculator.new
    ]]>
    </lang:inline-script>
    <lang:property name="rateCalculator" ref="rateCalculator" />
</lang:jruby>
```

Of course, you can also define the Groovy or BeanShell script sources inline using the `<lang:inline-script>` element.

```
<lang:groovy id="interestCalculator">
    <lang:inline-script>
    <![CDATA[
    import com.apress.springrecipes.interest.InterestCalculator;
    import com.apress.springrecipes.interest.RateCalculator;

    class SimpleInterestCalculator implements InterestCalculator {

        RateCalculator rateCalculator

        double calculate(double amount, double year) {
            return amount * year * rateCalculator.getAnnualRate()
        }
    }
    ]]>
    </lang:inline-script>
    <lang:property name="rateCalculator" ref="rateCalculator" />
</lang:groovy>
```

```
<lang:bsh id="interestCalculator"
    script-interfaces="com.apress.springrecipes.interest.InterestCalculator">
    <lang:inline-script>
    <![CDATA[
    import com.apress.springrecipes.interest.RateCalculator;

    RateCalculator rateCalculator;

    void setRateCalculator(RateCalculator aRateCalculator) {
        rateCalculator = aRateCalculator;
    }

    double calculate(double amount, double year) {
        return amount * year * rateCalculator.getAnnualRate();
    }
    ]]>
    </lang:inline-script>
    <lang:property name="rateCalculator" ref="rateCalculator" />
</lang:bsh>
```

Summary

In this chapter, you have learned how to use the scripting languages supported by Spring to implement your beans and how to declare them in the Spring IoC container. Spring supports three scripting languages: JRuby, Groovy, and BeanShell. You can specify the location for an external script source file or define an inline script source in the bean configuration file. As the script sources may require frequent and dynamic changes, Spring can detect and refresh changes from the script source files automatically. Finally, you can inject property values as well as bean references into your scripts.

CHAPTER 5

■■■

Spring Security

In this chapter, you will learn how to secure applications using the Spring Security framework, a subproject of the Spring framework. Spring Security was initially known as Acegi Security, but its name has been changed since joining with the Spring Portfolio projects. Spring Security can be used to secure any Java application, but it's mostly used for web-based applications. Web applications, especially those that can be accessed through the Internet, are vulnerable to hacker attacks if they are not secured properly.

If you've already used Spring Security, be advised there have been several changes introduced in the 3.0 release of the Spring Security framework, which was released almost in tandem with the 3.0 release of the Spring framework (i.e., core). These changes include feature enhancements like support for annotations and OpenID, as well as a restructuring that includes class name changes and package partitioning (i.e., multiple JARs). This is especially important if you are running Spring Security 2.x code, on which the first edition of the book was based.

If, on the other hand, you've never handled security in an application, there are several terms and concepts that you must understand first. *Authentication* is the process of verifying a principal's identity against what it claims to be. A *principal* can be a user, a device, or a system, but most typically, it's a user. A principal has to provide evidence of identity to be authenticated. This evidence is called a *credential*, which is usually a password when the target principal is a user.

Authorization is the process of granting *authorities* to an authenticated user so that this user is allowed to access particular resources of the target application. The authorization process must be performed after the authentication process. Typically, authorities are granted in terms of *roles*.

Access control means controlling access to an application's resources. It entails making a decision on whether a user is allowed to access a resource. This decision is called an *access control decision*, and it's made by comparing the resource's *access attributes* with the user's granted authorities or other characteristics.

After finishing this chapter, you will understand basic security concepts and know how to secure your web applications at the URL access level, the method invocation level, the view-rendering level, and the domain object level.

5-1. Securing URL Access

Problem

Many web applications have some particular URLs that are critically important and private. You must secure these URLs by preventing unauthorized access to them.

Solution

Spring Security enables you to secure a web application's URL access in a declarative way through simple configuration. It handles security by applying servlet filters to HTTP requests. You can configure these filters in Spring's bean configuration files using XML elements defined in the Spring Security schema. However, as servlet filters must be registered in the web deployment descriptor to take effect, you have to register a `DelegatingFilterProxy` instance in the web deployment descriptor, which is a servlet filter that delegates request filtering to a filter in Spring's application context.

Spring Security allows you to configure web application security through the `<http>` element. If your web application's security requirements are straightforward and typical, you can set this element's `auto-config` attribute to `true` so that Spring Security will automatically register and configure several basic security services, including the following:

- Form-based login service: This provides a default page that contains a login form for users to log into this application.

- Logout service: This provides a handler mapped with a URL for users to log out of this application.

- HTTP Basic authentication: This can process the Basic authentication credentials presented in HTTP request headers. It can also be used for authenticating requests made with remoting protocols and web services.

- Anonymous login: This assigns a principal and grants authorities to an anonymous user so that you can handle an anonymous user like a normal user.

- Remember-me support: This can remember a user's identity across multiple browser sessions, usually by storing a cookie in the user's browser.

- Servlet API integration: This allows you to access security information in your web application via standard Servlet APIs, such as `HttpServletRequest.isUserInRole()` and `HttpServletRequest.getUserPrincipal()`.

With these security services registered, you can specify the URL patterns that require particular authorities to access. Spring Security will perform security checks according to your configurations. A user must log into an application before accessing the secure URLs, unless these URLs are opened for anonymous access. Spring Security provides a set of authentication providers for you to choose from. An authentication provider authenticates a user and returns the authorities granted to this user.

How It Works

Suppose you are going to develop an online message board application for users to post their messages on. First, you create the domain class Message with three properties: author, title, and body:

```
package com.apress.springrecipes.board.domain;

public class Message {

    private Long id;
    private String author;
    private String title;
    private String body;

    // Getters and Setters
    ...
}
```

Next, you define the operations of your message board in a service interface, including listing all messages, posting a message, deleting a message, and finding a message by its ID:

```
package com.apress.springrecipes.board.service;
...
public interface MessageBoardService {

    public List<Message> listMessages();
    public void postMessage(Message message);
    public void deleteMessage(Message message);
    public Message findMessageById(Long messageId);
}
```

For testing purposes, let's implement this interface by using a list to store the posted messages. You can use the message posting time (in milliseconds) as a message's identifier. You also have to declare the postMessage() and deleteMessage() method as synchronized to make them thread-safe.

```
package com.apress.springrecipes.board.service;
...
public class MessageBoardServiceImpl implements MessageBoardService {

    private Map<Long, Message> messages = new LinkedHashMap<Long, Message>();

    public List<Message> listMessages() {
        return new ArrayList<Message>(messages.values());
    }

    public synchronized void postMessage(Message message) {
        message.setId(System.currentTimeMillis());
        messages.put(message.getId(), message);
    }
```

```
    public synchronized void deleteMessage(Message message) {
        messages.remove(message.getId());
    }

    public Message findMessageById(Long messageId) {
        return messages.get(messageId);
    }
}
```

Setting Up a Spring MVC Application That Uses Spring Security

To develop this application using Spring MVC as the web framework and Spring Security as the security framework, you first create the following directory structure for your web application.

■ **Note** Before using Spring Security, you have to have the relevant Spring Security jars on your classpath. If you are using Maven, add the following dependencies to your Maven project. We include here a few extra dependencies that you will need on a case-by-case basis, including LDAP support and ACL support. In this book, we have used a variable - ${spring.security.version} to extract the version out. In this book, we are building against **3.0.2.RELEASE**.

```
<dependency>
  <groupId>org.springframework.security</groupId>
  <artifactId>spring-security-core</artifactId>
  <version>${spring.security.version}</version>
</dependency>

<dependency>
  <groupId>org.springframework.security</groupId>
  <artifactId>spring-security-ldap</artifactId>
  <version>${spring.security.version}</version>
</dependency>

<dependency>
  <groupId>org.springframework.security</groupId>
  <artifactId>spring-security-config</artifactId>
  <version>${spring.security.version}</version>
</dependency>
```

```xml
<dependency>
  <groupId>org.springframework.security</groupId>
  <artifactId>spring-security-web</artifactId>
  <version>${spring.security.version}</version>
</dependency>

<dependency>
  <groupId>org.springframework.security</groupId>
  <artifactId>spring-security-taglibs</artifactId>
  <version>${spring.security.version}</version>
</dependency>

<dependency>
  <groupId>org.springframework.security</groupId>
  <artifactId>spring-security-acl</artifactId>
  <version>${spring.security.version}</version>
</dependency>
```

The Spring configurations for this application are separated into three different files: board-security.xml, board-service.xml, and board-servlet.xml. Each of them configures a particular layer.

Creating the Configuration Files

In the web deployment descriptor (i.e., web.xml), you register ContextLoaderListener to load the root application context at startup and Spring MVC's DispatcherServlet to dispatch requests:

```xml
<web-app version="2.4" xmlns="http://java.sun.com/xml/ns/j2ee"
    xmlns:xsi="http://www.w3.org/2001/XMLSchema-instance"
    xsi:schemaLocation="http://java.sun.com/xml/ns/j2ee
        http://java.sun.com/xml/ns/j2ee/web-app_2_4.xsd">

    <context-param>
        <param-name>contextConfigLocation</param-name>
        <param-value>/WEB-INF/board-service.xml</param-value>
    </context-param>

    <listener>
        <listener-class>
            org.springframework.web.context.ContextLoaderListener
        </listener-class>
    </listener>
```

```
<servlet>
    <servlet-name>board</servlet-name>
    <servlet-class>
        org.springframework.web.servlet.DispatcherServlet
    </servlet-class>
</servlet>

<servlet-mapping>
    <servlet-name>board</servlet-name>
    <url-pattern/></url-pattern>
</servlet-mapping>
</web-app>
```

If the root application context's configuration file doesn't have the default name (i.e., applicationContext.xml), or if you configure it with multiple configuration files, you'll have to specify the file locations in the contextConfigLocation context parameter. Also note that you have mapped the URL pattern / to DispatcherServlet, meaning everything under the application's root directory will be handled by this servlet

In the web layer configuration file (i.e., board-servlet.xml), you define a view resolver to resolve view names into JSP files located in the /WEB-INF/jsp/ directory. Later, you will have to configure your controllers in this file.

```
<beans xmlns="http://www.springframework.org/schema/beans"
    xmlns:xsi="http://www.w3.org/2001/XMLSchema-instance"
    xmlns:context="http://www.springframework.org/schema/context"
    xsi:schemaLocation="http://www.springframework.org/schema/beans
        http://www.springframework.org/schema/beans/spring-beans-3.0.xsd
        http://www.springframework.org/schema/context
        http://www.springframework.org/schema/context/spring-context-3.0.xsd">

  <context:component-scan base-package="com.apress.springrecipes.board.web" />

    <bean class="org.springframework.web.servlet.view.↩
        InternalResourceViewResolver">
        <property name="prefix" value="/WEB-INF/jsp/" />
        <property name="suffix" value=".jsp" />
    </bean>
</beans>
```

In the service layer configuration file (i.e., board-service.xml), you have to declare only the message board service:

```
<beans xmlns="http://www.springframework.org/schema/beans"
    xmlns:xsi="http://www.w3.org/2001/XMLSchema-instance"
    xsi:schemaLocation="http://www.springframework.org/schema/beans
        http://www.springframework.org/schema/beans/spring-beans-3.0.xsd">

    <bean id="messageBoardService"
        class="com.apress.springrecipes.board.service.MessageBoardServiceImpl" />
</beans>
```

Creating the Controllers and Page Views

Suppose you have to implement a function for listing all messages posted on the message board. The first step is to create the following controller.

```
package com.apress.springrecipes.board.web;
...

@Controller
@RequestMapping("/messageList*")
public class MessageListController {

    private MessageBoardService messageBoardService;

    @Autowired
    public MessageListController(MessageBoardService messageBoardService) {
        this.messageBoardService = messageBoardService;
    }


    @RequestMapping(method = RequestMethod.GET)
    public String generateList(Model model) {
        List<Message> messages = java.util.Collections.emptyList();
        messages = messageBoardService.listMessages();
        model.addAttribute("messages",messages);
        return "messageList";
    }
}
```

The controller is mapped to a URL in the form /messageList. The controller's main method—generateList()—obtains a list of messages from the messageBoardService, saves it to the model object under the messages named, and returns control to a logical view named messageList. In accordance with Spring MVC conventions, this last logical view is mapped to the JSP /WEB-INF/jsp/messageList.jsp showing all the messages passed from the controller:

```
<%@ taglib prefix="c" uri="http://java.sun.com/jsp/jstl/core" %>

<html>
<head>
<title>Message List</title>
</head>

<body>
<c:forEach items="${messages}" var="message">
<table>
  <tr>
    <td>Author</td>
    <td>${message.author}</td>
  </tr>
  <tr>
    <td>Title</td>
    <td>${message.title}</td>
  </tr>
  <tr>
    <td>Body</td>
    <td>${message.body}</td>
  </tr>
  <tr>
    <td colspan="2">
      <a href="messageDelete?messageId=${message.id}">Delete</a>
    </td>
  </tr>
</table>
<hr />
</c:forEach>
<a href="messagePost.htm">Post</a>
</body>
</html>
```

Another function you have to implement is for users to post messages on the message board. You create the following form controller for this purpose:

```
package com.apress.springrecipes.board.web;
...

@Controller
@RequestMapping("/messagePost*")
public class MessagePostController {

    private MessageBoardService messageBoardService;


    @Autowired
    public void MessagePostController(MessageBoardService messageBoardService) {
        this.messageBoardService = messageBoardService;
    }
```

```
@RequestMapping(method=RequestMethod.GET)
public String setupForm(Model model) {
    Message message = new Message();
    model.addAttribute("message",message);
    return "messagePost";
}

@RequestMapping(method=RequestMethod.POST)
public String onSubmit(@ModelAttribute("message") ↵
        Message message, BindingResult result) {
    if (result.hasErrors()) {
        return "messagePost";
    } else {
        messageBoardService.postMessage(message);
        return "redirect:messageList";
    }
}
}
```

A user must have logged into the message board before posting a message. You can get a user's login name with the getRemoteUser() method defined in HttpServletRequest. This login name will be used as the message's author name.

You then create the form view /WEB-INF/jsp/messagePost.jsp with Spring's form tags for users to input message contents:

```
<%@ taglib prefix="form" uri="http://www.springframework.org/tags/form" %>

<html>
<head>
<title>Message Post</title>
</head>

<body>
<form:form method="POST" modelAttribute="message">
<table>
  <tr>
    <td>Title</td>
    <td><form:input path="title" /></td>
  </tr>
  <tr>
    <td>Body</td>
    <td><form:textarea path="body" /></td>
  </tr>
  <tr>
    <td colspan="2"><input type="submit" value="Post" /></td>
  </tr>
</table>
</form:form>
</body>
</html>
```

The last function is to allow a user to delete a posted message by clicking the Delete link on the message list page. You create the following controller for this function:

```
package com.apress.springrecipes.board.web;
...


@Controller
@RequestMapping("/messageDelete*")
public class MessageDeleteController {

    private MessageBoardService messageBoardService;

    @Autowired
    public void MessageDeleteController(MessageBoardService messageBoardService) {
        this.messageBoardService = messageBoardService;
    }


    @RequestMapping(method= RequestMethod.GET)
    public String messageDelte(@RequestParam(required = true, ↵
        value = "messageId") Long messageId, Model model) {
        Message message = messageBoardService.findMessageById(messageId);
        messageBoardService.deleteMessage(message);
        model.addAttribute("messages", messageBoardService.listMessages());
        return "redirect:messageList";
    }
}
```

Now, you can deploy this application to a web container (e.g., Apache Tomcat 6.0). By default, Tomcat listens on port 8080, so if you deploy your application to the **board** context path, you can list all posted messages with the following URL:

```
http://localhost:8080/board/messageList.htm
```

Up to this time, you haven't configured any security service for this application, so you can access it directly without logging into it.

Securing URL Access

Now, let's secure this web application's URL access with Spring Security. First, you have to configure a `DelegatingFilterProxy` instance in `web.xml` to delegate HTTP request filtering to a filter defined in Spring Security:

```
<web-app ...>
    <context-param>
        <param-name>contextConfigLocation</param-name>
        <param-value>
            /WEB-INF/board-service.xml
            /WEB-INF/board-security.xml
        </param-value>
    </context-param>
    ...
    <filter>
        <filter-name>springSecurityFilterChain</filter-name>
        <filter-class>
            org.springframework.web.filter.DelegatingFilterProxy
        </filter-class>
    </filter>

    <filter-mapping>
        <filter-name>springSecurityFilterChain</filter-name>
        <url-pattern>/*</url-pattern>
    </filter-mapping>
    ...
</web-app>
```

The responsibility of `DelegatingFilterProxy` is simply to delegate HTTP request filtering to a Spring bean that implements the `java.util.logging.Filter` interface. By default, it delegates to a bean whose name is the same as its `<filter-name>` property, but you can override the bean name in its `targetBeanName` init parameter. As Spring Security will automatically configure a filter chain with the name `springSecurityFilterChain` when you enable web application security, you can simply use this name for your `DelegatingFilterProxy` instance.

Although you can configure Spring Security in the same configuration file as the web and service layers, it's better to separate the security configurations in an isolated file (e.g., `board-security.xml`). Inside `web.xml`, you have to add the file's location to the `contextConfigLocation` context parameter for `ContextLoaderListener` to load it at startup. Then, you create it with the following content:

```
<beans:beans xmlns="http://www.springframework.org/schema/security"
    xmlns:beans="http://www.springframework.org/schema/beans"
    xmlns:xsi="http://www.w3.org/2001/XMLSchema-instance"
    xsi:schemaLocation="http://www.springframework.org/schema/beans
        http://www.springframework.org/schema/beans/spring-beans-3.0.xsd
        http://www.springframework.org/schema/security
        http://www.springframework.org/schema/security/spring-security-3.0.xsd">

    <http auto-config="true">
        <intercept-url pattern="/messageList*"
            access="ROLE_USER,ROLE_ANONYMOUS" />
        <intercept-url pattern="/messagePost*" access="ROLE_USER" />
        <intercept-url pattern="/messageDelete*" access="ROLE_ADMIN" />
    </http>
```

```
    <authentication-manager>
    <authentication-provider>
        <user-service>
            <user name="admin" password="secret"
                authorities="ROLE_ADMIN,ROLE_USER" />
            <user name="user1" password="1111" authorities="ROLE_USER" />
        </user-service>
    </authentication-provider>
    </authentication-manager>
</beans:beans>
```

You may find that this file looks a bit different from a normal bean configuration file. Normally, the default namespace of a bean configuration file is beans, so you can use the <bean> and <property> elements without the beans prefix. However, if you use this style to declare the Spring Security services, all security elements must be appended with the security prefix. Because the elements in a security configuration file are mostly Spring Security's, you can define security as the default namespace instead, so you can use them without the security prefix. If you do it this way, however, when you declare normal Spring beans in this file, you have to include the beans prefix for the <bean> and <property> elements.

The <http auto-config="true"> element automatically configures the basic security services that a typical web application needs. You can fine-tune these services with the corresponding subelements inside it.

Inside the <http> configuration element, you can restrict access to particular URLs with one or more <intercept-url> elements. Each <intercept-url> element specifies a URL pattern and a set of access attributes required to access the URLs. Remember that you must always include a wildcard at the end of a URL pattern. Failing to do so will make the URL pattern unable to match a URL that has request parameters. As a result, hackers could easily skip the security check by appending an arbitrary request parameter.

Access attributes are compared with a user's authorities to decide if this user can access the URLs. In most cases, access attributes are defined in terms of roles. For example, users with the ROLE_USER role, or anonymous users, who have the ROLE_ANONYMOUS role by default, are able to access the URL /messageList to list all messages. However, a user must have the ROLE_USER role to post a new message via the URL /messagePost. Only an administrator who has the ROLE_ADMIN role can delete messages via /messageDelete.

You can configure authentication services in the <authentication-provider> element, which is nested inside the <authentication-manager> element. Spring Security supports several ways of authenticating users, including authenticating against a database or an LDAP repository. It also supports defining user details in <user-service> directly for simple security requirements. You can specify a username, a password, and a set of authorities for each user.

Now, you can redeploy this application to test its security configurations. You can enter the request path /messageList to list all posted messages as usual, because it's open to anonymous users. But if you click the link to post a new message, you will be redirected to the default login page generated by Spring Security. You must log into this application with a correct username and password to post a message. Finally, to delete a message, you must log in as an administrator.

5-2. Logging In to Web Applications

Problem

A secure application requires its users to log in before they can access certain secure functions. This is especially important for web applications running on the open Internet, because hackers can easily reach them. Most web applications have to provide a way for users to input their credentials to log in.

Solution

Spring Security supports multiple ways for users to log into a web application. It supports form-based login by providing a default web page that contains a login form. You can also provide a custom web page as the login page. In addition, Spring Security supports HTTP Basic authentication by processing the Basic authentication credentials presented in HTTP request headers. HTTP Basic authentication can also be used for authenticating requests made with remoting protocols and web services.

Some parts of your application may allow for anonymous access (e.g., access to the welcome page). Spring Security provides an anonymous login service that can assign a principal and grant authorities to an anonymous user so that you can handle an anonymous user like a normal user when defining security policies.

Spring Security also supports remember-me login, which is able to remember a user's identity across multiple browser sessions so that a user needn't log in again after logging in for the first time.

How It Works

To help you better understand the various login mechanisms in isolation, let's first disable HTTP auto-configuration by removing the `auto-config` attribute:

```
<http>
    <intercept-url pattern="/messageList*" access="ROLE_USER,ROLE_ANONYMOUS" />
    <intercept-url pattern="/messagePost*" access="ROLE_USER" />
    <intercept-url pattern="/messageDelete*" access="ROLE_ADMIN" />
</http>
```

Note that the login services introduced next will be registered automatically if you enable HTTP `auto-config`. However, if you disable HTTP `auto-config` or you want to customize these services, you have to configure the corresponding XML elements explicitly.

HTTP Basic Authentication

The HTTP Basic authentication support can be configured via the `<http-basic>` element. When HTTP Basic authentication is required, a browser will typically display a login dialog or a specific login page for users to log in.

```
<http>
    ...
    <http-basic />
</http>
```

Note that when HTTP Basic authentication and form-based login are enabled at the same time, the latter will be used. So, if you want your web application users to log in with this authentication type, you should not enable form-based login.

Form-Based Login

The form-based login service will render a web page that contains a login form for users to input their login details and process the login form submission. It's configured via the `<form-login>` element:

```
<http>
    ...
    <form-login />
</http>
```

By default, Spring Security automatically creates a login page and maps it to the URL /spring_security_login. So, you can add a link to your application (e.g., in messageList.jsp) referring to this URL for login:

```
<a href="<c:url value="/spring_security_login" />">Login</a>
```

If you don't prefer the default login page, you can provide a custom login page of your own. For example, you can create the following login.jsp file in the root directory of the web application. Note that you shouldn't put this file inside WEB-INF, which would prevent users from accessing it directly.

```
<%@ taglib prefix="c" uri="http://java.sun.com/jsp/jstl/core" %>

<html>
<head>
<title>Login</title>
</head>

<body>
<form method="POST" action="<c:url value="/j_spring_security_check" />">
<table>
  <tr>
    <td align="right">Username</td>
    <td><input type="text" name="j_username" /></td>
  </tr>
  <tr>
    <td align="right">Password</td>
    <td><input type="password" name="j_password" /></td>
  </tr>
```

```
<tr>
  <td align="right">Remember me</td>
  <td><input type="checkbox" name="_spring_security_remember_me" /></td>
</tr>
<tr>
  <td colspan="2" align="right">
    <input type="submit" value="Login" />
    <input type="reset" value="Reset" />
  </td>
</tr>
</table>
</form>
</body>
</html>
```

Note that the form action URL and the input field names are Spring Security–specific. However, the action URL can be customized with the `login-url` attribute of `<form-login>`.

Now, you have to change the previous login link (i.e., `messageList.jsp`) to refer to this URL for login:

```
<a href="<c:url value="/login.jsp" />">Login</a>
```

In order for Spring Security to display your custom login page when a login is requested, you have to specify its URL in the `login-page` attribute:

```
<http>
    ...
    <form-login login-page="/login.jsp" />
</http>
```

If the login page is displayed by Spring Security when a user requests a secure URL, the user will be redirected to the target URL once the login succeeds. However, if the user requests the login page directly via its URL, by default the user will be redirected to the context path's root (i.e., `http://localhost:8080/board/`) after a successful login. If you have not defined a welcome page in your web deployment descriptor, you may wish to redirect the user to a default target URL when the login succeeds:

```
<http>
    ....
    <form-login login-page="/login.jsp" default-target-url="/messageList" />
</http>
```

If you use the default login page created by Spring Security, then when a login fails, Spring Security will render the login page again with the error message. However, if you specify a custom login page, you will have to configure the `authentication-failure-url` attribute to specify which URL to redirect to on login error. For example, you can redirect to the custom login page again with the `error` request parameter:

```
<http>
    ....
    <form-login login-page="/login.jsp" default-target-url="/messageList"
        authentication-failure-url="/login.jsp?error=true" />
</http>
```

Then your login page should test whether the **error** request parameter is present. If an error has occurred, you will have to display the error message by accessing the session scope attribute SPRING_SECURITY_LAST_EXCEPTION, which stores the last exception for the current user.

```
<%@ taglib prefix="c" uri="http://java.sun.com/jsp/jstl/core" %>

<html>
<head>
<title>Login</title>
</head>

<body>
<c:if test="${not empty param.error}">
  <font color="red">
  Login error. <br />
  Reason : ${sessionScope["SPRING_SECURITY_LAST_EXCEPTION"].message}
  </font>
</c:if>
...
</body>
</html>
```

The Logout Service

The logout service provides a handler to handle logout requests. It can be configured via the `<logout>` element:

```
<http>
    ...
    <logout />
</http>
```

By default, it's mapped to the URL /j_spring_security_logout, so you can add a link to a page referring to this URL for logout. Note that this URL can be customized with the logout-url attribute of `<logout>`.

```
<a href="<c:url value="/j_spring_security_logout" />">Logout</a>
```

By default, a user will be redirected to the context path's root when the logout succeeds, but sometimes, you may wish to direct the user to another URL, which you can do as follows:

```
<http>
    ...
    <logout logout-success-url="/login.jsp" />
</http>
```

Anonymous Login

The anonymous login service can be configured via the `<anonymous>` element, where you can customize the username and authorities of an anonymous user, whose default values are `anonymousUser` and `ROLE_ANONYMOUS`:

```
<http>
    <intercept-url pattern="/messageList*" access="ROLE_USER,ROLE_GUEST" />
    <intercept-url pattern="/messagePost*" access="ROLE_USER" />
    <intercept-url pattern="/messageDelete*" access="ROLE_ADMIN" />
    ...
    <anonymous username="guest" granted-authority="ROLE_GUEST" />
</http>
```

Remember-Me Support

Remember-me support can be configured via the `<remember-me>` element. By default, it encodes the username, password, remember-me expiration time, and a private key as a token, and stores it as a cookie in the user's browser. The next time the user accesses the same web application, this token will be detected so that the user can log in automatically.

```
<http>
    ...
    <remember-me />
</http>
```

However, static remember-me tokens can cause security issues, because they may be captured by hackers. Spring Security supports rolling tokens for more advanced security needs, but this requires a database to persist the tokens. For details about rolling remember-me token deployment, please refer to the Spring Security reference documentation.

5-3. Authenticating Users

Problem

When a user attempts to log into your application to access its secure resources, you have to authenticate the user's principal and grant authorities to this user.

Solution

In Spring Security, authentication is performed by one or more *authentication providers*, connected as a chain. If any of these providers authenticates a user successfully, that user will be able to log into the application. If any provider reports that the user is disabled or locked or that the credential is incorrect, or if no provider can authenticate the user, then the user will be unable to log into this application.

Spring Security supports multiple ways of authenticating users and includes built-in provider implementations for them. You can easily configure these providers with the built-in XML elements. Most common authentication providers authenticate users against a user repository storing *user details* (e.g., in an application's memory, a relational database, or an LDAP repository).

When storing user details in a repository, you should avoid storing user passwords in clear text, because that makes them vulnerable to hackers. Instead, you should always store encrypted passwords in your repository. A typical way of encrypting passwords is to use a one-way hash function to encode the passwords. When a user enters a password to log in, you apply the same hash function to this password and compare the result with the one stored in the repository. Spring Security supports several algorithms for encoding passwords (including MD5 and SHA) and provides built-in password encoders for these algorithms.

If you retrieve a user's details from a user repository every time a user attempts to log in, your application may incur a performance impact. This is because a user repository is usually stored remotely, and it has to perform some kinds of queries in response to a request. For this reason, Spring Security supports caching user details in local memory and storage to save you the overhead of performing remote queries.

How It Works

Authenticating Users with In-Memory Definitions

If you have only a few users in your application and you seldom modify their details, you can consider defining the user details in Spring Security's configuration file so that they will be loaded into your application's memory:

```
<authentication-manager>
  <authentication-provider>
    <user-service>
        <user name="admin" password="secret" authorities="ROLE_ADMIN,ROLE_USER" />
        <user name="user1" password="1111" authorities="ROLE_USER" />
        <user name="user2" password="2222" disabled="true" authorities="ROLE_USER" />
    </user-service>
  </authentication-provider>
</authentication-manager>
```

You can define user details in `<user-service>` with multiple `<user>` elements. For each user, you can specify a username, a password, a disabled status, and a set of granted authorities. A disabled user cannot log into an application.

Spring Security also allows you to externalize user details in a properties file, such as `/WEB-INF/users.properties`:

```
<authentication-manager>
  <authentication-provider>
    <user-service properties="/WEB-INF/users.properties" />
  </authentication-provider>
</authentication-manager>
```

Then, you can create the specified properties file and define the user details in the form of properties:

```
admin=secret,ROLE_ADMIN,ROLE_USER
user1=1111,ROLE_USER
user2=2222,disabled,ROLE_USER
```

Each property in this file represents a user's details. The property key is the username, and the property value is divided into several parts separated by commas. The first part is the password, and the second part is the enabled status, which is optional; and the default status is **enabled**. The following parts are the authorities granted to the user.

Authenticating Users Against a Database

More typically, user details should be stored in a database for easy maintenance. Spring Security has built-in support for querying user details from a database. By default, it queries user details, including authorities, with the following SQL statements:

```
SELECT username, password, enabled
FROM   users
WHERE  username = ?

SELECT username, authority
FROM   authorities
WHERE  username = ?
```

In order for Spring Security to query user details with these SQL statements, you have to create the corresponding tables in your database. For example, you can create them in the **board** schema of Apache Derby with the following SQL statements:

```
CREATE TABLE USERS (
    USERNAME    VARCHAR(10)    NOT NULL,
    PASSWORD    VARCHAR(32)    NOT NULL,
    ENABLED     SMALLINT,
    PRIMARY KEY (USERNAME)
);

CREATE TABLE AUTHORITIES (
    USERNAME    VARCHAR(10)    NOT NULL,
    AUTHORITY   VARCHAR(10)    NOT NULL,
    FOREIGN KEY (USERNAME) REFERENCES USERS
);
```

Next, you can input some user details into these tables for testing purposes. The data for these two tables is shown in Tables 5-1 and 5-2.

Table 5-1. Testing User Data for the USERS Table

USERNAME	PASSWORD	ENABLED
Admin	Secret	1
user1	1111	1
user2	2222	0

Table 5-2. Testing User Data for the AUTHORITIES Table

USERNAME	AUTHORITY
Admin	ROLE_ADMIN
Admin	ROLE_USER
user1	ROLE_USER
user2	ROLE_USER

In order for Spring Security to access these tables, you have to declare a data source (e.g., in board-service.xml) for creating connections to this database.

___

■ **Note** To connect to a database in the Apache Derby server, you need the Derby client .jars, as well as the Spring JDBC support. If you are using Apache Maven, add the following dependencies to your project:

```
<dependency>
  <groupId>org.apache.derby</groupId>
  <artifactId>derbyclient</artifactId>
  <version>10.4.2.0</version>
</dependency>
```

```xml
<dependency>
  <groupId>org.springframework</groupId>
  <artifactId>spring-jdbc</artifactId>
  <version>${spring.version}</version>
</dependency>
```

```xml
<bean id="dataSource"
    class="org.springframework.jdbc.datasource.DriverManagerDataSource">
    <property name="driverClassName"
        value="org.apache.derby.jdbc.ClientDriver" />
    <property name="url"
        value="jdbc:derby://localhost:1527/board;create=true" />
    <property name="username" value="app" />
    <property name="password" value="app" />
</bean>
```

The final step is to configure an authentication provider that queries this database for user details. You can achieve this simply by using the `<jdbc-user-service>` element with a data source reference:

```xml
<authentication-manager>
  <authentication-provider>
    <jdbc-user-service data-source-ref="dataSource" />
  </authentication-provider>
</authentication-manager>
```

However, in some cases, you may already have your own user repository defined in a legacy database. For example, suppose that the tables are created with the following SQL statements, and that all users in the MEMBER table have the enabled status:

```sql
CREATE TABLE MEMBER (
    ID          BIGINT          NOT NULL,
    USERNAME    VARCHAR(10)     NOT NULL,
    PASSWORD    VARCHAR(32)     NOT NULL,
    PRIMARY KEY (ID)
);

CREATE TABLE MEMBER_ROLE (
    MEMBER_ID   BIGINT          NOT NULL,
    ROLE        VARCHAR(10)     NOT NULL,
    FOREIGN KEY (MEMBER_ID) REFERENCES MEMBER
);
```

Suppose you have the legacy user data stored in these tables as shown in Tables 5-3 and 5-4.

Table 5-3. *Legacy User Data in the MEMBER Table*

ID	USERNAME	PASSWORD
1	Admin	Secret
2	user1	1111

Table 5-4. *Legacy User Data in the MEMBER_ROLE Table*

MEMBER_ID	ROLE
1	ROLE_ADMIN
1	ROLE_USER
2	ROLE_USER

Fortunately, Spring Security also supports using custom SQL statements to query a legacy database for user details. You can specify the statements for querying a user's information and authorities in the `users-by-username-query` and `authorities-by-username-query` aauthorities-by-username-query attributes:

```
<jdbc-user-service data-source-ref="dataSource"
    users-by-username-query=
        "SELECT username, password, 'true' as enabled↵
        FROM    member↵
        WHERE   username = ?"
    authorities-by-username-query=
        "SELECT member.username, member_role.role as authorities↵
        FROM    member, member_role↵
        WHERE   member.username = ? AND member.id = member_role.member_id" />
```

Encrypting Passwords

Until now, you have been storing user details with clear-text passwords. But this approach is vulnerable to hacker attacks, so you should encrypt the passwords before storing them. Spring Security supports several algorithms for encrypting passwords. For example, you can choose MD5 (Message-Digest algorithm 5), a one-way hash algorithm, to encrypt your passwords.

■ **Note** You may need a utility to calculate MD5 digests for your passwords. One such utility is Jacksum, which you can download from `http://sourceforge.net/projects/jacksum/` and extract to a directory of your choice. Then execute the following command to calculate a digest for a text:

```
java -jar jacksum.jar -a md5 -q "txt:secret"
```

Now, you can store the encrypted passwords in your user repository. For example, if you are using in-memory user definitions, you can specify the encrypted passwords in the `password` attributes. Then, you can configure a `<password-encoder>` element with a hashing algorithm specified in the `hash` attribute.

```
<authentication-manager>
    <authentication-provider>
    <password-encoder hash="md5" />
        <user-service>
            <user name="admin" password="5ebe2294ecd0e0f08eab7690d2a6ee69"
                authorities="ROLE_ADMIN, ROLE_USER" />
            <user name="user1" password="b59c67bf196a4758191e42f76670ceba"
                authorities="ROLE_USER" />
            <user name="user2" password="934b535800b1cba8f96a5d72f72f1611"
                disabled="true" authorities="ROLE_USER" />
        </user-service>
    </authentication-provider>
</authentication-manager>
```

A password encoder is also applicable to a user repository stored in a database:

```
<authentication-manager>
    <authentication-provider>
    <password-encoder hash="md5" />
        <jdbc-user-service data-source-ref="dataSource" />
    </authentication-provider>
</authentication-manager>
```

Of course, you have to store the encrypted passwords in the database tables, instead of the clear-text passwords, as shown in Table 5-5.

Table 5-5. Testing User Data with Encrypted Passwords for the USERS Table

USERNAME	PASSWORD	ENABLED
Admin	5ebe2294ecd0e0f08eab7690d2a6ee69	1
user1	b59c67bf196a4758191e42f76670ceba	1
user2	934b535800b1cba8f96a5d72f72f1611	0

Authenticating Users Against an LDAP Repository

Spring Security also supports accessing an LDAP repository for authenticating users. First, you have to prepare some user data for populating the LDAP repository. Let's prepare the user data in the LDAP Data Interchange Format (LDIF), a standard plain-text data format for importing and exporting LDAP directory data. For example, create the users.ldif file containing the following contents:

```
dn: dc=springrecipes,dc=com
objectClass: top
objectClass: domain
dc: springrecipes

dn: ou=groups,dc=springrecipes,dc=com
objectclass: top
objectclass: organizationalUnit
ou: groups

dn: ou=people,dc=springrecipes,dc=com
objectclass: top
objectclass: organizationalUnit
ou: people

dn: uid=admin,ou=people,dc=springrecipes,dc=com
objectclass: top
objectclass: uidObject
objectclass: person
uid: admin
cn: admin
sn: admin
userPassword: secret
```

```
dn: uid=user1,ou=people,dc=springrecipes,dc=com
objectclass: top
objectclass: uidObject
objectclass: person
uid: user1
cn: user1
sn: user1
userPassword: 1111

dn: cn=admin,ou=groups,dc=springrecipes,dc=com
objectclass: top
objectclass: groupOfNames
cn: admin
member: uid=admin,ou=people,dc=springrecipes,dc=com

dn: cn=user,ou=groups,dc=springrecipes,dc=com
objectclass: top
objectclass: groupOfNames
cn: user
member: uid=admin,ou=people,dc=springrecipes,dc=com
member: uid=user1,ou=people,dc=springrecipes,dc=com
```

Don't worry if you don't understand this LDIF file very well. You probably won't need to use this file format to define LDAP data often, because most LDAP servers support GUI-based configuration. This users.ldif file includes the following contents:

- The default LDAP domain, dc=springrecipes,dc=com

- The groups and people organization units for storing groups and users

- The admin and user1 users with the passwords secret and 1111

- The admin group (including the admin user) and the user group (including the admin and user1 users)

For testing purposes, you can install an LDAP server on your local machine to host this user repository. For the sake of easy installation and configuration, we recommend installing OpenDS (http://www.opends.org/), a Java-based open source directory service engine that supports LDAP.

■ **Note** OpenDS supports two types of installation interfaces: command line and GUI. This example uses the command-line interface, so you have to download the ZIP distribution and extract it to an arbitrary directory (e.g., C:\OpenDS-2.2.0), and then execute the setup script from the root of this directory.

```
C:\OpenDS-2.2.0>setup --cli

OpenDS Directory Server 2.2.0
Please wait while the setup program initializes...

What would you like to use as the initial root user DN for the Directory
Server? [cn=Directory Manager]:
Please provide the password to use for the initial root user: ldap
Please re-enter the password for confirmation: ldap

On which port would you like the Directory Server to accept connections from
LDAP clients? [1389]:

On which port would you like the Administration Connector to accept
connections? [4444]:

What do you wish to use as the base DN for the directory data?
[dc=example,dc=com]:dc=springrecipes,dc=com
Options for populating the database:

    1)  Only create the base entry
    2)  Leave the database empty
    3)  Import data from an LDIF file
    4)  Load automatically-generated sample data

Enter choice [1]: 3

Please specify the path to the LDIF file containing the data to import: users.ldif

Do you want to enable SSL? (yes / no) [no]:

Do you want to enable Start TLS? (yes / no) [no]:

Do you want to start the server when the configuration is completed? (yes /
no) [yes]:

Enable OpenDS to run as a Windows Service? (yes / no) [no]:

Do you want to start the server when the configuration is completed? (yes /
no) [yes]:

What would you like to do?
    1)  Setup the server with the parameters above
    2)  Provide the setup parameters again
    3)  Cancel the setup

Enter choice [1]:

Configuring Directory Server ..... Done.
Importing LDIF file users.ldif ....... Done.
Starting Directory Server ........ Done.
```

Note that the root user and password for this LDAP server are `cn=Directory Manager` and `ldap`, respectively. Later, you will have to use this user to connect to this server.

After the LDAP server has started up, you can configure Spring Security to authenticate users against its repository.

■ **Note** To authenticate users against an LDAP repository, you have to have the Spring LDAP project on your CLASSPATH. If you are using Maven, add the following dependency to your Maven project:

```
<dependency>
  <groupId>org.springframework.ldap</groupId>
  <artifactId>spring-ldap</artifactId>
  <version>1.3.0.RELEASE</version>
</dependency>
```

```
<beans:beans ...>
    ...
    <authentication-manager>
      <authentication-provider>
        <password-encoder hash="{sha}" />
        <ldap-user-service server-ref="ldapServer"
            user-search-filter="uid={0}" user-search-base="ou=people"
            group-search-filter="member={0}" group-search-base="ou=groups" />
      </authentication-provider>
    </authentication-manager>

    <ldap-server id="ldapServer"
        url="ldap://localhost:389/dc=springrecipes,dc=com"
        manager-dn="cn=Directory Manager" manager-password="ldap" />
</beans:beans>
```

You have to configure an `<ldap-user-service>` element to define how to search users from an LDAP repository. You can specify the search filters and search bases for searching users and groups via several attributes, whose values must be consistent with the repository's directory structure. With the preceding attribute values, Spring Security will search a user from the `people` organization unit with a particular user ID and search a user's groups from the `groups` organization unit. Spring Security will automatically insert the `ROLE_` prefix to each group as an authority.

As OpenDS uses SSHA (Salted Secure Hash Algorithm) to encode user passwords by default, you have to specify `{sha}` as the hash algorithm in `<password-encoder>`. Note that this value is different from `sha`, as it's specific to LDAP password encoding.

Finally, `<ldap-user-service>` has to refer to an LDAP server definition, which defines how to create connections to an LDAP server. You can specify the root user's username and password to connect to the LDAP server running on localhost.

Caching User Details

Both `<jdbc-user-service>` and `<ldap-user-service>` support caching user details. First of all, you have to choose a cache implementation that provides a caching service. As Spring and Spring Security have built-in support for Ehcache (`http://ehcache.sourceforge.net/`), you can choose it as your cache implementation and create a configuration file for it (e.g., `ehcache.xml` in the classpath root) with the following contents:

```
<ehcache>
    <diskStore path="java.io.tmpdir"/>

    <defaultCache
        maxElementsInMemory="1000"
        eternal="false"
        timeToIdleSeconds="120"
        timeToLiveSeconds="120"
        overflowToDisk="true"
        />

    <cache name="userCache"
        maxElementsInMemory="100"
        eternal="false"
        timeToIdleSeconds="600"
        timeToLiveSeconds="3600"
        overflowToDisk="true"
        />
</ehcache>
```

■ **Note** To use Ehcache to cache objects, you have to have the Ehcache 1.7.2 library on your CLASSPATH. If you are using Maven, add the following dependency to your Maven project:

```
<dependency>
  <groupId>net.sf.ehcache</groupId>
  <version>1.7.2</version>
  <artifactId>ehcache-core</artifactId>
</dependency>
```

This Ehcache configuration file defines two types of cache configurations. One is for the default, and the other is for caching user details. If the user cache configuration is used, a cache instance will cache the details of at most 100 users in memory. The cached users will overflow to disk when this limit is exceeded. A cached user will expire if it has been idle for 10 minutes or live for 1 hour after its creation.

To enable caching user details in Spring Security, you can set the `cache-ref` attribute of either `<jdbc-user-service>` or `<ldap-user-service>` to refer to a `UserCache` object. For Ehcache, Spring Security comes with a `UserCache` implementation, `EhCacheBasedUserCache`, which has to refer to an Ehcache instance.

```
<beans:beans ...>
    ...
    <authentication-manager>
      <authentication-provider>
        ...
        <ldap-user-service server-ref="ldapServer"
            user-search-filter="uid={0}" user-search-base="ou=people"
            group-search-filter="member={0}" group-search-base="ou=groups"
            cache-ref="userCache" />
      </authentication-provider>
    </authentication-manager>

    <beans:bean id="userCache" class="org.springframework.security.providers.↵
        dao.cache.EhCacheBasedUserCache">
        <beans:property name="cache" ref="userEhCache" />
    </beans:bean>

    <beans:bean id="userEhCache"
        class="org.springframework.cache.ehcache.EhCacheFactoryBean">
        <beans:property name="cacheManager" ref="cacheManager" />
        <beans:property name="cacheName" value="userCache" />
    </beans:bean>
</beans:beans>
```

In Spring, an Ehcache instance can be created via `EhCacheFactoryBean` by providing a cache manager and a cache name. Spring also provides `EhCacheManagerFactoryBean` for you to create an Ehcache manager by loading a configuration file. By default, it loads `ehcache.xml` (located in the root of the classpath). As an Ehcache manager may be used by other service components, it should be defined in `board-service.xml`.

```
<bean id="cacheManager"
    class="org.springframework.security.core.userdetails.cache.EhCacheManagerFactoryBean" />
```

5-4. Making Access Control Decisions

Problem

In the authentication process, an application will grant a successfully authenticated user a set of authorities. When this user attempts to access a resource in the application, the application has to decide whether the resource is accessible with the granted authorities or other characteristics.

Solution

The decision on whether a user is allowed to access a resource in an application is called an access control decision. It is made based on the user's authentication status, and the resource's nature and access attributes. In Spring Security, access control decisions are made by access decision managers, which have to implement the `AccessDecisionManager` interface. You are free to create your own access decision managers by implementing this interface, but Spring Security comes with three convenient access decision managers based on the voting approach. They are shown in Table 5-6.

Table 5-6. *Access Decision Managers That Come with Spring Security*

Access Decision Manager	When to Grant Access
`AffirmativeBased`	At least one voter votes to grant access.
`ConsensusBased`	A consensus of voters votes to grant access.
`UnanimousBased`	All voters vote to abstain or grant access (no voter votes to deny access).

All these access decision managers require a group of *voters* to be configured for voting on access control decisions. Each voter has to implement the `AccessDecisionVoter` interface. A voter can vote to grant, abstain, or deny access to a resource. The voting results are represented by the `ACCESS_GRANTED`, `ACCESS_DENIED`, and `ACCESS_ABSTAIN` constant fields defined in the `AccessDecisionVoter` interface.

By default, if no access decision manager is specified explicitly, Spring Security will automatically configure an `AffirmativeBased` access decision manager with the following two voters configured:

`RoleVoter` votes for an access control decision based on a user's role. It will only process access attributes that start with the `ROLE_` prefix, but this prefix can be customized. It votes to grant access if the user has the same role as required to access the resource or to deny access if the user lacks any role required to access the resource. If the resource does not have an access attribute starting with `ROLE_`, it will abstain from voting.

`AuthenticatedVoter` votes for an access control decision based on a user's authentication level. It will only process the access attributes `IS_AUTHENTICATED_FULLY`, `IS_AUTHENTICATED_REMEMBERED`, and `IS_AUTHENTICATED_ANONYMOUSLY`. It votes to grant access if the user's authentication level is higher than the required attribute. From highest to lowest, authentication levels are fully authenticated, authentication remembered, and anonymously authenticated.

How It Works

By default, Spring Security will automatically configure an access decision manager if none is specified. This default access decision manager is equivalent to the one defined with the following bean configuration:

```
<bean id="_accessManager"
    class="org.springframework.security.access.vote.AffirmativeBased">
    <property name="decisionVoters">
        <list>
            <bean class="org.springframework.security.access.vote.RoleVoter" />
            <bean class="org.springframework.security.access.vote.AuthenticatedVoter" />
        </list>
    </property>
</bean>
```

This default access decision manager and its decision voters should satisfy most typical authorization requirements. However, if they don't satisfy yours, you can create your own. In most cases, you'll only need to create a custom voter. For example, you can create a voter to vote for a decision based on a user's IP address:

```
package com.apress.springrecipes.board.security;

import org.springframework.security.core.Authentication;
import org.springframework.security.access.ConfigAttribute;

import org.springframework.security.web.authentication.WebAuthenticationDetails;
import org.springframework.security.access.AccessDecisionVoter;

import java.util.Collection;

public class IpAddressVoter implements AccessDecisionVoter {

    public static final String IP_PREFIX = "IP_";
    public static final String IP_LOCAL_HOST = "IP_LOCAL_HOST";

    public boolean supports(ConfigAttribute attribute) {
        return attribute.getAttribute() != null
                && attribute.getAttribute().startsWith(IP_PREFIX);
    }

    public boolean supports(Class clazz) {
        return true;
    }

    public int vote(Authentication authentication, Object object,
            Collection<ConfigAttribute> configList) {
        if (!(authentication.getDetails() instanceof WebAuthenticationDetails)) {
            return ACCESS_DENIED;
        }

        WebAuthenticationDetails details =
            (WebAuthenticationDetails) authentication.getDetails();
        String address = details.getRemoteAddress();
```

```
        int result = ACCESS_ABSTAIN;
        for (ConfigAttribute config : configList) {

            result = ACCESS_DENIED;
            if (IP_LOCAL_HOST.equals(config.getAttribute())) {
                if (address.equals("127.0.0.1") || address.equals("0:0:0:0:0:0:0:1")) {
                    return ACCESS_GRANTED;
                }
            }

        }
        return result;
    }
}
```

Note that this voter will only process the access attributes that start with the IP_ prefix. At the moment, it only supports the IP_LOCAL_HOST access attribute. If the user is a web client whose IP address is equal to 127.0.0.1 or 0:0:0:0:0:0:0:1—the last value being returned by networkless Linux workstations—this voter will vote to grant access. Otherwise, it will vote to deny access. If the resource does not have an access attribute starting with IP_, it will abstain from voting.

Next, you have to define a custom access decision manager that includes this voter. If you define this access decision manager in board-security.xml, you will have to include the beans prefix, because the default schema is security.

```
<beans:bean id="accessDecisionManager"
    class="org.springframework.security.access.vote.AffirmativeBased">
    <beans:property name="decisionVoters">
        <beans:list>
            <beans:bean
                class="org.springframework.security.access.vote.RoleVoter" />
            <beans:bean
                class="org.springframework.security.acces.vote.AuthenticatedVoter" />
            <beans:bean
                class="com.apress.springrecipes.board.↵
                                security.IpAddressVoter" />
        </beans:list>
    </beans:property>
</beans:bean>
```

Now, suppose you would like to allow users of the machine running the web container (i.e., the server administrators) to delete messages without logging in. You have to refer to this access decision manager from the <http> configuration element and add the access attribute IP_LOCAL_HOST to the URL pattern /messageDelete.htm*:

```
<http access-decision-manager-ref="accessDecisionManager">
    <intercept-url pattern="/messageList*" access="ROLE_USER,ROLE_GUEST" />
    <intercept-url pattern="/messagePost*" access="ROLE_USER" />
    <intercept-url pattern="/messageDelete*"
        access="ROLE_ADMIN,IP_LOCAL_HOST" />
    ...
</http>
```

Then, if you access this message board application from localhost, you needn't log in as an administrator to delete a posted message.

5-5. Securing Method Invocations

Problem

As an alternative or a complement to securing URL access in the web layer, sometimes you may need to secure method invocations in the service layer. For example, in the case that a single controller has to invoke multiple methods in the service layer, you may wish to enforce fine-grained security controls on these methods.

Solution

Spring Security enables you to secure method invocations in a declarative way. First, you can embed a `<security:intercept-methods>` element in a bean definition to secure its methods. Alternatively, you can configure a global `<global-method-security>` element to secure multiple methods matched with AspectJ pointcut expressions. You can also annotate methods declared in a bean interface or an implementation class with the `@Secured` annotation and then enable security for them in `<<global-method-security>`.

How It Works

Securing Methods by Embedding a Security Interceptor

First, you can secure a bean's methods by embedding a `<security:intercept-methods>` element in the bean definition. For example, you can secure the methods of the `messageBoardService` bean defined in `board-service.xml`. As this element is defined in the `security` schema, you have to import it beforehand.

```
<beans xmlns="http://www.springframework.org/schema/beans"
    xmlns:xsi="http://www.w3.org/2001/XMLSchema-instance"
    xmlns:security="http://www.springframework.org/schema/security"
    xsi:schemaLocation="http://www.springframework.org/schema/beans
        http://www.springframework.org/schema/beans/spring-beans-3.0.xsd
        http://www.springframework.org/schema/security
        http://www.springframework.org/schema/security/spring-security-3.0..xsd">
```

```
    <bean id="messageBoardService"
        class="com.apress.springrecipes.board.service.MessageBoardServiceImpl">
        <security:intercept-methods
            access-decision-manager-ref="accessDecisionManager">
            <security:protect
                method="com.apress.springrecipes.board.service.↵
                    MessageBoardService.listMessages"
                access="ROLE_USER,ROLE_GUEST" />
            <security:protect
                method="com.apress.springrecipes.board.service.↵
                    MessageBoardService.postMessage"
                access="ROLE_USER" />
            <security:protect
                method="com.apress.springrecipes.board.service.↵
                    MessageBoardService.deleteMessage"
                access="ROLE_ADMIN,IP_LOCAL_HOST" />
            <security:protect
                method="com.apress.springrecipes.board.service.↵
                    MessageBoardService.findMessageById"
                access="ROLE_USER,ROLE_GUEST" />
        </security:intercept-methods>
    </bean>
    ...
</beans>
```

In a bean's `<security:intercept-methods>`, you can specify multiple `<security:protect>` elements to specify access attributes for this bean's methods. You can match multiple methods by specifying a method name pattern with wildcards. If you would like to use a custom access decision manager, you can specify it in the `access-decision-manager-ref` a`access-decision-manager-ref` attribute.

Securing Methods with Pointcuts

Second, you can define global pointcuts in `<global-method-security>` to secure methods using AspectJ pointcut expressions, instead of embedding a security interceptor in each bean whose methods require security. You should configure the `<global-method-security>` element in `board-security.xml` for centralizing security configurations. As the default namespace of this configuration file is `security`, you needn't specify a prefix for this element explicitly. You can also specify a custom access decision manager in the `access-decision-manager-ref` attribute.

```
<global-method-security
    access-decision-manager-ref="accessDecisionManager">
    <protect-pointcut expression=
        "execution(* com.apress.springrecipes.board.service.*Service.list*(..))"
        access="ROLE_USER,ROLE_GUEST" />
    <protect-pointcut expression=
        "execution(* com.apress.springrecipes.board.service.*Service.post*(..))"
        access="ROLE_USER" />
    <protect-pointcut expression=
        "execution(* com.apress.springrecipes.board.service.*Service.delete*(..))"
        access="ROLE_ADMIN,IP_LOCAL_HOST" />
```

```
    <protect-pointcut expression=
        "execution(* com.apress.springrecipes.board.service.*Service.find*(..))"
        access="ROLE_USER,ROLE_GUEST" />
</global-method-security>
```

To test this approach, you have to delete the preceding <security:intercept-methods> element.

Securing Methods with Annotations

The third approach to securing methods is by annotating them with @Secured. For example, you can annotate the methods in MessageBoardServiceImpl with the @Secured annotation and specify the access attributes as its value, whose type is String[].

```
package com.apress.springrecipes.board.service;
...
import org.springframework.security.access.annotation.Secured;

public class MessageBoardServiceImpl implements MessageBoardService {
    ...
    @Secured({"ROLE_USER", "ROLE_GUEST"})
    public List<Message> listMessages() {
        ...
    }

    @Secured("ROLE_USER")
    public synchronized void postMessage(Message message) {
        ...
    }

    @Secured({"ROLE_ADMIN", "IP_LOCAL_HOST"})
    public synchronized void deleteMessage(Message message) {
        ...
    }

    @Secured({"ROLE_USER", "ROLE_GUEST"})
    public Message findMessageById(Long messageId) {
        return messages.get(messageId);
    }
}
```

Then, in <global-method-security>, you have to enable security for methods annotated with ethods annotated with @Secured.

```
<global-method-security secured-annotations="enabled"
    access-decision-manager-ref="accessDecisionManager" />
```

5-6. Handling Security in Views

Problem

Sometimes, you may wish to display a user's authentication information, such as the principal name and the granted authorities, in the views of your web application. In addition, you would like to render the view contents conditionally according to the user's authorities.

Solution

Although you can write JSP scriptlets in your JSP files to retrieve authentication and authorization information through the Spring Security API, it's not an efficient solution. Spring Security provides a JSP tag library for you to handle security in JSP views. It includes tags that can display a user's authentication information and render the view contents conditionally according to the user's authorities.

How It Works

Displaying Authentication Information

Suppose you would like to display a user's principal name and granted authorities in the header of the message listing page (i.e., messageList.jsp). First of all, you have to import Spring Security's tag library definition.

```
<%@ taglib prefix="c" uri="http://java.sun.com/jsp/jstl/core" %>
<%@ taglib prefix="security" uri="http://www.springframework.org/security/tags" %>

<html>
<head>
<title>Message List</title>
</head>

<body>
<h2>Welcome! <security:authentication property="name" /></h2>

<security:authentication property="authorities" var="authorities" />
<ul>
<c:forEach items="${authorities}" var="authority">
  <li>${authority.authority}</li>
</c:forEach>
</ul>
<hr />
...
</body>
</html>
```

The `<security:authentication>` tag exposes the current user's `Authentication` object for you to render its properties. You can specify a property name or property path in its `property` attribute. For example, you can render a user's principal name through the `name` property.

In addition to rendering an authentication property directly, this tag supports storing the property in a JSP variable, whose name is specified in the `var` attribute. For example, you can store the `authorities` property, which contains the authorities granted to the user, in the JSP variable `authorities`, and render them one by one with a `<c:forEach>` tag. You can further specify the variable scope with the `scope ascope` attribute.

Rendering View Contents Conditionally

If you would like to render view contents conditionally according to a user's authorities, you can use the `<security:authorize>` tag. For example, you can decide whether to render the message authors according to the user's authorities:

```
<%@ taglib prefix="c" uri="http://java.sun.com/jsp/jstl/core" %>
<%@ taglib prefix="security" uri="http://www.springframework.org/security/tags" %>

<html>
<head>
<title>Message List</title>
</head>

<body>
...
<c:forEach items="${messages}" var="message">
<table>
  <security:authorize ifAllGranted="ROLE_ADMIN,ROLE_USER">
  <tr>
    <td>Author</td>
    <td>${message.author}</td>
  </tr>
  </security:authorize>
  ...
</table>
<hr />
</c:forEach>
...
</body>
</html>
```

If you want the enclosing content to be rendered only when the user has been granted certain authorities at the same time, you have to specify them in the `ifAllGranted` attribute. Otherwise, if the enclosing content can be rendered with any of the authorities, you have to specify them in the `ifAnyGranted` attribute:

```
<security:authorize ifAnyGranted="ROLE_ADMIN,ROLE_USER">
<tr>
  <td>Author</td>
  <td>${message.author}</td>
</tr>
</security:authorize>
```

You can also render the enclosing content when a user has not been granted any of the authorities specified in the ifNotGranted attribute:

```
<security:authorize ifNotGranted="ROLE_GUEST">
<tr>
  <td>Author</td>
  <td>${message.author}</td>
</tr>
</security:authorize>
```

5-7. Handling Domain Object Security

Problem

Sometimes, you may have complicated security requirements that require handling security at the domain object level. That means you have to allow each domain object to have different access attributes for different principals.

Solution

Spring Security provides a module named ACL that allows each domain object to have its own *access control list (ACL)*. An ACL contains a domain object's *object identity* to associate with the object, and also holds multiple *access control entries (ACEs)*, each of which contains the following two core parts:

- Permissions: An ACE's permissions are represented by a particular bit mask, with each bit value for a particular type of permission. The BasePermission class predefines five basic permissions as constant values for you to use: READ (bit 0 or integer 1), WRITE (bit 1 or integer 2), CREATE (bit 2 or integer 4), DELETE (bit 3 or integer 8), and ADMINISTRATION (bit 4 or integer 16). You can also define your own using other unused bits.

- Security Identity (SID): Each ACE contains permissions for a particular SID. An SID can be a principal (PrincipalSid) or an authority (GrantedAuthoritySid) to associate with permissions.

In addition to defining the ACL object model, Spring Security defines APIs for reading and maintaining the model, and provides high-performance JDBC implementations for these APIs. To simplify ACL's usages, Spring Security also provides facilities, such as access decision voters and JSP tags, for you to use ACL consistently with other security facilities in your application.

How It Works

Setting Up an ACL Service

Spring Security provides built-in support for storing ACL data in a relational database and accessing it with JDBC. First of all, you have to create the following tables in your database for storing ACL data:

```
CREATE TABLE ACL_SID(
    ID          BIGINT       NOT NULL GENERATED BY DEFAULT AS IDENTITY,
    SID         VARCHAR(100) NOT NULL,
    PRINCIPAL   SMALLINT     NOT NULL,
    PRIMARY KEY (ID),
    UNIQUE (SID, PRINCIPAL)
);

CREATE TABLE ACL_CLASS(
    ID    BIGINT       NOT NULL GENERATED BY DEFAULT AS IDENTITY,
    CLASS VARCHAR(100) NOT NULL,
    PRIMARY KEY (ID),
    UNIQUE (CLASS)
);

CREATE TABLE ACL_OBJECT_IDENTITY(
    ID                  BIGINT    NOT NULL GENERATED BY DEFAULT AS IDENTITY,
    OBJECT_ID_CLASS     BIGINT    NOT NULL,
    OBJECT_ID_IDENTITY  BIGINT    NOT NULL,
    PARENT_OBJECT       BIGINT,
    OWNER_SID           BIGINT,
    ENTRIES_INHERITING  SMALLINT  NOT NULL,
    PRIMARY KEY (ID),
    UNIQUE (OBJECT_ID_CLASS, OBJECT_ID_IDENTITY),
    FOREIGN KEY (PARENT_OBJECT)    REFERENCES ACL_OBJECT_IDENTITY,
    FOREIGN KEY (OBJECT_ID_CLASS) REFERENCES ACL_CLASS,
    FOREIGN KEY (OWNER_SID)        REFERENCES ACL_SID
);

CREATE TABLE ACL_ENTRY(
    ID                  BIGINT    NOT NULL GENERATED BY DEFAULT AS IDENTITY,
    ACL_OBJECT_IDENTITY BIGINT    NOT NULL,
    ACE_ORDER           INT       NOT NULL,
    SID                 BIGINT    NOT NULL,
    MASK                INTEGER   NOT NULL,
    GRANTING            SMALLINT  NOT NULL,
    AUDIT_SUCCESS       SMALLINT  NOT NULL,
    AUDIT_FAILURE       SMALLINT  NOT NULL,
    PRIMARY KEY (ID),
    UNIQUE (ACL_OBJECT_IDENTITY, ACE_ORDER),
    FOREIGN KEY (ACL_OBJECT_IDENTITY) REFERENCES ACL_OBJECT_IDENTITY,
    FOREIGN KEY (SID)                 REFERENCES ACL_SID
);
```

Spring Security defines APIs and provides high-performance JDBC implementations for you to access ACL data stored in these tables, so you'll seldom have a need to access ACL data from the database directly.

As each domain object can have its own ACL, there may be a large number of ACLs in your application. Fortunately, Spring Security supports caching ACL objects. You can continue to use Ehcache as your cache implementation and create a new configuration for ACL caching in ehcache.xml (located in the classpath root).

```
<ehcache>
    ...
    <cache name="aclCache"
        maxElementsInMemory="1000"
        eternal="false"
        timeToIdleSeconds="600"
        timeToLiveSeconds="3600"
        overflowToDisk="true"
        />
</ehcache>
```

Next, you have to set up an ACL service for your application. However, as Spring Security doesn't support configuring the ACL module with XML schema-based configurations, you have to configure this module with a group of normal Spring beans. As the default namespace of board-security.xml is security, it's cumbersome to configure an ACL in this file using the standard XML elements in the beans namespace. For this reason, let's create a separate bean configuration file named board-acl.xml, which will store ACL-specific configurations, and add its location in the web deployment descriptor:

```
<web-app ...>
    ...
    <context-param>
        <param-name>contextConfigLocation</param-name>
        <param-value>
            /WEB-INF/board-service.xml
            /WEB-INF/board-security.xml
            /WEB-INF/board-acl.xml
        </param-value>
    </context-param>
</web-app>
```

In an ACL configuration file, the core bean is an ACL service. In Spring Security, there are two interfaces that define operations of an ACL service: AclService and MutableAclService. AclService defines operations for you to read ACLs. MutableAclService is a subinterface of AclService that defines operations for you to create, update, and delete ACLs. If your application only needs to read ACLs, you can simply choose an AclService implementation, such as JdbcAclService. Otherwise, you should choose a MutableAclService implementation, such as JdbcMutableAclService.

```
<beans xmlns="http://www.springframework.org/schema/beans"
    xmlns:xsi="http://www.w3.org/2001/XMLSchema-instance"
    xsi:schemaLocation="http://www.springframework.org/schema/beans
        http://www.springframework.org/schema/beans/spring-beans-3.0.xsd">
```

```xml
<bean id="aclCache"
    class="org.springframework.security.acls.domain.EhCacheBasedAclCache">
    <constructor-arg ref="aclEhCache" />
</bean>

<bean id="aclEhCache"
    class="org.springframework.cache.ehcache.EhCacheFactoryBean">
    <property name="cacheManager" ref="cacheManager" />
    <property name="cacheName" value="aclCache" />
</bean>

<bean id="lookupStrategy"
    class="org.springframework.security.acls.jdbc.BasicLookupStrategy">
    <constructor-arg ref="dataSource" />
    <constructor-arg ref="aclCache" />
    <constructor-arg>
        <bean class="org.springframework.security.acls.domain. ↵
            AclAuthorizationStrategyImpl">
            <constructor-arg>
                <list>
                    <ref local="adminRole" />
                    <ref local="adminRole" />
                    <ref local="adminRole" />
                </list>
            </constructor-arg>
        </bean>
    </constructor-arg>
    <constructor-arg>
        <bean class="org.springframework.security.acls.domain. ↵
            ConsoleAuditLogger" />
    </constructor-arg>
</bean>

<bean id="adminRole"
    class="org.springframework.security.core.authority.GrantedAuthorityImpl">
    <constructor-arg value="ROLE_ADMIN" />
</bean>

<bean id="aclService"
    class="org.springframework.security.acls.jdbc.JdbcMutableAclService">
    <constructor-arg ref="dataSource" />
    <constructor-arg ref="lookupStrategy" />
    <constructor-arg ref="aclCache" />
    <property name="sidIdentityQuery" ↵
                value="values identity_val_local()" />
</bean>
</beans>
```

The core bean definition in this ACL configuration file is the ACL service, which is an instance of **JdbcMutableAclService** that allows you to maintain ACLs. This class requires three constructor arguments. The first is a data source for creating connections to a database that stores ACL data. You should have a data source defined in `board-service.xml` beforehand so that you can simply refer to it here (assuming that you have created the ACL tables in the same database). The third constructor argument is a cache instance to use with an ACL, which you can configure using Ehcache as the back-end cache implementation.

The second argument—`sidIdentityQuery`—is a lookup strategy that performs lookup for an ACL service. Note, if you're using HSQLDB, that the `sidIdentityQuery`'s property is not necessary, because it defaults to this database. If using another database—as in this case for Apache Derby—an explicit value is necessary.

The only implementation that comes with Spring Security is `BasicLookupStrategy`, which performs basic lookup using standard and compatible SQL statements. If you want to make use of advanced database features to increase lookup performance, you can create your own lookup strategy by implementing the `LookupStrategy` interface. A `BasicLookupStrategy` instance also requires a data source and a cache instance. Besides, it requires a constructor argument whose type is `AclAuthorizationStrategy`. This object determines whether a principal is authorized to change certain properties of an ACL, usually by specifying a required authority for each category of properties. For the preceding configurations, only a user who has the `ROLE_ADMIN` role can change an ACL's ownership, an ACE's auditing details, or other ACL and ACE details, respectively.

Finally, `JdbcMutableAclService` embeds standard SQL statements for maintaining ACL data in a relational database. However, those SQL statements may not be compatible with all database products. For example, you have to customize the identity query statement for Apache Derby.

Maintaining ACLs for Domain Objects

In your back-end services and DAOs, you can maintain ACLs for domain objects with the previously defined ACL service via dependency injection. For your message board, you have to create an ACL for a message when it is posted and delete the ACL when this message is deleted:

```
package com.apress.springrecipes.board.service;
...
import org.springframework.security.acls.model.MutableAcl;
import org.springframework.security.acls.model.MutableAclService;
import org.springframework.security.acls.domain.BasePermission;
import org.springframework.security.acls.model.ObjectIdentity;
import org.springframework.security.acls.domain.ObjectIdentityImpl;
import org.springframework.security.acls.domain.GrantedAuthoritySid;
import org.springframework.security.acls.domain.PrincipalSid;
import org.springframework.security.access.annotation.Secured;
import org.springframework.transaction.annotation.Transactional;

public class MessageBoardServiceImpl implements MessageBoardService {
    ...
    private MutableAclService mutableAclService;

    public void setMutableAclService(MutableAclService mutableAclService) {
        this.mutableAclService = mutableAclService;
    }
```

```
@Transactional
@Secured("ROLE_USER")
public synchronized void postMessage(Message message) {
    ...
    ObjectIdentity oid =
        new ObjectIdentityImpl(Message.class, message.getId());
    MutableAcl acl = mutableAclService.createAcl(oid);
    acl.insertAce(0, BasePermission.ADMINISTRATION,
            new PrincipalSid(message.getAuthor()), true);
    acl.insertAce(1, BasePermission.DELETE,
            new GrantedAuthoritySid("ROLE_ADMIN"), true);
    acl.insertAce(2, BasePermission.READ,
            new GrantedAuthoritySid("ROLE_USER"), true);
    mutableAclService.updateAcl(acl);
}

@Transactional
@Secured({"ROLE_ADMIN", "IP_LOCAL_HOST"})
public synchronized void deleteMessage(Message message) {
    ...
    ObjectIdentity oid =
        new ObjectIdentityImpl(Message.class, message.getId());
    mutableAclService.deleteAcl(oid, false);
}
}
```

When a user posts a message, you create a new ACL for this message at the same time, using the message ID as the ACL's object identity. When a user deletes a message, you delete the corresponding ACL as well. For a new message, you insert the following three ACEs into its ACL:

- The message author is permitted to administrate this message.

- A user who has the ROLE_ADMIN role is permitted to delete this message.

- A user who has the ROLE_USER role is permitted to read this message.

JdbcMutableAclService requires that the calling methods have transactions enabled so that its SQL statements can run within transactions. So, you annotate the two methods involving ACL maintenance with the @Transactional annotation and then define a transaction manager and <tx:annotation-driven> in board-service.xml. Also, don't forget to inject the ACL service into the message board service for it to maintain ACLs.

```
<beans xmlns="http://www.springframework.org/schema/beans"
    xmlns:xsi="http://www.w3.org/2001/XMLSchema-instance"
    xmlns:tx="http://www.springframework.org/schema/tx"
    xsi:schemaLocation="http://www.springframework.org/schema/beans
        http://www.springframework.org/schema/beans/spring-beans-3.0.xsd
        http://www.springframework.org/schema/tx
        http://www.springframework.org/schema/tx/spring-tx-3.0.xsd">
    ...
<tx:annotation-driven />
```

```xml
    <bean id="transactionManager"
        class="org.springframework.jdbc.datasource.DataSourceTransactionManager">
        <property name="dataSource" ref="dataSource" />
    </bean>

    <bean id="messageBoardService"
        class="com.apress.springrecipes.board.service.MessageBoardServiceImpl">
        <property name="mutableAclService" ref="aclService" />
    </bean>
</beans>
```

Making Access Control Decisions Based on ACLs

With an ACL for each domain object, you can use an object's ACL to make access control decisions on methods that involve this object. For example, when a user attempts to delete a posted message, you can consult this message's ACL about whether the user is permitted to delete this message.

Spring Security comes with the AclEntryVoter class, which allows you to define a decision voter that votes for decisions based on ACLs. The following ACL voter in board-acl.xml votes for an access control decision if a method has the ACL_MESSAGE_DELETE access attribute and a method argument whose type is Message. If the current user has the ADMINISTRATION or DELETE permissions in the message domain object's ACL, that user will be permitted to delete this message.

```xml
<beans xmlns="http://www.springframework.org/schema/beans"
    xmlns:xsi="http://www.w3.org/2001/XMLSchema-instance"
    xmlns:util="http://www.springframework.org/schema/util"
    xsi:schemaLocation="http://www.springframework.org/schema/beans
        http://www.springframework.org/schema/beans/spring-beans-3.0.xsd
        http://www.springframework.org/schema/util
        http://www.springframework.org/schema/util/spring-util-3.0.xsd">
    ...
    <bean id="aclMessageDeleteVoter"
        class="org.springframework.security.acls.AclEntryVoter">
        <constructor-arg ref="aclService" />
        <constructor-arg value="ACL_MESSAGE_DELETE" />
        <constructor-arg>
            <list>
                <util:constant static-field="org.springframework.security.↵
                    acls.domain.BasePermission.ADMINISTRATION" />
                <util:constant static-field="org.springframework.security.↵
                    acls.domain.BasePermission.DELETE" />
            </list>
        </constructor-arg>
        <property name="processDomainObjectClass"
            value="com.apress.springrecipes.board.domain.Message" />
    </bean>
```

```xml
<bean id="aclAccessDecisionManager"
    class="org.springframework.security.vote.AffirmativeBased">
    <property name="decisionVoters">
        <list>
            <bean class="org.springframework.security.vote.RoleVoter" />
            <ref local="aclMessageDeleteVoter" />
        </list>
    </property>
</bean>
</beans>
```

After configuring a voter, you have to include it in an access decision manager for it to vote for decisions. Because an ACL voter cannot vote for HTTP-based access decisions, you can't include it in the global access decision manager, as this manager is used for the <http> element. Instead, you should configure another access decision manager that is specific for method invocations (aclAccessDecisionManager in this case) and include the ACL voter in this manager. In board-security.xml, you have to modify the <global-method-security> element to use this access decision manager for method invocation security:

```xml
<global-method-security secured-annotations="enabled"
    access-decision-manager-ref="aclAccessDecisionManager" />
```

With the voter and access decision manager set up, the last step is to specify the access attribute ACL_MESSAGE_DELETE for the deleteMessage() method:

```java
package com.apress.springrecipes.board.service;
...
import org.springframework.security.access.annotation.Secured;

public class MessageBoardServiceImpl implements MessageBoardService {
    ...
    @Transactional
    @Secured("ACL_MESSAGE_DELETE")
    public synchronized void deleteMessage(Message message) {
        ...
    }
}
```

With this attribute, only a user who has the ADMINISTRATION permission (by default, the message author) or the DELETE permission (by default, an administrator who has the ROLE_ADMIN role) on the message argument can delete a message.

If you want to hide a message's Delete link when the current user isn't permitted to delete the message, you can wrap the link with the <security:accesscontrollist> tag, whose function is to render its body conditionally according to a domain object's ACL:

```
<%@ taglib prefix="c" uri="http://java.sun.com/jsp/jstl/core" %>
<%@ taglib prefix="security" uri="http://www.springframework.org/security/tags" %>

<html>
<head>
<title>Message List</title>
</head>

<body>
...
<c:forEach items="${messages}" var="message">
<table>
  ...
  <security:accesscontrollist domainObject="${message}" hasPermission="8,16">
  <tr>
    <td colspan="2">
      <a href="messageDelete.htm?messageId=${message.id}">Delete</a>
    </td>
  </tr>
  </security:accesscontrollist>
</table>
<hr />
</c:forEach>
...
</body>
</html>
```

The `<security:accesscontrollist>` tag consults the specified domain object's ACL to check whether the current user has the specified permissions. This tag will only render its body if the user has one of the required permissions. Note that, in this tag, permissions are defined as integers translated from their bit mask values. The values 8 and 16 represent the `DELETE` and `ADMINISTRATION` permissions, respectively.

Handling Domain Objects Returned from Methods

Spring Security can use *after invocation providers* to handle domain objects returned from methods according to the ACLs of these objects. For methods that return a single domain object, you can register an `AclEntryAfterInvocationProvider` instance to check whether the current user has specified permissions to access the returned domain object. If the user is not permitted to access the object, this provider will throw an exception to prevent the object from being returned.

On the other hand, for methods that return a collection of domain objects, you can register an `AclEntryAfterInvocationCollectionFilteringProvider` instance to filter the returned collection according to the ACLs of this collection's domain object elements. The domain objects that the current user doesn't have specified permissions on will be removed from the collection before it's returned to the calling method.

```xml
<beans xmlns="http://www.springframework.org/schema/beans"
    xmlns:xsi="http://www.w3.org/2001/XMLSchema-instance"
    xmlns:util="http://www.springframework.org/schema/util"
    xmlns:security="http://www.springframework.org/schema/security"
    xsi:schemaLocation="http://www.springframework.org/schema/beans
        http://www.springframework.org/schema/beans/spring-beans-3.0.xsd
        http://www.springframework.org/schema/util
        http://www.springframework.org/schema/util/spring-util-3.0.xsd
        http://www.springframework.org/schema/security
        http://www.springframework.org/schema/security/spring-security-3.0.xsd">
    ...
    <bean id="afterAclRead" class="org.springframework.security.↵
        acls.afterinvocation.AclEntryAfterInvocationProvider">
        <security:custom-after-invocation-provider />
        <constructor-arg ref="aclService" />
        <constructor-arg>
            <list>
                <util:constant static-field="org.springframework.security.↵
                    acls.domain.BasePermission.ADMINISTRATION" />
                <util:constant static-field="org.springframework.security.↵
                    acls.domain.BasePermission.READ" />
            </list>
        </constructor-arg>
    </bean>

    <bean id="afterAclCollectionRead" class="org.springframework.security.↵
        acls.afterinvocation.AclEntryAfterInvocationCollectionFilteringProvider">
        <security:custom-after-invocation-provider />
        <constructor-arg ref="aclService" />
        <constructor-arg>
            <list>
                <util:constant static-field="org.springframework.security.↵
                    acls.domain.BasePermission.ADMINISTRATION" />
                <util:constant static-field="org.springframework.security.↵
                    acls.domain.BasePermission.READ" />
            </list>
        </constructor-arg>
    </bean>
</beans>
```

To register a custom after invocation provider to Spring Security, you can simply embed a <custom-after-invocation-provider> element in the bean definition. This element is defined in the security schema, so you have to import it beforehand.

Now, you can specify the access attributes AFTER_ACL_COLLECTION_READ and AFTER_ACL_READ, which will be handled by the preceding after invocation providers, for the listMessages() and findMessageById() methods.

```
package com.apress.springrecipes.board.service;
...
import org.springframework.security.access.annotation.Secured;

public class MessageBoardServiceImpl implements MessageBoardService {
    ...
    @Secured({"ROLE_USER", "ROLE_GUEST", "AFTER_ACL_COLLECTION_READ"})
    public List<Message> listMessages() {
        ...
    }

    @Secured({"ROLE_USER", "ROLE_GUEST", "AFTER_ACL_READ"})
    public Message findMessageById(Long messageId) {
        ...
    }
}
```

Summary

In this chapter, you learned how to secure applications using Spring Security 3.0. It can be used to secure any Java application, but it's mostly used for web applications. The concepts of authentication, authorization, and access control are essential in the security area, so you should have a clear understanding of them.

You often have to secure critical URLs by preventing unauthorized access to them. Spring Security can help you to achieve this in a declarative way. It handles security by applying servlet filters, which can be configured with simple XML elements. If your web application's security requirements are simple and typical, you can enable the HTTP auto-config feature so that Spring Security will automatically configure the basic security services for you.

Spring Security supports multiple ways for users to log into a web application, such as form-based login and HTTP Basic authentication. It also provides an anonymous login service that allows you to handle an anonymous user just like a normal user. Remember-me support allows an application to remember a user's identity across multiple browser sessions.

Spring Security supports multiple ways of authenticating users and has built-in provider implementations for them. For example, it supports authenticating users against in-memory definitions, a relational database, and an LDAP repository. You should always store encrypted passwords in your user repository, because clear-text passwords are vulnerable to hacker attacks. Spring Security also supports caching user details locally to save you the overhead of performing remote queries.

Decisions on whether a user is allowed to access a given resource are made by access decision managers. Spring Security comes with three access decision managers that are based on the voting approach. All of them require a group of voters to be configured for voting on access control decisions.

Spring Security enables you to secure method invocations in a declarative way, either by embedding a security interceptor in a bean definition, or matching multiple methods with AspectJ pointcut expressions or annotations. Spring Security also allows you to display a user's authentication information in JSP views and render view contents conditionally according to a user's authorities.

Spring Security provides an ACL module that allows each domain object to have an ACL for controlling access. You can read and maintain an ACL for each domain object with Spring Security's high-performance APIs, which are implemented with JDBC. Spring Security also provides facilities such as access decision voters and JSP tags for you to use ACLs consistently with other security facilities.

CHAPTER 6

■■■

Integrating Spring with Other Web Frameworks

In this chapter, you will learn how to integrate the Spring framework with several popular web application frameworks, including Struts, JSF, and DWR. Spring's powerful IoC container and enterprise support features make it very suitable for implementing the service and persistence layers of your Java EE applications. However, for the presentation layer, you have a choice between many different web frameworks. So, you often need to integrate Spring with whatever web application framework you are using. The integration mainly focuses on accessing beans declared in the Spring IoC container within these frameworks.

Apache Struts (`http://struts.apache.org/`) is a popular open source web application framework based on the MVC design pattern. Struts has been used in many web-based projects in the Java community and thus has a large user base. Note that Spring's Struts support features target Struts 1.x only. This is because after Struts joined with WebWork in Struts version 2, it's very easy to configure Struts actions in Spring by using the Spring IoC container as the object factory of Struts 2.

JavaServer Faces, or JSF, (`http://java.sun.com/javaee/javaserverfaces/`) is an excellent component-based and event-driven web application framework included as part of the Java EE specification. You can use the rich set of standard JSF components and also develop custom components for reuse. JSF can cleanly separate presentation logic from UIs by encapsulating it in one or more managed beans. Due to its component-based approach and popularity, JSF is supported by a wide range of IDEs for visual development.

Direct Web Remoting, or DWR, (`http://getahead.org/dwr`) is a library that brings Ajax (Asynchronous JavaScript and XML) features to your web applications. It allows you to invoke Java objects on the server side by using JavaScript in a web browser. You can also update parts of a web page dynamically, without refreshing the entire page.

After finishing this chapter, you will be able to integrate Spring into web applications implemented with Servlet/JSP and popular web application frameworks such as Struts, JSF, and DWR.

6-1. Accessing Spring in Generic Web Applications

Problem

You would like to access beans declared in the Spring IoC container in a web application, regardless of which framework it uses.

Solution

A web application can load Spring's application context by registering the servlet listener `ContextLoaderListener`. This listener stores the loaded application context into the web application's servlet context. Later, a servlet, or any object that can access the servlet context, can also access Spring's application context through a utility method.

How It Works

Suppose you are going to develop a web application for users to find the distance (measured in kilometers) between two cities. First, you define the following service interface:

```
package com.apress.springrecipes.city;

public interface CityService {

    public double findDistance(String srcCity, String destCity);
}
```

For simplicity's sake, let's implement this interface by using a Java map to store the distance data. This map's keys are source cities while its values are nested maps that contain destination cities and their distances from the source city.

```
package com.apress.springrecipes.city;
...
public class CityServiceImpl implements CityService {

    private Map<String, Map<String, Double>> distanceMap;

    public void setDistanceMap(Map<String, Map<String, Double>> distanceMap) {
        this.distanceMap = distanceMap;
    }

    public double findDistance(String srcCity, String destCity) {
        Map<String, Double> destinationMap = distanceMap.get(srcCity);
        if (destinationMap == null) {
            throw new IllegalArgumentException("Source city not found");
        }
```

```
        Double distance = destinationMap.get(destCity);
        if (distance == null) {
            throw new IllegalArgumentException("Destination city not found");
        }
        return distance;
    }
}
```

Next, you create the following directory structure for your web application. As this application requires access to the Spring IoC container, you have to put the required Spring .jar files in your WEB-INF/lib folder. If you are using Maven, see chapter 1 for information on adding the correct .jars to your CLASSPATH.

```
city/
    WEB-INF/
        classes/
        lib/-*.jar
        jsp/
            distance.jsp
        applicationContext.xml
        web.xml
```

In Spring's bean configuration file, you can hard-code some distance data for several cities using the <map> element. You create this file with the name applicationContext.xml and put it in the root of WEB-INF.

```xml
<beans xmlns="http://www.springframework.org/schema/beans"
    xmlns:xsi="http://www.w3.org/2001/XMLSchema-instance"
    xsi:schemaLocation="http://www.springframework.org/schema/beans
        http://www.springframework.org/schema/beans/spring-beans-3.0.xsd">

    <bean id="cityService"
        class="com.apress.springrecipes.city.CityServiceImpl">
        <property name="distanceMap">
            <map>
                <entry key="New York">
                    <map>
                        <entry key="London" value="5574" />
                        <entry key="Beijing" value="10976" />
                    </map>
                </entry>
            </map>
        </property>
    </bean>
</beans>
```

In the web deployment descriptor (i.e., web.xml), you register the Spring-provided servlet listener ContextLoaderListener to load Spring's application context into the servlet context at startup. It will look for the context parameter contextConfigLocation for the location of the bean configuration file. You can specify multiple bean configuration files by separating them with either commas or spaces.

```
<web-app version="2.4" xmlns="http://java.sun.com/xml/ns/j2ee"
    xmlns:xsi="http://www.w3.org/2001/XMLSchema-instance"
    xsi:schemaLocation="http://java.sun.com/xml/ns/j2ee
        http://java.sun.com/xml/ns/j2ee/web-app_2_4.xsd">

    <context-param>
        <param-name>contextConfigLocation</param-name>
        <param-value>/WEB-INF/applicationContext.xml</param-value>
    </context-param>

    <listener>
        <listener-class>
            org.springframework.web.context.ContextLoaderListener
        </listener-class>
    </listener>
</web-app>
```

Actually, the default location where this listener will look for a bean configuration file is exactly what you specified (i.e., /WEB-INF/applicationContext.xml). So, you can simply omit this context parameter.

To allow users to query distances between cities, you have to create a JSP file that contains a form. You can name it distance.jsp and put it in the WEB-INF/jsp directory to prevent direct access to it. There are two text fields in this form for users to input the source and destination cities. There's also a table grid for showing the actual distance.

```
<html>
<head>
<title>City Distance</title>
</head>

<body>
<form method="POST">
<table>
  <tr>
    <td>Source City</td>
    <td><input type="text" name="srcCity" value="${param.srcCity}" /></td>
  </tr>
  <tr>
    <td>Destination City</td>
    <td><input type="text" name="destCity" value="${param.destCity}" /></td>
  </tr>
  <tr>
    <td>Distance</td>
    <td>${distance}</td>
  </tr>
  <tr>
    <td colspan="2"><input type="submit" value="Find" /></td>
  </tr>
</table>
</form>
</body>
</html>
```

You need a servlet to process the distance requests. When this servlet is accessed with the HTTP GET method, it simply displays the form. Later, when the form is submitted with the POST method, this servlet finds the distance between the two input cities and displays it in the form again.

■ **Note** To develop web applications that use the Servlet API, you have to include the Servlet API. If you are using Maven, add the following dependency to your project:

```
<dependency>
  <groupId>javax.servlet</groupId>
  <artifactId>servlet-api</artifactId>
  <version>2.5</version>
</dependency>
```

```
package com.apress.springrecipes.city.servlet;
...
import javax.servlet.RequestDispatcher;
import javax.servlet.ServletException;
import javax.servlet.http.HttpServlet;
import javax.servlet.http.HttpServletRequest;
import javax.servlet.http.HttpServletResponse;

import org.springframework.web.context.WebApplicationContext;
import org.springframework.web.context.support.WebApplicationContextUtils;

public class DistanceServlet extends HttpServlet {

    protected void doGet(HttpServletRequest request,
            HttpServletResponse response) throws ServletException, IOException {
        forward(request, response);
    }

    protected void doPost(HttpServletRequest request,
            HttpServletResponse response) throws ServletException, IOException {
        String srcCity = request.getParameter("srcCity");
        String destCity = request.getParameter("destCity");

        WebApplicationContext context =
            WebApplicationContextUtils.getRequiredWebApplicationContext(
                getServletContext());
        CityService cityService = (CityService) context.getBean("cityService");
        double distance = cityService.findDistance(srcCity, destCity);
        request.setAttribute("distance", distance);
```

```
        forward(request, response);
    }

    private void forward(HttpServletRequest request,
            HttpServletResponse response) throws ServletException, IOException {
        RequestDispatcher dispatcher =
            request.getRequestDispatcher("WEB-INF/jsp/distance.jsp");
        dispatcher.forward(request, response);
    }
}
```

This servlet needs to access the `cityService` bean declared in the Spring IoC container to find distances. As Spring's application context is stored in the servlet context, you can retrieve it through the `WebApplicationContextUtils.getRequiredWebApplicationContext()` method by passing in a servlet context.

Finally, you add this servlet declaration to `web.xml` and map it to the URL pattern `/distance`.

```
<web-app ...>
    ...
    <servlet>
        <servlet-name>distance</servlet-name>
        <servlet-class>
            com.apress.springrecipes.city.servlet.DistanceServlet
        </servlet-class>
    </servlet>

    <servlet-mapping>
        <servlet-name>distance</servlet-name>
        <url-pattern>/distance</url-pattern>
    </servlet-mapping>
</web-app>
```

Now, you can deploy this web application to a web container (e.g., Apache Tomcat 6.x). By default, Tomcat listens on port 8080, so if you deploy your application to the `city` context path, you can access it with the following URL once it has been started up:

```
http://localhost:8080/city/distance
```

6-2. Using Spring in Your Servlets and Filters

Problem

The servlet specification provides servlets and filters. Servlets handle requests and responses and are responsible ultimately for producing output and acting on the inbound request. Filters are given the opportunity to react to the state of a given request and response before and after the servlet to which a request is destined has processed it. Filters provide the same effect as aspect-oriented programming, which lets you intercept and modify the state of a method invocation. Filters can be added in arbitrary depths to any existing servlet. It is possible, thus, to reuse filters to provide generic functionality to any servlet, like for example gzip compression. These artifacts are declared in the `web.xml` file. The servlet container reads the configuration and instantiates the servlets or filters on your behalf and manages the life cycles of these objects inside the container. Because the life cycle is handled by the servlet container, and not by Spring, accessing the services of the Spring container—for example using traditional dependency injection and AOP—proves difficult. You can use `WebApplicationContextUtils` to look up and acquire the dependencies you need, but that defeats the value proposition of dependency injection—your code is required to acquire instances explicitly, which is not much better than using JNDI, for example. It is desirable to let Spring handle dependency injection for you and to let Spring manage the life cycles of your beans.

Solution

If you want to implement filter-like functionality but want to have full access to the Spring context's life cycle machinery and dependency injection, use the `DelegatingFilterProxy` class. Similarly, if you want to implement servlet-like functionality but want to have full access to the Spring context's life cycle machinery and dependency injection, use `HttpRequestHandlerServlet`. These classes are configured normally in `web.xml`, but they then delegate their obligations to a bean that you configure in the Spring application context.

How It Works

Servlets

Let's revisit our previous example. Suppose we wanted to rewrite the servlet functionality to leverage Spring's application context machinery and configuration. The `HttpRequestHandlerServlet` will handle this for us. It uses a little bit of indirection to achieve its work: you configure an instance of `org.springframework.web.context.support.HttpRequestHandlerServlet` in your `web.xml` and assign it a name. The servlet takes the name as configured in the `web.xml` file and looks up a bean in the root Spring application context. Assuming the bean exists and that it implements the `HttpRequestHandler` interface, the servlet delegates all requests to that bean by invoking the `handleRequest` method.

You must first write a bean that implements the `org.springframework.web.HttpRequestHandler` interface. We will endeavor to replace our existing `DistanceServlet` with a POJO that implements the `HttpRequestHandler` interface. The logic is identical; it's just been reorganized a bit. The POJO's definition is as follows:

```
package com.apress.springrecipes.city.servlet;

import com.apress.springrecipes.city.CityService;
import org.springframework.web.HttpRequestHandler;

import javax.servlet.RequestDispatcher;
import javax.servlet.ServletException;
import javax.servlet.http.HttpServletRequest;
import javax.servlet.http.HttpServletResponse;
import java.io.IOException;
```

```
public class DistanceHttpRequestHandler implements HttpRequestHandler {
    private CityService cityService;

    public void setCityService(final CityService cityService) {
        this.cityService = cityService;
    }

    @Override
    public void handleRequest(final HttpServletRequest request,
                final HttpServletResponse response)
        throws ServletException, IOException {
        if (request.getMethod().toUpperCase().equals("POST")) {
            String srcCity = request.getParameter("srcCity");
            String destCity = request.getParameter("destCity");
            double distance = cityService.findDistance(srcCity, destCity);
            request.setAttribute("distance", distance);
        }
        forward(request, response);
    }

    private void forward(HttpServletRequest request, HttpServletResponse response)
        throws ServletException, IOException {
        RequestDispatcher dispatcher = request.getRequestDispatcher↵
            ("WEB-INF/jsp/distance.jsp");
        dispatcher.forward(request, response);
    }
}
```

Now, we must wire the bean up in our applicationContext.xml file, like so:

```xml
<beans xmlns="http://www.springframework.org/schema/beans"
    xmlns:xsi="http://www.w3.org/2001/XMLSchema-instance"
    xsi:schemaLocation="http://www.springframework.org/schema/beans
        http://www.springframework.org/schema/beans/spring-beans-3.0.xsd">

    <bean id="cityService"
        class="com.apress.springrecipes.city.CityServiceImpl">
        <property name="distanceMap">
            <map>
                <entry key="New York">
                    <map>
                        <entry key="London" value="5574" />
                        <entry key="Beijing" value="10976" />
                    </map>
                </entry>
            </map>
        </property>
    </bean>
```

```
<bean id="distance"
    class="com.apress.springrecipes.city.servlet.DistanceHttpRequestHandler">
    <property name="cityService" ref="cityService"/>
</bean>

</beans>
```

Here, we've configured our bean and injected a reference to the `CityServiceImpl` instance. Note the bean id, `distance`, as it will be used to configure the servlet in the `web.xml` file.

```
<web-app version="2.4" xmlns="http://java.sun.com/xml/ns/j2ee"
    xmlns:xsi="http://www.w3.org/2001/XMLSchema-instance"
    xsi:schemaLocation="http://java.sun.com/xml/ns/j2ee
        http://java.sun.com/xml/ns/j2ee/web-app_2_4.xsd">

    <context-param>
        <param-name>contextConfigLocation</param-name>
        <param-value>/WEB-INF/applicationContext.xml</param-value>
    </context-param>

    <listener>
        <listener-class>
            org.springframework.web.context.ContextLoaderListener
        </listener-class>
    </listener>

    <servlet>
        <servlet-name>distance</servlet-name>
        <servlet-class>
            org.springframework.web.context.support.HttpRequestHandlerServlet
        </servlet-class>
    </servlet>

    <servlet-mapping>
        <servlet-name>distance</servlet-name>
        <url-pattern>/distance</url-pattern>
    </servlet-mapping>
</web-app>c
```

The use of the bean is identical as in the previous application—all code referencing the `/distance` endpoint will continue to work from the perspective of a bean. Try it yourself by launching your browser and pointing it to `http://localhost:8080/distance?srcCity=New%20York&destCity=London`.

Filters

The Spring framework provides a similar feature for filters. We will demonstrate a suitably simple filter configuration that simply iterates through the inbound request's request attributes and lists them. Here, we will use a collaborating object, of type `CityServiceRequestAuditor`, whose function it is to enumerate the request parameters (conceivably, such a filter could be used to send the data to syslog, to a

227

monitoring agent like Splunk™ or through JMX). The source code for `CityServiceRequestAuditor` is as follows:

```
package com.apress.springrecipes.city;

import java.util.Map;

public class CityServiceRequestAuditor {
    public void log(Map<String, String> attributes) {
        for (String k : attributes.keySet()) {
            System.out.println(String.format("%s=%s", k, attributes.get(k)));
        }
    }
}
```

In the servlet example, the `HttpRequestHandlerServlet` delegated to another object that implemented an interface—`HttpRequestHandler`—that was considerably simpler than that of a raw servlet. In the `javax.servlet.Filter` case, however, there is very little that can be done to simplify the interface, so we will instead delegate to an implementation of filter that's been configured using Spring.

Our filter implementation is as follows:

```
package com.apress.springrecipes.city.filter;

import com.apress.springrecipes.city.CityServiceRequestAuditor;

import javax.servlet.*;
import java.io.IOException;
import java.util.Map;


/**
 * This class is designed to intercept requests to the {@link
 com.apress.springrecipes.city.CityServiceImpl} and log them
 */
public class CityServiceRequestFilter implements Filter {
    private CityServiceRequestAuditor cityServiceRequestAuditor;

    @Override
    public void init(final FilterConfig filterConfig) throws ServletException {
    }

    @Override
    public void doFilter(final ServletRequest scervletRequest, final ↵
ServletResponse servletResponse, final FilterChain filterChain)
        throws IOException, ServletException {
        Map parameterMap = servletRequest.getParameterMap();

        this.cityServiceRequestAuditor.log(parameterMap);

        filterChain.doFilter(servletRequest, servletResponse);
    }
```

```
    @Override
    public void destroy() {
    }

    public void setCityServiceRequestAuditor(final CityServiceRequestAuditor↵
cityServiceRequestAuditor) {
        this.cityServiceRequestAuditor = cityServiceRequestAuditor;
    }
}
```

It has a dependency on a bean of type `CityServiceRequestAuditor`. We will inject it and configure this bean in our Spring application context, below the previous configuration.

```xml
<beans xmlns="http://www.springframework.org/schema/beans"
    xmlns:xsi="http://www.w3.org/2001/XMLSchema-instance"
    xsi:schemaLocation="http://www.springframework.org/schema/beans
        http://www.springframework.org/schema/beans/spring-beans-3.0.xsd">

    ...

    <bean id="cityServiceRequestAuditor"
            class="com.apress.springrecipes.city.CityServiceRequestAuditor" />

    <bean id="cityServiceRequestFilter"↵
class="com.apress.springrecipes.city.filter.CityServiceRequestFilter">
        <property name="cityServiceRequestAuditor" ref="cityServiceRequestAuditor" />
    </bean>

</beans>
```

Now, all that remains is to setup the Spring `org.springframework.web.filter.`
`DelegatingFilterProxy` instance in `web.xml`. This configuration maps the filter to the `distance` servlet we configured earlier.

```xml
<web-app version="2.4" xmlns="http://java.sun.com/xml/ns/j2ee"
    xmlns:xsi="http://www.w3.org/2001/XMLSchema-instance"
    xsi:schemaLocation="http://java.sun.com/xml/ns/j2ee
        http://java.sun.com/xml/ns/j2ee/web-app_2_4.xsd">

    ...

    <filter>
        <filter-name>cityServiceRequestFilter</filter-name>
        <filter-class>org.springframework.web.filter.DelegatingFilterProxy</filter-class>
    </filter>
```

```
<filter-mapping>
    <filter-name>cityServiceRequestFilter</filter-name>
    <servlet-name>distance</servlet-name>
</filter-mapping>

</web-app>
```

Again, note the use of engineered coincidence; the `filter-name` attribute is used to determine which bean in the root Spring application context to look up and delegate to. You might notice a bit of redundancy here: the filter interface exposes two methods for life cycle management—`init` and `destroy`—and the Spring context also provides life cycle management for your beans. The default behavior of the `DelegatingFilterProxy` is to *not* delegate those life cycle methods to your bean, preferring instead to let the Spring life cycle machinery (`InitializingBean`, `@PostConstruct`, etc. for initialization and `DisposableBean`, `@PreDestroy`, etc. for destruction) work instead. If you'd like to have Spring invoke those life cycle methods for you, set the `init-param` `targetFilterLifecycle` to true on the filter in the `web.xml` file:

```
<filter>
    <filter-name>cityServiceRequestFilter</filter-name>
    <filter-class>org.springframework.web.filter.DelegatingFilterProxy</filter-class>
    <init-param>
        <param-name>targetFilterLifecycle</param-name>
        <param-value>true</param-value>
    </init-param>
</filter>
```

6-3. Integrating Spring with Struts 1.x

Problem

You would like to access beans declared in the Spring IoC container in a web application developed with Apache Struts 1.x.

Solution

A Struts application is able to load Spring's application context by registering the servlet listener `ContextLoaderListener` and access it from the servlet context just like in a generic web application. However, Spring offers better Struts-specific solutions for accessing its application context.

First, Spring allows you to load an application context by registering a Struts plug-in in the Struts configuration file. This application context will automatically refer to the application context loaded by the servlet listener as its parent so that it can refer to beans declared in its parent application context.

Second, Spring provides the `ActionSupport` class, a subclass of the `Action` base class that has a convenient `getWebApplicationContext()` method for you to access Spring's application context.

Finally, your Struts actions can have Spring beans injected via dependency injection. The prerequisite is to declare them in Spring's application context and ask Struts to look them up from Spring.

How It Works

Now, let's implement your web application for finding city distances using Apache Struts. First, you create the following directory structure for your web application.

■ **Note** For a web application developed with Struts 1.3, you need to have Struts on your CLASSPATH. Additionally, to use Spring's support for Struts, you need to add a dependency to your CLASSPATH. If you are using Maven, add the following dependencies to your Maven project:

```
<dependency>
 <groupId>org.springframework</groupId>
 <artifactId>spring-struts</artifactId>
 <version>${spring.version}</version>
 <exclusions>
  <exclusion>
   <groupId>struts</groupId>
   <artifactId>struts</artifactId>
  </exclusion>
 </exclusions>
</dependency>

<dependency>
 <groupId>org.apache.struts</groupId>
 <artifactId>struts-core</artifactId>
 <version>1.3.10</version>
</dependency>
```

Note that we exclude the version of Struts that the spring-struts supports depends on and instead to include a newer version whose Maven coordinates differ with that defined by the Spring-Struts dependency.

```
city/
    WEB-INF/
        classes/
        lib/*-jar
        jsp/
            distance.jsp
        applicationContext.xml
        struts-config.xml
        web.xml
```

In the web deployment descriptor (i.e., `web.xml`) of a Struts application, you have to register the Struts servlet `ActionServlet` to handle web requests. You can map this servlet to the URL pattern `*.do`.

```
<web-app version="2.4" xmlns="http://java.sun.com/xml/ns/j2ee"
    xmlns:xsi="http://www.w3.org/2001/XMLSchema-instance"
    xsi:schemaLocation="http://java.sun.com/xml/ns/j2ee
        http://java.sun.com/xml/ns/j2ee/web-app_2_4.xsd">

    <servlet>
        <servlet-name>action</servlet-name>
        <servlet-class>
            org.apache.struts.action.ActionServlet
        </servlet-class>
    </servlet>

    <servlet-mapping>
        <servlet-name>action</servlet-name>
        <url-pattern>*.do</url-pattern>
    </servlet-mapping>
</web-app>
```

Loading Spring's Application Context into a Struts Application

There are two ways of loading Spring's application context into a Struts application. The first is to register the servlet listener `ContextLoaderListener` in `web.xml`. This is the generic approach that we've taken thus far for loading Spring application contexts into a Struts application. This listener loads `/WEB-INF/applicationContext.xml` as Spring's bean configuration file by default, so you don't need to specify its location explicitly.

```
<web-app ...>
    <listener>
        <listener-class>
            org.springframework.web.context.ContextLoaderListener
        </listener-class>
    </listener>
    ...
</web-app>
```

Another way is to register the Struts plug-in `ContextLoaderPlugin` in the Struts configuration file `struts-config.xml`. By default, this plug-in loads the bean configuration file using the name of the `ActionServlet` instance registered in `web.xml` with `-servlet.xml` as the suffix (`action-servlet.xml` in this case). If you would like to load another bean configuration file, you can specify its name in the `contextConfigLocation` property.

```
<!DOCTYPE struts-config PUBLIC
    "-//Apache Software Foundation//DTD Struts Configuration 1.1//EN"
    "http://jakarta.apache.org/struts/dtds/struts-config_1_1.dtd">

<struts-config>
    ...
    <plug-in className="org.springframework.web.struts.ContextLoaderPlugIn">
        <set-property property="contextConfigLocation"
            value="/WEB-INF/applicationContext.xml" />
    </plug-in>
</struts-config>
```

If both configurations exist at the same time, the Spring application context loaded by the Struts plug-in will automatically refer to the application context loaded by the servlet listener as its parent. Typically, business services should be declared in the application context loaded by the servlet listener, while web-related components should be separated in another application context loaded by the Struts plug-in. So let's omit the Struts plug-in setting for now.

Accessing Spring's Application Context in Struts Actions

Struts can help you to bind HTML form field values to a form bean's properties when a form is submitted. First, create a form class that extends `ActionForm` and includes two properties for a source city and a destination city.

```
package com.apress.springrecipes.city.struts;

import org.apache.struts.action.ActionForm;

public class DistanceForm extends ActionForm {

    private String srcCity;
    private String destCity;

    // Getters and Setters
    ...
}
```

Then, you'll create a JSP file that has a form for users to input a source and a destination city. You should define this form and its fields using the tag library provided by Struts so that these fields can be bound to a form bean's properties automatically. You can name this JSP file `distance.jsp` and put it in the `WEB-INF/jsp` directory to prevent direct access to it.

```
<%@ taglib prefix="html" uri="http://struts.apache.org/tags-html" %>

<html>
<head>
<title>City Distance</title>
</head>

<body>
<html:form method="POST" action="/distance.do">
<table>
  <tr>
    <td>Source City</td>
    <td><html:text property="srcCity" /></td>
  </tr>
  <tr>
    <td>Destination City</td>
    <td><html:text property="destCity" /></td>
  </tr>
  <tr>
    <td>Distance</td>
    <td>${distance}</td>
  </tr>
  <tr>
    <td colspan="2"><input type="submit" value="Find" /></td>
  </tr>
</table>
</html:form>
</body>
</html>
```

In Struts, each web request is processed by an action that extends the `Action` class. Sometimes, it's necessary for your Struts actions to access Spring beans. You can access the application context loaded by the servlet listener `ContextLoaderListener` through the static method `WebApplicationContextUtils.getRequiredWebApplicationContext()`.

However, there's a better way to access Spring's application context in a Struts action—by extending the `ActionSupport` class. This class is a subclass of `Action` that provides a convenient method, `getWebApplicationContext()`, for you to access Spring's application context. This method first attempts to return the application context loaded by `ContextLoaderPlugin`. If it doesn't exist, this method attempts to return its parent (i.e., the application context loaded by `ContextLoaderListener`).

```
package com.apress.springrecipes.city.struts;
...
import javax.servlet.http.HttpServletRequest;
import javax.servlet.http.HttpServletResponse;

import org.apache.struts.action.ActionForm;
import org.apache.struts.action.ActionForward;
import org.apache.struts.action.ActionMapping;
import org.springframework.web.struts.ActionSupport;
```

```
public class DistanceAction extends ActionSupport {

    public ActionForward execute(ActionMapping mapping, ActionForm form,
            HttpServletRequest request, HttpServletResponse response) {
        if (request.getMethod().equals("POST")) {
            DistanceForm distanceForm = (DistanceForm) form;
            String srcCity = distanceForm.getSrcCity();
            String destCity = distanceForm.getDestCity();

            CityService cityService =
                (CityService) getWebApplicationContext().getBean("cityService");
            double distance = cityService.findDistance(srcCity, destCity);
            request.setAttribute("distance", distance);
        }
        return mapping.findForward("success");
    }
}
```

In the Struts configuration file `struts-config.xml`, you declare the form beans as well as the actions and their mappings for your application.

```
<!DOCTYPE struts-config PUBLIC ↩
 "-//Apache Software Foundation//DTD Struts Configuration 1.1//EN"          ↩
 "http://jakarta.apache.org/struts/dtds/struts-config_1_1.dtd">↩
<struts-config>
    <form-beans>
        <form-bean name="distanceForm"
            type="com.apress.springrecipes.city.struts.DistanceForm" />
    </form-beans>

    <action-mappings>
        <action path="/distance"
            type="com.apress.springrecipes.city.struts.DistanceAction"
            name="distanceForm" validate="false">
            <forward name="success"
                path="/WEB-INF/jsp/distance.jsp" />
        </action>
    </action-mappings>
</struts-config>
```

Now, you can deploy this application to your web container and access it through the URL `http://localhost:8080/city/distance.do`.

Declaring Struts Actions in Spring's Bean Configuration File

In addition to looking up Spring beans in a Struts action actively via Spring's application context, you can apply the dependency injection pattern to inject Spring beans into your Struts action. In this case, your Struts action no longer needs to extend the `ActionSupport` class; it simply extends the `Action` class.

```
package com.apress.springrecipes.city.struts;
...
import javax.servlet.http.HttpServletRequest;
import javax.servlet.http.HttpServletResponse;

import org.apache.struts.action.Action;
import org.apache.struts.action.ActionForm;
import org.apache.struts.action.ActionForward;
import org.apache.struts.action.ActionMapping;

public class DistanceAction extends Action {

    private CityService cityService;

    public void setCityService(CityService cityService) {
        this.cityService = cityService;
    }

    public ActionForward execute(ActionMapping mapping, ActionForm form,
            HttpServletRequest request, HttpServletResponse response) {
        if (request.getMethod().equals("POST")) {
            ...
            double distance = cityService.findDistance(srcCity, destCity);
            request.setAttribute("distance", distance);
        }
        return mapping.findForward("success");
    }
}
```

However, this action must be under Spring's management to have its dependencies injected. You can choose to declare it in either applicationContext.xml or another bean configuration file loaded by ContextLoaderPlugin. To better separate business services and web components, I recommend declaring it in action-servlet.xml in the root of WEB-INF, which will be loaded by ContextLoaderPlugin by default, as your ActionServlet instance has the name action.

```
<beans xmlns="http://www.springframework.org/schema/beans"
    xmlns:xsi="http://www.w3.org/2001/XMLSchema-instance"
    xsi:schemaLocation="http://www.springframework.org/schema/beans
        http://www.springframework.org/schema/beans/spring-beans-3.0.xsd">

    <bean name="/distance"
        class="com.apress.springrecipes.city.struts.DistanceAction">
        <property name="cityService" ref="cityService" />
    </bean>
</beans>
```

This action's bean name must be identical to its action path in struts-config.xml. As a <bean> element's id attribute cannot contain the / character, you should use the name attribute instead. In this configuration file, you can refer to beans declared in its parent application context, which is loaded by ContextLoaderListener.

In `struts-config.xml`, you have to register `ContextLoaderPlugin` to load the preceding bean configuration file.

```
...
<struts-config>
    ...
    <action-mappings>
        <action path="/distance"
            name="distanceForm" validate="false">
            <forward name="success"
                path="/WEB-INF/jsp/distance.jsp" />
        </action>
    </action-mappings>

    <controller processorClass="org.springframework.web.struts.↵
        DelegatingRequestProcessor" />

    <plug-in className="org.springframework.web.struts.ContextLoaderPlugIn" />
</struts-config>
```

Also, you have to register the Struts request processor `DelegatingRequestProcessor` to ask Struts to look up its actions from Spring's application context by matching the action path with the bean name. With this request processor registered, you no longer need to specify the `type` attribute for an action.

Sometimes, you may already have another request processor registered so that you can't register `DelegatingRequestProcessor`. In this case, you can specify `DelegatingActionProxy` as your action's type to achieve the same effect.

```
<action path="/distance"
    type="org.springframework.web.struts.DelegatingActionProxy"
    name="distanceForm" validate="false">
    <forward name="success"
        path="/WEB-INF/jsp/distance.jsp" />
</action>
```

6-4. Integrating Spring with JSF

Problem

You would like to access beans declared in the Spring IoC container in a web application developed with JSF.

Solution

A JSF application is able to access Spring's application context just like a generic web application (i.e., by registering the servlet listener `ContextLoaderListener` and accessing it from the servlet context). However, due to the similarity between Spring's and JSF's bean models, it's very easy to integrate them by registering the Spring-provided JSF variable resolver `DelegatingVariableResolver` (for JSF 1.1) or the `SpringBeanFacesELResolver` (for JSF 1.2 and greater), which can resolve JSF variables into Spring beans.

Furthermore, you can even declare JSF managed beans in Spring's bean configuration file to centralize them with your Spring beans.

How It Works

Suppose you are going to implement your web application for finding city distances using JSF. First, you create the following directory structure for your web application.

■ **Note** Before you start developing a web application using JSF, you need a JSF implementation library. You can use the JSF Reference Implementation (JSF-RI) or a third party implementation. If you are using Maven, add the following dependencies to your Maven project:

```
<dependency>
  <groupId>javax.servlet</groupId>
  <artifactId>servlet-api</artifactId>
  <version>2.5</version>
</dependency>

<dependency>
  <groupId>javax.faces</groupId>
  <artifactId>jsf-api</artifactId>
  <version>1.2_13</version>
</dependency>

<dependency>
  <groupId>javax.servlet</groupId>
  <artifactId>jstl</artifactId>
  <version>1.1.2</version>
</dependency>

<dependency>
  <artifactId>jsf-impl</artifactId>
  <groupId>javax.faces</groupId>
  <version>1.2_13</version>
  <scope>provided</scope>
</dependency>
```

```
<dependency>
  <groupId>org.apache.myfaces.core</groupId>
  <artifactId>myfaces-api</artifactId>
  <version>1.2.8</version>
</dependency>

<dependency>
  <groupId>org.apache.myfaces.core</groupId>
  <artifactId>myfaces-impl</artifactId>
  <version>1.2.8</version>
</dependency>
```

```
city/
    WEB-INF/
        classes/
        lib/-*.jar
        applicationContext.xml
        faces-config.xml
        web.xml
    distance.jsp
```

In the web deployment descriptor (i.e., web.xml) of a JSF application, you have to register the JSF servlet FacesServlet to handle web requests. You can map this servlet to the URL pattern *.faces. To load Spring's application context at startup, you also have to register the servlet listener ContextLoaderListener.

```
<web-app version="2.4" xmlns="http://java.sun.com/xml/ns/j2ee"
        xmlns:xsi="http://www.w3.org/2001/XMLSchema-instance"
        xsi:schemaLocation="http://java.sun.com/xml/ns/j2ee
        http://java.sun.com/xml/ns/j2ee/web-app_2_4.xsd">
    <listener>
        <listener-class>
            org.springframework.web.context.ContextLoaderListener
        </listener-class>
    </listener>
    <context-param>
        <param-name>contextConfigLocation</param-name>
        <param-value>/WEB-INF/applicationContext.xml</param-value>
    </context-param>
    <listener>
        <listener-class>
            org.apache.myfaces.webapp.StartupServletContextListener
        </listener-class>
    </listener>
```

```
    <listener>
        <listener-class>
            org.springframework.web.context.request.RequestContextListener
        </listener-class>
    </listener>

    <servlet>
        <servlet-name>faces</servlet-name>
        <servlet-class>javax.faces.webapp.FacesServlet</servlet-class>
    </servlet>

    <servlet-mapping>
        <servlet-name>faces</servlet-name>
        <url-pattern>*.faces</url-pattern>
    </servlet-mapping>
</web-app>
```

The basic idea of JSF is to separate presentation logic from UIs by encapsulating it in one or more JSF managed beans. For your distance-finding function, you can create the following `DistanceBean` class for a JSF managed bean:

```
package com.apress.springrecipes.city.jsf;
...
public class DistanceBean {

    private String srcCity;
    private String destCity;
    private double distance;
    private CityService cityService;

    public String getSrcCity() {
        return srcCity;
    }

    public String getDestCity() {
        return destCity;
    }

    public double getDistance() {
        return distance;
    }

    public void setSrcCity(String srcCity) {
        this.srcCity = srcCity;
    }

    public void setDestCity(String destCity) {
        this.destCity = destCity;
    }
```

```
    public void setCityService(CityService cityService) {
        this.cityService = cityService;
    }

    public void find() {
        distance = cityService.findDistance(srcCity, destCity);
    }
}
```

There are four properties defined in this bean. As your page has to show the srcCity, destCity, and distance properties, you define a getter method for each of them. Users can only input the srcCity and destCity properties, so they require a setter method as well. The back-end CityService bean is injected via a setter method. When the find() method is called on this bean, it will invoke the back-end service to find the distance between these two cities and then store it in the distance property for subsequent display.

Then, you create distance.jsp in the root of your web application context. You have to put it here because when FacesServlet receives a request, it will map this request to a JSP file with the same name. For example, if you request the URL /distance.faces, then FacesServlet will load /distance.jsp accordingly.

```
<%@ taglib prefix="f" uri="http://java.sun.com/jsf/core" %>
<%@ taglib prefix="h" uri="http://java.sun.com/jsf/html" %>

<html>
<head>
<title>City Distance</title>
</head>

<body>
<f:view>
  <h:form>
    <h:panelGrid columns="2">
      <h:outputLabel for="srcCity">Source City</h:outputLabel>
      <h:inputText id="srcCity" value="#{distanceBean.srcCity}" />
      <h:outputLabel for="destCity">Destination City</h:outputLabel>
      <h:inputText id="destCity" value="#{distanceBean.destCity}" />
      <h:outputLabel>Distance</h:outputLabel>
      <h:outputText value="#{distanceBean.distance}" />
      <h:commandButton value="Find" action="#{distanceBean.find}" />
    </h:panelGrid>
  </h:form>
</f:view>
</body>
</html>
```

This JSP file contains an <h:form> component for users to input a source city and a destination city. These two fields are defined using two <h:inputText> components, whose values are bound to a JSF managed bean's properties. The distance result is defined using an <h:outputText> component because its value is read-only. Finally, you define an <h:commandButton> component whose action will be triggered on the server side when you click it.

Resolving Spring Beans in JSF

The JSF configuration file `faces-config.xml`, located in the root of `WEB-INF`, is where you configure your navigation rules and JSF managed beans. For this simple application with only one screen, there's no navigation rule to configure. You can simply configure the preceding `DistanceBean` here. Here is the configuration file we might use for JSF 1.1:

```
<faces-config xmlns="http://java.sun.com/xml/ns/javaee"
    xmlns:xsi="http://www.w3.org/2001/XMLSchema-instance"
    xsi:schemaLocation="http://java.sun.com/xml/ns/javaee
        http://java.sun.com/xml/ns/javaee/web-facesconfig_1_2.xsd"
    version="1.2">

    <application>
        <variable-resolver>
            org.springframework.web.jsf.DelegatingVariableResolver
        </variable-resolver>
    </application>

    <managed-bean>
        <managed-bean-name>distanceBean</managed-bean-name>
        <managed-bean-class>
            com.apress.springrecipes.city.jsf.DistanceBean
        </managed-bean-class>
        <managed-bean-scope>request</managed-bean-scope>
        <managed-property>
            <property-name>cityService</property-name>
            <value>#{cityService}</value>
        </managed-property>
    </managed-bean>
</faces-config>
```

Here is the same file, configured to use the JSF 1.2–exclusive `SpringBeanFacesELResolver`:

```
<?xml version="1.0" encoding="UTF-8"?>
<faces-config version="1.2" xmlns="http://java.sun.com/xml/ns/javaee"
            xmlns:xi="http://www.w3.org/2001/XInclude"
            xmlns:xsi="http://www.w3.org/2001/XMLSchema-instance"
            xsi:schemaLocation="http://java.sun.com/xml/ns/javaee
            http://java.sun.com/xml/ns/javaee/web-facesconfig_1_2.xsd">

    <application>
        <el-resolver>org.springframework.web.jsf.el.SpringBeanFacesELResolver</el-resolver>
    </application>

    <managed-bean>
        <managed-bean-name>distanceBean</managed-bean-name>
        <managed-bean-class>
            com.apress.springrecipes.city.jsf.DistanceBean
        </managed-bean-class>
        <managed-bean-scope>request</managed-bean-scope>
```

```
        <managed-property>
            <property-name>cityService</property-name>
            <value>#{cityService}</value>
        </managed-property>
    </managed-bean>

</faces-config>
```

The scope of `DistanceBean` is `request`, which means a new bean instance will be created on each request. Note that by registering the variable resolver `DelegatingVariableResolver` (or the `SpringBeanFacesELResolver`), you can easily refer to a bean declared in Spring's application context as a JSF variable in the form of `#{beanName}`. This variable resolver will first attempt to resolve variables from the original JSF variable resolver. If a variable cannot be resolved, this variable resolver will look up Spring's application context for a bean with the same name.

Now, you can deploy this application to your web container and access it through the URL `http://localhost:8080/city/distance.faces`.

Declaring JSF Managed Beans in Spring's Bean Configuration File

By registering `DelegatingVariableResolver`, you can refer to beans declared in Spring from JSF managed beans. However, they are managed by two different containers: JSF's and Spring's. A better solution is to centralize them under the management of Spring's IoC container. Let's remove the managed bean declaration from the JSF configuration file and add the following Spring bean declaration in `applicationContext.xml`:

```
<bean id="distanceBean"
    class="com.apress.springrecipes.city.jsf.DistanceBean"
    scope="request">
    <property name="cityService" ref="cityService" />
</bean>
```

To enable the `request` bean scope in Spring's application context, you have to register `RequestContextListener` in the web deployment descriptor.

```
<web-app ...>
    <listener>
        <listener-class>
            org.springframework.web.context.ContextLoaderListener
        </listener-class>
    </listener>

    <listener>
        <listener-class>
            org.springframework.web.context.request.RequestContextListener
        </listener-class>
    </listener>
    ...
</web-app>
```

6-5. Integrating Spring with DWR

Problem

You would like to access beans declared in the Spring IoC container in a web application developed with DWR.

Solution

DWR supports Spring by allowing you to expose Spring beans for remote invocation via its `spring` creator. Moreover, DWR 2.0 offers an XML schema for Spring that enables you to configure DWR inside Spring's bean configuration file. You can simply configure which beans to expose for remote invocation by embedding the `<dwr:remote>` tag without involving the DWR configuration file.

How It Works

Suppose you are going to use DWR to implement your web application for finding city distances with Ajax enabled. First, you create the following directory structure for your web application.

■ **Note** To develop a web application using DWR, you have to have DWR in your WEB-INF/lib folder. If you are using Maven, add the following dependencies to your Maven project:

```
<dependency>
  <groupId>org.directwebremoting</groupId>
  <artifactId>dwr</artifactId>
  <version>2.0.3</version>
</dependency>
```

```
city/
    WEB-INF/
        classes/
        lib/-*.jar
        applicationContext.xml
        dwr.xml
        web.xml
    distance.html
```

In the web deployment descriptor (i.e., `web.xml`) of a DWR application, you have to register the DWR servlet `DwrServlet` to handle Ajax web requests. You can map this servlet to the URL pattern `/dwr/*`. To load Spring's application context at startup, you also have to register the servlet listener `ContextLoaderListener`.

```
<web-app version="2.4" xmlns="http://java.sun.com/xml/ns/j2ee"
    xmlns:xsi="http://www.w3.org/2001/XMLSchema-instance"
    xsi:schemaLocation="http://java.sun.com/xml/ns/j2ee
        http://java.sun.com/xml/ns/j2ee/web-app_2_4.xsd">

    <listener>
        <listener-class>
            org.springframework.web.context.ContextLoaderListener
        </listener-class>
    </listener>

    <servlet>
        <servlet-name>dwr</servlet-name>
        <servlet-class>
            org.directwebremoting.servlet.DwrServlet
        </servlet-class>
    </servlet>

    <servlet-mapping>
        <servlet-name>dwr</servlet-name>
        <url-pattern>/dwr/*</url-pattern>
    </servlet-mapping>
</web-app>
```

A DWR application requires a configuration file to define which objects to expose for remote invocation by JavaScript. By default, `DwrServlet` loads `dwr.xml` from the root of `WEB-INF` as its configuration file.

```
<!DOCTYPE dwr PUBLIC
    "-//GetAhead Limited//DTD Direct Web Remoting 2.0//EN"
    "http://getahead.org/dwr/dwr20.dtd">

<dwr>
    <allow>
        <create creator="new" javascript="CityService">
            <param name="class"
                value="com.apress.springrecipes.city.CityServiceImpl" />
            <include method="findDistance" />
        </create>
    </allow>
</dwr>
```

This DWR configuration file exposes the `CityServiceImpl` class for remote invocation by JavaScript. The source of this class will be generated dynamically in `CityService.js`. The `new` creator is the most common DWR creator that will create a new instance of this class each time it's invoked. You only allow the `findDistance()` method of this class to be invoked remotely.

Exposing Spring Beans for Remote Invocation

DWR's new creator creates a new object instance each time it's invoked. If you would like to expose a bean in Spring's application context for remote invocation, you can make use of the spring creator and specify the name of the bean to expose.

```
<dwr>
    <allow>
        <create creator="spring" javascript="CityService">
            <param name="beanName" value="cityService" />
            <include method="findDistance" />
        </create>
    </allow>
</dwr>
```

Now, you can write a web page for users to find distances between cities. When using Ajax, your web page doesn't need to be refreshed like a traditional web page. So, you can simply create it as a static HTML page (e.g., distance.html, located in the root of your web application context).

```
<html>
<head>
<title>City Distance</title>
<script src='dwr/interface/CityService.js'></script>
<script src='dwr/engine.js'></script>
<script src='dwr/util.js'></script>
<script type="text/javascript">
function find() {
    var srcCity = dwr.util.getValue("srcCity");
    var destCity = dwr.util.getValue("destCity");
    CityService.findDistance(srcCity, destCity, function(data) {
        dwr.util.setValue("distance", data);
    });
}
</script>
</head>

<body>
<form>
<table>
  <tr>
    <td>Source City</td>
    <td><input type="text" id="srcCity" /></td>
  </tr>
  <tr>
    <td>Destination City</td>
    <td><input type="text" id="destCity" /></td>
  </tr>
  <tr>
    <td>Distance</td>
    <td><span id="distance" /></td>
  </tr>
</table>
```

```
    <tr>
        <td colspan="2"><input type="button" value="Find" onclick="find()" /></td>
    </tr>
</table>
</form>
</body>
</html>
```

When a user clicks the Find button, the JavaScript function `find()` will be called. It makes an Ajax request to the `CityService.findDistance()` method by passing the values in the source city and destination city fields. When the Ajax response arrives, it displays the distance result in the `distance` span. To make this function work, you have to include the JavaScript libraries generated dynamically by DWR.

Now, you can deploy this application to your web container and access it through the URL `http://localhost:8080/city/distance.html`.

Configuring DWR in Spring's Bean Configuration File

DWR 2.0 supports configuring itself directly in Spring's bean configuration file. Before this is possible, however, you have to replace the previously registered `DwrServlet` with `DwrSpringServlet` in the web deployment descriptor.

```
<web-app ...>
    ...
    <servlet>
        <servlet-name>dwr</servlet-name>
        <servlet-class>
            org.directwebremoting.spring.DwrSpringServlet
        </servlet-class>
    </servlet>
</web-app>
```

In Spring's bean configuration file `applicationContext.xml`, you can configure DWR with the XML elements defined in the DWR schema. First, you have to declare the `<dwr:configuration>` element to enable DWR in Spring. Then, for each bean that you would like to expose for remote invocation, you embed a `<dwr:remote>` element with the configuration information equivalent to that in `dwr.xml`.

```
<beans xmlns="http://www.springframework.org/schema/beans"
    xmlns:xsi="http://www.w3.org/2001/XMLSchema-instance"
    xmlns:dwr="http://www.directwebremoting.org/schema/spring-dwr"
    xsi:schemaLocation="http://www.springframework.org/schema/beans
        http://www.springframework.org/schema/beans/spring-beans-2.5.xsd
        http://www.directwebremoting.org/schema/spring-dwr
        http://www.directwebremoting.org/schema/spring-dwr-2.0.xsd">

    <dwr:configuration />
```

```
    <bean id="cityService"
        class="com.apress.springrecipes.city.CityServiceImpl">
        <dwr:remote javascript="CityService">
            <dwr:include method="findDistance" />
        </dwr:remote>
        ...
    </bean>
</beans>
```

Now, you can delete `dwr.xml` because all its configuration information has been ported to Spring's bean configuration file.

Summary

In this chapter, you have learned how to integrate Spring into web applications developed with Servlet/JSP and popular web application frameworks such as Struts, JSF, and DWR. The integration mainly focuses on accessing beans declared in the Spring IoC container within these frameworks.

In a generic web application, regardless of which framework it uses, you can register the Spring-provided servlet listener `ContextLoaderListener` to load Spring's application context into the servlet context of this web application. Later, a servlet or any object that can access the servlet context will also be able to access Spring's application context through a utility method.

In a web application developed with Struts, you can load Spring's application context by registering a Struts plug-in in addition to the servlet listener. This application context will automatically refer to the application context loaded by the servlet listener as its parent. Spring provides the `ActionSupport` class that has a convenient method for you to access Spring's application context. You can also declare Struts actions in Spring's application context to have Spring beans injected.

For JSF, you can register the variable resolver `DelegatingVariableResolver` to resolve JSF variables into Spring beans. Furthermore, you can even declare JSF managed beans in Spring's bean configuration file to centralize them with Spring beans.

DWR allows you to expose Spring beans for remote invocation by its spring creator. DWR 2.0 offers an XML schema for Spring that enables you to configure DWR inside Spring's bean configuration file.

CHAPTER 7

■■■

Spring Web Flow

In this chapter, you will learn how to use Spring Web Flow, a subproject of the Spring framework, to model and manage your web application's UI flows. Spring Web Flow's usage has changed significantly from version 1.0 to 2.0. Spring Web Flow 2.0 is simpler than 1.0 and makes a lot of convention-over-configuration improvements. This chapter will focus on Spring Web Flow 2.0 only. Note that Spring Web Flow 2.0 requires *the Spring framework 2.5.4 or higher*. Note also that Spring Web Flow 2.0.8 and later features slightly different configuration than in previous versions. For this chapter, we will work with Spring Web Flow 2.0.8 configuration.

In traditional web application development, developers often manage their UI flows programmatically, so these flows are hard to maintain and reuse. Spring Web Flow offers a flow definition language that can help separate UI flows from presentation logic in a highly configurable way, so the flows can be easily changed and reused. Spring Web Flow supports not just Spring Web MVC but also Spring Portlet MVC and other web application frameworks such as Struts and JSF.

After finishing this chapter, you will be able to develop basic Spring MVC–based and JSF–based web applications that use Spring Web Flow to manage their UI flows. This chapter only touches on the basic features and configurations of Spring Web Flow, so please consult the Spring Web Flow reference guide for further details.

7-1. Managing a Simple UI Flow with Spring Web Flow

Problem

You would like to manage a simple UI flow in a Spring MVC application using Spring Web Flow.

Solution

Spring Web Flow allows you to model UI activities as *flows*. It supports defining a flow either by Java or by XML. XML–based flow definitions are widely used due to the power and popularity of XML. You can also easily modify your XML–based flow definitions without recompiling your code. Moreover, Spring IDE supports Spring Web Flow by offering a visual editor for you to edit XML-based flow definitions.

A flow definition consists of one or more *states*, each of which corresponds to a step in the flow. Spring Web Flow builds in several state types, including view state, action state, decision state, subflow state, and end state. Once a state has completed its tasks, it fires an *event*. An event contains a source and an event ID, and perhaps some attributes. Each state may contain zero or more *transitions*, each of which maps a returned event ID to the next state.

When a user triggers a new flow, Spring Web Flow can auto-detect the start state of that flow (i.e., the state without transitions from other states), so you don't need to specify the start state explicitly. A flow can terminate at one of its defined end states. This marks the flow as ended and releases resources held by the flow.

How It Works

Suppose you are going to develop an online system for a library. The first page of this system is a welcome page. There are two links on this page. When a user clicks the Next link, the system will show the library introduction page. There's another Next link on this introduction page; clicking it will show the menu page. If a user clicks the Skip link on the welcome page, the system will skip the introduction page and show the menu page directly. This welcome UI flow is illustrated in Figure 7-1. This example will show you how to develop this application with Spring MVC and use Spring Web Flow to manage the flow.

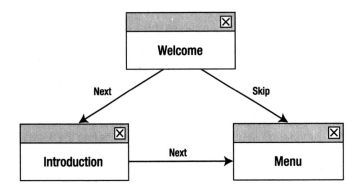

Figure 7-1. *The welcome UI flow*

In the library introduction page, you would like to show the public holidays on which this library will close. They are queried from a back-end service whose interface is defined as follows:

```
package com.apress.springwebrecipes.library.service;
...
public interface LibraryService {

    public List<Date> getHolidays();
}
```

For testing purposes, you can hard-code several holidays for this service implementation as follows:

```
package com.apress.springwebrecipes.library.service;
...
public class LibraryServiceImpl implements LibraryService {

    public List<Date> getHolidays() {
        List<Date> holidays = new ArrayList<Date>();
        holidays.add(new GregorianCalendar(2007, 11, 25).getTime());
        holidays.add(new GregorianCalendar(2008, 0, 1).getTime());
        return holidays;
    }
}
```

Setting Up a Spring MVC Application That Uses Spring Web Flow

To develop the library system using Spring MVC and Spring Web Flow, you first create the following directory structure for this web application.

■ **Note** To manage your web UI flows with Spring Web Flow, you neeed the Spring Web Flow distribution (e.g., v2.0.8) on your CLASSPATH. If you are using Maven, add the following dependency to your Maven project:

```
<dependency>

    <groupId>org.springframework.webflow</groupId>

    <artifactId>spring-faces</artifactId>

    <version>2.0.8.RELEASE</version>

</dependency>
```

```
library/
    WEB-INF/
        classes/
        flows/
            welcome/
                introduction.jsp
                menu.jsp
                welcome.jsp
                welcome.xml
        lib/-*jar
        library-service.xml
        library-servlet.xml
        library-webflow.xml
        web.xml
```

Spring Web Flow supports using an expression language in flow definitions to access its data model and invoke back-end services. Spring Web Flow supports using Unified EL (used in JSF 1.2 and JSP 2.1) and Object-Graph Navigation Language (OGNL), which is used in Tapestry, WebWork, and other frameworks, as its expression language. These two languages have a very similar syntax. For basic expressions such as property access and method invocations, the syntax is identical. The expressions used in this chapter are valid for both Unified EL and OGNL, so you are free to choose either of them as your expression language. Unified EL is recommended in a JSF environment, because it allows you to use the same expression language in flow definitions as in JSF views. However, developers using Spring Web Flow 1.0 may prefer OGNL, because it is the only supported expression language for the 1.0 version.

Spring Web Flow is able to detect the libraries of JBoss EL (as the default Unified EL implementation) and OGNL from the classpath. You can enable either of them (but not both) by including the corresponding JAR file in your classpath.

Note If you are going to use Unified EL as your Web Flow expression language, you can use JBoss EL (e.g., v2.0.0 GA) or OGNL (e.g., v2.6.9). If you are using Maven, add one of the following dependencies to your Maven project:

```
<dependency>
    <groupId>org.jboss.seam</groupId>
    <artifactId>jboss-el</artifactId>
    <version>2.0.0.GA</version>
</dependency>
```

or

```
<dependency>
    <groupId>ognl</groupId>
    <artifactId>ognl</artifactId>
    <version>2.6.9</version>
</dependency>
```

If you decide to use the JBoss EL, you will need to add a JBoss Maven repository to your Maven project:

```
<repositories>
 <repository>
   <url>http://repository.jboss.org/maven2/</url>
   <id>jboss</id>
   <name>JBoss Repository</name>
  </repository>
</repositories>
```

Creating the Configuration Files

In the web deployment descriptor (i.e., web.xml), you register ContextLoaderListener to load the root application context at startup, and also Spring MVC's DispatcherServlet for dispatching requests. You can map the URL pattern /flow/* to this servlet so that all requests under the request path flow will be handled by it.

```
<web-app version="2.4" xmlns="http://java.sun.com/xml/ns/j2ee"
    xmlns:xsi="http://www.w3.org/2001/XMLSchema-instance"
    xsi:schemaLocation="http://java.sun.com/xml/ns/j2ee
        http://java.sun.com/xml/ns/j2ee/web-app_2_4.xsd">

        <context-param>
                <param-name>contextConfigLocation</param-name>
                <param-value>
                                /WEB-INF/library-service.xml
                                /WEB-INF/library-security.xml
                </param-value>
        </context-param>

  <listener>
        <listener-class>
            org.springframework.web.context.ContextLoaderListener
        </listener-class>
    </listener>

    <filter>
        <filter-name>springSecurityFilterChain</filter-name>
        <filter-class>org.springframework.web.filter.DelegatingFilterProxy</filter-class>
    </filter>
```

```
    <filter-mapping>
        <filter-name>springSecurityFilterChain</filter-name>
        <url-pattern>/*</url-pattern>
    </filter-mapping>

    <servlet>
            <servlet-name>library</servlet-name>
            <servlet-class>org.springframework.web.servlet↵
.DispatcherServlet</servlet-class>
    </servlet>

    <servlet-mapping>
        <servlet-name>library</servlet-name>
        <url-pattern>/flows/*</url-pattern>
    </servlet-mapping>
</web-app>
```

ContextLoaderListener will load the root application context from the configuration file you specify in the contextConfigLocation context parameter (library-service.xml in this case). This configuration file declares beans in the service layer. For the welcome flow, you can declare the library service in this file for returning public holidays when queried.

```
<beans xmlns="http://www.springframework.org/schema/beans"
    xmlns:xsi="http://www.w3.org/2001/XMLSchema-instance"
    xsi:schemaLocation="http://www.springframework.org/schema/beans
        http://www.springframework.org/schema/beans/spring-beans-3.0.xsd">

    <bean name="libraryService"
        class="com.apress.springwebrecipes.library.service.LibraryServiceImpl" />
</beans>
```

As the DispatcherServlet instance in the web deployment descriptor has the name library, you create library-servlet.xml in the root of WEB-INF with the following content:

```
<beans xmlns="http://www.springframework.org/schema/beans"
    xmlns:xsi="http://www.w3.org/2001/XMLSchema-instance"
    xsi:schemaLocation="http://www.springframework.org/schema/beans
        http://www.springframework.org/schema/beans/spring-beans-3.0.xsd">

    <import resource="library-webflow.xml" />
</beans>
```

To separate the configurations of Spring MVC and Spring Web Flow, you can centralize Spring Web Flow's configurations in another file (e.g., library-webflow.xml) and import it into library-servlet.xml. Then, create this file with the following contents:

```xml
<beans xmlns="http://www.springframework.org/schema/beans"
    xmlns:xsi="http://www.w3.org/2001/XMLSchema-instance"
    xmlns:webflow="http://www.springframework.org/schema/webflow-config"
    xsi:schemaLocation="http://www.springframework.org/schema/beans
        http://www.springframework.org/schema/beans/spring-beans-3.0.xsd
        http://www.springframework.org/schema/webflow-config
        http://www.springframework.org/schema/webflow-config/~CCC
            spring-webflow-config-2.0.xsd">

    <webflow:flow-builder-services id="flowBuilderServices"
            development="true" view-factory-creator="flowResourceFlowViewResolver" />

    <bean id="flowResourceFlowViewResolver"
            class="org.springframework.webflow.mvc.builder.MvcViewFactoryCreator">
                <property name="useSpringBeanBinding" value="true"  />

    </bean>

    <webflow:flow-executor id="flowExecutor">
            <webflow:flow-execution-listeners>
            </webflow:flow-execution-listeners>
    </webflow:flow-executor>

    <webflow:flow-registry flow-builder-services="flowBuilderServices"
            id="flowRegistry" base-path="/WEB-INF/flows/">
                <webflow:flow-location path="/welcome/welcome.xml" />
</webflow:flow-registry>

    <bean class="org.springframework.webflow.mvc.servlet.FlowHandlerAdapter">
            <property name="flowExecutor" ref="flowExecutor" />
    </bean>

    <bean class="org.springframework.webflow.mvc.servlet.FlowHandlerMapping">
            <property name="flowRegistry" ref="flowRegistry" />
            <property name="order" value="0" />
    </bean>
    ...

</beans>
```

The FlowHandlerMapping follows a convention to create URL path mappings from the ids of registered flow definitions. This returns a FlowHandler that invokes web flows defined in the flowRegistry. Then you have to register your flow definitions in a flow registry by specifying their locations. The file name of a flow definition (e.g., welcome.xml) will be used as the flow ID by default (e.g., welcome), but you can specify a custom ID with the id attribute.

Creating Web Flow Definitions

Spring Web Flow offers an XML–based flow definition language that can be validated by Spring Web Flow's XSD and supported by Spring IDE or SpringSource Tool Suite (STS). Now, you can define your welcome flow in the definition file `/WEB-INF/flows/welcome/welcome.xml`:

```
<flow xmlns="http://www.springframework.org/schema/webflow"
    xmlns:xsi="http://www.w3.org/2001/XMLSchema-instance"
    xsi:schemaLocation="http://www.springframework.org/schema/webflow
        http://www.springframework.org/schema/webflow/spring-webflow-2.0.xsd">

    <view-state id="welcome">
        <transition on="next" to="introduction" />
        <transition on="skip" to="menu" />
    </view-state>

    <view-state id="introduction">
        <on-render>
            <evaluate expression="libraryService.getHolidays()"
                result="requestScope.holidays" />
        </on-render>
        <transition on="next" to="menu" />
    </view-state>

    <view-state id="menu" />
</flow>
```

In this welcome flow, you have defined three view states: `welcome`, `introduction`, and `menu`. As its name indicates, a view state will render a view to a user. Typically, in Spring MVC, a view is a JSP file. By default, a view state will render a JSP file with the state ID as the file name and `.jsp` as the file extension, located in the same path as this flow definition. If you want to render another view, you can specify its logical view name in the `view` attribute and define a corresponding Spring MVC view resolver to resolve it.

You can use the `<on-render>` element to trigger an action for a view state before its view renders. Spring Web Flow supports using an expression of Unified EL or OGNL to invoke a method. For more about Unified EL and OGNL, please refer to the article "Unified Expression Language," at `http://java.sun.com/products/jsp/reference/techart/unifiedEL.html`, and the OGNL language guide, at `http://www.ognl.org/`. The preceding expression is valid for both Unified EL and OGNL. It invokes the `getHolidays()` method on the `libraryService` bean and stores the result in the `holidays` variable in the request scope.

The flow diagram for this welcome flow is illustrated in Figure 7-2.

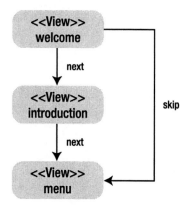

Figure 7-2. *The flow diagram for the welcome flow*

Creating the Page Views

Now, you have to create the JSP files for the preceding three view states. You can create them at the same location as the flow definition and with the same name as the view states so that they can be loaded by default. First, you create `welcome.jsp`:

```
<html>
<head>
<title>Welcome</title>
</head>

<body>
<h2>Welcome!</h2>
<a href="${flowExecutionUrl}&_eventId=next">Next</a>
<a href="${flowExecutionUrl}&_eventId=skip">Skip</a>
</body>
</html>
```

In this JSP file, there are two links to fire events, with **next** and **skip** as the event IDs. In Spring Web Flow, an event ID can be specified either as the _eventId request parameter's value (e.g., _eventId=next), or in a request parameter's name, with _eventId_ as the prefix (e.g., _eventId_next), no matter what the parameter value is. Also, you have to start the URLs with the variable ${flowExecutionUrl} to trigger a flow execution. This variable will be evaluated by Spring Web Flow at runtime.

Next, you create `introduction.jsp` to display the library holidays, which are loaded by the action specified in `<on-render>` before this view renders:

```
<%@ taglib prefix="c" uri="http://java.sun.com/jsp/jstl/core" %>
<%@ taglib prefix="fmt" uri="http://java.sun.com/jsp/jstl/fmt" %>

<html>
<head>
<title>Introduction</title>
</head>

<body>
<h2>Library Holidays</h2>
<c:forEach items="${holidays}" var="holiday">
  <fmt:formatDate value="${holiday}" pattern="yyyy-MM-dd" /><br />
</c:forEach>
<a href="${flowExecutionUrl}&_eventId=next">Next</a>
</body>
</html>
```

Finally, you create menu.jsp. This view is very simple, as there's no transition from this state to others.

```
<html>
<head>
<title>Menu</title>
</head>

<body>
<h2>Menu</h2>
</body>
</html>
```

Now, you can deploy this web flow application to a web container (e.g., Apache Tomcat 6.0 or Jetty.). By default, Tomcat and Jetty (and the Maven Jetty plug-in configured for this code) listen on port 8080, so if you deploy your application to the mvc context path, you can access this welcome web flow with the following URL, since the URLs under the flows request path will be mapped to DispatcherServlet:

```
http://localhost:8080/mvc/flows/welcome
```

7-2. Modeling Web Flows with Different State Types

Problem

You would like to model various types of UI activities as web flows to execute in Spring Web Flow.

Solution

In Spring Web Flow, each step of a flow is denoted by a state. A state may contain zero or more transitions to the next states according to an event ID. Spring Web Flow provides several built-in state types for you to model web flows. It also allows you to define custom state types. Table 7-1 shows the built-in state types in Spring Web Flow.

Table 7-1. *Built-In State Types in Spring Web Flow*

State Type	Description
View	Renders a view for a user to participate in the flow (e.g., by displaying information and gathering user input). The flow's execution pauses until an event is triggered to resume the flow (e.g., by a hyperlink click or a form submission).
Action	Executes actions for the flow, such as updating a database and gathering information for displaying.
Decision	Evaluates a Boolean expression to decide which state to transition to next.
Subflow	Launches another flow as a subflow of the current flow. The subflow will return to the launching flow when it ends.
End	Terminates the flow, after which all flow scope variables become invalid.

How It Works

Suppose you are going to build a web flow for library users to search books. First, a user has to enter the book criteria in the criteria page. If there's more than one book matching the criteria, the books will be displayed in the list page. In this page, the user can select a book to browse its details in the details page. However, if there's exactly one book matching the criteria, its details will be shown directly in the details page, without going through the list page. This book search UI flow is illustrated in Figure 7-3.

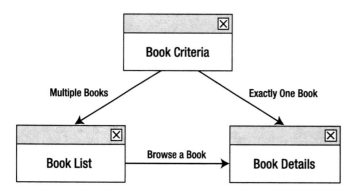

Figure 7-3. *The book search UI flow*

First of all, let's create the domain class Book. It should implement the Serializable interface, as its instances may need to be persisted in sessions.

```
package com.apress.springwebrecipes.library.domain;
...
public class Book implements Serializable {

    private String isbn;
    private String name;
    private String author;
    private Date publishDate;

    // Constructors, Getters and Setters
    ...
}
```

Next, you create the BookCriteria class, whose instances will act as form command objects for binding form fields. It should also implement the Serializable interface for the same reason.

```
package com.apress.springwebrecipes.library.domain;
...
public class BookCriteria implements Serializable {

    private String keyword;
    private String author;

    // Getters and Setters
    ...
}
```

In the service layer, you design a service interface for providing book search services to the presentation layer:

```
package com.apress.springwebrecipes.library.service;
...
public interface BookService {

    public List<Book> search(BookCriteria criteria);
    public Book findByIsbn(String isbn);
}
```

For testing purposes, let's hard-code some books and implement the search() method by matching the books one by one:

```
package com.apress.springwebrecipes.library.service;
...
public class BookServiceImpl implements BookService {

    private Map<String, Book> books;

    public BookServiceImpl() {
        books = new HashMap<String, Book>();
        books.put("0001", new Book("0001", "Spring Framework", "Ray",
                new GregorianCalendar(2007, 0, 1).getTime()));
        books.put("0002", new Book("0002", "Spring Web MVC", "Paul",
                new GregorianCalendar(2007, 3, 1).getTime()));
        books.put("0003", new Book("0003", "Spring Web Flow", "Ray",
                new GregorianCalendar(2007, 6, 1).getTime()));
    }

    public List<Book> search(BookCriteria criteria) {
        List<Book> results = new ArrayList<Book>();
        for (Book book : books.values()) {
            String keyword = criteria.getKeyword().trim();
            String author = criteria.getAuthor().trim();
            boolean keywordMatches = keyword.length() > 0
                    && book.getName().contains(keyword);
            boolean authorMatches = book.getAuthor().equals(author);
            if (keywordMatches || authorMatches) {
                results.add(book);
            }
        }
        return results;
    }

    public Book findByIsbn(String isbn) {
        return books.get(isbn);
    }
}
```

To make this book service accessible to all the library web flows, you declare it in the service layer configuration file (i.e., `library-service.xml`), which will be loaded for the root application context:

```
<bean name="bookService"
    class="com.apress.springwebrecipes.library.service.BookServiceImpl" />
```

Now, you can start with your book search flow development. First, you add the flow definition's location to the flow registry in `library-webflow.xml` and create the flow definition XML file as well:

```
<webflow:flow-registry id="flowRegistry" ...>
    ...
    <webflow:flow-location path="/bookSearch/bookSearch.xml" />
</webflow:flow-registry>
```

Next, let's build this web flow incrementally with different types of states offered by Spring Web Flow.

Defining View States

According to the requirement of the book search flow, you first need a view state to show a form so that a user can enter the book criteria. In Spring Web Flow, you can create an action corresponding to a controller in Spring MVC to handle flow requests. Spring Web Flow provides a `FormAction` class to assist you in handling forms. For complicated form processing, you can extend this class and add your own processing logic. But for a simple form's needs, you can use this class directly by populating its properties (e.g., the form object class, property editors, and validators). Now, you can define a form action with this class to handle the book criteria form in `library-webflow.xml`:

```
<bean id="bookCriteriaAction"
    class="org.springframework.webflow.action.FormAction">
    <property name="formObjectClass"
        value="com.apress.springwebrecipes.library.domain.BookCriteria" />
    <property name="propertyEditorRegistrar">
        <bean class="com.apress.springwebrecipes.library.web.PropertyEditors" />
    </property>
</bean>
```

A form action can bind form fields to a form object's properties of the same name. But you first have to specify the form object class in the `formObjectClass` property for this action to instantiate form objects. To convert form field values into proper data types, you have to register custom property editors to this form action. You can create a property editor registrar to register your own editors, and specify it in the `propertyEditorRegistrar` property:

```
package com.apress.springwebrecipes.library.web;
...
import org.springframework.beans.PropertyEditorRegistrar;
import org.springframework.beans.PropertyEditorRegistry;
import org.springframework.beans.propertyeditors.CustomDateEditor;

public class PropertyEditors implements PropertyEditorRegistrar {
```

```
    public void registerCustomEditors(PropertyEditorRegistry registry) {
        SimpleDateFormat dateFormat = new SimpleDateFormat("yyyy-MM-dd");
        dateFormat.setLenient(false);
        registry.registerCustomEditor(Date.class, new CustomDateEditor(
                dateFormat, true));
    }
}
```

With the form action ready, you can define the first view state for handling the book criteria form. To test your flow as soon as possible, you can directly display the search results in the list page, without considering the size of the results. You define the book search flow in the definition file /WEB-INF/flows/bookSearch/bookSearch.xml.

```
<flow xmlns="http://www.springframework.org/schema/webflow"
    xmlns:xsi="http://www.w3.org/2001/XMLSchema-instance"
    xsi:schemaLocation="http://www.springframework.org/schema/webflow
        http://www.springframework.org/schema/webflow/spring-webflow-2.0.xsd">

    <view-state id="bookCriteria">
        <on-render>
            <evaluate expression="bookCriteriaAction.setupForm" />
        </on-render>
        <transition on="search" to="bookList">
            <evaluate expression="bookCriteriaAction.bindAndValidate" />
            <evaluate expression="bookService.search(bookCriteria)"
                result="flowScope.books" />
        </transition>
    </view-state>
</flow>
```

Before this view state renders its view, it invokes the setupForm() method of the form action bookCriteriaAction defined previously. This method prepares the form object for this form by instantiating the form object class you specified. After a user submits the form with the event ID search, this state will transition to the bookList state, displaying all the search results.

Before the transition takes place, you have to invoke the bindAndValidate() method of the form action to bind the form field values to the form object's properties and then validate this object with the validators, if registered. Then, you call the back-end service to search books for the bound criteria object and store the results in the flow scope variable books so that it can be accessed by other states. Flow scope variables are stored in the session, so they must implement Serializable.

Next, you create the view for this view state in the JSP file with the same name as the view state and in the same location (i.e., /WEB-INF/flows/bookSearch/bookCriteria.jsp) so that it can be loaded by default.

```
<%@ taglib prefix="form" uri="http://www.springframework.org/tags/form" %>

<html>
<head>
<title>Book Criteria</title>
</head>
```

```
<body>
<form:form commandName="bookCriteria">
<table>
  <tr>
    <td>Keyword</td>
    <td><form:input path="keyword" /></td>
  </tr>
  <tr>
    <td>Author</td>
    <td><form:input path="author" /></td>
  </tr>
  <tr>
    <td colspan="2">
      <input type="submit" name="_eventId_search" value="Search" />
    </td>
  </tr>
</table>
</form:form>
</body>
</html>
```

This JSP file contains a form defined with Spring's form tags. It's bound to the form object with the name bookCriteria, which is generated automatically according to the form object's class name, BookCriteria. There's a submit button in this form, clicking which will trigger an event with search as the ID.

The second view state in this book search flow is for displaying the search results. It will render a view listing all results in a table, with links for showing book details. When the user clicks one of these links, it will trigger a select event that will cause a transition to the bookDetails state showing the book's details.

```
<view-state id="bookList">
    <transition on="select" to="bookDetails">
        <evaluate expression="bookService.findByIsbn(requestParameters.isbn)"
            result="flowScope.book" />
    </transition>
</view-state>
```

The link should pass the book ISBN as a request parameter, so you can find the book from the backend service and store it in the flow scope variable book.

The view for this state should be created in /WEB-INF/flows/bookSearch/bookList.jsp so that it will be loaded by default.

```
<%@ taglib prefix="c" uri="http://java.sun.com/jsp/jstl/core" %>
<%@ taglib prefix="fmt" uri="http://java.sun.com/jsp/jstl/fmt" %>

<html>
<head>
<title>Book List</title>
</head>
```

```
<body>
<table border="1">
  <tr>
    <th>ISBN</th>
    <th>Book Name</th>
    <th>Author</th>
    <th>Publish Date</th>
  </tr>
  <c:forEach items="${books}" var="book">
  <tr>
    <td>
      <a href="${flowExecutionUrl}&_eventId=select&isbn=${book.isbn}">
        ${book.isbn}
      </a>
    </td>
    <td>${book.name}</td>
    <td>${book.author}</td>
    <td><fmt:formatDate value="${book.publishDate}" pattern="yyyy-MM-dd" /></td>
  </tr>
  </c:forEach>
</table>
</body>
</html>
```

The ISBN column of each table row is a link that will trigger a `select` event with the book ISBN as a request parameter.

The last view state in this book search flow shows a selected book's details. It has no transition to other states at this moment.

```
<view-state id="bookDetails" />
```

You create the view for this state in `/WEB-INF/flows/bookSearch/bookDetails.jsp` so that it will be loaded by default.

```
<%@ taglib prefix="c" uri="http://java.sun.com/jsp/jstl/core" %>
<%@ taglib prefix="fmt" uri="http://java.sun.com/jsp/jstl/fmt" %>

<html>
<head>
<title>Book Details</title>
</head>

<body>
<table border="1">
  <tr>
    <td>ISBN</td>
    <td>${book.isbn}</td>
  </tr>
```

```
<tr>
  <td>Book Name</td>
  <td>${book.name}</td>
</tr>
<tr>
  <td>Author</td>
  <td>${book.author}</td>
</tr>
<tr>
  <td>Publish Date</td>
  <td><fmt:formatDate value="${book.publishDate}" pattern="yyyy-MM-dd" /></td>
</tr>
</table>
</body>
</html>
```

Now, you can deploy this application and test this simplified book search flow with the URL `http://localhost:8080/mvc/flows/bookSearch`. The current flow diagram for this book search flow is illustrated in Figure 7-4.

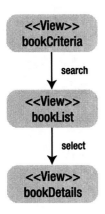

Figure 7-4. *The flow diagram for the book search flow with view states only*

Defining Action States

Although you can include the search action in the `bookCriteria` view state, this action cannot be reused for other states that require book searching. The best practice is to extract reusable actions into stand-alone action states. An action state simply defines one or more actions to perform in a flow, and these actions will be performed in the declared order. If an action returns an `Event` object containing an ID that matches a transition, the transition will take place immediately without performing the subsequent actions. But if all of the actions have been performed without a matching transition, the `success` transition will take place.

For the purposes of reuse, you can extract the book search action in a `searchBook` state. Then modify the transition of the `bookCriteria` state to go through this state.

```
<flow ...>
    <view-state id="bookCriteria">
        <on-render>
            <evaluate expression="bookCriteriaAction.setupForm" />
        </on-render>
        <transition on="search" to="searchBook">
            <evaluate expression="bookCriteriaAction.bindAndValidate" />
        </transition>
    </view-state>

    <action-state id="searchBook">
        <evaluate expression="bookService.search(bookCriteria)"
            result="flowScope.books" />
        <transition on="success" to="bookList" />
    </action-state>
    ...
</flow>
```

The current flow diagram for this book search flow is illustrated in Figure 7-5.

Figure 7-5. *The flow diagram for the book search flow with an action state*

Defining Decision States

Now, you are going to satisfy the book search flow's requirement: if there's more than one search result, display them in the list page; otherwise, show its details directly in the details page without going through the list page. For this purpose, you need a decision state that can evaluate a Boolean expression to determine the transition:

```
<flow ...>
    ...
    <action-state id="searchBook">
        <evaluate expression="bookService.search(bookCriteria)"
            result="flowScope.books" />
        <transition on="success" to="checkResultSize" />
    </action-state>

    <decision-state id="checkResultSize">
        <if test="books.size() == 1" then="extractResult" else="bookList" />
    </decision-state>

    <action-state id="extractResult">
        <set name="flowScope.book" value="books.get(0)" />
        <transition on="success" to="bookDetails" />
    </action-state>
    ...
</flow>
```

The success transition of the searchBook state has been changed to checkResultSize, a decision state that checks if there's exactly one search result. If true, it will transition to the extractResult action state to extract the first and only result into the flow scope variable book. Otherwise, it will transition to the bookList state to display all search results in the list page. The current flow diagram is illustrated in Figure 7-6.

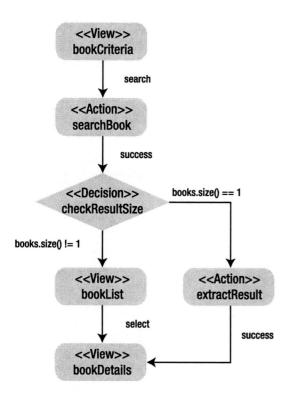

Figure 7-6. *The flow diagram for the book search flow with a decision state*

Defining End States

The basic requirement of the book search flow has been finished. However, you might be asked to provide a New Search link in both the book list page and the book details page for starting a new search. You can simply add the following link to both pages:

```
<a href="${flowExecutionUrl}&_eventId=newSearch">New Search</a>
```

As you can see, this link will trigger a newSearch event. Instead of transitioning to the first view state, bookCriteria, it's better to define an end state that restarts this flow. An end state will invalidate all flow scope variables to release their resources.

```
<flow ...>
    ...
    <view-state id="bookList">
        <transition on="select" to="bookDetails">
            <evaluate expression="bookService.findByIsbn(requestParameters.isbn)"
                result="flowScope.book" />
        </transition>
```

```
        <transition on="newSearch" to="newSearch" />
    </view-state>

    <view-state id="bookDetails">
        <transition on="newSearch" to="newSearch" />
    </view-state>

    <end-state id="newSearch" />
</flow>
```

By default, an end state restarts the current flow to the start state, but you can redirect to another flow by specifying the flow name with `flowRedirect` as the prefix in the end state's `view` attribute. The current flow diagram is illustrated in Figure 7-7.

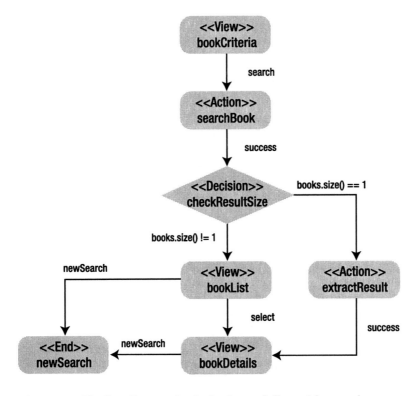

Figure 7-7. *The flow diagram for the book search flow with an end state*

Defining Subflow States

Suppose you have another web flow that also requires showing a book's details. For reuse purposes, you extract the `bookDetails` state into a new web flow that can be called by other flows as a subflow. First of all, you have to add the flow definition's location to the flow registry in library-webflow.xml and create the flow definition XML file as well:

```
<webflow:flow-registry id="flowRegistry">

    ...
    <webflow:flow-location path="/WEB-INF/flows/bookDetails/bookDetails.xml" />
</webflow:flow-registry>
```

Then, you move the bookDetails view state to this flow and bookDetails.jsp to this directory. As the bookDetails state has a transition to the newSearch state, you also define it in this flow as an end state.

```
<flow xmlns="http://www.springframework.org/schema/webflow"
    xmlns:xsi="http://www.w3.org/2001/XMLSchema-instance"
    xsi:schemaLocation="http://www.springframework.org/schema/webflow
        http://www.springframework.org/schema/webflow/spring-webflow-2.0.xsd">

    <input name="book" value="flowScope.book" />

    <view-state id="bookDetails">
        <transition on="newSearch" to="newSearch" />
    </view-state>

    <end-state id="newSearch" />
</flow>
```

The book instance to be shown is passed as an input parameter to this flow with the name book, and it is stored in the flow scope variable book. Note that the flow scope is only visible to the current flow.

Next, you define a subflow state in the bookSearch flow that launches the bookDetails flow to show a book's details:

```
<subflow-state id="bookDetails" subflow="bookDetails">
    <input name="book" value="flowScope.book" />
    <transition on="newSearch" to="newSearch" />
</subflow-state>
```

In this subflow state definition, you pass the book variable in the flow scope of the bookSearch flow to the bookDetails subflow as an input parameter. When the bookDetails subflow ends in its newSearch state, it will transition to the newSearch state of the parent flow, which happens to be the newSearch end state of the bookSearch flow in this case. The current flow diagram is illustrated in Figure 7-8.

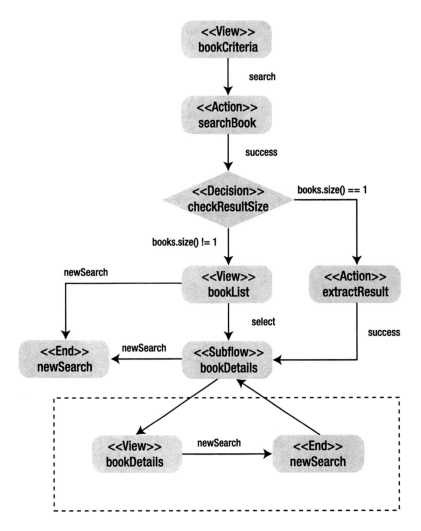

Figure 7-8. The flow diagram for the book search flow with a subflow

7-3. Securing Web Flows

Problem

You would like to secure certain web flows in your application by allowing access to authorized users only.

Solution

Spring Web Flow offers integration for Spring Security so that you can easily secure your web flows with Spring Security. With Spring Security configured properly, you can simply secure a flow, a state, or a transition by embedding the `<secured>` element with required access attributes specified.

How It Works

To secure web flows with Spring Security, you first have to configure a `DelegatingFilterProxy` filter in the web deployment descriptor (i.e., `web.xml`). This filter will delegate HTTP request filtering to a filter defined in Spring Security.

■ **Note** To use Spring Security in your web flow application, you have to add Spring Security to your CLASSPATH. If you are using Maven, add the following dependency to your Maven project:

```xml
<dependency>
    <groupId>org.springframework.security</groupId>
    <artifactId>spring-security-core</artifactId>
    <version>3.0.2.RELEASE</version>
</dependency>
```

```xml
<web-app ...>
    <context-param>
        <param-name>contextConfigLocation</param-name>
        <param-value>
            /WEB-INF/library-service.xml
            /WEB-INF/library-security.xml
        </param-value>
    </context-param>
    ...
    <filter>
        <filter-name>springSecurityFilterChain</filter-name>
        <filter-class>
            org.springframework.web.filter.DelegatingFilterProxy
        </filter-class>
    </filter>

    <filter-mapping>
        <filter-name>springSecurityFilterChain</filter-name>
        <url-pattern>/*</url-pattern>
    </filter-mapping>
    ...
</web-app>
```

As security configurations should be applied to the entire application, you centralize them in /WEB-INF/library-security.xml and load this file into the root application context. Then, you create this file with the following contents:

```
<beans:beans xmlns="http://www.springframework.org/schema/security"
    xmlns:beans="http://www.springframework.org/schema/beans"
    xmlns:xsi="http://www.w3.org/2001/XMLSchema-instance"
    xsi:schemaLocation="http://www.springframework.org/schema/beans
        http://www.springframework.org/schema/beans/spring-beans-3.0.xsd
        http://www.springframework.org/schema/security
        http://www.springframework.org/schema/security/spring-security-3.0.xsd">

    <http auto-config="true" />
<authentication-manager><authentication-provider>
        <user-service>
            <user name="user1" password="1111" authorities="ROLE_USER" />
            <user name="user2" password="2222" authorities="ROLE_USER" />
        </user-service>
    </authentication-provider>
</authentication-manager>
</beans:beans>
```

In the preceding security configurations, you enable Spring Security's HTTP auto-config, which provides a default form-based login service, an anonymous login service, and so on. You also define two user accounts for testing purposes.

In the web flow configuration file (i.e., library-webflow.xml), you have to register the flow execution listener SecurityFlowExecutionListener in the flow executor to enable Spring Security for web flows:

```
<beans ...>
    ...
    <webflow:flow-executor id="flowExecutor">
        <webflow:flow-execution-listeners>
            <webflow:listener ref="securityFlowExecutionListener" />
        </webflow:flow-execution-listeners>
    </webflow:flow-executor>

    <bean id="securityFlowExecutionListener" class="org.springframework.~CCC
        webflow.security.SecurityFlowExecutionListener" />
</beans>
```

Now, Spring Security has been configured for your web flow application. You can simply secure a web flow by embedding a <secured> element in a flow definition. For example, let's secure the bookSearch flow defined in /WEB-INF/flows/bookSearch/bookSearch.xml.

```
<flow xmlns="http://www.springframework.org/schema/webflow"
    xmlns:xsi="http://www.w3.org/2001/XMLSchema-instance"
    xsi:schemaLocation="http://www.springframework.org/schema/webflow
        http://www.springframework.org/schema/webflow/spring-webflow-2.0.xsd">
```

```
<secured attributes="ROLE_USER" />
    ...
</flow>
```

You can specify multiple access attributes required for accessing this web flow in the `attributes` attribute, separated by commas. By default, a user who has any of the attributes can access this web flow, but you can allow access only to users with all the attributes by setting the `match` attribute of `<secured>` to `all`.

Now if you deploy this application and test the book search flow, you will have to log into the application before you can access this flow. Similarly, you can finely secure a particular state or transaction by embedding a `<secured>` element.

7-4. Persisting Objects in Web Flows

Problem

In many cases, you may have to create and update persistent objects in different states of a web flow. According to the nature of a web flow, the changes made to these persistent objects should not be flushed to the database until the final state of this web flow, which either commits all these changes in a transaction or ignores them if the flow fails or is cancelled. You can maintain a persistence context across different web flow states, but it's hardly an efficient way.

Solution

Spring Web Flow is able to manage a persistence context across different states of a web flow without your involvement. You can simply access the managed persistence context with a flow scope variable exposed by Spring Web Flow. Spring Web Flow 2.0 comes with support for JPA and Hibernate.

To have Spring Web Flow manage the persistence contexts for your web flows, you have to register a flow execution listener (e.g., `JpaFlowExecutionListener` for JPA and `HibernateFlowExecutionListener` for Hibernate, both of which belong to the `org.springframework.webflow.persistence` package) in the flow executor. When a new flow starts, this listener creates a new persistence context (e.g., a JPA entity manager or a Hibernate session) and binds it to the flow scope. Then, you can persist your objects with this persistence context in different web flow states. Finally, you can define an end state that either commits the changes or ignores them.

How It Works

Suppose you are going to build a web flow for readers to borrow books from the library. You would like to store the borrowing records in a database managed by a database engine such as Apache Derby. You consider using JPA to persist the records, with Hibernate as the underlying PA engine. First of all, you define the `BorrowingRecord` entity class with JPA annotations.

■ **Note** To use Hibernate as the JPA engine, you have to add Hibernate 3, the Hibernate 3 EntityManager, the JPA API, and ehcache. As Hibernate `EntityManager` depends on Javassist, you also have to include `it` in your classpath. To use Apache Derby as the database engine, you also have to add a dependency on the Derby client jar. If you are using Maven, add the following declarations to your POM:

```xml
<dependency>
  <groupId>javax.persistence</groupId>
  <artifactId>persistence-api</artifactId>
  <version>1.0</version>
</dependency>

<dependency>
  <groupId>org.hibernate</groupId>
  <artifactId>hibernate-entitymanager</artifactId>
  <version>3.4.0.GA</version>
  <exclusions>
   <exclusion>
     <groupId>net.sf.ehcache</groupId>
     <artifactId>ehcache</artifactId>
   </exclusion>
   <exclusion>
     <groupId>javax.transaction</groupId>
     <artifactId>jta</artifactId>
   </exclusion>
  </exclusions>
</dependency>

<dependency>
  <groupId>org.apache.derby</groupId>
  <artifactId>derbyclient</artifactId>
  <version>10.4.2.0</version>
</dependency>
```

```
package com.apress.springwebrecipes.library.domain;
...
import javax.persistence.Entity;
import javax.persistence.GeneratedValue;
import javax.persistence.GenerationType;
import javax.persistence.Id;

@Entity
public class BorrowingRecord implements Serializable {

    @Id
    @GeneratedValue(strategy = GenerationType.IDENTITY)
    private Long id;

    private String isbn;
    private Date borrowDate;
    private Date returnDate;
    private String reader;

    // Getters and Setters
    ...
}
```

Next, you create the JPA configuration file persistence.xml in the META-INF directory of the classpath root:

```
<persistence xmlns="http://java.sun.com/xml/ns/persistence"
    xmlns:xsi="http://www.w3.org/2001/XMLSchema-instance"
    xsi:schemaLocation="http://java.sun.com/xml/ns/persistence
        http://java.sun.com/xml/ns/persistence/persistence_1_0.xsd"
    version="1.0">

    <persistence-unit name="library" />
</persistence>
```

In this configuration file, you only define the persistence unit library. The JPA provider information will be configured in Spring's application context.

Configuring JPA in Spring's Application Context

In the service layer configuration file (i.e., library-service.xml), you can configure a JPA entity manager factory by providing a data source and a JPA vendor adaptor, where you can configure JPA vendor-specific information. In addition, you have to configure a JPA transaction manager for managing JPA transactions. For details about configuring JPA, please see Chapter 17.

```
<beans ...>
    ...
    <bean id="dataSource"
        class="org.springframework.jdbc.datasource.DriverManagerDataSource">
        <property name="driverClassName"
            value="org.apache.derby.jdbc.ClientDriver" />
        <property name="url"
            value="jdbc:derby://localhost:1527/library;create=true" />
        <property name="username" value="app" />
        <property name="password" value="app" />
    </bean>

    <bean id="entityManagerFactory" class="org.springframework.orm.jpa.~CCC
        LocalContainerEntityManagerFactoryBean">
        <property name="dataSource" ref="dataSource" />
        <property name="jpaVendorAdapter">
            <bean class="org.springframework.orm.jpa.vendor.~CCC
                HibernateJpaVendorAdapter">
                <property name="databasePlatform"
                    value="org.hibernate.dialect.DerbyDialect" />
                <property name="showSql" value="true" />
                <property name="generateDdl" value="true" />
            </bean>
        </property>
    </bean>

    <bean id="transactionManager"
        class="org.springframework.orm.jpa.JpaTransactionManager">
        <property name="entityManagerFactory" ref="entityManagerFactory" />
    </bean>
</beans>
```

Setting Up JPA for Spring Web Flow

To have Spring Web Flow manage the persistence contexts for your web flows, you have to register a flow execution listener in the flow executor. As you are using JPA, you have to register JpaFlowExecutionListener in library-webflow.xml.

```
<beans ...>
    ...
    <webflow:flow-executor id="flowExecutor">
        <webflow:flow-execution-listeners>
            ...
            <webflow:listener ref="jpaFlowExecutionListener" />
        </webflow:flow-execution-listeners>
    </webflow:flow-executor>
```

```
<bean id="jpaFlowExecutionListener"
    class="org.springframework.webflow.persistence.JpaFlowExecutionListener">
    <constructor-arg ref="entityManagerFactory" />
    <constructor-arg ref="transactionManager" />
</bean>
</beans>
```

JpaFlowExecutionListener requires a JPA entity manager factory and a transaction manager as its constructor arguments, which you have configured in the service layer. You can filter the names of the flows to listen for in the criteria attribute, with commas as separators or an asterisk for all flows, which is the default value.

Using JPA in Web Flows

Now, let's define the flow for borrowing books from the library. First, you register a new flow definition in the flow registry:

```
<webflow:flow-registry flow-builder-services="flowBuilderServices" ~CCC
id="flowRegistry" base-path="/WEB-INF/flows/">
    ...
    <webflow:flow-location path="/borrowBook/borrowBook.xml" />
</webflow:flow-registry>
```

This flow's first state will show a form for library users to input the borrowing details, which will be bound to a form object of type BorrowingRecord. You can define a form action in library-webflow.xml to handle this borrowing form.

```
<bean id="borrowBookAction"
    class="org.springframework.webflow.action.FormAction">
    <property name="formObjectClass"
        value="com.apress.springwebrecipes.library.domain.BorrowingRecord" />
    <property name="propertyEditorRegistrar">
        <bean class="com.apress.springwebrecipes.library.web.PropertyEditors" />
    </property>
</bean>
```

In the flow definition file, /WEB-INF/flows/borrowBook/borrowBook.xml, you have to define a <persistence-context> element to ask Spring Web Flow to manage a persistence context for each flow instance:

```
<flow xmlns="http://www.springframework.org/schema/webflow"
    xmlns:xsi="http://www.w3.org/2001/XMLSchema-instance"
    xsi:schemaLocation="http://www.springframework.org/schema/webflow
        http://www.springframework.org/schema/webflow/spring-webflow-2.0.xsd">

    <persistence-context />
```

```
<view-state id="borrowForm">
    <on-render>
        <evaluate expression="borrowBookAction.setupForm" />
    </on-render>
    <transition on="proceed" to="borrowReview">
        <evaluate expression="borrowBookAction.bindAndValidate" />
    </transition>
    <transition on="cancel" to="cancel" />
</view-state>

<view-state id="borrowReview">
    <on-render>
        <evaluate expression="borrowBookAction.setupForm" />
    </on-render>
    <transition on="confirm" to="confirm">
        <evaluate expression="persistenceContext.persist(borrowingRecord)" />
    </transition>
    <transition on="revise" to="borrowForm" />
    <transition on="cancel" to="cancel" />
</view-state>

<end-state id="confirm" commit="true" />

<end-state id="cancel" />
</flow>
```

This flow includes two view states and two end states. The borrowForm state shows a form for a user to input the borrowing details, which will be bound to a flow scope object with the name borrowingRecord, derived from the form object's class name BorrowingRecord. If the user proceeds with the borrowing form, this state will transition to the borrowReview state, which shows the borrowing details for confirmation. If the user confirms the borrowing details, the form object in the flow scope will be persisted with the managed persistence context, and this state will transition to the end state confirm. As this state has its commit attribute set to true, it will commit the changes to the database. However, in either view state, the user can choose to cancel the borrowing form that will cause a transition to the end state cancel, which ignores the changes. The flow diagram for this book-borrowing flow is illustrated in Figure 7-9.

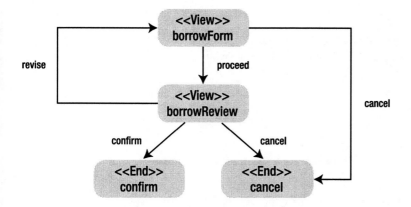

Figure 7-9. *The flow diagram for the book-borrowing flow*

The final step is to create the views for the two view states. For the borrowForm state, you create borrowForm.jsp in /WEB-INF/flows/borrowBook/ so that it will be loaded by default:

```
<%@ taglib prefix="form" uri="http://www.springframework.org/tags/form" %>

<html>
<head>
<title>Borrow Form</title>
</head>

<body>
<form:form commandName="borrowingRecord">
<table>
  <tr>
    <td>ISBN</td>
    <td><form:input path="isbn" /></td>
  </tr>
  <tr>
    <td>Borrow Date</td>
    <td><form:input path="borrowDate" /></td>
  </tr>
  <tr>
    <td>Return Date</td>
    <td><form:input path="returnDate" /></td>
  </tr>
  <tr>
    <td>Reader</td>
    <td><form:input path="reader" /></td>
  </tr>
```

281

```
   <tr>
     <td colspan="2">
       <input type="submit" name="_eventId_proceed" value="Proceed" />
       <input type="submit" name="_eventId_cancel" value="Cancel" />
     </td>
   </tr>
</table>
</form:form>
</body>
</html>
```

For the borrowReview state, you create borrowReview.jsp in the same location for confirming the borrowing details:

```
<%@ taglib prefix="fmt" uri="http://java.sun.com/jsp/jstl/fmt" %>

<html>
<head>
<title>Borrow Review</title>
</head>

<body>
<form method="POST">
<table>
  <tr>
    <td>ISBN</td>
    <td>${borrowingRecord.isbn}</td>
  </tr>
  <tr>
    <td>Borrow Date</td>
    <td>
      <fmt:formatDate value="${borrowingRecord.borrowDate}" pattern="yyyy-MM-dd" />
    </td>
  </tr>
  <tr>
    <td>Return Date</td>
    <td>
      <fmt:formatDate value="${borrowingRecord.returnDate}" pattern="yyyy-MM-dd" />
    </td>
  </tr>
  <tr>
    <td>Reader</td>
    <td>${borrowingRecord.reader}</td>
  </tr>
```

```
<tr>
  <td colspan="2">
    <input type="submit" name="_eventId_confirm" value="Confirm" />
    <input type="submit" name="_eventId_revise" value="Revise" />
    <input type="submit" name="_eventId_cancel" value="Cancel" />
  </td>
</tr>
</table>
</form>
</body>
</html>
```

Now, you can deploy the application and test this book-borrowing flow with the URL
`http://localhost:8080/library/flows/borrowBook`.

7-5. Integrating Spring Web Flow with JSF

Problem

By default, Spring Web Flow relies on Spring MVC's view technologies (e.g., JSP and Tiles) to render its views. However, you might wish to use JSF's rich set of UI components in your web flow's views or manage the UI flows of your existing JSF applications with Spring Web Flow. In either case, you have to integrate Spring Web Flow with JSF.

Solution

Spring Web Flow provides two submodules, Spring Faces and Spring JavaScript, to simplify using JSF and JavaScript in Spring. Spring Faces integrates Spring with JSF 1.2 or higher by allowing you to use JSF's UI components with Spring MVC and Spring Web Flow. Spring Faces supports rendering JSF views in Spring Web Flow and offers a number of JSF integration features for Spring Web Flow.

Spring JavaScript is a JavaScript abstraction framework that integrates the Dojo JavaScript toolkit (`http://www.dojotoolkit.org/`) as the underlying UI toolkit. Spring Faces provides a set of client-side validation components for standard JSF input components, building on top of Spring JavaScript. These components are provided as Facelets tags, so you have to use Facelets as your JSF view technology to use them.

How It Works

Rendering JSF Views for Spring Web Flow

Now, let's consider reimplementing the book-borrowing flow's views with JSF. In To use the JSF validation components provided by Spring Faces, you have to use Facelets to create your JSF views. First, configure JSF's `FacesServlet` in `web.xml`.

■ **Note** To integrate JSF and Facelets with Spring Web Flow, you have to add Spring Faces to your CLASSPATH. You will also need a JSF implementation, Facelets, and an Expression Language implementation. If you are using Maven, add the following dependencies to your Maven project:

```
<dependency>
  <groupId>org.springframework.webflow</groupId>
  <artifactId>spring-faces</artifactId>
  <version>2.0.8.RELEASE</version>
</dependency>
<dependency>
  <groupId>com.sun.facelets</groupId>
  <artifactId>jsf-facelets</artifactId>
  <version>1.1.15.B1</version>
</dependency>
<dependency>
  <groupId>org.apache.myfaces.core</groupId>
  <artifactId>myfaces-impl</artifactId>
  <version>1.2.7</version>
</dependency>

<dependency>
  <groupId>javax.servlet</groupId>
  <artifactId>jstl</artifactId>
  <version>1.2</version>
</dependency>
<dependency>
  <groupId>javax.servlet.jsp</groupId>
  <artifactId>jsp-api</artifactId>
  <version>2.1</version>
</dependency>

<dependency>
  <groupId>org.jboss.seam</groupId>
  <artifactId>jboss-el</artifactId>
  <version>2.0.0.GA</version>
```

```
  <exclusions>
    <exclusion>
     <groupId>javax.el</groupId>
     <artifactId>el-api</artifactId>
    </exclusion>
   </exclusions>
</dependency>
```

```
<web-app ...>
   ...
   <servlet>
       <servlet-name>faces</servlet-name>
       <servlet-class>javax.faces.webapp.FacesServlet</servlet-class>
   </servlet>
</web-app>
```

Note that this servlet is only registered for initializing a web application that uses JSF. It won't be used to handle web flow requests, so you needn't specify a `<servlet-mapping>` definition for it. However, if you are going to use the legacy JSF request handling at the same time, you will have to specify that.

In the JSF configuration file (i.e., `faces-config.xml` in the root of `WEB-INF`), you have to configure `FaceletViewHandler` as the JSF view handler to enable Facelets and a SpringBeanFacesELResolver to be able to access Spring beans through JSF's expression language.

```
<?xml version="1.0" encoding="UTF-8"?>
<faces-config version="1.2" xmlns="http://java.sun.com/xml/ns/javaee"
        xmlns:xi="http://www.w3.org/2001/XInclude"↵
 xmlns:xsi="http://www.w3.org/2001/XMLSchema-instance"
        xsi:schemaLocation="http://java.sun.com/xml/ns/javaee↵
 http://java.sun.com/xml/ns/javaee/web-facesconfig_1_2.xsd">
        <application>
                <view-handler>com.sun.facelets.FaceletViewHandler</view-handler>
                <el-resolver>org.springframework.web.jsf.el↵
.SpringBeanFacesELResolver</el-resolver>
        </application>
</faces-config>
```

In `library-webflow.xml`, you have to specify the JSF flow builder services for your flow registry, instead of the default Spring MVC flow builder services in use. This way, the JSF flow builder services can render JSF views for web flows. Additionally, we configure a `ViewResolver` to resolve Facelets views by conventions we dictate. This heuristic is what determines which Facelets view is used when a view state is encountered.

```
<beans xmlns="http://www.springframework.org/schema/beans"
        xmlns:xsi="http://www.w3.org/2001/XMLSchema-instance"
        xmlns:webflow="http://www.springframework.org/schema/webflow-config"
        xmlns:faces="http://www.springframework.org/schema/faces"
        xsi:schemaLocation="http://www.springframework.org/schema/beans
```

```
        http://www.springframework.org/schema/beans/spring-beans-3.0.xsd
        http://www.springframework.org/schema/webflow-config
        http://www.springframework.org/schema/webflow-config/spring-webflow-config-2.0.xsd
        http://www.springframework.org/schema/faces
        http://www.springframework.org/schema/faces/spring-faces-2.0.xsd">

        <webflow:flow-executor id="flowExecutor"
                flow-registry="flowRegistry">
                <webflow:flow-execution-listeners>
                        <webflow:listener ref="jpaFlowExecutionListener" />
                        <webflow:listener ref="securityFlowExecutionListener" />
                </webflow:flow-execution-listeners>
        </webflow:flow-executor>
        <webflow:flow-registry id="flowRegistry"
                flow-builder-services="facesFlowBuilderServices" base-path="/WEB-INF/flows">
                <webflow:flow-location-pattern value="/**/*.xml" />
        </webflow:flow-registry>
        <faces:flow-builder-services id="facesFlowBuilderServices"
                enable-managed-beans="true" development="true" />
        <bean
                class="org.springframework.web.servlet.mvc↵
.SimpleControllerHandlerAdapter" />
        <bean class="org.springframework.webflow.mvc.servlet.FlowHandlerAdapter">
                <property name="flowExecutor" ref="flowExecutor" />
        </bean>
        <bean class="org.springframework.webflow.mvc.servlet.FlowHandlerMapping">
                <property name="flowRegistry" ref="flowRegistry" />
                <property name="defaultHandler">
                        <bean class="org.springframework.web.servlet.mvc↵
.UrlFilenameViewController" />
                </property>
        </bean>
        <bean id="faceletsViewResolver"
                class="org.springframework.web.servlet.view.UrlBasedViewResolver">
                <property name="viewClass" value="org.springframework.faces.mvc.JsfView" />
                <property name="prefix" value="/WEB-INF/flows/" />
                <property name="suffix" value=".xhtml" />
        </bean>
        ...
</beans>
```

The JSF flow builder services internally use a JSF view factory, which will, by default, load a Facelets page using a view state's name and .xhtml as the file extension. Before you create the Facelets pages for the borrowForm and borrowReview states, you can define a page template to unify your web application's layout (e.g., in /WEB-INF/template.xhtml):

```
<!DOCTYPE html PUBLIC "-//W3C//DTD XHTML 1.0 Transitional//EN"
        "http://www.w3.org/TR/xhtml1/DTD/xhtml1-transitional.dtd">

<html xmlns="http://www.w3.org/1999/xhtml"
        xmlns:ui="http://java.sun.com/jsf/facelets">
```

```
<head>
<title><ui:insert name="title">Library</ui:insert></title>
</head>

<body>
<ui:insert name="content" />
</body>
</html>
```

The preceding template defines two areas, with the names `title` and `content`. The pages that use this template will insert their own contents into these two areas.

Now, let's create `/WEB-INF/flows/borrowBook/borrowForm.xhtml` for the `borrowForm` state so that it will be loaded by default:

```
<!DOCTYPE html PUBLIC "-//W3C//DTD XHTML 1.0 Transitional//EN"
    "http://www.w3.org/TR/xhtml1/DTD/xhtml1-transitional.dtd">

<ui:composition xmlns="http://www.w3.org/1999/xhtml"
                xmlns:f="http://java.sun.com/jsf/core"
                xmlns:h="http://java.sun.com/jsf/html"
                xmlns:ui="http://java.sun.com/jsf/facelets"
                template="/WEB-INF/template.xhtml">

  <ui:define name="title">Borrow Form</ui:define>

  <ui:define name="content">
    <h:form>
      <h:panelGrid columns="2">
        <h:outputLabel for="isbn">ISBN</h:outputLabel>
        <h:inputText id="isbn" value="#{borrowingRecord.isbn}" />

        <h:outputLabel for="borrowDate">Borrow Date</h:outputLabel>
        <h:inputText id="borrowDate" value="#{borrowingRecord.borrowDate}">
          <f:convertDateTime pattern="yyyy-MM-dd" />
        </h:inputText>

        <h:outputLabel for="returnDate">Return Date</h:outputLabel>
        <h:inputText id="returnDate" value="#{borrowingRecord.returnDate}">
          <f:convertDateTime pattern="yyyy-MM-dd" />
        </h:inputText>

        <h:outputLabel for="reader">Reader</h:outputLabel>
        <h:inputText id="reader" value="#{borrowingRecord.reader}" />
      </h:panelGrid>

      <h:commandButton value="Proceed" action="proceed" />
      <h:commandButton value="Cancel" action="cancel" />
    </h:form>
  </ui:define>
</ui:composition>
```

In this page, you use standard JSF components like `form`, `outputLabel`, `inputText`, and `commandButton` to create a form that binds the field values to a form object. The action triggered by a command button will be mapped to a Spring Web Flow event ID that will cause a transition.

Next, create `/WEB-INF/flows/borrowBook/borrowReview.` `xhtml` for the `borrowReview` state:

```
<!DOCTYPE html PUBLIC "-//W3C//DTD XHTML 1.0 Transitional//EN"
    "http://www.w3.org/TR/xhtml1/DTD/xhtml1-transitional.dtd">

<ui:composition xmlns="http://www.w3.org/1999/xhtml"
                xmlns:f="http://java.sun.com/jsf/core"
                xmlns:h="http://java.sun.com/jsf/html"
                xmlns:ui="http://java.sun.com/jsf/facelets"
                template="/WEB-INF/template.xhtml">

  <ui:define name="title">Borrow Review</ui:define>

  <ui:define name="content">
    <h:form>
      <h:panelGrid columns="2">
        <h:outputLabel for="isbn">ISBN</h:outputLabel>
        <h:outputText id="isbn" value="#{borrowingRecord.isbn}" />

        <h:outputLabel for="borrowDate">Borrow Date</h:outputLabel>
        <h:outputText id="borrowDate" value="#{borrowingRecord.borrowDate}">
          <f:convertDateTime pattern="yyyy-MM-dd" />
        </h:outputText>

        <h:outputLabel for="returnDate">Return Date</h:outputLabel>
        <h:outputText id="returnDate" value="#{borrowingRecord.returnDate}">
          <f:convertDateTime pattern="yyyy-MM-dd" />
        </h:outputText>

        <h:outputLabel for="reader">Reader</h:outputLabel>
        <h:outputText id="reader" value="#{borrowingRecord.reader}" />
      </h:panelGrid>

      <h:commandButton value="Confirm" action="confirm" />
      <h:commandButton value="Revise" action="revise" />
      <h:commandButton value="Cancel" action="cancel" />
    </h:form>
  </ui:define>
</ui:composition>
```

Actions and ActionListeners

Navigation in traditional JSF applications is handled by linking directly linking to a resource or by invoking an action (for example, on a `commandLink`). The action is a method on a backing bean that does some sort of processing (perhaps at the end of a form submission) and then returns a `String`. The `String` is mapped to a navigation outcome in `faces-config.xml`. When you use Spring Web Flow, it handles the mapping of the Strings to navigation outcomes for you, instead of `faces-config.xml`. This is true even when returning `Strings` from actions.

There are several reasons this is important to bear in mind. With Spring Web Flow, you can use the name of the transition in those action (or `actionListener`) parameters. Thus, if you click a button and want to cause an action to occur, you can use an event ID to start a flow. There, you might have an evaluate expression which calls Java functionality. This will work most of the time, but from those methods, the `FacesContext` is not available to you. There are many reasons to want to use the `FacesContext` from the action. If you have cross field validation, or perhaps even some sort of barrier to ensure state before you start a flow, then you should use the old, standard style of invoking a method and, from that method, return a `String` (which is an outcome) or `null` (which will let you stop procession of the navigation). Thus, you haven't lost your Spring Web Flow navigation, you're just using the action as a chance to invoke a method and perform some logic. If, from there, you decide you want to proceed with the navigation, do so as normal.

Thus, a `commandButton` whose action is mapped to a Spring Web Flow transition, like this

```
<h:commandButton value="Cancel" action="proceed" />
```

might become

```
<h:commandButton value="Cancel" action="#{backingBean.formSubmitted}" />
```

The code for `formSubmitted` is standard:

```
public String formSubmitted (){

    FacesContext fc = FacesContext.getCurrentInstance(); // won't be null
    // … do any kind of logic you want, or perhaps setup state
    return "proceed" ;
}
```

Using the JSF Components of Spring Faces

Before you can use the Spring Faces components, you have to register `ResourceServlet`, which is provided by Spring JavaScript for accessing static resources in JAR files, in the web deployment descriptor. These components will retrieve static JavaScript and CSS resources from Spring JavaScript through this servlet.

```
<web-app ...>
    ...
    <servlet>
        <servlet-name>resources</servlet-name>
        <servlet-class>
            org.springframework.js.resource.ResourceServlet
        </servlet-class>
    </servlet>

    <servlet-mapping>
        <servlet-name>resources</servlet-name>
        <url-pattern>/resources/*</url-pattern>
    </servlet-mapping>
</web-app>
```

Spring Faces provides a set of validation components to perform client-side validation for standard JSF input components. These components are provided as Facelets tags defined in the Spring Faces tag library, so you have to include this tag library in the root element beforehand. For example, you can enable client-side validation for the borrow form components in /WEB-INF/flows/borrowBook/ borrowForm.xhtml as follows:

```
<ui:composition xmlns="http://www.w3.org/1999/xhtml"
                xmlns:f="http://java.sun.com/jsf/core"
                xmlns:h="http://java.sun.com/jsf/html"
                xmlns:ui="http://java.sun.com/jsf/facelets"
                xmlns:sf="http://www.springframework.org/tags/faces"
                template="/WEB-INF/template.xhtml">

  <ui:define name="title">Borrow Form</ui:define>

  <ui:define name="content">
    <h:form>
      <h:panelGrid columns="2">
        <h:outputLabel for="isbn">ISBN</h:outputLabel>
        <sf:clientTextValidator required="true" regExp="[0-9]{10}">
          <h:inputText id="isbn" value="#{borrowingRecord.isbn}" />
        </sf:clientTextValidator>

        <h:outputLabel for="borrowDate">Borrow Date</h:outputLabel>
        <sf:clientDateValidator required="true">
          <h:inputText id="borrowDate" value="#{borrowingRecord.borrowDate}">
            <f:convertDateTime pattern="yyyy-MM-dd" />
          </h:inputText>
        </sf:clientDateValidator>

        <h:outputLabel for="returnDate">Return Date</h:outputLabel>
        <sf:clientDateValidator required="true">
          <h:inputText id="returnDate" value="#{borrowingRecord.returnDate}">
            <f:convertDateTime pattern="yyyy-MM-dd" />
          </h:inputText>
        </sf:clientDateValidator>

        <h:outputLabel for="reader">Reader</h:outputLabel>
        <sf:clientTextValidator required="true">
          <h:inputText id="reader" value="#{borrowingRecord.reader}" />
        </sf:clientTextValidator>
      </h:panelGrid>

      <sf:validateAllOnClick>
        <h:commandButton value="Proceed" action="proceed" />
      </sf:validateAllOnClick>

      <h:commandButton value="Cancel" action="cancel" />
    </h:form>
  </ui:define>
</ui:composition>
```

The validation components enable client-side validation for the `inputText` components. You will see that the `clientDateValidator` component additionally provides a pop-up date picker control for its enclosed input field. Finally, when a command button enclosed by a `validateAllInClick` component is clicked, it will trigger all validators in the same page to validate their fields.

Finally, you have to choose a Dojo theme for rendering these components. For example, you can specify using the `tundra` theme in the `<body>` element of the page template in `template.xhtml`:

```
<html xmlns="http://www.w3.org/1999/xhtml"
      xmlns:ui="http://java.sun.com/jsf/facelets">
<head>
<title><ui:insert name="title">Library</ui:insert></title>
</head>

<body class="tundra">
<ui:insert name="content"/>
</body>
</html>
```

7-6. Using RichFaces with Spring Web Flow

Problem

In the previous recipe, we leveraged some of the advanced components that ship with Spring Faces, most of which are based on the Dojo JavaScript framework. These components are a great start, but sometimes, you're going to want something slightly more powerful, like RichFaces.

Solution

There is integration support for using Spring Web Flow with RichFaces. RichFaces actually provides two libraries that each serve very different purposes. One, called Ajax4JSF, provides the ability to augment existing components and page elements with Ajax functionality. The other, RichFaces, provides an advanced component set with Ajax functionality baked into the core.

Approach

Because you can do things like return redirects and rerender partial pages using Ajax, it's important that the functionality is well integrated with Spring Web Flow. In our setup, we delegate all navigation to Spring Web Flow and let it manage the state of objects associated with those flows. Thus, for libraries wishing to integrate with Spring Web Flow, there are API hooks. One, for RichFaces, is provided out of the box.

Setting Up RichFaces With JSF

To setup RichFaces, you'll need to make a few changes to your `web.xml`, regardless of whether you're using Spring Web Flow. Most of the following `web.xml` should be familiar to you, as the code is repeated to provide a whole, working example. This example demonstrates setting up Spring Web Flow, RichFaces, and Facelets and the JSF framework using Apache's MyFaces.

```xml
<?xml version="1.0" encoding="UTF-8"?>
<web-app xmlns:xsi="http://www.w3.org/2001/XMLSchema-instance"
        xmlns="http://java.sun.com/xml/ns/javaee"↵
 xmlns:web="http://java.sun.com/xml/ns/javaee/web-app_2_5.xsd"
        xsi:schemaLocation="http://java.sun.com/xml/ns/javaee↵
 http://java.sun.com/xml/ns/javaee/web-app_2_5.xsd"
        version="2.5">
        <display-name>richfaces-swf-application</display-name>

        <listener>
                <listener-class>org.springframework.web.context↵
.ContextLoaderListener</listener-class>
        </listener>
        <listener>
                <listener-class>org.springframework.web.context↵
.request.RequestContextListener</listener-class>
        </listener>
        <context-param>
                <param-name>contextConfigLocation</param-name>
                <param-value>/WEB-INF/spring/web-application-context.xml</param-value>
        </context-param>
        <context-param>
                <param-name>org.ajax4jsf.VIEW_HANDLERS</param-name>
                <param-value>com.sun.facelets.FaceletViewHandler</param-value>
        </context-param>
        <listener>
                <listener-class>org.apache.myfaces.webapp↵
.StartupServletContextListener</listener-class>
        </listener>
        <filter>
                <display-name>RichFaces Filter</display-name>
                <filter-name>richfaces</filter-name>
                <filter-class>org.ajax4jsf.Filter</filter-class>
        </filter>
        <filter-mapping>
                <filter-name>richfaces</filter-name>
                <servlet-name>faces</servlet-name>
                <dispatcher>REQUEST</dispatcher>
                <dispatcher>FORWARD</dispatcher>
                <dispatcher>INCLUDE</dispatcher>
        </filter-mapping>
        <filter-mapping>
                <filter-name>richfaces</filter-name>
                <servlet-name>SwfServlet</servlet-name>
                <dispatcher>REQUEST</dispatcher>
                <dispatcher>FORWARD</dispatcher>
                <dispatcher>INCLUDE</dispatcher>
        </filter-mapping>
```

```xml
<servlet>
        <servlet-name>faces</servlet-name>
        <servlet-class>javax.faces.webapp.FacesServlet</servlet-class>
        <load-on-startup>1</load-on-startup>
</servlet>
<servlet>
        <servlet-name>SwfServlet</servlet-name>
        <servlet-class>org.springframework.web.servlet↩
.DispatcherServlet</servlet-class>
        <init-param>
                <param-name>contextConfigLocation</param-name>
                <param-value></param-value>
        </init-param>
        <load-on-startup>2</load-on-startup>
</servlet>
<servlet>
        <servlet-name>Resource Servlet</servlet-name>
        <servlet-class>org.springframework.js.resource↩
.ResourceServlet</servlet-class>
        <load-on-startup>0</load-on-startup>
</servlet>
<servlet-mapping>
        <servlet-name>Resource Servlet</servlet-name>
        <url-pattern>/resources/*</url-pattern>
</servlet-mapping>
<servlet-mapping>
        <servlet-name>SwfServlet</servlet-name>
        <url-pattern>/swf/*</url-pattern>
</servlet-mapping>
<servlet-mapping>
        <servlet-name>faces</servlet-name>
        <url-pattern>*.xhtml</url-pattern>
        <url-pattern>/faces/*</url-pattern>
</servlet-mapping>
</web-app>
```

Here, we have definitions for both the Spring Web Flow servlet and the JavaServer Faces (JSF) servlet. In addition, we've configured the RichFaces filter to handle requests destined for both servlets. The next step is to configure Spring Web Flow to be aware of the library. Everything remains as it was before, except that you need to tell Spring Web Flow about how to handle Ajax requests. You do this by configuring an instance of FlowHandlerAdapter in library-webflow.xml. Add the following toward the end, right before the closing beans element:

```xml
<bean class="org.springframework.webflow.mvc.servlet.FlowHandlerAdapter">
        <property name="flowExecutor" ref="flowExecutor" />
        <property name="ajaxHandler">
                <bean class="org.springframework.faces.richfaces.RichFacesAjaxHandler" />
        </property>
</bean>
```

At this point, almost everything's ready. The final nuance is in the application of Ajax partial page updates. When you use the RichFaces and Ajax4JSF libraries, there is the notion that actions that might affect server side state should also be able to rerender parts of the client. Let's examine the use case of updating a counter using Ajax. You click a button, and a number is incremented. In your flow, you'll simply return the user to the original view, re-rendering the updated value. In RichFaces, this looks like so:

```
<ui:composition template="/WEB-INF/template/default.xhtml"
        xmlns="http://www.w3.org/1999/xhtml"
        xmlns:ui="http://java.sun.com/jsf/facelets"
        xmlns:f="http://java.sun.com/jsf/core"
        xmlns:h="http://java.sun.com/jsf/html"
        xmlns:jawr="https://jawr.dev.java.net/jsf/facelets"
        xmlns:a4j="http://richfaces.org/a4j"
        xmlns:rich="http://richfaces.org/rich">
        <ui:define name="title"> Update Count  </ui:define>
        <ui:define name="content">
                <f:view>
                        <h:form id="counter">
                                <a4j:outputPanel id="countFragment">
                                        <h:outputText value = "#{counterBean.count}" />
                                </a4j:outputPanel>
                                <br />
                                <a4j:commandLink id="update" value="Update Count"↩
    action="updateCount" reRender="#{flowRenderFragments}" />
                        </h:form>
                </f:view>
        </ui:define>
</ui:composition>
```

When the link is clicked, method flow state is sent to the server (as the commandLink's action value) which triggers the advancement of the web flow. In this case, the state has a transition element, and a render element. When the transition is reached the expression is evaluated (triggering the logic that updates the counter) and the fragment to be rerendered is sent back to the client, where RichFaces rerenders components whose IDs are enumerated. Additionally, RichFaces will rerender a4j:outputPanel components whose ajaxRendered attribute is true, unless the limitToList attribute is specified. This is somewhat counterintuitive to the way Spring Web Flow's SpringFaces works, where you explicitly enumerate what to rerender on navigation.

```
<?xml version="1.0" encoding="UTF-8"?>
<flow xmlns="http://www.springframework.org/schema/webflow"
        xmlns:xsi="http://www.w3.org/2001/XMLSchema-instance"
        xsi:schemaLocation="http://www.springframework.org/schema/webflow
                        http://www.springframework.org/schema/webflow↩
/spring-webflow-2.0.xsd">
```

```
        <view-state id="counter">
                <transition on="updateCount">
                        <evaluate expression="counterBean.updateCount()" />
                        <render fragments="counter:countFragment" />
                </transition>
        </view-state>
</flow>
```

Spring Web Flow provides the `flowRenderFragments` context variable that Ajax4JSF can observe, which lets it rerender the fragments specified by the transition and thus avoid stepping on Spring Web Flow's toes. The preceding `commandLink` is rewritten to take advantage of this new transition. The result is not generic and moves any sort of transition and navigation logic into Spring Web Flow's control, where it belongs.

```
<a4j:commandLink id="update" value="Update Count" action="updateCount"
reRender="#{flowRenderFragments}" />
```

Summary

In this chapter, you learned how to manage a web application's UI flows using Spring Web Flow.

You started by building a flow definition using Spring Web Flow. A flow definition in Spring Web Flow consists of one or more *states*, which can include view, action , decision , subflow, and end states. Once a state has completed its tasks, it fires an *event*. An event contains a source and an event ID, and perhaps some attributes. Each state can also contain *transitions*, each of which maps a returned event ID to the next state.

Next, you learned how to secure a Spring Web Flow. Spring Web Flow offers integration for Spring Security. This allows you to easily secure your web flows using this Spring-related security project, thoroughly discussed in Chapter 7. With Spring Security configured properly, you can secure a flow, a state, or a transition by embedding the `<secured>` element with required access attributes specified.

You also explored how Spring Web Flow deals with persistence. Since Spring Web Flow 2.0 comes with support for JPA and Hibernate, you can easily access a persistence context across different states of a web flow. You just access the managed persistence context with a flow scope variable exposed by Spring Web Flow.

Finally, you learned that not only does Spring Web Flow work with Spring MVC's view technologies (e.g., JSP and Tiles) to render its views but it can also be configured to use JSF or RichFaces UI components in your web flow's views.

CHAPTER 8

■ ■ ■

Spring @MVC

In this chapter, you will learn web-based application development using the Spring MVC framework. Spring MVC is one of the most important modules of the Spring framework. It builds on the powerful Spring IoC container and makes extensive use of the container features to simplify its configuration.

Model-view-controller (MVC) is a common design pattern in UI design. It decouples business logic from UIs by separating the roles of model, view, and controller in an application. *Models* are responsible for encapsulating application data for views to present. *Views* should only present this data, without including any business logic. *Controllers* are responsible for receiving requests from users and invoking back-end services for business processing. After processing, back-end services may return some data for views to present. Controllers collect this data and prepare models for views to present. The core idea of the MVC pattern is to separate business logic from UIs to allow them to change independently without affecting each other.

In a Spring MVC application, models usually consist of domain objects that are processed by the service layer and persisted by the persistence layer. Views are usually JSP templates written with Java Standard Tag Library (JSTL). However, it's also possible to define views as PDF files, Excel files, RESTful web services or even Flex interfaces, the last of which are often dubbed a Rich Internet Application (RIA).

Upon finishing this chapter, you will be able to develop Java web applications using Spring MVC. You will also understand Spring MVC's common controller and view types. Including, what has become the de facto use of annotations for creating controllers as of Spring 3.0. Moreover, you will understand the basic principles of Spring MVC, that will serve as the foundations for more advanced topics covered in the upcoming chapters.

8-1. Developing a Simple Web Application with Spring MVC

Problem

You want to develop a simple web application with Spring MVC to learn the basic concepts and configurations of this framework.

Solution

The central component of Spring MVC is a controller. In the simplest Spring MVC application, a controller is the only servlet you need to configure in a Java web deployment descriptor (i.e., the web.xml file). A Spring MVC controller—often referred to as a Dispatcher Servlet—implements one of Sun's core

Java EE design patterns called *front controller*. It acts as the front controller of the Spring MVC framework, and every web request must go through it so that it can manage the entire request-handling process.

When a web request is sent to a Spring MVC application, a controller first receives the request. Then it organizes the different components configured in Spring's web application context or annotations present in the controller itself, all needed to handle the request. Figure 8-1 shows the primary flow of request handling in Spring MVC.

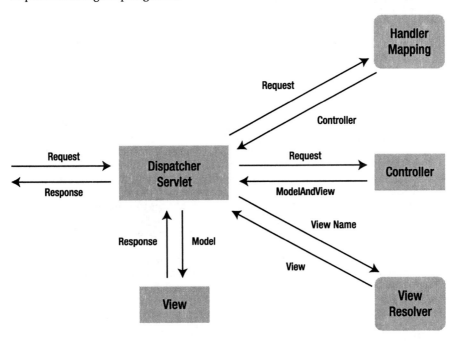

Figure 8-1. *Primary flow of request handling in Spring MVC*

To define a controller class in Spring 3.0, a class has to be marked with the `@Controller` annotation. In contrast to other framework controllers or earlier Spring versions, an annotated controller class needn't implement a framework-specific interface or extend a framework-specific base class.

For example, prior to Spring 3.0 one of a series of classes, such as `AbstractController`, were used to give a class the behavior of a Dispatcher Servlet. Starting from Spring 2.5, annotated classes for defining Dispatcher Servlets became available. As of Spring 3.0, these series of classes for giving a class the behavior of a Dispatcher Servlet have been deprecated in favor of annotated classes.

When a `@Controller` annotated class (i.e., a controller class) receives a request, it looks for an appropriate handler method to handle the request. This requires that a controller class map each request to a handler method by one or more handler mappings. In order to do so, a controller class's methods are decorated with the `@RequestMapping` annotation, making them handler methods.

The signature for these handler methods—like you can expect from any standard class—is open ended. You can specify an arbitrary name for a handler method and define a variety of method arguments. Equally, a handler method can return any of a series of values (e.g., `String` or `void`), depending on the application logic it fulfills.

As the book progresses, you will encounter the various method arguments that can be used in handler methods using the `@RequestMapping` annotation. The following is only a partial list of valid argument types, just to give you an idea.

- `HttpServletRequest` or `HttpServleResponse`

- Request parameters of arbitrary type, annotated with `@RequestParam`

- Model attributes of arbitrary type, annotated with `@ModelAttribute`

- Cookie values included in an incoming request, annotated with `@CookieValue`

- `Map` or `ModelMap`, for the handler method to add attributes to the model

- `Errors` or `BindingResult`, for the handler method to access the binding and validation result for the command object

- `SessionStatus`, for the handler method to notify its completion of session processing

Once the controller class has picked an appropriate handler method, it invokes the handle method's logic with the request. Usually, a controller's logic invokes back-end services to handle the request. In addition, a handler method's logic is likely to add or remove information from the numerous input arguments (e.g., `HttpServletRequest`, `Map`, `Errors`, or `SessionStatus`) that will form part of the ongoing Spring MVC flow.

After a handler method has finished processing the request, it delegates control to a view, which is represented as handler method's return value. To provide a flexible approach, a handler method's return value doesn't represent a view's implementation (e.g., `user.jsp` or `report.pdf`) but rather a *logical* view (e.g., `user` or `report`)—note the lack of file extension.

A handler method's return value can be either a `String`–representing a logical view name—or `void`, in which case a default logical view name is determined on the basis of a handler method's or controller name.

In order to pass information from a controller to a view, it's irrelevant that a handler's method returns a logical view name—`String` or a `void`–since the handler method input arguments will be available to a view.

For example, if a handler method takes a `Map` and `SessionStatus` objects as input parameters—modifying their contents inside the handler method's logic—these same objects will be accessible to the view returned by the handler method.

When the controller class receives a view, it resolves the *logical* view name into a specific view implementation (e.g., `user.jsp` or `report.pdf`) by means of a view resolver. A view resolver is a bean configured in the web application context that implements the `ViewResolver` interface. Its responsibility is to return a specific view implementation (HTML, JSP, PDF, or other) for a logical view name.

Once the controller class has resolved a view name into a view implementation, per the view implementation's design, it renders the objects (e.g., `HttpServletRequest`, `Map`, `Errors`, or `SessionStatus`) passed by the controller's handler method. The view's responsibility is to display the objects added in the handler method's logic to the user.

How It Works

Suppose you are going to develop a court reservation system for a sports center. The UIs of this application are web-based so that users can make online reservations through the Internet. You want to develop this application using Spring MVC. First of all, you create the following domain classes in the domain subpackage:

```
package com.apress.springrecipes.court.domain;
...
public class Reservation {

    private String courtName;
    private Date date;
    private int hour;
    private Player player;
    private SportType sportType;

    // Constructors, Getters and Setters
    ...
}
```

```
package com.apress.springrecipes.court.domain;

public class Player {

    private String name;
    private String phone;

    // Constructors, Getters and Setters
    ...
}
```

```
package com.apress.springrecipes.court.domain;

public class SportType {

    private int id;
    private String name;

    // Constructors, Getters and Setters
    ...
}
```

Then you define the following service interface in the **service** subpackage to provide reservation services to the presentation layer:

```
package com.apress.springrecipes.court.service;
...
public interface ReservationService {

    public List<Reservation> query(String courtName);
}
```

In a production application, you should implement this interface with database persistence. But for simplicity's sake, you can store the reservation records in a list and hard-code several reservations for testing purposes:

```
package com.apress.springrecipes.court.service;
...
public class ReservationServiceImpl implements ReservationService {

    public static final SportType TENNIS = new SportType(1, "Tennis");
    public static final SportType SOCCER = new SportType(2, "Soccer");

    private List<Reservation> reservations;

    public ReservationServiceImpl() {
        reservations = new ArrayList<Reservation>();
        reservations.add(new Reservation("Tennis #1",
                new GregorianCalendar(2008, 0, 14).getTime(), 16,
                new Player("Roger", "N/A"), TENNIS));
        reservations.add(new Reservation("Tennis #2",
                new GregorianCalendar(2008, 0, 14).getTime(), 20,
                new Player("James", "N/A"), TENNIS));
    }

    public List<Reservation> query(String courtName) {
        List<Reservation> result = new ArrayList<Reservation>();
        for (Reservation reservation : reservations) {
            if (reservation.getCourtName().equals(courtName)) {
                result.add(reservation);
            }
        }
        return result;
    }
}
```

Setting up a Spring MVC Application

Next, you need to create a Spring MVC application layout. In general, a web application developed with Spring MVC is set up in the same way as a standard Java web application, except that you have to add a couple of configuration files and required libraries specific to Spring MVC.

The Java EE specification defines the valid directory structure of a Java web application made up of a Web Archive or WAR file. For example, you have to provide a web deployment descriptor (i.e., web.xml) in the WEB-INF root. The class files and JAR files for this web application should be put in the WEB-INF/classes and WEB-INF/lib directories, respectively.

For your court reservation system, you create the following directory structure. Note that the highlighted files are Spring-specific configuration files.

■ **Note** To develop a web application with Spring MVC, you have to add all the normal Spring dependencies (see chapter 1 for more information) as well as the Spring Web and Spring MVC dependencies to your CLASSPATH. If you are using Maven, add the following dependencies to your Maven Project:

```
<dependency>
  <groupId>org.springframework</groupId>
  <artifactId>spring-webmvc</artifactId>
  <version>${spring.version}</version>
</dependency>

<dependency>
  <groupId>org.springframework</groupId>
  <artifactId>spring-web</artifactId>
  <version>${spring.version}</version>
</dependency>
```

```
court/
    css/
    images/
    WEB-INF/
        classes/
        lib/*.jar
        jsp/
            welcome.jsp
            reservationQuery.jsp
        court-service.xml
        court-servlet.xml
        web.xml
```

The files outside the WEB-INF directory are directly accessible to users via URLs, so the CSS files and image files must be put there. When using Spring MVC, the JSP files act as templates. They are read by the framework for generating dynamic content, so the JSP files should be put inside the WEB-INF directory to prevent direct access to them. However, some application servers don't allow the files inside WEB-INF to be read by a web application internally. In that case, you can only put them outside the WEB-INF directory.

Creating the Configuration Files

The web deployment descriptor web.xml is the essential configuration file for a Java web application. In this file, you define the servlets for your application and how web requests are mapped to them. For a

Spring MVC application, you only have to define a single `DispatcherServlet` instance that acts as the front controller for Spring MVC, although you are allowed to define more than one if required.

In large applications, it can be convenient to use multiple `DispatcherServlet` instances. This allows `DispatcherServlet` instances to be designated to specific URLs, making code management easier and letting individual team members work on an application's logic without getting in each other's way.

```
<web-app version="2.4" xmlns="http://java.sun.com/xml/ns/j2ee"
    xmlns:xsi="http://www.w3.org/2001/XMLSchema-instance"
    xsi:schemaLocation="http://java.sun.com/xml/ns/j2ee
        http://java.sun.com/xml/ns/j2ee/web-app_2_4.xsd">

    <display-name>Court Reservation System</display-name>

    <servlet>
        <servlet-name>court</servlet-name>
        <servlet-class>
            org.springframework.web.servlet.DispatcherServlet
        </servlet-class>
        <load-on-startup>1</load-on-startup>
    </servlet>

    <servlet-mapping>
        <servlet-name>court</servlet-name>
        <url-pattern>/</url-pattern>
    </servlet-mapping>
</web-app>
```

In this web deployment descriptor, you define a servlet of type `DispatcherServlet`. This is the core servlet class in Spring MVC that receives web requests and dispatches them to appropriate handlers. You set this servlet's name to court and map all URLs using a / (slash), with the slash representing the root directory. Note that the URL pattern can be set to more granular patterns. In larger application's it can make more sense to delegate patterns among various servlets, but for simplicity all URLs in the application are delegated to the single court servlet.

Another purpose of the servlet name is for `DispatcherServlet` to decide which file to load for Spring MVC configurations. By default, a look is made for a file by joining the servlet name with `-servlet.xml` as the file name. You can explicitly specify a configuration file in the `contextConfigLocation` servlet parameter. With the preceding setting, the court servlet loads the Spring MVC configuration file `court-servlet.xml` by default. This file should be a standard Spring bean configuration file, as shown following:

```
<beans xmlns="http://www.springframework.org/schema/beans"
    xmlns:xsi="http://www.w3.org/2001/XMLSchema-instance"
    xsi:schemaLocation="http://www.springframework.org/schema/beans
        http://www.springframework.org/schema/beans/spring-beans-3.0.xsd">
    ...
</beans>
```

Later, you can configure Spring MVC with a series of Spring beans declared in this configuration file. You may also declare other application components such as data access objects and service objects in this file. However, it's not a good practice to mix beans of different layers in a single configuration file. Instead, you should declare one bean configuration file per layer (e.g., `court-persistence.xml` for the persistence layer and `court-service.xml` for the service layer). For example, `court-service.xml` should include the following service object:

```
<beans xmlns="http://www.springframework.org/schema/beans"
    xmlns:xsi="http://www.w3.org/2001/XMLSchema-instance"
    xsi:schemaLocation="http://www.springframework.org/schema/beans
        http://www.springframework.org/schema/beans/spring-beans-3.0.xsd">

    <bean id="reservationService"
        class="com.apress.springrecipes.court.service.ReservationServiceImpl" />
</beans>
```

In order for Spring to load your configuration files besides `court-servlet.xml`, you need to define the servlet listener `ContextLoaderListener` in `web.xml`. By default, it loads the bean configuration file `/WEB-INF/applicationContext.xml`, but you can specify your own in the context parameter `contextConfigLocation`. You can specify multiple configuration files by separating their locations with either commas or spaces.

```
<web-app ...>
    <context-param>
        <param-name>contextConfigLocation</param-name>
        <param-value>/WEB-INF/court-service.xml</param-value>
    </context-param>

    <listener>
        <listener-class>
            org.springframework.web.context.ContextLoaderListener
        </listener-class>
    </listener>
    ...
</web-app>
```

Note that `ContextLoaderListener` loads the specified bean configuration files into the root application context, while each `DispatcherServlet` instance loads its configuration file into its own application context and refers to the root application context as its parent. So, the context loaded by each `DispatcherServlet` instance can access and even override beans declared in the root application context (but not vice versa). However, the contexts loaded by the `DispatcherServlet` instances cannot access each other.

Activating Spring MVC annotation scanning

Before you create an application's controllers, you have to set up the web application for classes to be scanned for the presence of `@Controller` and `@RequestMapping` annotations. Only then can they operate as controllers. First, for Spring to auto-detect annotations, you have to enable Spring's component scanning feature through the `<context:component-scan>` element.

In addition to this statement, since Spring MVC's `@RequestMapping` annotation maps URL requests to controller classes and their corresponding handler methods, this requires additional statements in a web application's context. To make this work, you have to register a `DefaultAnnotationHandlerMapping` instance and an `AnnotationMethodHandlerAdapter` instance in the web application context. These instances process the `@RequestMapping` annotations at the class level and the method level, respectively.

To enable support for annotation-based controllers, include the following configuration in the court-servlet.xml file:

```xml
<beans xmlns="http://www.springframework.org/schema/beans"
    xmlns:xsi="http://www.w3.org/2001/XMLSchema-instance"
    xmlns:context="http://www.springframework.org/schema/context"
    xsi:schemaLocation="http://www.springframework.org/schema/beans
        http://www.springframework.org/schema/beans/spring-beans-3.0.xsd
        http://www.springframework.org/schema/context
        http://www.springframework.org/schema/context/spring-context-3.0.xsd">

    <context:component-scan
        base-package="com.apress.springrecipes.court.web" />

    <bean class="org.springframework.web.servlet.mvc.annotation. ↵
        DefaultAnnotationHandlerMapping" />

    <bean class="org.springframework.web.servlet.mvc.annotation. ↵
        AnnotationMethodHandlerAdapter" />

</beans>
```

Notice the element <context:component-scan> with a base-package value of com.apress.springrecipes.court.web. This package corresponds to the same one used in the Spring MVC controller, which is illustrated next.

Next, the DefaultAnnotationHandlerMapping and AnnotationMethodHandlerAdapter bean classes are preregistered in the web application context by default.

Once you have the basic context configuration file for scanning Spring MVC annotations, you can proceed to creating the controller class itself, as well as finishing the configuration set-up for court-servlet.xml.

Creating Spring MVC Controllers

An annotation-based controller class can be an arbitrary class that doesn't implement a particular interface or extend a particular base class. You can annotate it with the @Controller annotation. There can be one or more handler methods defined in a controller to handle single or multiple actions. The signature of the handler methods is flexible enough to accept a range of arguments.

The @RequestMapping annotation can be applied to the class level or the method level. The first mapping strategy is to map a particular URL pattern to a controller class, and then a particular HTTP method to each handler method:

```java
package com.apress.springrecipes.court.web;
...
import org.springframework.stereotype.Controller;
import org.springframework.web.bind.annotation.RequestMapping;
import org.springframework.web.bind.annotation.RequestMethod;
import org.springframework.web.servlet.ModelAndView;
import org.springframework.ui.Model;
```

```
@Controller
@RequestMapping("/welcome")
public class WelcomeController {

    @RequestMapping(method = RequestMethod.GET)
    public String welcome(Model model) {
        Date today = new Date();
        model.addAttribute("today", today);
        return "welcome";
    }
}
```

This controller creates a `java.util.Date` object to retrieve the current date, and then adds it to the input `Model` object as an attribute so the target view can display it.

Since you've already activated annotation scanning on the `com.apress.springrecipes.court.web` package declared inside the `court-servlet.xml` file, the annotations for the controller class are detected upon deployment.

The `@Controller` annotation defines the class as a Spring MVC controller. The `@RequestMapping` annotation is more interesting since it contains properties and can be declared at the class or handler method level. The first value used in this class— `("/welcome")`–is used to specify the URL on which the controller is actionable, meaning any request received on the `/welcome` URL is attended by the `WelcomeController` class.

Once a request is attended by the controller class, it delegates the call to the default HTTP `GET` handler method declared in the controller. The reason for this behavior is that every initial request made on a URL is of the HTTP `GET` kind. So when the controller attends a request on the `/welcome` URL it subsequently delegates to the default HTTP `GET` handler method for processing.

The annotation `@RequestMapping(method = RequestMethod.GET)` is used to decorate the `welcome` method as the controller's default HTTP `GET` handler method. It's worth mentioning that if no default HTTP `GET` handler method is declared, a `ServletException` is thrown. Hence the importance of a Spring MVC controller having at a minimum a URL route and default HTTP `GET` handler method.

Another variation to this approach can be declaring both values—URL route and default HTTP `GET` handler method—in the `@RequestMapping` annotation used at the method level. This declaration is illustrated next:

```
@Controller
public class WelcomeController {

@RequestMapping(value = "/welcome", method=RequestMethod.GET)
public String welcome(Model model) {
….
```

This last declaration is equivalent to the earlier one. The `value` attribute indicates the URL to which the handler method is mapped and the `method` attribute defines the handler method as the controller's default HTTP `GET` method.

This last controller illustrates the basic principles of Spring MVC. However, a typical controller may invoke back-end services for business processing. For example, you can create a controller for querying reservations of a particular court as follows:

```
package com.apress.springrecipes.court.web;
...

import com.apress.springrecipes.court.domain.Reservation;
import com.apress.springrecipes.court.service.ReservationService;

import org.springframework.beans.factory.annotation.Autowired;
import org.springframework.stereotype.Controller;
import org.springframework.web.bind.annotation.RequestMapping;
import org.springframework.web.bind.annotation.RequestMethod;

import org.springframework.web.bind.annotation.RequestParam;

import org.springframework.ui.Model;

@Controller
@RequestMapping("/reservationQuery")
public class ReservationQueryController {

    private ReservationService reservationService;

    @Autowired
    public void ReservationQueryController(ReservationService reservationService) {
        this.reservationService = reservationService;
    }

    @RequestMapping(method = RequestMethod.GET)
    public void setupForm() {
    }

    @RequestMapping(method = RequestMethod.POST)
    public String sumbitForm(@RequestParam("courtName") String courtName,↵
                                        Model model) {
        List<Reservation> reservations = java.util.Collections.emptyList();
        if (courtName != null) {
            reservations = reservationService.query(courtName);
        }
        model.addAttribute("reservations", reservations);
        return "reservationQuery";
    }

}
```

This controller equally relies on the @Controller annotation to indicate the class in question is a Spring MVC controller. A new addition though is the @Autowired annotation assigned to the class's constructor. This allows a class's constructor to instantiate its fields from declarations made in the application's configuration files (i.e., court-service.xml). So for example, in this last controller an attempt is made to locate a bean named reservationService to instantiate the field by the same name.

If you recall from earlier, the court-service.xml file was used to define a service bean by this same name. This allows the service bean to be injected into the controller class and assigned to the field implicitly. Without the `@Autowired` annotation, the service bean can be injected explicitly inside the `court-servlet.xml` configuration using a statement like the following:

```
<bean
    class="com.apress.springrecipes.court.web.ReservationQueryController">
    <property name="reservationService" ref="reservationService" />
</bean>
```

Thus the `@Autowired` annotation saves you time by not having to inject properties using XML. Continuing with the controller class statements, you can find the `@RequestMapping("/reservationQuery")` statement used to indicate that any request on the `/reservationQuery` URL be attended by the controller.

As outlined earlier, the controller then looks for a default HTTP `GET` handler method. Since the public void `setupForm()` method is assigned the necessary `@RequestMapping` annotation for this purpose, it's called next.

Unlike the previous default HTTP `GET` handler method, notice that this method has no input parameters, no logic and also has a `void` return value. This means two things. By having no input parameters and no logic, a view only displays data hard-coded in the implementation template (e.g., JSP), since no data is being added by the controller. By having a `void` return value, a default view name based on the request URL is used, therefore since the requesting URL is `/reservationQuery` a return view named `reservationQuery` is assumed.

The remaining handler method is decorated with the `@RequestMapping(method = RequestMethod.POST)` annotation. At first sight, having two handler methods with only the class level `/reservationQuery` URL statement can be confusing, but it's really simple. One method is invoked when HTTP `GET` requests are made on the `/reservationQuery` URL, the other when HTTP `POST` requests are made on the same URL.

The majority of requests in web applications are of the HTTP `GET` kind, where as requests of the HTTP `POST` kind are generally made when a user submits an HTML form. So revealing more of the application's view (which we will describe shortly), one method is called when the HTML form is initially loaded (i.e., HTTP `GET`), where as the other is called when the HTML form is submitted (i.e., HTTP `POST`).

Looking closer at the HTTP `POST` default handler method, notice the two input parameters. First the `@RequestParam("courtName") String courtName` declaration, used to extract a request parameter named `courtName`. In this case, the HTTP `POST` request comes in the form `/reservationQuery?courtName=<value>`, this declaration makes said value available in the method under the variable named `courtName`. And second the `Model` declaration, used to define an object in which to pass data onto the returning view.

The logic executed by the handler method consists of using the controller's `reservationService` to perform a query using the `courtName` variable. The results obtained from this query are assigned to the `Model` object, that will later become available to the returning view for display.

Finally, note that the method returns a view named `reservationQuery`. This method could have also returned `void`, just like the default HTTP `GET`, and have been assigned to the same `reservationQuery` default view on account of the requesting URL. Both approaches are identical.

Now that you are aware of how Spring MVC controllers are constituted, it's time to explore the views to which a controller's handler methods delegate their results.

Creating JSP Views

Spring MVC supports many types of views for different presentation technologies. These include: JSPs, HTML, PDF, Excel worksheets (XLS), XML, JSON, Atom and RSS feeds, JasperReports and other third party view implementations.

In a Spring MVC application, views are most commonly JSP templates written with JSTL. When the DispatcherServlet—defined in an application's web.xml file—receives a view name returned from a handler, it resolves the *logical* view name into a view implementation for rendering. For example, you can configure the InternalResourceViewResolver bean, in this case inside court-servlet.xml, of a web application's context to resolve view names into JSP files in the /WEB-INF/jsp/ directory:

```
<bean class="org.springframework.web.servlet.view.InternalResourceViewResolver">
    <property name="prefix" value="/WEB-INF/jsp/" />
    <property name="suffix" value=".jsp" />
</bean>
```

By using this last configuration, a *logical* view named reservationQuery is delegated to a view implementation located at /WEB-INF/jsp/**reservationQuery**.jsp . Knowing this you can create the following JSP template for the welcome controller, naming it welcome.jsp and putting it in the /WEB-INF/jsp/ directory:

```
<%@ taglib prefix="fmt" uri="http://java.sun.com/jsp/jstl/fmt" %>

<html>
<head>
<title>Welcome</title>
</head>

<body>
<h2>Welcome to Court Reservation System</h2>
Today is <fmt:formatDate value="${today}" pattern="yyyy-MM-dd" />.
</body>
</html>
```

In this JSP template, you make use of the fmt tag library in JSTL to format the today model attribute into the pattern yyyy-MM-dd. Don't forget to include the fmt tag library definition at the top of this JSP template.

Next, you can create another JSP template for the reservation query controller and name it reservationQuery.jsp to match the view name:

```
<%@ taglib prefix="c" uri="http://java.sun.com/jsp/jstl/core" %>
<%@ taglib prefix="fmt" uri="http://java.sun.com/jsp/jstl/fmt" %>

<html>
<head>
<title>Reservation Query</title>
</head>

<body>
<form method="post">
Court Name
<input type="text" name="courtName" value="${courtName}" />
<input type="submit" value="Query" />
</form>
```

```
<table border="1">
  <tr>
    <th>Court Name</th>
    <th>Date</th>
    <th>Hour</th>
    <th>Player</th>
  </tr>
  <c:forEach items="${reservations}" var="reservation">
  <tr>
    <td>${reservation.courtName}</td>
    <td><fmt:formatDate value="${reservation.date}" pattern="yyyy-MM-dd" /></td>
    <td>${reservation.hour}</td>
    <td>${reservation.player.name}</td>
  </tr>
  </c:forEach>
</table>
</body>
</html>
```

In this JSP template, you include a form for users to input the court name they want to query, and then use the `<c:forEach>` tag to loop the `reservations` model attribute to generate the result table.

Deploying the Web Application

In a web application's development process, we strongly recommend installing a local Java EE application server that comes with a web container for testing and debugging purposes. For the sake of easy configuration and deployment, we have chosen Apache Tomcat 6.0.x as my web container.

The deployment directory for this web container is located under the `webapps` directory. By default, Tomcat listens on port 8080 and deploys applications onto a context by the same name of an application WAR. Therefore, if you package the application in a WAR named `court.war`, the welcome controller and the reservation query controller can be accessed through the following URLs:

```
http://localhost:8080/court/welcome
http://localhost:8080/court/reservationQuery
```

8-2. Mapping requests with @RequestMapping

Problem

When `DispatcherServlet` receives a web request, it attempts to dispatch requests to the various controllers classes that have been declared with the `@Controller` annotation. The dispatching process depends on the various `@RequestMapping` annotations declared in a controller class and its handler methods. You want to define a strategy for mapping requests using the `@RequestMapping` annotation.

Solution

In a Spring MVC application, web requests are mapped to handlers by one or more @RequestMapping annotations declared in controller classes.

Handler mappings match URLs according to their paths relative to the context path (i.e., the web application context's deployed path) and the servlet path (i.e., the path mapped to DispatcherServlet). So for example, in the URL http://localhost:8080/court/welcome the path to match is /welcome, as the context path is /court and there's no servlet path—recall the servlet path declared as / in web.xml.

How It Works

Mapping requests by method

The simplest strategy for using @RequestMapping annotations is to decorate the handler methods directly. For this strategy to work, you have to declare each handler method with the @RequestMapping annotation containing a URL pattern. If a handler's @RequestMapping annotation matches a request's URL, DispatcherServlet it dispatches the request to this handler for it to handle the request.

```
@Controller
public class MemberController {

    private MemberService memberService;

    @Autowired
    public MemberController(MemberService memberService) {
        this.memberService = memberService;
    }

    @RequestMapping("/member/add")
    public String addMember(Model model) {
        model.addAttribute("member", new Member());
        model.addAttribute("guests", memberService.list());
        return "memberList";
    }

    @RequestMapping(value={"/member/remove","/member/delete"},↵
                            method=RequestMethod.GET)
    public String removeMember(
            @RequestParam("memberName") String memberName) {
        memberService.remove(memberName);
        return "redirect:";
    }
}
```

This last listing illustrates how each handler method is mapped to a particular URL using the @RequestMapping annotation. The second handler method illustrates the assignment of multiple URLs, so both /member/remove and /member/delete trigger the execution of the handler method. By default, it's assumed all incoming requests to URLs are of the HTTP GET kind.

Mapping requests by class

The @RequestMapping annotation can also be used to decorate a controller class. This allows handler methods to either forgo the use of @RequestMapping annotations, as illustrated in the ReservationQueryController controller in recipe 8-1, or use finer grained URLs with their own @RequestMapping annotation. For broader URL matching, the @RequestMapping annotation also supports the use wildcards (i.e., *) .

The following listing illustrates the use of URL wildcards in a @RequestMapping annotation, as well as finer grained URL matching on @RequestMapping annotations for handler methods.

```
@Controller
@RequestMapping("/member/*")
public class MemberController {


    private MemberService memberService;

    @Autowired
    public MemberController(MemberService memberService) {
        this.memberService = memberService;
    }

    @RequestMapping("add")
    public String addMember(Model model) {
        model.addAttribute("member", new Member());
        model.addAttribute("guests", memberService.list());
        return "memberList";
    }

    @RequestMapping(value={"remove","delete"}, ↵
                                    method=RequestMethod.GET)
    public String removeMember(
            @RequestParam("memberName") String memberName) {
            memberService.remove(memberName);
            return "redirect:";
    }

    @RequestMapping("display/{user}")
    public String removeMember(
            @RequestParam("memberName") String memberName,
            @PathVariable("user") String user) {
        …..
    }
```

```
@RequestMapping
public void memberList() {
      …..
}

public void memberLogic(String memberName) {
      …..
}
}
```

Note the class level @RequestMapping annotation uses a URL wildcard: /member/* . This in turn delegates all requests under the /member/ URL to the controller's handler methods.

The first two handler methods make use of the @RequestMapping annotation. The addMember() method is invoked when an HTTP GET request is made on the /memeber/add URL. Whereas the removeMember() method is invoked when an HTTP GET request is made on either the /memeber/remove or /memeber/delete URL.

The third handler method uses the special notation {path_variable} to specify its @RequestMapping value. By doing so, a value present in the URL can be passed as input to the handler method. Notice the handler method declares @PathVariable("user") String user. In this manner, if a request is received in the form member/display/jdoe , the handler method has access to the user variable with a jdoe value. This is mainly a facility that allows you to avoid tinkering with a handler's request object and an approach that is especially helpful when you design RESTful web services.

The fourth handler method also uses the @RequestMapping annotation, but in this case lacks a URL value. Since the class level uses the /member/* URL wildcard, this handler method is executed as a catch-all. So any URL request (e.g., /member/abcdefg or /member/randomroute) triggers this method. Note the void return value, that in turn makes the handler method default to a view by its name(i.e., memeberList).

The last method—memberLogic—lacks any @RequestMapping annotations, this means the method is a utility for the class and has no influence on Spring MVC.

Mapping requests by HTTP request type

By default, @RequestMapping annotations assume all incoming requests are of the HTTP GET kind, which is the most common in web applications. However, if an incoming request is of another HTTP type, it's necessary to specify the type explicitly in the @RequestMapping annotation as follows:

```
@RequestMapping(method =  RequestMethod.POST)
public String submitForm(@ModelAttribute("member") Member member,↵
                                BindingResult result, Model model) {
…..
}
```

This last method is treated as the default handler method for any HTTP POST made on a controller class—with the triggering URL being the one specified at the class level @RequestMapping annotation. Of course, it's also possible to use the value attribute to specify an explicit URL for the handler method. This is illustrated next:

```
@RequestMapping(value= "processUser" method =  RequestMethod.POST)
public String submitForm(@ModelAttribute("member") Member member,↵
                                      BindingResult result, Model model) {
...
}
```

The extent to which you require specifying a handler method's HTTP type depends on how and what is interacting with a controller. For the most part, web browsers perform the bulk of their operations using HTTP GET and HTTP POST requests. However, other devices or applications(e.g., RESTful web services) may require support for other HTTP request types.

In all, there are eight different HTTP request types: HEAD, GET, POST, PUT, DELETE, TRACE, OPTIONS and CONNECT. However, support for handling all these request types goes beyond the scope of an MVC controller, since a web server, as well as the requesting party need to support such HTTP request types. Considering the majority of HTTP requests are of the GET or POST kind, you will rarely if ever require implementing support for these additional HTTP request types.

WHERE ARE THE URL EXTENSIONS LIKE .HTML AND .JSP ?

You might have noticed that in all the URLs specified in @RequestMapping annotations, there was no trace of a file extension like .html or .jsp. This is good practice in accordance with MVC design, even though it's not widely adopted.

A controller should not be tied to any type of extension that is indicative of a view technology, like HTML or JSP. This is why controllers return logical views and also why matching URLs should be declared without extensions.

In an age where it's common to have applications serve the same content in different formats, such as XML, JSON, PDF or XLS(Excel). It should be left to a view resolver to inspect the extension provided in a request—if any—and determine which view technology to use.

In this short introduction, you've seen how a resolver is configured in an MVC's configuration file (*-servlet.xml) to map logical views to JSP files, all without every using a URL file extension like .jsp.

In later recipes, you will learn how Spring MVC uses this same non-extension URL approach to serve content using different view technologies.

8-3. Intercepting Requests with Handler Interceptors

Problem

Servlet filters defined by the Servlet API can pre-handle and post-handle every web request before and after it's handled by a servlet. You want to configure something with similar functions as filters in Spring's web application context to take advantage of the container features.

Moreover, sometimes you may want to pre-handle and post-handle web requests that are handled by Spring MVC handlers, and manipulate the model attributes returned by these handlers before they are passed to the views.

Solution

Spring MVC allows you to intercept web requests for pre-handling and post-handling through *handler interceptors*. Handler interceptors are configured in Spring's web application context, so they can make use of any container features and refer to any beans declared in the container. A handler interceptor can be registered for particular URL mappings, so it only intercepts requests mapped to certain URLs.

Each handler interceptor must implement the HandlerInterceptor interface, which contains three callback methods for you to implement: preHandle(), postHandle(), and afterCompletion(). The first and second methods are called before and after a request is handled by a handler. The second method also allows you to get access to the returned ModelAndView object, so you can manipulate the model attributes in it. The last method is called after the completion of all request processing (i.e., after the view has been rendered).

How It Works

Suppose you are going to measure each web request's handling time by each request handler and allow the views to show this time to the user. You can create a custom handler interceptor for this purpose:

```
package com.apress.springrecipes.court.web;
...
import org.springframework.web.servlet.HandlerInterceptor;
import org.springframework.web.servlet.ModelAndView;

public class MeasurementInterceptor implements HandlerInterceptor {

    public boolean preHandle(HttpServletRequest request,
            HttpServletResponse response, Object handler) throws Exception {
        long startTime = System.currentTimeMillis();
        request.setAttribute("startTime", startTime);
        return true;
    }

    public void postHandle(HttpServletRequest request,
            HttpServletResponse response, Object handler,
            ModelAndView modelAndView) throws Exception {
        long startTime = (Long) request.getAttribute("startTime");
        request.removeAttribute("startTime");

        long endTime = System.currentTimeMillis();
        modelAndView.addObject("handlingTime", endTime - startTime);
    }

    public void afterCompletion(HttpServletRequest request,
            HttpServletResponse response, Object handler, Exception ex)
            throws Exception {
    }
}
```

In the preHandle() method of this interceptor, you record the start time and save it to a request attribute. This method should return true, allowing DispatcherServlet to proceed with request handling. Otherwise, DispatcherServlet assumes that this method has already handled the request, so DispatcherServlet returns the response to the user directly. Then, in the postHandle() method, you load the start time from the request attribute and compare it with the current time. You can calculate the total duration and then add this time to the model for passing to the view. Finally, as there is nothing for the afterCompletion() method to do, you can leave its body empty.

When implementing an interface, you must implement all the methods even though you may not have a need for all of them. A better way is to extend the interceptor adapter class instead. This class implements all the interceptor methods by default. You can override only the methods that you need.

```
package com.apress.springrecipes.court.web;
...
import org.springframework.web.servlet.ModelAndView;
import org.springframework.web.servlet.handler.HandlerInterceptorAdapter;

public class MeasurementInterceptor extends HandlerInterceptorAdapter {

    public boolean preHandle(HttpServletRequest request,
            HttpServletResponse response, Object handler) throws Exception {
        ...
    }

    public void postHandle(HttpServletRequest request,
            HttpServletResponse response, Object handler,
            ModelAndView modelAndView) throws Exception {
        ...
    }
}
```

A handler interceptor is registered to the DefaultAnnotationHandlerMapping bean, which is charged with applying interceptors to any class marked with a @Controller annotation. You can specify multiple interceptors in the interceptors property, whose type is an array.

```
<beans ...>
    ...
    <bean id="measurementInterceptor"
        class="com.apress.springrecipes.court.web.MeasurementInterceptor" />

    <bean
        class="org.springframework.web.servlet.mvc.annotation.↵
                DefaultAnnotationHandlerMapping">
        <property name="interceptors">
            <list>
                <ref bean="measurementInterceptor" />
            </list>
        </property>
        ...
    </bean>
</beans>
```

Then you can show this time in welcome.jsp to verify this interceptor's functionality. As WelcomeController doesn't have much to do, you may likely see that the handling time is 0 milliseconds. If this is the case, you may add a sleep statement to this class to see a longer handling time.

```
<%@ taglib prefix="fmt" uri="http://java.sun.com/jsp/jstl/fmt" %>

<html>
<head>
<title>Welcome</title>
</head>

<body>
...
<hr />
Handling time : ${handlingTime} ms
</body>
</html>
```

Using the DefaultAnnotationHandlerMapping bean in this form has one particular drawback, the interceptors is assigned to *every* class defined with a @Controller annotation. If you have a few pair of controllers, you may want to discriminate on which controllers interceptors are applied.

To do so, you need to define a custom handler interceptor. Fortunately, the situation is so common that a project is already available to support this scenario. Scott Murphy's spring-plugins project allows you to apply interceptors on a controller basis by using URLs.

You can download the project at http://code.google.com/p/springplugins/downloads/list. Once you download the project and place its JAR in the application's /WEB-INF/lib directory, you only need to incorporate its configuration alongside the DefaultAnnotationHandlerMapping bean, as illustrated next:

```
<beans ...>
    ...
    <bean id="measurementInterceptor"
        class="com.apress.springrecipes.court.web.MeasurementInterceptor" />

    <bean id="summaryReportInterceptor"
        class="com.apress.springrecipes.court.web.↵
                    ExtensionInterceptor" />

    <bean
        class="org.springframework.web.servlet.mvc.annotation.↵
                    DefaultAnnotationHandlerMapping">
        <property name="order" value="1"/>
        <property name="interceptors">
            <list>
                <ref bean="measurementInterceptor" />
            </list>
        </property>
        ...
    </bean>
```

```
<bean class="org.springplugins.web.↵
                SelectedAnnotationHandlerMapping">
    <property name="order" value="0" />
    <property name="urls">
        <list>
            <value>/reservationSummary*</value>
        </list>
    </property>
    <property name="interceptors">
        <list>
            <ref bean="summaryReportInterceptor" />
        </list>

    </property>

    </bean>
</beans>
```

First there is the addition of the interceptor bean summaryReportInterceptor. The structure of the backing class for this bean is identical to that of the measurementInterceptor. (i.e., it implements the HandlerInterceptor interface). However, this interceptor performs logic that should be restricted to a particular controller.

To allow this, the org.springplugins.web.SelectedAnnotationHandlerMapping bean which forms part of the spring-plugins project is used. In a similar fashion to the DefaultAnnotationHandlerMapping bean, this bean also declares an interceptors property element with a nested list of interceptor beans. But unlike this first bean, the SelectedAnnotationHandlerMapping has a url property element with nested list of URLs on which to apply the list of interceptors.

With these statements, the measurementInterceptor interceptor is applied to all controllers annotated with a @Controller annotation, where as the summaryReportInterceptor interceptor is only applied to those controllers annotated with a @Controller annotation that are mapped to URLs under /reservationSummary*.

One more aspect of these handler interceptor declarations has to do with the order property. Note that the DefaultAnnotationHandlerMapping bean now has a statement in the form <property name="order" value="1"/>. The purpose of the order property is to set a precedence between multiple handler interceptor beans. The lower the value—0 (zero_—the higher the precedence a handler interceptor bean has.

In this case, the SelectedAnnotationHandlerMapping bean has a lower order value—0 (zero)—and will therefore have a higher priority, than the DefaultAnnotationHandlerMapping bean. The process of assigning order values to handler interceptor beans is similar to the load-on-startup property assigned to servlets in web.xml fweb.xml files.

8-4. Resolving User Locales

Problem

In order for your web application to support internationalization, you have to identify each user's preferred locale and display contents according to this locale.

Solution

In a Spring MVC application, a user's locale is identified by a locale resolver, which has to implement the LocaleResolver interface. Spring MVC comes with several LocaleResolver implementations for you to resolve locales by different criteria. Alternatively, you may create your own custom locale resolver by implementing this interface.

You can define a locale resolver by registering a bean of type LocaleResolver in the web application context. You must set the bean name of the locale resolver to localeResolver for DispatcherServlet to auto-detect. Note that you can register only one locale resolver per DispatcherServlet.

How It Works

Resolving Locales by an HTTP Request Header

The default locale resolver used by Spring is AcceptHeaderLocaleResolver. It resolves locales by inspecting the accept-language header of an HTTP request. This header is set by a user's web browser according to the locale setting of the underlying operating system. Note that this locale resolver cannot change a user's locale because it is unable to modify the locale setting of the user's operating system.

Resolving Locales by a Session Attribute

Another option of resolving locales is by SessionLocaleResolver. It resolves locales by inspecting a predefined attribute in a user's session. If the session attribute doesn't exist, this locale resolver determines the default locale from the accept-language HTTP header.

```
<bean id="localeResolver"
    class="org.springframework.web.servlet.i18n.SessionLocaleResolver">
    <property name="defaultLocale" value="en" />
</bean>
```

You can set the defaultLocale property for this resolver in case the session attribute doesn't exist. Note that this locale resolver is able to change a user's locale by altering the session attribute that stores the locale.

Resolving Locales by a Cookie

You can also use CookieLocaleResolver to resolve locales by inspecting a cookie in a user's browser. If the cookie doesn't exist, this locale resolver determines the default locale from the accept-language HTTP header.

```
<bean id="localeResolver"
    class="org.springframework.web.servlet.i18n.CookieLocaleResolver" />
```

The cookie used by this locale resolver can be customized by setting the cookieName and cookieMaxAge properties. The cookieMaxAge property indicates how many seconds this cookie should be persisted. The value -1 indicates that this cookie will be invalid after the browser is closed.

```
<bean id="localeResolver"
    class="org.springframework.web.servlet.i18n.CookieLocaleResolver">
    <property name="cookieName" value="language" />
    <property name="cookieMaxAge" value="3600" />
    <property name="defaultLocale" value="en" />
</bean>
```

You can also set the defaultLocale property for this resolver in case the cookie doesn't exist in a user's browser. This locale resolver is able to change a user's locale by altering the cookie that stores the locale.

Changing a User's Locale

In addition to changing a user's locale by calling LocaleResolver.setLocale() explicitly, you can also apply LocaleChangeInterceptor to your handler mappings. This interceptor detects if a special parameter is present in the current HTTP request. The parameter name can be customized with the paramName property of this interceptor. If such a parameter is present in the current request, this interceptor changes the user's locale according to the parameter value.

```
<beans ...>
    ...
    <bean id="localeChangeInterceptor"
        class="org.springframework.web.servlet.i18n.LocaleChangeInterceptor">
        <property name="paramName" value="language" />
    </bean>

    <bean class="org.springframework.web.servlet.mvc.annotation.↵
        DefaultAnnotationHandlerMapping">
        <property name="interceptors">
            <list>
                ...
                <ref bean="localeChangeInterceptor" />
            </list>
        </property>
        ...
    </bean>
</beans>
```

LocaleChangeInterceptor can only detect the parameter for the handler mappings that enable it. So, if you have more than one handler mapping configured in your web application context, you have to register this interceptor to allow users to change their locales in any of the URLs.

Now a user's locale can be changed by any URLs with the language parameter. For example, the following two URLs change the user's locale to English for the United States, and to German, respectively:

```
http://localhost:8080/court/welcome?language=en_US
http://localhost:8080/court/welcome?language=de
```

Then you can show the HTTP response object's locale in welcome.jsp to verify the locale interceptor's configuration:

```
<%@ taglib prefix="fmt" uri="http://java.sun.com/jsp/jstl/fmt" %>

<html>
<head>
<title>Welcome</title>
</head>

<body>
...
<br />
Locale : ${pageContext.response.locale}
</body>
</html>
```

8-5. Externalizing Locale-Sensitive Text Messages

Problem

When developing an internationalized web application, you have to display your web pages in a user's preferred locale. You don't want to create different versions of the same page for different locales.

Solution

To avoid creating different versions of a page for different locales, you should make your web page independent of the locale by externalizing locale-sensitive text messages. Spring is able to resolve text messages for you by using a message source, which has to implement the `MessageSource` interface. Then your JSP files can use the `<spring:message>` tag, defined in Spring's tag library, to resolve a message given the code.

How It Works

You can define a message source by registering a bean of type `MessageSource` in the web application context. You must set the bean name of the message source to `messageSource` for `DispatcherServlet` to auto-detect. Note that you can register only one message source per `DispatcherServlet`.

The `ResourceBundleMessageSource` implementation resolves messages from different resource bundles for different locales. For example, you can register it in `court-servlet.xml` to load resource bundles whose base name is `messages`:

```
<bean id="messageSource"
    class="org.springframework.context.support.ResourceBundleMessageSource">
    <property name="basename" value="messages" />
</bean>
```

Then you create two resource bundles, `messages.properties` and `messages_de.properties`, to store messages for the default and German locales. These resource bundles should be put in the root of the classpath.

```
welcome.title=Welcome
welcome.message=Welcome to Court Reservation System

welcome.title=Willkommen
welcome.message=Willkommen zum Spielplatz-Reservierungssystem
```

Now, in a JSP file such as welcome.jsp, you can use the `<spring:message>` tag to resolve a message given the code. This tag automatically resolves the message according to a user's current locale. Note that this tag is defined in Spring's tag library, so you have to declare it at the top of your JSP file.

```
<%@ taglib prefix="spring" uri="http://www.springframework.org/tags" %>

<html>
<head>
<title><spring:message code="welcome.title" text="Welcome" /></title>
</head>

<body>
<h2><spring:message code="welcome.message"
        text="Welcome to Court Reservation System" /></h2>
...
</body>
</html>
```

In `<spring:message>`, you can specify the default text to output when a message for the given code cannot be resolved.

8-6. Resolving Views by Names

Problem

After a handler has finished handling a request, it returns a logical view name . In which case the `DispatcherServlet` has to delegate control to a view template so the information is rendered. You want to define a strategy for `DispatcherServlet` to resolve views by their logical names.

Solution

In a Spring MVC application, views are resolved by one or more view resolver beans declared in the web application context. These beans have to implement the `ViewResolver` interface for `DispatcherServlet` to auto-detect them. Spring MVC comes with several `ViewResolver` implementations for you to resolve views using different strategies.

How It Works

Resolving Views Based on a template's name and location

The basic strategy of resolving views is to map them to a template's name and location directly. The view resolver `InternalResourceViewResolver` maps each view name to an application's directory by means of a prefix and a suffix declaration. To register `InternalResourceViewResolver`, you can declare a bean of this type in the web application context.

```
<bean class="org.springframework.web.servlet.view.InternalResourceViewResolver">
    <property name="viewClass"
        value="org.springframework.web.servlet.view.JstlView" />
    <property name="prefix" value="/WEB-INF/jsp/" />
    <property name="suffix" value=".jsp" />
</bean>
```

For example, `InternalResourceViewResolver` resolves the view names `welcome` and `reservationQuery` in the following way:

```
welcome ' /WEB-INF/jsp/welcome.jsp
reservationQuery ' /WEB-INF/jsp/reservationQuery.jsp
```

The type of the resolved views can be specified by the `viewClass` property. By default, `InternalResourceViewResolver` resolves view names into view objects of type `JstlView` if the JSTL library (i.e., `jstl.jar`) is present in the classpath. So, you can omit the `viewClass` property if your views are JSP templates with JSTL tags.

`InternalResourceViewResolver` is simple, but it can only resolve internal resource views that can be forwarded by the Servlet API's `RequestDispatcher` (e.g., an internal JSP file or a servlet). As for other view types supported by Spring MVC, you have to resolve them using other strategies.

Resolving Views from an XML Configuration File

Another strategy for resolving views is to declare them as Spring beans and resolve them by their bean names. You can declare the view beans in the same configuration file as the web application context, but it's better to isolate them in a separate configuration file. By default, `XmlViewResolver` loads view beans from `/WEB-INF/views.xml`, but this location can be overridden through the `location` property.

```
<bean class="org.springframework.web.servlet.view.XmlViewResolver">
    <property name="location">
        <value>/WEB-INF/court-views.xml</value>
    </property>
</bean>
```

In the `court-views.xml` configuration file, you can declare each view as a normal Spring bean by setting the class name and properties. In this way, you can declare any types of views (e.g., `RedirectView` and even custom view types).

```
<beans xmlns="http://www.springframework.org/schema/beans"
    xmlns:xsi="http://www.w3.org/2001/XMLSchema-instance"
    xsi:schemaLocation="http://www.springframework.org/schema/beans
        http://www.springframework.org/schema/beans/spring-beans-3.0.xsd">

    <bean id="welcome"
        class="org.springframework.web.servlet.view.JstlView">
        <property name="url" value="/WEB-INF/jsp/welcome.jsp" />
    </bean>

    <bean id="reservationQuery"
        class="org.springframework.web.servlet.view.JstlView">
        <property name="url" value="/WEB-INF/jsp/reservationQuery.jsp" />
    </bean>

    <bean id="welcomeRedirect"
        class="org.springframework.web.servlet.view.RedirectView">
        <property name="url" value="welcome" />
    </bean>
</beans>
```

Resolving Views from a Resource Bundle

In addition to an XML configuration file, you can declare view beans in a resource bundle.
`ResourceBundleViewResolver` loads view beans from a resource bundle in the classpath root. Note that
`ResourceBundleViewResolver` can also take advantage of the resource bundle capability to load view
beans from different resource bundles for different locales.

```
<bean class="org.springframework.web.servlet.view.ResourceBundleViewResolver">
    <property name="basename" value="views" />
</bean>
```

As you specify `views` as the base name of `ResourceBundleViewResolver`, the default resource bundle
is `views.properties`. In this resource bundle, you can declare view beans in the format of properties.
This type of declaration is equivalent to the XML bean declaration.

```
welcome.(class)=org.springframework.web.servlet.view.JstlView
welcome.url=/WEB-INF/jsp/welcome.jsp

reservationQuery.(class)=org.springframework.web.servlet.view.JstlView
reservationQuery.url=/WEB-INF/jsp/reservationQuery.jsp

welcomeRedirect.(class)=org.springframework.web.servlet.view.RedirectView
welcomeRedirect.url=welcome
```

Resolving Views with Multiple Resolvers

If you have a lot of views in your web application, it is often insufficient to choose only one view-
resolving strategy. Typically, `InternalResourceViewResolver` can resolve most of the internal JSP views,

but there are usually other types of views that have to be resolved by ResourceBundleViewResolver. In this case, you have to combine both strategies for view resolution.

```
<beans ...>
    ...
    <bean class="org.springframework.web.servlet.view.ResourceBundleViewResolver">
        <property name="basename" value="views" />
        <property name="order" value="0" />
    </bean>

    <bean
        class="org.springframework.web.servlet.view.InternalResourceViewResolver">
        <property name="prefix" value="/WEB-INF/jsp/" />
        <property name="suffix" value=".jsp" />
        <property name="order" value="1" />
    </bean>
</beans>
```

When choosing more than one strategy at the same time, it's important to specify the resolving priority. You can set the order properties of the view resolver beans for this purpose. The lower order value represents the higher priority. Note that you should assign the lowest priority to InternalResourceViewResolver because it always resolves a view no matter whether it exists or not. So, other resolvers will have no chance to resolve a view if they have lower priorities.

Now the resource bundle views.properties should only contain the views that can't be resolved by InternalResourceViewResolver (e.g., the redirect views):

```
welcomeRedirect.(class)=org.springframework.web.servlet.view.RedirectView
welcomeRedirect.url=welcome
```

The Redirect Prefix

If you have InternalResourceViewResolver configured in your web application context, it can resolve redirect views by using the redirect prefix in the view name. Then the rest of the view name is treated as the redirect URL. For example, the view name redirect:welcome triggers a redirect to the relative URL welcome. You may also specify an absolute URL in the view name.

8-7. Views and Content Negotiation

Problem

You are relying on extension-less URLs in your controllers—welcome and not welcome.html or welcome.pdf. You want to devise a strategy so the correct content and type is returned for all requests.

Solution

When a request is received for a web application, it contains a series of properties that allow the processing framework, in this case Spring MVC, to determine the correct content and type to return to the requesting party. The main two properties include:

- The URL extension provided in a request

- The HTTP `Accept` header

For example, if a request is made to a URL in the form `/reservationSummary.xml`, a controller is capable of inspecting the extension and delegating it to a logical view representing an XML view.

However, the possibility can arise for a request to be made to a URL in the form `/reservationSummary`. Should this request be delegated to an XML view or an HTML view? Or perhaps some other type of view? It's impossible to tell through the URL. But instead of deciding on a default view for such requests, a request can be inspected for its HTTP Accept header to decide what type of view is more appropriate.

Inspecting HTTP Accept headers in a controller can be a messy process. So Spring MVC supports the inspection of headers through the `ContentNegotiatingViewResolver`

resolver, allowing view delegation to be made based on either a URL file extension or HTTP Accept header value.

How It Works

The first thing you need to realize about Spring MVC content negotiation is that it's configured as a resolver, just like those illustrated in the previous recipe "Resolving Views by Names."

The Spring MVC content negotiating resolver is based on the `ContentNegotiatingViewResolver` class. But before we describe how it works, we will illustrate how to integrate it with other resolvers.

```
<beans ...>
  ...
  <bean id="contentNegotiatingResolver"
            class="org.springframework.web.servlet.view.↵
                        ContentNegotiatingViewResolver">
      <property name="order" ↵
                        value="#{T(org.springframework.core.Ordered).↵
                                        HIGHEST_PRECEDENCE}" />
      <property name="mediaTypes">
          <map>
              <entry key="html" value="text/html"/>
              <entry key="pdf" value="application/pdf"/>
              <entry key="xsl" value="application/vnd.ms-excel"/>
              <entry key="xml" value="application/xml"/>
              <entry key="json" value="application/json"/>
          </map>
      </property>

      ....
  </bean>
```

```xml
<bean id="resourceBundleResolver"
            class="org.springframework.web.servlet.view. ↵
            ResourceBundleViewResolver">
    <property name="order" ↵
                      value="#{contentNegotiatingResolver.order+1}" />
    ….
</bean>

<bean id="secondaryResourceBundleResolver"
        class="org.springframework.web.servlet.view.ResourceBundleViewResolver">
    <property name="basename" value="secondaryviews" />
    <property name="order" ↵
                      value="#{resourceBundleResolver.order+1}" />

</bean>

<bean id="internalResourceResolver">
        class="org.springframework.web.servlet.view. ↵
                    InternalResourceViewResolver">
    <property name="order" ↵
                      value="#{secondaryResourceBundleResolver.order+1}" />
    ….
</bean>

</beans>
```

First of all, the resolver declarations in this last listing have a slight variation from the ones you saw in the earlier recipe. They rely on Spring Expression Language (SpEL) to specify their precedence order. In this case, the ContentNegotiatingViewResolver resolver is given the highest precedence by assigning it an order value based on a SpEL declaration #{T(org.springframework.core.Ordered).HIGHEST_PRECEDENCE}. Subsequent resolver beans use similar SpEL declarations for their order, relying on #{bean_name.order+1)}. This allows you to use a relative order weight for resolvers, instead of hard-coding values.

Turning our attention back to the ContentNegotiatingViewResolver resolver. This configuration sets up the resolver to have the highest priority among all resolvers, which **is necessary to make the content negotiating resolver work**. The reason for this resolver having the highest priority, is that it does not resolve views themselves, but rather delegates them to other view resolvers. Since a resolver that does not resolve views can be confusing, we will elaborate with an example.

Let's assume a controller receives a request for /reservationSummary.xml. Once the handler method finishes, it sends control to a logical view named reservation. At this point Spring MVC resolvers come into play, the first of which is the ContentNegotiatingViewResolver resolver, since it has the highest priority.

The `ContentNegotiatingViewResolver` resolver first determines the media type for a request based on the following criteria:

- It checks a request path extension (e.g., `.html`, `.xml`, or `.pdf`) against the default media types (e.g., `text/html`) specified in the `mediaTypes` section of the `ContentNegotiatingViewResolver` bean.

- If a request path has an extension but no match can be found in the default `mediaTypes` section of the `ContentNegotiatingViewResolver` bean, an attempt is made to determine an extension's media type using `FileTypeMap` belonging to Java Activation Framework.

- If no extension is present in a request path, the HTTP Accept header of the request is used.

For the case of a request made on `/reservationSummary.xml`, the media type is determined in step 1 to be `application/xml`. However, for a request made on a URL like `/reservationSummary`, the media type is not determined until step 3.

The HTTP Accept header contains values like `Accept: text/html` or `Accept:application/pdf`, these values help the resolver determine the media type a requester is expecting, given that no extension is present in the requesting URL.

At this juncture, the `ContentNegotiatingViewResolver` resolver has a media type and logical view named **reservation**. Based on this information, an iteration is performed over the remaining resolvers—based on their order—to determine what view best matches the logical name based on the detected media type.

This process allows you to have multiple logical views with the same name, each supporting a different media type (e.g., HTML, PDF, or XLS), with `ContentNegotiatingViewResolver` resolving which is the best match.

In such cases a controller's design is further simplified, since it won't be necessary to hard-code the logical view necessary to create a certain media type (e.g., `pdfReservation`, `xlsReservation`, or `htmlReservation`), but instead a single view (e.g., `reservation`), letting the `ContentNegotiatingViewResolver` resolver determine the best match.

A series of outcomes for this process can be the following:

- The media type is determined to be `application/pdf`. If the resolver with the highest priority (lower `order`) contains a mapping to a logical view named `reservation`, but such a view does not support the `application/pdf` type, no match occurs—the lookup process continues onto the remaining resolvers.

- The media type is determined to be `application/pdf`. The resolver with the highest priority(lower `order`) containing a mapping to a logical view named `reservation` and having support for `application/pdf` is matched.

- The media type is determined to be `text/html`. There are four resolvers with a logical view named `reservation`, but the views mapped to the two resolvers with highest priority do not support `text/html`. It's the remaining resolver containing a mapping for a view named `reservation` that supports `text/html` that is matched.

This search process for views automatically take place on all the resolvers configured in an application. It's also possible to configure—within the `ContentNegotiatingViewResolver` bean—default views and resolvers, in case you don't want to fall-back on configurations made outside the `ContentNegotiatingViewResolver` resolver.

Recipe 8-13, "Creating Excel and PDF Views," will illustrate a controller that relies on the ContentNegotiatingViewResolver resolver to determine an application's views.

8-8. Mapping Exceptions to Views

Problem

When an unknown exception occurs, your application server usually displays the evil exception stack trace to the user. Your users have nothing to do with this stack trace and complain that your application is not user friendly. Moreover, it's also a potential security risk, as you may expose the internal method call hierarchy to users.

Though a web application's web.xml can be configured to display friendly JSP pages in case an HTTP error or class exception occur. Spring MVC supports a more robust approach to managing views for class exceptions.

Solution

In a Spring MVC application, you can register one or more exception resolver beans in the web application context to resolve uncaught exceptions. These beans have to implement the HandlerExceptionResolver interface for DispatcherServlet to auto-detect them. Spring MVC comes with a simple exception resolver for you to map each category of exceptions to a view.

How It Works

Suppose your reservation service throws the following exception due to a reservation not being available:

```
package com.apress.springrecipes.court.service;
...
public class ReservationNotAvailableException extends RuntimeException {

    private String courtName;
    private Date date;
    private int hour;

    // Constructors and Getters
    ...
}
```

To resolve uncaught exceptions, you can write your custom exception resolver by implementing the HandlerExceptionResolver interface. Usually, you'll want to map different categories of exceptions into different error pages. Spring MVC comes with the exception resolver SimpleMappingExceptionResolver for you to configure the exception mappings in the web application context. For example, you can register the following exception resolver in **court-servlet.xml**:

```
<bean class="org.springframework.web.servlet.handler. ↵
    SimpleMappingExceptionResolver">
    <property name="exceptionMappings">
        <props>
            <prop key="com.apress.springrecipes.court.service. ↵
                ReservationNotAvailableException">
                reservationNotAvailable
            </prop>
        </props>
    </property>
     <property name="defaultErrorView" value="error"/>
</bean>
```

In this exception resolver, you define the logical view name reservationNotAvailable for ReservationNotAvailableException. You can add any number of exception classes using the <prop> element, all the way down to the more general exception class java.lang.Exception. In this manner, depending on the type of class exception, a user is served a view in accordance with the exception.

The last element, <property name="defaultErrorView" value="error"/>, is used to define a default view named error, used in case an exception class not mapped in the exceptionMapping element is raised.

Addressing the corresponding views, if the InternalResourceViewResolver is configured in your web application context, the following reservationNotAvailable.jsp page is shown in case of a reservation not being available:

```
<%@ taglib prefix="fmt" uri="http://java.sun.com/jsp/jstl/fmt" %>

<html>
<head>
<title>Reservation Not Available</title>
</head>

<body>
Your reservation for ${exception.courtName} is not available on
<fmt:formatDate value="${exception.date}" pattern="yyyy-MM-dd" /> at
${exception.hour}:00.
</body>
</html>
```

In an error page, the exception instance can be accessed by the variable ${exception}, so you can show the user more details on this exception.

It's a good practice to define a default error page for any unknown exceptions. You can use <property name="defaultErrorView" value="error"/> to define a default view or map a page to the key java.lang.Exception as the last entry of the mapping, so it will be shown if no other entry has been matched before. Then you can create this view's JSP— error.jsp—as follows:

```
<html>
<head>
<title>Error</title>
</head>

<body>
An error has occurred. Please contact our administrator for details.
</body>
</html>
```

8-9. Assigning values in a Controller with @Value

Problem

When creating a controller, you don't want to hard-code a field value. Instead, you want to assign a value present in a bean or properties file (i.e., `message.properties`)

Solution

The `@Value` annotation allows a controller's field to be assigned using Spring Expression Language(SpEL). You can use the `@Value` annotation along with SpEL to query beans present in an application's context and extract values to help you initialize controller fields.

How It Works

For example, suppose you have a simple controller whose purpose is only to render an about page, such as the following JSP:

```
<html>
<head>
<title>About</title>
</head>

<body>
<h2>Court Reservation System</h2>
<table>
  <tr>
    <td>Version:</td>
    <td>1.0</td>
  </tr>
</table>
</body>
</html>
```

Adding an administrator email for contact purposes is a common practice in about pages. But since an administrator email is likely to be displayed in various pages, this type of information is something that lends itself to being centralized in a location like an application's `message.properties` file. This way, if an administrator's email changes, you just modify one location and changes are propagated to all locations making use of the email. Therefore you can add the following property to an application's `message.properties` file:

```
admin.email=reservation@domain.com
```

Then you can modify the `about.jsp` to show the `email` attribute passed in by a controller as a model attribute:

```html
<html>
<head>
<title>About</title>
</head>

<body>
<h2>Court Reservation System</h2>
<table>
  ...
  <tr>
    <td>Email:</td>
    <td><a href="mailto:${email}">${email}</a></td>
  </tr>
</table>
</body>
</html>
```

After you create the `about.jsp` in an application's `/WEB-INF/jsp/`, you need to create the corresponding controller in order for the `email` attribute to be passed to the view. The following `AboutController` assigns the `email` field from an application's `message.properties` file using the `@Value` annotation:

```java
package com.apress.springrecipes.court.web;
...
import org.springframework.stereotype.Controller;
import org.springframework.ui.Model;
import org.springframework.web.bind.annotation.RequestMapping;
import org.springframework.beans.factory.annotation.Value;

@Controller(
public class AboutController

    @Value("#{ messageSource.getMessage('admin.email',null,'en')}")
    private String email;

    @RequestMapping("/about")
```

```
    public String courtReservation(Model model) {
        model.addAttribute("email", email);
        return "about";
    }
}
```

The value assigned to the @Value annotation is a SpEL statement. SpEL statements are recognizable because they use a notation in the form "#{ SpEL statement }".

In this case, messageSource represents the value of the bean org.springframework.context.support.ResourceBundleMessageSource which is declared in an application's context to access message.properties files. See recipe 8-5, "Externalizing Locale-Sensitive Text Message," for more details on this bean.

Added to the bean reference is getMessage('admin.email',null,'en'). This is a method that belongs to the backing bean class, that when called with these parameters returns the value of the admin.email property. Through the @Value annotation, the value is automatically assigned to the email field.

Next, you can find the controller's only handler method that defines a Model object as its input parameters. Inside the method, the email field0 is assigned to a model attribute named email, so it can later be referenced inside the corresponding view. The about return value represents the name of the logical view, that in this case is resolved to about.jsp.

Finally, on the basis of the handler method's @RequestMapping("/about") annotation, you can access this controller through the following URL:

http://localhost:8080/court/about

8-10. Handling Forms with Controllers

Problem

In a web application, you often have to deal with forms. A form controller has to show a form to a user and also handle the form submission. Form handling can be a complex and variable task.

Solution

When a user interacts with a form, it requires support for two operations from a controller. First when a form is initially requested, it asks the controller to show a form by an HTTP GET request, that renders the form view to the user. Then when the form is submitted, an HTTP POST request is made to handle things like validation and business processing for the data present in the form.
If the form is handled successfully, it renders the success view to the user. Otherwise, it renders the form view again with errors.

How It Works

Suppose you want to allow a user to make a court reservation by filling out a form. To give you a better idea of the data handled by a controller, we will introduce the controller's view (i.e., the form) first.

Creating a form's views

Let's create the form view `reservationForm.jsp`. The form relies on Spring's form tag library, as this simplifies a form's data binding, display of error messages and the re-display of original values entered by the user in case of errors.

```
<%@ taglib prefix="form" uri="http://www.springframework.org/tags/form"%>

<html>
<head>
<title>Reservation Form</title>
<style>
.error {
  color: #ff0000;
  font-weight: bold;
}
</style>
</head>

<body>
<form:form method="post" modelAttribute="reservation">
<form:errors path="*" cssClass="error" />
<table>
  <tr>
    <td>Court Name</td>
    <td><form:input path="courtName" /></td>
    <td><form:errors path="courtName" cssClass="error" /></td>
  </tr>
  <tr>
    <td>Date</td>
    <td><form:input path="date" /></td>
    <td><form:errors path="date" cssClass="error" /></td>
  </tr>
  <tr>
    <td>Hour</td>
    <td><form:input path="hour" /></td>
    <td><form:errors path="hour" cssClass="error" /></td>
  </tr>
  <tr>
    <td colspan="3"><input type="submit" /></td>
  </tr>
</table>
</form:form>
</body>
</html>
```

The Spring `<form:form>` declares two attributes. The `method="post"` attribute used to indicate a form performs an HTTP POST request upon submission. And the `modelAttribute="reservation"` attribute used to indicate the form data is bound to a model named `reservation`. The first attribute should be familiar to you since it's used on most HTML forms. The second attribute will become clearer once we describe the controller that handles the form.

Bear in mind the `<form:form>` tag is rendered into a standard HTML before it's sent to a user, so it's not that the `modelAttribute="reservation"` is of use to a browser, the attribute is used as facility to generate the actual HTML form.

Next, you can find the `<form:errors>` tag, used to define a location in which to place errors in case a form does not meet the rules set forth by a controller. The attribute `path="*"` is used to indicate the display of all errors—given the wildcard *—where as the attribute `cssClass="error"` is used to indicate a CSS formatting class to display the errors.

Next, you can find the form's various `<form:input>` tags accompanied by another set of corresponding `<form:errors>` tags. These tags make use of the attribute `path` to indicate the form's fields, which in this case are `courtName`, `date` and `hour`.

The `<form:input>` tags are bound to properties corresponding to the `modelAttribute` by using the `path` attribute. They show the user the original value of the field, which will either be the bound property value or the value rejected due to a binding error. They must be used inside the `<form:form>` tag, which defines a form that binds to the `modelAttribute` by its name.

Finally, you can find the standard HTML tag `<input type="submit" />` that generates a 'Submit' button and trigger the sending of data to the server, followed by the `</form:form>` tag that closes out the form.

In case the form and its data are processed correctly, you need to create a success view to notify the user of a successful reservation. The `reservationSuccess.jsp` illustrated next serves this purpose.

```
<html>
<head>
<title>Reservation Success</title>
</head>

<body>
Your reservation has been made successfully.
</body>
</html>
```

It's also possible for errors to occur due to invalid values being submitted in a form. For example, if the date is not in a valid format, or an alphabetic character is presented for the hour, the controller is designed to reject such field values. The controller will then generate a list of selective error codes for each error to be returned to the form view, values that are placed inside the `<form:errors>` tag.

For example, for an invalid value input in the `date` field, the following error codes are generated by a controller:

```
typeMismatch.command.date
typeMismatch.date
typeMismatch.java.util.Date
typeMismatch
```

If you have `ResourceBundleMessageSource` defined, you can include the following error messages in your resource bundle for the appropriate locale (e.g., `messages.properties` for the default locale):

```
typeMismatch.date=Invalid date format
typeMismatch.hour=Invalid hour format
```

The corresponding errors codes and their values are what is returned to a user if a failure occurs processing form data.

Now that you know the structure of the views involved with a form, as well as the data handled by it, let's take a look at the logic that handles the submitted data (i.e., the reservation) in a form.

Creating a form's service processing

This is not the controller, but rather the service used by the controller to process the form's data reservation. First define a make() method in the ReservationService interface:

```
package com.apress.springrecipes.court.service;
...
public interface ReservationService {
    ...
    public void make(Reservation reservation)
            throws ReservationNotAvailableException;
}
```

Then you implement this make() method by adding a Reservation item to the list that stores the reservations. You throw a ReservationNotAvailableException in case of a duplicate reservation.

```
package com.apress.springrecipes.court.service;
...
public class ReservationServiceImpl implements ReservationService {
    ...
    public void make(Reservation reservation)
            throws ReservationNotAvailableException {
        for (Reservation made : reservations) {
            if (made.getCourtName().equals(reservation.getCourtName())
                    && made.getDate().equals(reservation.getDate())
                    && made.getHour() == reservation.getHour()) {
                throw new ReservationNotAvailableException(
                        reservation.getCourtName(), reservation.getDate(),
                        reservation.getHour());
            }
        }
        reservations.add(reservation);
    }
}
```

Now that you have a better understanding of the two elements that interact with a controller—a form's views and the reservation service class—let's create a controller to handle the court reservation form.

Creating a form's controller

A controller used to handle forms makes use of practically the same annotations you've already used in the previous recipes. So let's get right to the code.

```
package com.apress.springrecipes.court.web;
...

@Controller
@RequestMapping("/reservationForm")
@SessionAttributes("reservation")
public class ReservationFormController extends SimpleFormController {

    private ReservationService reservationService;

    @Autowired
    public ReservationFormController() {
            this.reservationService = reservationService;
    }

    @RequestMapping(method = RequestMethod.GET)
    public String setupForm(Model model) {
        Reservation reservation = new Reservation();
        model.addAttribute("reservation", reservation);
        return "reservationForm";
    }

    @RequestMapping(method = RequestMethod.POST)
    public String submitForm(
            @ModelAttribute("reservation") Reservation reservation,
            BindingResult result, SessionStatus status) {
                reservationService.make(reservation);
                return "redirect:reservationSuccess";
}
```

The controller starts by using the standard @Controller annotation, as well as the @RequestMapping annotation that allows access to the controller through the following URL:

http://localhost:8080/court/reservationForm

When you enter this URL in your browser, it will send an HTTP GET request to your web application. This in turn triggers the execution of the setupForm method, which is designated to attend this type of request based on its @RequestMapping annotation.

The setupForm method defines a Model object as an input parameter, which serves to send model data to the view (i.e., the form). Inside the handler method, an empty Reservation object is created that is added as an attribute to the controller's Model object. Then the controller returns the execution flow to the reservationForm view, which in this case is resolved to reservationForm.jsp (i.e., the form).

The most important aspect of this last method is the addition of empty Reservation object. If you analyze the form reservationForm.jsp ,you will notice the <form:form> tag declares an attribute modelAttribute="reservation" . This means that upon rendering the view, the form expects an object named reservation to be available, which is achieved by placing it inside the handler method's Model. In fact further inspection, reveals that the path values for each <form:input> tag correspond to the field names belonging to the Reservation object. Since the form is being loaded for the first time, it should be evident that an empty Reservation object is expected.

Another aspect that is vital to describe prior to analyzing the other controller handler method is the `@SessionAttributes("reservation")` annotation—declared at the top of the controller class. Since it's possible for a form to contain errors, it can be an inconvenience to lose whatever valid data was already provided by a user on every subsequent submission. To solve this problem, the `@SessionAttributes` is used to save a `reservation` field to a user's session, so that any future reference to the `reservation` field is in fact made on the same reference, whether a form is submitted twice or more times. This is also the reason why only a single `Reservation` object is created and assigned to the `reservation` field in the entire controller. Once the empty `Reservation` object is created—inside the HTTP GET handler method—all actions are made on the same object, since it's assigned to a user's session.

Now let's turn our attention to submitting the form for the first time. After you have filled in the form fields, submitting the form triggers an HTTP POST request, that in turn invokes the `submitForm` method—on account of this method's `@RequestMapping` value.

The input fields declared for the `submitForm` method are three. The `@ModelAttribute("reservation")` `Reservation reservation` used to reference the `reservation` object. The `BindingResult` object that contains newly submitted data by the user. And the `SessionStatus` object used in case it's necessary to access a user's session.

At this juncture, the handler method doesn't incorporate validation or perform access to a user's session, which is the purpose of the `BindingResult` object and `SessionStatus` object—I will describe and incorporate them shortly.

The only operation performed by the handler method is `reservationService.make(reservation);`. This operation invokes the reservation service using the current state of the `reservation` object. Generally, controller objects are first validated prior to performing this type of operations on them.

Finally, note the handler method returns a view named `redirect:reservationSuccess`. The actual name of the view in this case is `reservationSuccess`, which is resolved to the `reservationSuccess.jsp` page you created earlier.

The `redirect:` prefix in the view name is used to avoid a problem known as *duplicate form submission*.

When you refresh the web page in the form success view, the form you just submitted is resubmitted again. To avoid this problem, you can apply the *post/redirect/get* design pattern, which recommends redirecting to another URL after a form submission is handled successfully, instead of returning an HTML page directly. This is the purpose of prefixing a view name with `redirect:`.

Initializing a model attribute object and pre-populating a form with values

The form is designed to let users make reservations. However, if you analyze the `Reservation` domain class, you will note the form is still missing two fields in order to create a complete reservation object. One of these fields is the `player` field, which corresponds to a `Player` object. Per the `Player` class definition, a `Player` object has both a `name` and `phone` fields.

So can the `player` field be incorporated into a form view and controller? Let's analyze the form view first:

```
<html>
<head>
<title>Reservation Form</title>
</head>
```

```
<body>
<form method="post" modelAttribute="reservation">
<table>
  ...
  <tr>
    <td>Player Name</td>
    <td><form:input path="player.name" /></td>
    <td><form:errors path="player.name" cssClass="error" /></td>
  </tr>
  <tr>
    <td>Player Phone</td>
    <td><form:input path="player.phone" /></td>
    <td><form:errors path="player.phone" cssClass="error" /></td>
  </tr>
  <tr>
    <td colspan="3"><input type="submit" /></td>
  </tr>
</table>
</form>
</body>
</html>
```

Straightforward, you add two additional `<form:input>` tags used to represent the `Player` object's fields. Though these forms declaration are simple, you also need to perform modifications to the controller. Recall that by using `<form:input>` tags, a view expects to have access to model objects passed by the controller, that match the `path` value for `<form:input>` tags.

Though the controller's HTTP `GET` handler method returns an empty reservation `Reservation` to this last view, the `player` property is `null`, so it causes an exception when rendering the form. To solve this problem, you have to initialize an empty `Player` object and assign it to the `Reservation` object returned to the view.

```
@RequestMapping(method = RequestMethod.GET)
public String setupForm(
@RequestParam(required = false, value = "username") String username, Model model) {
    Reservation reservation = new Reservation();
    reservation.setPlayer(new Player(username, null));
    model.addAttribute("reservation", reservation);
    return "reservationForm";
}
```

In this case, after creating the empty `Reservation` object, the `setPlayer` method is used to assign it an empty `Player` object.

Further note that the creation of the `Person` object relies on the `username` value. This particular value is obtained from the `@RequestParam` input value which was also added to the handler method. By doing so, the `Player` object can be created with a specific `username` value passed in as a request parameter, resulting in the `username` form field being pre-populated with this value.

So for example, if a request to the form is made in the following manner:

```
http://localhost:8080/court/reservationForm?username=Roger
```

This allows the handler method to extract the `username` parameter to create the `Player` object, in turn pre-populating the form's `username` form field with a `Roger` value. It's worth noting that the `@RequestParam` annotation for the `username` parameter uses the property `required=false`, this allows a form request to be processed even if such a request parameter is not present.

Providing form Reference Data

When a form controller is requested to render the form view, it may have some types of reference data to provide to the form (e.g., the items to display in an HTML selection). Now suppose you want to allow a user to select the sport type when reserving a court—which is the final unaccounted field for the `Reservation` class.

```
<html>
<head>
<title>Reservation Form</title>
</head>

<body>
<form method="post" modelAttribute="reservation">
<table>
  ...
 <tr>
    <td>Sport Type</td>
    <td>
      <form:select path="sportType" items="${sportTypes}"
        itemValue="id" itemLabel="name" />
    </td>
    <td><form:errors path="sportType" cssClass="error" /></td>
  </tr>
  <tr>
    <td colspan="3"><input type="submit" /></td>
  </tr>
</table>
</form>
</body>
</html>
```

The `<form:select>` tag provides a way to generate a drop-down list of values passed to the view by the controller. Thus the form represents the `sportType` field as a set of HTML `<select>` elements, instead of the previous open-ended fields—`<input>`—that require a user to introduce text values.

Next, let's take a look at how the controller assigns the `sportType` field as a model attribute, the process is a little different than the previous fields.

First let's define the `getAllSportTypes()` method in the `ReservationService` interface for retrieving all available sport types:

```
package com.apress.springrecipes.court.service;
...
public interface ReservationService {
    ...
    public List<SportType> getAllSportTypes();
}
```

Then you can implement this method by returning a hard-coded list:

```
package com.apress.springrecipes.court.service;
...
public class ReservationServiceImpl implements ReservationService {
    ...
    public static final SportType TENNIS = new SportType(1, "Tennis");
    public static final SportType SOCCER = new SportType(2, "Soccer");

    public List<SportType> getAllSportTypes() {
        return Arrays.asList(new SportType[] { TENNIS, SOCCER });
    }
}
```

Now that you have the an implementation that returns a hard-coded list of SportType objects, let's take a look at how the controller associates this list for it to be returned to the form view.

```
package com.apress.springrecipes.court.service;
…..
    @ModelAttribute("sportTypes")
    public List<SportType> populateSportTypes() {
        return reservationService.getAllSportTypes();
    }

    @RequestMapping(method = RequestMethod.GET)
    public String setupForm(
    @RequestParam(required = false, value = "username") String username, ↩
    Model model) {
        Reservation reservation = new Reservation();
        reservation.setPlayer(new Player(username, null));
        model.addAttribute("reservation", reservation);
        return "reservationForm";
    }
```

Notice that the setupForm handler method charged with returning the empty Reservation object to the form view remains unchanged.

The new addition and what is responsible for passing a SportType list as a model attribute to the form view is the method decorated with the @ModelAttribute("sportTypes") annotation.

The @ModelAttribute annotation is used to define global model attributes, available to any returning view used in handler methods. In the same way a handler method declares a Model object as an input parameter and assigns attributes that can be accessed in the returning view.

Since the method decorated with the `@ModelAttribute("sportTypes")` annotation has a return type of `List<SportType>` and makes a call to `reservationService.getAllSportTypes()`, the hard-coded `TENNIS` and `SOCCER` `SportType` objects are assigned to the model attribute named `sportTypes`. With this last model attribute used in the form view to populate a drop down list (i.e.`<form:select>` tag).

Binding Properties of Custom Types

When a form is submitted, a controller binds the form field values to model object's properties of the same name, in this case a `Reservation` object. However, for properties of custom types, a controller is not able to convert them unless you specify the corresponding property editors for them.

For example, the sport type selection field only submits the selected sport type ID—as this is the way HTML `<select>` fields operate. Therefore, you have to convert this ID into a `SportType` object with a property editor. First of all, you require the `getSportType()` method in `ReservationService` to retrieve a `SportType` object by its ID:

```
package com.apress.springrecipes.court.service;
...
public interface ReservationService {
    ...
    public SportType getSportType(int sportTypeId);
}
```

For testing purposes, you can implement this method with a switch/case statement:

```
package com.apress.springrecipes.court.service;
...
public class ReservationServiceImpl implements ReservationService {
    ...
    public SportType getSportType(int sportTypeId) {
        switch (sportTypeId) {
        case 1:
            return TENNIS;
        case 2:
            return SOCCER;
        default:
            return null;
        }
    }
}
```

Then you create the `SportTypeEditor` class to convert a sport type ID into a `SportType` object. This property editor requires `ReservationService` to perform the lookup.

```
package com.apress.springrecipes.court.domain;
...
import java.beans.PropertyEditorSupport;

public class SportTypeEditor extends PropertyEditorSupport {
```

```
    private ReservationService reservationService;

    public SportTypeEditor(ReservationService reservationService) {
        this.reservationService = reservationService;
    }

    public void setAsText(String text) throws IllegalArgumentException {
        int sportTypeId = Integer.parseInt(text);
        SportType sportType = reservationService.getSportType(sportTypeId);
        setValue(sportType);
    }
}
```

Now that you have the supporting SportTypeEditor class required to bind form properties to a custom class like SportType, you need to associate it with the controller. For this purpose, Spring MVC relies on custom classes that implement the WebBindingInitializer class.

By creating a custom class that implements WebBindingInitializer, supporting classes for binding form properties to custom types can be associated with a controller. This includes the SportTypeEditor class and other custom types like Date.

Though we didn't mention the date field earlier, it suffers from the same problem as the sport type selection field. A user introduces date fields as text values. In order for the controller to assign these text values to the Reservation object's date field, this requires the date fields be associated with a Date object,. Given the Date class is part of the Java language, it won't be necessary to create special a class like SportTypeEditor for this purpose, the Spring framework already includes a custom class for this purpose.

Knowing you need to bind both the SportTypeEditor class and a Date class to the underlying controller, the following listing illustrates the ReservationBindingInitializer class that implements WebBindingInitializer.

```
package com.apress.springrecipes.court.web;
...
import org.springframework.beans.factory.annotation.Autowired;
import org.springframework.beans.propertyeditors.CustomDateEditor;
import org.springframework.web.bind.WebDataBinder;
import org.springframework.web.bind.support.WebBindingInitializer;
import org.springframework.web.context.request.WebRequest;

public class ReservationBindingInitializer implements WebBindingInitializer {

    private ReservationService reservationService;

    @Autowired
    public ReservationBindingInitializer(ReservationService reservationService) {
        this.reservationService = reservationService;
    }

    public void initBinder(WebDataBinder binder, WebRequest request) {
        SimpleDateFormat dateFormat = new SimpleDateFormat("yyyy-MM-dd");
        dateFormat.setLenient(false);
        binder.registerCustomEditor(Date.class, new CustomDateEditor(
                dateFormat, true));
```

```
        binder.registerCustomEditor(SportType.class, new SportTypeEditor(
            reservationService));
    }
}
```

The only field for this last class corresponds to `reservationService`, used to access the application's `ReservationService` bean. Note the use of the `@Autowired` annotation that injects the bean through the class's constructor.

Next, you can find the `initBinder` method used to bind the `Date` and `SportTypeEditor` classes. Prior to binding these classes though, a `SimpleDateFormat` object is setup to specify the expected format for the date field, in addition to indicating a strict matching pattern by invoking the `setLenient(false)` method.

You can then find two calls to the `registerCustomEditor` method. This method belongs to the `WebDataBinder` object, which is passed as an input parameter to `initBinder` method.

The first call is used to bind a `Date` class to the `CustomDateEditor` class. The `CustomDateEditor` class is provided by the Spring framework and offers the same functionality as the `SportTypeEditor` class you created, except for `Date` objects. Its input parameters are a `SimpleDateFormat` object indicating the expected date format and a Boolean value to indicate if the value is allowed to be empty, in this case `true`.

The second call is used to bind a `SportType` class to the `SportTypeEditor` class. Since you created the `SportTypeEditor` class, you should be familiar that its only input parameter is a `ReservationService` bean.

Once you complete the `ReservationBindingInitializer` class, you have to register it with the application. To do this, you declare the binding initializer class as an `AnnotationMethodHandlerAdapter` property.

```xml
<bean class="org.springframework.web.servlet.mvc.annotation.↵
    AnnotationMethodHandlerAdapter">
    <property name="webBindingInitializer">
        <bean class="com.apress.springrecipes.court.web.↵
            ReservationBindingInitializer" />
    </property>
</bean>
```

By using this last declaration, every annotation-based controller (i.e., classes using the `@Controller` annotation) can have access to the same property editors in their handler methods.

Validating Form Data

When a form is submitted, it's standard practice to validate the data provided by a user before a submission is successful. Spring MVC supports validation by means of a validator object that implements the `Validator` interface. You can write the following validator to check if the required form fields are filled, and if the reservation hour is valid on holidays and weekdays:

```java
package com.apress.springrecipes.court.domain;
...
import org.springframework.validation.Errors;
import org.springframework.validation.ValidationUtils;
import org.springframework.validation.Validator;
```

```
import org.springframework.stereotype.Component;

@Component
public class ReservationValidator implements Validator {

    public boolean supports(Class clazz) {
        return Reservation.class.isAssignableFrom(clazz);
    }

    public void validate(Object target, Errors errors) {
        ValidationUtils.rejectIfEmptyOrWhitespace(errors, "courtName",
                "required.courtName", "Court name is required.");
        ValidationUtils.rejectIfEmpty(errors, "date",
                "required.date", "Date is required.");
        ValidationUtils.rejectIfEmpty(errors, "hour",
                "required.hour", "Hour is required.");
        ValidationUtils.rejectIfEmptyOrWhitespace(errors, "player.name",
                "required.playerName", "Player name is required.");
        ValidationUtils.rejectIfEmpty(errors, "sportType",
                "required.sportType", "Sport type is required.");

        Reservation reservation = (Reservation) target;
        Date date = reservation.getDate();
        int hour = reservation.getHour();
        if (date != null) {
            Calendar calendar = Calendar.getInstance();
            calendar.setTime(date);
            if (calendar.get(Calendar.DAY_OF_WEEK) == Calendar.SUNDAY) {
                if (hour < 8 || hour > 22) {
                    errors.reject("invalid.holidayHour", "Invalid holiday hour.");
                }
            } else {
                if (hour < 9 || hour > 21) {
                    errors.reject("invalid.weekdayHour", "Invalid weekday hour.");
                }
            }
        }
    }
}
```

In this validator, you use utility methods such as `rejectIfEmptyOrWhitespace()` and `rejectIfEmpty()` in the `ValidationUtils` class to validate the required form fields. If any of these form fields is empty, these methods will create a *field error* and bind it to the field. The second argument of these methods is the property name, while the third and fourth are the error code and default error message.

You also check whether the reservation hour is valid on holidays and weekdays. In case of invalidity, you should use the `reject()` method to create an *object error* to be bound to the reservation object, not to a field.

Since the validator class is annotated with the @Component annotation, Spring attempts to instantiate the class as a bean in accordance with the class name, in this case reservationValidator. In order for this process to work, remember that it's necessary to activate annotation scanning on the package containing such declarations. Therefore the following addition is necessary to the servlet-config.xml file:

```
<context:component-scan base-package="com.apress.↵
                        springrecipes.court.web" />
<context:component-scan base-package="com.apress.↵
springrecipes.court.domain" />
```

An alternative to using the @Component annotation is to manually register the validator class bean using the following notation in the servlet-config.xml file:

```
<bean id="reservationValidator" class="com.apress.↵
springrecipes.court.domain.ReservationValidator" />
```

Since validators may create errors during validation, you should define messages for the error codes for displaying to the user. If you have ResourceBundleMessageSource defined, you can include the following error messages in your resource bundle for the appropriate locale (e.g., messages. properties for the default locale):

```
required.courtName=Court name is required
required.date=Date is required
required.hour=Hour is required
required.playerName=Player name is required
required.sportType=Sport type is required
invalid.holidayHour=Invalid holiday hour
invalid.weekdayHour=Invalid weekday hour
```

To apply this validator, you need to perform the following modification to your controller:

```
package com.apress.springrecipes.court.service;
…..
    private ReservationService reservationService;
    private ReservationValidator reservationValidator;

    @Autowired
    public ReservationFormController(ReservationService reservationService,
            ReservationValidator reservationValidator) {
        this.reservationService = reservationService;
        this.reservationValidator = reservationValidator;
    }

    @RequestMapping(method = RequestMethod.POST)
    public String submitForm(
            @ModelAttribute("reservation") Reservation reservation,
            BindingResult result, SessionStatus status) {
        reservationValidator.validate(reservation, result);
```

```
        if (result.hasErrors()) {
            model.addAttribute("reservation", reservation);
            return "reservationForm";
        } else {
            reservationService.make(reservation);
            return "redirect:reservationSuccess";
        }
}
```

The first addition to the controller is the ReservationValidator field, that gives the controller access to an instance of the validator bean. By relying on the @Autowired annotation, a ReservationValidator bean is injected along with the pre-existing ReservationService bean.

The next modification takes place in the HTTP POST handler method, which is always called when a user submits a form. The initial action of the handler method now consists of calling the validate method belonging to the ReservationValidator bean. For parameters, this last method uses an instance of the Reservation object and the BindingResult object that contains data submitted in a user form.

Once the validate method returns, the result parameter—BindingResult object— contains the results for the validation process. So next, a conditional based on the value of result.hasErrors()is made. If the validation class detects errors this value is true.

In case errors are detected in the validation process, the newly modified Reservation object—as returned by the validator—is added to the method handler's Model object, so it can be displayed in the returning view. A Reservation instance is containing errors messages is returned informing a user what went wrong.

Finally, the method handler returns the view reservationForm , which corresponds to the same form that so a user can re-submit information. In case no errors are detected in the validation process, a call is made to perform the reservation— reservationService.make(reservation);—followed by a redirection to the success view reservationSuccess.

Expiring a controller's Session Data

In order to support the possibility of a form being submitted multiple times and not loose data provided by a user in between submissions, the controller relies on the use of the @SessionAttributes annotation. By doing so, a reference to the reservation field represented as a Reservation object is saved between requests.

However, once a form is submitted successfully and a reservation is made, there is no point in keeping the Reservation object in a user's session. In fact, if a user revisits the form within a short period of time, there is a possibility remnants of this old Reservation object emerge if not removed.

Values assigned using the @SessionAttributes annotation can be removed using the SessionStatus object, an object that can be passed as an input parameter to handler methods. The following listing illustrates how to expire the controller's session data.

```
package com.apress.springrecipes.court.web;
....
@Controller
@RequestMapping("/reservationForm")
@SessionAttributes("reservation")
public class ReservationFormController {
....
    @RequestMapping(method = RequestMethod.POST)
    public String submitForm(
```

```
        @ModelAttribute("reservation") Reservation reservation,
        BindingResult result, SessionStatus status) {
        reservationValidator.validate(reservation, result);

        if (result.hasErrors()) {
            model.addAttribute("reservation", reservation);
            return "reservationForm";
        } else {
        reservationService.make(reservation);
        status.setComplete();
        return "redirect:reservationSuccess";
        }
    }
```

Once the handler method performs the reservation by calling `reservationService.make(reservation);` and right before a user is redirected to a success page, it becomes an ideal time in which expire a controller's session data. This is done by calling the `setComplete()` method on the `SessionStatus` object. It's that simple.

8-11. Handling Multipage Forms with Wizard Form Controllers

Problem

In a web application, you sometimes have to deal with complex forms that span multiple pages. Forms like this are usually called *wizard forms*, as users have to fill them page by page—just like using a software wizard. Undoubtedly, you can create one or more form controllers to handle a wizard form.

Solution

As there are multiple form pages for a wizard form, you have to define multiple page views for a wizard form controller. A controller then manages the form status across all these form pages. In a wizard form, there can also be a single controller handler method for form submissions, just like an individual form. However, in order to distinguish between a user's action, a special request parameter needs to be embedded in each form, usually specified as the name of a submit button:

> `_finish`: Finish the wizard form.

> `_cancel`: Cancel the wizard form.

> `_targetx`: Step to the target page, where x is the zero-based page index.

Using these parameters. a controller's handler method can determine what steps to take based on the form and user's action.

How It Works

Suppose you want to provide a function that allows a user to reserve a court at fixed hours periodically. You first define the `PeriodicReservation` class in the **domain** subpackage:

```
package com.apress.springrecipes.court.domain;
...
public class PeriodicReservation {

    private String courtName;
    private Date fromDate;
    private Date toDate;
    private int period;
    private int hour;
    private Player player;

    // Getters and Setters
    ...
}
```

Then you add a `makePeriodic()` method to the `ReservationService` interface for making a periodic reservation:

```
package com.apress.springrecipes.court.service;
...
public interface ReservationService {
    ...
    public void makePeriodic(PeriodicReservation periodicReservation)
            throws ReservationNotAvailableException;
}
```

The implementation of this method involves generating a series of `Reservation` objects from `PeriodicReservation` and passing each reservation to the `make()` method. Obviously in this simple application, there's no transaction management support.

```
package com.apress.springrecipes.court.service;
...
public class ReservationServiceImpl implements ReservationService {
    ...
    public void makePeriodic(PeriodicReservation periodicReservation)
            throws ReservationNotAvailableException {
        Calendar fromCalendar = Calendar.getInstance();
        fromCalendar.setTime(periodicReservation.getFromDate());

        Calendar toCalendar = Calendar.getInstance();
        toCalendar.setTime(periodicReservation.getToDate());
```

```
        while (fromCalendar.before(toCalendar)) {
            Reservation reservation = new Reservation();
            reservation.setCourtName(periodicReservation.getCourtName());
            reservation.setDate(fromCalendar.getTime());
            reservation.setHour(periodicReservation.getHour());
            reservation.setPlayer(periodicReservation.getPlayer());
            make(reservation);

            fromCalendar.add(Calendar.DATE, periodicReservation.getPeriod());
        }
    }
}
```

Creating Wizard Form Pages

Suppose you want to show users the periodic reservation form split across three different pages. Each page has a portion of the form fields. The first page is reservationCourtForm.jsp, which contains only the court name field for the periodic reservation.

```
<%@ taglib prefix="form" uri="http://www.springframework.org/tags/form"%>

<html>
<head>
<title>Reservation Court Form</title>
<style>
.error {
  color: #ff0000;
  font-weight: bold;
}
</style>
</head>

<body>
<form:form method="post" modelAttribute="reservation">
<table>
  <tr>
    <td>Court Name</td>
    <td><form:input path="courtName" /></td>
    <td><form:errors path="courtName" cssClass="error" /></td>
  </tr>
```

```
    <tr>
      <td colspan="3">
        <input type="hidden" value="0" name="_page" />
        <input type="submit" value="Next" name="_target1" />
        <input type="submit" value="Cancel" name="_cancel" />
      </td>
    </tr>
  </table>
</form:form>
</body>
</html>
```

The form and input fields in this page are defined with Spring's <form:form> and <form:input> tags. They are bound to the model attribute **reservation** and its properties. There's also an error tag for displaying the field error message to the user. Note that there are two submit buttons in this page. The Next button's name must be **_target1**. It asks the wizard form controller to step forward to the second page, whose page index is 1 (zero-based). The Cancel button's name must be **_cancel**. It asks the controller to cancel this form. In addition, there is also a hidden form field to keep track of the page a user is on, in this case it corresponds to 0.

The second page is **reservationTimeForm.jsp**. It contains the date and time fields for a periodic reservation:

```
<%@ taglib prefix="form" uri="http://www.springframework.org/tags/form"%>

<html>
<head>
<title>Reservation Time Form</title>
<style>
.error {
  color: #ff0000;
  font-weight: bold;
}
</style>
</head>

<body>
<form:form method="post" modelAttribute="reservation">
<table>
  <tr>
    <td>From Date</td>
    <td><form:input path="fromDate" /></td>
    <td><form:errors path="fromDate" cssClass="error" /></td>
  </tr>
  <tr>
    <td>To Date</td>
    <td><form:input path="toDate" /></td>
    <td><form:errors path="toDate" cssClass="error" /></td>
  </tr>
```

```
<tr>
  <td>Period</td>
  <td><form:select path="period" items="${periods}" /></td>
  <td><form:errors path="period" cssClass="error" /></td>
</tr>
<tr>
  <td>Hour</td>
  <td><form:input path="hour" /></td>
  <td><form:errors path="hour" cssClass="error" /></td>
</tr>
<tr>
  <td colspan="3">
    <input type="hidden" value="1" name="_page"/>
    <input type="submit" value="Previous" name="_target0" />
    <input type="submit" value="Next" name="_target2" />
    <input type="submit" value="Cancel" name="_cancel" />
  </td>
</tr>
</table>
</form:form>
</body>
</html>
```

There are three submit buttons in this form. The names of the Previous and Next buttons must be _target0 and _target2, respectively. They ask the wizard form controller to step to the first page and the third page. The Cancel button asks the controller to cancel this form. In addition, there is also a hidden form field to keep track of the page a user is on, in this case it corresponds to 1.

The third page is reservationPlayerForm.jsp. It contains the player information fields for a periodic reservation:

```
<%@ taglib prefix="form" uri="http://www.springframework.org/tags/form"%>

<html>
<head>
<title>Reservation Player Form</title>
<style>
.error {
  color: #ff0000;
  font-weight: bold;
}
</style>
</head>

<body>
<form:form method="POST" commandName="reservation">
<table>
  <tr>
    <td>Player Name</td>
    <td><form:input path="player.name" /></td>
    <td><form:errors path="player.name" cssClass="error" /></td>
  </tr>
```

```
<tr>
  <td>Player Phone</td>
  <td><form:input path="player.phone" /></td>
  <td><form:errors path="player.phone" cssClass="error" /></td>
</tr>
<tr>
  <td colspan="3">
    <input type="hidden" value="2" name="_page"/>
    <input type="submit" value="Previous" name="_target1" />
    <input type="submit" value="Finish" name="_finish" />
    <input type="submit" value="Cancel" name="_cancel" />
  </td>
</tr>
</table>
</form:form>
</body>
</html>
```

There are three submit buttons in this form. The Previous button asks the wizard form controller to step back to the second page. The Finish button's name must be _finish. It asks the controller to finish this form. The Cancel button asks the controller to cancel this form. In addition, there is also a hidden form field to keep track of the page a user is on, in this case it corresponds to 2.

Creating a Wizard Form Controller

Now let's create a wizard form controller to handle this periodic reservation form. Like the previous Spring MVC controllers, this controller has two main handler methods—one for HTTP GET requests and another for HTTP POST requests—as well as make use of the same controller elements (e.g., annotations, validation, or sessions) used in prior controllers. For a wizard form controller, all the form fields in different pages are bound to a single model attribute Reservation object, that is stored in a user's session across multiple requests.

```
package com.apress.springrecipes.court.web;
...
@Controller
@RequestMapping("/periodicReservationForm")
@SessionAttributes("reservation")
public class PeriodicReservationController {

    private ReservationService reservationService;

    @Autowired
    public PeriodicReservationController(ReservationService reservationService) {
        this.reservationService = reservationService;
    }
```

```java
    @RequestMapping(method = RequestMethod.GET)
    public String setupForm(Model model) {
        PeriodicReservation reservation = new PeriodicReservation();
        reservation.setPlayer(new Player());
        model.addAttribute("reservation", reservation);
        return "reservationCourtForm"
    }

    @RequestMapping(method = RequestMethod.POST)
    public String submitForm(
            HttpServletRequest request, HttpServletResponse response,
            @ModelAttribute("reservation") PeriodicReservation reservation,
            BindingResult result, SessionStatus status,
            @RequestParam("_page") int currentPage, Model model) {

        Map pageForms = new HashMap();
        pageForms.put(0,"reservationCourtForm");
        pageForms.put(1,"reservationTimeForm");
        pageForms.put(2,"reservationPlayerForm");
        if (request.getParameter("_cancel") != null) {
            // Return to current page view, since user clicked cancel
            return (String)pageForms.get(currentPage);
        } else if (request.getParameter("_finish") != null) {
            // User is finished, make reservation
            reservationService.makePeriodic(reservation);
            return "redirect:reservationSuccess";
        } else {
        // User clicked Next or Previous(_target)

// Extract target page
        int targetPage = WebUtils.getTargetPage(request, "_target", currentPage);
        // If targetPage is lesser than current page, user clicked 'Previous'
        if (targetPage < currentPage) {

                return (String)pageForms.get(targetPage);
            }
        // User clicked 'Next', return target page
        return (String)pageForms.get(targetPage);
        }
      }

    @ModelAttribute("periods")
    public Map<Integer, String> periods() {
        Map<Integer, String> periods = new HashMap<Integer, String>();
        periods.put(1, "Daily");
        periods.put(7, "Weekly");
        return periods;
    }

}
```

This controller uses some of the same elements used in the previous `ReservationFormController` controller, so we won't go into specifics about what's already been explained. But just recapping. It uses the `@SessionAttributes` annotation to place the `reservation` object in a user's session. It uses the `@Autowired` annotation to inject a bean into the controller. And it has the same HTTP `GET` method used to assign an empty `Reservation` and `Player` object upon loading the first form view.

On the other hand, this controller's HTTP `POST` handler method is a little more elaborate, given it processes three distinct forms. We will start by the describing its input parameters.

This handler method declares as input parameters the standard `HttpServletRequest` and `HttpServletResponse` objects, allowing the handler method to access these object's contents. Previous handlers method used parameters like `@RequestParam` to input data that are typically by located in these standard objects, as a shortcut mechanism. In fact, this controller could have forgone using the `HttpServletRequest` and `HttpServletResponse` objects, instead using `@RequestParam`. But it demonstrates that full access to the standard `HttpServletRequest` and `HttpServletResponse` objects inside a handler method is possible. The names and notation for the remaining input parameters should be familiar to you from earlier controllers.

Next, the handler method defines a `HashMap` in which it associates page numbers to view names. This `HashMap` is used various times in the handler method, since the controller needs to determine target views for a variety of scenarios(e.g., validation or a user clicking Cancel or Next)

Then you can find the first conditional that attempts to extract the `_cancel` parameter from the `HttpServletRequest` object. The determination of this parameter could have also been made using an input parameter in the handler method in the following form: `@RequestParam("_cancel") String cancelButton`. If there is a `_cancel` parameter in the request, it means the user clicked the Cancel button on a form. Based on this, the handler method returns control to the view corresponding to the `currentPage`; this last variable is declared as an input parameter in the handler method.

The next conditional attempts to extract the `_finish` parameter from the `HttpServletRequest` object. If there is a `_finish` parameter in the request, it means the user clicked the 'Finish' button. Based on this, the handler method makes the reservation by calling `reservationService.makePeriodic(reservation);` and redirects the user the `reservationSuccess` view.

If the handler method enters the remaining conditional, it means the user clicked on either the Next or Previous button on either of the forms. As a consequence, this means that inside the `HttpServletRequest` object there is a parameter named `_target`. This is because each of the form's Next and Previous buttons are assigned this parameter.

Using the `WebUtils` class, which is included in the Spring framework as a utility, the value for the `_target` parameter is extracted, which corresponds to either `target0`, `target1` or `target2` and be trimmed to `0`, `1` or `2` representing the target page.

Once you have the target page number and the current page number you can determine if the user clicked on the Next or Previous button. If the target page is lower than the current page, this means a user clicked on the Previous button. If the target page number is greater than the current page number, this means the user clicked on the Next button.

At this juncture it isn't clear why you need to determine if a user clicked on the Next or Previous button, especially since a view corresponding to the target page is always returned. But the reason behind this logic is the following. If a user clicked on the Next button you will want to validate the data, where as if a user clicked on the Previous button there is no need to validate anything. This will become obvious in the next section when validation is incorporated into the controller.

Finally, you can find the last method decorated with the `@ModelAttribute("periods")` annotation. As it was illustrated in previous controllers, this declaration allows a list of values to be made available to any returning view place in the controller. If you look at the previous form `reservationTimeForm.jsp`, you can see that it expects to have access to a model attribute named `periods`.

As you have the `PeriodicReservationController` class decorated with the `@RequestMapping("/periodicReservationForm")` annotation, you can access this controller through the following URL:

```
http://localhost:8080/court/periodicReservation
```

Validating Wizard Form Data

In a simple form controller, you validate the entire model attribute object in one shot when the form is submitted. However, as there are multiple form pages for a wizard form controller, you have to validate each page when it's submitted. For this reason, you create the following validator, which splits the `validate()` method into several fine-grained validate methods, each of which validates fields in a particular page:

```
package com.apress.springrecipes.court.domain;

import org.springframework.validation.Errors;
import org.springframework.validation.ValidationUtils;
import org.springframework.validation.Validator;

public class PeriodicReservationValidator implements Validator {

    public boolean supports(Class clazz) {
        return PeriodicReservation.class.isAssignableFrom(clazz);
    }

    public void validate(Object target, Errors errors) {
        validateCourt(target, errors);
        validateTime(target, errors);
        validatePlayer(target, errors);
    }

    public void validateCourt(Object target, Errors errors) {
        ValidationUtils.rejectIfEmptyOrWhitespace(errors, "courtName",
                "required.courtName", "Court name is required.");
    }

    public void validateTime(Object target, Errors errors) {
        ValidationUtils.rejectIfEmpty(errors, "fromDate",
                "required.fromDate", "From date is required.");
        ValidationUtils.rejectIfEmpty(errors, "toDate", "required.toDate",
                "To date is required.");
        ValidationUtils.rejectIfEmpty(errors, "period",
                "required.period", "Period is required.");
        ValidationUtils.rejectIfEmpty(errors, "hour", "required.hour",
                "Hour is required.");
    }
```

```
    public void validatePlayer(Object target, Errors errors) {
        ValidationUtils.rejectIfEmptyOrWhitespace(errors, "player.name",
                "required.playerName", "Player name is required.");
    }
}
```

Similar to the earlier validator example, notice that this validator also relies on the @Component annotation to automatically register the validator class as a bean. Once the validator bean is registered, the only thing left to do is incorporate the validator into the controller. The changes needed to be made to the controller are illustrated next.

```
package com.apress.springrecipes.court.domain;

    private ReservationService reservationService;
    private PeriodicReservationValidator validator;

    @Autowired
    public PeriodicReservationController(ReservationService reservationService, ⏎
PeriodicReservationValidator validator) {
        this.reservationService = reservationService;
        this.validator = validator;
    }

....

    @RequestMapping(method = RequestMethod.POST)
    public String submitForm(
            HttpServletRequest request, HttpServletResponse response,
            @ModelAttribute("reservation") PeriodicReservation reservation,
            BindingResult result, SessionStatus status,
            @RequestParam("_page") int currentPage, Model model) {

        Map pageForms = new HashMap();
        pageForms.put(0,"reservationCourtForm");
        pageForms.put(1,"reservationTimeForm");
        pageForms.put(2,"reservationPlayerForm");
        if (request.getParameter("_cancel") != null) {
            // Return to current page view, since user clicked cancel
            return (String)pageForms.get(currentPage);
        } else if (request.getParameter("_finish") != null) {
            new PeriodicReservationValidator().validate(reservation, result);
            if (!result.hasErrors()) {
                reservationService.makePeriodic(reservation);
                status.setComplete();
                return "redirect:reservationSuccess";
            } else {
                // Errors
                return (String)pageForms.get(currentPage);
            }
```

```
        } else {
         int targetPage = WebUtils.getTargetPage(request, "_target", currentPage);
         // If targetPage is lesser than current page, user clicked 'Previous'
         if (targetPage < currentPage) {

                return (String)pageForms.get(targetPage);
        }
         // User clicked next
         // Validate data based on page
        switch (currentPage) {
                case 0:
                    new PeriodicReservationValidator().↵
                            validateCourt(reservation, result); break;
                case 1:
                    new PeriodicReservationValidator().↵
                            validateTime(reservation, result); break;
                case 2:
                    new PeriodicReservationValidator().↵
                            validatePlayer(reservation, result); break;
        }
        if (!result.hasErrors()) {
            // No errors, return target page
            return (String)pageForms.get(targetPage);
        } else {
            // Errors, return current page
            return (String)pageForms.get(currentPage);
        }
    }
 ....
}
```

The first addition to the controller is the validator field that is assigned an instance of the PeriodicReservationValidator validator bean via the class's constructor. You can then find two references to the validator in the controller.

The first one is when a user finishes submitting a form. In this case, the validator is called with the Reservation object and BindingResult object. If the validator returns no errors, the reservation is committed, a user's session is reset and he is redirected to the reservationSuccess view. If the validator return errors, a user is sent to the current view form in order for him to correct the errors.

The second occasion the validator is used in the controller is when a user clicks the 'Next' button on a form. Since a user is attempting to advance to the next form, it's necessary to validate whatever data a user provided. Given there are three possible form views to validate, a case statement is used to determine what validator method to invoke. Once the execution of a validator method returns, if errors are detected a user is sent to the currentPage view so he can correct the errors, if no errors are detected a user is sent to the targetPage view; note that these target pages numbers are mapped to a HashMap in the controller.

8-12. Bean validation with Annotations (JSR-303)

Problem

You want to validate Java beans in a web application using annotations based on the JSR-303 standard.

Solution

JSR-303 or bean validation is a specification whose objective is to standardize the validation of Java beans through annotations.

In the previous examples, you saw how the Spring framework supports an ad-hoc technique for validating beans. This requires you to extend one of the Spring framework's classes to create a validator class for a particular type of Java bean.

The objective of the JSR-303 standard is to use annotations directly in a Java bean class. This allows validation rules to be specified directly in the code they are intended to validate, instead of creating validation rules in separate classes—just like you did earlier using Spring a framework class.

How It Works

The first thing you need to do is decorate a Java bean with the necessary JSR-303 annotations. The following listing illustrates the **Player** domain class used in the court application decorated with three JSR-303 annotations:

```
package com.apress.springrecipes.court.domain;

import javax.validation.constraints.NotNull;
import javax.validation.constraints.Size;
import javax.validation.constraints.Pattern;

public class Member {

    @NotNull
    @Size(min=2)
    private String name;
    @NotNull
    @Size(min = 9, max = 14)
    private String phone;
    @Pattern(regexp=".+@.+\\.[a-z]+")
    private String email;

    // Getter/Setter methods ommited for brevity
}
```

The name field is assigned two annotations. The @NotNull annotation, which indicates a field cannot be null and the @Size annotation used to indicate a field has to have a minimum of 2 characters. The email field uses a similar approach to the name field, except it declares the @Size annotation with the value (min = 9, max = 14), this indicates that a field needs to have a minimum size of 9 characters and a maximum size of 14 characters.

The email field is declared with the @Pattern annotation. In this case, the @Pattern annotation receives a value in the form regexp=".+@.+\\.[a-z]+", this forces the value assigned to the email field to match this pattern, which is a regular expression for matching emails.

Now that you know how a Java bean class is decorated with annotations belonging to the JSR-303 standard. Let's take a look at how these validator annotations are enforced in a controller.

```
package com.apress.springrecipes.court.web;

import javax.validation.Validator;
import javax.validation.Validation;
import javax.validation.ValidatorFactory;
import javax.validation.ConstraintViolation;

@Controller
@RequestMapping("/member/*")
@SessionAttributes("guests")
public class MemberController {

    private MemberService memberService;
    private static Validator validator;

    @Autowired
    public MemberController(MemberService memberService) {
        this.memberService = memberService;
        ValidatorFactory validatorFactory = ↵
                        Validation.buildDefaultValidatorFactory();
        validator = validatorFactory.getValidator();
    }
...

    @RequestMapping(method = RequestMethod.POST)
    public String submitForm(@ModelAttribute("member") Member member,
                        BindingResult result, Model model) {
        Set<ConstraintViolation<Member>> violations = ↵
                                        validator.validate(member);
        for (ConstraintViolation<Member> violation : violations) {
            String propertyPath = violation.getPropertyPath().toString();
            String message = violation.getMessage();
            // Add JSR-303 errors to BindingResult
            // This allows Spring to display them in view via a FieldError
            result.addError(new FieldError("member",propertyPath, ↵
                            "Invalid "+ propertyPath + "(" + message + ")"));
        }
```

```
        if(!result.hasErrors()) {
            …..
        } else {
            …..
        }

    }
}
```

The first addition to the controller is a field named `validator` of the type `javax.validation.Validator`. However, unlike the earlier Spring specific validation approach, the `validator` field is not assigned to any bean, but rather a factory class of the type `javax.validation.ValidatorFactory`. This is how JSR-303 validation works. The assignment process is done inside the controller's constructor.

Next, you can find the controller's HTTP `POST` handler method used to handle the submission of user data. Since the handler method is expecting an instance of the `Person` object, which you decorated with JSR-303 annotations, you can validate its data.

The first step consists of creating a `Set` of the type `javax.validation.ConstraintViolation` to hold any errors detected from validating the instance of the `Person` object. The value assigned to this `Set` results from executing `validator.validate(member)`, which is used to run the validation process on the `member` field that is an instance of the `Person` object.

Once the validation process is complete, a loop is declared over the violations `Set` to extract any possible validation errors encountered in the `Person` object. Since the violations `Set` contains JSR-303 specific errors, it's necessary to extract the raw error messages and place them in a Spring MVC specific format. This allows validation errors to be displayed in a view managed by Spring as if they are generated by a Spring validator.

■ **Note** To use JSR-303 bean validation in a web application, you must add a dependency to an implementation to your CLASSPATH. If you are using Maven, add the following dependencies to your Maven Project:

```
<dependency>
  <groupId>javax.validation</groupId>
  <artifactId>validation-api</artifactId>
  <version>1.0.0.GA</version>
</dependency>

<dependency>
  <groupId>org.hibernate</groupId>
  <artifactId>hibernate-validator</artifactId>
  <version>4.0.0.GA</version>
</dependency>
```

8-13. Creating Excel and PDF Views

Problem

Although HTML is the most common method of displaying web contents, sometimes your users may wish to export contents from your web application in Excel or PDF format. In Java, there are several libraries that can help generate Excel and PDF files. However, to use these libraries directly in a web application, you have to generate the files behind the scenes and return them to users as binary attachments. You have to deal with HTTP response headers and output streams for this purpose.

Solution

Spring integrates the generation of Excel and PDF files into its MVC framework. You can consider Excel and PDF files as special kinds of views, so you can consistently handle a web request in a controller and add data to a model for passing to Excel and PDF views. In this way, you have no need to deal with HTTP response headers and output streams.

Spring MVC supports generating Excel files using either the Apache POI library (http://poi.apache.org/) or the JExcelAPI library (http://jexcelapi.sourceforge.net/). The corresponding view classes are `AbstractExcelView` and `AbstractJExcelView`. PDF files are generated by the iText library (http://www.lowagie.com/iText/), and the corresponding view class is `AbstractPdfView`.

How It Works

Suppose your users wish to generate a report of the reservation summary for a particular day. They want this report to be generated in either, Excel, PDF or the basic HTML format. For this report generation function, you need to declare a method in the service layer that returns all the reservations of a specified day:

```
package com.apress.springrecipes.court.service;
...
public interface ReservationService {
    ...
    public List<Reservation> findByDate(Date date);
}
```

Then you provide a simple implementation for this method by iterating over all the made reservations:

```
package com.apress.springrecipes.court.service;
...
public class ReservationServiceImpl implements ReservationService {
    ...
    public List<Reservation> findByDate(Date date) {
        List<Reservation> result = new ArrayList<Reservation>();
        for (Reservation reservation : reservations) {
```

```
            if (reservation.getDate().equals(date)) {
                result.add(reservation);
            }
        }
        return result;
    }
}
```

Now you can write a simple controller to get the date parameters from the URL. The date parameter is formatted into a date object and passed to the service layer for querying reservations. The controller relies on the content negotiation resolver described in recipe 8-7 "Views and Content Negotiation," therefore the controller returns a single logic view and lets the resolver determine if a report should be generated in Excel, PDF or a default HTML web page.

```
package com.apress.springrecipes.court.web;
...
@Controller
@RequestMapping("/reservationSummary*")
public class ReservationSummaryController {
    private ReservationService reservationService;

    @Autowired
    public ReservationSummaryController(ReservationService reservationService) {
        this.reservationService = reservationService;
    }

    @RequestMapping(method = RequestMethod.GET)
        public String generateSummary(
            @RequestParam(required = true, value = "date") String selectedDate,
            Model model) {
        List<Reservation> reservations = java.util.Collections.emptyList();
        try {
            Date summaryDate = ↩
                new SimpleDateFormat("yyyy-MM-dd").parse(selectedDate);
            reservations = reservationService.findByDate(summaryDate);
        } catch (java.text.ParseException ex) {
            StringWriter sw = new StringWriter();
            PrintWriter pw = new PrintWriter(sw);
            ex.printStackTrace(pw);
            throw new ReservationWebException("Invalid date format for reservation
summary",new Date(),sw.toString());
        }
        model.addAttribute("reservations",reservations);
        return "reservationSummary";
    }

}
```

This controller only contains a default HTTP GET handler method. The first action performed by this method is creating an empty Reservation list to place the results obtained from the reservation service. Next, you can find a try/catch block that attempts to create a Date object from the selectedDate @RequestParam, as well as invoke the reservation service with the created Date object. If creating the a Date object fails, a custom Spring exception named ReservationWebException is thrown.

If no errors are raised in the try/catch block, the Reservation list is placed into the controller's Model object. Once this is done, the method returns control to reservationSummary view.

Note that the controller returns a single view, even though it supports PDF, XLS and HTML views. This is possible due to the ContentNegotiatingViewResolver resolver, that determines on the basis of this single view name which of these multiple views to use. See recipe 8-7, "Views and Content Negotiation," for more information on this resolver.

Creating Excel Views

An Excel view can be created by extending the AbstractExcelView class (for Apache POI) or the AbstractJExcelView class (for JExcelAPI). Here, AbstractExcelView is used as an example. In the buildExcelDocument() method, you can access the model passed from the controller and also a precreated Excel workbook. Your task is to populate the workbook with the data in the model.

■ **Note** To generate Excel files with Apache POI in a web application, you must have the Apache POI dependencies on your CLASSPATH. If you are using Apache Maven, add the following dependencies to your Maven Project:

```
<dependency>
  <groupId>org.apache.poi</groupId>
  <artifactId>poi</artifactId>
  <version>3.0.2-FINAL</version>
</dependency>
```

```
package com.apress.springrecipes.court.web.view;
...
import org.apache.poi.hssf.usermodel.HSSFRow;
import org.apache.poi.hssf.usermodel.HSSFSheet;
import org.apache.poi.hssf.usermodel.HSSFWorkbook;

import org.springframework.web.servlet.view.document.AbstractExcelView;

public class ExcelReservationSummary extends AbstractExcelView {

    protected void buildExcelDocument(Map model, HSSFWorkbook workbook,
            HttpServletRequest request, HttpServletResponse response)
            throws Exception {
```

```
        List<Reservation> reservations = (List) model.get("reservations");
        DateFormat dateFormat = new SimpleDateFormat("yyyy-MM-dd");
        HSSFSheet sheet = workbook.createSheet();

        HSSFRow header = sheet.createRow(0);
        header.createCell((short) 0).setCellValue("Court Name");
        header.createCell((short) 1).setCellValue("Date");
        header.createCell((short) 2).setCellValue("Hour");
        header.createCell((short) 3).setCellValue("Player Name");
        header.createCell((short) 4).setCellValue("Player Phone");

        int rowNum = 1;
        for (Reservation reservation : reservations) {
            HSSFRow row = sheet.createRow(rowNum++);
            row.createCell((short) 0).setCellValue(reservation.getCourtName());
            row.createCell((short) 1).setCellValue(
                    dateFormat.format(reservation.getDate()));
            row.createCell((short) 2).setCellValue(reservation.getHour());
            row.createCell((short) 3).setCellValue(
                    reservation.getPlayer().getName());
            row.createCell((short) 4).setCellValue(
                    reservation.getPlayer().getPhone());
        }
    }
}
```

In the preceding Excel view, you first create a sheet in the workbook. In this sheet, you show the headers of this report in the first row. Then you iterate over the reservation list to create a row for each reservation.

As you have @RequestMapping("/reservationSummary*") configured in your controller and the handler method requires date as a request parameter. You can access this Excel view through the following URL. .

```
http://localhost:8080/court/reservationSummary.xls?date=2009-01-14
```

Creating PDF Views

A PDF view is created by extending the AbstractPdfView class. In the buildPdfDocument() method, you can access the model passed from the controller and also a precreated PDF document. Your task is to populate the document with the data in the model.

▓ **Note** To generate PDF files with iText in a web application, you must have the iText library on your CLASSPATH. If you are using Apache Maven, add the following dependency to your Maven Project:

```
<dependency>
  <groupId>com.lowagie</groupId>
  <artifactId>itext</artifactId>
  <version>2.0.8</version>
</dependency>
```

```java
package com.apress.springrecipes.court.web.view;
...
import org.springframework.web.servlet.view.document.AbstractPdfView;

import com.lowagie.text.Document;
import com.lowagie.text.Table;
import com.lowagie.text.pdf.PdfWriter;

public class PdfReservationSummary extends AbstractPdfView {

    protected void buildPdfDocument(Map model, Document document,
            PdfWriter writer, HttpServletRequest request,
            HttpServletResponse response) throws Exception {
        List<Reservation> reservations = (List) model.get("reservations");
        DateFormat dateFormat = new SimpleDateFormat("yyyy-MM-dd");
        Table table = new Table(5);

        table.addCell("Court Name");
        table.addCell("Date");
        table.addCell("Hour");
        table.addCell("Player Name");
        table.addCell("Player Phone");

        for (Reservation reservation : reservations) {
            table.addCell(reservation.getCourtName());
            table.addCell(dateFormat.format(reservation.getDate()));
            table.addCell(Integer.toString(reservation.getHour()));
            table.addCell(reservation.getPlayer().getName());
            table.addCell(reservation.getPlayer().getPhone());
        }

        document.add(table);
    }
}
```

As you have @RequestMapping("/reservationSummary*") configured in your controller and the handler method requires date as a request parameter. You can access this PDF view through the following URL. .

```
http://localhost:8080/court/reservationSummary.pdf?date=2009-01-14
```

Creating resolvers for Excel and PDF views

In recipe 8-6, "Resolving Views by Names," you learned different strategies for resolving logical view names to specific view implementations. One of these strategies was resolving views from a resource bundle, this is the better suited strategy for mapping logical view names to view implementations consisting of PDF or XLS classes.

Ensuring you have the ResourceBundleViewResolver bean configured in your web application context as a view resolver, you can then define views in the views.properties file included in a web application's classpath root

You can add the following entry to the views.properties in order to map the XLS view class to a logical view name:

```
reservationSummary.(class)=↵
com.apress.springrecipes.court.web.view.ExcelReservationSummary
```

Since the application relies on the process of content negotiation, this implies that the same view name is mapped to multiple view technologies. In addition, since it's not possible to have duplicate names in the same views.properties file, you need to create a separate file named secondaryviews.properties to map the PDF view class to a logical view name, as illustrated next:

```
reservationSummary.(class)=com.apress.springrecipes.court.web.view.PdfReservationSummary
```

Take note that this file—secondaryviews.properties—needs to be configured in its own ResourceBundleViewResolver resolver.

The property name—reservationSummary—corresponds to the views name returned by the controller. It's the task of the ContentNegotiatingViewResolver resolver to determine which of these classes to use based on a user's request. Once this is determined, the execution of the corresponding class generates either a PDF or XLS file.

Creating date based PDF and XLS file names

When a user makes a request for a PDF or XLS file using any of the following URLs:

```
http://localhost:8080/court/reservationSummary.pdf?date=2009-01-14
http://localhost:8080/court/reservationSummary.xls?date=2009-02-24
```

The browser prompts a user with a question like "Save as reservationSummary.pdf?" or "Save as reservationSummary.xls?". This convention is based on the URL a user is requesting a resource. However, given that a user is also providing a date in the URL, a nice feature can be an automatic prompt in the form "Save as ReservationSummary_2009_01_24.xls?" or "Save as ReservationSummary_2009_02_24.xls?". This can be done by applying an interceptor to rewrite the returning URL. The following listing illustrates this interceptor:

```
package com.apress.springrecipes.court.web
...

public class ExtensionInterceptor extends HandlerInterceptorAdapter {

    public void postHandle(HttpServletRequest request,
            HttpServletResponse response, Object handler,
                        ModelAndView modelAndView) throws Exception {
        // Report date is present in request
        String reportName = null;
        String reportDate = request.getQueryString().↵
                                        replace("date=","").replace("-","_");
        if(request.getServletPath().endsWith(".pdf")) {
            reportName= "ReservationSummary_" + reportDate + ".pdf";
        }
        if(request.getServletPath().endsWith(".xls")) {
            reportName= "ReservationSummary_" + reportDate + ".xls";
        }
        if (reportName != null) {
            // Set "Content-Disposition" HTTP Header
            // so a user gets a pretty 'Save as' address
            response.setHeader("Content-Disposition",↵
                                "attachment; filename="+reportName);
        }
    }
}
```

The interceptor extracts the entire URL if it contains a .pdf or .xls extension. If it detects such an extension, it creates a value for the return file name in the form ReservationSummary_<report_date>.<.pdf|.xls>. To ensure a user receives a download prompt in this form, the HTTP header Content-Disposition is set with this file name format.

In order to deploy this interceptor and that it only be applied to the URL corresponding to the controller charged with generating PDF and XLS files, we advise you to look over recipe 8-3, "Intercepting Requests with Handler Interceptors," which contains this particular configuration and more details about interceptor classes.

CONTENT NEGOTIATION AND SETTING HTTP HEADERS IN AN INTERCEPTOR

Though this application uses the ContentNegotiatingViewResolver resolver to select an appropriate view, the process of modifying a return URL is outside the scope of resolvers.

Therefore, it's necessary to use an interceptor to manually inspect a request extension, as well as set the necessary HTTP headers to modify the outgoing URL.

Summary

In this chapter, you have learned how to develop a Java web application using the Spring MVC framework. The central component of Spring MVC is `DispatcherServlet`, which acts as a front controller that dispatches requests to appropriate handlers for them to handle requests.

In Spring MVC, controllers are standard Java classes that are decorated with the `@Controller` annotation. Throughout the various recipes, you learned how to leverage other annotations used in Spring MVC controllers, which included: `@RequestMapping` to indicate access URLs, `@Autowired` to automatically inject bean references and `@SessionAttributes` to maintain objects in a user's session, among many others.

You also learned how to incorporate interceptors into an application, which allow you to alter request and response objects in a controller. In addition, you explored how Spring MVC supports form processing, including data validation using both Spring validators and the JSR-303 bean validation standard.

You also explored how Spring MVC incorporates SpEL to facilitate certain configuration tasks and how Spring MVC supports different types of views for different presentation technologies. Finally, you also learned how Spring supports content negotiation in order to determine a view based on a request's extensions or HTTP headers.

CHAPTER 9

■■■

Spring REST

In this chapter, you will learn how Spring addresses Representational State Transfer, usually referred to by its acronym REST. REST has had an important impact on web applications since the term was coined by Roy Fielding (http://en.wikipedia.org/wiki/Roy_Fielding) in the year 2000.

Based on the foundations of the web's protocol Hypertext Transfer Protocol (HTTP), the architecture set forth by REST has become increasingly popular in the implementation of web services.

Web services in and of themselves have become the cornerstone for much machine-to-machine communication taking place on the Web. It's the fragmented technology choices (e.g., Java, Python, Ruby, .NET) made by many organizations that have necessitated a solution capable of bridging the gaps between these disparate environments. How is information in an application backed by Java accessed by one written in Python? How can a Java application obtain information from an application written in .NET? Web services fill this void.

There are various approaches to implementing web services, but RESTful web services have become the most common choice in web applications. They are used by some of the largest Internet portals (e.g., Google and Yahoo) to provide access to their information, used to back access to Ajax calls made by browsers, in addition to providing the foundations for the distribution of information like news feeds (e.g., RSS).

In this chapter, you will learn how Spring applications can use REST, so you can both access and provide information using this popular approach.

9-1. Publishing a REST Service with Spring

Problem

You want to publish a REST service with Spring.

Solution

There are two possibilities when designing REST services in Spring. One involves *publishing* an application's data as a REST service, the other one involves *accessing* data from third-party REST services to be used in an application. This recipe describes how to publish an application's data as a REST service. Recipe 9-2 describes how to access data from third-party REST services.

Publishing an application's data as a REST service revolves around the use of the Spring MVC annotations @RequestMapping and @PathVariable. By using these annotations to decorate a Spring MVC handler method, a Spring application is capable of publishing an application's data as a REST service.

In addition, Spring supports a series of mechanisms to generate a REST service's payload. This recipe will explore the simplest mechanism, which involves the use of Spring's MarshallingView class. As the recipes in this chapter progress, you will learn about more advanced mechanisms supported by Spring to generate REST service payloads.

How It Works

Publishing a web application's data as a REST service, or as it's more technically known in web services parlance "creating an end point," is strongly tied to Spring MVC, which you explored in Chapter 8.

Since Spring MVC relies on the annotation @RequestMapping to decorate handler methods and define access points (i.e., URLs), it's the preferred way in which to define a REST service's end point. The following listing illustrates a Spring MVC controller class with a handler method that defines a REST service end point:

```
package com.apress.springrecipes.court.web;

import org.springframework.stereotype.Controller;
import org.springframework.ui.Model;
import org.springframework.web.bind.annotation.RequestMapping;

import com.apress.springrecipes.court.domain.Member;

@Controller
public class RestMemberController {

    @RequestMapping("/members")
     public String getRestMembers(Model model) {
         // Return view membertemplate. Via resolver the view
         // will be mapped to a JAXB Marshler bound to the Member class
         Member member = new Member();
         member.setName("John Doe");
         member.setPhone("1-800-800-800");
         member.setEmail("john@doe.com");
         model.addAttribute("member", member);
         return "membertemplate";
     }
}
```

By using @RequestMapping("/members") to decorate a controller's handler method, a REST service end point is made accessible at http://[host_name]/[app-name]/members. Before elaborating on the body of this last handler method, it's worth mentioning other variations you can use for declaring REST service end points.

It's also common for REST service requests to have parameters. This is done to limit or filter a service's payload. For example, a request in the form http://[host_name]/[app-name]/member/353/ can be used to retrieve information exclusively on member 353. Another variation can be a request like http://[host_name]/[app-name]/reservations/07-07-2010/ to retrieve reservations made on the date 07-07-2010.

In order to use parameters for constructing a REST service in Spring, you use the `@PathVariable` annotation. The `@PathVariable` annotation is added as an input parameter to the handler method, per Spring's MVC conventions, in order for it to be used inside the handler method body. The following snippet illustrates a handler method for a REST service using the `@PathVariable` annotation.

```
Import org.springframework.web.bind.annotation.PathVariable;

@RequestMapping("/member/{memberid}")
    public void getMember(@PathVariable("memberid") long memberID) {
}
```

Notice the `@RequestMapping` value contains {memberid}. Values surrounded by { } are used to indicate URL parameters are variables. Further note the handler method is defined with the input parameter `@PathVariable("memberid") long memberID`. This last declaration associates whatever memberid value forms part of the URL and assigns it to a variable named memberID that can be accessible inside the handler method.

Therefore, REST end points in the form /member/353/ and /member/777/ will be processed by this last handler method, with the memberID variable being assigned values of 353 and 777, respectively. Inside the handler method, the appropriate queries can be made for members 353 and 777—via the memberID variable—and returned as the REST service's payload. Even though void is the return value for the method, the REST service's payload is not void. Recall that per Spring MVC conventions, a method returning void is still mapped to a template that returns a payload.

In addition to supporting the { } notation, it's also possible to use a wildcard * notation for defining REST end points. This is often the case when a design team has opted to use expressive URLs (often called *pretty URLs*) or opts to use search engine optimization (SEO) techniques to make a REST URL search engine friendly. The following snippet illustrates a declaration for a REST service using the wildcard notation.

```
@RequestMapping("/member/*/{memberid}")
    public void getMember(@PathVariable("memberid") long memberID) {
}
```

In this case, the addition of a wildcard doesn't have any influence over the logic performed by the REST service. But it will match end point requests in the form /member/John+Smith/353/ and /member/Mary+Jones/353/, which can have an important impact on end user readability or SEO.

It's also worth mentioning that data binding can be used in the definition of handler methods for REST end points. The following snippet illustrates a declaration for a REST service using data binding:

```
@InitBinder
public void initBinder(WebDataBinder binder) {
    SimpleDateFormat dateFormat = new SimpleDateFormat("yyyy-MM-dd");
    binder.registerCustomEditor(Date.class, new CustomDateEditor(dateFormat, false));
}
@RequestMapping("/reservations/{date}")
    public void getReservation(@PathVariable("date") Date resDate) {
}
```

In this case, a request in the form http://[host_name]/[app-name]/reservations/07-07-2010/ is matched by this last handler method, with the value 07-07-2010 passed into the handler method—as the variable resDate– where it can be used to filter the REST web service payload.

Turning your attention back to the handler method decorated with the @RequestMapping("/members") annotation and its body, note that the handler method creates a Member object that is then assigned to the method's Model object. By associating data with a handler method's Model object, it becomes accessible to the view associated with the handler method—per Spring MVC conventions.

In this case, this single Member object is hard-coded to be the REST service's payload. More sophisticated REST service's can include querying a RDBMS or accessing class methods.

All handler methods in Spring MVC end up being delegated to logical views, which are used to render content passed in by handler methods, and that content is finally dispatched to requesting users.

In the case of RESTful services, the payload expected by requesting users is generally that of XML. Therefore, Spring MVC handler methods designed to attend REST end points are delegated to view technologies that generate XML-type payloads.

In the case of the handler method decorated with @RequestMapping("/members"), you can observe that control is relinquished to a logical view named membertemplate. Logical views, per Spring MVC conventions, are defined inside a Spring application's *-servlet.xml files. The following listing illustrates the declaration used to define the logical view named membertemplate:

```
<bean id="membertemplate" class="org.springframework.web.servlet.view.xml.MarshallingView">
    <constructor-arg>
        <bean class="org.springframework.oxm.jaxb.Jaxb2Marshaller">
            <property name="classesToBeBound">
                <list>
                    <value>com.apress.springrecipes.court.domain.Member</value>
                </list>
            </property>
        </bean>
    </constructor-arg>
</bean>
```

The membertemplate view is defined as a MarshallingView type, which is a general-purpose class that allows a response to be rendered using a marshaller. Marshalling is the process of transforming an in-memory representation of an object into a data format. Therefore, for this particular case, a marshaller is charged with transforming a Member object into an XML data format.

The marshaller used by MarshallingView belongs to one of a series of XML marshallers provided by Spring—Jaxb2Marshaller. Other marshallers provided by Spring include CastorMarshaller, JibxMarshaller, XmlBeansMarshaller, and XStreamMarshaller.

Marshallers themselves also require configuration. We opted to use the Jaxb2Marshaller marshaller due to its simplicity and Java Architecture for XML Binding (JAXB) foundations. However, if you're more comfortable using the Castor XML framework, you might find it easier to use the CastorMarshaller, and you would likely find it easier to use the XStreamMarshaller if your more at ease using XStream, with the same case applying for the rest of the available marshallers.

The Jaxb2Marshaller marshaller requires to be configured with either a property named classesToBeBound or contextPath. In the case of classesToBeBound, the classes assigned to this property, indicate the class (i.e., object) structure that is to be transformed into XML. The following listing illustrates the Member class assigned to the Jaxb2Marshaller:

```
package com.apress.springrecipes.court.domain;

import javax.xml.bind.annotation.XmlRootElement;

@XmlRootElement
public class Member {
    private String name;
    private String phone;
    private String email;

    public String getEmail() {
        return email;
    }

    public String getName() {
        return name;
    }

    public String getPhone() {
        return phone;
    }

    public void setEmail(String email) {
        this.email = email;
    }

    public void setName(String name) {
        this.name = name;
    }

    public void setPhone(String phone) {
        this.phone = phone;
    }
}
```

Note the Member class is a POJO decorated with the @XmlRootElement annotation. This annotation allows the Jaxb2Marshaller marshaller to detect a class's (i.e., object's) fields and transform them into XML data (e.g., name=John into <name>john</name>, email=john@doe.com into <email>john@doe.com</email>).

To recap what's been described, this means that when a request is made to a URL in the form http://[host_name]//app-name]/members.xml, the corresponding handler is charged with creating a Memeber object, which is then passed to a logical view named membertemplate. Based on this last view's definition, a marshaller is used to convert a Memeber object into an XML payload that is returned to the REST service's requesting party. The XML payload returned by the REST service is illustrated in the following listing:

```
<?xml version="1.0" encoding="UTF-8" standalone="yes">
<member>
<email>john@doe.com</email>
<name>John Doe</name>
<phone>1-800-800-800</phone>
</member>
```

This last XML payload represents a very simple approach to generating a REST service's response. As the recipes in this chapter progress, you will learn more sophisticated approaches, such as the ability to create widely used REST service payloads like RSS, Atom, and JSON.

If you look closely at the REST service end point or URL described in the previous paragraph, you'll note that it has an .xml extension. If you try another extension—or even omit the extension—this particular REST service may not be triggered. This last behavior is directly tied to Spring MVC and how it handles view resolution. It has nothing do with REST services per se.

By default, since the view associated with this particular REST service handler method returns XML, it's triggered by an .xml extension. This allows the same handler method to support multiple views. For example, it can be convenient for a request like http://[host_name]/[app-name]/members.pdf to return the same information in a PDF document, as well as a request like http://[host_name]/[app-name]/members.html to return content in HTML or a request like http://[host_name]/[app-name]/members.xml to return XML for a REST request.

So what happens to a request with no URL extension, like http://[host_name]/[app-name]/members? This also depends heavily on Spring MVC view resolution. For this purpose, Spring MVC supports a process called *content negotiation*, by which a view is determined based on a request's extension or HTTP headers.

Since REST service requests typically have HTTP headers in the form Accept: application/xml, Spring MVC configured to use content negotiation can determine to serve XML (REST) payloads to such requests even if requests are made extensionless. This also allows extensionless requests to be made in formats like HTML, PDF and XLS, all simply based on HTTP headers. Recipe 8-7 in Chapter 8 discusses content negotiation.

9-2. Accessing a REST Service with Spring

Problem

You want to access a REST service from a third party (e.g., Google, Yahoo, another business partner) and use its payload inside a Spring application.

Solution

Accessing a third-party REST service inside a Spring application revolves around the use of the Spring RestTemplate class.

The RestTemplate class is designed on the same principles as the many other Spring *Template classes (e.g., JdbcTemplate, JmsTemplate), providing a simplified approach with default behaviors for performing lengthy tasks.

This means the processes of invoking a REST service and using its returning payload are streamlined in Spring applications.

How It Works

Before describing the particularities of the `RestTemplate` class, it's worth exploring the life cycle of a REST service, so you're aware of the actual work the `RestTemplate` class performs. Exploring the life cycle of a REST service can best be done from a browser, so open your favorite browser on your workstation to get started.

The first thing that's needed is a REST service end point. The following URL represents a REST service end point provided by Yahoo that returns sports news results:

```
http://search.yahooapis.com/NewsSearchService/V1/newsSearch?appid=↵
YahooDemo&query=sports&results=2&language=en
```

The structure of the REST service end point comprises an address, which starts with `http://` and ends with ?, as well as a series of parameters that start with ? and are delimited by &, each represented by a key and value divided by =.

If you load this last REST service end point on your browser, the browser performs a `GET` request, which is one of the most popular HTTP requests supported by REST services. Upon loading the REST service, the browser displays a responding payload like the following:

```
<ResultSet xsi:schemaLocation="urn:yahoo:yn ↵
http://api.search.yahoo.com/NewsSearchService/V1/↵
NewsSearchResponse.xsd" totalResultsAvailable="55494"↵
 totalResultsReturned="2" firstResultPosition="1">
    <Result>
        <Title>Toyota Recalls Will Slam Sports</Title>
        <Summary>
          All the big sports are likely to see their sponsorship revenue ↵
          go down as a result of the Toytota de
        </Summary>
        <Url>
      http://blogs.forbes.com/sportsmoney/2010/02/toyota-recalls-will-slam-sports/
        </Url>
        ...Remaining code omitted for brevity...
    </Result>
</ResultSet>
```

This last payload represents a well-formed XML fragment, which is in line with most REST service's responses. The actual meaning of the payload is highly dependent on a REST service. In this case, the XML tags (e.g., <Result>, <Title>) are definitions set forth by Yahoo, while the character data enclosed in each XML tag represents information related to a REST service's request.

It's the task of a REST service consumer (i.e., you) to know the payload structure—sometimes referred to as *vocabulary*—of a REST service to appropriately process its information. Though this last REST service relies on what can be considered a custom vocabulary, a series of REST services often rely on standardized vocabularies (e.g., RSS), which make the processing of REST service payloads uniform. In addition, it's also worth noting that some REST services provide Web Application Description Language (WADL) contracts to facilitate the discovery and consumption of payloads.

Now that your familiar with a REST service's life cycle using your browser, we can take a look at how to use the Spring `RestTemplate` class in order to incorporate a REST service's payload into a Spring application.

Given that the `RestTemplate` class is designed to call REST services, it should come as no surprise that its main methods are closely tied to REST's underpinnings, which are the HTTP protocol's methods: HEAD, GET, POST, PUT, DELETE, and OPTIONS. Table 9-1 contains the main methods supported by the `RestTemplate` class.

Table 9-1. RestTemplate class methods based on HTTP protocol's request methods

Method	Description
headForHeaders(String, Object...)	Performs an HTTP HEAD operation
getForObject(String, Class, Object...)	Performs an HTTP GET operation
postForLocation(String, Object, Object...)	Performs an HTTP POST operation using an object
postForObject(String, Object, Class, Object...)	Performs an HTTP POST operation using a class.
put(String, Object, Object...)	Performs an HTTP PUT operation
delete(String, Object...)	Performs an HTTP DELETE operation
optionsForAllow(String, Object...)	Performs an HTTP OPTIONS operation
execute(String, HttpMethod, RequestCallback, ResponseExtractor, Object...)	Can perform any HTTP operation with the exception of CONNECT

As you can observe in Table 9-1, the `RestTemplate` class methods are prefixed with a series of HTTP protocol methods that include HEAD, GET, POST, PUT, DELETE, and OPTIONS. In addition, the `execute` method serves as a general-purpose method that can perform any HTTP operation, including the more esoteric HTTP protocol TRACE method, albeit not the CONNECT method, the last of which is not supported by the underlying `HttpMethod enum` used by the `execute` method.

■ **Note** By far the most common HTTP method used in REST services is GET, since it represents a safe operation to obtain information (i.e., it doesn't modify any data). On the other hand, HTTP methods such as POST and DELETE are designed to modify a provider's information, which makes them less likely to be supported by a REST service provider. For cases in which data modification needs to take place, many providers opt for the SOAP protocol, which is an alternative mechanism to using REST services.

Now that you're aware of the `RestTemplate` class methods, we can move onto invoking the same REST service you did with your browser previously, except this time using Java code from the Spring framework. The following listing illustrates a Spring MVC controller class with a handler method that accesses the REST service and returns its contents to a standard HTML page:

```
package com.apress.springrecipes.court.web;

import org.springframework.stereotype.Controller;
import org.springframework.ui.Model;
import org.springframework.web.bind.annotation.RequestMapping;
import org.springframework.beans.factory.annotation.Autowired;

import org.springframework.web.client.RestTemplate;


@Controller
public class RestNewsController {

    @Autowired
    protected RestTemplate restTemplate;

    @RequestMapping("/sportsnews")
    public String getYahooNews(Model model) {
        // Return view newstemplate. Via resolver the view
        // will be mapped to /WEB-INF/jsp/newstemplate.jsp
        String result = restTemplate.getForObject("↵
                http://search.yahooapis.com/↵
                NewsSearchService/V1/newsSearch?appid={appid}&↵
                query={query}&results={results}&language={language}",↵
                String.class, "YahooDemo","sports","2","en");
        model.addAttribute("newsfeed", result);
        return "newstemplate";
    }
}
```

■ **Caution** Some REST service providers restrict access to their data feeds depending on the requesting party. Access is generally denied by relying on data present in a request (e.g., HTTP headers or IP address). So depending on the circumstances, a provider can return an access denied response even when a data feed appears to be working in another medium (e.g., you might be able to access a REST service in a browser but get an accessed denied response when attempting to access the same feed from a Spring application). This depends on the terms of use set forth by a REST provider.

The first line marked in bold declares the import statement needed to access the RestTemplate class within a class's body. The second statement in bold represents this same class decorated with the @Autowired annotation, which allows the Spring framework to wire the class. The following listing illustrates the related configuration code needed inside a web application's Spring configuration file to wire the RestTemplate class:

```
<bean id="restTemplate" class="org.springframework.web.client.RestTemplate">
</bean>
```

If you're unfamiliar with the process of Spring wiring a class, we recommend you read Chapters 1 through 3, which introduce this fundamental process of the framework. If you're unfamiliar with the `@Autowired` annotation, we recommend you read Chapter 8, which introduces you to Spring MVC, a part of the framework that relies on this annotation.

Next, you'll find a handler method decorated with the `@RequestMapping("/sportsnews")` annotation. This last method represents a basic Spring MVC declaration, indicating the method is triggered when a request is made on a URL in the form `http://[host_name]/[app-name]/sportsnews`.

In the first line of the handler method, you can find a call made to the `getForObject` method that belongs to the `RestTemplate` class, which as described in Table 9-1 is used to perform an HTTP `GET` operation—just like the one performed by a browser to obtain a REST service's payload. There are two important aspects related to this last method, its response and its parameters.

The response of calling the `getForObject` method is assigned to a `String` object. This means the same output you saw on your browser for this REST service (i.e., the XML structure) is assigned to a `String`. Even if you've never processed XML in Java, you're likely aware that extracting and manipulating data as a Java `String` is not an easy task. In other words, there are classes better suited for processing XML data, and with it a REST service's payload, than a `String` object. For the moment just keep this in mind; other recipes in the chapter illustrate how to better extract and manipulate the data obtained from a REST service.

The parameters passed to the `getForObject` method consist of the actual REST service end point. The first parameter corresponds to the URL (i.e., end point) declaration with a series of placeholders using { and }. Notice the URL is identical to the one used when you relied on a browser to call it, except now it doesn't have any hard-coded values and instead uses placeholders where these values were once declared.

In this case, each of the placeholder declarations (e.g., `{appid}` and `{query}`) are substituted by one of the remaining parameters passed to the `getForObject` method. With the first parameter representing the return type class—`String.class`—and the remaining parameters corresponding to the placeholder values mapped in the same order in which they're declared (e.g., the `YahooDemo` value assigned to `{appid}` or the `sports` value assigned to `{query}`).

Even though this process allows a REST service to be parameterized on a case-by-case basis (i.e., for each web application visitor), passing a series of `String` objects and keeping track of their order can be an error-prone process. The various `RestTemplate` class methods described in Table 9-1 also support a more compact parameter passing strategy using the Java collections framework. This process is illustrated in the following snippet:

```
Map<String, String> params = new HashMap<String, String>();
params.put("appid","YahooDemo");
params.put("query","sports");
params.put("results", "2");
params.put("language", "en");

String result = restTemplate.getForObject("http://search.yahooapis.com/↵
            NewsSearchService/V1/newsSearch?appid={appid}↵
            &query={query}&results={results}&language={language}",↵
            String.class, params);
```

This last snippet makes use of the `HashMap` class—part of the Java collections framework—creating an instance with the corresponding REST service parameters, which is later passed to the `getForObject` method of the `RestTemplate` class. The results obtained by passing either a series of `String` parameters or a single `Map` parameter to the various `RestTemplate` methods is identical.

Turning our attention back to the remaining part of the handler method, once the REST service's XML payload is assigned to a `String` object, it's then associated with the handler's `Model` object through the `newsfeed` keyword, so it can be accessed and displayed from the view linked to the handler method. In this case, the handler method relinquishes control to a logical view named `newstemplate`.

Since configuring logical views is a concept related Spring MVC, we advise you to read Chapter 8 if you're unfamiliar with the topic. The `newstemplate` logical view would finally be mapped to a JSP capable of displaying the contents of the REST service's XML payload, that in accordance with the Spring MVC mapping would be accessible at `http://[host_name]/[app-name]/sportsnews.html`. The following listing illustrates such a JSP:

```
<html>
  <head>
    <title>Sports news feed by Yahoo</title>
  </head>
<body>
    <h2>Sports news feed by Yahoo</h2>
      <table>
      <tr>
        <td>${newsfeed}</td>
      </tr>
      </table>
</body>
</html>
```

The REST service's XML payload is substituted into the `${newsfeed}` placeholder, in accordance with the key value defined inside the handler method.

As we already mentioned, future recipes will address more elaborate ways to extract and manipulate data belonging to a REST service's XML payload than this approach, which simply dumps the entire feed's contents verbatim on an HTML page.

9-3. Publishing RSS and Atom feeds

Problem

You want to publish an RSS or Atom feed in a Spring application.

Solution

RSS and Atom feeds have become a popular means by which to publish information. Access to these types of feeds is provided by means of a REST service, which means building a REST service is a prerequisite to publishing RSS and Atom feeds.

In addition to relying on Spring's REST support, it's also convenient to rely on a third-party library especially designed to deal with the particularities of RSS and Atom feeds. This makes it easier for a REST service to publish this type of XML payload. For this last purpose, we will use Project Rome, an open source library available at `https://rome.dev.java.net/`.

■ **Note** Project Rome depends on the JDOM library that can be downloaded at http://www.jdom.org/. If you are using Maven, you can add the following dependency to your pom.xml file:

<dependency>
  <groupId>org.jdom</groupId>
  <artifactId>jdom</artifactId>
  <version>1.1</version>
</dependency>

■ **Tip** Even though RSS and Atom feeds are often categorized as news feeds, they have surpassed this initial usage scenario of providing just news. Nowadays, RSS and Atom feeds are used to publish information related to blogs, weather, travel, and many other things in a cross-platform manner (i.e., using XML). Hence, if you require publishing information of any sort that's to be accessible in a cross-platform manner, doing so as RSS or Atom feeds can be an excellent choice given their wide adoption (e.g., many applications support them and many developers know their structure).

How It Works

The first thing you need to do is determine the information you wish to publish as an RSS or Atom news feed. This information can be located in an RDBMS or text file, accessed through JDBC or ORM, inclusively be part of a Spring bean or some other type of construct. Describing how to obtain this information would go beyond the scope of this recipe, so we will assume you'll use whatever means you deem appropriate to access it.

Once you've pinpointed the information you wish to publish, it's necessary to structure it as either an RSS or Atom feed, which is where Project Rome comes into the picture.

In case you're unfamiliar with an Atom feed's structure, the following snippet illustrates a fragment of this format:

```
<?xml version="1.0" encoding="utf-8"?>
<feed xmlns="http://www.w3.org/2005/Atom">

  <title>Example Feed</title>
  <link href="http://example.org/"/>
  <updated>2010-08-31T18:30:02Z</updated>
  <author>
    <name>John Doe</name>
  </author>
  <id>urn:uuid:60a76c80-d399-11d9-b93C-0003939e0af6</id>
```

```
<entry>
  <title>Atom-Powered Robots Run Amok</title>
  <link href="http://example.org/2010/08/31/atom03"/>
  <id>urn:uuid:1225c695-cfb8-4ebb-aaaa-80da344efa6a</id>
  <updated>2010-08-31T18:30:02Z</updated>
  <summary>Some text.</summary>
</entry>

</feed>
```

The following snippet illustrates a fragment of an RSS feed's structure:

```
<?xml version="1.0" encoding="UTF-8" ?>

<rss version="2.0">
<channel>
<title>RSS Example</title>
<description>This is an example of an RSS feed</description>
<link>http://www.example.org/link.htm</link>
<lastBuildDate>Mon, 28 Aug 2006 11:12:55 -0400 </lastBuildDate>
<pubDate>Tue, 31 Aug 2010 09:00:00 -0400</pubDate>

<item>
<title>Item Example</title>
<description>This is an example of an Item</description>
<link>http://www.example.org/link.htm</link>
<guid isPermaLink="false"> 1102345</guid>
<pubDate>Tue, 31 Aug 2010 09:00:00 -0400</pubDate>
</item>


</channel>


</rss>
```

As you can observe from these last two snippets, RSS and Atom feeds are just XML payloads that rely on a series of elements to publish information. Though going into the finer details of either an RSS or Atom feed structure would require a book in itself, both formats possess a series of common characteristics; chief among them are these:

- They have a metadata section to describe the contents of a feed. (e.g., the `<author>` and `<title>` elements for the Atom format and the `<description>` and `<pubDate>` elements for the RSS format)

- They have recurring elements to describe information (e.g., the `<entry>` element for the Atom feed format and the `<item>` element for the RSS feed format). In addition, each recurring element also has its own set of elements with which to further describe information.

- They have multiple versions. RSS versions include 0.90, 0.91 Netscape, 0.91 Userland, 0.92, 0.93, 0.94, 1.0, and 2.0. Atom versions include 0.3 and 1.0.

Project Rome allows you to create a feed's metadata section, recurring elements, as well as any of the previously mentioned versions, from information available in Java code (e.g., Strings, Maps, or other such constructs).

Now that you're aware of the structure of an RSS and Atom feed, as well as the role Project Rome plays in this recipe, let's take a look at a Spring MVC controller charged with presenting a feed to an end user.

```
package com.apress.springrecipes.court.web;

import org.springframework.stereotype.Controller;
import org.springframework.ui.Model;
import org.springframework.web.bind.annotation.RequestMapping;

import com.apress.springrecipes.court.feeds.TournamentContent;

import com.apress.springrecipes.court.domain.Member;
import java.util.List;
import java.util.Date;
import java.util.ArrayList;

@Controller
public class FeedController {

    @RequestMapping("/atomfeed")
    public String getAtomFeed(Model model) {
        List<TournamentContent> tournamentList = new ArrayList<TournamentContent>();
        tournamentList.add(TournamentContent.generateContent("ATP", ↩
                            new Date(),"Australian Open","www.australianopen.com"));
        tournamentList.add(TournamentContent.generateContent("ATP", ↩
                            new Date(),"Roland Garros","www.rolandgarros.com"));
        tournamentList.add(TournamentContent.generateContent("ATP", ↩
                            new Date(),"Wimbledon","www.wimbledon.org"));
        tournamentList.add(TournamentContent.generateContent("ATP", ↩
                            new Date(),"US Open","www.usopen.org"));
        model.addAttribute("feedContent",tournamentList);
        return "atomfeedtemplate";
    }


    @RequestMapping("/rssfeed")
    public String getRSSFeed(Model model) {
        List<TournamentContent> tournamentList = new ArrayList<TournamentContent>();
        tournamentList.add(TournamentContent.generateContent("FIFA", ↩
                new Date(),"World Cup","www.fifa.com/worldcup/"));
        tournamentList.add(TournamentContent.generateContent("FIFA", ↩
                new Date(),"U-20 World Cup","www.fifa.com/u20worldcup/"));
        tournamentList.add(TournamentContent.generateContent("FIFA", ↩
                new Date(),"U-17 World Cup","www.fifa.com/u17worldcup/"));
        tournamentList.add(TournamentContent.generateContent("FIFA", ↩
                new Date(),"Confederations Cup","www.fifa.com/confederationscup/"));
```

```
        model.addAttribute("feedContent",tournamentList);
        return "rssfeedtemplate";

    }
}
```

This last Spring MVC controller has two handler methods. One called getAtomFeed(), which is mapped to a URL in the form http://[host_name]/[app-name]/atomfeed, and another called getRSSFeed(), which is mapped to a URL in the form http://[host_name]/[app-name]/rssfeed.

Each handler method defines a List of TournamentContent objects, where the backing class for a TournamentContent object is a POJO. This List is then assigned to the handler method's Model object in order for it to become accessible to the returning view. The returning logical views for each handler methods are atomfeedtemplate and rssfeedtemplate, respectively. These logical views are defined in the following manner inside a Spring XML configuration file:

```
<bean id="atomfeedtemplate" ↩
class="com.apress.springrecipes.court.feeds.AtomFeedView"/>

<bean id="rssfeedtemplate" ↩
 class="com.apress.springrecipes.court.feeds.RSSFeedView"/>
```

As you can observe, each logical view is mapped to a class. Each of these classes is charged with implementing the necessary logic to build either an Atom or RSS view. If you recall from Chapter 8, you used an identical approach (i.e., using classes) for implementing PDF and Excel views.

In the case of Atom and RSS views, Spring comes equipped with two classes specially equipped and built on the foundations of Project Rome. These classes are AbstractAtomFeedView and AbstractRssFeedView. Such classes provide the foundations to build an Atom or RSS feed, without dealing in the finer details of each of these formats.

The following listing illustrates the AtomFeedView class which implements the AbstractAtomFeedView class and is used to back the atomfeedtemplate logical view:

```
package com.apress.springrecipes.court.feeds;

import javax.servlet.http.HttpServletRequest;
import javax.servlet.http.HttpServletResponse;

import com.sun.syndication.feed.atom.Feed;
import com.sun.syndication.feed.atom.Entry;
import com.sun.syndication.feed.atom.Content;

import org.springframework.web.servlet. ↩
view.feed.AbstractAtomFeedView;

import java.util.Date;
import java.util.List;
import java.util.ArrayList;
import java.util.Map;

public class AtomFeedView extends AbstractAtomFeedView {
    protected void buildFeedMetadata(Map model, ↩
    Feed feed, HttpServletRequest request) {
```

```
            feed.setId("tag:tennis.org");
            feed.setTitle("Grand Slam Tournaments");
            List<TournamentContent> tournamentList = (List<TournamentContent>)model.↵
get("feedContent");
            for (TournamentContent tournament : tournamentList) {
                Date date = tournament.getPublicationDate();
                if (feed.getUpdated() == null || date.compareTo(feed.getUpdated()) > 0) {
                    feed.setUpdated(date);
                }
            }

        }

    protected List buildFeedEntries(Map model,↵
    HttpServletRequest request, HttpServletResponse response) ↵
    throws Exception {
            List<TournamentContent> tournamentList = ↵
                        (List<TournamentContent>)model.get("feedContent");
            List<Entry> entries = new ArrayList<Entry>(tournamentList.size());
            for (TournamentContent tournament : tournamentList) {
                Entry entry = new Entry();
                String date = String.format("%1$tY-%1$tm-%1$td",↵
                                            tournament.getPublicationDate());
                entry.setId(String.format("tag:tennis.org,%s:%d", date,↵
                                            tournament.getId()));
                entry.setTitle(String.format("%s - Posted by %s", ↵
                                            tournament.getName(), tournament.getAuthor()));
                entry.setUpdated(tournament.getPublicationDate());
                Content summary = new Content();
                summary.setValue(String.format("%s - %s",↵
                                            tournament.getName(),tournament.getLink()));
                entry.setSummary(summary);
                entries.add(entry);
            }
        return entries;
    }
}
```

The first thing to notice about this class is that it imports several Project Rome classes from the com.sun.syndication.feed.atom package, in addition to implementing the AbstractAtomFeedView class provided by the Spring framework. In doing so, the only thing that's needed next is to provide a feed's implementation details for two methods inherited from the AbstractAtomFeedView class: buildFeedMetadata and buildFeedEntries.

The buildFeedMetadata has three input parameters. A Map object which represents the data used to build the feed (i.e., data assigned inside the handler method, in this case a List of TournamentContent objects), a Feed object based on a Project Rome class that is used to manipulate the feed itself, and an HttpServletRequest object in case it's necessary to manipulate the HTTP request.

Inside the buildFeedMetadata method, you can observe several calls are made to the Feed object's setter methods (e.g., setId, setTitle, setUpdated). Two of these calls are made using hard-coded strings, while another is made with a value determined after looping over a feed's data (i.e., the Map object). All these calls represent the assignment of an Atom feed's metadata information.

■ **Note** Consult Project Rome's API if you want to assign more values to an Atom feed's metadata section, as well as specify a particular Atom version. The default version is Atom 1.0.

The `buildFeedEntries` method also has three input parameters: a `Map` object that represents the data used to build the feed (i.e., data assigned inside the handler method, in this case a `List` of `TournamentContent` objects), an `HttpServletRequest` object in case it's necessary to manipulate the HTTP request, and an `HttpServletResponse` object in case it's necessary to manipulate the HTTP response. It's also important to note the `buildFeedEntries` method returns a `List` objects, which in this case corresponds to a `List` of `Entry` objects based on a Project Rome class and containing an Atom feed's recurring elements.

Inside the `buildFeedEntries` method, you can observe that the `Map` object is accessed to obtain the `feedContent` object assigned inside the handler method. Once this is done, an empty `List` of `Entry` objects is created. Next, a loop is performed on the `feedContent` object, which contains a list of a `List` of `TournamentContent` objects, and for each element, an `Entry` object is created that is assigned to the top-level `List` of `Entry` objects. Once the loop is finished, the method returns a filled `List` of `Entry` objects.

■ **Note** Consult Project Rome's API if you want to assign more values to an Atom feed's recurring elements section.

Upon deploying this last class, in addition to the previously cited Spring MVC controller, accessing a URL in the form `http://[host_name]/[app-name]/atomfeed.atom` (or `http://[host_name]/atomfeed.xml`) would result in the following response:

```
<?xml version="1.0" encoding="UTF-8"?>
<feed xmlns="http://www.w3.org/2005/Atom">
  <title>Grand Slam Tournaments</title>
  <id>tag:tennis.org</id>
  <updated>2010-03-04T20:51:50Z</updated>
  <entry>
    <title>Australian Open - Posted by ATP</title>
    <id>tag:tennis.org,2010-03-04:0</id>
    <updated>2010-03-04T20:51:50Z</updated>
    <summary>Australian Open - www.australianopen.com</summary>
  </entry>
  <entry>
    <title>Roland Garros - Posted by ATP</title>
    <id>tag:tennis.org,2010-03-04:1</id>
    <updated>2010-03-04T20:51:50Z</updated>
    <summary>Roland Garros - www.rolandgarros.com</summary>
  </entry>
```

```
<entry>
  <title>Wimbledon - Posted by ATP</title>
  <id>tag:tennis.org,2010-03-04:2</id>
  <updated>2010-03-04T20:51:50Z</updated>
  <summary>Wimbledon - www.wimbledon.org</summary>
</entry>
<entry>
  <title>US Open - Posted by ATP</title>
  <id>tag:tennis.org,2010-03-04:3</id>
  <updated>2010-03-04T20:51:50Z</updated>
  <summary>US Open - www.usopen.org</summary>
</entry>
</feed>
```

Turning your attention to the remaining handler method—getRSSFeed—from the previous Spring MVC controller charged with building an RSS feed, you'll see that the process is similar to the one just described for building Atom feeds.

The handler methods also creates a List of TournamentContent objects, which is then assigned to the handler method's Model object for it to become accessible to the returning view. The returning logical view in this case though, now corresponds to one named **rssfeedtemplate**. As described earlier, this logical view is mapped to a class named RssFeedView.

The following listing illustrates the RssFeedView class, which implements the AbstractRssFeedView class:

```
package com.apress.springrecipes.court.feeds;

import javax.servlet.http.HttpServletRequest;
import javax.servlet.http.HttpServletResponse;

import com.sun.syndication.feed.rss.Channel;
import com.sun.syndication.feed.rss.Item;
import org.springframework.web.servlet.↵
view.feed.AbstractRssFeedView;

import java.util.Date;
import java.util.List;
import java.util.ArrayList;
import java.util.Map;

public class RSSFeedView extends AbstractRssFeedView {
    protected void buildFeedMetadata(Map model, ↵
    Channel feed, HttpServletRequest request) {
        feed.setTitle("World Soccer Tournaments");
        feed.setDescription("FIFA World Soccer Tournament Calendar");
        feed.setLink("tennis.org");
        List<TournamentContent> tournamentList = (List<TournamentContent>)model.↵
get("feedContent");
        for (TournamentContent tournament : tournamentList) {
            Date date = tournament.getPublicationDate();
```

```
            if (feed.getLastBuildDate() == null || date.compareTo(feed.↵
getLastBuildDate()) > 0) {
                feed.setLastBuildDate(date);
            }
        }
    }

    protected List buildFeedItems(Map model,↵
    HttpServletRequest request, HttpServletResponse response) ↵
    throws Exception {
        List<TournamentContent> tournamentList = (List<TournamentContent>)model.get↵
("feedContent");
        List<Item> items = new ArrayList<Item>(tournamentList.size());
        for (TournamentContent tournament : tournamentList) {
            Item item = new Item();
            String date = String.format("%1$tY-%1$tm-%1$td", tournament.get↵
PublicationDate());
            item.setAuthor(tournament.getAuthor());
            item.setTitle(String.format("%s - Posted by %s", tournament.getName(),↵
 tournament.getAuthor())));
            item.setPubDate(tournament.getPublicationDate());
            item.setLink(tournament.getLink());
            items.add(item);
            }
        return items;
        }
    }
```

The first thing to notice about this class is that it imports several Project Rome classes from the com.sun.syndication.feed.rss package, in addition to implementing the AbstractRssFeedView class provided by the Spring framework. Once it does so, the only thing that's needed next is to provide a feed's implementation details for two methods inherited from the AbstractRssFeedView class: buildFeedMetadata and buildFeedItems.

The buildFeedMetadata method is similar in nature to the one by the same name used in building an Atom feed. Notice the buildFeedMetadata method manipulates a Channel object based on a Project Rome class, which is used to build RSS feeds, instead of a Feed object, which is used to build Atom feeds. The setter method calls made on the Channel object (e.g., setTitle, setDescription, setLink) represent the assignment of an RSS feed's metadata information.

The buildFeedItems method, which differs in name to its Atom counterpart buildFeedEntries, is so named because an Atom feed's recurring elements are called *entries* and an RSS feed's recurring elements are *items*. Naming conventions aside, their logic is similar.

Inside the buildFeedItems method, you can observe that the Map object is accessed to obtain the feedContent object assigned inside the handler method. Once this is done, an empty List of Item objects is created. Next, a loop is performed on the feedContent object, which contains a list of a List of TournamentContent objects, and for each element, an Item object is created which is assigned to the top level List of Item objects. Once the loop is finished, the method returns a filled List of Item objects.

■ **Note** Consult Project Rome's API if you want to assign more values to an RSS feed's metadata and recurring element sections, as well as specify a particular RSS version. The default version is RSS 2.0.

When you deploy this last class, in addition to the previously cited Spring MVC controller, accessing a URL in the form `http://[host_name]/rssfeed.rss` (or `http://[host_name]/rssfeed.xml`) results in the following response:

```
<?xml version="1.0" encoding="UTF-8"?>
<rss version="2.0">
  <channel>
    <title>World Soccer Tournaments</title>
    <link>tennis.org</link>
    <description>FIFA World Soccer Tournament Calendar</description>
    <lastBuildDate>Thu, 04 Mar 2010 21:45:08 GMT</lastBuildDate>
    <item>
      <title>World Cup - Posted by FIFA</title>
      <link>www.fifa.com/worldcup/</link>
      <pubDate>Thu, 04 Mar 2010 21:45:08 GMT</pubDate>
      <author>FIFA</author>
    </item>
    <item>
      <title>U-20 World Cup - Posted by FIFA</title>
      <link>www.fifa.com/u20worldcup/</link>
      <pubDate>Thu, 04 Mar 2010 21:45:08 GMT</pubDate>
      <author>FIFA</author>
    </item>
    <item>
      <title>U-17 World Cup - Posted by FIFA</title>
      <link>www.fifa.com/u17worldcup/</link>
      <pubDate>Thu, 04 Mar 2010 21:45:08 GMT</pubDate>
      <author>FIFA</author>
    </item>
    <item>
      <title>Confederations Cup - Posted by FIFA</title>
      <link>www.fifa.com/confederationscup/</link>
      <pubDate>Thu, 04 Mar 2010 21:45:08 GMT</pubDate>
      <author>FIFA</author>
    </item>
  </channel>
</rss>
```

9-4. Publishing JSON with REST services

Problem

You want to publish JavaScript Object Notation (JSON) in a Spring application.

Solution

JSON, in addition to RSS and Atom, has blossomed into a favorite payload format for REST services. However, unlike most REST service payloads, which rely on XML markup, JSON is different in the sense that its content is a special notation based on the JavaScript language.

For this recipe, in addition to relying on Spring's REST support, we will also use the `MappingJacksonJsonView` class that forms part of Spring to facilitate the publication of JSON content.

■ **Note** The `MappingJacksonJsonView` class depends on the presence of the Jackson JSON processor library which can be downloaded at `http://wiki.fasterxml.com/JacksonDownload`. If you're using Maven, add the following dependency to your project:

```
<dependency>
  <groupId>org.codehaus.jackson</groupId>
  <artifactId>jackson-mapper-asl</artifactId>
  <version>1.4.2</version>
</dependency>
```

WHY PUBLISH JSON?

If your Spring application's incorporate Ajax designs, it's very likely that you'll find yourself designing REST services that publish JSON as their payload. This is mainly due to the limited processing capabilities in browsers.

Although browsers can process and extract information from REST services that publish XML payloads, it's not very efficient. By instead delivering payloads in JSON, which is based on a language for which browsers have a native interpreter—JavaScript—the processing and extraction of data becomes more efficient.

Unlike RSS and Atom feeds, which are standards, JSON has no specific structure it needs to follow—except its syntax which you'll explore shortly. Therefore, a JSON element's payload structure is likely to be determined in coordination with the team members charged with an application's Ajax design.

How It Works

The first thing you need to do is determine the information you wish to publish as a JSON payload. This information can be located in a RDBMS or text file, accessed through JDBC or ORM, inclusively be part of a Spring bean or some other type of construct. Describing how to obtain this information would go beyond the scope of this recipe, so we will assume you'll use whatever means you deem appropriate to access it.

In case you're unfamiliar with JSON, the following snippet illustrates a fragment of this format:

```
{
    "glossary": {
        "title": "example glossary",
            "GlossDiv": {
            "title": "S",
                    "GlossList": {
                "GlossEntry": {
                    "ID": "SGML",
                                "SortAs": "SGML",
                                "GlossTerm": "Standard Generalized Markup Language",
                                "Acronym": "SGML",
                                "Abbrev": "ISO 8879:1986",
                                "GlossDef": {
                        "para": "A meta-markup language, used to create markup ⏎
                                languages such as DocBook.",
                                        "GlossSeeAlso": ["GML", "XML"]
                    },
                                "GlossSee": "markup"
                }
            }
        }
    }
}
```

As you can observe, a JSON payload consists of text and separators like { , } ,[,] , : and ". We won't go into details about using one separator over another, but it suffices to say this type of syntax makes it easier for a JavaScript engine to access and manipulate data than if it was to process it in an XML type format.

Since you've already explored how to publish data using a REST service in recipes 9-1 and 9-3, we'll cut to the chase and show you the actual handler method needed in a Spring MVC controller to achieve this process.

```
@RequestMapping("/jsontournament")
    public String getJSON(Model model) {
        List<TournamentContent> tournamentList = new ArrayList<TournamentContent>();
        tournamentList.add(TournamentContent.generateContent("FIFA", ⏎
            new Date(),"World Cup","www.fifa.com/worldcup/"));
        tournamentList.add(TournamentContent.generateContent("FIFA", ⏎
            new Date(),"U-20 World Cup","www.fifa.com/u20worldcup/"));
        tournamentList.add(TournamentContent.generateContent("FIFA", ⏎
            new Date(),"U-17 World Cup","www.fifa.com/u17worldcup/"));
```

```
        tournamentList.add(TournamentContent.generateContent("FIFA", ↵
            new Date(),"Confederations Cup","www.fifa.com/confederationscup/"));
        model.addAttribute("feedContent",tournamentList);
        return "jsontournamenttemplate";
}
```

This last handler method is mapped to a URL in the form http://[host_name]/[app-name]/jsontournament. Similar to the handler methods used in recipe 9-3 to publish Atom and RSS feeds, this handler method defines a List of TournamentContent objects, where the backing class for a TournamentContent object is a POJO. This List is then assigned to the handler method's Model object, so it becomes accessible to the returning view. The returning logical view in this case is named jsontournamenttemplate.

This last logical view is defined in the following manner inside a Spring XML configuration file:

```
<bean id="jsontournamenttemplate" ↵
class="org.springframework.web.servlet.view.json.MappingJacksonJsonView"/>
```

Note the logical view jsontournamenttemplate is mapped to the MappingJacksonJsonView class provided by the Spring framework. This last class converts the entire contents of the model map (i.e., the one assigned inside the handler method) and encodes it as JSON.

In this manner, if you access a URL in the form http://[host_name]/jsontournament.json (or http://[host_name]/jsontournament.xml), you will obtain the following response:

```
{
    "handlingTime":1,
"feedContent":
        [
            {"link":"www.fifa.com/worldcup/",
             "publicationDate":1267758100256,
             "author":"FIFA",
             "name":"World Cup",
             "id":16},
            {"link":"www.fifa.com/u20worldcup/",
             "publicationDate":1267758100256,
             "author":"FIFA",
             "name":"U-20 World Cup",
             "id":17},
            {"link":"www.fifa.com/u17worldcup/",
             "publicationDate":1267758100256,
             "author":"FIFA",
             "name":"U-17 World Cup",
             "id":18},
            {"link":"www.fifa.com/confederationscup/",
             "publicationDate":1267758100256,
             "author":"FIFA",
             "name":"Confederations Cup",
             "id":19}
        ]
}
```

WHAT ABOUT ACCESSING JSON WITH REST?

Even though JSON is common as a publishing format for REST services, it's not so popular as a consumption format outside of a browser. In other words, you are more likely to publish JSON in a Spring application than to access JSON in a Spring application.

Though it's technically possible to access JSON in a Spring application (i.e., on the server side), using a third-party Java library like JSON-LIB (http://json-lib.sourceforge.net/). You are often better served accessing and manipulating REST services with XML payloads in Spring applications, given the Java platform's native support for XML, in addition to the fact that XML is more intuitive and does not have the same processing limitations as browsers.

9-5. Accessing REST Services with Elaborate XML Responses

Problem

You want to access a REST service with an elaborate XML response and use its data inside a Spring application.

Solution

REST services have become a popular means by which to publish information. However, the data structures returned by certain REST services can turn out to be quite complex.

Though the Spring `RestTemplate` class is capable of performing a multitude of operations on REST services in order for their payloads to be used inside Spring applications, processing elaborate XML responses requires using a set of approaches beyond those of this last class.

These approaches include relying on data streams, XPath—an XML query language for selecting nodes from an XML document— knowledge about Spring's `HttpConverterMessage`, as well as supporting facilities like Spring's `XPathTemplate`.

How It Works

Since you've already explored how to access a REST service in recipe 9-2 using the Spring `RestTemplate` class, what we'll do next is concentrate on the particularities of processing a REST service that returns a more elaborate XML response, in this case an RSS feed.

Let's start with the case of accessing an RSS feed containing weather information, with the RSS feed having the following end point: `http://rss.weather.com/rss/national/rss_nwf_rss.xml?cm_ven=NWF&cm_cat=rss&par=NWF_rss`.

Based on what you learned in recipe 9-2, the Spring MVC controller handler method used to access the RSS feed would be the following:

```
@RequestMapping("/nationalweather")
    public String getWeatherNews(Model model) {
        // Return view nationalweathertemplate. Via resolver the view
        // will be mapped to /WEB-INF/jsp/nationalweathertemplate.jsp
        String result = restTemplate.getForObject("http://rss.weather.com/rss/↵
                    national/rss_nwf_rss.xml?cm_ven={cm_ven}&cm_cat={cm_cat}↵
                    &par={par}", String.class, "NWF","rss","NWF_rss");
        model.addAttribute("nationalweatherfeed",result);
        return "nationalweathertemplate";
}
```

The handler method makes use of the `getForObject` method of the `RestTemplate` class and assigns the returning XML payload to a `String`, which is then added to the handler method's `Model` object. Once the `String` is added, the method relinquishes control to the logical view named `nationalweathertemplate`, so the XML payload can be displayed to the requesting party.

This logic is identical to that of recipe 9-2. However, since we're now dealing with a more elaborate payload—in this case RSS—it's convenient to assign the REST service's payload to something other than a `String`. Why? So it becomes easier to extract and manipulate the contents of the REST service.

To extract and manipulate payloads in Spring REST in a format other than a `String`, it's necessary to discuss the `HttpConverterMessage` interface. All objects that are returned and inclusively passed to the methods belonging to the `RestTemplate` class—those described in Table 9-1—are converted to and from HTTP messages using a class which implements the `HttpConverterMessage` interface.

The default `HttpConverterMessage` implementations registered with the `RestTemplate` class are `ByteArrayHttpMessageConverter`, `StringHttpMessageConverter`, `FormHttpMessageConverter`, and `SourceHttpMessageConverter`. This means that it's possible to cast a REST service's payload into a byte array, string array, form data, or a source, respectively.

▓ **Tip** It's also possible to write your own converters relying on the `MarshallingHttpMessageConverter` interface that would allow the use of custom marshallers. Using custom converters requires registering them with the `messageConverters` bean property in a Spring application. In addition, it's also possible to override the default implementations registered with the `RestTemplate` class using the same `messageConverters` bean property.

For example, the following snippet illustrates how a REST service's payload is cast into a stream source (i.e., `javax.xml.transform.stream.StreamSource`), which is an implementation of a source type (i.e., `javax.xml.transform.Source`):

```
StreamSource result = restTemplate.getForObject("↵
http://rss.weather.com/rss/national/rss_nwf_rss.xml?↵
cm_ven={cm_ven}&cm_cat={cm_cat}&par={par}", ↵
StreamSource.class, "NWF","rss","NWF_rss");
```

By performing this last task, it becomes easier to extract and manipulate the contents of a REST service's payload, since it can be done through the more flexible `StreamSource` class.

One approach involving a StreamSource payload consists of further transforming it into a better data-manipulation class such as Java's Document Object Model (DOM) interface (i.e. org.w3c.dom.Document). By going down this route, a REST service's content can be extracted in a more granular fashion. The following listing illustrates the body of a Spring MVC handler method, which extracts a REST service's payload using the Document interface and parts from a StreamSource class obtained using the RestTemplate class:

```
StreamSource source = restTemplate.getForObject("↵
http://rss.weather.com/rss/national/rss_nwf_rss.xml?↵
cm_ven={cm_ven}&cm_cat={cm_cat}&par={par}", ↵
StreamSource.class, "NWF","rss","NWF_rss");

// Define DocumentBuilderFactory
DocumentBuilderFactory dbf = DocumentBuilderFactory.newInstance();
dbf.setValidating(false);
dbf.setIgnoringComments(false);
dbf.setIgnoringElementContentWhitespace(true);
dbf.setNamespaceAware(true);

// Define DocumentBuilder
DocumentBuilder db = null;
db = dbf.newDocumentBuilder();

// Define InputSource
InputSource is = new InputSource();
is.setSystemId(source.getSystemId());
is.setByteStream(source.getInputStream());
is.setCharacterStream(source.getReader());
is.setEncoding("ISO-8859-1");

// Define DOM W3C Document
Document doc = db.parse(is);
// Get items
NodeList itemElements = doc.getElementsByTagName("item");
// Define lists for titles and links
List feedtitles = new ArrayList();
List feedlinks = new ArrayList();
// Loop over all item elements
int length = itemElements.getLength();
  for ( int n = 0; n < length; ++n )   {
     NodeList childElements = itemElements.item(n).getChildNodes();
     int lengthnested = childElements.getLength();
         for ( int k = 0; k < lengthnested; ++k ) {
            if (childElements.item(k).getNodeName() == "title") {
feedtitles.add(childElements.item(k).getChildNodes().item(0).getNodeValue());
            }
            if (childElements.item(k).getNodeName() == "link") {
feedlinks.add(childElements.item(k).getChildNodes().item(0).getNodeValue());
            }
         }
     }
```

```
// List for content
List feedcontent = new ArrayList();
int titlelength = feedtitles.size();
// Loop over extracted titles and links
for  ( int x = 0; x < titlelength; ++x ) {
  feedcontent.add(new FeedContent((String)feedtitles.get(x),(String)feedlinks.get(x)));
}
// Place feed type, version and content in model object
model.addAttribute("feedtype",↩
        doc.getDocumentElement().getNodeName());
model.addAttribute("feedversion",↩
        doc.getDocumentElement().getAttribute("version"));
model.addAttribute("feedcontent",feedcontent);
return "nationalweathertemplate";
```

■ **Caution** Processing REST service payloads (i.e., XML) is often fraught with encoding issues. The majority of XML payloads are preceded with a statements like `<?xml version="1.0" encoding="UTF-8"?>` or `<?xml version="1.0" encoding="ISO-8859-1" ?>`—meaning the payload is encoded as UTF-8 or ISO-8859-1, respectively. Or the payload may simply have no encoding statement at all. These statements, or lack thereof, can make it difficult for a consuming party to process data appropriately. Processing errors such as "Invalid byte 1 of 1-byte UTF-8 sequence" are fairly common when encoding information conflicts with how the payload is actually encoded. To deal with these type of conflicts, it can be necessary to coerce a payload to a certain encoding or explicitly specify the encoding in a transformation class in order for it to be processed correctly.

There are multiple steps involved using this last approach. Once a REST service's payload is cast into a `StreamSource` class, a `DocumentBuilderFactory`, `DocumentBuilder`, and `InputSource` class are created. These last classes are standard in the manipulation of XML data in Java applications, as they allow the data extraction process to be highly customized (e.g., specify an encoding, validate it, and transform it using something like XSL). With the aid of these classes, a REST service's payload is placed inside a `Document` object.

Once the payload is available as a `Document` object, several iterations are performed on the data using classes and methods related to the DOM (e.g., `NodeList`, `Node`, `getChildNodes()`). Upon finishing the data extraction process, three objects—`feedtype`, `feedversion`, and `feedcontent`—are assigned to the handler method's `Model` object to display the values inside the returning view. In this case, the returning view is mapped to a JSP that displays the object values to an end user.

As you can attest, the process of extracting a REST service's payload can be done at a more granular level than using a Java String as it was done in recipe 9-2.

Another approach to extracting a REST service's payload involves using XPath. XPath is a query language for XML data. Similar in nature to SQL, which is used to extract granular data sets in RDBMS, XPath serves the same purpose but for XML. XPath's syntax and usage scenarios can become elaborate since it's a full-fledged language. Given this fact, we will concentrate on the basics of XPath and how it integrates with REST services and Spring. You can consult the XPath specification at http://www.w3.org/TR/xpath/ for more details on its syntax and usage scenarios.

Just like the DOM, XPath is supported in the core Java platform. The following listing illustrates the previous Spring MVC handler method using Java's `javax.xml.xpath.XPathExpression` interface:

```java
// Omitted for brevity- REST payload transformation to W3C Document
// Define W3C Document
Document doc = db.parse(is);

// Define lists for titles and links
List feedtitles = new ArrayList();
List feedlinks = new ArrayList();

// Defin XPath constructs
XPathFactory factory = XPathFactory.newInstance();
XPath xpath = factory.newXPath();

// Define XPath expression to extract titles
XPathExpression titleexpr = xpath.compile("//item/title");
// Define XPath expression to extract links
XPathExpression linkexpr = xpath.compile("//item/link");

// Evaluate XPath expressions
Object titleresult = titleexpr.evaluate(doc, XPathConstants.NODESET);
Object linkresult = linkexpr.evaluate(doc, XPathConstants.NODESET);

// Loop over extracted title elements using DOM
NodeList titlenodes = (NodeList) titleresult;
for (int i = 0; i < titlenodes.getLength(); i++) {
  feedtitles.add(titlenodes.item(i).getChildNodes().item(0).getNodeValue());
}

// Loop over extracted link elements using DOM
NodeList linknodes = (NodeList) linkresult;
for (int j = 0; j < linknodes.getLength(); j++) {
  feedlinks.add(linknodes.item(j).getChildNodes().item(0).getNodeValue());
}
    // Omitted for brevity- Values placed in Model object and returned to view
return "nationalweathertemplate";
```

Though this last approach also relies on the transformation of a REST service's payload into a `Document` object, notice how XPath makes the data extraction process simpler than just using the DOM. In one case, the XPath expression `//item/title` is used to extract all the `<title>`elements nested inside `<item>` elements. In another case, the XPath expression `//item/link` is used to extract all the `<link>` elements nested inside `<item>` elements.

Once XPath is used to obtain the elements, the elements are cast into a DOM `NodeList` object, where their data is finally extracted and assigned to the handler method's `Model` object to be displayed to the requesting user.

In addition to using Java's built-in XPath class, it's also possible to use another series of XPath-related approaches using Spring classes. These approaches form part of Spring's XML project.

■ **Note** The Spring XML project JAR is distributed separately from Spring's core distribution and can be obtained at `http://www.springsource.com/repository/app/bundle/version/download?name=org.springframework.xml&version=1.5.9.A&type=binary`. If you are using Maven, add the following dependencies to your project:

<dependency>
  <groupId>org.springframework.ws</groupId>
  <artifactId>spring-xml</artifactId>
  <version>1.5.9</version>
</dependency>

<dependency>
  <groupId>org.springframework.ws</groupId>
  <artifactId>spring-oxm</artifactId>
  <version>1.5.9</version>
</dependency>

The first approach involving XPath and Spring classes involves defining XPath expressions as Spring beans. This allows XPath expressions to be reused throughout an application, in addition to limiting the need to use additional XPath instantiation classes (e.g., **XPathFactory**, **XPath**) and instead rely on Spring's bean injection.

For example, the previous XPath expression can be defined in the following manner inside an application's Spring configuration file:

```
<bean id="feedtitleExpression" ↵
  class="org.springframework.xml.xpath.XPathExpressionFactoryBean">
        <property name="expression" value="//item/title"/>
    </bean>

<bean id="feedlinkExpression" class="org.springframework.xml.xpath. ↵
XPathExpressionFactoryBean">
        <property name="expression" value="//item/link"/>
  </bean>
```

Once these XPath expression beans are defined, they can be injected into a Spring MVC controller class and used inside a handler method, just as if they were declared using Java's core XPath classes (e.g., **XPathFactory**, **XPath**.). The following listing illustrates the contents of a Spring MVC controller using this process:

```
@Autowired
protected XPathExpression feedtitleExpression;
@Autowired
protected XPathExpression feedlinkExpression;

// START HANDLER METHOD
// Omitted for brevity- REST payload transformation to W3C Document
// Define W3C Document
Document doc = db.parse(is);

// Define lists for titles and links
List feedtitles = new ArrayList();
List feedlinks = new ArrayList();

List<Node> titlenodes =  feedtitleExpression.↵
                         evaluateAsNodeList(doc.getDocumentElement());
List<Node> linknodes = feedlinkExpression.↵
                         evaluateAsNodeList(doc.getDocumentElement());

for (Node node : titlenodes) {
  feedtitles.add(node.getChildNodes().item(0).getNodeValue());
}

for (Node node : linknodes) {
 feedlinks.add(node.getChildNodes().item(0).getNodeValue());
}

 // Omitted for brevity- Values placed in Model object and returned to view
return "nationalweathertemplate";
```

Notice that by using Spring's XPathExpressionFactoryBean as well as Spring's XPathExpression, the code to extract a REST service's payload becomes simpler. First of all, the XPath expression beans are injected into the class using the @Autowired annotation. Once available, the XPath expression beans are evaluated by passing the REST service's payload in the form of a Document object.

Further note how the results of evaluating the evaluateAsNodeList, which belongs to Spring's XPathExpression class, are cast into a List of Node objects, instead of the DOM's NodeList class, something which also makes the data-extraction process simpler by being able to use a short-handed Java loop.

Another alternative available using Spring's XML project consists of the NodeMapper class. The purpose of the NodeMapper class is to directly map XML nodes into Java objects.

For the NodeMapper case, let's assume you have the following XPath expression bean defined inside your Spring configuration file:

```
<bean id="feeditemExpression" ↵
 class="org.springframework.xml.xpath.XPathExpressionFactoryBean">
        <property name="expression" value="//item"/>
    </bean>
```

This XPath expression bean is defined with a value //item. This XPath value indicates to extract all the <item> elements that belong to an XML payload. In case you don't recall, <item> elements represent the recurring elements of an RSS feed, which further contain elements such as <title> and <link>.

The following listing illustrates how to use the NodeMapper class using this last XPath expression bean in the context of a Spring MVC controller:

```
@Autowired
protected XPathExpression feeditemExpression;

// START HANDLER METHOD
// Omitted for brevity- REST payload transformation to W3C Document
// Define W3C Document
Document doc = db.parse(is);

// Define lists for titles and links
List feedtitles = new ArrayList();
List feedlinks = new ArrayList();

List feedcontent = feeditemExpression.evaluate(doc, ↵
    new NodeMapper() {
        public Object mapNode(Node node, int nodeNum) ↵
            throws DOMException {
                Element itemElement = (Element) node;
                Element titleElement = ↵
    (Element) itemElement.getElementsByTagName("title").item(0);
                Element linkElement = ↵
    (Element) itemElement.getElementsByTagName("link").item(0);
            return new FeedContent(titleElement.getTextContent(), ↵
                linkElement.getTextContent());
            }
    }
);

// Place feed type, version and content in model object
model.addAttribute("feedtype", ↵
                    doc.getDocumentElement().getNodeName());
model.addAttribute("feedversion", ↵
                    doc.getDocumentElement().getAttribute("version"));
model.addAttribute("feedcontent", feedcontent);
return "nationalweathertemplate";
```

The XPath expression bean is injected into the controller class using the @Autowired annotation, just as the previous example. However, notice the XPath expression bean reference—feedItemExpression—is passed a Document object as well as a NodeMapper instance. The Document object represents the XML payload cast from a StreamSource class obtained using the RestTemplate class, which is identical to the previous approaches. The NodeMapper instance, though, deserves further explanation.

The NodeMapper loops over the elements that match the XPath expression bean, in this case <item> elements. On each iteration, it relies on the DOM's Element to extract each <item> element's nested <title> and <link> values. Further note that, after each iteration, a POJO backed by the class FeedContent and containing these values is returned. As a consequence of this step, the results of evaluating the XPath expression—feedItemExpression—are a List of FeedContent objects and not List DOM Node objects, making the data available for immediate assignment to the handler method's Model object instead of requiring further processing of DOM Node objects.

As you can see, using the Spring `NodeMapper` class further shortens the process of extracting data in a granular fashion from a REST service.

Finally, another approach involving Spring classes based on XPath involves using `XPathTemplate`. `XPathTemplate` is by far the shortest—syntax-wise—of all the approaches available to extract data from a REST service in a Spring application.

The first thing that's needed to use the `XPathTemplate` is to define a `XPathTemplate` Spring bean to make it available (i.e. inject it) into a Spring MVC controller. The following snippet illustrates this configuration, which needs to be placed inside a Spring configuration file:

```
<bean id="feedXPathTemplate" ↵
        class="org.springframework.xml.xpath.Jaxp13XPathTemplate">
</bean>
```

■ **Note** `Jaxp13XPathTemplate` is an implementation of `XPathTemplate`, another implementation is `JaxenXPathTemplate`. Both are included in Spring's XML project ,and you can use either one. The difference is that one is built on JAXP 1.3 (which is part of the Java 5 core platform), and the other is built on Jaxen, an open source Java XPath library.

Once an `XPathTemplate` Spring bean is defined, it's possible to inject it into a Spring MVC controller using the `@Autowired` annotation and then use it inside a handler method's body. The following listing illustrates this process:

```
@Autowired
protected org.springframework.xml.xpath.AbstractXPathTemplate feedXPathTemplate;

@RequestMapping("/nationalweather")
public String getWeatherNews(Model model) {
Source source = restTemplate.getForObject(" ↵
        http://rss.weather.com/rss/national/rss_nwf_rss.xml? ↵
        cm_ven={cm_ven}&cm_cat={cm_cat}&par={par}", ↵
        Source.class, "NWF","rss","NWF_rss");

// Define lists for titles and links
List feedtitles = new ArrayList();
List feedlinks = new ArrayList();

List feedcontent = feedXPathTemplate.evaluate("//item", source, ↵
                new NodeMapper() {
        public Object mapNode(Node node, int nodeNum) throws DOMException {
                Element itemElement = (Element) node;
                Element titleElement = (Element)
                itemElement.getElementsByTagName("title").item(0);
                Element linkElement = (Element)
                itemElement.getElementsByTagName("link").item(0);
```

```
                      return new FeedContent(titleElement.getTextContent(),↵
                               linkElement.getTextContent());
            }
         }
);

// No Document, so just hard-code feed type and version
model.addAttribute("feedtype","rss");
model.addAttribute("feedversion","2.0");
// Place feedcontent obtained using XPathTemplate
model.addAttribute("feedcontent",feedcontent);
return "nationalweathertemplate";
}
```

Notice the response of the getForObject method—part of the RestTemplate class. Unlike the previous approaches, it is assigned to a Source interface, instead of a StreamSource class, because the XPathTemplate expects to work with an XML payload built as a Source reference. It's worth mentioning that the StreamSource class implements the Source interface, so they're compatible.

If you then look at the XPathTemplate reference, feedXPathTemplate, you will note the call to the evaluate method takes three input parameters: //item, which represents an XPath query for all <item> elements; source, which represents a reference to the XML payload on which the XPath query is applied; and a NodeMapper instance used to loop over the elements extracted in applying the XPath query. The return value of calling the evaluate method corresponds to a List of FeedContent objects, making the data available for immediate assignment to the handler method's Model object.

As you can observe, by using Spring's XPathTemplate, the process of extracting a REST service's payload is further shortened, by forgoing the use of a DOM Document object and the capability of declaring XPath expression in line.

Even though Spring's XPathTemplate approach can seem like an obvious choice over all the previous methods given its succinctness, it's important to realize that flexibility can also be an important factor in processing REST service payloads. By using some of the earlier and more general-purpose approaches to processing XML, you have the ability to choose from a wider set of techniques for processing and manipulating XML (e.g., using filters, explicitly specifying encodings, or applying XSL style-sheets), which under certain circumstances, can prove to be more powerful than using Spring's XPathTemplate.

Finally, it's worth mentioning that in addition to the approaches described here—which are among the most popular for processing XML payloads—a multitude of libraries are available for processing XML in Java. Some of these other libraries include JDOM, Castor XML, and Project Rome. Depending on your previous experience with some of these libraries, you can opt to use them instead or in conjunction with the techniques described here.

USING PROJECT ROME TO ACCESS RSS AND ATOM REST SERVICES

In recipe 9-3, you learned how to publish Atom and RSS feeds using Project Rome. Project Rome also offers support to access Atom and RSS feeds from Java code. The following snippet illustrates how to access a REST services using Project Rome's API:

```
URL feedSource = new URL("http://rss.weather.com/↵
        rss/national/rss_nwf_rss.xml?cm_ven=NWF&↵
        cm_cat=rss&par=NWF_rss");
SyndFeedInput input = new SyndFeedInput();
SyndFeed feed = input.build(new XmlReader(feedSource));
```

As you can see, Project Rome is able to perform an HTTP GET on a REST service and assign its payload to a SyndFeed class, from where it can be further manipulated using Project Rome's API.

Though this approach forgoes using Spring's built-in and more general-purpose support for REST services, it's an alternative that can serve you if your more comfortable using Project Rome and only require accessing RSS and Atom feeds.

Summary

In this chapter, you have learned how to develop and access REST services using Spring. REST services are closely tied to Spring MVC, whereby a controller acts to dispatch requests made to REST services, as well as access third-party REST services to use this information for application content.

You learned how REST services leverage annotations used in Spring MVC controllers, which included @RequestMapping to indicate service end points, as well as @PathVariable to specify access parameters for filtering a service's payload. In addition, you learned about Spring's XML marshallers, such as Jaxb2Marshaller, which allow application objects to be transformed into XML and be output as a REST service's payload.

You also learned about Spring's RestTemplate class and how it supports the series of HTTP protocol methods that include HEAD, GET, POST, PUT, and DELETE—all of which allow you to access and perform operations on third-party REST services directly from the context of a Spring application.

You also explored how to publish Atom and RSS feeds in a Spring application by leveraging the Project Rome API. Additionally, you learned how to publish JSON payloads in a Spring application.

Finally, you learned how to access REST services with elaborate XML payloads using a variety of techniques that included data streams, XPath, marshallers, Spring's HttpMessageConverter, and Spring's XPathTemplate.

CHAPTER 10

■ ■ ■

Spring and Flex

It's an interesting time for web developers. The decade of the 2000s saw the rise of the rich Internet application. The idea of an Internet application as we know it is essentially a series of tradeoffs made by developers for the Internet, the ultimate platform. In the early '90s when client/server architectures ruled the day, every application communicated with its server differently, and most clients were operating system specific. Java came around and promised to unshackle the client from the operating system, but the fact remains that the fundamental interface between client and server was variable.

Along came the Internet and then the Web, and with it HTTP. The Internet wasn't designed to be an application platform; in fact, the earliest versions of what we know as the Internet didn't prescribe any of the things a Visual Basic or Delphi user would've expected, for example. If the Internet was going to work as a platform, it would need to be made to work.

The Internet is the largest platform on earth. It's application neutral—you can do whatever you want that needs connectivity. The Web, built on top of the Internet, was originally conceived as just a mesh of hyperlinks, forming a huge reference library: don't knock that; it's immensely useful. To make applications run over the Web, you need to do a lot of work and—more than likely—dilute some of the original notions extended about the Web. Developers have made do with it. We plugged the gaps where required; we took an inherently stateless platform and created "sessions;" we took SGML and added markup for describing presentation to get HTML; we took incompatible browser clients and abstracted away the considerable differences behind libraries, which we deploy with religious zealotry. We evolved the ideas behind the venerable MVC pattern to yield model 2 MVC (the MVC variant as espoused by Struts and a lot of early Java MVC frameworks) and the model-view-presenter (MVP) pattern (this variant seems more common in the .NET world). In short, we've done a lot to bend the Web to our will, and it *still* isn't easy to figure out all the constituent parts of a working web application.

A skilled developer can work with all the technologies built on the Internet and assemble an impressive application—one that feels coherent and quick and that looks good—leveraging HTML, CSS, JavaScript, DOM, XML, JSON, REST, and—of course—a server-side programming language. A really skilled developer will endeavor to also build an application that works on all browsers and that works consistently. A really, really skilled developer (indeed, a whole team) might even endeavor to completely hide all the fragility of the underlying platform altogether. This developer will build a compiler that emits JavaScript given input Java code and perhaps work to change the HTML specification to better support requirements.

For the rest of us wanting to simply ship a working application, we can let somebody else do the work. We can't remove all problems, but we can remove the ones that are not sufficiently abstracted already. We can't obfuscate the need for HTTP—that's the part that makes the Web a worthy platform. We need that part. If you've chosen a server-side programming language, then you've also already got a working abstraction for sessions, for example, so there's no need to "fix" that. It's a problem that's already been solved for you. Most of what we need is there already. The only irksome bit is how we will actually build the user-facing application. We have web frameworks that handle a lot of the minutiae on the server, and we've built component libraries that take us a long way in abstracting away the differences between browsers, but the fact remains that these approaches are common-ground solutions, designed to work across many clients by not exceeding the capabilities of any one client.

The modern day web programmer (as of 2010) contends with a long list of things he or she can't (readily) do that a client/server programmer of the 1990s (20 or more years ago!) took for granted: file system access, multimedia, cutting edge graphics, persistent local storage, skinning, and so on. Worse, while applications are increasingly quicker in today's browsers, few provide compiled-code execution speed. The idioms we use today for form validation, server communication, and rendering change with every web framework.

When Macromedia, now owned by Adobe, initially released Flash, it was to bring the animation finesse of Macromedia Shockwave to the Internet. As time progressed, the animation facilities grew to include a sophisticated programming environment. The only thing missing was support for data-intensive applications, the niche formerly occupied by Visual Basic. It was no surprise then that, in 2004, when Macromedia announced Flex, an environment with a generous complement of data-bound controls and full support for RPC, that developers in the Java camp were curious. There were early adopters, even if the interest was muted. The problem—the platform was closed source and expensive. The tooling, SDK, and integration middleware were all costly, and Flex was an unproven architecture few were willing to risk and prove at cost. The barrier to entry was too high.

Adobe, which bought Macromedia in 2005, eventually started opening up the bits. The Flex platform's SDK itself was made available so that you could compile from the command line. Flash offers a binary protocol called Action Message Format (AMF) by which Flash VMs talk to servers: it's quick and compact, especially when compared to JSON and SOAP. While many open source projects had reverse-engineered the protocol and exposed similar, alternative integrations for their favorite platform (PHP, Python, and in the Java world, Granite DS), the ideal solution was a proper implementation like that exposed by Adobe's expensive Lifecycle Data Services (LDS) middle project. Key bits of LDS were released under an open source license (various bits are licensed differently: BlazeDS proper is LGPL) in 2007 and renamed BlazeDS.

The tooling—an Eclipse derivative called Adobe Flex Builder—is still a pay-for-use product, but this doesn't impede others from creating their own tooling. Particularly, IntelliJ's IDEA product, versions 8 and 9, support Flex and AIR development with aplomb. Additionally, it is entirely possible to build entire Flex and AIR applications using only the command line, or with third-party tools, like the Maven 2 FlexMojos project, which supports building Flex applications using Maven.

As the platform's become more open, so too has the groundswell of open source projects supporting the Flex environment gown. If you want to leverage BlazeDS to consume Spring services, there is specialized support built in cooperation between SpringSource and Adobe available called the Spring BlazeDS Integration. The integration makes working in Spring and exposing services using a Spring a piece of cake. On the client side, in ActionScript, the Spring ActionScript project provides a lot of the familiar niceties provided by the Spring platform for Java developers. We'll use this project to explore dependency injection (DI) in ActionScript, wiring up remote services, and wiring in services to your Flex components.

10-1. Getting started with Flex

Problem

The Flex platform is huge, and it helps to have a sense of the landscape. How does one know what tool does what and why?

Solution

We will explore the tools and technologies that make up the Flex platform. First, we'll look at the SDK and the tooling offerings. Then, we'll explore the middleware technologies and the state of the platform itself today.

How It Works

The first thing to realize when working with Flex is that it is, technically, a library implemented on top of the Flash virtual machine. If you've ever been victim to an annoying animated ad of late, then you've probably seen Flash. Flash maintains a frame-based timeline. Every second that ticks by causes the Flash runtime to paint the screen at a fixed interval. If you are using regular Flash code, then you will need to concern yourself with the frames of the animation, since these play into values like the duration of an animation or time. In Flash, the displayed area where animation and rendering occurs is called the stage. Components are added to the stage and given a life cycle, very much like objects in the DOM of your browser.

Flash uses a language called ActionScript 3.0. ActionScript is a variant of JavaScript that has drawn inspiration from the various specifications for JavaScript. You'll likely encounter two variants of ActionScript code in the wild: ActionScript 2, which shipped with the Flash 8 VM, and ActionScript 3, which is what's been available since Flash 9. The two versions are *very* different beasts: ActionScript 2 is more similar to the JavaScript variant in your web browser, and ActionScript 3 is more similar to JScript.NET or C#/Java. Unlike the JavaScript variant most developers are probably familiar with in the browser, ActionScript is compiled. ActionScript code pages end in `.as`, and ActionScript binaries are `.swf` files. You can use ActionScript tools to build linkable libraries, much like a `.dll` on Windows, or a `.so` on Linux. These linkable libraries have the extension `.swc`. This can be a strange thing to grasp for a Java developer with no history in C/C++ or even .NET; in Java all "binaries" are `.jars`. The ability for `.jar` "a" to use another `.jar`, "b," is not dictated at compile time. We will see later when we use Spring ActionScript that the library is shipped as a `.swc` file.

Flex is implemented on top of the Flash VM as a library. You can inspect the source code, and you'll see that most of it is written using ActionScript. It enjoys a special status among libraries, however, in that most people will get their instance of the Flex library directly from their player.

Flash, and Flex, run inside of a web page in your browser, in the same way as Java applets run. Flex applications can't install themselves in the OS's application menus or manipulate the file system (except when doing things like uploading files, in which case there's no control surfaced to the programmer; it's an isolated use case). Similarly, the life cycle of a Flex application is constrained by that of the host browser: when the browser stops, so does Flex. To address these issues, Adobe released AIR. AIR is a superset of Flex that has APIs for manipulating the file system, installation, automatic updates, and more. The AIR runtime, like the Flex runtime, will typically come from Adobe. AIR deployments are more akin to Java Web Start deployments than applets. It is very easy to write a Flex application and change the outermost container component to run it in AIR. Thus, Flex applications are AIR applications, though AIR applications aren't Flex applications, per se.

Flex Development Basics

Whereas Flash provides an animation-centric environment with support for creating timelines and importing graphics and the like (with the expectation that script that was added would be done so as event handling logic in ActionScript), Flex is a code-centric platform. The two source artifacts of a Flex application are the ActionScript files (ending in `.as`) and the `.mxml` files.

ActionScript files can contain classes, public functions and variables, and annotations. Indeed, ActionScript files may house any number of public classes. The look and feel of the language will feel familiar to anyone who's used Java, C#, or Scala.

MXML files are an XML variant that describe the UI components and provide a DOM. Scripts may be inline, which we will do for this chapter's trivial examples in the name of expediency. Each tag in MXML describes a component or object that is registered with its container. In the case of Flex applications, the outermost tag is the `<mx:Application/>` tag; in AIR, it's `<mx:WindowedApplication/>`. These tags describe containers that themselves handle all the minutiae of creating components on the Flash **Stage** object.

You can use MXML to instantiate regular ActionScript objects, like you might in Spring, but you'll find that some uses will more naturally lend themselves to code and some to MXML. You could create an entire Flex application using only ActionScript with no MXML. When the MXML files are compiled, they are converted to ActionScript expressions as an intermediary format, and *that* is what is ultimately compiled. MXML files support a limited form of expression language binding (*limited* when compared to the EL support in frameworks like Tapestry or JSF, anyway). Flex components are wired together using the expression binding support, as well as with powerful event mechanism.

Let's look at a simple MXML file:

```
<?xml version="1.0" encoding="utf-8"?>
<mx:Application
xmlns:mx="http://www.adobe.com/2006/mxml"
applicationComplete="applicationCompleteCallback(event)">

    <mx:Script>
        <![CDATA[

            import mx.events.FlexEvent;
            import mx.controls.Alert;

            public function applicationCompleteCallback(fe:FlexEvent):void
            {
                Alert.show('Hello World!');
            }

        ]]>
    </mx:Script>

</mx:Application>
```

This MXML describes the simplest possible Flex application. As soon as the application has been loaded and all the objects configured, an event will be fired—the `applicationComplete` event. Just as you can in the browser, you have two choices for listening to events in Flex: programmatic registration and through MXML attributes on the component that fires the event. Here, we've installed our listener using the `applicationComplete` attribute on the `mx:Application` tag. It's very convenient to use MXML event subscription in most cases, though sometimes, you want to programmatically register listeners.

Let's try another example with a button that displays an alert when clicked. We'll register the event through ActionScript, instead.

```
<?xml version="1.0" encoding="utf-8"?>
<mx:Application
        xmlns:mx="http://www.adobe.com/2006/mxml"
        applicationComplete="applicationCompleteHandler(event)">

    <mx:Script>
        <![CDATA[

        import mx.controls.Alert;
        import mx.events.FlexEvent;

        private function applicationCompleteHandler(evt:FlexEvent):void
        {
            button.addEventListener(MouseEvent.CLICK, onClick);
        }

        private function onClick(me:MouseEvent):void
        {
            Alert.show('Hello, world!');
        }

        ]]>
    </mx:Script>
    <mx:Button id="button" label="Say Hello"/>
</mx:Application>
```

I won't belabor the point but for one more example; this *is* a JavaScript variant, after all! The previous example could have been rewritten to use an anonymous function:

```
<?xml version="1.0" encoding="utf-8"?>
<mx:Application
        xmlns:mx="http://www.adobe.com/2006/mxml"
        applicationComplete="applicationCompleteHandler(event)">

    <mx:Script>
        <![CDATA[

        import mx.controls.Alert;
        import mx.events.FlexEvent;
```

```
            private function applicationCompleteHandler(evt:FlexEvent):void
            {
                button.addEventListener(MouseEvent.CLICK,
                function (me:MouseEvent):void  {
                  Alert.show('Hello, world!');
                });
            }

        ]]>
    </mx:Script>
    <mx:Button id="button" label="Say Hello"/>
</mx:Application>
```

In the preceding examples, we did nothing special to access the object created by the `<mx:Button />` tag, except to refer to it by its `id` attribute, `button`. We didn't need to use something like `document.getElementById(String)`, as you might expect from the browser.

Now, let's look at a simple ActionScript class. We'll flesh out this class more later, but for now, it's helpful to see what it looks like to define a Plain Old ActionScript Object (yes, Virginia, that is what it's called!):

```
package com.apress.springwebrecipes.auction.model
{
public class Item
{
    private var _sellerEmail:String;
    private var _basePrice:Number;
    private var _sold:Date;
    private var _description:String;
    private var _id:Number;

    public function get id():Number {
        return _id;
    }

    public function set id(value:Number):void {
        _id = value;
    }

    // ...

}
}
```

This should seem pretty intuitive. Most striking is the C++/C#–style package syntax; the package declaration wraps the classes. Here, we only have one, but we could have as easily defined 20. We won't get into the gory details of visibility rules, but suffice it to say that `public` and `private` work pretty much the way you'd expect them to. The next element to note is that ActionScript has a proper property syntax. We declared a private class variable `_id`, of type `Number`. Then, we declared two functions that look a little different than the other functions you've seen thus far. These functions have the keyword `get` and `set` and share the same function name. This is the language support for defining accessors and mutators, just like with Java's JavaBeans. Unlike JavaBeans, however, there is syntactic support to let the users manipulate properties like they would public instance variables. To use the preceding class, we could write something like this:

```
package com.apress.springwebrecipes
{
    import com.apress.springwebrecipes.auction.model.Item;

    public class ItemDemo
    {
        public function ItemDemo()
        {
            var item:Item = new Item();
            item.id = 232;
        }
    }
}
```

The Tools

The most common tool for building Flex applications, by far, is Adobe's Flex Builder tooling. It is what we'll use in this chapter. Flex Builder is an Eclipse-based IDE. The IDE provides compilation, debugging, and wizard support for developing ActionScript- and Flex-based applications. It also has a visual designer, but experience has shown that it serves little purpose for moderate-sized applications. Flex Builder features support for working with other tools in the Adobe Creative Suite, including Flash Professional (which, as indicated previously, is useful for timeline based applications and components), Photoshop, and Illustrator.

Arguably, Flex's most powerful feature is its integration with other Adobe tools, in support of Adobe's vision of the designer/developer workflow.

Flex supports the concept of states. With a state, you can assign arbitrary names to given sets of components and configuration and, by setting the currentState property, have the engine activate that state. A state can prescribe that components be added or removed a display. It can also outright replace the current display. There is a lot of potential here. These states are used to describe a widget's state on screen, too. The Adobe Creative Suite facilitates exporting Photoshop or Illustrator assets, for example, and mapping the layers of those assets to states in a Flex component. You might imagine a button whose mouse-over, mouse-down, mouse-up, hover, focus, and other states each are each assigned a layer in a Photoshop file—a layer for the focus state might render the button with a glow; the layer for mouse down might darken the colors, and so on.

There are many other such niceties, but ultimately, they are all available even without Flex Builder, using the stand-alone compiler, if you know where to look.

Indeed, the single simplest and most cost-effective way to get started with Flex is to use the SDK. You can download the SDK from Adobe's site for free. At the time of this writing, the most current version of the SDK is 3.5. You may download it at http://www.adobe.com/cfusion/entitlement/index.cfm?e=flex3sdk.

To use the SDK, download it, and extract the archive. Put the bin folder inside the SDK on your system's PATH variable, just as you might with Ant, Maven, and the Java SDK. The Flex SDK offers two compilers: one for components, and one for Flex applications. If you want to compile components, you will use compc. If you want to compile an application, you will use mxmlc. An example invocation of the mxmlc says it all:

```
mxmlc main.mxml
```

The Flex SDK compilers are written in Java, so you could also invoke them using the `java` command. What follows is an invocation of the compiler using Java. This does the same thing as the preceding command. The following invocation is assumed to be in the `bin` directory of the SDK. There should be no breaks in your command, though; it should all be on one line.

```
java -jar ../lib/mxmlc.jar +flexlib ../frameworks test1.mxml
```

Another approach for developing application is to use Maven. The FlexMojos project (`http://flexmojos.sonatype.org/`) is a set of plug-ins supporting building Flex projects and handing dependency resolution, just as Maven does for Java projects.

Because the runtime and compiler are available, other IDEs have built support for Flex. One very good integration is IntelliJ's IDEA 9.0. It supports coding, compiling, refactoring, debugging, and all the basics you'd expect of a good IDE. While it doesn't support the visual design mechanism or many of the wizards that Flex Builder has, it does excel in some areas where Flex Builder falls short: IDEA supports formatting code, for example, import of Maven FlexMojos projects, and refactoring (renaming) of MXML fragments. Flex Builder is a set of plug-ins built on Eclipse. You may run Flex Builder stand-alone or integrated with an existing Eclipse installation. By itself, Flex Builder lacks an XML editor, support for Subversion, and any kind of support for Java. Additionally, Flex Builder is usually coupled with an older revision of Eclipse.

Clearly, there is no shortage of ways to approach the problem. If you can swing it, the Flex Builder tooling will be familiar to Adobe users. IntelliJ users have no need to switch. Failing those options, the SDK and various build systems welcome any would-be Flex developers.

10-2. Leaving the Sandbox

Problem

You know you want to integrate Flex and Java, but there are many options. What technologies work best, and when? Which—if any—is preferable?

Solution

The Flex platform is nothing if not *flexible!* The answer, of course, is "it depends." You have several options to talk to a remote service from Flex including HTTP requests, AMF communication, JSON serialization, and even specialized support for consuming services exposed with REST, XML, and SOAP.

Flex also talks plays nicely with the web page hosting the Flex application using JavaScript. This communication is bidirectional: Flex may manipulate the containing page, and the containing page may manipulate the Flex application.

Your main limitation in all of these options is the Flash sandbox which—much like the applet sandbox—was put in place to assure that Flex applications are well-behaved.

With Flex, breaking outside of the sandbox means ensuring permission with the `crossdomain.xml` file, proxying access to services on hosts not otherwise available using something like BlazeDS, and ensuring proper host-of-origin etiquette in all other cases.

How It Works

We will spend most of the balance of this chapter exploring the Spring BlazeDS integration. However, there are other options, and it pays to be aware of them. Perhaps they offer an easier path.

FlashVars

Let's start with the simplest option: talking to the host page. Often, a Flex application will need to be configured at launch. You can launch a Flash application using `FlashVars` as parameters, just as you can launch a Java application with arguments.

Before diving into that, let's talk about Flex deployment. To deploy a Flex application, you need to embed markup in the browser to enable the browser to display the Flash content, since it is not part of browser's native capabilities. There are many ways to generate this configuration. The configuration for the `embed` and `object` tags can be quite convoluted because no single configuration works reliably over the many target browsers. Flex Builder will generate a default version, but this markup is fragile and can quickly become unmaintainable. To save space, we won't bother reprinting it. Instead, we recommend using the SWF Object JavaScript library (`http://code.google.com/p/swfobject/wiki/documentation`). Simply download the JavaScript library and put it in your web application. The library dynamically generates the relevant `object` and `plugin` tags, along with the FlashVars parameters. Because the JavaScript library dynamically adds the plug-in content to the page, it triggered the "Dynamic Content" warning in Internet Explorer 6 for a few years. This is, in practice, less and less of an issue now that newer versions of Internet Explorer 6 (and indeed, all subsequent versions, too) no longer have this issue.

Here is a minimalistic use:

```html
<html>
    <head>
        <title> Hello World </title>
        <meta http-equiv="Content-Type"
            content="text/html; charset=iso-8859-1" />
        <style>
            body,html { padding:0; margin:0 }
        </style>
        <script type="text/javascript" src="swfobject/swfobject.js"> </script>
        <script type="text/javascript">
            var flashVars = {
              parameter1: 'parameter1',
              parameter2: 'parameter2'
            };
            swfobject.embedSWF(
              "helloworld.swf",
              "helloworld",
              "500",
              "500",
              "9.0.0",
              "swfobject/expressInstall.swf",
              flashVars );
        </script>
    </head>
```

```
    <body>
        <div id="helloworld"></div>
    </body>
</html>
```

The first bold line shows the inclusion of the script. Further down, you see the invocation of the swfobject.embedSWF method. The first parameter is the name of the SWF asset (relative to the current page, of course). The second parameter is the id of the HTML element on the page that should be replaced when the SWFObject tries to *paint* the Flex application. Here, we want the Flash application to render where the div element with the ID of "helloworld" is, which is shown further in the following example in bold. The plug-in and object instances will be created with an ID of helloworld.

Finally, coming around to the original point, toward the top, we define a variable (flashVars) that is an associative array of keys and values. These keys and values are passed as parameters to the Flex application (note that it is passed as the last parameter to the swfobject.embedSWF method). The Flex application may get at these variables from inside using the Application instance:

```
<?xml version="1.0" encoding="utf-8"?>
<mx:Application
        xmlns:mx="http://www.adobe.com/2006/mxml"
        applicationComplete="setup(event)">

    <mx:Script>
        <![CDATA[

        import mx.controls.Alert;
        import mx.events.FlexEvent;

        private function setup(evt:FlexEvent):void
        {
            Alert.show (
' param1='+Application.application.parameters['parameter1'] +
' param2='+Application.application.parameters['parameter2'] );

        }
        ]]>
    </mx:Script>
</mx:Application>
```

You can use these variables to configure the state of your Flash (and Flex) applications. This works well for configuration options—which may be all you need to communicate from the host application. It is, tragically, only a one-way solution. If you want a bi-directional channel from the containing application (in our case, a Spring web application) to the Flex application, you need to pursue other options.

ExternalInterface

Because Flex lives inside the Flash VM, it's easy to think of it as being confined, when in fact, it is freely able to talk to the host environment. To talk to the containing HTML page, you can use the flash.external.ExternalInterface class. This class defines two static methods, call() (which lets the Flex application talk to the host) and addCallback() (which lets the host talk to Flex). The

ExternalInterface class provides a communication line going both directions: Flex-to-host and host-to-Flex. This solution is appropriate when you don't have a lot you need to inside the Flex environment—perhaps you need to notify the host page of some events when drawing some graph, or perhaps your Flex environment only needs to make one Ajax call. Similarly, perhaps you're embedding Flex to take advantage of its multimedia support or its rendering capabilities, but you want to drive that rendering through events in the host container. This indirection is slower (naturally) than doing something directly from the host page or directly from the Flex application, but it can be quite appropriate in many situations.

If we want to talk to the host environment, we can use the call() method on ExternalInterface. It is a blocking call. Assume we have a function defined in the host HTML page called updateStatus:

```
<html>
  <head><title>Addition</title></head>
 <body>
  <div id ='status'></div>
  <script language='JavaScript'>
   function updateStatus (msg){
      document.getElementById('status').innerHTML = msg;
   }
  </script>

  <!--
    …
    Flex/flash
    …
  -->
 </body>
</html>
```

We could, of course, call methods that are already in the host environment, like window.alert(String). To call the updateStatus function from within Flex, you might do something like the following:

```
<?xml version="1.0" encoding="utf-8"?>
<mx:Application
        xmlns:mx="http://www.adobe.com/2006/mxml"
        applicationComplete="setup(event)">

    <mx:Script>
        <![CDATA[
        import mx.events.FlexEvent;
```

```
            private function setup(evt:FlexEvent):void
            {
                ExternalInterface.call(
                   'updateStatus',
                   'Hello, from the future! '+
                   'The Flex application has '+
                   'finished loading.');
            }
         ]]>
      </mx:Script>
</mx:Application>
```

Now, to go the other way—from the host environment to the Flex application—you have to register the functions that you want the host environment to see using the ExternalInterface's addCallback method. Perhaps we surface a method in our Flex application to play a track of music given the String path to an .mp3 file. Let's first build the Flex code:

```
<?xml version="1.0" encoding="utf-8"?>
<mx:Application
         xmlns:mx="http://www.adobe.com/2006/mxml"
         applicationComplete="setup(event)">

   <mx:Script>
      <![CDATA[
      import mx.events.FlexEvent;

      public function enqueueMP3Track( trackName:String) : void
      {
          //...
      }

      private function setup(evt:FlexEvent):void
      {
          ExternalInterface.addCallback('playTrack', enqueueMP3Track );
      }
      ]]>
   </mx:Script>
</mx:Application>
```

The first parameter to ExternalInterface.addCallback is the alias used to reference the function from the host page. On the host, calling the function *should* be pretty easy, but isn't, unless you're aware of the nuances between browsers. The following is a fairly fail-safe way of invoking the playTrack function from the host page:

```html
<html>

  <head>
  <title>Our Jukebox</title>
  <script language='JavaScript'>
   function getFlexApplicationReference( flexAppId ){
       return navigator.appName.indexOf('Microsoft')!= -1 ?
        window[flexAppId] : document[flexAppId];
   }

   function startTheMusic(evt){
       getFlexApplicationReference('jukebox').playTrack(
                      'La_Camisa_Negra.mp3');
   }
  </script>

  </head>

  <body onload='startTheMusic(event)'>

  <!--
    …
    Flex/flash setup using the swfobject
      as before, with an ID of 'jukebox'

    …
  -->
  </body>
</html>
```

This option works well when you need to expose functionality in one direction or another. You
might have an application that's predominantly built using conventional web frameworks (Struts, Spring
MVC, JSF, etc.) and Ajax (perhaps you've exposed Spring services using DWR). If you have an island of
functionality that's better suited to Flex, you can use this integration to provide the few touch points
your application needs to talk to the containing application.

HTTP and HTTPS

Talking to HTTP or HTTPS resources is one of the simplest mechanisms for talking to other systems, yet
it remains one of the most powerful. With the rapid adoption of REST-based services, HTTP is even more
powerful an option for many architectures. Additionally, HTTP support opens the door to the numerous
services exposing JSON or XML data. Fortunately, Flex provides robust support HTTP. Actually, it
provides **two** robust options for HTTP.

The first option is the Flex class mx.rpc.http.HTTPService. You can employ the HTTPService using
ActionScript or using MXML. The HTTPService works like wget or curl. You specify a URL (or a resource)
to request and then specify a listener to react to the retrieved data. The HTTPService supports GET and
POST methods. If you use a proxy, you can also use PUT and DELETE (which you're more likely to use when
consuming REST-ian services.) You cannot request an HTTP resource unless the resource is on the same
domain as the .SWF or that resource's domain's crossdomain.xml file is open to requests from your
domain.

To use the object from code, you create an instance of `mx.rpc.http.HTTPService`. Let's look at an example usage:

```
<?xml version="1.0" encoding="utf-8"?>
<mx:Application
        xmlns:mx="http://www.adobe.com/2006/mxml"
        applicationComplete="applicationCompleteHandler(event)">

    <mx:Script>
        <![CDATA[
        import mx.controls.Alert;
        import mx.events.FlexEvent;
        import mx.rpc.events.FaultEvent;
        import mx.rpc.events.ResultEvent;
        import mx.rpc.http.HTTPService;

        private function applicationCompleteHandler(evt:FlexEvent):void
        {
            var service:HTTPService = new HTTPService('http://127.0.0.1:8080/');
            service.url = 'test.txt';
            service.method ='GET'; // redundant
            service.addEventListener(ResultEvent.RESULT,
             function(re:ResultEvent):void {
                Alert.show('the response is ' + re.result);
            });
            service.addEventListener(FaultEvent.FAULT,
  function(fe:FaultEvent):void {
    Alert.show('the error is ' + fe.fault.content);
            });
            service.send();
        }
        ]]>
    </mx:Script>
</mx:Application>
```

Here, we construct an instance of `HTTPService` and pass the root URL against which subsequent requests should be evaluated. You can, of course, leave this blank and specify an absolute URL for the url property. We're using relative requests, so the url, which is `test.txt`, is relative to `http://127.0.0.1:8080`. Therefore, the fully qualified URL for the asset is `http://127.0.0.1:8080/test.txt`. If you have placed the web application under a different context than the root one (/), be sure to prefix `test.txt`. Here, the method property lets us specify which HTTP verb to use. There's no need to specify GET though, because it's redundant. To receive notification that the HTTP request was successful, we configure an event listener (for the result event). From this listener, we can access the payload of the response via the `ResultEvent` object instance's result property, `re`. If the request is not successful, we can get a notification by specifying an event listener for the `fault` event. Here, we interrogate the fault from the `FaultEvent` instance's `fault` property. Finally, we send the request. We could optionally specify headers as parameter to the send method using an associative array. Thus:

```
...
service.send({customerID: '23232432sssh543'});
```

There are other options available, including support for HTTPS, cookies, more sophisticated encoding of requests and responses, and so on.

If you prefer a more declarative approach, there is MXML support for declaring and configuring an HTTPService. To do what we did previously, we might configure the following:

```
<mx:HTTPService
id="service"
   rootURL="http://127.0.0.1:8080/"
   url="test.txt"
   method="GET"
   result="Alert.show( 'the response is ' + event.result )"
   fault="Alert.show('the error is ' + event.fault.content )"
/>
```

The HTTPService can now be referenced using the id property. Invoke the request just as you did before, in ActionScript code: the event listeners (for a result or a fault) specified in MXML will be invoked.

```
...
service.send();
```

The second option for creating HTTP requests is to use the class flash.net.URLLoader. There is little difference between the two options, but both are worth knowing about. To use flash.net.URLLoader, instantiate an instance, configure it, and invoke the load method with a parameter of type flash.net.URLRequest, in much the same way as you used the HTTPService.

To access the same resource as in the HTTPService examples, we might write the following:

```
<?xml version="1.0" encoding="utf-8"?>
<mx:Application
        xmlns:mx="http://www.adobe.com/2006/mxml"
        applicationComplete="applicationCompleteHandler(event)">

    <mx:Script>
        <![CDATA[
        import mx.controls.Alert;
        import mx.events.FlexEvent;

        private function applicationCompleteHandler(evt:FlexEvent):void
        {
            var urlLoader:URLLoader = new URLLoader();
                urlLoader.addEventListener(Event.COMPLETE, function(evt:Event):void  {
                Alert.show('the response is ' + urlLoader.data);
            });
            urlLoader.load(
                new URLRequest('http://127.0.0.1:8080/test.txt'));
        }
        ]]>
    </mx:Script>
</mx:Application>
```

There are a few key differences here. First, the reference to the result data came from the `urlLoader` variable itself, and not as a reference on the event dispatched when result data became available. Second, instead of configuring the URL to be accessed on the `urlLoader`, we passed it as a parameter to the `urlLoader.load` method. Depending on your tastes, this API may feel more natural to use. It's a slightly more lower level API and slightly less verbose.

HTTP services provide a generic mechanism to talk to many other resources, including REST services. You might also prefer REST—generic and platform neutral—to exposing AMF- and Flex-specific services. With Java EE 6.0 and/or Spring 3.0, creating REST services is a snap, and you may prefer to interact with them over traditional remoting APIs like SOAP going forward.

If you do need to interface with SOAP services, however, manually consuming XML resources and parsing them using ActionScript's XML support can be tedious. Instead, it's better to use something more suited to the task.

Consuming SOAP Services

Sometimes, you need to consume SOAP. It happens. Spring makes it dead simple to expose SOAP services. If your application is charged with consuming them, then you'll find the Flex framework is well equipped to do so. It works very much like the `HTTPService`: instantiate an instance, configure it, and then send a request.

Using the `WebService` object from MXML is only a bit more tedious than using the `HTTPService`. Here, we have to enumerate which operations on the SOAP endpoint to expose.

```
<?xml version="1.0" encoding="utf-8"?>
<mx:Application
        xmlns:mx="http://www.adobe.com/2006/mxml"
        applicationComplete="applicationCompleteHandler(event)">


    <mx:WebService id="echoService"
                wsdl="http://localhost:8080/echoService?wsdl">
        <mx:operation name="echo"/>
    </mx:WebService>

    <mx:Script>
        <![CDATA[
        import mx.controls.Alert;
        import mx.events.FlexEvent;
        import mx.rpc.AsyncToken;
        import mx.rpc.events.FaultEvent;
        import mx.rpc.events.ResultEvent;

        private function applicationCompleteHandler(evt:FlexEvent):void
        {
            var at:AsyncToken =
                    echoService.echo.send('Hello, World!');
            at.addEventListener(ResultEvent.RESULT,
              function(re:ResultEvent) :void {
                Alert.show('the result is ' + re.result + '');
                // 'Echo: Hello, World!'
            });
```

```
            at.addEventListener(FaultEvent.FAULT,
                function(fe:FaultEvent) :void {
                    Alert.show(fe.fault.toString());
            });
        }
        ]]>
    </mx:Script>
</mx:Application>
```

Using the WebService functionality from JavaScript is plain and fundamentally the same.

```
<?xml version="1.0" encoding="utf-8"?>
<mx:Application
        xmlns:mx="http://www.adobe.com/2006/mxml"
        applicationComplete="setup(event)">
    <mx:Script>
        <![CDATA[
        import mx.controls.Alert;
        import mx.events.FlexEvent;
        import mx.rpc.AsyncToken;
        import mx.rpc.events.FaultEvent;
        import mx.rpc.events.ResultEvent;
        import mx.rpc.soap.WebService;

        private function setup(evt:FlexEvent):void
        {
            var echoService:WebService = new WebService();
            echoService.wsdl = 'http://localhost:8080/echoService?wsdl';
            echoService.loadWSDL();

            var at:AsyncToken = echoService.echo.send('Hello, World!');

            at.addEventListener(ResultEvent.RESULT,
                function(re:ResultEvent):void {
                Alert.show('the result is ' + re.result + '');
                        // 'Echo: Hello, World!'
            });
            at.addEventListener(FaultEvent.FAULT,
                function(fe:FaultEvent):void {
                    Alert.show(fe.fault.toString());
            });
        }
        ]]>
    </mx:Script>
</mx:Application>
```

Here, we import the base class (whereas the first example uses an MXML-friendly subclass) and have to remember to call loadWSDL() once we've configured the WebService. SOAP services work fine for integrating legacy systems, but we think few people would be interested in setting them up for new projects, specifically for Flex, if there's a better alternative. What's required is something really quick and compressed with binary, something that plays well with Flex and Flash itself so that marshalling complex types isn't an issue. It should also be easy to support from the Java end. Creating SOAP is decidedly *not* easy to support.

This is where AMF comes in.

Flash Remoting with AMF

This is the most powerful option. AMF is a format that Flash clients can read efficiently. Because it's just binary data, it's efficient when sent across the wire (especially when compared to porous text formats like SOAP, XML, or JSON). Basically, AMF is everything you could ask for! It's compact, efficient, plays well with Flash, and it's easy to use. It's got everything! Well, *almost everything*, anyway. The first problem is that AMF services aren't ubiquitous, and even if they were, that doesn't mean you're exposing AMF services inside the enterprise. We'll discuss solving that problem in recipes to come, but first, let's look at how we might consume an AMF endpoint in Flex, both in MXML, and ActionScript.

Using an AMF service from MXML is a matter of configuring it and sending requests, similar to the other options you've seen so far.

```
<?xml version="1.0" encoding="utf-8"?>
<mx:Application
        xmlns:mx="http://www.adobe.com/2006/mxml"
        applicationComplete="setup(event)">

    <mx:RemoteObject
     endpoint="http://yourhost:8080/mb/amf"
     showBusyCursor="true"
     destination="auctionService"
     id="auctionService"
    />

    <mx:Script>
        <![CDATA[
        import mx.controls.Alert;
        import mx.events.FlexEvent;
        import mx.rpc.AsyncResponder;
        import mx.rpc.AsyncToken;
        import mx.rpc.events.FaultEvent;
        import mx.rpc.events.ResultEvent;

        private function setup(evt:FlexEvent):void
        {

            var resultHandler:Function = function(
                resultEvent:ResultEvent, asyncToken:AsyncToken) :void {
                Alert.show('result = ' + resultEvent.result);
            };
            var faultHandler:Function = function(
                faultEvent:FaultEvent, asyncToken:AsyncToken) :void {
                Alert.show('fault = ' + faultEvent.fault);
            };
```

```
        auctionService.getItemsForAuction().addResponder(
            new AsyncResponder(resultHandler, faultHandler));
    }
    ]]>
</mx:Script>
</mx:Application>
```

Toward the top, we configure an instance of a `<mx:RemoteObject />`. We don't tell it specifically which service endpoint to connect to. Instead, we tell it the address of the broker (in this case, BlazeDS) and the destination (the destination is, roughly, the abstract name of the resource that's exposed). A destination is where we send messages. Whether the message is ultimately routed to a service or a JMS queue, for example, is configured on the server, but the client doesn't necessarily know either way. IN the following example, we invoke services by calling them asynchronously. To be notified of a result or of a remoting fault, we configure callback functions. The functions are used as arguments for the `AsyncResponder`. It is the responder that ultimately handles the results of an invocation of a method. There are two callbacks: one to receive notifications that a result was returned from the server and another to receive notifications of errors in the messaging.

To achieve the same thing using ActionScript, we need only move the configuration of the objet from MXML to ActionScript code. This, as usual, involves removing "mxml" from the package name and simply constructing the object in ActionScript.

```
<?xml version="1.0" encoding="utf-8"?>
<mx:Application
        xmlns:mx="http://www.adobe.com/2006/mxml"
        applicationComplete="setup(event)">

    <mx:Script>
        <![CDATA[
        import mx.controls.Alert;
        import mx.events.FlexEvent;
        import mx.rpc.AsyncResponder;
        import mx.rpc.AsyncToken;
        import mx.rpc.events.FaultEvent;
        import mx.rpc.events.ResultEvent;
        import mx.rpc.remoting.RemoteObject;

        private function setup(evt:FlexEvent):void
        {

            var auctionService:RemoteObject = new RemoteObject();
            auctionService.endpoint = 'http://localhost:8080/mb/amf';
            auctionService.showBusyCursor = true;
            auctionService.destination = 'auctionService';

            var resultHandler:Function = function(
                resultEvent:ResultEvent, asyncToken:AsyncToken) :void {
                Alert.show('result = ' + resultEvent.result);
            };
```

```
            var faultHandler:Function = function(
                faultEvent:FaultEvent, asyncToken:AsyncToken) :void {
                Alert.show('fault = ' + faultEvent.fault);
            };

            auctionService.getItemsForAuction().addResponder(
                    new AsyncResponder(resultHandler, faultHandler));
        }
        ]]>
    </mx:Script>
</mx:Application>
```

So, AMF is a very convenient protocol. If you've got an easy connectivity layer that works with one of the protocols described in this recipe, then you might consider using those. In all other cases, AMF is a very solid option. The issue is then, "how do I expose my services in AMF?" You can expose an AMF endpoint using a broker like Adobe's LiveCycle Data Services product, a commercial offering; an open source offering like Granite DS; or as we'll discuss in this chapter, an open source project that is a subset of Lifecycle Data Services called BlazeDS. BlazeDS sits on your domain and can be used to expose Java objects and services as AMF-friendly services. It can also expose messaging middleware (like JMS) in such a way that a Flex client can consume messages asynchronously, very much in the same way Ajax clients can use Comet to receive messages *pushed* from the server. Finally, it can be used to simply proxy other services on other domains if required. There are servers like this that implement the AMF endpoint functionality for most platforms, including Python, PHP, Perl, and Ruby.

If you're using Java, and Spring, you may want to consider BlazeDS. It's a very powerful broker, has good support, and—as you'll see—is an absolute breeze to configure. BlazeDS can actually be downloaded and run stand-alone as a `.war` project. But, this introduces at minimum an unnecessary deployment into your architecture and at worse an extra server. So, most people tend to pick apart BlazeDS and install the relevant bits in their own web applications. This process was tedious, but worked. It didn't play well with Spring or EJB, however, so other brokers like GraniteDS presented a stronger alternative. Now, with the Spring BlazeDS integration, you can have your cake and eat it too: the Spring BlazeDS integration lets you *easily* install BlazeDS into your application *and* works perfectly with all the things you can imagine wanting to work with from Spring: messaging (both straight JMS and with the Spring Integration service bus) and Spring components or services.

10-3. Adding the Spring BlazeDS support to an application

Problem

Now that we've gone through the options, and you've decided you want to install the Spring BlazeDS integration in an existing web application, the installation itself can vary depending on the target integration.

Solution

If you've installed any of the standard Spring web infrastructure (Spring MVC) into your application already, then installing the Spring BlazeDS support will seem trivial. If not, we'll need to explore configuring the Spring BlazeDS integration, as well as configuring BlazeDS itself.

How It Works

There are two parts to work through when installing the Spring BlazeDS integration. First, we need to install the Spring support, namely the Spring MVC `DispatcherServlet`. Then, we need to configure BlazeDS itself. The balance of the work to configure BlazeDS is minimal. I'll include it here, but you can as easily download the resulting file from this book's web site and plug it in to your own code, unchanged.

Installing the Spring Support

The Spring BlazeDS integration requires us to set up the same infrastructure we'd set up if we were using Spring Faces, Spring Web Flow, Spring MVC, and so on: the `DispatchServlet`. There is no need for any custom BlazeDS servlet or `web.xml` configuration at all. The configuration lives in the `web.xml` file, and we provide a mapping so that we know where to send Flex requests. Note that the following configuration *could* be used in setting up Spring MVC or Spring Web Flow, too! There is nothing BlazeDS-specific, or even specific to the Spring BlazeDS integration, in the following code:

```
<web-app version="2.4"
xmlns="http://java.sun.com/xml/ns/j2ee"
xmlns:xsi="http://www.w3.org/2001/XMLSchema-instance"
xsi:schemaLocation="http://java.sun.com/xml/ns/j2ee
    http://java.sun.com/xml/ns/j2ee/web-app_2_4.xsd">

    <display-name>Spring Flex BlazeDS integration example</display-name>

    <servlet>
        <servlet-name>spring-flex</servlet-name>
        <servlet-class>
            org.springframework.web.servlet.DispatcherServlet
        </servlet-class>
        <init-param>
            <param-name>contextConfigLocation</param-name>
            <param-value>/WEB-INF/auction-flex-context.xml</param-value>
        </init-param>
        <load-on-startup>1</load-on-startup>
    </servlet>

    <servlet-mapping>
        <servlet-name>spring-flex</servlet-name>
        <url-pattern>/mb/*</url-pattern>
    </servlet-mapping>
</web-app>
```

This configuration is the simplest configuration possible, but it is enough to install support for Spring in your web application. You need to set up the Flex message broker and so forth, which we do inside a Spring context file. Here, we reference `/WEB-INF/auction-flex-context.xml`, where we set up the message broker.

The contents of the `auction-flex-context.xml` file follow. We won't expose any services or messaging endpoints, yet. Let's leave those for the next few recipes.

```xml
<?xml version="1.0" encoding="UTF-8"?>
<beans xmlns:file= http://www.springframework.org/schema/integration/file
xmlns:integration="http://www.springframework.org/schema/integration"
xmlns="http://www.springframework.org/schema/beans"
xmlns:context="http://www.springframework.org/schema/context"
xmlns:xsi="http://www.w3.org/2001/XMLSchema-instance"
xmlns:p="http://www.springframework.org/schema/p"
xmlns:util="http://www.springframework.org/schema/util"
xmlns:tool="http://www.springframework.org/schema/tool"
xmlns:lang="http://www.springframework.org/schema/lang"
xmlns:jms="http://www.springframework.org/schema/integration/jms"
xmlns:amq="http://activemq.apache.org/schema/core"
xmlns:flex="http://www.springframework.org/schema/flex"
xsi:schemaLocation="
    http://www.springframework.org/schema/util
    http://www.springframework.org/schema/util/spring-util-3.0.xsd
    http://www.springframework.org/schema/tool
    http://www.springframework.org/schema/tool/spring-tool-3.0.xsd
    http://www.springframework.org/schema/lang
    http://www.springframework.org/schema/lang/spring-lang-3.0.xsd
    http://www.springframework.org/schema/beans
    http://www.springframework.org/schema/beans/spring-beans-3.0.xsd
    http://www.springframework.org/schema/context
    http://www.springframework.org/schema/context/spring-context-3.0.xsd
    http://www.springframework.org/schema/integration
    http://www.springframework.org/schema/integration/spring-integration-1.0.xsd
    http://www.springframework.org/schema/integration/file
    http://www.springframework.org/schema/integration/file/spring-integration-file-1.0.xsd
    http://www.springframework.org/schema/integration/jms
    http://www.springframework.org/schema/integration/jms/spring-integration-jms-1.0.xsd
    http://activemq.apache.org/schema/core
    http://activemq.apache.org/schema/core/activemq-core-5.3.0.xsd
    http://www.springframework.org/schema/flex
    http://www.springframework.org/schema/flex/spring-flex-1.0.xsd
">

    <context:annotation-config />
    <context:component-scan base-package="com.apress.springwebrecipes.flex.auction" />

    <flex:message-broker services-config-path="/WEB-INF/flex/services-config.xml">
        <flex:message-service default-channels="my-amf" />
    </flex:message-broker>

</beans>
```

This context file imports quite a few namespaces because we'll use them later as we integrate services and messaging channels. Technically, though, you don't need them right now. You could import the context namespace and the flex namespace and be done with it.

Here, we use the context element to enable annotation configuration and to tell the Spring framework in which package to scan for, and automatically register, components (beans). Again, we'll use those as part of using standard Spring. So, the only thing we've configured of any interest here is the

BlazeDS message broker. The message broker, in turn, creates channels, which are like named ports where messages may be sent or received from. We configure the specifics of the channel—like polling frequency, timeout settings, the specific sub-URL, streaming, and so on, all from the services configuration file. The message broker will, by default, look for the `services-config.xml` file in `/WEB-INF/flex/services-config.xml`. You can thus remove our explicit declaration, as it is redundant. We only mention it because you may want to vary that location, though the default (WEB-INF/flex) is a very broad de-facto standard.

Let's look at a very sophisticated `services-config.xml` configuration file. We'll reuse only a very small subset of all of the configuration in this file throughout this chapter. There are numerous configurations, some of which you may reuse to great effect. It will give you an idea of some of the things that you can support, however, to study this file.

```xml
<?xml version="1.0" encoding="UTF-8"?>
<services-config>
    <services>
        <default-channels>
            <channel ref="my-amf"/>
        </default-channels>
    </services>

    <channels>
        <channel-definition id="my-amf" class="mx.messaging.channels.AMFChannel">
            <endpoint url="http://{server.name}:{server.port}/{context.root}/mb/amf"
                    class="flex.messaging.endpoints.AMFEndpoint"/>
        </channel-definition>
        <channel-definition id="my-secure-amf"
                class="mx.messaging.channels.SecureAMFChannel">
            <endpoint url="https://{server.name}:{server.port}/{context.root}/mb/amfsecure"
                    class="flex.messaging.endpoints.SecureAMFEndpoint"/>
            <properties>
                <add-no-cache-headers>false</add-no-cache-headers>
            </properties>
        </channel-definition>
        <channel-definition id="my-polling-amf" class="mx.messaging.channels.AMFChannel">
            <endpoint url="http://{server.name}:{server.port}/{context.root}/mb/amfpolling"
                    class="flex.messaging.endpoints.AMFEndpoint"/>
            <properties>
                <polling-enabled>true</polling-enabled>
                <polling-interval-seconds>4</polling-interval-seconds>
            </properties>
        </channel-definition>
        <channel-definition id="my-longpolling-amf"
                        class="mx.messaging.channels.AMFChannel">
            <endpoint
                url="http://{server.name}:{server.port}/{context.root}/mb/amflongpolling"
                class="flex.messaging.endpoints.AMFEndpoint"/>
```

```
        <properties>
            <polling-enabled>true</polling-enabled>
            <polling-interval-seconds>5</polling-interval-seconds>
            <wait-interval-millis>60000</wait-interval-millis>
            <client-wait-interval-millis>1</client-wait-interval-millis>
            <max-waiting-poll-requests>200</max-waiting-poll-requests>
        </properties>
    </channel-definition>
    <channel-definition id="my-streaming-amf"
                        class="mx.messaging.channels.StreamingAMFChannel">
        <endpoint
            url="http://{server.name}:{server.port}/{context.root}/mb/streamingamf"
            class="flex.messaging.endpoints.StreamingAMFEndpoint"/>
    </channel-definition>
 </channels>

<logging>
    <target class="flex.messaging.log.ConsoleTarget" level="Warn">
        <properties>
            <prefix>[BlazeDS] </prefix>
            <includeDate>false</includeDate>
            <includeTime>false</includeTime>
            <includeLevel>false</includeLevel>
            <includeCategory>false</includeCategory>
        </properties>
        <filters>
            <pattern>Endpoint.*</pattern>
            <pattern>Service.*</pattern>
            <pattern>Configuration</pattern>
        </filters>
    </target>
</logging>

<system>
    <redeploy>
        <enabled>false</enabled>
    </redeploy>
</system>
</services-config>
```

We won't review every line here. You may look into these options specifically in greater detail on your own, as required. For our purposes, we can use the following configuration, which comes in at a *staggering* dozen or so lines of XML!

```xml
<?xml version="1.0" encoding="UTF-8"?>
<services-config>
    <channels>
        <channel-definition id="my-amf" class="mx.messaging.channels.AMFChannel">
            <endpoint url="http://{server.name}:{server.port}/{context.root}/mb/amf"
                      class="flex.messaging.endpoints.AMFEndpoint"/>
        </channel-definition>
    </channels>
</services-config>
```

The endpoint's url attribute defines where we should expect this service to be mounted. Any service that's exposed using the my-amf channel will be available via that URL. You'll need this value in the client Flex application. For the sample auction application we'll develop in this chapter, we deploy the application at the root web context. You'll use the URL http://127.0.0.1:8080/mb/amf in your Flex client code.

To keep our code as ready-to-deploy as possible, you should parameterize the URL of the service in the client. Alternatively, if you know the domain name for your application, you might add an entry to your /etc/hosts file on Unix derivatives or, on Windows, to your C:\WINDOWS\system32\drivers\ etc\hosts file mapping 127.0.0.1 to your target domain. Thus, all references to the server—whether in production or in development—will resolve to the correct host. In this chapter, we are explicitly referencing localhost, but only because we're writing a book and don't have a separate domain we control the rights to that we can print here.

Our sample application's interface is very simple (see Figure 10-1). We'll use two synchronous services and consume one asynchronous message. Our application displays a UI with items in a grid. We also have a form with which new items may be posted. As soon as the items are posted, an asynchronous message will trigger an update of the view on all the clients who are looking at the grid, so that their display updates immediately.

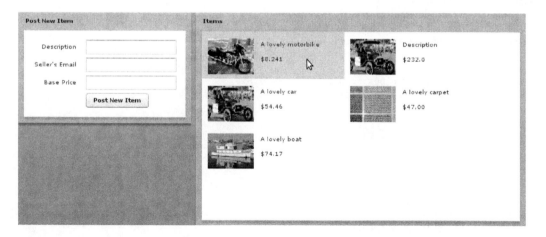

Figure 10-1. *This is the UI of the Flex client. On the left is the form with which clients may post new items that appear in the grid (to the right), and they appear nearly instantly thanks to our integration with Spring BlazeDS's messaging support.*

With our message broker up and running, we'll look next at how to create those services and how to build the Flex client above to consume them.

10-4. Exposing Services Through BlazeDS / Spring

Problem

You've got the message broker up and running. Now, you want to deploy a Spring service as an AMF service, much like we might use a Spring exporter to export our service as an RMI service. You'll also want to put it together with what you learned before about consuming AMF services.

Solution

We'll use Spring BlazeDS to set up a simple service and demonstrate its invocation from the client—a simple auction application that we'll build on in subsequent recipes. The service, in this case, will simply fetch all the items that are for auction and return the description, a photo, and price for each item. Our implementation is a simple in-memory, POJO service, but you easily build any kind of other service, just as you would for any other application.

How It Works

Spring BlazeDS lets you expose existing Spring beans as AMF endpoints. To do this, you define your service as usual, and then modify the configuration of the service itself, or independently create a reference.

Let's look at our sample service's interface first.

```
package com.apress.springwebrecipes.flex.auction;

import java.util.Set;
import com.apress.springwebrecipes.flex.auction.model.Bid;
import com.apress.springwebrecipes.flex.auction.model.Item;

/**
 * provides an implementation of an auction house
 *
 **/
public interface AuctionService {

/**
Create a new item and post it.
In our client we use this to demonstrate messaging
*/
```

```
Item postItem(
    String sellerEmail,
    String item,
    String description,
    double price,
    String imageUrl);

/**
 * Returns a view of all the items that
 * are available (which, in the sample, is everything, always).
 * We'll use this to demonstrate services.
 */
Set<Item> getItemsForAuction() ;

/** We don't use this in the sample
 * client, but we include it for posterity
 */
Bid bid(Item item, double price);

/** We don't use this in the sample
 * client, but we include it for posterity
 */
void acceptBid(Item item, Bid bid);

}
```

Let's look now at the implementation:

```
package com.apress.springwebrecipes.flex.auction;

import com.apress.springwebrecipes.flex.auction.model.Bid;
import com.apress.springwebrecipes.flex.auction.model.Item;
import org.apache.commons.collections.CollectionUtils;
import org.apache.commons.collections.Predicate;
import org.apache.commons.lang.StringUtils;
import org.apache.commons.lang.builder.ToStringBuilder;
import org.springframework.beans.factory.annotation.Autowired;
import org.springframework.jms.core.JmsTemplate;
import org.springframework.jms.core.MessageCreator;
import org.springframework.stereotype.Service;
import org.springframework.util.Assert;

import javax.annotation.PostConstruct;
import javax.annotation.Resource;
import javax.jms.*;
import java.util.Date;
import java.util.HashSet;
import java.util.Set;
import java.util.concurrent.ConcurrentSkipListSet;
import java.util.concurrent.atomic.AtomicInteger;
import java.util.logging.Logger;
```

```
@Service("auctionService")
public class AuctionServiceImpl implements AuctionService {

    static private Logger logger = Logger.getLogger(AuctionServiceImpl.class.getName());

    private ConcurrentSkipListSet<Item> items = new ConcurrentSkipListSet<Item>();
    private AtomicInteger uuidForBids = new AtomicInteger(0);
    private AtomicInteger uuidForItems = new AtomicInteger(0);
    private String images[] = "boat,car,carpet,motorbike".split(",");

    @Resource(name = "itemPosted")
    private Topic itemPostedDestination;

    @Resource(name = "bidPosted")
    private Topic bidPostedTopic;

    @Resource(name = "bidAccepted")
    private Topic bidAcceptedTopic;

    @Autowired
    private JmsTemplate jmsTemplate;

    @PostConstruct
    public void setupFakeItems() {
        Assert.isTrue(jmsTemplate != null);

        String[] items = "boat,car,carpet,motorbike".split(",");
        String[] sellerEmails = "gary@gary.com,daniel@daniel.com,josh@josh.com, ↵
george@george.com,srinvas@srinvas.com,manuel@manuel.com".split(",");

        for (String item : items) {
            String sellerEmail = sellerEmails[(int)
        Math.floor(Math.random() * sellerEmails.length)];
            String description = String.format("A lovely %s", item);
            double basePrice = Math.random() * 100;
            String imageUrl = String.format("/images/%s.jpg", item);
            postItem(sellerEmail, item,
description, basePrice, imageUrl);
        }
        logger.info(String.format("setupFakeItems(): there are %s items", "" +
                this.items.size()));
    }
```

```java
      private Message mapFromBid(javax.jms.Session session, Bid b)
   throws JMSException {
        MapMessage mm = session.createMapMessage();
        mm.setLong("itemId", b.getItem().getId());
        mm.setLong("bidId", b.getId());
        mm.setLong("acceptedTimestamp",
 b.getAccepted() == null ? 0 : b.getAccepted().getTime());
        mm.setDouble("amount", b.getAmount());
        return mm;
     }

private Message mapFromItem(javax.jms.Session session, Item item)
throws JMSException {
        MapMessage mapMessage = session.createMapMessage();
        mapMessage.setLong("itemId", item.getId());
        mapMessage.setDouble("threshold", item.getThreshold());
        mapMessage.setDouble("basePrice", item.getBasePrice());
        mapMessage.setString("sellerEmail", item.getSellerEmail());
        mapMessage.setString("description", item.getDescription());
        return mapMessage;
     }

    @Override
    public synchronized void acceptBid(Item item, final Bid bid) {
        Date accepted = new Date();
        item.setSold(accepted);
        bid.setAccepted(accepted);
        jmsTemplate.send(bidAcceptedTopic, new MessageCreator() {
            public Message createMessage(Session session)
              throws JMSException {
                return mapFromBid(session, bid);
            }
        });

    }


    @Override
    public synchronized Bid bid(Item item, double price) {
        final Bid bid = new Bid();
        bid.setAmount(price);
        bid.setItem(item);
        bid.setId(uuidForBids.getAndIncrement());
        item.addBid(bid);
        jmsTemplate.send(bidPostedTopic, new MessageCreator() {
            @Override
            public Message createMessage(Session session)
```

```
  throws JMSException {
                return mapFromBid(session, bid);
          }
      });
      if (item.getThreshold() <= bid.getAmount()) {
          acceptBid(item, bid);
      }
      return bid;
  }


  private String randomImage() {
      int indexOfImage = (int)
(Math.random() * (this.images.length - 1));
      return this.images[indexOfImage];
  }


  @Override
  public Item postItem(
      String sellerEmail,
      String itemTitle,
      String description,
      double basePrice,
      String imageUrlParam) {

      String imageUrl = imageUrlParam;
      if (StringUtils.isEmpty(imageUrl)) {
          imageUrl = String.format("/images/%s.jpg", randomImage());
      }

      final Item item = new Item();
      item.setItem(itemTitle);
      item.setBasePrice(basePrice);
      item.setId(uuidForItems.getAndIncrement());
      item.setImageUrl(imageUrl);
      item.setThreshold(10 * 1000);
      item.setDescription(description);
      item.setSellerEmail(sellerEmail);

      System.out.println("adding " + ToStringBuilder.reflectionToString(item));
```

```
        items.add(item);
        jmsTemplate.send(itemPostedDestination, new MessageCreator() {
            @Override
            public Message createMessage(Session session)
                throws JMSException {
                return mapFromItem(session, item);
            }
        });
        return item;
    }

    @Override
    public Set<Item> getItemsForAuction() {
        Set<Item> uniqueItemsForAuction = new HashSet<Item>();
        uniqueItemsForAuction.addAll(this.items);
        CollectionUtils.filter(uniqueItemsForAuction, new Predicate() {
            @Override
            public boolean evaluate(Object object) {
                Item itm = (Item) object;
                return itm.getSold() == null;
            }
        });
        return uniqueItemsForAuction;
    }
}
```

There's a lot going on here, but nothing too unusual. We're not using Hibernate or any backing data store to keep the code simpler. Instead, the service uses a `ConcurrentSkipListSet<Item>` instance variable (imaginatively named `items`). Because there's no real backing store, we spend some time constructing seed data in the `setupFakeItems` method, which is called after the component's been configured by Spring. Because we want to notify other viewers of any new items posted, we use JMS and a `javax.jms.Topic`. We'll get into the configuration for those bits in a bot, but suffice it to say that we need a simple way of issuing JMS messages. This is why we inject an instance of Spring's `org.springframework.jms.core.JmsTemplate` class. The `acceptBid` and `bid` methods aren't used in this example, though they are left in for posterity. Finally, toward the bottom, we get to the real meat of the service: the `postBid` and `getItemsForAuction` methods.

The `bid` method takes parameters required to describe a bid and creates it. A less trivial example might do validation on the object. In our case, we simply add it to the `items` collection and publish news of its addition to the `itemPosted javax.jms.Topic`.

The `getItemsForAuction` method returns all the items that haven't been sold (and thus, should be displayed in the grid on the client). For our application, this effectively always returns every item in the collection, as we don't use the bidding functionality and thus no item will ever be sold.

With the Java out of the way, let's examine the Spring configuration a bit. There are two parts to the configuration: the standard services configuration, and the Spring BlazeDS configuration. We've already gone a long way to configuring the standard Spring beans with the addition of the `context:component-scan` element from the last recipe. We'll skip the configuration of the JMS functionality for now, as we'll cover that in the next recipe. All that leaves us with is the service itself.

If you add the Spring `org.springframework.stereotype.Service("auctionService")`to the `AuctionServiceImpl`, then you don't need to do anything to configure the Spring service itself. Otherwise, add the following to your Spring XML context (`/WEB-INF/auction-flex-context.xml`):

```
<bean id="auctionService"
  class="com.apress.springwebrecipes.flex.auction.AuctionServiceImpl"/>
```

Finally, we tell Spring BlazeDS about the bean using the following XML:

```
<flex:remoting-destination ref="auctionService"/>
```

This allows you to take existing beans and expose them as endpoints on BlazeDS. If you're defining a bean in the same logical tier as your BlazeDS services, perhaps as a more coarse-grained service façade inside your web application, then you can simply annotate that:

```
<bean id="auctionService"
      class="com.apress.springwebrecipes.flex.auction.AuctionServiceImpl">
      <flex:remoting-destination destination-id="auctionService"/>
</bean>
```

Here, we don't need the `ref` attribute on the `remoting-destination` element.

You can exercise quite a bit of control over how the bean is exported. The `remoting-destination` tag will let you exclude and/or include methods on the bean that should be accessible from remote clients. Use the `exclude-methods` and `include-methods` attributes to excluded methods and include methods, respectively.

Additionally, you can configure what exported service should be exposed as under BlazeDS. By default it uses the bean name to set the `destination-id`. If you want something else, you can configure that here using the `destination-id` attribute.

Recall that in our Spring context XML for the message broker, we had a `flex:message-broker` element, in which we had a `flex:message-service` element. That element had an attribute, `default-channels`. If specified, `<flex:remoting-destination />` may omit the `channel` they'd like to use when communicating with the server, as the default will be used. If, however, you'd like to use a different channel, then you may override it on the `flex:remoting-destination` element.

```
<flex:remoting-destination ref="auctionService"
                           exclude-methods="acceptBid, bid"
                           destination="theBestAuctionService"
/>
```

Under the hood, this support is simply instantiating an instance of the class `org.springframework.flex.remoting.RemotingDestinationExporter`. If you'd like to debug it and see how it works, that's the class to look at. Finally, if you—for some reason—wanted to configure it explicitly and avoid the namespace support, then that's the bean to look at.

So, given our earlier and simplest definition of the remoting destination (`<flex:remoting-destination ref="auctionService"/>`), we can make a call to the service from the client, just as we did before. You've already seen the full code for this example, so we won't rehash the entire thing. Here are the salient bits of ActionScript code, though:

```
var auctionService:RemoteObject = new RemoteObject();
auctionService.endpoint = 'http://localhost:8080/mb/amf';
auctionService.showBusyCursor = true;
auctionService.destination = 'auctionService';
var resultHandler:Function = function(
    resultEvent:ResultEvent, asyncToken:AsyncToken) :void {
        Alert.show('result = ' + resultEvent.result);
};
var faultHandler:Function = function(
    faultEvent:FaultEvent, asyncToken:AsyncToken) :void {
        Alert.show('fault = ' + faultEvent.fault);
};
auctionService.getItemsForAuction().addResponder(
    new AsyncResponder(resultHandler, faultHandler));
```

10-5. Working With Server-Side Objects

Problem

In the last recipe, you built a service that returned a result by invoking an operation on a server-side Spring service. The service returned a Collection of Items (Collection<Item>). The ActionScript code didn't have any type information, so your client code could have accessed incorrect properties with no warning.

Solution

You can tell the Flex runtime how to preserve the type information of objects that are serialized in the AMF format using the ActionScript [RemoteClass] attribute on a client-side mapping of the Java object.

How It Works

On the Java side, the getItemsForAuction method returns a collection of Item objects. In ActionScript, this translates into a collection of dynamic Object instances. In ActionScript, "dynamic" means that you can arbitrarily add or reference fields and methods on an object without type information. Essentially, ActionScript treats a class just like you could in the standard JavaScript you're no doubt familiar with from the browser. In the browser, this behavior is called expando properties and these are useful for us because Flash doesn't have any built-in way of knowing (and surfacing to tools like your IDE's auto-completion) the type information of the returned object. There's no mapping anywhere by default.

So, to iterate over the code inside the preceding `resultHandler` function, we might write

```
import mx.collections.ArrayCollection;
...

var acOfItems:ArrayCollection = resultEvent.result as ArrayCollection;
for each(var item:* in acOfItems)
      Alert.show( 'item.id = '+ item.id +
          ', item.description='+ item.description);
```

Here, we cast the `resultEvent` instance's result property into an `mx.collections.ArrayCollection` instance. We access the JavaBean properties of the `Item` class (an entity on the server) as properties on the `Object` reference on the client. This works well enough for small applications.

There are many occasions where an application is better suited to the type safety we enjoy on the server-side Java environment. We need to provide a client-side double of the server-side Java object. This object provides a mapping. We create this by a building a client-side version of the server-side entity. Here's our declaration of the Java `Item` class in ActionScript code:

```
package com.apress.springwebrecipes.auction.model
{

[Bindable]
[RemoteClass(alias="com.apress.springwebrecipes.flex.auction.model.Item")]
public class Item
{
    private var _sellerEmail:String;
    private var _basePrice:Number;
    private var _threshold:Number;
    private var _sold:Date;
    private var _item:String;
    private var _description:String;
    private var _imageUrl:String;
    private var _id:Number;

    public function get sellerEmail():String {
        return _sellerEmail;
    }

    public function set sellerEmail(value:String):void {
        _sellerEmail = value;
    }

    public function get basePrice():Number {
        return _basePrice;
    }

    public function set basePrice(value:Number):void {
        _basePrice = value;
    }
```

```
    public function get threshold():Number {
        return _threshold;
    }

    public function set threshold(value:Number):void {
        _threshold = value;
    }

    public function get sold():Date {
        return _sold;
    }

    public function set sold(value:Date):void {
        _sold = value;
    }

    public function get item():String {
        return _item;
    }

    public function set item(value:String):void {
        _item = value;
    }

    public function get description():String {
        return _description;
    }

    public function set description(value:String):void {
        _description = value;
    }

    public function get imageUrl():String {
        return _imageUrl;
    }

    public function set imageUrl(value:String):void {
        _imageUrl = value;
    }

    public function get id():Number {
        return _id;
    }

    public function set id(value:Number):void {
        _id = value;
    }
}
}
```

Importantly, the class is annotated with the RemoteClass tag. Usually, this tag is used to tell the Flex runtime to preserve type information when serializing Flash objects into and out of the AMF format.

Here, in conjunction with the `alias` attribute, it tells the Flex runtime the type information it should imbue AMF data coming from the server. The `alias` attribute should be set with the Java object for which this class is a mapping.

Our previous code snippet may now be rewritten as:

```
import mx.collections.ArrayCollection;

import com.apress.springwebrecipes.auction.model.Item;
...
var acOfItems:ArrayCollection = resultEvent.result as ArrayCollection;
for each(var item:Item in acOfItems)
        Alert.show( 'item.id = '+ item.id +
            ', item.description='+ item.description);
```

This doesn't represent a giant change in the code by any stretch, but now, auto-completion works in your favorite IDE, and you can refactor. Additionally, you may define methods on the ActionScript object—perhaps to update state in peculiar ways. Additionally, you now have a place to put some validation or constraints.

It can quickly become tedious to have to define ActionScript classes for every entity on the server side. There are solutions that can help, however. We mention the Granite DS entity broker earlier, for example. It has an Eclipse plug-in or Ant task (the Ant task can, in turn, be used with Maven if you'd like) that can be used to scan compiled Java classes and emit equivalent ActionScript. For every Java class, the plug-in will emit two ActionScript classes of the form `XBase.as`, and `X.as`, where X is the name of your Java class.

The plug-in will write all the accessor/mutator code and some optimized serialization logic in the `XBase` class and have the X class extend the `XBase` one. As an example, if you want to add logic to ensure that phone numbers comply with some sort of validation routine, you may put an override in the X class and have it call super once the property has been validated. If you rerun the generator, it will not overwrite the X class, only the `XBase` one, so your changes survive iterations. There are other such features like this in various projects. We've had good experience with the Granite Data Services Gas3 plug-in described here. Note that the code generated by the Granite Data Services plug-in works well with BlazeDS, too. To find out more about the generator, refer to `http://www.graniteds.org/confluence/display/DOC/2.+Gas3+Code+Generator`.

10-6. Consuming Message-Oriented Services Using BlazeDS and Spring

Problem

How do you build solutions that can handle so-called push-oriented messaging? In the Ajax world, these are called Comet–style applications. How do you connect Flex clients to each in an asynchronous manner? How do you work with message-oriented middleware (MOM) services like JMS to send and receive messages? Finally, how do you architect solutions that talk to a more sophisticated event bus like Spring Integration?

Solution

We'll use Spring BlazeDS to connect our client to the BlazeDS messaging facilities. BlazeDS supports JMS, as well as a regular BlazeDS messaging facility already. The Spring BlazeDS integration simplifies both integrations and provides a third to let client applications send and receive messages on Spring Integration channels. Spring BlazeDS works with Spring Integration to let you bind any arbitrary endpoint (be it an e-mail server, a Twitter user's update feed, an FTP server, a file system, or anything for which you want to write an adapter) to the Spring BlazeDS messaging facilities.

How It Works

Thus far, our auction application has talked to the server, but it's not really been a conversation, has it? If the client asks the server for something, the server responds. What if the server has something more to say? This question is ignored in most web applications because the answer is usually "we can't afford to find out." HTTP itself is stateless and a pull-only protocol. It has no way of pushing data to clients. This a problem in that many applications are better served by being able to push data, like for example chat rooms, or stock tickers, or generally anything whose frequency of change is variable and out of the client's control (which, if we're honest, applies to most applications).

We've built abstractions to solve all sorts of oddities with HTTP to make it more suitable as application platform, why not solve the push problem? It turns out, people have tried; it's just *not* that easy to solve. In the web browser environment, people use polling, Comet, and piggybacking to mimic push-style architectures. Polling works by polling a well-known server resource at a consistent interval and retrieving updates. Comet works by opening a request and keeping it open, pushing out a ping byte whenever there's updated state on the server. Another option is to send data only when a request is sent to the server (not polling, in that the request isn't specifically designed to ascertain whether some resource has pushed data, so much as it is to request some other resource). The pushed data—if any—piggybacks the request.

Each of these options has its own advantages and disadvantages: Polling can overwhelm a server if the request is processing intensive, time intensive, or too frequent. Comet can quickly bog down a server because it requires keeping open a thread for each client. Piggyback treats the server nicely but can be unreliable or untenable for an application requiring guarantees of freshness of data: what happens if the client doesn't ever send a request to piggyback on?

People have tried to bake in support for these architectures at the server level. Newer servers have built more efficient threading options so that threads can be passivated or so that threads require minimal amounts of memory. Jetty, for example, supports asynchronous and Comet-friendly threading models through its continuations support. Tomcat eventually added similar support for this through its `CometProcessor` class. Grizzly (Glassfish 3) has the `CometEngine` class. Languages like Google's Go offer solid support for spawning numerous lightweight threads with almost no cost. Indeed, HTML 5 itself offers the WebSocket standard, which provides a way to solve these problems. The third edition of the Servlets specification, part of Java EE 6, offers support for asynchronous servlets too. But none of these is quite there yet, and in the meantime, there are applications to build. So, we're back to simulating the effect.

We use the word "simulate" here because for a Java developer in the enterprise world or even in the world of regular protocols, this stuff seems like a horrid hack. In the enterprise world, if one service publishes a message, any subscriber can register as a listener, and as soon as there's a message, the subscriber is notified instantly. Sure, we know that behind the scenes there's some sort of very efficient polling happening, but we don't have to work in terms of the polling. We work in terms of the event raised by the arrival of a new message. This is called an event-driven architecture (EDA). When Spring developers write message-driven POJOs, or EJB developers write message-driven beans, the objects are isolated from the means by which messages arrive.

It seems a shame then that web developers don't enjoy such elegance. The only way to restore it is to make the use of message-oriented services, which are an aspect in the framework code, not the client code. If you use the DWR project (a popular Ajax project), then you know that you can create "reverse Ajax" applications, where your client code enjoys essentially the same benefits.

Flex too enjoys a framework–level solution for handling push messaging when working in concert with a message broker like BlazeDS. Messages are routed to and from BlazeDS, which talks to your Flash client. The advantage of this solution is that Flex and BlazeDS are smart enough to keep track of the state of the client. Also, they can do things to help you out, even when you don't realize you need it. For example, most browsers cannot open more than a certain number of HTTP connections. Behind the scenes, though, when a Flex client opens a connection to listen for push messages, it is, in fact, doing one of the three techniques we described before—Comet, piggybacking, or polling—or some combination thereof. Thus, were a Flex client to open a channel for consuming push messages using long-lived connection (Comet), it's using the browser's HTTP connections, and the number of available HTTP connections is decremented by one. If you then try to invoke an RPC call, that's another connection that's used. This works because most browsers support two concurrent connections. If, however, the limit were two, and you instead created two connections for consuming push messages, there would be no connection available for invoking services. In this situation, you can configure BlazeDS to vary the type of functionality it provides by configuring the BlazeDS `services-config.xml` file. Here, you can specify that requests against a destination "a" are handled using Comet and requests against a lesser-priority destination "b" are handled using polling. Thus, connections to the server are intermittent on that destination, but the client is still able to perform RPC invocations.

Let's look at how you consume messages pushed from the server in Flex before we dig into the nitty-gritty configuration behind the scenes. In our auction application, we want the UI notified whenever any new message is published on the `itemPosted` topic. In our client's setup method (called when the `applicationComplete` event fires), we initialize the consumer:

```
import mx.controls.Alert;
import mx.events.FlexEvent;
import mx.messaging.*;
import mx.messaging.channels.AMFChannel;
import mx.messaging.events.*;
import mx.rpc.*;
import mx.rpc.events.*;

...

private var itemPostedDestinationConsumer:Consumer;

...

public function onApplicationComplete(flexEvent:FlexEvent):void
{
    var aChannelSet:ChannelSet = new ChannelSet();
    aChannelSet.channels = [new AMFChannel('my-amf','http://localhost:8080/mb/amf')];
    itemPostedDestinationConsumer  = new Consumer() ;
    itemPostedDestinationConsumer.channelSet = aChannelSet;
    itemPostedDestinationConsumer.destination='itemPostedDestination' ;
```

```
itemPostedDestinationConsumer.addEventListener(
    MessageEvent.MESSAGE, function(me:MessageEvent):void {
        // react to the new item (perhaps re-paint the UI)
        layoutGridOfItems();
        Alert.show('A new item has arrived!');
    });
    itemPostedDestinationConsumer.subscribe();
}
```

First, while this may seem verbose compared to the rest of the examples in this chapter, we dare you to write all the code you need to set up a `MessageContainer` and subscribe to messages using raw JMS! Second, we *can* improve on even this Spartan code, as you'll see in the next recipe.

The code is about what you'd expect. We create a Flex `Consumer` and tell it the BlazeDS destination it should consume messages from, and on what channel the client should communicate. The destination, in this case, is the BlazeDS assigned name for the resource from which we will consume messages. The destination, on the BlazeDS side, could in turn be linked to a JMS queue, a Spring Integration channel, and so on. This indirection is valuable because it keeps our client code flexible and unaware of how messages are being produced. Then, we register a listener in exactly the same manner as we would listen for a button click. Finally, we issue the `subscribe` method, telling the client to start consuming messages as they come in. It doesn't get *much* simpler than this!

Now, let's see how we configure the server side Spring BlazeDS message broker. No matter which option you choose, you'll use the Spring BlazeDS namespace support to declare a destination in Spring and assign it an ID of `itemPostedDestination` (because that's what the client code we just created is subscribed to).

We already looked at the code for the service before, so we know that we're using JMS in this particular integration. Let's first look at using Spring BlazeDS to talk directly to JMS. In our example, we want to react to messages declared on the `javax.jms.Topic` named `itemPosted`. In JMS, a `javax.jms.Topic` is used to describe a named channel in a JMS server whose messages are sent to *all* clients that are subscribed to it. This option is the enterprise equivalent of adding an action listener using Flex. This is as opposed to a `javax.jms.Queue`, where each message sent to the queue is read by one client and then removed.

In our example, we're using the freely available `ActiveMQ` JMS broker because it provides good support for Spring. You can configure connection factories as you might with any JMS broker, but you can also use a Spring namespace to configure options on the server like your destinations (`javax.jms.Topic`, `javax.jms.Queue`), and it's got many best-of-breed messaging-oriented-middleware (MOM) features like clustering and XMPP support. Plus, it's easy to get started with. Here are the steps you'll need to get it installed:

1. Download the freely available Apache Active MQ project (`http://activemq.apache.org/`). We're using version 5.3 for this book, but you should have no trouble with later versions (or even earlier ones, especially if only off by a few point releases).

2. Unzip it.

3. Start the project by executing the appropriate `activemq` script (there's one for Unix-variants and one for Windows) in the unzipped project's `bin` directory.

We'll use the `ActiveMQ` broker for both the JMS example and the Spring Integration example. Let's explore the various ways to produce and consume messages from Flex.

JMS

The support for JMS on the BlazeDS involves configuring a JMS connection factory in Spring. We want to ensure we are using a `javax.jms.Topic`, and not a `javax.jms.Queue`, so we will use the ActiveMQ library namespace support for Spring to create it. This is standard configuration that you will do no matter what your ultimate use is for JMS.

Add the following to the `/WEB-INF/auction-flex-context.xml` file that we defined in the previous recipe. We have already imported the `amq` (Active MQ) namespace in that file.

```
<bean id="connectionFactory"
  class="org.springframework.jms.connection.CachingConnectionFactory"
  p:sessionCacheSize="10"
  p:cacheProducers="false">
    <property name="targetConnectionFactory">
        <amq:connectionFactory brokerURL="tcp://localhost:61616" />
    </property>
</bean>
```

The inner `amq:connectionFactory` element defines a `org.apache.activemq.spring.ActiveMQConnectionFactory` instance. This defines the connection factory, but to add an extra layer of robustness, we create a connection factoring pool, `org.springframework.jms.connection.CachingConnectionFactory`.

To be able to work with the JMS connection factory from our services, we create a `JmsTemplate`, wiring in the connection factory proxy that we've just configured.

```
<bean id="jmsTemplate"
      class="org.springframework.jms.core.JmsTemplate"
      p:connectionFactory-ref="connectionFactory" />
```

Finally, we use the `ActiveMQ` namespace support to create the `javax.jms.Topic` instances that we'll need (if they don't already exist).

```
<amq:topic id="itemPosted" name="itemPosted" physicalName="itemPosted" />
<amq:topic id="bidPosted" name="bidPosted" physicalName="bidPosted" />
<amq:topic id="bidAccepted" name="bidAccepted" physicalName="bidAccepted" />
```

With all this in place, our service has what it needs to be able to talk to JMS. We've not configured any piece that's specific to Flex. Let's get that out of the way now. Add the following, near where you defined the message broker previously:

```
<flex:jms-message-destination id="itemPostedDestination"
            jms-destination="itemPosted" channels="my-amf"
            connection-factory="connectionFactory"  />
```

And that's it! The `id` defines the string that we use to connect to the JMS destination from the Flex client. That's the only part that permeates your code. The `jms-destination` attribute correlates to an ID used in defining the topics with the `amq:topic` element. So, the form to post a new item is completed and submitted. The form invokes the `postItem` method on the Spring service, which in turn sends a message, using the `jmsTemplate`, out to the `itemPosted` destination. We've then configured Flex to listen for that message here using the `flex:jms-message-destination`. Because it's being sent on a `Topic`, it will multicast the message, so that everyone who's using the application will see the message. To try it, open the Flex application from multiple browsers, or computers, and log in. You want to use different browsers so you can avoid reusing the same session. Post an Item from one of them. Watch as all the others are updated instantaneously. You should see an alert message saying, "A new item has arrived!"

Spring Integration

In the previous example, we used JMS to create a publish-and-subscribe style architecture. Because it was a sort of circuit, it worked fine. However, there is often a requirement to have Flex user interfaces be aware of other events besides ones that the Flex UI itself generates—events that are either specific to your business or don't talk to JMS by default. The list of such applications is infinite. You don't have to think long before the possibilities become overwhelming, and exciting. What if you could have your user-interface update each time e-mail arrives? Or an RSS feed updates? Or what if somebody logged in via a Jabber server (XMPP; for example, using Google Talk)? What if your Flex client was designed to facilitate an editorial workflow and needed to load up new entries from a content management system for approval when ever any changes were made? Or perhaps it is the user interface for an audit system, so new customer loan applications need to be reviewed as they arrive. Need to load up the contents of files dropped on a shared mount? What about reacting to Twitter or Facebook status updates? What about when new rows are inserted in a watched view on the database?

These kinds of integration problems require an extra piece of middleware to let our code consume these various events while remaining indifferent to their source. The prescription for these kinds of solutions is usually an enterprise service bus (ESB). So, we will use one too, of a sort. We will use Spring Integration. Spring Integration is great because it's not a proper server, but instead an embeddable set of components that you configure using Spring. It lets you consume and produce messages for arbitrary endpoints, and if there's no support out of the box, it's trivially easy to build your own.

In our example, we will simply rework the JMS example: instead of sending messages to the JMS topic and then consuming them in Flex, we'll provide two ways to add items: one from JMS, as before, and one from a shared file system where new files are to be processed and their contents transformed into new Items, which get added via a call to the service. Either input source will ultimately be sent to JMS, where Spring Integration will consume the messages and forward it to the BlazeDS destination. Our Flex client will consume messages from this destination, as usual, and remain unchanged. We'll work entirely in our Spring application context to achieve these changes, using Spring Integration.

The way Spring Integration works is it lets you establish a sort of gauntlet for your message to pass through. It has to go through each component until the goal is finished. It lets us configure as much as possible about the way messages get into a pipeline and about where they ultimately end up. You use adapters to read and write to external systems. You use other specialized components to handle transformation of the message and so on. Each component has an input message and an output message. Some components let you take an input and transform it, so the resulting output is different than the input. Others let you do things like forking control on the process: perhaps one message (a File object) enters and multiple messages (each line of the file) leave the component. Just as you do with Spring Web Flow or Struts, Spring Integration adds a layer of indirection between components. Given two components, component "a" and component "b," a product for component "a" may be passed to component "b." Perhaps in the future it's decided that there needs to be processing between the two components, so you introduce component "c" and stick it between them. In normal solutions, this would present a problem. With Spring Integration, however, there's a level of indirection. Components are connected by channels, which are basically named pipes. The pipe takes the output of a component and pipes it as the input of another. You can rearrange the components in a pipeline by simply changing the pipes going into and out of it, in much the same way that you can isolate your Spring Web Flow pages of the knowledge of what page will succeed the current one.

The files should have a payload with a well-known format: here, for the sake of simplicity, we'll assume that the contents of the file are on one line and that the line can be split into columns along comma (,) characters. The first column will be the seller's e-mail, the second will be the item, the third description, and the fourth base price. We'll then call the service to add this item and send it to JMS, as usual. So, we have two contributories feeding into the JMS topic that eventually gets consumed and piped to the BlazeDS destination: the file system integration and the service, which sends the event directly to the JMS topic.

To make these changes, we'll configure a few Spring Integration components: We need a way of reading files from a well-known directory, so we'll use an inbound file adapter. We'll need a way to convert the `java.io.File` from the file system into a `String` with the contents of the `java.io.File`, so we'll use a file-to-string transformer. We'll need a way of converting the `String` into an `Item` that we can call the service with, so we'll create a transformer. We'll need a component to actually call the `postItem` method on the service, which will send the `Item` to JMS. We'll have a component consume all messages that come off the JMS topic—regardless of source—and then feed those to the BlazeDS destination. Should be simple enough! In this process, all that we need to do is tell the Spring Integration message bus how to convert our simple CSV format into an `Item` and how to invoke our service. For that purpose, we'll create two Java classes: `FileToItemTransformer` and `ItemCreationServiceActivator` to transform the CSV String and to invoke our service, respectively.

There is a lot of power here.

Let's look at our initial solution. First, we must declare the channels that connect the components.

```
<integration:channel id="inboundItemFiles"/>
<integration:channel id="inboundItemFileStrings"/>
<integration:channel id="inboundItems"/>
<integration:channel id="inboundItemsPosted"/>
<integration:publish-subscribe-channel id="inboundItemsAudited"/>
```

With the channels introduced, let's start analyzing the components that the channels connect.

```
<bean id="itemFilesMount"
      class="org.springframework.core.io.FileSystemResource"   >
   <constructor-arg
   value="#{ systemProperties['user.home']+'/flexCsvFiles' }"/>
</bean>

<file:inbound-channel-adapter
      auto-create-directory="true"
      directory="file:#{itemFilesMount.file.absolutePath}"
      channel="inboundItemFiles">
        <integration:poller>
<integration:interval-trigger interval="1000"/>
        </integration:poller>
</file:inbound-channel-adapter>
```

First, we create a Spring framework `Resource` to declare the directory where we will look for new files. We avail ourselves of the new Spring 3.0 expression language to use a standard System property, `user.home`, to determine the home directory of the current user. The folder we want will be in the home directory, under a folder named `flexCsvFiles`. Now, we can create a `file:inbound-channel-adapter` to poll that directory and consume new files as they become available. To ensure that the directory is created when the integration is deployed, we set the `auto-create-directory` attribute to `true`. To tell the adapter which directory to use, we again employ the Spring Expression Language to reference access the

String representation of the Resource we created by dereferencing the Resource's file property, which we dereference again to get the absolutePath. The <file:inbound-channel-adapter /> is configured here to scan the directory at an interval of 1,000 milliseconds (every second) and if it sees any new files, it creates a message, which it puts through the inboundItemFiles channel. Note that you can also specify a glob for the inbound channel adapter, though we don't here.

```
<file:file-to-string-transformer
    input-channel="inboundItemFiles"
    output-channel="inboundItemFileStrings"
    delete-files="true" />
```

The next two components in the pipeline are instances of a standard Spring Integration component called a transformer. The first one, shown in the preceding snippet, is a standard transformer that we'll reuse. It knows how to take a java.io.File object and read its contents into a String. The String contents are returned on the inboundItemFileStrings channel where the next component, another transformer, will be expecting it. Since we don't want to throw the integration processing into an infinite loop, we use the delete-files option on the file-to-string-transformer component to remove the file from the directory once it has read the file and sent it.

```
<integration:transformer
    input-channel="inboundItemFileStrings"
    ref="fileToItemTransformer"
    output-channel="inboundItems"/>
```

The next component, shown in the preceding snippet, is a customer transformer because Spring Integration has no way of knowing how to transform that String into an Item object. It takes the input of the input-channel and transforms it using transformation logic that we supply.

```
package com.apress.springwebrecipes.flex.auction.integrations;

import com.apress.springwebrecipes.flex.auction.model.Item;
import org.apache.commons.lang.StringUtils;
import org.springframework.integration.annotation.Transformer;
import org.springframework.stereotype.Component;

import java.io.IOException;

@Component
public class FileToItemTransformer {

    @Transformer
    public Item transformFromFileStringToItem(String fileContent)
      throws IOException {


        if (StringUtils.isEmpty(fileContent))
            throw new RuntimeException(
                "the file content is empty; can't create Item");
```

```
        String[] parts = fileContent.split(",");

        if (parts.length != 4)
            throw new RuntimeException(
              "couldn't parse the file; can't create Item");

        String seller = parts[0],
               item = parts[1],
               description = parts[2],
               basePrice = parts[3];

        Item itemObj = new Item();
        itemObj.setDescription(description);
        itemObj.setItem(item);
        itemObj.setSellerEmail(seller);
        itemObj.setBasePrice(Double.parseDouble(basePrice));
        return itemObj;
    }
}
```

Spring Integration looks at the Spring bean configured with the `ref` attribute—as in the preceding code—to get our transformation logic. It scans the class for any methods annotated with a `@Transformer` annotation, and it invokes that. It takes the result and sends it out on another channel, `inboundItems`. Because this is a simple demonstration, the code is intentionally and artificially optimistic and simple; no error handling or validation is done at all.

```
    <integration:service-activator
        input-channel="inboundItems"
        ref="itemCreationServiceActivator"/>
```

The next component in the pipeline—in the preceding snippet—actually calls our Spring service, `AuctionService`, to insert the `Item` into our repository. Note that the component has no `output-channel` configured here. This is because we know that the service invokes JMS directly, sending the `Item` to the `itemPosted javax.jms.Topic`.

```
package com.apress.springwebrecipes.flex.auction.integrations;

import com.apress.springwebrecipes.flex.auction.AuctionService;
import com.apress.springwebrecipes.flex.auction.model.Item;
import org.springframework.beans.factory.annotation.Autowired;
import org.springframework.integration.annotation.ServiceActivator;
import org.springframework.stereotype.Component;

@Component
public class ItemCreationServiceActivator {

    @Autowired
    private AuctionService auctionService;
```

```
@ServiceActivator
public void postItem(Item item) throws RuntimeException {
    auctionService.postItem(
        item.getSellerEmail(),
        item.getItem(),
        item.getDescription(),
        item.getBasePrice(),
        null);
    }
}
```

The preceding code is very simple. It takes the input message, an Item, and uses it to call the postItem method on our AuctionService instance.

Our next step then is to consume those messages and funnel them to BlazeDS. We don't care if the JMS messages came from postings inside our Flex application or if they came from this file integration. We need to send them to the BlazeDS middleware, so it can publish the new Item to all the logged in Flex clients.

```
<jms:message-driven-channel-adapter
    connection-factory="connectionFactory"
    destination="itemPosted"
    channel="inboundItemsPosted"
/>
```

We'll set up a jms:message-driven-channel-adapter, as shown in the preceding code, which will consume messages and send them on the inboundItemsPosted channel, in much the same way as our file:inbound-channel-adapter consumed files and sent them out on its channel attribute. Because this is JMS-specific, we need to configure the connection factory, as well as what destination it should look at. We simply use references to the connection factory and ActiveMQ topics that we declared earlier.

Normally, we would send each message received from JMS directly to the BlazeDS integration. There is one small fly in the ointment, however. A Spring Integration pipeline works on the assumption that each component in the pipeline is available. In this case, we'll do all this processing and then send it to BlazeDS where we hope the event will be consumed. If there is no one logged into a Flex client consuming messages, then the message itself can't be consumed, and we get an exception. So, what we do is send the message ourselves and ignore the failure result. We don't actually care if BlazeDS consumes it. Remember, JMS is being used here to send event messages, not document messages that need to be consistent and honored. We can ignore the events, as we reload the UI with the latest data on the Flex client's load, anyway. So, we'll add a middleman who can swallow the error state for us:

```
<integration:service-activator
    input-channel="inboundItemsPosted"
    ref="messageAbsorber"
    output-channel="inboundItemsAudited" />
```

Our component is a service-activator. As before, the service-activator takes input on the input-channel and delegates the heavy lifting to the Spring bean referenced by the ref attribute. Again, we could send the result out through an output-channel, but that may, in some cases, cause an Exception when there is no consumer on the other end. So, we'll cheat and simply handle the send operation by ourselves. You can inject any Spring Integration component just as you would any other bean. We use this to good effect to inject the implementation class for the inboundItemsAudited channel itself.

```
package com.apress.springwebrecipes.flex.auction.integrations;

import org.apache.commons.lang.builder.ToStringBuilder;
import org.springframework.integration.annotation.ServiceActivator;
import org.springframework.integration.core.Message;
import org.springframework.integration.core.MessageChannel;
import org.springframework.stereotype.Component;

import javax.annotation.Resource;
import java.util.Map;

@Component
public class MessageAbsorber {

    @Resource(name = "inboundItemsAudited")
    private MessageChannel publishSubscribeChannel;

    @ServiceActivator
    public void handle(Message<Map<String, Object>> msg) {
        boolean status = publishSubscribeChannel.send(msg);
        // do not care about status
    }
}
```

Here, we simply swallow the status—throwing no exceptions or anything. If there's a consumer for this message, then the status will be true. If not, it's no problem either.

Ultimately, the BlazeDS needs to know to look for messages coming from a Spring Integration channel. Just as we told BlazeDS where to look for new JMS messages, we will tell BlazeDS where to look for new messages coming from a Spring Integration channel.

```
<flex:integration-message-destination
 channels="my-amf"
 id="itemPostedDestination"
 message-channel="inboundItemsAudited"
/>
```

The channels attribute and the id attribute should appear familiar. The only thing different here is the use of the flex:integration-message-destination and the message-channel attribute. These simply tell BlazeDS to consume messages being sent from the MessageAbsorber.

BlazeDS

You've seen the incredibly rich support the Spring BlazeDS project offers for tying your application to existing MOM and integrations. Sometimes, however, you have no other messaging middleware or integration processing. Sometimes, you simply want other Flex clients to be notified of something. BlazeDS supports this use case as well. To declare a destination that can only receive messages from Flex clients simply configure a <<flex:message-destination />.

```
<flex:message-destination channels="my-amf" id="myDestination"/>
```

Sending Messages from Flex

Such a destination can only be used by clients who know how to talk to BlazeDS, like Flex. So, how does Flex send messages to this destination, or indeed any of the destinations you've seen? The API, like the one for consuming messages, is minimalistic. Let's walk through the nominal BlazeDS messaging example: the chat room!

```
<?xml version="1.0" encoding="iso-8859-1"?>
<mx:Application xmlns:mx="http://www.adobe.com/2006/mxml" xmlns="*"
                pageTitle="Chat" creationComplete="setup(event)">

    <mx:Panel title="Chat" >
        <mx:TextArea id="output" height="200" />
        <mx:TextInput id="input" />
        <mx:ControlBar horizontalAlign="center" >
            <mx:Button id="send" label="Send" click="sendChatMessage(event)"/>
            <mx:Button id="clear" label="Clear" click="output.text =''" />
        </mx:ControlBar>
    </mx:Panel>

    <mx:Script>
        <![CDATA[

        import mx.events.FlexEvent;
        import mx.messaging.ChannelSet;
        import mx.messaging.Consumer;
        import mx.messaging.Producer;
        import mx.messaging.channels.AMFChannel;
        import mx.messaging.events.MessageEvent;
        import mx.messaging.messages.AsyncMessage;

        private var chatPublisher:Producer;
        private var chatConsumer:Consumer ;

        public function setup(fe:FlexEvent):void
        {

            var chatDestination:String = 'chatDestination';

            var cs:ChannelSet = new ChannelSet();
            cs.channels=[ new AMFChannel(
                'my-amf','http://localhost:8080/mb/amf') ];

            chatPublisher = new Producer();
            chatPublisher.channelSet =cs;
            chatPublisher.destination = chatDestination;
            chatPublisher.connect();
```

```
            chatConsumer = new Consumer();
            chatConsumer.channelSet = cs;
            chatConsumer.destination = chatDestination;
            chatConsumer.addEventListener(MessageEvent.MESSAGE,
              function (msgEvent:MessageEvent):void {
                  var msg:AsyncMessage = msgEvent.message as AsyncMessage;
                  output.text += msg.body + "\n";
              }
            );
            chatConsumer.subscribe();
        }

        private function sendChatMessage(me:MouseEvent):void
        {
            var msg:AsyncMessage = new AsyncMessage();
            msg.body = input.text;
            chatPublisher.send(msg);
            input.text = "";
        }
        ]]>
    </mx:Script>
</mx:Application>
```

This application connects a `Consumer` and a `Producer` to the same BlazeDS destination, `chatDestination`. The definition of the `chatDestination` in the Spring BlazeDS configuration is as follows:

```
<flex:message-destination channels="my-amf" id="chatDestination"/>
```

In the application, we set up a simple text area in which text may be entered. When the text is submitted, we use the `Producer` to send the message to BlazeDS. If you open up this example in multiple browsers, you'll see that all the other browsers update their view of the chat instantly.

10-7. Bringing Dependency Injection to your ActionScript Client

Problem

How do you use dependency injection on the Flex client? Spring has long made Java and .NET applications cleaner by providing a powerful way to configure your components. How do you do the same for your ActionScript code? In Flash or Flex? In the previous examples, whether we configured the `Producer`s and `Consumer`s and `RemoteObject`s using MXML or ActionScript, it still represented a source of code duplication. If we wanted to connect to the same services in a component, for example, we'd have to worry about passing around references, or rewrite the resource acquisition logic. Because ActionScript is statically typed and Flex is a component-oriented system, it is very easy to build sophisticated applications with hundreds of components that communicate. It is thus very important to put in place best practices for isolating that which changes from that which stays the same. In the Java world, we've solved this problem using Spring.

Solution

We'll use the Spring ActionScript project (formerly called Prana) to rebuild the simple Flex chat client with remote services and consumers configured externally, where it may be reused and reacqquired by components in the application in much the same manner as you're familiar with from Spring in Java. The similarities run deep between the two; Spring ActionScript even includes an [Autowired] annotation!

How It Works

The Spring ActionScript project is an ActionScript implementation of the ideas behind the Spring framework. It is a Spring extension project whose homepage is http://www.springsource.org/extensions/se-springactionscript-as (additionally, the main project page is http://www.springactionscript.org). Spring ActionScript can be used in regular Flash, Flex, or AIR environments. We'll concentrate on using it with Flex. Spring ActionScript won't help us reuse Spring services from Java in ActionScript, but it will help us clean up our ActionScript code. The Spring ActionScript project works in much the same way as a Spring project: you configure objects (*not* beans!) in an XML file and load the XML file in ApplicationContext subclass. There are two ApplicationContext implementations: one for Flex environments (org.springextensions.actionscript.context.support.FlexXMLApplicationContext) and one for pure Flash environments (org.springextensions.actionscript.context.support.XMLApplicationContext).

   The Flex one has some extra niceties that support automatic injection of objects into Flex components. This is powerful because Flex components are managed by the Flex runtime, not the Spring container, and so being able to have variables tagged with the [Autowired] tag resolve correctly is a powerful win, even despite those limitations.

   Let's put them to use and rework our chat example to get its mx.messaging.Producer and mx.messaging.Consumer references from the Spring application context. First, we need to instantiate the application context.

```
<?xml version="1.0" encoding="iso-8859-1"?>
<mx:Application xmlns:mx="http://www.adobe.com/2006/mxml" xmlns:*="" pageTitle="Chat"↵
  applicationComplete="setup(event)">

    <mx:Panel title="Chat">
        <mx:TextArea id="output" height="200"/>
        <mx:TextInput id="input"/>
        <mx:ControlBar horizontalAlign="center">
            <mx:Button id="send" label="Send" click="sendChatMessage(event)"/>
            <mx:Button id="clear" label="Clear" click="output.text =''"/>
        </mx:ControlBar>
    </mx:Panel>

    <mx:Script>
        <![CDATA[
```

```
        import mx.controls.Alert;
        import mx.events.FlexEvent;
        import mx.messaging.Consumer;
        import mx.messaging.Producer;
        import mx.messaging.channels.AMFChannel;
        import mx.messaging.events.MessageEvent;
        import mx.messaging.messages.AsyncMessage;

        import org.springextensions.actionscript.context.support.FlexXMLApplicationContext;
        import org.springextensions.actionscript.context.support.XMLApplicationContext;

        private var chatProducer:Producer;
        private var chatConsumer:Consumer;

        private var _applicationContext:XMLApplicationContext;

        [Bindable]
        [Embed(source="app-context4.xml",
mimeType ="application/octet-stream")]
        public var contextConfig:Class;

        public function setup(fe:FlexEvent):void
        {
            _applicationContext = new FlexXMLApplicationContext();
            _applicationContext.addEmbeddedConfig(contextConfig);
            _applicationContext.load();

        }

        private function sendChatMessage(me:MouseEvent):void
        {
            var msg:AsyncMessage = new AsyncMessage();
            msg.body = input.text;
            chatProducer.send(msg);
            input.text = "";
        }
        ]]>
    </mx:Script>
</mx:Application>
```

We've torn out all the initialization logic in our chat application and focus in this example on bootstrapping a Spring ActionScript application context. There are many ways to load an XML context, including via remote URL or with an embedded resource. The simplest and most reliable is probably the embedded resource approach—to simply have the compiler embed the contents of the resource in the compiled SWF file itself. To access it, we use the [Embed] attribute to tell Flex which resource to embed and the MIME type of that resource. Flex injects the content of that resource into the variable that's been tagged. Then, in our listener for the applicationComplete event dispatched by the Application, we initialize the FlexXMLApplicationContext instance. We call the addEmbeddedConfig method to tell it to bootstrap the XML context using the contents of that embedded XML file resource. Finally, we call the load method on the context.

In other scenarios, when using some other kind of resource besides an embedded one, loading is an asynchronous operation. In those cases, you need to attach a listener and have it tell you when the XML file has been loaded. This is why the load operation is pivotal and why instantiation of the context doesn't happen on the construction of the `FlexXMLApplicationContext` itself.

Now, let's flesh out our first Spring XML application context file, `app-context4.xml`.

The configuration support for Flex ActionScript is very powerful and become even more with every release. As of version 0.8.1, there is preliminary support for namespaces, for example. If we're honest, you're not going to need a lot of the complex functionality you have in the Java version, either. Put another way: in Java Spring, we use the configuration options to both enforce the DRY principle *and* to abstract away complex object construction scenarios like those involved in declarative transaction management, and so on. Flex can be tedious, but it's far more likely you'll use Flex to avoid duplicated code.

The simplest possible application context looks like this:

```
<?xml version="1.0" encoding="UTF-8"?>

<objects
xmlns="http://www.springactionscript.org/schema/objects"
xmlns:xsi="http://www.w3.org/2001/XMLSchema-instance"
xsi:schemaLocation="http://www.springactionscript.org/schema/objects
http://www.springactionscript.org/schema/objects/spring-actionscript-objects-1.0.xsd"
>

<!-- hello, world! -->

</objects>
```

It should be clear what's happening here. In lieu of `beans` elements, we're using `objects` elements. The namespaces have been changed a bit, too. This should be familiar ground for us Spring developers!

Let's add some features to our Spring application context to support us. One thing we will want is the ability to resolve Flex runtime properties made available by the `Application` class. These properties give your application an idea of its context—where and how fast it is running, at what URL, and so on. Among the properties supported are `applicationurl.port`, `application.url`, `application.url.host`, and `application.url.protocol`. To resolve the properties, we'll add the Spring ActionScript analog of a `BeanPostProcessor`. Add the following in between the `objects` elements:

```
<object class="org.springextensions.actionscript.ioc.factory.config.flex.
ApplicationPropertiesResolver"/>
```

Now, just as you'd expect, you can refer to these properties in your configuration using the variable interpolation syntax, like this: `${application.url}`.

The next thing to do is add support for having Spring ActionScript automatically wire dependencies on all components it adds to the stage. To do this, add the following:

```
<object class="org.springextensions.actionscript.stage.DefaultAutowiringStageProcessor"
        id="defaultAutowiringStageProcessor" />
```

To use this, you need only declare a variable on a component that you add to the stage, like so:

```
import mx.rpc.remoting.RemoteObject;
// ...
Autowired(name = "auctionService")]
public var auctionService:RemoteObject ;
```

Remember, the main .mxml file is not a component. Creating components is not very difficult but is out of the scope of this book. A component lets you create functionality (and the view for that functionality, if you want), and reuse it elsewhere. An example of this is the buttons that you use in the framework. You use XML and a button (whose behavior is completely hidden from you) shows up on the user interface, ready to use.

This initial setup should precede any work you do in ActionScript, because it saves a lot of time for almost no cost. Let's now turn to actually configuring objects worth injecting!

In our chat application, we created an mx.messaging.Consumer and an mx.messaging.Producer. To create those objects, we need a valid mx.messaging.ChannelSet. Let's configure that first. Add the following to your application context:

```
<object id="channelSet" class="mx.messaging.ChannelSet">
    <property name="channels" >
        <array>
            <object class="mx.messaging.channels.AMFChannel">
                <constructor-arg value="my-amf"/>
                <constructor-arg value="http://localhost:8080/mb/amf"/>
            </object>
        </array>
    </property>
</object>
```

This example is small but demonstrates a lot. We demonstrate how to create an array in the Spring ActionScript XML, how to do constructor configuration, and even how an object is configured. Creating the Producer and Consumer are similarly easy, dispatched with three lines of XML each:

```
<object id="consumer" class="mx.messaging.Consumer" scope="prototype">
    <property name="channelSet" ref="channelSet"/>
    <property name="destination" value="chatDestination"/>
</object>

<object id="producer" class="mx.messaging.Producer" scope="prototype">
    <property name="channelSet" ref="channelSet"/>
    <property name="destination" value="chatDestination"/>
</object>
```

So far, this should all read very naturally. In fact, for the most part, you could swap out object and replace it with bean to get a valid Java Spring XML context!

All that's left now is to use them. We'll revisit the chat application and obtain references to the Producer and Consumer from the application context when the application's completely loaded.

Using beans from Spring is slightly different with Spring ActionScript because of the way the Flex compiler works. The obvious first thing to do is replace the old initialization logic with acquisition logic after the FlexXMLApplicationContext has been realized in the setup method that we've wired to react to the applicationComplete event.

```
chatConsumer = _applicationContext.getObject('consumer') as Consumer;
chatConsumer.addEventListener(MessageEvent.MESSAGE,
   function (msgEvent:MessageEvent):void {
            var msg:AsyncMessage = msgEvent.message as AsyncMessage;
               output.text += msg.body + "\n";
});

chatConsumer.subscribe();
chatProducer = _applicationContext.getObject('producer') as Producer;
chatProducer.connect();
```

This should be all that we need to do to realize an equivalent program to the one we started with, but it isn't. The problem is that the Flex compiler prunes classes that aren't used to minimize the size of the resultant compiled binary. This includes classes in the base framework library. Normally, this would be laudable. However, because we're constructing a lot of our objects using Spring, it has no way of knowing what classes are being used. Since we aren't declaring any variables anywhere of type AMFChannel, for example, it won't include that class—even though we're constructing an instance of it using Spring! There are many solutions, but the simplest is an explicit reference to any class you want to retain in the compiled code. Our habit is to simply create anonymous blocks. You can put them in different modules, or at higher places like the main class. Here's how ours looks:

```
<mx:Script>
<![CDATA[
 import mx.messaging.channels.AMFChannel; // imports
 {  // anonymous block
    AMFChannel  // class reference
    // , OtherClass, OtherClass
 }
]]>
</mx:Script>
```

Now, you have something that replaces the earlier code and keeps you from needlessly reintroducing the same logic as before. Run the Flex client as before in different browsers and confirm that a message produced in one session is reflected instantly in another window.

Summary

In this chapter, you've learned about Flash, and the Flex architecture. You've learned about how the Flash/Flex/AIR trifecta should fit into your architecture. You've learned about the features, and limitations, that may change the way your application works when talking to other services. We explored different ways to interoperate from Flex and then finally looked at setting up BlazeDS, an open source middleware project from Adobe. You learned how BlazeDS can help overcome inherent limitations (or, features) in the Flash platform and how to use the Spring BlazeDS integration to simplify deployment of the BlazeDS middleware with your application. We explored the push and pill types of services models that a client/server application might use and how we could take advantage of those using BlazeDS and Flex; this included how to expose Spring services to Flex clients in a synchronous and asynchronous fashion using messaging-based, JMS-based, and Spring Integration–based services. Finally, you learned about using the Spring ActionScript container to bring the same discipline and elegance to ActionScript programming that Spring Java brings to Java developers.

CHAPTER 11

Grails

When you embark on the creation of a Java web application, you need to put together a series of Java classes, create configuration files, and establish a particular layout, all of which have little to do with the problems an application solves. Such pieces are often called "scaffolding code" or "scaffolding steps," since they are just the means to an end—the end being what an application actually accomplishes.

Grails is a framework designed to limit the amount of scaffolding steps you need to take in Java applications. Based on the Groovy language, which is a Java Virtual Machine–compatible language, Grails automates many steps that need to be undertaken in a Java application on the basis of conventions.

For example, when you create application controllers, they are eventually accompanied by a series of views (e.g., JavaServer Pages [JSP] pages), in addition to requiring some type of configuration file to make them work. If you generate a controller using Grails, Grails automates numerous steps using conventions (e.g., creating views and configuration files). You can later modify whatever Grails generates to more specific scenarios, but Grails undoubtedly shortens your development time since you won't need to write everything from scratch (e.g., write XML configuration files and prepare a project directory structure).

Grails is fully integrated with Spring 3.0, so you can use it to kick-start your Spring applications and thus reduce your development efforts.

11-1. Getting and Installing Grails

Problem

You want to start creating a Grails application but don't know where to get Grails and how to set it up.

Solution

You can download Grails at http://www.grails.org/. Ensure that you download Grails version 1.2 or higher, since only those versions support Spring 3.0. Grails is a self-contained framework that comes with various scripts to automate the creation of Java applications. In this sense, you simply need to unpack the distribution and perform a few installation steps in order to create Java applications on your workstation.

How It Works

After you unpack Grails on your workstation, define two environment variables on your operating system: GRAILS_HOME and PATH. This allows you to invoke Grails operations from anywhere on your workstation.

If you use a Linux workstation, you can edit the global bashrc file– located under the /etc/ directory, or a use's .bashrc file, located under a user's home directory. Note that, depending on the Linux distribution, these last file names can vary (e.g., bash.bashrc). Both files use identical syntax to define environment variables, with one file used to define variables for all users and another for a single user. Place the following contents in either one:

```
GRAILS_HOME=/<installation_directory>/grails
export GRAILS_HOME
export PATH=$PATH:$GRAILS_HOME/bin
```

If you use a Windows workstation, go to the Control Panel, and click the System icon. On the window that emerges, click the Advanced Options tab. Next, click the "Environment variables" box to bring up the environment variable editor. From there, you can add or modify environment variables for either a single user or all users, using the following steps:

1. Click the New box.

2. Create an environment variable with the name GRAILS_HOME and a value corresponding to the Grails installation directory (e.g., /<installation_directory>/grails).

3. Select the PATH environment variable, and click the Modify box.

4. Add the ;%GRAILS_HOME%\bin value to the end of the PATH environment variable.

▪ **Caution** Be sure to *add* this last value and not modify the PATH environment variable in any other way, as this may cause certain applications to stop working.

Once you perform these steps in either a Windows or Linux workstation, you can start creating Grails applications. If you execute the command grails help from any directory on your workstation, you should see Grails's numerous commands.

11-2. Creating a Grails Application

Problem

You want to create a Grails application.

Solution

To create a Grails application, invoke the following command wherever you wish to create an application: grails create-app <grailsappname>. This creates a Grails application directory, with a project structure in accordance to the framework's design.

If this last command fails, consult recipe 11-1, on "Getting and Installing Grails." The grails command should be available from any console or terminal if Grails was installed correctly.

How It Works

For example, typing grails create-app court creates a Grails application under a directory named court. Inside this directory, you will find a series of files and directories generated by Grails on the basis of conventions. The initial project structure for a Grails application is the following:

```
application.properties
build.xml
court.iml
court.iws
court-test.launch
court.ipr
court.launch
court.tmproj
ivy.xml
ivysettings.xml
  grails-app/
  lib/
  scripts/
  src/
  test/
  web-app/
```

■ **Note** In addition to this last layout, Grails also creates a series of working directories and files (i.e., not intended to be modified directly) for an application. These working directories and files are placed under a user's home directory under the name.grails/<grails_version>/.

As you can note from this last listing, Grails generates a series of files and directories that are common in most Java applications. This includes, an Apache Ant file (build.xml) and an Apache Ivy file (ivy.xml), as well as common directories like src for placing source code files and a web-app directory that includes the common layout for Java web application(e.g., /WEB-INF/, /META-INF/, css, images, and js).

So right out of the box, Grails saves you time by putting these common Java application constructs together using a single command.

A Grails Application's File and Directory Structure

Since some of these files and directories are Grails specific, we will describe the purpose behind each one:

- `application.properties`: Used to define an application's properties, including the Grails version, servlet version, and an application's name

- `build.xml`: An Apache Ant script with a series of predefined tasks designed to create a Grails application

- `court.iml`: An XML file containing configuration parameters for an application, such as directory locations and treatment of JARs

- `court.iws`: An XML file containing configuration parameters for an application's deployment, such as web container port and project views

- `court-test.launch`: An XML file containing configuration parameters for an application's test process

- `court.ipr`: An XML file containing configuration parameters for an application's library table (i.e., JARs)

- `court.launch`: An XML file containing configuration parameters for an application's launch, such as JVM arguments

- `court.tmproj`: An XML file containing configuration parameters for an application's temporary working properties

- `ivy.xml`: An Apache Ivy configuration file used for defining an application's dependencies

- `ivysettings.xml`: An Apache Ivy configuration file used for defining repositories in order to download dependencies

- `grails-app`: A directory containing the core of an application, which further contains the following folders:

  1. `conf`: A directory containing an application's configuration sources

  2. `controllers`: A directory containing an application's controllers files

  3. `domain`: A directory containing an application's domain files

  4. `i18n`: A directory containing an application's internationalization (i18n) files

  5. `services`: A directory containing an application's service files

  6. `taglib`: A directory containing an application's tag libraries

  7. `utils`: A directory containing an application's utility files

  8. `views`: A directory containing an application's view files

- `lib`: Directory used for libraries (i.e., JARs)

- `scripts`: Directory used for scripts

- `src`: Directory used for an application's source code files; contains two subfolders named groovy and java, for sources written in these respective languages

- `test`: Directory used for an application's test files. Contains two subfolders named integration and unit, for tests belonging to these respective types

- `web-app`: Directory used for an application's deployment structure; contains the standard web archive (WAR) files and directory structure (e.g., /WEB-INF/, /META-INF/, css, images, and js)

■ **Note** Grails does not support Apache Maven out of the box. However, if you prefer to use Maven as your build tool, there is support for using Maven with Grails. Consult `http://www.grails.org/Maven+Integration`.

Running an Application

Grails come preconfigured to run application's on an Apache Tomcat web container. Note the files pertaining to the Apache Tomcat container are one of those placed under a user's home directory (i.e., .grails/<grails_version>/), they are not visible. Similar to the creation of creating a Grails application, the process of running Grails applications is highly automated.

Placed under the root directory of a Grails application, invoke `grails run-app`. This command will trigger the build process for an application if it's needed, as well as start the Apache Tomcat web container and deploy the application.

Since Grails operates on conventions, an application is deployed under a context named after the project name. So for example, the application named court is deployed to the URL `http://localhost:8080/court/`. Figure 11-1 illustrates the default main screen for Grails applications.

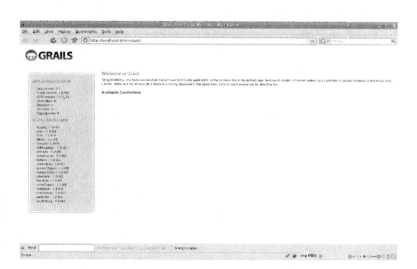

Figure 11-1. *Default main screen for court Grails application*

The application is still in its out of the box state. Next, we will illustrate how to create your first Grails construct in order to realize more time saving procedures.

Creating Your First Grails Application Construct

Now that you have seen how easy it is to create a Grails application, let's incorporate an application construct in the form of a controller. This will further illustrate how Grails automates a series of steps in the development process of Java applications.

Placed under the root directory of a Grails application, invoke grails create-controller welcome. Executing this command will perform the following steps:

1. Create a controller named WelcomeController.groovy under the application directory grails-app/controllers.

2. Create a directory named welcome under the application directory grails-app/views.

3. Create a test class named WelcomeControllerTests.groovy under the application directory test/unit.

As a first step, let's analyze the contents of the controller generated by Grails. The contents of the WelcomeController.groovy controller are the following:

```
class WelcomeController {
 def index = {}
}
```

If you're unfamiliar with Groovy, the syntax will seem awkward. But it's simply a class named WelcomeController with a method named index. The purpose is the same as the Spring MVC controllers you created back in Chapter 8, WelcomeController, represents a controller class where as the method, index, represents a handler method. However, in this state the controller isn't doing anything. Modify it to reflect the following:

```
class WelcomeController {
  Date now = new Date()
  def index = {[today:now]}
}
```

The first addition is a Date object assigned to the now class field, to represent the system date. Since def index = {} represents a handler method, the addition of [today:now] is used as a return value. In this case, the return value represents a variable named today with the now class field, and that variable's value will be passed onto to the view associated with the handler method.

Having a controller and a handler method that returns the current date, you can create a corresponding view. If you place yourself under the directory grails-app/views/welcome, you will not find any views. However, Grails attempts to locate a view for the WelcomeController controller inside this directory, in accordance with the name of the handler method; this, once again, is one of the many conventions used by Grails.

Therefore, create a JSP page named index.jsp inside this directory with the following contents:

```
<%@ taglib prefix="fmt" uri="http://java.sun.com/jsp/jstl/fmt" %>
<html>
<head>
<title>Welcome</title>
</head>

<body>
<h2>Welcome to Court Reservation System</h2>
Today is <fmt:formatDate value="${today}" pattern="yyyy-MM-dd" />
</body>

</html>
```

As you can see, this is a standard JSP page that makes use of a JSTL tag. The JSTL tag renders a variable named ${today}, which is precisely the name of the variable returned by the controller handler method named index. It's important to note that even though you've added a JSP page with a JSTL tag to the application, Grails automatically fulfils dependencies (i.e., JARs) for this component; you don't have to manually obtain and manage these common dependencies,

Next, from the root directory of the Grails application, invoke the command grails run-app. This automatically builds the application, compiling the controller class and copying files where they are needed as well as starting the Apache Tomcat web container and deploying the application.

Following the same Grails convention process, the WelcomeController along with its handler methods and views will be accessible from the context path http://localhost:8080/court/welcome/. Since index is the default page used for context paths, if you open a browser and visit http://localhost:8080/court/welcome/ or the explicit URL http://localhost:8080/court/welcome/index, you will see the previous JSP page that renders the current date as returned by the controller. Note the lack of view extensions in the URLs (i.e., .jsp). Grails hides the view technology by default, the reasons for this will become more evident in more advanced Grails scenarios.

As you repeat the simple steps needed to create an application controller and view, bear in mind you didn't have to create or modify any configuration files, manually copy files to different locations, or set up a web container to run the application. As an application moves forward, avoiding these scaffolding steps that are common in Java web applications can be a great way to reduce development time.

Exporting a Grails Application to a WAR

The previous steps were all performed in the confines of a Grails environment. That is to say, you relied on Grails to bootstrap a web container and run applications. However, when you want to run a Grails application in a production environment, you will undoubtedly need to generate a format in which to deploy the application to an external web container, which is a WAR file in the case of Java applications.

Placed under the root directory of a Grails application, invoke grails war. Executing this command generates a WAR file under the root directory in the form <application-name>-<application-version>.war. This WAR is a self-contained file with all the necessary elements needed to run a Grails application on any Java standard web container

In the case of the court application, a file named court-0.1.war is generated in the root directory of the Grails application, and the application version is taken from the parameter app.version defined in the application.properties file.

In accordance with Apache Tomcat deployment conventions, a WAR named `court-0.1.war` would be accessible at a URL in the form `http://localhost:8080/court-0.1/`. WAR deployment to URL conventions may vary depending on the Java web container (e.g., Jetty or Oracle WebLogic).

11-3. Grails Plug-Ins

Problem

You want to use functionality from a Java framework or Java API inside Grails applications, while taking advantage of the same Grails techniques to save scaffolding.

The problem isn't simply using a Java framework or Java API in an application; this can be achieved by simply dropping the corresponding JARs into an application's `lib` directory. But rather having a Java framework or Java API *tightly* integrated with Grails, something that is provided in the form of Grails plug-ins.

By *tightly* integrated with Grails, we mean having the capacity to use short-cut instructions (e.g., `grails <plug-in-task>`) for performing a particular Java framework or Java API task or the ability to use functionality inside an application's classes or configuration files without resorting to scaffolding steps.

Solution

Grails actually comes with a few preinstalled plug-ins, even though this is not evident if you stick to using Grails out of the box functionality. However, there are many Grails plug-ins that can make working with a particular Java framework or Java API as productive a process as using Grails core functionality. Some of the more popular Grails plug-ins follow:

- *App Engine*: Integrates Google's App Engine SDK and tools with Grails.

- *Quartz*: Integrates the Quartz Enterprise Job Scheduler to schedule jobs and have them executed using a specified interval or cron expression

- *Spring WS*: Integrates and supports the provisioning of web services, based on the Spring Web Services project

- Clojure: Integrates Clojure and allows Clojure code to be executed in Grails artifacts

To obtain a complete list of Grails plug-ins you can execute the command: `grails list-plugins`. This last command connects to the Grails plug-in repository and displays all the available Grails plug-ins. In addition, the command `grails plugin-info <plugin_name>` can be used to obtain detailed information about a particular plug-in. As an alternative, you can visit the Grails plug-in page located at `http://grails.org/plugin/home`.

Installing a Grails plug-in requires invoking the following command from a Grails application's root directory: `grails install-plugin <plugin_name>`.

Removing a Grails plug-in requires invoking the following command from a Grails application's root directory: `grails uninstall-plugin <plugin_name>`.

How It Works

A Grails plug-in follows a series of conventions that allow it to tightly integrate a particular Java framework or Java API with Grails. By default, Grails comes with the Apache Tomcat and Hibernate plug-ins preinstalled, and both of these are located under the `plugins` directory of the Grails distribution.

When you first create a Grails application, these plug-ins are copied to the Grails working directory `.grails/<grails_version>/plugins` located under a user's home directory. In addition, two files are generated under this same directory: `plugins-list-core.xml` and `plugins-list-default.xml`. The first of which contains plug-ins included in every Grails application, by default Apache Tomcat and Hibernate, and the second containing the entire list of available Grails plug-ins.

Every Grails application you create afterward includes the plug-ins defined in the `plugins-list-core.xml` file. This inclusion takes place by unzipping each plug-in under an application's working directory under `.grails/<grails_version>/projects/<project_name>/plugins/`. Once the plug-ins are unzipped, a Grails application is equipped to support whatever functionality is provided by a plug-in.

Besides these default plug-ins, additional plug-ins can be installed on a per-application basis. For example, to install the Clojure plug-in, you would execute the following command from an application's root directory:

```
grails install-plugin clojure
```

This last command downloads and initially copies the Clojure plug-in to the same Grails working directory, `.grails/<grails_version>/plugins`, located under a user's home directory. Once downloaded, the plug-in is copied as a zip file, as well as unzipped under an application's working directory under.`grails/<grails_version>/projects/<project_name>/plugins/`.

To remove a plug-in from a Grails application, you can invoke the following command:

```
grails uninstall-plugin clojure
```

This last command removes the unzipped plug-in from an application's working directory under.`grails/<grails_version>/projects/<project_name>/plugins/`, though the zipped plug-in file will remain. In addition, the downloaded plug-in remains under the Grails working directory `.grails/<grails_version>/plugins`, located under a user's home directory.

This installation and uninstallation of plug-ins is done on a per-application basis. In order for a plug-in to be automatically added to a Grails application upon creation, you need to modify the `plugins-list-core.xml` file manually. This copies whatever plug-ins you deem necessary on all subsequent application you create, along with the default Apache Tomcat and Hibernate plug-ins.

■ **Caution** Besides the steps outlined here, we do not recommend you modify the structure of a plug-in or a Grails application working directory. Plug-ins always alter the structure of a Grails application to provide it with the necessary functionality. If you encounter problems with a Grails plug-in, we recommend you consult the plug-in's documentation or ask the plug-in maintainers on the Grails development mailing list at `http://grails.org/Mailing%20lists`.

11-4. Developing, Producing, and Testing in Grails Environments

Problem

You want to use different parameters for the same application on the basis of the environment (e.g., development, production, and testing) it's being run in.

Solution

Grails anticipates that a Java application can undergo various phases that require different parameters. These phases, or "environments" as they are called by Grails, can be, for instance, development, production, and testing.

The most obvious scenario involves data sources, where you are likely to use a different permanent storage system for development, production, and testing environments. Since each of these storage systems will use different connection parameters, it's easier to configure parameters for multiple environments and let Grails connect to each one depending on an application's operations.

In addition to data sources, Grails provides the same feature for other parameters that can change in between application environments, such as server URLs for creating an application's absolute links.

Configuration parameters for a Grails application environment are specified in the files located under an application's /grails-app/conf/ directory.

How It Works

Depending on the operation your performing, Grails automatically selects the most suitable environment: development, production, or testing.

For example, when you invoke the command grails run-app, this implies that you are still developing an application locally, so a development environment is assumed. In fact, when you execute this command, among the output you can see a line that reads:

```
Environment set to development
```

This means that whatever parameters are set for a development environment are used to build, configure and run the application.

Another example is the grails war command. Since exporting a Grails application to a stand-alone WAR implies you will be running it on an external web container, Grails assumes a production environment. In the output generated for this command, you will find a line that reads

```
Environment set to production
```

This means that whatever parameters are set for a production environment are used to build, configure, and export the application.

Finally, if you run a command like grails test-app, Grails assumes a testing environment. This means that whatever parameters are set for a testing environment are used to build, configure, and run tests. In the output generated for this command, you will find a line that reads

```
Environment set to test
```

Inside the configuration files located in an application's directory /grails-app/conf/, you can find sections in the following form:

```
environments {
    production {
        grails.serverURL = "http://www.domain.com"
    }
    development {
        grails.serverURL = "http://localhost:8080/${appName}"
    }
    test {
        grails.serverURL = "http://localhost:8080/${appName}"
    }
}
```

This last listing belongs to the Config.groovy file. It's used to specify different server URLs for creating an application's absolute links on the basis of an application's environment. Another example would be the section contained in the DataSource.groovy file, which is used to define data sources and illustrated next:

```
environments {
    development {
        dataSource {
            dbCreate = "create-drop" // one of 'create', 'create-drop','update'
            url = "jdbc:hsqldb:mem:devDB"
        }
    }
    test {
        dataSource {
            dbCreate = "update"
            url = "jdbc:hsqldb:mem:testDb"
        }
    }
    production {
        dataSource {
            dbCreate = "update"
            url = "jdbc:hsqldb:file:prodDb;shutdown=true"
        }
    }
}
```

In this last listing, different connection parameters are specified for permanent storage systems on the basis of an application's environment. This allows an application to operate on different data sets, as you will surely not want development modifications to take place on the same data set used in a production environment. It should be noted that this doesn't mean these last examples are the only parameters that are allowed to be configured on the basis of an application's environment. You can equally place any parameter inside the corresponding environments { <environment_phase> } section. These last examples simply represent the most likely parameters to change in between an application's environments.

It's also possible to perform programming logic (e.g., within a class or script) on the basis of a given application's environment. This is achieved through the grails.util.Environment class. The following listing illustrates this process.

```
import grails.util.Environment
…

…
switch(Environment.current) {
        case Environment.DEVELOPMENT:
            // Execute development logic
        break
        case Environment.PRODUCTION:
            // Execute production logic
        break
}
```

This last code snippet illustrates how a class first imports the grails.util.Environment class. Then, on the basis of the Environment.current value, which contains the environment an application is being run on, the code uses a switch conditional to execute logic depending on this value.

Such a scenario can be common in areas like sending out emails or performing geolocation. It would not make sense to send out e-mails or determine where a user is located on a development environment, given that a development team's location is irrelevant in addition to not requiring an application's e-mail notifications.

Finally, it's worth mentioning that you can override the default environment used for any Grails command.

For example, by default, the grails run-app command uses the parameters specified for a development environment. If for some reason you want to run this command with the parameters specified for a production environment, you can do so using the following instruction: grails prod run-app. If you wish to use the parameters specified for a test environment, you can also do so by using the following instruction: grails test run-app.

By the same token, for a command like grails test-app, which uses the parameters specified for a test environment, you can use the parameters belonging to a development environment by using the command grails dev test-app. The same case applies for all other commands, by simply inserting the prod, test, or dev keyword after the grails command.

11-5. Creating an Application's Domain Classes

Problem

You need to define an application's domain classes.

Solution

Domain classes are used to describe an application's primary elements and characteristics. If an application is designed to attend reservations, it's likely to have a domain class for holding reservations. Equally, if reservations are associated with a person, an application will have a domain class for holding persons.

In web applications, domain classes are generally the first things to be defined, because these classes represent data that is saved for posterity—in a permanent storage system—so it interacts with controllers, as well as representing data displayed in views.

In Grails, domain classes are placed under the /grails-app/domain/ directory. The creation of domain classes, like most other things in Grails, can be carried out by executing a simple command in the following form:

```
grails create-domain-class <domain_class_name>
```

This last command generates a skeleton domain class file named <domain_class_name>.groovy inside the /grails-app/domain/ directory.

How It Works

Grails creates skeleton domain classes, but you still need to modify each domain class to reflect the purpose of an application.

Let's create a reservation system, similar to the one you created back in Chapter 8 to experiment with Spring MVC. Create two domain classes, one named Reservation and another named Player. To do so, execute the following commands:

```
grails create-domain-class Player
grails create-domain-class Reservation
```

By executing these last commands, a class file named Player.groovy and another one named Reservation.groovy1 are placed under an application's /grails-app/domain/ directory. In addition, corresponding unit tests files are also generated for each domain class under an application's test/unit directory, though testing will be addressed in a recipe 11-10.

Next, open the Player.groovy class to edit its contents. The following statements in bold represent the declarations you need to add to this domain class:

```
class Player {
    static hasMany = [ reservations : Reservation ]
    String name
    String phone
    static constraints = {
      name(blank:false)
      phone(blank:false)
    }
}
```

The first addition, static hasMany = [reservations : Reservation], represents a relationship among domain classes. This statement indicates that the Player domain class has a reservations field that has many Reservation objects associated with it. The following statements indicate that the Player domain class also has two String fields, one called name and another called phone.

The remaining element, static constraints = { }, defines constraints on the domain class. In this case, the declaration name(blank:false) indicates that a Player object's name field cannot be left blank. While the declaration phone(blank:false) indicates that a Player object cannot be created unless the phone field is provided with a value.

Once you modify the Player domain class, open the Reservation.groovy class to edit its contents. The following statements in bold represent the declarations you need to add to this domain class:

```
class Reservation {
    static belongsTo = Player
    String courtName;
    Date date;
    Player player;
    String sportType;
    static constraints = {
        sportType(inList:["Tennis", "Soccer"] )
        date(validator: {
            if (it.getAt(Calendar.DAY_OF_WEEK) == "SUNDAY" &&↵
                            ( it.getAt(Calendar.HOUR_OF_DAY) < 8 || ↵
                          it.getAt(Calendar.HOUR_OF_DAY) > 22)) { ↵
                            return ['invalid.holidayHour']
            } else if ( it.getAt(Calendar.HOUR_OF_DAY) < 9 || ↵
                        it.getAt(Calendar.HOUR_OF_DAY) > 21) { ↵
                            return ['invalid.weekdayHour']
            }
        })
    }
}
```

The first statement added to the Reservation domain class, static belongsTo = Player, indicates that a Reservation object always belongs to a Player object. The following statements indicate the Reservation domain class has a field named courtName of the type String, a field named date of the type Date, a field named player of the type Player and another field named sportType of the type String.

The constraints for the Reservation domain class are a little more elaborate than the Player domain class. The first constraint, sportType(inList:["Tennis", "Soccer"]), restricts the sportType field of a Reservation object to a string value of either Tennis or Soccer. The second constraint is a custom-made validator to ensure the date field of a Reservation object is within a certain hour range depending on the day of the week.

Now that you have an application's domain classes, you can create the corresponding views and controllers for an application.

Before proceeding, though, a word on Grails domain classes is in order. While the domain classes you created in this recipe provide you with a basic understanding of the syntax used to define Grails domain classes, they illustrate only a fraction of the features available in Grails domain classes.

As the relationship between domain classes grows more elaborate, more sophisticated constructs are likely to be required for defining Grails domain classes. This comes as a consequence of Grails relying on domain classes for various application functionalities.

For example, if a domain object is updated or deleted from an application's permanent storage system, the relationships between domain classes need to be well established. If relationships are not well established, there is a possibility for inconsistent data to arise in an application (e.g., if a person object is deleted, its corresponding reservations also need to be deleted to avoid an inconsistent state in an application's reservations).

Equally, a variety of constraints can be used to enforce a domain class's structure. Under certain circumstances, if a constraint is too elaborate, it's often incorporated within an application's controller prior to creating an object of a certain domain class. Though for this recipe, model constraints were used to illustrate the design of Grails domain classes.

11-6. Generating CRUD Controllers and Views for an Application's Domain Classes

Problem

You need to generate create, read, update, and delete (CRUD) controllers and views for an application's domain classes.

Solution

An application's domain classes by themselves are of little use. The data mapped to domain classes still needs to be created, presented to end users, and potentially saved for future use in a permanent storage system.

In web applications backed by permanent storage systems, these operations on domain classes are often referred to as CRUD operations. In the majority of web frameworks, generating CRUD controllers and views entails a substantial amount of work. This is on account of needing controllers capable of creating, reading, updating, and deleting domain objects to a permanent storage systems, as well as creating the corresponding views (e.g., JSP pages) for an end user to create, read, update, and delete these same objects.

However, since Grails operates on the basis of conventions, the mechanism for generating CRUD controllers and views for an application's domain classes is easy. You can execute the following command to generate the corresponding CRUD controller and views for an application's domain class:

```
grails generate-all <domain_class_name>
```

How It Works

Grails is capable of inspecting an application's domain classes and generating the corresponding controllers and views necessary to create, read, update, and delete instances belonging to an application's domain classes.

For example, take the case of the Player domain class you created earlier. In order to generate its CRUD controller and views, you only need to execute the following command from an application's root directory:

```
grails generate-all Player
```

A similar command would apply to the Reservation domain class. Simply execute the following command to generate its CRUD controller and views:

```
grails generate-all Reservation
```

So what is actually generated by executing these steps? If you saw the output for these commands you will have a pretty good idea, but I will recap the process here nonetheless.

1. Compile an application's classes.

2. Generate 12 properties files under the directory grails-app/i18n to support an application's internationalization(e.g., messages_<language>.properties).

3. Create a controller named <domain_class>Controller.groovy with CRUD operations designed for an RDBMS, placed under an application's grails-app/controllers directory.

4. Create four views corresponding to a controller class's CRUD operations named create.gsp, edit.gsp, list.gsp, and show.gsp. Note that the .gsp extension stands for "Groovy Server Pages," which is equivalent to JavaServer Pages except it uses Groovy to declare programmatic statements instead of Java. These views are placed under an application's grails-app/views/<domain_class> directory.

Once you finish these steps, you can start the Grails application using grails run-app and work as an end user with the application. Yes, you read correctly; after performing these simple commands, the application is now ready to for end users. This is the mantra of Grails operating on conventions, to simplify the creation of scaffolding code through one word commands

After the application is started, you can perform CRUD operations on the Player domain class at the following URLs:

- Create: http://localhost:8080/court/player/create

- Read: http://localhost:8080/court/player/list (for all players) or http://localhost:8080/court/player/show/<player_id>

- Update: http://localhost:8080/court/player/edit/<player_id>

- Delete: http://localhost:8080/court/player/delete/<player_id>

The page navigation between each view is more intuitive than these URLs have it to be, but we will illustrate with a few screen shots shortly. An important thing to be aware about these URLs is their conventions. Notice the pattern <domain>/<app_name>/<domain_class>/<crud_action>/<object_id>, where <object_id> is optional depending on the operation.

In addition to being used to define URL patterns, these conventions are used throughout an application's artifacts. For example, if you inspect the PlayerController.groovy controller, you can observe there are handler methods named like the various <crud_action> values. Similarly, if you inspect an application's backing RDBMS, you can note that the domain class objects are saved using the same <player_id> used in a URL.

Now that your aware of how CRUD operations are structured in Grails applications, create a Player object by visiting the address http://localhost:8080/court/player/create. Once you visit this page, you can see an HTML form with the same field values you defined for the Player domain class.

Introduce any two values for the name and phone fields and submit the form. You've just persisted a Player object to a RDBMS. By default, Grails come preconfigured to use HSQLDB, an in-memory RDBMS. A future recipe will illustrate how to change this to another RDBMS, for now HSQLDB will suffice.

Next, try submitting the same form but, this time, without any values. Grails will not persist the Player object, it will instead show two warning messages indicating that the name and phone fields cannot be blank. Figure 11-2 illustrates this screen shot.

Figure 11-2. *Grails domain class validation taking place in a view (in this case, an HTML form)*

This validation process is being enforced on account of the statements, name(blank:false) and phone(blank:false), which you placed in the Player domain class. You didn't need to modify an application's controllers or views or even create properties files for these error messages; everything was taken care of by Grails convention based approach.

Experiment with the remaining views available for the Player domain class, creating, reading, updating, and deleting objects directly from a web browser to get a feel for how Grails handles these tasks.

Moving along the application, you can also perform CRUD operations on the Reservation domain class at the following URLs:

- Create: http://localhost:8080/court/reservation/create

- Read: http://localhost:8080/court/reservation/list (for all reservations) or http://localhost:8080/court/reservation/show/<reservation_id>

- Update: http://localhost:8080/court/reservation/edit/<reservation_id>

- Delete: http://localhost:8080/court/reservation/delete/<reservation_id>

These last URLs serve the same purpose as those for the Player domain class. The ability to create, read, update, and delete objects belonging to the Reservation domain class from a web interface.

Next, let's analyze the HTML form used for creating Reservation objects, available at the URL http://localhost:8080/court/reservation/create. Figure 11-3 illustrates this form.

Figure 11-3. Grails domain class HTML form, populated with domain objects from separate class

Figure 11-3 is interesting in various ways. Though the HTML form is still created on the basis of the fields of the Reservation domain class, just like the HTML form for the Player domain class, notice that it has various prepopulated HTML select menus.

The first select menu belongs to the sportType field. Since this particular field has a definition constraint to have a string value of either Soccer or Tennis, Grails automatically provides a user with these options instead of allowing open-ended strings and validating them afterward.

The second select menu belongs to the date field. In this case, Grails generates various HTML select menus representing a date and time to make the date-selection process easier, instead of allowing open-ended dates and validating them afterward.

The third select menu belongs to the player field. This select menu's options are different in the sense they are taken from the Player objects you've created for the application. The values are being extracted from querying the application's RDBMS; if you add another Player object, it will automatically become available in this select menu.

In addition, a validation process is performed on the date field. If the selected date does not conform to a certain range, the Reservation object cannot be persisted and a warning message appears on the form.

Try experimenting with the remaining views available for the Reservation domain class, creating, reading, updating, and deleting objects directly from a web browser.

Finally, just to keep things into perspective, realize what your application is already doing in a few steps: validating input; creating, reading, updating and deleting objects from a RDBMS; completing HTML forms from data in a RDBMS; and supporting internationalization. And you haven't even modified a configuration file, been required to use HTML, or needed to deal with SQL or object-relational mappers (ORMs).

11-7. Internationalization (I18n) Message Properties

Problem

You need to internationalize values used throughout a Grails application.

Solution

By default, all Grails applications are equipped to support internationalization. Inside an application's /grails-app/i18n/ folder, you can find series of *.properties files used to define messages in 12 languages.

The values declared in these *.properties files allow Grails applications to display messages based on a user's languages preferences or an application's default language. Within a Grails application, the values declared in *.properties files can be accessed from places that include views (JSP or GSP pages) or an application's context.

How it works

Grails determines which locale (i.e., from an internationalization properties file) to use for a user based on two criteria:

- The explicit configuration inside an application's /grails-app/conf/spring/ resource.groovy file

- A user's browser language preferences

Since the explicit configuration of an application's locale takes precedence over a user's browser language preferences, there is no default configuration present in an application's resource.groovy file.

This ensures that if a user's browser language preferences are set to Spanish (es) or German (de), a user is served messages from the Spanish or German properties files (e.g., messages_es.properties or messages_de.properties). On the other hand, if an application's resource.groovy file is configured to use Italian (it), it won't matter what a user's browser language preferences are; a user will always be served messages from the Italian properties file (e.g., messages_it.properties)

Therefore, you should define an explicit configuration inside an application's /grails-app/conf/spring/resource.groovy file, only if you want to coerce users into using a specific language locale. For example, maybe you don't want to update several internationalization properties files or maybe you simply value uniformity.

Since Grails internationalization is based on Spring's Locale Resolver, you need to place the following contents inside an application's /grails-app/conf/spring/resource.groovy file, in order to force a specific language on users:

```
import org.springframework.web.servlet.i18n.SessionLocaleResolver

beans = {
  localeResolver(SessionLocaleResolver) {
     defaultLocale= Locale.ENGLISH
     Locale.setDefault (Locale.ENGLISH)
   }
}
```

By using this last declaration, any visitor is served messages from the English properties files (e.g. messages_en.properties) irrespective of his or her browser's language preferences.

It's also worth mentioning that if you specify a locale for which there are no available properties files, Grails falls-back to using the default messages.properties file, which by default is written in English though you can easily modify its values to reflect another language if you prefer. This same scenario applies when a user's browser language preferences are the defining selection criteria (e.g., if a user browser's language preferences are set for Chinese and there is no Chinese properties file, Grails falls back to using the default messages.properties file).

Now that you know how Grails determines which properties file to choose from in order to serve localized content, let's take a look at the syntax of a Grails *.properties file.

```
default.paginate.next=Next
typeMismatch.java.net.URL=Property {0} must be a valid URL
default.blank.message=Property [{0}] of class [{1}] cannot be blank
default.invalid.email.message=Property [{0}] of class [{1}] with value ↩
[{2}] is not a valid e-mail address
default.invalid.range.message=Property [{0}] of class [{1}] with value ↩
[{2}] does not fall within the valid range from [{3}] to [{4}]
```

The first line is the simplest declaration possible in a *.properties file. If Grails encounters the property named default.paginate.next in an application, it will substitute it for the value Next, or whatever other value is specified for this same property based on a user's determining locale.

On certain occasions, it can be necessary to provide more explicit messages that are best determined from wherever a localized message is being called. This is the purpose of the keys {0}, {1}, {2}, {3}, and {4}, they are parameters used in conjunction with a localized property. In this manner, the localized message displayed to a user can convey more detailed information. Figure 11-4 illustrates localized and parameterized messages for the court application determined on a user browser's language preferences.

Figure 11-4. Grails localized and parameterized messages, determined on a user browser's language preferences (Left-Right, Top-Down: Spanish, German, Italian, and French)

Armed with this knowledge, define the following four properties inside Grails `message.properties` files:

```
invalid.holidayHour=Invalid holiday hour
invalid.weekdayHour=Invalid weekday hour
welcome.title=Welcome to Grails
welcome.message=Welcome to Court Reservation System
```

Next, it's time to explore how property placeholders are defined in Grails applications.

Back in recipe 11-5, "Defining an Application's Domain Classes," you might not have realized it, but you declared a localized property for the `Reservation` domain class. In the validation section (`static constraints = { }`), you created this statement in the form:

```
return ['invalid.weekdayHour']
```

If this statement is reached, Grails attempts to locate a property named `invalid.weekdayHour` inside a properties file and substitute its value on the basis of a user's determining locale.

It's also possible to introduce localized properties into an application's views. For example, you can modify the JSP page created in recipe 11-2 and located under `/court/grails-app/views/welcome/index.jsp` to use the following

```
<%@ taglib prefix="fmt" uri="http://java.sun.com/jsp/jstl/fmt" %>
<%@ taglib prefix="g" uri="http://grails.codehaus.org/tags" %>
<html>
<head>
<title><g:message code="welcome.title"/></title>
</head>
```

```
<body>
<h2><g:message code="welcome.message"/></h2>
Today is <fmt:formatDate value="${today}" pattern="yyyy-MM-dd" />
</body>

</html>
```

This JSP page first imports the Groovy tag library and later declares two statements using the Groovy `<g:message/>` tag. Then using the code attribute, the properties `welcome.title` and `welcome.messsage` are defined, both of which will be replaced with the corresponding localized values once the JSP is rendered.

The `<g:message/>` tag can also be used in GSP pages views, but note that it's not necessary to import the tag library explicitly, since it's available by default on all Grails GSP pages.

11-8. Changing Permanent Storage Systems

Problem

You want to change a Grails application's permanent storage system to your favorite RDBMS.

Solution

Grails is designed to use a RDBMS as a permanent storage system. By default, Grails comes preconfigured to use HSQLDB. HSQLDB is a database that is automatically started by Grails upon deploying an application (i.e., executing `grails run-app`).

However, the simplicity of HSQLDB can also be its primary drawback. Every time an application is restarted in development and testing environments, HSQLDB loses all its data since it's configured to operate in memory. And even though Grails applications in a production environment are configured with HSQLDB to store data permanently on a file, HSQLDB feature set may be seen as a limited for certain application demands.

You can configure Grails to use another RDBMS by modifying an application's `DataSource.groovy` file, located under the `grails-app/conf` directory. Inside this file, you can configure up to three RDBMS, one for each environment—development, production, and testing— undertaken by an application. See recipe 11-4, "Developing, producing, and testing Grails Environments," for more on development, production, and testing environments in Grails applications.

How It Works

Grails relies on the standard Java JDBC notation to specify RDBMS connection parameters, as well as on the corresponding JDBC drivers provided by each RDBMS vendor, to create, read, update, and delete information.

One important aspect you need to aware if you change RDBMS, is that Grails uses an ORM called Groovy Object Relational Mapper (GROM) to interact with a RDBMS.

The purpose behind GROM is the same as all other ORM solutions—to allow you to concentrate on an application's business logic, without worrying about the particularities of an RDBMS implementation, which can range from discrepancies in data types to working with SQL directly. GROM allows you to design an application's domain classes and maps your design to the RDBMS of your choice.

Setting Up an RDBMS Driver

The first step you need to take in changing Grails default RDBMS is to install the JDBC driver for the RDBMS of your choice inside an application's lib directory. This allows the application access to the JDBC classes needed to persist objects to a particular RDBMS.

Configuring an RDBMS Instance

The second step consists of modifying the DataSource.groovy file located under an application's grails-app/conf directory. Inside this file, there are three sections for defining an RDBMS instance.

Each RDBMS instance corresponds to a different possible application environment: development, production, and testing. Depending on the actions you take, Grails chooses one of these instances to perform any permanent storage operations an application is designed to do. See recipe 11-4, "Developing, producing, and testing Grails Environments," for more on development, production, and testing environments in Grails applications.

However, the syntax used for declaring a RDBMS in each of these sections is the same. Table 11-1 contains the various properties that can be used in a dataSource definition for the purpose of configuring a RDBMS.

Table 11-1. *dataSource properties for configuring a RDBMS*

Property	Definition
driverClassName	Class name for the JDBC driver
username	Username to establish a connection to a RDBMS
password	Password to establish a connection to a RDBMS
url	URL connection parameters for a RDBMS
pooled	Indicates whether to use connection pooling for a RDMBS; defaults to true
jndiName	Indicates a JNDI connection string for a data source. (This is an alternative to configuring driverClassName, username, password, and url directly in Grails and instead relying on a data source being configured in a web container.)
logSql	Indicates whether to enable SQL logging
dialect	Indicates the RDBMS dialect to perform operations.

Continued

Property	Definition
properties	Used to indicate extra parameters for RDBMS operation
dbCreate	Indicates auto-generation of RDBMS data definition language (DDL)
dbCreate value	Definition
create-drop	Drops and recreates the RDBMS DDL when Grails is run (Warning: Deletes all existing data in the RDBMS.)
create	Creates the RDBMS DDL if it doesn't exist, but doesn't modify if it does (Warning: Deletes all existing data in the RDBMS.)
update	Creates the RDBMS DDL if it doesn't exist or update if it does

If you've used a Java ORM, such as Hibernate or EclipseLink, the parameters in Table 11-1 should be fairly familiar. The following listing illustrates the dataSource definition for a MySQL RDBMS:

```
dataSource {
        dbCreate = "update"
        url = "jdbc:mysql://localhost/grailsDB"
        driverClassName = "com.mysql.jdbc.Driver"
        username = "grails"
        password = "groovy"
}
```

Of the properties in this last definition, the one you should be most careful with is dbCreate, since it can destroy data in a RDBMS. In this case, the update value is the most conservative of all three available values, as explained in Table 11-1.

If you're using a production RDBMS, then dbCreate="update" is surely to be your preferred strategy, since it doesn't destroy any data in the RDBMS. If, on the other hand, a Grails application is undergoing testing, you are likely *to want* data in a RDBMS being cleaned out on every test run, thus a value like dbCreate="create" or dbCreate="create-drop" would be more common. For a development RDBMS, which of these options you select as the better strategy depends on how advanced a Grails application is in terms of development.

Grails also allows you to use a RDBMS configured on a web container. In such cases, a web container, such as Apache Tomcat, is set up with the corresponding RDBMS connection parameters and access to the RDBMS is made available through JNDI. The following listing illustrates the dataSource definition to access RDBMS via JNDI:

```
dataSource {
    jndiName = "java:comp/env/grailsDataSource"
}
```

Finally, it's worth mentioning that you can configure a dataSource definition to take effect on an application's various environments, while further specifying properties for each specific environment. This configuration is illustrated in the following listing:

```
dataSource {
        driverClassName = "com.mysql.jdbc.Driver"
        username = "grails"
}
environments {
  production {
     dataSource {
        url = "jdbc:mysql://localhost/grailsDBPro"
                password = "production"
     }
  }
    development {
     dataSource {
        url = "jdbc:mysql://localhost/grailsDBDev"
                password = "development"
     }
  }
}
```

As this last listing illustrates, a dataSource's driverClassName and username properties are defined globally, taking effect on all environments, while other dataSource properties are declared specifically for each individual environment.

11-9. Logging

Problem

You want to customize the logging output generated by a Grails application.

Solution

Grails relies on Java Log4J to perform its logging operations. In doing so, all Log4J configuration parameters are specified inside the Config.groovy file located under an application's /grails-app/conf directory.

Given Log4J's logging versatility, a Grails application logging can be configured in various ways. This includes creating custom appenders, logging levels, console output, logging by artifacts and custom logging layouts.

How It Works

Grails comes preconfigured with a basic set of Log4J parameters. Defined inside the Config.groovy file located under an application's /grails-app/conf directory, these Log4J parameters are the following:

```
log4j = {
    error       'org.codehaus.groovy.grails.web.servlet', // controllers
                'org.codehaus.groovy.grails.web.pages', // GSP
                'org.codehaus.groovy.grails.web.sitemesh', // layouts
                'org.codehaus.groovy.grails.web.mapping.filter', // URL mapping
                'org.codehaus.groovy.grails.web.mapping', // URL mapping
                'org.codehaus.groovy.grails.commons', // core / classloading
                'org.codehaus.groovy.grails.plugins', // plugins
                'org.codehaus.groovy.grails.orm.hibernate', // hibernate integration
                'org.springframework',
                'org.hibernate'
    warn        'org.mortbay.log'
}
```

The notation for this last listing follows the convention <logging_level> '<package_name>'. This implies that any logging operation occurring at any of the cited packages will be logged so long as it occurs within the specified logging level or a more severe level.

In Log4J parlance, each package is known as a *logger*. Log4J also has the following logging levels: fatal, error, warn, info, debug, and trace. fatal is the most severe. Grails thus follows a conservative default logging policy by using the error level on most of its packages. Specifying a less severe level (e.g., debug) would result in greater volumes of logging information, which may not be practical for most cases.

By default, all logging message are sent to the stacktrace.log file located under an application's root directory. And if applicable, to the standard output (i.e., console) of a running application. When you execute a grails command, you will observe logging messages sent to standard output.

Configuring Custom Appenders and Loggers

Log4J relies on appenders and loggers to offer versatile logging functionality. An appender is a location where logging information is sent (e.g., a file or standard output), whereas a logger is a location where logging information is generated (e.g., a class or package).

Grails is configured with a root Log4J logger, from which all other loggers inherit their behavior. The default Log4J logger can be customized in a Grails application using the following statement within the log4j { } section of an application's Config.groovy file:

```
root {
    error()
    additivity = true
}
```

This last statement defines a logger so that messages of an error level, or a more severe one, are logged to standard output. This is the reason you can see logging message from other loggers (e.g., a class or package) being sent to standard output, they all inherit the root logger's behavior, in addition to specifying their own log level.

On the other hand, Log4J appenders provide a means to send logging messages to various locations. There are four types of appenders available by default:

- jdbc : An appender that logs to a JDBC connection
- console: An appender that logs to standard output
- file: An appender that logs to a file.
- rollingFile: An appender that logs to a rolling set of files

In order to define Log4J appenders in a Grails application, you need to declare them within the log4j { } section of an application's Config.groovy file, as follows:

```
appenders {
        file            name:'customlogfile', file:'/logs/grails.log'
        rollingFile  name:'rollinglogfile', maxFileSize:1024,↵
                        file:'/logs/rollinggrails.log'
}
```

As you can see, Log4J appenders are defined in the form <appender_type> name:<appender_name> <additional_appender_options>. In order to use appenders, you simply need to add them to a corresponding logger where they can receive input.

The following declaration illustrates how to put together the use of appenders, loggers and logging levels:

```
root {
    debug 'stdout', 'customlogfile'
    additivity = true
}
```

This last listing overrides the default root Log4J logger. It indicates to use a debug level for outputting logging messages to both to the stdout appender (i.e., standard output or console) as well as the customlogfile appender, the last of which represent a file defined in the appender section. Be aware that a debug level generates a lot of logging information.

If you simply want to use an appender for a particular package (i.e., logger), you can do so using the following syntax:

```
error customlogfile:'com.apress.springwebrecipes.grails'
```

This last syntax is similar to the default notation included in Grails <logging_level> '<package_name>', except it prefixes the name of an appender to the package.

Configuring Layouts

In addition to custom loggers and appenders, Log4J can also be customized to use a particular logging layout. There are four types of layouts available by default:

- `xml` : An XML log file

- `html`: An HTML log file

- `simple`: A simple textual log

- `pattern`: A pattern layout

By default, Log4J uses a `pattern` layout. However, you can configure a different logging layout on a per-appender basis. The following listing illustrates how to assign layouts to appenders:

```
appenders {
        file            name:'customlogfile', file:'/logs/grails.log' ↵
                                layout:pattern(conversionPattern: '%c{2} %m%n')
        console     name:'stdout', layout:simple
}
```

The first appender, `customlogfile`, is assigned a `pattern` layout. Whereas the second appender, `stdout`, is assigned a `simple` layout. Note that `stdout` is the built-in appender for standard output (i.e., console).

11-10. Running Unit and Integration Tests

Problem

To make sure that your application's classes are working as specified, you need to perform unit and integration tests on them.

Solution

Grails has built-in support for running both unit and integration tests on an application. Earlier when you generated Grails artifacts, such as an application's domain classes, you might recall a series of test classes were automatically generated.

In a Grails application, tests are placed under an application's `test` directory. Inside this directory, you will find three more folders: `unit` used to place an application's unit test classes, `integration` used to place an application's integration test classes, and `reports` used to place the results of performing an application's tests.

Similar to other functionality offered by Grails, much of the drudgery involved in setting up and configuring application tests is handled by Grails. You simply need to concentrate on designing tests.

Once you've designed an application's tests, running tests in Grails is as simple as executing the `grails test-app` command from an application's root directory.

How It Works

Grails bootstraps an environment necessary to perform application tests. This environment includes the libraries (i.e., JARs), permanent storage system (i.e., RDBMS), as well as any other artifact necessary to carry out unit and integration tests.

Let's start by analyzing the output of executing the grails test-app command, illustrated next:

```
Running script /springrecipes/grails-1.2/scripts/TestApp.groovy
Environment set to test
    [mkdir] Created dir: /springrecipes/Ch11/court/test/reports/html
    [mkdir] Created dir: /springrecipes/Ch11/court/test/reports/plain

Starting unit tests ...
Running tests of type 'unit'
  [groovyc] Compiling 3 source files to /home/web/.grails/1.2/↵
              projects/court/test-classes/unit
--------------------------------------------------------
Running 3 unit tests...
Running test WelcomeControllerTests...PASSED
Running test ReservationTests...PASSED
Running test PlayerTests...PASSED
Tests Completed in 2302ms ...
--------------------------------------------------------
Tests passed: 3
Tests failed: 0


--------------------------------------------------------
Starting integration tests ...
      [copy] Copying 1 file to /home/web/.grails/1.2/↵
              projects/court/test-classes/integration
      [copy] Copying 1 file to /home/web/.grails/1.2/↵
              projects/court/test-classes
Running tests of type 'integration'
No tests found in test/integration to execute ...

[junitreport] Processing /springrecipes/sourcecode/Ch11/↵
              court/test/reports/TESTS-TestSuites.xml to /tmp/null993113113
[junitreport] Loading stylesheet jar:file:/springrecipes/grails-1.2/↵
          lib/ant-junit-1.7.1.jar!/org/apache/tools/ant/taskdefs/optional/↵
          junit/xsl/junit-frames.xsl
[junitreport] Transform time: 2154ms
[junitreport] Deleting: /tmp/null993113113
```

The script TestApp.groovy, included in the Grails distribution, starts the testing process. Immediately after, you can see the Grails environment is set to set test, meaning configuration parameters are taken from this type of environment (e.g. test RDBMS parameters). Next, there are three sections.

The first section indicates the execution of unit tests, which are taken from the test/unit directory under an application's root directory. In this case, three successful unit tests are performed, which correspond to the three skeleton test classes generated upon the creation of an application's domain classes. Since these test classes contain an empty test, they automatically validate one unit test.

The second section indicates the execution of integration tests, which are taken from the test/integration directory under an application's root directory. In this case, there are no classes found in this last directory, so no integration tests are performed.

The third and last section indicates the creation of reports for both unit and integration tests. In this case, reports are placed in an XML format under the test/reports directory of an application's root directory, as well as reports in the more user-friendly HTML and plain text formats under the corresponding test/reports/html and test/reports/plain subdirectories of an application's root directory.

Now that you know how Grails executes tests, let's modify the preexisting unit test classes to incorporate unit tests based on a domain class's logic. Given that Grails testing is based on the foundations of the JUnit testing framework (http://www.junit.org/), if your unfamiliar with this framework, we advise you to look over its documentation to grasp its syntax and approach. The following sections assume a basic understanding of JUnit.

Add the following methods (i.e., unit tests) to the PlayerTests.groovy class located under an application's /test/unit/ directory:

```
void testNonEmptyPlayer() {
        def player = new Player(name:'James',phone:'111-1111')
        mockForConstraintsTests(Player, [player])
        assertTrue player.validate()
}
void testEmptyName() {
        def player = new Player(name:'',phone:'111-1111')
        mockForConstraintsTests(Player, [player])
        assertFalse player.validate()
        assertEquals 'Name cannot be blank', 'blank',player.errors['name']
}

void testEmptyPhone() {
        def player = new Player(name:'James',phone:'')
        mockForConstraintsTests(Player, [player])
        assertFalse player.validate()
        assertEquals 'Phone cannot be blank', 'blank',player.errors['phone']
}
```

The first unit test creates a Player object and instantiates it with both a name and phone fields. In accordance with the constraints declared in the Player domain class, this type of an instance should always be valid. Therefore, the statement assertTrue player.validate() confirms the validation of this object is always true.

The second and third unit tests also create a Player object. However, notice in one test the Player object is instantiated with a blank name field, and in another, the Player object is instantiated with a blank phone field. In accordance with the constraints declared in the Player domain class, both instances should always be invalid. Therefore, the statements assertFalse player.validate() confirm the validation of such objects are always false. The assertEquals statements provide detailed results as to why the assertFalse declarations are false.

Next, add the following methods (i.e., unit tests) to the ReservationTests.groovy class located under an application's /test/unit/ directory:

```
void testReservation() {
      def calendar = Calendar.instance
      calendar.with {
        clear()
        set MONTH, OCTOBER
        set DATE, 15
        set YEAR, 2009
        set HOUR, 15
        set MINUTE, 00
      }

      def validDateReservation = calendar.getTime()
      def reservation = new Reservation(↵
                            sportType:'Tennis',courtName:'',↵
                            date:validDateReservation,player:new Player())
      mockForConstraintsTests(Reservation, [reservation])
      assertTrue reservation.validate()
  }

  void testOutOfRangeDateReservation() {
      def calendar = Calendar.instance
      calendar.with {
        clear()
        set MONTH, OCTOBER
        set DATE, 15
        set YEAR, 2009
        set HOUR, 23
        set MINUTE, 00
      }

      def invalidDateReservation = calendar.getTime()
      def reservation = new Reservation(↵
                            sportType:'Tennis',courtName:'',↵
                            date:invalidDateReservation,player:new Player())
      mockForConstraintsTests(Reservation, [reservation])
      assertFalse reservation.validate()
      assertEquals 'Reservation date is out of range', 'invalid.weekdayHour',↵
reservation.errors['date']
  }

  void testOutOfRangeSportTypeReservation() {
      def calendar = Calendar.instance
      calendar.with {
        clear()
        set MONTH, OCTOBER
        set DATE, 15
        set YEAR, 2009
        set HOUR, 15
        set MINUTE, 00
      }
```

```
        def validDateReservation = calendar.getTime()
        def reservation = new Reservation(↵
                            sportType:'Baseball',courtName:'',↵
                            date:validDateReservation,player:new Player())
        mockForConstraintsTests(Reservation, [reservation])
        assertFalse reservation.validate()
        assertEquals 'SportType is not valid', 'inList',reservation.errors['sportType']
    }
```

This last listing contains three unit tests designed to validate the integrity of Reservation objects. The first test creates a Reservation object instance and confirms that its corresponding values pass through the Reservation domain class's constraints. The second test creates a Reservation object that violates the domain class's date constraint and confirms such an instance is invalid. The third test creates a Reservation object that violates the domain class's sportType constraint and confirms such an instance is invalid.

If you execute the grails test-app command, Grails automatically executes all the previous tests and outputs the test results to the application's /test/reports/ directory.

Now that you've created unit tests for a Grails application, let's explore the creation of integration tests.

Unlike unit tests, integration tests validate more elaborate logic undertaken by an application. Interactions between various domain classes or operations performed against a RDBMS are the realm of integration testing. In this sense, Grails aids the integration testing process by automatically bootstrapping a RDBMS and other application properties to perform integration tests. The "Grails Differences for Running Unit and Integration Tests" sidebar contains more details on the different aspects provided by Grails for running both unit and integration tests.

GRAILS DIFFERENCES FOR RUNNING UNIT AND INTEGRATION TESTS

Unit tests are designed to validate the logic contained in a single domain class. Because of this fact, besides automating the execution of such tests, Grails provides no type of bootstrapping properties for performing these type of tests.

This is the reason the previous unit tests relied on the special method mockForConstraintsTests. This method creates a mock object from a domain class that is used to access a class's dynamic methods (e.g., validate) needed to perform unit tests. In this manner, Grails maintains a low overhead for performing unit tests by not bootstrapping anything, leaving even the creation of mock objects to the creator of a test.

Integration tests are designed to validate more elaborate logic that can span a series of application classes. Therefore, Grails bootstraps not only a RDBMS for the purpose of running tests against this type of permanent storage system but also bootstraps a domain class's dynamic methods to simplify the creation of such tests. This of course entails additional overhead for performing such tests, compared to unit tests.

It's also worth mentioning that if you look closely at the skeleton test classes generated by Grails for both unit and integration tests, there aren't any difference among them. The only difference is that tests placed inside the integration directory have access to the series of provisions mentioned earlier, whereas those inside the unit directory do not. You could go down the route of placing unit tests inside the integration directory, but this is a matter for you to decide by considering convenience versus overhead.

Next, create an integration class for the application by executing the following command: grails create-integration-test CourtIntegrationTest. This generates an integration test class inside the application's /test/integration/ directory.

Incorporate the following method (i.e., the integration test) into this last class to validate the RDBMS operations performed by the application:

```
void testQueries() {
    // Define and save players
    def players = [ new Player(name:'James',phone:'111-1111'),↵
                         new Player(name:'Martha',phone:'999-9999')]
    players*.save()

    // Confirm two players are saved in the database
    assertEquals 2, Player.list().size()

    // Get player from the database by name
    def testPlayer = Player.findByName('James')

    // Confirm phone
    assertEquals '111-1111', testPlayer.phone

    // Update player name
    testPlayer.name = 'Marcus'
    testPlayer.save()

    // Get updated player from the database, but now by phone
    def updatedPlayer = Player.findByPhone('111-1111')

    // Confirm name
    assertEquals 'Marcus', updatedPlayer.name

    // Delete player
    updatedPlayer.delete()

    // Confirm one player is left in the database
    assertEquals 1, Player.list().size()

    // Confirm updatedPlayer is deleted
    def nonexistantPlayer = Player.findByPhone('111-1111')
    assertNull nonexistantPlayer
}
```

This last listing performs a series of operations against an application's RDBMS, starting from saving two Player objects and then querying, updating, and deleting those objects from the RDBMS. After each operation, a validation step (e.g., assertEquals, assertNull) is performed to ensure the logic—in this case contained in the PlayerController controller class—operates as expected (i.e., the controller list() method returns the correct number of objects in the RDBMS).

By default, Grails performs RDBMS test operations against HSQLDB. However, you can use any RDBMS you like. See recipe 11-8, "Changing Permanent Storage Systems," for details on changing Grails RDBMS.

Finally, it's worth mentioning that if you wish to execute a single type of test (i.e., unit or integration), you can rely on the command flags -unit or -integration. Executing the grails test-app -unit command performs only an application's unit tests, whereas executing the grails test-app -integration command performs only an application's integration tests. This can be helpful if you have a large amount of both tests, since it can cut down on the overall time needed to perform tests.

11-11. Using Custom Layouts and Templates

Problem

You need to customize layouts and templates to display an application's content.

Solution

By default, Grails applies a global layout to display an application's content. This allows views to have a minimal set of display elements (e.g., HTML, CSS, and JavaScript) and inherit their layout behavior from a separate location.

This inheritance process allows application designers and graphic designers to perform their work separately, with application designers concentrating on creating views with the necessary data and graphic designers concentrating on the layout (i.e., aesthetics) of such data.

You can create custom layouts to include elaborate HTML displays, as well as custom CSS or JavaScript libraries.

Grails also supports the concept of templates, which serve the same purpose as layouts, except applied at a more granular level. In addition, it's also possible to use templates for rendering a controller's output, instead of a view as in most controllers.

How It Works

Inside the /grails-app/view/ directory of an application, you can find a subdirectory called layouts, containing the layouts available to an application. By default, there is a file named main.gsp whose contents are the following:

```
<html>
    <head>
        <title><g:layoutTitle default="Grails" /></title>
        <link rel="stylesheet" ↵
            href="${resource(dir:'css',file:'main.css')}" />
        <link rel="shortcut icon" ↵
            href="${resource(dir:'images',file:'favicon.ico')}" ↵
            type="image/x-icon" />
        <g:layoutHead />
        <g:javascript library="application" />
    </head>
```

```
<body>
    <div id="spinner" class="spinner" style="display:none;">
        <img src="${resource(dir:'images',file:'spinner.gif')}" ↵
            alt="Spinner" />
    </div>
    <div id="grailsLogo" class="logo"><a href="http://grails.org">
        <img src="${resource(dir:'images',file:'grails_logo.png')}" ↵
            alt="Grails" border="0" /></a></div>
    <g:layoutBody />
</body>
</html>
```

Though apparently a simple HTML file, this last listing contains several elements that are used as placeholders in order for application views (i.e., JSP and GSP pages) to inherit the same layout.

The first of such elements are Groovy tags appended to the `<g:*>` namespace. The `<g:layoutTitle>` tag is used to define the contents of a layout's title section. If a view inherits the behavior from this layout and lacks such a value, Grails automatically assigns the Grails value, as indicated by the `default` attribute. On the other hand, if an inheriting view has such a value, it's displayed in its place.

The `<g:layoutHead>` tag is used to define the contents of a layout's head section. Any values declared in the head of a view head inheriting this layout are placed in this location upon rendering.

The `<g:javascript library="application">` tag allows any view inheriting this layout automatic access to JavaScript libraries. Upon rendering, this element is transformed into the following: `<script type="text/javascript" src="/court/js/application.js"></script>`. Notice the `library` attribute value points to the name of the JavaScript library, whereas the prefix route, `court/js`, corresponds to the name of the application and the default directory used by Grails to place JavaScript libraries. Bear in mind JavaScript libraries have to be placed inside the Grails `/<app-name>/web-app/js` subdirectory; `<app-name>` in this case corresponds to court.

Moving along, you will also find several declarations in the form `${resource*}` with a `dir` and `file` attribute. Such statements are translated by Grails to reflect a resource contained in an application. So for example, the statement `${resource(dir:'images',file:'grails_logo.png')}` is transformed into `/court/images/grails_logo.png`. Notice the addition of the application's name (i.e., context path) to the transformed values. This allows the layout to be reused in several applications while referencing the same image, the last of which should be placed under the Grails `/court/web-app/img` subdirectory.

Now that you know how a Grails layout is structured, let's take a look at how a view inherits its behavior. If you open any of the views generated by the application controllers created earlier—player, reservation or welcome (also located under the views directory)— you will find the following statement used to inherit behavior from a Grails layout:

```
<meta name="layout" content="main"/>
```

The `<meta>` tag is a standard HTML tag that has no effect on a page's display but is used by Grails to detect the layout from which a view should inherit its behavior. By using this last statement, a view is automatically rendered with the layout named main, which is precisely the template described earlier.

Looking further into a view's structure, you will notice that all generated views are structured as standalone HTML pages; they contain `<html>`, `<body>` and other such HTML tags, similar to the layout template. This doesn't mean, however, that a page will contain duplicate HTML tags upon rendering. Grails automatically sorts out the substitution process by placing a view's `<title>` content inside the `<g:layoutTitle>` tag, a view's `<body>` content inside the `<g:layoutBody />` tag, and so on.

What happens if you remove <meta> tag from a Grails view? On the face of it, the answer to this question is obvious: no layout is applied upon rendering a view, which also implies no visual elements are rendered (e.g., images, menus, and CSS borders). However, since Grails operates on the basis of conventions, Grails always attempts to apply a layout on the basis of a controller's name.

For example, even if the views corresponding to the reservation controller have no <meta name="layout"> tag declaration's associated with them, if a layout named reservation.gsp is present inside an application's layout directory, it will be applied to all views corresponding to the controller.

Though layouts provide an excellent foundation on which to modularize an application's views, they are only applicable to a view's entire page. Providing a more granular approach, templates allow certain chunks of a view's page be made reusable.

Take the case of an HTML section used to display a player's reservations. You'd like to display this information on all views corresponding to this controller as a reminder. Placing this HTML section explicitly on all views not only results in more initial work but can also result in more ongoing work in case such an HTML section changes. To facilitate this inclusion process, a template can be used. The following listing illustrates the contents of a template named _reservationList.gsp:

```
<table>
  <g:each in="${reservationInstanceList}" status="i" var="reservationInstance">
      <tr class="${(i % 2) == 0 ? 'odd' : 'even'}">
         <td><g:link action="show" id="${reservationInstance.id}">
               ${fieldValue(bean:reservationInstance, field:'id')}</g:link></td>
            <td>${fieldValue(bean:reservationInstance, field:'sportType')}</td>
            <td>${fieldValue(bean:reservationInstance, field:'date')}</td>
            <td>${fieldValue(bean:reservationInstance, field:'courtName')}</td>
            <td>${fieldValue(bean:reservationInstance, field:'player')}</td>
         </tr>
  </g:each>
</table>
```

This last template generates an HTML table relying on the Groovy tag <g:each> with a list of reservations. The underscore (_) prefix used to name the file is a notation by Grails to different between templates and stand-alone views; templates are always prefixed with an underscore.

In order to use this template inside a view, you need to use the <g:render> tag illustrated here:

```
<g:render template="reservationList"↵
                                model="[reservationList:reservationInstanceList]" />
```

In this case, the <g:render> tag takes two attributes: the template attribute to indicate the name of a template and the model attribute to pass reference data needed by a template.

Another variation of the <g:render> tag includes a template's relative and absolute locations. By declaring template="reservationList", Grails attempts to locate a template in the same directory as the view in which it's declared. To facilitate reuse, templates can be loaded from a common directory for which absolute directories are used. For example, a view with a statement in the form template="/common/reservationList" would attempt to locate a template named _reservationList.gsp under an application's grails-app/views/common directory.

Finally, it's worth mentioning that a template can also be used by a controller to render its output. For example, most controllers return control to a view using the following syntax:

```
render view:'reservations', model:[reservationList:reservationList]
```

However, it's also possible to return control to a template using the following syntax:

```
render template:'reservationList', model:[reservationList:reservationList]
```

By using this last render statement, Grails attempts to locate a template by the name
`_reservationList.gsp`.

11-12. Using GORM Queries

Problem

You want to perform queries against an application's RDBMS.

Solution

Grails performs RDBMS operations using GORM. GORM is based on the popular Java ORM Hibernate, allowing Grails applications to perform queries using Hibernate Query Language (HQL).

However, in addition to supporting the use of HQL, GORM also has a series of built-in functionalities that make querying a RDBMS very simple.

How It Works

In Grails, queries against a RDBMS are generally performed from within controllers. If you inspect any of the court application controllers, one of the simplest queries is the following:

```
Player.get(id)
```

This query is used to obtain a `Player` object with a particular ID. Under certain circumstances though, an application can be required to perform queries on another set of criteria.

For example, `Player` objects in the court application have the `name` and `phone` fields, as defined in the `Player` domain class. GORM supports the querying of domain objects on the basis of its field names. It does so by offering methods in the form `findBy<field_name>`, as illustrated here:

```
Player.findByName('Henry')
Player.findByPhone('111-1111')
```

These two statements are used to query a RDBMS and obtain a `Player` object on the basis of a name and phone. These methods are called dynamic finders, since they are made available by GORM on the basis of a domain class's fields.

In a similar fashion, the `Reservation` domain class having its own field names will have dynamic finders like `findByPlayer()`, `findByCourtName()`, and `findByDate()`. As you can see, this process simplifies the creation of queries against an RDBMS in Java applications.

In addition, dynamic finder methods can also use comparators to further refine a query's results. The following snippet illustrates how to use a comparator to extract `Reservation` objects in a particular date range:

```
def now = new Date()
def tomorrow = now + 1
def reservations = Reservation.findByDateBetween( now, tomorrow )
```

Besides the Between comparator, another comparator that can be of use in the court application is the Like comparator. The following snippet illustrates the use of the Like comparator to extract Player objects with names starting with the letter A.

```
def letterAPlayers = Player.findByNameLike('A%')
```

Table 11-2 describes the various comparators available for dynamic finder methods.

Table 11-2. *GORM dynamic finder comparators*

GORM comparator	Query
InList	If value is present in a given list of values
LessThan	For lesser object(s) than the given value
LessThanEquals	For lesser or equal object(s) than the given value
GreaterThan	For greater object(s) than the given value
GreaterThanEquals	For greater or equal object(s) than the given value
Like	For object(s) like the given value
Ilike	For object(s) like the given value in a case insensitive manner
NotEqual	For object(s) not equal to the given value
Between	For object(s) between to the two given values
IsNotNull	For not null object(s); uses no arguments
IsNull	For null object(s); uses no arguments

GORM also supports the use of Boolean logic (and/or) in the construction of dynamic finder methods. The following snippet demonstrates how to perform a query for Reservation objects that satisfy both a certain court name and a date in the future.

```
def reservations = Reservation.findAllByCourtNameLike↵
                        AndDateGreaterThan("%main%", new Date()+7)
```

In a similar fashion, the Or statement (instead of And) could have been used in this last dynamic finder method to extract Reservation objects that satisfy at least one of the criteria.

Finally, dynamic finder methods also support the use of pagination and sorting to further refine queries. This is achieved by appending a map to the dynamic finder method. The following snippet illustrates how to limit the number of results in a query, as well as define its sorting and order properties:

```
def reservations = Reservation.findAllByCourtName("%main%", ↵
                            [ max: 3, sort: "date", order: "desc"] )
```

As outlined at the start of this recipe, GORM also supports the use HQL to execute queries against a RDBMS. Though more verbose and error prone than the preceding listing, the following one illustrates several equivalent queries using HQL:

```
def letterAPlayers = Player.findAll("from Player as p where p.name like 'A%'")
def reservations = Reservation.findAll("from Reservation as r ↵
        where r.courtName like '%main%' order by r.date desc", [ max: 3] )
```

11-13. Creating Custom Tags

Problem

You want to execute logic inside a Grails view that is not available through a prebuilt GSP or JSTL tag and yet not resort to the inclusion of code in a view.

Solution

A Grails view can contain display elements (e.g., HTML tags), business logic elements (e.g., GSP or JSTL tags) or straightforward Groovy or Java code to achieve its display objectives.

On certain occasions, a view can require a unique combination of display elements and business logic. For example, displaying the reservations of a particular player on a monthly basis requires the use of custom code. To simplify the inclusion of such a combination and facilitate its reuse in multiple views a custom tag can be used.

How It Works

To create custom tags, you can use the `grails create-tag-lib <tag-lib-name>` command. This command creates a skeleton class for a custom tag library under an application's `/grails-app/tag-lib/` directory.

Knowing this, let's create a custom tag library for the court application designed to display special reservation offers. The first custom tag will detect the current date and based on this information display special reservation offers. The end result being the capacity to use a tag like `<g:promoDailyAd/>` inside an application's view, instead of placing in-line code in a view or performing this logic in a controller.

Execute the `grails create-tag-lib DailyNotice` command to create the custom tag library class. Next, open the generated `DailyNoticeTagLib.groovy` class located under an application's `/grails-app/tag-lib/` directory, and add the following method (i.e., custom tag):

```
def promoDailyAd = { attrs, body ->
    def dayoftheweek = Calendar.getInstance().get(Calendar.DAY_OF_WEEK)
    out << body() << (dayoftheweek == 7 ?
        "We have special reservation offers for Sunday!": "No special offers")
}
```

The name of this method defines the name of the custom tag. The first declarations of the method (attrs, body) represent the input values of a custom tag—its attributes and body. Next, the day of the week is determined using a Calendar object.

After that, you can find a conditional statement based on the day of the week. If the day of the week is 7 (Saturday), the conditional statement resolves to the string "We have special reservation offers for Saturday!"; otherwise, it resolves to "No special offers".

The string is outputted through << and is first assigned through to the body() method, which represents the custom tag's body, then through out, which represents the custom tag's output. In this manner, you declare the custom tag in an application's view using the following syntax:

```
<h3><g:promoDailyAd/></h3>
```

When the view containing this custom tag is rendered, Grails executes the logic in the backing class method and supplants it with the results. This allows a view to display results based on more elaborate logic by means of a simple declaration.

■ **Caution** This type of tag is automatically available in GSP pages but not JSP pages. In order for this custom tag to function properly in JSP, it's necessary to add it to the corresponding Tag Library Definition (TLD) grails.tld . TLDs are located in an application's /web-app/WEB-INF/tld/ directory.

Custom tags can also rely on input parameters passed in as tag attributes to perform a backing class's logic. The following listing illustrates another custom tag that expects an attribute named offerdate to determine its results:

```
def upcomingPromos  = { attrs, body ->
    def dayoftheweek = attrs['offerdate']
    out << body() << (dayoftheweek == 7 ?
        "We have special reservation offers for Saturday!": "No special offers")
}
```

Though similar to the earlier custom tag, this last listing uses the statement attrs['offerdate'] to determine the day of the week. In this case, attrs represents the attributes passed as input parameters to the class method (i.e., those declared in the view). Therefore, to use this last custom tag, a declaration like the following is used:

```
<h3><g:upcomingPromos offerdate='saturday'/></h3>
```

This type of custom tag allows more flexibility, since its logic is executed on the basis of data provided in a view. Inclusively, it's also possible to use a variable representing data passed by a controller into a view, as illustrated here:

```
<h3><g:upcomingPromos offerdate='${promoDay}'/></h3>
```

Finally, a word about the namespace used in Grails custom tags—by default, Grails assigns custom tags to the `<g:>` namespace. To use a custom namespace, it's necessary to declare the namespace field a top the custom tag library class.

```
class DailyNoticeTagLib {
    static namespace = 'court'
    def promoDailyAd = { attrs, body ->
      ...
    }
    def upcomingPromos  = { attrs, body ->
      ...
    }
}
```

By using this last statement, a class's custom tags are assigned their own custom namespace named court. With the custom tag declarations made in a view requiring to be changed to the following:

```
<h3><court:promoDailyAd/></h3>
<h3><court:upcomingPromos offerdate='${promoDay}'/></h3>
```

▨ **Tip** The Grails project has several contributed custom tags you can use in your applications. Consult:
http://www.grails.org/Contribute+a+Tag

Summary

In this chapter, you learned how to develop Java web applications using the Grails framework. You started by learning the structure of a Grails application and quickly followed that by working with a sample application that demonstrated the automation of several steps undertaken in a web application.

Throughout the various recipes, you also learned how Grails uses conventions in its automation process to create an application's views, controllers, models, and configuration files.

In addition, you also learned about the existence of Grails plug-ins to automate tasks for related Java APIs or frameworks in the context of Grails. You then explored how Grails separates configuration parameters and executes tasks on the basis of an application's working environment, which can be development, testing, or production.

You then learned how, from an application's domain classes, Grails generates the corresponding controller and views used to perform CRUD operations against a RDBMS. Next, you explored Grails internationalization, logging, and testing facilities.

Finally, you explored Grails layouts and templates used to modularize an application's display and followed that with a look at the Grails Object Relational Mapping (GORM) facilities, as well as the creation of custom tags.

CHAPTER 12

Spring Roo

Java has a long history and has become very popular. The language itself is still considered fairly simple when compared to languages like C, C++, COBOL, Pascal, or even C#. The tooling support for Java is second to none, and nothing offers a larger compliment of compelling libraries for more use cases than the rich ecosystem surrounding Java. Indeed, there are also many virtues attached to Java, not the least of which is its widespread use and employment. You already know this, or you wouldn't be looking to simplifying, enabling frameworks like Spring to help you build applications.

That is not to say that there aren't compelling alternatives. Java has some warts, of course. Many languages, and frameworks evolved in those languages, have emerged in the last decade. These platforms are often built on top of the JVM and promise unparalleled integration ease with existing Java libraries. These platforms are furthered by the strength of their frameworks—"killer apps" that hit a sweet spot, enabling developers with a unique blend of runtime libraries, APIs, domain-specific languages, and code generation. Some of these frameworks, like JRuby on Rails and SpringSource's Grails, offer a compelling story for developers on the JVM who want to build a web application that babysits a database, which, if we're honest, represents a very significant percentage of the new applications being developed today. Grails users also benefit from the robustness of open source frameworks in the Java space, like the Spring framework and Hibernate, because these also underpin much of the Grails stack.

However, these underlying frameworks are still hidden for the most part. The developer deals with high-level APIs that sit between the lower Java frameworks and the developer, often at the cost of a runtime performance penalty. When something breaks, the levels of indirection between Java, Groovy, and Grails, for example, can be dizzying, and the stack traces even more so! There are other concerns, too. Some of the biggest complaints against JRuby or Grails concern their relatively poor performance and their reliance on reflection-intensive APIs and brittle code generation. That's all assuming you've mastered the Ruby or Groovy languages. They are simple languages, and Groovy can feel very familiar to Java developers, but that doesn't mean there's no cost associated with learning them. Ruby, with its use of domain-specific languages, can become very difficult to decipher, relying on magic APIs.

Clearly, there's a middle ground to be had: what's needed is a way of breaking through the ceremony associated with Java development (good tools do help, but the fact remains that generating accessor/mutator pairs is an extra step to somebody coming from languages with real property support like C#, Ruby, Delphi, Scala, Visual Basic, or Python!) and optimizing for certain classes of applications; enterprise web applications are a good place to start. What's needed is something that will feel familiar to users of existing Java frameworks and libraries—like the Spring framework, JMS, Hibernate, JPA, Spring MVC, or Spring Web Flow—while freeing the developer of the burden of integrating them.

Enter Spring Roo. Spring Roo, created by Ben Alex of Spring Security fame, is both an evolution of and a radical departure from all the existing attempts at enhancing Java developer productivity. The objective of Spring Roo, as enumerated in the mission statement (`http://static.springsource.org/spring-roo/reference/html/background.html#background-mission`) is to "fundamentally and sustainably improve Java developer productivity without compromising engineering integrity or flexibility." This has a lot of implications. Applications built in Roo are Java applications that benefit from the mature Java language and platform. Roo applications are easier to develop at every level, owing to a pervasive adherence to convention-over-configuration.

You can always go home again. Using Roo doesn't mean you cede any control over your application. Roo is a development-time only framework and imposes no runtime model on your application. Ultimately, Roo applications are just plain old Java and Spring applications. There's no Roo library to deploy; it delegates all the runtime handling to Spring and other frameworks you were already using. Roo applications are ultimately the code you would write if you were writing it by hand; the framework espouses best-practice–oriented code. If you disagree with the implementation, the code is ultimately yours to change and is fully malleable. If you choose to override Roo, it will stand down, never overwriting or interfering with your changes. If you don't want Roo in your application, it takes all of five minutes to remove it completely without sacrificing any functionality. If you want to continue using to evolve the application, even after considerable customizations to the generated code, it'll adapt—happily helping in any way it can. So it fully supports round-tripping of generated Roo artifacts through updates by the developer.

Spring Roo is powerful and has support out of the box for many of the libraries and frameworks you're likely to need, including JPA or Hibernate, JMS, Spring MVC, Spring Web Flow, and GWT. For scenarios that aren't supported, Roo ships with a powerful plug-in model, enabling third parties to ship integrations that play well with Spring Roo. Examples of this include a Flex add-on for Flex-based RIA clients and a Surf add-on to enable content-management–centric applications using the Spring Surf framework. If something is not available, developing a Roo add-on is very simple.

With the sales pitch out of the way, let's talk about what Roo is in practice. Spring Roo provides a shell, which sits in the background and monitors your code. You interact with the shell and, when you want a helping hand building something, ask it to act on your behalf. If you've asked it to write something brand new, it'll simply generate the required artifacts and then silently monitor them for interesting changes where it might lend a hand. It tends to stay out of your Java code after it has initially generated it, unless you ask it to intercede.

It will often generate code in response to your changes, however, and put those changes in AspectJ inter-type declarations (ITD), which take the form of files adjacent to your Java code ending in the `.aj` extension. So, for example, suppose you've introduced a variable. You're going to need an accessor/mutator pair, right? It'll generate that accessor/mutator and store it in an ITD. These files—AspectJ aspects—are merged at build time with Java code you've written. The result at runtime is the same as if you had written the Java class with the accessor/mutators pair by hand. There is no reflection or magic.

Spring Roo is not merely a code-generation tool, however. The same shell that was kind enough to generate the accessor/mutators pair for you on the introduction of a private variable in an entity will also remove the accessor/mutators pair upon removal of the variable. Similarly, if you explicitly code the accessor or mutators in your Java code, Roo drops the generated one, favoring the one you've written, all transparent to you.

If your tool understands these ITDs, it can let you code against their synthetic interface. Eclipse, through the AspectJ Development Toolkit, does understand them, so their use in your code is transparent in that environment. Additionally, because the generated Roo project uses Maven, you may build a working version of your application at any time, regardless of whether or not you use Eclipse. At the time of this writing, IntelliJ IDEA 9.0.2 supports compilation (using the AspectJ weaver) and code-completion of ITDs through a plug-in (see: `http://plugins.intellij.net/plugin/?idea&id=4679`), which makes coding Spring Roo projects pleasant. There is no particular support for Roo specifically however, so for this chapter, we will, where relevant, assume you are using the SpringSource Tool Suite. At the time of this writing, we are unaware of any support for ITDs or for Roo for Netbeans. Even if your IDE doesn't support ITDs, Spring Roo might still be compelling as a way to bootstrap the development process, because as we'll discuss later, Spring Roo (and AspectJ) can be completely removed, leaving a standard Java and Spring application with its full functionality intact that can be edited using IntelliJ or Netbeans.

This chapter is a short one, which speaks to the power of Spring Roo. Once you've gotten started, there's very little that's unfamiliar or unintuitive. If ever you feel out on a lurch, you can simply ask Roo for help! Your resulting project is Spring-based, but if you've read this book, you'll have no problem there!

12-1. Setting Up the Spring Roo Development Environment

Problem

You want to use Roo, but don't know where to start. After all, Roo is not a library, and it's not a framework. It's a lightweight developer tool. You want to know what tools are required to get the best development experience and, more precisely, how to set start using those tools.

Solution

Setting up Spring Roo is fairly painless, but there are some caveats. Theoretically, there's nothing stopping you from using Spring Roo, a JDK, and Vim by themselves. Practically, however, you need to set up an appropriate version of Eclipse, Java 6 Spring Roo itself, and Maven.

How It Works

To achieve its promise of increasing developer productivity, Spring Roo relies on many standard tools—tools with which you're certainly at least somewhat familiar. Even in this book, we've worked through examples using Spring, of course, and you're no doubt aware of Maven, the ubiquitous project comprehension and build tool. If you've set up Maven, Ant, or the JDK, you've likely added something to your operating system's PATH variable before, too. Similarly, if you've worked with Java, you've more than likely used an IDE, like IntelliJ IDEA or Eclipse. So none of what we're about to enumerate should be unfamiliar to you. There are very specific things that need to happen, so please review all the steps, even if you feel like you've already taken care of these before.

It is also worth noting that while most features work on all platforms, Spring Roo makes heavy use of the command line shell. The shell is quite smart, featuring tab completion, line history, and much more. These features are surfaced pretty consistently on all platforms, thanks to the excellent JLine library (http://jline.sourceforge.net). JLine handles some features inconsistently, however, on Windows—nothing fundamentally irresolvable, mind you, just nuisances like shell color differences and line history glitches. Proceed full speed ahead, but if you're not using a Unix-like operating system, be aware of the (ever diminishing) possibility of issues.

Let's get started!

Maven

You need Apache Maven, version 2.0.9 or greater. Maven isn't strictly necessary if you've already got an existing Spring Roo project, but it's definitely convenient and is required to do things like use Roo's commands for dependency management, builds, project bootstrapping, and so on.

1. To obtain Maven, visit `http://maven.apache.org/download.html`, and download it.

2. Unzip the archive into a directory of your choosing. At this point, you might create an environment variable to record its location; `MAVEN_HOME` is a pretty standard (but not required) name.

3. Add the `bin` folder under the directory to your system's `PATH` variable. If you gave the folder an environment variable like `MAVEN_HOME`, you can simply modify the `PATH` to reference `MAVEN_HOME/bin`. On a Unix-like environment, you would modify a system shell script (like `/etc/profile`, or `~/.profile`, or `~/.bashrc`) to have an entry like `export PATH=$PATH:$MAVEN_HOME/bin`.

4. Start a new shell session and confirm that you can issue the following command without error, in any directory on your system: `mvn --version`

SpringSource Tool Suite

Eclipse is an ideal environment, because it has support for the AspectJ Development Tools (AJDT). This support lets you code in Eclipse with aspects as a first class member of the language; aspects are transparently woven in and everything compiles. All mechanisms—refactoring, class inspection and IDE pop ups—work as you'd expect. Unfortunately, this support is limited to Eclipse, at the moment. If you're a Spring user, and in particular if you want a guaranteed stable integration for development with Roo, no Eclipse distribution can offer you more than the SpringSource Tool Suite.

You can download the IDE from `http://www.springsource.com/products/sts`. It is not open-source, but it is free of cost ("as in beer"). The SpringSource Tool Suite integrates all the Eclipse plug-ins you would typically download and set up manually if you were to download the stock install of the Java EE edition of Eclipse. So, from that perspective, this is a compelling download all by itself, regardless of whether or not you plan on using Spring Roo: it's got Maven, Subversion, unmatched Spring support, enterprise OSGi, support for all of SpringSource's deployment targets (above and beyond stock adapters like Tomcat and JBoss) and much, much more.

1. To obtain the SpringSource Tool Suite, visit `http://www.springsource.com/products/sts`, and click Download STS.

2. Once STS is downloaded, extract the distribution to the directory of your choosing. If you navigate the directory structure, you'll note that these are in the directory:

    •   A directory for a bundled version of SpringSource's tc Server (in my installation, version 6.0.20)—a world-class, developer-friendly, and operations-enabled web server

- A directory for SpringSource Tool Suite itself (in my installation, version 2.3.2)

- A directory for Spring Roo (in my installation, version 1.0.2)

Spring Roo

You need Spring Roo itself. If you've downloaded the SpringSource Tool Suite, then you already have Spring Roo in the folder adjacent to the folder in which the IDE lives. If you simply wish to upgrade Roo independent of SpringSource Tool Suite or wish to use Roo with another tooling option, proceed reading this.

Visit http://www.springsource.org/roo for a plethora of information, helpful tutorials, and, of course, the distribution. While all the SpringSource projects are easy to get into—owing in large part to their excellent, world-class documentation—Spring Roo particularly excels at providing a compelling out-of-the-box developer experience. If, by chance, there is any question about how to do something even after reading this chapter (perish the thought!), you'll find ample resources on this site. To set up Roo, follow these steps:

1. To obtain Spring Roo, visit http://www.springsource.org/roo/start, and download it by clicking the Download link on the page.

2. Once you have the distribution on your system, unzip it to a directory of your choosing. At this point, create an environment variable called ROO_HOME to record its location.

3. Add the bin folder under the directory to your system's PATH variable. If you gave the folder of an environment variable like ROO_HOME, you can simply modify the PATH to reference ROO_HOME/bin. For example, in a Unix-like environment, you would modify a system shell script (like /etc/profile or ~/.profile or ~/.bashrc) to have an entry like export PATH=$PATH:$ROO_HOME/bin.

4. On the command line, type the following sequence. If you are running on Windows, issue roo.bat instead of roo.sh:

   ```
   mkdir first_flight ;
   cd first_flight ;
   roo.sh quit;
   rm first_flight ;
   ```

5. Confirm that you saw output. On my system, the output looked like this:

   ```
   $ roo.sh quit
   ```

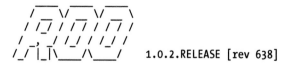

   ```
   1.0.2.RELEASE [rev 638]
   ```

   ```
   Welcome to Spring Roo. For assistance press TAB or type "hint" then hit ENTER.
   ```

Now, you're ready to get to the business of building your application! Launch a shell instance and then launch the SpringSource Tool Suite by executing the STS binary in the SpringSource Tool Suite folder.

12-2. Creating Your First Spring Roo Project

Problem

There are at least a couple of good ways to start a Spring Roo project, but none are obvious if you haven't used it before. This isn't a library, of course, so you don't just add the relevant .jar files to your classpath like you might the Spring framework. How do you begin?

Solution

As was famously uttered in no science-fiction movie, ever, the answer is, "Use the shell, Luke." The Spring Roo shell provides everything you need to get started. An alternative approach is to use STS's wizard, which may be familiar to users accustomed to tooling-based support.

How It Works

The first option—using the shell—is the most obvious, worthwhile, and potentially powerful. Let's start there.

The Spring Roo shell is a blank slate. It represents the ultimate user interface for Spring Roo to facilitate development. The Spring Roo team did a lot of research before building Roo on how to advance the Java developer experience, best expose the tool to the developers, and avoid being overly coupled to any single technology. The team came up with a custom command line shell to facilitate the developer. This shell can be intimidating to the uninitiated.

The shell is initially empty and replete with untapped potential; to make the shell intuitive, the Spring Roo team gave it lots of smarts. It supports tab completion, which will enable you to tab your way to a completely specified command. You can ask it questions using the hint command, and it does its best to direct you in response.

Additionally, the shell keeps context. It knows that a command run to modify an entity, or to add a field to an entity, must affect an entity and that it's likely you, the developer, intended to update the last entity you created earlier in the shell session. After a while, the shell starts to feel like an extra arm; you might find yourself feeling disappointed when the shell *can't* solve a problem for you!

SCRIPT ONCE, RUN ANYWHERE

The Spring Roo shell is pretty darned handy, and even fun, but on the surface, it would appear to lack the reusability we developers have come to expect from our tools. If you have built the next big thing but want to be able to reproduce it, you can create a Roo shell script. Simply create a file whose name ends with `.roo`. An example might be `myapp.roo`. Put the shell commands as exactly as you have issued them inside the shell in this file, separated by a newline character and then save.

To run the script, simply invoke the Roo shell as follows (changing the path of the file as appropriate):

```
roo.sh script --file ~/Desktop/myapp.roo
```

This will cause the commands in the script to be run—instant reproducible build! This can be very handy if you want to enforce consistency in your company's applications by seeding them with a common base project and configuration.

There is, at the time of this writing, no simple command to create a Roo script from an interactive shell session. Your best bet is to simply copy the buffer into a text file and find and remove the `roo>` prompts.

First, let's create a new Spring Roo project using the Spring shell. First, create an empty directory in which to work and then, on the command line, change your current directory to the directory you just created. Then launch Roo (much as we did in the first recipe):

```
$ roo.sh
```

At this point, you'll be greeted by a welcome message:

```
Welcome to Spring Roo. For assistance press TAB or type "hint" then hit ENTER.
```

Type hint, and press the Enter key.

```
roo> hint
Welcome to Roo! We hope you enjoy your stay!

Before you can use many features of Roo, you need to start a new project.

To do this, type 'project' (without the quotes) and then hit TAB.

Enter a --topLevelPackage like 'com.mycompany.projectname' (no quotes).
When you've finished completing your --topLevelPackage, press ENTER.
Your new project will then be created in the current working directory.

Note that Roo frequently allows the use of TAB, so press TAB regularly.
Once your project is created, type 'hint' and ENTER for the next suggestion.
You're also welcome to visit http://forum.springframework.org for Roo help.
roo>
```

And we're off! It's done all but lay out a welcome mat for us! Let's oblige it: enter the **project** command as follows and then press Enter:

```
$ project –topLevelPackage com.apress.springrecipes.roo.test1
```

Output will flash across your screen. In the preceding example, you could have just typed project and pressed Tab. Tab signals to the Roo shell that you want suggestions, just as Ctrl + space bar does in your IDE for auto-completion. If you had pressed Tab in this case, Roo would have simply filled in the required (and unique) argument to the project command, the --topLevelPackage argument, and you could have then simply typed your package. Here's what it looked like on my shell:

```
Created /home/jlong/Documents/code/roo/t1/pom.xml
Created SRC_MAIN_JAVA
Created SRC_MAIN_RESOURCES
Created SRC_TEST_JAVA
Created SRC_TEST_RESOURCES
Created SRC_MAIN_WEBAPP
Created SRC_MAIN_RESOURCES/META-INF/spring
Created SRC_MAIN_RESOURCES/META-INF/spring/applicationContext.xml
Created SRC_MAIN_RESOURCES/META-INF/spring/log4j.properties
```

At this point, you've got a skeletal installation all set up and ready to use. If you attempt to type project again, it won't auto-complete or provide any suggestions or feedback, because it knows that the command is inappropriate for this project, at this point.

Quit the Roo shell, and inspect the output. You've got a directory with a Maven 2 (or greater) project preconfigured already with Spring and more. Here's what is in my directory structure:

```
jlong@studio:~/Documents/code/roo/t1$ find
.
./log.roo
./src
./src/main
./src/main/webapp
./src/main/java
./src/main/resources
./src/main/resources/META-INF
./src/main/resources/META-INF/spring
./src/main/resources/META-INF/spring/log4j.properties
./src/main/resources/META-INF/spring/applicationContext.xml
./src/test
./src/test/java
./src/test/resources
./pom.xml
jlong@studio:~/Documents/code/roo/t1$
```

This is a Maven project.

Exploring the Maven Project

If you've used Maven before, you will know that the directory structure is consistent for all Maven projects, and it's shown in Table 12-1.

Table 12-1. *Maven Directories*

Directory	Use
src/main/java	A directory to hold the non–unit-test Java files for your application.
src/main/resources	Holds classpath resources that aren't Java class files. You can see in the previous output that it's appropriate to put the META-INF/ directory as well as any other artifacts (like Spring application contexts) there. Note, this is for classpath resources and is not appropriate, for example, for web application resources. For that you need src/main/webapp.
src/main/webapp	This directory is used to hold the *rest* of a web application's structure. If you were going to develop a web application, put everything except what you would put in WEB-INF/classes in this folder. Examples include the WEB-INF folder itself, as well as JSP (*.jsp, *.jspx) artifacts, WEB-INF/web.xml, JavaScript (*.js), .css, or HTML artifacts.
src/test/java	This directory holds artifacts intended to test the Java classes under the src/main/java folder. Typically, the package structures mirrors the package structure in src/main/java, allowing your tests to have package-friendly visibility to the classes under test.
src/test/resources	This directory holds resources needed by your test classes at test time, in the same way that src/main/resources works.

Maven projects are described by the pom.xml file in the root of the project. They store metadata about the dependencies required in the application, as well as their scope: .jar files that are required only for unit testing are not included in the final build intended for deployment. Similarly, .jar files that provide interfaces needed only at compile time, such as the Spring Roo aspects (since the Spring Roo annotations are source-level only) and the various standard interfaces (you need to compile against javax.servlet.*, for example, but your deployment server already has those libraries on its path and there's no need to furnish them.)

Maven builds, much like Roo, work on the notion of convention-over-configuration. You only need to modify the Maven pom.xml file when you want to augment or change some existing behavior in the build. A minimal pom.xml is fully functional, however.

Maven already knows how to compile, deploy, document, run tests for, and share your project artifacts for you. It exposes life cycle hooks like compile, test, and so on. Plug-ins can be written to hook into those life cycle phases for different types of projects. There are defaults, however. For a standard .jar file, you don't need to specify any of these plug-ins. If you invoke a plug-in that exists in a specific phase, Maven will run all earlier phases and then invoke that plug-in. Thus, to build a working .jar of your Maven application, run the following command in the same folder as the pom.xml file lives for your project:

```
mvn package
```

This will invoke the compiler phase, the test phase, and so on, and finally the package plug-in. The package plug-in will generate a `.jar` file that lives in the `target` folder of your project (all outputs, including code generation, will live somewhere in this folder). Spring Roo also lets you perform certain operations using Maven from within the Roo shell. To package the project using the Roo shell, launch it again (using `roo.sh`), and invoke the following command:

```
$ roo> perform package
```

When you are using Spring Roo, there's almost no reason to directly modify the Maven `pom.xml` file if you don't wish to. However, it doesn't hurt to understand what Spring Roo has done for us. Open up the `pom.xml` file in your favorite text editor. You'll note that it has imported standard `.jar` files like JUnit 4.x, Apache Commons Logging, AspectJ, and the Java Servlet APIs. It has also declared a dependency on many Spring framework libraries like the core, AOP support, transaction support and test support. More than likely, you would have added most of these to your own Spring project, whether you're using Spring Roo or not. In addition, you'll note a solitary Spring Roo–specific dependency:

```
<dependency>
          <groupId>org.springframework.roo</groupId>
          <artifactId>org.springframework.roo.annotations</artifactId>
          <version>1.0.2.RELEASE</version>
          <scope>provided</scope>
     </dependency>
```

The scope is `provided`, which simply means it won't exist at runtime and is there only for the compiler. Spring Roo has no runtime footprint at all.

Getting Started Using STS

We've created our project using the shell. STS also provides a fast and convenient way to bootstrap a new Spring Roo project.

1. To start, open up SpringSource Tool Suite.

2. Go to File ➤ New ➤ Roo Project.

3. You will be greeted with the dialog box shown in Figure 12-1. Note the field for the project name, as well as the "Top level package name" field. This wizard establishes the same setup as you did by creating a directory and then using the Roo shell to create a project and requires virtually identical inputs. You need only specify the project and top-level package names; everything else may remain as specified by default.

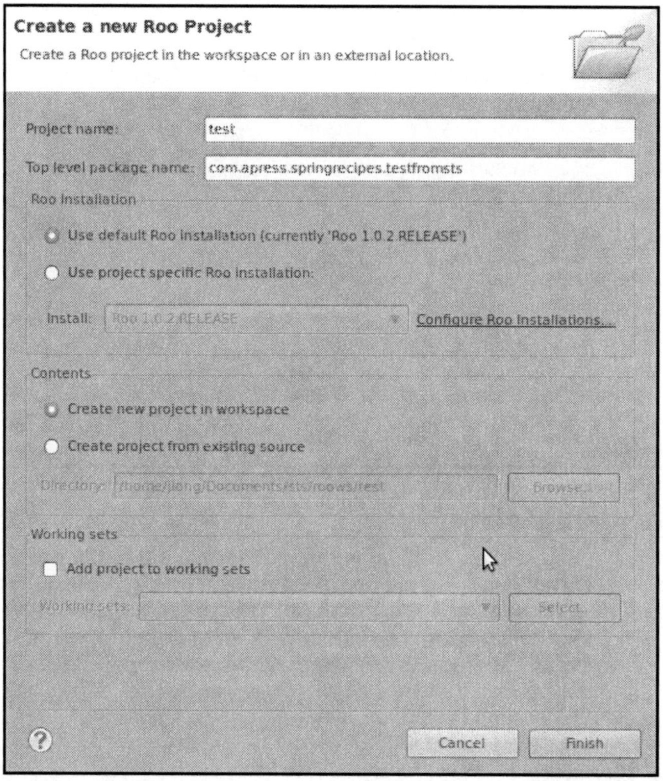

Figure 12-1. The New Roo Project dialog in SpringSource Tool Suite

You should have a new project. Go to the Eclipse Project Explorer. Your project should be very similar to the project you created on the command line.

SpringSource Tool Suite provides a shell to let you interact with Roo from within the IDE environment. To use it, go to Window ➤ Show View ➤ Roo Shell. This should bring a tab up as shown in Figure 12-2 (typically in the same rack of tabs as the Console and Markers editors, though of course, this may change according to the customizations in your environment).

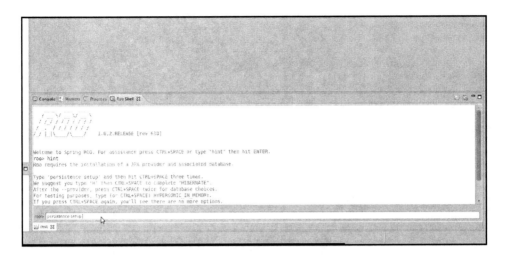

Figure 12-2. *The Spring Roo shell from within STS*

Here, you may enter the same commands as you did on the command line to proceed. Note that when entering commands in the STS shell, use Ctrl + space bar, not Tab, to get auto-completion and suggestions. Ctrl + space bar is used because it's more consistent with a developer's expectations for auto-completion when in Eclipse, whereas Tab is more consistent within a terminal (Bash provides tab completion, for example).

12-3. Importing an Existing Project into SpringSource Tool Suite

Problem

You've walked through the two approaches to creating a Spring Roo project, but what happens if you want to import the project created on the command line into SpringSource Tool Suite?

Solution

The m2eclipse plug-in, which provides Maven support to Eclipse (and thus to SpringSource Tool Suite), can do all the heavy lifting of importing your project, since it is just a stock-standard Maven project. Then, simply use SpringSource Tool Suite to add the Roo nature to your project.

How It Works

SpringSource Tool Suite bundles the m2eclipse plug-in (http://m2eclipse.sonatype.org/), which provides a convenient integration between Maven and Eclipse. You can import an existing Maven project, and the plug-in takes care of mapping the dependencies specified in the Maven project to Eclipse classpath libraries, specifying which folders are source folders, which Java compiler to use, and more. The plug-in also provides a convenient way of working with Maven projects and updating them.

Here's how to import an existing Spring Roo into SpringSource Tool Suite (or any Eclipse variant with the m2eclipse plug-in already installed).

1. Go to File ➤ Import ➤ Maven ➤ Existing Maven Projects (see Figure 12-3).

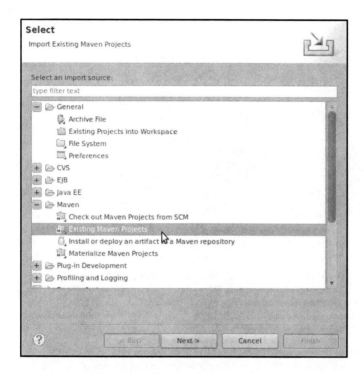

Figure 12-3. *The m2eclipse plugin adds a "Maven" folder. This lets you import a Maven project by pointing to its pom.xml file.*

2. Browse to select the folder where you created the Spring Roo project. It should list the projects available under the folder selected by showing you the `pom.xml` it wants to import. Confirm the selection by choosing Finish (see Figure 12-4).

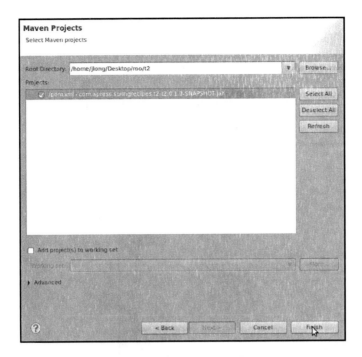

Figure 12-4. Confirm your import selection by choosing Finish.

3. At this point, you have a working Eclipse project, but it will complain of compiler errors if you've introduced any AspectJ ITDs. The project hasn't been configured to know what to do with them, yet. In SpringSource Tool Suite, you need only right click on the project in the Eclipse Project Explorer. Choose Spring Tools ➤ Add Roo Project Nature.

4. If you're using IntelliJ IDEA Ultimate Edition (it should work with Community Edition, too) version 9.0.2 or better, and already have the aforementioned AspectJ support plug-in installed, you can simply open the project just as you would any IntelliJ project, selecting the **pom.xml** instead of a standard IntelliJ IDEA project file.

12-4. Building A Better Application, Quicker

Problem

You have Roo set up and now want to see the storied productivity gains had by using Spring Roo. For starters, how do you build a web application using our existing Spring Roo project as a base? How do you add entities, controllers, services, messaging, and any of a myriad of other concerns?

Solution

Use the shell, of course! Spring Roo provides very powerful support to bootstrap most solutions, and if it doesn't, it's entirely possible there's a plug-in that will do the job for you. Failing that, it is just a stock-standard Spring project, after all, so you can simply add it as you would normally. At no point will you (or could you) code yourself into a corner where the Spring Roo way is impeding you from solving a problem!

How It Works

Spring Roo provides intuitive support for building applications. In this recipe, we'll explore the rhythm of Spring Roo development. This recipe is not so much about picking apart the nuances of the technologies we're using to build this application as about understanding the Roo development life cycle. As you'll see, once you embrace the Roo shell, you may see the finish line approach with startling suddenness.

Let's build a simple customer relationship management (CRM) application. We want to store, update, view, and (hopefully very rarely!) delete customers. We shall work using a sort of domain-driven design approach to generate useful components in the higher view tier from the data present in the model and services tiers.

Coding the Backend

You should have a freshly created Spring Roo application to follow along. If you haven't already done so, in either STS or on the command line, start the Roo shell (if it wasn't already running) for the project you wish to edit and update.

I think that, before we can build any kind of web application or UI layer, we need to build some sort of entity to model our records. There are many ways to do that, but for the very large majority of applications, it will involve a database and some sort of object/relational mapping (ORM) solution. That can get tedious very quickly.

If Spring Roo's so smart, let's ask it! In the Roo shell, type hint to see what to do next before we can get started. On my console, it responded:

```
roo> hint
Roo requires the installation of a JPA provider and associated database.

Type 'persistence setup' and then hit CTRL+SPACE three times.
We suggest you type 'H' then CTRL+SPACE to complete "HIBERNATE".
After the --provider, press CTRL+SPACE twice for database choices.
For testing purposes, type (or CTRL+SPACE) HYPERSONIC_IN_MEMORY.
If you press CTRL+SPACE again, you'll see there are no more options.
As such, you're ready to press ENTER to execute the command.

Once JPA is installed, type 'hint' and ENTER for the next suggestion.
```

Geez! It's a step ahead of us! It already knows we need a database and some sort of persistence mechanism. If this sort of thing carries on too long, it might give us Spring book authors a complex! Fine, enter persistence setup as it suggests. On my console, I ended up entering the following command:

```
roo> persistence setup --database HYPERSONIC_IN_MEMORY --provider HIBERNATE
```

In my project, the command created two new files (`src/main/resources/META-INF/persistence.xml` and `src/main/resources/META-INF/spring/database.properties`), and it updated two files (`src/main/resources/META-INF/spring/applicationContext.xml` and `pom.xml`).

The file `src/main/resources/META-INF/spring/database.properties` contains useful configuration to facilitate connection to the Hypersonic in-memory database. The `pom.mxl` file has been updated to contain dependencies for Hibernate and for JPA, as well as the Hypersonic embedded database `.jar` files. The file `src/main/resources/META-INF/persistence.xml` is the standard JPA configuration file to enable the Hibernate-based JPA implementation to do its work. Finally, the Spring application context, `src/main/resources/META-INF/spring/applicationContext.xml`, has been updated to have a data source, a JPA transaction manager, and a JPA entity manager factory.

That wasn't so bad after all! Now, we need only code a `Customer` entity, write a DAO and maybe a service, set up Spring MVC, add a controller, and design the UI. This should be easy. We could have a first draft up in no time—in a day or two, maximum, if we start now. Right?

I, for one, think it's fantastic that Spring Roo got us this far. It might be worth it to see if it can, by some infinitesimally small chance, get us further along and perhaps spare us the next few days' worth of development.

In the Spring Roo shell, type `hint` again. Here's what it said in my shell:

```
roo> hint
You can create entities either via Roo or your IDE.
Using the Roo shell is fast and easy, especially thanks
 to the CTRL+SPACE completion.

Start by typing 'ent' and then hitting CTRL+SPACE twice.
Enter the --class in the form '~.domain.MyEntityClassName'
In Roo, '~' means the --topLevelPackage you specified via 'create project'.

After specify a --class argument, press SPACE then CTRL+SPACE. Note nothing appears.
Because nothing appears, it means you've entered all mandatory arguments.
However, optional arguments do exist for this command (and most others in Roo).
To see the optional arguments, type '--' and then hit CTRL+SPACE. Mostly you won't
need any optional arguments, but let's select the --testAutomatically option
and hit ENTER. You can always use this approach to view optional arguments.

After creating an entity, use 'hint' for the next suggestion.
roo>
```

Huh! Why, Will wonders never cease?

It *can* help us with the entities! Right then, let's oblige it again: type ent, and press Ctrl + space bar twice. Roo should prompt you to specify a class name. Typically, the entity class should be in a subpackage of the root package. Spring Roo has a special convention, which it announces in the console message, to avoid having to retype the entire base package when specifying a class in a sub package of the application: simply use ~ in place of the entire package. If your root project was `com.apress.springrecipes.test.t3`, then ~ will resolve to that, and `~.domain.Customer` would resolve to `com.apress.springrecipes.test.t3.domain.Customer`. So, the full mandatory command to generate a Customer entity, is as follows:

```
roo> ent --class ~.domain.Customer
```

However, we should also take advantage of the fact that Spring Roo can generate unit tests and integration tests for us. Let's suffix the command with the optional **-testAutomatically** argument. In the Spring Roo shell, to see all the optional arguments, simply type -- and then press Ctrl + space bar or Tab (for STS or the regular old Spring Roo shell, respectively) to see all the options. The command now looks like this, instead:

```
roo> ent --class ~.domain.Customer --testAutomatically
```

On my console, I can see that it added a **Customer** class, as expected, complete with the base JPA annotations as well as three Roo-specific annotations.

```
package com.apress.springrecipes.test.t3.domain;

import javax.persistence.Entity;
import org.springframework.roo.addon.javabean.RooJavaBean;
import org.springframework.roo.addon.tostring.RooToString;
import org.springframework.roo.addon.entity.RooEntity;

@Entity
@RooJavaBean
@RooToString
@RooEntity
public class Customer {
}
```

These annotations tell the Roo shell what services to provide to the **Customer** class while you're developing. Yes, you read that correctly—while you are developing! These annotations never make it past the compiler. They are there for the benefit of the Spring Roo shell, so that it knows what things you want it to help you with.

You'll note that Spring Roo also created three other files in the same package, **Customer_Roo_Configurable.aj**, **Customer_Roo_Entity.aj**, and **Customer_Roo_ToString.aj**. These are AspectJ ITDs. They are where Spring Roo does its magic to help you. You should not modify them. Spring Roo modifies them, and only in response to changes you make on the Customer entity. The annotations tell Spring Roo that you would like its help.

Open the **Customer_Roo_ToString.aj** file. In my application, the file looks like this:

```
package com.apress.springrecipes.test.t3.domain;

import java.lang.String;

privileged aspect Customer_Roo_ToString {

    public String Customer.toString() {
        StringBuilder sb = new StringBuilder();
        sb.append("Id: ").append(getId()).append(", ");
        sb.append("Version: ").append(getVersion());
        return sb.toString();
    }

}
```

It's pretty clear that this is intended to be the `toString` method for our `Customer` class, even if it is a bit strange looking. If the syntax is off-putting or confusing, don't worry. You don't need to edit these files yourself; Spring Roo modifies them for you, as you make changes to the `Customer` java class.

To see this effect in action, open `Customer.java`, and comment out the `@RooToString` annotation. Instantly, the `Customer_Roo_ToString.aj` file disappears! Uncomment the annotation, and observe that the ITD reappears instantly. Alright, I'm sure you're impressed. What happens if you write your own `toString` method on the `Customer` class? Who wins? You do, of course! Try it, and observe the ITD again disappear, deferring to your custom `toString` implementation first.

Remove the overridden `toString` implementation, for now.

If you open `Customer_Roo_Entity.aj`, you'll observe that Roo has already created an ID and a version field for your entity, and that it has created methods to facilitate persisting, finding, updating, and removing the entity.

Let's introduce a field. The first way we'll do so is by simply adding the filed into the `Customer` java class. Modify the file to look like this:

```
package com.apress.springrecipes.test.t3.domain;

import javax.persistence.Entity;
import org.springframework.roo.addon.javabean.RooJavaBean;
import org.springframework.roo.addon.tostring.RooToString;
import org.springframework.roo.addon.entity.RooEntity;

@Entity
@RooJavaBean
@RooToString
@RooEntity
public class Customer {
    private String name;
}
```

As soon as you do, you can confirm that the `toString` method has been updated to include the new field, and that a new ITD, called `Customer_Roo_JavaBean.aj`, has been introduced. This new ITD should contain the declaration of an accessor/mutator pair for the field. Convenient!

Remove the field. Let's get back to the business of letting Spring Roo do things for us. We need a few fields: a first name, a last name, and an e-mail at least. We should probably try to record the date they first bought the product and whether or not the `Customer` is considered still active for revenue-recognition purposes.

Spring Roo provides a command just for this scenario: the `field` command. Here are the commands to generate our fields. We won't hash out the gory specifics of the invocations, as they're pretty self-explanatory.

```
field string --fieldName firstName --notNull
field string --fieldName lastName --notNull
field string --fieldName email --notNull
field date --fieldName signupDate --type java.util.Date
field boolean --fieldName active
```

As you enter these, Spring Roo adds the fields to the `Customer` java class, complete with JSR-303 (the JSR specifying validation in the tradition of frameworks like the Hibernate Validation framework) validations, accessor/mutators, and an updated `toString` method. It's important to note that we aren't specifying to which entity the fields changes be applied. Spring Roo remembers what entity you last created and applies the changes to that. It has context. If you want to explicitly spell it out, use the --entity parameter.

At this point, we have everything we need in the backend (and then some!). Let's turn our focus to building the front-end—a web application.

Coding the Front-end

The goal here is to generate some simple support code that we can tune and tweak later. We'd just like to get a proof-of-concept example working. We want to build a web application that can manipulate `Customer` entities. We know that this would take the form of a controller in Spring MVC, so let's take a stab in the dark. Type `hint controllers` at the Spring Roo shell. You can see that there is indeed support for generating scaffolding controllers. Type the following command to create a Spring MVC controller that provides a UI to manipulate `Customer` entities (and stand back!):

```
controller scaff --class ~.web.CustomerController --entity ~.domain.Customer
```

That command packs a wallop! Our pedestrian application was just transformed from a simple service tier to a full-blown Spring MVC application with a very sane Spring MVC setup; controller support for RESTful endpoints to create, update, retrieve or delete entities; URL rewriting logic; and much more. Let's test out the application!

Let's deploy the application to a web container. If you're on the standard command line, you have a couple of options.

- In the project directory, in the standard shell, run `mvn tomcat:run` or `mvn jetty:run`, and open `http://localhost:8080` in your browser.

- In the Spring Roo shell, invoke `perform package`, and deploy the resulting `.war` file in the target folder of your project to any web server of your choice.

If you're in an IDE, you can use your IDE's support for deploying web applications. In SpringSource Tool Suite, two preconfigured servers are already available to you. Let's use the tcServer instance (which is ultimately based on Tomcat, so it should perform similarly). To do so, go to Window ➤ Show View ➤ Servers. The Servers tab should become visible. Right-click the icon labeled "SpringSource tc Server v6.0", and choose "Add and Remove" to open the dialog shown in Figure 12-5.

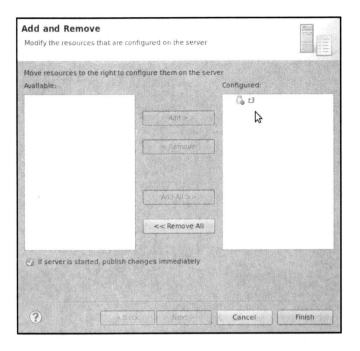

Figure 12-5. *This is the "Add and Remove" dialog inside of STS (or almost any Eclipse distribution with WTP support). Here, t3 is the name of my Spring Roo project.*

Finally, just launch the instance by clicking on the icon with the white arrow inside a green circle; see Figure 12-6.

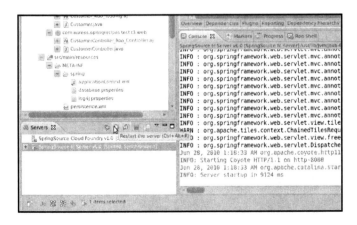

Figure 12-6. *The Servers tab lets you launch the application from within your IDE.*

When the server comes up, launch your browser and point it to `http://localhost:8080/t3`. Replace `t3` with your application's project name.

In Figure 12-7, you can see the default welcome page for our CRM. If you click around, you'll find there is a page to create a new customer record and another to list them all. Click the "Create new Customer" link, and fill out the form to create a new `Customer` record. Then, click the "List all Customers" link on the left-hand side of the page to see that very record. On this page, you have the ability to update or delete the record. Paging of the results is already provided out of the box, too.

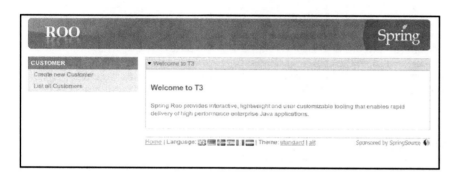

Figure 12-7. *The default welcome page for your newly minted CRM*

If you're astute, you will notice that the application also supports themes and is internationalized already. The application is leveraging Spring MVC's integration with Apache Tiles to support the themes and modularization, and it's leveraging Spring MVC's excellent internationalization and localization capabilities to support the various languages.

Finally, you'll note that there are RESTful endpoints that support manipulating the Customer entity. Not bad for a minute of work!

This may not be finished enough for you, but it's definitely a good start. The project is familiar Spring MVC and Spring. There are many options from here. You can continue using Roo to add Spring Security, Spring Web Flow, and even GWT support, for example. Or you can tune the pages by hand and update the themes yourself; that's also a good option.

12-5. Removing Spring Roo from Your Project

Problem

Your application is working like a charm, and you got home in time for dinner. Now, you're ready to deploy to production (hard to believe you just started this project only a few pages ago!), but you're getting pushback against having Spring Roo in your build (even though it won't get deployed, since it's not retained beyond the compiler anyway). Or, perhaps you just want to shed the training wheels and get a non-Rooified project.

Solution

It takes about five minutes to remove Spring Roo from your entire project. You need only remove the annotations, remove the solitary dependency on the Spring Roo annotations `.jar`, and use the Eclipse-based AspectJ Development Toolkit's support for push-in refactoring.

How It Works

Let's start with the single largest change: the removal of the AspectJ ITDs. To achieve this, you need to use AJDT's push-in refactoring. This refactor will merge the Aspects with their owning class. Note that this capability isn't available in the IntelliJ IDEA AspectJ support, at the time of this writing.

Right-click the root folder (or any of the source packages, e.g., `src/main/java`, `src/main/resources`, `src/test/java`, or `src/test/resources`) in Eclipse under the Java Resources tab in the Project Explorer. Choose Refactor ➤ Push In. You'll be presented with all the changes (see Figure 12-8). Simply select OK to continue.

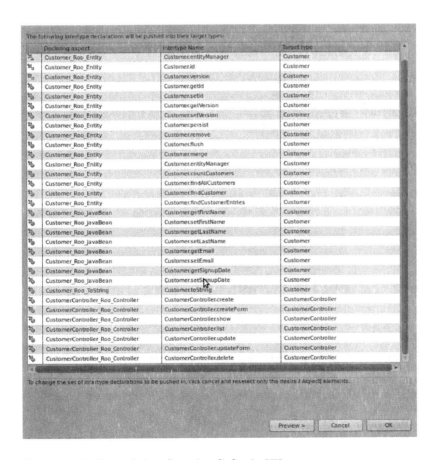

Figure 12-8. *The push-in refactoring dialog in STS*

Once this is done, 99 percent of the remnants of Spring Roo are already gone. As it is, your application is already 100 percent editable in Netbeans, IntelliJ, or any other editor that doesn't support AspectJ. However, technically, Spring Roo is still a part of your application. You need to remove the annotations from your build. Open up your `pom.xml` file, and search for the comment that reads

```
<!-- ROO dependencies -->
```

Right below it, you should see the following:

```
<dependency>
        <groupId>org.springframework.roo</groupId>
        <artifactId>org.springframework.roo.annotations</artifactId>
        <version>1.0.2.RELEASE</version>
        <scope>provided</scope>
</dependency>
```

Delete that dependency, and save the file. At this point, your application will not build because the compiler cannot resolve which library contains the Spring Roo annotations left on classes that were formerly managed by Spring Roo. You can simply remove the annotations from the `Customer` class and the `CustomerController` class. Alternatively, you might use the Find and Replace feature of your favorite text editor or IDE and find and remove all texts starting with `@Roo`.

Your application is now 100 percent Roo-free. This is obviously not desirable, since you lose Roo's support. However, if one day you decide that you want to bring Roo back, you simply need to add the annotations again and declare the Maven dependency once more. If you want to leave the existing classes as they are but want Spring Roo's help adding new components, simply start up the Spring Roo shell as usual and issue invocations as usual. It can even work with projects that were never Spring Roo projects, so long as they follow the directory layout conventions of a Maven project. Spring Roo takes inventory of what's happened and which beans have annotations on it when it starts up. So, if you add the annotations to a bean it had nothing to do with creating, Spring Roo will catch up; it will generate the AspectJ ITDs, just as if it had generated the class in the first place.

Summary

In this chapter, we worked through Spring Roo, an excellent framework on which to build best-of-breed Spring applications with hitherto unmatched productivity for Java developers. You learned how to get started, set up a project, and take that project all the way to the point where you could use start playing around with the web pages. Then, once we were satisfied we'd gotten enough mileage out of Spring Roo, we removed it from the Spring project.

CHAPTER 13

■ ■ ■

Spring Testing

In this chapter, you will learn about basic techniques you can use to test Java applications, and the testing support features offered by the Spring framework. These features can make your testing tasks easier and lead you to better application design. In general, applications developed with the Spring framework and the dependency injection pattern are easy to test.

Testing is a key activity for ensuring quality in software development. There are many types of testing, including unit testing, integration testing, functional testing, system testing, performance testing, and acceptance testing. Spring's testing support focuses on unit and integration testing, but it can also help with other types of testing. Testing can be performed either manually or automatically. However, since automated tests can be run repeatedly and continuously at different phases of a development process, they are highly recommended, especially in agile development processes. The Spring framework is an agile framework that fits these kinds of processes.

Many testing frameworks are available on the Java platform. Currently, JUnit and TestNG are the most popular. JUnit has a long history and a large user group in the Java community. TestNG is another popular Java testing framework. Compared to JUnit, TestNG offers additional powerful features such as test grouping, dependent test methods, and data-driven tests.

In releases prior to 2.5, Spring offered testing support specific to JUnit 3, which is now referred to as "JUnit 3 legacy support." Since Spring 2.5 testing support features have been offered by the Spring TestContext framework, which requires Java 1.5 or higher. This framework abstracts the underlying testing framework with the following concepts:

- *Test context*: This encapsulates the context of a test's execution, including the application context, test class, current test instance, current test method, and current test exception.

- *Test context manager*: This manages a test context for a test and triggers test execution listeners at predefined test execution points, including when preparing a test instance, before executing a test method (before any framework-specific initialization methods), and after executing a test method (after any framework-specific cleanup methods).

- *Test execution listener*: This defines a listener interface; by implementing this, you can listen to test execution events. The TestContext framework provides several test execution listeners for common testing features, but you are free to create your own.

Spring provides convenient TestContext support classes for JUnit 3, JUnit 4, and TestNG 5, with particular test execution listeners preregistered. You can simply extend these support classes to use the TestContext framework without having to know much about the framework details.

After finishing this chapter, you will understand the basic concepts and techniques of testing and the popular Java testing frameworks JUnit and TestNG. You will also be able to create unit tests and integration tests using both the JUnit 3 legacy support and the Spring TestContext framework.

13-1. Creating Tests with JUnit and TestNG

Problem

You would like to create automated tests for your Java application so that they can be run repeatedly to ensure the correctness of your application.

Solution

The most popular testing frameworks on the Java platform are JUnit and TestNG. JUnit 4 incorporates several major improvements over JUnit 3, which relies on the base class (i.e., `TestCase`) and the method signature (i.e., methods whose names begin with `test`) to identify test cases—an approach that lacks flexibility. JUnit 4 allows you to annotate your test methods with JUnit's `@Test` annotation, so an arbitrary public method can be run as a test case. TestNG is another powerful testing framework that makes use of annotations. It also provides a `@Test` annotation type for you to identify test cases.

How It Works

Suppose you are going to develop a system for a bank. To ensure the system's quality, you have to test every part of it. First, let's consider an interest calculator, whose interface is defined as follows:

```
package com.apress.springrecipes.bank;

public interface InterestCalculator {

    public void setRate(double rate);
    public double calculate(double amount, double year);
}
```

Each interest calculator requires a fixed interest rate to be set. Now, you can implement this calculator with a simple interest formula:

```
package com.apress.springrecipes.bank;

public class SimpleInterestCalculator implements InterestCalculator {

    private double rate;

    public void setRate(double rate) {
        this.rate = rate;
    }
```

```
    public double calculate(double amount, double year) {
        if (amount < 0 || year < 0) {
            throw new IllegalArgumentException("Amount or year must be positive");
        }
        return amount * year * rate;
    }
}
```

Next, you will test this simple interest calculator with the popular testing frameworks JUnit (both versions 3 and 4) and TestNG (version 5).

▨ **Tip** Usually, a test and its target class are located in the same package, but the source files of tests are stored in a separate directory (e.g., test) from the source files of other classes (e.g., src).

Testing with JUnit 3

In JUnit 3, a class that contains test cases must extend the framework class TestCase. Each test case must be a public method and its name must begin with test. Each test case should run in a fixed environment, which is made up of a particular set of objects called *test fixtures*. In JUnit 3, you can initialize test fixtures by overriding the setUp() method defined in TestCase. This method will be called by JUnit before each test case's execution. Accordingly, you can override the tearDown() method to perform cleanup tasks, such as releasing permanent resources. This method will be called by JUnit after each test case's execution. You can create the following JUnit 3 test cases to test your simple interest calculator.

▨ **Note** To compile and run test cases created for JUnit 3, you have to include the libraries for either JUnit 3 or JUnit 4. If you are using Maven, add one of the following dependencies to your project:

```
<dependency>
  <groupId>junit</groupId>
  <artifactId>junit</artifactId>
  <version>3.7</version>
</dependency>
```

or

```
<dependency>
  <groupId>junit</groupId>
```

```
<artifactId>junit</artifactId>
<version>4.7</version>
</dependency>
```

```java
package com.apress.springrecipes.bank;

import junit.framework.TestCase;

public class SimpleInterestCalculatorJUnit38Tests extends TestCase {

    private InterestCalculator interestCalculator;

    protected void setUp() throws Exception {
        interestCalculator = new SimpleInterestCalculator();
        interestCalculator.setRate(0.05);
    }

    public void testCalculate() {
        double interest = interestCalculator.calculate(10000, 2);
        assertEquals(interest, 1000.0);
    }

    public void testIllegalCalculate() {
        try {
            interestCalculator.calculate(-10000, 2);
            fail("No exception on illegal argument");
        }
        catch (IllegalArgumentException e) {}
    }
}
```

In addition to normal cases, a typical test should include exceptional cases, which are usually expected to throw an exception. To test if a method throws an exception in JUnit 3, you can surround that method call with a try/catch block. Then, at the next line of the method call in the try block, the test should fail if there's no exception thrown.

■ **Note** Most Java IDEs - Eclipse, IntelliJ IDEA, and Netbeans among them - provide JUnit test runners for you to run JUnit test cases. You will see a green bar if all your tests pass, and you will see a red bar if any of the tests fail. However, if you are not using an IDE that supports JUnit, you can still run JUnit tests at the command line. JUnit 3 provides both GUI–based and text-based test runners, but JUnit 4 doesn't come with a GUI–based test runner anymore.

Testing with JUnit 4

In JUnit 4, a class that contains test cases no longer needs to extend the TestCase class. It can be an arbitrary class. A test case is simply a public method with the @Test annotation. Similarly, you no longer need to override the setUp() and tearDown() methods, but rather annotate a public method with the @Before or @After annotation. You can also annotate a public static method with @BeforeClass or @AfterClass to have it run once before or after all test cases in the class.

Since your class doesn't extend TestCase, it doesn't inherit the assert methods. So, you have to call the static assert methods declared in the org.junit.Assert class directly. However, you can import all assert methods via a static import statement in Java 1.5. You can create the following JUnit 4 test cases to test your simple interest calculator.

■ **Note** To compile and run test cases created for JUnit 4, you have to include JUnit 4 on your CLASSPATH. If you are using Maven, add the following dependency to your project:

```
<dependency>
  <groupId>junit</groupId>
  <artifactId>junit</artifactId>
  <version>4.7</version>
</dependency>
```

```java
package com.apress.springrecipes.bank;

import static org.junit.Assert.*;

import org.junit.Before;
import org.junit.Test;

public class SimpleInterestCalculatorJUnit4Tests {

    private InterestCalculator interestCalculator;

    @Before
    public void init() {
        interestCalculator = new SimpleInterestCalculator();
        interestCalculator.setRate(0.05);
    }

    @Test
    public void calculate() {
        double interest = interestCalculator.calculate(10000, 2);
        assertEquals(interest, 1000.0, 0);
    }
```

```
@Test(expected = IllegalArgumentException.class)
public void illegalCalculate() {
    interestCalculator.calculate(-10000, 2);
}
}
```

JUnit 4 offers a powerful feature that allows you to expect an exception to be thrown in a test case. You can simply specify the exception type in the `expected` attribute of the `@Test` annotation.

Testing with TestNG

A TestNG test looks very similar to a JUnit 4 one, except that you have to use the classes and annotation types defined by the TestNG framework.

■ **Note** To compile and run test cases created for TestNG 5, you have to add TestNG to your CLASSPATH. If you are using Maven, add the following dependency to your project.

```
<dependency>
  <groupId>org.testng</groupId>
  <artifactId>testng</artifactId>
  <version>5.7</version>
  <classifier>jdk15</classifier>
</dependency>
```

```
package com.apress.springrecipes.bank;

import static org.testng.Assert.*;

import org.testng.annotations.BeforeMethod;
import org.testng.annotations.Test;

public class SimpleInterestCalculatorTestNG5Tests {

    private InterestCalculator interestCalculator;

    @BeforeMethod
    public void init() {
        interestCalculator = new SimpleInterestCalculator();
        interestCalculator.setRate(0.05);
    }
```

```
@Test
public void calculate() {
    double interest = interestCalculator.calculate(10000, 2);
    assertEquals(interest, 1000.0);
}

@Test(expectedExceptions = IllegalArgumentException.class)
public void illegalCalculate() {
    interestCalculator.calculate(-10000, 2);
}
}
```

■ **Note** If you are using Eclipse for development, you can download and install the TestNG Eclipse plug-in from http://testng.org/doc/eclipse.html to run TestNG tests in Eclipse. Again, you will see a green bar if all your tests pass and a red bar otherwise.

One of the powerful features of TestNG is its built-in support for data-driven testing. TestNG cleanly separates test data from test logic so that you can run a test method multiple times for different data sets. In TestNG, test data sets are provided by data providers, which are methods with the @DataProvider annotation.

```
package com.apress.springrecipes.bank;

import static org.testng.Assert.*;

import org.testng.annotations.BeforeMethod;
import org.testng.annotations.DataProvider;
import org.testng.annotations.Test;

public class SimpleInterestCalculatorTestNG5Tests {

    private InterestCalculator interestCalculator;

    @BeforeMethod
    public void init() {
        interestCalculator = new SimpleInterestCalculator();
        interestCalculator.setRate(0.05);
    }

    @DataProvider(name = "legal")
    public Object[][] createLegalInterestParameters() {
        return new Object[][] { new Object[] { 10000, 2, 1000.0 } };
    }
```

```
@DataProvider(name = "illegal")
public Object[][] createIllegalInterestParameters() {
    return new Object[][] {new Object[] { -10000, 2 },
            new Object[] { 10000, -2 }, new Object[] { -10000, -2 }};
}

@Test(dataProvider = "legal")
public void calculate(double amount, double year, double result) {
    double interest = interestCalculator.calculate(amount, year);
    assertEquals(interest, result);
}

@Test(
    dataProvider = "illegal",
    expectedExceptions = IllegalArgumentException.class)
public void illegalCalculate(double amount, double year) {
    interestCalculator.calculate(amount, year);
}
}
```

If you run the preceding test with TestNG, the `calculate()` method will be executed once, while the `illegalCalculate()` method will be executed three times, as there are three data sets returned by the `illegal` data provider.

13-2. Creating Unit Tests and Integration Tests

Problem

A common testing technique is to test each module of your application in isolation and then test them in combination. You would like to apply this skill in testing your Java applications.

Solution

Unit tests are used to test a single programming unit. In object-oriented languages, a *unit* is usually a class or a method. The scope of a unit test is a single unit, but in the real world, most units won't work in isolation. They often need to cooperate with others to complete their tasks. When testing a unit that depends on other units, a common technique you can apply is to simulate the unit's dependencies with stubs and mock objects, both of which can reduce complexity of your unit tests caused by dependencies.

A *stub* is an object that simulates a dependent object with the minimum number of methods required for a test. The methods are implemented in a predetermined way, usually with hard-coded data. A stub also exposes methods for a test to verify the stub's internal states. In contrast to a stub, a *mock object* usually knows how its methods are expected to be called in a test. The mock object then verifies the methods actually called against the expected ones. In Java, there are several libraries that can help create mock objects, including EasyMock and jMock. The main difference between a stub and a mock object is that a stub is usually used for *state verification*, while a mock object is used for *behavior verification*.

Integration tests, in contrast, are used to test several units in combination as a whole. They test if the integration and interaction between units are correct. Each of these units should already have been tested with unit tests, so integration testing is usually performed after unit testing.

Finally, note that applications developed using the principle of "separating interface from implementation" and the dependency injection pattern are easy to test, both for unit testing and integration testing. This is because that principle and pattern can reduce coupling between different units of your application.

How It Works

Creating Unit Tests for Isolated Classes

The core functions of your bank system should be designed around customer accounts. First of all, you create the following domain class, Account, with a custom equals() method:

```
package com.apress.springrecipes.bank;

public class Account {

    private String accountNo;
    private double balance;

    // Constructors, Getters and Setters
    ...

    public boolean equals(Object obj) {
        if (!(obj instanceof Account)) {
            return false;
        }
        Account account = (Account) obj;
        return account.accountNo.equals(accountNo) && account.balance == balance;
    }
}
```

Next, you define the following DAO interface for persisting account objects in your bank system's persistence layer:

```
package com.apress.springrecipes.bank;

public interface AccountDao {

    public void createAccount(Account account);
    public void updateAccount(Account account);
    public void removeAccount(Account account);
    public Account findAccount(String accountNo);
}
```

To demonstrate the unit testing concept, let's implement this interface by using a map to store account objects. The AccountNotFoundException and DuplicateAccountException classes are subclasses of RuntimeException that you should be able to create yourself.

```
package com.apress.springrecipes.bank;
...
public class InMemoryAccountDao implements AccountDao {

    private Map<String, Account> accounts;

    public InMemoryAccountDao() {
        accounts = Collections.synchronizedMap(new HashMap<String, Account>());
    }

    public boolean accountExists(String accountNo) {
        return accounts.containsKey(accountNo);
    }

    public void createAccount(Account account) {
        if (accountExists(account.getAccountNo())) {
            throw new DuplicateAccountException();
        }
        accounts.put(account.getAccountNo(), account);
    }

    public void updateAccount(Account account) {
        if (!accountExists(account.getAccountNo())) {
            throw new AccountNotFoundException();
        }
        accounts.put(account.getAccountNo(), account);
    }

    public void removeAccount(Account account) {
        if (!accountExists(account.getAccountNo())) {
            throw new AccountNotFoundException();
        }
        accounts.remove(account.getAccountNo());
    }

    public Account findAccount(String accountNo) {
        Account account = accounts.get(accountNo);
        if (account == null) {
            throw new AccountNotFoundException();
        }
        return account;
    }
}
```

Obviously, this simple DAO implementation doesn't support transactions. However, to make it thread-safe, you can wrap the map storing accounts with a synchronized map so that it will be accessed serially.

Now, let's create unit tests for this DAO implementation with JUnit 4. As this class doesn't depend directly on other classes, it's easy to test. To ensure that this class works properly for exceptional cases as well as normal cases, you should also create exceptional test cases for it. Typically, exceptional test cases expect an exception to be thrown.

```java
package com.apress.springrecipes.bank;

import static org.junit.Assert.*;

import org.junit.Before;
import org.junit.Test;

public class InMemoryAccountDaoTests {

    private static final String EXISTING_ACCOUNT_NO = "1234";
    private static final String NEW_ACCOUNT_NO = "5678";

    private Account existingAccount;
    private Account newAccount;
    private InMemoryAccountDao accountDao;

    @Before
    public void init() {
        existingAccount = new Account(EXISTING_ACCOUNT_NO, 100);
        newAccount = new Account(NEW_ACCOUNT_NO, 200);
        accountDao = new InMemoryAccountDao();
        accountDao.createAccount(existingAccount);
    }

    @Test
    public void accountExists() {
        assertTrue(accountDao.accountExists(EXISTING_ACCOUNT_NO));
        assertFalse(accountDao.accountExists(NEW_ACCOUNT_NO));
    }

    @Test
    public void createNewAccount() {
        accountDao.createAccount(newAccount);
        assertEquals(accountDao.findAccount(NEW_ACCOUNT_NO), newAccount);
    }

    @Test(expected = DuplicateAccountException.class)
    public void createDuplicateAccount() {
        accountDao.createAccount(existingAccount);
    }
}
```

```
@Test
public void updateExistedAccount() {
    existingAccount.setBalance(150);
    accountDao.updateAccount(existingAccount);
    assertEquals(accountDao.findAccount(EXISTING_ACCOUNT_NO), existingAccount);
}

@Test(expected = AccountNotFoundException.class)
public void updateNotExistedAccount() {
    accountDao.updateAccount(newAccount);
}

@Test
public void removeExistedAccount() {
    accountDao.removeAccount(existingAccount);
    assertFalse(accountDao.accountExists(EXISTING_ACCOUNT_NO));
}

@Test(expected = AccountNotFoundException.class)
public void removeNotExistedAccount() {
    accountDao.removeAccount(newAccount);
}

@Test
public void findExistedAccount() {
    Account account = accountDao.findAccount(EXISTING_ACCOUNT_NO);
    assertEquals(account, existingAccount);
}

@Test(expected = AccountNotFoundException.class)
public void findNotExistedAccount() {
    accountDao.findAccount(NEW_ACCOUNT_NO);
}
}
```

Creating Unit Tests for Dependent Classes Using Stubs and Mock Objects

Testing an independent class is easy, because you needn't consider how its dependencies work and how to set them up properly. However, testing a class that depends on results of other classes or services (e.g., database services and network services) would be a little bit difficult. For example, let's consider the following AccountService interface in the service layer:

```
package com.apress.springrecipes.bank;

public interface AccountService {

    public void createAccount(String accountNo);
    public void removeAccount(String accountNo);
```

```
    public void deposit(String accountNo, double amount);
    public void withdraw(String accountNo, double amount);
    public double getBalance(String accountNo);
}
```

The implementation of this service interface has to depend on an `AccountDao` object in the persistence layer to persist account objects. The `InsufficientBalanceException` class is also a subclass of `RuntimeException` that you have to create.

```
package com.apress.springrecipes.bank;

public class AccountServiceImpl implements AccountService {

    private AccountDao accountDao;

    public AccountServiceImpl(AccountDao accountDao) {
        this.accountDao = accountDao;
    }

    public void createAccount(String accountNo) {
        accountDao.createAccount(new Account(accountNo, 0));
    }

    public void removeAccount(String accountNo) {
        Account account = accountDao.findAccount(accountNo);
        accountDao.removeAccount(account);
    }

    public void deposit(String accountNo, double amount) {
        Account account = accountDao.findAccount(accountNo);
        account.setBalance(account.getBalance() + amount);
        accountDao.updateAccount(account);
    }

    public void withdraw(String accountNo, double amount) {
        Account account = accountDao.findAccount(accountNo);
        if (account.getBalance() < amount) {
            throw new InsufficientBalanceException();
        }
        account.setBalance(account.getBalance() - amount);
        accountDao.updateAccount(account);
    }

    public double getBalance(String accountNo) {
        return accountDao.findAccount(accountNo).getBalance();
    }
}
```

A common technique used in unit testing to reduce complexity caused by dependencies is using stubs. A stub must implement the same interface as the target object so that it can substitute for the target object. For example, you can create a stub for `AccountDao` that stores a single customer account and implements only the findAccount() and updateAccount() methods, as they are required for deposit() and withdraw():

```
package com.apress.springrecipes.bank;

import static org.junit.Assert.*;

import org.junit.Before;
import org.junit.Test;

public class AccountServiceImplStubTests {

    private static final String TEST_ACCOUNT_NO = "1234";
    private AccountDaoStub accountDaoStub;
    private AccountService accountService;

    private class AccountDaoStub implements AccountDao {

        private String accountNo;
        private double balance;

        public void createAccount(Account account) {}
        public void removeAccount(Account account) {}

        public Account findAccount(String accountNo) {
            return new Account(this.accountNo, this.balance);
        }

        public void updateAccount(Account account) {
            this.accountNo = account.getAccountNo();
            this.balance = account.getBalance();
        }
    }

    @Before
    public void init() {
        accountDaoStub = new AccountDaoStub();
        accountDaoStub.accountNo = TEST_ACCOUNT_NO;
        accountDaoStub.balance = 100;
        accountService = new AccountServiceImpl(accountDaoStub);
    }

    @Test
    public void deposit() {
        accountService.deposit(TEST_ACCOUNT_NO, 50);
        assertEquals(accountDaoStub.accountNo, TEST_ACCOUNT_NO);
        assertEquals(accountDaoStub.balance, 150, 0);
    }
```

```
    @Test
    public void withdrawWithSufficientBalance() {
        accountService.withdraw(TEST_ACCOUNT_NO, 50);
        assertEquals(accountDaoStub.accountNo, TEST_ACCOUNT_NO);
        assertEquals(accountDaoStub.balance, 50, 0);
    }

    @Test(expected = InsufficientBalanceException.class)
    public void withdrawWithInsufficientBalance() {
        accountService.withdraw(TEST_ACCOUNT_NO, 150);
    }
}
```

However, writing stubs yourself requires a lot of coding. A more efficient technique is to use mock objects. The EasyMock library is able to dynamically create mock objects that work in a record/playback mechanism.

■ **Note** To use EasyMock for testing, you have to add it to your CLASSPATH. If you are using Maven, add the following dependency to your project.

```
<dependency>
 <groupId>org.easymock</groupId>
 <artifactId>easymock</artifactId>
 <version>2.4</version>
</dependency>
```

```
package com.apress.springrecipes.bank;

import org.easymock.EasyMock;
import org.junit.Before;
import org.junit.Test;

public class AccountServiceImplMockTests {

    private static final String TEST_ACCOUNT_NO = "1234";
    private EasyMock easyMock;
    private AccountDao accountDao;
    private AccountService accountService;

    @Before
    public void init() {
```

```
        accountDao = easyMock.createMock(AccountDao.class) ;
        accountService = new AccountServiceImpl(accountDao);
    }

    @Test
    public void deposit() {
        Account account = new Account(TEST_ACCOUNT_NO, 100);
        accountDao.findAccount(TEST_ACCOUNT_NO);
        easyMock.expectLastCall().andReturn(account);
        account.setBalance(150);
        accountDao.updateAccount(account);
        easyMock.replay();

        accountService.deposit(TEST_ACCOUNT_NO, 50);
        easyMock.verify();
    }

    @Test
    public void withdrawWithSufficientBalance() {
        Account account = new Account(TEST_ACCOUNT_NO, 100);
        accountDao.findAccount(TEST_ACCOUNT_NO);
        easyMock.expectLastCall().andReturn(account);
        account.setBalance(50);
        accountDao.updateAccount(account);
        easyMock.replay();

        accountService.withdraw(TEST_ACCOUNT_NO, 50);
        easyMock.verify();
    }

    @Test(expected = InsufficientBalanceException.class)
    public void testWithdrawWithInsufficientBalance() {
        Account account = new Account(TEST_ACCOUNT_NO, 100);
        accountDao.findAccount(TEST_ACCOUNT_NO);
        easyMock.expectLastCall().andReturn(account);
        easyMock.replay();

        accountService.withdraw(TEST_ACCOUNT_NO, 150);
        easyMock.verify();
    }
}
```

With EasyMock, you can create a mock object dynamically for an arbitrary interface or class. Once created by EasyMock, a mock object is in the *record* state. Any method calls made to it will be recorded for future verification. During recording, you can also specify the value that you want to return for a method. After calling the **replay()** method, a mock object will be in the *replay* state. Any method calls then made to it will be verified against the recorded ones. Finally, you can call the **verify()** method to check if all the recorded method calls have been made completely. Finally, you can call the **reset()** method to reset a mock object so that it can be reused again. But since you create a new mock object in the method with @Before, which will be called before each test method, you have no need to reuse a mock object.

Creating Integration Tests

Integration tests are used to test several units in combination to ensure that the units are properly integrated and can interact correctly. For example, you can create an integration test to test AccountServiceImpl using InMemoryAccountDao as the DAO implementation:

```java
package com.apress.springrecipes.bank;

import static org.junit.Assert.*;

import org.junit.After;
import org.junit.Before;
import org.junit.Test;

public class AccountServiceTests {

    private static final String TEST_ACCOUNT_NO = "1234";
    private AccountService accountService;

    @Before
    public void init() {
        accountService = new AccountServiceImpl(new InMemoryAccountDao());
        accountService.createAccount(TEST_ACCOUNT_NO);
        accountService.deposit(TEST_ACCOUNT_NO, 100);
    }

    @Test
    public void deposit() {
        accountService.deposit(TEST_ACCOUNT_NO, 50);
        assertEquals(accountService.getBalance(TEST_ACCOUNT_NO), 150, 0);
    }

    @Test
    public void withDraw() {
        accountService.withdraw(TEST_ACCOUNT_NO, 50);
        assertEquals(accountService.getBalance(TEST_ACCOUNT_NO), 50, 0);
    }

    @After
    public void cleanup() {
        accountService.removeAccount(TEST_ACCOUNT_NO);
    }
}
```

13-3. Unit Testing Spring MVC Controllers

Problem

In a web application, you would like to test the web controllers developed with the Spring MVC framework.

Solution

A Spring MVC controller is invoked by `DispatcherServlet` with an HTTP request object and an HTTP response object. After processing a request, the controller returns it to `DispatcherServlet` for rendering the view. The main challenge of unit testing Spring MVC controllers, as well as web controllers in other web application frameworks, is simulating HTTP request objects and response objects in a unit testing environment. Fortunately, Spring supports web controller testing by providing a set of mock objects for the Servlet API (including `MockHttpServletRequest`, `MockHttpServletResponse`, and `MockHttpSession`).

To test a Spring MVC controller's output, you need to check if the object returned to `DispatcherServlet` is correct. Spring also provides a set of assertion utilities for checking the contents of an object.

How It Works

In your bank system, suppose you are going to develop a web interface for bank staff to input the account number and amount of a deposit. You create a controller named `DepositController` using the techniques you already know from Spring MVC:

```
package com.apress.springrecipes.bank;

import org.springframework.beans.factory.annotation.Autowired;
import org.springframework.stereotype.Controller;
import org.springframework.ui.ModelMap;
import org.springframework.web.bind.annotation.RequestMapping;
import org.springframework.web.bind.annotation.RequestParam;

@Controller
public class DepositController {

    private AccountService accountService;

    @Autowired
    public DepositController(AccountService accountService) {
        this.accountService = accountService;
    }
```

```
@RequestMapping("/deposit.do")
protected String deposit(
        @RequestParam("accountNo") String accountNo,
        @RequestParam("amount") double amount,
        ModelMap model) {
    accountService.deposit(accountNo, amount);
    model.addAttribute("accountNo", accountNo);
    model.addAttribute("balance", accountService.getBalance(accountNo));
    return "success";
}
}
```

Because this controller doesn't deal with the Servlet API, testing it is very easy. You can test it just like a simple Java class:

```
package com.apress.springrecipes.bank;

import static org.junit.Assert.*;

import org.easymock.MockControl;
import org.junit.Before;
import org.junit.Test;
import org.springframework.ui.ModelMap;

public class DepositControllerTests {

    private static final String TEST_ACCOUNT_NO = "1234";
    private static final double TEST_AMOUNT = 50;
    private MockControl mockControl;
    private AccountService accountService;
    private DepositController depositController;

    @Before
    public void init() {
        mockControl = MockControl.createControl(AccountService.class);
        accountService = (AccountService) mockControl.getMock();
        depositController = new DepositController(accountService);
    }

    @Test
    public void deposit() {
        accountService.deposit(TEST_ACCOUNT_NO, 50);
        accountService.getBalance(TEST_ACCOUNT_NO);
        mockControl.setReturnValue(150.0);
        mockControl.replay();
```

```
        ModelMap model = new ModelMap();
        String viewName =
            depositController.deposit(TEST_ACCOUNT_NO, TEST_AMOUNT, model);
        mockControl.verify();

        assertEquals(viewName, "success");
        assertEquals(model.get("accountNo"), TEST_ACCOUNT_NO);
        assertEquals(model.get("balance"), 150.0);
    }
}
```

13-4. Managing Application Contexts in Integration Tests

Problem

When creating integration tests for a Spring application, you have to access beans declared in the application context. Without Spring's testing support, you have to load the application context manually in an initialization method of your tests, such as `setUp()` in JUnit 3, or a method with `@Before` or `@BeforeClass` in JUnit 4. However, as an initialization method is called before each test method or test class, the same application context may be reloaded many times. In a large application with many beans, loading an application context may require a lot of time, which causes your tests to run slowly.

Solution

Spring's testing support facilities can help you manage the application context for your tests, including loading it from one or more bean configuration files and caching it across multiple test executions. An application context will be cached across all tests within a single JVM, using the configuration file locations as the key. As a result, your tests can run much faster without reloading the same application context many times.

With Spring's JUnit 3 legacy support in releases prior to 2.5, your test class can extend the `AbstractSingleSpringContextTests` base class to access the managed application context through the inherited `getApplicationContext()` method.

Starting from Spring 2.5, the TestContext framework provides two test execution listeners related to context management. They will be registered with a test context manager by default if you don't specify your own explicitly.

- `DependencyInjectionTestExecutionListener`: This injects dependencies, including the managed application context, into your tests.

- `DirtiesContextTestExecutionListener`: This handles the `@DirtiesContext` annotation and reloads the application context when necessary.

To have the TestContext framework manage the application context, your test class has to integrate with a test context manager internally. For your convenience, the TestContext framework provides support classes that do this, as shown in Table 13-1. These classes integrate with a test context manager and implement the `ApplicationContextAware` interface, so they can provide access to the managed application context through the protected field `applicationContext`. Your test class can simply extend the corresponding TestContext support class for your testing framework.

Table 13-1. *TestContext Support Classes for Context Management*

Testing Framework	TestContext Support Class*
JUnit 3	`AbstractJUnit38SpringContextTests`
JUnit 4	`AbstractJUnit4SpringContextTests`
TestNG	`AbstractTestNGSpringContextTests`

* These three TestContext support classes have only `DependencyInjectionTestExecutionListener` and `DirtiesContextTestExecutionListener` enabled.

If you are using JUnit 4 or TestNG, you can integrate your test class with a test context manager by yourself and implement the `ApplicationContextAware` interface directly, without extending a TestContext support class. In this way, your test class doesn't bind to the TestContext framework class hierarchy, so you can extend your own base class. In JUnit 4, you can simply run your test with the test runner `SpringJUnit4ClassRunner` to have a test context manager integrated. However, in TestNG, you have to integrate with a test context manager manually.

How It Works

First, let's declare an `AccountService` instance and an `AccountDao` instance in the bean configuration file (e.g., `beans.xml`) as follows. Later, you will create integration tests for them.

```
<beans xmlns="http://www.springframework.org/schema/beans"
    xmlns:xsi="http://www.w3.org/2001/XMLSchema-instance"
    xsi:schemaLocation="http://www.springframework.org/schema/beans
        http://www.springframework.org/schema/beans/spring-beans-3.0.xsd">

    <bean id="accountDao"
        class="com.apress.springrecipes.bank.InMemoryAccountDao" />

    <bean id="accountService"
        class="com.apress.springrecipes.bank.AccountServiceImpl">
        <constructor-arg ref="accountDao" />
    </bean>
</beans>
```

Accessing the Context with JUnit 3 Legacy Support

When using Spring's JUnit 3 legacy support to create tests, your test class can extend `AbstractSingleSpringContextTests` to access the managed application context:

```
package com.apress.springrecipes.bank;

import org.springframework.test.AbstractSingleSpringContextTests;

public class AccountServiceJUnit38LegacyTests extends
        AbstractSingleSpringContextTests {

    private static final String TEST_ACCOUNT_NO = "1234";
    private AccountService accountService;

    protected String[] getConfigLocations() {
        return new String[] { "beans.xml" };
    }

    protected void onSetUp() throws Exception {
        accountService =
            (AccountService) getApplicationContext().getBean("accountService");
        accountService.createAccount(TEST_ACCOUNT_NO);
        accountService.deposit(TEST_ACCOUNT_NO, 100);
    }

    public void testDeposit() {
        accountService.deposit(TEST_ACCOUNT_NO, 50);
        assertEquals(accountService.getBalance(TEST_ACCOUNT_NO), 150.0);
    }

    public void testWithDraw() {
        accountService.withdraw(TEST_ACCOUNT_NO, 50);
        assertEquals(accountService.getBalance(TEST_ACCOUNT_NO), 50.0);
    }

    protected void onTearDown() throws Exception {
        accountService.removeAccount(TEST_ACCOUNT_NO);
    }
}
```

In this class, you can override the getConfigLocations() method to return a list of bean
configuration file locations, which are classpath locations relative to the root by default, but they
support Spring's resource prefixes (e.g., file and classpath). Alternatively, you can override the
getConfigPath() method or the getConfigPaths() method to return one or more bean configuration file
paths, which can be absolute classpath locations starting with a slash, or paths relative to the package of
the current test class.

By default, the application context will be cached and reused for each test method once loaded for
the first time. However, in some cases, such as when you have modified the bean configurations or
changed a bean's state in a test method, you have to reload the application context. You can call the
setDirty() method to indicate that the application context is dirty so that it will be reloaded
automatically for the next test method.

Finally, note that you cannot override the setUp() and tearDown() methods of the base class, since
they are declared as final. To perform initialization and cleanup tasks, you have to override the
onSetUp() and onTearDown() methods instead, which will be called by the parent's setUp() and
tearDown() methods.

Accessing the Context with the TestContext Framework in JUnit 4

If you are using JUnit 4 to create tests with the TestContext framework, you will have two options to access the managed application context. The first option is by implementing the ApplicationContextAware interface. For this option, you have to explicitly specify a Spring-specific test runner for running your test—SpringJUnit4ClassRunner. You can specify this in the @RunWith annotation at the class level.

```java
package com.apress.springrecipes.bank;

import static org.junit.Assert.*;

import org.junit.After;
import org.junit.Before;
import org.junit.Test;
import org.junit.runner.RunWith;
import org.springframework.context.ApplicationContext;
import org.springframework.context.ApplicationContextAware;
import org.springframework.test.context.ContextConfiguration;
import org.springframework.test.context.junit4.SpringJUnit4ClassRunner;

@RunWith(SpringJUnit4ClassRunner.class)
@ContextConfiguration(locations = "/beans.xml")
public class AccountServiceJUnit4ContextTests implements ApplicationContextAware {

    private static final String TEST_ACCOUNT_NO = "1234";
    private ApplicationContext applicationContext;
    private AccountService accountService;

    public void setApplicationContext(ApplicationContext applicationContext) {
        this.applicationContext = applicationContext;
    }

    @Before
    public void init() {
        accountService =
            (AccountService) applicationContext.getBean("accountService");
        accountService.createAccount(TEST_ACCOUNT_NO);
        accountService.deposit(TEST_ACCOUNT_NO, 100);
    }

    @Test
    public void deposit() {
        accountService.deposit(TEST_ACCOUNT_NO, 50);
        assertEquals(accountService.getBalance(TEST_ACCOUNT_NO), 150, 0);
    }
```

```
    @Test
    public void withDraw() {
        accountService.withdraw(TEST_ACCOUNT_NO, 50);
        assertEquals(accountService.getBalance(TEST_ACCOUNT_NO), 50, 0);
    }

    @After
    public void cleanup() {
        accountService.removeAccount(TEST_ACCOUNT_NO);
    }
}
```

You can specify the bean configuration file locations in the `locations` attribute of the `@ContextConfiguration` annotation at the class level. These locations are classpath locations relative to the test class by default, but they support Spring's resource prefixes. If you don't specify this attribute explicitly, the TestContext framework will load the file by joining the test class name with `-context.xml` as the suffix (i.e., `AccountServiceJUnit4Tests-context.xml`) from the same package as the test class.

By default, the application context will be cached and reused for each test method, but if you want it to be reloaded after a particular test method, you can annotate the test method with the `@DirtiesContext` annotation so that the application context will be reloaded for the next test method.

The second option to access the managed application context is by extending the TestContext support class specific to JUnit 4: `AbstractJUnit4SpringContextTests`. This class implements the `ApplicationContextAware` interface, so you can extend it to get access to the managed application context via the protected field `applicationContext`. However, you first have to delete the private field `applicationContext` and its setter method. Note that if you extend this support class, you don't need to specify `SpringJUnit4ClassRunner` in the `@RunWith` annotation, because this annotation is inherited from the parent.

```
package com.apress.springrecipes.bank;
...
import org.springframework.test.context.ContextConfiguration;
import org.springframework.test.context.junit4.AbstractJUnit4SpringContextTests;

@ContextConfiguration(locations = "/beans.xml")
public class AccountServiceJUnit4ContextTests extends
        AbstractJUnit4SpringContextTests {

    private static final String TEST_ACCOUNT_NO = "1234";
    private AccountService accountService;

    @Before
    public void init() {
        accountService =
            (AccountService) applicationContext.getBean("accountService");
        accountService.createAccount(TEST_ACCOUNT_NO);
        accountService.deposit(TEST_ACCOUNT_NO, 100);
    }
    ...
}
```

Accessing the Context with the TestContext Framework in JUnit 3

If you want to access the managed application context with the TestContext framework in JUnit 3, you must extend the TestContext support class AbstractJUnit38SpringContextTests. This class implements the ApplicationContextAware interface, so you can get access to the managed application context via the protected field applicationContext.

```
package com.apress.springrecipes.bank;

import org.springframework.test.context.ContextConfiguration;
import org.springframework.test.context.junit38.AbstractJUnit38SpringContextTests;

@ContextConfiguration(locations = "/beans.xml")
public class AccountServiceJUnit38ContextTests extends
        AbstractJUnit38SpringContextTests {

    private static final String TEST_ACCOUNT_NO = "1234";
    private AccountService accountService;

    protected void setUp() throws Exception {
        accountService =
            (AccountService) applicationContext.getBean("accountService");
        accountService.createAccount(TEST_ACCOUNT_NO);
        accountService.deposit(TEST_ACCOUNT_NO, 100);
    }

    public void testDeposit() {
        accountService.deposit(TEST_ACCOUNT_NO, 50);
        assertEquals(accountService.getBalance(TEST_ACCOUNT_NO), 150.0);
    }

    public void testWithDraw() {
        accountService.withdraw(TEST_ACCOUNT_NO, 50);
        assertEquals(accountService.getBalance(TEST_ACCOUNT_NO), 50.0);
    }

    protected void tearDown() throws Exception {
        accountService.removeAccount(TEST_ACCOUNT_NO);
    }
}
```

Accessing the Context with the TestContext Framework in TestNG

To access the managed application context with the TestContext framework in TestNG, you can extend the TestContext support class AbstractTestNGSpringContextTests. This class also implements the ApplicationContextAware interface.

```
package com.apress.springrecipes.bank;

import static org.testng.Assert.*;

import org.springframework.test.context.ContextConfiguration;
import org.springframework.test.context.testng.AbstractTestNGSpringContextTests;
import org.testng.annotations.AfterMethod;
import org.testng.annotations.BeforeMethod;
import org.testng.annotations.Test;

@ContextConfiguration(locations = "/beans.xml")
public class AccountServiceTestNGContextTests extends
        AbstractTestNGSpringContextTests {

    private static final String TEST_ACCOUNT_NO = "1234";
    private AccountService accountService;

    @BeforeMethod
    public void init() {
        accountService =
            (AccountService) applicationContext.getBean("accountService");
        accountService.createAccount(TEST_ACCOUNT_NO);
        accountService.deposit(TEST_ACCOUNT_NO, 100);
    }

    @Test
    public void deposit() {
        accountService.deposit(TEST_ACCOUNT_NO, 50);
        assertEquals(accountService.getBalance(TEST_ACCOUNT_NO), 150, 0);
    }

    @Test
    public void withDraw() {
        accountService.withdraw(TEST_ACCOUNT_NO, 50);
        assertEquals(accountService.getBalance(TEST_ACCOUNT_NO), 50, 0);
    }

    @AfterMethod
    public void cleanup() {
        accountService.removeAccount(TEST_ACCOUNT_NO);
    }
}
```

If you don't want your TestNG test class to extend a TestContext support class, you can implement the ApplicationContextAware interface just as you did for JUnit 4.4. However, you have to integrate with a test context manager by yourself. Please refer to the source code of AbstractTestNGSpringContextTests for details.

13-5. Injecting Test Fixtures into Integration Tests

Problem

The test fixtures of an integration test for a Spring application are mostly beans declared in the application context. You might wish to have the test fixtures automatically injected by Spring via dependency injection, which saves you the trouble of retrieving them from the application context manually.

Solution

Spring's testing support facilities can inject beans automatically from the managed application context into your tests as test fixtures.

When using Spring's JUnit 3 legacy support in releases prior to 2.5, your test class can extend the `AbstractDependencyInjectionSpringContextTests` base class, which is a subclass of `AbstractSingleSpringContextTests`, to have its test fixtures injected automatically. This class supports two ways of performing dependency injection. The first auto-wires beans by type via setter methods. The second auto-wires beans by name via protected fields.

Starting in Spring 2.5's TestContext framework, `DependencyInjectionTestExecutionListener` can automatically inject dependencies into your tests. If you have this listener registered, you can simply annotate a setter method or field of your test with Spring's `@Autowired` annotation or JSR-250's `@Resource` annotation to have a fixture injected automatically. For `@Autowired`, the fixture will be injected by type, and for `@Resource`, it will be injected by name.

How It Works

Injecting Test Fixtures with JUnit 3 Legacy Support

When using Spring's JUnit 3 legacy support to create tests, your test class can extend `AbstractDependencyInjectionSpringContextTests` to have its test fixtures injected from beans in the managed application context. You can define a setter method for the fixture you want to be injected.

```
package com.apress.springrecipes.bank;

import org.springframework.test.AbstractDependencyInjectionSpringContextTests;

public class AccountServiceJUnit38LegacyTests extends
        AbstractDependencyInjectionSpringContextTests {

    private AccountService accountService;
    private static final String TEST_ACCOUNT_NO = "1234";

    public void setAccountService(AccountService accountService) {
        this.accountService = accountService;
    }
```

```
    protected void onSetUp() throws Exception {
        accountService.createAccount(TEST_ACCOUNT_NO);
        accountService.deposit(TEST_ACCOUNT_NO, 100);
    }
    ...
}
```

The `AbstractDependencyInjectionSpringContextTests` class you extend is a subclass of `AbstractSingleSpringContextTests`, so it also manages an application context loaded from your bean configuration files specified in the `getConfigLocations()` method. By default, this class uses auto-wiring by type to inject beans from the application context. However, if there's more than one bean of the target type in the application context, this auto-wiring will not work. In this case, you have to look up the bean explicitly from the application context retrieved from `getApplicationContext()` and remove the setter method that causes ambiguity.

Another method of injecting test fixtures using JUnit 3 legacy support is via protected fields. To make this work, you must enable the `populateProtectedVariables` property in a constructor. In this case, you needn't provide a setter method for each field that you want to be injected.

```
package com.apress.springrecipes.bank;

import org.springframework.test.AbstractDependencyInjectionSpringContextTests;

public class AccountServiceJUnit38LegacyTests extends
        AbstractDependencyInjectionSpringContextTests {

    protected AccountService accountService;

    public AccountServiceJUnit38LegacyTests() {
        setPopulateProtectedVariables(true);
    }
    ...
}
```

This protected field's name will be used to look up a bean with the same name from the managed application context.

Injecting Test Fixtures with the TestContext Framework in JUnit 4

When using the TestContext framework to create tests, you can have their test fixtures injected from the managed application context by annotating a field or setter method with the `@Autowired` or `@Resource` annotations. In JUnit 4, you can specify `SpringJUnit4ClassRunner` as your test runner without extending a support class.

```
package com.apress.springrecipes.bank;
...
import org.springframework.beans.factory.annotation.Autowired;
import org.springframework.test.context.ContextConfiguration;
import org.springframework.test.context.junit4.SpringJUnit4ClassRunner;
```

```
@RunWith(SpringJUnit4ClassRunner.class)
@ContextConfiguration(locations = "/beans.xml")
public class AccountServiceJUnit4ContextTests {

    private static final String TEST_ACCOUNT_NO = "1234";

    @Autowired
    private AccountService accountService;

    @Before
    public void init() {
        accountService.createAccount(TEST_ACCOUNT_NO);
        accountService.deposit(TEST_ACCOUNT_NO, 100);
    }
    ...
}
```

If you annotate a field or setter method of a test with @Autowired, it will be injected using auto-wiring by type. You can further specify a candidate bean for auto-wiring by providing its name in the @Qualifier annotation. However, if you want a field or setter method to be auto-wired by name, you can annotate it with @Resource.

By extending the TestContext support class AbstractJUnit4SpringContextTests, you can also have test fixtures injected from the managed application context. In this case, you don't need to specify SpringJUnit4ClassRunner for your test, as it is inherited from the parent.

```
package com.apress.springrecipes.bank;
...
import org.springframework.beans.factory.annotation.Autowired;
import org.springframework.test.context.ContextConfiguration;
import org.springframework.test.context.junit4.AbstractJUnit4SpringContextTests;

@ContextConfiguration(locations = "/beans.xml")
public class AccountServiceJUnit4ContextTests extends
        AbstractJUnit4SpringContextTests {

    private static final String TEST_ACCOUNT_NO = "1234";

    @Autowired
    private AccountService accountService;
    ...
}
```

Injecting Test Fixtures with the TestContext Framework in JUnit 3

In JUnit 3, you can also use the TestContext framework to create tests with the same test fixture–injection approach. However, your test class has to extend the TestContext support class AbstractJUnit38SpringContextTests.

```
package com.apress.springrecipes.bank;

import org.springframework.beans.factory.annotation.Autowired;
import org.springframework.test.context.ContextConfiguration;
import org.springframework.test.context.junit38.AbstractJUnit38SpringContextTests;

@ContextConfiguration(locations = "/beans.xml")
public class AccountServiceJUnit38ContextTests extends
        AbstractJUnit38SpringContextTests {

    private static final String TEST_ACCOUNT_NO = "1234";

    @Autowired
    private AccountService accountService;

    protected void setUp() throws Exception {
        accountService.createAccount(TEST_ACCOUNT_NO);
        accountService.deposit(TEST_ACCOUNT_NO, 100);
    }
    ...
}
```

Injecting Test Fixtures with the TestContext Framework in TestNG

In TestNG, you can extend the TestContext support class `AbstractTestNGSpringContextTests` to have test fixtures injected from the managed application context:

```
package com.apress.springrecipes.bank;
...
import org.springframework.beans.factory.annotation.Autowired;
import org.springframework.test.context.ContextConfiguration;
import org.springframework.test.context.testng.AbstractTestNGSpringContextTests;

@ContextConfiguration(locations = "/beans.xml")
public class AccountServiceTestNGContextTests extends
        AbstractTestNGSpringContextTests {

    private static final String TEST_ACCOUNT_NO = "1234";

    @Autowired
    private AccountService accountService;

    @BeforeMethod
    public void init() {
        accountService.createAccount(TEST_ACCOUNT_NO);
        accountService.deposit(TEST_ACCOUNT_NO, 100);
    }
    ...
}
```

13-6. Managing Transactions in Integration Tests

Problem

When creating integration tests for an application that accesses a database, you usually prepare the test data in the initialization method. After each test method runs, it may have modified the data in the database. So, you have to clean up the database to ensure that the next test method will run from a consistent state. As a result, you have to develop many database cleanup tasks.

Solution

Spring's testing support facilities can create and roll back a transaction for each test method, so the changes you make in a test method won't affect the next one. This can also save you the trouble of developing cleanup tasks to clean up the database.

When using Spring's JUnit 3 legacy support in releases prior to 2.5, your test class can extend the `AbstractTransactionalSpringContextTests` base class, which is a subclass of `AbstractDependencyInjectionSpringContextTests`, to create and roll back a transaction for each test method. This class requires a transaction manager to be configured properly in the bean configuration file.

Starting from Spring 2.5, the TestContext framework provides a test execution listener related to transaction management. It will be registered with a test context manager by default if you don't specify your own explicitly.

- `TransactionalTestExecutionListener`: This handles the `@Transactional` annotation at the class or method level and has the methods run within transactions automatically.

Your test class can extend the corresponding TestContext support class for your testing framework, as shown in Table 13-2, to have its test methods run within transactions. These classes integrate with a test context manager and have `@Transactional` enabled at the class level. Note that a transaction manager is also required in the bean configuration file.

Table 13-2. TestContext Support Classes for Transaction Management

Testing Framework	TestContext Support Class*
JUnit 3	`AbstractTransactionalJUnit38SpringContextTests`
JUnit 4	`AbstractTransactionalJUnit4SpringContextTests`
TestNG	`AbstractTransactionalTestNGSpringContextTests`

* These three TestContext support classes have `TransactionalTestExecutionListener` enabled in addition to `DependencyInjectionTestExecutionListener` and `DirtiesContextTestExecutionListener`.

In JUnit 4 and TestNG, you can simply annotate @Transactional at the class level or the method level to have the test methods run within transactions, without extending a TestContext support class. However, to integrate with a test context manager, you have to run the JUnit 4 test with the test runner SpringJUnit4ClassRunner, and you have to do it manually for a TestNG test.

How It Works

Let's consider storing your bank system's accounts in a relational database. You can choose any JDBC-compliant database engine that supports transactions and then execute the following SQL statement on it to create the ACCOUNT table. Here, we have chosen Apache Derby as our database engine and created the table in the bank instance.

```
CREATE TABLE ACCOUNT (
    ACCOUNT_NO    VARCHAR(10)    NOT NULL,
    BALANCE       DOUBLE         NOT NULL,
    PRIMARY KEY (ACCOUNT_NO)
);
```

Next, you create a new DAO implementation that uses JDBC to access the database. You can take advantage of SimpleJdbcTemplate to simplify your operations.

```
package com.apress.springrecipes.bank;

import org.springframework.jdbc.core.simple.SimpleJdbcDaoSupport;

public class JdbcAccountDao extends SimpleJdbcDaoSupport implements AccountDao {

    public void createAccount(Account account) {
        String sql = "INSERT INTO ACCOUNT (ACCOUNT_NO, BALANCE) VALUES (?, ?)";
        getSimpleJdbcTemplate().update(
                sql, account.getAccountNo(), account.getBalance());
    }

    public void updateAccount(Account account) {
        String sql = "UPDATE ACCOUNT SET BALANCE = ? WHERE ACCOUNT_NO = ?";
        getSimpleJdbcTemplate().update(
                sql, account.getBalance(), account.getAccountNo());
    }

    public void removeAccount(Account account) {
        String sql = "DELETE FROM ACCOUNT WHERE ACCOUNT_NO = ?";
        getSimpleJdbcTemplate().update(sql, account.getAccountNo());
    }
```

```
    public Account findAccount(String accountNo) {
        String sql = "SELECT BALANCE FROM ACCOUNT WHERE ACCOUNT_NO = ?";
        double balance = getSimpleJdbcTemplate().queryForObject(
                sql, Double.class, accountNo);
        return new Account(accountNo, balance);
    }
}
```

Before you create integration tests to test the `AccountService` instance that uses this DAO to persist account objects, you have to replace `InMemoryAccountDao` with this DAO in the bean configuration file, and configure the target data source as well.

■ **Note** To access a database running on the Derby server, you have to add the client library to the CLASSPATH of your application. If you are using Maven, add the following dependency to your project.

```
<dependency>
 <groupId>org.apache.derby</groupId>
 <artifactId>derbyclient</artifactId>
 <version>10.4.2.0</version>
</dependency>
```

```
<beans ...>
    <bean id="dataSource"
        class="org.springframework.jdbc.datasource.DriverManagerDataSource">
        <property name="driverClassName"
            value="org.apache.derby.jdbc.ClientDriver" />
        <property name="url"
            value="jdbc:derby://localhost:1527/bank;create=true" />
        <property name="username" value="app" />
        <property name="password" value="app" />
    </bean>

    <bean id="accountDao"
        class="com.apress.springrecipes.bank.JdbcAccountDao">
        <property name="dataSource" ref="dataSource" />
    </bean>
    ...
</beans>
```

Managing Transactions with JUnit 3 Legacy Support

When using Spring's JUnit 3 legacy support to create tests, your test class can extend `AbstractTransactionalSpringContextTests` to have its test methods run within transactions:

```
package com.apress.springrecipes.bank;

import org.springframework.test.AbstractTransactionalDataSourceSpringContextTests;

public class AccountServiceJUnit38LegacyTests extends
        AbstractTransactionalSpringContextTests {

    private AccountService accountService;
    private static final String TEST_ACCOUNT_NO = "1234";

    public void setAccountService(AccountService accountService) {
        this.accountService = accountService;
    }

    protected void onSetUpInTransaction() throws Exception {
        executeSqlScript("classpath:/bank.sql",true);
        accountService.createAccount(TEST_ACCOUNT_NO);
        accountService.deposit(TEST_ACCOUNT_NO, 100);
    }

    // Don't need onTearDown() any more
    ...
}
```

By default, each test method will run within a transaction that will be rolled back at the end of this method. So, you needn't perform database cleanup tasks in the onTearDown() method, and therefore you can simply delete it. Note that the data preparation tasks must be performed in the onSetUpInTransaction() method—not onSetUp()—to have them run within the same transactions as test methods, which will be rolled back at the end. This is why the executeSqlScript method is invoked in this same method, since it will call the script bank.sql to create the necessary database table (i.e., the ACCOUNT table) to ensure the database is equipped to run each test.

However, if you would like a transaction to commit at the end of a test method, you can call the setComplete() method explicitly to cause it to commit instead of rolling back. Also, you can end a transaction during a test method by calling the endTransaction() method, which causes a transaction to roll back normally, or commit if you have called setComplete() before.

This class requires a transaction manager to be configured in the bean configuration file. By default, it looks for a bean whose type is PlatformTransactionManager and uses this bean to manage transactions for your test methods.

```
<bean id="transactionManager"
    class="org.springframework.jdbc.datasource.DataSourceTransactionManager">
    <property name="dataSource" ref="dataSource" />
</bean>
```

Managing Transactions with the TestContext Framework in JUnit 4

When using the TestContext framework to create tests, you can have the tests' methods run within transactions by annotating @Transactional at the class or method level. In JUnit 4, you can specify SpringJUnit4ClassRunner for your test class so that it doesn't need to extend a support class.

```
package com.apress.springrecipes.bank;
...
import org.springframework.beans.factory.annotation.Autowired;
import org.springframework.test.context.ContextConfiguration;
import org.springframework.test.context.junit4.SpringJUnit4ClassRunner;
import org.springframework.transaction.annotation.Transactional;

@RunWith(SpringJUnit4ClassRunner.class)
@ContextConfiguration(locations = "/beans.xml")
@Transactional
public class AccountServiceJUnit4ContextTests {

    private static final String TEST_ACCOUNT_NO = "1234";

    @Autowired
    private AccountService accountService;

    @Before
    public void init() {
        executeSqlScript("classpath:/bank.sql",true);
        accountService.createAccount(TEST_ACCOUNT_NO);
        accountService.deposit(TEST_ACCOUNT_NO, 100);
    }

    // Don't need cleanup() anymore
    ...
}
```

If you annotate a test class with @Transactional, all of its test methods will run within transactions. If you would like a particular method not to run within a transaction, you can annotate it with @NotTransactional. An alternative is to annotate individual methods with @Transactional, not the entire class.

By default, transactions for test methods will be rolled back at the end. You can alter this behavior by disabling the defaultRollback attribute of @TransactionConfiguration, which should be applied to the class level. Also, you can override this class-level rollback behavior at the method level with the @Rollback annotation, which requires a Boolean value.

Note that methods with the @Before or @After annotation will be executed within the same transactions as test methods. If you have methods that need to perform initialization or cleanup tasks before or after a transaction, you have to annotate them with @BeforeTransaction or @AfterTransaction. Notice that these methods will not be executed for test methods annotated with @NotTransactional.

Finally, you also need a transaction manager configured in the bean configuration file. By default, a bean whose type is PlatformTransactionManager will be used, but you can specify another one in the transactionManager attribute of the @TransactionConfiguration annotation by giving its name.

```
<bean id="transactionManager"
    class="org.springframework.jdbc.datasource.DataSourceTransactionManager">
    <property name="dataSource" ref="dataSource" />
</bean>
```

In JUnit 4, an alternative to managing transactions for test methods is to extend the transactional TestContext support class `AbstractTransactionalJUnit4SpringContextTests`, which has `@Transactional` enabled at the class level so that you don't need to enable it again. By extending this support class, you don't need to specify `SpringJUnit4ClassRunner` for your test, as it is inherited from the parent.

```
package com.apress.springrecipes.bank;
...
import org.springframework.test.context.ContextConfiguration;
import org.springframework.test.context.junit4.~CCC
        AbstractTransactionalJUnit4SpringContextTests;

@ContextConfiguration(locations = "/beans.xml")
public class AccountServiceJUnit4ContextTests extends
        AbstractTransactionalJUnit4SpringContextTests {
    ...
}
```

Managing Transactions with the TestContext Framework in JUnit 3

In JUnit 3, you can also use the TestContext framework to create tests that run within transactions. However, your test class has to extend the corresponding TestContext support class `AbstractTransactionalJUnit38SpringContextTests`.

```
package com.apress.springrecipes.bank;

import org.springframework.beans.factory.annotation.Autowired;
import org.springframework.test.context.ContextConfiguration;
import org.springframework.test.context.junit38.~CCC
        AbstractTransactionalJUnit38SpringContextTests;

@ContextConfiguration(locations = "/beans.xml")
public class AccountServiceJUnit38ContextTests extends
        AbstractTransactionalJUnit38SpringContextTests {

    private static final String TEST_ACCOUNT_NO = "1234";

    @Autowired
    private AccountService accountService;

    protected void setUp() throws Exception {
        executeSqlScript("classpath:/bank.sql",true);
        accountService.createAccount(TEST_ACCOUNT_NO);
        accountService.deposit(TEST_ACCOUNT_NO, 100);
    }

    // Don't need tearDown() anymore
    ...
}
```

Managing Transactions with the TestContext Framework in TestNG

To create TestNG tests that run within transactions, your test class can extend the TestContext support class `AbstractTransactionalTestNGSpringContextTests` to have its methods run within transactions:

```
package com.apress.springrecipes.bank;
...
import org.springframework.beans.factory.annotation.Autowired;
import org.springframework.test.context.ContextConfiguration;
import org.springframework.test.context.testng.~CCC
        AbstractTransactionalTestNGSpringContextTests;

@ContextConfiguration(locations = "/beans.xml")
public class AccountServiceTestNGContextTests extends
        AbstractTransactionalTestNGSpringContextTests {

    private static final String TEST_ACCOUNT_NO = "1234";

    @Autowired
    private AccountService accountService;

    @BeforeMethod
    public void init() {
        executeSqlScript("classpath:/bank.sql",true);
        accountService.createAccount(TEST_ACCOUNT_NO);
        accountService.deposit(TEST_ACCOUNT_NO, 100);
    }

    // Don't need cleanup() anymore
    ...
}
```

13-7. Accessing a Database in Integration Tests

Problem

When creating integration tests for an application that accesses a database, especially one developed with an ORM framework, you might wish to access the database directly to prepare test data and validate the data after a test method runs.

Solution

Spring's testing support facilities can create and provide a JDBC template for you to perform database-related tasks in your tests.

When using Spring's JUnit 3 legacy support in releases prior to 2.5, your test class can extend the AbstractTransactionalDataSourceSpringContextTests base class, which is a subclass of AbstractTransactionalDataSourceSpringContextTests, to access the precreated JdbcTemplate instance via the getJdbcTemplate() method. This class requires a data source and a transaction manager to be configured properly in the bean configuration file.

Starting in Spring 2.5's TestContext framework, your test class can extend one of the transactional TestContext support classes to access the precreated SimpleJdbcTemplate instance. These classes also require a data source and a transaction manager in the bean configuration file.

How It Works

Accessing a Database with JUnit 3 Legacy Support

When creating tests with Spring's JUnit 3 legacy support, your test class can extend AbstractTransactionalDataSourceSpringContextTests to use a JdbcTemplate instance through the getJdbcTemplate() method to prepare and validate test data:

```
package com.apress.springrecipes.bank;

import org.springframework.test.AbstractTransactionalDataSourceSpringContextTests;

public class AccountServiceJUnit38LegacyTests extends
        AbstractTransactionalDataSourceSpringContextTests {
    ...
    protected void onSetUpInTransaction() throws Exception {
        executeSqlScript("classpath:/bank.sql",true);
        getJdbcTemplate().update(
                "INSERT INTO ACCOUNT (ACCOUNT_NO, BALANCE) VALUES (?, ?)",
                new Object[] { TEST_ACCOUNT_NO, 100 });
    }

    public void testDeposit() {
        accountService.deposit(TEST_ACCOUNT_NO, 50);
        double balance = (Double) getJdbcTemplate().queryForObject(
                "SELECT BALANCE FROM ACCOUNT WHERE ACCOUNT_NO = ?",
                new Object[] { TEST_ACCOUNT_NO }, Double.class);
        assertEquals(balance, 150.0);
    }

    public void testWithDraw() {
        accountService.withdraw(TEST_ACCOUNT_NO, 50);
        double balance = (Double) getJdbcTemplate().queryForObject(
                "SELECT BALANCE FROM ACCOUNT WHERE ACCOUNT_NO = ?",
                new Object[] { TEST_ACCOUNT_NO }, Double.class);
        assertEquals(balance, 50.0);
    }
}
```

In addition to the getJdbcTemplate() method, this class offers convenient methods for you to count the number of rows in a table, delete rows from a table, and execute a SQL script. Please refer to the Javadoc of this class for details.

Accessing a Database with the TestContext Framework

When using the TestContext framework to create tests, you can extend the corresponding TestContext support class to use a SimpleJdbcTemplate instance via a protected field. For JUnit 4, this class is AbstractTransactionalJUnit4SpringContextTests, which provides similar convenient methods for you to count the number of rows in a table, delete rows from a table, and execute a SQL script:

```
package com.apress.springrecipes.bank;
...
import org.springframework.test.context.ContextConfiguration;
import org.springframework.test.context.junit4.~CCC
        AbstractTransactionalJUnit4SpringContextTests;

@ContextConfiguration(locations = "/beans.xml")
public class AccountServiceJUnit4ContextTests extends
        AbstractTransactionalJUnit4SpringContextTests {
    ...
    @Before
    public void init() {
        executeSqlScript("classpath:/bank.sql",true);
        simpleJdbcTemplate.update(
                "INSERT INTO ACCOUNT (ACCOUNT_NO, BALANCE) VALUES (?, ?)",
                TEST_ACCOUNT_NO, 100);
    }

    @Test
    public void deposit() {
        accountService.deposit(TEST_ACCOUNT_NO, 50);
        double balance = simpleJdbcTemplate.queryForObject(
                "SELECT BALANCE FROM ACCOUNT WHERE ACCOUNT_NO = ?",
                Double.class, TEST_ACCOUNT_NO);
        assertEquals(balance, 150.0, 0);
    }

    @Test
    public void withDraw() {
        accountService.withdraw(TEST_ACCOUNT_NO, 50);
        double balance = simpleJdbcTemplate.queryForObject(
                "SELECT BALANCE FROM ACCOUNT WHERE ACCOUNT_NO = ?",
                Double.class, TEST_ACCOUNT_NO);
        assertEquals(balance, 50.0, 0);
    }
}
```

In JUnit 3, you can extend AbstractTransactionalJUnit38SpringContextTests to use a SimpleJdbcTemplate instance through a protected field:

```
package com.apress.springrecipes.bank;
...
import org.springframework.test.context.ContextConfiguration;
import org.springframework.test.context.junit38.~CCC
        AbstractTransactionalJUnit38SpringContextTests;

@ContextConfiguration(locations = "/beans.xml")
public class AccountServiceJUnit38ContextTests extends
        AbstractTransactionalJUnit38SpringContextTests {
    ...
    protected void setUp() throws Exception {
        executeSqlScript("classpath:/bank.sql",true);
        simpleJdbcTemplate.update(
                "INSERT INTO ACCOUNT (ACCOUNT_NO, BALANCE) VALUES (?, ?)",
                TEST_ACCOUNT_NO, 100);
    }

    public void testDeposit() {
        accountService.deposit(TEST_ACCOUNT_NO, 50);
        double balance = simpleJdbcTemplate.queryForObject(
                "SELECT BALANCE FROM ACCOUNT WHERE ACCOUNT_NO = ?",
                Double.class, TEST_ACCOUNT_NO);
        assertEquals(balance, 150.0);
    }

    public void testWithDraw() {
        accountService.withdraw(TEST_ACCOUNT_NO, 50);
        double balance = simpleJdbcTemplate.queryForObject(
                "SELECT BALANCE FROM ACCOUNT WHERE ACCOUNT_NO = ?",
                Double.class, TEST_ACCOUNT_NO);
        assertEquals(balance, 50.0);
    }
}
```

In TestNG, you can extend AbstractTransactionalTestNGSpringContextTests to use a SimpleJdbcTemplate instance SimpleJdbcTemplate instance:

```
package com.apress.springrecipes.bank;
...
import org.springframework.beans.factory.annotation.Autowired;
import org.springframework.test.context.ContextConfiguration;
import org.springframework.test.context.testng.~CCC
        AbstractTransactionalTestNGSpringContextTests;

@ContextConfiguration(locations = "/beans.xml")
public class AccountServiceTestNGContextTests extends
        AbstractTransactionalTestNGSpringContextTests {
    ...
    @BeforeMethod
    public void init() {
        executeSqlScript("classpath:/bank.sql",true);
```

```
        simpleJdbcTemplate.update(
                "INSERT INTO ACCOUNT (ACCOUNT_NO, BALANCE) VALUES (?, ?)",
                TEST_ACCOUNT_NO, 100);
    }

    @Test
    public void deposit() {
        accountService.deposit(TEST_ACCOUNT_NO, 50);
        double balance = simpleJdbcTemplate.queryForObject(
                "SELECT BALANCE FROM ACCOUNT WHERE ACCOUNT_NO = ?",
                Double.class, TEST_ACCOUNT_NO);
        assertEquals(balance, 150, 0);
    }

    @Test
    public void withDraw() {
        accountService.withdraw(TEST_ACCOUNT_NO, 50);
        double balance = simpleJdbcTemplate.queryForObject(
                "SELECT BALANCE FROM ACCOUNT WHERE ACCOUNT_NO = ?",
                Double.class, TEST_ACCOUNT_NO);
        assertEquals(balance, 50, 0);
    }
}
```

13-8. Using Spring's Common Testing Annotations

Problem

Because JUnit 3 doesn't provide built-in testing annotations like JUnit 4, you often have to manually implement common testing tasks, such as expecting an exception to be thrown, repeating a test method multiple times, ensuring that a test method will complete in a particular time period, and so on.

Solution

Spring's testing support provides a common set of testing annotations to simplify your test creation. These annotations are Spring-specific but independent of the underlying testing framework. Of these, the following annotations are very useful for common testing tasks. However, they are only supported for use with JUnit (both 3 and 4):

- @Repeat: This indicates that a test method has to run multiple times. The number of times it will run is specified as the annotation value.

- @Timed: This indicates that a test method must complete in a specified time period (in milliseconds). Otherwise, the test fails. Note that the time period includes the repetitions of the test method and any initialization and cleanup methods.

- **@IfProfileValue**: This indicates that a test method can only run in a specific testing environment. This test method will run only when the actual profile value matches the specified one. You can also specify multiple values so that the test method will run if any of the values is matched. By default, **SystemProfileValueSource** is used to retrieve system properties as profile values, but you can create your own **ProfileValueSource** implementation and specify it in the **@ProfileValueSourceConfiguration** annotation.

- **@ExpectedException**: This has the same effect as JUnit 4 and TestNG's expected exception support. However, as JUnit 3 doesn't have similar support, this is a good complement for testing exceptions in JUnit 3.

When using Spring's JUnit 3 legacy support in releases prior to 2.5, your test class can extend the **AbstractAnnotationAwareTransactionalTests** base class, which is a subclass of **AbstractTransactionalDataSourceSpringContextTests**, to use Spring's common testing annotations.

Starting from Spring 2.5's TestContext framework, you can use Spring's testing annotations by extending one of the TestContext support classes. If you don't extend a support class but run your JUnit 4 test with the test runner **SpringJUnit4ClassRunner**, you can also use these annotations.

How It Works

Using Common Testing Annotations with JUnit 3 Legacy Support

When creating tests with Spring's JUnit 3 legacy support, your test class can extend **AbstractAnnotationAwareTransactionalTests** to use Spring's common testing annotations:

```
package com.apress.springrecipes.bank;

import org.springframework.test.annotation.↩
        AbstractAnnotationAwareTransactionalTests;
import org.springframework.test.annotation.Repeat;
import org.springframework.test.annotation.Timed;

public class AccountServiceJUnit38LegacyTests extends
        AbstractAnnotationAwareTransactionalTests {
    ...
    @Timed(millis = 1000)
    public void testDeposit() {
        ...
    }

    @Repeat(5)
    public void testWithDraw() {
        ...
    }
}
```

Using Common Testing Annotations with the TestContext Framework

When using the TestContext framework to create tests for JUnit 4, you can use Spring's testing annotations if you run your test with SpringJUnit4ClassRunner or extend a JUnit 4 TestContext support class:

```
package com.apress.springrecipes.bank;
...
import org.springframework.test.annotation.Repeat;
import org.springframework.test.annotation.Timed;
import org.springframework.test.context.ContextConfiguration;
import org.springframework.test.context.junit4.
        AbstractTransactionalJUnit4SpringContextTests;

@ContextConfiguration(locations = "/beans.xml")
public class AccountServiceJUnit4ContextTests extends
        AbstractTransactionalJUnit4SpringContextTests {

    ...
    @Test
    @Timed(millis = 1000)
    public void deposit() {
        ...
    }

    @Test
    @Repeat(5)
    public void withDraw() {
        ...
    }
}
```

When using the TestContext framework to create tests for JUnit 3, you must extend a TestContext support class to use Spring's testing annotations:

```
package com.apress.springrecipes.bank;
...
import org.springframework.test.annotation.Repeat;
import org.springframework.test.annotation.Timed;
import org.springframework.test.context.ContextConfiguration;
import org.springframework.test.context.junit38.~CCC
        AbstractTransactionalJUnit38SpringContextTests;

@ContextConfiguration(locations = "/beans.xml")
public class AccountServiceJUnit38ContextTests extends
        AbstractTransactionalJUnit38SpringContextTests {
    ...
```

```
@Timed(millis = 1000)
public void testDeposit() {
    ...
}

@Repeat(5)
public void testWithDraw() {
    ...
}
}
```

Summary

In this chapter, you learned about the basic concepts and techniques used in testing Java applications. JUnit and TestNG are the most popular testing frameworks on the Java platform. JUnit 4 introduces several major improvements over JUnit 3. The most important of these is annotation support. TestNG is also a powerful annotation-based testing framework.

Unit tests are used for testing a single programming unit, which is typically a class or a method in object-oriented languages. When testing a unit that depends on other units, you can use stubs and mock objects to simulate its dependencies, thus making the tests simpler. In contrast, integration tests are used to test several units as a whole.

In the web layer, controllers are usually hard to test. Spring offers mock objects for the Servlet API so that you can easily simulate web request and response objects to test a web controller.

Spring's testing support facilities can manage application contexts for your tests by loading them from bean configuration files and caching them across multiple test executions. In releases prior to 2.5, Spring offered testing support specific to JUnit 3. Starting from version 2.5, Spring provides similar support through the TestContext framework.

You can access the managed application context in your tests, as well as have your test fixtures injected from the application context automatically. In addition, if your tests involve database updates, Spring can manage transactions for them so that changes made in one test method will be rolled back and thus won't affect the next test method. Spring can also create a JDBC template for you to prepare and validate your test data in the database.

Spring provides a common set of testing annotations to simplify your test creation. These annotations are Spring-specific but independent of the underlying testing framework. However, some of these are only supported for use with JUnit.

■ ■ ■

Spring Portlet MVC Framework

In this chapter, you will learn about portlet development using the Spring Portlet MVC framework, which is very similar to the Spring MVC framework discussed in Chapter 14.

Portlets are common in web applications that have a wide array of features, with each feature belonging to a different stakeholder. Since the integration of features belonging to different stakeholders into a single application can create considerable administrative overhead, each stakeholder is charged with creating a more user-friendly integration component, a portlet.

A *portlet* is a servlet-like web component that can process requests and generate responses dynamically. The content generated by a portlet is usually an HTML fragment that is aggregated into a portal page. Portlets need to be managed by a portlet container. The Java Portlet specification defines the contract between a portlet and a portlet container to ensure interoperability between different portal servers. In Spring 3.0, the Portlet MVC framework supports version 2.0 of this specification: JSR-286.

A *portal* is a web site that collects information from different sources and presents it to users in a unified, centralized, and personalized way. This gives users a single access point to various information sources, such as applications and systems. In Java, a portal can use portlets to generate its contents.

Due to its similarities with Spring MVC, we are not going to cover Spring Portlet MVC feature by feature, but rather focus on those portlet-specific features that are different from Spring MVC. Before reading this chapter, please be sure that you have gone through Chapter 8 or have a basic understanding of Spring MVC.

After finishing this chapter, you will be able to develop portlet applications using the Spring Portlet MVC framework and understand the differences between portlet and servlet development.

14-1. Developing a Simple Portlet with Spring Portlet MVC

Problem

You would like to develop a simple portlet with Spring Portlet MVC to learn the basic concepts and configurations of this framework.

Solution

The central component of Spring Portlet MVC is `DispatcherPortlet`. It dispatches portlet requests to appropriate handlers that handle the requests. It acts as the front controller of Spring Portlet MVC, and every portlet request must go through it so that it can manage the entire request-handling process.

When DispatcherPortlet receives a portlet request, it will organize different components configured in the portlet application context to handle this request. Figure 14-1 shows the primary flow of request handling in Spring Portlet MVC.

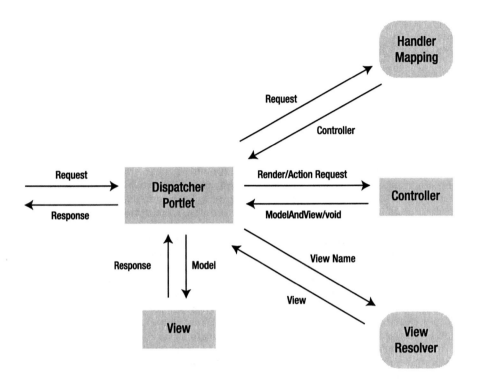

Figure 14-1. *Primary flow of request handling in Spring Portlet MVC*

When DispatcherPortlet receives a portlet request, it first looks for an appropriate handler to handle the request. DispatcherPortlet maps each request to a handler through one or more handler mapping beans. Once it has picked an appropriate handler, it will invoke this handler to handle the request. The most typical handler used in Spring Portlet MVC is a controller.

In portlets, there are two types of URLs: *render URLs* and *action URLs*. In most cases, multiple portlets will be displayed in a page. When a user triggers a render URL, the portlet container will ask all the portlets in the same page to handle a *render request* to render its view, unless the view's content has been cached. A controller should return an object in response to a render request. However, when a user triggers an action URL in a portlet, the portlet container will first ask the target portlet to handle an *action request*. A controller needn't return anything for an action request. When the action request finishes, the portlet container will ask all the portlets in the same page, including the target portlet, to handle a render request to render its view.

After a controller has finished handling a render request, it returns a model and a view name, or sometimes a view object, to DispatcherPortlet. If a view name is returned, it will be resolved into a view object for rendering. DispatcherPortlet resolves a view name from one or more view resolver beans.

Finally, `DispatcherPortlet` renders the view and passes in the model returned by the controller. Note that an action request doesn't need to render a view.

How It Works

Suppose you are going to develop a travel portal for a travel agency. In this portal is a portlet displaying weather information such as the temperatures of major cities. First of all, you design the service interface as follows:

```
package com.apress.springrecipes.travel.weather;
...
public interface WeatherService {

    public Map<String, Double> getMajorCityTemperatures();
}
```

For testing purposes, you can return some hard-coded data for the implementation of this service interface.

```
package com.apress.springrecipes.travel.weather;
...
public class WeatherServiceImpl implements WeatherService {

    public Map<String, Double> getMajorCityTemperatures() {
        Map<String, Double> temperatures = new HashMap<String, Double>();
        temperatures.put("New York", 6.0);
        temperatures.put("London", 10.0);
        temperatures.put("Beijing", 5.0);
        return temperatures;
    }
}
```

Setting Up a Portlet Application

The Java Portlet specification defines the valid structure of a portlet application, which is very similar to that of a web application, but with the addition of a portlet deployment descriptor (i.e., `portlet.xml`). Now, let's create the following directory structure for your travel portlet application.

■ **Note** To develop a portlet application with Spring Portlet MVC, you have to add the appropriate Spring support library to your CLASSPATH, along with other common Spring web libraries. If you are using Maven, add the following dependency to your project.

```
<dependency>
  <groupId>org.springframework</groupId>
```

```
<artifactId>spring-webmvc-portlet</artifactId>
<version>${spring.version}</version>
</dependency>
```

```
travel/
    WEB-INF/
        classes/
        lib/*jar
        jsp/
            weatherView.jsp
        applicationContext.xml
        portlet.xml
        weather-portlet.xml
        web.xml
```

Creating the Configuration Files

Next, you define the weather service in the root application context's bean configuration file (i.e., applicationContext.xml). Beans in this context are accessible to the contexts of all portlets within this application.

```
<beans xmlns="http://www.springframework.org/schema/beans"
    xmlns:xsi="http://www.w3.org/2001/XMLSchema-instance"
    xsi:schemaLocation="http://www.springframework.org/schema/beans
        http://www.springframework.org/schema/beans/spring-beans-3.0.xsd">

    <bean id="weatherService"
        class="com.apress.springrecipes.travel.weather.WeatherServiceImpl" />
</beans>
```

In the web deployment descriptor (i.e., web.xml), you have to register the servlet listener ContextLoaderListener to load the root application context at startup. By default, it loads applicationContext.xml from the root of WEB-INF, but you can override this location with the context parameter contextConfigLocation.

```
<web-app version="2.4" xmlns="http://java.sun.com/xml/ns/j2ee"
    xmlns:xsi="http://www.w3.org/2001/XMLSchema-instance"
    xsi:schemaLocation="http://java.sun.com/xml/ns/j2ee
        http://java.sun.com/xml/ns/j2ee/web-app_2_4.xsd">

    <display-name>Travel Portal</display-name>

    <listener>
        <listener-class>
            org.springframework.web.context.ContextLoaderListener
        </listener-class>
    </listener>
```

```
<servlet>
    <servlet-name>view</servlet-name>
    <servlet-class>
        org.springframework.web.servlet.ViewRendererServlet
    </servlet-class>
</servlet>

<servlet-mapping>
    <servlet-name>view</servlet-name>
    <url-pattern>/WEB-INF/servlet/view</url-pattern>
</servlet-mapping>
</web-app>
```

In order for Spring Portlet MVC to reuse the view technologies of Spring Web MVC, you have to configure the bridge servlet `ViewRendererServlet` in the portlet application's web deployment descriptor. This servlet converts portlet requests and responses into servlet requests and responses so that you can render Spring Web MVC's servlet-based views for portlets. By default, `DispatcherPortlet` will request the relative URL `/WEB-INF/servlet/view` for view rendering.

In the portlet development descriptor (i.e., `portlet.xml`), you declare a weather portlet for displaying weather information.

```
<portlet-app version="1.0"
    xmlns="http://java.sun.com/xml/ns/portlet/portlet-app_2_0.xsd"
    xmlns:xsi="http://www.w3.org/2001/XMLSchema-instance"
    xsi:schemaLocation="http://java.sun.com/xml/ns/portlet/portlet-app_2_0.xsd
        http://java.sun.com/xml/ns/portlet/portlet-app_2_0.xsd">

    <portlet>
        <portlet-name>weather</portlet-name>
        <portlet-class>
            org.springframework.web.portlet.DispatcherPortlet
        </portlet-class>
        <supports>
            <mime-type>text/html</mime-type>
            <portlet-mode>view</portlet-mode>
        </supports>
        <portlet-info>
            <title>Weather</title>
        </portlet-info>
    </portlet>
</portlet-app>
```

For a portlet developed with Spring Portlet MVC, you specify `DispatcherPortlet` as its portlet class. It acts as the front controller of Spring Portlet MVC, dispatching requests to appropriate controllers. It's the central component of Spring Portlet MVC, just as `DispatcherServlet` is for Spring Web MVC. Each `DispatcherPortlet` instance also has its own Spring application context that is able to access and even override beans declared in the root application context (but not vice versa).

By default, `DispatcherPortlet` loads its configuration file from the root of `WEB-INF` by joining the portlet name with `-portlet.xml` as the file name (e.g., `weather-portlet.xml`). You can override its location with the `contextConfigLocation` parameter.

The JSR-286 specification defines three standard portlet modes: *view, edit,* and *help.* The view mode usually displays information to users and handles user inputs. Typically, portlets in the edit mode allow users to update their preferences. Finally, help information should be displayed in the help mode. You can specify which modes your portlet supports in the portlet deployment descriptor. For example, your weather portlet only supports the view mode.

Creating Portlet Controllers

The controllers in Spring Portlet MVC are very similar to those in Spring Web MVC, so it is very easy to port controller code from Web MVC to Portlet MVC.

Your portlet controller can rely on the same annotations (e.g., @Controller or @RequestMapping) used to define servlet controllers, as is illustrated in the following listing.

■ **Note** To compile portlet controllers, you have to include `portlet-api.jar` (included in the `lib` directory of the Portlet reference implementation Apache Pluto, for example) in your CLASSPATH. **Do not include this JAR** in your application WAR (i.e., inside `/WEB-INF/lib/`), as it will cause class-loading errors. Apache Pluto already includes this JAR for you. Use it only for compile purposes. If you use Apache Maven, add the following dependency to your project. Note that we use the *compile* scope.

```
<dependency>
  <groupId>javax.portlet</groupId>
  <artifactId>portlet-api</artifactId>
  <version>2.0</version>
  <scope>compile</scope>
</dependency>
```

```
package com.apress.springrecipes.travel.weather;


import org.springframework.beans.factory.annotation.Autowired;
import org.springframework.web.bind.annotation.RequestMapping;
import org.springframework.web.bind.annotation.RequestMethod;
import org.springframework.stereotype.Controller;
import org.springframework.ui.Model;


@Controller
@RequestMapping("VIEW")
public class WeatherController  {
```

```
    private WeatherService weatherService;

    @Autowired
    public void WeatherController(WeatherService weatherService) {
        this.weatherService = weatherService;
    }
    @RequestMapping
    public String handleRenderRequestInternal(
            Model model) throws Exception {
        model.addAttribute("temperatures", ↵
                                    weatherService.getMajorCityTemperatures());
        return "weatherView";

    }
}
```

The WeatherController classcontains a single handler method, which queries the weather service and returns its results to a view named weatherView.

The code is strikingly similar to the one you used to define Spring MVC controllers in Chapter 8. This includes the handler method definitions, the use of annotations, as well as the constructor method used to inject a service.

The only distinction you need to be aware of is the @RequestMapping("VIEW") declaration. In Spring MVC Portlet controllers, the value assigned to the @RequestMapping annotation represents a portlet's mode—unlike Spring MVC controllers, which represent access URLs.

This means the preceding WeatherController only handles a portlet's *view mode*. You can define additional handler methods to support a portlet's additional modes' render requests. Note that since there is one handler method, the @RequestMapping annotation can be used to decorate a class (i.e., globally), and it will take effect on the only available handler method.

Next, you declare this controller in the configuration file weather-portlet.xml.

```
<beans xmlns="http://www.springframework.org/schema/beans"
    xmlns:xsi="http://www.w3.org/2001/XMLSchema-instance"
    xsi:schemaLocation="http://www.springframework.org/schema/beans
        http://www.springframework.org/schema/beans/spring-beans-3.0.xsd">

    <context:annotation-config/>

    <bean id="weatherController"
        class="com.apress.springrecipes.travel.weather.WeatherController"/>

    </bean>
    <bean class="org.springframework.web.portlet.mvc.↵
                    annotation.DefaultAnnotationHandlerMapping"/>



</beans>
```

This controller has to inspect the annotations defined in the controller, for this it uses the `<context:annotation-config>` declaration. In addition, it has to map a controller's handler methods to portlet requests.

When a portlet controller receives a portlet request, it will first look for an appropriate handler to handle the request. In Spring Web MVC, handler mappings are typically based on URLs. However, unlike in web applications, you don't deal with URLs in portlets; portlets rely on modes. This particular portlet controller defines one handler method mapped to a view mode. In order for the Spring framework to realize a controller's annotation mappings refer to portlet modes, a bean based on the `DefaultAnnotationHandlerMapping` class is used.

By declaring a bean based on the `DefaultAnnotationHandlerMapping` class, you can assign a controller's handler methods `@RequestMapping` annotations each referring to different portlet modes.

Resolving View Names into Views

When a portlet controller receives a view name returned from a handler, it will resolve the logical view name into a view object for rendering. Spring Portlet MVC reuses all the view technologies from Spring Web MVC so that you can use the same view resolvers in a portlet. For example, you can declare an `InternalResourceViewResolver` bean to resolve view names into JSP files inside the `WEB-INF` directory. Putting the JSP files here can prevent direct access to them for security reasons.

```
<bean class="org.springframework.web.servlet.view.InternalResourceViewResolver">
    <property name="viewClass"
        value="org.springframework.web.servlet.view.JstlView" />
    <property name="prefix" value="/WEB-INF/jsp/" />
    <property name="suffix" value=".jsp" />
</bean>
```

Creating Portlet Views

Although Spring Portlet MVC reuses the view technologies from Spring Web MVC, portlets don't support HTTP redirect, so you can't use `RedirectView` and the `redirect` prefix. Typically, a portlet view should be an HTML fragment, not a complete HTML page. Let's create the weather portlet view in `/WEB-INF/jsp/weatherView.jsp` to show weather information.

```
<%@ taglib prefix="c" uri="http://java.sun.com/jsp/jstl/core" %>

<table border="1">
  <tr>
    <th>City</th>
    <th>Temperature</th>
  </tr>
  <c:forEach items="${temperatures}" var="temperature">
  <tr>
    <td>${temperature.key}</td>
    <td>${temperature.value}</td>
  </tr>
  </c:forEach>
</table>
```

Deploying the Portlet Application

Now, your portlet application is almost ready to deploy to a Java portal server that supports JSR-286. For the sake of easy installation and configuration, we recommend installing Apache Pluto (http://portals.apache.org/pluto/), a subproject of the Apache Portals project. Pluto is the reference implementation of the Java Portlet specification. Pluto 2.x supports JSR-286, version 2.0 of this specification.

■ **Note** You can download the Apache Pluto distribution bundled with Tomcat (`pluto-current-bundle.zip`) from the Apache Pluto web site and extract it to a directory of your choice to complete the installation.

Typically, a portal server or a portlet container is deployed in a servlet container as a web application, and your portlet applications are deployed as other web applications in the same servlet container. The portlet container will make cross-context calls to your portlet applications. For this to work, you have to register one or more vendor-specific servlets in your portlet applications to handle the calls from the portlet container.

Pluto follows this practice if deployment is performed from its administrative console.

It's also necessary to register each portlet of a portlet application with a Pluto provided class: `org.apache.pluto.container.driver.PortletServlet`. For your weather portlet, you register this servlet in your `web.xml` and map it to the `/PlutoInvoker/weather` URL pattern.

```
<web-app ...>
    ...
    <servlet>
        <servlet-name>weather</servlet-name>
        <servlet-class>
            org.apache.pluto.container.driver.PortletServlet
        </servlet-class>
        <init-param>
            <param-name>portlet-name</param-name>
            <param-value>weather</param-value>
        </init-param>
        <load-on-startup>1</load-on-startup>
    </servlet>
    ...
    <servlet-mapping>
        <servlet-name>weather</servlet-name>
        <url-pattern>/PlutoInvoker/weather</url-pattern>
    </servlet-mapping>
</web-app>
```

■ **Note** To start up Pluto, just execute its `startup` script for your platform (located in the `bin` directory).

After Pluto has started, you can open the URL `http://localhost:8080/pluto/` in your browser and log in with the default username `pluto` and password `pluto`. From the Pluto Admin page, you can then deploy your weather portlet.

If you click the Pluto Admin tab on Pluto's main page, you will observe the Pluto Admin page illustrated in Figure 14-2.

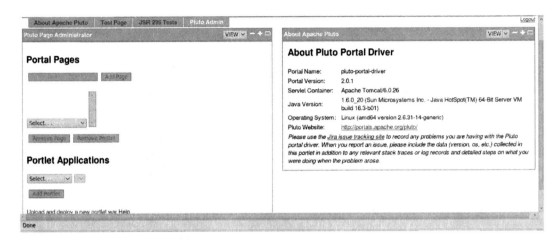

Figure 14-2. *Apache Pluto Admin Page*

At the bottom of the Pluto Admin page, you will find a link named "Upload and deploy a new portlet war". Clicking this link will take you to Pluto's upload and deployment page. If you scroll to the bottom of this last page, you will find a selection box from where you can browse and upload the portlet WARs to Pluto. Once you upload the weather portlet (i.e., the WAR file), you can add it to a portal page.

In the same Pluto Admin page (illustrated in Figure 14-2), if you select the list next to the Portlet Applications title, you will find an option by the name you gave to the weather portlet application (e.g., a WAR named `spring-travel.war` will show an option named `spring-travel`). Once you do this, an adjacent list is generated containing the available portlets of the selected portlet application. In this case, the weather portlet application contains only a portlet named `weather`. Select the portlet named weather and click the Add Portlet button.

Since no Apache Pluto portlet page was preselected, by default Apache Pluto will add portlets to the About Apache Pluto page. If you click the tab by this same name, visible in Apache Pluto's main page, and scroll to the bottom page, you can observe the weather portlet built with Spring's Portlet framework in Figure 14-3.

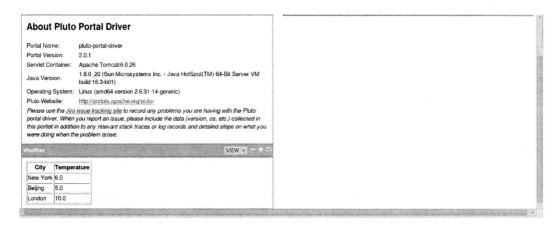

Figure 14-3. The weather portlet built with the Spring framework deployed on an Apache Pluto page

14-2. Mapping Portlet Requests to Handlers

Problem

When a portlet controller receives a portlet request, it will dispatch this request to an appropriate handler. You have to define how a portlet controller maps portlet requests to handlers.

Solution

In a portlet application developed with Spring Portlet MVC, portlet requests are mapped to handlers by one or more annotations. You can chain multiple handler mapping annotations as required. Spring Portlet MVC comes with several strategies for you to map portlet requests.

Unlike in a web application, you can't control URLs directly in a portlet. So the main strategies offered by Spring Portlet MVC for mapping portlet requests are based on the portlet mode and a request parameter. Of course, you can combine them together or even develop your own custom strategies.

How It Works

Suppose you are going to develop another portlet in your travel portal for showing flight information. First of all, you define the `Flight` domain class.

```
package com.apress.springrecipes.travel.flight;
...
public class Flight {

    private String number;
    private String origin;
    private String destination;
    private Date departureTime;

    // Constructors, Getters and Setters
    ...
}
```

Next, you define the service interface for querying all flights departing today and for a particular flight by its flight number.

```
package com.apress.springrecipes.travel.flight;
...
public interface FlightService {

    public List<Flight> findTodayFlights();
    public Flight findFlight(String flightNo);
}
```

For testing purposes, you can store the flights in a map and hard-code some flights for the service implementation.

```
package com.apress.springrecipes.travel.flight;
...
public class FlightServiceImpl implements FlightService {

    private Map<String, Flight> flights;

    public FlightServiceImpl() {
        flights = new HashMap<String, Flight>();
        flights.put("CX888", new Flight("CX888", "HKG", "YVR", new Date()));
        flights.put("CX889", new Flight("CX889", "HKG", "JFK", new Date()));
    }

    public List<Flight> findTodayFlights() {
        return new ArrayList<Flight>(flights.values());
    }

    public Flight findFlight(String flightNo) {
        return flights.get(flightNo);
    }
}
```

Then, you define the flight service in the root application context's bean configuration file (i.e., applicationContext.xml) so that it can be accessed by all portlet contexts.

```
<bean id="flightService"
    class="com.apress.springrecipes.travel.flight.FlightServiceImpl" />
```

To add a new portlet to your portlet application, you create a `<portlet>` entry in the portlet deployment descriptor `portlet.xml`.

```
<portlet-app ...>
    ...
    <portlet>
        <portlet-name>flight</portlet-name>
        <portlet-class>
            org.springframework.web.portlet.DispatcherPortlet
        </portlet-class>
        <supports>
            <mime-type>text/html</mime-type>
            <portlet-mode>view</portlet-mode>
            <portlet-mode>edit</portlet-mode>
            <portlet-mode>help</portlet-mode>
        </supports>
        <portlet-info>
            <title>Flight</title>
        </portlet-info>
        <portlet-preferences>
            <preference>
                <name>timeZone</name>
                <value>GMT-08:00</value>
            </preference>
        </portlet-preferences>
    </portlet>
</portlet-app>
```

This portlet supports the standard portlet modes: view, edit, and help. In addition, you set the default time zone for this portlet as a custom preference attribute. It will be used by JSTL to format departure dates. Please refer to the Javadoc of `java.util. TimeZone` for its valid formats.

Mapping Requests by the Portlet Mode

The simplest strategy to map portlet requests is by the portlet mode. Because this flight portlet supports all three standard portlet modes, let's create a portlet controller for each of these modes. First, you create a controller for displaying all flights departing today. It will be used for the view mode.

```
package com.apress.springrecipes.travel.flight;
...
import javax.portlet.PortletPreferences;



import org.springframework.beans.factory.annotation.Autowired;
```

```
import org.springframework.stereotype.Controller;

import org.springframework.ui.Model;

import org.springframework.web.bind.annotation.ModelAttribute;

import org.springframework.web.bind.annotation.RequestMapping;

import org.springframework.web.bind.annotation.RequestParam;

@Controller
@RequestMapping("VIEW")
public class FlightViewController {

    private FlightService flightService;

    @Autowired
    public FlightViewController(FlightService flightService) {
        this.flightService = flightService;
    }

    @ModelAttribute("timeZone")
    public String getTimeZone(PortletPreferences preferences) {
        return preferences.getValue("timeZone", null);
    }

    @RequestMapping
     public String flightList(Model model) {
            model.addAttribute("flights", flightService.findTodayFlights());
            return "flightList";
    }

}
```

This controller is mapped to the view mode at the class level, so its handler methods will handle only view mode requests. The `flightList()` method is annotated with `@RequestMapping`, which has no value or attribute, so it will handle default view mode requests. Then, you create the JSP file `/WEB-INF/jsp/flightList.jsp` to list all flights returned by this controller.

```
<%@ taglib prefix="c" uri="http://java.sun.com/jsp/jstl/core" %>
<%@ taglib prefix="fmt" uri="http://java.sun.com/jsp/jstl/fmt" %>

<table border="1">
  <tr>
    <th>Flight Number</th>
    <th>Origin</th>
    <th>Destination</th>
    <th>Departure Time</th>
  </tr>
  <c:forEach items="${flights}" var="flight">
    <tr>
```

```
    <td>${flight.number}</td>
    <td>${flight.origin}</td>
    <td>${flight.destination}</td>
    <td><fmt:formatDate value="${flight.departureTime}"
            pattern="yyyy-MM-dd HH:mm" timeZone="${timeZone}" /></td>
  </tr>
  </c:forEach>
</table>
```

In this JSP, you use the `<fmt:formatDate>` tag to format each flight's departure time, using the time zone attribute passed from the controller.

Most portlets allow users to set their preferences in the edit mode. For example, your flight portlet may allow users to edit their preferred time zone.

```
package com.apress.springrecipes.travel.flight;

import javax.portlet.PortletPreferences;

import org.springframework.stereotype.Controller;
import org.springframework.ui.Model;
import org.springframework.web.bind.annotation.RequestMapping;
import org.springframework.web.bind.annotation.RequestParam;

@Controller
@RequestMapping("EDIT")
public class FlightPreferencesController {

    @RequestMapping
    public String showPreferences(PortletPreferences preferences, Model model) {
        model.addAttribute("timeZone", preferences.getValue("timeZone", null));
        return "flightPreferences";
    }

    @RequestMapping
    public void changePreference(PortletPreferences preferences,
            @RequestParam("timeZone") String timeZone) throws Exception {
        preferences.setValue("timeZone", timeZone);
        preferences.store();
    }

}
```

The preceding controller handles two types of portlet requests: render requests and action requests. When handling a render request, it gets the time zone attribute from the portlet preferences and passes it to the view for editing. When handling an action request, it gets the time zone parameter from the portlet request and stores it in the portlet preferences as an attribute, which will override the existing one.

In addition, this controller is mapped to the edit mode, so its methods will only handle edit mode requests. Both `showPreferences()` and `changePreference()` are annotated with `@RequestMapping`, which has no value or attribute. In this case, the method whose return type is `void` will handle action requests. Otherwise, it will handle render requests.

The view for this controller is as simple as an HTML form. Let's create it in the JSP file /WEB-INF/jsp/flightPreferences.jsp.

```
<%@ taglib prefix="portlet" uri="http://java.sun.com/portlet" %>

<form method="post" action="<portlet:actionURL />">
  Time Zone
  <input type="text" name="timeZone" value="${timeZone}" />
  <input type="submit" value="Modify" />
</form>
```

The submission URL of this form should be a portlet action URL that will trigger an action request to the current portlet. In portlets, you have to construct an action URL with the <portlet:actionURL> tag defined in the portlet tag library.

In the help mode, a portlet usually displays some help information about itself. The following controller is used to display help information in help mode.

```
package com.apress.springrecipes.travel.flight;

import org.springframework.stereotype.Controller;
import org.springframework.web.bind.annotation.RequestMapping;

@Controller
@RequestMapping("HELP")
public class FlightHelpController {

    @RequestMapping
    public String showHelp() {
        return "flightHelp";
    }
}
```

Note how the @RequestingMapping annotation is assigned a HELP value. This indicates the controller is charged with handling a portlet's help mode. Next, let's create the view for this controller in the JSP file /WEB-INF/jsp/flightHelp.jsp to include the following message:

```
This portlet lists flights departing today.
```

In order for Spring to auto-detect your controllers and handler mappings, you have to enable Spring's component scan feature through the <component-scan> element defined in the context schema. To enable this, you need to create a file named flight-portlet.xml—in accordance with the portlet's name—with the following contents:

```
<beans xmlns="http://www.springframework.org/schema/beans"
    xmlns:xsi="http://www.w3.org/2001/XMLSchema-instance"
    xmlns:context="http://www.springframework.org/schema/context"
    xsi:schemaLocation="http://www.springframework.org/schema/beans
        http://www.springframework.org/schema/beans/spring-beans-3.0.xsd
        http://www.springframework.org/schema/context
        http://www.springframework.org/schema/context/spring-context-3.0.xsd">
```

```
<context:component-scan
    base-package="com.apress.springrecipes.travel.flight" />
```

```
</beans>
```

To deploy this portlet in Pluto, you add a `PortletServlet` instance for this portlet in `web.xml` and map it to the corresponding URL pattern.

```
<web-app ...>
    ...
    <servlet>
        <servlet-name>flight</servlet-name>
        <servlet-class>
            org.apache.pluto.container.driver.PortletServlet
        </servlet-class>
        <init-param>
            <param-name>portlet-name</param-name>
            <param-value>flight</param-value>
        </init-param>
      <load-on-startup>1</load-on-startup>
    </servlet>
    ...
    <servlet-mapping>
        <servlet-name>flight</servlet-name>
        <url-pattern>/PlutoInvoker/flight</url-pattern>
    </servlet-mapping>
</web-app>
```

After starting up and logging into Pluto, you can add your flight portlet to a portal page from the Pluto Admin page. You can switch the mode of this portlet using the icons in its upper-right corner.

Mapping Requests by a Parameter

Another strategy for mapping portlet requests is by a particular request parameter. To illustrate how this is done, let's make each of the flight numbers in the flight list view a hyperlink that will show the flight's details when clicked.

```
<%@ taglib prefix="portlet" uri="http://java.sun.com/portlet" %>
...
<table border="1">
  ...
  <c:forEach items="${flights}" var="flight">
  <tr>
    <td>
      <portlet:renderURL var="detailUrl">
        <portlet:param name="action" value="flightDetail" />
        <portlet:param name="flightNo" value="${flight.number}" />
      </portlet:renderURL>
      <a href="${detailUrl}">${flight.number}</a>
```

```
      </td>
      ...
   </tr>
   </c:forEach>
</table>
```

A portlet render URL has to be constructed by the `<portlet:renderURL>` tag defined in the portlet tag library. You can specify parameters for this URL with the `<portlet:param>` element. Note that you have set the `action` parameter value to `flightDetail`, which will be mapped to the controller showing flight details later. Finally, you can store the generated URL in a JSP variable such as `detailUrl` and use it for the flight number hyperlink.

To show flight details, you need to add another handler method to the portlet controller you created earlier, `FlightViewController`, which handles a portlet's view mode. This new handler method will query for a flight by the flight number specified in the request parameter. This new handler method looks like the following:

```
@RequestMapping(params = "action=flightDetail")
public String flightDetail( @RequestParam("flightNo") String flightNo, Model model) {
    model.addAttribute("flight", flightService.findFlight(flightNo));

    return "flightDetail";
}
```

Note how this handler method handles view mode requests with an `action` parameter whose value is `flightDetail`. Then, you create the detail view in the JSP file `/WEB-INF/jsp/flightDetail.jsp` to show the details of a selected flight.

```
<%@ taglib prefix="fmt" uri="http://java.sun.com/jsp/jstl/fmt" %>
<%@ taglib prefix="portlet" uri="http://java.sun.com/portlet" %>

<table>
  <tr>
    <td>Flight Number</td>
    <td>${flight.number}</td>
  </tr>
  <tr>
    <td>Origin</td>
    <td>${flight.origin}</td>
  </tr>
  <tr>
    <td>Destination</td>
    <td>${flight.destination}</td>
  </tr>
  <tr>
    <td>Departure Time</td>
    <td><fmt:formatDate value="${flight.departureTime}"
            pattern="yyyy-MM-dd HH:mm" timeZone="${timeZone}" /></td>
  </tr>
```

```
  <tr>
    <td colspan="2">
      <a href="<portlet:renderURL portletMode="view" />">Return</a>
    </td>
  </tr>
</table>
```

In this JSP, you provide a link for users to return to the flight list page. The URL for this link should be a render URL constructed by the `<portlet:renderURL>` tag. You set its portlet mode to view, which has already been mapped to the controller listing all flights departing today.

14-3. Handling Portlet Forms with Simple Form Controllers

Problem

In portlet applications, you sometimes have to deal with forms. In order for a controller to handle forms, it has to render the form view to a user and also handle the form submission. You will get involved in too many form-handling details if you build your form controller from scratch.

Solution

Spring Portlet MVC can use the same annotation mechanism used in Spring Web MVC to handle forms.

When a portlet controller is asked to show a form by a portlet render request, it will render the form view to the user. Later, when the form is submitted by a portlet action request, the controller binds the form field values and then validates them against any validators that exist. If no error occurs, it will invoke the submission method. After the action request completes, the controller will be asked to handle a render request. If the form has been handled successfully, it will render the success view to the user. Otherwise, it will render the form view again with the errors.

How It Works

Suppose you are going to create a portlet for users to book tours through your travel portal. First of all, you define the following `BookingForm` domain class, whose instances will be used as a form's values. Because command objects may be persisted in sessions, this class should implement the `Serializable` interface.

```
package com.apress.springrecipes.travel.tour;
...
public class BookingForm implements Serializable {

    private String tourist;
    private String phone;
    private String origin;
    private String destination;
```

```
    private Date departureDate;
    private Date returnDate;

    // Getters and Setters
    ...
}
```

Next, you define the interface for the back-end tour service as follows. In addition to the processBooking() method, there's also a getLocations() method for returning all available tour locations.

```
package com.apress.springrecipes.travel.tour;
...
public interface TourService {

    public List<String> getLocations();
    public void processBooking(BookingForm form);
}
```

For simplicity's sake, let's implement this interface by storing the completed booking forms in a list and providing a setter method for the location list.

```
package com.apress.springrecipes.travel.tour;
...
public class TourServiceImpl implements TourService {

    private List<BookingForm> forms = new ArrayList<BookingForm>();
    private List<String> locations;

    public List<String> getLocations() {
        return locations;
    }

    public void setLocations(List<String> locations) {
        this.locations = locations;
    }

    public void processBooking(BookingForm form) {
        forms.add(form);
    }
}
```

Now, you define the tour service in the root application context's bean configuration file (i.e., applicationContext.xml) so that it can be accessed by all portlet contexts. You can also hard-code some locations for testing purposes.

```xml
<bean id="tourService"
    class="com.apress.springrecipes.travel.tour.TourServiceImpl">
    <property name="locations">
        <list>
            <value>France</value>
            <value>Switzerland</value>
            <value>New Zealand</value>
        </list>
    </property>
</bean>
```

To add a new portlet to your portlet application, you create a `<portlet>` entry in the portlet deployment descriptor `portlet.xml`. Note that this portlet supports the view mode only.

```xml
<portlet-app ...>
    ...
    <portlet>
        <portlet-name>tour</portlet-name>
        <portlet-class>
            org.springframework.web.portlet.DispatcherPortlet
        </portlet-class>
        <supports>
            <mime-type>text/html</mime-type>
            <portlet-mode>view</portlet-mode>
        </supports>
        <portlet-info>
            <title>Tour</title>
        </portlet-info>
    </portlet>
</portlet-app>
```

Creating Form Controllers

Now, let's create a controller to handle the tour booking forms. An annotation-based portlet form controller has to provide two handler methods, one for handling render requests and another for handling action requests. For example, you can implement the booking form controller as follows:

```java
package com.apress.springrecipes.travel.tour;
...
import javax.portlet.ActionResponse;

import org.springframework.beans.factory.annotation.Autowired;
import org.springframework.beans.propertyeditors.CustomDateEditor;
import org.springframework.stereotype.Controller;
import org.springframework.ui.ModelMap;
import org.springframework.validation.BindingResult;
import org.springframework.web.bind.WebDataBinder;
import org.springframework.web.bind.annotation.InitBinder;
import org.springframework.web.bind.annotation.ModelAttribute;
import org.springframework.web.bind.annotation.RequestMapping;
```

```java
import org.springframework.web.bind.annotation.RequestParam;
import org.springframework.web.bind.annotation.SessionAttributes;
import org.springframework.web.bind.support.SessionStatus;

@Controller
@RequestMapping("VIEW")
@SessionAttributes("bookingForm")
public class BookingFormController {

    private TourService tourService;

    @Autowired
    public BookingFormController(TourService tourService) {
            this.tourService = tourService;
    }

    @InitBinder
    public void initBinder(WebDataBinder binder) {
        SimpleDateFormat dateFormat = new SimpleDateFormat("yyyy-MM-dd");
        dateFormat.setLenient(false);
        binder.registerCustomEditor(Date.class, new CustomDateEditor(
                dateFormat, true));
    }

    @ModelAttribute("locations")
    protected List<String> getLocations() {
        return tourService.getLocations();
    }

    @RequestMapping
    public String showForm(
            @RequestParam(required = false, value = "form-submit")
            Boolean isFormSubmission, ModelMap model) {
        if (isFormSubmission == null) {
            BookingForm bookingForm = new BookingForm();
            model.addAttribute("bookingForm", bookingForm);
            return "bookingForm";
        }
        return "bookingSuccess";
    }

    @RequestMapping
    public void processSubmit(
            @ModelAttribute("bookingForm") BookingForm form,
            BindingResult result, SessionStatus status,
            ActionResponse response) {
            tourService.processBooking(form);
            status.setComplete();
            response.setRenderParameter("form-submit", "true");
    }
}
```

Portlet MVC differs from its Web MVC counterpart in that it has to handle both types of portlet requests: render requests and action requests.

When a form is submitted by an action request mapped to a form controller without errors, its submit method—processSumbit() in this case—is called to handle the form submission. In this method, you have to process the form data, for instance by storing it in a database. However, unlike when using forms dealing with Web MVC, you don't need to return a view object for this method, because an action request doesn't expect a view to be rendered. After the action request finishes, the portlet container will ask each portlet in the same page to handle a render request. The render method of the form controller—showForm() in this case—will be called if no error occurs in form handling. By default, it simply renders the form success view, so you don't need to override it in most cases.

In portlet form controllers, you also have to use a request parameter, such as form-submit, to distinguish whether a render request is made before or after a form submission. When this form controller is asked to show the form by a portlet render request, the showForm() method will be called, since its return type is not void, and it will handle a render request. In this case, the form-submit parameter is null, so you simply render the form view to the user.

When the form is submitted by a portlet action request, the processSubmit() method will be called, since its return type is void, and it will handle an action request. If the form is handled successfully, you will call the setRenderParameter() method on the response to set the form-submit request parameter for the next render request. After the action request finishes, the portlet container will ask this controller to handle a new render request. This time, the request should contain the form-submit parameter, so the showForm() method will render the success view.

Next, you can create the form view for this controller using the Spring form tag library. Let's create it in the JSP file /WEB-INF/jsp/bookingForm.jsp. Note that this form will be submitted to the action URL.

```jsp
<%@ taglib prefix="portlet" uri="http://java.sun.com/portlet" %>
<%@ taglib prefix="form" uri="http://www.springframework.org/tags/form" %>

<portlet:actionURL var="formAction" />

<form:form method="POST" action="${formAction}" commandName="bookingForm">
<table>
  <tr>
    <td>Tourist</td>
    <td><form:input path="tourist" /></td>
    <td><form:errors path="tourist" cssClass="portlet-msg-error" /></td>
  </tr>
  <tr>
    <td>Phone</td>
    <td><form:input path="phone" /></td>
    <td><form:errors path="phone" cssClass="portlet-msg-error" /></td>
  </tr>
  <tr>
    <td>Origin</td>
    <td><form:select path="origin" items="${locations}" /></td>
    <td><form:errors path="origin" cssClass="portlet-msg-error" /></td>
  </tr>
  <tr>
    <td>Destination</td>
    <td><form:select path="destination" items="${locations}" /></td>
    <td><form:errors path="destination" cssClass="portlet-msg-error" /></td>
  </tr>
```

```
<tr>
  <td>Departure Date</td>
  <td><form:input path="departureDate" /></td>
  <td><form:errors path="departureDate" cssClass="portlet-msg-error" /></td>
</tr>
<tr>
  <td>Return Date</td>
  <td><form:input path="returnDate" /></td>
  <td><form:errors path="returnDate" cssClass="portlet-msg-error" /></td>
</tr>
<tr>
  <td colspan="3"><input type="submit" /></td>
</tr>
</table>
</form:form>
```

Note that you will output the error messages with the CSS class `portlet-msg-error`, which is defined by the Java Portlet specification for you to display error messages.

The success view for this form controller is very simple. Let's create it in the JSP file `/WEB-INF/jsp/bookingSuccess.jsp`. From this view, users can return to the form view by a render URL, which will trigger all the portlets in the same page to handle a new render request. Then, the form controller will render its form view in response.

```
<%@ taglib prefix="portlet" uri="http://java.sun.com/portlet" %>

Your booking has been made successfully.
<br />
<a href="<portlet:renderURL />">Return</a>
```

Finally, you create the Spring configuration file for this portlet. As we're dealing with a **tour** portlet, create a file named `tour-portlet.xml` in the `WEB-INF` root with the following content:

```
<beans xmlns="http://www.springframework.org/schema/beans"
    xmlns:xsi="http://www.w3.org/2001/XMLSchema-instance"
    xmlns:context="http://www.springframework.org/schema/context"
    xsi:schemaLocation="http://www.springframework.org/schema/beans
        http://www.springframework.org/schema/beans/spring-beans-3.0.xsd
        http://www.springframework.org/schema/context
        http://www.springframework.org/schema/context/spring-context-3.0.xsd">

    <context:component-scan
        base-package="com.apress.springrecipes.travel.tour" />

</beans>
```

In this configuration file, you enable the component scan feature through the `<context:component-scan>` element for Spring to auto-detect your controllers and handler mappings.

To deploy this portlet in Pluto, you add a `PortletServlet` instance for this portlet in `web.xml` and map it to the corresponding URL pattern.

```
<web-app ...>
    ...
    <servlet>
        <servlet-name>tour</servlet-name>
        <servlet-class>
            org.apache.pluto.container.driver.PortletServlet
        </servlet-class>
        <init-param>
            <param-name>portlet-name</param-name>
            <param-value>tour</param-value>
        </init-param>
      <load-on-startup>1</load-on-startup>
    </servlet>
    ...
    <servlet-mapping>
        <servlet-name>tour</servlet-name>
        <url-pattern>/PlutoInvoker/tour</url-pattern>
    </servlet-mapping>
</web-app>
```

After starting up and logging into Pluto, you can add your tour portlet to a portal page from the Pluto Admin page.

Validating Form Data

Validation in Portlet MVC is performed in the same way as in Web MVC—typically by registering a validator that implements the Validator interface or another validation variation, as described in Chapter 8. By relying on validation, a controller can validate data after it's bound to the form field values. For example, you can create the following validator class to validate the booking form:

```
package com.apress.springrecipes.travel.tour;

import org.springframework.validation.Errors;
import org.springframework.validation.ValidationUtils;
import org.springframework.validation.Validator;

public class BookingFormValidator implements Validator {

    public boolean supports(Class clazz) {
        return BookingForm.class.isAssignableFrom(clazz);
    }

    public void validate(Object target, Errors errors) {
        ValidationUtils.rejectIfEmptyOrWhitespace(errors, "tourist",
                "required.tourist");
        ValidationUtils.rejectIfEmptyOrWhitespace(errors, "phone",
                "required.phone");
        ValidationUtils.rejectIfEmpty(errors, "origin",
                "required.origin");
```

```
        ValidationUtils.rejectIfEmpty(errors, "destination",
                "required.destination");
        ValidationUtils.rejectIfEmpty(errors, "departureDate",
                "required.departureDate");
        ValidationUtils.rejectIfEmpty(errors, "returnDate",
                "required.returnDate");

        BookingForm form = (BookingForm) target;
        if (form.getOrigin().equals(form.getDestination())) {
            errors.rejectValue("destination", "invalid.destination");
        }
        if (form.getDepartureDate() != null && form.getReturnDate() != null
                && !form.getDepartureDate().before(form.getReturnDate())) {
            errors.rejectValue("returnDate", "invalid.returnDate");
        }
    }
}
```

To apply this validator to your form controller, you first need to declare it in a Spring configuration file, just like you do in Spring MVC. In this case, open the `tour-portlet.xml` file and add the following declaration:

```
<bean id="bookingFormValidator" ↵
        class="com.apress.springrecipes.travel.tour.BookingFormValidator" />
```

This declaration makes the validator available to the portlet under the bean named bookingFormValidator. Once this is finished, you can inject the validator into the controller using the same Spring Web MVC technique. The following snippets illustrate the modifications you need to make to the `BookingFormController` controller to enable validation:

```
public class BookingFormController {

    private TourService tourService;
    private BookingFormValidator bookingFormValidator;

    @Autowired
    public BookingFormController(TourService tourService,
            BookingFormValidator bookingFormValidator) {
        this.tourService = tourService;
        this.validator = bookingFormValidator;
    }

    // Other controller handler methods omitted for brevity
    // …..

    @RequestMapping
    public void processSubmit(
            @ModelAttribute("bookingForm") BookingForm form,
            BindingResult result, SessionStatus status,
            ActionResponse response) {
        bookingFormvalidator.validate(form, result);
```

```
        if (!result.hasErrors()) {
            tourService.processBooking(form);
            status.setComplete();
            response.setRenderParameter("form-submit", "true");
        }
    }
}
```

Note that the validator is injected via the @Autowired annotation, just like the controller tourService. In addition, note that the validator instance is called inside the processSubmit method, prior to calling the hasErrors() method on the BindingResult object. Finally, to display user-friendly messages in case of binding or validation errors, you have to define the error messages in resource bundles of appropriate locales in the root of the classpath (e.g., messages. properties for the default locale).

```
typeMismatch.java.util.Date=Invalid date format.
required.tourist=Tourist is required.
required.phone=Phone is required.
required.origin=Origin is required.
required.destination=Destination is required.
required.departureDate=Departure date is required.
required.returnDate=Return date is required.
invalid.destination=Destination cannot be the same as origin.
invalid.returnDate=Return date must be later than departure date.
```

In order for these user-friendly messages to be used in the application, you need to declare the ResourceBundleMessageSource bean in the Spring configuration file for this portlet (i.e., tour-portlet.xml), whose bean name must be messageSource.

```
<bean id="messageSource"
    class="org.springframework.context.support.ResourceBundleMessageSource">
    <property name="basename"value="messages"/>
</bean>
```

Once this is done, you can proceed to Pluto's Admin page and deploy the tour portlet.

Summary

In this chapter, you have learned how to develop a portlet application using Spring Portlet MVC, which is very similar to Spring Web MVC (because most of it is ported from Web MVC). The main difference between portlets and servlets is that portlets have two types of URLs: render URLs and action URLs. When a user triggers a render URL, the portlet container will ask all the portlets in the same page to handle a render request to render its view. However, when a user triggers an action URL, the portlet container will first ask the target portlet to handle an action request. When the action request finishes, the portlet container will ask all the portlets in the same page, including the target portlet, to handle a render request to render its view.

Unlike in a web application, portlets don't allow you to control URLs directly. So the main strategies for mapping portlet requests in Spring Portlet MVC are based on the portlet mode and a request parameter or both combined. You can also chain multiple handler mappings to meet your needs. Spring Portlet MVC provides a form controller that is very similar to that in Spring Web MVC. However, as there are two types of portlet requests, the form-handling flow is a bit different from the form controller in Spring Web MVC.

CHAPTER 15

■ ■ ■

Data Access

In this chapter, you will learn how Spring can simplify your database access tasks. Data access is a common requirement for most enterprise applications, which usually require accessing data stored in relational databases. As an essential part of Java SE, Java Database Connectivity (JDBC) defines a set of standard APIs for you to access relational databases in a vendor-independent fashion.

The purpose of JDBC is to provide APIs through which you can execute SQL statements against a database. However, when using JDBC, you have to manage database-related resources by yourself and handle database exceptions explicitly. To make JDBC easier to use, Spring provides an abstraction framework for interfacing with JDBC. As the heart of the Spring JDBC framework, JDBC templates are designed to provide template methods for different types of JDBC operations. Each template method is responsible for controlling the overall process and allows you to override particular tasks of the process.

If raw JDBC doesn't satisfy your requirement or you feel your application would benefit from something slightly higher level, then Spring's support for ORM solutions will interest you. In this chapter, you will also learn how to integrate *object/relational mapping (ORM)* frameworks into your Spring applications. Spring supports most of the popular ORM (or data mapper) frameworks, including Hibernate, JDO, iBATIS, and the Java Persistence API (JPA). Classic TopLink isn't supported starting from Spring 3.0 (the JPA implementation's still supported, of course). However, the JPA support is varied and has support for many implementations of JPA, including the Hibernate and TopLink-based versions. The focus of this chapter will be on Hibernate and JPA. However, Spring's support for ORM frameworks is consistent, so you can easily apply the techniques in this chapter to other ORM frameworks as well.

ORM is a modern technology for persisting objects into a relational database. An ORM framework persists your objects according to the mapping metadata you provide (XML- or annotation-based), such as the mappings between classes and tables, properties and columns, and so on. It generates SQL statements for object persistence at runtime, so you needn't write database-specific SQL statements unless you want to take advantage of database-specific features or provide optimized SQL statements of your own. As a result, your application will be database independent, and it can be easily migrated to another database in the future. Compared to the direct use of JDBC, an ORM framework can significantly reduce the data access effort of your applications.

Hibernate is a popular open source and high-performance ORM framework in the Java community. Hibernate supports most JDBC-compliant databases and can use specific dialects to access particular databases. Beyond the basic ORM features, Hibernate supports more advanced features such as caching, cascading, and lazy loading. It also defines a querying language called Hibernate Query Language (HQL) for you to write simple but powerful object queries.

JPA defines a set of standard annotations and APIs for object persistence in both the Java SE and Java EE platforms. JPA is defined as part of the EJB 3.0 specification in JSR-220. JPA is just a set of standard APIs that require a JPA-compliant engine to provide persistence services. You can compare JPA with the JDBC API and a JPA engine with a JDBC driver. Hibernate can be configured as a JPA-compliant engine through an extension module called Hibernate EntityManager. This chapter will mainly demonstrate JPA with Hibernate as the underlying engine. JPA 2.0 debuted with Java EE6. Spring supports JPA 2.0 with no problems, and Spring 3.0.1 was the first release to declare a dependency on Hibernate 3.5 RC1, which in turn was the first in the Hibernate line to support JPA 2.0.

Problems with Direct JDBC

Suppose that you are going to develop an application for vehicle registration, whose major functions are the basic create, read, update, and delete (CRUD) operations on vehicle records. These records will be stored in a relational database and accessed with JDBC. First, you design the following Vehicle class, which represents a vehicle in Java:

```
package com.apress.springrecipes.vehicle;

public class Vehicle {

    private String vehicleNo;
    private String color;
    private int wheel;
    private int seat;

    // Constructors, Getters and Setters
    ...
}
```

Setting Up the Application Database

Before developing your vehicle registration application, you have to set up the database for it. For the sake of low memory consumption and easy configuration, I have chosen Apache Derby (http://db.apache.org/derby/) as my database engine. Derby is an open source relational database engine provided under the Apache License and implemented in pure Java.

Derby can run in either the embedded mode or the client/server mode. For testing purposes, the client/server mode is more appropriate because it allows you to inspect and edit data with any visual database tools that support JDBC—for example, the Eclipse Data Tools Platform (DTP).

■ **Note** To start the Derby server in the client/server mode, just execute the startNetworkServer script for your platform (located in the bin directory of the Derby installation).

After starting up the Derby network server on localhost, you can connect to it with the JDBC properties shown in Table 15-1.

■ **Note** You require Derby's client JDBC driver. If you are using Maven, add the following dependency to your project.

```
<dependency>
  <groupId>org.apache.derby</groupId>
  <artifactId>derbyclient</artifactId>
  <version>10.4.2.0</version>
</dependency>
```

Table 15-1. *JDBC Properties for Connecting to the Application Database*

Property	Value
Driver class	`org.apache.derby.jdbc.ClientDriver`
URL	`jdbc:derby://localhost:1527/vehicle;create=true`
Username	`app`
Password	`app`

The first time you connect to this database, the database instance `vehicle` will be created, if it did not exist before, because you specified `create=true` in the URL. Note that the specification of this parameter will not cause the re-creation of the database if it already exists.

Follow these steps to connect to Derby:

1. Open a shell on your platform.

2. Type `java -jar $DERBY_HOME/lib/derbyrun.jar ij` on Unix variants or `%DERBY_HOME%/lib/derbyrun.jar ij` on Windows.

3. Issue the command `CONNECT 'jdbc:derby://localhost:1527/vehicle;create=true';`.

You can provide any values for the username and password because Derby disables authentication by default. Next, you have to create the `VEHICLE` table for storing vehicle records with the following SQL statement. By default, this table will be created in the `APP` database sAPP database schema.

```
CREATE TABLE VEHICLE (
    VEHICLE_NO    VARCHAR(10)    NOT NULL,
    COLOR         VARCHAR(10),
    WHEEL         INT,
    SEAT          INT,
    PRIMARY KEY (VEHICLE_NO)
);
```

Understanding the Data Access Object Design Pattern

A typical design mistake made by inexperienced developers is to mix different types of logic (e.g., presentation logic, business logic, and data access logic) in a single large module. This reduces the module's reusability and maintainability because of the tight coupling it introduces. The general purpose of the Data Access Object (DAO) pattern is to avoid these problems by separating data access logic from business logic and presentation logic. This pattern recommends that data access logic be encapsulated in independent modules called data access objects.

For your vehicle registration application, you can abstract the data access operations to insert, update, delete, and query a vehicle. These operations should be declared in a DAO interface to allow for different DAO implementation technologies.

```
package com.apress.springrecipes.vehicle;

public interface VehicleDao {

    public void insert(Vehicle vehicle);
    public void update(Vehicle vehicle);
    public void delete(Vehicle vehicle);
    public Vehicle findByVehicleNo(String vehicleNo);
}
```

Most parts of the JDBC APIs declare throwing `java.sql.SQLException`. But because this interface aims to abstract the data access operations only, it should not depend on the implementation technology. So, it's unwise for this general interface to declare throwing the JDBC-specific `SQLException`. A common practice when implementing a DAO interface is to wrap this kind of exception with a runtime exception (either your own business `Exception` subclass or a generic one).

Implementing the DAO with JDBC

To access the database with JDBC, you create an implementation for this DAO interface (e.g., `JdbcVehicleDao`). Because your DAO implementation has to connect to the database to execute SQL statements, you may establish database connections by specifying the driver class name, database URL, username, and password. However, in JDBC 2.0 or higher, you can obtain database connections from a preconfigured `javax.sql.DataSource` object without knowing about the connection details.

```
package com.apress.springrecipes.vehicle;

import java.sql.Connection;
import java.sql.PreparedStatement;
import java.sql.ResultSet;
import java.sql.SQLException;

import javax.sql.DataSource;

public class JdbcVehicleDao implements VehicleDao {

    private DataSource dataSource;
```

```java
public void setDataSource(DataSource dataSource) {
    this.dataSource = dataSource;
}

public void insert(Vehicle vehicle) {
    String sql = "INSERT INTO VEHICLE (VEHICLE_NO, COLOR, WHEEL, SEAT) "
            + "VALUES (?, ?, ?, ?)";
    Connection conn = null;
    try {
        conn = dataSource.getConnection();
        PreparedStatement ps = conn.prepareStatement(sql);
        ps.setString(1, vehicle.getVehicleNo());
        ps.setString(2, vehicle.getColor());
        ps.setInt(3, vehicle.getWheel());
        ps.setInt(4, vehicle.getSeat());
        ps.executeUpdate();
        ps.close();
    } catch (SQLException e) {
        throw new RuntimeException(e);
    } finally {
        if (conn != null) {
            try {
                conn.close();
            } catch (SQLException e) {}
        }
    }
}

public Vehicle findByVehicleNo(String vehicleNo) {
    String sql = "SELECT * FROM VEHICLE WHERE VEHICLE_NO = ?";
    Connection conn = null;
    try {
        conn = dataSource.getConnection();
        PreparedStatement ps = conn.prepareStatement(sql);
        ps.setString(1, vehicleNo);

        Vehicle vehicle = null;
        ResultSet rs = ps.executeQuery();
        if (rs.next()) {
            vehicle = new Vehicle(rs.getString("VEHICLE_NO"),
                    rs.getString("COLOR"), rs.getInt("WHEEL"),
                    rs.getInt("SEAT"));
        }
        rs.close();
        ps.close();
        return vehicle;
    } catch (SQLException e) {
        throw new RuntimeException(e);
    } finally {
```

```
        if (conn != null) {
            try {
                conn.close();
            } catch (SQLException e) {}
        }
    }
}

    public void update(Vehicle vehicle) {/* … */}

    public void delete(Vehicle vehicle) {/* … */}
}
```

The vehicle insert operation is a typical JDBC update scenario. Each time this method is called, you obtain a connection from the data source and execute the SQL statement on this connection. Your DAO interface doesn't declare throwing any checked exceptions, so if a `SQLException` occurs, you have to wrap it with an unchecked `RuntimeException`. (There is a detailed discussion on handling exceptions in your DAOs later in this chapter). Don't forget to release the connection in the `finally` block. Failing to do so may cause your application to run out of connections.

Here, the update and delete operations will be skipped, because they are much the same as the insert operation from a technical point of view. For the query operation, you have to extract the data from the returned result set to build a vehicle object in addition to executing the SQL statement.

Configuring a Data Source in Spring

The `javax.sql.DataSource` interface is a standard interface defined by the JDBC specification that factories `Connection` instances. There are many data source implementations provided by different vendors and projects: C3PO and Apache Commons DBCP are popular open source options, and most applications servers will provide their own implementation. It is very easy to switch between different data source implementations, because they implement the common `DataSource` interface. As a Java application framework, Spring also provides several convenient but less powerful data source implementations. The simplest one is `DriverManagerDataSource`, which opens a new connection every time one is requested.

```
<beans xmlns="http://www.springframework.org/schema/beans"
    xmlns:xsi="http://www.w3.org/2001/XMLSchema-instance"
    xsi:schemaLocation="http://www.springframework.org/schema/beans
        http://www.springframework.org/schema/beans/spring-beans-3.0.xsd">

    <bean id="dataSource"
        class="org.springframework.jdbc.datasource.DriverManagerDataSource">
        <property name="driverClassName"
            value="org.apache.derby.jdbc.ClientDriver" />
        <property name="url"
            value="jdbc:derby://localhost:1527/vehicle;create=true" />
        <property name="username" value="app" />
        <property name="password" value="app" />
    </bean>
```

```
    <bean id="vehicleDao"
        class="com.apress.springrecipes.vehicle.JdbcVehicleDao">
        <property name="dataSource" ref="dataSource" />
    </bean>
</beans>
```

DriverManagerDataSource is not an efficient data source implementation because it opens a new connection for the client every time it's requested. Another data source implementation provided by Spring is SingleConnectionDataSource (a DriverManagerDataSource subclass). As its name indicates, this maintains only a single connection that's reused all the time and never closed. Obviously, it is not suitable in a multithreaded environment.

Spring's own data source implementations are mainly used for testing purposes. However, many production data source implementations support connection pooling. For example, the Database Connection Pooling Services (DBCP) module of the Apache Commons Library has several data source implementations that support connection pooling. Of these, BasicDataSource accepts the same connection properties as DriverManagerDataSource and allows you to specify the initial connection size and maximum active connections for the connection pool.

```
<bean id="dataSource"
    class="org.apache.commons.dbcp.BasicDataSource">
    <property name="driverClassName"
        value="org.apache.derby.jdbc.ClientDriver" />
    <property name="url"
        value="jdbc:derby://localhost:1527/vehicle;create=true" />
    <property name="username" value="app" />
    <property name="password" value="app" />
    <property name="initialSize" value="2" />
    <property name="maxActive" value="5" />
</bean>
```

bean configuration file.

Table 13-2. *TestContext Support Classes for Transaction Management*

Testing Framework	TestContext Support Class*
JUnit 3	AbstractTransactionalJUnit38SpringContextTests
JUnit 4	AbstractTransactionalJUnit4SpringContextTests
TestNG	AbstractTransactionalTestNGSpringContextTests

** These three TestContext support classes have **TransactionalTestExecutionListener** enabled in addition to DependencyInjectionTestExecutionListener and DirtiesContextTestExecutionListener.*

In JUnit 4 and TestNG, you can simply annotate @Transactional at the class level or the method level to have the test methods run within transactions, without extending a TestContext support class. However, to integrate with a test context manager, you have to run the JUnit 4 test with the test runner SpringJUnit4ClassRunner, and you have to do it manually for a TestNG test.

How It Works

Let's consider storing your bank system's accounts in a relational database. You can choose any JDBC-compliant database engine that supports transactions and then execute the following SQL statement on it to create the ACCOUNT table. Here, we have chosen Apache Derby as our database engine and created the table in the bank instance.

```
CREATE TABLE ACCOUNT (
    ACCOUNT_NO    VARCHAR(10)    NOT NULL,
    BALANCE       DOUBLE         NOT NULL,
    PRIMARY KEY (ACCOUNT_NO)
);
```

Next, you create a new DAO implementation that uses JDBC to access the database. You can take advantage of SimpleJdbcTemplate to simplify your operations.

```
package com.apress.springrecipes.bank;

import org.springframework.jdbc.core.simple.SimpleJdbcDaoSupport;

public class JdbcAccountDao extends SimpleJdbcDaoSupport implements AccountDao {

    public void createAccount(Account account) {
        String sql = "INSERT INTO ACCOUNT (ACCOUNT_NO, BALANCE) VALUES (?, ?)";
        getSimpleJdbcTemplate().update(
                sql, account.getAccountNo(), account.getBalance());
    }

    public void updateAccount(Account account) {
        String sql = "UPDATE ACCOUNT SET BALANCE = ? WHERE ACCOUNT_NO = ?";
        getSimpleJdbcTemplate().update(
                sql, account.getBalance(), account.getAccountNo());
    }

    public void removeAccount(Account account) {
        String sql = "DELETE FROM ACCOUNT WHERE ACCOUNT_NO = ?";
        getSimpleJdbcTemplate().update(sql, account.getAccountNo());
    }

    public Account findAccount(String accountNo) {
        String sql = "SELECT BALANCE FROM ACCOUNT WHERE ACCOUNT_NO = ?";
        double balance = getSimpleJdbcTemplate().queryForObject(
                sql, Double.class, accountNo);
        return new Account(accountNo, balance);
    }
}
```

Before you create integration tests to test the AccountService instance that uses this DAO to persist account objects, you have to replace InMemoryAccountDao with this DAO in the bean configuration file, and configure the target data source as well.

■ **Note** To use the data source implementations provided by DBCP, you have to add them to your CLASSPATH. If you are using Maven, add the following dependency to your project:

```
<dependency>
  <groupId>commons-dbcp</groupId>
  <artifactId>commons-dbcp</artifactId>
  <version>1.2.1</version>
</dependency>
```

Many Java EE application servers build in data source implementations that you can configure from the server console or in configuration files. If you have a data source configured in an application server and exposed for JNDI lookup, you can use `JndiObjectFactoryBean` to look it up.

```
<bean id="dataSource"
    class="org.springframework.jndi.JndiObjectFactoryBean">
    <property name="jndiName" value="jdbc/VehicleDS" />
</bean>
```

In Spring, a JNDI lookup can be simplified by the `jndi-lookup` element defined in the `jee` sjee schema.

```
<beans xmlns="http://www.springframework.org/schema/beans"
    xmlns:xsi="http://www.w3.org/2001/XMLSchema-instance"
    xmlns:jee="http://www.springframework.org/schema/jee"
    xsi:schemaLocation="http://www.springframework.org/schema/beans
        http://www.springframework.org/schema/beans/spring-beans-3.0.xsd
        http://www.springframework.org/schema/jee
        http://www.springframework.org/schema/jee/spring-jee-3.0.xsd">

    <jee:jndi-lookup id="dataSource" jndi-name="jdbc/VehicleDS" />
    ...
</beans>
```

Running the DAO

The following `Main` class tests your DAO by using it to insert a new vehicle to the database. If it succeeds, you can query the vehicle from the database immediately.

```
package com.apress.springrecipes.vehicle;

import org.springframework.context.ApplicationContext;
import org.springframework.context.support.ClassPathXmlApplicationContext;
```

```
public class Main {

    public static void main(String[] args) {
        ApplicationContext context =
            new ClassPathXmlApplicationContext("beans.xml");

        VehicleDao vehicleDao = (VehicleDao) context.getBean("vehicleDao");
        Vehicle vehicle = new Vehicle("TEM0001", "Red", 4, 4);
        vehicleDao.insert(vehicle);

        vehicle = vehicleDao.findByVehicleNo("TEM0001");
        System.out.println("Vehicle No: " + vehicle.getVehicleNo());
        System.out.println("Color: " + vehicle.getColor());
        System.out.println("Wheel: " + vehicle.getWheel());
        System.out.println("Seat: " + vehicle.getSeat());
    }
}
```

Now you can implement a DAO using JDBC directly. However, as you can see from the preceding DAO implementation, most of the JDBC code is similar and needs to be repeated for each database operation. Such redundant code will make your DAO methods much longer and less readable.

Taking It A Step Further

An alternative approach is to use an ORM (an object/relational mapping) tool, which lets you code the logic specifically for mapping an entity in your domain model to a database table. The ORM will, in turn, figure out how to write the logic to usefully persist your class's data to the database. This can be very liberating: you are suddenly beholden only to your business and domain model, not to whims of your database' SQL parser. The flip side, of course, is that you are also divesting yourself from the complete control over the communication between your client and the database—you have to trust that the ORM layer will do the right thing.

15-1. Using a JDBC Template to Update a Database

Problem

Using JDBC is tedious and fraught with redundant API calls, many of which could be managed for you. To implement a JDBC update operation, you have to perform the following tasks, most of which are redundant:

1. Obtain a database connection from the data source.

2. Create a PreparedStatement object from the connection.

3. Bind the parameters to the PreparedStatement object.

4. Execute the PreparedStatement object.

5. Handle SQLException.

6. Clean up the statement object and connection.

JDBC is a very low-level API, but with the JDBC template, the surface area of the API that you need to work with becomes more expressive (you spend less time in the weeds and more time working on your application logic) and is simpler to work with safely.

Solution

The `org.springframework.jdbc.core.JdbcTemplate` class declares a number of overloaded `update()` template methods to control the overall update process. Different versions of the `update()` method allow you to override different task subsets of the default process. The Spring JDBC framework predefines several callback interfaces to encapsulate different task subsets. You can implement one of these callback interfaces and pass its instance to the corresponding `update()` method to complete the process.

How It Works

Updating a Database with a Statement Creator

The first callback interface to introduce is `PreparedStatementCreator`. You implement this interface to override the statement creation task (task 2) and the parameter binding task (task 3) of the overall update process. To insert a vehicle into the database, you implement the `PreparedStatementCreator` interface as follows:

```
package com.apress.springrecipes.vehicle;

import java.sql.Connection;
import java.sql.PreparedStatement;
import java.sql.SQLException;

import org.springframework.jdbc.core.PreparedStatementCreator;

public class InsertVehicleStatementCreator implements PreparedStatementCreator {

    private Vehicle vehicle;

    public InsertVehicleStatementCreator(Vehicle vehicle) {
        this.vehicle = vehicle;
    }

    public PreparedStatement createPreparedStatement(Connection conn)
            throws SQLException {
        String sql = "INSERT INTO VEHICLE (VEHICLE_NO, COLOR, WHEEL, SEAT) "
                + "VALUES (?, ?, ?, ?)";
        PreparedStatement ps = conn.prepareStatement(sql);
        ps.setString(1, vehicle.getVehicleNo());
        ps.setString(2, vehicle.getColor());
```

```
            ps.setInt(3, vehicle.getWheel());
            ps.setInt(4, vehicle.getSeat());
            return ps;
        }
    }
```

When implementing the `PreparedStatementCreator` interface, you will get the database connection as the `createPreparedStatement()` method's argument. All you have to do in this method is to create a `PreparedStatement` object on this connection and bind your parameters to this object. Finally, you have to return the `PreparedStatement` object as the method's return value. Notice that the method signature declares throwing `SQLException`, which means that you don't need to handle this kind of exception yourself.

Now, you can use this statement creator to simplify the vehicle insert operation. First of all, you have to create an instance of the `JdbcTemplate` class and pass in the data source for this template to obtain a connection from it. Then, you just make a call to the `update()` method and pass in your statement creator for the template to complete the update process.

```
package com.apress.springrecipes.vehicle;
...
import org.springframework.jdbc.core.JdbcTemplate;

public class JdbcVehicleDao implements VehicleDao {
    ...
    public void insert(Vehicle vehicle) {
        JdbcTemplate jdbcTemplate = new JdbcTemplate(dataSource);
        jdbcTemplate.update(new InsertVehicleStatementCreator(vehicle));
    }
}
```

Typically, it is better to implement the `PreparedStatementCreator` interface and other callback interfaces as inner classes if they are used within one method only. This is because you can get access to the local variables and method arguments directly from the inner class, instead of passing them as constructor arguments. The only constraint on such variables and arguments is that they must be declared as `final`.

```
package com.apress.springrecipes.vehicle;
...
import org.springframework.jdbc.core.JdbcTemplate;
import org.springframework.jdbc.core.PreparedStatementCreator;

public class JdbcVehicleDao implements VehicleDao {
    ...
    public void insert(final Vehicle vehicle) {
        JdbcTemplate jdbcTemplate = new JdbcTemplate(dataSource);

        jdbcTemplate.update(new PreparedStatementCreator() {
```

```
    public PreparedStatement createPreparedStatement(Connection conn)
            throws SQLException {
        String sql = "INSERT INTO VEHICLE "
                + "(VEHICLE_NO, COLOR, WHEEL, SEAT) "
                + "VALUES (?, ?, ?, ?)";
        PreparedStatement ps = conn.prepareStatement(sql);
        ps.setString(1, vehicle.getVehicleNo());
        ps.setString(2, vehicle.getColor());
        ps.setInt(3, vehicle.getWheel());
        ps.setInt(4, vehicle.getSeat());
        return ps;
    }
});
    }
}
```

Now, you can delete the preceding InsertVehicleStatementCreator class, because it will not be used anymore.

Updating a Database with a Statement Setter

The second callback interface, PreparedStatementSetter, as its name indicates, performs only the parameter binding task (task 3) of the overall update process.

```
package com.apress.springrecipes.vehicle;
...
import org.springframework.jdbc.core.JdbcTemplate;
import org.springframework.jdbc.core.PreparedStatementSetter;

public class JdbcVehicleDao implements VehicleDao {
    ...
    public void insert(final Vehicle vehicle) {
        String sql = "INSERT INTO VEHICLE (VEHICLE_NO, COLOR, WHEEL, SEAT) "
                + "VALUES (?, ?, ?, ?)";
        JdbcTemplate jdbcTemplate = new JdbcTemplate(dataSource);

        jdbcTemplate.update(sql, new PreparedStatementSetter() {

                public void setValues(PreparedStatement ps)
                        throws SQLException {
                    ps.setString(1, vehicle.getVehicleNo());
                    ps.setString(2, vehicle.getColor());
                    ps.setInt(3, vehicle.getWheel());
                    ps.setInt(4, vehicle.getSeat());
                }
            });
    }
}
```

Another version of the update() template method accepts a SQL statement and a PreparedStatementSetter object as arguments. This method will create a PreparedStatement object for you from your SQL statement. All you have to do with this interface is to bind your parameters to the PreparedStatement object.

Updating a Database with a SQL Statement and Parameter Values

Finally, the simplest version of the update() method accepts a SQL statement and an object array as statement parameters. It will create a PreparedStatement object from your SQL statement and bind the parameters for you. Therefore, you don't have to override any of the tasks in the update process.

```
package com.apress.springrecipes.vehicle;
...
import org.springframework.jdbc.core.JdbcTemplate;

public class JdbcVehicleDao implements VehicleDao {
    ...
    public void insert(final Vehicle vehicle) {
        String sql = "INSERT INTO VEHICLE (VEHICLE_NO, COLOR, WHEEL, SEAT) "
                + "VALUES (?, ?, ?, ?)";
        JdbcTemplate jdbcTemplate = new JdbcTemplate(dataSource);

        jdbcTemplate.update(sql, new Object[] { vehicle.getVehicleNo(),
                vehicle.getColor(),vehicle.getWheel(), vehicle.getSeat() });
    }
}
```

Of the three different versions of the update() method introduced, the last is the simplest because you don't have to implement any callback interfaces. Additionally, we've managed to remove all setX (setInt, setString, etc.)–style methods for parameterizing the query. In contrast, the first is the most flexible because you can do any preprocessing of the PreparedStatement object before its execution. In practice, you should always choose the simplest version that meets all your needs.

There are also other overloaded update() methods provided by the JdbcTemplate class. Please refer to Javadoc for details.

Batch Updating a Database

Suppose that you want to insert a batch of vehicles into the database. If you call the insert() method multiple times, the update will be very slow as the SQL statement will be compiled repeatedly. So, it would be better to add a new method to the DAO interface for inserting a batch of vehicles.

```
package com.apress.springrecipes.vehicle;
...
public interface VehicleDao {
    ...
    public void insertBatch(List<Vehicle> vehicles);
}
```

The `JdbcTemplate` class also offers the `batchUpdate()` template method for batch update operations. It requires a SQL statement and a `BatchPreparedStatementSetter` object as arguments. In this method, the statement is compiled (prepared) only once and executed multiple times. If your database driver supports JDBC 2.0, this method automatically makes use of the batch update features to increase performance.

```java
package com.apress.springrecipes.vehicle;
...
import org.springframework.jdbc.core.BatchPreparedStatementSetter;
import org.springframework.jdbc.core.JdbcTemplate;

public class JdbcVehicleDao implements VehicleDao {
    ...
    public void insertBatch(final List<Vehicle> vehicles) {
        String sql = "INSERT INTO VEHICLE (VEHICLE_NO, COLOR, WHEEL, SEAT) "
                + "VALUES (?, ?, ?, ?)";
        JdbcTemplate jdbcTemplate = new JdbcTemplate(dataSource);

        jdbcTemplate.batchUpdate(sql, new BatchPreparedStatementSetter() {

                    public int getBatchSize() {
                        return vehicles.size();
                    }

                    public void setValues(PreparedStatement ps, int i)
                            throws SQLException {
                        Vehicle vehicle = vehicles.get(i);
                        ps.setString(1, vehicle.getVehicleNo());
                        ps.setString(2, vehicle.getColor());
                        ps.setInt(3, vehicle.getWheel());
                        ps.setInt(4, vehicle.getSeat());
                    }
                });
    }
}
```

You can test your batch insert operation with the following code snippet in the `Main cMain` class:

```java
package com.apress.springrecipes.vehicle;
...
public class Main {

    public static void main(String[] args) {
        ...
        VehicleDao vehicleDao = (VehicleDao) context.getBean("vehicleDao");
        Vehicle vehicle1 = new Vehicle("TEM0002", "Blue", 4, 4);
        Vehicle vehicle2 = new Vehicle("TEM0003", "Black", 4, 6);
        vehicleDao.insertBatch(
                Arrays.asList(new Vehicle[] { vehicle1, vehicle2 }));
    }
}
```

15-2. Using a JDBC Template to Query a Database

Problem

To implement a JDBC query operation, you have to perform the following tasks, two of which (tasks 5 and 6) are additional as compared to an update operation:

1. Obtain a database connection from the data source.

2. Create a `PreparedStatement` object from the connection.

3. Bind the parameters to the `PreparedStatement` object.

4. Execute the `PreparedStatement` object.

5. Iterate the returned result set.

6. Extract data from the result set.

7. Handle `SQLException`.

8. Clean up the statement object and connection.

The only steps relevant to your business logic, however, are the definition of the query and the extraction of the results from the result set! The rest is better handled by the JDBC template.

Solution

The `JdbcTemplate` class declares a number of overloaded `query()` template methods to control the overall query process. You can override the statement creation (task 2) and the parameter binding (task 3) by implementing the `PreparedStatementCreator` and `PreparedStatementSetter` interfaces, just as you did for the update operations. Moreover, the Spring JDBC framework supports multiple ways for you to override the data extraction (task 6).

How It Works

Extracting Data with Row Callback Handler

`RowCallbackHandler` is the is the primary interface that allows you to process the current row of the result set. One of the `query()` methods iterates the result set for you and calls your `RowCallbackHandler` for each row. So, the `processRow()` method will be called once for each row of the returned result set.

```
package com.apress.springrecipes.vehicle;
...
import org.springframework.jdbc.core.JdbcTemplate;
import org.springframework.jdbc.core.RowCallbackHandler;
```

```
public class JdbcVehicleDao implements VehicleDao {
    ...
    public Vehicle findByVehicleNo(String vehicleNo) {
        String sql = "SELECT * FROM VEHICLE WHERE VEHICLE_NO = ?";
        JdbcTemplate jdbcTemplate = new JdbcTemplate(dataSource);

        final Vehicle vehicle = new Vehicle();
        jdbcTemplate.query(sql, new Object[] { vehicleNo },
                new RowCallbackHandler() {
                    public void processRow(ResultSet rs) throws SQLException {
                        vehicle.setVehicleNo(rs.getString("VEHICLE_NO"));
                        vehicle.setColor(rs.getString("COLOR"));
                        vehicle.setWheel(rs.getInt("WHEEL"));
                        vehicle.setSeat(rs.getInt("SEAT"));
                    }
                });
        return vehicle;
    }
}
```

As there will be one row returned for the SQL query at maximum, you can create a vehicle object as a local variable and set its properties by extracting data from the result set. For a result set with more than one row, you should collect the objects as a list.

Extracting Data with a Row Mapper

The RowMapper<T> interface is more general than RowCallbackHandler. Its purpose is to map a single row of the result set to a customized object, so it can be applied to a single-row result set as well as a multiple-row result set. From the viewpoint of reuse, it's better to implement the RowMapper<T> interface as a normal class than as an inner class. In the mapRow() method of this interface, you have to construct the object that represents a row and return it as the method's return value.

```
package com.apress.springrecipes.vehicle;

import java.sql.ResultSet;
import java.sql.SQLException;

import org.springframework.jdbc.core.RowMapper;

public class VehicleRowMapper implements RowMapper<Vehicle> {

    public Vehicle mapRow(ResultSet rs, int rowNum) throws SQLException {
        Vehicle vehicle = new Vehicle();
        vehicle.setVehicleNo(rs.getString("VEHICLE_NO"));
        vehicle.setColor(rs.getString("COLOR"));
        vehicle.setWheel(rs.getInt("WHEEL"));
        vehicle.setSeat(rs.getInt("SEAT"));
        return vehicle;
    }
}
```

As mentioned, RowMapper<T> can be used for either a single-row or multiple-row result set. When querying for a unique object like in findByVehicleNo(), you have to make a call to the queryForObject() method of JdbcTemplate.

```
package com.apress.springrecipes.vehicle;
...
import org.springframework.jdbc.core.JdbcTemplate;

public class JdbcVehicleDao implements VehicleDao {
    ...
    public Vehicle findByVehicleNo(String vehicleNo) {
        String sql = "SELECT * FROM VEHICLE WHERE VEHICLE_NO = ?";
        JdbcTemplate jdbcTemplate = new JdbcTemplate(dataSource);

        Vehicle vehicle = (Vehicle) jdbcTemplate.queryForObject(sql,
                new Object[] { vehicleNo }, new VehicleRowMapper());
        return vehicle;
    }
}
```

Spring comes with a convenient RowMapper<T> implementation, BeanPropertyRowMapper<T>, which can automatically map a row to a new instance of the specified class. Note that the specified class must be a top-level class and must have a default or no-argument constructor. It first instantiates this class and then maps each column value to a property by matching their names. It supports matching a property name (e.g., vehicleNo) to the same column name or the column name with underscores (e.g., VEHICLE_NO).

```
package com.apress.springrecipes.vehicle;
...
import org.springframework.jdbc.core.BeanPropertyRowMapper;
import org.springframework.jdbc.core.JdbcTemplate;

public class JdbcVehicleDao implements VehicleDao {

    ...

    public Vehicle findByVehicleNo(String vehicleNo) {
        String sql = "SELECT * FROM VEHICLE WHERE VEHICLE_NO = ?";
        BeanPropertyRowMapper<Vehicle> vehicleRowMapper =
                BeanPropertyRowMapper.newInstance(Vehicle.class);
        Vehicle vehicle = getSimpleJdbcTemplate().queryForObject(
                sql, vehicleRowMapper, vehicleNo);
         return vehicle;
    }
}
```

Querying for Multiple Rows

Now, let's look at how to query for a result set with multiple rows. For example, suppose that you need a findAll() method in the DAO interface to get all vehicles.

```
package com.apress.springrecipes.vehicle;
...
public interface VehicleDao {
    ...
    public List<Vehicle> findAll();
}
```

Without the help of `RowMapper<T>`, you can still call the `queryForList()` method and pass in a SQL statement. The returned result will be a list of maps. Each map stores a row of the result set with the column names as the keys.

```
package com.apress.springrecipes.vehicle;
...
import org.springframework.jdbc.core.JdbcTemplate;

public class JdbcVehicleDao implements VehicleDao {
    ...
    public List<Vehicle> findAll() {
        String sql = "SELECT * FROM VEHICLE";
        JdbcTemplate jdbcTemplate = new JdbcTemplate(dataSource);

        List<Vehicle> vehicles = new ArrayList<Vehicle>();
        List<Map<String,Object>> rows = jdbcTemplate.queryForList(sql);
        for (Map<String, Object> row : rows) {
            Vehicle vehicle = new Vehicle();
            vehicle.setVehicleNo((String) row.get("VEHICLE_NO"));
            vehicle.setColor((String) row.get("COLOR"));
            vehicle.setWheel((Integer) row.get("WHEEL"));
            vehicle.setSeat((Integer) row.get("SEAT"));
            vehicles.add(vehicle);
        }
        return vehicles;
    }
}
```

You can test your `findAll()` method with the following code snippet in the `Main` class:

```
package com.apress.springrecipes.vehicle;
...
public class Main {

    public static void main(String[] args) {
        ...
        VehicleDao vehicleDao = (VehicleDao) context.getBean("vehicleDao");
        List<Vehicle> vehicles = vehicleDao.findAll();
        for (Vehicle vehicle : vehicles) {
            System.out.println("Vehicle No: " + vehicle.getVehicleNo());
            System.out.println("Color: " + vehicle.getColor());
```

```
            System.out.println("Wheel: " + vehicle.getWheel());
            System.out.println("Seat: " + vehicle.getSeat());
        }
    }
}
```

If you use a RowMapper<T> object to map the rows in a result set, you will get a list of mapped objects from the query() mquery() method.

```
package com.apress.springrecipes.vehicle;
...
import org.springframework.jdbc.core.BeanPropertyRowMapper;
import org.springframework.jdbc.core.JdbcTemplate;

public class JdbcVehicleDao implements VehicleDao {
    ...
    public List<Vehicle> findAll() {
        String sql = "SELECT * FROM VEHICLE";
        RowMapper<Vehicle> rm =
BeanPropertyRowMapper.newInstance(Vehicle.class);
        List<Vehicle> vehicles = getSimpleJdbcTemplate().query(sql, rm);
        return vehicles;
    }
}
```

Querying for a Single Value

Finally, let's consider to query for a single-row and single-column result set. As an example, add the following operations to the DAO interface:

```
package com.apress.springrecipes.vehicle;
...
public interface VehicleDao {
    ...
    public String getColor(String vehicleNo);
    public int countAll();
}
```

To query for a single string value, you can call the overloaded queryForObject() method, which requires an argument of java.lang.Class type. This method will help you to map the result value to the type you specified. For integer values, you can call the convenient method queryForInt().

```
package com.apress.springrecipes.vehicle;
...
import org.springframework.jdbc.core.JdbcTemplate;

public class JdbcVehicleDao implements VehicleDao {
    ...
```

```
    public String getColor(String vehicleNo) {
        String sql = "SELECT COLOR FROM VEHICLE WHERE VEHICLE_NO = ?";
        JdbcTemplate jdbcTemplate = new JdbcTemplate(dataSource);

        String color = (String) jdbcTemplate.queryForObject(sql,
                new Object[] { vehicleNo }, String.class);
        return color;
    }

    public int countAll() {
        String sql = "SELECT COUNT(*) FROM VEHICLE";
        JdbcTemplate jdbcTemplate = new JdbcTemplate(dataSource);

        int count = jdbcTemplate.queryForInt(sql);
        return count;
    }
}
```

You can test these two methods with the following code snippet in the Main cMain class:

```
package com.apress.springrecipes.vehicle;
...
public class Main {

    public static void main(String[] args) {
        ...
        VehicleDao vehicleDao = (VehicleDao) context.getBean("vehicleDao");
        int count = vehicleDao.countAll();
        System.out.println("Vehicle Count: " + count);
        String color = vehicleDao.getColor("TEM0001");
        System.out.println("Color for [TEM0001]: " + color);
    }
}
```

15-3. Simplifying JDBC Template Creation

Problem

It's not efficient to create a new instance of JdbcTemplate every time you use it, because you have to repeat the creation statement and incur the cost of creating a new object.

Solution

The JdbcTemplate class is designed to be thread-safe, so you can declare a single instance of it in the IoC container and inject this instance into all your DAO instances. Furthermore, the Spring JDBC framework offers a convenient class, org.springframework.jdbc.core.support.JdbcDaoSupport, to simplify your DAO implementation. This class declares a jdbcTemplate property, which can be injected from the IoC container or created automatically from a data source, for example, `JdbcTemplate jdbcTemplate = new JdbcTemplate(dataSource)`. Your DAO can extend this class to have this property inherited.

How It Works

Injecting a JDBC Template

Until now, you have created a new instance of `JdbcTemplate` in each DAO method. Actually, you can have it injected at the class level and use this injected instance in all DAO methods. For simplicity's sake, the following code shows only the change to the `insert()` method:

```
package com.apress.springrecipes.vehicle;
...
import org.springframework.jdbc.core.JdbcTemplate;

public class JdbcVehicleDao implements VehicleDao {

    private JdbcTemplate jdbcTemplate;

    public void setJdbcTemplate(JdbcTemplate jdbcTemplate) {
        this.jdbcTemplate = jdbcTemplate;
    }

    public void insert(final Vehicle vehicle) {
        String sql = "INSERT INTO VEHICLE (VEHICLE_NO, COLOR, WHEEL, SEAT) "
                + "VALUES (?, ?, ?, ?)";

        jdbcTemplate.update(sql, new Object[] { vehicle.getVehicleNo(),
                vehicle.getColor(), vehicle.getWheel(), vehicle.getSeat() });

    }
    ...
}
```

A JDBC template requires a data source to be set. You can inject this property by either a setter method or a constructor argument. Then, you can inject this JDBC template into your DAO.

```
<beans ...>
    ...
    <bean id="jdbcTemplate"
        class="org.springframework.jdbc.core.JdbcTemplate">
        <property name="dataSource" ref="dataSource" />
    </bean>

    <bean id="vehicleDao"
        class="com.apress.springrecipes.vehicle.JdbcVehicleDao">
        <property name="jdbcTemplate" ref="jdbcTemplate" />
    </bean>
</beans>
```

Extending the JdbcDaoSupport Class

The `org.springframework.jdbc.core.support.JdbcDaoSupport` class has a `setDataSource()` method and a `setJdbcTemplate()` method. Your DAO class can extend this class to have these methods inherited. Then, you can either inject a JDBC template directly or inject a data source for it to create a JDBC template. The following code fragment is taken from Spring's `JdbcDaoSupport` class:

```
package org.springframework.jdbc.core.support;
...
public abstract class JdbcDaoSupport extends DaoSupport {

    private JdbcTemplate jdbcTemplate;

    public final void setDataSource(DataSource dataSource) {
        if( this.jdbcTemplate == null || dataSource != this.jdbcTemplate.↩
getDataSource() ){
            this.jdbcTemplate = createJdbcTemplate(dataSource);
            initTemplateConfig();
        }
    }
    ...
    public final void setJdbcTemplate(JdbcTemplate jdbcTemplate) {
        this.jdbcTemplate = jdbcTemplate;
        initTemplateConfig();
    }

    public final JdbcTemplate getJdbcTemplate() {
        return this.jdbcTemplate;
    }
    ...
}
```

In your DAO methods, you can simply call the `getJdbcTemplate()` method to retrieve the JDBC template. You also have to delete the `dataSource` and `jdbcTemplate` properties, as well as their setter methods, from your DAO class, because they have already been inherited. Again, for simplicity's sake, only the change to the `insert()` method is shown.

```
package com.apress.springrecipes.vehicle;
...
import org.springframework.jdbc.core.support.JdbcDaoSupport;

public class JdbcVehicleDao extends JdbcDaoSupport implements VehicleDao {

    public void insert(final Vehicle vehicle) {
        String sql = "INSERT INTO VEHICLE (VEHICLE_NO, COLOR, WHEEL, SEAT) "
                + "VALUES (?, ?, ?, ?)";
```

```
        getJdbcTemplate().update(sql, new Object[] { vehicle.getVehicleNo(),
                vehicle.getColor(), vehicle.getWheel(), vehicle.getSeat() });
    }
    ...
}
```

By extending JdbcDaoSupport, your DAO class inherits the setDataSource() method. You can inject a data source into your DAO instance for it to create a JDBC template.

```
<beans ...>
    ...
    <bean id="vehicleDao"
        class="com.apress.springrecipes.vehicle.JdbcVehicleDao">
        <property name="dataSource" ref="dataSource" />
    </bean>
</beans>
```

15-4. Using the Simple JDBC Template with Java 1.5

Problem

The JdbcTemplate class works fine in most circumstances, but it can be further improved to take advantage of the Java 1.5 features.

Solution

org.springframework.jdbc.core.simple.SimpleJdbcTemplate is an evolution of JdbcTemplate that takes advantage of Java 1.5 features such as auto-boxing, generics, and variable-length arguments to simplify its usage.

How It Works

Using a Simple JDBC Template to Update a Database

Many of the methods in the classic JdbcTemplate require statement parameters to be passed as an object array. In SimpleJdbcTemplate, they can be passed as variable-length arguments; this saves you the trouble of wrapping them in an array. To use SimpleJdbcTemplate, you can either instantiate it directly or retrieve its instance by extending the SimpleJdbcDaoSupport class.

```
package com.apress.springrecipes.vehicle;
...
import org.springframework.jdbc.core.simple.SimpleJdbcDaoSupport;
```

```
public class JdbcVehicleDao extends SimpleJdbcDaoSupport implements
        VehicleDao {

    public void insert(Vehicle vehicle) {
        String sql = "INSERT INTO VEHICLE (VEHICLE_NO, COLOR, WHEEL, SEAT) "
                + "VALUES (?, ?, ?, ?)";

        getSimpleJdbcTemplate().update(sql, vehicle.getVehicleNo(),
                vehicle.getColor(), vehicle.getWheel(), vehicle.getSeat());
    }
    ...
}
```

SimpleJdbcTemplate offers a convenient batch update method for you to specify a SQL statement and a batch of parameters in the form of List<Object[]> so that you don't need to implement the BatchPreparedStatementSetter interface. Note that SimpleJdbcTemplate requires either a DataSourceor a JdbcTemplate.

```
package com.apress.springrecipes.vehicle;
...
import org.springframework.jdbc.core.simple.SimpleJdbcDaoSupport;

public class JdbcVehicleDao extends SimpleJdbcDaoSupport implements VehicleDao {
    ...
    public void insertBatch(List<Vehicle> vehicles) {
        String sql = "INSERT INTO VEHICLE (VEHICLE_NO, COLOR, WHEEL, SEAT) "
                + "VALUES (?, ?, ?, ?)";

        List<Object[]> parameters = new ArrayList<Object[]>();
        for (Vehicle vehicle : vehicles) {
            parameters.add(new Object[] { vehicle.getVehicleNo(),
                    vehicle.getColor(), vehicle.getWheel(), vehicle.getSeat() });
        }
        getSimpleJdbcTemplate().batchUpdate(sql, parameters);
    }
}
```

Using a Simple JDBC Template to Query a Database

When implementing the RowMapper<T> interface, the return type of the mapRow() method is java.lang.Object. ParameterizedRowMapper<T> is a subinterface that takes a type parameter as the return type of the mapRow() method.

```
package com.apress.springrecipes.vehicle;
...
import org.springframework.jdbc.core.simple.ParameterizedRowMapper;

public class VehicleRowMapper implements ParameterizedRowMapper<Vehicle> {
```

```
    public Vehicle mapRow(ResultSet rs, int rowNum) throws SQLException {
        Vehicle vehicle = new Vehicle();
        vehicle.setVehicleNo(rs.getString("VEHICLE_NO"));
        vehicle.setColor(rs.getString("COLOR"));
        vehicle.setWheel(rs.getInt("WHEEL"));
        vehicle.setSeat(rs.getInt("SEAT"));
        return vehicle;
    }
}
```

Using `SimpleJdbcTemplate` with `ParameterizedRowMapper<T>` can save you the trouble of casting the type of the returned result. For the `queryForObject()` method, the return type is determined by the `ParameterizedRowMapper<T>` object's type parameter, which is `Vehicle` in this case. Note that the statement parameters must be supplied at the end of the argument list since they are of variable length.

```
package com.apress.springrecipes.vehicle;
...
import org.springframework.jdbc.core.simple.SimpleJdbcDaoSupport;

public class JdbcVehicleDao extends SimpleJdbcDaoSupport implements
        VehicleDao {
    ...
    public Vehicle findByVehicleNo(String vehicleNo) {
        String sql = "SELECT * FROM VEHICLE WHERE VEHICLE_NO = ?";

        // No need to cast into Vehicle anymore.
        Vehicle vehicle = getSimpleJdbcTemplate().queryForObject(sql,
                new VehicleRowMapper(), vehicleNo);
        return vehicle;
    }
}
```

Spring also comes with a convenient `ParameterizedRowMapper<T>` implementation, `ParameterizedBeanPropertyRowMapper<T>`, which can automatically map a row to a new instance of the specified class.

```
package com.apress.springrecipes.vehicle;
...
import org.springframework.jdbc.core.simple.ParameterizedBeanPropertyRowMapper;
import org.springframework.jdbc.core.simple.SimpleJdbcDaoSupport;

public class JdbcVehicleDao extends SimpleJdbcDaoSupport implements
        VehicleDao {
    ...
    public Vehicle findByVehicleNo(String vehicleNo) {
        String sql = "SELECT * FROM VEHICLE WHERE VEHICLE_NO = ?";
```

```
        Vehicle vehicle = getSimpleJdbcTemplate().queryForObject(sql,
                ParameterizedBeanPropertyRowMapper.newInstance(Vehicle.class),
                vehicleNo);
        return vehicle;
    }
}
```

When using the classic `JdbcTemplate`, the `findAll()` method has a warning from the Java compiler because of an unchecked conversion from `List` to `List<Vehicle>`. This is because the return type of the `query()` method is `List` rather than the type-safe `List<Vehicle>`. After switching to `SimpleJdbcTemplate` and `ParameterizedBeanPropertyRowMapper<T>`, the warning will be eliminated immediately because the returned `List` is parameterized with the same type as the `ParameterizedRowMapper<T>` argument.

```
package com.apress.springrecipes.vehicle;
...
import org.springframework.jdbc.core.simple.ParameterizedBeanPropertyRowMapper;
import org.springframework.jdbc.core.simple.SimpleJdbcDaoSupport;

public class JdbcVehicleDao extends SimpleJdbcDaoSupport implements
        VehicleDao {
    ...
    public List<Vehicle> findAll() {
        String sql = "SELECT * FROM VEHICLE";

        List<Vehicle> vehicles = getSimpleJdbcTemplate().query(sql,
                ParameterizedBeanPropertyRowMapper.newInstance(Vehicle.class));
        return vehicles;
    }
}
```

When querying for a single value with `SimpleJdbcTemplate`, the return type of the `queryForObject()` method will be determined by the `class` argument (e.g., `String.class`). So, there's no need for you to perform type casting manually. Note that the statement parameters of variable length must also be supplied at the end of the argument list.

```
package com.apress.springrecipes.vehicle;
...
import org.springframework.jdbc.core.simple.SimpleJdbcDaoSupport;

public class JdbcVehicleDao extends SimpleJdbcDaoSupport implements
        VehicleDao {
    ...
    public String getColor(String vehicleNo) {
        String sql = "SELECT COLOR FROM VEHICLE WHERE VEHICLE_NO = ?";

        // No need to cast into String anymore.
        String color = getSimpleJdbcTemplate().queryForObject(sql,
                String.class, vehicleNo);
        return color;
    }
}
```

623

15-5. Using Named Parameters in a JDBC Template

Problem

In classic JDBC usage, SQL parameters are represented by the placeholder ? and are bound by position. The trouble with positional parameters is that whenever the parameter order is changed, you have to change the parameter bindings as well. For a SQL statement with many parameters, it is very cumbersome to match the parameters by position.

Solution

Another option when binding SQL parameters in the Spring JDBC framework is to use named parameters. As the term implies, named SQL parameters are specified by name (starting with a colon) rather than by position. Named parameters are easier to maintain and also improve readability. At runtime, the framework classes replace named parameters with placeholders. Named parameters are supported only in `SimpleJdbcTemplate` and `NamedParameterJdbcTemplate`.

How It Works

When using named parameters in your SQL statement, you can provide the parameter values in a map with the parameter names as the keys.

```
package com.apress.springrecipes.vehicle;
...
import org.springframework.jdbc.core.simple.SimpleJdbcDaoSupport;

public class JdbcVehicleDao extends SimpleJdbcDaoSupport implements
        VehicleDao {

    public void insert(Vehicle vehicle) {
        String sql = "INSERT INTO VEHICLE (VEHICLE_NO, COLOR, WHEEL, SEAT) "
                + "VALUES (:vehicleNo, :color, :wheel, :seat)";

        Map<String, Object> parameters = new HashMap<String, Object>();
        parameters.put("vehicleNo", vehicle.getVehicleNo());
        parameters.put("color", vehicle.getColor());
        parameters.put("wheel", vehicle.getWheel());
        parameters.put("seat", vehicle.getSeat());

        getSimpleJdbcTemplate().update(sql, parameters);
    }
    ...
}
```

You can also provide a SQL parameter source, whose responsibility is to offer SQL parameter values for named SQL parameters. There are three implementations of the SqlParameterSource interface. The basic one is MapSqlParameterSource, which wraps a map as its parameter source. In this example, this is a net-loss compared to the previous example, as we've introduced one extra object—the SqlParameterSource:

```
package com.apress.springrecipes.vehicle;
...
import org.springframework.jdbc.core.namedparam.MapSqlParameterSource;
import org.springframework.jdbc.core.namedparam.SqlParameterSource;
import org.springframework.jdbc.core.simple.SimpleJdbcDaoSupport;

public class JdbcVehicleDao extends SimpleJdbcDaoSupport implements
        VehicleDao {

    public void insert(Vehicle vehicle) {
        String sql = "INSERT INTO VEHICLE (VEHICLE_NO, COLOR, WHEEL, SEAT) "
                + "VALUES (:vehicleNo, :color, :wheel, :seat)";

        Map<String, Object> parameters = new HashMap<String, Object>();
        ...
        SqlParameterSource parameterSource =
            new MapSqlParameterSource(parameters);

        getSimpleJdbcTemplate().update(sql, parameterSource);
    }
    ...
}
```

The power comes when we need an extra level of indirection between the parameters passed into the update method and the source of their values. For example, what if we want to get properties from a JavaBean? Here is where the SqlParameterSource intermediary starts to benefit us! SqlParameterSource is BeanPropertySqlParameterSource, which wraps a normal Java object as a SQL parameter source. For each of the named parameters, the property with the same name will be used as the parameter value.

```
package com.apress.springrecipes.vehicle;
...
import org.springframework.jdbc.core.namedparam.BeanPropertySqlParameterSource;
import org.springframework.jdbc.core.namedparam.SqlParameterSource;
import org.springframework.jdbc.core.simple.SimpleJdbcDaoSupport;

public class JdbcVehicleDao extends SimpleJdbcDaoSupport implements
        VehicleDao {

    public void insert(Vehicle vehicle) {
        String sql = "INSERT INTO VEHICLE (VEHICLE_NO, COLOR, WHEEL, SEAT) "
                + "VALUES (:vehicleNo, :color, :wheel, :seat)";
```

```
        SqlParameterSource parameterSource =
            new BeanPropertySqlParameterSource(vehicle);

        getSimpleJdbcTemplate().update(sql, parameterSource);
    }
    ...
}
```

Named parameters can also be used in batch update. You can provide either a `Map` array or a `SqlParameterSource` array for the parameter values.

```
package com.apress.springrecipes.vehicle;
...
import org.springframework.jdbc.core.namedparam.BeanPropertySqlParameterSource;
import org.springframework.jdbc.core.namedparam.SqlParameterSource;
import org.springframework.jdbc.core.simple.SimpleJdbcDaoSupport;

public class JdbcVehicleDao extends SimpleJdbcDaoSupport implements VehicleDao {
    ...
    public void insertBatch(List<Vehicle> vehicles) {
        String sql = "INSERT INTO VEHICLE (VEHICLE_NO, COLOR, WHEEL, SEAT) "
                + "VALUES (:vehicleNo, :color, :wheel, :seat)";

        List<SqlParameterSource> parameters = new ArrayList<SqlParameterSource>();
        for (Vehicle vehicle : vehicles) {
            parameters.add(new BeanPropertySqlParameterSource(vehicle));
        }

        getSimpleJdbcTemplate().batchUpdate(sql,
                parameters.toArray(new SqlParameterSource[0]));
    }
}
```

15-6. Handling Exceptions in the Spring JDBC Framework

Problem

Many of the JDBC APIs declare throwing `java.sql.SQLException`, a checked exception that must be caught. It's very troublesome to handle this kind of exception every time you perform a database operation. You often have to define your own policy to handle this kind of exception. Failure to do so may lead to inconsistent exception handling.

Solution

The Spring framework offers a consistent data access exception-handling mechanism for its data access module, including the JDBC framework. In general, all exceptions thrown by the Spring JDBC framework are subclasses of org.springframework.dao.DataAccessException, a type of RuntimeException that you are not forced to catch. It's the root exception class for all exceptions in Spring's data access module.

Figure 15-1 shows only part of the DataAccessException hierarchy in Spring's data access module. In total, there are more than 30 exception classes defined for different categories of data access exceptions.

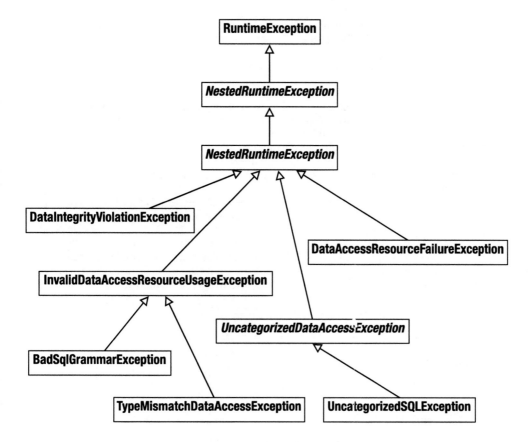

***Figure 15-1.** Common exception classes in the DataAccessException hierarchy*

How It Works

Understanding Exception Handling in the Spring JDBC Framework

Until now, you haven't handled JDBC exceptions explicitly when using a JDBC template or JDBC operation objects. To help you understand the Spring JDBC framework's exception-handling mechanism, let's consider the following code fragment in the Main class, which inserts a vehicle. What happens if you insert a vehicle with a duplicate vehicle number?

```
package com.apress.springrecipes.vehicle;
...
public class Main {

    public static void main(String[] args) {
        ...
        VehicleDao vehicleDao = (VehicleDao) context.getBean("vehicleDao");
        Vehicle vehicle = new Vehicle("EX0001", "Green", 4, 4);
        vehicleDao.insert(vehicle);
    }
}
```

If you run the method twice, or the vehicle has already been inserted into the database, it will throw a DuplicateKeyException, an indirect subclass of DataAccessException. In your DAO methods, you neither need to surround the code with a try/catch block nor declare throwing an exception in the method signature. This is because DataAccessException (and therefore its subclasses, including DuplicateKeyException) is an unchecked exception that you are not forced to catch. The direct parent class of DataAccessException is NestedRuntimeException, a core Spring exception class that wraps another exception in a RuntimeException.

When you use the classes of the Spring JDBC framework, they will catch SQLException for you and wrap it with one of the subclasses of DataAccessException. As this exception is a RuntimeException, you are not required to catch it.

But how does the Spring JDBC framework know which concrete exception in the DataAccessException hierarchy should be thrown? It's by looking at the errorCode and SQLState properties of the caught SQLException. As a DataAccessException wraps the underlying SQLException as the root cause, you can inspect the errorCode and SQLState properties with the following catch block:

```
package com.apress.springrecipes.vehicle;
...
import java.sql.SQLException;

import org.springframework.dao.DataAccessException;

public class Main {

    public static void main(String[] args) {
        ...
        VehicleDao vehicleDao = (VehicleDao) context.getBean("vehicleDao");
        Vehicle vehicle = new Vehicle("EX0001", "Green", 4, 4);
        try {
            vehicleDao.insert(vehicle);
        } catch (DataAccessException e) {
            SQLException sqle = (SQLException) e.getCause();
            System.out.println("Error code: " + sqle.getErrorCode());
            System.out.println("SQL state: " + sqle.getSQLState());
        }
    }
}
```

When you insert the duplicate vehicle again, notice that Apache Derby returns the following error code and SQL state:

```
Error code : -1

SQL state : 23505
```

If you refer to the Apache Derby reference manual, you will find the error code description shown in Table 15-2.

Table 15-2. *Apache Derby's Error Code Description*

SQL State	Message Text
23505	The statement was aborted because it would have caused a duplicate key value in a unique or primary key constraint or unique index identified by '*<value>*' defined on '*<value>*'.

How does the Spring JDBC framework know that state 23505 should be mapped to DuplicateKeyException? The error code and SQL state are database specific, which means different database products may return different codes for the same kind of error. Moreover, some database products will specify the error in the errorCode property, while others (like Derby) will do so in the SQLState property.

As an open Java application framework, Spring understands the error codes of most popular database products. Because of the large number of error codes, however, it can only maintain mappings for the most frequently encountered errors. The mapping is defined in the sql-error-codes.xml file, located in the org.springframework.jdbc.support package. The following snippet for Apache Derby is taken from this file:

```xml
<?xml version="1.0" encoding="UTF-8"?>
<!DOCTYPE beans PUBLIC "-//SPRING//DTD BEAN 3.0//EN"
    "http://www.springframework.org/dtd/spring-beans-3.0.dtd">

<beans>
    ...

<bean id="Derby" class="org.springframework.jdbc.support.SQLErrorCodes">
                <property name="databaseProductName">
                            <value>Apache Derby</value>
                </property>
                <property name="useSqlStateForTranslation">
                            <value>true</value>
                </property>
                <property name="badSqlGrammarCodes">
        <value>42802,42821,42X01,42X02,42X03,42X04,42X05,42X06,↩
42X07,42X08</value>
                </property>
                <property name="duplicateKeyCodes">
                            <value>23505</value>
                </property>
```

```
                        <property name="dataIntegrityViolationCodes">
                                <value>22001,22005,23502,23503,23513, ↵
X0Y32</value>
                        </property>
                        <property name="dataAccessResourceFailureCodes">
                                <value>04501,08004,42Y07</value>
                        </property>
                        <property name="cannotAcquireLockCodes">
                                <value>40XL1</value>
                        </property>
                        <property name="deadlockLoserCodes">
                                <value>40001</value>
                        </property>
                </bean>
        </beans>
```

Note that the databaseProductName property is used to match the database product name returned by Connection.getMetaData().getDatabaseProductName(). This enables Spring to know which type of database is currently connecting. The useSqlStateForTranslation property means that the SQLState property, rather than the errorCode property, should be used to match the error code. Finally, the SQLErrorCodes class defines several categories for you to map database error codes. The code 23505 lies in the dataIntegrityViolationCodes cdataIntegrityViolationCodes category.

Customizing Data Access Exception Handling

The Spring JDBC framework only maps well-known error codes. Sometimes, you may wish to customize the mapping yourself. For example, you might decide to add more codes to an existing category or define a custom exception for particular error codes.

In Table 15-2, the error code 23505 indicates a duplicate key error in Apache Derby. It is mapped by default to DataIntegrityViolationException. Suppose that you want to create a custom exception type, MyDuplicateKeyException, for this kind of error. It should extend DataIntegrityViolationException because it is also a kind of data integrity violation error. Remember that for an exception to be thrown by the Spring JDBC framework, it must be compatible with the root exception class DataAccessException.

```
package com.apress.springrecipes.vehicle;

import org.springframework.dao.DataIntegrityViolationException;

public class MyDuplicateKeyException extends DataIntegrityViolationException {

    public MyDuplicateKeyException(String msg) {
        super(msg);
    }

    public MyDuplicateKeyException(String msg, Throwable cause) {
        super(msg, cause);
    }
}
```

By default, Spring will look up an exception from the `sql-error-codes.xml` file located in the `org.springframework.jdbc.support` package. However, you can override some of the mappings by providing a file with the same name in the root of the classpath. If Spring can find your custom file, it will look up an exception from your mapping first. However, if it does not find a suitable exception there, Spring will look up the default mapping.

For example, suppose that you want to map your custom `DuplicateKeyException` type to error code `23505`. You have to add the binding via a `CustomSQLErrorCodesTranslation` bean, and then add this bean to the `customTranslations` category.

```xml
<?xml version="1.0" encoding="UTF-8"?>
<!DOCTYPE beans PUBLIC "-//SPRING//DTD BEAN 2.0//EN"
    "http://www.springframework.org/dtd/spring-beans-2.0.dtd">

<beans>
    <bean id="Derby"
        class="org.springframework.jdbc.support.SQLErrorCodes">
        <property name="databaseProductName">
            <value>Apache Derby</value>
        </property>
        <property name="useSqlStateForTranslation">
            <value>true</value>
        </property>
        <property name="customTranslations">
            <list>
                <ref local="myDuplicateKeyTranslation" />
            </list>
        </property>
    </bean>

    <bean id="myDuplicateKeyTranslation"
        class="org.springframework.jdbc.support.CustomSQLErrorCodesTranslation">
        <property name="errorCodes">
            <value>23505</value>
        </property>
        <property name="exceptionClass">
            <value>
                com.apress.springrecipes.vehicle.MyDuplicateKeyException
            </value>
        </property>
    </bean>
</beans>
```

Now, if you remove the try/catch block surrounding the vehicle insert operation and insert a duplicate vehicle, the Spring JDBC framework will throw a MyDuplicateKeyException instead.

However, if you are not satisfied with the basic code-to-exception mapping strategy used by the `SQLErrorCodes` class, you may further implement the `SQLExceptionTranslator` interface and inject its instance into a JDBC template via the `setExceptionTranslator()` method.

15-7. Problems with Using ORM Frameworks Directly

Problem

You've decided to go to the next level—you have a sufficiently complex domain model, and manually writing all the code for each entity is getting tedious, so you begin to investigate a few alternatives, like Hibernate. You're stunned to find that while they're powerful, they can be anything but simple!

Solution

Let Spring lend a hand; it has facilities for dealing with ORM layers that rival those available for plain ol' JDBC access.

How It Works

Suppose you are developing a course management system for a training center. The first class you create for this system is Course. This class is called an *entity class* or a *persistent class* because it represents a real-world entity and its instances will be persisted to a database. Remember that for each entity class to be persisted by an ORM framework, a default constructor with no argument is required.

```
package com.apress.springrecipes.course;
...
public class Course {

    private Long id;
    private String title;
    private Date beginDate;
    private Date endDate;
    private int fee;

    // Constructors, Getters and Setters
    ...
}
```

For each entity class, you must define an identifier property to uniquely identify an entity. It's a best practice to define an auto-generated identifier because this has no business meaning and thus won't be changed under any circumstances. Moreover, this identifier will be used by the ORM framework to determine an entity's state. If the identifier value is null, this entity will be treated as a new and unsaved entity. When this entity is persisted, an insert SQL statement will be issued; otherwise, an update statement will. To allow the identifier to be null, you should choose a primitive wrapper type like java.lang.Integer and java.lang.Long for the identifier.

In your course management system, you need a DAO interface to encapsulate the data access logic. Let's define the following operations in the CourseDao interface:

```
package com.apress.springrecipes.course;
...
public interface CourseDao {

    public void store(Course course);
    public void delete(Long courseId);
    public Course findById(Long courseId);
    public List<Course> findAll();
}
```

Usually, when using ORM for persisting objects, the insert and update operations are combined into a single operation (e.g., store). This is to let the ORM framework (not you) decide whether an object should be inserted or updated.

In order for an ORM framework to persist your objects to a database, it must know the mapping metadata for the entity classes. You have to provide mapping metadata to it in its supported format. The native format for Hibernate is XML. However, because each ORM framework may have its own format for defining mapping metadata, JPA defines a set of persistent annotations for you to define mapping metadata in a standard format that is more likely to be reusable in other ORM frameworks.

Hibernate also supports the use of JPA annotations to define mapping metadata, so there are essentially three different strategies for mapping and persisting your objects with Hibernate and JPA:

- Using the Hibernate API to persist objects with Hibernate XML mappings

- Using the Hibernate API to persist objects with JPA annotations

- Using JPA to persist objects with JPA annotations

The core programming elements of Hibernate, JPA, and other ORM frameworks resemble those of JDBC. They are summarized in Table 15-3.

Table 15-3. Core Programming Elements for Different Data Access Strategies

Concept	JDBC	Hibernate	JPA
Resource	Connection	Session	EntityManager
Resource factory	DataSource	SessionFactory	EntityManagerFactory
Exception	SQLException	HibernateException	PersistenceException

In Hibernate, the core interface for object persistence is Session, whose instances can be obtained from a SessionFactory instance. In JPA, the corresponding interface is EntityManager, whose instances can be obtained from an EntityManagerFactory instance. The exceptions thrown by Hibernate are of type HibernateException, while those thrown by JPA may be of type PersistenceException or other Java SE exceptions like IllegalArgumentException and IllegalStateException. Note that all these exceptions are subclasses of RuntimeException, which you are not forced to catch and handle.

Persisting Objects Using the Hibernate API with Hibernate XML Mappings

To map entity classes with Hibernate XML mappings, you can provide a single mapping file for each class or a large file for several classes. Practically, you should define one for each class by joining the class name with `.hbm.xml` as the file extension for ease of maintenance. The middle extension `hbm` stands for "Hibernate metadata."

The mapping file for the `Course` class should be named `Course.hbm.xml` and put in the same package as the entity class.

```
<!DOCTYPE hibernate-mapping
    PUBLIC "-//Hibernate/Hibernate Mapping DTD 3.0//EN"
    "http://hibernate.sourceforge.net/hibernate-mapping-3.0.dtd">

<hibernate-mapping package="com.apress.springrecipes.course">
    <class name="Course" table="COURSE">
        <id name="id" type="long" column="ID">
            <generator class="identity" />
        </id>
        <property name="title" type="string">
            <column name="TITLE" length="100" not-null="true" />
        </property>
        <property name="beginDate" type="date" column="BEGIN_DATE" />
        <property name="endDate" type="date" column="END_DATE" />
        <property name="fee" type="int" column="FEE" />
    </class>
</hibernate-mapping>
```

In the mapping file, you can specify a table name for this entity class and a table column for each simple property. You can also specify the column details such as column length, not-null constraints, and unique constraints. In addition, each entity must have an identifier defined, which can be generated automatically or assigned manually. In this example, the identifier will be generated using a table identity column.

Each application that uses Hibernate requires a global configuration file to configure properties such as the database settings (either JDBC connection properties or a data source's JNDI name), the database dialect, the mapping metadata's locations, and so on. When using XML mapping files to define mapping metadata, you have to specify the locations of the XML files. By default, Hibernate will read the `hibernate.cfg.xml` file from the root of the classpath. The middle extension `cfg` stands for "configuration." If there is a `hibernate.properties` file on the classpath, that file will be consulted first and overridden by `hibernate.cfg.xml`.

```
<!DOCTYPE hibernate-configuration PUBLIC
    "-//Hibernate/Hibernate Configuration DTD 3.0//EN"
    "http://hibernate.sourceforge.net/hibernate-configuration-3.0.dtd">

<hibernate-configuration>
    <session-factory>
        <property name="connection.driver_class">
            org.apache.derby.jdbc.ClientDriver
        </property>
```

```
        <property name="connection.url">
            jdbc:derby://localhost:1527/course;create=true
        </property>
        <property name="connection.username">app</property>
        <property name="connection.password">app</property>
        <property name="dialect">org.hibernate.dialect.DerbyDialect</property>
        <property name="show_sql">true</property>
        <property name="hbm2ddl.auto">update</property>

        <mapping resource="com/apress/springrecipes/course/↵
Course.hbm.xml" />
    </session-factory>
</hibernate-configuration>
```

Before you can persist your objects, you have to create tables in a database schema to store the object data. When using an ORM framework like Hibernate, you usually needn't design the tables by yourself. If you set the `hbm2ddl.auto` property to `update`, Hibernate can help you to update the database schema and create the tables when necessary. Naturally, you shouldn't enable this in production, but it can be a great speed boost for development.

Now, let's implement the DAO interface in the `hibernate` subpackage using the plain Hibernate API. Before you call the Hibernate API for object persistence, you have to initialize a Hibernate session factory (e.g., in the constructor).

```
package com.apress.springrecipes.course.hibernate;
...
import org.hibernate.Query;
import org.hibernate.Session;
import org.hibernate.SessionFactory;
import org.hibernate.Transaction;
import org.hibernate.cfg.Configuration;

public class HibernateCourseDao implements CourseDao {

    private SessionFactory sessionFactory;

    public HibernateCourseDao() {
        Configuration configuration = new Configuration().configure();
        sessionFactory = configuration.buildSessionFactory();
    }

    public void store(Course course) {
        Session session = sessionFactory.openSession();
        Transaction tx = session.getTransaction();
        try {
            tx.begin();
            session.saveOrUpdate(course);
            tx.commit();
        } catch (RuntimeException e) {
            tx.rollback();
            throw e;
```

```
        } finally {
            session.close();
        }
    }

    public void delete(Long courseId) {
        Session session = sessionFactory.openSession();
        Transaction tx = session.getTransaction();
        try {
            tx.begin();
            Course course = (Course) session.get(Course.class, courseId);
            session.delete(course);
            tx.commit();
        } catch (RuntimeException e) {
            tx.rollback();
            throw e;
        } finally {
            session.close();
        }
    }

    public Course findById(Long courseId) {
        Session session = sessionFactory.openSession();
        try {
            return (Course) session.get(Course.class, courseId);
        } finally {
            session.close();
        }
    }

    public List<Course> findAll() {
        Session session = sessionFactory.openSession();
        try {
            Query query = session.createQuery("from Course");
            return query.list();
        } finally {
            session.close();
        }
    }
}
```

The first step in using Hibernate is to create a Configuration object and ask it to load the Hibernate configuration file. By default, it loads hibernate.cfg.xml from the classpath root when you call the configure() method. Then, you build a Hibernate session factory from this Configuration object. The purpose of a session factory is to produce sessions for you to persist your objects.

In the preceding DAO methods, you first open a session from the session factory. For any operation that involves database update, such as saveOrUpdate() and delete(), you must start a Hibernate transaction on that session. If the operation completes successfully, you commit the transaction. Otherwise, you roll it back if any RuntimeException happens. For read-only operations such as get() and HQL queries, there's no need to start a transaction. Finally, you must remember to close a session to release the resources held by this session.

You can create the following Main class to test run all the DAO methods. It also demonstrates an entity's typical life cycle.

```
package com.apress.springrecipes.course;
...
public class Main {

    public static void main(String[] args) {
        CourseDao courseDao = new HibernateCourseDao();

        Course course = new Course();
        course.setTitle("Core Spring");
        course.setBeginDate(new GregorianCalendar(2007, 8, 1).getTime());
        course.setEndDate(new GregorianCalendar(2007, 9, 1).getTime());
        course.setFee(1000);
        courseDao.store(course);

        List<Course> courses = courseDao.findAll();
        Long courseId = courses.get(0).getId();

        course = courseDao.findById(courseId);
        System.out.println("Course Title: " + course.getTitle());
        System.out.println("Begin Date: " + course.getBeginDate());
        System.out.println("End Date: " + course.getEndDate());
        System.out.println("Fee: " + course.getFee());

        courseDao.delete(courseId);
    }
}
```

Persisting Objects Using the Hibernate API with JPA Annotations

JPA annotations are standardized in the JSR-220 specification, so they're supported by all JPA-compliant ORM frameworks, including Hibernate. Moreover, the use of annotations will be more convenient for you to edit mapping metadata in the same source file.

The following Course class illustrates the use of JPA annotations to define mapping metadata:

```
package com.apress.springrecipes.course;
...
import javax.persistence.Column;
import javax.persistence.Entity;
import javax.persistence.GeneratedValue;
import javax.persistence.GenerationType;
import javax.persistence.Id;
import javax.persistence.Table;
```

```
@Entity
@Table(name = "COURSE")
public class Course {

    @Id
    @GeneratedValue(strategy = GenerationType.IDENTITY)
    @Column(name = "ID")
    private Long id;

    @Column(name = "TITLE", length = 100, nullable = false)
    private String title;

    @Column(name = "BEGIN_DATE")
    private Date beginDate;

    @Column(name = "END_DATE")
    private Date endDate;

    @Column(name = "FEE")
    private int fee;

    // Constructors, Getters and Setters
    ...
}
```

Each entity class must be annotated with the @Entity annotation. You can assign a table name for an entity class in this annotation. For each property, you can specify a column name and column details using the @Column annotation. Each entity class must have an identifier defined by the @Id annotation. You can choose a strategy for identifier generation using the @GeneratedValue annotation. Here, the identifier will be generated by a table identity column.

Hibernate supports both native XML mapping files and JPA annotations as ways of defining mapping metadata. For JPA annotations, you have to specify the fully qualified names of the entity classes in hibernate.cfg.xml for Hibernate to read the annotations.

```
<hibernate-configuration>
    <session-factory>
        ...
        <!-- For Hibernate XML mappings -->
        <!--
        <mapping resource="com/apress/springrecipes/course/↩
Course.hbm.xml" />
        -->

        <!-- For JPA annotations -->
        <mapping class="com.apress.springrecipes.course.Course" />
    </session-factory>
</hibernate-configuration>
```

In the Hibernate DAO implementation, the Configuration class you used is for reading XML mappings. If you use JPA annotations to define mapping metadata for Hibernate, you have to use its subclass, AnnotationConfiguration, instead.

```
package com.apress.springrecipes.course.hibernate;
...
import org.hibernate.SessionFactory;
import org.hibernate.cfg.AnnotationConfiguration;

public class HibernateCourseDao implements CourseDao {

    private SessionFactory sessionFactory;

    public HibernateCourseDao() {
        // For Hibernate XML mapping
        // Configuration configuration = new Configuration().configure();

        // For JPA annotation
        Configuration configuration = new AnnotationConfiguration().configure();

        sessionFactory = configuration.buildSessionFactory();
    }
    ...
}
```

Persisting Objects Using JPA with Hibernate as the Engine

In addition to persistent annotations, JPA defines a set of programming interfaces for object persistence. However, JPA is not a persistence implementation; you have to pick up a JPA-compliant engine to provide persistence services. Hibernate can be JPA-compliant through the Hibernate EntityManager extension module. With this extension, Hibernate can work as an underlying JPA engine to persist objects. This lets you retain both the valuable investment in Hibernate (perhaps it's faster or handles certain operations more to your satisfaction) and write code that is JPA-compliant and portable among other JPA engines. This can also be a useful way to transition a code base to JPA. New code is written strictly against the JPA APIs, and older code is transitioned to the JPA interfaces.

In a Java EE environment, you can configure the JPA engine in a Java EE container. But in a Java SE application, you have to set up the engine locally. The configuration of JPA is through the central XML file persistence.xml, located in the META-INF directory of the classpath root. In this file, you can set any vendor-specific properties for the underlying engine configuration.

Now, let's create the JPA configuration file persistence.xml in the META-INF directory of the classpath root. Each JPA configuration file contains one or more <persistence-unit> elements. A *persistence unit* defines a set of persistent classes and how they should be persisted. Each persistence unit requires a name for identification. Here, you assign the name course to this persistence unit.

```
<persistence xmlns="http://java.sun.com/xml/ns/persistence"
    xmlns:xsi="http://www.w3.org/2001/XMLSchema-instance"
    xsi:schemaLocation="http://java.sun.com/xml/ns/persistence
        http://java.sun.com/xml/ns/persistence/persistence_1_0.xsd"
    version="1.0">
```

```
        <persistence-unit name="course">
            <properties>
                <property name="hibernate.ejb.cfgfile" value="/hibernate.cfg.xml" />
            </properties>
        </persistence-unit>
    </persistence>
```

In this JPA configuration file, you configure Hibernate as your underlying JPA engine by referring to the Hibernate configuration file located in the classpath root. However, because Hibernate EntityManager will automatically detect XML mapping files and JPA annotations as mapping metadata, you have no need to specify them explicitly. Otherwise, you will encounter an **org.hibernate. DuplicateMappingException**.

```
<hibernate-configuration>
    <session-factory>
        ...
        <!-- Don't need to specify mapping files and annotated classes -->
        <!--
        <mapping resource="com/apress/springrecipes/course/↵
Course.hbm.xml" />
        <mapping class="com.apress.springrecipes.course.Course" />
        -->
    </session-factory>
</hibernate-configuration>
```

As an alternative to referring to the Hibernate configuration file, you can also centralize all the Hibernate configurations in persistence.xml.

```
<persistence ...>
    <persistence-unit name="course">
        <properties>
            <property name="hibernate.connection.driver_class"
                value="org.apache.derby.jdbc.ClientDriver" />
            <property name="hibernate.connection.url"
                value="jdbc:derby://localhost:1527/course;create=true" />
            <property name="hibernate.connection.username" value="app" />
            <property name="hibernate.connection.password" value="app" />
            <property name="hibernate.dialect"
                value="org.hibernate.dialect.DerbyDialect" />
            <property name="hibernate.show_sql" value="true" />
            <property name="hibernate.hbm2ddl.auto" value="update" />
        </properties>
    </persistence-unit>
</persistence>'
```

In a Java EE environment, a Java EE container is able to manage the entity manager for you and inject it into your EJB components directly. But when you use JPA outside of a Java EE container (e.g., in a Java SE application), you have to create and maintain the entity manager by yourself.

■ **Note** To use Hibernate as the underlying JPA engine, you have to include the Hibernate Entity Manager libraries to your CLASSPATH. If you're using Maven, add the following dependency to your project:

```
<dependency>
  <groupId>org.hibernate</groupId>
  <artifactId>hibernate-entitymanager</artifactId>
  <version>${hibernate.version}</version>
</dependency>
```

Now, let's implement the `CourseDao` interface in the **jpa** subpackage using JPA in a Java SE application. Before you call JPA for object persistence, you have to initialize an entity manager factory. The purpose of an entity manager factory is to produce entity managers for you to persist your objects.

```
package com.apress.springrecipes.course.jpa;
...
import javax.persistence.EntityManager;
import javax.persistence.EntityManagerFactory;
import javax.persistence.EntityTransaction;
import javax.persistence.Persistence;
import javax.persistence.Query;

public class JpaCourseDao implements CourseDao {

    private EntityManagerFactory entityManagerFactory;

    public JpaCourseDao() {
        entityManagerFactory = Persistence.createEntityManagerFactory("course");
    }

    public void store(Course course) {
        EntityManager manager = entityManagerFactory.createEntityManager();
        EntityTransaction tx = manager.getTransaction();
        try {
            tx.begin();
            manager.merge(course);
            tx.commit();
        } catch (RuntimeException e) {
            tx.rollback();
            throw e;
        } finally {
            manager.close();
        }
    }
}
```

```
    public void delete(Long courseId) {
        EntityManager manager = entityManagerFactory.createEntityManager();
        EntityTransaction tx = manager.getTransaction();
        try {
            tx.begin();
            Course course = manager.find(Course.class, courseId);
            manager.remove(course);
            tx.commit();
        } catch (RuntimeException e) {
            tx.rollback();
            throw e;
        } finally {
            manager.close();
        }
    }

    public Course findById(Long courseId) {
        EntityManager manager = entityManagerFactory.createEntityManager();
        try {
            return manager.find(Course.class, courseId);
        } finally {
            manager.close();
        }
    }

    public List<Course> findAll() {
        EntityManager manager = entityManagerFactory.createEntityManager();
        try {
            Query query = manager.createQuery(
                "select course from Course course");
            return query.getResultList();
        } finally {
            manager.close();
        }
    }
}
```

The entity manager factory is built by the static method createEntityManagerFactory() of the
javax.persistence.Persistence class. You have to pass in a persistence unit name defined in
persistence.xml for an entity manager factory.

In the preceding DAO methods, you first create an entity manager from the entity manager factory.
For any operation that involves database update, such as merge() and remove(), you must start a JPA
transaction on the entity manager. For read-only operations such as find() and JPA queries, there's no
need to start a transaction. Finally, you must close an entity manager to release the resources.

You can test this DAO with the similar Main class, but this time, you instantiate the JPA DAO
implementation instead.

```
package com.apress.springrecipes.course;
...
public class Main {

    public static void main(String[] args) {
        CourseDao courseDao = new JpaCourseDao();
        ...
    }
}
```

In the preceding DAO implementations for both Hibernate and JPA, there are only one or two lines that are different for each DAO method. The rest of the lines are boilerplate routine tasks that you have to repeat. Moreover, each ORM framework has its own API for local transaction management.

15-8. Configuring ORM Resource Factories in Spring

Problem

When using an ORM framework on its own, you have to configure its resource factory with its API. For Hibernate and JPA, you have to build a session factory and an entity manager factory from the native Hibernate API and JPA. You have no choice but to manage these objects manually, without Spring's support.

Solution

Spring provides several factory beans for you to create a Hibernate session factory or a JPA entity manager factory as a singleton bean in the IoC container. These factories can be shared between multiple beans via dependency injection. Moreover, this allows the session factory and the entity manager factory to integrate with other Spring data access facilities, such as data sources and transaction managers.

How It Works

Configuring a Hibernate Session Factory in Spring

First of all, let's modify HibernateCourseDao to accept a session factory via dependency injection, instead of creating it directly with the native Hibernate API in the constructor.

```
package com.apress.springrecipes.course.hibernate;
...
import org.hibernate.SessionFactory;

public class HibernateCourseDao implements CourseDao {
```

```
    private SessionFactory sessionFactory;

    public void setSessionFactory(SessionFactory sessionFactory) {
        this.sessionFactory = sessionFactory;
    }
    ...
}
```

Now, let's look at how to declare a session factory that uses XML mapping files in Spring. For this purpose, you have to enable the XML mapping file definition in `hibernate.cfg.xml` again.

```
<hibernate-configuration>
    <session-factory>

        ...
        <!-- For Hibernate XML mappings -->
        <mapping resource="com/apress/springrecipes/course/↵
Course.hbm.xml" />
    </session-factory>
</hibernate-configuration>
```

Then, you create a bean configuration file for using Hibernate as the ORM framework (e.g., beans-hibernate.xml in the classpath root). You can declare a session factory that uses XML mapping files with the factory bean `LocalSessionFactoryBean`. You can also declare a `HibernateCourseDao` instance under Spring's management.

```
<beans xmlns="http://www.springframework.org/schema/beans"
    xmlns:xsi="http://www.w3.org/2001/XMLSchema-instance"
    xsi:schemaLocation="http://www.springframework.org/schema/beans
        http://www.springframework.org/schema/beans/spring-beans-3.0.xsd">

    <bean id="sessionFactory"
        class="org.springframework.orm.hibernate3.LocalSessionFactoryBean">
        <property name="configLocation" value="classpath:hibernate.cfg.xml" />
    </bean>

    <bean id="courseDao"
        class="com.apress.springrecipes.course.hibernate. ↵
HibernateCourseDao">
        <property name="sessionFactory" ref="sessionFactory" />
    </bean>
</beans>
```

Note that you can specify the `configLocation` property for this factory bean to load the Hibernate configuration file. The `configLocation` property is of type `Resource`, but you can assign a string value to it. The built-in property editor `ResourceEditor` will convert it into a `Resource` object. The preceding factory bean loads the configuration file from the root of the classpath.

Now, you can modify the `Main` class to retrieve the `HibernateCourseDao` instance from the Spring IoC container.

```
package com.apress.springrecipes.course;
...
import org.springframework.context.ApplicationContext;
import org.springframework.context.support.ClassPathXmlApplicationContext;

public class Main {

    public static void main(String[] args) {
        ApplicationContext context =
            new ClassPathXmlApplicationContext("beans-hibernate.xml");

        CourseDao courseDao = (CourseDao) context.getBean("courseDao");
        ...
    }
}
```

The preceding factory bean creates a session factory by loading the Hibernate configuration file, which includes the database settings (either JDBC connection properties or a data source's JNDI name). Now, suppose that you have a data source defined in the Spring IoC container. If you want to use this data source for your session factory, you can inject it into the dataSource property of LocalSessionFactoryBean. The data source specified in this property will override the database settings in the Hibernate configuration file. If this is set, the Hibernate settings should not define a connection provider to avoid meaningless double configuration.

```
<beans ...>
    ...
    <bean id="dataSource"
        class="org.springframework.jdbc.datasource.DriverManagerDataSource">
        <property name="driverClassName"
            value="org.apache.derby.jdbc.ClientDriver" />
        <property name="url"
            value="jdbc:derby://localhost:1527/course;create=true" />
        <property name="username" value="app" />
        <property name="password" value="app" />
    </bean>

    <bean id="sessionFactory"
        class="org.springframework.orm.hibernate3.LocalSessionFactoryBean">
        <property name="dataSource" ref="dataSource" />
        <property name="configLocation" value="classpath:hibernate.cfg.xml" />
    </bean>
</beans>
```

Or you can even ignore the Hibernate configuration file by merging all the configurations into LocalSessionFactoryBean. For example, you can specify the locations of the XML mapping files in the mappingResources property and other Hibernate properties such as the database dialect in the hibernateProperties property.

```
<bean id="sessionFactory"
    class="org.springframework.orm.hibernate3.LocalSessionFactoryBean">
    <property name="dataSource" ref="dataSource" />
    <property name="mappingResources">
        <list>
            <value>com/apress/springrecipes/course/Course.hbm.xml</value>
        </list>
    </property>
    <property name="hibernateProperties">
        <props>
            <prop key="hibernate.dialect">org.hibernate.dialect.DerbyDialect</prop>
            <prop key="hibernate.show_sql">true</prop>
            <prop key="hibernate.hbm2ddl.auto">update</prop>
        </props>
    </property>
</bean>
```

The mappingResources property's type is String[], so you can specify a set of mapping files in the classpath. LocalSessionFactoryBean also allows you take advantage of Spring's resource-loading support to load mapping files from various types of locations. You can specify the resource paths of the mapping files in the mappingLocations property, whose type is Resource[].

```
<bean id="sessionFactory"
    class="org.springframework.orm.hibernate3.LocalSessionFactoryBean">
    ...
    <property name="mappingLocations">
        <list>
            <value>classpath:com/apress/springrecipes/course/Course.hbm.xml</value>
        </list>
    </property>
    ...
</bean>
```

With Spring's resource-loading support, you can also use wildcards in a resource path to match multiple mapping files so that you don't need to configure their locations every time you add a new entity class. Spring's preregistered ResourceArrayPropertyEditor will convert this path into a Resource array.

```
<bean id="sessionFactory"
    class="org.springframework.orm.hibernate3.LocalSessionFactoryBean">
    ...
    <property name="mappingLocations"
        value="classpath:com/apress/springrecipes/course/*.hbm.xml" />
    ...
</bean>
```

If your mapping metadata is provided through JPA annotations, you have to make use of AnnotationSessionFactoryBean instead. You have to specify the persistent classes in the annotatedClasses property of AnnotationSessionFactoryBean, or use the packagesToScan property to tell the AnnotationSessionFactoryBean which packages to scan for beans with JPA annotations.

```
<bean id="sessionFactory" class="org.springframework.orm.hibernate3. ↵
    annotation.AnnotationSessionFactoryBean">
    <property name="dataSource" ref="dataSource" />
    <property name="annotatedClasses">
        <list>
            <value>com.apress.springrecipes.course.Course</value>
        </list>
    </property>
    <property name="hibernateProperties">
        <props>
            <prop key="hibernate.dialect">org.hibernate.dialect.DerbyDialect</prop>
            <prop key="hibernate.show_sql">true</prop>
            <prop key="hibernate.hbm2ddl.auto">update</prop>
        </props>
    </property>
</bean>
```

Now you can delete the Hibernate configuration file (i.e., `hibernate.cfg.xml`) because its configurations have been ported to Spring.

Configuring a JPA Entity Manager Factory in Spring

First of all, let's modify `JpaCourseDao` to accept an entity manager factory via dependency injection, instead of creating it directly in the constructor.

```
package com.apress.springrecipes.course.jpa;
...
import javax.persistence.EntityManagerFactory;
import javax.persistence.Persistence;

public class JpaCourseDao implements CourseDao {

    private EntityManagerFactory entityManagerFactory;

    public void setEntityManagerFactory(
            EntityManagerFactory entityManagerFactory) {
        this.entityManagerFactory = entityManagerFactory;
    }
    ...
}
```

The JPA specification defines how you should obtain an entity manager factory in Java SE and Java EE environments. In a Java SE environment, an entity manager factory is created manually by calling the `createEntityManagerFactory()` static method of the `Persistence` class.

Let's create a bean configuration file for using JPA (e.g., `beans-jpa.xml` in the classpath root). Spring provides a factory bean, `LocalEntityManagerFactoryBean`, for you to create an entity manager factory in the IoC container. You must specify the persistence unit name defined in the JPA configuration file. You can also declare a `JpaCourseDao` instance under Spring's management.

```
<beans xmlns="http://www.springframework.org/schema/beans"
    xmlns:xsi="http://www.w3.org/2001/XMLSchema-instance"
    xsi:schemaLocation="http://www.springframework.org/schema/beans
        http://www.springframework.org/schema/beans/spring-beans-3.0.xsd">

    <bean id="entityManagerFactory"
        class="org.springframework.orm.jpa.LocalEntityManagerFactoryBean">
        <property name="persistenceUnitName" value="course" />
    </bean>

    <bean id="courseDao"
        class="com.apress.springrecipes.course.jpa.JpaCourseDao">
        <property name="entityManagerFactory" ref="entityManagerFactory" />
    </bean>
</beans>
```

Now, you can test this JpaCourseDao instance with the Main class by retrieving it from the Spring IoC container.

```
package com.apress.springrecipes.course;
...
import org.springframework.context.ApplicationContext;
import org.springframework.context.support.ClassPathXmlApplicationContext;

public class Main {

    public static void main(String[] args) {
        ApplicationContext context =
            new ClassPathXmlApplicationContext("beans-jpa.xml");

        CourseDao courseDao = (CourseDao) context.getBean("courseDao");
        ...
    }
}
```

In a Java EE environment, you can look up an entity manager factory from a Java EE container with JNDI. In Spring, you can perform a JNDI lookup by using the <jee:jndi-lookup> element.

```
<jee:jndi-lookup id="entityManagerFactory" jndi-name="jpa/coursePU" />
```

LocalEntityManagerFactoryBean creates an entity manager factory by loading the JPA configuration file (i.e., persistence.xml). Spring supports a more flexible way to create an entity manager factory by another factory bean, LocalContainerEntityManagerFactoryBean. It allows you to override some of the configurations in the JPA configuration file, such as the data source and database dialect. So, you can take advantage of Spring's data access facilities to configure the entity manager factory.

```
<beans ...>
    ...
    <bean id="dataSource"
        class="org.springframework.jdbc.datasource.DriverManagerDataSource">
        <property name="driverClassName"
            value="org.apache.derby.jdbc.ClientDriver" />
        <property name="url"
            value="jdbc:derby://localhost:1527/course;create=true" />
        <property name="username" value="app" />
        <property name="password" value="app" />
    </bean>

    <bean id="entityManagerFactory" class="org.springframework.orm.jpa.
        LocalContainerEntityManagerFactoryBean">
        <property name="persistenceUnitName" value="course" />
        <property name="dataSource" ref="dataSource" />
        <property name="jpaVendorAdapter">
            <bean class="org.springframework.orm.jpa.vendor.↵
                HibernateJpaVendorAdapter">
                <property name="databasePlatform"
                    value="org.hibernate.dialect.DerbyDialect" />
                <property name="showSql" value="true" />
                <property name="generateDdl" value="true" />
            </bean>
        </property>
    </bean>
</beans>
```

In the preceding bean configurations, you inject a data source into this entity manager factory. It will override the database settings in the JPA configuration file. You can set a JPA vendor adapter to LocalContainerEntityManagerFactoryBean to specify JPA engine–specific properties. With Hibernate as the underlying JPA engine, you should choose HibernateJpaVendorAdapter. Other properties that are not supported by this adapter can be specified in the jpaProperties property.

Now your JPA configuration file (i.e., persistence.xml) can be simplified as follows because its configurations have been ported to Spring:

```
<persistence ...>
    <persistence-unit name="course" />
</persistence>
```

15-9. Persisting Objects with Spring's ORM Templates

Problem

When using an ORM framework on its own, you have to repeat certain routine tasks for each DAO operation. For example, in a DAO operation implemented with Hibernate or JPA, you have to open and close a session or an entity manager, and begin, commit, and roll back a transaction with the native API.

Solution

Spring's approach to simplifying an ORM framework's usage is the same as JDBC's—by defining template classes and DAO support classes. Also, Spring defines an abstract layer on top of different transaction management APIs. For different ORM frameworks, you only have to pick up a corresponding transaction manager implementation. Then, you can manage transactions for them in a similar way.

In Spring's data access module, the support for different data access strategies is consistent. Table 15-4 compares the support classes for JDBC, Hibernate, and JPA.

Table 15-4. *Spring's Support Classes for Different Data Access Strategies*

Support Class	JDBC	Hibernate	JPA
Template class	JdbcTemplate	HibernateTemplate	JpaTemplate
DAO support	JdbcDaoSupport	HibernateDaoSupport	JpaDaoSupport
Transaction	DataSourceTransaction	HibernateTransaction	JpaTransactionManager

Spring defines the HibernateTemplate and JpaTemplate classes to provide template methods for different types of Hibernate and JPA operations to minimize the effort involved in using them. The template methods in HibernateTemplate and JpaTemplate ensure that Hibernate sessions and JPA entity managers will be opened and closed properly. They will also have native Hibernate and JPA transactions participate in Spring-managed transactions. As a result, you will be able to manage transactions declaratively for your Hibernate and JPA DAOs without any boilerplate transaction code.

How It Works

Using a Hibernate Template and a JPA Template

First, the HibernateCourseDao class can be simplified as follows with the help of Spring's HibernateTemplate:

```
package com.apress.springrecipes.course.hibernate;
...
import org.springframework.orm.hibernate3.HibernateTemplate;
import org.springframework.transaction.annotation.Transactional;

public class HibernateCourseDao implements CourseDao {

    private HibernateTemplate hibernateTemplate;

    public void setHibernateTemplate(HibernateTemplate hibernateTemplate) {
        this.hibernateTemplate = hibernateTemplate;
    }
```

```
@Transactional
public void store(Course course) {
    hibernateTemplate.saveOrUpdate(course);
}

@Transactional
public void delete(Long courseId) {
    Course course = (Course) hibernateTemplate.get(Course.class, courseId);
    hibernateTemplate.delete(course);
}

@Transactional(readOnly = true)
public Course findById(Long courseId) {
    return (Course) hibernateTemplate.get(Course.class, courseId);
}

@Transactional(readOnly = true)
public List<Course> findAll() {
    return hibernateTemplate.find("from Course");
}
}
```

In this DAO implementation, you declare all the DAO methods to be transactional with the `@Transactional` annotation. Among these methods, `findById()` and `findAll()` are read-only. The template methods in `HibernateTemplate` are responsible for managing the sessions and transactions. If there are multiple Hibernate operations in a transactional DAO method, the template methods will ensure that they will run within the same session and transaction. As a result, you have no need to deal with the Hibernate API for session and transaction management.

The `HibernateTemplate` class is thread-safe, so you can declare a single instance of it in the bean configuration file for Hibernate (i.e., `beans-hibernate.xml`) and inject this instance into all Hibernate DAOs. A `HibernateTemplate` instance requires the `sessionFactory` property to be set. You can inject this property by either setter method or constructor argument.

```
<beans xmlns="http://www.springframework.org/schema/beans"
    xmlns:xsi="http://www.w3.org/2001/XMLSchema-instance"
    xmlns:tx="http://www.springframework.org/schema/tx"
    xsi:schemaLocation="http://www.springframework.org/schema/beans
        http://www.springframework.org/schema/beans/spring-beans-3.0.xsd
        http://www.springframework.org/schema/tx
        http://www.springframework.org/schema/tx/spring-tx-3.0.xsd">
    ...
    <tx:annotation-driven />

    <bean id="transactionManager"
        class="org.springframework.orm.hibernate3.HibernateTransactionManager">
        <property name="sessionFactory" ref="sessionFactory" />
    </bean>
```

```
    <bean id="hibernateTemplate"
        class="org.springframework.orm.hibernate3.HibernateTemplate">
        <property name="sessionFactory" ref="sessionFactory" />
    </bean>

    <bean name="courseDao"
        class="com.apress.springrecipes.course.hibernate. ↵
HibernateCourseDao">
        <property name="hibernateTemplate" ref="hibernateTemplate" />
    </bean>
</beans>
```

To enable declarative transaction management for the methods annotated with @Transactional, you have to enable the <tx:annotation-driven> element in your bean configuration file. By default, it will look for a transaction manager with the name transactionManager, so you have to declare a HibernateTransactionManager instance with that name. HibernateTransactionManager requires the session factory property to be set. It will manage transactions for sessions opened through this session factory.

Similarly, you can simplify the JpaCourseDao class as follows with the help of Spring's JpaTemplate. You also declare all the DAO methods to be transactional.

```
package com.apress.springrecipes.course.jpa;
...
import org.springframework.orm.jpa.JpaTemplate;
import org.springframework.transaction.annotation.Transactional;

public class JpaCourseDao implements CourseDao {

    private JpaTemplate jpaTemplate;

    public void setJpaTemplate(JpaTemplate jpaTemplate) {
        this.jpaTemplate = jpaTemplate;
    }

    @Transactional
    public void store(Course course) {
        jpaTemplate.merge(course);
    }

    @Transactional
    public void delete(Long courseId) {
        Course course = jpaTemplate.find(Course.class, courseId);
        jpaTemplate.remove(course);
    }

    @Transactional(readOnly = true)
    public Course findById(Long courseId) {
        return jpaTemplate.find(Course.class, courseId);
    }
```

```
    @Transactional(readOnly = true)
    public List<Course> findAll() {
        return jpaTemplate.find("from Course");
    }
}
```

In the bean configuration file for JPA (i.e., `beans-jpa.xml`), you can declare a `JpaTemplate` instance and inject it into all JPA DAOs. Also, you have to declare a `JpaTransactionManager` instance for managing JPA transactions.

```xml
<beans xmlns="http://www.springframework.org/schema/beans"
    xmlns:xsi="http://www.w3.org/2001/XMLSchema-instance"
    xmlns:tx="http://www.springframework.org/schema/tx"
    xsi:schemaLocation="http://www.springframework.org/schema/beans
        http://www.springframework.org/schema/beans/spring-beans-3.0.xsd
        http://www.springframework.org/schema/tx
        http://www.springframework.org/schema/tx/spring-tx-3.0.xsd">
    ...
    <tx:annotation-driven />

    <bean id="transactionManager"
        class="org.springframework.orm.jpa.JpaTransactionManager">
        <property name="entityManagerFactory" ref="entityManagerFactory" />
    </bean>

    <bean id="jpaTemplate"
        class="org.springframework.orm.jpa.JpaTemplate">
        <property name="entityManagerFactory" ref="entityManagerFactory" />
    </bean>

    <bean name="courseDao"
        class="com.apress.springrecipes.course.jpa.JpaCourseDao">
        <property name="jpaTemplate" ref="jpaTemplate" />
    </bean>
</beans>
```

Another advantage of `HibernateTemplate` and `JpaTemplate` is that they will translate native Hibernate and JPA exceptions into exceptions in Spring's `DataAccessException` hierarchy. This allows consistent exception handling for all the data access strategies in Spring. For instance, if a database constraint is violated when persisting an object, Hibernate will throw an `org.hibernate.exception.ConstraintViolationException`, while JPA will throw a `javax.persistence.EntityExistsException`. These exceptions will be translated by `HibernateTemplate` and `JpaTemplate` into `DataIntegrityViolationException`, which is a subclass of Spring's `DataAccessException`.

If you want to get access to the underlying Hibernate session or JPA entity manager in `HibernateTemplate` or `JpaTemplate` in order to perform native Hibernate or JPA operations, you can implement the `HibernateCallback` or `JpaCallback` interface and pass its instance to the `execute()` method of the template. This will give you a chance to use any implementation-specific features directly if there's not sufficient support already available from the template implementations.

```
hibernateTemplate.execute(new HibernateCallback() {
    public Object doInHibernate(Session session) throws HibernateException,
            SQLException {
        // ... anything you can imagine doing can be done here. ↵
        // Cache invalidation, for example...
    }
};
```

```
jpaTemplate.execute(new JpaCallback() {
    public Object doInJpa(EntityManager em) throws PersistenceException {
// ... anything you can imagine doing can be done here.     }
};
```

Extending the Hibernate and JPA DAO Support Classes

Your Hibernate DAO can extend HibernateDaoSupport to have the setSessionFactory() and setHibernateTemplate() methods inherited. Then, in your DAO methods, you can simply call the getHibernateTemplate() method to retrieve the template instance.

```
package com.apress.springrecipes.course.hibernate;
...
import org.springframework.orm.hibernate3.support.HibernateDaoSupport;
import org.springframework.transaction.annotation.Transactional;

public class HibernateCourseDao extends HibernateDaoSupport implements
        CourseDao {

    @Transactional
    public void store(Course course) {
        getHibernateTemplate().saveOrUpdate(course);
    }

    @Transactional
    public void delete(Long courseId) {
        Course course = (Course) getHibernateTemplate().get(Course.class,
                courseId);
        getHibernateTemplate().delete(course);
    }

    @Transactional(readOnly = true)
    public Course findById(Long courseId) {
        return (Course) getHibernateTemplate().get(Course.class, courseId);
    }

    @Transactional(readOnly = true)
    public List<Course> findAll() {
        return getHibernateTemplate().find("from Course");
    }
}
```

Because `HibernateCourseDao` inherits the `setSessionFactory()` and `setHibernateTemplate()` methods, you can inject either of them into your DAO so that you can retrieve the `HibernateTemplate` instance. If you inject a session factory, you will be able to delete the `HibernateTemplate` declaration.

```
<bean name="courseDao"
    class="com.apress.springrecipes.course.hibernate.HibernateCourseDao">
    <property name="sessionFactory" ref="sessionFactory" />
</bean>
```

Similarly, your JPA DAO can extend `JpaDaoSupport` to have `setEntityManagerFactory()` and `setJpaTemplate()` inherited. In your DAO methods, you can simply call the `getJpaTemplate()` method to retrieve the template instance. This instance will contain the pre-initialized `EntityManagerFactory`.

```
package com.apress.springrecipes.course.jpa;
...
import org.springframework.orm.jpa.support.JpaDaoSupport:
import org.springframework.transaction.annotation.Transactional;

public class JpaCourseDao extends JpaDaoSupport implements CourseDao {

    @Transactional
    public void store(Course course) {
        getJpaTemplate().merge(course);
    }

    @Transactional
    public void delete(Long courseId) {
        Course course = getJpaTemplate().find(Course.class, courseId);
        getJpaTemplate().remove(course);
    }

    @Transactional(readOnly = true)
    public Course findById(Long courseId) {
        return getJpaTemplate().find(Course.class, courseId);
    }

    @Transactional(readOnly = true)
    public List<Course> findAll() {
        return getJpaTemplate().find("from Course");
    }
}
```

Because `JpaCourseDao` inherits both `setEntityManagerFactory()` and `setJpaTemplate()`, you can inject either of them into your DAO. If you inject an entity manager factory, you will be able to delete the `JpaTemplate` he `JpaTemplate` declaration.

```
<bean name="courseDao"
    class="com.apress.springrecipes.course.jpa.JpaCourseDao">
    <property name="entityManagerFactory" ref="entityManagerFactory" />
</bean>
```

15-10. Persisting Objects with Hibernate's Contextual Sessions

Problem

Spring's `HibernateTemplate` can simplify your DAO implementation by managing sessions and transactions for you. However, using `HibernateTemplate` means your DAO has to depend on Spring's API.

Solution

An alternative to Spring's `HibernateTemplate` is to use Hibernate's contextual sessions. In Hibernate 3, a session factory can manage contextual sessions for you and allows you to retrieve them by the `getCurrentSession()` method on `org.hibernate.SessionFactory`. Within a single transaction, you will get the same session for each `getCurrentSession()` method call. This ensures that there will be only one Hibernate session per transaction, so it works nicely with Spring's transaction management support.

How It Works

To use the contextual session approach, your DAO methods require access to the session factory, which can be injected via a setter method or a constructor argument. Then, in each DAO method, you get the contextual session from the session factory and use it for object persistence.

```
package com.apress.springrecipes.course.hibernate;
...
import org.hibernate.Query;
import org.hibernate.SessionFactory;
import org.springframework.transaction.annotation.Transactional;

public class HibernateCourseDao implements CourseDao {

    private SessionFactory sessionFactory;

    public void setSessionFactory(SessionFactory sessionFactory) {
        this.sessionFactory = sessionFactory;
    }

    @Transactional
    public void store(Course course) {
        sessionFactory.getCurrentSession().saveOrUpdate(course);
    }
```

```
@Transactional
public void delete(Long courseId) {
    Course course = (Course) sessionFactory.getCurrentSession().get(
            Course.class, courseId);
    sessionFactory.getCurrentSession().delete(course);
}

@Transactional(readOnly = true)
public Course findById(Long courseId) {
    return (Course) sessionFactory.getCurrentSession().get(
            Course.class, courseId);
}

@Transactional(readOnly = true)
public List<Course> findAll() {
    Query query = sessionFactory.getCurrentSession().createQuery(
            "from Course");
    return query.list();
}
}
```

Note that all your DAO methods must be made transactional. This is required because Spring wraps the `SessionFactory` with a proxy that expects that Spring's transaction management is in play when methods on a session are made. It will attempt to find a transaction and then fail, complaining that no Hibernate session's been bound to the thread. You can achieve this by annotating each method or the entire class with `@Transactional`. This ensures that the persistence operations within a DAO method will be executed in the same transaction and hence by the same session. Moreover, if a service layer component's method calls multiple DAO methods, and it propagates its own transaction to these methods, then all these DAO methods will run within the same session as well.

In the bean configuration file for Hibernate (i.e., `beans-hibernate.xml`), you have to declare a `HibernateTransactionManager` instance for this application and enable declarative transaction management via `<tx:annotation-driven>`.

```xml
<beans xmlns="http://www.springframework.org/schema/beans"
    xmlns:xsi="http://www.w3.org/2001/XMLSchema-instance"
    xmlns:tx="http://www.springframework.org/schema/tx"
    xsi:schemaLocation="http://www.springframework.org/schema/beans
        http://www.springframework.org/schema/beans/spring-beans-3.0.xsd
        http://www.springframework.org/schema/tx
        http://www.springframework.org/schema/tx/spring-tx-3.0.xsd">
...
<tx:annotation-driven />

<bean id="transactionManager"
    class="org.springframework.orm.hibernate3.HibernateTransactionManager">
    <property name="sessionFactory" ref="sessionFactory" />
</bean>
```

```
    <bean name="courseDao"
        class="com.apress.springrecipes.course.hibernate.HibernateCourseDao">
        <property name="sessionFactory" ref="sessionFactory" />
    </bean>
</beans>
```

Remember that `HibernateTemplate` will translate the native Hibernate exceptions into exceptions in Spring's `DataAccessException` hierarchy. This allows consistent exception handling for different data access strategies in Spring. However, when calling the native methods on a Hibernate session, the exceptions thrown will be of native type `HibernateException`. If you want the Hibernate exceptions to be translated into Spring's `DataAccessException` for consistent exception handling, you have to apply the `@Repository` annotation to your DAO class that requires exception translation.

```
package com.apress.springrecipes.course.hibernate;
...
import org.springframework.stereotype.Repository;

@Repository
public class HibernateCourseDao implements CourseDao {
    ...
}
```

Then, register a `PersistenceExceptionTranslationPostProcessor` instance to translate the native Hibernate exceptions into data access exceptions in Spring's `DataAccessException` hierarchy. This bean post processor will only translate exceptions for beans annotated with `@Repository`.

```
<beans ...>
    ...
    <bean class="org.springframework.dao.annotation.↵
        PersistenceExceptionTranslationPostProcessor" />
</beans>
```

In Spring, `@Repository` is a stereotype annotation. By annotating it, a component class can be auto-detected through component scanning. You can assign a component name in this annotation and have the session factory auto-wired by the Spring IoC container with `@Autowired`.

```
package com.apress.springrecipes.course.hibernate;
...
import org.hibernate.SessionFactory;
import org.springframework.beans.factory.annotation.Autowired;
import org.springframework.stereotype.Repository;

@Repository("courseDao")
public class HibernateCourseDao implements CourseDao {

    private SessionFactory sessionFactory;
```

```
@Autowired
public void setSessionFactory(SessionFactory sessionFactory) {
    this.sessionFactory = sessionFactory;
}
...
}
```

Then, you can simply enable the `<context:component-scan>` element and delete the original HibernateCourseDao bean declaration.

```
<beans xmlns="http://www.springframework.org/schema/beans"
    xmlns:xsi="http://www.w3.org/2001/XMLSchema-instance"
    xmlns:context="http://www.springframework.org/schema/context"
    xmlns:tx="http://www.springframework.org/schema/tx"
    xsi:schemaLocation="http://www.springframework.org/schema/beans
        http://www.springframework.org/schema/beans/spring-beans-3.0.xsd
        http://www.springframework.org/schema/context
        http://www.springframework.org/schema/context/spring-context-3.0.xsd
        http://www.springframework.org/schema/tx
        http://www.springframework.org/schema/tx/spring-tx-3.0.xsd">

    <context:component-scan
        base-package="com.apress.springrecipes.course.hibernate" />
    ...
</beans>
```

15-11. Persisting Objects with JPA's Context Injection

Problem

In a Java EE environment, a Java EE container can manage entity managers for you and inject them into your EJB components directly. An EJB component can simply perform persistence operations on an injected entity manager without caring much about the entity manager creation and transaction management.

Similarly, Spring provides JpaTemplate to simplify your DAO implementation by managing entity managers and transactions for you. However, using Spring's JpaTemplate means your DAO is dependent on Spring's API.

Solution

An alternative to Spring's JpaTemplate is to use JPA's context injection. Originally, the @PersistenceContext annotation is used for entity manager injection in EJB components. Spring can also interpret this annotation by means of a bean post processor. It will inject an entity manager into a property with this annotation. Spring ensures that all your persistence operations within a single transaction will be handled by the same entity manager.

How It Works

To use the context injection approach, you can declare an entity manager field in your DAO and annotate it with the @PersistenceContext annotation. Spring will inject an entity manager into this field for you to persist your objects.

```
package com.apress.springrecipes.course.jpa;
...
import javax.persistence.EntityManager;
import javax.persistence.PersistenceContext;
import javax.persistence.Query;

import org.springframework.transaction.annotation.Transactional;

public class JpaCourseDao implements CourseDao {

    @PersistenceContext
    private EntityManager entityManager;

    @Transactional
    public void store(Course course) {
        entityManager.merge(course);
    }

    @Transactional
    public void delete(Long courseId) {
        Course course = entityManager.find(Course.class, courseId);
        entityManager.remove(course);
    }

    @Transactional(readOnly = true)
    public Course findById(Long courseId) {
        return entityManager.find(Course.class, courseId);
    }

    @Transactional(readOnly = true)
    public List<Course> findAll() {
        Query query = entityManager.createQuery("from Course");
        return query.getResultList();
    }
}
```

You can annotate each DAO method or the entire DAO class with @Transactional to make all these methods transactional. It ensures that the persistence operations within a DAO method will by executed in the same transaction and hence by the same entity manager.

In the bean configuration file for JPA (i.e., beans-jpa.xml), you have to declare a JpaTransactionManager instance and enable declarative transaction management via <tx:annotation-driven>. You have to register a PersistenceAnnotationBeanPostProcessor instance to inject entity managers into properties annotated with @PersistenceContext.

```
<beans xmlns="http://www.springframework.org/schema/beans"
    xmlns:xsi="http://www.w3.org/2001/XMLSchema-instance"
    xmlns:tx="http://www.springframework.org/schema/tx"
    xsi:schemaLocation="http://www.springframework.org/schema/beans
        http://www.springframework.org/schema/beans/spring-beans-3.0.xsd
        http://www.springframework.org/schema/tx
        http://www.springframework.org/schema/tx/spring-tx-3.0.xsd">
    ...
    <tx:annotation-driven />

    <bean id="transactionManager"
        class="org.springframework.orm.jpa.JpaTransactionManager">
        <property name="entityManagerFactory" ref="entityManagerFactory" />
    </bean>

    <bean name="courseDao"
        class="com.apress.springrecipes.course.jpa.JpaCourseDao" />

    <bean class="org.springframework.orm.jpa.support.PersistenceAnnotationBeanPostProcessor" />
</beans>
```

A PersistenceAnnotationBeanPostProcessor instance will be registered automatically once you enable the <context:annotation-config> element. So, you can delete its explicit bean declaration.

```
<beans xmlns="http://www.springframework.org/schema/beans"
    xmlns:xsi="http://www.w3.org/2001/XMLSchema-instance"
    xmlns:context="http://www.springframework.org/schema/context"
    xmlns:tx="http://www.springframework.org/schema/tx"
    xsi:schemaLocation="http://www.springframework.org/schema/beans
        http://www.springframework.org/schema/beans/spring-beans-3.0.xsd
        http://www.springframework.org/schema/context
        http://www.springframework.org/schema/context/spring-context-3.0.xsd
        http://www.springframework.org/schema/tx
        http://www.springframework.org/schema/tx/spring-tx-3.0.xsd">

    <context:annotation-config />
    ...
</beans>
```

This bean post processor can also inject the entity manager factory into a property with the @PersistenceUnit annotation. This allows you to create entity managers and manage transactions by yourself. It's no different from injecting the entity manager factory via a setter method.

```
package com.apress.springrecipes.course.jpa;
...
import javax.persistence.EntityManagerFactory;
import javax.persistence.PersistenceUnit;
```

```
public class JpaCourseDao implements CourseDao {
    @PersistenceContext
    private EntityManager entityManager;

    @PersistenceUnit
    private EntityManagerFactory entityManagerFactory;
    ...
}
```

Remember that `JpaTemplate` will translate the native JPA exceptions into exceptions in Spring's `DataAccessException` hierarchy. However, when calling native methods on a JPA entity manager, the exceptions thrown will be of native type `PersistenceException`, or other Java SE exceptions like `IllegalArgumentException` and `IllegalStateException`. If you want JPA exceptions to be translated into Spring's `DataAccessException`, you have to apply the `@Repository` annotation to your DAO class.

```
package com.apress.springrecipes.course.jpa;
...
import org.springframework.stereotype.Repository;

@Repository("courseDao")
public class JpaCourseDao implements CourseDao {
    ...
}
```

Then, register a `PersistenceExceptionTranslationPostProcessor` instance to translate the native JPA exceptions into exceptions in Spring's `DataAccessException` hierarchy. You can also enable `<context:component-scan>` and delete the original `JpaCourseDao` bean declaration because `@Repository` is a stereotype annotation in Spring 2.5 and beyond.

```
<beans ...>
    ...
    <context:component-scan
        base-package="com.apress.springrecipes.course.jpa" />

    <bean class="org.springframework.dao.annotation.PersistenceException
TranslationPostProcessor" />
</beans>
```

Summary

This chapter discussed how to use Spring's support for JDBC, Hibernate, and JPA. You learned how to configure a `DataSource` to connect to a database and how to use Spring's `JdbcTemplate`, `HibernateTemplate`, and `JpaTemplate` to rid your code of tedious boilerplate handling. You saw how to use the utility base classes to build DAO classes with JDBC, Hibernate, and JPA, as well as how to use Spring's support for stereotype annotations and component scanning to easily build new DAOs and Services with a minimum of XML.

In the next chapter, you will learn how to use transactions (i.e., for JMS or a database) with Spring to help ensure consistent state in your services.

■ ■ ■

CHAPTER 16

Transaction Management in Spring

In this chapter, you will learn about the basic concept of transactions and Spring's capabilities in the area of transaction management. Transaction management is an essential technique in enterprise applications to ensure data integrity and consistency. Spring, as an enterprise application framework, provides an abstract layer on top of different transaction management APIs. As an application developer, you can use Spring's transaction management facilities without having to know much about the underlying transaction management APIs.

Like the *bean-managed transaction (BMT)* and *container-managed transaction (CMT)* approaches in EJB, Spring supports both programmatic and declarative transaction management. The aim of Spring's transaction support is to provide an alternative to EJB transactions by adding transaction capabilities to POJOs.

Programmatic transaction management is achieved by embedding transaction management code in your business methods to control the commit and rollback of transactions. You usually commit a transaction if a method completes normally and roll back a transaction if a method throws certain types of exceptions. With programmatic transaction management, you can define your own rules to commit and roll back transactions.

However, when managing transactions programmatically, you have to include transaction management code in each transactional operation. As a result, the boilerplate transaction code is repeated in each of these operations. Moreover, it's hard for you to enable and disable transaction management for different applications. If you have a solid understanding of AOP, you may already have noticed that transaction management is a kind of crosscutting concern.

Declarative transaction management is preferable to programmatic transaction management in most cases. It's achieved by separating transaction management code from your business methods via declarations. Transaction management, as a kind of crosscutting concern, can be modularized with the AOP approach. Spring supports declarative transaction management through the Spring AOP framework. This can help you to enable transactions for your applications more easily and define a consistent transaction policy. Declarative transaction management is less flexible than programmatic transaction management. Programmatic transaction management allows you to control transactions through your code—explicitly starting, committing, and joining them as you see fit. You can specify a set of transaction attributes to define your transactions at a fine level of granularity. The transaction attributes supported by Spring include the propagation behavior, isolation level, rollback rules, transaction timeout, and whether or not the transaction is read-only. These attributes allow you to further customize the behavior of your transactions.

Upon finishing this chapter, you will be able to apply different transaction management strategies in your application. Moreover, you will be familiar with different transaction attributes to finely define your transactions.

Programmatic transaction management is a good idea in certain cases where you don't feel the addition of Spring proxies is worth the trouble or negligible performance loss. Here, you might access the native transaction yourself and control the transaction manually. A more convenient option that avoids the overhead of Spring proxies is the TransactionTemplate class, which provides a template method around which a transactional boundary is started and then committed.

16-1. Problems with Transaction Management

Transaction management is an essential technique in enterprise application development to ensure data integrity and consistency. Without transaction management, your data and resources may be corrupted and left in an inconsistent state. Transaction management is particularly important for recovering from unexpected errors in a concurrent and distributed environment .

In simple words, a *transaction* is a series of actions that are treated as a single unit of work. These actions should either complete entirely or take no effect at all. If all the actions go well, the transaction should be committed permanently. In contrast, if any of them goes wrong, the transaction should be rolled back to the initial state as if nothing had happened.

The concept of transactions can be described with four key properties: *atomicity, consistency, isolation, and durability (ACID)*.

- *Atomicity.* A *transaction* is an atomic operation that consists of a series of actions. The atomicity of a transaction ensures that the actions either complete entirely or take no effect at all.

- *Consistency.* Once all actions of a transaction have completed, the transaction is committed. Then your data and resources will be in a consistent state that conforms to business rules.

- *Isolation.* Because there may be many transactions processing with the same data set at the same time, each transaction should be isolated from others to prevent data corruption.

- *Durability.* Once a transaction has completed, its result should be durable to survive any system failure (imagine if the power to your machine was cut right in the middle of a transaction's commit). Usually, the result of a transaction is written to persistent storage.

To understand the importance of transaction management, let's begin with an example about purchasing books from an online bookshop. First, you have to create a new schema for this application in your database. If you are choosing Apache Derby as your database engine, you can connect to it with the JDBC properties shown in Table 16-1. For the examples in this book, we're using Derby 10.4.2.0.

Table 16-1. JDBC Properties for Connecting to the Application Database

Property	Value
Driver class	`org.apache.derby.jdbc.ClientDriver`
URL	`jdbc:derby://localhost:1527/bookshop;create=true`
Username	`App`
Password	`App`

With the preceding configuration, the database will be created for you because of the parameter on the JDBC URL: `create=true`. For your bookshop application, you need a place to store the data. You'll create a simple database to manage books and accounts.

The entity relational (ER) diagram for the tables looks like Figure 16-1.

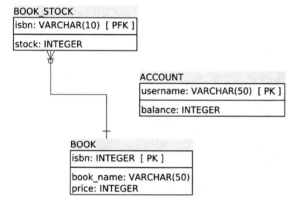

Figure 16-1. BOOK_STOCK describes how many given BOOKs exist.

Now, let's create the SQL for the preceding model. You'll use the `ij` tool that ships with Derby. On a command line, proceed to the directory where Derby is installed (usually just where you unzipped it when you downloaded it.). Descend to the `bin` directory. If Derby's not already started, run `startNetworkServer` (or `startNetworkServer.bat` on Windows). Now, you need to log in and execute the SQL DDL. Background the Derby Server process or open up a second shell and return to the same `bin` directory in the Derby installation directory. Execute `ij`. In the shell, execute the following:

```
connect 'jdbc:derby://localhost:1527/bookshop;create=true' ;
```

Paste the following SQL into the shell and verify its success:

```
CREATE TABLE BOOK (
    ISBN          VARCHAR(50)    NOT NULL,
    BOOK_NAME     VARCHAR(100)   NOT NULL,
    PRICE         INT,
    PRIMARY KEY (ISBN)
);

CREATE TABLE BOOK_STOCK (
    ISBN     VARCHAR(50)    NOT NULL,
    STOCK    INT            NOT NULL,
    PRIMARY KEY (ISBN),
    CHECK (STOCK >= 0)
);

CREATE TABLE ACCOUNT (
    USERNAME    VARCHAR(50)    NOT NULL,
    BALANCE     INT            NOT NULL,
    PRIMARY KEY (USERNAME),
    CHECK (BALANCE >= 0)
);
```

A real-world application of this type would probably feature a price field with a decimal type, but using an int makes the programming simpler to follow, so leave it as an int.

The BOOK table stores basic book information such as the name and price, with the book ISBN as the primary key. The BOOK_STOCK table keeps track of each book's stock. The stock value is restricted by a CHECK constraint to be a positive number. Although the CHECK constraint type is defined in SQL-99, not all database engines support it. At the time of this writing, this limitation is mainly true of MySQL because Sybase, Derby, HSQL, Oracle, DB2, SQL Server, Access, PostgreSQL, and FireBird all support it. If your database engine doesn't support CHECK constraints, please consult its documentation for similar constraint support. Finally, the ACCOUNT table stores customer accounts and their balances. Again, the balance is restricted to be positive.

The operations of your bookshop are defined in the following BookShop interface. For now, there is only one operation: purchase().

```
package com.apress.springrecipes.bookshop.spring;

public interface BookShop {

    public void purchase(String isbn, String username);
}
```

Because you will implement this interface with JDBC, you create the following JdbcBookShop class. To better understand the nature of transactions, let's implement this class without the help of Spring's JDBC support.

```java
package com.apress.springrecipes.bookshop.spring;

import java.sql.Connection;
import java.sql.PreparedStatement;
import java.sql.ResultSet;
import java.sql.SQLException;

import javax.sql.DataSource;

public class JdbcBookShop implements BookShop {

    private DataSource dataSource;

    public void setDataSource(DataSource dataSource) {
        this.dataSource = dataSource;
    }

    public void purchase(String isbn, String username) {
        Connection conn = null;
        try {
            conn = dataSource.getConnection();

            PreparedStatement stmt1 = conn.prepareStatement(
                    "SELECT PRICE FROM BOOK WHERE ISBN = ?");
            stmt1.setString(1, isbn);
            ResultSet rs = stmt1.executeQuery();
            rs.next();
            int price = rs.getInt("PRICE");
            stmt1.close();

            PreparedStatement stmt2 = conn.prepareStatement(
                    "UPDATE BOOK_STOCK SET STOCK = STOCK - 1 "+
                    "WHERE ISBN = ?");
            stmt2.setString(1, isbn);
            stmt2.executeUpdate();
            stmt2.close();

            PreparedStatement stmt3 = conn.prepareStatement(
                    "UPDATE ACCOUNT SET BALANCE = BALANCE - ? "+
                    "WHERE USERNAME = ?");
            stmt3.setInt(1, price);
            stmt3.setString(2, username);
            stmt3.executeUpdate();
            stmt3.close();
        } catch (SQLException e) {
            throw new RuntimeException(e);
```

```
        } finally {
            if (conn != null) {
                try {
                    conn.close();
                } catch (SQLException e) {}
            }
        }
    }
}
```

For the purchase() operation, you have to execute three SQL statements in total. The first is to query the book price. The second and third update the book stock and account balance accordingly.

Then, you can declare a bookshop instance in the Spring IoC container to provide purchasing services. For simplicity's sake, you can use DriverManagerDataSource, which opens a new connection to the database for every request.

■ **Note** To access a database running on the Derby server, you have to the Derby client library to your CLASSPATH. If you're using Maven, add the following dependency to your project.

```
<dependency>
    <groupId>org.apache.derby</groupId>
    <artifactId>derbyclient</artifactId>
    <version>10.4.2.0</version>
</dependency>
```

```
<beans xmlns="http://www.springframework.org/schema/beans"
    xmlns:xsi="http://www.w3.org/2001/XMLSchema-instance"
    xsi:schemaLocation="http://www.springframework.org/schema/beans
        http://www.springframework.org/schema/beans/spring-beans-3.0.xsd">

    <bean id="dataSource"
        class="org.springframework.jdbc.datasource.DriverManagerDataSource">
        <property name="driverClassName"
            value="org.apache.derby.jdbc.ClientDriver"/>
        <property name="url"
            value="jdbc:derby://localhost:1527/bookshop;create=true"/>
        <property name="username"value="app"/>
        <property name="password"value="app"/>
    </bean>
```

```
    <bean id="bookShop"
class="com.apress.springrecipes.bookshop.spring.JdbcBookShop">
        <property name="dataSource"ref="dataSource"/>
    </bean>
</beans>
```

To demonstrate the problems that can arise without transaction management, suppose you have the data shown in Tables 16-2, 16-3, and 16-4 entered in your bookshop database.

Table 16-2. Sample Data in the BOOK Table for Testing Transactions

ISBN	BOOK_NAME	PRICE
0001	The First Book	30

Table 16-3. Sample Data in the BOOK_STOCK Table for Testing Transactions

ISBN	STOCK
0001	10

Table 16-4. Sample Data in the ACCOUNT Table for Testing Transactions

USERNAME	BALANCE
user1	20

Then, write the following Main class for purchasing the book with ISBN 0001 by the user user1. Because that user's account has only $20, is the funds are not sufficient to purchase the book.

```
package com.apress.springrecipes.bookshop.spring;

import org.springframework.context.ApplicationContext;
import org.springframework.context.support.ClassPathXmlApplicationContext;

public class Main {

    public static void main(String[] args) {
        ApplicationContext context =
            new ClassPathXmlApplicationContext("beans.xml");

        BookShop bookShop = (BookShop) context.getBean("bookShop");
        bookShop.purchase("0001", "user1");
    }
}
```

When you run this application, you will encounter a SQLException, because the CHECK constraint of the ACCOUNT table has been violated. This is an expected result because you were trying to debit more than the account balance. However, if you check the stock for this book in the BOOK_STOCK table, you will find that it was accidentally deducted by this unsuccessful operation! The reason is that you executed the second SQL statement to deduct the stock before you got an exception in the third statement.

As you can see, the lack of transaction management causes your data to be left in an inconsistent state. To avoid this inconsistency, your three SQL statements for the purchase() operation should be executed within a single transaction. Once any of the actions in a transaction fail, the entire transaction should be rolled back to undo all changes made by the executed actions.

Managing Transactions with JDBC Commit and Rollback

When using JDBC to update a database, by default, each SQL statement will be committed immediately after its execution. This behavior is known as *auto-commit*. However, it does not allow you to manage transactions for your operations.

JDBC supports the primitive transaction management strategy of explicitly calling the commit() and rollback() methods on a connection. But before you can do that, you must turn off auto-commit, which is turned on by default.

```
package com.apress.springrecipes.bookshop.spring;
...
public class JdbcBookShop implements BookShop {
    ...
    public void purchase(String isbn, String username) {
        Connection conn = null;
        try {
            conn = dataSource.getConnection();
            conn.setAutoCommit(false);
            ...
            conn.commit();
        } catch (SQLException e) {
            if (conn != null) {
                try {
                    conn.rollback();
                } catch (SQLException e1) {}
            }
            throw new RuntimeException(e);
        } finally {
            if (conn != null) {
                try {
                    conn.close();
                } catch (SQLException e) {}
            }
        }
    }
}
```

The auto-commit behavior of a database connection can be altered by calling the setAutoCommit() method. By default, auto-commit is turned on to commit each SQL statement immediately after its execution. To enable transaction management, you must turn off this default behavior and commit the connection only when all the SQL statements have been executed successfully. If any of the statements go wrong, you must roll back all changes made by this connection.

Now, if you run your application again, the book stock will not be deducted when the user's balance is insufficient to purchase the book.

Although you can manage transactions by explicitly committing and rolling back JDBC connections, the code required for this purpose is boilerplate code that you have to repeat for different methods. Moreover, this code is JDBC specific, so once you have chosen another data access technology, it needs to be changed also. Spring's transaction support offers a set of technology-independent facilities, including transaction managers (e.g., `org.springframework.transaction.PlatformTransactionManager`), a transaction template (e.g., `org.springframework.transaction.support.TransactionTemplate`), and transaction declaration support to simplify your transaction management tasks.

16-2. Choosing a Transaction Manager Implementation

Problem

Typically, if your application involves only a single data source, you can simply manage transactions by calling the `commit()` and `rollback()` methods on a database connection. However, if your transactions extend across multiple data sources or you prefer to make use of the transaction management capabilities provided by your Java EE application server, you may choose the Java Transaction API (JTA). Besides, you may have to call different proprietary transaction APIs for different object/relational mapping frameworks such as Hibernate and JPA.

As a result, you have to deal with different transaction APIs for different technologies. It would be hard for you to switch from one set of APIs to another.

Solution

Spring abstracts a general set of transaction facilities from different transaction management APIs. As an application developer, you can simply utilize Spring's transaction facilities without having to know much about the underlying transaction APIs. With these facilities, your transaction management code will be independent of any specific transaction technology.

Spring's core transaction management abstraction is based on the interface `PlatformTransactionManager`. It encapsulates a set of technology-independent methods for transaction management. Remember that a transaction manager is needed no matter which transaction management strategy (programmatic or declarative) you choose in Spring. The `PlatformTransactionManager` interface provides three methods for working with transactions:

- `TransactionStatus getTransaction(TransactionDefinition definition) throws TransactionException`

- `void commit(TransactionStatus status) throws TransactionException;`

- `void rollback(TransactionStatus status) throws TransactionException;`

How It Works

`PlatformTransactionManager` is a general interface for all Spring transaction managers. Spring has several built-in implementations of this interface for use with different transaction management APIs:

- If you have to deal with only a single data source in your application and access it with JDBC, `DataSourceTransactionManager` should meet your needs.

- If you are using JTA for transaction management on a Java EE application server, you should use `JtaTransactionManager` to look up a transaction from the application server. Additionally, `JtaTransactionManager` is appropriate for distributed transactions (transactions that span multiple resources). Note that while it's common to use a JTA transaction manager to integrate the application servers' transaction manager, there's nothing stopping you from using a stand-alone JTA transaction manager such as Atomikos.

- If you are using an object/relational mapping framework to access a database, you should choose a corresponding transaction manager for this framework, such as `HibernateTransactionManager` and `JpaTransactionManager`.

Figure 16-2 shows the common implementations of the `PlatformTransactionManager` interface in Spring.

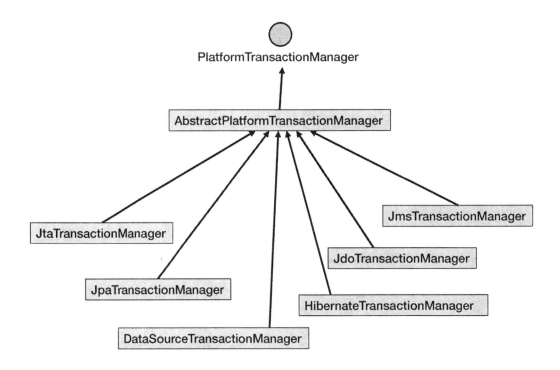

Figure 16-2. *Common implementations of the PlatformTransactionManager interface*

A transaction manager is declared in the Spring IoC container as a normal bean. For example, the following bean configuration declares a DataSourceTransactionManager instance. It requires the dataSource property to be set so that it can manage transactions for connections made by this data source.

```
<bean id="transactionManager"
    class="org.springframework.jdbc.datasource.DataSourceTransactionManager">
    <property name="dataSource" ref="dataSource"/>
</bean>
```

16-3. Managing Transactions Programmatically with the Transaction Manager API

Problem

You need to precisely control when to commit and roll back transactions in your business methods, but you don't want to deal with the underlying transaction API directly.

Solution

Spring's transaction manager provides a technology-independent API that allows you to start a new transaction (or obtain the currently active transaction) by calling the getTransaction() method and manage it by calling the commit() and rollback() methods. Because PlatformTransactionManager is an abstract unit for transaction management, the methods you called for transaction management are guaranteed to be technology independent.

How It Works

To demonstrate how to use the transaction manager API, let's create a new class, TransactionalJdbcBookShop, which will make use of the Spring JDBC template. Because it has to deal with a transaction manager, you add a property of type PlatformTransactionManager and allow it to be injected via a setter method.

```
package com.apress.springrecipes.bookshop.spring;

import org.springframework.dao.DataAccessException;
import org.springframework.jdbc.core.support.JdbcDaoSupport;
import org.springframework.transaction.PlatformTransactionManager;
import org.springframework.transaction.TransactionDefinition;
import org.springframework.transaction.TransactionStatus;
import org.springframework.transaction.support.DefaultTransactionDefinition;
```

```
public class TransactionalJdbcBookShop extends JdbcDaoSupport implements
        BookShop {

    private PlatformTransactionManager transactionManager;

    public void setTransactionManager(
            PlatformTransactionManager transactionManager) {
        this.transactionManager = transactionManager;
    }

    public void purchase(String isbn, String username) {
        TransactionDefinition def = new DefaultTransactionDefinition();
        TransactionStatus status = transactionManager.getTransaction(def);

        try {
            int price = getJdbcTemplate().queryForInt(
                    "SELECT PRICE FROM BOOK WHERE ISBN = ?",
                    new Object[] { isbn });

            getJdbcTemplate().update(
                    "UPDATE BOOK_STOCK SET STOCK = STOCK - 1 "+
                    "WHERE ISBN = ?", new Object[] { isbn });

            getJdbcTemplate().update(
                    "UPDATE ACCOUNT SET BALANCE = BALANCE - ? "+
                    "WHERE USERNAME = ?",
                    new Object[] { price, username });

            transactionManager.commit(status);
        } catch (DataAccessException e) {
            transactionManager.rollback(status);
            throw e;
        }
    }
}
```

Before you start a new transaction, you have to specify the transaction attributes in a transaction definition object of type TransactionDefinition. For this example, you can simply create an instance of DefaultTransactionDefinition to use the default transaction attributes.

Once you have a transaction definition, you can ask the transaction manager to start a new transaction with that definition by calling the getTransaction() method. Then, it will return a TransactionStatus object to keep track of the transaction status. If all the statements execute successfully, you ask the transaction manager to commit this transaction by passing in the transaction status. Because all exceptions thrown by the Spring JDBC template are subclasses of DataAccessException, you ask the transaction manager to roll back the transaction when this kind of exception is caught.

In this class, you have declared the transaction manager property of the general type PlatformTransactionManager. Now, you have to inject an appropriate transaction manager implementation. Because you are dealing with only a single data source and accessing it with JDBC, you should choose DataSourceTransactionManager. Here, you also wire a dataSource because the class is a subclass of Spring's JdbcDaoSupport, which requires it.

```
<beans ...>
    ...
    <bean id="transactionManager"
        class="org.springframework.jdbc.datasource.DataSourceTransactionManager">
        <property name="dataSource" ref="dataSource"/>
    </bean>

    <bean id="bookShop"
        class="com.apress.springrecipes.bookshop.spring.TransactionalJdbcBookShop">
        <property name="dataSource" ref="dataSource"/>
        <property name="transactionManager" ref="transactionManager"/>
    </bean>
</beans>
```

16-4. Managing Transactions Programmatically with a Transaction Template

Problem

Suppose that you have a code block, but not the entire body, of a business method that has the following transaction requirements:

- Start a new transaction at the beginning of the block.

- Commit the transaction after the block completes successfully.

- Roll back the transaction if an exception is thrown in the block.

If you call Spring's transaction manager API directly, the transaction management code can be generalized in a technology-independent manner. However, you may not want to repeat the boilerplate code for each similar code block.

Solution

As with the JDBC template, Spring also provides a TransactionTemplate to help you control the overall transaction management process and transaction exception handling. You just have to encapsulate your code block in a callback class that implements the TransactionCallback<T> interface and pass it to the TransactionTemplate's execute method for execution. In this way, you don't need to repeat the boilerplate transaction management code for this block. The template objects that Spring provides are lightweight and usually can be discarded or re-created with no performance impact. A JDBC template can be re-created on the fly with a DataSource reference, for example, and so too can a TransactionTemplate be re-created by providing a reference to a transaction manager. You can, of course, simply create one in your Spring application context, too.

How It Works

A TransactionTemplate is created on a transaction manager just as a JDBC template is created on a data source. A transaction template executes a transaction callback object that encapsulates a transactional code block. You can implement the callback interface either as a separate class or as an inner class. If it's implemented as an inner class, you have to make the method arguments final for it to access.

```
package com.apress.springrecipes.bookshop.spring;
...
import org.springframework.transaction.PlatformTransactionManager;
import org.springframework.transaction.TransactionStatus;
import org.springframework.transaction.support.TransactionCallbackWithoutResult;
import org.springframework.transaction.support.TransactionTemplate;

public class TransactionalJdbcBookShop extends JdbcDaoSupport implements
        BookShop {

    private PlatformTransactionManager transactionManager;

    public void setTransactionManager(
            PlatformTransactionManager transactionManager) {
        this.transactionManager = transactionManager;
    }

    public void purchase(final String isbn, final String username) {
        TransactionTemplate transactionTemplate =
            new TransactionTemplate(transactionManager);

        transactionTemplate.execute(new TransactionCallbackWithoutResult() {

            protected void doInTransactionWithoutResult(
                    TransactionStatus status) {

                int price = getJdbcTemplate().queryForInt(
                        "SELECT PRICE FROM BOOK WHERE ISBN = ?",
                        new Object[] { isbn });

                getJdbcTemplate().update(
                        "UPDATE BOOK_STOCK SET STOCK = STOCK - 1 "+
                        "WHERE ISBN = ?", new Object[] { isbn });

                getJdbcTemplate().update(
                        "UPDATE ACCOUNT SET BALANCE = BALANCE - ? "+
                        "WHERE USERNAME = ?",
                        new Object[] { price, username });
            }
        });
    }
}
```

A TransactionTemplate can accept a transaction callback object that implements either the TransactionCallback<T> or an instance of the one implementor of that interface provided by the framework, the TransactionCallbackWithoutResult class. For the code block in the purchase() method for deducting the book stock and account balance, there's no result to be returned, so TransactionCallbackWithoutResult is fine. For any code blocks with return values, you should implement the TransactionCallback<T> interface instead. The return value of the callback object will finally be returned by the template's T execute() method. The main benefit is that the responsibility of starting, rolling back, or committing the transaction has been removed.

During the execution of the callback object, if it throws an unchecked exception (e.g., RuntimeException and DataAccessException fall into this category), or if you explicitly called setRollbackOnly() on the TransactionStatus argument in the doInTransactionWithoutResult method, the transaction will be rolled back. Otherwise, it will be committed after the callback object completes.

In the bean configuration file, the bookshop bean still requires a transaction manager to create a TransactionTemplate.

```
<beans ...>
    ...
    <bean id="transactionManager"
        class="org.springframework.jdbc.datasource.DataSourceTransactionManager">
        <property name="dataSource"ref="dataSource"/>
    </bean>

    <bean id="bookShop"
        class="com.apress.springrecipes.bookshop.spring.
TransactionalJdbcBookShop">
        <property name="dataSource" ref="dataSource"/>
        <property name="transactionManager" ref="transactionManager"/>
    </bean>
</beans>
```

You can also have the IoC container inject a transaction template instead of creating it directly. Because a transaction template handles all transactions, there's no need for your class to refer to the transaction manager any more.

```
package com.apress.springrecipes.bookshop.spring;
...
import org.springframework.transaction.support.TransactionTemplate;

public class TransactionalJdbcBookShop extends JdbcDaoSupport implements
        BookShop {

    private TransactionTemplate transactionTemplate;

    public void setTransactionTemplate(
            TransactionTemplate transactionTemplate) {
        this.transactionTemplate = transactionTemplate;
    }
```

```
public void purchase(final String isbn, final String username) {
    transactionTemplate.execute(new TransactionCallbackWithoutResult() {
        protected void doInTransactionWithoutResult(TransactionStatus status) {
            ...
        }
    });
}
}
```

Then you define a transaction template in the bean configuration file and inject it, instead of the transaction manager, into your bookshop bean. Notice that the transaction template instance can be used for more than one transactional bean because it is a thread-safe object. Finally, don't forget to set the transaction manager property for your transaction template.

```
<beans ...>
    ...
    <bean id="transactionManager"
        class="org.springframework.jdbc.datasource.DataSourceTransactionManager">
        <property name="dataSource" ref="dataSource"/>
    </bean>

    <bean id="transactionTemplate"
        class="org.springframework.transaction.support.TransactionTemplate">
        <property name="transactionManager" ref="transactionManager"/>
    </bean>

    <bean id="bookShop"
        class="com.apress.springrecipes.bookshop.spring.TransactionalJdbcBookShop">
        <property name="dataSource" ref="dataSource"/>
        <property name="transactionTemplate" ref="transactionTemplate"/>
    </bean>
</beans>
```

16-5. Managing Transactions Declaratively with Transaction Advices

Problem

Because transaction management is a kind of crosscutting concern, you should manage transactions declaratively with the AOP approach available from Spring 2.x onward. Managing transactions manually can be tedious and error prone. It is simpler to specify, declaratively, what behavior you are expecting and to not prescribe *how* that behavior is to be achieved.

Solution

Spring (since version 2.0) offers a transaction advice that can be easily configured via the <tx:advice> element defined in the tx schema. This advice can be enabled with the AOP configuration facilities defined in the aop saop schema.

How It Works

To enable declarative transaction management, you can declare a transaction advice via the <tx:advice> element defined in the tx schema, so you have to add this schema definition to the <beans> root element beforehand. Once you have declared this advice, you need to associate it with a pointcut. Because a transaction advice is declared outside the <aop:config> element, it cannot link with a pointcut directly. You have to declare an advisor in the <aop:config> element to associate an advice with a pointcut.

■ **Note** Because Spring AOP uses the AspectJ pointcut expressions to define pointcuts, you have to include the AspectJ Weaver support on your CLASSPATH. If you're using Maven, add the following dependency to your project.

```
<dependency>
    <groupId>org.aspectj</groupId>
    <artifactId>aspectjweaver</artifactId>
    <version>1.6.8</version>
</dependency>
```

```
<beans xmlns="http://www.springframework.org/schema/beans"
    xmlns:xsi="http://www.w3.org/2001/XMLSchema-instance"
    xmlns:tx="http://www.springframework.org/schema/tx"
    xmlns:aop="http://www.springframework.org/schema/aop"
    xsi:schemaLocation="http://www.springframework.org/schema/beans
        http://www.springframework.org/schema/beans/spring-beans-3.0.xsd
        http://www.springframework.org/schema/tx
        http://www.springframework.org/schema/tx/spring-tx-3.0.xsd
        http://www.springframework.org/schema/aop
        http://www.springframework.org/schema/aop/spring-aop-3.0.xsd">

    <tx:advice id="bookShopTxAdvice"
        transaction-manager="transactionManager">
        <tx:attributes>
            <tx:method name="purchase"/>
        </tx:attributes>
    </tx:advice>
```

```
    <aop:config>
        <aop:pointcut id="bookShopOperation" expression=
            "execution(* com.apress.springrecipes.bookshop.spring.
BookShop.*(..))"/>
        <aop:advisor advice-ref="bookShopTxAdvice"
            pointcut-ref="bookShopOperation"/>
    </aop:config>
    ...
    <bean id="transactionManager"
        class="org.springframework.jdbc.datasource.DataSourceTransactionManager">
        <property name="dataSource"ref="dataSource"/>
    </bean>

    <bean id="bookShop"
        class="com.apress.springrecipes.bookshop.spring.JdbcBookShop">
        <property name="dataSource" ref="dataSource"/>
    </bean>
</beans>
```

The preceding AspectJ pointcut expression matches all the methods declared in the BookShop interface. However, because Spring AOP is based on proxies, it can apply only to public methods. Thus only public methods can be made transactional with Spring AOP.

Each transaction advice requires an identifier and a reference to a transaction manager in the IoC container. If you don't specify a transaction manager explicitly, Spring will search the application context for a TransactionManager with a bean name of transactionManager. The methods that require transaction management are specified with multiple <tx:method> elements inside the <tx:attributes> element. The method name supports wildcards for you to match a group of methods. You can also define transaction attributes for each group of methods, but let's use the default attributes for simplicity's sake. The defaults are shown in Table 16-5.

Table 16-5. *Attributes Used with tx:attributes*

Attribute	Required	Default	Description
name	Yes	n/a	The name of the methods against which the advice will be applied. You can use wildcards (*).
propagation	No	REQUIRED	The propagation specification for the transaction.
isolation	No	DEFAULT	The isolation level specification for the transaction.
timeout	No	-1	How long (in seconds) the transaction will attempt to commit before it times out.

Attribute	Required	Default	Description
read-only	No	False	Tells the container whether the transaction is read-only or not. This is a Spring-specific setting. If you're used to standard Java EE transaction configuration, you won't have seen this setting before. Its meaning is different for different resources (e.g., databases have a different notion of "read-only" than a JMS queue does).
rollback-for	No	N/A	Comma-delimited list of fully qualified Exception types that, when thrown from the method, the transaction should rollback for.
no-rollback-for	No	N/A	A comma-delimited list of Exception types that, when thrown from the method, the transaction should ignore and not roll back for.

Now, you can retrieve the bookShop bean from the Spring IoC container to use. Because this bean's methods are matched by the pointcut, Spring will return a proxy that has transaction management enabled for this bean.

```
package com.apress.springrecipes.bookshop.spring;
...
public class Main {

    public static void main(String[] args) {
        ...
        BookShop bookShop = (BookShop) context.getBean("bookShop");
        bookShop.purchase("0001", "user1");
    }
}
```

16-6. Managing Transactions Declaratively with the @Transactional Annotation

Problem

Declaring transactions in the bean configuration file requires knowledge of AOP concepts such as pointcuts, advices, and advisors. Developers who lack this knowledge might find it hard to enable declarative transaction management.

Solution

In addition to declaring transactions in the bean configuration file with pointcuts, advices, and advisors, Spring allows you to declare transactions simply by annotating your transactional methods with

@Transactional and enabling the <tx:annotation-driven> element. However, Java 1.5 or higher is required to use this approach. Note that although you could apply the annotation to an interface method, it's not a recommended practice.

How It Works

To define a method as transactional, you can simply annotate it with @Transactional. Note that you should only annotate public methods due to the proxy-based limitations of Spring AOP.

```
package com.apress.springrecipes.bookshop.spring;
...
import org.springframework.transaction.annotation.Transactional;
import org.springframework.jdbc.core.support.JdbcDaoSupport;

public class JdbcBookShop extends JdbcDaoSupport implements BookShop {

    @Transactional
    public void purchase(String isbn, String username) {

        int price = getJdbcTemplate().queryForInt(
            "SELECT PRICE FROM BOOK WHERE ISBN = ?",
            new Object[] { isbn });

        getJdbcTemplate().update(
            "UPDATE BOOK_STOCK SET STOCK = STOCK - 1 "+
            "WHERE ISBN = ?", new Object[] { isbn });

        getJdbcTemplate().update(
            "UPDATE ACCOUNT SET BALANCE = BALANCE - ? "+
            "WHERE USERNAME = ?",
            new Object[] { price, username });
    }
}
```

Note that, as we are extending JdbcDaoSupport, we no longer need the mutators for the DataSource; remove it from your DAO class.

You may apply the @Transactional annotation at the method level or the class level. When applying this annotation to a class, all of the public methods within this class will be defined as transactional. Although you can apply @Transactional to interfaces or method declarations in an interface, it's not recommended because it may not work properly with class-based proxies (i.e., CGLIB proxies).

In the bean configuration file, you only have to enable the <tx:annotation-driven> element and specify a transaction manager for it. That's all you need to make it work. Spring will advise methods with @Transactional, or methods in a class with @Transactional, from beans declared in the IoC container. As a result, Spring can manage transactions for these methods.

```
<beans xmlns="http://www.springframework.org/schema/beans"
  xmlns:xsi="http://www.w3.org/2001/XMLSchema-instance"
  xmlns:tx="http://www.springframework.org/schema/tx"
  xsi:schemaLocation="http://www.springframework.org/schema/beans
 http://www.springframework.org/schema/beans/spring-beans-3.0.xsd
    http://www.springframework.org/schema/tx
http://www.springframework.org/schema/tx/spring-tx-3.0.xsd">
    <tx:annotation-driven transaction-manager="transactionManager"/>
    ...
    <bean id="transactionManager"
        class="org.springframework.jdbc.datasource.DataSourceTransactionManager">
        <property name="dataSource" ref="dataSource"/>
    </bean>

    <bean id="bookShop"
        class="com.apress.springrecipes.bookshop.spring.JdbcBookShop">
        <property name="dataSource" ref="dataSource"/>
    </bean>
</beans>
```

In fact, you can omit the `transaction-manager` attribute in the `<tx:annotation-driven>` element if your transaction manager has the name `transactionManager`. This element will automatically detect a transaction manager with this name. You have to specify a transaction manager only when it has a different name.

```
<beans ...>
    <tx:annotation-driven />
    ...
</beans>
```

16-7. Setting the Propagation Transaction Attribute

Problem

When a transactional method is called by another method, it is necessary to specify how the transaction should be propagated. For example, the method may continue to run within the existing transaction, or it may start a new transaction and run within its own transaction.

Solution

A transaction's propagation behavior can be specified by the *propagation* transaction attribute. Spring defines seven propagation behaviors, as shown in Table 16-6. These behaviors are defined in the `org.springframework.transaction.TransactionDefinition` interface. Note that not all types of transaction managers support all of these propagation behaviors. Their behavior is contingent on the underlying resource. Databases, for example, may support varying isolation levels, which constrains what propagation behaviors the transaction manager can support.

Table 16-6. Propagation Behaviors Supported by Spring

Propagation	Description
REQUIRED	If there's an existing transaction in progress, the current method should run within this transaction. Otherwise, it should start a new transaction and run within its own transaction.
REQUIRES_NEW	The current method must start a new transaction and run within its own transaction. If there's an existing transaction in progress, it should be suspended.
SUPPORTS	If there's an existing transaction in progress, the current method can run within this transaction. Otherwise, it is not necessary to run within a transaction.
NOT_SUPPORTED	The current method should not run within a transaction. If there's an existing transaction in progress, it should be suspended.
MANDATORY	The current method must run within a transaction. If there's no existing transaction in progress, an exception will be thrown.
NEVER	The current method should not run within a transaction. If there's an existing transaction in progress, an exception will be thrown.
NESTED	If there's an existing transaction in progress, the current method should run within the nested transaction (supported by the JDBC 3.0 save point feature) of this transaction. Otherwise, it should start a new transaction and run within its own transaction. This feature is unique to Spring (whereas the previous propagation behaviors have analogs in Java EE transaction propagation). The behavior is useful for situations such as batch processing, in which you've got a long running process (imagine processing 1 million records) and you want to chunk the commits on the batch. So you commit every 10,000 records. If something goes wrong, you roll back the nested transaction and you've lost only 10,000 records' worth of work (as opposed to the entire 1 million).

How It Works

Transaction propagation happens when a transactional method is called by another method. For example, suppose that a customer would like to check out all books to purchase at the bookshop cashier. To support this operation, you define the Cashier interface as follows:

```
package com.apress.springrecipes.bookshop.spring;
...
public interface Cashier {

    public void checkout(List<String> isbns, String username);
}
```

You can implement this interface by delegating the purchases to a bookshop bean by calling its purchase() method multiple times. Note that the checkout() method is made transactional by applying the @Transactional annotation.

```
package com.apress.springrecipes.bookshop.spring;
...
import org.springframework.transaction.annotation.Transactional;

public class BookShopCashier implements Cashier {

    private BookShop bookShop;

    public void setBookShop(BookShop bookShop) {
        this.bookShop = bookShop;
    }

    @Transactional
    public void checkout(List<String> isbns, String username) {
        for (String isbn : isbns) {
            bookShop.purchase(isbn, username);
        }
    }
}
```

Then define a cashier bean in your bean configuration file and refer to the bookshop bean for purchasing books.

```
<bean id="cashier"
    class="com.apress.springrecipes.bookshop.spring.BookShopCashier">
    <property name="bookShop" ref="bookShop"/>
</bean>
```

To illustrate the propagation behavior of a transaction, enter the data shown in Tables 16-7, 16-8, and 16-9 in your bookshop database.

Table 16-7. Sample Data in the BOOK Table for Testing Propagation Behaviors

ISBN	BOOK_NAME	PRICE
0001	The First Book	30
0002	The Second Book	50

Table 16-8. Sample Data in the BOOK_STOCK Table for Testing Propagation Behaviors

ISBN	STOCK
0001	10
0002	10

Table 16-9. Sample Data in the ACCOUNT Table for Testing Propagation Behaviors

USERNAME	BALANCE
user1	40

The REQUIRED Propagation Behavior

When the user user1 checks out the two books from the cashier, the balance is sufficient to purchase the first book but not the second.

```
package com.apress.springrecipes.bookshop.spring;
...
public class Main {

    public static void main(String[] args) {
        ...
        Cashier cashier = (Cashier) context.getBean("cashier");
        List<String> isbnList =
                Arrays.asList(new String[] { "0001", "0002"});
        cashier.checkout(isbnList, "user1");
    }
}
```

When the bookshop's purchase() method is called by another transactional method, such as checkout(), it will run within the existing transaction by default. This default propagation behavior is called REQUIRED. That means there will be only one transaction whose boundary is the beginning and ending of the checkout() method. This transaction will be committed only at the end of the checkout() method. As a result, the user can purchase none of the books. Figure 16-3 illustrates the REQUIRED propagation behavior.

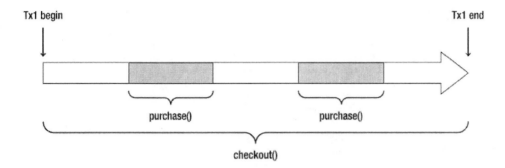

Figure 16-3. *The REQUIRED transaction propagation behavior*

However, if the purchase() method is called by a non-transactional method and there's no existing transaction in progress, it will start a new transaction and run within its own transaction.

The propagation transaction attribute can be defined in the @Transactional annotation. For example, you can set the REQUIRED behavior for this attribute as follows. In fact, this is unnecessary, because it's the default behavior.

```
package com.apress.springrecipes.bookshop.spring;
...
import org.springframework.transaction.annotation.Propagation;
import org.springframework.transaction.annotation.Transactional;

public class JdbcBookShop extends JdbcDaoSupport implements BookShop {
    @Transactional(propagation = Propagation.REQUIRED)
    public void purchase(String isbn, String username) {
        ...
    }
}
```

```
package com.apress.springrecipes.bookshop.spring;
...
import org.springframework.transaction.annotation.Propagation;
import org.springframework.transaction.annotation.Transactional;

public class BookShopCashier implements Cashier {
    ...
    @Transactional(propagation = Propagation.REQUIRED)
    public void checkout(List<String> isbns, String username) {
        ...
    }
}
```

The REQUIRES_NEW Propagation Behavior

Another common propagation behavior is REQUIRES_NEW. It indicates that the method must start a new transaction and run within its new transaction. If there's an existing transaction in progress, it should be suspended first (as, for example, with the checkout method on BookShopCashier, with a propagation of REQUIRED).

```
package com.apress.springrecipes.bookshop.spring;
...
import org.springframework.transaction.annotation.Propagation;
import org.springframework.transaction.annotation.Transactional;

public class JdbcBookShop extends JdbcDaoSupport implements BookShop {
    @Transactional(propagation = Propagation.REQUIRES_NEW)
    public void purchase(String isbn, String username) {
        ...
    }
}
```

In this case, there will be three transactions started in total. The first transaction is started by the checkout() method, but when the first purchase() method is called, the first transaction will be suspended and a new transaction will be started. At the end of the first purchase() method, the new transaction completes and commits. When the second purchase() method is called, another new transaction will be started. However, this transaction will fail and roll back. As a result, the first book will be purchased successfully, while the second will not. Figure 16-4 illustrates the REQUIRES_NEW propagation behavior.

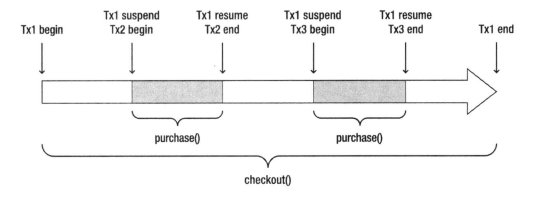

Figure16-4. *The REQUIRES_NEW transaction propagation behavior*

Setting the Propagation Attribute in Transaction Advices, Proxies, and APIs

In a Spring transaction advice, the propagation transaction attribute can be specified in the `<tx:method>` element as follows:

```
<tx:advice ...>
    <tx:attributes>
        <tx:method name="..."
            propagation="REQUIRES_NEW"/>
    </tx:attributes>
</tx:advice>
```

In classic Spring AOP, the propagation transaction attribute can be specified in the transaction attributes of `TransactionInterceptor` and `TransactionProxyFactoryBean` as follows:

```
<property name="transactionAttributes">
    <props>
        <prop key="...">PROPAGATION_REQUIRES_NEW</prop>
    </props>
</property>
```

In Spring's transaction management API, the propagation transaction attribute can be specified in a `DefaultTransactionDefinition` object and then passed to a transaction manager's `getTransaction()` method or a transaction template's constructor.

```
DefaultTransactionDefinition def = new DefaultTransactionDefinition();
def.setPropagationBehavior(TransactionDefinition.PROPAGATION_REQUIRES_NEW);
```

16-8. Setting the Isolation Transaction Attribute

Problem

When multiple transactions of the same application or different applications are operating concurrently on the same dataset, many unexpected problems may arise. You must specify how you expect your transactions to be isolated from one another.

Solution

The problems caused by concurrent transactions can be categorized into four types:

- *Dirty read*: For two *transactions* T1 and T2, T1 reads a field that has been updated by T2 but not yet committed. Later, if T2 rolls back, the field read by T1 will be temporary and invalid.

- *Nonrepeatable read*: For two transactions T1 and T2, T1 reads a field and then T2 updates the field. Later, if T1 reads the same field again, the value will be different.

- *Phantom read*: For two transactions T1 and T2, T1 reads some rows from a table and then T2 inserts new rows into the table. Later, if T1 reads the same table again, there will be additional rows.

- *Lost updates*: For two transactions T1 and T2, they both select a row for update, and based on the state of that row, make an update to it. Thus, one overwrites the other when the second transaction to commit should have waited until the first one committed before performing its selection.

In theory, transactions should be completely isolated from each other (i.e., serializable) to avoid all the mentioned problems. However, this isolation level will have great impact on performance, because transactions have to run in serial order. In practice, transactions can run in lower isolation levels in order to improve performance.

A transaction's isolation level can be specified by the *isolation* transaction attribute. Spring supports five isolation levels, as shown in Table 16-10. These levels are defined in the org.springframework.transaction.TransactionDefinition interface.

Table 16-10. *Isolation Levels Supported by Spring*

Isolation	Description
DEFAULT	Uses the default isolation level of the underlying database. For most databases, the default isolation level is READ_COMMITTED.
READ_UNCOMMITTED	Allows a transaction to read uncommitted changes by other transactions. The dirty read, nonrepeatable read, and phantom read problems may occur.
READ_COMMITTED	Allows a transaction to read only those changes that have been committed by other transactions. The dirty read problem can be avoided, but the nonrepeatable read and phantom read problems may still occur.
REPEATABLE_READ	Ensures that a transaction can read identical values from a field multiple times. For the duration of this transaction, updates made by other transactions to this field are prohibited. The dirty read and nonrepeatable read problems can be avoided, but the phantom read problem may still occur.
SERIALIZABLE	Ensures that a transaction can read identical rows from a table multiple times. For the duration of this transaction, inserts, updates, and deletes made by other transactions to this table are prohibited. All the concurrency problems can be avoided, but the performance will be low.

Note that transaction isolation is supported by the underlying database engine but not an application or a framework. However, not all database engines support all these isolation levels. You can change the isolation level of a JDBC connection by calling the setTransactionIsolation() method on the java.sql.Connection ijava.sql.Connection interface.

How It Works

To illustrate the problems caused by concurrent transactions, let's add two new operations to your bookshop for increasing and checking the book stock.

```
package com.apress.springrecipes.bookshop.spring;

public interface BookShop {
    ...
    public void increaseStock(String isbn, int stock);
    public int checkStock(String isbn);
}
```

Then, you implement these operations as follows. Note that these two operations should also be declared as transactional.

```
package com.apress.springrecipes.bookshop.spring;
...
import org.springframework.transaction.annotation.Transactional;

public class JdbcBookShop extends JdbcDaoSupport implements BookShop {
    ...
    @Transactional
    public void increaseStock(String isbn, int stock) {
        String threadName = Thread.currentThread().getName();
        System.out.println(threadName + "- Prepare to increase book stock");

        getJdbcTemplate().update(
                "UPDATE BOOK_STOCK SET STOCK = STOCK + ? "+
                "WHERE ISBN = ?",
                new Object[] { stock, isbn });

        System.out.println(threadName + "- Book stock increased by "+ stock);
        sleep(threadName);

        System.out.println(threadName + "- Book stock rolled back");
        throw new RuntimeException("Increased by mistake");
    }

    @Transactional
    public int checkStock(String isbn) {
        String threadName = Thread.currentThread().getName();
        System.out.println(threadName + "- Prepare to check book stock");

        int stock = getJdbcTemplate().queryForInt(
                "SELECT STOCK FROM BOOK_STOCK WHERE ISBN = ?",
                new Object[] { isbn });

        System.out.println(threadName + "- Book stock is "+ stock);
        sleep(threadName);

        return stock;
    }
```

```
        private void sleep(String threadName) {
            System.out.println(threadName + "- Sleeping");
            try {
                Thread.sleep(10000);
            } catch (InterruptedException e) {}
            System.out.println(threadName + "- Wake up");
        }
    }
}
```

To simulate concurrency, your operations need to be executed by multiple threads. You can track the current status of the operations through the println statements. For each operation, you print a couple of messages to the console around the SQL statement's execution. The messages should include the thread name for you to know which thread is currently executing the operation.

After each operation executes the SQL statement, you ask the thread to sleep for 10 seconds. As you know, the transaction will be committed or rolled back immediately once the operation completes. Inserting a sleep statement can help to postpone the commit or rollback. For the increase() operation, you eventually throw a RuntimeException to cause the transaction to roll back. Let's look at a simple client that runs these examples.

Before you start with the isolation level examples, enter the data from Tables 16-11 and 16-12 into your bookshop database. (Note that the ACCOUNT table isn't needed in this example.)

Table 16-11. *Sample Data in the BOOK Table for Testing Isolation Levels*

ISBN	BOOK_NAME	PRICE
0001	The First Book	30

Table 16-12. *Sample Data in the BOOK_STOCK Table for Testing Isolation Levels*

ISBN	STOCK
0001	10

The READ_UNCOMMITTED and READ_COMMITTED Isolation Levels

READ_UNCOMMITTED is the lowest isolation level that allows a transaction to read uncommitted changes made by other transactions. You can set this isolation level in the @Transaction annotation of your checkStock() method.

```
package com.apress.springrecipes.bookshop.spring;
...
import org.springframework.transaction.annotation.Isolation;
import org.springframework.transaction.annotation.Transactional;
```

```
public class JdbcBookShop extends JdbcDaoSupport implements BookShop {
    ...
    @Transactional(isolation = Isolation.READ_UNCOMMITTED)
    public int checkStock(String isbn) {
        ...
    }
}
```

You can create some threads to experiment on this transaction isolation level. In the following Main class, there are two threads you are going to create. Thread 1 increases the book stock, while thread 2 checks the book stock. Thread 1 starts 5 seconds before thread 2.

```
package com.apress.springrecipes.bookshop.spring;
...
public class Main {

    public static void main(String[] args) {
        ...
        final BookShop bookShop = (BookShop) context.getBean("bookShop");

        Thread thread1 = new Thread(new Runnable() {
            public void run() {
                try {
                    bookShop.increaseStock("0001", 5);
                } catch (RuntimeException e) {}
            }
        }, "Thread 1");

        Thread thread2 = new Thread(new Runnable() {
            public void run() {
                bookShop.checkStock("0001");
            }
        }, "Thread 2");

        thread1.start();
        try {
            Thread.sleep(5000);
        } catch (InterruptedException e) {}
        thread2.start();
    }
}
```

If you run the application, you will get the following result:

```
Thread 1—Prepare to increase book stock

Thread 1—Book stock increased by 5

Thread 1—Sleeping

Thread 2—Prepare to check book stock

Thread 2—Book stock is 15

Thread 2—Sleeping

Thread 1—Wake up

Thread 1—Book stock rolled back

Thread 2—Wake up
```

First, thread 1 increased the book stock and then went to sleep. At that time, thread 1's transaction had not yet been rolled back. While thread 1 was sleeping, thread 2 started and attempted to read the book stock. With the READ_UNCOMMITTED isolation level, thread 2 would be able to read the stock value that had been updated by an uncommitted transaction.

However, when thread 1 wakes up, its transaction will be rolled back due to a RuntimeException, so the value read by thread 2 is temporary and invalid. This problem is known as *dirty read*, because a transaction may read values that are "dirty."

To avoid the dirty read problem, you should raise the isolation level of checkStock() to READ_COMMITTED.

```java
package com.apress.springrecipes.bookshop.spring;
...
import org.springframework.transaction.annotation.Isolation;
import org.springframework.transaction.annotation.Transactional;

public class JdbcBookShop extends JdbcDaoSupport implements BookShop {
    ...
    @Transactional(isolation = Isolation.READ_COMMITTED)
    public int checkStock(String isbn) {
        ...
    }
}
```

If you run the application again, thread 2 won't be able to read the book stock until thread 1 has rolled back the transaction. In this way, the dirty read problem can be avoided by preventing a transaction from reading a field that has been updated by another uncommitted transaction.

Thread 1—Prepare to increase book stock

Thread 1—Book stock increased by 5

Thread 1—Sleeping

Thread 2—Prepare to check book stock

Thread 1—Wake up

Thread 1—Book stock rolled back

Thread 2—Book stock is 10

Thread 2—Sleeping

Thread 2—Wake up

In order for the underlying database to support the READ_COMMITTED isolation level, it may acquire an *update lock* on a row that was updated but not yet committed. Then, other transactions must wait to read that row until the update lock is released, which happens when the locking transaction commits or rolls back.

The REPEATABLE_READ Isolation Level

Now, let's restructure the threads to demonstrate another concurrency problem. Swap the tasks of the two threads so that thread 1 checks the book stock before thread 2 increases the book stock.

```
package com.apress.springrecipes.bookshop.spring;
...
public class Main {

    public static void main(String[] args) {
        ...
        final BookShop bookShop = (BookShop) context.getBean("bookShop");

        Thread thread1 = new Thread(new Runnable() {
            public void run() {
                bookShop.checkStock("0001");
            }
        }, "Thread 1");
```

```
            Thread thread2 = new Thread(new Runnable() {
                public void run() {
                    try {
                        bookShop.increaseStock("0001", 5);
                    } catch (RuntimeException e) {}
                }
            }, "Thread 2");

            thread1.start();
            try {
                Thread.sleep(5000);
            } catch (InterruptedException e) {}
            thread2.start();
        }
    }
```

If you run the application, you will get the following result:

```
Thread 1—Prepare to check book stock

Thread 1—Book stock is 10

Thread 1—Sleeping

Thread 2—Prepare to increase book stock

Thread 2—Book stock increased by 5

Thread 2—Sleeping

Thread 1—Wake up

Thread 2—Wake up

Thread 2—Book stock rolled back
```

First, thread 1 read the book stock and then went to sleep. At that time, thread 1's transaction had not yet been committed. While thread 1 was sleeping, thread 2 started and attempted to increase the book stock. With the READ_COMMITTED isolation level, thread 2 would be able to update the stock value that was read by an uncommitted transaction.

However, if thread 1 reads the book stock again, the value will be different from its first read. This problem is known as *nonrepeatable read* because a transaction may read different values for the same field.

To avoid the nonrepeatable read problem, you should raise the isolation level of checkStock() to REPEATABLE_READ.

```
package com.apress.springrecipes.bookshop.spring;
...
import org.springframework.transaction.annotation.Isolation;
import org.springframework.transaction.annotation.Transactional;

public class JdbcBookShop extends JdbcDaoSupport implements BookShop {
    ...
    @Transactional(isolation = Isolation.REPEATABLE_READ)
    public int checkStock(String isbn) {
        ...
    }
}
```

If you run the application again, thread 2 won't be able to update the book stock until thread 1 has committed the transaction. In this way, the nonrepeatable read problem can be avoided by preventing a transaction from updating a value that has been read by another uncommitted transaction.

```
Thread 1–Prepare to check book stock

Thread 1–Book stock is 10

Thread 1–Sleeping

Thread 2–Prepare to increase book stock

Thread 1–Wake up

Thread 2–Book stock increased by 5

Thread 2–Sleeping

Thread 2–Wake up

Thread 2–Book stock rolled back
```

In order for the underlying database to support the REPEATABLE_READ isolation level, it may acquire a *read lock* on a row that was read but not yet committed. Then, other transactions must wait to update the row until the read lock is released, which happens when the locking transaction commits or rolls back.

The SERIALIZABLE Isolation Level

After a transaction has read several rows from a table, another transaction inserts new rows into the same table. If the first transaction reads the same table again, it will find additional rows that are different from the first read. This problem is known as *phantom read*. Actually, phantom read is very similar to nonrepeatable read but involves multiple rows.

To avoid the phantom read problem, you should raise the isolation level to the highest: SERIALIZABLE. Notice that this isolation level is the slowest because it may acquire a read lock on the full table. In practice, you should always choose the lowest isolation level that can satisfy your requirements.

Setting the Isolation Level Attribute in Transaction Advices, Proxies, and APIs

In a Spring transaction advice, the isolation level can be specified in the <tx:method> element as follows:

```
<tx:advice ...>
    <tx:attributes>
        <tx:method name="*"
            isolation="REPEATABLE_READ"/>
    </tx:attributes>
</tx:advice>
```

In classic Spring AOP, the isolation level can be specified in the transaction attributes of TransactionInterceptor and TransactionProxyFactoryBean as follows:

```
<property name="transactionAttributes">
    <props>
        <prop key="...">
            PROPAGATION_REQUIRED, ISOLATION_REPEATABLE_READ
        </prop>
    </props>
</property>
```

In Spring's transaction management API, the isolation level can be specified in a DefaultTransactionDefinition object and then passed to a transaction manager's getTransaction() method or a transaction template's constructor.

```
DefaultTransactionDefinition def = new DefaultTransactionDefinition();
def.setIsolationLevel(TransactionDefinition.ISOLATION_REPEATABLE_READ);
```

16-9. Setting the Rollback Transaction Attribute

Problem

By default, only unchecked exceptions (i.e., of type RuntimeException and Error) will cause a transaction to roll back, while checked exceptions will not. Sometimes, you may wish to break this rule and set your own exceptions for rolling back.

Solution

The exceptions that cause a transaction to roll back or not can be specified by the *rollback* transaction attribute. Any exceptions not explicitly specified in this attribute will be handled by the default rollback rule (i.e., rolling back for unchecked exceptions and not rolling back for checked exceptions).

How It Works

A transaction's rollback rule can be defined in the @Transactional annotation via the rollbackFor and noRollbackFor attributes. These two attributes are declared as Class[], so you can specify more than one exception for each attribute.

```
package com.apress.springrecipes.bookshop.spring;
...
import org.springframework.transaction.annotation.Propagation;
import org.springframework.transaction.annotation.Transactional;
import java.io.IOException;

public class JdbcBookShop extends JdbcDaoSupport implements BookShop {
    ...
    @Transactional(
            propagation = Propagation.REQUIRES_NEW,
            rollbackFor = IOException.class,
            noRollbackFor = ArithmeticException.class)
    public void purchase(String isbn, String username) throws Exception{
    throw new ArithmeticException();
            //throw new IOException();
    }
}
```

In a Spring transaction advice, the rollback rule can be specified in the <tx:method> element. You can separate the exceptions with commas if there's more than one exception.

```
<tx:advice ...>
    <tx:attributes>
        <tx:method name="..."
            rollback-for="java.io.IOException"
            no-rollback-for="java.lang.ArithmeticException"/>
        ...
    </tx:attributes>
</tx:advice>
```

In classic Spring AOP, the rollback rule can be specified in the transaction attributes of TransactionInterceptor and TransactionProxyFactoryBean. The minus sign indicates an exception to cause a transaction to roll back, while the plus sign indicates an exception to cause a transaction to commit.

```
<property name="transactionAttributes">
    <props>
        <prop key="...">
            PROPAGATION_REQUIRED, -java.io.IOException,
            +java.lang.ArithmeticException
        </prop>
    </props>
</property>
```

In Spring's transaction management API, the rollback rule can be specified in a RuleBasedTransactionAttribute object. Because it implements the TransactionDefinition interface, it can be passed to a transaction manager's getTransaction() method or a transaction template's constructor.

```
RuleBasedTransactionAttribute attr = new RuleBasedTransactionAttribute();
attr.getRollbackRules().add(
    new RollbackRuleAttribute(IOException.class));
attr.getRollbackRules().add(
    new NoRollbackRuleAttribute(SendFailedException.class));
```

16-10. Setting the Timeout and Read-Only Transaction Attributes

Problem

Because a transaction may acquire locks on rows and tables, a long transaction will tie up resources and have an impact on overall performance. Besides, if a transaction only reads but does not update data, the database engine could optimize this transaction. You can specify these attributes to increase the performance of your application.

Solution

The *timeout* transaction attribute (an integer that describes seconds) indicates how long your transaction can survive before it is forced to roll back. This can prevent a long transaction from tying up resources. The *read-only* attribute indicates that this transaction will only read but not update data. The read-only flag is just a hint to enable a resource to optimize the transaction, and a resource might not necessarily cause a failure if a write is attempted.

How It Works

The timeout and read-only transaction attributes can be defined in the @Transactional annotation. Note that timeout is measured in seconds.

```
package com.apress.springrecipes.bookshop.spring;
...
import org.springframework.transaction.annotation.Isolation;
import org.springframework.transaction.annotation.Transactional;

public class JdbcBookShop extends JdbcDaoSupport implements BookShop {
    ...
    @Transactional(
            isolation = Isolation.REPEATABLE_READ,
            timeout = 30,
            readOnly = true)
```

```
    public int checkStock(String isbn) {
        ...
    }
}
```

In a Spring 2.0 transactional advice, the timeout and read-only transaction attributes can be specified in the <tx:method> element.

```
<tx:advice ...>
    <tx:attributes>
        <tx:method name="checkStock"
            timeout="30"
            read-only="true"/>
    </tx:attributes>
</tx:advice>
```

In classic Spring AOP, the timeout and read-only transaction attributes can be specified in the transaction attributes of TransactionInterceptor and TransactionProxyFactoryBean.

```
<property name="transactionAttributes">
    <props>
        <prop key="...">
            PROPAGATION_REQUIRED, timeout_30, readOnly
        </prop>
    </props>
</property>
```

In Spring's transaction management API, the timeout and read-only transaction attributes can be specified in a DefaultTransactionDefinition object and then passed to a transaction manager's getTransaction() method or a transaction template's constructor.

```
DefaultTransactionDefinition def = new DefaultTransactionDefinition();
def.setTimeout(30);
def.setReadOnly(true);
```

16-11. Managing Transactions with Load-Time Weaving

Problem

By default, Spring's declarative transaction management is enabled via its AOP framework. However, as Spring AOP can only advise public methods of beans declared in the IoC container, you are restricted to managing transactions within this scope using Spring AOP. Sometimes, you may wish to manage transactions for nonpublic methods, or methods of objects created outside the Spring IoC container (e.g., domain objects).

Solution

Spring 2.5 also provides an AspectJ aspect named AnnotationTransactionAspect that can manage transactions for any methods of any objects, even if the methods are non-public or the objects are created outside the Spring IoC container. This aspect will manage transactions for any methods with the @Transactional annotation. You can choose either AspectJ's compile-time weaving or load-time weaving to enable this aspect.

How It Works

First of all, let's create a domain class Book, whose instances (i.e., domain objects) may be created outside the Spring IoC container.

```
package com.apress.springrecipes.bookshop.spring;

import org.springframework.beans.factory.annotation.Autowired;
import org.springframework.beans.factory.annotation.Configurable;
import org.springframework.jdbc.core.JdbcTemplate;

@Configurable
public class Book {

    private String isbn;
    private String name;
    private int price;

    // Constructors, Getters and Setters
    ...

    private JdbcTemplate jdbcTemplate;

    @Autowired
    public void setJdbcTemplate(JdbcTemplate jdbcTemplate) {
        this.jdbcTemplate = jdbcTemplate;
    }

    public void purchase(String username) {
        jdbcTemplate.update(
                "UPDATE BOOK_STOCK SET STOCK = STOCK - 1 "+
                "WHERE ISBN = ?",
                new Object[] { isbn });

        jdbcTemplate.update(
                "UPDATE ACCOUNT SET BALANCE = BALANCE - ? "+
                "WHERE USERNAME = ?",
                new Object[] { price, username });
    }
}
```

This domain class has a purchase() method that will deduct the current book instance's stock and the user account's balance from the database. To utilize Spring's powerful JDBC support features, you can inject the JDBC template via setter injection.

You can use Spring's load-time weaving support to inject a JDBC template into book domain objects. You have to annotate this class with @Configurable to declare that this type of object is configurable in the Spring IoC container. Moreover, you can annotate the JDBC template's setter method with @Autowired to have it auto-wired.

Spring includes an AspectJ aspect, AnnotationBeanConfigurerAspect, in its aspect library for configuring object dependencies even if these objects are created outside the IoC container. To enable this aspect, you just define the <context:spring-configured> element in your bean configuration file. To weave this aspect into your domain classes at load time, you also have to define <context:load-time-weaver>. Finally, to auto-wire the JDBC template into book domain objects via @Autowired, you need <context:annotation-config> also.

■ **Note** To use the Spring aspect library for AspectJ in Spring 2.0 and 2.5, you have to include **spring-aspects** module on your CLASSPATH. In Spring 3.0, the library has been renamed **spring-instrument**. If you're using Maven, add the following dependency to your project.

```
<dependency>
  <groupId>org.springframework</groupId>
  <artifactId>spring-instrument</artifactId>
  <version>${spring.version}</version>
</dependency>
```

```
<beans xmlns="http://www.springframework.org/schema/beans"
    xmlns:xsi="http://www.w3.org/2001/XMLSchema-instance"
    xmlns:context="http://www.springframework.org/schema/context"
    xsi:schemaLocation="http://www.springframework.org/schema/beans
        http://www.springframework.org/schema/beans/spring-beans-3.0.xsd
        http://www.springframework.org/schema/context
        http://www.springframework.org/schema/context/spring-context-3.0.xsd">

    <context:load-time-weaver />

    <context:annotation-config />

    <context:spring-configured />

    <bean id="dataSource"
        class="org.springframework.jdbc.datasource.DriverManagerDataSource">
        <property name="driverClassName"
            value="org.apache.derby.jdbc.ClientDriver"/>
```

```
            <property name="url"
                value="jdbc:derby://localhost:1527/bookshop;create=true"/>
            <property name="username" value="app"/>
            <property name="password" value="app"/>
        </bean>

        <bean id="jdbcTemplate"
            class="org.springframework.jdbc.core.JdbcTemplate">
            <property name="dataSource" ref="dataSource"/>
        </bean>
</beans>
```

In this bean configuration file, you can define a JDBC template on a data source, and then, it will be auto-wired into book domain objects for them to access the database.

Now, you can create the following Main class to test this domain class. Of course, there's no transaction support at this moment.

```
package com.apress.springrecipes.bookshop.spring;

import org.springframework.context.ApplicationContext;
import org.springframework.context.support.ClassPathXmlApplicationContext;

public class Main {

    public static void main(String[] args) {
        ApplicationContext context =
            new ClassPathXmlApplicationContext("beans.xml");

        Book book = new Book("0001", "My First Book", 30);
        book.purchase("user1");
    }
}
```

For a simple Java application, you can weave this aspect into your classes at load time with the Spring agent specified as a VM argument.

```
java -javaagent: spring-instrument.jar
com.apress.springrecipes.bookshop.spring.Main
```

To enable transaction management for a domain object's method, you can simply annotate it with @Transactional, just as you did for methods of Spring beans.

```
package com.apress.springrecipes.bookshop.spring;
...
import org.springframework.beans.factory.annotation.Configurable;
import org.springframework.transaction.annotation.Transactional;
```

```
@Configurable
public class Book {
    ...
    @Transactional
    public void purchase(String username) {
        ...
    }
}
```

Finally, to enable Spring's AnnotationTransactionAspect for transaction management, you just define the <tx:annotation-driven> element and set its mode to aspectj. The <tx:annotation-driven> element takes two values for the mode attribute: aspectj and proxy. aspect stipulates that the container should use load-time or compile-time weaving to enable the transaction advice. This requires the spring-instrument jar to be on the classpath, as well as the appropriate configuration at load time or compile time. Alternatively, proxy stipulates that the container should use the Spring AOP mechanisms. It's important to note that the aspect mode doesn't support configuration of the @Transactional annotation on interfaces. Then the transaction aspect will automatically get enabled. You also have to provide a transaction manager for this aspect. By default, it will look for a transaction manager whose name is transactionManager.

```
<beans xmlns="http://www.springframework.org/schema/beans"
    xmlns:xsi="http://www.w3.org/2001/XMLSchema-instance"
    xmlns:context="http://www.springframework.org/schema/context"
    xmlns:tx="http://www.springframework.org/schema/tx"
    xsi:schemaLocation="http://www.springframework.org/schema/beans
        http://www.springframework.org/schema/beans/spring-beans-3.0.xsd
        http://www.springframework.org/schema/context
        http://www.springframework.org/schema/context/spring-context-3.0.xsd
        http://www.springframework.org/schema/tx
        http://www.springframework.org/schema/tx/spring-tx-3.0.xsd">
    ...
    <tx:annotation-driven mode="aspectj"/>

    <bean id="transactionManager"
        class="org.springframework.jdbc.datasource.DataSourceTransactionManager">
        <property name="dataSource" ref="dataSource"/>
    </bean>
</beans>
```

Summary

This chapter discussed transactions and why you should use them. You explored the approach taken for transaction management historically in Java EE and then learned how the approach the Spring framework offers differs. You explored explicit use of transactions in your code as well as implicit use with annotation-driven aspects. You set up a database and used transactions to enforce valid state in the database.

In the next chapter, you will explore Spring's remoting support. Spring provides a layer to isolate your POJOs from the protocol and platform over which they are exposed to remote clients. You will explore the approach in general as well as see it applied to a few key technologies on the Java EE and Spring platforms.

CHAPTER 17

■ ■ ■

EJB, Spring Remoting, and Web Services

In this chapter, you will learn about Spring's support for various remoting technologies, such as EJB, RMI, Hessian, Burlap, HTTP Invoker, and web services. *Remoting* is a key technology in developing distributed applications, especially multitier enterprise applications. It allows different applications or components, running in different JVMs or on different machines, to communicate with each other using a specific protocol.

Spring's remoting support is consistent across different remoting technologies. On the server side, Spring allows you to expose an arbitrary bean as a remote service through a service exporter. On the client side, Spring provides various proxy factory beans for you to create a local proxy for a remote service so that you can use the remote service as if it were a local bean.

Nowadays, there are two main approaches to developing web services: *contract-first* and *contract-last*. Automatically exposing a bean from the IoC container as a web service means that the service is contract-last because the service contract is generated from an existing bean. The Spring team has created a subproject called Spring Web Services (Spring-WS), which focuses on the development of contract-first web services. In this approach, a service contract is defined first, and code is then written to fulfill this contract.

17-1. Exposing and Invoking Services Through RMI

Problem

You want to expose a service from your Java application for other Java-based clients to invoke remotely. Because both parties are running on the Java platform, you can choose a pure Java-based solution without considering cross-platform portability.

Solution

Remote Method Invocation (RMI) is a Java-based remoting technology that allows two Java applications running in different JVMs to communicate with each other. With RMI, an object can invoke the methods of a remote object. RMI relies on object serialization to marshall and unmarshall method arguments and return values.

Considering the typical RMI usage scenario, to expose a service through RMI, you have to create the service interface that extends `java.rmi.Remote` and whose methods declare throwing `java.rmi.RemoteException`. Then, you create the service implementation for this interface. After that, you start an RMI registry and register your service to it. As you can see, there are quite a lot of steps required for exposing a simple service.

To invoke a service through RMI, you first look up the remote service reference in an RMI registry, and then, you can call the methods on it. However, to call the methods on a remote service, you must handle `java.rmi.RemoteException` in case any exception is thrown by the remote service.

Fortunately, Spring's remoting facilities can significantly simplify the RMI usage on both the server and client sides. On the server side, you can use `RmiServiceExporter` to export a Spring bean as an RMI service whose methods can be invoked remotely. It's just several lines of bean configuration without any programming. Beans exported in this way don't need to implement `java.rmi.Remote` or throw `java.rmi.RemoteException`. On the client side, you can simply use `RmiProxyFactoryBean` to create a proxy for the remote service. It allows you to use the remote service as if it were a local bean. Again, it requires no additional programming at all.

How It Works

Suppose you are going to build a weather web service for clients running on different platforms to invoke. This service includes an operation for querying a city's temperatures on multiple dates. First, you create the `TemperatureInfo` class representing the minimum, maximum, and average temperatures of a particular city and date.

```
package com.apress.springrecipes.weather;
...
public class TemperatureInfo implements Serializable {

    private String city;
    private Date date;
    private double min;
    private double max;
    private double average;

    // Constructors, Getters and Setters
    ...
}
```

Next, you define the service interface that includes the `getTemperatures()` operation, which returns a city's temperatures on multiple dates as requested.

```
package com.apress.springrecipes.weather;
...
public interface WeatherService {

    public List<TemperatureInfo> getTemperatures(String city, List<Date> dates);
}
```

You have to provide an implementation for this interface. In a production application, you probably want to implement this service interface by querying the database. Here, you may hard-code the temperatures for testing purposes.

```
package com.apress.springrecipes.weather;
...
public class WeatherServiceImpl implements WeatherService {

    public List<TemperatureInfo> getTemperatures(String city, List<Date> dates) {
        List<TemperatureInfo> temperatures = new ArrayList<TemperatureInfo>();
        for (Date date : dates) {
            temperatures.add(new TemperatureInfo(city, date, 5.0, 10.0, 8.0));
        }
        return temperatures;
    }
}
```

Exposing an RMI Service

Suppose you want to expose the weather service as an RMI service. To use Spring's remoting facilities for this purpose, create a bean configuration file such as `rmi-server.xml` in the classpath root to define the service. In this file, you declare a bean for the weather service implementation and export it as an RMI service by using `RmiServiceExporter`.

```
<beans xmlns="http://www.springframework.org/schema/beans"
    xmlns:xsi="http://www.w3.org/2001/XMLSchema-instance"
    xsi:schemaLocation="http://www.springframework.org/schema/beans
        http://www.springframework.org/schema/beans/spring-beans-3.0.xsd">

    <bean id="weatherService"
        class="com.apress.springrecipes.weather.WeatherServiceImpl" />

    <bean class="org.springframework.remoting.rmi.RmiServiceExporter">
        <property name="serviceName" value="WeatherService" />
        <property name="serviceInterface"
            value="com.apress.springrecipes.weather.WeatherService" />
        <property name="service" ref="weatherService" />
    </bean>
</beans>
```

There are several properties you must configure for an `RmiServiceExporter` instance, including the service name, the service interface, and the service object to export. You can export any bean configured in the IoC container as an RMI service. `RmiServiceExporter` will create an RMI proxy to wrap this bean and bind it to the RMI registry. When the proxy receives an invocation request from the RMI registry, it will invoke the corresponding method on the bean.

By default, `RmiServiceExporter` attempts to look up an RMI registry at `localhost` port 1099. If it can't find the RMI registry, it will start a new one. However, if you want to bind your service to another running RMI registry, you can specify the host and port of that registry in the `registryHost` and `registryPort` properties. Note that once you specify the registry host, `RmiServiceExporter` will not start a new registry, even if the specified registry doesn't exist.

To start a server that provides the RMI weather service, run the following class to create an application context for the preceding bean configuration file:

```
package com.apress.springrecipes.weather;

import org.springframework.context.support.ClassPathXmlApplicationContext;

public class RmiServer {

    public static void main(String[] args) {
        new ClassPathXmlApplicationContext("rmi-server.xml");
    }
}
```

In this configuration, the server will launch; among the output, you should see a message indicating that an existing RMI registry could not be found.

Invoking an RMI Service

By using Spring's remoting facilities, you can invoke a remote service just like a local bean. For example, you can create a client that refers to the weather service by its interface.

```
package com.apress.springrecipes.weather;
...
public class WeatherServiceClient {

    private WeatherService weatherService;

    public void setWeatherService(WeatherService weatherService) {
        this.weatherService = weatherService;
    }

    public TemperatureInfo getTodayTemperature(String city) {
        List<Date> dates = Arrays.asList(new Date[] { new Date() });
        List<TemperatureInfo> temperatures =
            weatherService.getTemperatures(city, dates);
        return temperatures.get(0);
    }
}
```

In a client bean configuration file, such as `client.xml` located in the classpath root, you can use `RmiProxyFactoryBean` to create a proxy for the remote service. Then, you can use this service as if it were a local bean (e.g., inject it into the weather service client).

```
<beans xmlns="http://www.springframework.org/schema/beans"
    xmlns:xsi="http://www.w3.org/2001/XMLSchema-instance"
    xsi:schemaLocation="http://www.springframework.org/schema/beans
        http://www.springframework.org/schema/beans/spring-beans-3.0.xsd">
```

```xml
<bean id="client"
    class="com.apress.springrecipes.weather.WeatherServiceClient">
    <property name="weatherService" ref="weatherService" />
</bean>

<bean id="weatherService"
    class="org.springframework.remoting.rmi.RmiProxyFactoryBean">
    <property name="serviceUrl"
        value="rmi://localhost:1099/WeatherService" />
    <property name="serviceInterface"
        value="com.apress.springrecipes.weather.WeatherService" />
</bean>
</beans>
```

There are two properties you must configure for an `RmiProxyFactoryBean` instance. The service URL property specifies the host and port of the RMI registry, as well as the service name. The service interface allows this factory bean to create a proxy for the remote service against a known, shared Java interface. The proxy will transfer the invocation requests to the remote service transparently. You can test this service with the following `Client` main class:

```java
package com.apress.springrecipes.weather;

import org.springframework.context.ApplicationContext;
import org.springframework.context.support.ClassPathXmlApplicationContext;

public class Client {

    public static void main(String[] args) {
        ApplicationContext context =
            new ClassPathXmlApplicationContext("client.xml");
        WeatherServiceClient client =
            (WeatherServiceClient) context.getBean("client");

        TemperatureInfo temperature = client.getTodayTemperature("Houston");
        System.out.println("Min temperature : " + temperature.getMin());
        System.out.println("Max temperature : " + temperature.getMax());
        System.out.println("Average temperature : " + temperature.getAverage());
    }
}
```

17-2. Creating EJB 2.x Components with Spring

Problem

In EJB 2.x, as opposed to the current EJB 3.1 and what you may know from Spring, each EJB component requires a remote/local interface, a remote/local home interface, and a bean implementation class, in which you must implement all EJB life cycle callback methods even if you don't need them.

Solution

Sometimes, the proxy approach isn't 100 percent tenable for both clients and servers, but Spring still tries to lighten the load wherever possible. Spring even supports legacy component models like EJB 2.x, in addition to its support for the current EJB 3.x series. Examples in this chapter will also cover EJB 2.x integration, but it should be forewarned that you should avoid at all costs any new development on EJB 2.x. Newer iterations of the EJB specification are already deprecating large swathes of the older specification. Spring's remoting support can't completely remove the burden of all these requirements, but it does provide powerful support for building legacy EJB2.x components with Spring. The Spring support classes facilitate building session beans—*stateful session beans (SFSBs)* and *stateless session beans (SLSBs)*—and *message-driven beans (MDBs)* with Spring. Classic entity beans have no direct support in Spring, presumably because they map more usefully to something like Hibernate or JDO. These classes provide empty implementation for all EJB life cycle callback methods.

Your EJB classes can extend these classes to inherit the methods. Table 17-1 shows Spring's EJB support classes for different types of EJB.

Table 17-1. Spring's EJB Support Classes for Different Types of EJB

EJB Support Class	EJB Type
AbstractStatelessSessionBean	Stateless session bean
AbstractStatefulSessionBean	Stateful session bean
AbstractMessageDrivenBean	General message-driven bean that may not use JMS
AbstractJmsMessageDrivenBean	Message-driven bean that uses JMS

Moreover, the EJB support classes provide access to the Spring IoC container for you to implement your business logic in POJOs and wrap them with EJB components. Because POJOs are easier to develop and test, implementing business logic in POJOs can accelerate your EJB development.

How It Works

Suppose you are going to develop a system for a post office. You are asked to develop a stateless session bean for calculating postage based on the destination country and the weight. The target runtime environment is an application server that supports EJB 2.x only, so you have to develop the EJB component that will work with this version. Obviously, this scenario is not ideal, but there are still quite a few shops that are stuck on EJB 2.x!

Compared with lightweight POJOs, EJB 2.x components are more difficult to build, deploy, and test. A good practice for developing EJB 2.x components is to implement business logic in POJOs and then wrap them with EJB components. First, you define the following business interface for postage calculation:

```
package com.apress.springrecipes.post;

public interface PostageService {

    public double calculatePostage(String country, double weight);
}
```

Next, you have to implement this interface. Typically, it should query the database for the postage and perform some calculation. Here, you may hard-code the result for testing purposes.

```
package com.apress.springrecipes.post;

public class PostageServiceImpl implements PostageService {

    public double calculatePostage(String country, double weight) {
        return 1.0;
    }
}
```

Before you start creating your EJB component, you might like to have a simple EJB container for testing purposes. For simplicity's sake, we have chosen Apache OpenEJB (http://openejb.apache.org/) as the EJB container, which is very easy to install, configure, and deploy. OpenEJB is an open source EJB container. OpenEJB was designed for the Apache Geronimo server project (http://geronimo.apache.org/), but you don't need Apache Geronimo to run OpenEJB.

■ **Note** You can download OpenEJB Standalone Server (e.g., v3.1.2) from the OpenEJB web site and extract it to a directory of your choice to complete the installation.

Creating EJB 2.x Components Without Spring's Support

First, let's create the EJB component without Spring's support. To allow remote access to this EJB component, you expose the following remote interface to clients.

■ **Note** To compile and build your EJB component, you have to include a library that contains standard EJB classes and interfaces in your classpath. OpenEJB 3.1.1 supports both legacy EJB 2.x components as well as newer EJB 3.0 and EJB 3.1 components, so we'll use its implementation library. If you are using Maven, add the following dependency to your classpath.

```
<dependency>
  <groupId>org.apache.openejb</groupId>
  <artifactId>openejb-client</artifactId>
```

```
<version>3.1</version>
</dependency>

<dependency>
 <groupId>org.apache.openejb</groupId>
 <artifactId>openejb-jee</artifactId>
 <version>3.1</version>
</dependency>
```

```
package com.apress.springrecipes.post;

import java.rmi.RemoteException;

import javax.ejb.EJBObject;

public interface PostageServiceRemote extends EJBObject {

    public double calculatePostage(String country, double weight)
        throws RemoteException;
}
```

This `calculatePostage()` method has a signature similar to that in the business interface, except it declares throwing `RemoteException`.

Also, you need a remote home interface for clients to retrieve a remote reference to this EJB component, whose methods must declare throwing `RemoteException` and `CreateException`.

```
package com.apress.springrecipes.post;

import java.rmi.RemoteException;

import javax.ejb.CreateException;
import javax.ejb.EJBHome;

public interface PostageServiceHome extends EJBHome {

    public PostageServiceRemote create() throws RemoteException, CreateException;
}
```

If you want to expose this EJB component for local access within an enterprise application, the preceding two interfaces should extend `EJBLocalObject` and `EJBLocalHome` instead, whose methods don't need to throw `RemoteException`. For simplicity's sake, we're omitting the local and local home interfaces here.

Note that the following EJB implementation class also implements the `PostageService` business interface so that you can delegate requests to the POJO service implementation.

```
package com.apress.springrecipes.post;

import javax.ejb.SessionBean;
import javax.ejb.SessionContext;

public class PostageServiceBean implements SessionBean, PostageService {

    private PostageService postageService;
    private SessionContext sessionContext;
  // this isn't part of the interface, but is required
    public void ejbCreate() {
        postageService = new PostageServiceImpl();
    }

    public void ejbActivate() {}
    public void ejbPassivate() {}
    public void ejbRemove() {}

    public void setSessionContext(SessionContext sessionContext) {
        this.sessionContext = sessionContext;
    }

    public double calculatePostage(String country, double weight) {
        return postageService.calculatePostage(country, weight);
    }
}
```

In the `ejbCreate()` life cycle method, you instantiate the POJO service implementation class. It's up to this object to perform the actual postage calculation. The EJB component just delegates requests to this object.

The astute reader will note that the `ejbCreate()` method is nowhere to be found on the `SessionBean` interface. Instead, it's a convention. Stateless session beans can contain one version of `ejbCreate()`. If the method has any arguments, the corresponding **create** method on the `EJBHome` bean must have the same arguments. The `ejbCreate()` method is the EJB hook for initialization of state, much as a JSR-250 annotated `@PostConstruct()` method or `afterPropertiesSet()` method work in Java EE 5 and Spring. If you have a stateful session bean, then there may be multiple overloaded `ejbCreate()` methods. Similarly, for each overloaded form of `ejbCreate()` on the `SessionBean`, there must be a create method with the same arguments on the `EJBHome`. We mention all this (which, if we're honest, doesn't even begin to cover the nuances involved) to put in stark relief the Spring container's lightweight approach *and* to show that even the Spring abstractions for EJB 2.x are incredible improvements.

Finally, you require an EJB deployment descriptor for your EJB component. You create the file `ejb-jar.xml` in the `META-INF` directory of your classpath and add the following contents to describe your EJB component:

```
<ejb-jar>
    <enterprise-beans>
        <session>
            <display-name>PostageService</display-name>
            <ejb-name>PostageService</ejb-name>
        <home>com.apress.springrecipes.post.PostageServiceHome</home>
```

```
        <remote>com.apress.springrecipes.post.PostageServiceRemote</remote>
            <ejb-class>
                com.apress.springrecipes.post.PostageServiceBean
            </ejb-class>
            <session-type>Stateless</session-type>
            <transaction-type>Bean</transaction-type>
        </session>
    </enterprise-beans>
</ejb-jar>
```

Now, your EJB component is finished, and you should pack your interfaces, classes, and deployment descriptors in a JAR file. Then start up your EJB container, and deploy this EJB component to it.

■ **Note** To start the OpenEJB container, you first set the OPENEJB_HOME environment variable to point to your OpenEJB installation directory. Then execute the OpenEJB startup script (located in the bin directory) with the parameter start (e.g., openejb start). In another shell, to deploy an EJB component, you also execute the OpenEJB startup script, but this time, you pass deploy and the location of your EJB JAR file as parameters. (e.g., openejb deploy ./PostService.jar).

For OpenEJB, the default JNDI name for a remote home interface of an EJB 2.x component is the EJB name with RemoteHome as its suffix (PostageServiceRemoteHome in this case). If the deployment is successful, you should see the following output:

```
Application deployed successfully at "c:\PostageService.jar"

App(id=C:\openejb-3.1.2\apps\PostageService.jar)

    EjbJar(id=PostageService.jar, path=C:\openejb-3.1.2\apps\PostageService.jar)

        Ejb(ejb-name=PostageService, id=PostageService)

            Jndi(name=PostageServiceRemoteHome)

            Jndi(name=PostageServiceLocal)
```

Creating EJB 2.x Components with Spring's Support

As you can see, your EJB implementation class needs to implement all EJB life cycle methods even if you don't need them. It should extend Spring's EJB support class to get the life cycle methods implemented by default. The support class for stateless session beans is AbstractStatelessSessionBean.

■ **Note** To use Spring's EJB support for your EJB implementation classes, you have to include a few Spring framework JARs, including `spring-beans`, `spring-core`, `spring-context`, `spring-asm`, and `spring-expression` in the classpath of your EJB container. For OpenEJB, you can copy these JAR files to the `lib` directory of the OpenEJB installation directory. If your OpenEJB container is running, you will have to restart it.

```
package com.apress.springrecipes.post;

import javax.ejb.CreateException;

import org.springframework.ejb.support.AbstractStatelessSessionBean;

public class PostageServiceBean extends AbstractStatelessSessionBean
        implements PostageService {

    private PostageService postageService;

    protected void onEjbCreate() throws CreateException {
        postageService = (PostageService)
                getBeanFactory().getBean("postageService");
    }

    public double calculatePostage(String country, double weight) {
        return postageService.calculatePostage(country, weight);
    }
}
```

When you extend the `AbstractStatelessSessionBean` class, your EJB class no longer needs to implement any EJB life cycle methods, but you can still override them if necessary. Note that this class has an `onEjbCreate()` method that you must implement to perform initialization tasks. Here, you just retrieve the `postageService` bean from the Spring IoC container for this EJB component to use. Of course, you must define it in a bean configuration file. This file can have an arbitrary name but must be located in the classpath. For example, you can create it as `beans-ejb.xml` in the root of the classpath.

```
<beans xmlns=http://www.springframework.org/schema/beans
xmlns:xsi="http://www.w3.org/2001/XMLSchema-instance"
    xsi:schemaLocation="http://www.springframework.org/schema/beans
        http://www.springframework.org/schema/beans/spring-beans-3.0.xsd">

    <bean id="postageService"
        class="com.apress.springrecipes.post.PostageServiceImpl" />
</beans>
```

The final step is to tell the EJB support class where your bean configuration is. By default, it looks at the JNDI environment variable `java:comp/env/ejb/BeanFactoryPath` for the file location. So, you add an environment entry to your EJB deployment descriptor for this location.

```
<ejb-jar>
    <enterprise-beans>
        <session>
            <display-name>PostageService</display-name>
            <ejb-name>PostageService</ejb-name>
            <home>com.apress.springrecipes.post.PostageServiceHome</home>
            <remote>com.apress.springrecipes.post.PostageServiceRemote
</remote>
            <ejb-class>
                com.apress.springrecipes.post.PostageServiceBean
            </ejb-class>
            <session-type>Stateless</session-type>
            <transaction-type>Bean</transaction-type>
            <env-entry>
                <env-entry-name>ejb/BeanFactoryPath</env-entry-name>
                <env-entry-type>java.lang.String</env-entry-type>
                <env-entry-value>beans-ejb.xml</env-entry-value>
            </env-entry>
        </session>
    </enterprise-beans>
</ejb-jar>
```

The EJB support classes instantiate the Spring IoC container using `BeanFactoryLocator`. The default `BeanFactoryLocator` they use is `ContextJndiBeanFactoryLocator`, which instantiates the IoC (a regular `BeanFactory` implementation such as `ApplicationContext`) container using a bean configuration file specified by the JNDI environment variable `java:comp/env/ejb/BeanFactoryPath`. You can override this variable name by calling the `setBeanFactoryLocatorKey()` method in a constructor or in the `setSessionContext()` method.

Now, you can repack your EJB JAR file to include the preceding bean configuration file and redeploy it to your EJB container. In OpenEJB, this is a simple undeploy and redeploy sequence. It will vary from container to container.

17-3. Accessing Legacy EJB 2.x Components in Spring

Problem

In EJB 2.x, you have to perform the following tasks to invoke a method on a remote EJB component. Invoking a method on a local EJB component is very similar, except that you have no need to handle `RemoteException`.

- Initialize the JNDI lookup context, which may throw a `NamingException`.

- Look up the home interface from JNDI, which may throw a `NamingException`.

- Retrieve a remote EJB reference from the home interface, which may throw a `CreateException` or a `RemoteException`.

- Invoke the method on the remote interface, which may throw a `RemoteException`.

As you can see, invoking a method on an EJB component requires a lot of coding. The exceptions `NamingException`, `CreateException`, and `RemoteException` are all checked exceptions that you must handle. Moreover, your client is bound to EJB and would require a lot of changes if you ever switched the service implementation from EJB to another technology.

Solution

Spring offers two factory beans, `SimpleRemoteStatelessSessionProxyFactoryBean` and `LocalStatelessSessionProxyFactoryBean`, for creating a proxy for a remote and local stateless session bean respectively. They allow EJB clients to invoke an EJB component by the business interface as if it were a simple local object. The proxy handles the JNDI context initialization, home interface lookup, and invocation of local/remote EJB methods behind the scenes.

The EJB proxy also converts exceptions such as `NamingException`, `CreateException`, and `RemoteException` into runtime exceptions, so the client code is not required to handle them. For example, if a `RemoteException` is thrown when accessing a remote EJB component, the EJB proxy will convert it into Spring's runtime exception `RemoteAccessException`.

How It Works

Suppose that there's a front desk subsystem in your post office system that requires postage calculation. First, let's define the `FrontDesk` interface as follows:

```
package com.apress.springrecipes.post;

public interface FrontDesk {

    public double calculatePostage(String country, double weight);
}
```

Because there's an EJB 2.x remote stateless session bean for calculating postage, you only have to access it in your front desk subsystem. To talk to the remote service, you interface in terms of the `EJBHome` and the `EJB Remote` (`PostageServiceRemote`) interface. It is against these interfaces that a client-side proxy will be created. You are given the following remote interface and home interface for this EJB component:

```
package com.apress.springrecipes.post;

import java.rmi.RemoteException;

import javax.ejb.EJBObject;

public interface PostageServiceRemote extends EJBObject {

    public double calculatePostage(String country, double weight)
        throws RemoteException;
}
```

```
package com.apress.springrecipes.post;

import java.rmi.RemoteException;

import javax.ejb.CreateException;
import javax.ejb.EJBHome;

public interface PostageServiceHome extends EJBHome {

    public PostageServiceRemote create() throws RemoteException, CreateException;
}
```

Suppose this EJB component has already been deployed in an EJB container (e.g., an OpenEJB container started up on localhost). The JNDI name of this EJB component is PostageServiceRemoteHome.

■ **Note** To access an EJB component deployed in an EJB container, you have to include the EJB container's client library in your classpath. If you are using Maven, add the following dependency to your project.

```
<dependency>
  <groupId>org.apache.openejb</groupId>
  <artifactId>openejb-client</artifactId>
  <version>3.1</version>
</dependency>
```

Accessing EJB 2.x Components

With Spring's support, accessing an EJB component can be significantly simplified. You can access an EJB component by its business interface. A business interface differs from an EJB remote interface in that it doesn't extend EJBObject, and its method declarations don't throw RemoteException, which means that the client doesn't have to handle this type of exception, and it doesn't know that the service is implemented by an EJB component. The business interface for postage calculation is shown following:

```
package com.apress.springrecipes.post;

public interface PostageService {
    public double calculatePostage(String country, double weight);
}
```

Now, in FrontDeskImpl, you can define a setter method for the PostageService business interface to let Spring inject the service implementation so that your FrontDeskImpl will no longer be EJB specific. Later, if you reimplement the PostageService interface with another technology (SOAP, RMI, Hessian/Burlap, Flash AMF, etc.), you won't need to modify a single line of code.

```
package com.apress.springrecipes.post;

public class FrontDeskImpl implements FrontDesk {

    private PostageService postageService;

    public void setPostageService(PostageService postageService) {
        this.postageService = postageService;
    }

    public double calculatePostage(String country, double weight) {
        return postageService.calculatePostage(country, weight);
    }
}
```

Spring offers the proxy factory bean SimpleRemoteStatelessSessionProxyFactoryBean to create a local proxy for a remote stateless session bean.

```
<beans xmlns="http://www.springframework.org/schema/beans"
    xmlns:xsi="http://www.w3.org/2001/XMLSchema-instance"
    xsi:schemaLocation="http://www.springframework.org/schema/beans
        http://www.springframework.org/schema/beans/spring-beans-3.0.xsd">

    <bean id="postageService"
class="org.springframework.ejb.access.SimpleRemoteStatelessSession↵
ProxyFactoryBean">
        <property name="jndiEnvironment">
            <props>
                <prop key="java.naming.factory.initial">
                    org.apache.openejb.client.RemoteInitialContextFactory
                </prop>
                <prop key="java.naming.provider.url">
                    ejbd://localhost:4201
                </prop>
            </props>
        </property>
        <property name="jndiName" value="PostageServiceRemoteHome" />
        <property name="businessInterface"
            value="com.apress.springrecipes.post.PostageService" />
    </bean>

    <bean id="frontDesk"
        class="com.apress.springrecipes.post.FrontDeskImpl">
        <property name="postageService" ref="postageService" />
    </bean>
</beans>
```

You have to configure the JNDI details for this EJB proxy in the jndiEnvironment and jndiName properties. The most important is to specify the business interface for this proxy to implement. The calls to methods declared in this interface will be translated into remote method calls to the remote EJB component. You can inject this proxy into FrontDeskImpl in the same way as a normal bean.

EJB proxies can also be defined using the `<jee:remote-slsb>` and `<jee:local-slsb>` elements in the jee schema. You must add the jee schema definition to the `<beans>` root element beforehand.

```
<beans xmlns="http://www.springframework.org/schema/beans"
    xmlns:xsi="http://www.w3.org/2001/XMLSchema-instance"
    xmlns:jee="http://www.springframework.org/schema/jee"
    xsi:schemaLocation="http://www.springframework.org/schema/beans
        http://www.springframework.org/schema/beans/spring-beans-3.0.xsd
        http://www.springframework.org/schema/jee
        http://www.springframework.org/schema/jee/spring-jee-3.0.xsd">

    <jee:remote-slsb id="postageService"
        jndi-name="PostageServiceRemoteHome"
        business-interface="com.apress.springrecipes.post.PostageService">
        <jee:environment>
            java.naming.factory.initial=↵
                org.apache.openejb.client.RemoteInitialContextFactory
            java.naming.provider.url=ejbd://localhost:4201
        </jee:environment>
    </jee:remote-slsb>
    ...
</bean>
```

To access the EJB from a client, your code looks like almost any example demonstrating accessing beans from a Spring context. It describes the instantiation of a Spring `ApplicationContext` and the use of a bean that's interface-compatible with your service's POJO interface.

```
package com.apress.springrecipes.post;
import org.springframework.context.ApplicationContext;
import org.springframework.context.support.ClassPathXmlApplicationContext;

public class FrontDeskMain {

    public static void main(String[] args) {
        ApplicationContext context =
            new ClassPathXmlApplicationContext("beans-front.xml");

        FrontDesk frontDesk = (FrontDesk) context.getBean("frontDesk");
        double postage = frontDesk.calculatePostage("US", 1.5);
        System.out.println(postage);
    }
}
```

17-4. Creating EJB 3.0 Components in Spring

Problem

Happily, creating EJB 3.0 components is much simpler than with EJB 2.x. Indeed, an EJB can be as simple as a business interface and a POJO implementation class. In EJB 3.1, even this restriction is lifted, so that, like with Spring, you can simply specify a POJO and expose that a service. However, writing EJB 3 beans could be unpleasant if you need access to beans in a Spring application context. Without special support, there is no way to have beans auto-wired into the EJB.

Solution

Use the `org.springframework.ejb.interceptor.SpringBeanAutowiringInterceptor` interceptor to let Spring configure `@Autowired` elements on your EJB.

How It Works

First, build an EJB component. You will need to specify an implementation and at minimum a remote interface. The business interface for our EJB 3.0 stateless session bean will be the same as for the EJB 2.0 example. The bean implementation class can be a simple Java class that implements this interface and is annotated with the EJB annotations. A remote stateless session bean requires the `@Stateless` and `@Remote` annotations. In the `@Remote` annotation, you have to specify the remote interface for this EJB component.

```
package com.apress.springrecipes.post;

public interface PostageService {
    public double calculatePostage(String country, double weight);
}
```

Next, we must create an implementation.

```
package com.apress.springrecipes.post;

import javax.ejb.Remote;
import javax.ejb.Stateless;

@Stateless
@Remote( { PostageService.class })
public class PostageServiceBean implements PostageService {

    public double calculatePostage(String country, double weight) {
        return 1.0;
    }
}
```

You specify the remote interface for the session bean using the @Remote annotation that decorates the class. That is all that's required for the coding to create a working EJB3 bean. Compile and then package these classes into a .jar. Then, deploy them to OpenEJB in the same manner as for the EJB 2.x example.

Thus far, you've created a very simple working service in almost no code and haven't needed to use Spring. Let's have Spring inject a resource, which might be useful for a host of reasons: proxying Spring services with EJB3s, injecting custom resources configured in Spring, or even using Spring to isolate your EJBs from acquiring references to other distributed resources such as a REST endpoint or an RMI endpoint.

To do this, use Spring's SpringBeanAutowiringInterceptor class to provide configuration for the EJB. Here is the implementation class (PostageServiceBean) with a few extra lines. First, an @Interceptors annotation decorates the PostageServiceBean. This tells Spring to handle @Autowired injection points in the class. The interceptor obtains beans, by default, from a ContextSingletonBeanFactoryLocation, which in turn looks for an XML application context named beanRefContext.xml, which is presumed to be on the classpath. The second new line of interest here is an example injection of a Spring JdbcTemplate instance.

```
package com.apress.springrecipes.post;

import javax.ejb.Remote;
import javax.ejb.Stateless;
import javax.interceptor.Interceptors;

import org.springframework.jdbc.core.JdbcTemplate;
import org.springframework.ejb.interceptor.SpringBeanAutowiringInterceptor;

@Stateless
@Remote( { PostageService.class })
@Interceptors(SpringBeanAutowiringInterceptor.class)
public class PostageServiceBean implements PostageService {

        @Autowired
        private JdbcTemplate jdbcTemplate;

        public double calculatePostage(String country, double weight) {
                // use the jdbcTemplate …
                return 1.0;
        }
}
```

There are few provisos associated with the use of the SpringBeanAutowiringIntereptor: First, don't use the same name for your Spring bean as you do your EJB name using this interceptor. Second, you'll need to extend the SpringBeanAutowiringInterceptor and override the getBeanFactoryLocatorKey method if you have more than one ApplicationContext on your EJB's class loader.

17-5. Accessing EJB 3.0 Components in Spring

Problem

EJB 3.0 offers some improvements on EJB 2.x. First, the EJB interface is a simple Java interface whose methods don't throw `RemoteException`, while the implementation class is a simple Java class annotated with EJB annotations. Moreover, the concept of home interface has been eliminated to simplify the EJB lookup process. You can look up an EJB reference from JNDI directly in EJB 3.0. However, the JNDI lookup code is still complex, and you also have to handle `NamingException`.

Solution

By using Spring's `JndiObjectFactoryBean`, you can easily declare a JNDI object reference in the Spring IoC container. You can use this factory bean to declare a reference to an EJB 3.0 component.

How It Works

Now that you've created and deployed an EJB component, you can create a client. If you have chosen OpenEJB as your EJB container, the default JNDI name for a remote EJB 3.0 component is the EJB class name with `Remote` as its suffix (`PostageServiceBeanRemote`, in this case). Note that the JNDI name formulation isn't specified in the standard in EJB 3.0, so this may change from container to container. In EJB 3.1, this is remedied, and beans are prescribed a predictable naming scheme so that bean JNDI names are portable across implementations.

Accessing EJB 3.0 Components with Spring's Support

Accessing EJB 3.0 components is simpler than EJB 2.x. You can look up an EJB reference from JNDI directly without looking up its home interface first, so you don't need to handle `CreateException`. Moreover, the EJB interface is a business interface that doesn't throw a `RemoteException`.

Although accessing EJB 3.0 components is simpler than EJB 2.x, the JNDI lookup code is still too complex, and you have to handle `NamingException`. With Spring's support, your `FrontDeskImpl` class can define a setter method for this EJB component's business interface for Spring to inject the EJB reference that is looked up from JNDI.

```
package com.apress.springrecipes.post;

public class FrontDeskImpl implements FrontDesk {

    private PostageService postageService;

    public void setPostageService(PostageService postageService) {
        this.postageService = postageService;
    }
```

```
        public double calculatePostage(String country, double weight) {
            return postageService.calculatePostage(country, weight);
        }
    }
```

Spring offers the factory bean JndiObjectFactoryBean to declare a JNDI object reference in its IoC container. You declare this bean in the front desk system's bean configuration file.

```
<beans xmlns="http://www.springframework.org/schema/beans"
    xmlns:xsi="http://www.w3.org/2001/XMLSchema-instance"
    xsi:schemaLocation="http://www.springframework.org/schema/beans
        http://www.springframework.org/schema/beans/spring-beans-3.0.xsd">

    <bean id="postageService"
        class="org.springframework.jndi.JndiObjectFactoryBean">
        <property name="jndiEnvironment">
            <props>
                <prop key="java.naming.factory.initial">
                    org.apache.openejb.client.RemoteInitialContextFactory
                </prop>
                <prop key="java.naming.provider.url">
                    ejbd://localhost:4201
                </prop>
            </props>
        </property>
        <property name="jndiName" value="PostageServiceBeanRemote" />
    </bean>

    <bean id="frontDesk"
        class="com.apress.springrecipes.post.FrontDeskImpl">
        <property name="postageService" ref="postageService" />
    </bean>
</beans>
```

You can configure the JNDI details for this factory bean in the jndiEnvironment and jndiName properties. Then, you can inject this proxy into FrontDeskImpl in the same way as a normal bean.

In Spring, JNDI objects can also be defined using the <jee:jndi-lookup> element in the jee schema.

```
<beans xmlns="http://www.springframework.org/schema/beans"
    xmlns:xsi="http://www.w3.org/2001/XMLSchema-instance"
    xmlns:jee="http://www.springframework.org/schema/jee"
    xsi:schemaLocation="http://www.springframework.org/schema/beans
        http://www.springframework.org/schema/beans/spring-beans-3.0.xsd
        http://www.springframework.org/schema/jee
        http://www.springframework.org/schema/jee/spring-jee-3.0.xsd">

    <jee:jndi-lookup id="postageService"
        jndi-name="PostageServiceBeanRemote">
        <jee:environment>
            java.naming.factory.initial=org.apache.openejb.client.RemoteInitialContextFactory
```

```
            java.naming.provider.url=ejbd://localhost:4201
        </jee:environment>
    </jee:jndi-lookup>
    ...
</beans>
```

17-6. Exposing and Invoking Services Through HTTP

Problem

RMI and EJB communicate through their own protocol, which may not pass through firewalls. Ideally, you'd like to communicate over HTTP.

Solution

Hessian and Burlap are two simple lightweight remoting technologies developed by Caucho Technology (http://www.caucho.com/). They both communicate using proprietary messages over HTTP and have their own serialization mechanism, but they are much simpler than web services. The only difference between them is that Hessian communicates using binary messages, and Burlap communicates using XML messages. The message formats of both Hessian and Burlap are also supported on other platforms besides Java, such as PHP, Python, C#, and Ruby. This allows your Java applications to communicate with applications running on the other platforms.

In addition to the preceding two technologies, the Spring framework itself also offers a remoting technology called HTTP Invoker. It also communicates over HTTP, but uses Java's object serialization mechanism to serialize objects. Unlike Hessian and Burlap, HTTP Invoker requires both sides of a service to be running on the Java platform and using the Spring framework. However, it can serialize all kinds of Java objects, some of which may not be serialized by Hessian/Burlap's proprietary mechanism.

Spring's remoting facilities are consistent in exposing and invoking remote services with these technologies. On the server side, you can create a service exporter such as HessianServiceExporter, BurlapServiceExporter, or HttpInvokerServiceExporter to export a Spring bean as a remote service whose methods can be invoked remotely. It's just several lines of bean configurations without any programming. On the client side, you can simply configure a proxy factory bean such as HessianProxyFactoryBean, BurlapProxyFactoryBean, or HttpInvokerProxyFactoryBean to create a proxy for a remote service. It allows you to use the remote service as if it were a local bean. Again, it requires no additional programming at all.

How It Works

Exposing a Hessian Service

To expose a Hessian service with Spring, you have to create a web application using Spring MVC. First, you create the following directory structure for your web application context.

■ **Note** To expose a Hessian or Burlap service, you have to add the Hessian library to your classpath. If you are using Maven, add one or both of the following dependencies to your project.

```
<dependency>
    <groupId>com.caucho</groupId>
    <artifactId>hessian</artifactId>
    <version>3.1.5</version>
</dependency>

<dependency>
    <groupId>com.caucho</groupId>
    <artifactId>burlap</artifactId>
    <version>2.1.12</version>
</dependency>
```

```
weather/
    WEB-INF/
        classes/
        lib/*jar
        weather-servlet.xml
        web.xml
```

In the web deployment descriptor (i.e., web.xml), you have to configure Spring MVC's DispatcherServlet.

```
<web-app version="2.4" xmlns="http://java.sun.com/xml/ns/j2ee"
    xmlns:xsi="http://www.w3.org/2001/XMLSchema-instance"
    xsi:schemaLocation="http://java.sun.com/xml/ns/j2ee
        http://java.sun.com/xml/ns/j2ee/web-app_2_4.xsd">

    <servlet>
        <servlet-name>weather</servlet-name>
        <servlet-class>
            org.springframework.web.servlet.DispatcherServlet
        </servlet-class>
        <load-on-startup>1</load-on-startup>
    </servlet>

    <servlet-mapping>
        <servlet-name>weather</servlet-name>
        <url-pattern>/services/*</url-pattern>
    </servlet-mapping>
</web-app>
```

In the preceding servlet mapping definition, you map all URLs under the `services` path to `DispatcherServlet`. Because the name of this servlet is `weather`, you create the following Spring MVC configuration file, `weather-servlet.xml`, in the root of `WEB-INF`. In this file, you declare a bean for the weather service implementation and export it as a Hessian service using `HessianServiceExporter`.

```xml
<beans xmlns="http://www.springframework.org/schema/beans"
    xmlns:xsi="http://www.w3.org/2001/XMLSchema-instance"
    xsi:schemaLocation="http://www.springframework.org/schema/beans
        http://www.springframework.org/schema/beans/spring-beans-3.0.xsd">

    <bean id="weatherService"
        class="com.apress.springrecipes.weather.WeatherServiceImpl" />

    <bean name="/WeatherService"
        class="org.springframework.remoting.caucho.HessianServiceExporter">
        <property name="service" ref="weatherService" />
        <property name="serviceInterface"
            value="com.apress.springrecipes.weather.WeatherService" />
    </bean>
</beans>
```

For a `HessianServiceExporter` instance, you have to configure a service object to export and its service interface. You can export any bean configured in the IoC container as a Hessian service, and `HessianServiceExporter` will create a proxy to wrap this bean. When the proxy receives an invocation request, it will invoke the corresponding method on that bean. By default, `BeanNameUrlHandlerMapping` is preconfigured for a Spring MVC application. It maps requests to handlers according to the URL patterns specified as bean names. The preceding configuration maps the URL pattern `/WeatherService` to this exporter.

Now, you can deploy this web application to a web container (e.g., Apache Tomcat 6.0). By default, Tomcat listens on port 8080, so if you deploy your application to the `weather` context path, you can access this service with the following URL:

```
http://localhost:8080/weather/services/WeatherService
```

Invoking a Hessian Service

By using Spring's remoting facilities, you can invoke a remote service just like a local bean. In the client bean configuration file `client.xml`, you can use `HessianProxyFactoryBean` to create a proxy for the remote Hessian service. Then you can use this service as if it were a local bean.

```xml
<bean id="weatherService"
    class="org.springframework.remoting.caucho.HessianProxyFactoryBean">
    <property name="serviceUrl"
        value="http://localhost:8080/weather/services/WeatherService" />
    <property name="serviceInterface"
        value="com.apress.springrecipes.weather.WeatherService" />
</bean>
```

You have to configure two properties for a `HessianProxyFactoryBean` instance. The service URL property specifies the URL for the target service. The service interface property is for this factory bean to create a local proxy for the remote service. The proxy will send the invocation requests to the remote service transparently.

Exposing a Burlap Service

The configuration for exposing a Burlap service is similar to that for Hessian, except you should use `BurlapServiceExporter` instead.

```
<bean name="/WeatherService"
    class="org.springframework.remoting.caucho.BurlapServiceExporter">
    <property name="service" ref="weatherService" />
    <property name="serviceInterface"
        value="com.apress.springrecipes.weather.WeatherService" />
</bean>
```

Invoking a Burlap Service

Invoking a Burlap service is very similar to Hessian. The only difference is that you should use `BurlapProxyFactoryBean`.

```
<bean id="weatherService"
    class="org.springframework.remoting.caucho.BurlapProxyFactoryBean">
    <property name="serviceUrl"
        value="http://localhost:8080/weather/services/WeatherService" />
    <property name="serviceInterface"
        value="com.apress.springrecipes.weather.WeatherService" />
</bean>
```

Exposing an HTTP Invoker Service

Again, the configuration for exposing a service using HTTP Invoker is similar to that for Hessian and Burlap, except you have to use `HttpInvokerServiceExporter` instead.

```
<bean name="/WeatherService"
    class="org.springframework.remoting.httpinvoker.HttpInvokerServiceExporter">
    <property name="service" ref="weatherService" />
    <property name="serviceInterface"
        value="com.apress.springrecipes.weather.WeatherService" />
</bean>
```

Invoking an HTTP Invoker Service

Invoking a service exposed by HTTP Invoker is also similar to Hessian and Burlap. This time, you have to use `HttpInvokerProxyFactoryBean`.

```
<bean id="weatherService"
    class="org.springframework.remoting.httpinvoker.HttpInvokerProxyFactoryBean">
    <property name="serviceUrl"
        value="http://localhost:8080/weather/services/WeatherService" />
    <property name="serviceInterface"
        value="com.apress.springrecipes.weather.WeatherService" />
</bean>
```

17-7. Choosing a SOAP Web Service Development Approach

Problem

When you are asked to develop a web service, you first have to consider which web service development approach you are going to use.

Solution

There are two approaches to developing a web service, depending on whether you define the contract first or last. A web service contract is described using *Web Services Description Language (WSDL)*. In contract-last, you expose an existing service interface as a web service whose service contract is generated automatically. In contract-first, you design the service contract in terms of XML and then write code to fulfill it.

How It Works

Contract-Last Web Services

In contract-last web service development, you expose an existing service interface as a web service. Many tools and libraries can help expose a Java class/interface as a web service. They can generate the WSDL file for the class/interface by applying rules, such as turning the class/interface into a port type, turning the methods into operations, and generating the request/response message formats according to the method arguments and return value. All in all, everything is generated from a service interface like the following:

```
package com.apress.springrecipes.weather;
...
public interface WeatherService {

    public List<TemperatureInfo> getTemperatures(String city, List<Date> dates);
}
```

This approach is called contract-last because you define the contract for this web service as the last step in the development process by generating it from Java code. In other words, you are designing the service with Java, not with WSDL or XML.

Contract-First Web Services

In contrast, the contract-first approach encourages you to think of the service contract first, in terms of XML, using XML schema (`.xsd`) and WSDL. In this approach, you design the request and response messages for your service first. The messages are designed with XML, which is very good at representing complex data structures in a platform- and language-independent way. The next step is to implement this contract in a particular platform and programming language.

For example, the request message of your weather service contains a `city` element and multiple `date` elements. Note that you should specify the namespace for your messages to avoid naming conflicts with other XML documents.

```
<GetTemperaturesRequest
    xmlns="http://springrecipes.apress.com/weather/schemas">
    <city>Houston</city>
    <date>2007-12-01</date>
    <date>2007-12-08</date>
    <date>2007-12-15</date>
</GetTemperaturesRequest>
```

Then, the response message would contain multiple `Temperature` elements in response to the requested city and dates.

```
<GetTemperaturesResponse
    xmlns="http://springrecipes.apress.com/weather/schemas">
    <TemperatureInfo city="Houston" date="2007-12-01">
        <min>5.0</min>
        <max>10.0</max>
        <average>8.0</average>
    </TemperatureInfo>
    <TemperatureInfo city="Houston" date="2007-12-08">
        <min>4.0</min>
        <max>13.0</max>
        <average>7.0</average>
    </TemperatureInfo>
    <TemperatureInfo city="Houston" date="2007-12-15">
        <min>10.0</min>
        <max>18.0</max>
        <average>15.0</average>
    </TemperatureInfo>
</GetTemperaturesResponse>
```

After designing the sample request and response messages, you can start creating the contract for this web service using XSD and WSDL. Many tools and IDEs can help generate the default XSD and WSDL files for an XML document. You only need to carry out a few optimizations to have it fit your requirements.

Comparison

When developing a contract-last web service, you are actually exposing the internal API of your application to clients. But this API is likely to be changed—and after it's changed, you will also have to change the contract of your web service, which may involve changing all the clients. However, if you design the contract first, it reflects the external API that you want to expose. It's not as likely to need changing as the internal API.

Although many tools and libraries can expose a Java class/interface as a web service, the fact is that the contract generated from Java is not always portable to other platforms. For example, a Java map may not be portable to other programming languages without a similar data structure. Sometimes, you have to change the method signature to make a service contract portable. In some cases, it's also hard to map an object to XML (e.g., an object graph with cyclic references) because there's actually an *impedance mismatch* between an object model and an XML model, just like that between an object model and a relational model.

XML is good at representing complex data structures in a platform- and language-independent way. A service contract defined with XML is 100 percent portable to any platform. In addition, you can define constraints in the XSD file for your messages so that they can be validated automatically. For these reasons, it's more efficient to design a service contract with XML and implement it with a programming language such as Java. There are many libraries in Java for processing XML efficiently.

From a performance viewpoint, generating a service contract from Java code may lead to an inefficient design. This is because you might not consider the message granularity carefully (specifically, the typical granularity of a Java method invocation is going to be considerably finer than that of an optimum network message. This is restated by Martin Fowler as Fowler's First Law of Distributed Object Design: "Don't distribute your objects (any more than you *really* have to)"), as it's derived from the method signature directly. In contrast, defining the service contract first is more likely to lead to an efficient design.

Finally, the biggest reason for choosing the contract-last approach is its simplicity. Exposing a Java class/interface as a web service doesn't require you to know much about XML, WSDL, SOAP, and so on. You can expose a web service very quickly.

17-8. Exposing and Invoking a Contract-Last SOAP Web Services Using JAX-WS

Problem

Because web services is a standard and cross-platform application communication technology, you want to expose a web service from your Java application for clients on different platforms to invoke.

Solution

Spring comes with several service exporters that can export a bean as a remote service based on the RMI, Hessian, Burlap, or HTTP Invoker remoting technologies, but Spring doesn't come with a service exporter that can export a bean as a SOAP web service. We will use Apache CXF, which is the de facto successor to XFire.

How It Works

The standard for deploying web services on the Java EE platform as of Java EE 1.4 was called JAX-RPC. It supported SOAP 1.0 and 1.1, but didn't support message-oriented web services. This standard was surfaced in the Servlet and EJB tiers in Java EE—you could take an EJB stateless session bean, for example, and have the container expose a SOAP endpoint. Java 5 saw the debut of support for annotations. When the architects behind JAX-RPC sought to create their next generation SOAP stack, JAX-RPC 2.0, they designed it with a significantly different approach that would support POJOs. Also, because this new stack would support message-oriented services—as opposed to simple synchronous RPC calls—it was decided the old name was no longer suitable. JAX-WS 2.0 was the result. It enjoys support in Java EE 5, as well as in JDK 1.6; you can expose an endpoint using the regular JDK with no need for Java EE. Java EE 6 (or, rather, JDK 1.6.0_04 or better) supports JAX-WS 2.1. So, while Spring has provided JAX-RPC support for a long time, we will focus on JAX-WS here, as it is clearly the intended path for services.

To send objects across the wire, beans need to be encoded using the Java Architecture for XML Binding (JAXB). JAXB supports many class types out of the box with no special support. A complex object graph may require some extra help. You can use JAXB annotations to give hints to the runtime as to the correct interpretation of the object graph.

Even within the world of JAX-WS, we have many choices for creating web services. If you are deploying into a Java EE 5 (or better) container, you may simply create a bean that is annotated with `javax.jws.WebService` or `javax.jws.WebServiceProvider` and deploy that into a container in your web application. From there, you'll have some intermediary steps. If you are using the JAX-RS Reference Implementation, this intermediary step will involve a tool called `wsgen`, which will generate the configuration (a file called `sun-jaxws.xml`) and wrapper beans required to expose your service. More contemporary frameworks like Apache CXF have no such step; your bean and web service implementation are generated at startup in your runtime: deployment of the annotated bean is the final step. In this scenario, there's little Spring needs to do for you, except perhaps enable access to the application context and so on. For this purpose, you may have your service extend `org.springframework.web.context.support.SpringBeanAutowiringSupport`. Your service endpoint then benefits from `@Autowired` and the like.

Exposing a Web Service Using The JAX-WS Endpoint Support in the JDK

Another option is to deploy JAX-WS services outside of a container, using, for example, the stand-alone HTTP server. Spring provides a factory that can export beans annotated with `javax.jws.WebService` or `javax.jws.WebServiceProvider` inside the Spring context and then publishes the services using the JAX-WS runtime. If you have no runtime configured and are running on JDK 6, Spring will use the existing HTTP server support and JAX-WS RI in the JDK. Let's look at our example from previous recipes, the `WeatherService` service.

We need to annotate our service to indicate to the provider what should be exposed. Note the application of the `javax.jws.WebMethod` annotation to the method itself and the application of `javax.jws.WebService` to the service interface. You don't need to provide an `endpointInterface` or a `serviceName`, but we do here for the sake of demonstration. Similarly, you don't need to provide an `operationName` on the `@WebMethod` annotation, but we do for demonstration. This is generally good practice anyway, because it insulates clients of the SOAP endpoint from any refactoring you may do on the Java implementation.

The revised `WeatherServiceImpl` is as follows:

```
package com.apress.springrecipes.weather;

import javax.jws.WebMethod;
import javax.jws.WebService;
import java.util.ArrayList;
import java.util.Date;
import java.util.List;

@WebService(serviceName = "WeatherService", endpointInterface = WeatherService.class+"")
public class WeatherServiceImpl implements WeatherService {

        @WebMethod(operationName = "getTemperatures")
    public List<TemperatureInfo> getTemperatures(String city, List<Date> dates) {
        List<TemperatureInfo> temperatures = new ArrayList<TemperatureInfo>();

        for (Date date : dates) {
            temperatures.add(new TemperatureInfo(city, date, 5.0, 10.0, 8.0));
        }

        return temperatures;
    }
}
```

To then install the service and create the endpoint, we rely on Spring's `SimpleJaxWsServiceExporter`.

```
<?xml version="1.0" encoding="UTF-8"?>
<beans xmlns="http://www.springframework.org/schema/beans"
       xmlns:xsi="http://www.w3.org/2001/XMLSchema-instance"
       xmlns:aop="http://www.springframework.org/schema/aop"
       xsi:schemaLocation="
       http://www.springframework.org/schema/beans↩
 http://www.springframework.org/schema/beans/spring-beans-3.0.xsd
       http://www.springframework.org/schema/aop ↩
 http://www.springframework.org/schema/aop/spring-aop-3.0.xsd
     ">

    <bean id="weatherServiceImpl"↩
 class="com.apress.springrecipes.weather.WeatherServiceImpl"/>

    <bean class="org.springframework.remoting.jaxws.SimpleJaxWsServiceExporter"/>
</beans>
```

If you launch a browser and inspect the results at `http://localhost:8080/WeatherService?wsdl`, you'll see the generated WSDL, which you can feed to clients to access the service. Remoting, even with Spring, doesn't get much simpler than this! The generated WSDL is pretty tame, all things considered.

```xml
<?xml version="1.0" encoding="UTF-8"?>
<!-- Generated by JAX-WS RI at http://jax-ws.dev.java.net. RI's version is JAX-WS RI 2.1.6↵
 in JDK 6. -->
<definitions xmlns:soap="http://schemas.xmlsoap.org/wsdl/soap/"↵
 xmlns:tns="http://weather.springrecipes.apress.com/"
            xmlns:xsd="http://www.w3.org/2001/XMLSchema"↵
 xmlns="http://schemas.xmlsoap.org/wsdl/"
            targetNamespace="http://weather.springrecipes.apress.com/"↵
 name="WeatherService">
    <types>
        <xsd:schema>
            <xsd:import namespace="http://weather.springrecipes.apress.com/"
                schemaLocation="http://localhost:8080/WeatherService?xsd=1"></xsd:import>
        </xsd:schema>
    </types>
    <message name="getTemperatures">
        <part name="parameters" element="tns:getTemperatures"></part>
    </message>
    <message name="getTemperaturesResponse">
        <part name="parameters" element="tns:getTemperaturesResponse"></part>
    </message>
    <portType name="WeatherServiceImpl">
        <operation name="getTemperatures">
            <input message="tns:getTemperatures"></input>
            <output message="tns:getTemperaturesResponse"></output>
        </operation>

    </portType>
    <binding name="WeatherServiceImplPortBinding" type="tns:WeatherServiceImpl">
        <soap:binding transport="http://schemas.xmlsoap.org/soap/http" style="document">
        </soap:binding>
        <operation name="getTemperatures">
            <soap:operation soapAction=""></soap:operation>
            <input>
                <soap:body use="literal"></soap:body>
            </input>
            <output>
                <soap:body use="literal"></soap:body>
            </output>
        </operation>
    </binding>
    <service name="WeatherService">
        <port name="WeatherServiceImplPort" binding="tns:WeatherServiceImplPortBinding">
            <soap:address location="http://localhost:8080/WeatherService"></soap:address>
        </port>

    </service>
</definitions>
```

Exposing a Web Service Using CXF

Exposing a stand-alone SOAP endpoint using the `SimpleJaxWsServiceExporter` or the support for JAX-WS in a Java EE container in conjunction with Spring is simple, but these solutions ignore the largest cross-section of developers—people developing on Tomcat. Here again, we have plenty of options. Tomcat doesn't support JAX-WS by itself, so we need to help it by embedding a JAX-WS runtime. There are many choices, and you're free to take your pick. Two popular choices are Axis2 and CXF, both of which are Apache projects. CXF represents the consolidation of the Celtix and XFire projects, which each had useful SOAP support. For our example, we'll embed CXF since it's robust, fairly well tested, and provides support for other important standards like JAX-RS, the API for REST-ful endpoints. Setup is fairly straightforward. You'll need to include the CXF dependencies on your classpath, as well as the Spring dependencies.

Let's walk through the moving pieces for configuration. A good place to start is the `web.xml` file. In our simple example, `web.xml` looks like this:

```
<web-app version="2.4" xmlns="http://java.sun.com/xml/ns/j2ee"
        xmlns:xsi="http://www.w3.org/2001/XMLSchema-instance"
        xsi:schemaLocation="http://java.sun.com/xml/ns/j2ee
        http://java.sun.com/xml/ns/j2ee/web-app_2_4.xsd">


    <context-param>
        <param-name>contextConfigLocation</param-name>
        <param-value>
            /WEB-INF/weather-servlet.xml
        </param-value>
    </context-param>

    <listener>
        <listener-class>
            org.springframework.web.context.ContextLoaderListener
        </listener-class>
    </listener>

    <servlet>
        <servlet-name>spring</servlet-name>
        <servlet-class>
            org.springframework.web.servlet.DispatcherServlet
        </servlet-class>
        <init-param>
            <param-name>contextConfigLocation</param-name>
            <param-value>
            </param-value>
        </init-param>
        <load-on-startup>1</load-on-startup>

    </servlet>
```

```
<servlet-mapping>
    <servlet-name>spring</servlet-name>
    <url-pattern>/dispatch/*</url-pattern>
</servlet-mapping>

<servlet>
    <servlet-name>cxf</servlet-name>
    <servlet-class>org.apache.cxf.transport.servlet.CXFServlet</servlet-class>
    <load-on-startup>1</load-on-startup>
</servlet>

<servlet-mapping>
    <servlet-name>cxf</servlet-name>
    <url-pattern>/*</url-pattern>
</servlet-mapping>

</web-app>
```

This `web.xml` file will look pretty much as all Spring MVC applications do. The only exception here is that we've also configured a `CXFServlet`, which handles a lot of the heavy lifting required to expose our service. In the Spring MVC configuration file, `weather-servlet.xml`, we'll declare a bean for the weather service implementation and export it as a web service by using the Spring namespace support that CXF provides for configuring services (as well as clients, which we'll soon see).

The Spring context file is underwhelming; most of it is boilerplate XML namespace and Spring context file imports. The only two salient stanzas are below, where we first configure the service itself as usual. Finally, we use the CXF `jaxws:endpoint` namespace to configure our endpoint.

```
<?xml version="1.0" encoding="UTF-8"?>
<beans xmlns="http://www.springframework.org/schema/beans"
       xmlns:xsi="http://www.w3.org/2001/XMLSchema-instance"
       xmlns:aop="http://www.springframework.org/schema/aop"
       xmlns:jaxrs="http://cxf.apache.org/jaxrs"
       xmlns:simple="http://cxf.apache.org/simple"
       xmlns:soap="http://cxf.apache.org/bindings/soap"
       xmlns:jaxws="http://cxf.apache.org/jaxws"
       xsi:schemaLocation="
       http://www.springframework.org/schema/beans⏎
  http://www.springframework.org/schema/beans/spring-beans-3.0.xsd
       http://www.springframework.org/schema/aop⏎
  http://www.springframework.org/schema/aop/spring-aop-3.0.xsd
       http://cxf.apache.org/jaxrs http://cxf.apache.org/schemas/jaxrs.xsd
       http://cxf.apache.org/simple http://cxf.apache.org/schemas/simple.xsd
       http://cxf.apache.org/bindings/soap⏎
  http://cxf.apache.org/schemas/configuration/soap.xsd
       http://cxf.apache.org/jaxws http://cxf.apache.org/schemas/jaxws.xsd
       ">
```

```
<import resource="classpath:META-INF/cxf/cxf-servlet.xml"/>
<import resource="classpath:META-INF/cxf/cxf.xml"/>
<import resource="classpath:META-INF/cxf/cxf-extension-soap.xml"/>

<bean id="weatherServiceImpl"↩
class="com.apress.springrecipes.weather.WeatherServiceImpl"/>

<jaxws:endpoint implementor="#weatherServiceImpl" address="/weatherService">
    <jaxws:binding>
        <soap:soapBinding style="document" use="literal" version="1.1"/>
    </jaxws:binding>
</jaxws:endpoint>

</beans>
```

We tell the `jaxws:endpoint` factory to use our Spring bean as the implementation. We tell it at what address to publish the service using the address element. Note that we've found that using a forward slash at the beginning of the address is the only way to get the endpoint to work reliably across both Jetty and Tomcat; your mileage may vary. We also specify some extra niceties like what binding style to use. You don't need to, of course. This is mainly for illustration. The Java code stays the same as before, with the `javax.jws.WebService` method and `javax.jws.WebMethod` annotations in place. Launch the application and your web container, and then bring up the application in your browser. In this example, the application is deployed at the root context (/), so the SOAP endpoint is available at http://localhost:8080/weatherService. If you bring up the page at http://localhost:8080/, you'll see a directory of the available services and their operations. Click the link for the service's WSDL—or simply append `?wsdl` to the service endpoint—to see the WSDL for the service. WSDL describes the messages and endpoint to clients. You can use it to infer a client to the service on most platforms.

Invoking a Web Service Using CXF

Let's now use CXF to define a web service client. We'll want one to work with our new weather service, after all! Our client is the same as in previous recipes, and there is no special Java configuration or coding to be done. We simply need the interface of the service on the classpath. Once that's done, you can use CXF's namespace support to create a client.

```
<?xml version="1.0" encoding="UTF-8"?>
<beans xmlns="http://www.springframework.org/schema/beans"
       xmlns:xsi="http://www.w3.org/2001/XMLSchema-instance"
       xmlns:aop="http://www.springframework.org/schema/aop"
       xmlns:jaxws="http://cxf.apache.org/jaxws"
       xsi:schemaLocation="
          http://www.springframework.org/schema/beans↩
 http://www.springframework.org/schema/beans/spring-beans-3.0.xsd
          http://www.springframework.org/schema/aop ↩
 http://www.springframework.org/schema/aop/spring-aop-3.0.xsd
        http://cxf.apache.org/jaxws http://cxf.apache.org/schemas/jaxws.xsd
     ">
```

```
<import resource="classpath:META-INF/cxf/cxf-extension-soap.xml"/>
<import resource="classpath:META-INF/cxf/cxf.xml"/>
<import resource="classpath:META-INF/cxf/cxf-servlet.xml"/>
<jaxws:client serviceClass="com.apress.springrecipes.weather.WeatherService"
        address="http://localhost:8080/weatherService" id="weatherService"/>
<bean class="com.apress.springrecipes.weather.WeatherServiceClient" id="client">
    <property name="weatherService" ref="weatherService"/>
</bean>
</beans>
```

We use the `jaxws:client` namespace support to define to which interface the proxy should be bound, and the endpoint of the service itself. That is all that's required. Our examples from previous recipes works otherwise unchanged: here we inject the client into the `WeatherServiceClient` and invoke it.

17-9. Defining the Contract of a Web Service

Problem

According to the contract-first web service approach, the first step of developing a web service is to define the service contract. How should you go about this?

Solution

A web service's contract consists of two parts: the data contract and the service contract. They are both defined with the XML technology in a platform- and language-independent way.

> *Data contract*: Describes the complex data types and request and response messages of this web service. A data contract is typically defined with XSD, although you can also use DTDs, RELAX NG, or Schematron.

> *Service contract*: Describes the operations of this web service. A web service may have multiple operations. A service contract is defined with WSDL.

When using a comprehensive web service development framework like Spring-WS, the service contract can usually be generated automatically. But you must create the data contract yourself.

To create the data contract for your web service, you can start by creating the XSD file. Because there are many powerful XML tools available in the community, this won't be too hard. However, most developers prefer to start by creating some sample XML messages and then generate the XSD file from them. Of course, you need to optimize the generated XSD file yourself, as it may not fit your requirements entirely, and sometimes, you may wish to add more constraints to it.

How It Works

Creating Sample XML Messages

For your weather service, you can represent the temperature of a particular city and date as in the following XML message:

```
<TemperatureInfo city="Houston" date="2007-12-01">
    <min>5.0</min>
    <max>10.0</max>
    <average>8.0</average>
</TemperatureInfo>
```

Then, you can define the data contract for your weather service. Suppose you want to define an operation that allows clients to query the temperatures of a particular city for multiple dates. Each request consists of a `city` element and multiple `date` elements. You should also specify the namespace for this request to avoid naming conflicts with other XML documents. Let's save this XML message to `request.xml`.

```
<GetTemperaturesRequest
    xmlns="http://springrecipes.apress.com/weather/schemas">
    <city>Houston</city>
    <date>2007-12-01</date>
    <date>2007-12-08</date>
    <date>2007-12-15</date>
</GetTemperaturesRequest>
```

The response consists of multiple `TemperatureInfo` elements, each of which represents the temperature of a particular city and date, in accordance with the requested dates. Let's save this XML message to `response.xml`.

```
<GetTemperaturesResponse
    xmlns="http://springrecipes.apress.com/weather/schemas">
    <TemperatureInfo city="Houston" date="2007-12-01">
        <min>5.0</min>
        <max>10.0</max>
        <average>8.0</average>
    </TemperatureInfo>
    <TemperatureInfo city="Houston" date="2007-12-08">
        <min>4.0</min>
        <max>13.0</max>
        <average>7.0</average>
    </TemperatureInfo>
    <TemperatureInfo city="Houston" date="2007-12-15">
        <min>10.0</min>
        <max>18.0</max>
        <average>15.0</average>
    </TemperatureInfo>
</GetTemperaturesResponse>
```

Generating an XSD File from Sample XML Messages

Now, you can generate the XSD file from the preceding sample XML messages. Most popular XML tools and enterprise Java IDEs can generate an XSD file from a couple of XML files. Here, I have chosen Apache XMLBeans (`http://xmlbeans.apache.org/`) to generate my XSD file.

■ **Note** You can download Apache XMLBeans (e.g., v2.4.0) from the Apache XMLBeans web site and extract it to a directory of your choice to complete the installation.

Apache XMLBeans provides a tool called `inst2xsd` for generating XSD files from XML instance files. It supports several design types for generating XSD files. The simplest is called *Russian doll design*, which generates local elements and local types for the target XSD file. Because there's no enumeration type used in your XML messages, you should also disable the enumeration generation feature. You can execute the following command to generate the XSD file for your data contract:

```
inst2xsd -design rd -enumerations never request.xml response.xml
```

The generated XSD file will have the default name `schema0.xsd`, located in the same directory. Let's rename it to `temperature.xsd`.

```xml
<?xml version="1.0" encoding="UTF-8"?>
<xs:schema attributeFormDefault="unqualified"
    elementFormDefault="qualified"
    targetNamespace="http://springrecipes.apress.com/weather/schemas"
    xmlns:xs="http://www.w3.org/2001/XMLSchema">

    <xs:element name="GetTemperaturesRequest">
        <xs:complexType>
            <xs:sequence>
                <xs:element type="xs:string" name="city" />
                <xs:element type="xs:date" name="date"
                    maxOccurs="unbounded" minOccurs="0" />
            </xs:sequence>
        </xs:complexType>
    </xs:element>

    <xs:element name="GetTemperaturesResponse">
        <xs:complexType>
            <xs:sequence>
                <xs:element name="TemperatureInfo"
                    maxOccurs="unbounded" minOccurs="0">
                    <xs:complexType>
                        <xs:sequence>
                            <xs:element type="xs:float" name="min" />
                            <xs:element type="xs:float" name="max" />
                            <xs:element type="xs:float" name="average" />
                        </xs:sequence>
```

```
                        <xs:attribute type="xs:string" name="city"
                            use="optional" />
                        <xs:attribute type="xs:date" name="date"
                            use="optional" />
                    </xs:complexType>
                </xs:element>
            </xs:sequence>
        </xs:complexType>
    </xs:element>
</xs:schema>
```

Optimizing the Generated XSD File

As you can see, the generated XSD file allows clients to query temperatures of unlimited dates. If you want to add a constraint on the maximum and minimum query dates, you can modify the maxOccurs and minOccurs a minOccurs attributes.

```
<?xml version="1.0" encoding="UTF-8"?>
<xs:schema attributeFormDefault="unqualified"
    elementFormDefault="qualified"
    targetNamespace="http://springrecipes.apress.com/weather/schemas"
    xmlns:xs="http://www.w3.org/2001/XMLSchema">

    <xs:element name="GetTemperaturesRequest">
        <xs:complexType>
            <xs:sequence>
                <xs:element type="xs:string" name="city" />
                <xs:element type="xs:date" name="date"
                    maxOccurs="5" minOccurs="1" />
            </xs:sequence>
        </xs:complexType>
    </xs:element>

    <xs:element name="GetTemperaturesResponse">
        <xs:complexType>
            <xs:sequence>
                <xs:element name="TemperatureInfo"
                    maxOccurs="5" minOccurs="1">
                    ...
                </xs:element>
            </xs:sequence>
        </xs:complexType>
    </xs:element>
</xs:schema>
```

Previewing the Generated WSDL File

As you will learn later, Spring-WS can automatically generate the service contract for you, based on the data contract and some conventions that you can override. Here, you can preview the generated WSDL file to better understand the service contract. For simplicity's sake, the less important parts are omitted.

```
<?xml version="1.0" encoding="UTF-8" ?>
<wsdl:definitions ...
    targetNamespace="http://springrecipes.apress.com/weather/schemas">
    <wsdl:types>
        <!-- Copied from the XSD file -->
        ...
    </wsdl:types>
    <wsdl:message name="GetTemperaturesResponse">
        <wsdl:part element="schema:GetTemperaturesResponse"
            name="GetTemperaturesResponse">
        </wsdl:part>
    </wsdl:message>
    <wsdl:message name="GetTemperaturesRequest">
        <wsdl:part element="schema:GetTemperaturesRequest"
            name="GetTemperaturesRequest">
        </wsdl:part>
    </wsdl:message>
    <wsdl:portType name="Weather">
        <wsdl:operation name="GetTemperatures">
            <wsdl:input message="schema:GetTemperaturesRequest"
                name="GetTemperaturesRequest">
            </wsdl:input>
            <wsdl:output message="schema:GetTemperaturesResponse"
                name="GetTemperaturesResponse">
            </wsdl:output>
        </wsdl:operation>
    </wsdl:portType>
    ...
    <wsdl:service name="WeatherService">
        <wsdl:port binding="schema:WeatherBinding" name="WeatherPort">
            <soap:address
                location="http://localhost:8080/weather/services" />
        </wsdl:port>
    </wsdl:service>
</wsdl:definitions>
```

In the Weather port type, a GetTemperatures operation is defined whose name is derived from the prefix of the input and output messages (i.e., <GetTemperaturesRequest> and <GetTemperaturesResponse>). The definitions of these two elements are included in the <wsdl:types> part, as defined in the data contract.

17-10. Implementing Web Services Using Spring-WS

Problem

Once you have defined the contract for your web service, you can start implementing the service itself according to this contract. You want to use Spring-WS to implement this service.

Solution

Spring-WS provides a set of facilities for you to develop contract-first web services. The essential tasks for building a Spring-WS web service include the following:

- Setting up and configuring a Spring MVC application for Spring-WS

- Mapping web service requests to endpoints

- Creating service endpoints to handle the request messages and return the response messages

- Publishing the WSDL file for this web service

The concept of an *endpoint* in web services is much like that of a controller in web applications. The difference is that a web controller deals with HTTP requests and HTTP responses, while a service endpoint deals with XML request messages and XML response messages. They both need to invoke other back-end services to handle the requests.

Spring-WS provides various abstract endpoint classes for you to process the request and response XML messages using different XML processing technologies and APIs. These classes are all located in the `org.springframework.ws.server.endpoint` package. You can simply extend one of them to process the XML messages with a particular technology or API. Table 17-2 lists these endpoint classes.

Table 17-2. Endpoint Classes for Different XML Processing Technologies/APIs

Technology/API	Endpoint Class
DOM	`AbstractDomPayloadEndpoint`
JDOM	`AbstractJDomPayloadEndpoint`
dom4j	`AbstractDom4jPayloadEndpoint`
XOM	`AbstractXomPayloadEndpoint`
SAX	`AbstractSaxPayloadEndpoint`
Event-based StAX	`AbstractStaxEventPayloadEndpoint`
Streaming StAX	`AbstractStaxStreamPayloadEndpoint`
XML marshalling	`AbstractMarshallingPayloadEndpoint`

Note that the preceding endpoint classes are all for creating payload endpoints. That means you can access only the payloads of the request and response messages (i.e., the contents in the SOAP body but not other parts of a message like the SOAP headers). If you need to get access to the entire SOAP message, you should write an endpoint class by implementing the `org.springframework.ws.server.endpoint.MessageEndpoint org.springframework.ws.server.endpoint.MessageEndpoint` interface.

How It Works

Setting Up a Spring-WS Application

To implement a web service using Spring-WS, you first create the following directory structure for your web application context. Ensure that your `lib` directory contains the latest version of Spring-WS.

```
weather/
    WEB-INF/
        classes/
        lib/*jar
        temperature.xsd
        weather-servlet.xml
        web.xml
```

In `web.xml`, you have to configure the `MessageDispatcherServlet` servlet of Spring-WS, which is different from `DispatcherServlet` for a typical Spring MVC application. This servlet specializes in dispatching web service messages to appropriate endpoints and detecting the framework facilities of Spring-WS.

```xml
<web-app version="2.4" xmlns="http://java.sun.com/xml/ns/j2ee"
    xmlns:xsi="http://www.w3.org/2001/XMLSchema-instance"
    xsi:schemaLocation="http://java.sun.com/xml/ns/j2ee
        http://java.sun.com/xml/ns/j2ee/web-app_2_4.xsd">

    <servlet>
        <servlet-name>weather</servlet-name>
        <servlet-class>
            org.springframework.ws.transport.http.MessageDispatcherServlet
        </servlet-class>
        <load-on-startup>1</load-on-startup>
    </servlet>

    <servlet-mapping>
        <servlet-name>weather</servlet-name>
        <url-pattern>/services/*</url-pattern>
    </servlet-mapping>
</web-app>
```

In the Spring MVC configuration file, `weather-servlet.xml`, you first declare a bean for the weather service implementation. Later, you will define endpoints and mappings to handle the web service requests.

```
<beans xmlns="http://www.springframework.org/schema/beans"
    xmlns:xsi="http://www.w3.org/2001/XMLSchema-instance"
    xsi:schemaLocation="http://www.springframework.org/schema/beans
        http://www.springframework.org/schema/beans/spring-beans-3.0.xsd">

    <bean id="weatherService"
        class="com.apress.springrecipes.weather.WeatherServiceImpl" />
</beans>
```

Mapping Web Service Requests to Endpoints

In a Spring MVC application, you use handler mapping to map web requests to handlers. But in a Spring-WS application, you should use endpoint mapping to map web service requests to endpoints.

The most common endpoint mapping is `PayloadRootQNameEndpointMapping`. It maps web service requests to endpoints according to the name of the request payload's root element. The name used by this endpoint mapping is the qualified name (i.e., including the namespace). So you must include the namespace in the mapping keys, which is presented inside a brace.

```
<bean class="org.springframework.ws.server.endpoint.mapping.↵
    PayloadRootQNameEndpointMapping">
    <property name="mappings">
        <props>
            <prop key="{http://springrecipes.apress.com/weather/schemas}↵
                GetTemperaturesRequest">
                temperatureEndpoint
            </prop>
        </props>
    </property>
</bean>
```

Creating Service Endpoints

Spring-WS supports various XML parsing APIs, including DOM, JDOM, dom4j, SAX, StAX, and XOM. As an example, we will use dom4j (www.dom4j.org) to create a service endpoint. Creating an endpoint using other XML parsing APIs is very similar.

You can create a dom4j endpoint by extending the `AbstractDom4jPayloadEndpoint` class. The core method defined in this class that you must override is `invokeInternal()`. In this method, you can access the request XML element, whose type is `org.dom4j.Element`, and the response document, whose type is `org.dom4j.Document`, as method arguments. The purpose of the response document is for you to create the response element from it. Now, all you have to do in this method is handle the request message and return the response message.

■ **Note** To create a service endpoint using dom4j with XPath, you have to add it to your classpath. If you are using Maven, add the following dependency to your project.

```
<dependency>
  <groupId>dom4j</groupId>
  <artifactId>dom4j</artifactId>
  <version>1.6.1</version>
</dependency>
```

```java
package com.apress.springrecipes.weather;
...
import org.dom4j.Document;
import org.dom4j.Element;
import org.dom4j.XPath;
import org.dom4j.xpath.DefaultXPath;
import org.springframework.ws.server.endpoint.AbstractDom4jPayloadEndpoint;

public class TemperatureDom4jEndpoint extends AbstractDom4jPayloadEndpoint {

    private static final String namespaceUri =
        "http://springrecipes.apress.com/weather/schemas";

    private XPath cityPath;
    private XPath datePath;
    private DateFormat dateFormat;
    private WeatherService weatherService;

    public TemperatureDom4jEndpoint() {

        // Create the XPath objects, including the namespace
        Map<String, String> namespaceUris = new HashMap<String, String>();
        namespaceUris.put("weather", namespaceUri);
        cityPath = new DefaultXPath(
            "/weather:GetTemperaturesRequest/weather:city");
        cityPath.setNamespaceURIs(namespaceUris);
        datePath = new DefaultXPath(
            "/weather:GetTemperaturesRequest/weather:date");
        datePath.setNamespaceURIs(namespaceUris);

        dateFormat = new SimpleDateFormat("yyyy-MM-dd");
    }
```

```
public void setWeatherService(WeatherService weatherService) {
    this.weatherService = weatherService;
}

protected Element invokeInternal(Element requestElement,
        Document responseDocument) throws Exception {

    // Extract the service parameters from the request message
    String city = cityPath.valueOf(requestElement);
    List<Date> dates = new ArrayList<Date>();
    for (Object node : datePath.selectNodes(requestElement)) {
        Element element = (Element) node;
        dates.add(dateFormat.parse(element.getText()));
    }

    // Invoke the back-end service to handle the request
    List<TemperatureInfo> temperatures =
        weatherService.getTemperatures(city, dates);

    // Build the response message from the result of back-end service
    Element responseElement = responseDocument.addElement(
            "GetTemperaturesResponse", namespaceUri);
    for (TemperatureInfo temperature : temperatures) {
        Element temperatureElement = responseElement.addElement(
                "TemperatureInfo");
        temperatureElement.addAttribute("city", temperature.getCity());
        temperatureElement.addAttribute(
                "date", dateFormat.format(temperature.getDate()));
        temperatureElement.addElement("min").setText(
                Double.toString(temperature.getMin()));
        temperatureElement.addElement("max").setText(
                Double.toString(temperature.getMax()));
        temperatureElement.addElement("average").setText(
                Double.toString(temperature.getAverage()));
    }
    return responseElement;
}
}
```

In the preceding invokeInternal() method, you first extract the service parameters from the request message. Here, you use XPath to help locate the elements. The XPath objects are created in the constructor so that they can be reused for subsequent request handling. Note that you must also include the namespace in the XPath expressions, or else they will not be able to locate the elements correctly.

After extracting the service parameters, you invoke the back-end service to handle the request. Because this endpoint is configured in the Spring IoC container, it can easily refer to other beans through dependency injection.

Finally, you build the response message from the back-end service's result. The dom4j library provides a rich set of APIs for you to build an XML message. Remember that you must include the default namespace in your response element.

With the service endpoint written, you can declare it in weather-servlet.xml. Because this endpoint needs the weather service bean's help to query temperatures, you have to make a reference to it.

```
<bean id="temperatureEndpoint"
    class="com.apress.springrecipes.weather.TemperatureDom4jEndpoint">
    <property name="weatherService" ref="weatherService" />
</bean>
```

Publishing the WSDL File

The last step to complete your web service is to publish the WSDL file. In Spring-WS, it's not necessary for you to write the WSDL file manually, although you may still supply a manually written WSDL file. You only declare a DynamicWsdl11Definition bean in the web application context, and then it can generate the WSDL file dynamically. MessageDispatcherServlet can also detect this bean by the WsdlDefinition interface.

```
<bean id="temperature"
    class="org.springframework.ws.wsdl.wsdl11.DynamicWsdl11Definition">
    <property name="builder">
        <bean class="org.springframework.ws.wsdl.wsdl11.builder.↵
            XsdBasedSoap11Wsdl4jDefinitionBuilder">
            <property name="schema" value="/WEB-INF/temperature.xsd" />
            <property name="portTypeName" value="Weather" />
            <property name="locationUri"
                value="http://localhost:8080/weather/services" />
        </bean>
    </property>
</bean>
```

The only property you must configure for this WSDL definition bean is a builder that builds the WSDL file from your XSD file. XsdBasedSoap11Wsdl4jDefinitionBuilder builds the WSDL file using the WSDL4J library. Suppose that you have put your XSD file in the WEB-INF directory—you specify this location in the schema property. This builder scans the XSD file for elements that end with the Request or Response suffix. Then, it generates WSDL operations using these elements as input and output messages, inside a WSDL port type specified by the portTypeName property.

Because you have defined <GetTemperaturesRequest> and <GetTemperatureseResponse> in your XSD file, and you have specified the port type name as Weather, the WSDL builder will generate the following WSDL port type and operation for you. The following snippet is taken from the generated WSDL file:

```
<wsdl:portType name="Weather">
    <wsdl:operation name="GetTemperatures">
        <wsdl:input message="schema:GetTemperaturesRequest"
            name="GetTemperaturesRequest" />
        <wsdl:output message="schema:GetTemperaturesResponse"
            name="GetTemperaturesResponse" />
    </wsdl:operation>
</wsdl:portType>
```

The last property, locationUri, is for you to include this web service's deployed location in the WSDL file. To allow an easy switch to a production URI, you should externalize this URI in a properties file and use Spring's PropertyPlaceholderConfigurer to read the properties from it.

Finally, you can access this WSDL file by joining its definition's bean name and the `.wsdl` suffix. Supposing that your service is deployed in `http://localhost:8080/weather/services`, this WSDL file's URL would be `http://localhost:8080/weather/services/temperature.wsdl`, given that the bean name of the WSDL definition is `temperature`.

17-11. Invoking Web Services Using Spring-WS

Problem

Given the contract of a web service, you can start creating a service client to invoke this service according to the contract. You want to use Spring-WS to create the service client.

Solution

When using Spring-WS on the client side, web services can be invoked through the core template class `org.springframework.ws.client.core.WebServiceTemplate`. It's very like the `JdbcTemplate` class and other data access templates in that it defines template methods for sending and receiving request and response messages.

How It Works

Now, let's create a Spring-WS client to invoke the weather service according to the contract it publishes. You can create a Spring-WS client by parsing the request and response XML messages. As an example, we will use dom4j to implement it. You are free to choose other XML parsing APIs for it, however.

To shield the client from the low-level invocation details, you can create a local proxy for the remote web service. This proxy also implements the `WeatherService` interface, and it will translate local method calls into remote web service calls.

■ **Note** To invoke a web service using Spring-WS, you need to add Spring-WS to your classpath. If you are using Maven, add the following dependency to your project.

```
<dependency>
  <groupId>org.springframework.ws</groupId>
  <artifactId>spring-oxm</artifactId>
  <version>1.5.2</version>
</dependency>
```

```xml
<dependency>
 <groupId>org.springframework.ws</groupId>
 <artifactId>spring-ws-core</artifactId>
 <version>1.5.2</version>
</dependency>

<dependency>
 <groupId>org.springframework.ws</groupId>
 <artifactId>spring-xml</artifactId>
 <version>1.5.2</version>
</dependency>

<dependency>
 <groupId>org.springframework.ws</groupId>
 <artifactId>spring-oxm</artifactId>
 <version>1.5.2</version>
</dependency>
```

```java
package com.apress.springrecipes.weather;
...
import org.dom4j.Document;
import org.dom4j.DocumentHelper;
import org.dom4j.Element;
import org.dom4j.io.DocumentResult;
import org.dom4j.io.DocumentSource;
import org.springframework.ws.client.core.WebServiceTemplate;

public class WeatherServiceProxy implements WeatherService {

    private static final String namespaceUri =
        "http://springrecipes.apress.com/weather/schemas";

    private DateFormat dateFormat;
    private WebServiceTemplate webServiceTemplate;

    public WeatherServiceProxy() throws Exception {
        dateFormat = new SimpleDateFormat("yyyy-MM-dd");
    }

    public void setWebServiceTemplate(WebServiceTemplate webServiceTemplate) {
        this.webServiceTemplate = webServiceTemplate;
    }
```

```java
public List<TemperatureInfo> getTemperatures(String city, List<Date> dates) {

    // Build the request document from the method arguments
    Document requestDocument = DocumentHelper.createDocument();
    Element requestElement = requestDocument.addElement(
            "GetTemperaturesRequest", namespaceUri);
    requestElement.addElement("city").setText(city);
    for (Date date : dates) {
        requestElement.addElement("date").setText(dateFormat.format(date));
    }

    // Invoke the remote web service
    DocumentSource source = new DocumentSource(requestDocument);
    DocumentResult result = new DocumentResult();
    webServiceTemplate.sendSourceAndReceiveToResult(source, result);

    // Extract the result from the response document
    Document responsetDocument = result.getDocument();
    Element responseElement = responsetDocument.getRootElement();
    List<TemperatureInfo> temperatures = new ArrayList<TemperatureInfo>();
    for (Object node : responseElement.elements("TemperatureInfo")) {
        Element element = (Element) node;
        try {
            Date date = dateFormat.parse(element.attributeValue("date"));
            double min = Double.parseDouble(element.elementText("min"));
            double max = Double.parseDouble(element.elementText("max"));
            double average = Double.parseDouble(
                    element.elementText("average"));
            temperatures.add(
                    new TemperatureInfo(city, date, min, max, average));
        } catch (ParseException e) {
            throw new RuntimeException(e);
        }
    }
    return temperatures;
}
}
```

In the getTemperatures() method, you first build the request message using the dom4j API. WebServiceTemplate provides a sendSourceAndReceiveToResult() method that accepts a java.xml.transform.Source and a java.xml.transform.Result object as arguments. You have to build a dom4j DocumentSource object to wrap your request document and create a new dom4j DocumentResult object for the method to write the response document to it. Finally, you get the response message and extract the results from it.

With the service proxy written, you can declare it in a client bean configuration file such as client.xml. Because this proxy requires an instance of WebServiceTemplate for sending and receiving the messages, you have to instantiate it and inject this instance into the proxy. Also, you specify the default service URI for the template so that all the requests will be sent to this URI by default.

```
<beans xmlns="http://www.springframework.org/schema/beans"
    xmlns:xsi="http://www.w3.org/2001/XMLSchema-instance"
    xsi:schemaLocation="http://www.springframework.org/schema/beans
        http://www.springframework.org/schema/beans/spring-beans-3.0.xsd">

    <bean id="client"
        class="com.apress.springrecipes.weather.WeatherServiceClient">
        <property name="weatherService" ref="weatherServiceProxy" />
    </bean>

    <bean id="weatherServiceProxy"
        class="com.apress.springrecipes.weather.WeatherServiceProxy">
        <property name="webServiceTemplate" ref="webServiceTemplate" />
    </bean>

    <bean id="webServiceTemplate"
        class="org.springframework.ws.client.core.WebServiceTemplate">
        <property name="defaultUri"
            value="http://localhost:8080/weather/services" />
    </bean>
</beans>
```

Now, you can inject this manually written proxy into `WeatherServiceClient` and run it with the `Client` main class.

Because your DAO class can extend `JdbcDaoSupport` to get a precreated `JdbcTemplate` instance, your web service client can similarly extend the `WebServiceGatewaySupport` class to retrieve a `WebServiceTemplate` instance without explicit injection. At this point, you can comment out the `webServiceTemplate` variable and setter method.

```
package com.apress.springrecipes.weather;
...
import org.springframework.ws.client.core.support.WebServiceGatewaySupport;

public class WeatherServiceProxy extends WebServiceGatewaySupport
        implements WeatherService {

    public List<TemperatureInfo> getTemperatures(String city, List<Date> dates) {
        ...
        // Invoke the remote web service
        DocumentSource source = new DocumentSource(requestDocument);
        DocumentResult result = new DocumentResult();
        getWebServiceTemplate().sendSourceAndReceiveToResult(source, result);
        ...
    }
}
```

However, without a `WebServiceTemplate` bean declared explicitly, you have to inject the default URI to the proxy directly. The setter method for this property is inherited from the `WebServiceGatewaySupport` class.

```
<beans ...>
    ...
    <bean id="weatherServiceProxy"
        class="com.apress.springrecipes.weather.WeatherServiceProxy">
        <property name="defaultUri"
            value="http://localhost:8080/weather/services" />
    </bean>
</beans>
```

17-12. Developing Web Services with XML Marshalling

Problem

To develop web services with the contract-first approach, you have to process request and response XML messages. If you parse the XML messages with XML parsing APIs directly, you'll have to deal with the XML elements one by one with low-level APIs, which is a cumbersome and inefficient task.

Solution

Spring-WS supports using XML marshalling technology to marshal and unmarshall objects to and from XML documents. In this way, you can deal with object properties instead of XML elements. This technology is also known as *object/XML mapping (OXM)*, because you are actually mapping objects to and from XML documents.

To implement endpoints with an XML marshalling technology, you have to extend the `AbstractMarshallingPayloadEndpoint` class and configure an XML marshaller for it. Table 17-3 lists the marshallers provided by Spring-WS for different XML marshalling APIs.

Table 17-3. *Marshallers for Different XML Marshalling APIs*

API	Marshaller
JAXB 1.0	`org.springframework.oxm.jaxb.Jaxb1Marshaller`
JAXB 2.0	`org.springframework.oxm.jaxb.Jaxb2Marshaller`
Castor	`org.springframework.oxm.castor.CastorMarshaller`
XMLBeans	`org.springframework.oxm.xmlbeans.XmlBeansMarshaller`
JiBX	`org.springframework.oxm.jibx.JibxMarshaller`
XStream	`org.springframework.oxm.xstream.XStreamMarshaller`

To invoke a web service, `WebServiceTemplate` also allows you to choose an XML marshalling technology to process the request and response XML messages.

How It Works

Creating Service Endpoints with XML Marshalling

Spring-WS supports various XML marshalling APIs, including JAXB 1.0, JAXB 2.0, Castor, XMLBeans, JiBX, and XStream. As an example, I will create a service endpoint using Castor (www.castor.org) as the marshaller. Using other XML marshalling APIs is very similar.

The first step in using XML marshalling is creating the object model according to the XML message formats. This model can usually be generated by the marshalling API. For some marshalling APIs, the object model must be generated by them so that they can insert marshalling-specific information. Because Castor supports marshalling between XML messages and arbitrary Java objects, you can start creating the following classes by yourself.

```
package com.apress.springrecipes.weather;
...
public class GetTemperaturesRequest {

    private String city;
    private List<Date> dates;

    // Constructors, Getters and Setters
    ...
}

package com.apress.springrecipes.weather;
...
public class GetTemperaturesResponse {

    private List<TemperatureInfo> temperatures;

    // Constructors, Getters and Setters
    ...
}
```

With the object model created, you can write a marshalling endpoint by extending the AbstractMarshallingPayloadEndpoint class. The core method defined in this class that you must override is invokeInternal(). In this method, you can access the request object, which is unmarshalled from the request message, as the method argument. Now, all you have to do in this method is handle the request object and return the response object. Then, it will be marshalled to the response XML message.

■ **Note** To create a service endpoint using Castor, you need to add Castor to your classpath. If you are using Maven, add the following dependency to your project.

```
<dependency>
  <groupId>org.codehaus.castor</groupId>
  <artifactId>castor</artifactId>
  <version>1.2</version>
</dependency>
```

```
package com.apress.springrecipes.weather;
...
import org.springframework.ws.server.endpoint.AbstractMarshallingPayloadEndpoint;

public class TemperatureMarshallingEndpoint extends
        AbstractMarshallingPayloadEndpoint {

    private WeatherService weatherService;

    public void setWeatherService(WeatherService weatherService) {
        this.weatherService = weatherService;
    }

    protected Object invokeInternal(Object requestObject) throws Exception {
        GetTemperaturesRequest request = (GetTemperaturesRequest) requestObject;

        List<TemperatureInfo> temperatures =
            weatherService.getTemperatures(request.getCity(), request.getDates());

        return new GetTemperaturesResponse(temperatures);
    }
}
```

A marshalling endpoint requires both the `marshaller` and `unmarshaller` properties to be set. Usually, you can specify a single marshaller for both properties. For Castor, you declare a `CastorMarshaller` bean as the marshaller.

```
<beans ...>
    ...
    <bean id="temperatureEndpoint"
        class="com.apress.springrecipes.weather.Temperature↵
MarshallingEndpoint">
        <property name="marshaller" ref="marshaller" />
        <property name="unmarshaller" ref="marshaller" />
        <property name="weatherService" ref="weatherService" />
    </bean>

    <bean id="marshaller"
        class="org.springframework.oxm.castor.CastorMarshaller">
        <property name="mappingLocation" value="classpath:mapping.xml" />
    </bean>
</beans>
```

Note that Castor requires a mapping configuration file to know how to map objects to and from XML documents. You can create this file in the classpath root and specify it in the mappingLocation property (e.g., mapping.xml). The following Castor mapping file defines the mappings for the GetTemperaturesRequest, GetTemperaturesResponse, and TemperatureInfo classes:

```
<!DOCTYPE mapping PUBLIC "-//EXOLAB/Castor Mapping DTD Version 1.0//EN"
    "http://castor.org/mapping.dtd">

<mapping>
    <class name="com.apress.springrecipes.weather.GetTemperaturesRequest">
        <map-to xml="GetTemperaturesRequest"
            ns-uri="http://springrecipes.apress.com/weather/schemas" />
        <field name="city" type="string">
            <bind-xml name="city" node="element" />
        </field>
        <field name="dates" collection="arraylist" type="string"
            handler="com.apress.springrecipes.weather.DateFieldHandler">
            <bind-xml name="date" node="element" />
        </field>
    </class>

    <class name="com.apress.springrecipes.weather.↵
GetTemperaturesResponse">
        <map-to xml="GetTemperaturesResponse"
            ns-uri="http://springrecipes.apress.com/weather/schemas" />
        <field name="temperatures" collection="arraylist"
            type="com.apress.springrecipes.weather.TemperatureInfo">
            <bind-xml name="TemperatureInfo" node="element" />
        </field>
    </class>
```

```
<class name="com.apress.springrecipes.weather.TemperatureInfo">
    <map-to xml="TemperatureInfo"
        ns-uri="http://springrecipes.apress.com/weather/schemas" />
    <field name="city" type="string">
        <bind-xml name="city" node="attribute" />
    </field>
    <field name="date" type="string"
        handler="com.apress.springrecipes.weather.DateFieldHandler">
        <bind-xml name="date" node="attribute" />
    </field>
    <field name="min" type="double">
        <bind-xml name="min" node="element" />
    </field>
    <field name="max" type="double">
        <bind-xml name="max" node="element" />
    </field>
    <field name="average" type="double">
        <bind-xml name="average" node="element" />
    </field>
</class>
</mapping>
```

Remember that for each class mapping, you must specify the namespace URI for the element. Besides, for all the date fields, you have to specify a handler to convert the dates with a particular date format. The handler is implemented as shown following:

```
package com.apress.springrecipes.weather;
...
import org.exolab.castor.mapping.GeneralizedFieldHandler;

public class DateFieldHandler extends GeneralizedFieldHandler {

    private DateFormat format = new SimpleDateFormat("yyyy-MM-dd");

    public Object convertUponGet(Object value) {
        return format.format((Date) value);
    }

    public Object convertUponSet(Object value) {
        try {
            return format.parse((String) value);
        } catch (ParseException e) {
            throw new RuntimeException(e);
        }
    }

    public Class getFieldType() {
        return Date.class;
    }
}
```

Invoking Web Services with XML Marshalling

A Spring-WS client can also marshall and unmarshall the request and response objects to and from XML messages. As an example, we will create a client using Castor as the marshaller so that you can reuse the object models GetTemperaturesRequest, GetTemperaturesResponse, and TemperatureInfo, and the mapping configuration file, mapping.xml, from the service endpoint.

Let's implement the service proxy with XML marshalling. WebServiceTemplate provides a marshalSendAndReceive() method that accepts a request object as the method argument, which will be marshalled to the request message. This method has to return a response object that will be unmarshalled from the response message.

■ **Note** To create a service client using Castor, you need to add Castor to your classpath. If you are using Maven, add the following dependency to your project.

```
<dependency>
  <groupId>org.codehaus.castor</groupId>
  <artifactId>castor</artifactId>
  <version>1.2</version>
</dependency>
```

```
package com.apress.springrecipes.weather;
...
import org.springframework.ws.client.core.support.WebServiceGatewaySupport;

public class WeatherServiceProxy extends WebServiceGatewaySupport
        implements WeatherService {

    public List<TemperatureInfo> getTemperatures(String city, List<Date> dates) {
        GetTemperaturesRequest request = new GetTemperaturesRequest(city, dates);
        GetTemperaturesResponse response = (GetTemperaturesResponse)
            getWebServiceTemplate().marshalSendAndReceive(request);
        return response.getTemperatures();
    }
}
```

When you are using XML marshalling, WebServiceTemplate requires both the marshaller and unmarshaller properties to be set. You can also set them to WebServiceGatewaySupport if you extend this class to have WebServiceTemplate auto-created. Usually, you can specify a single marshaller for both properties. For Castor, you declare a CastorMarshaller bean as the marshaller.

```
<beans ...>
    <bean id="client"
        class="com.apress.springrecipes.weather.WeatherServiceClient">
        <property name="weatherService" ref="weatherServiceProxy" />
    </bean>

    <bean id="weatherServiceProxy"
        class="com.apress.springrecipes.weather.WeatherServiceProxy">
        <property name="defaultUri"
            value="http://localhost:8080/weather/services" />
        <property name="marshaller" ref="marshaller" />
        <property name="unmarshaller" ref="marshaller" />
    </bean>

    <bean id="marshaller"
        class="org.springframework.oxm.castor.CastorMarshaller">
        <property name="mappingLocation" value="classpath:mapping.xml" />
    </bean>
</beans>
```

17-13. Creating Service Endpoints with Annotations

Problem

By extending a Spring-WS base endpoint class, your endpoint class will be bound to the Spring-WS class hierarchy, and each endpoint class will only be able to handle one type of web service request.

Solution

Spring-WS supports annotating an arbitrary class as a service endpoint by the @Endpoint annotation, without extending a framework-specific class. You can also group multiple handler methods in an endpoint class so that it can handle multiple types of web service requests.

How It Works

For example, you can annotate your temperature endpoint with the @Endpoint annotation so that it doesn't need to extend a Spring-WS base endpoint class. The signature of the handler methods can also be more flexible.

```
package com.apress.springrecipes.weather;
...
import org.springframework.ws.server.endpoint.annotation.Endpoint;
import org.springframework.ws.server.endpoint.annotation.PayloadRoot;
```

```
@Endpoint
public class TemperatureMarshallingEndpoint {

    private static final String namespaceUri =
        "http://springrecipes.apress.com/weather/schemas";

    private WeatherService weatherService;

    public void setWeatherService(WeatherService weatherService) {
        this.weatherService = weatherService;
    }

    @PayloadRoot(
            localPart = "GetTemperaturesRequest",
            namespace = namespaceUri)
    public GetTemperaturesResponse getTemperature(GetTemperaturesRequest request) {
        List<TemperatureInfo> temperatures =
            weatherService.getTemperatures(request.getCity(), request.getDates());
        return new GetTemperaturesResponse(temperatures);
    }
}
```

Besides the @Endpoint annotation, you have to annotate each handler method with the @PayloadRoot annotation for mapping a service request. In this annotation, you specify the local name (localPort) and namespace of the payload root element to be handled. Then you just declare a PayloadRootAnnotationMethodEndpointMapping bean, and it will be able to detect the mapping from the @PayloadRoot annotation automatically.

```
<beans ...>
    ...
    <bean class="org.springframework.ws.server.endpoint.↵
mapping.PayloadRootAnnotationMethodEndpointMapping" />

    <bean id="temperatureEndpoint"
        class="com.apress.springrecipes.weather.Temperature↵
MarshallingEndpoint">
        <property name="weatherService" ref="weatherService" />
    </bean>

    <bean class="org.springframework.ws.server.endpoint.adapter.↵
GenericMarshallingMethodEndpointAdapter">
        <property name="marshaller" ref="marshaller" />
        <property name="unmarshaller" ref="marshaller" />
    </bean>

    <bean id="marshaller"
        class="org.springframework.oxm.castor.CastorMarshaller">
        <property name="mappingLocation" value="classpath:mapping.xml" />
    </bean>
</beans>
```

Because your endpoint class no longer extends a base endpoint class, it doesn't inherit the capabilities of marshalling and unmarshalling XML messages. You have to configure a `GenericMarshallingMethodEndpointAdapter` to do so.

Summary

This chapter discussed how to use Spring's remoting support. You learned how to both publish and consume an RMI service. You learned about Spring's support for legacy EJB 2.x services, as well as the support available for both EJB 3.0 and EJB 3.1 services. We also discussed building web services. We introduced using CXF, a third-party framework for building services. We used then used Spring-WS, Spring's excellent support for web service creation, to build the schema and then the web service.

CHAPTER 18

Spring in the Enterprise

In this chapter, you will learn about Spring's support for three common technologies on the Java EE platform: *Java Management Extensions (JMX)*, sending e-mail, and scheduling tasks.

JMX is a technology or managing and monitoring system resources such as devices, applications, objects, and service-driven networks. The specification offers powerful features for managing systems at runtime and for adapting legacy systems. These resources are represented by *managed beans (MBeans)*. Originally, JMX was distributed separately, but it has been part of Java SE since version 5.0. JMX has seen many improvements, but the original specification JSR 03 is very old! Spring supports JMX by allowing you to export any Spring beans as *model MBeans* (a kind of *dynamic MBean*), without programming against the JMX API. In addition, Spring enables you to access remote MBeans easily.

JavaMail is the standard API and implementation for sending e-mail in Java. Spring further provides an abstract layer for you to send e-mail in an implementation-independent fashion.

There are two main options for scheduling tasks on the Java platform: JDK Timer and Quartz Scheduler (`http://www.opensymphony.com/quartz/`). JDK Timer offers simple task scheduling features that you can use conveniently because the features are bundled with JDK. Compared with JDK Timer, Quartz offers more powerful job scheduling features. For both options, Spring supplies utility classes for you to configure scheduling tasks in the bean configuration file, without programming against their APIs.

Upon finishing this chapter, you will be able to export and access MBeans in a Spring application. You will also be able to utilize Spring's supporting features to simplify sending e-mail and scheduling tasks.

18-1. Exporting Spring Beans as JMX MBeans

Problem

You want to register an object from your Java application as a JMX MBean to allow management and monitoring. In this sense, management is the capability to look at services that are running and manipulate their runtime state on the fly. Imagine being able to do these tasks from a web page: rerun batch jobs, invoke methods, and change configuration metadata that you'd normally be able to do only at runtime. However, if you use the JMX API for this purpose, a lot of coding will be required, and you'll have to deal with JMX's complexity.

Solution

Spring supports JMX by allowing you to export any beans in its IoC container as model MBeans. This can be done simply by declaring an `MBeanExporter` instance. With Spring's JMX support, you no longer need to deal with the JMX API directly, so you can write code that is not JMX specific. In addition, Spring enables you to declare JSR-160 (Java Management Extensions Remote API) connectors to expose your MBeans for remote access over a specific protocol by using a factory bean. Spring provides factory beans for both servers and clients.

Spring's JMX support comes with other mechanisms by which you can assemble an MBean's management interface. These options include using exporting beans by method names, interfaces, and annotations. Spring can also detect and export your MBeans automatically from beans declared in the IoC container and annotated with JMX-specific annotations defined by Spring. The `MBeanExporter` class exports beans, delegating to an instance of `MBeanInfoAssembler` to do the heavy lifting.

How It Works

Suppose that you are developing a utility for replicating files from a source directory to a destination directory. Let's design the interface for this utility as follows:

```
package com.apress.springrecipes.replicator;
...
public interface FileReplicator {

    public String getSrcDir();
    public void setSrcDir(String srcDir);

    public String getDestDir();
    public void setDestDir(String destDir);

    public void replicate() throws IOException;
}
```

The source and destination directories are designed as properties of a replicator object, not method arguments. That means each file replicator instance replicates files only for a particular source and destination directory. You can create multiple replicator instances in your application.

Before you implement this replicator, you need another class that copies a file from one directory to another, given its name.

```
package com.apress.springrecipes.replicator;
...
public interface FileCopier {

    public void copyFile(String srcDir, String destDir, String filename)
            throws IOException;
}
```

There are many strategies for implementing this file copier. For instance, you can make use of the `FileCopyUtils` class provided by Spring.

```
package com.apress.springrecipes.replicator;
...
import org.springframework.util.FileCopyUtils;

public class FileCopierJMXImpl implements FileCopier {

    public void copyFile(String srcDir, String destDir, String filename)
            throws IOException {
        File srcFile = new File(srcDir, filename);
        File destFile = new File(destDir, filename);
        FileCopyUtils.copy(srcFile, destFile);
    }
}
```

With the help of a file copier, you can implement your file replicator, as shown in the following code sample. Each time you call the replicate() method, all files in the source directory will be replicated to the destination directory. To avoid unexpected problems caused by concurrent replication, you declare this method as synchronized.

```
package com.apress.springrecipes.replicator;

import java.io.File;
import java.io.IOException;

public class FileReplicatorImpl implements FileReplicator {

    private String srcDir;
    private String destDir;
    private FileCopier fileCopier;

    // accessors …
    // mutators …

    public void setSrcDir(String srcDir) {
        this.srcDir = srcDir;
        revaluateDirectories();
    }

    public void setDestDir(String destDir) {
        this.destDir = destDir;
        revaluateDirectories();
    }

    public void setFileCopier(FileCopier fileCopier) {
                this.fileCopier = fileCopier;
    }
```

```
    public synchronized void replicate() throws IOException {
        File[] files = new File(srcDir).listFiles();
        for (File file : files) {
            if (file.isFile()) {
                fileCopier.copyFile(srcDir, destDir, file.getName());
            }
        }
    }
    private void revaluateDirectories() {
        File src = new File(srcDir);
        File dest = new File(destDir);
        if (!src.exists())
            src.mkdirs();
        if (!dest.exists())
            dest.mkdirs();
    }
}
```

Now, you can configure one or more file replicator instances in the bean configuration file for your needs (in the example, this file is called beans-jmx.xml). The documentReplicator instance needs references to two directories: a source directory from which files are read and a target directory to which files are backed up. The code in this example attempts to read from a directory called docs in your operating system user's home directory and then copy to a folder called docs_backup in your operating system user's home directory. When this bean starts up, it creates the two directories if they don't already exist there.

■ **Tip** The "home directory" is different for each operating system, but typically on Unix it's the directory that ~ resolves to. On a Linux box, the folder might be /home/user. On Mac OS X, the folder might be /Users/user, and on Windows it might be similar to C:\Documents and Settings\user.

```
<beans xmlns="http://www.springframework.org/schema/beans"
    xmlns:xsi="http://www.w3.org/2001/XMLSchema-instance"
    xsi:schemaLocation="http://www.springframework.org/schema/beans
        http://www.springframework.org/schema/beans/spring-beans-3.0.xsd">

    <bean id="fileCopier"
        class="com.apress.springrecipes.replicator.FileCopierJMXImpl" />

    <bean id="documentReplicator"
        class="com.apress.springrecipes.replicator.FileReplicatorImpl">
        <property name="srcDir" value="#{systemProperties['user.home']}/docs" />
        <property name="destDir" value="#{systemProperties['user.home']}↵
/docs_backup" />
        <property name="fileCopier" ref="fileCopier" />
    </bean>
</beans>
```

Registering MBeans Without Spring's Support

First, let's see how to register a model MBean using the JMX API directly. In the following Main class, you get the documentReplicator bean from the IoC container and register it as an MBean for management and monitoring. All properties and methods are included in the MBean's management interface.

```
package com.apress.springrecipes.replicator;
...
import java.lang.management.ManagementFactory;

import javax.management.Descriptor;
import javax.management.JMException;
import javax.management.MBeanServer;
import javax.management.ObjectName;
import javax.management.modelmbean.DescriptorSupport;
import javax.management.modelmbean.InvalidTargetObjectTypeException;
import javax.management.modelmbean.ModelMBeanAttributeInfo;
import javax.management.modelmbean.ModelMBeanInfo;
import javax.management.modelmbean.ModelMBeanInfoSupport;
import javax.management.modelmbean.ModelMBeanOperationInfo;
import javax.management.modelmbean.RequiredModelMBean;

import org.springframework.context.ApplicationContext;
import org.springframework.context.support.ClassPathXmlApplicationContext;

public class Main {

    public static void main(String[] args) throws IOException {
        ApplicationContext context =
            new ClassPathXmlApplicationContext("beans-jmx.xml");

        FileReplicator documentReplicator =
            (FileReplicator) context.getBean("documentReplicator");

        try {
            MBeanServer mbeanServer = ManagementFactory.getPlatformMBeanServer();
            ObjectName objectName = new ObjectName("bean:name=documentReplicator");

            RequiredModelMBean mbean = new RequiredModelMBean();
            mbean.setManagedResource(documentReplicator, "objectReference");

            Descriptor srcDirDescriptor = new DescriptorSupport(new String[] {
                    "name=SrcDir", "descriptorType=attribute",
                    "getMethod=getSrcDir", "setMethod=setSrcDir" });
            ModelMBeanAttributeInfo srcDirInfo = new ModelMBeanAttributeInfo(
                    "SrcDir", "java.lang.String", "Source directory",
                    true, true, false, srcDirDescriptor);

            Descriptor destDirDescriptor = new DescriptorSupport(new String[] {
                    "name=DestDir", "descriptorType=attribute",
                    "getMethod=getDestDir", "setMethod=setDestDir" });
```

```
        ModelMBeanAttributeInfo destDirInfo = new ModelMBeanAttributeInfo(
                "DestDir", "java.lang.String", "Destination directory",
                true, true, false, destDirDescriptor);

        ModelMBeanOperationInfo getSrcDirInfo = new ModelMBeanOperationInfo(
                "Get source directory",
                FileReplicator.class.getMethod("getSrcDir"));
        ModelMBeanOperationInfo setSrcDirInfo = new ModelMBeanOperationInfo(
                "Set source directory",
                FileReplicator.class.getMethod("setSrcDir", String.class));
        ModelMBeanOperationInfo getDestDirInfo = new ModelMBeanOperationInfo(
                "Get destination directory",
                FileReplicator.class.getMethod("getDestDir"));
        ModelMBeanOperationInfo setDestDirInfo = new ModelMBeanOperationInfo(
                "Set destination directory",
                FileReplicator.class.getMethod("setDestDir", String.class));
        ModelMBeanOperationInfo replicateInfo = new ModelMBeanOperationInfo(
                "Replicate files",
                FileReplicator.class.getMethod("replicate"));

        ModelMBeanInfo mbeanInfo = new ModelMBeanInfoSupport(
                "FileReplicator", "File replicator",
                new ModelMBeanAttributeInfo[] { srcDirInfo, destDirInfo },
                null,
                new ModelMBeanOperationInfo[] { getSrcDirInfo, setSrcDirInfo,
                        getDestDirInfo, setDestDirInfo, replicateInfo },
                null);
        mbean.setModelMBeanInfo(mbeanInfo);

        mbeanServer.registerMBean(mbean, objectName);
    } catch (JMException e) {
        ...
    } catch (InvalidTargetObjectTypeException e) {
        ...
    } catch (NoSuchMethodException e) {
        ...
    }

    System.in.read();
    }
}
```

To register an MBean, you need an instance of the interface `javax.managment.MBeanServer`. In JDK 1.5, you can call the static method `ManagementFactory.getPlatformMBeanServer()` to locate a platform MBean server. It will create an MBean server if none exists and then register this server instance for future use. Each MBean requires an MBean *object name* that includes a domain. The preceding MBean is registered under the domain bean with the name `documentReplicator`.

From the preceding code, you can see that for each MBean attribute and MBean operation, you need to create a `ModelMBeanAttributeInfo` object and a `ModelMBeanOperationInfo` object for describing it. After those, you have to create a `ModelMBeanInfo` object for describing the MBean's management interface by assembling the preceding information. For details about using these classes, you can consult their Javadocs.

Moreover, you have to handle the JMX-specific exceptions when calling the JMX API. These exceptions are checked exceptions that you must handle.

Note that you must prevent your application from terminating before you look inside it with a JMX client tool. Requesting a key from the console using `System.in.read()` would be a good choice.

Finally, you have to add the VM argument -Dcom.sun.management.jmxremote to enable local monitoring of this application. You should also include all other options for your command, such as the classpath, as necessary.

```
Java –classpath … -Dcom.sun.management.jmxremote com.apress.springrecipes.replicator.Main
```

Now, you can use any JMX client tools to monitor your MBeans locally. The simplest one may be JConsole, which comes with JDK 1.5.

■ **Note** To start JConsole, just execute the `jconsole` executable file (located in the `bin` directory of the JDK installation).

When JConsole starts, you can see a list of JMX-enabled applications on the Local tab of the connection window. After connecting to the replicator application, you can see your `documentReplicator` MBean under the `bean` domain. If you want to invoke `replicate()`, simply click the button "replicate."

Exporting Spring Beans as MBeans

To export beans configured in the Spring IoC container as MBeans, you simply declare an `MBeanExporter` instance and specify the beans to export, with their MBean object names as the keys.

```xml
<bean id="mbeanExporter"
    class="org.springframework.jmx.export.MBeanExporter">
    <property name="beans">
        <map>
            <entry key="bean:name=documentReplicator"
                value-ref="documentReplicator" />
        </map>
    </property>
</bean>
```

The preceding configuration exports the `documentReplicator` bean as an MBean, under the domain `bean` and with the name `documentReplicator`. By default, all public properties are included as attributes and all public methods (with the exception of those from `java.lang.Object`) are included as operations in the MBean's management interface.

`MBeanExporter` attempts to locate an MBean server instance and register your MBeans with it implicitly. If your application is running in an environment that provides an MBean server (e.g., most Java EE application servers), `MBeanExporter` will be able to locate this MBean server instance.

However, in an environment with no MBean server available, you have to create one explicitly using Spring's `MBeanServerFactoryBean`. To make your application portable to different runtime environments, you should enable the `locateExistingServerIfPossible` property so that this factory bean will create an MBean server only if none is available.

■ **Note** JDK 1.5 will create an MBean server for the first time when you locate it. So, if you're using JDK 1.5 or above, you needn't create an MBean server explicitly.

```
<bean id="mbeanServer"
    class="org.springframework.jmx.support.MBeanServerFactoryBean">
    <property name="locateExistingServerIfPossible" value="true" />
</bean>
```

If, on the other hand, you have multiple MBeans servers running, you need to tell the `mbeanServer` bean to which server it should bind. You do this by specifying the `agentId` of the server. To figure out the `agentId` of a given server, browse to the `JMImplementation/MBeanServerDelegate/Attributes/MBeanServerId` node of the server you're inspecting in JConsole. There, you'll see the string value. On our local machine, the value is `workstation_1253860476443`. To enable it, configure the `agentId` property of the MBeanServer.

```
<bean id="mbeanServer"
    class="org.springframework.jmx.support.MBeanServerFactoryBean">
    <property name="locateExistingServerIfPossible" value="true" />
    <property name="agentId" value="workstation_1253860476443" />
</bean>
```

If you have multiple MBean server instances in your context, you can explicitly specify a specific MBean server for `MBeanExporter` to export your MBeans to. In this case, `MBeanExporter` will not locate an MBean server; it will use the specified MBean server instance. This property is for you to specify a particular MBean server when more than one is available.

```
<beans ...>
    ...
    <bean id="mbeanServer"
        class="org.springframework.jmx.support.MBeanServerFactoryBean">
        <property name="locateExistingServerIfPossible" value="true" />
    </bean>

    <bean id="mbeanExporter"
        class="org.springframework.jmx.export.MBeanExporter">
        ...
        <property name="server" ref="mbeanServer" />
    </bean>
</beans>
```

The `Main` class for exporting an MBean can be simplified as shown following. You have to retain the key-requesting statement to prevent your application from terminating.

```
package com.apress.springrecipes.replicator;
...
import org.springframework.context.support.ClassPathXmlApplicationContext;

public class Main {

    public static void main(String[] args) throws IOException {
        new ClassPathXmlApplicationContext("beans-jmx.xml");
        System.in.read();
    }
}
```

Exposing MBeans for Remote Access

If you want your MBeans to be accessed remotely, you need to enable a remoting protocol for JMX. JSR-160 defines a standard for JMX remoting through a JMX connector. Spring allows you to create a JMX connector server through ConnectorServerFactoryBean.

By default, ConnectorServerFactoryBean creates and starts a JMX connector server bound to the service URL service:jmx:jmxmp://localhost:9875, which exposes the JMX connector through the JMX Messaging Protocol (JMXMP). However, most JMX implementations, including JDK 1.5's, don't support JMXMP. Therefore, you should choose a widely supported remoting protocol for your JMX connector, such as RMI. To expose your JMX connector through a specific protocol, you just provide the service URL for it.

```
<beans ...>
    ...
    <bean id="rmiRegistry"
        class="org.springframework.remoting.rmi.RmiRegistryFactoryBean" />

    <bean id="connectorServer"
        class="org.springframework.jmx.support.ConnectorServerFactoryBean"
        depends-on="rmiRegistry">
        <property name="serviceUrl" value=
            "service:jmx:rmi://localhost/jndi/rmi://localhost:1099/replicator" />
    </bean>
</beans>
```

You specify the preceding URL to bind your JMX connector to an RMI registry listening on port 1099 of localhost. If no RMI registry has been created externally, you should create one by using RmiRegistryFactoryBean. The default port for this registry is 1099, but you can specify another one in its port property. Note that ConnectorServerFactoryBean must create the connector server after the RMI registry is created and ready. You can set the depends-on attribute for this purpose.

Now, your MBeans can be accessed remotely via RMI. When JConsole starts, you can enter the following service URL on the Advanced tab of the connection window.

```
service:jmx:rmi://localhost/jndi/rmi://localhost:1099/replicator
```

Assembling the Management Interface of MBeans

Recall that, by default, the Spring `MBeanExporter` exports all public properties of a bean as MBean attributes and all public methods as MBean operations. In fact, you can assemble the management interface of your MBeans using an MBean assembler. The simplest MBean assembler in Spring is `MethodNameBasedMBeanInfoAssembler`, which allows you to specify the names of the methods to export.

```
<beans ...>
    ...
    <bean id="mbeanExporter"
        class="org.springframework.jmx.export.MBeanExporter">
        ...
        <property name="assembler" ref="assembler" />
    </bean>

    <bean id="assembler" class="org.springframework.jmx.export.assembler.
        MethodNameBasedMBeanInfoAssembler">
        <property name="managedMethods">
            <list>
                <value>getSrcDir</value>
                <value>setSrcDir</value>
                <value>getDestDir</value>
                <value>setDestDir</value>
                <value>replicate</value>
            </list>
        </property>
    </bean>
</beans>
```

Another MBean assembler is `InterfaceBasedMBeanInfoAssembler`, which exports all methods defined in the interfaces you specified.

```
<bean id="assembler" class="org.springframework.jmx.export.assembler.
InterfaceBasedMBeanInfoAssembler">
    <property name="managedInterfaces">
        <list>
            <value>com.apress.springrecipes.replicator.FileReplicator</value>
        </list>
    </property>
</bean>
```

Spring also provides `MetadataMBeanInfoAssembler` to assemble an MBean's management interface based on the metadata in the bean class. It supports two types of metadata: JDK annotations and Apache Commons Attributes (behind the scenes, this is accomplished using a strategy interface `JmxAttributeSource`). For a bean class annotated with JDK annotations, you specify an `AnnotationJmxAttributeSource` instance as the attribute source of `MetadataMBeanInfoAssembler`.

```xml
<bean id="assembler" class="org.springframework.jmx.export.assembler.↵
    MetadataMBeanInfoAssembler">
    <property name="attributeSource">
        <bean class="org.springframework.jmx.export.annotation.AnnotationJmxAttributeSource" />
    </property>
</bean>
```

Then, you annotate your bean class and methods with the annotations @ManagedResource, @ManagedAttribute, and @ManagedOperation for MetadataMBeanInfoAssembler to assemble the management interface for this bean. The annotations are easily interpreted. They expose the element that they annotate. If you have a JavaBeans-compliant property, JMX will use the term *attribute*. Classes themselves are referred to as *resources*. In JMX, methods will be called *operations*. Knowing that, it's easy to see what the following code does:

```java
package com.apress.springrecipes.replicator;
...
import org.springframework.jmx.export.annotation.ManagedAttribute;
import org.springframework.jmx.export.annotation.ManagedOperation;
import org.springframework.jmx.export.annotation.ManagedResource;

@ManagedResource(description = "File replicator")
public class FileReplicatorImpl implements FileReplicator {
    ...
    @ManagedAttribute(description = "Get source directory")
    public String getSrcDir() {
        ...
    }

    @ManagedAttribute(description = "Set source directory")
    public void setSrcDir(String srcDir) {
        ...
    }

    @ManagedAttribute(description = "Get destination directory")
    public String getDestDir() {
        ...
    }

    @ManagedAttribute(description = "Set destination directory")
    public void setDestDir(String destDir) {
        ...
    }

    ...

    @ManagedOperation(description = "Replicate files")
    public synchronized void replicate() throws IOException {
        ...
    }
}
```

Auto-Detecting MBeans by Annotations

In addition to exporting a bean explicitly with `MBeanExporter`, you can simply configure its subclass `AnnotationMBeanExporter` to auto-detect MBeans from beans declared in the IoC container. You needn't configure an MBean assembler for this exporter, because it uses `MetadataMBeanInfoAssembler` with `AnnotationJmxAttributeSource` by default. You can delete the previous `beans` and `assembler` properties for this exporter.

```
<bean id="mbeanExporter"
    class="org.springframework.jmx.export.annotation.AnnotationMBeanExporter">
    ...
</bean>
```

`AnnotationMBeanExporter` detects any beans configured in the IoC container with the `@ManagedResource` annotation and exports them as MBeans. By default, this exporter exports a bean to the domain whose name is the same as its package name. Also, it uses the bean's name in the IoC container as its MBean name, and the bean's short class name as its type. So your `documentReplicator` bean will be exported under the following MBean object name:

```
com.apress.springrecipes.replicator:name=documentReplicator,
type=FileReplicatorImpl
```

If you don't want to use the package name as the domain name, you can set the default domain for this exporter.

```
<bean id="mbeanExporter"
    class="org.springframework.jmx.export.annotation.AnnotationMBeanExporter">
    ...
    <property name="defaultDomain" value="bean" />
</bean>
```

After setting the default domain to `bean`, the `documentReplicator` bean will be exported under the following MBean object name:

```
bean:name=documentReplicator,type=FileReplicatorImpl
```

Moreover, you can specify a bean's MBean object name in the `objectName` attribute of the `@ManagedResource` annotation. For example, you can export your file copier as an MBean by annotating it with the following annotations:

```
package com.apress.springrecipes.replicator;
...
import org.springframework.jmx.export.annotation.ManagedOperation;
import org.springframework.jmx.export.annotation.ManagedOperationParameter;
import org.springframework.jmx.export.annotation.ManagedOperationParameters;
import org.springframework.jmx.export.annotation.ManagedResource;
```

```
@ManagedResource(
    objectName = "bean:name=fileCopier,type=FileCopierImpl",
    description = "File Copier")
public class FileCopierImpl implements FileCopier {

    @ManagedOperation(
        description = "Copy file from source directory to destination directory")
    @ManagedOperationParameters( {
        @ManagedOperationParameter(
            name = "srcDir", description = "Source directory"),
        @ManagedOperationParameter(
            name = "destDir", description = "Destination directory"),
        @ManagedOperationParameter(
            name = "filename", description = "File to copy") })
    public void copyFile(String srcDir, String destDir, String filename)
            throws IOException {
        ...
    }
}
```

However, specifying the object name in this way works only for classes that you're going to create a single instance of in the IoC container (e.g., file copier), not for classes that you may create multiple instances of (e.g., file replicator). This is because you can only specify a single object name for a class. As a result, you shouldn't try and run the same server multiple times without changing the names.

You can simply declare a `<context:mbean-export>` element in your bean configuration file, instead of the AnnotationMBeanExporter declaration, which you can omit.

```
<beans xmlns="http://www.springframework.org/schema/beans"
    xmlns:xsi="http://www.w3.org/2001/XMLSchema-instance"
    xmlns:context="http://www.springframework.org/schema/context"
    xsi:schemaLocation="http://www.springframework.org/schema/beans
        http://www.springframework.org/schema/beans/spring-beans-3.0.xsd
        http://www.springframework.org/schema/context
        http://www.springframework.org/schema/context/spring-context-3.0.xsd">

    <context:mbean-export server="mbeanServer" default-domain="bean" />
    ...
</beans>
```

You can specify an MBean server and a default domain name for this element through the server and default-domain attributes. However, you won't be able to set other MBean exporter properties such as notification listener mappings. Whenever you have to set these properties, you need to declare an AnnotationMBeanExporter instance explicitly.

18-2. Publishing and Listening to JMX Notifications

Problem

You want to publish JMX notifications from your MBeans and listen to them with JMX notification listeners.

Solution

Spring allows your beans to publish JMX notifications through the `NotificationPublisher interface`. You can also register standard JMX notification listeners in the IoC container to listen to JMX notifications.

How It Works

Publishing JMX Notifications

The Spring IoC container supports the beans that are going to be exported as MBeans to publish JMX notifications. These beans must implement the `NotificationPublisherAware` interface (as you might implement `ApplicationContextAware` to receive a reference to the current bean's containing `ApplicatonContext` instance) to get access to `NotificationPublisher` so that they can publish notifications.

```
package com.apress.springrecipes.replicator;
...
import javax.management.Notification;

import org.springframework.jmx.export.notification.NotificationPublisher;
import org.springframework.jmx.export.notification.NotificationPublisherAware;

@ManagedResource(description = "File replicator")
public class FileReplicatorImpl implements FileReplicator,
        NotificationPublisherAware {
    ...
    private int sequenceNumber;
    private NotificationPublisher notificationPublisher;

    public void setNotificationPublisher(
            NotificationPublisher notificationPublisher) {
        this.notificationPublisher = notificationPublisher;
    }
  @ManagedOperation(description = "Replicate files")
    public void replicate() throws IOException {
        notificationPublisher.sendNotification(
                new Notification("replication.start", this, sequenceNumber));
        ...
```

```
    notificationPublisher.sendNotification(
            new Notification("replication.complete", this, sequenceNumber));
    sequenceNumber++;
  }
}
```

In this file replicator, you send a JMX notification whenever a replication starts or completes. The notification is visible both in the standard output in the console as well as in the Notifications node for your service in JConsole. To see them, you must click Subscribe. Then, invoke the `replicate()` method, and you'll see two new notifications arrive, much like your e-mail's inbox. The first argument in the `Notification` constructor is the notification type, while the second is the notification source. Each notification requires a sequence number. You can use the same sequence for a notification pair to keep track of them.

Listening to JMX Notifications

Now, let's create a notification listener to listen to JMX notifications. Because a listener will be notified of many different types of notifications, such as `javax.management.AttributeChangeNotification` when an MBean's attribute has changed, you have to filter those notifications that you are interested in handling.

```
package com.apress.springrecipes.replicator;

import javax.management.Notification;
import javax.management.NotificationListener;

public class ReplicationNotificationListener implements NotificationListener {

    public void handleNotification(Notification notification, Object handback) {
        if (notification.getType().startsWith("replication")) {
            System.out.println(
                    notification.getSource() + " " +
                    notification.getType() + " #" +
                    notification.getSequenceNumber());
        }
    }
}
```

Then, you can register this notification listener with your MBean exporter to listen to notifications emitted from certain MBeans.

```
<bean id="mbeanExporter"
    class="org.springframework.jmx.export.annotation.AnnotationMBeanExporter">
    <property name="defaultDomain" value="bean" />
    <property name="notificationListenerMappings">
        <map>
            <entry key="bean:name=documentReplicator,type=FileReplicatorImpl">
                <bean class="com.apress.springrecipes.replicator.↵
                ReplicationNotificationListener" />
            </entry>
        </map>
    </property>
</bean>
```

18-3. Accessing Remote JMX MBeans in Spring

Problem

You want to access JMX MBeans running on a remote MBean server exposed by a JMX connector. When accessing remote MBeans directly with the JMX API, you have to write complex JMX-specific code.

Solution

Spring offers two approaches to simplify your remote MBean access. First, it provides a factory bean for you to create an MBean server connection declaratively. With this server connection, you can query and update an MBean's attributes, as well as invoke its operations. Second, Spring provides another factory bean that allows you to create a proxy for a remote MBean. With this proxy, you can operate a remote MBean as if it were a local bean.

How It Works

Accessing Remote MBeans Through an MBean Server Connection

A JMX client requires an MBean server connection to access MBeans running on a remote MBean server. Spring provides `org.springframework.jmx.support.MBeanServerConnectionFactoryBean` for you to create a connection to a remote JSR-160–enabled MBean server declaratively. You only have to provide the service URL for it to locate the MBean server. Now let's declare this factory bean in your client bean configuration file (e.g., `beans-jmx-client.xml`).

```
<beans xmlns="http://www.springframework.org/schema/beans"
    xmlns:xsi="http://www.w3.org/2001/XMLSchema-instance"
    xsi:schemaLocation="http://www.springframework.org/schema/beans
        http://www.springframework.org/schema/beans/spring-beans-3.0.xsd">
```

```
    <bean id="mbeanServerConnection"
        class="org.springframework.jmx.support.MBeanServerConnectionFactoryBean">
        <property name="serviceUrl" value=
            "service:jmx:rmi://localhost/jndi/rmi://localhost:1099/replicator" />
    </bean>
</beans>
```

With the MBean server connection created by this factory bean, you can access and operate the MBeans running on this server. For example, you can query and update an MBean's attributes through the getAttribute() and setAttribute() methods, giving the MBean's object name and attribute name. You can also invoke an MBean's operations by using the invoke() method.

```
package com.apress.springrecipes.replicator;

import javax.management.Attribute;
import javax.management.MBeanServerConnection;
import javax.management.ObjectName;

import org.springframework.context.ApplicationContext;
import org.springframework.context.support.ClassPathXmlApplicationContext;

public class Client {

    public static void main(String[] args) throws Exception {
        ApplicationContext context =
            new ClassPathXmlApplicationContext("beans-jmx-client.xml");

        MBeanServerConnection mbeanServerConnection =
            (MBeanServerConnection) context.getBean("mbeanServerConnection");

        ObjectName mbeanName = new ObjectName(
                "bean:name=documentReplicator,type=FileReplicatorImpl");

        String srcDir = (String) mbeanServerConnection.getAttribute(
                mbeanName, "SrcDir");

        mbeanServerConnection.setAttribute(
                mbeanName, new Attribute("DestDir", srcDir + "_1"));

        mbeanServerConnection.invoke(
                mbeanName, "replicate", new Object[] {}, new String[] {});
    }
}
```

Suppose that you've created the following JMX notification listener, which listens to file replication notifications:

```
package com.apress.springrecipes.replicator;

import javax.management.Notification;
import javax.management.NotificationListener;

public class ReplicationNotificationListener implements NotificationListener {

    public void handleNotification(Notification notification, Object handback) {
        if (notification.getType().startsWith("replication")) {
            System.out.println(
                    notification.getSource() + " " +
                    notification.getType() + " #" +
                    notification.getSequenceNumber());
        }
    }
}
```

You can register this notification listener to the MBean server connection to listen to notifications emitted from this MBean server.

```
package com.apress.springrecipes.replicator;
...
import javax.management.MBeanServerConnection;
import javax.management.ObjectName;

public class Client {

    public static void main(String[] args) throws Exception {
        ...
        MBeanServerConnection mbeanServerConnection =
            (MBeanServerConnection) context.getBean("mbeanServerConnection");

        ObjectName mbeanName = new ObjectName(
                "bean:name=documentReplicator,type=FileReplicatorImpl");

        mbeanServerConnection.addNotificationListener(
                mbeanName, new ReplicationNotificationListener(), null, null);
        ...
    }
}
```

After you run this, check JConsole again under the Notifications node. You'll see the same two notifications as before and an interesting, new notification of type `jmx.attribute.change`.

Accessing Remote MBeans Through an MBean Proxy

Another approach that Spring offers for remote MBean access is through `MBeanProxy`, which can be created by `MBeanProxyFactoryBean`.

```
<beans ...>
    <bean id="mbeanServerConnection"
        class="org.springframework.jmx.support.MBeanServerConnectionFactoryBean">
        <property name="serviceUrl" value=
            "service:jmx:rmi://localhost/jndi/rmi://localhost:1099/replicator" />
    </bean>

    <bean id="fileReplicatorProxy"
        class="org.springframework.jmx.access.MBeanProxyFactoryBean">
        <property name="server" ref="mbeanServerConnection" />
        <property name="objectName"
            value="bean:name=documentReplicator,type=FileReplicatorImpl" />
        <property name="proxyInterface"
            value="com.apress.springrecipes.replicator.FileReplicator" />
    </bean>
</beans>
```

You need to specify the object name and the server connection for the MBean you are going to proxy. The most important is the proxy interface, whose local method calls will be translated into remote MBean calls behind the scenes.

Now, you can operate the remote MBean through this proxy as if it were a local bean. The preceding MBean operations invoked on the MBean server connection directly can be simplified as follows:

```
package com.apress.springrecipes.replicator;
...
public class Client {

    public static void main(String[] args) throws Exception {
        ...
        FileReplicator fileReplicatorProxy =
            (FileReplicator) context.getBean("fileReplicatorProxy");

        String srcDir = fileReplicatorProxy.getSrcDir();
        fileReplicatorProxy.setDestDir(srcDir + "_1");
        fileReplicatorProxy.replicate();
    }
}
```

18-4. Sending E-mail with Spring's E-mail Support

Problem

Many applications need to send e-mail. In a Java application, you can send e-mail with the JavaMail API. However, when using JavaMail, you have to handle the JavaMail-specific mail sessions and exceptions. As a result, your application becomes JavaMail dependent and hard to switch to another e-mail API.

Solution

Spring's e-mail support makes it easier to send e-mail by providing an abstract and implementation-independent API for sending e-mail. The core interface of Spring's e-mail support is `MailSender`.

The `JavaMailSender` interface is a subinterface of `MailSender` that includes specialized JavaMail features such as *Multipurpose Internet Mail Extensions (MIME)* message support. To send an e-mail message with HTML content, inline images, or attachments, you have to send it as a MIME message.

How It Works

Suppose that you want your file replicator application to notify the administrator of any error. First, you create the following `ErrorNotifier` interface, which includes a method for notifying of a file copy error:

```
package com.apress.springrecipes.replicator;

public interface ErrorNotifier {

    public void notifyCopyError(String srcDir, String destDir, String filename);
}
```

■ **Note** Invoking this notifier in case of error is left for you to accomplish. As you can consider error handling a crosscutting concern, AOP would be an ideal solution to this problem. You can write an after throwing advice to invoke this notifier.

Next, you can implement this interface to send a notification in a way of your choice. The most common way is to send e-mail. Before you implement the interface in this way, you may need a local e-mail server that supports the *Simple Mail Transfer Protocol (SMTP)* for testing purposes. We recommend installing Apache James Server (`http://james.apache.org/server/index.html`), which is very easy to install and configure.

■ **Note** You can download Apache James Server (e.g., version 2.3.2) from the Apache James web site and extract it to a directory of your choice to complete the installation. To start it, just execute the `run` script (located in the `bin` directory).

Let's create two user accounts for sending and receiving e-mail with this server. By default, the remote manager service of James listens on port 4555. You can telnet, using a console, to this port and run the following commands (displayed in bold) to add the users `system` and `admin`, whose passwords are `12345`:

```
JAMES Remote Administration Tool 2.3.1
Please enter your login and password
Login id:
root
Password:
root
Welcome root. HELP for a list of commands
adduser system 12345
User system added
adduser admin 12345
User admin added
listusers
Existing accounts 2
user: admin
user: system
quit
Bye
```

Sending E-mail Using the JavaMail API

Now, let's take a look at how to send e-mail using the JavaMail API. You can implement the
ErrorNotifier interface to send e-mail notifications in case of errors.

■ **Note** To use JavaMail in your application, you need the JavaMail library, as well as the Activation library. If you
are using Maven, add the following dependency to your project.

```xml
<dependency>
    <groupId>javax.mail</groupId>
    <artifactId>mail</artifactId>
    <version>1.4</version>
</dependency>
```

```java
package com.apress.springrecipes.replicator;

import java.util.Properties;

import javax.mail.Message;
import javax.mail.MessagingException;
import javax.mail.Session;
import javax.mail.Transport;
import javax.mail.internet.InternetAddress;
import javax.mail.internet.MimeMessage;
```

```java
public class EmailErrorNotifier implements ErrorNotifier {

    public void notifyCopyError(String srcDir, String destDir, String filename) {
        Properties props = new Properties();
        props.put("mail.smtp.host", "localhost");
        props.put("mail.smtp.port", "25");
        props.put("mail.smtp.username", "system");
        props.put("mail.smtp.password", "12345");
        Session session = Session.getDefaultInstance(props, null);
        try {
            Message message = new MimeMessage(session);
            message.setFrom(new InternetAddress("system@localhost"));
            message.setRecipients(Message.RecipientType.TO,
                    InternetAddress.parse("admin@localhost"));
            message.setSubject("File Copy Error");
            message.setText(
                "Dear Administrator,\n\n" +
                "An error occurred when copying the following file :\n" +
                "Source directory : " + srcDir + "\n" +
                "Destination directory : " + destDir + "\n" +
                "Filename : " + filename);
            Transport.send(message);
        } catch (MessagingException e) {
            throw new RuntimeException(e);
        }
    }
}
```

You first open a mail session connecting to an SMTP server by defining the properties. Then, you create a message from this session for constructing your e-mail. After that, you send the e-mail by making a call to Transport.send(). When dealing with the JavaMail API, you have to handle the checked exception MessagingException. Note that all these classes, interfaces, and exceptions are defined by JavaMail.

Next, declare an instance of EmailErrorNotifier in the Spring IoC container for sending e-mail notifications in case of file replication errors.

```xml
<bean id="errorNotifier"
    class="com.apress.springrecipes.replicator.EmailErrorNotifier" />
```

You can write the following Main class to test EmailErrorNotifier. After running it, you can configure your e-mail application to receive the e-mail from your James Server via POP3.

```java
package com.apress.springrecipes.replicator;

import org.springframework.context.ApplicationContext;
import org.springframework.context.support.ClassPathXmlApplicationContext;
```

```
public class Main {

    public static void main(String[] args) {
        ApplicationContext context =
            new ClassPathXmlApplicationContext("beans.xml");

        ErrorNotifier errorNotifier =
            (ErrorNotifier) context.getBean("errorNotifier");
        errorNotifier.notifyCopyError(
            "c:/documents", "d:/documents", "spring.doc");
    }
}
```

Sending E-mail with Spring's MailSender

Now, let's look at how to send e-mail with the help of Spring's MailSender interface, which can send SimpleMailMessage in its send() method. With this interface, your code is no longer JavaMail specific, and now it's easier to test.

```
package com.apress.springrecipes.replicator;

import org.springframework.mail.MailSender;
import org.springframework.mail.SimpleMailMessage;

public class EmailErrorNotifier implements ErrorNotifier {

    private MailSender mailSender;

    public void setMailSender(MailSender mailSender) {
        this.mailSender = mailSender;
    }

    public void notifyCopyError(String srcDir, String destDir, String filename) {
        SimpleMailMessage message = new SimpleMailMessage();
        message.setFrom("system@localhost");
        message.setTo("admin@localhost");
        message.setSubject("File Copy Error");
        message.setText(
                "Dear Administrator,\n\n" +
                "An error occurred when copying the following file :\n" +
                "Source directory : " + srcDir + "\n" +
                "Destination directory : " + destDir + "\n" +
                "Filename : " + filename);
        mailSender.send(message);
    }
}
```

Next, you have to configure a MailSender implementation in the bean configuration file and inject it into EmailErrorNotifier. In Spring, the unique implementation of this interface is JavaMailSenderImpl, which uses JavaMail to send e-mail.

```
<beans ...>
    ...
    <bean id="mailSender"
        class="org.springframework.mail.javamail.JavaMailSenderImpl">
        <property name="host" value="localhost" />
        <property name="port" value="25" />
        <property name="username" value="system" />
        <property name="password" value="12345" />
    </bean>

    <bean id="errorNotifier"
        class="com.apress.springrecipes.replicator.EmailErrorNotifier">
        <property name="mailSender" ref="mailSender" />
    </bean>
</beans>
```

The default port used by JavaMailSenderImpl is the standard SMTP port 25, so if your e-mail server listens on this port for SMTP, you can simply omit this property. Also, if your SMTP server doesn't require user authentication, you needn't set the username and password.

If you have a JavaMail session configured in your Java EE application server, you can first look it up with the help of JndiObjectFactoryBean.

```
<bean id="mailSession"
    class="org.springframework.jndi.JndiObjectFactoryBean">
    <property name="jndiName" value="mail/Session" />
</bean>
```

Or you can look up a JavaMail session through the <jee:jndi-lookup> element if you are using Spring 2.0 or later.

```
<jee:jndi-lookup id="mailSession" jndi-name="mail/Session" />
```

You can inject the JavaMail session into JavaMailSenderImpl for its use. In this case, you no longer need to set the host, port, username, or password.

```
<bean id="mailSender"
    class="org.springframework.mail.javamail.JavaMailSenderImpl">
    <property name="session" ref="mailSession" />
</bean>
```

Defining an E-mail Template

Constructing an e-mail message from scratch in the method body is not efficient, because you have to hard-code the e-mail properties. Also, you may have difficulty in writing the e-mail text in terms of Java strings. You can consider defining an e-mail message template in the bean configuration file and construct a new e-mail message from it.

```xml
<beans ...>
    ...
    <bean id="copyErrorMailMessage"
        class="org.springframework.mail.SimpleMailMessage">
        <property name="from" value="system@localhost" />
        <property name="to" value="admin@localhost" />
        <property name="subject" value="File Copy Error" />
        <property name="text">
            <value>
<![CDATA[
Dear Administrator,

An error occurred when copying the following file :
Source directory : %s
Destination directory : %s
Filename : %s
]]>
            </value>
        </property>
    </bean>

    <bean id="errorNotifier"
        class="com.apress.springrecipes.replicator.EmailErrorNotifier">
        <property name="mailSender" ref="mailSender" />
        <property name="copyErrorMailMessage" ref="copyErrorMailMessage" />
    </bean>
</beans>
```

Note that in the preceding message text, you include the placeholders %s, which will be replaced by message parameters through String.format(). Of course, you can also use a powerful templating language such as Velocity or FreeMarker to generate the message text according to a template. It's also a good practice to separate mail message templates from bean configuration files.

Each time you send e-mail, you can construct a new SimpleMailMessage instance from this injected template. Then you can generate the message text using String.format() to replace the %s placeholders with your message parameters.

```java
package com.apress.springrecipes.replicator;
...
import org.springframework.mail.SimpleMailMessage;

public class EmailErrorNotifier implements ErrorNotifier {
    ...
    private SimpleMailMessage copyErrorMailMessage;

    public void setCopyErrorMailMessage(SimpleMailMessage copyErrorMailMessage) {
        this.copyErrorMailMessage = copyErrorMailMessage;
    }
```

```
    public void notifyCopyError(String srcDir, String destDir, String filename) {
        SimpleMailMessage message = new SimpleMailMessage(copyErrorMailMessage);
        message.setText(String.format(
                copyErrorMailMessage.getText(), srcDir, destDir, filename));
        mailSender.send(message);
    }
}
```

Sending MIME Messages

So far, the SimpleMailMessage class you used can send only a simple plain text e-mail message. To send e-mail that contains HTML content, inline images, or attachments, you have to construct and send a MIME message instead. MIME is supported by JavaMail through the javax.mail.internet.MimeMessage class.

First of all, you have to use the JavaMailSender interface instead of its parent interface MailSender. The JavaMailSenderImpl instance you injected does implement this interface, so you needn't modify your bean configurations. The following notifier sends Spring's bean configuration file as an e-mail attachment to the administrator:

```
package com.apress.springrecipes.replicator;

import javax.mail.MessagingException;
import javax.mail.internet.MimeMessage;

import org.springframework.core.io.ClassPathResource;
import org.springframework.mail.MailParseException;
import org.springframework.mail.SimpleMailMessage;
import org.springframework.mail.javamail.JavaMailSender;
import org.springframework.mail.javamail.MimeMessageHelper;

public class EmailErrorNotifier implements ErrorNotifier {

    private JavaMailSender mailSender;
    private SimpleMailMessage copyErrorMailMessage;

    public void setMailSender(JavaMailSender mailSender) {
        this.mailSender = mailSender;
    }

    public void setCopyErrorMailMessage(SimpleMailMessage copyErrorMailMessage) {
        this.copyErrorMailMessage = copyErrorMailMessage;
    }

    public void notifyCopyError(String srcDir, String destDir, String filename) {
        MimeMessage message = mailSender.createMimeMessage();
        try {
            MimeMessageHelper helper = new MimeMessageHelper(message, true);
            helper.setFrom(copyErrorMailMessage.getFrom());
            helper.setTo(copyErrorMailMessage.getTo());
```

```
            helper.setSubject(copyErrorMailMessage.getSubject());
            helper.setText(String.format(
                    copyErrorMailMessage.getText(), srcDir, destDir, filename));

            ClassPathResource config = new ClassPathResource("beans.xml");
            helper.addAttachment("beans.xml", config);
        } catch (MessagingException e) {
            throw new MailParseException(e);
        }
        mailSender.send(message);
    }
}
```

Unlike `SimpleMailMessage`, the `MimeMessage` class is defined by JavaMail, so you can only instantiate it by calling `mailSender.createMimeMessage()`. Spring provides the helper class `MimeMessageHelper` to simplify the operations of `MimeMessage`. It allows you to add an attachment from a Spring `Resource` object. However, the operations of this helper class still throw JavaMail's `MessagingException`. You have to convert this exception into Spring's mail runtime exception for consistency.

Spring offers another method for you to construct a MIME message, which is through implementing the `MimeMessagePreparator` interface.

```
package com.apress.springrecipes.replicator;
...
import javax.mail.internet.MimeMessage;

import org.springframework.mail.javamail.MimeMessagePreparator;

public class EmailErrorNotifier implements ErrorNotifier {
    ...
    public void notifyCopyError(
            final String srcDir, final String destDir, final String filename) {
        MimeMessagePreparator preparator = new MimeMessagePreparator() {

            public void prepare(MimeMessage mimeMessage) throws Exception {
                MimeMessageHelper helper =
                    new MimeMessageHelper(mimeMessage, true);
                helper.setFrom(copyErrorMailMessage.getFrom());
                helper.setTo(copyErrorMailMessage.getTo());
                helper.setSubject(copyErrorMailMessage.getSubject());
                helper.setText(String.format(
                    copyErrorMailMessage.getText(), srcDir, destDir, filename));

                ClassPathResource config = new ClassPathResource("beans.xml");
                helper.addAttachment("beans.xml", config);
            }
        };
        mailSender.send(preparator);
    }
}
```

In the `prepare()` method, you can prepare the `MimeMessage` object, which is precreated for `JavaMailSender`. If there's any exception thrown, it will be converted into Spring's mail runtime exception automatically.

18-5. Scheduling with Spring's Quartz Support

Problem

Your application has an advanced scheduling requirement that you want to fulfill using Quartz Scheduler. Such a requirement might be something seemingly complex like the ability to run at arbitrary times, or at strange intervals ("every other Thursday, but only after 10 am and before 2 pm"). Moreover, you want to configure your scheduling jobs in a declarative way.

Solution

Spring provides utility classes for Quartz to enable you to configure scheduling jobs in the bean configuration file, without programming against the Quartz API.

How It Works

Using Quartz Without Spring's Support

To use Quartz for scheduling, first create your job by implementing the `Job` interface. For example, the following job executes the `replicate()` method of a file replicator, retrieved from the job data map through the `JobExecutionContext` object that's passed in.

■ **Note** To use Quartz in your application, you must add it to your classpath. If you are using Maven, add the following dependency to your project.

```
<dependency>
  <groupId>org.opensymphony.quartz</groupId>
  <artifactId>quartz</artifactId>
  <version>1.6.1</version>
</dependency>
```

```
package com.apress.springrecipes.replicator;
...
import org.quartz.Job;
import org.quartz.JobExecutionContext;
import org.quartz.JobExecutionException;

public class FileReplicationJob implements Job {

    public void execute(JobExecutionContext context)
            throws JobExecutionException {
        Map dataMap = context.getJobDetail().getJobDataMap();
        FileReplicator fileReplicator =
            (FileReplicator) dataMap.get("fileReplicator");
        try {
            fileReplicator.replicate();
        } catch (IOException e) {
            throw new JobExecutionException(e);
        }
    }
}
```

After creating the job, you configure and schedule it with the Quartz API. For instance, the following scheduler runs your file replication job every 60 seconds with a 5-second delay for the first time of execution:

```
package com.apress.springrecipes.replicator;
...
import org.quartz.JobDetail;
import org.quartz.Scheduler;
import org.quartz.SimpleTrigger;
import org.quartz.impl.StdSchedulerFactory;
import org.springframework.context.ApplicationContext;
import org.springframework.context.support.ClassPathXmlApplicationContext;

public class Main {

    public static void main(String[] args) throws Exception {
        ApplicationContext context =
            new ClassPathXmlApplicationContext("beans.xml");

        FileReplicator documentReplicator =
            (FileReplicator) context.getBean("documentReplicator");

        JobDetail job = new JobDetail();
        job.setName("documentReplicationJob");
        job.setJobClass(FileReplicationJob.class);
        Map dataMap = job.getJobDataMap();
        dataMap.put("fileReplicator", documentReplicator);
```

```
            SimpleTrigger trigger = new SimpleTrigger();
            trigger.setName("documentReplicationJob");
            trigger.setStartTime(new Date(System.currentTimeMillis() + 5000));
            trigger.setRepeatCount(SimpleTrigger.REPEAT_INDEFINITELY);
            trigger.setRepeatInterval(60000);

            Scheduler scheduler = new StdSchedulerFactory().getScheduler();
            scheduler.start();
            scheduler.scheduleJob(job, trigger);
        }
}
```

In the Main class, you first configure the job details for your file replication job in a JobDetail object and prepare job data in its jobDataMap property. Next, you create a SimpleTrigger object to configure the scheduling properties. Finally, you create a scheduler to run your job using this trigger.

Quartz supports two types of triggers: SimpleTrigger and CronTrigger. SimpleTrigger allows you to set trigger properties such as start time, end time, repeat interval, and repeat count. CronTrigger accepts a Unix *cron* expression for you to specify the times to run your job. For example, you can replace the preceding SimpleTrigger with the following CronTrigger to run your job at 17:30 every day:

```
CronTrigger trigger = new CronTrigger();
trigger.setName("documentReplicationJob");
trigger.setCronExpression("0 30 17 * * ?");
```

A cron expression is made up of seven fields (the last field is optional), separated by spaces. Table 18-1 shows the field description for a cron expression.

Table 18-1. *Field Description for a Cron Expression*

Position	Field Name	Range
1	Second	0–59
2	Minute	0–59
3	Hour	0–23
4	Day of month	1–31
5	Month	1–12 or JAN–DEC
6	Day of week	1–7 or SUN–SAT
7	Year (optional)	1970–2099

Each part of a cron expression can be assigned a specific value (e.g. 3), a range (e.g. 1–5), a list (e.g. 1,3,5), a wildcard (* matches all values), or a question mark (? is used in either of the "Day of month" and "Day of week" fields for matching one of these fields but not both). For more information on the cron expressions supported by `CronTrigger`, refer to its Javadoc `http://quartz.sourceforge.net/javadoc/org/quartz/CronTrigger.html`).

Using Quartz with Spring's Support

When using Quartz, you can create a job by implementing the `Job` interface and retrieve job data from the job data map through `JobExecutionContext`. To decouple your job class from the Quartz API, Spring provides `QuartzJobBean`, which you can extend to retrieve job data through setter methods. `QuartzJobBean` converts the job data map into properties and injects them via the setter methods.

```
package com.apress.springrecipes.replicator;
...
import org.quartz.JobExecutionContext;
import org.quartz.JobExecutionException;
import org.springframework.scheduling.quartz.QuartzJobBean;

public class FileReplicationJob extends QuartzJobBean {

    private FileReplicator fileReplicator;

    public void setFileReplicator(FileReplicator fileReplicator) {
        this.fileReplicator = fileReplicator;
    }

    protected void executeInternal(JobExecutionContext context)
            throws JobExecutionException {
        try {
            fileReplicator.replicate();
        } catch (IOException e) {
            throw new JobExecutionException(e);
        }
    }
}
```

Then, you can configure a Quartz `JobDetail` object in Spring's bean configuration file through `JobDetailBean`. By default, Spring uses this bean's name as the job name. You can modify it by setting the `name` property.

```
<bean name="documentReplicationJob"
    class="org.springframework.scheduling.quartz.JobDetailBean">
    <property name="jobClass"
        value="com.apress.springrecipes.replicator.FileReplicationJob" />
    <property name="jobDataAsMap">
        <map>
            <entry key="fileReplicator" value-ref="documentReplicator" />
        </map>
    </property>
</bean>
```

Spring also offers MethodInvokingJobDetailFactoryBean for you to define a job that executes a single method of a particular object. This saves you the trouble of creating a job class. You can use the following job detail to replace the previous:

```
<bean id="documentReplicationJob" class="org.springframework.↵
    scheduling.quartz.MethodInvokingJobDetailFactoryBean">
    <property name="targetObject" ref="documentReplicator" />
    <property name="targetMethod" value="replicate" />
</bean>
```

You can configure a Quartz SimpleTrigger object in Spring's bean configuration file through SimpleTriggerBean, which requires a reference to a JobDetail object. This bean provides common default values for certain trigger properties, such as using the bean name as the job name and setting indefinite repeat count.

```
<bean id="documentReplicationTrigger"
    class="org.springframework.scheduling.quartz.SimpleTriggerBean">
    <property name="jobDetail" ref="documentReplicationJob" />
    <property name="repeatInterval" value="60000" />
    <property name="startDelay" value="5000" />
</bean>
```

You can also configure a Quartz CronTrigger object in the bean configuration file through CronTriggerBean.

```
<bean id="documentReplicationTrigger"
    class="org.springframework.scheduling.quartz.CronTriggerBean">
    <property name="jobDetail" ref="documentReplicationJob" />
    <property name="cronExpression" value=" 0 * * * * ? " />
</bean>
```

Finally, you can configure a SchedulerFactoryBean instance to create a Scheduler object for running your trigger. You can specify multiple triggers in this factory bean.

```
<bean class="org.springframework.scheduling.quartz.SchedulerFactoryBean">
    <property name="triggers">
        <list>
            <ref bean="documentReplicationTrigger" />
            <!-- other triggers you have may be included here -->
        </list>
    </property>
</bean>
```

Now, you can simply start your scheduler with the following `Main` class. In this way, you don't require a single line of code for scheduling jobs.

```
package com.apress.springrecipes.replicator;

import org.springframework.context.support.ClassPathXmlApplicationContext;

public class Main {

    public static void main(String[] args) throws Exception {
        new ClassPathXmlApplicationContext("beans.xml");
    }
}
```

18-6. Scheduling With Spring 3.0's Scheduling Namespace

Problem

You want to schedule a method invocation in a consistent manner, using either a cron expression, an interval, or a rate, and you don't want to have to go through Quartz just to do it.

Solution

Spring 3.0 debuts new support for configuring `TaskExecutors and TaskSchedulers.` This capability, coupled with the ability to schedule method execution using the `@Scheduled` annotation, makes Spring 3.0 very capable of meeting this challenge. The scheduling support works with a minimal of fuss: all you need are a method, an annotation, and to have switched on the scanner for annotations, in the simplest case.

How It Works

Let's revisit the example in the last recipe: we want to schedule a call to the replication method on the bean using a cron expression. Our XML file looks familiar:

```xml
<beans xmlns="http://www.springframework.org/schema/beans"
       xmlns:xsi="http://www.w3.org/2001/XMLSchema-instance"
       xmlns:context="http://www.springframework.org/schema/context"
       xmlns:task="http://www.springframework.org/schema/task"
xsi:schemaLocation="http://www.springframework.org/schema/beans
          http://www.springframework.org/schema/beans/spring-beans-3.0.xsd
          http://www.springframework.org/schema/context
http://www.springframework.org/schema/context/spring-context-3.0.xsd
          http://www.springframework.org/schema/task
http://www.springframework.org/schema/task/spring-task-3.0.xsd
          ">

<context:component-scan annotation-config="true"
                        base-package="com.apress.springrecipes.replicator"/>

        <task:scheduler id="scheduler" pool-size="10"/>
        <task:executor id="executor" pool-size="10"/>

        <task:annotation-driven scheduler="scheduler" executor="executor"/>

<bean id="fileCopier"
      class="com.apress.springrecipes.replicator.FileCopierJMXImpl" />

        <bean id="documentReplicator"
                class="com.apress.springrecipes.replicator.FileReplicatorImpl">
                <property name="srcDir" value="#{systemProperties['user.home']}/docs" />
                <property name="destDir"
                        value="#{systemProperties['user.home']}/docs_backup" />
                <property name="fileCopier" ref="fileCopier" />
        </bean>

</beans>
```

We have our two beans from the previous example. At the top, however, we've added some configuration to support the scheduling features. We've drawn out the configuration of each element here, but you don't need to. Once that's done, we switch on general annotation support with the task:annotation-driven element. Let's look at our code now.

```java
package com.apress.springrecipes.replicator;

import org.springframework.scheduling.annotation.Scheduled;

import java.io.File;
import java.io.IOException;


public class FileReplicatorImpl implements FileReplicator {
    private String srcDir;
    private String destDir;
    private FileCopier fileCopier;
```

```java
    public String getSrcDir() {
        return srcDir;
    }

    public void setSrcDir(String srcDir) {
        this.srcDir = srcDir;
        revaluateDirectories();
    }

    public String getDestDir() {
        return destDir;
    }

    public void setDestDir(String destDir) {
        this.destDir = destDir;
        revaluateDirectories();
    }

    public void setFileCopier(FileCopier fileCopier) {
        this.fileCopier = fileCopier;
    }

    @Scheduled(fixedDelay = 60 * 1000)
    public synchronized void replicate() throws IOException {
        File[] files = new File(srcDir).listFiles();

        for (File file : files) {
            if (file.isFile()) {
                fileCopier.copyFile(srcDir, destDir, file.getName());
            }
        }
    }

    private void revaluateDirectories() {
        File src = new File(srcDir);
        File dest = new File(destDir);

        if (!src.exists()) {
            src.mkdirs();
        }

        if (!dest.exists()) {
            dest.mkdirs();
        }
    }
}
```

Note that we've annotated the replicate() method with a @Scheduled annotation. Here, we've told the scheduler to execute the method every 30 seconds, as measured from the completion time of the previous invocation. Alternateively, we might specify a `fixedRate` value for the `@Scheduled` annotation, which would measure the time between successive starts and then trigger another run.

```
@Scheduled(fixedRate = 60 * 1000)
public synchronized void replicate() throws IOException {
    File[] files = new File(srcDir).listFiles();

    for (File file : files) {
        if (file.isFile()) {
            fileCopier.copyFile(srcDir, destDir, file.getName());
        }
    }
}
```

Finally, we might want more complex control over the execution of the method. In this case, we can use a cron expression, just as we did in the Quartz example.

```
@Scheduled( cron = " 0 * * * * ? " )
public synchronized void replicate() throws IOException {
    File[] files = new File(srcDir).listFiles();

    for (File file : files) {
        if (file.isFile()) {
            fileCopier.copyFile(srcDir, destDir, file.getName());
        }
    }
}
```

There is support for configuring all of this in the XML too. This might be useful if you didn't want to, or couldn't, add an annotation to an existing bean method. Here's a look at how we might re-create the preceding annotation-centric examples using the Spring **task** XML namespace.

```
<beans xmlns="http://www.springframework.org/schema/beans"
       xmlns:xsi="http://www.w3.org/2001/XMLSchema-instance"
       xmlns:context="http://www.springframework.org/schema/context"
       xmlns:task="http://www.springframework.org/schema/task"↵
  xsi:schemaLocation="http://www.springframework.org/schema/beans
       http://www.springframework.org/schema/beans/spring-beans-3.0.xsd
       http://www.springframework.org/schema/context↵
http://www.springframework.org/schema/context/spring-context-3.0.xsd
       http://www.springframework.org/schema/task↵
http://www.springframework.org/schema/task/spring-task-3.0.xsd
       ">

<context:component-scan annotation-config="true"↵
 base-package="com.apress.springrecipes.replicator"/>
<task:scheduler id="scheduler" pool-size="10"/>
<task:executor id="executor" pool-size="10"/>
<task:annotation-driven scheduler="scheduler" executor="executor"/>
```

```xml
<task:scheduled-tasks scheduler="scheduler">
        <task:scheduled ref="documentReplicator" method="replicate" fixed-rate="60000"/>
        <task:scheduled ref="documentReplicator" method="replicate" fixed-delay="60000"/>
        <task:scheduled ref="documentReplicator" method="replicate" cron="0 * * * * ? "/>
</task:scheduled-tasks>

<bean id="fileCopier" class="com.apress.springrecipes.replicator.FileCopierJMXImpl" />

        <bean id="documentReplicator"
                class="com.apress.springrecipes.replicator.FileReplicatorImpl">
                <property name="srcDir" value="#{systemProperties['user.home']}/docs" />
                <property name="destDir"↵
 value="#{systemProperties['user.home']}/docs_backup" />
                <property name="fileCopier" ref="fileCopier" />
        </bean>

</beans>
```

Summary

This chapter discussed JMX and a few of the surrounding specifications. You learned how to export Spring beans as JMX MBeans and how to use those MBeans from a client, both remotely and locally by using Spring's proxies. You published and listened to notification events on a JMX server from Spring. You built a simple replicator and exposed its configuration through JMX. You learned how to schedule the replication using the Quartz Scheduler, as well as Spring 3.0's new **task** namespace.

CHAPTER 19

∎∎∎

Messaging

In this chapter, you will learn about Spring's support for *Java Message Service (JMS)*. JMS defines a set of standard APIs for message-oriented communication (using message-oriented middleware, a.k.a MOM) in the Java EE platform. With JMS, different applications can communicate in a loosely coupled way compared with other remoting technologies such as RMI. However, when using the JMS API to send and receive messages, you have to manage the JMS resources yourself and handle the JMS API's exceptions, which results in many lines of JMS-specific code. Spring simplifies JMS's usage with a template-based approach, just as it does for JDBC. Moreover, Spring enables beans declared in its IoC container to listen for JMS messages and react to them.

Messaging is a very powerful technique for scaling out your application. It allows work that would otherwise overwhelm a service to be queued up. It also encourages a very decoupled architecture. A component, for example, might only consume messages with a single `java.util.Map`-based key/value pair. This loose contract makes it a viable hub of communication for multiple, disparate systems, without requiring that they share object types.

Today's messaging middleware stacks are very powerful. There are many factors that apply to messaging middleware performs, including how (or *if*) the messages are persisted, how they are transmitted en route, and how they are made available to the client. Another factor to consider is how IO occurs. Some commercial message queues (and even a few open source ones) use Java NIO when available or, in some cases—such as with JBoss' HornetQ project or the as-yet-unreleased ActiveMQ 6— they use a native asynchronous IO layer to notch up performance to levels you wouldn't think possible. News of HornetQ's having handily bested other message queues in the SPECjms2007 benchmark in February, 2010 has just emerged as of this writing. These kinds of advances can make it possible to transmit hundreds of thousands of messages *per second*; today's message queues are *definitely* not your father's message queues!

Some message queues, like Amazon SQS, provide RESTful interfaces. Amazon's SQS interface is proprietary but powerful. It's also very scalable, backed by Amazon's expertise in cloud-readiness. On the other hand, since it is a REST-based API, some of the plumbing required to use it (polling and consuming messages in Java, for example) is left to the developer to write; there is no JMS API. Another aspect to consider is that message queues are only available to Java clients if they only surface a JMS API. A nascent standard, AMQP, aims to provide a language-neutral specification of a message queue, which any language might consume. Apache's ActiveMQ has some support for this. ActiveMQ's a very fast message queue, but a common sentiment is that RabbitMQ (implemented in Erlang) is faster. Because it surfaces an AMQP-compliant interface, any client language can benefit from its speed.

Going the other way, ActiveMQ might still be the better choice precisely because it supports both JMS and AMQP: Java EE and Spring clients can take advantage of the JMS interface, and other languages can interface through AMQP.

Clearly, there are lots of choices. With all this in mind, we can begin to tackle using JMS with Spring.

By the end of this chapter, you will be able to create and access message-based middleware using Spring and JMS. This chapter will also provide you with a working knowledge of messaging in general, which will help you when we discuss Spring Integration. You will also know how to use Spring's JMS support to simplify sending, receiving, and listening for JMS messages.

19-1. Sending and Receiving JMS Messages with Spring

Problem

In the Java EE platform, applications often need to communicate using JMS. To send or receive a JMS message, you have to perform the following tasks:

1. Create a JMS connection factory on a message broker.

2. Create a JMS destination, which can be either a queue or a topic.

3. Open a JMS connection from the connection factory.

4. Obtain a JMS session from the connection.

5. Send or receive the JMS message with a message producer or consumer.

6. Handle JMSException, which is a checked exception that must be handled.

7. Close the JMS session and connection.

As you can see, a lot of coding is required to send or receive a simple JMS message. In fact, most of these tasks are boilerplate and require you to repeat them each time when dealing with JMS.

ON THE TOPIC OF TOPICS . . .

In this chapter, we'll refer quite a bit to "topics" and "queues." Messaging solutions are designed to solve two types of architecture requirements: messaging from one point in an application to another known point, and messaging from one point in an application to many other unknown points. These patterns are the middleware equivalents of telling somebody something face to face and saying something over a loud speaker to a room of people, respectively.

If you want messages sent on a message queue to be broadcast to an unknown set of clients who are "listening" for the message (as in the loud speaker analogy), send the message on a *topic.* If you want the message sent to a single, known client, then you send it over a *queue.*

Solution

Spring offers a template-based solution for simplifying your JMS code. With a JMS template (Spring framework class JmsTemplate), you can send and receive JMS messages with much less code. The template handles the boilerplate tasks for you and also converts the JMS API's JMSException hierarchy into Spring's runtime exception `org.springframework.jms.JmsException` hierarchy. The translation converts exceptions to a mirrored hierarchy of unchecked exceptions.

In JMS 1.0.2, topics and queues are known as *domains* and are handled with a different API that is provided for legacy reasons, so you'll find JARs or implementations of the JMS API in different application servers: one for 1.1, and one for 1.0.2. In Spring 3.0, this 1.0.2 support in Spring is considered deprecated.

JMS 1.1 provides a domain-independent API, treating topic and queue as alternative message destinations. To address different JMS APIs, Spring provides two JMS template classes, `JmsTemplate` and `JmsTemplate102`, for these two versions of JMS. This chapter will focus on JMS 1.1, which is available for Java EE 1.4 and higher versions.

How It Works

Suppose that you are developing a post office system that includes two subsystems: the front desk subsystem and the back office subsystem. When the front desk receives mail from a citizen, it passes the mail to the back office for categorizing and delivering. At the same time, the front desk subsystem sends a JMS message to the back office subsystem, notifying it of new mail. The mail information is represented by the following class:

```
package com.apress.springrecipes.post;

public class Mail {

    private String mailId;
    private String country;
    private double weight;

    // Constructors, Getters and Setters
    ...
}
```

The methods for sending and receiving mail information are defined in the `FrontDesk` and `BackOffice` interfaces as follows:

```
package com.apress.springrecipes.post;

public interface FrontDesk {

    public void sendMail(Mail mail);
}
```

```
package com.apress.springrecipes.post;

public interface BackOffice {

    public Mail receiveMail();
}
```

Before you can send and receive JMS messages, you need to install a JMS message broker. For simplicity's sake, we have chosen Apache ActiveMQ (http://activemq.apache.org/) as our message broker, which is very easy to install and configure. ActiveMQ is an open source message broker that fully supports JMS 1.1.

■ **Note** You can download ActiveMQ (e.g., v5.3.0) from the ActiveMQ web site and extract it to a directory of your choice to complete the installation.

Sending and Receiving Messages Without Spring's Support

First, let's look at how to send and receive JMS messages without Spring's support. The following `FrontDeskImpl` class sends JMS messages with the JMS API directly.

■ **Note** To send and receive JMS messages to and from a JMS message broker, you have to include the client library for the message broker, as well as the JMS APIs in your classpath. If you are using Maven, add the following dependencies to your classpath.

```
<dependency>
  <groupId>javax.jms</groupId>
  <artifactId>jms</artifactId>
  <version>1.1</version>
</dependency>

<dependency>
  <groupId>org.apache.activemq</groupId>
  <version>5.3.0</version>
  <artifactId>activemq-all</artifactId>
</dependency>
```

```
package com.apress.springrecipes.post;

import javax.jms.Connection;
import javax.jms.ConnectionFactory;
import javax.jms.Destination;
import javax.jms.JMSException;
import javax.jms.MapMessage;
```

```
import javax.jms.MessageProducer;
import javax.jms.Session;

import org.apache.activemq.ActiveMQConnectionFactory;
import org.apache.activemq.command.ActiveMQQueue;

public class FrontDeskImpl implements FrontDesk {

    public void sendMail(Mail mail) {
        ConnectionFactory cf =
            new ActiveMQConnectionFactory("tcp://localhost:61616");
        Destination destination = new ActiveMQQueue("mail.queue");

        Connection conn = null;
        try {
            conn = cf.createConnection();
            Session session =
                conn.createSession(false, Session.AUTO_ACKNOWLEDGE);
            MessageProducer producer = session.createProducer(destination);

            MapMessage message = session.createMapMessage();
            message.setString("mailId", mail.getMailId());
            message.setString("country", mail.getCountry());
            message.setDouble("weight", mail.getWeight());
            producer.send(message);

            session.close();
        } catch (JMSException e) {
            throw new RuntimeException(e);
        } finally {
            if (conn != null) {
                try {
                    conn.close();
                } catch (JMSException e) {
                }
            }
        }
    }
}
```

In the preceding sendMail() method, you first create JMS-specific ConnectionFactory and
Destination objects with the classes provided by ActiveMQ. The message broker URL is the default for
ActiveMQ if you run it on localhost. In JMS, there are two types of destinations: queue and topic. As
explained before, a *queue* is for the point-to-point communication model, while *topic* is for the publish-
subscribe communication model. Because you are sending JMS messages point to point from front desk
to back office, you should use a message queue. You can easily create a topic as a destination using the
ActiveMQTopic class.

Next, you have to create a connection, session, and message producer before you can send your message. There are several types of messages defined in the JMS API, including **TextMessage**, **MapMessage**, **BytesMessage**, **ObjectMessage**, and **StreamMessage**. **MapMessage** contains message content in key/value pairs like a map. All of them are interfaces, whose super class is simply **Message**. In the meantime, you have to handle **JMSException**, which may be thrown by the JMS API. Finally, you must remember to close the session and connection to release system resources. Every time a JMS connection is closed, all its opened sessions will be closed automatically. So you only have to ensure that the JMS connection is closed properly in the **finally** block.

On the other hand, the following **BackOfficeImpl** class receives JMS messages with the JMS API directly:

```
package com.apress.springrecipes.post;

import javax.jms.Connection;
import javax.jms.ConnectionFactory;
import javax.jms.Destination;
import javax.jms.JMSException;
import javax.jms.MapMessage;
import javax.jms.MessageConsumer;
import javax.jms.Session;

import org.apache.activemq.ActiveMQConnectionFactory;
import org.apache.activemq.command.ActiveMQQueue;

public class BackOfficeImpl implements BackOffice {

    public Mail receiveMail() {
        ConnectionFactory cf =
            new ActiveMQConnectionFactory("tcp://localhost:61616");
        Destination destination = new ActiveMQQueue("mail.queue");

        Connection conn = null;
        try {
            conn = cf.createConnection();
            Session session =
                conn.createSession(false, Session.AUTO_ACKNOWLEDGE);
            MessageConsumer consumer = session.createConsumer(destination);

            conn.start();
            MapMessage message = (MapMessage) consumer.receive();
            Mail mail = new Mail();
            mail.setMailId(message.getString("mailId"));
            mail.setCountry(message.getString("country"));
            mail.setWeight(message.getDouble("weight"));
```

```
                session.close();
                return mail;
        } catch (JMSException e) {
                throw new RuntimeException(e);
        } finally {
                if (conn != null) {
                        try {
                                conn.close();
                        } catch (JMSException e) {
                        }
                }
        }
    }
}
```

Most of the code in this method is similar to that for sending JMS messages, except that you create a message consumer and receive a JMS message from it. Note that we used the connection's **start()** method here, although we didn't in the **FrontDeskImpl** example before. When using a **Connection** to receive messages, you can add listeners to the connection that are invoked on receipt of a message, or you can block synchronously, waiting for a message to arrive. The container has no way of knowing which approach you will take and so it doesn't start polling for messages until you've explicitly called **start()**. If you add listeners or do any kind of configuration, you do so before you invoke **start()**.

Finally, you create two bean configuration files—one for the front desk subsystem (e.g., **beans-front.xml**), and one for the back office subsystem (e.g., **beans-back.xml**)—in the root of the classpath.

```xml
<beans xmlns="http://www.springframework.org/schema/beans"
    xmlns:xsi="http://www.w3.org/2001/XMLSchema-instance"
    xsi:schemaLocation="http://www.springframework.org/schema/beans
        http://www.springframework.org/schema/beans/spring-beans-3.0.xsd">

    <bean id="frontDesk"
        class="com.apress.springrecipes.post.FrontDeskImpl" />
</beans>
```

```xml
<beans xmlns="http://www.springframework.org/schema/beans"
    xmlns:xsi="http://www.w3.org/2001/XMLSchema-instance"
    xsi:schemaLocation="http://www.springframework.org/schema/beans
        http://www.springframework.org/schema/beans/spring-beans-3.0.xsd">

    <bean id="backOffice"
        class="com.apress.springrecipes.post.BackOfficeImpl" />
</beans>
```

Now, your front desk and back office subsystems are ready to send and receive JMS messages. You must start up your message broker before sending and receiving messages with the following main classes. To run them, first run **FrontDeskMain** and then run **BackOfficeMain** in another window or console.

> ■ **Note** To start ActiveMQ, you just execute one of the ActiveMQ startup scripts for your operating system. The script itself is called activemq.sh or activemq.bat for Unix variants or Windows, respectively, and is located in the bin directory.

```
package com.apress.springrecipes.post;

import org.springframework.context.ApplicationContext;
import org.springframework.context.support.ClassPathXmlApplicationContext;

public class FrontDeskMain {

    public static void main(String[] args) {
        ApplicationContext context =
            new ClassPathXmlApplicationContext("beans-front.xml");

        FrontDesk frontDesk = (FrontDesk) context.getBean("frontDesk");
        frontDesk.sendMail(new Mail("1234", "US", 1.5));
    }
}

package com.apress.springrecipes.post;

import org.springframework.context.ApplicationContext;
import org.springframework.context.support.ClassPathXmlApplicationContext;

public class BackOfficeMain {

    public static void main(String[] args) {
        ApplicationContext context =
            new ClassPathXmlApplicationContext("beans-back.xml");

        BackOffice backOffice = (BackOffice) context.getBean("backOffice");
        Mail mail = backOffice.receiveMail();
        System.out.println("Mail #" + mail.getMailId() + " received");
    }
}
```

> ■ **Note** You're encouraged to use your messaging middleware's reporting functionality. In these examples, we're using ActiveMQ. With the default installation, you can open http://localhost:8161/admin/queueGraph.jsp to see what's happening with mail.queue, the queue used in these examples. Alternatively, ActiveMQ exposes very useful beans and statistics from JMX. Simply run jconsole, and drill down to org.apache.activemq in the MBeans tab.

Sending and Receiving Messages with Spring's JMS Template

Spring offers a JMS template that can significantly simplify your JMS code. To send a JMS message with this template, you simply call the send() method and provide a message destination, as well as a MessageCreator object, which creates the JMS message you are going to send. The MessageCreator object is usually implemented as an anonymous inner class.

```
package com.apress.springrecipes.post;

import javax.jms.Destination;
import javax.jms.JMSException;
import javax.jms.MapMessage;
import javax.jms.Message;
import javax.jms.Session;

import org.springframework.jms.core.JmsTemplate;
import org.springframework.jms.core.MessageCreator;

public class FrontDeskImpl implements FrontDesk {

    private JmsTemplate jmsTemplate;
    private Destination destination;

    public void setJmsTemplate(JmsTemplate jmsTemplate) {
        this.jmsTemplate = jmsTemplate;
    }

    public void setDestination(Destination destination) {
        this.destination = destination;
    }

    public void sendMail(final Mail mail) {
        jmsTemplate.send(destination, new MessageCreator() {
            public Message createMessage(Session session) throws JMSException {
                MapMessage message = session.createMapMessage();
                message.setString("mailId", mail.getMailId());
                message.setString("country", mail.getCountry());
                message.setDouble("weight", mail.getWeight());
                return message;
            }
        });
    }
}
```

Note that an inner class can access only arguments or variables of the enclosing method that are declared as final. The MessageCreator interface declares only a createMessage() method for you to implement. In this method, you create and return your JMS message with the JMS session provided.

A JMS template helps you to obtain and release the JMS connection and session, and it sends the JMS message created by your MessageCreator object. Moreover, it converts the JMS API's JMSException hierarchy into Spring's JMS runtime exception hierarchy, whose base exception class is org.springframework.jms.JmsException. You can catch the JmsException thrown from send and the other send variants and then take action in the catch block if you want.

In the front desk subsystem's bean configuration file, you declare a JMS template that refers to the JMS connection factory for opening connections. Then, you inject this template as well as the message destination into your front desk bean.

```
<beans ...>
    <bean id="connectionFactory"
        class="org.apache.activemq.ActiveMQConnectionFactory">
        <property name="brokerURL" value="tcp://localhost:61616" />
    </bean>

    <bean id="mailDestination"
        class="org.apache.activemq.command.ActiveMQQueue">
        <constructor-arg value="mail.queue" />
    </bean>

    <bean id="jmsTemplate"
        class="org.springframework.jms.core.JmsTemplate">
        <property name="connectionFactory" ref="connectionFactory" />
    </bean>

    <bean id="frontDesk"
        class="com.apress.springrecipes.post.FrontDeskImpl">
        <property name="destination" ref="mailDestination" />
        <property name="jmsTemplate" ref="jmsTemplate" />
    </bean>
</beans>
```

To receive a JMS message with a JMS template, you call the receive() method by providing a message destination. This method returns a JMS message, javax.jms.Message, whose type is the base JMS message type (that is, an interface), so you have to cast it into proper type before further processing.

```
package com.apress.springrecipes.post;

import javax.jms.Destination;
import javax.jms.JMSException;
import javax.jms.MapMessage;

import org.springframework.jms.core.JmsTemplate;
import org.springframework.jms.support.JmsUtils;

public class BackOfficeImpl implements BackOffice {

    private JmsTemplate jmsTemplate;
    private Destination destination;

    public void setJmsTemplate(JmsTemplate jmsTemplate) {
        this.jmsTemplate = jmsTemplate;
    }
```

```
    public void setDestination(Destination destination) {
        this.destination = destination;
    }

    public Mail receiveMail() {
        MapMessage message = (MapMessage) jmsTemplate.receive(destination);
        try {
            if (message == null) {
                return null;
            }
            Mail mail = new Mail();
            mail.setMailId(message.getString("mailId"));
            mail.setCountry(message.getString("country"));
            mail.setWeight(message.getDouble("weight"));
            return mail;
        } catch (JMSException e) {
            throw JmsUtils.convertJmsAccessException(e);
        }
    }
}
```

However, when extracting information from the received MapMessage object, you still have to handle the JMS API's JMSException. This is in stark contrast to the default behavior of the framework, where it automatically maps exceptions for you when invoking methods on the JmsTemplate. To make the type of the exception thrown by this method consistent, you have to make a call to JmsUtils.convertJmsAccessException() to convert the JMS API's JMSException into Spring's JmsException.

In the back office subsystem's bean configuration file, you declare a JMS template and inject it together with the message destination into your back office bean.

```
<beans ...>
    <bean id="connectionFactory"
        class="org.apache.activemq.ActiveMQConnectionFactory">
        <property name="brokerURL" value="tcp://localhost:61616" />
    </bean>

    <bean id="mailDestination"
        class="org.apache.activemq.command.ActiveMQQueue">
        <constructor-arg value="mail.queue" />
    </bean>

    <bean id="jmsTemplate"
        class="org.springframework.jms.core.JmsTemplate">
        <property name="connectionFactory" ref="connectionFactory" />
        <property name="receiveTimeout" value="10000" />
    </bean>
```

```
    <bean id="backOffice"
        class="com.apress.springrecipes.post.BackOfficeImpl">
        <property name="destination" ref="mailDestination" />
        <property name="jmsTemplate" ref="jmsTemplate" />
    </bean>
</beans>
```

Pay special attention to the `receiveTimeout` (which specifies how long to wait in milliseconds) property of the JMS template. By default, this template will wait for a JMS message at the destination forever, and the calling thread is blocked in the meantime. To avoid waiting for a message so long, you should specify a receive timeout for this template. If there's no message available at the destination in the duration, the JMS template's `receive()` method will return a `null` message.

In your applications, the main use of receiving a message might be because you're expecting a response to something or want to check for messages at an interval, handling the messages and then spinning down until the next interval. If you intend to receive messages and respond to them as a service, you're likely going to want to use the message-driven POJO functionality described later in this chapter. There, we discuss a mechanism that will constantly sit and wait for messages, handling them by calling back into your application as the messages arrive.

Sending and Receiving Messages to and from a Default Destination

Instead of specifying a message destination for each JMS template's `send()` and `receive()` method call, you can specify a default destination for a JMS template. Then, you will no longer need to inject it into your message sender and receiver beans again.

```
<beans ...>
    ...
    <bean id="jmsTemplate"
        class="org.springframework.jms.core.JmsTemplate">
        <property name="connectionFactory" ref="connectionFactory" />
            <property name="defaultDestination" ref="mailDestination" />
    </bean>

    <bean id="frontDesk"
        class="com.apress.springrecipes.post.FrontDeskImpl">
        <property name="jmsTemplate" ref="jmsTemplate" />
    </bean>
</beans>

<beans ...>
    ...
    <bean id="jmsTemplate"
        class="org.springframework.jms.core.JmsTemplate">
        <property name="receiveTimeout" value ="10000"/>
        <property name="connectionFactory" ref="connectionFactory" />
        <property name="defaultDestination" ref="mailDestination" />
    </bean>
```

```
    <bean id="backOffice"
        class="com.apress.springrecipes.post.BackOfficeImpl">
        <property name="jmsTemplate" ref="jmsTemplate" />
    </bean>
</beans>
```

With the default destination specified for a JMS template, you can delete the setter method for a message destination from your message sender and receiver classes. Now, when you call the send() and receive() methods, you no longer need to specify a message destination.

```
package com.apress.springrecipes.post;
...
import org.springframework.jms.core.MessageCreator;

public class FrontDeskImpl implements FrontDesk {
    ...
    public void sendMail(final Mail mail) {
        jmsTemplate.send(new MessageCreator() {
            ...
        });
    }
}

package com.apress.springrecipes.post;
...
import javax.jms.MapMessage;
...

public class BackOfficeImpl implements BackOffice {
    ...
    public Mail receiveMail() {
        MapMessage message = (MapMessage) jmsTemplate.receive();
        ...
    }
}
```

Instead of specifying an instance of the Destination interface for a JMS template, you can specify the destination name to let the JMS template resolve it for you, so you can delete the Destination object's declaration from both bean configuration files.

```
<bean id="jmsTemplate"
    class="org.springframework.jms.core.JmsTemplate">
    ...
    <property name="defaultDestinationName" value="mail.queue" />
</bean>
```

Extending the JmsGatewaySupport Class

Just like your DAO class can extend `JdbcDaoSupport` to retrieve a JDBC template, your JMS sender and receiver classes can also extend `JmsGatewaySupport` to retrieve a JMS template. You have the following two options for classes that extend `JmsGatewaySupport` to create their JMS template:

- Inject a JMS connection factory for `JmsGatewaySupport` to create a JMS template on it automatically. However, if you do it this way, you won't be able to configure the details of the JMS template.

- Inject a JMS template for `JmsGatewaySupport` that is created and configured by you.

Of them, the second approach is more suitable if you have to configure the JMS template yourself. You can delete the private field `jmsTemplate` and its setter method from both your sender and receiver classes. When you need access to the JMS template, you just make a call to `getJmsTemplate()`.

```
package com.apress.springrecipes.post;

import org.springframework.jms.core.support.JmsGatewaySupport;
...

public class FrontDeskImpl extends JmsGatewaySupport implements FrontDesk {
    ...
    public void sendMail(final Mail mail) {
        getJmsTemplate().send(new MessageCreator() {
            ...
        });
    }
}

package com.apress.springrecipes.post;
...

import org.springframework.jms.core.support.JmsGatewaySupport;

public class BackOfficeImpl extends JmsGatewaySupport implements BackOffice {
    public Mail receiveMail() {
        MapMessage message = (MapMessage) getJmsTemplate().receive();
        ...
    }
}
```

19-2. Converting JMS Messages

Problem

Your application receives messages from your message queue but also should transform those messages from the JMS-specific type to a business-specific class.

Solution

Spring provides an implementation of `SimpleMessageConvertor` to handle the translation of a JMS message received to a business object and the translation of a business object to a JMS message. You can leverage the default or provide your own.

Approach

So far, you have been handling the raw JMS messages by yourself. Spring's JMS template can help you convert JMS messages to and from Java objects using a message converter. By default, the JMS template uses `SimpleMessageConverter` for converting `TextMessage` to or from a string, `BytesMessage` to or from a byte array, `MapMessage` to or from a map, and `ObjectMessage` to or from a serializable object. For your front desk and back office classes, you can send and receive a map using the `convertAndSend()` and `receiveAndConvert()` methods, and the map will be converted to/from `MapMessage`.

```
package com.apress.springrecipes.post;
...
public class FrontDeskImpl extends JmsGatewaySupport implements FrontDesk {
    public void sendMail(Mail mail) {
        Map<String, Object> map = new HashMap<String, Object>();
        map.put("mailId", mail.getMailId());
        map.put("country", mail.getCountry());
        map.put("weight", mail.getWeight());
        getJmsTemplate().convertAndSend(map);
    }
}
```

```
package com.apress.springrecipes.post;
...
public class BackOfficeImpl extends JmsGatewaySupport implements BackOffice {
    public Mail receiveMail() {
        Map map = (Map) getJmsTemplate().receiveAndConvert();
        Mail mail = new Mail();
        mail.setMailId((String) map.get("mailId"));
        mail.setCountry((String) map.get("country"));
        mail.setWeight((Double) map.get("weight"));
        return mail;
    }
}
```

You can also create a custom message converter by implementing the `MessageConverter` interface for converting mail objects.

```
package com.apress.springrecipes.post;

import javax.jms.JMSException;
import javax.jms.MapMessage;
import javax.jms.Message;
import javax.jms.Session;

import org.springframework.jms.support.converter.MessageConversionException;
import org.springframework.jms.support.converter.MessageConverter;

public class MailMessageConverter implements MessageConverter {

    public Object fromMessage(Message message) throws JMSException,
            MessageConversionException {
        MapMessage mapMessage = (MapMessage) message;
        Mail mail = new Mail();
        mail.setMailId(mapMessage.getString("mailId"));
        mail.setCountry(mapMessage.getString("country"));
        mail.setWeight(mapMessage.getDouble("weight"));
        return mail;
    }

    public Message toMessage(Object object, Session session) throws JMSException,
            MessageConversionException {
        Mail mail = (Mail) object;
        MapMessage message = session.createMapMessage();
        message.setString("mailId", mail.getMailId());
        message.setString("country", mail.getCountry());
        message.setDouble("weight", mail.getWeight());
        return message;
    }
}
```

To apply this message converter, you have to declare it in both bean configuration files and inject it into the JMS template.

```
<beans ...>
    ...
    <bean id="mailMessageConverter"
        class="com.apress.springrecipes.post.MailMessageConverter" />

    <bean id="jmsTemplate"
        class="org.springframework.jms.core.JmsTemplate">
        ...
        <property name="messageConverter" ref="mailMessageConverter" />
    </bean>
</beans>
```

When you set a message converter for a JMS template explicitly, it will override the default SimpleMessageConverter. Now, you can call the JMS template's convertAndSend() and receiveAndConvert() methods to send and receive mail objects.

```
package com.apress.springrecipes.post;
...
public class FrontDeskImpl extends JmsGatewaySupport implements FrontDesk {
    public void sendMail(Mail mail) {
        getJmsTemplate().convertAndSend(mail);
    }
}
```

```
package com.apress.springrecipes.post;
...
public class BackOfficeImpl extends JmsGatewaySupport implements BackOffice {
    public Mail receiveMail() {
        return (Mail) getJmsTemplate().receiveAndConvert();
    }
}
```

19-3. Managing JMS Transactions

Problem

You want to participate in transactions with JMS so that the receipt and sending of messages are transactional.

Approach

You can use the same strategy as you will everywhere else in Spring: leveraging Spring's many `TransactionManager` implementations as needed and wiring the behavior into your beans.

Solution

When producing or consuming multiple JMS messages in a single method, if an error occurs in the middle, the JMS messages produced or consumed at the destination may be left in an inconsistent state. You have to surround the method with a transaction to avoid this problem.

In Spring, JMS transaction management is consistent with other data access strategies. For example, you can annotate the methods that require transaction management with the `@Transactional` annotation.

```
package com.apress.springrecipes.post;

import org.springframework.jms.core.support.JmsGatewaySupport;
import org.springframework.transaction.annotation.Transactional;
...
public class FrontDeskImpl extends JmsGatewaySupport implements FrontDesk {
```

```
    @Transactional
    public void sendMail(Mail mail) {
        ...
    }
}

package com.apress.springrecipes.post;

import org.springframework.jms.core.support.JmsGatewaySupport;
import org.springframework.transaction.annotation.Transactional;
...
public class BackOfficeImpl extends JmsGatewaySupport implements BackOffice {

    @Transactional
    public Mail receiveMail() {
        ...
    }
}
```

Then, in both bean configuration files, you add the `<tx:annotation-driven />` element and declare a transaction manager. The corresponding transaction manager for local JMS transactions is `JmsTransactionManager`, which requires a reference to the JMS connection factory.

```
<beans xmlns="http://www.springframework.org/schema/beans"
    xmlns:xsi="http://www.w3.org/2001/XMLSchema-instance"
    xmlns:tx="http://www.springframework.org/schema/tx"
    xsi:schemaLocation="http://www.springframework.org/schema/beans
        http://www.springframework.org/schema/beans/spring-beans-3.0.xsd
        http://www.springframework.org/schema/tx
        http://www.springframework.org/schema/tx/spring-tx-3.0.xsd">
    ...
    <tx:annotation-driven />

    <bean id="transactionManager"
        class="org.springframework.jms.connection.JmsTransactionManager">
        <property name="connectionFactory">
            <ref bean="connectionFactory" />
        </property>
    </bean>
</beans>
```

If you require transaction management across multiple resources, such as a data source and an ORM resource factory, or if you need distributed transaction management, you have to configure JTA transaction in your application server and use `JtaTransactionManager`. Of course, your JMS connection factory must be XA compliant (i.e., supporting distributed transactions).

19-4. Creating Message-Driven POJOs in Spring

Problem

When you call the `receive()` method on a JMS message consumer to receive a message, the calling thread is blocked until a message is available. The thread can do nothing but wait. This type of message reception is called *synchronous reception*, because your application must wait for the message to arrive before it can finish its work.

Starting with EJB 2.0, a new kind of EJB component called a *message-driven bean (MDB)* was introduced for *asynchronous reception* of JMS messages. An EJB container can listen for JMS messages at a message destination and trigger MDBs to react to these messages so that your application no longer has to wait for messages. In EJB 2.x, besides being a nonabstract, nonfinal public class with a public constructor and no `finalize` method, an MDB must implement both the `javax.ejb.MessageDrivenBean` and `javax.jms.MessageListener` interfaces and override all EJB life cycle methods (`ejbCreate` and `ejbRemove`). In EJB 3.0, an MDB can be a POJO that implements the `MessageListener` interface and is annotated with the `@MessageDriven` annotation.

Although MDBs can listen for JMS messages, they must be deployed in an EJB container to run. You may prefer to add the same capability to POJOs so that they can listen for JMS messages without an EJB container.

Solution

Spring allows beans declared in its IoC container to listen for JMS messages in the same way as MDBs. Because Spring adds message-listening capabilities to POJOs, they are called *message-driven POJOs (MDPs)*.

How It Works

Suppose that you want to add an electronic board to the post office's back office to display mail information in real time as it arrives from the front desk. As the front desk sends a JMS message along with mail, the back office subsystem can listen for these messages and display them on the electronic board. For better system performance, you should apply the asynchronous JMS reception approach to avoid blocking the thread that receives these JMS messages.

Listening for JMS Messages with Message Listeners

First, you create a message listener to listen for JMS messages. This negates the need for the approach taken in `BackOfficeImpl` in previous recipes. For example, the following `MailListener` listens for JMS messages that contain mail information:

```
package com.apress.springrecipes.post;

import javax.jms.JMSException;
import javax.jms.MapMessage;
import javax.jms.Message;
import javax.jms.MessageListener;

import org.springframework.jms.support.JmsUtils;

public class MailListener implements MessageListener {

    public void onMessage(Message message) {
        MapMessage mapMessage = (MapMessage) message;
        try {
            Mail mail = new Mail();
            mail.setMailId(mapMessage.getString("mailId"));
            mail.setCountry(mapMessage.getString("country"));
            mail.setWeight(mapMessage.getDouble("weight"));
            displayMail(mail);
        } catch (JMSException e) {
            throw JmsUtils.convertJmsAccessException(e);
        }
    }

    private void displayMail(Mail mail) {
        System.out.println("Mail #" + mail.getMailId() + " received");
    }
}
```

A message listener must implement the `javax.jms.MessageListener` interface. When a JMS message arrives, the `onMessage()` method will be called with the message as the method argument. In this sample, you simply display the mail information to the console. Note that when extracting message information from a `MapMessage` object, you need to handle the JMS API's `JMSException`. You can make a call to `JmsUtils.convertJmsAccessException()` to convert it into Spring's runtime exception `JmsException`.

Next, you have to configure this listener in the back office's bean configuration file. Declaring this listener alone is not enough to listen for JMS messages. You need a message listener container to monitor JMS messages at a message destination and trigger your message listener on message arrival.

```
<beans xmlns="http://www.springframework.org/schema/beans"
    xmlns:xsi="http://www.w3.org/2001/XMLSchema-instance"
    xsi:schemaLocation="http://www.springframework.org/schema/beans
        http://www.springframework.org/schema/beans/spring-beans-3.0.xsd">

    <bean id="connectionFactory"
        class="org.apache.activemq.ActiveMQConnectionFactory">
        <property name="brokerURL" value="tcp://localhost:61616" />
    </bean>
```

```
<bean id="mailListener"
    class="com.apress.springrecipes.post.MailListener" />

<bean
    class="org.springframework.jms.listener.SimpleMessageListenerContainer">
    <property name="connectionFactory" ref="connectionFactory" />
    <property name="destinationName" value="mail.queue" />
    <property name="messageListener" ref="mailListener" />
</bean>
</beans>
```

Spring provides several types of message listener containers for you to choose from in the `org.springframework.jms.listener` package, of which `SimpleMessageListenerContainer` and `DefaultMessageListenerContainer` are the most commonly used. `SimpleMessageListenerContainer` is the simplest one that doesn't support transaction. If you have a transaction requirement in receiving messages, you have to use `DefaultMessageListenerContainer`.

Now, you can start your message listener with the following main class, which starts the Spring IoC container only:

```
package com.apress.springrecipes.post;

import org.springframework.context.support.ClassPathXmlApplicationContext;

public class BackOfficeMain {

    public static void main(String[] args) {
        new ClassPathXmlApplicationContext("beans-back.xml");
    }
}
```

Listening for JMS Messages with POJOs

While a listener that implements the `MessageListener` interface can listen for messages, so can an arbitrary bean declared in the Spring IoC container. Doing so means that beans are decoupled from the Spring framework interfaces as well as the JMS `MessageListener` interface. For a method of this bean to be triggered on message arrival, it must accept one of the following types as its sole method argument:

> *Raw JMS message type*: For `TextMessage`, `MapMessage`, `BytesMessage`, and `ObjectMessage`
>
> *String*: For `TextMessage` only
>
> *Map*: For `MapMessage` only
>
> *byte[]*: For `BytesMessage` only
>
> *Serializable*: For `ObjectMessage` only

For example, to listen for `MapMessage`, you declare a method that accepts a map as its argument. This listener no longer needs to implement the `MessageListener` interface.

```
package com.apress.springrecipes.post;
...
public class MailListener {

    public void displayMail(Map map) {
        Mail mail = new Mail();
        mail.setMailId((String) map.get("mailId"));
        mail.setCountry((String) map.get("country"));
        mail.setWeight((Double) map.get("weight"));
        System.out.println("Mail #" + mail.getMailId() + " received");
    }
}
```

A POJO is registered to a listener container through a `MessageListenerAdapter` instance. This adapter implements the `MessageListener` interface and will delegate message handling to the target bean's method via reflection.

```
<beans ...>
    ...
    <bean id="mailListener"
        class="com.apress.springrecipes.post.MailListener" />

    <bean id="mailListenerAdapter"
        class="org.springframework.jms.listener.adapter.MessageListenerAdapter">
        <property name="delegate" ref="mailListener" />
        <property name="defaultListenerMethod" value="displayMail" />
    </bean>

    <bean
        class="org.springframework.jms.listener.SimpleMessageListenerContainer">
        <property name="connectionFactory" ref="connectionFactory" />
        <property name="destinationName" value="mail.queue" />
        <property name="messageListener" ref="mailListenerAdapter" />
    </bean>
</beans>
```

You have to set the `delegate` property of `MessageListenerAdapter` to your target bean. By default, this adapter will call the method whose name is `handleMessage` on that bean. If you want to call another method, you can specify it in the `defaultListenerMethod` property. Finally, notice that you have to register the listener adapter, not the target bean, with the listener container.

Converting JMS Messages

You can also create a message converter for converting mail objects from JMS messages that contain mail information. Because message listeners receive messages only, the method `toMessage()` will not be called, so you can simply return `null` for it. However, if you use this message converter for sending messages too, you have to implement this method. The following example reprints the `MailMessageConvertor` class written earlier:

```
package com.apress.springrecipes.post;

import javax.jms.JMSException;
import javax.jms.MapMessage;
import javax.jms.Message;
import javax.jms.Session;

import org.springframework.jms.support.converter.MessageConversionException;
import org.springframework.jms.support.converter.MessageConverter;

public class MailMessageConverter implements MessageConverter {

    public Object fromMessage(Message message) throws JMSException,
            MessageConversionException {
        MapMessage mapMessage = (MapMessage) message;
        Mail mail = new Mail();
        mail.setMailId(mapMessage.getString("mailId"));
        mail.setCountry(mapMessage.getString("country"));
        mail.setWeight(mapMessage.getDouble("weight"));
        return mail;
    }

    public Message toMessage(Object object, Session session) throws JMSException,
            MessageConversionException {
        ...
    }
}
```

A message converter should be applied to a listener adapter for it to convert messages into objects before calling your POJO's methods.

```
<beans ...>
    ...
    <bean id="mailMessageConverter"
        class="com.apress.springrecipes.post.MailMessageConverter" />

    <bean id="mailListenerAdapter"
        class="org.springframework.jms.listener.adapter.MessageListenerAdapter">
        <property name="delegate" ref="mailListener" />
        <property name="defaultListenerMethod" value="displayMail" />
        <property name="messageConverter" ref="mailMessageConverter" />
    </bean>
</beans>
```

With this message converter, the listener method of your POJO can accept a mail object as the method argument.

```
package com.apress.springrecipes.post;

public class MailListener {

    public void displayMail(Mail mail) {
        System.out.println("Mail #" + mail.getMailId() + " received");
    }
}
```

Managing JMS Transactions

As mentioned before, `SimpleMessageListenerContainer` doesn't support transactions. So, if you need transaction management for your message listener method, you have to use `DefaultMessageListenerContainer` instead. For local JMS transactions, you can simply enable its `sessionTransacted` property, and your listener method will run within a local JMS transaction (as opposed to XA transactions).

```xml
<bean
    class="org.springframework.jms.listener.DefaultMessageListenerContainer">
    <property name="connectionFactory" ref="connectionFactory" />
    <property name="destinationName" value="mail.queue" />
    <property name="messageListener" ref="mailListenerAdapter" />
    <property name="sessionTransacted" value="true" />
</bean>
```

However, if you want your listener to participate in a JTA transaction, you need to declare a `JtaTransactionManager` instance and inject it into your listener container.

Using Spring's JMS Schema

Spring, from 2.5 and onward, offers a new JMS schema to simplify your JMS listener and listener container configuration. You must add the `jms` schema definition to the `<beans>` root element beforehand.

```xml
<beans xmlns="http://www.springframework.org/schema/beans"
    xmlns:xsi="http://www.w3.org/2001/XMLSchema-instance"
    xmlns:jms="http://www.springframework.org/schema/jms"
    xsi:schemaLocation="http://www.springframework.org/schema/beans
        http://www.springframework.org/schema/beans/spring-beans-3.0.xsd
        http://www.springframework.org/schema/jms
        http://www.springframework.org/schema/jms/spring-jms-3.0.xsd">

    <bean id="connectionFactory"
        class="org.apache.activemq.ActiveMQConnectionFactory">
        <property name="brokerURL" value="tcp://localhost:61616" />
    </bean>
```

```
<bean id="transactionManager"
    class="org.springframework.jms.connection.JmsTransactionManager">
    <property name="connectionFactory">
        <ref bean="connectionFactory" />
    </property>
</bean>

<bean id="mailMessageConverter"
    class="com.apress.springrecipes.post.MailMessageConverter" />

<bean id="mailListener"
    class="com.apress.springrecipes.post.MailListener" />

<jms:listener-container
    connection-factory="connectionFactory"
    transaction-manager="transactionManager"
    message-converter="mailMessageConverter">
    <jms:listener
        destination="mail.queue"
        ref="mailListener" method="displayMail" />
</jms:listener-container>
</beans>
```

Actually, you don't need to specify the `connection-factory` attribute for a listener container explicitly if your JMS connection factory's name is `connectionFactory`, which can be located by default.

19-5. Making the Connection

Problem

Throughout this chapter, for the sake of simplicity, we've explored using Spring's JMS support with a very simple instance of `org.apache.activemq.ActiveMQConnectionFactory` as our connection factory. This isn't the best choice in practice. As with all things, there are performance considerations. In this recipe, we will discuss these considerations. Part of the issue stems from the judicious resource management task the Spring `JmsTemplate` performs on behalf of the client. The crux of it is that `JmsTemplate` closes sessions and consumers on each invocation. This means that it tears down all those objects and restores frees the memory. This is "safe," but not performant, as some of the objects created—like Consumers—are meant to be long lived. This behavior stems from the use of the `JmsTemplate` in EJB-like environments, where typically the application server's Connection Factory is used, and it, internally, provides connection pooling. In this environment, restoring all the objects simply returns it to the pool, which is the desirable behavior.

Solution

There's no "one size fits all" solution to this. You need to weigh the qualities you're looking for and react appropriately.

How It Works

Generally, you want a connection factory that provides pooling and caching of some sort when publishing messages using `JmsTemplate`. The first place to look for a pooled connection factory might be your application server (if you're using one). It may very well provide one by default.

In the examples in this chapter ,we use ActiveMQ in a stand-alone configuration. ActiveMQ, like many vendors, provides a pooled connection factory class alternative (ActiveMQ provides two, actually: one for use consuming messages with a JCA connector and another one for use outside of a JCA container), we can use these instead to handle caching producers and sessions when sending messages. The following configuration pools a connection factory in a stand-alone configuration. It is a drop-in replacement for the previous examples when publishing messages.

```
<bean id="connectionFactory" class="org.apache.activemq.pool.PooledConnectionFactory"
    destroy-method="stop">
  <property name="connectionFactory">
    <bean class="org.apache.activemq.ActiveMQConnectionFactory">
      <property name="brokerURL">
        <value>tcp://localhost:61616</value>
      </property>
    </bean>
  </property>
</bean>
```

If you are receiving messages, you could still stand some more efficiency, because the `JmsTemplate` constructs a new `MessageConsumer` each time as well. In this situation, you have a few alternatives: use Spring's various `*MessageListenerContainer` implementations mechanism (MDPs), because it caches consumers correctly, or use Spring's `ConnectionFactory` implementations. The first implementation, `org.springframework.jms.connection.SingleConnectionFactory`, returns the same underlying JMS connection each time (which is thread-safe according to the JMS API) and ignores calls to the `close()` method. Generally, this implementation works well with the JMS 1.0.2 API *and* the JMS 1.1 API. A much newer alternative is the `org.springframework.jms.connection.CachingConnectionFactory`. This one works only with the 1.1 API but has a few advantages. First, the obvious advantage is that it provides the ability to cache multiple instances. Second, it caches sessions, `MessageProducers`, and `MessageConsumers`. This makes the `JmsTemplate` a suitable choice for all messaging needs, even if you can't use the `MessageListenerContainer`.

Summary

This chapter explored Spring's support for JMS: how JMS fits in an architecture and how to use Spring to build message-oriented architectures. You learned how to both produce and consume messages using a message queue. You worked with Active MQ, a reliable open source message queue. Finally, you learned how to build message-driven POJOs.

The next chapter will explore Spring Integration, which is an ESB-like framework for building application integration solutions, similar to Mule ESB and ServiceMix. You will be able to leverage the knowledge gained in this chapter to take your message-oriented applications to new heights with Spring integration.

■ ■ ■

CHAPTER 20

Spring Integration

In this chapter, you will learn the principles behind enterprise application integration (EAI), used by many modern applications to decouple dependencies between components. The Spring framework provides a powerful and extensible framework called Spring Integration. Spring Integration provides the same level of decoupling for disparate systems and data that the core Spring framework provides for components within an application.

This chapter aims to give you all the required knowledge to understand the patterns involved in *EAI*, to understand what an *enterprise service bus (ESB)* is, and - ultimately - how to build solutions using Spring Integration. If you've used an EAI server or an ESB, you'll find that Spring Integration is markedly simpler than anything you're likely to have used before.

After finishing this chapter, you will be able to write fairly sophisticated Spring Integration solutions to integrate applications, to let them to share services and data. You will learn Spring Integration's many options for configuration, too. Spring Integration can be configured entirely in a standard XML namespace, if you like, but you'll probably find that a hybrid approach, using annotations and XML, is more natural. You will also learn why Spring Integration is a very attractive alternative for people coming from a classic enterprise application integration background. If you've used an ESB before, such as Mule or ServiceMix, or a classical EAI server such as Axway's Integrator or TIBCO's ActiveMatrix, the idioms explained here should be familiar, and the configuration refreshingly straightforward.

■ **Note** To use Spring Integration, you need to have the requisite framework libraries and adapters on the classpath. If you are using Apache Maven, you should add - at a minimum for this chapter - the following dependencies to your project.

```
<dependency>
  <groupId>org.springframework.integration</groupId>
  <artifactId>spring-integration-core</artifactId>
  <version>1.0.3.RELEASE</version>
</dependency>
```

```
<dependency>
  <groupId>org.springframework.integration</groupId>
  <artifactId>spring-integration-httpinvoker</artifactId>
  <version>1.0.3.RELEASE</version>
</dependency>

<dependency>
  <groupId>org.springframework.integration</groupId>
  <artifactId>spring-integration-file</artifactId>
  <version>1.0.3.RELEASE</version>
</dependency>

<dependency>
  <groupId>org.springframework.integration</groupId>
  <artifactId>spring-integration-jms</artifactId>
  <version>1.0.3.RELEASE</version>
</dependency>

<dependency>
  <groupId>org.springframework.integration</groupId>
  <artifactId>spring-integration-adapter</artifactId>
  <version>1.0.3.RELEASE</version>
</dependency>
```

20-1. Integrating One System with Another Using EAI

Problem

You have two applications that need to talk to each other through external interfaces. You need to establish a connection between the applications' services and/or their data.

Solution

You need to employ *enterprise application integration (EAI)*, which is the discipline of integrating applications and data using a set of well-known patterns. These patterns are usefully summarized and embodied in a landmark book called *Enterprise Integration Patterns*, by Gregor Hohpe, Bobby Woolf, et al. Today the patterns are canonical and are the lingua franca of the modern-day ESB.

How It Works

Picking an Integration Style

There are multiple integration styles, each best suited for certain types of applications and requirements. The basic premise is simple: your application can't speak directly to the other system using the native mechanism in one system. So you can devise a bridging connection, something to build on top of, abstract, or work around some characteristic about the other system in a way that's advantageous to the invoking system. What you abstract is different for each application. Sometimes it's the location, sometimes it's the synchronous or asynchronous nature of the call, and sometimes it's the messaging protocol. There are many criteria for choosing an integration style, related to how tightly coupled you want your application to be, to server affinity, to the demands of the messaging formats, and so on. In a way, TCP/IP is the most famous of all integration techniques because it decouples one application from another's server.

You have probably built applications that use some or all of the following integration styles (using Spring, no less!). Shared Database, for example, is easily achieved using Spring's JDBC support; Remote Procedure Invocation is easily achieved using Spring's exporter functionality.

The four integration styles are as follows:

- *File transfer.* Have each application produce files of shared data for others to consume and consume files that others have produced.

- *Shared database.* Have the applications store the data they want to share in a common database. This usually takes the form of a database to which different applications have access. This is not usually a favored approach because it means exposing your data to different clients who might not respect the constraints you have in place (but not codified). Using views and stored procedures can often make this option possible, but it's not ideal. There's no particular support for talking to a database, per se, but you can build an endpoint that deals with new results in a SQL database as message payloads. Integration with databases doesn't tend to be granular or message-oriented, but batch-oriented instead. After all, a million new rows in a database isn't an event so much as a batch! It's no surprise then that Spring Batch (discussed in Chapter 21) included terrific support for JDBC-oriented input and output.

- *Remote Procedure Invocation.* Have each application expose some of its procedures so that they can be invoked remotely and have applications invoke them to initiate behavior and exchange data. There is specific support for optimizing RPC (remote procedure calls such as SOAP, RMI, and HTTP Invoker) exchanges using Spring Integration.

- *Messaging.* Have each application connect to a common messaging system and exchange data and invoke behavior using messages. This style, most enabled by JMS in the JEE world, also describes other asynchronous or multicast publish/subscribe architectures. In a way, an ESB or an EAI container such as Spring Integration lets you handle most of the other styles as though you were dealing with a messaging queue: a request comes in on a queue and is managed, responded to, or forwarded onward on another queue.

Building on an ESB Solution

Now that you know how you want to approach the integration, it's all about actually implementing it. You have many choices in today's world. If the requirement is common enough, most middleware or frameworks will accommodate it in some way. JEE, .NET, and others handle common cases very well: SOAP, XMLRPC, a binary layer such as EJB or binary remoting, JMS, or a MQ abstraction. If, however, the requirement is somewhat exotic, or you have a lot of configuration to do, then perhaps an ESB is required. An ESB is middleware that provides a high-level approach to modeling integrations, in the spirit of the patterns described by EAI. The ESB provides and manageable configuration format for orchestrating the different pieces of an integration in a simple high-level format.

Spring Integration, an API in the SpringSource Portfolio, provides a robust mechanism for modeling a lot of these integration scenarios that work well with Spring. Spring Integration has many advantages over a lot of other ESBs, especially the lightweight nature of the framework. The nascent ESB market is filled with choices. Some are former EAI servers, reworked to address the ESB-centric architectures. Some are genuine ESBs, built with that in mind. Some are little more than message queues with adapters.

Indeed, if you're looking for an extraordinarily powerful EAI server (with almost integration with the JEE platform and a very hefty price tag), you might consider Axway Integrator. There's very little it can't do. Vendors such as TIBCO and WebMethods made their marks (and were subsequently acquired) because they provided excellent tools for dealing with integration in the enterprise. These options, although powerful, are usually very expensive and middleware-centric: your integrations are deployed to the middleware.

Standardization attempts, such as Java Business Integration (JBI), have proven successful to an extent, and there are good compliant ESBs based on these standards (OpenESB and ServiceMix for example). One of the thought leaders in the ESB market is the Mule ESB, which has a good reputation; it is free/open source friendly, community-friendly, and lightweight. These characteristics also make Spring Integration attractive. Often, you simply need to talk to another open system, and you don't want to requisition a purchase approval for middleware that's more expensive than some houses!

Each Spring Integration application is completely embedded and needs no server infrastructure. In fact, you could deploy an integration inside another application, perhaps in your web application endpoint. Spring Integration flips the deployment paradigms of most ESBs on their head: you deploy Spring Integration into your application; you don't deploy your application into Spring Integration. There are no start and stop scripts and no ports to guard.

The simplest possible working Spring Integration application is a simple Java `public static void main()` method to bootstrap a Spring context:

```
package com.apress.springrecipes.springintegration;

import org.springframework.context.support.ClassPathXmlApplicationContext;

public class Main {
    public static void main(String [] args){
        String nameOfSpringIntegrationXmlConfigurationFile = args[0];
        ClassPathXmlApplicationContext applicationContext = new ↩
ClassPathXmlApplicationContext(
                nameOfSpringIntegrationXmlConfigurationFile) ;
        applicationContext.start();
    }
}
```

You created a standard Spring application context and started it. The contents of the Spring application context will be discussed in subsequent recipes, but it's helpful to see how simple it is. You might decide to hoist the context up in a web application, an EJB container, or anything else you want. Indeed, you can use Spring Integration to power the e-mail polling functionality in a Swing/JavaFX application! It's as lightweight as you want it to be.

In subsequent examples, the configuration shown should be put in an XML file and that XML file referenced as the first parameter when running this class. When the main method runs to completion, your context will start up the Spring Integration bus and start responding to requests on the components configured in the application context's XML.

20-2. Integrating Two Systems Using JMS

Problem

You want to build an integration to connect one application to another using JMS, which provides locational and temporal decoupling on modern middleware for Java applications. You're interested in applying more sophisticated routing and want to isolate your code from the specifics of the origin of the message (in this case, the JMS queue or topic).

Solution

While you can do this by using regular JMS code or EJB's support for message-driven beans (MDBs), or using core Spring's message-driven POJO (MDP) support, all are necessarily coded for handling messages coming specifically from JMS. Your code is tied to JMS. Using an ESB lets you hide the origin of the message from the code that's handling it. You'll use this solution as an easy way to see how a Spring Integration solution can be built. Spring Integration provides an easy way to work with JMS, just as you might using MDPs in the core Spring container. Here, however, you could conceivably replace the JMS middleware with an e-mail, and the code that reacts to the message could stay the same.

How it Works

Building an Message Driven Pojo (MDP) Using Spring Integration

As you recall from Chapter 19, Spring can replace EJB's MDB functionality by using MDPs. This is a powerful solution for anyone wanting to build something that handles messages on a message queue. You'll build an MDP, but you will configure it using Spring Integration's more concise configuration and provide an example of a very rudimentary integration. All this integration will do is take an inbound JMS message (whose payload is of type `Map<String,Object>`).

As with a standard MDP, configuration for the `ConnectionFactory` exists. There's also a lot of other schema required for using the configuration elements available in Spring Integration. Shown following is a configuration file. You can store in on the classpath and pass it in as a parameter to the Spring `ApplicationContext` on creation (as you did in the previous recipe, in the `Main` class.)

```xml
<?xml version="1.0" encoding="UTF-8"?>

<beans:beans xmlns:beans="http://www.springframework.org/schema/beans"
             xmlns:xsi="http://www.w3.org/2001/XMLSchema-instance"
             xmlns="http://www.springframework.org/schema/integration"
             xmlns:context="http://www.springframework.org/schema/context"
             xmlns:jms="http://www.springframework.org/schema/integration/jms"
             xsi:schemaLocation="http://www.springframework.org/schema/beans
http://www.springframework.org/schema/beans/spring-beans-3.0.xsd
http://www.springframework.org/schema/context
http://www.springframework.org/schema/context/spring-context-3.0.xsd
http://www.springframework.org/schema/integration
http://www.springframework.org/schema/integration/spring-integration-1.0.xsd
http://www.springframework.org/schema/integration/jms
http://www.springframework.org/schema/integration/jms/spring-integration-
jms-1.0.xsd">

    <context:annotation-config/>

    <beans:bean id="connectionFactory"  class="org.springframework.↵
jms.connection.CachingConnectionFactory">
        <beans:property name="targetConnectionFactory">
            <beans:bean class="org.apache.activemq.ActiveMQConnectionFactory">
                <beans:property name="brokerURL" value="tcp://localhost:8753"/>
            </beans:bean>
        </beans:property>
        <beans:property name="sessionCacheSize" value="10"/>
        <beans:property name="cacheProducers" value="false"/>
    </beans:bean>

    <beans:bean id="inboundHelloWorldJMSPingServiceActivator"
class="com.apress.springrecipes.springintegration.↵
InboundHelloWorldJMSMessageProcessor"/>

    <channel id="inboundHelloJMSMessageChannel"/>

    <jms:message-driven-channel-adapter
        channel="inboundHelloJMSMessageChannel"
        extract-payload="true"
        connection-factory="connectionFactory"
        destination-name="solution011"/>

    <service-activator input-channel="inboundHelloJMSMessageChannel"
ref="inboundHelloWorldJMSPingServiceActivator"/>
</beans:beans>
```

As you can see, the most intimidating part is the schema import! The rest of the code is standard boilerplate. You define a connectionFactory exactly as if you were configuring a standard MDP.

Then, you define any beans specific to this solution: in this case a bean that responds to messages coming in to the bus from the message queue, inboundHelloWorldJMSPingServiceActivator. A service-activator is a generic endpoint in Spring Integration that's used to invoke functionality whether it be an operation in a service, or some routine in a regular POJO, or anything you want instead in response to a message sent in on an input channel. Although this will be covered in some detail, it's interesting here only because you are using it to respond to messages. These beans taken together are the collaborators in the solution, and this example is fairly representative of how most integrations look: you define your collaborating components; then you define the configuration using Spring Integration schema that configures the solution itself.

The configuration starts with the inboundHelloJMSMessageChannel channel, which tells Spring Integration what to name the point-to-point connection from the message queue to the service-activator. You typically define a new channel for every point-to-point connection.

Next is a jms:message-driven-channel-adapter configuration element that instructs Spring Integration to send messages coming from the message queue destination solution011 to Spring Integration inboundHelloJMSMessageChannel. An *adapter* is a component that knows how to speak to a specific type of subsystem and translate messages on that subsystem into something that can be used in the Spring Integration bus. Adapters also do the same in reverse, taking messages on the Spring Integration bus and translating them into something a specific subsystem will understand. This is different from a service-activator (covered next) in that it's meant to be a general connection between the bus and the foreign endpoint. A service-activator, however, only helps you invoke your application's business logic on receipt of a message. What you do in the business logic, connecting to another system or not, is up to you.

The next component, a service-activator, listens for messages coming into that channel and invokes the bean referenced by the ref attribute, which in this case is the bean defined previously: inboundHelloWorldJMSPingServiceActivator.

As you can see, there's quite a bit of configuration, but the only custom Java code needed was the inboundHelloWorldJMSPingServiceActivator, which is the part of the solution that Spring can't infer by itself.

```
package com.apress.springrecipes.springintegration;

import org.apache.log4j.Logger;
import org.springframework.integration.annotation.ServiceActivator;
import org.springframework.integration.core.Message;
import java.util.Map;

public class InboundHelloWorldJMSMessageProcessor {
    private static final Logger logger =
Logger.getLogger(
InboundHelloWorldJMSMessageProcessor.class);

    @ServiceActivator
    public void handleIncomingJmsMessage(
        Message<Map<String, Object>> inboundJmsMessage
        ) throws Throwable {
        Map<String, Object> msg = inboundJmsMessage.getPayload();
        logger.debug(String.format(
```

```
        "firstName: %s, lastName: %s, id:%s",
        msg.get("firstName"), msg.get("lastName"),  ↵
        msg.get("id")));

// you can imagine what we could do here: put
// the record into the database, call a websrvice,
// write it to a file, etc, etc

    }
}
```

Notice that there is an annotation, @ServiceActivator, that tells Spring to configure this component, and this method as the recipient of the message payload from the channel, which is passed to the method as Message<Map<String, Object>> inboundJmsMessage. In the previous configuration, extract-payload="true", which tells Spring Integration to take the payload of the message from the JMS queue (in this case, a Map<String,Object>) and extract it and pass *that* as the payload of the message that's being moved through Spring Integration's channels as a org.springframework.integration.core.Message<T>. The Spring Integration Message is not to be confused with the JMS Message interface, although they have some similarities. Had you not specified the extract-payload option, the type of payload on the Spring Integration Message interface would have been javax.jms.Message. The onus of extracting the payload would have been on you, the developer, but sometimes getting access to that information is useful. Rewritten to handle unwrapping the javax.jms.Message, the example would look a little different:

```
package com.apress.springrecipes.springintegration;

import org.apache.log4j.Logger;
import org.springframework.integration.annotation.ServiceActivator;
import org.springframework.integration.core.Message;
import java.util.Map;

public class InboundHelloWorldJMSMessageProcessor {
    private static final Logger logger =
Logger.getLogger(InboundHelloWorldJMSMessageProcessor.class);

  @ServiceActivator
    public void handleIncomingJmsMessageWithPayloadNotExtracted(
            Message<javax.jms.Message> msgWithJmsMessageAsPayload
    ) throws Throwable {
        javax.jms.MapMessage jmsMessage = (MapMessage)↵
msgWithJmsMessageAsPayload.getPayload();
        logger.debug(String.format("firstName: %s, lastName: %s, id:%s",
jmsMessage.getString("firstName"),
                jmsMessage.getString("lastName"), jmsMessage.getLong("id")));
    }
}
```

You could have specified the payload type as the type of the parameter passed into the method. If the payload of the message coming from JMS was of type `Cat`, for example, the method prototype could just as well have been `public void handleIncomingJmsMessageWithPayloadNotExtracted( Cat inboundJmsMessage) throws Throwable`. Spring Integration will figure out the right thing to do. In this case, we prefer access to the Spring Integration `Message<T>`, which has header values that can be useful to interrogate.

Also note that you don't need to specify `throws Throwable`. Error handling can be as generic or as specific as you want in Spring Integration.

In the example, you use the `@ServiceActivator` to invoke the functionality where the integration ends. However, you can forward the response from the activation on to the next channel by returning a value from the method. The type of the return value is what will be used to determine the next message sent in the system. If you return a `Message<T>`, that will be sent directly. If you return something other than `Message<T>`, that value will be wrapped as a payload in a `Message<T>` instance, and that will become the next Message that is ultimately sent to the next component in the processing pipeline. This `Message<T>` will be sent on the output channel that's configured on the `service-activator`. There is no requirement to send a message on the output channel with the same type as the message that came on in the input channel; this is an effective way to *transform* the message type. A `service-activator` is a very flexible component in which to put hooks to your system and to help mold the integration.

This solution is pretty straightforward, and in terms of configuration for one JMS queue, it's not really a win over straight MDPs because there's an extra level of indirection to overcome. The Spring Integration facilities make building complex integrations easier than Spring Core or EJB3 could because the configuration is centralized. You have a birds-eye view of the entire integration, with routing and processing centralized, so you can better reposition the components in your integration. However, as you'll see, Spring Integration wasn't meant to compete with EJB and Spring Core; it shines at solutions that couldn't naturally be built using EJB3 or Spring Core.

20-3. Interrogating Spring Integration Messages for Context Information

Problem

You want more information about the message coming into the Spring Integration processing pipeline than the type of the message implicitly can give you.

Solution

Interrogate the Spring Integration `Message<T>` for header information specific to the message. These values are enumerated as header values in a map (of type `Map<String,Object>`).

How it Works

Using MessageHeaders for Fun and Profit

The Spring Integration Message<T> interface is a generic wrapper that contains a pointer to the actual payload of the message as well as to headers that provide contextual message metadata. You can manipulate or augment this metadata to enable/enhance the functionality of components that are downstream, too; for example, when sending a message through e-mail it's useful to specify the TO/FROM headers.

Any time you expose a class to the framework to handle some requirement (such as the logic you provide for the service-activator component or a transformer component), there will be some chance to interact with the Message<T> and with the message headers. Remember that Spring Integration pushes a Message<T> through a processing pipeline. Each component that interfaces with the Message<T> instance has to act on it, do something with it, or forward it on. One way of providing information to those components, and of getting information about what's happened in the components up until that point, is to interrogate the MessageHeaders.

There are several values that you should be aware of when working with Spring Integration (see Table 20-1). These constants are exposed on the org.springframework.integration.core.MessageHeaders interface.

Table 20-1. *Some Common Headers Found in Spring Integration Messages*

Constant	Description
ID	This is a unique value assigned to the message by the Spring Integration engine.
TIMESTAMP	Timestamp assigned to the message.
CORRELATION_ID	This is optional. It is used by some components (such as aggregators) to group messages together in some sort of processing pipeline.
REPLY_CHANNEL	The String name of the channel to which the output of the current component should be sent. This can be overridden.
ERROR_CHANNEL	The String name of the channel to which the output of the current component should be sent if an exception bubbles up into the runtime. This can be overridden.
EXPIRATION_DATE	Used by some components as a threshold for processing after which a component can wait no longer in processing.
SEQUENCE_NUMBER	The order in which the message is to be sequenced; typically used with a sequencer.
SEQUENCE_SIZE	The size of the sequence so that an aggregator can know when to stop waiting for more messages and move forward. This is useful in implementing "join" functionality.

Some header values are specific to the type of the source message's payload; for example, payloads sourced from a file on the file system are different from those coming in from a JMS queue, which are different from messages coming from an e-mail system. These different components are typically packaged in their own JARs, and there's usually some class that provides constants for accessing these headers. An example of component-specific headers are the constants defined for files on `org.springframework.integration.file.FileHeaders`: `FILENAME` and `PREFIX`. Naturally, when in doubt, you can just enumerate the values manually because the headers are just a `java.util.Map` instance.

```java
public void interrogateMessage(Message<?> message) {
        MessageHeaders headers = message.getHeaders();
        for (String key : headers.keySet()) {
            logger.debug(String.format("%s : %s", key, headers.get(key)));
        }
    }
```

These headers let you interrogate the specific features of these messages without surfacing them as a concrete interface dependency if you don't want them. They can also be used to help processing and allow you to specify custom metadata to downstream components. The act of providing extra data for the benefit of a downstream component is called *message enrichment*. Message enrichment is when you take the headers of a given `Message` and add to them, usually to the benefit of components in the processing pipeline downstream. You might imagine processing a message to add a customer to a customer relationship management (CRM) system that makes a call to a third-party web site to establish credit ratings. This credit is added to the headers so the component downstream is tasked with either adding the customer or rejecting it can make its decisions.

Another way to get access to header metadata is to simply have it passed as parameters to your component's method. You simply annotate the parameter with the `@Header` annotation, and Spring Integration will take care of the rest.

```java
package com.apress.springrecipes.springintegration;

import org.springframework.integration.annotation.Header;
import org.springframework.integration.annotation.ServiceActivator;
import org.springframework.integration.core.MessageHeaders;
import org.springframework.integration.file.FileHeaders;
import org.apache.log4j.Logger;
import java.io.File;

public class InboundFileMessageServiceActivator {
    private static final  Logger logger = Logger.getLogger(
InboundFileMessageServiceActivator.class);

    @ServiceActivator
    public void interrogateMessage(
        @Header(MessageHeaders.ID)   String uuid,
        @Header(FileHeaders.FILENAME) String fileName, File file ) {
        logger.debug(String.format( "the id of the message is %s, and name "+
                                    "of the file payload is %s", uuid, fileName));
    }
}
```

You can also have Spring Integration simply pass the `Map<String,Object>`:

```
package com.apress.springrecipes.springintegration;

import org.springframework.integration.annotation.Headers;
import org.springframework.integration.annotation.ServiceActivator;
import org.springframework.integration.core.MessageHeaders;
import org.springframework.integration.file.FileHeaders;

...

import java.io.File;
import java.util.Map;

public class InboundFileMessageServiceActivatorWithHeadersMap {
    private static final Logger logger = Logger.getLogger(
            InboundFileMessageServiceActivatorWithHeadersMap.class);

    @ServiceActivator
    public void interrogateMessage(
    @Headers Map<String, Object>
 headers, File file) {
        logger.debug(String.format(
                "the id of the message is %s, and name of the file payload is %s",
                    headers.get(MessageHeaders.ID),
                    headers.get(FileHeaders.FILENAME)));
    }
}
```

20-4. Integrating Two Systems Using a File System

Problem

You want to build a solution that takes files on a well-known, shared file system and uses them as the conduit for integration with another system. An example might be that your application produces a comma-separated value (CSV) dump of all the customers added to a system every hour. The company's third-party financial system is updated with these sales by a process that checks a shared folder, mounted over a network file system, and processes the CSV records. What's required is a way to treat the presence of a new file as an event on the bus.

Solution

You have an idea of how this could be built by using standard techniques, but you want something more elegant. Let Spring Integration isolate you from the event-driven nature of the file system and from the file input/output requirements and instead let's use it to focus on writing the code that deals with the `java.io.File` payload itself. With this approach, you can write unit-testable code that accepts an input and responds by adding the customers to the financial system. When the functionality is finished, you configure it in the Spring Integration pipeline and let Spring Integration invoke your functionality whenever a new file is recognized on the file system. This is an example of an event-driven architecture (EDA). EDAs let you ignore how an event was generated and focus instead on reacting to them, in much the same way that event-driven GUIs let you change the focus of your code from controlling how a user triggers an action to actually reacting to the invocation itself. Spring Integration makes it a natural approach for loosely coupled solutions. In fact, this code should look very similar to the solution you built for the JMS queue because it's just another class that takes a parameter (a Spring Integration `Message<T>`, and a parameter of the same type as the payload of the message, and so on).

How It Works

Concerns in Dealing with a File System

Building a solution to talk to JMS is old hat. Instead, let's consider what building a solution using a shared file system might look like. Imagine how to build it without an ESB solution. You need some mechanism by which to poll the file system periodically and detect new files. Perhaps Quartz and some sort of cache? You need something to read in these files quickly and then pass the payload to your processing logic efficiently. Finally, your system needs to work with that payload.

Spring Integration frees you from all that infrastructure code; all you need to do is configure it. There are some issues with dealing with file-system–based processing, however, that are up to you to resolve. Behind the scenes, Spring Integration is still dealing with polling the file system and detecting new files. It can't possibly have a semantically correct idea for your application of when a file is "completely" written, and thus providing a way around that is up to you.

Several approaches exist. You might write out a file and then write another zero-byte file. The presence of that file would mean it's safe to assume that the real payload is present. Configure Spring Integration to look for that file. If it finds it, it knows that there's another file (perhaps with the same name and a different file extension?) and that it can start reading it/working with it. Another solution along the same line is to have the client ("producer") write the file to the directory using a name that the glob pattern Spring Integration is using to poll the directory won't detect. Then, when it's finished writing, issue an `mv` command if you trust your file system to do the right thing there.

Let's revisit the first solution, but this time with a file-based adapter. The configuration looks conceptually the same as before, except the configuration for the adapter has changed, and with that has gone a lot of the configuration for the JMS adapter, like the connection factory. Instead, you tell Spring Integration about a different source from whence messages will come: the file system.

```xml
<?xml version="1.0" encoding="UTF-8"?>

<beans:beans xmlns:beans="http://www.springframework.org/schema/beans"
            xmlns:xsi="http://www.w3.org/2001/XMLSchema-instance"
            xmlns="http://www.springframework.org/schema/integration"
             xmlns:context="http://www.springframework.org/schema/context"
            xmlns:file="http://www.springframework.org/schema/integration/file"
            xsi:schemaLocation="http://www.springframework.org/schema/beans
http://www.springframework.org/schema/beans/
spring-beans-3.0.xsd http://www.springframework.org/schema/context
http://www.springframework.org/schema/context/
spring-context-3.0.xsd http://www.springframework.org/schema/integration
http://www.springframework.org/schema/integration/
```

```
spring-integration-1.0.xsd
http://www.springframework.org/schema/integration/jms
http://www.springframework.org/schema/integration/jms/↵
spring-integration-jms-1.0.xsd http://www.springframework.org/↵
schema/integration/file
http://www.springframework.org/schema/integration/file/↵
spring-integration-file-1.0.xsd">

  <context:annotation-config/>

    <poller id="poller" default="true">
        <interval-trigger time-unit="SECONDS" interval="10"/>
    </poller>

    <beans:bean id="inboundHelloWorldFileMessageProcessor"
        class="com.apress.springrecipes.springintegration.↵
                InboundHelloWorldFileMessageProcessor"/>

    <channel id="inboundFileChannel"/>

    <file:inbound-channel-adapter directory="${user.home}/inboundFiles/new/"
                                    channel="inboundFileChannel"
                                    filename-pattern="^new.*csv"
                                    />
    <service-activator input-channel="inboundFileChannel"↵
ref="inboundHelloWorldFileMessageProcessor"/>

</beans:beans>
```

Nothing you haven't already seen, really. The code for file:inbound-channel-adapter is the only new element, and it comes with its own schema, which is in the prologue for the XML itself.

The code for the service-activator has changed to reflect the fact that you're expecting a message containing a message of type Message<java.io.File>.

```
package com.apress.springrecipes.springintegration;

import org.apache.log4j.Logger;
import org.springframework.integration.annotation.ServiceActivator;
import org.springframework.integration.core.Message;

import java.io.File;

public class InboundHelloWorldFileMessageProcessor {
    private static final Logger logger =
 Logger.getLogger(InboundHelloWorldFileMessageProcessor.class);
```

```
@ServiceActivator
public void handleIncomingFileMessage(
    Message<File> inboundJmsMessage) throws Throwable {
    File filePayload = inboundJmsMessage.getPayload();
    logger.debug(String.format("absolute path: %s, size: %s",
        filePayload.getAbsolutePath(), filePayload.length()));
    }
}
```

20-5. Transforming a Message from One Type to Another

Problem

You want to send a message into the bus and transform it before working with it further. Usually, this is done to adapt the message to the requirements of a component downstream. You might also want to transform a message by enriching it—adding extra headers or augmenting the payload so that components downstream in the processing pipeline can benefit from it.

Solution

Use a `transformer` component to take a `Message<T>` of a payload and send the `Message<T>` out with a payload of a different type. You can also use the transformer to add extra headers or update the values of headers for the benefit of components downstream in the processing pipeline.

How It Works

Spring Integration provides a `transformer` message endpoint to permit the augmentation of the message headers or the transformation of the message itself. In Spring Integration, components are chained together, and output from one component is returned by way of the method invoked for that component. The return value of the method is passed out on the "reply channel" for the component to the next component, which receives it as an input parameter.

A `transformer` component lets you change the type of the object being returned or add extra headers and that updated object is what is passed to the next component in the chain.

Modifying a Message's Payload

The configuration of a transformer component is very much in keeping with everything you've seen so far:

```
package com.apress.springrecipes.springintegration;
import org.springframework.integration.annotation.Transformer;
import org.springframework.integration.core.Message;
import java.util.Map;
```

```java
public class InboundJMSMessageToCustomerTransformer {
    @Transformer
    public Customer transformJMSMapToCustomer(
        Message<Map<String, Object>> inboundSpringIntegrationMessage) {
        Map<String, Object> jmsMessagePayload = ↵
inboundSpringIntegrationMessage.getPayload();
        Customer customer = new Customer();
        customer.setFirstName((String) jmsMessagePayload.get("firstName"));
        customer.setLastName((String) jmsMessagePayload.get("lastName"));
        customer.setId((Long) jmsMessagePayload.get("id"));
        return customer;
    }
}
```

Nothing terribly complex is happening here: a `Message<T>` of type `Map<String,Object>` is passed in. The values are manually extracted and used to build an object of type `Customer`. The `Customer` object is returned, which has the effect of passing it out on the reply channel for this component. The next component in the configuration will receive this object as its input `Message<T>`.

The solution is mostly the same as you've seen, but there is a new **transformer** element:

```xml
<?xml version="1.0" encoding="UTF-8"?>

<beans:beans xmlns:beans="http://www.springframework.org/schema/beans"

 …
>

    <context:annotation-config/>

    <beans:bean id="connectionFactory"
 class="org.springframework.jms.connection.CachingConnectionFactory">
        <beans:property name="targetConnectionFactory">
            <beans:bean class="org.apache.activemq.ActiveMQConnectionFactory">
                <beans:property name="brokerURL" value="tcp://localhost:8753"/>
            </beans:bean>
        </beans:property>
        <beans:property name="sessionCacheSize" value="10"/>
        <beans:property name="cacheProducers" value="false"/>
    </beans:bean>
    <beans:bean id="jmsTemplate" class="org.springframework.jms.core.JmsTemplate">
        <beans:property name="connectionFactory" ref="connectionFactory"/>
    </beans:bean>

    <beans:bean id="inboundJMSMessageToCustomerTransformer"
            class="com.apress.springrecipes.springintegration.↵
InboundJMSMessageToCustomerTransformer"/>
```

```xml
    <beans:bean id="inboundCustomerServiceActivator"
class="com.apress.springrecipes.springintegration. ↵
InboundCustomerServiceActivator"/>
    <channel id="inboundHelloJMSMessageChannel"/>
    <channel id="inboundCustomerChannel"/>
    <jms:message-driven-channel-adapter channel="inbound ↵
HelloJMSMessageChannel" extract-payload="true"  connection-factory ↵
="connectionFactory" destination-name="solution015"/>
    <transformer input-channel="inboundHelloJMSMessageChannel"
ref="inboundJMSMessageToCustomerTransformer" output- ↵
channel="inboundCustomerChannel"/>
    <service-activator input-channel="inboundCustomerChannel"
 ref="inboundCustomerServiceActivator" />

</beans:beans>
```

Here, you're also specifying an `output-channel` attribute on the component, which tells a component on what channel to send the component's response output, in this case, the `Customer`.

The code in the next component can now declare a dependency on the `Customer` interface with impunity. You can, with transformers, receive messages from any number of sources and transform into a `Customer` so that you can reuse the `InboundCustomerServiceActivator`:

```java
package com.apress.springrecipes.springintegration;

import org.apache.log4j.Logger;
import org.springframework.integration.annotation.ServiceActivator;
import org.springframework.integration.core.Message;


public class InboundCustomerServiceActivator {
    private static final Logger logger =
      Logger.getLogger(InboundCustomerServiceActivator.class);

    @ServiceActivator
            public void doSomethingWithCustomer(
                Message<Customer> customerMessage) {
        Customer customer = customerMessage.getPayload();
        logger.debug(String.format("id=%s, firstName:%s, lastName:%s",
                                customer.getId(),
                                customer.getFirstName(),
                                customer.getLastName()));


    }
}
```

Modifying a Message's Headers

Sometimes changing a message's payload isn't enough. Sometimes you want to update the payload as well as the headers. Doing this is slightly more interesting because it involves using the `MessageBuilder<T>` class, which allows you to create new `Message<T>` objects with any specified payload and any specified header data. The XML configuration is identical in this case.

```
package com.apress.springrecipes.springintegration;

import org.springframework.integration.annotation.Transformer;
import org.springframework.integration.core.Message;
import org.springframework.integration.message.MessageBuilder;

import java.util.Map;

public class InboundJMSMessageToCustomerWithExtraMetadataTransformer {
    @Transformer
    public Message<Customer> transformJMSMapToCustomer(
        Message<Map<String, Object>> inboundSpringIntegrationMessage) {
        Map<String, Object> jmsMessagePayload =
                inboundSpringIntegrationMessage.getPayload();
        Customer customer = new Customer();
        customer.setFirstName((String) jmsMessagePayload.get("firstName"));
        customer.setLastName((String) jmsMessagePayload.get("lastName"));
        customer.setId((Long) jmsMessagePayload.get("id"));
        return MessageBuilder.withPayload(customer)
                .copyHeadersIfAbsent( inboundSpringIntegrationMessage.getHeaders())
                .setHeaderIfAbsent("randomlySelectedForSurvey", Math.random() > .5)
                .build();
    }
}
```

As before, this code is simply a method with an input and an output. The output is constructed dynamically using `MessageBuilder<T>` to create a message that has the same payload as the input message as well as copy the existing headers and adds an extra header: `randomlySelectedForSurvey`.

20-6. Error Handling Using Spring Integration

Problem

Spring Integration brings together systems distributed across different nodes; computers; and services, protocol, and language stacks. Indeed, a Spring Integration solution might not even finish in remotely the same time period as when it started. Exception handling, then, can never be as simple as a language-level try/catch block in a single thread for any component with asynchronous behavior. This implies that many of the kinds of solutions you're likely to build, with channels and queues of any kind, need a way of signaling an error that is distributed and natural to the component that created the error. Thus, an error might get sent over a JMS queue on a different continent, or in process, on a queue in a different thread.

Solution

Use Spring Integration's support for an error channel, both implicit and explicitly via code. This solution works only for solutions that employ channels whose messages are received out of the client's thread.

How It Works

Spring Integration provides the ability to catch exceptions and send them to an error channel of your choosing. By default, it's a global channel called `errorChannel`. You can have components subscribe to messages from this channel to override the exception handling behavior. You can create a class that will be invoked whenever a message comes in on the `errorChannel` channel:

```xml
<?xml version="1.0" encoding="UTF-8"?>

<beans:beans xmlns:beans="http://www.springframework.org/schema/beans"
 ...
>

    <context:annotation-config/>

    <beans:bean id="defaultErrorHandlingServiceActivator"
 class="com.apress.springrecipes.springintegration.DefaultError
HandlingServiceActivator"/>

    <service-activator input-channel="errorChannel" ref="defaultErrorHandling↲
ServiceActivator"/>

</beans:beans>
```

The Java code is exactly as you'd expect it to be. Of course, the component that receives the error message from the `errorChannel` doesn't need to be a `service-activator`. We just use it for convenience here. The code for the following `service-activator` depicts some of the machinations you might go through to build a handler for the `errorChannel`:

```java
package com.apress.springrecipes.springintegration;

import org.apache.commons.lang.exception.ExceptionUtils;
import org.apache.log4j.Logger;
import org.springframework.integration.annotation.ServiceActivator;
import org.springframework.integration.core.Message;
import org.springframework.integration.core.MessagingException;

public class DefaultErrorHandlingServiceActivator {
    private static final Logger logger =
      Logger.getLogger( DefaultErrorHandlingServiceActivator.class );

    @ServiceActivator
    public void handleThrowable(Message<Throwable> errorMessage) throws Throwable {
        Throwable throwable = errorMessage.getPayload();
        logger.debug(String.format("message: %s, stack trace :%s",
            throwable.getMessage(),
```

```
            ExceptionUtils.getFullStackTrace(throwable)));
        if (throwable instanceof MessagingException) {
            Message<?> failedMessage =
                ((MessagingException) throwable).getFailedMessage();
            if (failedMessage != null) {
                // do something with the original message
            }
        } else {
            // it's something that was thrown in the
            // execution of code in some component you created
        }
    }
}
```

All errors thrown from Spring Integration components will be a subclass of `MessagingException`. `MessagingException` carries a pointer to the original `Message` that caused an error, which you can dissect for more context information. In the example, you're doing a nasty `instanceof`. Clearly, being able to delegate to custom exception handlers based on the type of exception would be useful.

Routing to Custom Handlers Based on the Type of Exception

Sometimes, more specific error handling is required. One way to discriminate by `Exception` type is to use the `org.springframework.integration.router.ErrorMessageExceptionTypeRouter` class. In the following code, this router is configured as a router component, which in turn listens to `errorChannel`. It then splinters off, using the type of the exception as the predicate in determining which channel should get the results.

```xml
<?xml version="1.0" encoding="UTF-8"?>

<beans:beans xmlns:beans="http://www.springframework.org/schema/beans"
  …
>
    <context:annotation-config/>
    <channel id="customErrorChannelForMyCustomException"/>
    <beans:bean id="myCustomErrorRouter"
  class="org.springframework.integration.router.↵
ErrorMessageExceptionTypeRouter">
        <beans:property name="exceptionTypeChannelMap">
            <beans:map key-type="java.lang.Class">
                <beans:entry
     key="com.apress.springrecipes.springintegration.MyCustomException"
     value-ref="customErrorChannelForMyCustomException" />
            </beans:map>
        </beans:property>
    </beans:bean>
    <router input-channel="errorChannel" ref="myCustomErrorRouter"/>
</beans:beans>
```

Building a Solution with Multiple Error Channels

The preceding example might work fine for simple cases, but often different integrations require different error-handling approaches, which implies that sending all the errors to the same channel can eventually lead to a large switch-laden class that's too complex to maintain. Instead, it's better to selectively route error messages to the error channel most appropriate to each integration. This avoids centralizing all error handling. One way to do that is to explicitly specify on what channel errors for a given integration should go. The following example shows a component (service-activator) that upon receiving a message, adds a header indicating the name of the error channel. Spring Integration will use that header and forward errors encountered in the processing of this message to that channel.

```
package com.apress.springrecipes.springintegration;

import org.apache.log4j.Logger;
import org.springframework.integration.annotation.ServiceActivator;
import org.springframework.integration.core.Message;
import org.springframework.integration.core.MessageHeaders;
import org.springframework.integration.message.MessageBuilder;

public class ServiceActivatorThatSpecifiesErrorChannel {
    private static final Logger logger = Logger.getLogger(
        ServiceActivatorThatSpecifiesErrorChannel.class);

    @ServiceActivator
    public Message<?> startIntegrationFlow(Message<?> firstMessage)
        throws Throwable {
        return MessageBuilder.fromMessage(firstMessage).
            setHeaderIfAbsent( MessageHeaders.ERROR_CHANNEL,
                "errorChannelForMySolution").build();
    }
}
```

Thus, all errors that come from the integration in which this component is used will be directed to customErrorChannel, to which you can subscribe any component you like.

20-7. Forking Integration Control: Splitters and Aggregators

Problem

You want to fork the process flow from one component to many, either all at once or to a single one based on a predicate condition.

Solution

You can use a splitter component (and maybe its cohort, the aggregator component) to fork and join (respectively) control of processing.

How it Works

One of the fundamental cornerstones of an ESB is routing. You've seen how components can be chained together to create sequences in which progression is mostly linear. Some solutions require the capability to split a message into many constituent parts. One reason why this might be is that some problems are parallel in nature and don't depend on each other in order to complete. You should strive to achieve the efficiencies of parallelism wherever possible.

Using a Splitter

It's often useful to divide large payloads into separate messages with separate processing flows. In Spring Integration, this is accomplished by using a `splitter` component. A `splitter` takes an input message and asks you, the user of the component, on what basis it should split the `Message<T>`: you're responsible for providing the split functionality. Once you've told Spring Integration how to split a `Message<T>`, it forwards each result out on the `output-channel` of the `splitter` component. In a few cases, Spring Integration ships with useful splitters that require no customization. One example is the splitter provided to partition an XML payload along an XPath query, `XPathMessageSplitter`.

One example of a useful application of a splitter might be a text file with rows of data, each of which must be processed. Your goal is to be able to submit each row to a service that will handle the processing. What's required is a way to extract each row and forward each row as a new `Message<T>`.

The configuration for such a solution looks like this:

```xml
<?xml version="1.0" encoding="UTF-8"?>

<beans:beans xmlns:beans="http://www.springframework.org/schema/beans"
             xmlns:xsi="http://www.w3.org/2001/XMLSchema-instance"
             xmlns="http://www.springframework.org/schema/integration"
             xmlns:context="http://www.springframework.org/schema/context"
             xmlns:jms="http://www.springframework.org/schema/integration/jms"
             xmlns:file="http://www.springframework.org/schema/integration/file"
             xsi:schemaLocation="http://www.springframework.org/schema/beans
http://www.springframework.org/schema/beans/↵
spring-beans-3.0.xsd
http://www.springframework.org/schema/context
http://www.springframework.org/schema/context/↵
spring-context-3.0.xsd http://www.springframework.org/schema/integration
http://www.springframework.org/schema/integration/↵
spring-integration-1.0.xsd
http://www.springframework.org/schema/integration/jms
http://www.springframework.org/schema/integration/jms/↵
spring-integration-jms-1.0.xsd
http://www.springframework.org/schema/integration/file
http://www.springframework.org/schema/integration/file/
spring-integration-file-1.0.xsd">

    <context:annotation-config/>
```

```
    <poller id="poller" default="true">
        <interval-trigger interval="1000"/>
    </poller>
    <beans:bean id="fileSplitter"
                class="com.apress.springrecipes.↩
springintegration.CustomerBatchFileSplitter"/>
    <beans:bean id="customerDeletionServiceActivator"
            class="com.apress.springrecipes.↩
springintegration.CustomerDeletionServiceActivator"/>
    <channel id="customerBatchChannel"/>
    <channel id="customerIdChannel"/>
    <file:inbound-channel-adapter
        directory="file:${user.home}/customerstoremove/new/"
        channel="customerBatchChannel"  filename-pattern="^new.*txt$"/>

    <splitter input-channel="customerBatchChannel"
            ref="fileSplitter" output-channel="customerIdChannel" />

    <service-activator input-channel="customerIdChannel"
                    ref="customerDeletionServiceActivator"/>

</beans:beans>
```

The configuration for this is not terribly different from the previous solutions. The Java code is just about the same as well, except that the return type of the method annotated by the @Splitter annotation is of type java.util.Collection.

```
package com.apress.springrecipes.springintegration;

import org.apache.commons.io.IOUtils;
import org.springframework.integration.annotation.Splitter;
import java.io.File;
import java.io.FileReader;
import java.io.Reader;
import java.util.Collection;

public class CustomerBatchFileSplitter {
    @Splitter
    public Collection<String> splitAFile(File file) throws Throwable {
        Reader reader = new FileReader(file);
        Collection<String> lines = IOUtils.readLines(reader);
        IOUtils.closeQuietly(reader);
        return lines;
    }
}
```

A message payload is passed in as a java.io.File and the contents are read. The result (a collection or array value; in this case, a Collection<String>) is returned. Spring Integration executes a kind of foreach on the results, sending each value in the collection out on the output-channel configured for the splitter. Often, you split messages so that the individual pieces can be forwarded to processing that's more focused. Because the message is more manageable, the processing requirements are dampened.

This is true in many different architectures: in map/reduce solutions tasks are split and then processed in parallel, and the fork/join constructs in a BPM system (see Chapter 23) let control flow proceed in parallel so that the total work product can be achieved quicker.

Using Aggregators

Ineluctably, you'll need to do the reverse: combine many messages into one, and create a single result that can be returned on the `output-channel`. An `@Aggregator` collects a series of messages (based on some correlation that you help Spring Integration make between the messages) and publishes a single message to the components downstream. Suppose that you know that you're expecting 22 different messages from 22 actors in the system, but you don't know when. This is similar to a company that auctions off a contract and collects all the bids from different vendors before choosing the ultimate vendor. The company can't accept a bid until all bids have been received from all companies. Otherwise, there's the risk of prematurely signing a contract that would not be in the best interest of the company. An `aggregator` is perfect for building this type of logic.

There are many ways for Spring Integration to correlate incoming messages. To determine how many messages to read until it can stop, it uses the class `SequenceSizeCompletionStrategy`, which reads a well known header value (aggregators are often used after a `splitter`. Thus, the default header value is provided by the `splitter`, though there's nothing stopping you from creating the header parameters yourself) to calculate how many it should look for and to note the index of the message relative to the expected total count (e.g., 3/22).

For correlation when you might not have a size but know that you're expecting messages that share a common header value within a known time, Spring Integration provides the `HeaderAttributeCorrelationStrategy`. In this way, it knows that all messages with that value are from the same group, in the same way that your last name identifies you as being part of a larger group.

Let's revisit the last example. Suppose that the file was split (by lines, each belonging to a new customer) and subsequently processed. You now want to reunite the customers and do some cleanup with everyone at the same time. In this example, you use the default `completion-strategy` and `correlation-strategy`. The only custom logic is a POJO with an `@Aggregator` annotation on a method expecting a collection of `Message<T>` objects. It could, of course, be a collection of `Customer` objects, because they are what you're expecting as output from the previous `splitter`. You return on the reply channel a `Message<T>` that has the entire collection as its payload:

```
    <beans:bean id="customAggregator" class="com.apress.springrecipes. ↵
springintegration.MessagePayloadAggregator"/>
...
    <channel id="messagePayloadAggregatorChannel"/>
    <channel id="summaryChannel"/>
...
    <aggregator input-channel="messagePayloadAggregatorChannel"
        ref="customAggregator"
        output-channel="summaryChannel" />
```

The Java code is even simpler:

```
package com.apress.springrecipes.springintegration;

import org.springframework.integration.annotation.Aggregator;
import org.springframework.integration.core.Message;
import org.springframework.integration.message.MessageBuilder;


import java.util.List;

public class MessagePayloadAggregator {
    @Aggregator
    public Message<?> joinMessages(
    List<Message<Customer>> customers
    ) {
        if (customers.size() > 0) {
            return MessageBuilder.withPayload(customers).copyHeadersIfAbsent(
                        customers.get(0).getHeaders()).build();
        }
        return null;
    }
}
```

20-8. Conditional Routing with Routers

Problem

You want to conditionally move a message through different processes based on some criteria. This is the EAI equivalent to an if/else branch.

Solution

You can use a `router` component to alter the processing flow based on some predicate. You can also use a router to multicast a message to many subscribers (as you did with the `splitter`).

How It Works

With a router you can specify a known list of channels on which the incoming `Message` should be passed. This has some powerful implications. It means you can change the flow of a process conditionally, and it also means that you can forward a `Message` to as many (or as few) channels as you want. There are some convenient default routers available to fill common needs, such as payload-type–based routing (`PayloadTypeRouter`) and routing to a group or list of channels (`RecipientListRouter`).

Imagine, for example, a processing pipeline that routes customers with high credit scores to one service and customers with lower credit scores to another process in which the information is queued up for a human audit and verification cycle. The configuration is, as usual, very straightforward. In the following example, you show the configuration. One router element, which in turn delegates the routing logic to a class, is CustomerCreditScoreRouter.

```
<beans:bean id="customerCreditScoreRouter"
  class="com.apress.springrecipes.springintegration.CustomerCreditScoreRouter"/>
...
<channel id="safeCustomerChannel"/>
<channel id="riskyCustomerChannel"/>
...
<router input-channel="customerIdChannel" ref="customerCreditScoreRouter"/>
```

The Java code is similarly approachable. It feels a lot like a workflow engine's conditional element, or even a JSF backing-bean method, in that it extricates the routing logic into the XML configuration, away from code, delaying the decision until runtime. In the example, the Strings returned are the names of the channels on which the Message should pass.

```
package com.apress.springrecipes.springintegration;
import org.springframework.integration.annotation.Router;

public class CustomerCreditScoreRouter {
    @Router
    public String routeByCustomerCreditScore(Customer customer) {
        if (customer.getCreditScore() > 770) {
            return "safeCustomerChannel";
        } else {
            return "riskyCustomerChannel";
        }
    }
}
```

If you decide that you'd rather not let the Message<T> pass and want to arrest processing, you can return null instead of a String.

20-9. Adapting External Systems to the Bus

Problem

You want to receive messages from an external system and process them using Spring Integration. The external system doesn't expose any messaging functionality.

Solution

The answer is a channel adapter that comes straight from the EIP book. Spring Integration makes it trivially easy to build one.

How It Works

You use a channel adapter to access an application's API or data. Typically, this is done by publishing data from the application on a channel or receiving messages and invoking functionality on the application's API. Channels can also be used to broadcast events from an application to interested, external systems.

Adapters are opaque in nature. Your external system interfaces with the adapter. What functionality or scope of access the application provides to the adapter varies based on the requirements.

Some systems are insurmountable "walled gardens," and sometimes, the worst solution is the only solution. Imagine, for example, a legacy terminal application based on curses that surfaces application functionality and data only via the user interface. In this case, a *user interface adapter* is required. This situation also presents itself often with web sites, which become data silos. These applications require an adapter to parse the emitted HTML for data or "screen-scrape" them.

Sometimes, functionality is made available from within the application via a cohesive, stable API but in a component model or form that isn't directly accessible to the bus. This type of adapter is called a *business logic adapter*. An application built in C++ that provides CORBA endpoints but needs to support SOAP endpoints is a good candidate for this approach.

A third type of adapter, which sits on the database and adapts an external system by way of the schema, is also an option. This is essentially an implementation of the *shared database* integration pattern.

An Inbound Twitter Adapter

Spring Integration already provides many useful implementations of channel adapters, as you have seen in previous exercises. You will build an example to receive messages from an external system for which there is no existing support (yet): Twitter. In Spring Integration, you use an implementation of the interface MessageSource<T> to model components that can produce messages for consumption on the bus and that should be polled. There is also a MessageEndpoint interface, which you'd overwrite to build an endpoint that might support pushing the event onto the bus—and thus has no need for polling. We will use the MessageSource<T>, since it solves our requirement and, generally, will be used more often than not.

Although you are probably familiar with Twitter, please indulge us in a quick overview and introduction, just to be thorough. Twitter is a social networking site founded in 2006. It allows users to broadcast a message (a *status* or a *tweet*) to all people who have subscribed to these status updates. The updates are limited to 140 characters. Subscribing to a person's status updates is called *following* that person.

Support for inspecting other peoples' updates and updating your own status is provided by the web site itself. Additionally, support is offered by a telephone integration that takes messages sent via a mobile phone (SMS) and correlates the phone number of the inbound message to a user's account and updates that person's status on her behalf.

Many people, from the everyman to the super famous, use Twitter. Reports have it as the third biggest social networking site at the time of this writing. Some people (presidents, celebrities, and so on) have hundreds of thousands of followers, and some have millions. As you can imagine, the difficulties and logistics of managing a graph as complex and sprawling as the one Twitter manages can be frustrating and has been the source of many well publicized outages for the service.

Twitter furnishes a REST API through which users can interact with the system. The API lets users do anything they might do from the web site: follow users, stop following users, update status, and so on. The API is concise and has many language bindings already available. In this recipe, you'll use one project's API, called Twitter4J, which nicely wraps the REST API in simple approachable API calls.

Twitter4J was created by Yusuke Yamamoto and is available under the BSD license. It's available in the Maven repositories, and it has a fairly active support mailing list. If you want to find more about Twitter4J, visit http://yusuke.homeip.net.

Twitter Messages

In the first example, you'll build support for receiving messages, not for sending them. The second example will feature support for outbound messages. In particular, you'll build support for receiving the status updates of the people to which a particular account is subscribed, or *following*.

There are other types of Twitter messages. Although you won't build adapters for every type, it won't be difficult to imagine how it's done once you've completed the examples. Twitter supports direct messaging, in which you can specify that only one recipient sees the contents of the message; this is *peer-to-peer messaging*, roughly analogous to using SMS messaging. Twitter also supports receiving messages in which your screen handle was mentioned. These messages can often be messages directed to you and others, messages discussing you, or messages reposting (*retweeting*) something you said already.

A Simple MessageSource

To build an adapter, you either write a class that implements MessageSource<T> and reference that as a bean, or you can reference any arbitrary method on any arbitrary bean if you specify the method in configuration. The method needs to return a value. In this example, you'll implement MessageSource, whose interface is very succinct.

```
package org.springframework.integration.message;
import org.springframework.integration.core.Message;

public interface MessageSource<T> {
    Message<T> receive();
}
```

In the example, you're building a solution that can pull status updates and return them in a simple POJO object called Tweet.

```
package com.apress.springrecipes.springintegration.twitter;

import java.io.Serializable;
import java.util.Date;
// …

public class Tweet implements Serializable, Comparable<Tweet> {
    private long tweetId;
     private String message;
    private Date received;
    private String user;
     // constructors, accessor/mutators, compareTo,
                // toString/equals/hashCode methods all ommited for brevity.
                // …
}
```

Thus, the implementation for the `MessageSource<T>` will return `Messages` containing an object of type `Tweet` as the payload. Examining the outline of the implementation is telling because the approach for satisfying the interface becomes evident now that you know what interface requirements you're trying to meet. With any luck, the beginnings of the final solution will crystallize.

```
package com.apress.springrecipes.springintegration.twitter;

public class TwitterMessageSource
     implements MessageSource<Tweet>,  InitializingBean {
   public Message<Tweet> receive() {
     return … ;
   }
   // …
 }
```

As you can see, the `MessageSource<T>` contract dictates that you provide "one" message each time the method is called. This message is read from the external system of your choice, in this case Twitter. There are no other interfaces to implement. You do, however, have some design constraints imposed on you not by Spring Integration, but by the Twitter API. The Twitter API limits how many requests you can make to it per hour. The operative word here is *requests* because the limitation doesn't apply to updates. As of this writing, the API limits you to 100 requests per hour. After that, you are stalled until the top of the next hour.

So, what you want is to be able to handle 100 messages on each pull if you get 100 messages, but to not exceed the API request limit, which means using the API every 36 seconds at most. To be safe, let's just assume that the `poller` will be scheduled to run every minute.

Before diving into the code, let's examine the configuration:

```
<?xml version="1.0" encoding="UTF-8"?>
<beans:beans
    xmlns="http://www.springframework.org/schema/integration"
    xmlns:beans="http://www.springframework.org/schema/beans"
    xmlns:xsi="http://www.w3.org/2001/XMLSchema-instance"
    xmlns:p="http://www.springframework.org/schema/p"
    xmlns:context="http://www.springframework.org/schema/context"
    xmlns:util="http://www.springframework.org/schema/util"
    xmlns:tool="http://www.springframework.org/schema/tool"
    xmlns:lang="http://www.springframework.org/schema/lang"
    xsi:schemaLocation="http://www.springframework.org/schema/beans
http://www.springframework.org/schema/beans/spring-beans.xsd
http://www.springframework.org/schema/integration
http://www.springframework.org/schema/integration/spring-integration-1.0.xsd
http://www.springframework.org/schema/context
http://www.springframework.org/schema/context/spring-context-3.0.xsd
http://www.springframework.org/schema/util
http://www.springframework.org/schema/util/spring-util-3.0.xsd
http://www.springframework.org/schema/tool
http://www.springframework.org/schema/tool/spring-tool-3.0.xsd
http://www.springframework.org/schema/lang
http://www.springframework.org/schema/lang/spring-lang-3.0.xsd">
```

```
<beans:bean class="org.springframework.beans.factory.↵
config.PropertyPlaceholderConfigurer"
  p:location="08-adaptingexternalsystemstothebus.properties"
  p:ignoreUnresolvablePlaceholders="true" />

<channel id="inboundTweets" />

<beans:bean
    id="twitterMessageSource"
    class="com.apress.springrecipes.↵
springintegration.twitter.TwitterMessageSource"
    p:password="${twitter.password}"
    p:userId="${twitter.userId}"
 />

<inbound-channel-adapter ref="twitterMessageSource" channel="inboundTweets">
    <poller receive-timeout="10000"  max-messages-per-poll="100">
        <interval-trigger interval="10" time-unit="SECONDS" />
    </poller>
</inbound-channel-adapter>

<service-activator
    input-channel="inboundTweets" ref="twitterMessageOutput" method="announce" />

</beans:beans>
```

The bold parts are the only salient bits. As in previous examples, you start by declaring a channel ("inboundTweets"). Next, you configure an instance of the custom MessageSource<T> implementation TwitterMessageSource. Finally, you use Spring Integration's inbound-channel-adapter element to wire the TwitterMessageSource and a poller element. The poller element is configured to run every 10 seconds and to consume as many as 100 messages each time it runs. That is, if it runs 10 seconds from now, it will call read() without pause on the MessageSource<T> implementation until it's given a null value, at which point it will idle until the scheduler starts the cycle again at the next 10-second interval. Thus, if you have 100 messages, this will consume all of them as quick as possible. Ideally, all the messages will be processed before the next scheduled pull occurs.

All this is provided by Spring Integration. All you have to do is avoid wastefully calling the service by caching the results and feeding the results back until the cache is exhausted. Then, you just wait for the next scheduled run. Simple, right? Let's look at the final result:

```
package com.apress.springrecipes.springintegration.twitter;

import java.util.Date;
import java.util.List;
import java.util.Queue;
import java.util.concurrent.ConcurrentLinkedQueue;

import org.apache.commons.lang.StringUtils;
import org.apache.commons.lang.exception.ExceptionUtils;
import org.apache.log4j.Logger;
import org.springframework.beans.factory.InitializingBean;
import org.springframework.context.support.ClassPathXmlApplicationContext;
```

```java
import org.springframework.integration.channel.DirectChannel;
import org.springframework.integration.core.Message;
import org.springframework.integration.message.MessageBuilder;
import org.springframework.integration.message.MessageHandler;
import org.springframework.integration.message.MessageSource;
import org.springframework.util.Assert;

import twitter4j.Paging;
import twitter4j.Status;
import twitter4j.Twitter;
import twitter4j.TwitterException;

public class TwitterMessageSource implements MessageSource<Tweet>,
        InitializingBean {

    static private Logger logger = Logger.getLogger(TwitterMessageSource.class);

    private volatile Queue<Tweet> cachedStatuses;
    private volatile String userId;
    private volatile String password;
    private volatile Twitter twitter;
    private volatile long lastStatusIdRetrieved = -1;

    private Tweet buildTweetFromStatus(Status firstPost) {
        Tweet tweet = new Tweet(firstPost.getId(), firstPost.getUser()
                .getName(), firstPost.getCreatedAt(), firstPost.getText());
        return tweet;
    }

    public Message<Tweet> receive() {
        Assert.state(cachedStatuses != null);

        if (cachedStatuses.peek() == null) {
            Paging paging = new Paging();

            if (-1 != lastStatusIdRetrieved) {
                paging.sinceId(lastStatusIdRetrieved);

            }
            try {
                List<Status> statuses = twitter.getFriendsTimeline(paging);
                Assert.state(cachedStatuses.peek() == null);// size() isn't
                // constant time
                for (Status status : statuses)
                    this.cachedStatuses.add(buildTweetFromStatus(status));

            } catch (TwitterException e) {
                logger.info(ExceptionUtils.getFullStackTrace(e));
                throw new RuntimeException(e);
            }
        }
```

```java
        if (cachedStatuses.peek() != null) {
            // size() == 0 would be more obvious
            // a test, but size() isn't constant time
            Tweet cachedStatus = cachedStatuses.poll();
            lastStatusIdRetrieved = cachedStatus.getTweetId();
            return MessageBuilder.withPayload(cachedStatus).build();
        }
        return null;
    }

    public void afterPropertiesSet() throws Exception {

        if (twitter == null) {
            Assert.state(!StringUtils.isEmpty(userId));
            Assert.state(!StringUtils.isEmpty(password));

            twitter = new Twitter();
            twitter.setUserId(userId);
            twitter.setPassword(password);

        } else { // it isnt null, in which case it becomes canonical memory
            setPassword(twitter.getPassword());
            setUserId(twitter.getUserId());
        }

        cachedStatuses = new ConcurrentLinkedQueue<Tweet>();
        lastStatusIdRetrieved = -1;

    }

    public String getUserId() {
        return userId;
    }

    public void setUserId(String userId) {
        this.userId = userId;
    }

    public String getPassword() {
        return password;
    }

    public void setPassword(String password) {
        this.password = password;
    }

    public Twitter getTwitter() {
        return twitter;
    }
```

```
public void setTwitter(Twitter twitter) {
    this.twitter = twitter;
}

}
```

The bulk of the class is in the accessors and mutators for configuration. The class takes a userId and password, or can be configured with an instance of Twitter4J's Twitter class (which itself has userId and password properties). The read() method is the crux of the implementation. It attempts to take items off of the Queue, which it then returns. If it finds there's nothing to return which it will when it either is first run or has exhausted all the cache items it will attempt a query on the API. The API surfaces a Paging object, which works something like Criteria in Hibernate. You can configure how many results to return using the count property. The most interesting option is called the *sinceId*, which lets you search for all records occurring after the Status having the ID equal to the value given as the *sinceId*. It's a built-in duplication-prevention mechanism.

This means that while you are caching Status updates in the MessageSource<T>, you can bound the growth because you don't have to forever store every previous message and test each new one for equality. This implementation does note the last ID that was processed and returned from the read() method. This value is then used in any subsequent queries to preclude it, and any Statuses before it, from appearing in the search results.

Note that there is no support in this implementation for durably storing the ID of the last read status between runtimes. That is, if you kill the Java process running Spring Integration, this MessageSource<T> will simply start again with the last 100 messages from the instant it makes the query, regardless of whether they've been read or not in a previous or concurrent process. Care should be taken to either guard that state in something durable and transactional like a database, or at the very least to implement duplicate detection further on down the line.

A quick test of the component might look like the following:

```
public static void main(String[] args) throws Throwable {
    ClassPathXmlApplicationContext classPathXmlApplicationContext =
                    new ClassPathXmlApplicationContext↵
( "08-1-adaptingexternalsystemstothebus.xml");
    classPathXmlApplicationContext.start();
    DirectChannel channel = (DirectChannel) classPathXmlApplicationContext
            .getBean("inboundTweets");
    channel.subscribe(new MessageHandler() {
        public void handleMessage(Message<?> message) {
            Tweet tweet = (Tweet) message.getPayload();
            logger.debug(String.format("Received %s at %s ", tweet
                    .toString(), new Date().toString()));
        }
    });
}
```

Here, you've done very little except manually subscribe (which is what components do behind the scenes when you configure it in XML, although it's quite succinct) to messages that come onto the channel (from the MessageSource<T>) and print them out.

An Outbound Twitter Example

You've seen how to consume Twitter status updates on the bus. Now, let's explore how to send messages from the bus to Twitter. You will build an outbound Twitter adapter. This component will accept status updates (messages of type Tweet) coming in a channel and update the configured account with the new status.

In the last example, you built a class that implemented MessageSource, and we explained that you could optionally configure a regular POJO and simply instruct Spring Integration to use a particular method in lieu of relying on the interface-enforced receive method of the MessageSource<T> interface. The same is true in the opposite direction. You can implement MessageHandler<T> which gives you a hook to react to inbound messages (instead of publishing outbound messages using MessageSource<T>), whose API is similarly simple:

```
package org.springframework.integration.message
public interface MessageHandler {
        void handleMessage(Message<?> message)
                throws MessageRejectedException,
                        MessageHandlingException,
                        MessageDeliveryException;
}
```

This time, you won't implement the interface (as we'll pursue the alternative approach of simply configuring a regular POJO), but knowing it's there is useful. These two interfaces are symmetrical in a way. The code for the outbound adapter is much simpler than the code for the inbound adapter, because you have no quirks to contend with and the mapping from Spring Integration to Twitter is sane: one message to one status update.

```
package com.apress.springrecipes.springintegration.twitter;

import org.apache.commons.lang.StringUtils;
import org.apache.commons.lang.exception.ExceptionUtils;
import org.apache.log4j.Logger;
import org.springframework.beans.factory.InitializingBean;
import org.springframework.context.support.ClassPathXmlApplicationContext;
import org.springframework.integration.channel.DirectChannel;
import org.springframework.integration.core.Message;
import org.springframework.integration.message.MessageBuilder;
import org.springframework.util.Assert;

import twitter4j.Twitter;
import twitter4j.TwitterException;

public class TwitterMessageProducer implements InitializingBean {

    static private Logger logger = Logger.getLogger(TwitterMessageProducer.class);

    private volatile String userId;
    private volatile String password;
    private volatile Twitter twitter;
```

```java
    public void tweet(String tweet) {
        try {
            twitter.updateStatus(tweet);
        } catch (TwitterException e) {
            logger.debug(ExceptionUtils.getFullStackTrace(e));
        }
    }

    public String getUserId() {
        return userId;
    }

    public void setUserId(String userId) {
        this.userId = userId;
    }

    public String getPassword() {
        return password;
    }

    public void setPassword(String password) {
        this.password = password;
    }

    public Twitter getTwitter() {
        return twitter;
    }

    public void setTwitter(Twitter twitter) {
        this.twitter = twitter;
    }

    public void afterPropertiesSet() throws Exception {
        if (twitter == null) {
            Assert.state(!StringUtils.isEmpty(userId));
            Assert.state(!StringUtils.isEmpty(password));

            twitter = new Twitter();
            twitter.setUserId(userId);
            twitter.setPassword(password);

        } else { // it isnt null, in which case it becomes canonical memory
            setPassword(twitter.getPassword());
            setUserId(twitter.getUserId());
        }
    }
}
```

Most of the code is boilerplate—exposed for configuration. Of note the method called tweet(Tweet). As you've seen in other places, you're relying on Spring Integration to unbundle the payload from the Message<T> coming in on a channel and to pass the payload as a parameter to this method.

The configuration inside the XML application context is strikingly similar to the configuration for the outbound adapter:

```xml
<?xml version="1.0" encoding="UTF-8"?>
<beans:beans
    xmlns="http://www.springframework.org/schema/integration"
    xmlns:beans="http://www.springframework.org/schema/beans"
    xmlns:xsi="http://www.w3.org/2001/XMLSchema-instance"
    xmlns:p="http://www.springframework.org/schema/p"
    xmlns:context="http://www.springframework.org/schema/context"
    xmlns:util="http://www.springframework.org/schema/util"
    xmlns:tool="http://www.springframework.org/schema/tool"
    xmlns:lang="http://www.springframework.org/schema/lang"
    xsi:schemaLocation="http://www.springframework.org/schema/beans
http://www.springframework.org/schema/beans/↵
spring-beans.xsd
http://www.springframework.org/schema/integration
 http://www.springframework.org/schema/integration/↵
spring-integration-1.0.xsd
http://www.springframework.org/schema/context
 http://www.springframework.org/schema/context/spring-context-3.0.xsd
 http://www.springframework.org/schema/util
http://www.springframework.org/schema/util/spring-util-3.0.xsd
http://www.springframework.org/schema/tool
http://www.springframework.org/schema/tool/spring-tool-3.0.xsd
http://www.springframework.org/schema/lang
http://www.springframework.org/schema/lang/spring-lang-3.0.xsd">

    <beans:bean class="org.springframework.beans.factory.↵
config.PropertyPlaceholderConfigurer"
        p:location="08-adaptingexternalsystemstothebus.properties"
        p:ignoreUnresolvablePlaceholders="true" />

    <beans:bean id="twitterMessageProducer"
  class="com.apress.springrecipes.springintegration.twitter.TwitterMessageProducer"
        p:password="${twitter.password}"
        p:userId="${twitter.userId}"
    />

    <channel id="outboundTweets" />

    <outbound-channel-adapter ref="twitterMessageProducer"
                method="tweet"
                channel="outboundTweets" />

</beans:beans>
```

You renamed the channel and employed an `outbound-channel-adapter` instead of an `inbound-channel-adapter`. Indeed, the only thing novel is that you're employing the method attribute on the `outbound-channel-adapter` element to give the component an extra level of insulation from the Spring Integration APIs.

Using the component is easy, and a quick test might look like this:

```
public static void main(String[] args) throws Throwable {
    ClassPathXmlApplicationContext classPathXmlApplicationContext = new
                ClassPathXmlApplicationContext( "solution032.xml");
    classPathXmlApplicationContext.start();
    DirectChannel channel = (DirectChannel)
                classPathXmlApplicationContext.getBean("outboundTweets");
    Message<String> helloWorldMessage =
                MessageBuilder.withPayload( "Hello, world!").build();
    channel.send(helloWorldMessage);
}
```

The example's even simpler than the test code for the inbound adapter! The code goes through the motions of setting up a Message<T> and then simply sends it. Confirm by checking your status on twitter.com.

20-10. Staging Events Using Spring Batch

Problem

You have a file with a million records in it. This file's too big to handle as one event; it's far more natural to react to each row as an event.

Solution

Spring Batch works very well with these types of solutions. It allows you to take an input file or a payload and reliably, and systematically, decompose it into events that an ESB can work with.

How It Works

Spring Integration does support reading files into the bus, and Spring Batch does support providing custom, unique endpoints for data. However, just like Mom always says, "just because you can, it doesn't mean you *should*."

Although it seems as if there's a lot of overlap here, it turns out that there is a distinction (albeit a fine one). While both systems will work with files and message queues, or anything else you could conceivably write code to talk to, Spring Integration doesn't do well with large payloads because it's hard to deal with something as large as a file with a million rows that might require hours of work as an *event*. That's simply too big a burden for an ESB. At that point, the term *event* has no meaning. A million records in a CSV file isn't an event on a bus, it's a file with a million records, each of which might in turn *be* events. It's a subtle distinction.

A file with a million rows needs to be decomposed into smaller events. Spring Batch can help here: it allows you to systematically read through, apply validations, and optionally skip and retry invalid records. The processing can begin on an ESB such as Spring Integration. Spring Batch and Spring Integration can be used together to build truly scalable decoupled systems.

Staged event-driven architecture (SEDA) is an architecture style that deals with this sort of processing situation. In SEDA, you dampen the load on components of the architecture by staging it in queues, and let advance only what the components downstream can handle. Put another way, imagine video processing. If you ran a site with a million users uploading video that in turn needed to be transcoded and you only had ten servers, your system would fail if your system attempted to process each video as soon as it received the uploaded video. Transcoding can take hours and pegs a CPU (or multiple CPUs!) while it works. The most sensible thing to do would be to store the file and then, as capacity permits, process each one. In this way, the load on the nodes that handle transcoding is managed. There's always only enough work to keep the machine humming, but not overrun.

Similarly, no processing system (such as an ESB) can deal with a million records at once efficiently. Strive to decompose bigger events and messages into smaller ones. Let's imagine a hypothetical solution designed to accommodate a drop of batch files representing hourly sales destined for fulfillment. The batch files are dropped onto a mount that Spring Integration is monitoring. Spring Integration kicks off processing as soon as it sees a new file. Spring Integration tells Spring Batch about the file and launches a Spring Batch job asynchronously.

Spring Batch reads the file, transforms the records into objects, and writes the output to a JMS topic with a key correlating the original batch to the JMS message. Naturally, this takes half a day to get done, but it does get done. Spring Integration, completely unaware that the job it started half a day ago is now finished, begins popping messages off the topic, one by one. Processing to fulfill the records would begin. Simple processing involving multiple components might begin on the ESB.

If fulfillment is a long-lived process with a long-lived, conversational state involving many actors, perhaps the fulfillment for each record could be farmed to a BPM engine. The BPM engine would thread together the different actors and work lists, allow work to continue over the course of days instead of the small millisecond timeframes Spring Integration is more geared to. In this example, we talked about using Spring Batch as a springboard to dampen the load for components downstream. In this case, the component downstream was again a Spring Integration process that took the work and set it up to be funneled into a BPM engine where final processing could begin.

20-11. Using Gateways

Problem

You want to expose an interface to clients of your service, without betraying the fact that your service is implemented in terms of messaging middleware.

Solution

Use a gateway—a pattern from the classic book *Enterprise Integration Patterns* by Gregor Hohpe and Bobby Woolf (Addison-Wesley, 2004) that enjoys rich support in Spring Integration.

How It Works

A *gateway* is a distinct animal, similar to a lot of other patterns but ultimately different enough to warrant its own consideration. You used adapters in previous examples to enable two systems to speak in terms of foreign, loosely coupled, middleware components. This foreign component can be anything: the file system, JMS queues/topics, Twitter, and so on.

You also know what a *façade* is, serving to abstract away the functionality of other components in an abbreviated interface to provide courser functionality. You might use a façade to build an interface oriented around vacation planning that in turn abstracts away the minutiae of using a car rental, hotel reservation, and airline reservation system.

You build a gateway, on the other hand, to provide an interface for your system that insulates clients from the middleware or messaging in your system, so that they're not dependent on JMS or Spring Integration APIs, for example. A gateway allows you to express compile time constraints on the inputs and outputs of your system.

There are several reasons why you might want to do this. First, it's cleaner. If you have the latitude to insist that clients comply with an interface, this is a good way to provide that interface. Your use of middleware can be an implementation detail. Perhaps your architectures messaging middleware can be to exploit the performance increases had by leveraging asynchronous messaging, but you didn't intend for those performance gains to come at the cost of a precise, explicit external facing interface.

This feature—the capability to hide messaging behind a POJO interface—is very interesting and has been the focus of several other projects. Lingo, a project from Codehaus.org that is no longer under active development, had such a feature that was specific to JMS and the Java EE Connector Architecture (JCA –it was originally used to talk about the Java Cryptography Architecture, but is more commonly used for The Java EE Connector Architecture now). Since then, the developers have moved on to work on Apache Camel.

In this recipe, you'll explore Spring Integration's core support for messaging gateways and explore its support for message exchange patterns. Then, you'll see how to completely remove implementation details from the client-facing interface.

SimpleMessagingGateway

The most fundamental support for gateways comes from the Spring Integration class `SimpleMessagingGateway`. The class provides the ability to specify a channel on which requests should be sent and a channel on which responses are expected. Finally, the channel on which replies are sent can be specified. This gives you the ability to express in-out and in-only patterns on top of your existing messaging systems. This class supports working in terms of payloads, isolating you from the gory details of the messages being sent and received. This is already one level of abstraction. You could, conceivably, use the `SimpleMessagingGateway` and Spring Integration's concept of channels to interface with file systems, JMS, e-mail, or any other system and deal simply with payloads and channels. There are implementations already provided for you to support some of these common endpoints such as web services and JMS.

Let's look at using a generic messaging gateway. In this example, you'll send messages to a `service-activator` and then receive the response. You manually interface with the `SimpleMessageGateway` so that you can see how convenient it is.

```
package com.apress.springrecipes.springintegration;

import org.springframework.context.support.ClassPathXmlApplicationContext;
import org.springframework.integration.core.MessageChannel;
import org.springframework.integration.gateway.SimpleMessagingGateway;

public class SimpleMessagingGatewayExample {
    public static void main(String[] args) {
        ClassPathXmlApplicationContext ctx =
                        new ClassPathXmlApplicationContext("solution042.xml");
        MessageChannel request = (MessageChannel) ctx.getBean("request");
        MessageChannel response = (MessageChannel) ctx.getBean("response");
        SimpleMessagingGateway msgGateway = new SimpleMessagingGateway();
        msgGateway.setRequestChannel(request);
        msgGateway.setReplyChannel(response);
        Number result = (Number) msgGateway.sendAndReceive(new Operands(22, 4));
        System.out.println("Result: " + result.floatValue());

    }
}
```

The interface is very straightforward. The SimpleMessagingGateway needs a request and a response channel, and it coordinates the rest. In this case, you're doing nothing but forwarding the request to a service-activator, which in turn adds the operands and sends them out on the reply channel. The configuration XML is sparse because most of the work is done in those five lines of Java code.

```
<?xml version="1.0" encoding="UTF-8"?>
<beans:beans … >
    <beans:bean id="additionService" class="com.apress.springrecipes.↵
springintegration.AdditionService" />
    <channel id="request" />
    <channel id="response" />
    <service-activator  ref="additionService"
        method="add"
        input-channel="request"
        output-channel="response" />
</beans:beans>
```

Breaking the Interface Dependency

The previous example demonstrates what's happening behind the scenes. You're dealing only with Spring Integration interfaces and are isolated from the nuances of the endpoints. However, there are still plenty of inferred constraints that a client might easily fail to comply with. The simplest solution is to hide the messaging behind an interface. Let's look at building a fictional hotel reservation search engine. Searching for a hotel might take a long time, and ideally processing should be offloaded to a separate server. An ideal solution is JMS because you could implement the aggressive consumer pattern and scale simply by adding more consumers. The client would still block waiting for the result, in this example, but the server(s) would not be overloaded or in a blocking state.

You'll build two Spring Integration solutions. One for the client (which will in turn contain the gateway) and one for the service itself, which, presumably, is on a separate host connected to the client only by way of well-known message queues.

Let's look at the client configuration first. The first thing that the client configuration does is import a shared application context (to save typing if nothing else) that declares a JMS connection factory that you reference in the client and service application contexts. (We won't repeat all of that here because it's not relevant or noteworthy.)

Then, you declare two channels, imaginatively named **requests** and **responses**. Messages sent on the **requests** channel are forwarded to the **jms:outbound-gateway** that you've declared. The **jms:outbound-gateway** is the component that does most of the work. It takes the message you created and sends it to the request JMS destination, setting up the reply headers and so on. Finally, you declare a generic gateway **element**, which does most of the magic. The gateway **element** simply exists to identify the component and the interface, to which the proxy is cast and made available to clients.

```xml
<?xml version="1.0" encoding="UTF-8"?>
<beans:beans
    xmlns:beans="http://www.springframework.org/schema/beans"
    xmlns:xsi="http://www.w3.org/2001/XMLSchema-instance"
    xmlns="http://www.springframework.org/schema/integration"
    xmlns:context="http://www.springframework.org/schema/context"
    xmlns:jms="http://www.springframework.org/schema/integration/jms"
    xsi:schemaLocation="http://www.springframework.org/schema/beans
http://www.springframework.org/schema/beans/ ↵
spring-beans-3.0.xsd
http://www.springframework.org/schema/context
http://www.springframework.org/schema/context/spring-context-3.0.xsd
http://www.springframework.org/schema/integration
http://www.springframework.org/schema/integration/ ↵
spring-integration-1.0.xsd
http://www.springframework.org/schema/integration/jms
http://www.springframework.org/schema/integration/jms/ ↵
spring-integration-jms-1.0.xsd
            ">

    <beans:import resource="09-gateways.xml" />
        <context:annotation-config />

    <channel id="requests" />
    <channel id="responses" />

    <jms:outbound-gateway
        request-destination-name="inboundHotelReservationSearchDestination"
        request-channel="requests"
        reply-destination-name="outboundHotelReservationSearchResultsDestination"
        reply-channel="responses"
        connection-factory="connectionFactory" />
```

```
<gateway id="vacationService"
                service-interface="com.apress.springrecipes.⏎
springintegration.myholiday.VacationService" />

</beans:beans>
```

One thing that's conspicuously absent is any mention of an output or input channel from and to the gateway element. While it is possible to declare default request/reply message queues in the configuration for the gateway, realistically, most methods on an interface will require their own request/reply queues. So, you configure the channels on the interface itself.

```
package com.apress.springrecipes.springintegration.myholiday;

import java.util.List;
import org.springframework.integration.annotation.Gateway;

public interface VacationService {

    @Gateway(requestChannel = "requests", replyChannel = "responses")
    List<HotelReservation> findHotels(HotelReservationSearch hotelReservationSearch);

}
```

This is the client facing interface. There is no coupling between the client facing interface exposed via the gateway component and the interface of the service that ultimately handles the messages. We use the interface for the service and the client to simplify the names needed to understand everything that's going on. This is not like traditional, synchronous remoting in which the service interface and the client interface match.

In this example, you're using two very simple objects for demonstration: HotelReservationSearch and HotelReservation. There is nothing interesting about these objects in the slightest; they are simple POJOs that implement Serializable and contain a few accessor/mutators to flesh out the example domain.

The client Java code demonstrates how all of this comes together:

```
package com.apress.springrecipes.springintegration.myholiday;

import java.util.Calendar;
import java.util.Date;
import java.util.List;

import org.apache.commons.lang.time.DateUtils;
import org.springframework.context.support.ClassPathXmlApplicationContext;

public class Main {
    public static void main(String[] args) throws Throwable {
        ClassPathXmlApplicationContext classPathXmlApplicationContext = new
                ClassPathXmlApplicationContext("09-1-gateways_service.xml");
        classPathXmlApplicationContext.start();
```

```
    // setup the input parameter
        Date now = new Date();
    HotelReservationSearch hotelReservationSearch =  new HotelReservationSearch(
            200f, 2,
            DateUtils.add(now, Calendar.DATE, 1),
            DateUtils.add(now, Calendar.DATE, 8));

    ClassPathXmlApplicationContext classPathXmlApplicationContext1 =
                new ClassPathXmlApplicationContext("09-1-gateways_client.xml");
    classPathXmlApplicationContext1.start();

    // get a hold of our gateway proxy (you might
        // imagine injecting this into another service just like
        // you would a Hibernate DAO, for example)
    VacationService vacationService = (VacationService)
                classPathXmlApplicationContext1.getBean("vacationService");
    List<HotelReservation> results = vacationService.findHotels(
                        hotelReservationSearch);
    System.out.printf("Found %s results.", results.size());
    System.out.println();
    for (HotelReservation reservation : results) {
        System.out.printf("\t%s", reservation.toString());
        System.out.println();
    }
  }
}
```

It just doesn't get any cleaner than that! No Spring Integration interfaces whatsoever. You make a request, searching is done, and you get the result back when the processing is done.

The service implementation for this setup is interesting, not because of what you've added, but because of what's not there:

```
<?xml version="1.0" encoding="UTF-8"?>
<beans:beans
    xmlns:beans="http://www.springframework.org/schema/beans"
    xmlns:xsi="http://www.w3.org/2001/XMLSchema-instance"
    xmlns="http://www.springframework.org/schema/integration"
    xmlns:context="http://www.springframework.org/schema/context"
    xmlns:jms="http://www.springframework.org/schema/integration/jms"
    xsi:schemaLocation="http://www.springframework.org/schema/beans
http://www.springframework.org/schema/beans/spring-beans-3.0.xsd
http://www.springframework.org/schema/context
http://www.springframework.org/schema/context/  ↵
spring-context-3.0.xsd
http://www.springframework.org/schema/integration
http://www.springframework.org/schema/integration/spring-integration-1.0.xsd
http://www.springframework.org/schema/integration/jms
http://www.springframework.org/schema/integration/jms/↵
```

```
spring-integration-jms-1.0.xsd">
    <beans:import resource="09-gateways.xml" />
    <context:annotation-config />

    <channel id="inboundHotelReservationSearchChannel" />
    <channel id="outboundHotelReservationSearchResultsChannel" />

    <beans:bean id="vacationServiceImpl"  ↵
    class="com.apress.springrecipes.springintegration. ↵
myholiday.VacationServiceImpl" />

    <jms:inbound-gateway
        request-channel="inboundHotelReservationSearchChannel"
        request-destination-name="inboundHotelReservationSearchDestination"
        connection-factory="connectionFactory" />

    <service-activator
        input-channel="inboundHotelReservationSearchChannel"
        ref="vacationServiceImpl"
        method="findHotels" />

</beans:beans>
```

Here, you've defined an inbound JMS gateway element. The messages from the inbound JMS gateway are put on a channel, inboundHotelReservationSearchChannel, whose messages are forwarded to a service-activator, as you would expect. The service-activator is what handles actual processing. What's interesting here is that there's no mention of a response channel, for either the service-activator, or for the inbound JMS gateway. The service-activator looks, and fails to find, a reply channel and so uses the reply channel created by the inbound JMS gateway component, which in turn has created the reply channel based on the header metadata in the inbound JMS message. Thus, everything just works without specification.

The implementation is a simple useless implementation of the interface:

```
package com.apress.springrecipes.springintegration.myholiday;
import java.util.Arrays;
import java.util.List;
import org.springframework.beans.factory.InitializingBean;

public class VacationServiceImpl implements VacationService, InitializingBean {
    private List<HotelReservation> hotelReservations;
    public void afterPropertiesSet() throws Exception {
        hotelReservations = Arrays.asList(
    new HotelReservation("Bilton", 243.200F),
    new HotelReservation("West Western", 75.0F),
    new HotelReservation("Theirfield Inn", 70F),
    new HotelReservation("Park Inn", 200.00F));
    }
```

```
    public List<HotelReservation> findHotels(HotelReservationSearch searchMsg) {
        try {
            Thread.sleep(1000);
        } catch (Throwable th) {
          // eat the exception
        }
        return hotelReservations;
    }

}
```

Summary

This chapter discussed building an integration solution using Spring Integration, an ESB-like framework built on top of the Spring framework. You were introduced to the core concepts of enterprise application integration (EAI). You learned how to handle a few integration scenarios, including JMS and file polling. You saw how to build a custom endpoint to talk to Twitter and how to hide the integration functionality behind a POJO service interface using a gateway so that clients can interface synchronously while the server still enjoys the benefits of a decoupled, asynchronous, message-oriented architecture.

While this chapter has focused on Spring Integration 1.0, Spring Integration 2.0 is nearing completion. Spring Integration is largely the same – and should not be backwards incompatible. Where Spring Integration 2.0 is clearly an improvement is in the plethora of new adapters and integration possibilities. Spring Integration 2.0 debuts support for integration with XMPP (the protocol used behind Facebook Chat and Google Talk, for example), Twitter, TCP/IP, and much more. There are adapters that will tentatively be included for IRC, SFTP, RSS/ATOM, and more. Finally, one might speculate that Spring Integration 2.0 will play a key part in the recent SpringSource acquisitions of GemStone Systems (a company that makes a distributed cache, very much like Oracle's Coherence or Terracotta) and Rabbit Technologies (the company that makes the AMQP-compliant, Erlang-based RabbitMQ message broker). Indeed, work has already begun apace on a Spring-AMQP project, and that support will no doubt manifest itself as adapters in Spring Integration 2.0. Your grasp of Spring Integration 1.0 will serve you well in Spring Integration 2.0; you'll simply have more tools in your toolbox!

In the next chapter, you will work with Spring Batch, a batch-processing framework built on top of the Spring platform to handle long-running jobs.

◼ ◼ ◼

CHAPTER 21

Spring Batch

Previous chapters discussed JMS and Spring Integration, which provide essential framework infrastructure for very common types of problems in an event-driven architecture (EDA). Another common kind of processing requirement is batch processing, which is both a complement and sometimes necessary extension to event-driven processing.

Batch processing has been around for decades. The earliest widespread applications of technology for managing information (information technology) were applications of batch processing. These environments didn't have interactive sessions and usually didn't have the capability to load multiple applications in memory. Computers were expensive and bore no resemblance to today's servers. Typically, machines were multiuser and in use during the day (time-shared). During the evening, however, the machines would sit idle, which was a tremendous waste. Businesses invested in ways to utilize the offline time to do work aggregated through the course of the day. Out of this practice emerged batch processing.

Batch processing solutions typically run offline, indifferent to events in the system. In the past, batch processes ran offline out of necessity. Today, however, most batch processes are run offline because having work done at a predictable time and having chunks of work done is a requirement for a lot of architectures. A batch processing solution doesn't usually respond to requests, although there's no reason it couldn't be started as a consequence of a message or request. Batch processing solutions tend to be used on large datasets where the duration of the processing is a critical factor in its architecture and implementation. A process might run for minutes, hours, or days! Jobs may have unbounded durations (i.e., run until all work is finished, even if this means running for a few days), or they may be strictly bounded (jobs must proceed in constant time, with each row taking the same amount of time regardless of bound, which lets you say predict that a given job will finish in a certain time window.)

Batch processing has had a long history that informs even modern batch processing solutions.

Mainframe applications used batch processing, and one of the largest modern day environments for batch processing, CICS on z/OS, is still fundamentally a mainframe operating system. Customer Information Control System (CICS) is very well suited to a particular type of task: take input, process it, and write it to output. CICS is a transaction server used most in financial institutions and government that runs programs in a number of languages (COBOL, C, PLI, and so on). It can easily support thousands of transactions per second. CICS was one of the first *containers*, a concept familiar to Spring and Java EE users, even though CICS itself debuted in 1969! A CICS installation is very expensive, and although IBM still sells and installs CICS, many other solutions have come along since then. These solutions are usually specific to a particular environment: COBOL/CICS on mainframes, C on Unix, and, today, Java on any number of environments. The problem is that there's very little standardized infrastructure for dealing with these types of batch processing solutions. Very few people are even aware of what they're missing because there's very little native support on the Java platform for batch processing. Businesses that need a solution typically end up writing it in-house, resulting in fragile, domain-specific code.

The pieces are there, however: transaction support, fast I/O, schedulers such as Quartz, and solid threading support, as well as a very powerful concept of an application container in Java EE and Spring. It was only natural that Dave Syer and his team would come along and build Spring Batch, a batch processing solution for the Spring platform.

It's important to think about the kinds of problems this framework solves before diving into the details. A technology is defined by its solution space. A typical Spring Batch application typically reads in a lot of data and then writes it back out in a modified form. Decisions about transactional barriers, input size, concurrency, and order of steps in processing are all dimensions of a typical integration.

A common requirement is loading data from a comma-separated value (CSV) file, perhaps as a business-to-business (B2B) transaction, perhaps as an integration technique with an older legacy application. Another common application is nontrivial processing on records in a database. Perhaps the output is an update of the database record itself. An example might be resizing of images on the file system whose metadata is stored in a database or needing to trigger another process based on some condition.

■ **Note** *Fixed-width data* is a format of rows and cells, quite like a CSV file. CSV file cells are separated by commas or tabs however, and fixed-width data works by presuming certain lengths for each value. The first value might be the first nine characters, the second value the next four characters after that, and so on.

Fixed-width data, which is often used with legacy or embedded systems, is a fine candidate for batch processing. Processing that deals with a resource that's fundamentally nontransactional (e.g., a web service or a file) begs for batch processing, because batch processing provides retry/skip/fail functionality that most web services will not.

It's also important to understand what Spring Batch *doesn't* do. Spring Batch is a flexible but not all-encompassing solution. Just as Spring doesn't reinvent the wheel when it can be avoided, Spring Batch leaves a few important pieces to the discretion of the implementor. Case in point: Spring Batch provides a generic mechanism by which to launch a job, be it by the command line, a Unix `cron`, an operating system service, Quartz (discussed in Chapter 18), or in response to an event on an enterprise service bus (for example, the Mule ESB or Spring's own ESB-like solution, Spring Integration, which is discussed in Chapter 20). Another example is the way Spring Batch manages the state of batch processes. Spring Batch requires a durable store. The only useful implementation of a `JobRepository` (an interface provided by Spring Batch for storing runtime data) requires a database, because a database is transactional and there's no need to reinvent it. To which database you should deploy, however, is largely unspecified, although there are useful defaults provided for you, of course.

Runtime Metadata Model

Spring Batch works with a `JobRepository`, which is the keeper of all the knowledge and metadata for each `job` (including component parts such as `JobInstances`, `JobExecution`, and `StepExecution`). Each `job` is composed of one or more `steps`, one after another. With Spring Batch 2.0, a `step` can conditionally follow another `step`, allowing for primitive workflows. These `steps` can also be concurrent: two `steps` can run at the same time.

When a job is run, it's often coupled with JobParameters to parameterize the behavior of the job itself. For example, a job might take a date parameter to determine which records to process. This coupling is called a JobInstance. A JobInstance is unique because of the JobParameters associated with it. Each time the same JobInstance (i.e., the same job and JobParameters) is run, it's called a JobExecution. This is a runtime context for a version of the job. Ideally, for every JobInstance there'd be only one JobExecution: the JobExecution that was created the first time the JobInstance ran. However, if there were any errors, the JobInstance should be restarted; the subsequent run would create another JobExecution. For every step in the original job, there is a StepExecution in the JobExecution.

Thus, you can see that Spring Batch has a mirrored object graph, one reflecting the design/build time view of a job, and another reflecting the runtime view of a job. This split between the prototype and the instance is very similar to the way many workflow engines—including jBPM—work.

For example, suppose that a daily report is generated at 2 AM. The parameter to the job would be the date (most likely the previous day's date). The job, in this case, would model a loading step, a summary step, and an output step. Each day the job is run, a new JobInstance and JobExecution would be created. If there are any retries of the same JobInstance, conceivably many JobExecutions would be created.

Note if you want to use Spring Batch, you need to add the appropriate libraries to the classpath. If you are using Maven, add the following dependency to your project.

```
<dependency>
  <groupId>org.springframework.batch</groupId>
  <version>2.1.1.RELEASE</version>
  <artifactId>spring-batch-core</artifactId>
</dependency>
```

21-1. Setting Up Spring Batch's Infrastructure

Problem

Spring Batch provides a lot of flexibility and guarantees to your application, but it cannot work in a vacuum. To do its work, the JobRepository requires a database. Additionally, there are several collaborators required for Spring Batch to do its work. This configuration is mostly boilerplate.

Solution

In this recipe, you'll set up the Spring Batch database and also create a Spring XML application context that can be imported by subsequent solutions. This configuration is repetitive and largely uninteresting. It will also tell Spring Batch what database to use for the metadata it stores.

How It Works

The JobRepository interface is the first thing that you'll have to deal with when setting up a Spring Batch process. You usually don't deal with it in code, but in Spring configuration it is key to getting everything else working. There's only one really useful implementation of the JobRepository interface called SimpleJobRepository, which stores information about the state of the batch processes in a database. Creation is done through a JobRepositoryFactoryBean. Another standard factory, MapJobRepositoryFactoryBean is useful mainly for testing because its state is not durable – it's an in-memory implementation. Both factories create an instance of SimpleJobRepository.

Because this JobRepository instance works on your database, you need to set up the schema for Spring Batch to work with. The simplest way to get that schema was to simply download the spring-batch-2.1.1.RELEASE-no-dependencies.zip and look in the sources folder at spring-batch-2.1.1.RELEASE/dist/org/springframework/batch/core. There you'll find a slew of .sql files, each containing the data definition language (DDL, the subset of SQL used for defining and examining the structure of a database) for the required schema for the database of your choice. In these examples, we will use PostgreSQL, so we will use the DDL for PostgreSQL: schema-postgresql.sql. Make sure you configure it and tell Spring Batch about it as in the following configuration:

```xml
<?xml version="1.0" encoding="UTF-8"?>
<beans:beans
    xmlns="http://www.springframework.org/schema/batch"
    xmlns:beans="http://www.springframework.org/schema/beans"
    xmlns:aop="http://www.springframework.org/schema/aop"
    xmlns:tx="http://www.springframework.org/schema/tx"
    xmlns:p="http://www.springframework.org/schema/p"
    xmlns:xsi="http://www.w3.org/2001/XMLSchema-instance"
    xmlns:util="http://www.springframework.org/schema/util"
    xsi:schemaLocation="
    http://www.springframework.org/schema/beans ↵
http://www.springframework.org/schema/beans/spring-beans-3.0.xsd
    http://www.springframework.org/schema/batch ↵
http://www.springframework.org/schema/batch/spring-batch-2.1.xsd
    http://www.springframework.org/schema/aop ↵
http://www.springframework.org/schema/aop/spring-aop-3.0.xsd
    http://www.springframework.org/schema/tx ↵
http://www.springframework.org/schema/tx/spring-tx-3.0.xsd
    http://www.springframework.org/schema/util ↵
http://www.springframework.org/schema/util/spring-util-3.0.xsd">

<context:component-scan base-package="com.apress.springrecipes.springbatch"/>

<beans:bean          class="org.springframework.beans.factory.config.↵
PropertyPlaceholderConfigurer"
        p:location="batch.properties"
        p:ignoreUnresolvablePlaceholders="true"/>

<beans:bean
        id="dataSource"
        class="org.apache.commons.dbcp.BasicDataSource"
        destroy-method="close"
        p:driverClassName="${dataSource.driverClassName}"
```

```
        p:username="${dataSource.username}"
        p:password="${dataSource.password}"
        p:url="${dataSource.url}"/>

<beans:bean
        id="transactionManager"            class="org.springframework.jdbc.↵
datasource.DataSourceTransactionManager"
        p:dataSource-ref="dataSource"/>

<beans:bean
        id="jobRegistry"            class="org.springframework.batch.core.configuration.↵
support.MapJobRegistry"/>

<beans:bean
        id="jobLauncher"            class="org.springframework.batch.core.launch.↵
support.SimpleJobLauncher"
        p:jobRepository-ref="jobRepository"/>

<beans:bean
        id="jobRegistryBeanPostProcessor"            class="org.springframework.batch.core.↵
configuration.support.JobRegistryBeanPostProcessor"
        p:jobRegistry-ref="jobRegistry"/>

<beans:bean
        id="jobRepository"            class="org.springframework.batch.core.↵
repository.support.JobRepositoryFactoryBean"
        p:dataSource-ref="dataSource"
        p:transactionManager-ref="transactionManager"/>


</beans:beans>
```

Because the implementation uses a database to persist the metadata, take care to configure a DataSource as well as a TransactionManager. In this example, you're using a PropertyPlaceholderConfigurer to load the contents of a properties file (batch.properties) whose values you use to configure the data source. You need to place values for your particular database in this file. This example uses Spring's property schema ("p") to abbreviate the tedious configuration. In subsequent examples, this file will be referenced as batch.xml. The properties file looks like this for us:

```
hibernate.configFile=hibernate.cfg.xml
dataSource.password=sep
dataSource.username=sep
dataSource.databaseName=sep
dataSource.driverClassName=org.postgresql.Driver
dataSource.dialect=org.hibernate.dialect.PostgreSQLDialect
dataSource.serverName=studio:5432
dataSource.url=jdbc:postgresql://${dataSource.serverName}/${dataSource.databaseName}
dataSource.properties=user=${dataSource.username};databaseName=${dataSource.databaseName};se
rverName=${dataSource.serverName};password=${dataSource.password}
```

The first few beans are related strictly to configuration – nothing particularly novel or peculiar to Spring Batch: a data source, a transaction manager and a properties resolver.

Eventually, we get to the declaration of a `MapJobRegistry` instance. This is critical—it is the central store for information regarding a given `Job`, and it controls the "big picture" about all `Jobs` in the system. Everything else works with this instance.

Next, we have a `SimpleJobLauncher`, whose sole purpose is to give you a mechanism to launch batch jobs, where a "job" in this case is our batch solution. The `jobLauncher` is used to specify the name of the batch solution to run as well as any parameters required. We'll follow up more on that in the next recipe.

Next, you define a `JobRegistryBeanPostProcessor`. This bean scans your Spring context file and associates any configured `Jobs` with the `MapJobRegistry`.

Finally, we get to the `SimpleJobRepository` (that is, in turn, factoried by the `JobRepositoryFactoryBean`). The `JobRepository` is an implementation of "repository (in the *Patterns of Enterprise Application Architecture* sense of the word): it handles persistence and retrieval for the domain models surrounding `Steps`, `Jobs`, etc.

21-2. Reading and Writing (but No Arithmetic)

Problem

You want to insert data from a file into a database. This solution will be one of the simplest solutions and will give you a chance to explore the moving pieces of a typical solution.

Solution

You'll build a solution that does a minimal amount of work, while being a viable application of the technology. The solution will read in a file of arbitrary length and write out the data into a database. The end result will be almost 100 percent code free. You will rely on an existing model class and write one class (a class containing the `public static void main(String [] args()` method) to round out the example. There's no reason why the model class couldn't be a Hibernate class or something from your DAO layer, though in this case it's a brainless POJO. This solution will use the components we configured in batch.xml.

How It Works

This example demonstrates the simplest possible use of a Spring Batch: to provide scalability. This program will do nothing but read data from a CSV file, with fields delimited by commas and rows delimited by new lines. It then inserts the records into a table. You are exploiting the intelligent infrastructure that Spring Batch provides to avoid worrying about scaling. This application could easily be done manually. You will not exploit any of the smart transactional functionality made available to you, nor will you worry about retries for the time being.

This solution is as simple as Spring Batch solutions get. Spring Batch models solutions using XML schema. This schema is new to Spring Batch 2.1. The abstractions and terms are in the spirit of classical batch processing solutions so will be portable from previous technologies and perhaps to subsequent technologies. Spring Batch provides useful default classes that you can override or selectively adjust. In the following example, you'll use a lot of the utility implementations provided by Spring Batch.

Fundamentally, most solutions look about the same and feature a combination of the same set of interfaces. It's usually just a matter of picking and choosing the right ones.

When I ran this program, it worked on files with 20,000 rows, and it worked on files with 1 million rows. I experienced no increase in memory, which indicates there were no memory leaks. Naturally, it took a lot longer! (The application ran for several hours with the 1-million-row insert.)

■ **Tip** Of course, it would be catastrophic if you worked with a million rows and it failed on the penultimate record, because you'd lose all your work when the transaction rolled back! Read on for examples on chunking. Additionally, you might want to read through Chapter 16 to brush up on transactions.

The following example inserts records into a table. I'm using PostgreSQL, which is a good mature open source database; you can use any database you want. (More information and downloads are available at www.postgresql.org.) The schema for the table is simple:

```
create table USER_REGISTRATION
(
  ID bigserial  not null  ,
  FIRST_NAME character varying(255) not null,
  LAST_NAME character varying(255) not null,
  COMPANY character varying(255) not null,
  ADDRESS character varying(255) not null,
  CITY character varying(255) not null,
  STATE character varying(255) not null,
  ZIP character varying(255) not null,
  COUNTY character varying(255) not null,
  URL character varying(255) not null,
  PHONE_NUMBER character varying(255) not null,
  FAX character varying(255) not null,
  constraint USER_REGISTRATION_PKEY primary key (id)
) ;
```

DATA LOADS AND DATA WAREHOUSES

In Recipe 21-3, I didn't tune the table at all. For example, there are no indexes on any of the columns besides the primary key. This is to avoid complicating the example. Great care should be taken with a table like this one in a nontrivial, production-bound application.

Spring Batch applications are workhorse applications and have the potential to reveal bottlenecks in your application you didn't know you had. Imagine suddenly being able to achieve 1 million new database insertions every 10 minutes. Would your database grind to a halt? Insert speed can be a critical factor in the speed of your application. Software developers will (hopefully) think about their database schema in terms of how well it enforces the constraints of the business logic and how well it serves the overall business model. However, it's important to wear another hat, that of a DBA, when writing applications such as this one. A common solution is to create a denormalized table whose contents can be coerced into valid data once inside the database, perhaps by a trigger on inserts. This is typical in data warehousing. Later, you'll explore using Spring Batch to do processing on a record before insertion. This lets the developer verify or override the input into the database. This processing, in tandem with a conservative application of constraints that are best expressed in the database, can make for applications that are very robust *and* quick.

The Job Configuration

The configuration for the job is as follows:

```
<job
  job-repository="jobRepository"
  id="insertIntoDbFromCsvJob">
  <step id="step1">
      <tasklet transaction-manager="transactionManager">
      <chunk
              reader="csvFileReader"
              writer="jdbcItemWriter"
              commit-interval="5"
          />
      </tasklet>
    </step>
</job>
```

As described earlier, a job consists of steps, which are the real workhorse of a given job. The steps can be as complex or as simple as you like. Indeed, a step could be considered the smallest unit of work for a job. Input (what's read) is passed to the Step and potentially processed; then output (what's written) is created from the step. This processing is spelled out using a Tasklet. You can provide your own Tasklet implementation or simply use some of the preconfigured configurations for different processing scenarios. These implementations are made available in terms of subelements of the Tasklet element. One of the most important aspects of batch processing is chunk-oriented processing, which is employed here using the chunk element.

In chunk-oriented processing, input is read from a reader, optionally processed, and then aggregated. Finally, at a configurable interval as specified by the commit-interval attribute to configure how many items will be processed before the transaction is committed all the input is sent to the writer. If there is a transaction manager in play, the transaction is also committed. Right before a commit, the metadata in the database is updated to mark the progress of the job.

There are some nuances surrounding the aggregation of the input (read) values when a transaction-aware writer (or processor) rolls back. Spring Batch caches the values it reads and writes them to the writer. If the writer component is transactional, like a database, and the reader is not, there's nothing inherently wrong with caching the read values and perhaps retrying or taking some alternative approach. If the reader itself is also transactional, then the values read from the resource will be rolled back and could conceivably change, rendering the in-memory cached values stale. If this happens, you can configure the chunk to not cache the values using reader-transactional-queue="true" on the chunk element.

Input

The first responsibility is reading a file from the file system. You use a provided implementation for the example. Reading CSV files is a very common scenario, and Spring Batch's support does not disappoint. The `org.springframework.batch.item.file.FlatFileItemReader<T>` class delegates the task of delimiting fields and records within a file to a `LineMapper<T>`, which in turn delegates the task of identifying the fields within that record, to `LineTokenizer`. You use a `org.springframework.batch.item.file.transform.DelimitedLineTokenizer`, which is configured to delineate fields separated by a "," character.

The `FlatFileItemReader` also declares a `fieldSetMapper` attribute that requires an implementation of `FieldSetMapper`. This bean is responsible for taking the input name/value pairs and producing a type that will be given to the writer component.

In this case, you use an `BeanWrapperFieldSetMapper` that will create a JavaBean POJO of type `UserRegistration`. You name the fields so that you can reference them later in the configuration. These names don't have to be the values of some header row in the input file; they just have to correspond to the order in which the fields are found in the input file. These names are also used by the `FieldSetMapper` to match properties on a POJO. As each record is read, the values are applied to an instance of a POJO, and that POJO is returned.

```
<beans:bean
  id="csvFileReader"
  class="org.springframework.batch.item.file.FlatFileItemReader"
  p:resource="file:${user.home}/batches/registrations.csv">
  <beans:property
   name="lineMapper">
   <beans:bean
    class="org.springframework.batch.item.file.mapping.DefaultLineMapper">
    <beans:property
     name="lineTokenizer">
     <beans:bean        class="org.springframework.batch.item.file.↵
transform.DelimitedLineTokenizer"
      p:delimiter=","        p:names="firstName,lastName,company,address,↵
city,state,zip,county,url,phoneNumber,fax" />
    </beans:property>
    <beans:property
     name="fieldSetMapper">
     <beans:bean
class="org.springframework.batch.item.file.mapping.BeanWrapperFieldSetMapper"↵
      p:targetType="com.apress.springrecipes.springbatch.UserRegistration" />
    </beans:property>
   </beans:bean>
  </beans:property>
 </beans:bean>
```

The class returned from the reader, `UserRegistration`, is a rather plain JavaBean.

```
package com.apress.springrecipes.springbatch.solution1;

public class UserRegistration implements Serializable {

    private String firstName;
    private String lastName;
    private String company;
    private String address;
    private String city;
    private String state;
    private String zip;
    private String county;
    private String url;
    private String phoneNumber;
    private String fax;

    //… accessor / mutators omitted for brevity …

}
```

Output

The next component to do work is the writer, which is responsible for taking the aggregated collection of items read from the reader. In this case, you might imagine that a new collection (java.util.List<UserRegistration>) is created, then written, and then reset each time the collection exceeds the commit-interval attribute on the chunk element. Because you're trying to write to a database, you use Spring Batch's org.springframework.batch.item.database.JdbcBatchItemWriter. This class contains support for taking input and writing it to a database. It is up to the developer to provide the input and to specify what SQL should be run for the input. It will run the SQL specified by the sql property, in essence reading from the database, as many times as specified by the chunk element's commit-interval, and then commit the whole transaction. Here, you're doing a simple insert. The names and values for the named parameters are being created by the bean configured for the itemSqlParameterSourceProvider property, an instance of the interface BeanPropertyItemSqlParameterSourceProvider, whose sole job it is to take JavaBean properties and make them available as named parameters corresponding to the property name on the JavaBean.

```
<beans:bean id="jdbcItemWriter"class="org.springframework.batch.item.↩
database.JdbcBatchItemWriter"          p:assertUpdates="true"
      p:dataSource-ref="dataSource">
      <beans:property name="sql">
       <beans:value>
           <![CDATA[
     insert into USER_REGISTRATION(
FIRST_NAME, LAST_NAME, COMPANY, ADDRESS,
CITY, STATE, ZIP, COUNTY,
URL, PHONE_NUMBER, FAX )
values (  :firstName, :lastName, :company, :address,  :city , :state, :↩
zip, :county,  :url, :phoneNumber, :fax  )
]]> </beans:value>
</beans:property>
```

```
<beans:property name="itemSqlParameterSourceProvider">
<beans:bean
    class="org.springframework.batch.item.database.BeanPropertyItemSql
ParameterSourceProvider" />
</beans:property>
</beans:bean>
```

And that's it! A working solution. With little configuration and no custom code, you've built a solution for taking large CSV files and reading them into a database. This solution is bare bones and leaves a lot of edge cases uncared for. You might want to do processing on the item as it's read (before it's inserted), for example.

This exemplifies a simple job. It's important to remember that there are similar classes for doing the exact opposite transformation: reading from a database and writing to a CSV file.

21-3. Writing a Custom ItemWriter and ItemReader

Problem

You want to talk to a resource (you might imagine an RSS feed, or any other custom data format) that Spring Batch doesn't know how to connect to.

Solution

You can easily write your own `ItemWriter` or `ItemReader`. The interfaces are drop dead simple, and there's not a lot of responsibility placed on the implementations.

How It Works

As easy and trivial as this process is to do, it's still not better than just reusing any of the numerous provided options. If you look, you'll likely find something. There's support for writing JMS (`JmsItemWriter<T>`), JPA (`JpaItemWriter<T>`), JDBC (`JdbcBatchItemWriter<T>`), Files (`FlatFileItemWriter<T>`), iBatis (`IbatisBatchItemWriter<T>`), Hibernate (`HibernateItemWriter<T>`), and more. There's even support for writing by invoking a method on a bean (`PropertyExtractingDelegatingItemWriter<T>`) and passing to it as arguments the properties on the `Item` to be written! One of the more useful writers lets you write to a set of files that are numbered. This implementation—`MultiResourceItemWriter<T>`—delegates to other proper `ItemWriter<T>` implementation for the work, but lets you write to multiple files, not just one very large one. There's a slightly smaller but impressive set of implementations for `ItemReader` implementations. If it doesn't exist, look again. If you *still* can't find one, consider writing your own. In this recipe, we will do just that.

Writing a Custom ItemReader

The `ItemReader` example is trivial. Here, an `ItemReader` is created that knows how to retrieve `UserRegistration` objects from a remote procedure call (RPC) endpoint:

```
package com.apress.springrecipes.springbatch.solution2;

import java.util.Collection;
import java.util.Date;

import org.springframework.batch.item.ItemReader;
import org.springframework.batch.item.ParseException;
import org.springframework.batch.item.UnexpectedInputException;
import org.springframework.beans.factory.annotation.Autowired;

import com.apress.springrecipes.springbatch.UserRegistrationService;
import com.apress.springrecipes.springbatch.solution1.UserRegistration;

public class UserRegistrationItemReader
    implements ItemReader<UserRegistration> {

    @Autowired
    private UserRegistrationService userRegistrationService;
    public UserRegistration read() throws Exception,UnexpectedInputException,
    ParseException {
        Date today = new Date();
        Collection<UserRegistration> registrations =

          userRegistrationService.getOutstandingUserRegistrationBatchForDate(
                  1, today);
        if (registrations!=null && registrations.size() >= 1)
            return registrations.iterator().next();
        return null;
    }
}
```

As you can see, the interface is trivial. In this case, you defer most work to a remote service to provide you with the input. The interface requires that you return one record. The interface is parameterized to the type of object (the "item") to be returned. All the read items will be aggregated and then passed to the ItemWriter.

Writing a Custom ItemWriter

The ItemWriter example is also trivial. Imagine wanting to write by invoking a remote service using any of the numerous options for remoting that Spring provides. The ItemWriter<T> interface is parameterized by the type of item you're expecting to write. Here, you expect a UserRegistration object from the ItemReader<T>. The interface consists of one method, which expects a List of the class's parameterized type. These are the objects read from ItemReader<T> and aggregated. If your commit-interval were ten, you might expect ten or fewer items in the List.

```java
package com.apress.springrecipes.springbatch.solution2;

import java.util.List;

import org.apache.commons.lang.builder.ToStringBuilder;
import org.apache.log4j.Logger;
import org.springframework.batch.item.ItemWriter;
import org.springframework.beans.factory.annotation.Autowired;

import com.apress.springrecipes.springbatch.User;
import com.apress.springrecipes.springbatch.UserRegistrationService;
import com.apress.springrecipes.springbatch.solution1.UserRegistration;

public class UserRegistrationServiceItemWriter implements
        ItemWriter<UserRegistration> {

    private static final Logger logger = Logger
        .getLogger(UserRegistrationServiceItemWriter.class);

    // this is the client interface to an HTTP Invoker service.
    @Autowired
    private UserRegistrationService userRegistrationService;

    /**
     * takes aggregated input from the reader and 'writes' them using a custom
     * implementation.
     */
    public void write(List<? extends UserRegistration> items)
    throws Exception {
        for (final UserRegistration userRegistration : items) {
            UserRegistration registeredUser = userRegistrationService
                .registerUser(userRegistration);
            logger.debug("Registered:"
                + ToStringBuilder.reflectionToString(registeredUser));
        }
    }
}
```

Here, you've wired in the service's client interface. You simply loop through the UserRegistration objects and invoke the service, which in turn hands you back an identical instance of UserRegistration. If you remove the gratuitous spacing, curly brackets and logging output, it becomes two lines of code to satisfy the requirement.

The interface for UserRegistrationService follows:

```java
package com.apress.springrecipes.springbatch;

import java.util.Collection;
import java.util.Date;

public interface UserRegistrationService {
```

```
Collection<UserRegistration> getOutstandingUserRegistrationBatchForDate(
    int quantity, Date date);

UserRegistration registerUser(
    UserRegistration userRegistrationRegistration);
}
```

In our example, we have no particular implementation for the interface, as it is irrelevant: it could be any interface that Spring Batch doesn't know about already.

21-4. Processing Input Before Writing

Problem

While transferring data directly from a spreadsheet or CSV dump might be useful, one can imagine having to do some sort of processing on the data before it's written. Data in a CSV file, and more generally from any source, is not usually exactly the way you expect it to be or immediately suitable for writing. Just because Spring Batch can coerce it into a POJO on your behalf, that doesn't mean the state of the data is correct. There may be additional data that you need to infer or fill in from other services before the data is suitable for writing.

Solution

Spring Batch will let you do processing on **reader** output. This processing can do virtually anything to the output before it gets passed to the **writer**, including changing the type of the data.

How It Works

Spring Batch gives the implementor a chance to perform any custom logic on the data read from **reader**. The **processor** attribute on the **chunk** element expects a reference to a bean of the interface `org.springframework.batch.item.ItemProcessor<I,O>`. Thus, the revised definition for the **job** from the previous recipe looks like this:

```
        <job
job-repository="jobRepository"
id="insertIntoDbFromCsvJob">
<step id="step1">
    <tasklet transaction-manager="transactionManager">
                <chunk
            reader="csvFileReader"
```

```
            processor = "userRegistrationValidationProcessor"
            writer="jdbcItemWriter"
            commit-interval="5"
         />
      </tasklet>
   </step>
</job>
```

The goal is to do certain validations on the data before you authorize it to be written to the database. If you determine the record is invalid, you can stop further processing by returning null from the ItemProcessor<I,O>. This is crucial and provides a necessary safeguard. One thing that you want to do is ensure that the data is the right format (for example, the schema may require a valid two-letter state name instead of the longer full state name). Telephone numbers are expected to follow a certain format, and you can use this processor to strip the telephone number of any extraneous characters, leaving only a valid (in the United States) ten-digit phone number. The same applies for U. S. zip codes, which consist of five characters and optionally a hyphen followed by a four-digit code. Finally, while a constraint guarding against duplicates is best implemented in the database, there may very well be some other eligibility criteria for a record that can be met only by querying the system before insertion.

Here's the configuration for the ItemProcessor:

```
<beans:bean id="userRegistrationValidationProcessor"
class="com.apress.springrecipes.springbatch.solution2.↵
    UserRegistrationValidationItemProcessor" />
```

In the interest of keeping this class short, I won't reprint it in its entirety, but the salient bits should be obvious:

```
package com.apress.springrecipes.springbatch.solution2;
import java.util.Arrays;
import java.util.Collection;

import org.apache.commons.lang.StringUtils;
import org.springframework.batch.core.StepExecution;
import org.springframework.batch.item.ItemProcessor;
import com.apress.springrecipes.springbatch.solution1.UserRegistration;

public class UserRegistrationValidationItemProcessor
   implements ItemProcessor<UserRegistration, UserRegistration> {

   private String stripNonNumbers(String input) { /* … */ }

   private boolean isTelephoneValid(String telephone) { /* … */ }

   private boolean isZipCodeValid(String zip) { /* … */ }

   private boolean isValidState(String state) { /* … */ }

   public UserRegistration process(UserRegistration input) throws Exception {
      String zipCode = stripNonNumbers(input.getZip());
      String telephone = stripNonNumbers(input.getPhoneNumber());
      String state = StringUtils.defaultString(input.getState());
```

```
        if (isTelephoneValid(telephone) && isZipCodeValid(zipCode) ↵
&& isValidState(state)) {
            input.setZip(zipCode);
            input.setPhoneNumber(telephone );
            return input;
        }
        return null;
    }
}
```

The class is a parameterized type. The type information is the type of the input, as well as the type of the output. The input is what's given to the method for processing, and the output is the returned data from the method. Because you're not transforming anything in this example, the two parameterized types are the same.

Once this process has completed, there's a lot of useful information to be had in the Spring Batch metadata tables. Issue the following query on your database:

```
select * from BATCH_STEP_EXECUTION;
```

Among other things, you'll get back the exit status of the job, how many commits occurred, how many items were read, and how many items were filtered. So if the preceding job was run on a batch with a 100 rows, each item was read and passed through the processor, and it found 10 items invalid (it returned null 10 times), the value for the `filter_count` column would be 10. You could see that a 100 items were read from the `read_count`. The `write_count` column would reflect that 10 items didn't make it and would show 90.

Chaining Processors Together

Sometimes you might want to add extra processing that isn't congruous with the goals of the processor you've already set up. Spring Batch provides a convenience class, `CompositeItemProcessor<I,O>`, which forwards the output of the filter to the input of the successive filter. In this way, you can write many, singly focused `ItemProcessor<I,O>`s and then reuse them and chain them as necessary:

```
<beans:bean id="compositeBankCustomerProcessor"
    class="org.springframework.batch.↵
item.support.CompositeItemProcessor">
<beans:property name="delegates">
<beans:list>
<bean ref="creditScoreValidationProcessor"  />
<bean ref="salaryValidationProcessor" />
<bean ref="customerEligibilityProcessor" />
</beans:list>
</beans:property>
</beans:bean>
<job job-repository="jobRepository" id="insertIntoDbFromCsvJob">
<step id="step1">
        <tasklet transaction-manager="transactionManager">
```

```
            <chunk
                reader="csvFileReader"
                processor="compositeBankCustomerProcessor"
                writer="jdbcItemWriter"
                commit-interval="5"
            />
        </tasklet>
    </step>
</job>
```

The example created a very simple workflow. The first `ItemProcessor<T>` will take an input of whatever's coming from the `ItemReader<T>` configured for this job, presumably a `Customer` object. It will check the credit score of the `Customer` and, if approved, forward the `Customer` to the salary and income validation processor. If everything checks out there, the `Customer` will be forwarded to the eligibility processor, where the system is checked for duplicates or any other invalid data. It will finally be forwarded to the `writer` to be added to the output. If at any point in the three processors the `Customer` fails a check, the executing `ItemProcessor` can simply return `null` and arrest processing.

21-5. Better Living through Transactions

Problem

You want your reads and writes to be robust. Ideally, they'll use transactions where appropriate and correctly react to exceptions.

Solution

Transaction capabilities are built on top of the first class support already provided by the core Spring framework. Where relevant, Spring Batch surfaces the configuration so that you can control it. Within the context of chunk-oriented processing, it also exposes a lot of control over the frequency of commits, rollback semantics, and so on.

How It Works

Transactions

Spring's core framework provides first-class support for transactions. You simply wire up a `TransactionManager` and give Spring Batch a reference, just as you would in any regular `JdbcTemplate` or `HibernateTemplate` solution. As you build your Spring Batch solutions, you'll be given opportunities to control how `steps` behave in a transaction. You've already seen some of the support for transactions baked right in.

The `batch.xml` file, used in all these examples, established a BasicDataSource and a DataSourceTransactionManager bean. The `TransactionManager` and `BasicDataSource` were then wired to the `JobRepository`, which was in turn wired to the `JobLauncher`, which you used to launch all jobs thus far. This enabled all the metadata your `jobs` create to be written to the database in a transactional way.

You might wonder why there is no explicit mention of the `TransactionManager` when you configured the `JdbcItemWriter` with a reference to `dataSource`. The transaction manager reference can be specified, but in your solutions, it wasn't required because Spring Batch will, by default, try to pluck the `PlatformTransactionManager` named `transactionManager` from the context and use it. If you want to explicitly configure this, you can specify the `transactionManager` property on the `tasklet` element. A simple `TransactionManager` for JDBC work might look like this:

```
<bean id="myCustomTransactionManager" class="org.springframework.jdbc.datasource.⏎
DataSourceTransactionManager"
p:dataSource-ref="dataSource" />

<job job-repository="jobRepository" id="insertIntoDbFromCsvJob">
      <step id="step1">
          <tasklet transaction-manager="myCustomTransactionManager" >
              <!-- ... -->
          </tasklet>
      </step>
</job>
  ...
```

Items read from an `ItemReader<T>` are normally aggregated. If a commit on the `ItemWriter<T>` fails, the aggregated items are kept and then resubmitted. This process is efficient and works most of the time. One place where it breaks semantics is when reading from a transactional message queue. Reads from a message queue can and should be rolled back if the transaction they participate in (in this case, the transaction for the `writer`) fails:

```
<tasklet transaction-manager="customTransactionManager" >
    <chunk
        reader="jmsItemReader" is-reader-transactional-queue="true"
        processor="userRegistrationValidationProcessor"
        writer="jdbcItemWriter"
        commit-interval="5" />
</tasklet>
```

Rollbacks

Handling the simple case ("read X items, and every Y items, commit a database transaction every Y items") is easy. Spring Batch excels in the robustness it surfaces as simple configuration options for the edge and failure cases.

If a write fails on an `ItemWriter`, or some other exception occurs in processing, Spring Batch will roll back the transaction. This is valid handling for a majority of the cases. There may be some scenarios when you want to control which exceptional cases cause the transaction to roll back.

You can use the `no-rollback-exception-classes` element to configure this for the `step`. The value is a list of `Exception` classes that should not cause the transaction to roll back:

```
<step id = "step2">
        <tasklet>
                <chunk reader="reader" writer="writer" commit-interval="10" />
                    <no-rollback-exception-classes>
                        <include class="com.yourdomain.exceptions.YourBusinessException"/>
                    </no-rollback-exception-classes>
        </tasklet>
</step>
```

21-6. Retrying

Problem

You are dealing with a requirement for functionality that may fail but is not transactional. Perhaps it is transactional but unreliable. You want to work with a resource that may fail when you try to read from or write to it. It may fail because of networking connectivity because an endpoint is down or for any other number of reasons. You know that it will likely be back up soon, though, and that it should be retried.

Solution

Use Spring Batch's retry capabilities to systematically retry the read or write.

How It Works

As you saw in the last recipe, it's easy to handle transactional resources with Spring Batch. When it comes to transient or unreliable resources, a different tack is required. Such resources tend to be distributed or manifest problems that eventually resolve themselves. Some (such as web services) cannot inherently participate in a transaction because of their distributed nature. There are products that can start a transaction on one server and propagate the transactional context to a distributed server and complete it there, although this tends to be very rare and inefficient. Alternatively, there's good support for distributed ("global" or XA) transactions if you can use it. Sometimes, however, you may be dealing with a resource that isn't either of those. A common example might be a call made to a remote service, such as an RMI service or a REST endpoint. Some invocations will fail but may be retried with some likelihood of success in a transactional scenario. For example, an update to the database resulting in `org.springframework.dao.DeadlockLoserDataAccessException` might be usefully retried.

Configuring a Step

The simplest example is in the configuration of a `step`. Here, you can specify exception classes on which to retry the operation. As with the rollback exceptions, you can delimit this list of exceptions with newlines or commas:

```
<step id = "step23">
<tasklet transaction-manager="transactionManager">
        <chunk reader="csvFileReader" writer="jdbcItemWriter" commit-interval="10" ↵
 retry-limit="3" cache-capacity="10">
              <retryable-exception-classes>
        <include class="org.springframework.dao.DeadlockLoserDataAccessException"/>
                  </retryable-exception-classes>
        </chunk>
    </tasklet>
</step>
```

Retry Template

Alternatively, you can leverage Spring Batch's support for retries and recovery in your own code. For example, you can have a custom `ItemWriter<T>` in which retry functionality is desired or even an entire service interface for which retry support is desired.

Spring Batch supports these scenarios through the `RetryTemplate` that (much like its various other `Template` cousins) isolates your logic from the nuances of retries and instead enables you to write the code as though you were only going to attempt it once. Let Spring Batch handle everything else through declarative configuration.

The `RetryTemplate` supports many use cases, with convenient APIs to wrap otherwise tedious retry/fail/recover cycles in concise, single-method invocations.

Let's take a look at the modified version of a simple `ItemWriter<T>` from Recipe 9.4 on how to write a custom `ItemWriter<T>`. The solution was simple enough and would ideally work all the time. It fails to handle the error cases for the service, however. When dealing with RPC, always proceed as if it's almost impossible for things to go right; the service itself may surface a semantic or system violation. An example might be a duplicate database key, invalid credit card number, and so on. This is true whether the service is distributed or in-VM, of course.

Next, the RPC layer below the system may also fault. Here's the rewritten code, this time allowing for retries:

```
package com.apress.springrecipes.springbatch.solution2;

import java.util.List;

import org.apache.commons.lang.builder.ToStringBuilder;
import org.apache.log4j.Logger;
import org.springframework.batch.item.ItemWriter;
import org.springframework.batch.retry.RetryCallback;
import org.springframework.batch.retry.RetryContext;
import org.springframework.batch.retry.support.RetryTemplate;
import org.springframework.beans.factory.annotation.Autowired;

import com.apress.springrecipes.springbatch.User;
import com.apress.springrecipes.springbatch.UserRegistrationService;
import com.apress.springrecipes.springbatch.solution1.UserRegistration;
```

```
/**
 *
 *
 * This class writes the user registration by calling an RPC service (whose
 * client interface is wired in using Spring
 */
public class RetryableUserRegistrationServiceItemWriter implements
      ItemWriter<UserRegistration> {

   private static final Logger logger = Logger
       .getLogger(RetryableUserRegistrationServiceItemWriter.class);

   // this is the client interface to an HTTP Invoker service.
   @Autowired
   private UserRegistrationService userRegistrationService;

   @Autowired
   private RetryTemplate retryTemplate;

   /**
    * takes aggregated input from the reader and 'writes' them using a custom
    * implementation.
    */
   public void write(List<? extends UserRegistration> items)
     throws Exception {
       for (final UserRegistration userRegistration : items) {
          User registeredUser = retryTemplate.execute(
          new RetryCallback<User>() {
             public User doWithRetry(RetryContext context) throws Exception {
                return userRegistrationService.registerUser(userRegistration);
             }
          });
          logger.debug("Registered:"
              + ToStringBuilder.reflectionToString(registeredUser));
      }
    }
  }
}
```

As you can see, the code hasn't changed much, and the result is much more robust. The
RetryTemplate itself is configured in the Spring context, although it's trivial to create in code. I declare it
in the Spring context only because there is some surface area for configuration when creating the object,
and I try to let Spring handle the configuration.

One of the more useful settings for the RetryTemplate is the BackOffPolicy in use. The
BackOffPolicy dictates how long the RetryTemplate should back off between retries. Indeed, there's even
support for growing the delay between retries after each failed attempt to avoid lock stepping with other
clients attempting the same invocation. This is great for situations in which there are potentially many
concurrent attempts on the same resource and a race condition may ensue. There are other
BackOffPolicies, including one that delays retries by a fixed amount called FixedBackOffPolicy.

```
<beans:bean id="retryTemplate" class="org.springframework.batch.retry.
support.RetryTemplate">
    <beans:property name="backOffPolicy" >
        <beans:bean  class="org.springframework.batch.retry.backoff.↵
            ExponentialBackOffPolicy"
        p:initialInterval="1000" p:maxInterval="10000" p:multiplier="2" />
    </beans:property>
</beans:bean>
```

You have configured a `RetryTemplate`'s `backOffPolicy` so that the `backOffPolicy` will wait 1 second (1,000 milliseconds) before the initial retry. Subsequent attempts will double that value (the growth is influenced by the multiplier). It'll continue until the `maxInterval` is met, at which point all subsequent retry intervals will level off, retrying at a consistent interval.

AOP-Based Retries

An alternative is an AOP advisor provided by Spring Batch that will wrap invocations of methods whose success is not guaranteed in retries, as you did with the `RetryTemplate`. In the previous example, you rewrote an `ItemWriter<T>` to make use of the template. Another approach might be to merely advise the entire `userRegistrationService` proxy with this retry logic. In this case, the code could go back to the way it was in the original example, with no `RetryTemplate`!

```
<aop:config>
    <aop:pointcut id="remote"
        expression="execution(* com..*RetryableUserRegistrationServiceItemWriter.*(..))" />
    <aop:advisor pointcut-ref="remote"  advice-ref="retryAdvice" order="-1"/>
</aop:config>

<beans:bean id="retryAdvice" class="org.springframework.batch.retry.interceptor.↵
RetryOperationsInterceptor"/>
```

21-7. Controlling Step Execution

Problem

You want to control how `steps` are executed, perhaps to eliminate a needless waste of time by introducing concurrency or by executing `steps` only if a condition is `true`.

Solution

There are different ways to change the runtime profile of your `jobs`, mainly by exerting control over the way `steps` are executed: concurrent `steps`, decisions, and sequential `steps`.

How It Works

Thus far, you have explored running one step in a job. Typical jobs of almost any complexity will have multiple steps, however. A step provides a boundary (transactional or not) to the beans and logic it encloses. A step can have its own reader, writer, and processor. Each step helps decide what the next step will be. A step is isolated and provides focused functionality that can be assembled using the updated schema and configuration options in Spring Batch 2.1 in very sophisticated workflows. In fact, some of the concepts and patterns you're about to see will be very familiar if you have an interest in business process management (BPM) systems and workflows. (To learn more about BPM, and jBPM in particular, see Chapter 23.) BPM provides many constructs for process or job control that are similar to what you're seeing here.

A step often corresponds to a bullet point when you outline the definition of a job on paper. For example, a batch job to load the daily sales and produce a report might be proposed as follows:

Daily Sales Report Job

1. Load customers from the CSV file into the database.

2. Calculate daily statistics, and write to a report file.

3. Send messages to the message queue to notify an external system of the successful registration for each of the newly loaded customers.

Sequential Steps

In the previous example, there's an implied sequence between the first two steps: the audit file can't be written until all the registrations have completed. This sort of relationship is the default relationship between two steps. One occurs after the other. Each step executes with its own execution context and shares only a parent job execution context and an order.

```
<job    id="nightlyRegistrationsJob"
    job-repository="jobRepository">
    <step id="loadRegistrations" next="reportStatistics" >
    <tasklet ref = "tasklet1"/>
    </step>
    <step id="reportStatistics" next="…" >
    <tasklet ref ="tasklet2"/>
    </step>
    <!-- … other steps … -->
</job>
```

Notice that you specify the next attribute on the step elements to tell processing which step to go to next.

Concurrency

The first version of Spring Batch was oriented toward batch processing inside the same thread and, with some alteration, perhaps inside the virtual machine. There were workarounds, of course, but the situation was less than ideal.

In the outline for this example job, the first step had to come before the second two because the second two are dependent on the first. The second two, however, do not share any such dependencies. There's no reason why the audit log couldn't be written at the same time as the JMS messages are being delivered. Spring Batch provides the capability to fork processing to enable just this sort of arrangement:

```
<job job-repository="jobRepository" id="insertIntoDbFromCsvJob">
    <step id="loadRegistrations" next="finalizeRegistrations">
    <!-- ... -->
    </step>
    <split id="finalizeRegistrations" >
        <flow>
            <step id="reportStatistics" ><!-- ... --></step>
        </flow>
        <flow>
            <step id="sendJmsNotifications" > <!-- ... --></step>
        </flow>
    </split>
</job>
```

In this example, there's nothing to prevent you from having many steps within the flow elements, nor was there anything preventing you from having more steps after the split element. The split element, like the step elements, takes a next attribute as well.

Spring Batch provides a mechanism to offload processing to another process. This feature, called *remote chunking*, is new in Spring Batch 2.x. This distribution requires some sort of durable, reliable connection. This is a perfect use of JMS because it's rock-solid and transactional, fast, and reliable. Spring Batch support is modeled at a slightly higher level, on top of the Spring Integration abstractions for Spring Integration channels. This support is not in the main Spring Batch code, though. Remote chunking lets individual steps read and aggregate items as usual in the main thread. This step is called the Master. Items read are sent to the ItemProcessor<I,O>/ItemWriter<T> running in another process (this is called the Slave). If the Slave is an aggressive consumer, you have a simple, generic mechanism to scale: work is instantly farmed out over as many JMS clients as you can throw at it. The aggressive-consumer pattern refers to the arrangement of multiple JMS clients all consuming the same queue's messages. If one client consumes a message and is busy processing, other idle queues will get the message instead. As long as there's a client that's idle, the message will be processed instantly.

Additionally, Spring Batch supports implicitly scaling out using a feature called *partitioning*. This feature is interesting because it's built in and generally very flexible. You replace your instance of a step with a subclass, PartitionStep, which knows how to coordinate distributed executors and maintains the metadata for the execution of the step, thus eliminating the need for a durable medium of communication as in the "remote chunking" technology.

The functionality here is also very generic. It could, conceivably, be used with any sort of grid fabric technology such as GridGain or Hadoop. (For more on GridGain, see Chapter 22.) Spring Batch ships with only a TaskExecutorPartitionHandler, which executes steps in multiple threads using a TaskExecutor strategy. This simple improvement might be enough of a justification for this feature! If you're really hurting, however, you can extend it.

Conditional Steps with Statuses

Using the ExitStatus of a given job or step to determine the next step is the simplest example of a conditional flow. Spring Batch facilitates this through the use of the stop, next, fail, and end elements. By default, assuming no intervention, a step will have an ExitStatus that matches its BatchStatus, which is a property whose values are defined in an enum and may be any of the following: COMPLETED, STARTING, STARTED, STOPPING, STOPPED, FAILED, ABANDONED, or UNKNOWN.

Let's look at an example that executes one of two steps based on the success of a preceding step:

```
<step id="step1" >
    <next on="COMPLETED" to="step2" > <!-- ... --></step>
        <next on="FAILED" to="failureStep" > <!-- ... --></step>
</step>
```

It's also possible to provide a wildcard. This is useful if you want to ensure a certain behavior for any number of BatchStatus, perhaps in tandem with a more specific next element that matches only one BatchStatus.

```
<step id="step1" >
    <next on="COMPLETED" to="step2" > <!-- ... --></step>
        <next on="*" to="failureStep" > <!-- ... --></step>
</step>
```

In this example, you are instructing Spring Batch to perform some step based on any unaccounted-for ExitStatus. Another option is to just stop processing altogether with a BatchStatus of FAILED. You can do this using the fail element. A less aggressive rewrite of the preceding example might be the following:

```
<step id="step1" >
    <next on="COMPLETED" to="step2" />
        <fail  on="FAILED"  />
        <!-- ... -->
</step>
```

In all these examples, you're reacting to the standard BatchStatuses that the Spring Batch framework provides. But it's also possible to raise your own ExitStatus. If, for example, you wanted the whole job to fail with a custom ExitStatus of "MAN DOWN", you might do something like this:

```
<step id="step1" next="step2"><!-- ... --></step>
<step id="step2" …>
  <fail on="FAILED" exit-code="MAN DOWN "/>
  <next on="*" to="step3"/>
</step>
<step id="step3"><!-- ... --></step>
```

Finally, if all you want to do is end processing with a BatchStatus of COMPLETED, you can use the end element. This is an explicit way of ending a flow as if it had run out of steps and incurred no errors.

```
<next on="COMPLETED" to="step2" />
<step id="step2" >
  <end on="COMPLETED"/>
  <next on="FAILED" to="errorStep"/>
  <!-- ... -->
</step>
```

Conditional Steps with Decisions

If you want to vary the execution flow based on some logic more complex than a `job`'s `ExitStatuses`, you may give Spring Batch a helping hand by using a `decision` element and providing it with an implementation of a `JobExecutionDecider`.

```
package com.apress.springrecipes.springbatch.solution2;

import org.springframework.batch.core.JobExecution;
import org.springframework.batch.core.StepExecution;
import org.springframework.batch.core.job.flow.FlowExecutionStatus;
import org.springframework.batch.core.job.flow.JobExecutionDecider;

public class HoroscopeDecider implements JobExecutionDecider {

    private boolean isMercuryIsInRetrograde (){ return Math.random() > .9 ; }

    public FlowExecutionStatus decide(JobExecution jobExecution, ↵
                                      StepExecution stepExecution) {
        if (isMercuryIsInRetrograde()) {
            return new FlowExecutionStatus("MERCURY_IN_RETROGRADE");
        }
        return FlowExecutionStatus.COMPLETED;
    }
}
```

All that remains is the XML configuration:

```
  <beans:bean id="horoscopeDecider" class="com.apress.springrecipes.
springbatch.solution2.HoroscopeDecider"/>

 <job id="job">
    <step id="step1"  next="decision"  ><!-- ... --></step>
    <decision id="decision" decider="horoscopeDecider">
      <next on="MERCURY_IN_RETROGRADE" to="step2" />
      <next on="COMPLETED" to="step3" />
    </decision>
    <step id="step2" next="step3"> <!-- ... --> </step>
    <step id="step3" parent="s3"> <!-- ... --> </step>
 </job>
```

21-8. Launching a Job

Problem

What deployment scenarios does Spring Batch support? How does Spring Batch launch? How does Spring Batch work with a system scheduler such as `cron` or `autosys`, or from a web application?

Solution

Spring Batch works well in all environments that Spring runs: your public static void main, OSGi, a web application—anywhere! Some use cases are uniquely challenging, though: it is rarely practical to run Spring Batch in the same thread as an HTTP response because it might end up stalling execution, for example. Spring Batch supports asynchronous execution for just this scenario. Spring Batch also provides a convenience class that can be readily used with cron or autosys to support launching jobs. Additionally, Spring 3.0's excellent scheduler namespace provides a great mechanism to schedule jobs.

How It Works

Before you get into creating a solution, it's important to know what options are available for deploying and running these solutions. All solutions require, at minimum, a job and a JobLauncher. You already configured these components in the previous recipe. The job is configured in your Spring XML application context, as you'll see later. The simplest example of launching a Spring Batch solution from Java code is about five lines of Java code, three if you've already got a handle to the ApplicationContext!

```
package com.apress.springrecipes.springbatch.solution1;

import org.springframework.batch.core.Job;
import org.springframework.batch.core.JobParameters;
import org.springframework.batch.core.JobParametersBuilder;
import org.springframework.batch.core.launch.JobLauncher;
import org.springframework.context.support.ClassPathXmlApplicationContext;

import java.util.Date;


public class Main {
    public static void main(String[] args) throws Throwable {
        ClassPathXmlApplicationContext ctx = new↵
 ClassPathXmlApplicationContext("solution2.xml");
        ctx.start();

        JobLauncher jobLauncher = (JobLauncher) ctx.getBean("jobLauncher");
        Job job = (Job) ctx.getBean("myJobName");
        JobExecution jobExecution = jobLauncher.run(job, new JobParameters());
    }
}
```

As you can see, the JobLauncher reference you configured previously is obtained and used to then launch an instance of a Job. The result is a JobExecution. You can interrogate the JobExecution for information on the state of the Job, including its exit status and runtime status.

```
JobExecution jobExecution = jobLauncher.run(job, jobParameters);
BatchStatus batchStatus = jobExecution.getStatus();
while(batchStatus.isRunning()) {
        System.out.println( "Still running...");
        Thread.sleep( 10 * 1000 ); // 10 seconds
}
```

You can also get the ExitStatus:

```
System.out.println( "Exit code: "+ jobExecution.getExitStatus().getExitCode());
```

The JobExecution also provides a lot of other very useful information like the create time of the Job, the start time, the last updated date, and the end time—all as java.util.Date instances. If you want to correlate the job back to the database, you'll need the jobInstance and the ID:

```
JobInstance jobInstance = jobExecution.getJobInstance();
System.out.println( "job instance Id: "+ jobInstance.getId());
```

In our simple example, we use an empty JobParameters instance. In practice, this will only work once. Spring Batch builds a unique key based on the parameters and uses to keep uniquely identify one run of a given Job from another. You'll learn about parameterizing a Job in detail in the next recipe.

Launching From a Web Application

Launching a job from a web application requires a slightly different approach, because the client thread (presumably an HTTP request) can't usually wait for a batch job to finish. The ideal solution is to have the job execute asynchronously when launched from a controller or action in the web tier, unattended by the client thread. Spring Batch supports this scenario through the use of a Spring TaskExecutor. This requires a simple change to the configuration for the JobLauncher, although the Java code can stay the same. Here, we will use a SimpleAsyncTaskExecutor that will spawn a thread of execution and manage that thread without blocking.

```
<beans:bean id="jobLauncher"
class="org.springframework.batch.execution.launch.support.SimpleJobLauncher"
        p:jobRepository-ref="jobRepository" >
    <beans:property name="taskExecutor">
    <beans:bean class="org.springframework.core.task.SimpleAsyncTaskExecutor" />
    </beans:property>
</beans:bean>
```

Running from the Command Line

Another common use case is deployment of a batch process from a system scheduler such as cron or autosys, or even Window's event scheduler. Spring Batch provides a convenience class that takes as its parameters the name of the XML application context (that contains *everything* required to run a job) as well as the name of the job bean itself. Additional parameters may be provided and used to parameterize the job. These parameters must be in the form name=value. An example invocation of this class on the command line (on a Linux/Unix system), assuming that you set up the classpath, might look like this:

```
java CommandLineJobRunner jobs.xml hourlyReport date=`date +%m/%d/%Y` time=`date +%H`
```

The `CommandLineJobRunner` will even return system error codes (0 for success, 1 for failure, and 2 for an issue with loading the batch job) so that a shell (such as used by most system schedulers) can react or do something about the failure. More complicated return codes can be returned by creating and declaring a top-level bean that implements the interface `ExitCodeMapper`, in which you can specify a more useful translation of exit status messages to integer-based error codes that the shell will see on process exit.

Running On A Schedule

Spring 3.0 debuts support for a scheduling framework. This framework lends itself perfectly to running Spring Batch. First, let's modify our existing application context `batch.xml` to use the Spring scheduling namespace. The additions consist mainly of changes to schema imports, as well as the declaration of a few beans. The application context file now starts off like so:

```
<?xml version="1.0" encoding="UTF-8"?>
<beans:beans
        xmlns="http://www.springframework.org/schema/batch"
        xmlns:beans="http://www.springframework.org/schema/beans"
        xmlns:aop="http://www.springframework.org/schema/aop"
        xmlns:task="http://www.springframework.org/schema/task"
        xmlns:tx="http://www.springframework.org/schema/tx"
        xmlns:p="http://www.springframework.org/schema/p"
        xmlns:xsi="http://www.w3.org/2001/XMLSchema-instance"
        xmlns:util="http://www.springframework.org/schema/util"
        xmlns:context="http://www.springframework.org/schema/context"
        xsi:schemaLocation="http://www.springframework.org/schema/beans ↵
http://www.springframework.org/schema/beans/spring-beans-3.0.xsd
    http://www.springframework.org/schema/batch ↵
http://www.springframework.org/schema/batch/spring-batch-2.1.xsd
    http://www.springframework.org/schema/aop ↵
http://www.springframework.org/schema/aop/spring-aop-3.0.xsd
    http://www.springframework.org/schema/tx ↵
http://www.springframework.org/schema/tx/spring-tx-3.0.xsd
    http://www.springframework.org/schema/task ↵
http://www.springframework.org/schema/task/spring-task-3.0.xsd
    http://www.springframework.org/schema/util ↵
http://www.springframework.org/schema/util/spring-util-3.0.xsd ↵
http://www.springframework.org/schema/context ↵
http://www.springframework.org/schema/context/spring-context.xsd">

    <context:component-scan annotation-config="true"
      base-package="com.apress.springrecipes.springbatch"/>

    <task:scheduler id="scheduler" pool-size="10"/>
    <task:executor id="executor" pool-size="10"/>

    <task:annotation-driven scheduler="scheduler" executor="executor"/>

...
```

These imports enable the simplest possible support for scheduling. The preceding declaration ensures that any bean under the package com.apress.springrecipes.springbatch will be configured and scheduled as required. Our bean is as follows:

```
package com.apress.springrecipes.springbatch.scheduler;

import org.apache.commons.lang.StringUtils;
import org.springframework.batch.core.Job;
import org.springframework.batch.core.JobExecution;
import org.springframework.batch.core.JobParameters;
import org.springframework.batch.core.JobParametersBuilder;
import org.springframework.batch.core.launch.JobLauncher;
import org.springframework.beans.factory.annotation.Autowired;
import org.springframework.context.support.ClassPathXmlApplicationContext;
import org.springframework.scheduling.annotation.Scheduled;
import org.springframework.stereotype.Component;

import java.util.Date;

@Component
public class ScheduledMain {

    @Autowired private JobLauncher jobLauncher;

    @Autowired private Job job;

    public void runRegistrationsJob(Date date) throws Throwable {
        System.out.println(StringUtils.repeat("-", 100));
        System.out.println("Starting job at " + date.toString());
        JobParametersBuilder jobParametersBuilder = new JobParametersBuilder();
        jobParametersBuilder.addDate("date", date);
        jobParametersBuilder.addString("input.file", "registrations");
        JobParameters jobParameters = jobParametersBuilder.toJobParameters();
        JobExecution jobExecution = jobLauncher.run(job, jobParameters);
        System.out.println("jobExecution finished, exit code: " +
                jobExecution.getExitStatus().getExitCode());
    }

    @Scheduled(fixedDelay = 1000 * 10)
    void runRegistrationsJobOnASchedule() throws Throwable {
        runRegistrationsJob(new Date());
    }

    public static void main(String[] args) throws Throwable {
        ClassPathXmlApplicationContext classPathXmlApplicationContext =
                new ClassPathXmlApplicationContext("scheduled_batch.xml", "solution1.xml");
        classPathXmlApplicationContext.start();
    }
}
```

There is nothing particularly novel; it's a good study of how the different components of the Spring framework work well together. The bean is recognized and becomes part of the application context because of the `@Component` annotation, which we enabled with the `context:component-scan` element in our reworked `batch.xml` (which we're calling `scheduled_batch.xml`). There's only one Job in the `solution1.xml` file and only one `JobLauncher`, so we simply have those auto-wired into our bean. Finally, the logic for kicking off a batch run is inside the `runRegistrationsJob(java.util.Date date)` method. This method could be called from anywhere. Our only client for this functionality is the scheduled method `runRegistrationsJobOnASchedule`. The framework will invoke this method for us, according to the timeline dictated by the `@Scheduled` annotation.

There are other options for this sort of thing; traditionally in the Java and Spring world, this sort of problem would be a good fit for Quartz. It might still be, as the Spring scheduling support isn't designed to be as extensible as Quartz. If you are in an environment requiring more traditional, ops-friendly scheduling tools, there are of course old standbys like `cron`, `autosys`, and BMC, too.

21-9. Parameterizing a Job

Problem

The previous examples work well enough, but they leave something to be desired in terms of flexibility. To apply the batch code to some other file, you'd have to edit the configuration and hard-code the name in there. The ability to parameterize the batch solution would be very helpful.

Solution

Use `JobParameters` to parameterize a `job`, which is then available to your `step`s through Spring Batch's expression language or via API calls.

How It Works

Launching a Job with Parameters

A `job` is a prototype of a `JobInstance`. `JobParameters` are used to provide a way of identifying a unique run of a job (a `JobInstance`). These `JobParameters` allow you to give input to your batch process, just as you would with a method definition in Java. You've seen the `JobParameters` in previous examples but not in detail. The `JobParameters` object is created as you launch the job using the `JobLauncher`. To launch a job called `dailySalesFigures`, with the date for the job to work with, you would write something like this:

```
ClassPathXmlApplicationContext classPathXmlApplicationContext = new
ClassPathXmlApplicationContext("solution2.xml");
classPathXmlApplicationContext.start();
JobLauncher jobLauncher = (JobLauncher) classPathXmlApplicationContext.↵
getBean("jobLauncher");
Job job = (Job) classPathXmlApplicationContext.getBean("dailySalesFigures");
jobLauncher.run(job, new JobParametersBuilder().addDate( "date",
    new Date() ).toJobParameters());
```

Accessing JobParameters

Technically, you can get at `JobParameters` via any of the `ExecutionContexts` (`step` and `job`). Once you have it, you can access the parameters in a type-safe way by calling `getLong()`, `getString()`, and so on. A simple way to do this is to bind to the `@BeforeStep` event, save the `StepExecution`, and iterate over the parameters this way. From here, you can inspect the parameters and do anything you want with them. Let's look at that in terms of the `ItemProcessor<I,O>` you wrote earlier:

```
// …
private StepExecution stepExecution;

@BeforeStep
public void saveStepExecution(StepExecution stepExecution) {
  this.stepExecution = stepExecution;
}

public UserRegistration process(UserRegistration input) throws Exception {

    Map<String, JobParameter> params =  stepExecution.getJobParameters().↵
getParameters();

  // iterate over all of the parameters
  for (String jobParameterKey : params.keySet()) {
     System.out.println(String.format("%s=%s", jobParameterKey,
  params.get(jobParameterKey).getValue().toString()));
  }

  // access specific parameters in a type safe way
  Date date = stepExecution.getJobParameters().getDate("date");
  // etc …
}
```

This turns out to be of limited value. The 80 percent case is that you'll need to bind parameters from the `job`'s launch to the Spring beans in the application context. These parameters are available only at runtime, whereas the `steps` in the XML application context are configured at design time. This happens in many places. Previous examples demonstrated `ItemWriters<T>` and `ItemReaders <T>` with hard-coded paths. That works fine unless you want to parameterize the file name. This is hardly acceptable unless you plan on using a `job` just once!

The core Spring Framework 3.0 features an enhanced expression language that Spring Batch 2.0 (depending on Spring Framework 3.0) uses to defer binding of the parameter until the correct time. Or, in this case, until the bean is in the correct scope. Spring Batch 2.0 introduces the `"step"` scope for just this purpose. Let's take a look at how you'd rework the previous example to use a parameterized file name for the `ItemReader`'s resource:

```
<beans:bean
        scope="step"
        id="csvFileReader"
        class="org.springframework.batch.item.file.FlatFileItemReader"
        p:resource="file:${user.home}/batches/#{jobParameters['input.fileName']}.csv">
  <!-- … this is the same as before…-->
</beans:bean>
```

All you did is scope the bean (the `FlatFileItemReader<T>`) to the life cycle of a `step` (at which point those `JobParameters` will resolve correctly) and then used the EL syntax to parameterize the path to work off of.

Note that the earlier versions of Spring Batch 2.0 featured an expression language in advance of the Spring Expression Language that debuted in the core framework for 3.0 (SpEL). This expression language is by and large similar to SpEL but is not exact. In the preceding example, we reference the input variable as `#{jobParameters['input.fileName']}`, which works in Spring Batch with SpEL. In the original Spring Batch expression language, however, you could have left off the quotes.

Summary

This chapter introduced you to the concepts of batch processing, some of its history, and why it fits in a modern day architecture. You learned about Spring Batch, the batch processing from SpringSource, and how to do reading and writing with `ItemReader<T>` and `ItemWriter<T>` implementations in your batch jobs. You wrote your own `ItemReader<T>`, and `ItemWriter` `<T>`implementations as needed and saw how to control the execution of `steps` inside a `job`.

The next chapter will discuss Terracotta and GridGain. You'll learn how to use Terracotta to build a distributed cache and take your Spring applications onto the grid with GridGain.

CHAPTER 22

■ ■ ■

Spring on the Grid

In this chapter, you will learn the principles behind various distributed computing concepts and how to use Spring in conjunction with some very powerful, open-source–ish third-party products to build solutions leveraging those concepts. There are many different types of distributed computing. In this chapter, we talk about grid computing, which can be defined as an application of many systems in service to a task greater than any single system could usefully handle. Grid computing solves many problems, some more ephemeral than others:

- *Scalability*: The distribution of work enables more requests to be handled. Distribution expands an application's ability to scale, as required, to meet demand. This is the quintessential reason behind clustering and load balancing.

- *Redundancy*: Computers fail. It's built in. The only thing you can guarantee about a hard disk of any make? That it will, at some point or another, fail, and more than likely in your lifetime. Being able to have a computer take over when something else becomes ineffective, or to have a computer's load lessened by adjoining members in a cluster, is a valuable benefit of distribution. Distribution provides built in resilience, if architected carefully.

- *Parallelization*: Distribution enables solutions designed to split problems into more manageable chunks or to expedite processing by bringing more power to bear on the problem. Some problems are inherently, embarrassingly parallelizable. These often reflect real life. Take, for example, a process that's designed to check hotels, car rentals, and airline accommodations and show you the best possible options. All three checks can be done concurrently, as they share no state and have no dependencies on each other. It would be a crime not to parallelize this logic. Some problem domains are not naturally, embarrassingly parallel, so it as at your discretion that you seek to apply parallelization.

The other reasons are more subtle, but very real. Over the course of computing, we've clung to the notion that computers will constantly expand in processing speed with time. This has come to be known as Moore's Law, named for Gordon Moore of Intel. Looking at history, you might remark that we've, in fact, done quite well along that scale. Servers in the early '80s were an order of magnitude slower than computers in the early '90s, and computers at the turn of the millennium were roughly an order of magnitude faster than those in the early '90s. At the time of this writing, in 2009, however, computers are not, strictly speaking, an order of magnitude faster than computers in the late '90s. They've become better parallelized and can better serve software designed to run in parallel. Thus, parallelization isn't just a good idea for big problems; it's a necessity if you want to take full advantage of modern-day processing power.

Additionally, parallelization defeats another trend, as described by Wirth's Law (named for Niklaus Wirth): "Software gets slower faster than hardware gets faster." In the Java landscape, this problem is even more pronounced because of Java's difficulty in addressing large amounts of RAM (anecdotally, 2GB to 4GB is about the most a single JVM can usefully address without pronounced garbage collection pauses). There are garbage collectors in the works that seek to fix some of these issues, but the fact remains that a single computer can have far more RAM than a single JVM could ever utilize. Parallelization is a must. Today, more and more enterprises are deploying entire virtualized operating system stacks on one server simply to isolate Java applications and fully exploit the hardware.

Thus, distribution isn't just a function of resilience or capability; it's a function of common-sense investing.

There are costs to parallelization, as well. There's always going to be some constraint, and very rarely is an entire system uniformly scalable. The cost of coordinating state between nodes, for example, might be too high because the network or hard disks impose latency. Additionally, not all operations are parallelizable. It's important to design systems with this in mind. An example might be the overall processing of a person's uploaded photos (as happens in many web sites today). You might take the moment at which they upload the batch to the moment a process has watermarked them and added them to an online photo album and measure the time during which the whole process is executed serially. Some of these steps are not parallelizable. The one part that is parallelizable—the watermarking —will only lead to a fixed increase, and little can be done beyond that.

You can describe these potential gains. Amdahl's law, also known as Amdahl's argument, is a formula to find the maximum expected improvement to an overall system when only part of the system is improved. It is shown here:

$$\frac{1}{(1 - P) + \left(\frac{P}{N}\right)}$$

It describes the relationship between a solution's execution time when serially executed and when executed in parallel with the same problem set. Thus, for 90 photos, if we know that it takes a minute for each photo, and that uploading takes 5 minutes, and that posting the resulting photos to the repository takes 5 minutes, the total time is 100 minutes when executed serially. Let's assume we add 9 workers to the watermarking process, for a total of 10 processes that watermark. In the equation, P is the portion of the process that can be parallelized, and N is the factor by which that portion might be parallelized (that is, the number of workers, in this case). For the process described, 90 percent of the process can be parallelized: each photo could be given to a different worker, which means it's parallelizable, which means that 90 percent of the serial execution is parallelizable. If you have 10 nodes working together, the equation is: 1/((1-.9) + (.9 / 10)), or 5.263. So, with 10 workers, the process could be 5 times faster. With 100 workers, the equation yields 9.174, or 9 times faster. It may not make sense to continue adding nodes past a certain point, as you'll achieve progressively smaller gains.

Building an effective distributed solution, then, is an application of cost/benefit analysis. Spring has no direct support for distributed paradigms, *per se*, because plenty of other solutions do a great job already. Often, these solutions make Spring integration a first priority because it's a de-facto standard. In some cases, these projects have forgone their own configuration format and use Spring itself as the configuration mechanism. If you decide to employ distribution, you'll be glad to know that there are many projects designed to meet the call, whatever it may be.

In this chapter, we discuss a few solutions that are Spring-friendly and ready. A lot of these solutions are possible because of Spring's support for "components," such as its XML schema support and runtime class detection. These technologies often require you to change your frame of mind when building solutions, even if ever so slightly, as compared to solutions built using Java EE, but being able to rely on your Spring skills is powerful. Other times, these solutions may not even be visible, except as configuration. Further still, a lot of these solutions expose themselves as standard interfaces familiar to

Java EE developers, or as infrastructure (such as, for example, backing for an HTTP session, or as a cluster-ready message queue) that goes unnoticed and isolated, except at the configuration level, thanks to Spring's dependency injection.

22-1. Clustering Object State Using Terracotta

Problem

You want to share object state across multiple virtual machines. For example, you'd like to be able to load the names of all the cities in the United States into memory for faster lookup, or load all the products in your company's catalog, or the entire stock market's trading history for the last decade for online calculation and analysis. Any other nodes in the cluster that need access to those objects should be able to get them from the cache and not reload them.

Solution

You can use Terracotta to build such a solution. Terracotta (http://www.terracotta.org) is a free, open source clustering solution. The company, Terracotta, has also recently become the corporate sponsor of the Ehcache and Quartz projects. Terracotta works like many other clustered caches, except that, in addition to being a good Hibernate clustered cache, it also works as a mostly unnoticeable engine to enable API-free shared state across a cluster. Terracotta doesn't use serialization of objects (not even highly compact serialization like Swift, Google's Protocol Buffers, Coherence Pofs, or Hazelcast DataSerializables), and instead ferries around deltas of VM memory across the cluster. It provides a VM-level view of other objects, as if they were in the same VM.

How It Works

Terracotta works as a JVM agent that monitors the object graph of a given JVM instance and ensures replication of object state across a cluster. It does this by referring to a configuration file in which you specify which classes, methods, and fields should be clustered.

It does this for any object in the JVM, not just Hibernate entities or session entries, or objects otherwise updated by some caching API. It's as simple as using a property on an object or updating a shared variable on an object. Instantly, across as many nodes as you want, that updated state is reflected in reads to that property on other instances.

To illustrate, it's best to imagine a threaded application. Imagine a shared integer value in a threaded application. Three threads increment the value of an integer in lockstep, delayed every five seconds. Each thread acquires the lock, increments the integer, and then releases the lock. Other threads see the updated value and print it out. Eventually, as this goes on, the number rises and rises until some condition is met (e.g., you exit the program) to stop it. This is a very effective example of where Java's support for threading is useful, because it guarantees state through concurrent access. Now, imagine perhaps that you have that same integer, and each time a server hits a page, that integer is accessed and incremented. This page is deployed across several nodes, so that hitting the page on each of the nodes causes the integer, and thus the state, to change. Other servers see the new value on refresh, even though the change was last made on another server. The state is visible to all nodes in the cluster, and at the same times as the state would be visible to threads. This is what Terracotta does: it clusters object state.

On the whole, your code will remain simple code (perhaps multithreaded in nature) that works across multiple VMs.

Terracotta is different than most clustered caches today because it has no visible API, and because it's far more efficient in conveying the changed state to nodes across the cluster. Most systems use some sort of Java serialization or broadcast mechanism, wherein each other node is given the entire object, or object graph, that's changed, regardless of whether they even they need to be aware of the new state. Terracotta does it differently: it deltas the memory of the object graphs itself and synchronizes other nodes in the cluster as they need a consistent view of the object state. Succinctly, it can do something tantamount to transmitting just one updated variable in an object, and not the entire object.

Deploying a Simple Example with Terracotta

You want to deploy Terracotta and see what a simple application looks like. This example is a simple client that responds to certain commands that you can give it. After each command, it prompts for another command. It, in turn, uses a service implementation that keeps state. We cluster this state using Terracotta. A client manipulates the CustomerServiceImpl class, shown here, which is an implementation of CustomerService, which implements the following interface:

```
package com.apress.springrecipes.distributedspring.terracotta.customerconsole.service;

import com.apress.springrecipes.distributedspring.terracotta.customerconsole.↵
entity.Customer;

import java.util.Date;
import java.util.Collection;

public interface CustomerService {
    Customer getCustomerById( String id ) ;
    Customer createCustomer(
        String id, String firstName,
        String lastName, Date birthdate ) ;
    Customer removeCustomer( String id ) ;
    Customer updateCustomer( String id, String firstName, String lastName, Date↵
 birthdate ) ;
    Collection<Customer > getAllCustomers() ;
}
```

As this is meant to be a gentle introduction to Terracotta, I'll forego building a complete Hibernate- and Spring-based solution. The implementation will be in-memory, using nothing but primitives from the JDK.

```
package com.apress.springrecipes.distributedspring.terracotta.customerconsole.service;

import com.apress.springrecipes.distributedspring.terracotta.↵
customerconsole.entity.Customer;
import org.apache.commons.collections.CollectionUtils;
import org.apache.commons.collections.Predicate;
```

```java
import java.util.*;

public class CustomerServiceImpl implements CustomerService {

    private volatile Set<Customer> customers;

    public CustomerServiceImpl() {
        customers = Collections.synchronizedSet(new HashSet<Customer>());
    }

    public Customer updateCustomer(String id, String firstName,
                String lastName, Date birthdate) {
        Customer customer;
        synchronized (customers) {
            customer = getCustomerById(id);
            customer.setBirthday(birthdate);
            customer.setFirstName(firstName);
            customer.setLastName(lastName);
            removeCustomer(id);
            customers.add(customer);
        }
        return customer;
    }

    public Collection<Customer> getAllCustomers() {
        return (customers);
    }

    public Customer removeCustomer(String id) {
        Customer customerToRemove;
        synchronized (customers) {
            customerToRemove = getCustomerById(id);
            if (null != customerToRemove)
                customers.remove(customerToRemove);
        }
        return customerToRemove;
    }

    public Customer getCustomerById(final String id) {
        return (Customer) CollectionUtils.find(customers, new Predicate() {
            public boolean evaluate(Object o) {
                Customer customer = (Customer) o;
                return customer.getId().equals(id);
            }
        });
    }
```

```
public Customer createCustomer(String firstName, String lastName, Date birthdate ){
    synchronized (customers) {
        final Customer newCustomer = new Customer(
                firstName, lastName, birthdate);
        if (!customers.contains(newCustomer)) {
            customers.add(newCustomer);
            return newCustomer;
        } else {
            return (Customer) CollectionUtils.find(
                customers, new Predicate() {
                public boolean evaluate(Object o) {
                    Customer customer = (Customer) o;
                    return customer.equals(newCustomer);
                }
            });
        }
    }
}
```

The entity, Customer, is a simple POJO with accessors and mutators, and it works equals, hashCode, toString methods.

```
package com.apress.springrecipes.distributedspring.terracotta.customerconsole.entity;

import org.apache.commons.lang.builder.EqualsBuilder;
import org.apache.commons.lang.builder.HashCodeBuilder;
import org.apache.commons.lang.builder.ReflectionToStringBuilder;

import java.io.Serializable;

import java.util.Date;
import java.util.UUID;

public class Customer implements Serializable {
    private String id;
    private String firstName, lastName;
    private Date birthday;
    // …
    // accessor/mutators, id, equals, and hashCode.
    // …
}
```

Note first that nothing we do in that class has any effect on Terracotta. We implement Serializable, ostensibly because the class may very well be serialized in, for example, an HTTP session, not for Terracotta's benefit. The hashCode/equals implementations are good practice because they help our entity play well and comply with the contract of various JDK utilities like the collections implementations.

The client that will allow us to interact with this service class is as follows:

```
package com.apress.springrecipes.distributedspring.terracotta.↵
customerconsole.view;

import com.apress.springrecipes.distributedspring.↵
terracotta.customerconsole.entity.Customer;
import com.apress.springrecipes.distributedspring.↵
terracotta.customerconsole.service.CustomerService;
import org.apache.commons.lang.StringUtils;
import org.apache.commons.lang.SystemUtils;
import org.apache.commons.lang.exception.ExceptionUtils;

import javax.swing.*;
import java.text.DateFormat;
import java.text.ParseException;
import java.util.Date;

public class CustomerConsole {

        private CustomerService customerService;

        private void log(String msg) {
                System.out.println(msg);
        }

        private void list() {
                for (Customer customer : customerService.getAllCustomers())
                        log(customer.toString());
                log(SystemUtils.LINE_SEPARATOR);
        }

        private void create(String customerCreationString) {
                String cmd = StringUtils.defaultString(
                        customerCreationString).trim();
                String[] parts = cmd.split(" ");
                String firstName = parts[1], lastName = parts[2];
                Date date = null;
                try {

                    date = DateFormat.getDateInstance(
                        DateFormat.SHORT).parse(parts[3]);

                } catch (ParseException e) {
                  log(ExceptionUtils.getFullStackTrace(e));
                }
                customerService.createCustomer(
                        firstName, lastName, date);
                list();
        }
```

```java
        private void delete(String c) {
                log("delete:" + c);
                String id = StringUtils.defaultString(c).trim().split(" ")[1];
                customerService.removeCustomer(id);
                list();
        }

        private void update(String stringToUpdate) {
                String[] parts = StringUtils.defaultString(stringToUpdate).trim()
                                .split(" ");
                String idOfCustomerAsPrintedOnConsole = parts[1],
                    firstName = parts[2],
                    lastName = parts[3];
                Date date = null;
                try {
                    date = DateFormat.getDateInstance(
                        DateFormat.SHORT).parse(parts[4]);
                } catch (ParseException e) {
                        log(ExceptionUtils.getFullStackTrace(e));
                }
                customerService.updateCustomer(
                        idOfCustomerAsPrintedOnConsole,
                        firstName, lastName, date);
                list();
        }


        public CustomerService getCustomerService() {
                return customerService;
        }

        public void setCustomerService(
                CustomerService customerService) {
                this.customerService = customerService;
        }

        enum Commands {
                LIST, UPDATE, DELETE, CREATE
        }

        public void handleNextCommand(String prompt) {
                System.out.println(prompt);

                String nextLine = JOptionPane.showInputDialog(
                        null, prompt);

                if (StringUtils.isEmpty(nextLine)) {
                        System.exit(1);
                        return;
                }

                log(nextLine);
```

```
        if ((StringUtils.trim(nextLine).toUpperCase())
                        .startsWith(Commands.UPDATE.name())) {
            update(nextLine);
            return;
        }
        if ((StringUtils.trim(nextLine).toUpperCase())
                        .startsWith(Commands.DELETE.name())) {
            delete(nextLine);
            return;
        }
        if ((StringUtils.trim(nextLine).toUpperCase())
                        .startsWith(Commands.CREATE.name())) {
            create(nextLine);
            return;
        }

        if((StringUtils.trim(nextLine).toUpperCase()).startsWith(
          Commands.LIST.name())) {
            list();
            return;
        }
        System.exit(1);
    }
}
```

Terracotta Architecture and Deployment

The client code is simple as well. It's basically a dumb loop waiting for input. The client reacts to commands such as create First Last 12/02/78. You can test it out, without Terracotta, if you like. Simply run the class containing the public static void main(String [] args) method, as you would any other main class. If you're using Maven, you may simply execute the following:

```
mvn exec:java
-Dexec.mainClass=com.apress.springrecipes.distributedspring.terracotta.↵
customerconsole.MainWithSpring
```

You can imagine how the client would work with Terracotta. The data managed by the CustomerService implementation is shared across a cluster. Changes to the data via an instance of the CustomerConsole on one machine should propagate to other machines instantly, and issuing a call to list() should reflect as much.

Let's dissect deployment. Terracotta has a client/server architecture. The server, in this case, is the one that contains the original working memory. It's what hands out deltas of changed memory to other nodes in the cluster. Other nodes "fault" in that memory as they need it. To deploy a Terracotta application, you first download the distribution. The distribution provides utility scripts, as well as JARs. You may download Terracotta from http://www.terracotta.org.

For Terracotta to work, you need to provide it with a configuration file. This file is an XML file that we'll review shortly. On Unix-like operating systems, you start Terracotta as follows:

```
$TERRACOTTA_HOME/bin/start-tc-server.sh −f $PATH_TO_TERRACOTTA_CONFIGURATION
```

If you're on Windows, use the equivalent .bat file instead.

For each virtual machine client that you want to "see" and share that state, start it with a customized bootclasspath parameter when starting Java. The arguments for this vary per operating system, so Terracotta provides a handy script for determining the correct arguments, dso-env.sh. When provided with the host and port of the Terracotta server, it can ensure that all configuration data for each client virtual machine is loaded dynamically from the server. As you might imagine, this greatly eases deployment over a grid of any substantive size! Here's how to use the script on Unix-like operating systems:

```
$TERRACOTTA_HOME/bin/dso-env.sh $HOST:$PORT
```

Replace $TERRACOTTA_HOME with the Terracotta's installation directory, and replace $HOST and $PORT with the host and port of the server instance. When run, it will print out the correct arguments, which you then need to feed into each client virtual machine's invocation scripts, for example in the $JAVA_OPTS section for Tomcat or any standard java invocation.

```
$ dso-env.sh localhost:9510
```

When executed, this will produce something like the following (naturally, this changes from operating system and environment), which you need to ensure is used in your invocation of the java cjava command:

```
-Xbootclasspath/p:../../lib/dso-boot/dso-boot-hotspot_linux_160_20.jar -Dtc.install-root=./..
```

The XML Configuration File

The XML for the Terracotta configuration is verbose but self evident. Terracotta is a 99 percent code-incursion-free solution. Because Terracotta works at such a low level, you don't need to know about it when programming. The only thing of concern may be the introduction of threading issues, which you would not have to deal with in strictly serialized execution. You would, however, have to deal with them if you wrote multithreaded code on your local machine. Think of Terracotta as a layer that lets your thread-safe single VM code work across a cluster. There are no annotations, and no APIs, to direct Terracotta. Instead, Terracotta gets its information from the XML configuration file that you provide it. Our example XML file (tc-customerconsole-w-spring.xml) is as follows:

```
<?xml version="1.0" encoding="UTF-8"?>
<tc:tc-config xsi:schemaLocation="http://www.terracotta.org/schema/terracotta-5.xsd"
              xmlns:tc="http://www.terracotta.org/config"
 xmlns:xsi="http://www.w3.org/2001/XMLSchema-instance">

    <servers>
        <server host="%i" name="server1">
            <dso-port>9510</dso-port>
            <jmx-port>9520</jmx-port>
            <data>target/terracotta/server/data</data>
            <logs>target/terracotta/server/logs</logs>
            <statistics>target/terracotta/server/statistics</statistics>
        </server>
```

```xml
        <update-check>
            <enabled>true</enabled>
        </update-check>
    </servers>
    <system>
        <configuration-model>development</configuration-model>
    </system>
    <clients>
        <logs>target/terracotta/clients/logs/%(tc.nodeName)</logs>
        <statistics>target/terracotta/clients/statistics/%(tc.nodeName)</statistics>
    </clients>
    <application>

        <dso>
            <instrumented-classes>
                <include>
                    <class-expression>
                        com.apress.springrecipes.distributedspring.terracotta.↵
customerconsole.entity.*
                    </class-expression>
                </include>
                <include>
                    <class-expression>
                        com.apress.springrecipes.distributedspring.terracotta.↵
customerconsole.service.CustomerServiceImpl
                    </class-expression>
                </include>
            </instrumented-classes>
            <roots>
                <root>
                    <root-name>customers</root-name>
                    <field-name>
                        com.apress.springrecipes.distributedspring.terracotta.↵
customerconsole.service.CustomerServiceImpl.customers
                    </field-name>
                </root>
            </roots>
            <locks>
                <autolock>
                    <method-expression>*
                        com.apress.springrecipes.distributedspring.terracotta.↵
customerconsole.service.CustomerServiceImpl.*(..)
                    </method-expression>
                </autolock>
            </locks>
        </dso>
    </application>


</tc:tc-config>
```

The servers element tells Terracotta about how to the server behaves: on what port it listens, where logs are, and so forth. The application instance is what's of concern to us. Here, we first spell out which classes are to be clusterable in the instrumented-classes element.

The locks element lets us prescribe what behavior to ensure with regard to concurrent access of fields on classes. The last element, the field-name element, is the most interesting. This instruction tells Terrracotta to ensure that the changes to the customers field in the CustomerServiceImpl class are visible cluster-wide. An element inserted into the collection on one host is visible on other hosts, and this is the crux of our functionality.

At this point, you might be expecting some Spring-specific configuration, but there is none. It just works. Here's a Spring context (called customerconsole-context.xml), as you'd expect.

```xml
<?xml version="1.0" encoding="UTF-8"?>
<beans xmlns="http://www.springframework.org/schema/beans"
       xmlns:xsi="http://www.w3.org/2001/XMLSchema-instance"
       xmlns:context="http://www.springframework.org/schema/context"
       xsi:schemaLocation="http://www.springframework.org/schema/beans
            http://www.springframework.org/schema/beans/spring-beans-3.0.xsd
            http://www.springframework.org/schema/context
            http://www.springframework.org/schema/context/spring-context-3.0.xsd">

    <bean id="customerService"
          class="com.apress.springrecipes.distributedspring.terracotta.
customerconsole.service.CustomerServiceImpl"/>

    <bean id="customerConsole"
          class="com.apress.springrecipes.distributedspring.terracotta.
customerconsole.view.CustomerConsole">
        <property name="customerService" ref="customerService"/>
    </bean>
</beans>
```

Let's now look at a client to this Spring bean:

```java
package com.apress.springrecipes.distributedspring.terracotta.customerconsole;

import com.apress.springrecipes.distributedspring.terracotta.
customerconsole.view.CustomerConsole;
import org.springframework.context.ApplicationContext;
import org.springframework.context.support.ClassPathXmlApplicationContext;

public class MainWithSpring {
    public static void main(String[] args) {
        ApplicationContext context = new ClassPathXmlApplicationContext
("customerconsole-context.xml");
        CustomerConsole customerConsole =
        (CustomerConsole) context.getBean("customerConsole");
```

```
        while (true) {
            customerConsole.handleNextCommand(
                    "Welcome to the customer console: your choices are DELETE,↵
UPDATE, CREATE or LIST");
        }
    }
}
```

You can run this client as many times as you'd like using the dso-env.sh script previously mentioned (or use the drop-in Terracotta replacement for Java called dso-java.sh, which effectively does what dso-env.sh does, as well as then executing the java command for you). It doesn't matter on how many clients you launch the application; all changes made to the customers collection will be visible cluster wide. For example, you might create a customer and put that person's information in the cache of one node (using a command in the form of "create first last MM/DD/YYYY") and then list the contents of the cache on another (using "list") to verify that there are entries in the cache.

Often, you will use Terracotta behind some other product, which you interface with Spring. Additionally, Terracotta supports a customized integration to cluster your web sessions, and sports specific support for Spring Web Flow and Spring Security. Generally, Terracotta is a good way to bring enterprise-level caching to your application at all tiers. If you need to manipulate something in a cluster directly, there's no need to hesitate. After all, Terracotta doesn't have an API—just configuration. As you've seen in this recipe, creating a useful, clustered Spring bean is very straightforward.

22-2. Farming Out Execution to a Grid

Problem

You want to distribute processing over many nodes, perhaps to increase result speed through the use of concurrences, perhaps merely to provide load balance and fault tolerance.

Solution

You can use something like GridGain, which was designed to transparently offload processing to a grid. This can be done many ways: one is to use the grid as a load alleviation mechanism, something to absorb the extra work. Another, if possible, is to split the job up in such a way that many nodes can work on it concurrently.

Approach

GridGain is an implementation of a processing grid. GridGain differs from data grids like Terracotta or Coherence, although data grids and processing grids are often used together, and in point of fact, GridGain encourages the use of any number of data grids with its processing functionality. There are many data grids, such as Coherence, Terracotta, and Hadoop's HFS, and these are designed to be fault-tolerant, memory-based RAM disks, essentially. These sorts of grids are natural compliments to a processing grid such as GridGain in that they can field massive amounts of data fast enough for a processing grid to keep busy. GridGain allows code to be farmed out to a grid for execution and then the results returned to the client, transparently. You can do this in many ways. The easiest route is to merely annotate the methods you want to be farmed out and then configure some mechanism to detect and act on those annotations, and then you're done!

The other approach is slightly more involved, but it is where solutions such as GridGain and Hadoop really shine: use the map/reduce pattern to partition a job into smaller pieces and then concurrently run those pieces on the grid. Map/reduce is a pattern that was popularized by Google, and it comes from functional programming languages, which often have map() and reduce() functions. The idea is that you somehow partition a job and send those pieces to be processed. Finally, you take the results and join them, and those results are then sent back. Often, you won't have results *per se*; instead, you'll have sought only to distribute the processing asynchronously.

GridGain packs a lot of power in the few interfaces you're required to ever deal with. Its internal configuration system is Spring, and when you wish to avail yourself of anything besides the absolute minimum configuration options—for example, configuring a certain node with characteristics upon which job routing might be predicated—you do so using Spring. GridGain provides a Spring AOP Aspect for use on beans with the @Gridify annotation for the very simple cases.

Deployment

To get started, download GridGain from the web site, http://www.gridgain.com. Unzip the distribution, descend into the bin directory, and run gridgain.(bat|sh). If you're running a Unix/Linux instance, you may need to make the scripts executable:

```
chmod a+x *sh
```

You need to set up an environment variable, GRIDGAIN_HOME, pointing to the directory in which you installed the distribution for it to function correctly. If you're running Unix, you need to set the variable in your shell environment. Usually, this happens in something like ~/.bashrc or ~/.bash_profile:

```
export GRIDGAIN_HOME=<YOUR DIRECTORY>
```

If you are running Windows, you will need to go to System Properties ~TRA Advanced ~TRA Environment Variables and add a new system variable, GRIDGAIN_HOME, pointing to the directory of your installation. Regardless of what operating system you're using, you need to ensure that there are no trailing slashes or backslashes on the variable's path.

Finally, run the script.

```
./gridgain.sh
```

If you have more than a few hundred megabytes of RAM, you might run the script several times. Each invocation creates a new node, so that, in essence, you'll have started a grid on your local machine. GridGain uses multicast, so you could put GridGain on several boxes and run numerous instances on each machine, and they'd all join the same grid. If you want to expand your grid to 10 boxes, simply repeat the installation of the GridGain software and set up the environment variable on each. You can partition the grid and characteristics of the nodes if you want, but for now, we'll concern ourselves with the defaults.

Astonishingly, this is all that's required for deployment. Shortly, you'll create executable code (with numerous .jars, no doubt), make changes on your local development machine, and then run the changed job, and the rest of the nodes in the grid will just notice the updated job and participate in running it thanks to its first-rate class-loading magic. This mechanism, peer-to-peer class loading, means that you don't need to do anything to deploy a job besides run the code with the job itself once.

22-3. Load Balancing a Method

Problem

You want to quickly grid-enable a method on a bean using GridGain. You can see doing this, for example, to expose service methods that, in turn, instantiate longer running jobs on the grid. One example might be sending notification e-mails, or image processing, or any process you don't want bogging down a single machine or VM instance or whose results you need quickly.

Solution

You can use GridGain's @Gridify annotation along with some Spring AOP configuration to let GridGain know that it can parallelize the execution of the method across the grid.

Approach

The first use case you're likely to have is to simply be able to farm out functionality in a bean to other nodes, as a load-balancing precaution, for example. GridGain provides load balancing as well as fault tolerance and routing out of the box, which you get for free by adding this annotation. Let's take a look at a simple service bean with a single method that we want to farm out to the grid. The interface contract looks like the following:

```
package com.apress.springrecipes.distributedspring.gridgain;

public interface SalutationService {
    String saluteSomeoneInForeignLanguage( String recipient);
    String[] saluteManyPeopleInRandomForeignLanguage( String[] recipients);

}
```

The only salient requirement here is the saluteSomeoneInForeignLanguage method. Naturally, this is also the method we want to be run on the grid when possible. The implementation looks like this:

```
package com.apress.springrecipes.distributedspring.gridgain;

import java.io.Serializable;
import java.util.HashMap;
import java.util.Locale;
import java.util.Map;
import java.util.Set;

import org.apache.commons.lang.StringUtils;
import org.gridgain.grid.gridify.Gridify;
import org.springframework.beans.BeansException;
import org.springframework.context.ApplicationContext;
import org.springframework.context.ApplicationContextAware;
```

```java
/**
 * Admittedly trivial example of saying 'hello' in a few languages
 *
 */
public class SalutationServiceImpl
implements SalutationService, Serializable {

        private static final long serialVersionUID = 1L;

        private Map<String, String> salutations;

    public SalutationServiceImpl() {
        salutations = new HashMap<String, String>();
        salutations.put(
                Locale.FRENCH.getLanguage().toLowerCase(),
                "bonjour %s!");
                salutations.put(
                Locale.ITALIAN.getLanguage().toLowerCase(),
                "buongiorno %s!");
        salutations.put(
                Locale.ENGLISH.getLanguage().toLowerCase(),
                "hello %s!");
    }

    @Gridify
    public String saluteSomeoneInForeignLanguage(
                String recipient) {
        Locale[] locales = new Locale[]{
            Locale.FRENCH, Locale.ENGLISH, Locale.ITALIAN};
        Locale locale = locales[
            (int) Math.floor(
                        Math.random() * locales.length)];
        String language = locale.getLanguage();
        Set<String> languages = salutations.keySet();
        if (!languages.contains(language))
            throw new java.lang.RuntimeException(
                String.format(
        "this isn't supported! You need to choose " +
        "from among the accepted languages: %s",↵
                        StringUtils.join(languages.iterator(), ",")));
        String salutation = String.format(
                salutations.get(language), recipient);
        System.out.println(
                String.format("returning: %s " ,salutation));
        return salutation;
    }

    @Gridify(taskClass = MultipleSalutationTask.class)
    public String[] saluteManyPeopleInRandomForeignLanguage(
                String[] recipients) {
        return recipients;
    }
}
```

There are no telltale signs that this code is Grid-enabled except for the @Gridify annotation. Otherwise, the functionality is self-evident and infinitely testable. We use Spring to ensure that this bean is given a chance to run. The configuration of the Spring file (gridservice.xml, located at the classpath root) side looks like this:

```xml
<?xml version="1.0" encoding="UTF-8"?>
<beans xmlns="http://www.springframework.org/schema/beans"
       xmlns:xsi="http://www.w3.org/2001/XMLSchema-instance"
       xmlns:util="http://www.springframework.org/schema/util"
       xmlns:aop="http://www.springframework.org/schema/aop"
       xsi:schemaLocation="
       http://www.springframework.org/schema/beans ↵
http://www.springframework.org/schema/beans/spring-beans-3.0.xsd
       http://www.springframework.org/schema/aop
       http://www.springframework.org/schema/aop/spring-aop-3.0.xsd
       http://www.springframework.org/schema/util
       http://www.springframework.org/schema/util/spring-util-3.0.xsd">

    <bean id="myGrid" class="org.gridgain.grid.GridSpringBean"  scope="singleton">
        <property name="configuration">
            <bean id="grid.cfg" class="org.gridgain.grid.GridConfigurationAdapter"↵
  scope="singleton">
                <property name="topologySpi">
                    <bean class="org.gridgain.grid.spi.topology.basic.GridBasicTopologySpi">
                        <property name="localNode" value="false"/>
                    </bean>
                </property>
            </bean>
        </property>
    </bean>

    <bean id="interceptor" class="org.gridgain.grid.gridify.aop.spring.↵
    GridifySpringAspect"/>

    <bean depends-on="myGrid" id="salutationService" class="org.springframework.aop.↵
    framework.ProxyFactoryBean">
        <property name="autodetectInterfaces" value="false"/>
        <property name="target">
            <bean class="com.apress.springrecipes.distributedspring.gridgain.↵
            SalutationServiceImpl"/>
        </property>
        <property name="interceptorNames">
            <list>
                <value>interceptor</value>
            </list>
        </property>
    </bean>
</beans>
```

Here, we use a plain, old-style AOP Proxy in conjunction with the GridGain aspect to proxy our humble service class. I override `topologySpi` to set `localNode` to `false`, which has the effect of stopping jobs from being run on the invoking node—in this case, our service bean's node. The idea is that this node is, locally, the front for application services, and it's inappropriate to run jobs on that virtual machine, which may be handling highly transactional workloads. You might set the value to true if you don't mind a node bearing the load of both handling the services *and* acting as a grid node. Because you usually set up an instance of the interface `Grid` to offload work to some other node, this is usually not desirable. We know that invoking that service will cause it to be farmed out. Here's a simple client. The parameter is the only context we have, and it's the only thing you can rely on being present on the node that's run. You can't, if you're running the nodes via the startup script mentioned previously, rely on the Spring beans being wired up. We'll explore this further, but in the meantime, witness our client:

```
package com.apress.springrecipes.distributedspring.gridgain;

import org.springframework.context.ApplicationContext;
import org.springframework.context.support.ClassPathXmlApplicationContext;

import java.util.Locale;

public class Main {

    public static void main(String[] args)
        throws Throwable {

        ApplicationContext applicationContext =
new ClassPathXmlApplicationContext("gridservice.xml");
        SalutationService salutationServiceImpl =
(SalutationService) applicationContext.getBean("salutationService");

        String[] names =("Alan,Arin,Clark,Craig,Drew,Duncan,Gary,Gordon,Fumiko,"+
"Hicham,James,Jordon,Kathy,Ken,Makani,Manuel,Mario, "+
"Mark,Mia,Mike,Nick,Richard,Richelle, "+
"Rod,Ron,Scott,Shaun,Srinivas,Valerie,Venkatesh").split(",");

        Locale[] locales = new Locale[]{
          Locale.FRENCH, Locale.ENGLISH, Locale.ITALIAN};

        for (String name : names) {
           System.out.println("Result: " +
              salutationServiceImpl.saluteSomeoneInForeignLanguage(name));
        }
    }
}
```

When you run this, you'll notice—on as many command-line consoles as you've opened by clicking on the startup script—the jobs being handled in a round-robin fashion, each on its own node. If you had 100 names and 10 nodes, you'd notice that each node gets about 10 names listed on the command line, for example.

22-4. Parallelizing Processing

Problem

You want to build a parallelized solution for a problem that's intrinsically better-suited to parallelization or that, for want of resources, needs to be chunked.

Solution

Use map/reduce to approach the problem concurrently. As was mentioned earlier, decisions to parallelize shouldn't be taken lightly but with an eye on the ultimate performance expectations and tradeoffs.

Approach

Underneath the hood, GridGain works with a GridTask<T>, which specifies how to handle the main unit of work of the interface type GridJob. Sometimes, GridTask splits up and reconciles large jobs. This process is simplified by abstract adapter classes. In this case, we'll use one called GridifyTaskSplitAdapter<T>, which abstracts away most of the minutiae of building a map/reduce–oriented solution. It provides two template methods that we need to override.

In this example, we'll build a modified version of the previous solution that takes an array of String parameters. We intend for all entries in the array to be farmed out to the grid. Let's add the call from the client, which is the Main class we used earlier:

```
        System.out.println("Results:" + StringUtils.join↵
(   salutationServiceImpl.saluteManyPeopleInRandomForeignLanguage(names), ","));
```

We add one method to the original service interface and implementation.

```
@Gridify( taskClass = MultipleSalutationTask.class )
    public String[] saluteManyPeopleInRandomForeignLanguage(String[] recipients) {
        return recipients;
    }
```

As you can see, the method is simple. The only salient piece is the modified @Gridify annotation, which in this case has a taskClass parameter pointing to a MultipleSalutationTask class.

```
import java.io.Serializable;
import java.util.ArrayList;
import java.util.Collection;
import java.util.List;

import org.gridgain.grid.GridException;
import org.gridgain.grid.GridJob;
import org.gridgain.grid.GridJobAdapter;
import org.gridgain.grid.GridJobResult;
import org.gridgain.grid.gridify.GridifyArgument;
```

```
import org.gridgain.grid.gridify.GridifyTaskSplitAdapter;

public class MultipleSalutationTask extends GridifyTaskSplitAdapter<String[]> {

    private static final long serialVersionUID = 1L;

    protected Collection<? extends GridJob> split(int i,
            final GridifyArgument gridifyArgument) throws GridException {

        Collection<GridJob> jobs = new ArrayList<GridJob>();
        Object[] params = gridifyArgument.getMethodParameters();
        String[] names = (String[]) params[0];
        for (final String n : names)
            jobs.add(new GridJobAdapter<String>(n) {
                private static final long serialVersionUID = 1L;

                public Serializable execute() throws GridException {
                    SalutationService service =
                        (SalutationService) gridifyArgument.getTarget();
                    return service.saluteSomeoneInForeignLanguage(n);
                }
            });

        return jobs;

    }

    public String[] reduce(List<GridJobResult> gridJobResults)
        throws GridException {
        Collection<String> res = new ArrayList<String>();
        for (GridJobResult result : gridJobResults) {
            String data = result.getData();
            res.add(data);
        }
        return res.toArray(new String[res.size()]);

    }
}
```

Although this code is pretty straightforward, there is some magic going on that you need to be aware of. When you call the method on the service with the @Gridify annotation pointing to this GridTask implementation, it stops execution of method and loads an instance of this implementation. The parameters, as passed to the method with the annotation, are passed to: split(int i, final GridifyArgument gridifyArgument), which is used to dole out GridJob instances, each one taking as its payload a name from the array. In this code, we create the GridJob instances inline using GridJobAdapter, which is a template class. The work of each GridJob instance is trivial; in this case, we actually just delegate to the first method on the service that we created: saluteSomeoneInForeignLanguage. Note that the invocation of the service in this case does *not* run the job on the grid again, as we're already on a node. The result is returned to the calling context, which in this case is another virtual machine altogether.

All the results are collected and then passed to the reduce method on the Task class. This method is responsible for doing something with the final results. In this case, the results are simply unwrapped and returned as an array of Strings. Those results are then again sent to the calling context, which in this case is our original method invocation on the service. The results returned from that invocation are the results of all the processing. Thus, if you invoke saluteManyPeopleInRandomForeignLanguage with new String[]{"Steve"}, you're likely to get "Bonjour Steve!" (or something like that), even though it appears you're merely returning the input parameter.

22-5. Deploying on GridGain

Problem

There are several issues to be aware of when deploying applications using GridGain. How do you configure nodes with specific properties that can be used for determining its eligibility for a certain job? How do you inject Spring beans into a node? What is a .gar?

Solution

The issues you're likely to confront when using GridGain stem mostly from the fact that what you develop on one node can't always automatically work on another node with no additional configuration. It becomes helpful to think about these deployment issues ahead of time, before you run into a wall in production.

How It Works

In the previous examples, we deployed simple processing solutions that are deployable using GridGain's peer-to-peer class-loading mechanism. We haven't done anything too complex, however, and as they say, the devil's in the details.

Creating a Grid Node

Let's look at the infrastructural components of GridGain in detail. First, let's consider how a node is started up. As you saw before, GridGain lets you start up nodes using the startup script in the bin directory of the distribution. This script invokes a class of interface type GridLoader, of which there are many. The GridLoader's job is to hoist a grid node into existence. It responds to the life cycle events and knows how to work in specific environments. The one that gets started when you use the script that comes with the distribution is the class GridCommandLineLoader. There are others, though, including several for loading a grid instance from within a servlet container or application server instance. A GridLoader instance is responsible for many things, not the least of which is correctly calling GridFactory.start and GridFactory.stop.

GridFactory.start can take as its first parameter a GridConfiguration object or a Spring application context or a path to a Spring application context. This GridConfiguration object is what tells GridGain what is unique about a given node and the grid's topology. By default, it uses $GRIDGAIN_HOME/config/default-spring.xml, which, in turn, does things such as load a Grid object and configure user parameters about a specific node. These parameters may be queried to determine the candidacy of a node to handle a specific job. GridGain, because it is so deeply rooted in Spring, is very flexible and configurable. Different subsystems may be swapped out and replaced. GridGain provides several options via its service provider interfaces (SPIs). In the directory where default-spring.xml is located, there are several other Spring configurations for grids demonstrating integrations with many other technologies. Perhaps you'd like to use JMS as your message exchange platform? There are examples there for three different vendors. Perhaps you'd like to use Mule, or JBoss Cache?

Provisioning a Grid Node

In the previous examples, we deployed instances that were self-contained and had no dependency on any other components. When you do start introducing dependency—and you will, naturally—you'll want to be able to leverage Spring for dependency injection. At this point, you lose some of the elegance of GridGain's peer-to-peer class loading.

You can deploy a.gar archive for which there is an ant task; it will package your .jars and resources and deploy everything to every node's $GRIDGAIN_HOME/work/deployment/file folder. This is far easier than it sounds if you can get away with an NFS mount or something like that to simplify deployment. Additionally, you can tell GridGain to load a resource from an HTTP location, or another remote, URL.

This mechanism has a lot of advantages for production: your extra .jars are visible to the node (which means you won't have to transfer megabytes of libraries over the wire each time you hot redeploy a node instance), and most importantly, the custom beans inside the Spring application context we've been working with will be visible should you need them. When using this method, you can disable peer-to-peer class loading; this, while not significant, represents a gain in startup time.

A GAR archive looks like a standard .jar or .war. It provides several things that are mainly of concern for production. The first is that the libraries are already present, which we discussed. Second, the gridgain.xml file, which is optional, enables you to tell GridGain about which GridTask<T,R> classes are deployed. The structure is as follows:

```
*class
lib/*jar
META-INF/{gridgain.xml,*}
```

gridgain.xml is a simple Spring application context. An example configuration follows:

```
<?xml version="1.0" encoding="UTF-8"?>

<beans xmlns="http://www.springframework.org/schema/beans"
       xmlns:xsi="http://www.w3.org/2001/XMLSchema-instance"
       xmlns:util="http://www.springframework.org/schema/util"
       xsi:schemaLocation="
        http://www.springframework.org/schema/beans↵
  http://www.springframework.org/schema/beans/spring-beans-3.0.xsd
        http://www.springframework.org/schema/util↵
  http://www.springframework.org/schema/util/spring-util-3.0.xsd">
    <description>Gridgain configuration file in gar-file.</description>

    <util:list id="tasks">
        <value>org.gridgain.examples.gar.GridGarHelloWorldTask</value>
    </util:list>
</beans>
```

In this file, we provide a list with ID `tasks`. This file is consulted to help load any tasks contained in the GAR file. If you don't specify anything, GridGain will simply search for tasks itself.

Getting Access to the Spring Container from a Task

Instances of the `ApplicationContext` can be injected into the various GridGain class instances (`GridTask<T,R>`, `GridJob`, and so forth) using GridGain's `@GridSpringApplicationContextResource` annotation. This example shows the Spring application context being injected using the `@GridSpringApplicationContextResource` annotation. This works like `@Autowired` or `@Resource`:

@GridSpringApplicationContextResource
```
private ApplicationContext applicationContext ;
```

Additionally, you can get components injected directly, using the `@GridSpringResource`:

@GridSpringResource(resourceName = "customerServiceBean")
```
private transient CustomerService customerService ;
```

Note the use of `transient`. These resources aren't copied across the wire, but rather, reinjected on each node's initialization. This is a crucial tool in your tool belt, especially with volatile resources that aren't amenable to being sent over the wire, such as `DataSources`.

Node-Specific GridGain Configuration

When you start GridGain via the `gridgain.sh` script, it provides very good defaults. However, sometimes you will want to exercise more control over the process.

When `gridgain.sh` is run, it consults (of all things!) a Spring application context for its configuration information. This file, located at `$GRIDGAIN_HOME/config/default-spring.xml`, contains all the information for GridGain to do what it does—communicate with other nodes. Usually, this works well enough. However, there are *many* things you may want to configure, and because GridGain is Spring-friendly from the core, configuration is very easy. If, instead, you'd like to override the settings in that file, pass in your own application context:

```
./gridgain.sh my-application-context.xml
```

If you want even further control over the process, down to the last shell script, you can bootstrap the GridGain grid nodes yourself. The shell scripts as they ship also, essentially, use the following code to launch the grid from Java. You can as well:

```
org.gridgain.grid.GridFactory.start( "my-application-context.xml") ;
```

There are many versions of the `start` method, but most of them take a Spring application context (either an instance of `ApplicationContext`, or a `String` or URL to an XML application context). The application context is where you configure the grid node.

There are many prebuilt implementations for starting a `Grid` instance however, and you'll rarely need to write your own. The implementations, called grid loaders, provide the necessary integration to start the `Grid` in many different environments. Summarized in Table 22-1 are some of the common ones.

Table 22-1. *Description of the various* GridLoader *implementations.*

Class	Description
org.gridgain.grid.loaders.cmdline.GridCommandLineLoader	This is the default implementation. It is used when you run gridgain.sh or gridgain.bat.
org.gridgain.grid.loaders.servlet.GridServletLoader	This is likely the second most useful implementation. It provides a servlet that bootstraps the GridGain instance inside any web container as a servlet.
org.gridgain.grid.loaders.jboss.GridJbossLoader	Provides a hook for running a Grid inside of JBoss as JMX MBean.
org.gridgain.grid.loaders.weblogic.GridWeblogicStartup, org.gridgain.grid.loaders.weblogic.GridWeblogicShutdown	Provides integration with WebLogic's infrastructure for JMX (monitoring), logging, and the WorkManager implementation.
org.gridgain.grid.loaders.websphere.GridWebsphereLoader	This GridGain loader is implemented as a JMX MBean. This, like the WebLogic integration, provides integration with logging, and the WorkManager implementation.
org.gridgain.grid.loaders.glassfish.GridGlassfishLoader	Provides integration with Glassfish as a life cycle listener that works on both Glassfish 1 and 2.

In most of the loaders in Table 22-1 will be some sort of parameter that lets you provide the URL to a Spring XML application context file.

GridGain is imminently configurable. You might, for example, want to use a JMS queue for the communications layer between nodes. You might want to override the discovery mechanism. You might want to make use of any of numerous caching solutions on the market. There are too many permutations to list, but the distribution itself will contain a config/ directory in which you can find numerous example configurations.

One common requirement is sharing one LAN with multiple grids. You could conceivably have five nodes doing one kind of processing and another ten doing another type for a different project, without requiring a separate subnet.

You partition the cluster by setting the gridName property. gridName enables you to start several grids on the same LAN without fear of one grid stealing another grid's jobs.

An example might be as follows:

```xml
<?xml version="1.0" encoding="UTF-8"?>

<beans xmlns="http://www.springframework.org/schema/beans"
       xmlns:xsi="http://www.w3.org/2001/XMLSchema-instance"
       xmlns:util="http://www.springframework.org/schema/util"
       xsi:schemaLocation="
        http://www.springframework.org/schema/beans↵
 http://www.springframework.org/schema/beans/spring-beans-3.0.xsd
        http://www.springframework.org/schema/util↵
 http://www.springframework.org/schema/util/spring-util-3.0.xsd">

    <bean id="grid.cfg" class="org.gridgain.grid.GridConfigurationAdapter"↵
scope="singleton">
        <property name="gridName" value="mygrid-001"/>

            <!-- ... other configuration … -->

    </bean>
</beans>
```

The next level of parameterization is user attributes. These parameters are specific to the node on which they're configured. You might imagine using these to partition your grid jobs, or to provide box-specific metadata like a NFS mount, or specify which FireWire or USB device to consult for something. In the following example, we use it to describe to the node on which countries' data it should concern itself with:

```xml
<?xml version="1.0" encoding="UTF-8"?>

<beans xmlns="http://www.springframework.org/schema/beans"
       xmlns:xsi="http://www.w3.org/2001/XMLSchema-instance"
       xmlns:util="http://www.springframework.org/schema/util"
       xsi:schemaLocation="
        http://www.springframework.org/schema/beans↵
 http://www.springframework.org/schema/beans/spring-beans-3.0.xsd
        http://www.springframework.org/schema/util↵
 http://www.springframework.org/schema/util/spring-util-3.0.xsd">
    <bean id="grid.cfg" class="org.gridgain.grid.GridConfigurationAdapter"↵
scope="singleton">
        <property name="userAttributes">
            <map>
                <entry key="countries">
                  <util:list>
                        <value>FR</value>
                        <value>MX</value>
                        <value>CA</value>
```

```
                    <value>BG</value>
                    <value>JP</value>
                    <value>PH</value>
</util:list>
                  </entry>
            </map>
        </property>
    </bean>
</beans>
```

You may access parameters configured in this way using the `GridNode` interface:

```
GridNode gridNode = GridFactory.getGrid().getLocalNode();
Serializable attribute = gridNode.getAttribute("countries");
```

Summary

In this chapter, you explored the foundations of distributed computing and the use of grids for both processing and storage. You learned how to use Terracotta to synchronize your application's memory over a cluster so that it is highly available and in memory. You learned how to use GridGain to build a processing grid to distribute the load of a large job over smaller, more plentiful nodes. You learned about the basics of the map/reduce pattern, which enables you to build a parallelized solution for better performance, and you learned how to use GridGain's annotation-based approach to easily leverage a bean's methods on a cluster. Last, you learned how clustered GridGain jobs can access beans from a Spring application context.

■ ■ ■

CHAPTER 23

jBPM and Spring

A business is only as good as its processes. Often, businesses will thread together the contributions of multiple resources (people, automated computer processes, and so forth) to achieve a greater result. These individual contributions by people and automatic services are most efficient when single-focused and, ideally, reused. The simplest example of this might be a conveyor belt in a car factory, where work enters the line at the beginning of the conveyer belt and is worked on by any number of individuals or machines until finally the output of the work reaches the end of the line, at which point the job is done. One machine paints the chassis; another machine lowers the engine into the car. A person screws in and attaches the chairs and another person installs the radio. These people and machines do their work without worrying about what's going to happen to the car next.

A more complicated, interesting process—to take the car example even further—can be seen at a car dealership. There are many workers whose job depends on playing their role in selling you a car. It starts when you enter the car dealership and salesmen descend on you like wolves. Somebody walks with you, showing off models and features and answering questions. Finally, your eye catches the glimmer of a silver Porsche sitting an aisle over. You're sold. The next part of the process begins.

You're whisked away into the office where somebody starts prompting you for information to purchase the vehicle. You either have cash on hand, or you require a loan, or you've already got a loan from another bank. If you have cash on hand, you give it to them and wait an hour for them to count it. Perhaps you've got a check from the bank, in which case you give them that. Or, you begin the process of applying for a loan with the dealership. Eventually, the pecuniary details are sorted, credit scores checked, driver's license and insurance verified, and you begin signing paper work. If you've already paid for the car, the paper work to ensure proper title and registration is drawn up. If you're establishing a loan with the dealership, you fill out that paperwork, then work on registration, and so on.

Eventually, you're given the keys, the car, and the relevant paperwork, and you're done. Or so you think. You make a break for the door, just itching to see how fast you can get the car to 65, which is the maximum speed limit in your area freeway, conditions permitting. As you arrive at the door, you're all but assaulted with one last packet of brochures and business cards and a branded pen and the good wishes of the grinning salesmen.

Baffled, you shrug them off and break for the car, jumping into the sporty convertible's driver's seat. As you leave, you turn the music up and speed off into the horizon. You'll remember that you left your wife at the dealership eventually, but for now, the fruit of all that bureaucracy is too sweet to ignore.

The process to buy the car may seem like it takes forever, and indeed, it does take a long time. However, the process is efficient in that all things that can be done at the same time are done at the same time, by multiple workers. Further, because each actor knows the part, each individual step is as efficient as possible. Being able to orchestrate a process like this is crucial in the enterprise.

You can extrapolate here, too. These examples are relatively small, though perhaps the inefficiencies of the worst-case scenario for the process are tolerable. The inefficiencies are overwhelmingly untenable in even slightly larger business processes, though! For example, imagine the new-hire process at a large company. Beyond the initial process of interviewing and a background security check, there's the provisioning that's required to get the new employee installed. The IT department needs to repurpose a laptop, image it, and install an operating system. Somebody needs to create a user account for that employee and ensure that LDAP and e-mail are accessible. Somebody needs to ready a security card so that the employee can use the elevator or enter the building. Somebody needs to make sure the employee's desk station or office is cleaned and that remnants from the previous occupant are gone. Somebody needs to get forms for the health insurance or benefits, and somebody needs to give the new employee a walk around the office, introducing the employee to staff.

Imagine having only one person to do all of that for each employee! In a bigger company (such as a bank, for example) this process would soon become overwhelming! Indeed, many of the tasks mentioned themselves require several steps to achieve the goal. Thus, the main process—integrating a new employee in the company—has multiple subprocesses. If all the tasks are performed concurrently by many people however, the process becomes manageable. Additionally, not all people are suited to doing all of those tasks. A little specialization makes for a lot of efficiency here.

We see that processes, and the understanding of those processes, are *crucial* to a business. It is from this revelation that the study of business management emerged, called Business Process Management (BPM). BPM originally described how to best orchestrate technology and people to the betterment of the business, but it was a businessman's preoccupation, not a technologist's. As it became apparent that businesses were already leveraging technology, the next hurdle was to codify the notion of a business process. How could software systems know—and react to—what the immovable enterprises and unbending market forces demanded? BPM provides the answer. It describes, in higher-level diagrams, the flow a given process takes from start to finish. These diagrams are useful both to the business analyst and to the programmer, because they describe two sides of the same coin. Once a process is codified, it can be reused and reapplied in the same way a programmer reuses a class in Java.

Software Processes

Thus, the unit of work—that which is required to achieve a quantifiable goal—for a business is rarely a single request/response. Even the simplest of processes in a business requires at least a few steps. This is true not just in business but in your users' use cases. Short of simple read-only scenarios such as looking at a web page for the news, most meaningful processes require multiple steps. Think through the sign-up process of your typical web application. It begins with a user visiting a site and filling out a form. The user completes the form and submits the finalized data, after satisfying validation. If you think about it, however, this is just the beginning of the work for this very simple process. Typically, to avoid spam, a verification e-mail will be sent to the user. When the e-mail is read, the user clicks a link, which confirms the intentions of the registrant and that the registrant is not a robot. This tells the server that the user is a valid user, and that a welcome e-mail should be sent. A welcome e-mail is then sent. Here alone, we had four steps with two different roles! This involved process, when translated into an activity diagram, is shown in Figure 23-1.

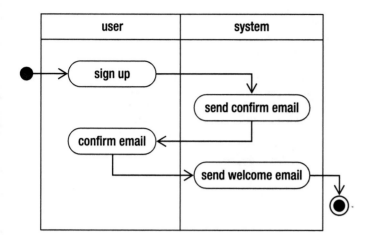

Figure 23-1. *The two roles (user and system) are shown as swimlanes. Rounded shapes inside the swimlanes are states. Process flows from one state to another, following the path of the connecting lines.*

For such a simple process, it might be tempting to keep track of the state of the process in the domain model. After all, some of the state, such as the sign-up date, can certainly be regarded as business data, belonging to model entities. Such a date is valuable for revenue recognition. The date when the welcome e-mail was sent is probably not very important, though. The situation will escalate if you send out more e-mail. If you build other kinds of processes involving the user, management of the user's state within those processes will become a burden on your system and will complicate the schema.

A workflow system extricates that process state from the domain and into a separate layer, called a business process. A workflow system also typically models which agents in the system do what work, providing work lists for different agents in the system.

A workflow engine lets you model the process in a higher-level form, roughly corresponding in code to what a UML activity diagram can describe. Because a workflow is high-level, specifying how a business process is leveraged as an executable component of a system is a dizzyingly vast task. In industry, there are standards for the language used to model a business process as well as the model of the engine that's used to run the business process. Additionally, there are standards specifying interoperability, how endpoints are mapped to the agents being orchestrated by the process, and much more. All this can quickly become overwhelming.

Let's look at some of these standards in Table 23-1.

Table 23-1. Some of the Myriad, Significant Standards Surrounding BPM

Standard Name	Standards Group	Description
WS-BPEL (BPEL)	OASIS	A language that, when deployed to a BPEL container, describes the execution of a process. It interfaces with the outside world via the invocation of external web services. This language describes the runtime behavior of a process. It has several flaws, not the least of which is the reliance on web service technology and the lack of work list support.
WS-BPEL (BPEL 2.0)	OASIS	This is largely an upgrade to its predecessor, clarifying the behavior at runtime of certain elements and adding more expressive elements to the language.
WS-BPEL for People (BPEL4People)	OASIS	The main feature common to traditional workflow systems is the ability to support work lists for actors in a process. BPEL had no such support, as it didn't support human tasks (that is, wait states for people). This specification addresses that exact shortcoming.
Business Process Modeling Notation (BPMN)	Originally BPMI, then OMG, as the two organizations merged	This provides a set of diagramming notations that describe a business process. This notation is akin to UML's activity diagram, though the specification also describes how the notations relate to runtime languages such as BPEL. The notation is sometimes ambiguous, however, and one of the formidable challenges facing BPM vendors is creating a drawing tool that can take a round-trip to BPEL and back, providing seamless authoring.
XML Process Definition Language	Workflow Management Coalition (WfMC)	This one describes the interchange of diagrams between modeling tools, especially how elements are displayed and the semantics of those elements to the target notation.

As you can see, there are some problems. Some of these standards are ill suited to real business needs, even once the busywork is surmounted. And some of them lack adequate support for work lists—essentially making the processes useless for anything that models human interaction, a fairly typical requirement.

While a lot of this is slowly getting better, there's no reason to wait. There are viable *de facto* standards that meet a lot of these problems and offer a compelling alternative. In this chapter, we will review jBPM, a popular open source environment. You might take a look at the alternative open source workflow engines (e.g., Enhydra Shark or OpenWFE) or, indeed, the proprietary engines from Tibco, IBM, Oracle, WebMethods, and so forth, before you decide on jBPM. In our opinion, it's powerful enough for easily 80 percent of the situations you're likely to encounter and can at least facilitate solutions for another 10 percent.

Ultimately, jBPM integrates well with Spring, and it provides a very powerful complement to the features of the things we've discussed in this book and to the core Spring framework itself. Just as a page-flow description language threads together multiple requests in a web application, workflows thread together many disparate actors (both people and automatic computer processes) into a process, keeping track of state. Workflow support becomes far more compelling in an architecture using even a few of the technologies we've covered in this book: messaging, distributed computing, ESB endpoints, web services, and long-lived processing infrastructure, for example! Workflow orchestrates these different, powerful tools and provides cohesion. Eventually, you'll even begin to reuse processes much like you might reuse a class or a Spring Integration endpoint.

23-1. Understanding Workflow Models

Problem

You understand the "why" behind business processes and have identified types of problems that might be well suited to this technology. Now, you want to understand how—after all, it all sounds so nebulous and abstract. How do you describe and speak about a workflow, exactly?

Solution

It turns out, happily, that you probably already know most of what you need to describe a workflow engine. This is part of why a workflow engine is so powerful—it formalizes and facilitates solutions you're already struggling to build in other technologies. In fact, when you draw an activity diagram, the result is likely directly translatable into a workflow. As you'll see, a lot of the constructs used to build a business process are familiar. We've discussed many of them in our discussions of Spring Integration and Spring Batch and of the map/reduce pattern with GridGain.

How It Works

One metric by which you might judge an engine is how well it lets you express workflow patterns. The workflow patterns describe different idioms that you might apply to a pattern. All patterns ultimately are built out of any mixture of a few key concepts (see Table 23-2), many of which we've discussed in other chapters of this book, as with Spring Batch and Spring Integration.

Table 23-2. *Kinds of Constructs You Will Use When Working with a BPM or Workflow System*

Concept	Description
State	"State" can mean many things, but simply, it's a pause or window in the action. It's a way of letting your process rest in a known condition indefinitely. Perhaps during this time, an external event might take place, or the system might wait for an input. Perhaps the state is entered and left as quickly as can be, serving only to provide record of the event. This is one of the simplest and most powerful functions of a workflow engine. Indeed, all discussions of long-lived state, of conversational state, and of continuations are centered on this concept. It allows your process to stop and wait for an event that tells it to proceed. This is powerful because it implies that no resources need to be wasted waiting for that event and that the process can effectively sleep, or passivate, until such an event, at which point the workflow engine will wake the process up and start it moving.
Activity	An *activity* is a pause in the action that can only move forward when a known actor or agent in the system moves it forward. You might imagine the moderator or group administrator who has to OK your subscription to a news group. In that case, only specified agents or roles may say the process may move forward.
Sequence	A *sequence* is simply an aggregation of states, activities, and other types of constructs that serializes them. You might have three states and an activity. You might imagine them as steps on a ladder, where the ladder is the sequence directing the process upwards to the ultimate goal.
Fork or concurrence or split	A sequence is important because it implies there's another way of threading things along. A *fork* is a concurrent execution of multiple threads of execution at the same time, originating from a common thread. Some parts of a business process are inherently sequential, and some are readily concurrent. In the new employee example explored previously, you might imagine the security clearance, laptop provisioning, and other tasks could be done at the same time, thus increasing the speed of the process.
Subprocess	In the new employee example, we discuss several tasks that need to be performed by representatives of different departments. Each department may have its own task list to complete in order to achieve the goals of the overarching process. These subtasks (basically a separate process unto their own) may be modeled as a *subprocess*. Subprocesses afford your workflows the same flexibility through reuse that composition through functions or classes affords your programs.
Decision	A *decision* describes a node that is conditional, based on some logic that you inject. You might use this to vary the execution based on some fact that you provide the process as a parameter.

23-2. Installing jBPM

Problem

You want to build a jBPM solution and need to know the simplest way to get the JARs. There are many supported workflows for jBPM, so it isn't clear where to begin for what role. For a business analyst, the path is different than for a programmer, whose task it will be to employ jBPM, not deploy it. You will need a few libraries first.

Solution

You can use jBPM as an API, rather than as a server or service. This integration is the most natural to a developer, but not, for example, to a business user. We'll use Maven to get the dependencies.

While we'll focus on embedding jBPM in this chapter, it's useful to see the other ways you can integrate jBPM into your architecture.

- A developer may embed jBPM as services and Hibernate entities.

- A developer may deploy jBPM into a stand-alone server and then use the administration console to deploy and test processes.

- jBPM 4.3 ships with a web application in which a user can diagram and test processes.

How It Works

For this example, we're using a few libraries for AOP, transactions, the core Spring context, and, of course, jBPM itself.

If you're looking to find out more, read the documentation, and get the downloadable binaries for exploration, check out http://jboss.org/jbossjbpm/. There, you can find a lot of useful information.

Because we're looking to embed it, we'll simply use the libraries.

▨ **Note** If you're using Maven, you should add the following dependencies to your project.

```
<dependency>
  <groupId>org.jbpm.jbpm4</groupId>
  <artifactId>jbpm-jpdl</artifactId>
  <version>4.3</version>
</dependency>
```

```xml
<dependency>
  <groupId>javax.annotation</groupId>
  <artifactId>jsr250-api</artifactId>
  <version>1.0</version>
</dependency>

<dependency>
  <groupId>commons-dbcp</groupId>
  <artifactId>commons-dbcp</artifactId>
  <version>1.2.1</version>
  <exclusions>
    <exclusion>
      <groupId>xerces</groupId>
      <artifactId>xercesImpl</artifactId>
    </exclusion>
  </exclusions>
</dependency>

<dependency>
  <groupId>xerces</groupId>
  <artifactId>xercesImpl</artifactId>
  <version>2.7.1</version>
</dependency>

<dependency>
  <groupId>commons-lang</groupId>
  <artifactId>commons-lang</artifactId>
  <version>2.2</version>
</dependency>

<dependency>
  <groupId>commons-io</groupId>
  <artifactId>commons-io</artifactId>
  <version>1.1</version>
</dependency>
```

```
<dependency>
  <groupId>org.hibernate</groupId>
  <artifactId>hibernate-entitymanager</artifactId>
  <version>3.4.0.GA</version>
</dependency>

<dependency>
  <groupId>javax.persistence</groupId>
  <artifactId>persistence-api</artifactId>
  <version>1.0</version>
</dependency>
```

Some of these dependencies are from the JBoss Maven repository. You should add a reference to the JBoss Maven repository to your Maven project.

```
<repository>
  <id>jboss</id>
  <url>http://repository.jboss.com/maven2/</url>
</repository>
```

It's hard to find an exhaustive or conclusive list of supported databases for jBPM, but because it's built on Hibernate, you can expect it's going to work on the big-name databases: Oracle, SQL Server, MySQL, PostgreSQL, and so forth. In this example, we're using PostgreSQL 8.3.

■ **Note** To use PostgreSQL, you need to add a the driver library to the classpath. If you are using Maven, add the following dependency to your project.

```
<dependency>
  <groupId>postgresql</groupId>
  <artifactId>postgresql</artifactId>
  <version>8.3-603.jdbc3</version>
</dependency>
```

23-3. Integrating jBPM 4 with Spring

Problem

You want to use jBPM 4 (the newest, and current, release at the time of this writing) but you've got a Spring-based architecture and want to make use of jBPM from within a Spring application context.

Solution

Earlier versions of Spring shipped with a custom bean for use with Spring (`org.jbpm.pvm.internal.cfg.SpringConfiguration`). Now, however, the initialization is so simple there's no real need, and the class has been removed. We'll create a factory for our jBPM configuration that can be reused across projects. The balance of the configuration is fairly boilerplate transaction management and Hibernate integration, with some caveats. Andries Inzé started the project to integrate Spring and jBPM, and so much of the great work here is because of his efforts, on top of the great work behind jBPM itself, of course.

How It Works

There are many ways to use jBPM. One approach is to use it as a stand-alone process server, perhaps deployed using JBoss. This solution exposes a console into which you can deploy business processes and even test out the process and watch it move state forward. As it's written using Hibernate, it's not too difficult to get it working on JBoss's EJB environment. So, you might use it as a service. Indeed, JBoss itself supports deploying processes to a directory and loading those, with some configuration.

For our purposes, we want to flip that deployment on its head. We want to embed, rather than deploy to, jBPM, in the same way that we can use Spring to invert control for other things such as remote services, message driven POJOs, and the `HibernateTemplate`.

In this example, we'll host jBPM's services in the Spring context, just like we might any other Hibernate services. jBPM is, fundamentally, a runtime that stores its state and jobs in a database. It uses Hibernate as its persistence mechanism (though it may eventually move to a strict JPA–based model). When jBPM, with Hibernate, interacts with the database, it uses transactions and avails itself of many of the features that Hibernate provides to build a sophisticated object graph mapped to a database schema. Naturally, this isn't so bad, except that in order to use jBPM with other services inside of Spring, particularly ones that leverage transactions (other database resources, XA functionality including but not limited to JMS, other Hibernate models, and so forth), you need to exert control over jBPM's transactions. Otherwise, jBPM will commit and begin transactions independent of the Spring container's transaction lifecycle.

jBPM 4 is built cleanly, in such a way that delegating the life cycle of the system to another container (such as JBoss's microcontainer or Spring) is feasible. The jBPM 4 and Spring integration builds on top of this, providing a recipe for accessing key services that jBPM provides at runtime. This is the key to the integration. With jBPM available to your beans as just another bean in the container, you can leverage it just like you might a Hibernate session or a JMS queue connection. Similarly, you can hide its use behind service methods that you expose to your applications clients.

Imagine exposing a service method for creating customer entities. It might use Hibernate to save the new record to the database, use JMS to trigger integration with an external financial system the company uses, and use jBPM to start a business process for fulfillment. This is a very robust, well-rounded service.

You can use the services like you might any other transactional service—confident that the containing transaction will envelope the transactions of the jBPM process.

We will build a simple application context that contains the common elements you'll need to start using jBPM in your application, and then see where you may want to customize the solution to your environment.

In the example for jBPM 4, we will build a solution that models a simple customer registration workflow. In so doing, you will get a feeling for how you would set up the example, as well as get a chance to see a (very simple) jBPM solution. The namespaces of the work we'll do will sit below `com.apress.springrecipes.jbpm.jbpm4`.

The Application Context

The first thing to do is to set up basic database and Hibernate configuration. We will use the `tx`, `p`, `aop`, and `context` namespaces to build this solution. The skeletal frame for our Spring XML configuration is as follows:

```
<?xml version="1.0" encoding="UTF-8"?>
<beans xmlns="http://www.springframework.org/schema/beans"
       xmlns:tx="http://www.springframework.org/schema/tx" ↵
xmlns:p="http://www.springframework.org/schema/p"
       xmlns:util="http://www.springframework.org/schema/util" ↵
xmlns:xsi="http://www.w3.org/2001/XMLSchema-instance"
       xmlns:aop="http://www.springframework.org/schema/aop" ↵
xmlns:context="http://www.springframework.org/schema/context"
       xsi:schemaLocation="http://www.springframework.org/schema/beans
http://www.springframework.org/schema/beans/spring-beans-3.0.xsd
http://www.springframework.org/schema/util
http://www.springframework.org/schema/util/spring-util-3.0.xsd
http://www.springframework.org/schema/context
http://www.springframework.org/schema/context/spring-context-3.0.xsd
http://www.springframework.org/schema/aop
http://www.springframework.org/schema/aop/spring-aop-3.0.xsd
http://www.springframework.org/schema/tx
http://www.springframework.org/schema/tx/spring-tx-3.0.xsd">

    ...

</beans>
```

In this example, we'll use two Spring application contexts. One application context will configure jBPM (`jbpm4-context.xml`), and the other will configure our sample application (simply, `context.xml`). The first application context is geared around configuring jBPM. You should be able to reuse this file later with no changes to the file itself. Mainly, you'd have to update the property file (naturally) and you'd have to tell the session factory about any annotated classes that you want it to know about from your own domain model. In this example, doing so is simple, as it involves overriding an existing `List` bean named `annotatedHibernateClasses` in a separate context. It's been done this way because it's not possible to have two sets of Hibernate classes that are registered with the Hibernate `SessionFactory`. To have an annotated class be registered as a Hibernate entity, it needs to be registered with the `AnnotationSessionFactoryBean`. The `annotatedClasses` property expects a list of class names. Because our jBPM configuration uses Hibernate, we have to configure the `AnnotatedSessionFactoryBean` on behalf of jBPM, which means that you can't create a separate one if you're using the `jbpm4-context.xml` and want only one Hibernate session in your application. This is probably the case, because there's rarely a need for two Hibernate sessions, because they can't share transactions and so on. So, we provide a template configuration, referencing a list that's created in the context. The list is empty, but you can in your Spring application context include (`jbpm4-context.xml`) and create your own list bean with the same bean name ("`annotatedHibernateClasses`"), effectively overriding the configuration. This delegation scheme works in much the same way an abstract method in a base class does.

Because we want this to be as automatic as possible, we'll exploit Spring's AOP schema support and transaction schema support. The first few lines of the application context are boilerplate: they instruct the context to enable annotation configuration and use a property file as values for placeholders in the application context's XML itself. The file `jbpm4.properties` is included and its values resolved. Those values are then available as expressions to other beans in the context file.

```
<context:annotation-config />

<bean class="org.springframework.beans.factory.config.PropertyPlaceholderConfigurer"
p:location="jbpm4.properties" p:ignoreUnresolvablePlaceholders="true" />
```

Next comes the `sessionFactory`. It's key to get this right: we need to tell Spring about our database and give it the information on our schema. It does this by resolving the properties in the property file. When we configure the `mappingLocations` property, we are pointing it to classpath Hibernate mapping files so that it may resolve the various entities that ship with jBPM 4. These entities will exist in your database. They persist such information as process definitions, process variables, and so forth that are important to the successful execution of the jBPM engine.

The final property we've configured here is the `annotatedClasses` property, which we basically punt. Providing an empty list object here allows us to override it in another context file, so we don't even need to modify the original one. If you don't want to provide any classes, the original empty list declaration will still work, and you won't get any errors from Spring at runtime.

Note that we've specified `p:schemaUpdate="true"`, which let's Hibernate generate the schema for us on load. Naturally, you probably want to disable this in production.

```
<bean id="sessionFactory"
class="org.springframework.orm.hibernate3.annotation.AnnotationSessionFactoryBean"
p:dataSource-ref="dataSource"
p:schemaUpdate="true">
        <property name="hibernateProperties">
            <props>
                    <prop key="hibernate.dialect">${dataSource.dialect}</prop>
                    <prop key="hibernate.show_sql">true</prop>
                    <prop key="hibernate.hbm2ddl.auto">create-drop</prop>
                    <prop key="hibernate.jdbc.batch_size">20</prop>
                    <prop key="hibernate.show_sql">true</prop>
                    <prop key="hibernate.use_sql_comments">true</prop>
            </props>
        </property>
```

```
        <property name="mappingLocations">
                <list>
                        <value>classpath:jbpm.execution.hbm.xml</value>
                        <value>classpath:jbpm.repository.hbm.xml</value>
                        <value>classpath:jbpm.task.hbm.xml</value>
                        <value>classpath:jbpm.history.hbm.xml</value>
                </list>
        </property>
        <property name="annotatedClasses" ref="annotatedHibernateClasses" />
    </bean>

    <util:list id="annotatedHibernateClasses" />
```

The next bean—the dataSource—is configured entirely at your discretion. The properties are set using properties in the properties file jbpm4.properties. The contents of jbpm4.properties:

```
hibernate.configFile=hibernate.cfg.xml
dataSource.password=sep
dataSource.username=sep
dataSource.databaseName=sep
dataSource.driverClassName=org.postgresql.Driver
dataSource.dialect=org.hibernate.dialect.PostgreSQLDialect
dataSource.serverName=sep
dataSource.url=jdbc:postgresql://${dataSource.serverName}/${dataSource.databaseName}
dataSource.properties=user=${dataSource.username};databaseName=${dataSource.databaseName};se
rverName=${dataSource.serverName};password=${dataSource.password}
```

Modify the values there to reflect your database of choice. As mentioned before, there are lots of supported databases. If you're using MySQL, I'd suggest something like the InnoDB table type to take advantage of transactions. In our experience, PostgreSQL, MySQL, Oracle, and so forth all work fine. You'll also want to configure a transaction manager. You will use this later when setting up AOP–advised transaction management for our beans.

```
    <bean id="dataSource" class="org.apache.commons.dbcp.BasicDataSource"
            destroy-method="close" p:driverClassName="${dataSource.driverClassName}"
            p:username="${dataSource.username}" p:password="${dataSource.password}"
            p:url="${dataSource.url}" />

    <bean id="transactionManager"
            class="org.springframework.orm.hibernate3.HibernateTransactionManager"
            p:sessionFactory-ref="sessionFactory" />
```

Additionally, add a HibernateTemplate, as you'll need it to interact with both your and jBPM's entities.

```
    <bean    id="hibernateTemplate"
            class="org.springframework.orm.hibernate3.HibernateTemplate"
            p:sessionFactory-ref="sessionFactory"  />
```

Finally, we configure the actual factory that sets everything up for us. This class is our own, simple implementation.

```
    <bean id="processEngine"
class="com.apress.springrecipes.jbpm.jbpm4.CustomSpringFactory">
        <property name="jbpmCfg" value="jbpm.cfg.xml"/>
    </bean>
```

Here's the definition of the class:

```
package com.apress.springrecipes.jbpm.jbpm4;

import org.jbpm.api.ProcessEngine;
import org.jbpm.pvm.internal.cfg.ConfigurationImpl;

import org.springframework.beans.BeansException;
import org.springframework.beans.factory.FactoryBean;
import org.springframework.beans.factory.InitializingBean;

import org.springframework.context.ApplicationContext;
import org.springframework.context.ApplicationContextAware;


/**
 * A custom {@link org.springframework.beans.factory.BeanFactory} that we can
 * use to setup the {@link org.jbpm.api.ProcessEngine}. This is based on jBPM's {@link ↵
org.jbpm.pvm.internal.processengine.SpringHelper}.
 */
public class CustomSpringFactory implements FactoryBean, InitializingBean, ↵
ApplicationContextAware {
    private ApplicationContext applicationContext;
    private ProcessEngine processEngine;
    private String jbpmCfg;

    public void setJbpmCfg(final String jbpmCfg) {
        this.jbpmCfg = jbpmCfg;
    }

    @Override
    public Object getObject() throws Exception {
        return processEngine;
    }

    @Override
    public Class<?> getObjectType() {
        return ProcessEngine.class;
    }

    @Override
    public boolean isSingleton() {
        return true;
    }
```

```
    @Override
    public void afterPropertiesSet() throws Exception {
        processEngine = new ConfigurationImpl().springInitiated(applicationContext).↵
setResource(jbpmCfg).buildProcessEngine();
    }

    @Override
    public void setApplicationContext(final ApplicationContext applicationContext)
        throws BeansException {
        this.applicationContext = applicationContext;
    }
}
```

At this point, all that remains is to specify the following jBPM configuration itself (jbpm.cfg.xml), which is fairly boilerplate and you can use, unchanged, for a vast many solutions:

```
<?xml version="1.0" encoding="UTF-8"?>
<jbpm-configuration>
    <import resource="jbpm.default.cfg.xml"/>
    <import resource="jbpm.jpdl.cfg.xml"/>
    <import resource="jbpm.identity.cfg.xml"/>
    <import resource="jbpm.tx.spring.cfg.xml"/>

    <process-engine-context>
        <repository-service/>
        <repository-cache/>
        <execution-service/>
        <history-service/>
        <management-service/>
        <identity-service/>
        <task-service/>
        <command-service>
            <retry-interceptor/>
            <environment-interceptor/>
            <spring-transaction-interceptor/>
        </command-service>
        <script-manager default-expression-language="juel" default-script-language="juel" ↵
read-contexts="execution, environment, process-engine, spring" write-context="">
            <script-language name="juel" factory="org.jbpm.pvm.internal.script.↵
JuelScriptEngineFactory"/>
        </script-manager>
        <id-generator/>
        <types resource="jbpm.variable.types.xml"/>
        <address-resolver/>
        <business-calendar>
            <monday hours="9:00-12:00 and 12:30-17:00"/>
            <tuesday hours="9:00-12:00 and 12:30-17:00"/>
            <wednesday hours="9:00-12:00 and 12:30-17:00"/>
```

```
                <thursday hours="9:00-12:00 and 12:30-17:00"/>
                <friday hours="9:00-12:00 and 12:30-17:00"/>
                <holiday period="01/07/2008 - 31/08/2008"/>
            </business-calendar>
        </process-engine-context>
        <transaction-context>
            <repository-session/>
            <db-session/>
            <message-session/>
            <timer-session/>
            <history-session/>
            <hibernate-session current="true"/>
        </transaction-context>
</jbpm-configuration>
```

By and large, this is a pretty standard configuration for jBPM. It specifies many things that are safe defaults and largely out of the scope of this book. Mainly, the configuration tells jBPM which services to bring up and defines some configuration for those services. Because we're integrating with Spring, we modify the transaction-context element and the command-service element, as those are the touch points with Spring. The hibernate-session element tells jBPM to reuse an existing Hibernate session (the one we created with our Hibernate session factory) instead of creating its own. The spring-transaction-interceptor element is a special element to enable jBPM to defer to the TransactionManager defined in our application context. Here again, jBPM integrates by delegating to the Spring services, making for a very eloquent solution.

23-4. Building a Service with Spring

Problem

In the previous recipe, you configured Spring and jBPM, such that Spring's is successfully hosting jBPM. You set about writing a business process and now want to work with jBPM inside of your service code and to be able to delegate actions to Spring beans from within a business process.

Solution

Use Spring normally, injecting the services as you need them. For access within your business process, you can simply reference the services as you would any other process or environment variable in a business process. jBPM will expose beans using the jBPM expression language, and you can then just reference them by name.

How It Works

In this recipe, we'll work through a simple example so you can see the pieces of a typical integration with Spring and jBPM. We've already laid the groundwork in the previous example. Here, we'll actually build a simple Java service that works with Spring to move the process state forward.

The use case is a user registration, like the one described in Figure 23-1.

There are four steps:

1. A prospective customer (modeled here as a Hibernate entity, Customer) signs up via a form. (We'll leave the web page interactions to your imagination for this example; suffice it to say that the form, when submitted, invokes a service method, which we'll define.)

2. A verification e-mail is sent.

3. The user (ideally) will confirm the receipt of the e-mail by clicking a link, which authorizes the user. This could happen in a minute, or in a decade, so the system can't afford to waste resources waiting.

4. Upon confirmation, the user will receive a "Welcome!" e-mail.

This is a simple use of a business process. It abstracts away the process of incorporating and processing a new Customer. Conceivably, the Customer object could have come from any number of channels: somebody sitting taking phone calls inputs them manually, the user self-subscribes to the system, in a batch process, and so on. All of these different channels can create and reuse this business process, though. When the processing for a new customer is standardized, the challenge becomes about surfacing the functionality for as many end users as possible.

Because the user could conceivably wait a few days or weeks (it's arbitrary) before checking the e-mail and clicking the confirm link, state needs to be maintained but not burden the system. jBPM, and indeed most workflow engines, passivate state for you, allowing a process to wait on external events (*signals*). Indeed, because you've decomposed your process into a series of isolated steps, each of which contributes to the larger goal while remaining independently useful, you get the best of both worlds: stateful processes and stateless scalability. The state of the global business process is maintained and is persistent throughout the state of customer's sign-up, but you get the benefits of not keeping things in memory when there's no progress in the business process, thus freeing up the memory to handle other requests.

To build our solution, we need to build a simple CustomerService class and configure it appropriately. We'll integrate jBPM and tailor transaction management for the CustomerService class. We'll also make our bean responsible for deploying the process definitions for us as the bean starts up, so that if they weren't already deployed, they will be.

The XML for the application context is stark and simple.

```
<?xml version="1.0" encoding="UTF-8"?>
<beans xmlns="http://www.springframework.org/schema/beans"
       xmlns:tx="http://www.springframework.org/schema/tx" ↵
xmlns:p="http://www.springframework.org/schema/p"
       xmlns:util="http://www.springframework.org/schema/util" ↵
xmlns:xsi="http://www.w3.org/2001/XMLSchema-instance"
       xmlns:aop="http://www.springframework.org/schema/aop"
       xmlns:context="http://www.springframework.org/schema/context"
       xsi:schemaLocation="
http://www.springframework.org/schema/beans
http://www.springframework.org/schema/beans/spring-beans-3.0.xsd
http://www.springframework.org/schema/context
http://www.springframework.org/schema/context/spring-context-3.0.xsd
http://www.springframework.org/schema/util
http://www.springframework.org/schema/util/spring-util-3.0.xsd
http://www.springframework.org/schema/aop
http://www.springframework.org/schema/aop/spring-aop-3.0.xsd
```

```
http://www.springframework.org/schema/tx
http://www.springframework.org/schema/tx/spring-tx-3.0.xsd
                                            ">
    <import resource="jbpm4-context.xml"/>

    <context:annotation-config/>

    <tx:advice id="txAdvice" transaction-manager="transactionManager">
        <tx:attributes>
            <tx:method propagation="REQUIRED" name="*"/>
        </tx:attributes>
    </tx:advice>

    <aop:config>
        <aop:advisor advice-ref="txAdvice" pointcut="execution(* ↵
com.apress.springrecipes..jbpm4.*.*(..))"/>
    </aop:config>

    <util:list id="annotatedHibernateClasses">
        <value>com.apress.springrecipes.jbpm.jbpm4.customers.Customer</value>
    </util:list>

    <bean id="customerService" class="com.apress.springrecipes.jbpm.jbpm4.customers.↵
CustomerServiceImpl">
        <property name="processDefinitions">
            <list>
                <value>/process-definitions/RegisterCustomer.jpdl.xml</value>
            </list>
        </property>
    </bean>
</beans>
```

The first few elements are familiar: we set up the AOP–based transaction management and apply it to the services deployed under the jbpm4 package in our solution. Next, we override the List bean (with id annotatedHibernateClasses) that we created for the last recipe (jbpm4-context.xml) to provide the session factory with a collection of annotated entities, here, the Customer entity. Finally, we have a bean to handle the customerService bean. This bean leverages Hibernate (through the HibernateTemplate instance) to handle persistence, and it leverages jBPM (through the SpringConfiguration instance) to handle BPM. We provide the customerService bean with a list of business processes we want to ensure are deployed, which the bean handles as part of its duties in its post-initialization phase (the method annotated with @PostConstruct will be run after the bean's been configured to let the user inject custom initialization logic). In this case, we're deploying only one business process. Note that the business process file's name needs to end in jpdl.xml; otherwise, jBPM won't deploy it. The customerService bean is an implementation of the interface CustomerService, whose definition is as follows:

```
package com.apress.springrecipes.jbpm.jbpm4.customers;

public interface CustomerService {

        void sendWelcomeEmail(Long customerId);

        void deauthorizeCustomer(Long customerId);

        void authorizeCustomer(Long customerId);

        Customer getCustomerById(Long customerId);

        Customer createCustomer(String email, String password, String firstName, ⏎
String lastName);

        void sendCustomerVerificationEmail(Long customerId);
}
```

The interface is trivial and only provides creation and mutation services for a Customer record. The implementation is where we see all the pieces come together.

```
package com.apress.springrecipes.jbpm.jbpm4.customers;
```

CustomerServiceImpl is a simple class. At the top, we've injected three dependencies: springConfiguration (which doesn't get used, though its configuration is worth noting because you may use it to access other services), repositoryService, and executionService. The class provides a few salient methods (some of which are required by its interface, CustomerService):

- void setupProcessDefinitions()

- Customer createCustomer(String email, String passphrase, String firstName, String lastName)

- void sendCustomerVerificationEmail(Long customerId)

- void authorizeCustomer(Long customerId)

In the bean, setupProcessDefinitions is run when the bean is created. It iterates through the processDefinitions collection and deploys the resource whose path it is given. If you monitor the logs, you'll witness SQL being issued against the database, creating the runtime structure of your process definition inside the database.

23-5. Building a Business Process

Problem

You've built a service that uses jBPM to create a working service. We've seen how jBPM is configured, and we've even built a service for a business requirement (the sign-up of customers). The last element that remains is the process definition itself. What does a business process definition look like? How does a process definition reference Spring beans?

Solution

We'll build a process definition that codifies the steps diagrammed in Figure 23-1 at the beginning of the chapter. This process definition will reference Spring beans using the JBoss expression language. Finally, we'll walk through how the business process uses our customerService bean and how the customerService bean uses the business process to handle the customer's sign-up.

How It Works

Let's examine the business process itself (RegisterCustomer.jpdl.xml). In jBPM, a business process is built using jPDL. You can use the Eclipse plug-in to model jBPM processes, but the jPDL schema is so simple that you don't really need it. This is not like BPEL where it can become all but intolerably complicated to write the code by hand. What follows is the XML for the business process:

```xml
<?xml version="1.0" encoding="UTF-8"?>
<process name="RegisterCustomer" xmlns="http://jbpm.org/4.0/jpdl">

        <start>
                <transition to="send-verification-email" />
        </start>

        <java name="send-verification-email" expr="#{customerService}"
                method="sendCustomerVerificationEmail">
                <arg> <object expr="#{customerId}" /> </arg>
                <transition to="confirm-receipt-of-verification-email" />
        </java>

        <state name="confirm-receipt-of-verification-email">
                <transition to="send-welcome-email" />
        </state>

        <java name="send-welcome-email"
                        expr="#{customerService}" method="sendWelcomeEmail">
                <arg> <object expr="#{customerId}" /> </arg>
        </java>

</process>
```

In the customerService bean, a client will use createCustomer to create a customer record. In a real-world example, you might imagine exposing these services as a SOAP endpoint to be consumed by various clients, such as a web application or other business applications. You can imagine it being called as a result of a successful form on a web site. When it executes, it creates a new Customer object and uses Hibernate to persist it. Inside the createCustomer method, we use jBPM to start the business process to track the Customer. This is done with the startProcessInstanceByKey method. In the invocation, we give jBPM variables through a Map<String,Object> instance (acting as something of a context for the process variables). Those variables are accessible inside the business process as Expression Language expressions and allow you to parameterize the business process in much the same way you might parameterize a macro or a Java method. We give the process instance a custom business key, instead of letting it generate its own.

```
executionService.startProcessInstanceByKey(
    REGISTER_CUSTOMER_PROCESS_KEY, vars, Long.toString(customer.getId()));
```

The last parameter is the key. Here, we're using the String ID of the customer as the key. This makes it easy to find the process instance later, though you could also query for the process instance, predicating on process variables that, taken together, should make the process instance unique. You might also query by roles or users assigned to certain tasks, or simply note the ID of the business process itself in your domain model and reference that later when looking up the process instance. Here, we know that there's only ever going to be one sign-up process for a customer, so we key it with a valid ID that will work only once: the Customer's id value.

When the process starts, it will start executing the steps in your process definition. First, it will go to the <start> element. It will evaluate the one transition it has and proceed through that transition to the next step, send-verification-email.

Once in the java element named send-verification-email, jBPM will invoke the method sendCustomerVerificationEmail on the customerService bean in Spring. It uses an Expression Language construct to reference the Spring bean by name:

```
<java name="send-verification-email"
      expr="#{customerService}"
      method="sendCustomerVerificationEmail">
    ...
</java>
```

The sendCustomerVerificationEmail method takes the customer's ID and sends a notification. We leave the functionality of actually sending the e-mail to you—just imagine a unique, hashed link being generated and embedded in the body of the e-mail that lets the server trace the request back to a customer.

Once the process has left the send-verification-email java element, it'll proceed to confirm-receipt-of-verification-email state, where it will wait indefinitely before proceeding. This is called a *wait state*. An external event is needed to tell it to proceed. In our scenario, this event will come when the user clicks on the link in the e-mail, which, for the sake of the demonstration, will trigger the invocation of the authorizeCustomer method on our customerService bean. This method expects a customer ID as a parameter.

Inside authorizeCustomer, the service queries the server for the any processes waiting at the confirm-receipt-of-verification-email state and having this customer's ID. We know that there's only one instance of this process, but the query returns a collection of Execution instances. We then iterate through the collection, signaling (with the Execution instance's signalExecutionById method) the transition from a wait state to the next state. When a node in jBPM moves from one to another, it takes a transition. As you've seen before, it does so implicitly. Here, however, in the wait state, we have to explicitly tell it to take a transition to signal that it can proceed to the next node.

```
for (Execution execution : executions) {
    Execution subExecution = execution.findActiveExecutionIn(
        "confirm-receipt-of-verification-email");
    executionService.signalExecutionById(subExecution.getId());
}
```

The authorizeCustomer method also updates the Customer entity, marking it as authorized.

From there, execution proceeds to the send-welcome-email java element. As before, the java element will be used to invoke a method on the customerService bean. This time, it will invoke sendWelcomeEmail to send the newly registered Customer a welcome e-mail.

The name of the process (what we use when we call startProcessInstanceByKey) is in the process element. Here, that name is RegisterCustomer.

Many of the expressions are in the JBoss expression language, which works very similarly to the unified Expression Language (EL) found in JavaServer Faces, or the Spring EL. You can use the EL here to reference parameters to the process.

You'll recall that when we invoked the service method for createCustomer, it, in turn, kicked off a business process whose progression the rest of the code followed. We use a Map<String,Object> to parameterize the business process. In this case, our Map<String,Object> was called vars.

```
Map<String, Object> vars = new HashMap<String, Object>();
vars.put("customerId", customer.getId());
executionService.startProcessInstanceByKey(
 REGISTER_CUSTOMER_PROCESS_KEY,
 vars,
 Long.toString(customer.getId()));
```

From within the running process, you can access the parameters from Java or as an EL expression. To access the parameter using the EL, use something like: #{customerId}. To access the parameter from Java code at runtime, use the following:

```
Number customerId = (Number) executionService.getVariable(subExecution.getId(), ↵
"customerId") ;
```

At this point, you've got a working business process that lives inside of a Spring context, and you've got a working grasp of the constructs required to build a process.

Summary

In this chapter, you were given an introduction to business process management as a technology. You should have a big-picture view of the technology. There's much more to learn, because BPM can become a key piece of architecture, providing a spine to otherwise isolated functionality. No single introduction to one particular brand of BPM will ever be adequate. There are lots of resources out there, though it helps to keep an eye on the bookshelf at your local bookstore, because often these technologies become irrelevant as quickly as the sands of the markets shift.

BPM is a discipline that's rooted in many decades of growth and concepts. The earliest tenants of workflow engines have their bases in a branch of mathematics called *Petri nets*. The discipline's become more mainstream over the years, and the focus evolved from using BPM as a record-keeping mechanism to an enabling orchestration mechanism.

There are several very good discussions of BPM if you're curious, including several good sites on the Internet and many more good books readily had by searching for "BPM" in a search engine. For a deeper treatment of the discipline (though not necessarily the technology), we recommend the following:

- *Production Workflow: Concepts and Techniques* by Frank Leymann and Dieter Roller (Prentice Hall, 2000)

- *Essential Business Process Modeling* by Michael Havey (O'Reilly, 2005)

- http://www.workflowpatterns.com/ (a comprehensive introduction to the patterns of workflow)

In the next chapter, you will learn about OSGi and how to build OSGi solutions using Spring Dynamic Modules and SpringSource dm Server.

CHAPTER 24

OSGi and Spring

OSGi and Spring are, in many ways, a very natural technology combination. They approach different problems from different directions, but they do so in a similar spirit. It's only natural, then, that SpringSource, the company that stewards the Spring framework, should turn its eye to OSGi.

OSGi—which was formerly known as the Open Services Gateway initiative, though the name's obsolete now—has its roots in the embedded space, where dynamic service provisioning is far more important than it is in the gridiron world of enterprise applications. It provides a services registry as well as an application life cycle management framework. Beyond this, OSGi provides such features as granular component visibility via a highly specialized class-loading environment, service versioning and reconciliation, and security. OSGi provides a layer on top of the JVM's default class loader. The deployment unit for OSGi is a bundle, which is essentially a JAR with an augmented `MANIFEST.MF`. This manifest contains declarations that specify, among other things, on what other services the bundle depends, and what service the bundle exports.

OSGi has gained some notoriety because of Eclipse, which uses it for the plug-in model. This is a natural choice, because Eclipse needs to allow plug-ins to load and unload, and to guarantee that certain resources are made available to plug-ins. Indeed, the hope of an enhanced "module" system for Java has loomed large for many years, manifesting in at least a few JSRs: JSR-277, "Java Module System," and JSR-291, "Dynamic Component Support for Java SE." OSGi is a natural fit because it's been around for many years, matured, and has been improved on by many more vendors still. It is already the basis of the architecture of a few application servers.

OSGi is important today, more than ever, in the enterprise space because it represents a solution that can be gracefully layered on top of the Java Virtual Machine (JVM) (if not existing application servers) that can solve problems frequently encountered in today's environments. "`.jar` hell," the collision of two different versions of the same JAR in the same class loader, is something most developers have encountered. Application footprint reduction provides another compelling use of OSGi. Applications today, be they `.war` or `.ear`, are typically bundled with numerous `.jars` that exist solely to service that application's requirements. It may be that other applications on the same application server are using the same jars and services. This implies that there are duplicated instances of the same libraries loaded into memory. This situation's even worse when you consider how large typical deployed `.wars` are today. Most `.wars` are 90% third-party JARs, with a little application-specific code rounding out the mix. Imagine three `.wars` of 50 MBs, or 100 MBs, where only 5 MBs are application-specific code and libraries. This implies that the application server needs to field 300 MBs just to meet the requirements of a 15-30 unique MBs. OSGi provides a way of sharing components, loading them once, and reducing the footprint of the application.

Just as you may be paying an undue price for redundant libraries, so too are you likely paying for unused application server services, such as EJB1.x and 2.x support, or JCA. Here again, OSGi can help by providing a "server à la carte" model, where your application is provisioned by the container only with the services it needs.

OSGi is, on the large, a deployment concern. However, using it effectively requires changes to your code, as well. It affects how you acquire dependencies for your application. Naturally, this is where Spring is strongest and where dependency-injection in general can be a very powerful tool. SpringSource has made several forays into the OSGi market, first with Spring Dynamic Modules, which is an enhanced OSGi framework that provides support for Spring and much more. Then, on top of Spring Dynamic Modules, SpringSource built SpringSource dm Server, which is a server wired from top to bottom with OSGi and Spring. SpringSource dm Server supports dynamic deployment, enhanced tooling, HTTP, and native .war deployment. It also sports superb administrative features.

OSGi is a specification, not a framework. There are many implementations of the specification, just as there are many implementations of the Java EE specification. Additionally, OSGi is not a user component model, like Spring or EJB 3. Instead, it sits below your components, providing life-cycle management for Java classes. It is, conceptually, possible to deploy to an OSGi runtime in the same way that you deploy to a Java EE runtime, completely unaware of how Java consumes your .jar files and manifests and so on. As you'll see in this chapter, however, there's a lot of power to be had in specifically targeting OSGi and exploiting it in your application. In this chapter, we will discuss Spring Dynamic Modules, and to a lesser extent, Spring dm Server.

24-1. Getting Started with OSGi

Problem

You understand OSGi conceptually, but you want to see what a basic, working example with raw OSGi looks like. It's hard to appreciate the sun, after all, if you've never seen the rain.

Solution

In this solution, we'll build a simple service and then use it in a client. Remember, in OSGi, anything used by something else is a service. "Service" doesn't imply any concrete inheritance; it doesn't imply transactional qualities, and it doesn't imply RPC. It's merely a class on whose concrete, black-box functionality and interface your class relies.

How It Works

In this example, we'll use Eclipse's OSGi distribution, Eclipse Equinox. There are many distributions to choose from. Popular ones include Apache's Felix and Eclipse's Equinox. You may use any distribution you want, but for this example, the instructions will be for Felix. The concepts should be the same across implementations, but the specifics may vary wildly in both commands and mechanism.

OSGi and JavaBeans

This is sort of like what a JavaBean was originally intended to be. These days, OSGi is starting to take on the very vivid marketing life that JavaBeans did before it. You'll occasionally note products promoting chief among their upgrades their new, internal use of OSGi, as products did years ago with JavaBeans and object-oriented programming ("Now object-oriented!"). Be mindful of the hype.

The helloworld-service Service

Let's first examine the Java code for the service's interface. It describes a service whose sole function is to take as inputs a target language and a name and to return as output a greeting.

```
package com.apress.springrecipes.osgi.helloworld.service;

public interface GreeterService {
    String greet(String language, String name);
}
```

The implementation's similarly plain. It hard-codes the greetings for three languages and satisfies the interface.

```
package com.apress.springrecipes.osgi.helloworld.service;

import java.util.HashMap;
import java.util.Locale;
import java.util.Map;

public class GreeterServiceImpl implements GreeterService {

    private Map<String, String> salutation;

    public GreeterServiceImpl() {
        salutation  = new HashMap<String, String>();
        salutation.put(Locale.ENGLISH.toString(), "Hello, %s");
        salutation.put(Locale.FRENCH.toString(), "Bonjour, %s");
        salutation.put(Locale.ITALIAN.toString(), "Buongiorno, %s");
    }

    /**
     * @param language Can be any language you want, so long as that language is one of
     *                 <code>Locale.ENGLISH.toString()</code>,
     *                 <code>Locale.ITALIAN.toString()</code>, or
     *                 <code>Locale.FRENCH.toString()</code>.
     *                 :-)
     * @param name     the name of the person you'd like to address
     * @return the greeting, in the language you want, tailored to the name you specified
     */
```

```
    public String greet(String language, String name) {
        if (salutation.containsKey(language))
            return String.format(salutation.get(language), name);
        throw new RuntimeException(String.format("The language you specified "+ ↵
" (%s) doesn't exist", language));
    }
}
```

As you can see, the code is simple and, in point of fact, does nothing to betray the fact that we're going to deploy it on top of OSGi. The next class, called an Activator, is required for every bundle. The Activator registers services and receives a life cycle hook to set the stage for the service. Similarly, it reacts to events and register listeners.

```
package com.apress.springrecipes.osgi.helloworld.service;

import org.osgi.framework.BundleActivator;
import org.osgi.framework.BundleContext;
import java.util.Properties;

public class Activator implements BundleActivator {

    public void start(BundleContext bundleContext) throws Exception {
        System.out.println("Start: ");
        bundleContext.registerService(
        GreeterService.class.getName(),
                new GreeterServiceImpl(),
                new Properties());
    }

    public void stop(BundleContext bundleContext) throws Exception {
        System.out.println("Stop: ");   // NOOP
    }
}
```

The Activator implements BundleActivator, which has a few life cycle callback methods. We avail ourselves of the start method when the JAR is installed to register the service that's contained. We could register many services. The first parameter, a String, is the service name, sort of like a JNDI name or a Spring beanName. The second parameter is the implementation of the service. The third parameter— the java.util.Properties object being passed to the registerService—are key/value pairs, called service attributes. The client can use them together as a predicate to qualify what service should be returned when looking the service up in the registry. Here, we specify nothing.

This is all the Java code for this service, but we do need to expand on the MANIFEST itself a little bit, to specify extra metadata that OSGi uses in deploying the service. How you do this is entirely at your discretion, and it's simple enough that you could get away with doing it by hand. We use a Maven plug-in that handles the minutiae for us, though there are other approaches as well. Remember, OSGi bundles are simply standard .jar files with customized MANIFESTs that OSGi consumes at runtime. The configuration of the Maven plug-in is simple. The plug-in wraps the bnd command line tool. The bnd tool dynamically interrogates classes for their imports and generates OSGi–compliant entries. We repeat it here mainly for illustrative purposes. For fully working code, see the source code for this book. Note that the plug-in produces OSGi–compliant bundles that work in any container. To read more on the plug-in itself, see http://felix.apache.org/site/apache-felix-maven-bundle-plugin-bnd.html.

```
...
<plugin>
                <groupId>org.apache.felix</groupId>
                <artifactId>maven-bundle-plugin</artifactId>
                <extensions>true</extensions>
                <configuration>
                    <instructions>
<Export-Package>com.apress.springrecipes.osgi.helloworld.service</Export-Package>
<Bundle-Activator>com.apress.springrecipes.osgi.helloworld.service.Activator↵
</Bundle-Activator>
                    </instructions>
                </configuration>
</plugin>
...
```

The relevant bits are in bold. It tells the plug-in to add to our MANIFEST certain properties: an Export-Package directive and a Bundle-Activator header. The Export-Package directive tells the OSGi environment that this JAR, a bundle, vends the classes in that package, and that those classes should be made visible to the client. The Bundle-Activator directive describes to the OSGi environment, which class implements BundleActivator, and should be consulted when life cycle events occur.

The preceding plug-in takes care of specifying on which other bundles our bundle depends, using the Import-Package directive. The final, resulting MANIFEST.MF (in target/classes/META-INF) is telling.

```
Manifest-Version: 1.0
Export-Package: com.apress.springrecipes.osgi.
helloworld.service;uses:="org.osgi.framework"
Private-Package: com.apress.springrecipes.osgi.helloworld.service,
Built-By: Owner
Tool: Bnd-0.0.311
Bundle-Name: helloworld-service
Created-By: Apache Maven Bundle Plugin
Bundle-Version: 1.0.0.SNAPSHOT
Build-Jdk: 1.6.0_14-ea
Bnd-LastModified: 1243157994625
Bundle-ManifestVersion: 2
Bundle-Activator: com.apress.springrecipes.osgi.
helloworld.service.Activator
Import-Package: com.apress.springrecipes.osgi.helloworld.service,
org.osgi.framework;version="1.3"
Bundle-SymbolicName: com.apress.springrecipes.osgi.helloworld.service.
helloworld-service
```

This describes the dependencies, exports, and layout of the bundle fully to the OSGi runtime, and makes it easy for clients to know what they're getting when they use this bundle. This rounds out the code for the service. Let's install it into the OSGi environment and then start in using it as a client. The installation procedure is very specific to each tool.

Installing Equinox

Assuming that you've downloaded Equinox from http://www.eclipse.org/equinox/ (this book was written against 3.4.2) and unzipped it, change to the installation directory and, on the command line, type the following:

```
java -jar eclipse/plugins/org.eclipse.osgi_YOUR_VERSION.jar -console
```

Naturally, substitute YOUR_VERSION for the one that applies to the version of the distribution that you downloaded. We're using 3.4, which is the latest stable release. This will start an interactive session. You can type help to see the list of available commands. You can issue the services command to list the bundles already installed. To install the bundle, assuming you've put the JAR produced from previous steps for the service at the root of your file system (C:/, or /) issue:

```
install file://helloworld-service-1.0-SNAPSHOT.jar or install file:/C:↵
/helloworld-service-1.0-SNAPSHOT.jar
```

This installs the JAR in the OSGi registry and produces an ID that can be used to refer to the bundle. Use it as the operand to the start command.

```
start 3
```

This will start the bundle and ready it for use by other bundles.

Using the Service in a Client Bundle

Using the service is almost exactly the same as creating the service, except that we need to specify our dependence on the service in the bundle. Let's first review the client-side Java code. In this case, we simply look up the service and demonstrate it in the Activator for the client bundle. This is simple, and to the point, though not necessarily typical. In the source code for the book, this is a different Maven project, called helloworld-client.

```
package com.apress.springrecipes.osgi.helloworld.client;

import com.apress.springrecipes.osgi.helloworld.service.GreeterService;
import org.osgi.framework.BundleActivator;
import org.osgi.framework.BundleContext;
import org.osgi.framework.ServiceReference;
import java.util.Arrays;
import java.util.Locale;

public class Activator implements BundleActivator {

    public void start(BundleContext bundleContext) throws Exception {
        ServiceReference refs[] = bundleContext.getServiceReferences(
                        GreeterService.class.getName(), null);
        if (null == refs || refs.length == 0) {
            System.out.println("there is no service by this description!");
            return;
        }
```

```
GreeterService greeterService = (GreeterService)
        bundleContext.getService(refs[0]);

    String[] names = {"Gary", "Steve", "Josh", "Mario",
        "Srinivas", "Tom", "James", "Manuel"};

    for (String language : Arrays.asList(
            Locale.ENGLISH.toString(),
            Locale.FRENCH.toString(),
            Locale.ITALIAN.toString())) {
        for (String name : names) {
            System.out.println(greeterService.greet(language, name));
        }
    }
}

public void stop(BundleContext bundleContext) throws Exception {
    // NOOP
}
}
```

The salient code is in bold. Here, we look up a ServiceReference in the OSGi registry. We use the same name as we provided when we registered the class in the registry. The second argument, null, is where we would specify any values to narrow the criteria for the search for a service. Because there's only one that could possibly match in this case, we won't specify anything. Note that there is no guarantee you'll get a reference to the service, or that you'll get only one. Indeed, you may be given any number of ServiceReferences, which is why the return type is scalar. This is a very different paradigm than more traditional component models such as EJB, which treat the inability to return a handle to a service as an error. This is also somewhat counterintuitive from how traditional service registries (such as JNDI) work. When we're sure we have a handle to a service, we redeem it for an interface to the actual service itself, somewhat like an EJBHome, using the bundleContext.getService(ServiceReference) method. You can see, already, where Spring might be able to lend a hand—in this resource lookup and acquisition logic.

Let's examine the final MANIFEST for the client. It's not much different from what we've done before. It differs mainly in that it lists our service as a dependency. Apart from that, it's pretty boilerplate. The Activator is the only thing that's changed from the previous example. If you're following with Maven, don't forget to specify the changed Activator class in the plug-in. Additionally, we're using the interface from the service JAR we produced in the last example. The Maven plug-in automatically adds this to your Import-Package MANIFEST header.

```
Manifest-Version: 1.0
Export-Package: com.apress.springrecipes.osgi.helloworld.client;
uses:="com.apress.springrecipes.osgi.helloworld.service,org.osgi.framework"
Private-Package: com.apress.springrecipes.osgi.helloworld.client,
Built-By: Owner
Tool: Bnd-0.0.311
Bundle-Name: helloworld-client
Created-By: Apache Maven Bundle Plugin
Bundle-Version: 1.0.0.SNAPSHOT
Build-Jdk: 1.6.0_14-ea
Bnd-LastModified: 1243159626828
```

```
Bundle-ManifestVersion: 2
Bundle-Activator: com.apress.springrecipes.osgi.
helloworld.client.Activator
```
Import-Package: com.apress.springrecipes.osgi.
helloworld.client,com.apress.springrecipes.osgi.
helloworld.service,org.osgi.framework;version="1.3"
```
Bundle-SymbolicName: com.apress.springrecipes.osgi.helloworld.client.helloworld-client
```

Nothing too exceptional here, except the aforementioned Import-Package. Install the bundle as we did for the service. When the bundle begins to load and start, it calls the start method of the Activator. You should see greetings being enumerated on the console. You've successfully completed your first OSGi deployment.

```
install file://helloworld-client-1.0-SNAPSHOT.jar.
start 2
```

You should see the output, as expected, greeting each name.

```
osgi> install file://helloworld-client-1.0-SNAPSHOT.jar.

Bundle id is 2

osgi> start 2
Hello, Gary
Hello, Steve
Hello, Josh
Hello, Mario
Hello, Srinivas
Hello, Tom
Hello, James
Hello, Manuel
Bonjour, Gary
Bonjour, Steve
Bonjour, Josh
Bonjour, Mario
Bonjour, Srinivas
Bonjour, Tom
Bonjour, James
Bonjour, Manuel
Buongiorno, Gary
Buongiorno, Steve
Buongiorno, Josh
Buongiorno, Mario
Buongiorno, Srinivas
Buongiorno, Tom
Buongiorno, James
Buongiorno, Manuel
osgi>
```

24-2. Getting Started Using Spring Dynamic Modules

Problem

You've got a feeling for how OSGi works, what it's capable of, and even how to go about creating a simple "hello, world!" example. Now, you want to start using Spring to smooth over some of the minutiae of resource acquisition and to help build more reliable systems in an OSGi environment.

Solution

Use Spring Dynamic Modules to provide the integration. Spring Dynamic Modules is a framework on top of OSGi that works with any OSGi environment. It provides tight integration for Spring dependency injection in the world of OSGi, which includes support for things like application context discovery, interface-based service injection, and versioning.

How It Works

Spring Dynamic Modules is a very powerful API for integration with the OSGi environment. You need the Spring framework itself, and the Spring OSGi JARs, as well. If you're following along using Maven, the JARs can be added by using SpringSource's OSGi bundle repository. This repository exports the Spring framework JARs, as well as those of countless other open source projects, in an OSGi–friendly format under a Maven/Ivy–friendly repository. For more information on the repositories, see `http://www.springsource.com/repository/app/faq`. To get access to them from Maven, add the repositories to your `pom.xml` configuration file, at the bottom, before the closing `</project>` element:

```
<repository>
          <id>com.springsource.repository.bundles.release</id>
          <name>SpringSource Enterprise Bundle Repository - SpringSource Bundle ↩
Releases</name>
          <url>http://repository.springsource.com/maven/bundles/release</url>
     </repository>
     <repository>
          <id>com.springsource.repository.bundles.external</id>
          <name>SpringSource Enterprise Bundle Repository - External Bundle ↩
Releases</name>
          <url>http://repository.springsource.com/maven/bundles/external</url>
</repository>
```

The SpringSource Enterprise Bundle Repository provides numerous OSGi–friendly jars files. To see if yours is already supported, search for it at `http://www.springsource.com/repository`.

We'll use this infrastructure to rebuild our previous "hello, world!" example, this time relying on Spring to provide the injection of the service itself and to make writing the client more in line with what we've come to expect from Spring development. We've already deployed the service, so we don't need to rework any of that. Let's instead concentrate on a new client bundle.

Let's explore our revised client code. The entirety of the client is one Java class and two Spring XML application context files. One file has the OSGi–friendly Spring Dynamic Modules namespace imported; the other is a standard Spring application context.

When we're finished and deploy the final bundle to Equinox, the XML context files loaded in the META-INF directory will be loaded. It is through the magic of OSGi extender models that this works. OSGi enables deployed bundles to scan other deployed bundles and react to qualities of those bundles. In particular, this is sort of like what Spring does when it scans a package for classes with annotations. Here, Spring Dynamic Modules scans our deployed bundles and loads an ApplicationContext (actually, the specific type of the ApplicationContext is OsgiBundleXmlApplicationContext) into memory based on an event, or a trigger. There are two ways to trigger this behavior. The first is to explicitly specify in the META-INF/MANIFEST.MF file the attribute Spring-Context, which allows you to override the default location it consults. Otherwise, by default, Spring Dynamic Modules will look for the XML file in the META-INF/spring directory of a bundle. Typically, you'll split your OSGi–specific Spring configuration and your plain-vanilla Spring configuration into two different files, of the form: *modulename*-context.xml and *modulename*-osgi-context.xml.

The Java code is like that of any other standard Spring bean. In fact, for all intents and purposes, this code has no knowledge of OSGi. It *does* have knowledge of Spring itself, though there's no reason it needs to. The @Autowired field-injection and InitializingBean interface are just for convenience and brevity's sake.

```
package com.apress.springrecipes.osgi.springdmhelloworld.impl;

import com.apress.springrecipes.osgi.helloworld.service.GreeterService;
import org.springframework.beans.factory.InitializingBean;
import org.springframework.beans.factory.annotation.Autowired;

import java.util.Arrays;
import java.util.Locale;

public class SpringDMGreeterClient implements InitializingBean {

    @Autowired
    private GreeterService greeterService;

    public void afterPropertiesSet() throws Exception {
      for (String name : Arrays.asList("Mario", "Fumiko", "Makani"))
        System.out.println(greeterService.greet(Locale.FRENCH.toString(), name));
    }
}
```

Let's explore the Spring XML files. The first one, src/main/resources/META-INF/spring/bundle-context.xml, a standard Spring XML application context, should not be very surprising. It contains just one bean definition.

```xml
<?xml version="1.0" encoding="UTF-8"?>
<beans xmlns="http://www.springframework.org/schema/beans"
       xmlns:xsi="http://www.w3.org/2001/XMLSchema-instance"
       xmlns:context="http://www.springframework.org/schema/context"
       xsi:schemaLocation="http://www.springframework.org/schema/beans ↵
http://www.springframework.org/schema/beans/spring-beans.xsd
                           http://www.springframework.org/schema/context ↵
http://www.springframework.org/schema/context/spring-context.xsd">

    <context:annotation-config/>

    <bean name="springDMGreeterClient"
     class="com.apress.springrecipes.osgi.springdmhelloworld.impl.SpringDMGreeterClient"/>

</beans>
```

Exploring the Spring Dynamic Modules application context (src/main/resources/META-INF/spring/bundle-context-osgi.xml), we see little that's different or unusual, except an osgi namespace.

```xml
<?xml version="1.0" encoding="UTF-8"?>
<beans xmlns="http://www.springframework.org/schema/beans"
  xmlns:xsi="http://www.w3.org/2001/XMLSchema-instance"
  xmlns:osgi="http://www.springframework.org/schema/osgi"
  xsi:schemaLocation="http://www.springframework.org/schema/beans ↵
http://www.springframework.org/schema/beans/spring-beans-2.5.xsd
                    http://www.springframework.org/schema/osgi ↵
http://www.springframework.org/schema/osgi/spring-osgi.xsd">

  <osgi:reference id="greeterService"
interface="com.apress.springrecipes.osgi.helloworld.service.GreeterService"/>

</beans>
```

Here, we've imported a new namespace, osgi, which enables us to use the osgi:reference element. The osgi:reference element proxies an OSGi service. The proxy manages awareness of whether the service has been removed or not. This might happen, for example, if you unload the service to replace it. If the service is removed and you make a call against the proxy, it will block, waiting for the service to be reinstalled. This is called *damping*. Furthermore, the proxy itself can be referenced for standard dependency injection into other beans. Remember: when we registered the service with OSGi in the Activator for the greeter service, we passed in an interface as well as the implementation to the bundleContext.registerService invocation. This interface is what we're using to look up the service here.

Already, we've reaped the benefits of OSGi and Spring Dynamic Modules. This application is infinitely more robust because, as a client to a service, it's immune to outages in the service itself and because any number of other clients can now also use the service in the same way, without loading duplicate versions of the jar.

In order for this example to run, we need to deploy all the dependencies of the client into Equinox so that they can be managed. In this case, that implies that we have to install all the bundles for Spring and all the dependencies that Spring itself has. To simplify this process, we'll have Equinox automatically load the JARs at startup. The simplest way to do this is to modify Equinox's config.ini file. The file will be located under the configuration directory, under the eclipse/plugins folder. The folder won't be present if you haven't run the console as explained in previous exercises. The configuration folder is where Equinox keeps state between sessions. Create the file with a text editor. We're going to reference the JARs that are required by this project. To obtain those JARs using the Maven project, you can issue mvn dependency:copy-dependencies, which will place the jars in the target/lib folder of the current project, where you can grab them. I would put them in a folder under the OSGi Equinox directory so that you may reference them quickly, using relative paths. You can visit the source code for this book to see the exact Maven configuration I've used. Now that you've got the JARs, modify the config.ini file and list the JARs. My config.ini looks like this:

```
osgi.bundles=spring/com.springsource.org.aopalliance-1.0.0.jar@start, ↵
spring/com.springsource.org.apache.commons.logging-1.1.1.jar@start,
spring/helloworld-service-1.0-SNAPSHOT.jar@start,
spring/org.osgi.core-1.0.0.jar@start,
spring/org.osgi.core-4.0.jar@start,
spring/org.springframework.aop-2.5.6.A.jar@start,
spring/org.springframework.beans-2.5.6.A.jar@start,
spring/org.springframework.context-2.5.6.A.jar@start,
spring/org.springframework.core-2.5.6.A.jar@start,
spring/org.springframework.osgi.core-1.1.3.RELEASE.jar@start,
spring/org.springframework.osgi.extender-1.1.3.RELEASE.jar@start, ↵
spring/org.springframework.osgi.io-1.1.3.RELEASE.jar@start
eclipse.ignoreApp=true
```

These declarations tell Equinox to load and start the JARs at launch time. We put the JARs in a folder called spring, which itself is located under the eclipse/plugins folder.

We have one last thing to do to see it all working. We need to install and start the client. There is no change in this process from before. We repeat it here for clarity. Run the Equinox console:

```
java -jar eclipse/plugins/org.eclipse.osgi_YOUR_VERSION.jar -console
```

Then, install and start the client:

```
install file:/path/to/your/client/jar.jar
start 12
```

If everything goes to plan, you should see the application contexts recognized by Spring, and you should, toward the end of the output, see the output from the invocation of the service.

```
…terService,org.springframework.context.annotation.internalAutowiredAnnotationPro…
equiredAnnotationProcessor,springDMGreeterClient]; root of factory hierarchy
Bonjour, Mario
Bonjour, Fumiko
Bonjour, Makani
May 25, 2009 11:26:04 PM org.springframework.osgi.context.support.AbstractOsgiBu…
INFO: Publishing application context as OSGi service with properties {org.spring…
iserecipes.springdmhelloworld, Bundle-SymbolicName=com.apress.springenterprisere…
```

24-3. Exporting a Service Using Spring Dynamic Modules

Problem

You want to create services and have those automatically installed in the registry, as we did in the first recipe, available for other services to depend on. This process is different because we will no longer register the services in Java code, and instead will let Spring export the service on our behalf.

Solution

You can use Spring Dynamic Modules configuration schema to export a service. The service will be made available to other beans as well as other OSGi components.

How It Works

The approach is similar to that of the other configurations. We will create a bundle and deploy it. Create a Spring XML configuration (src/main/resources/META-INF/spring/bundle-context.xml) for our regular Spring beans, just as we did in the previous recipe.

```
<?xml version="1.0" encoding="UTF-8"?>
<beans xmlns="http://www.springframework.org/schema/beans"
       xmlns:xsi="http://www.w3.org/2001/XMLSchema-instance"
       xmlns:osgi="http://www.springframework.org/schema/osgi"
       xsi:schemaLocation=" http://www.springframework.org/schema/beans
                           http://www.springframework.org/schema/beans/spring-beans-3.0.xsd
                           http://www.springframework.org/schema/osgi
                           http://www.springframework.org/schema/osgi/spring-osgi.xsd">

    <osgi:reference id="greeterService"
        interface="com.apress.springrecipes.osgi.helloworld.service.GreeterService"/>

</beans>
```

Here, we declare a bean named greeterService that we will reference.

In a separate file (src/main/resources/META-INF/spring/bundle-osgi-context.xml), we will export the service using the Spring Dynamic Modules configuration schema. Here, we'll use the osgi:service element to export the bean as an OSGi service, classified by the interface we specify. Note that we could, technically, have specified a concrete class for the value of interface, though it's not recommended. In our example, we want our service to advertise that it supports multiple interfaces, so we'll specify both of them.

```
<?xml version="1.0" encoding="UTF-8"?>
<beans xmlns="http://www.springframework.org/schema/beans"
      xmlns:xsi="http://www.w3.org/2001/XMLSchema-instance"
        xmlns:osgi="http://www.springframework.org/schema/osgi"
      xmlns:util="http://www.springframework.org/schema/util"
      xmlns:context="http://www.springframework.org/schema/context"
      xsi:schemaLocation="http://www.springframework.org/schema/beans ↵
http://www.springframework.org/schema/beans/spring-beans.xsd
http://www.springframework.org/schema/util
http://www.springframework.org/schema/beans/spring-util.xsd
http://www.springframework.org/schema/context
http://www.springframework.org/schema/context/spring-context.xsd
http://www.springframework.org/schema/osgi
http://www.springframework.org/schema/osgi/spring-osgi.xsd">

    <context:annotation-config/>

    <osgi:service auto-export="all-classes" ref="greeterService">
     <osgi:interfaces>
     <value>com.apress.springrecipes.osgi.helloworld.service.GreeterService</value>
     <value>com.apress.springrecipes.osgi.helloworld.service.GreetingRecorderService</value>
     </osgi:interfaces>
    </osgi:service>

</beans>
```

You can abbreviate the syntax by using an anonymous bean. An anonymous bean specified inside of the osgi:service element allows you to avoid cluttering the namespace. The previous salient pieces, slightly changed to use an anonymous bean, look like this:

```
<osgi:service   interface="com.apress.springrecipes.
osgi.helloworld.service.GreeterService">
    <bean class="com.apress.springrecipes.osgi.helloworld.
service.GreeterServiceImpl"/>
</osgi:service>
```

Remember, as these beans are proxies, some may load asynchronously or take a longer time to register. This implies that you may have timing issues to resolve in configuring your service. For this, Spring Dynamic Modules provides the depends-on attribute, which lets your bean *wait* for another bean. Suppose our greeterService depended on a dictionaryService, which itself took a long time to load:

```
<osgi:service  depends-on="dictionaryService"
interface="com.apress.springrecipes.osgi.helloworld.service.GreeterService">
    <bean class="com.apress.springrecipes.osgi.helloworld.service.GreeterServiceImpl"/>
</osgi:service>
```

Interfacing with the OSGi Runtime

You can interact with the OSGi infrastructure in some interesting, more metaprogramming-oriented ways. Spring surfaces a lot of this functionality if you want to use it. The first, most direct connection to OSGi is the bean that's created on your behalf when you export a service. This bean, an instance of org.osgi.framework.ServiceRegistration, is in turn a delegate to the Spring bean you have defined. You can inject this instance if you want and manipulate it, just as with any other Spring bean. Define an ID on the osgi:service element to be able to reference it.

By default, beans created in a Spring application context are global to the entire OSGi runtime, including all clients that use it. Sometimes, you may want to limit the visibility of a service so that multiple clients each get their own instance of the bean. Spring Dynamic Modules provides a clever use of the scope attribute here, allowing you to limit beans exported as services to the client, or service importer.

```
    <bean scope ="bundle"  id="greeterService"
class="com.apress.springrecipes.osgi.helloworld.service.GreeterServiceImpl"/>

    <osgi:service
interface="com.apress.springrecipes.osgi.helloworld.service.GreeterService"
ref="greeterService"      />
```

The OSGi runtime surfaces events based on the life cycle of services. You can register a listener to react to the life cycle of a service. There are two ways to do this, one using anonymous inner beans and one using a named reference.

```
<osgi:service  id="greeterServiceReference"
interface="com.apress.springrecipes.osgi.helloworld.
service.GreeterService">
    <registration-listener registration-method="greeterServiceRegistered"
                                unregistration-method="greeterServiceUnRegistered">
  <bean class="com.apress.springrecipes.osgi.helloworld.service.↵
            GreeterServiceLifeCycleListener"/>
    </registration-listener>
</osgi:service>
```

Spring Dynamic Modules is relatively flexible with respect to the prototype of the method:

```
public void serviceRegistered( ServiceInstance serviceInstance, Map serviceProperties)
public void serviceUnregistered(ServiceInstance serviceInstance, Dictionary
serviceProperties)
```

Naturally, there's a similar feature for client-side proxies. The feature is a listener on the osgi:reference element. Here, we use an inner bean inside the osgi:listener element, though you can also use the ref attribute on the osgi:listener element and avoid the inner bean if you wish.

```
<osgi:reference id="greeterService"
interface="com.apress.springrecipes.osgi.
helloworld.service.GreeterService">
    <osgi:listener bind-method="greeterServiceOnBind"
            unbind-method="greeterServiceOnUnbind" >
        <bean class = "com.apress.springrecipes.osgi.↵
                      helloworld.client.GreeterClientBindListener"/>
    </osgi:listener>
</osgi:reference>
```

Spring Dynamic Modules also supports injection and manipulation of bundles themselves. An injected bundle is of type org.osgi.framework.Bundle instances. The simplest use case is that you want to obtain an instance of the org.osgi.framework.Bundle class from an already loaded bundle in the system. You specify the symbolic name to help Spring look it up. The Symbolic-Name is a MANIFEST.MF attribute that every bundle should specify. Once acquired, the Bundle can be interrogated to introspect information about the bundle itself, including any entries, its current state (which can be any of: UNINSTALLED, INSTALLED, RESOLVED, STARTING, STOPPING, or ACTIVE), and any headers specified on the bundle. The Bundle class also exposes methods to dynamically control the life cycle of the bundle, in much the same way as you might from the Equinox shell. This includes things like stopping a bundle, starting it, uninstalling it, and updating it (that is, replacing it with a new version at runtime, for example.)

```
<osgi:bundle id ="greeterServiceBundle"
            symbolic-name="symbolic-name-from-greeter-service" />
```

You can inject into a variable of type org.osgi.framework.Bundle, just as you would any other bean. More powerful, however, is the prospect of dynamically loading and starting bundles using Spring. This sidesteps the shell we used earlier to install a service. Now, that configuration is built into your application and it will be enforced on your application context's startup. To do this, you need to specify the location of the .jar to be installed and optionally an action to take, such as start, when the bundle is installed into the system.

```
<osgi:bundle
        id ="greeterServiceBundle"
            location= "file:/home/user/jars/greeter-service.jar"
            symbolic-name="symbolic-name-from-greeter-service"
            action="start"
/>
```

You can specify what action the bundle should take on the event that the OSGi runtime is shut down using the destroy-action attribute.

24-4. Finding a Specific Service in the OSGi Registry

Problem

OSGi will let you maintain multiple versions of a service in your registry at the same time. While it is possible to ask the registry to simply return all instances of the services that match (i.e., by interface), it can be useful to qualify them when searching.

Solution

OSGi, and Spring Dynamic Modules on top of it, provides many tools for discriminating services both in publishing and consuming services.

How It Works

Multiple services of the same interface may be registered inside of an OSGi environment, which necessitates a conflict-resolution process. To aid in that, Spring Dynamic Modules provides a few features to help.

Ranking

The first feature is ranking. *Ranking*, when specified on a service element, allows the ascription of a rank relative to other beans with the same interface. Ranking is specified on the service element itself. When encountered, the OSGi runtime will return the service with the highest-ranking integer value. If a version of a service is published with a higher integer, any references will rebind to that.

```
<osgi:service
ranking="1"
interface="com.apress.springrecipes.osgi.helloworld.service.GreeterService">
    <bean class="com.apress.springrecipes.osgi.helloworld.service.GreeterServiceImpl" />
</osgi:service>
...
<osgi:service
ranking="2"
interface="com.apress.springrecipes.osgi.
helloworld.service.GreeterService">
    <bean class="com.apress.springrecipes.osgi.helloworld.service.GreeterServiceImpl"/>
</osgi:service>
```

If you want to bind to a specific service of a particular ranking, you can use a `filter` on your `osgi:reference` element.

```
<osgi:reference id="greeterServiceReference"
   interface="com.apress.springrecipes.osgi.helloworld.service.GreeterService"
  filter="( service.ranking = 1 )"
  />
```

Service Attributes

A more robust solution to service discrimination is service attributes. A service attribute is an arbitrary key and value pair that the service exports, and on which lookups for a service with multiple matches can be predicated. The service properties are specified as a `Map` element. You may have as many keys as you want.

```
<osgi:service  ref="greeterService"  interface="com.apress.springrecipes.
osgi.helloworld.service.GreeterService">
  <osgi:service-properties>
    <entry key="region" value = "europe"/>
  </osgi:service-properties>
  </osgi:service>
```

If you wanted to look this service up, you would use a `filter` attribute for the client. Here's how you might specify the `osgi:reference` element to find this service as a client.

```
<osgi:reference id="greeterService" interface="com.apress.springrecipes.
osgi.helloworld.service.GreeterService"
filter="(region=europe)"
  />
```

There are also many standard attributes that the runtime configures for all services. For a good list, consult `http://www.osgi.org/javadoc/r2/org/osgi/framework/Constants.html`. You may also use the bean name of the original service as a predicate for finding a service. This will be very familiar.

```
<osgi:reference id="greeterServiceReference"
interface="com.apress.springrecipes.osgi.helloworld.service.GreeterService"
bean-name="greeterService"
  />
```

Cardinality

There are frequently situations where OSGi will return more than one instance of a service that satisfies the interface, especially if you aren't able to specify which one you're looking for using the methods discussed before. Take, for example, a deployment where you have multiple GreeterServices deployed for various regions. Spring Dynamic Modules provides the set and list interfaces to retrieve multiple references and populate a java.util.Set and java.util.List, respectively.

```
<list id="greeterServices"
    interface ="com.apress.springrecipes.osgi.helloworld.service.GreeterService"
    cardinality="1..N" />
```

Note the cardinality element, which stipulates how many instances are expected. 0..N stipulates that any number of references are expected. 1..N stipulates that at least one instance is expected. On a single reference element, only two values for cardinality are acceptable: 0..1, and 1..1. This has the effect of saying that fulfillment of the dependency for a reference is not mandatory (0..1) or that it's mandatory (1..1).

You may fine-tune the collections returned to you. For example, you might specify a comparator element or attribute to sort the collection returned. The bean you reference should implement java.util.Comparator. Unless this logic is extraordinarily involved, it might be an ideal place for using Spring's scripting support to inline the java.util.Comparator implementation in the Spring application-context XML file.

```
<list id="greeterServices"
    interface ="com.apress.springrecipes.osgi.helloworld.service.GreeterService"
    cardinality="1..N"  comparator-ref="comparatorReference" />
```

24-5. Publishing a Service Under Multiple Interfaces

Problem

Your bean implements many interfaces, and you want those interfaces to be visible to clients of the service.

Solution

Spring Dynamic Modules supports registering beans under multiple interfaces. It also provides extra flexibility in auto-detecting the interfaces.

How It Works

Spring Dynamic Modules creates a proxy for you based on the interface you specify. A side effect is that the other interfaces your bean implements won't be visible. To be able to access a bean by other interfaces, you may enumerate the other interfaces in the bean's registration, which will make it available under all of those interfaces. Note that it's illegal to specify both the interface attribute *and* the interfaces attribute: use one or the other.

```xml
<?xml version="1.0" encoding="UTF-8"?>
<beans xmlns="http://www.springframework.org/schema/beans"
       xmlns:xsi="http://www.w3.org/2001/XMLSchema-instance"
       xmlns:osgi="http://www.springframework.org/schema/osgi"
       xmlns:context="http://www.springframework.org/schema/context"
       xsi:schemaLocation="http://www.springframework.org/schema/beans ↵
http://www.springframework.org/schema/beans/spring-beans-3.0.xsd ↵
ttp://www.springframework.org/schema/context
http://www.springframework.org/schema/context/spring-context-3.0.xsd ↵
ttp://www.springframework.org/schema/osgi
http://www.springframework.org/schema/osgi/spring-osgi.xsd">

    <context:annotation-config/>

    <bean id="greeterService" class="com.apress.springrecipes.osgi.helloworld.↵
service.GreeterServiceImpl"/>

    <osgi:service ref="greeterService">
        <osgi:interfaces>
<value>com.apress.springrecipes.osgi.helloworld.service.GreeterService</value>
<value>com.apress.springrecipes.osgi.helloworld.service.GreetingRecorderService</value>
        </osgi:interfaces>
    </osgi:service>
</beans>
```

This is powerful in its own right, but Spring Dynamic Modules can help even more. The service element supports an auto-export attribute, which starts auto-detection of interfaces on the bean and publishes them under the detected interfaces. There are four options: disabled, interfaces, class-hierarchy, and all-classes.

The first option, disabled, is the default behavior. It works with whatever interfaces you've explicitly configured on the bean using the interfaces element or the interface attribute. The second, interfaces, registers the service using the interfaces implemented by a bean but not its superclasses or the implementation class. If you want to include all superclasses as well as the current implementation class, use class-hierarchy. If you want everything: superclasses, implementation class, as well as all interfaces on the implementation class, choose all-classes.

Having said this, you should probably stick to explicitly specifying the interfaces of your bean. The auto-detection may overexpose your bean, revealing crucial private implementation knowledge. More to the point, sometimes it may not expose enough. Perhaps you forgot that the functionality that you're trying to export is specified on an interface on a superclass? Don't risk either, and instead prefer explicit configuration.

24-6. Customizing Spring Dynamic Modules

Problem

Spring Dynamic Modules is a powerful tool, and it provides reasonable defaults (and results) for very little investment. The main work of Spring Dynamic Modules is done through extenders, which sometimes require customization.

Solution

Spring Dynamic Modules provides strong support for fragments, part of the OSGi specification, to override key infrastructure beans Spring uses in service of the extenders.

How It Works

Extenders provide a way to let a bundle control the loading process of another bundle. This magic is most clearly exemplified in Spring Dynamic Modules's ability to auto-load Spring XML application contexts detected in the META-INF/spring/ folder, or those configured by the Spring-Context MANIFEST.MF attribute. Spring provides two extenders: one for web-based bundles (spring-osgi-web-extender, whose trigger is being deployed in a bundle ending in .WAR) and one for normal bundles (spring-osgi-extender).

Customizing these extenders is key to customizing Spring Dynamic Modules's behavior at runtime. Fragments permit the injection of resources, classes, and functionality into a bundle on the same ClassLoader as the host bundle. Fragments do not, however, let you remove functionality or override MANIFEST.MF values that are already established. Additionally, a fragment cannot contain its own Activator. The OSGi runtime knows a bundle is a fragment if it encounters a Fragment-Host header in the MANIFEST.MF file. The Fragment-Host attribute, in turn, is the symbolic name of another bundle. In this case, because we are interested in configuring the two bundles with the extenders, we will reference one of org.springframework.bundle.osgi.extender or org.springframework.bundle.osgi.web.extender.

Spring will check bundles that are configured this way and look for Spring XML application contexts inside the META-INF/spring/extender folder. These Spring XML application contexts are loaded and any beans with the same names as well known beans used by Spring will be given priority and used instead. Let's go through some examples of where this might be useful.

Making Spring Process OSGi Annotations on Beans

Spring provides the ability to inject OSGi services using annotations. This functionality is available as an extension and requires a little configuration to enable it. The annotation serves the same function as the reference element discussed earlier.

```
@ServiceReference
public void  setGreeterService(GreeterService greeterService) {
 // …
}
```

To see this work, you need to enable it using a fragment. Let's first take a look at the Spring XML configuration. Here, we declare a properties bean that, in turn, contains our property key, `process.annotations`.

```
<?xml version="1.0" encoding="UTF-8"?>
<beans xmlns="http://www.springframework.org/schema/beans"
       xmlns:xsi="http://www.w3.org/2001/XMLSchema-instance"
        xmlns:context="http://www.springframework.org/schema/context"
       xsi:schemaLocation="http://www.springframework.org/schema/beans ↵
http://www.springframework.org/schema/beans/spring-beans-3.0.xsd ↵
http://www.springframework.org/schema/context ↵
http://www.springframework.org/schema/context/spring-context-3.0.xsd">

 <bean name="extenderProperties" class="org.springframework.beans.factory.↵
config.PropertiesFactoryBean">
        <property name="properties">
            <props>
                <prop key="process.annotations">true</prop>
            </props>
        </property>
    </bean>
 </beans>
```

Changing the Default HTTP Server That Spring Uses When Deploying a .war

Spring Dynamic Modules provides the ability to install OSGi bundles as web applications. It uses an instance of `org.springframework.osgi.web.deployer.WarDeployer` to perform this feat. Currently, the default is `org.springframework.osgi.web.deployer.tomcat.TomcatWarDeployer`. You can change this to use Jetty:

```
<?xml version="1.0" encoding="UTF-8"?>
<beans xmlns="http://www.springframework.org/schema/beans"
       xmlns:xsi="http://www.w3.org/2001/XMLSchema-instance"
        xmlns:context="http://www.springframework.org/schema/context"
       xsi:schemaLocation="http://www.springframework.org/schema/beans ↵
http://www.springframework.org/schema/beans/spring-beans-3.0.xsd ↵
```

```
http://www.springframework.org/schema/context ↵
http://www.springframework.org/schema/context/spring-context-3.0.xsd">

<bean name="warDeployer"
class="org.springframework.osgi.web.deployer.jetty.JettyWarDeployer"/>

</beans>
```

24-7. Using SpringSource dm Server

Problem

You're convinced of the potential of OSGi, but you feel that perhaps, even with Spring Dynamic Modules, the investment might be hard to justify without some serious upgrades to the tooling and a general smoothing out of the road. Such upgrades would enhance monitoring, provide better, more thoroughly baked support for deployment of traditional `.war` artifacts, enable use of some of the standard Java EE libraries, provide useful defaults for many *de facto* standard libraries, and provide fully integrated support for Spring Dynamic Modules.

Solution

Use Spring dm Server, SpringSource's tried and true OSGi–oriented server built on many technologies including Equinox and the Spring framework itself.

How It Works

OSGi is a framework, on top of which more sophisticated solutions are built. OSGi doesn't solve framework concerns, instead focusing on infrastructure requirements for Java applications. OSGi is a specification that is well-represented in implementations. Spring Dynamic Modules provides functionality that sits on top of those implementations, providing very powerful runtime sophistication for developers looking to produce and consume OSGi services in a Spring-friendly fashion.

Realizing that Spring Dynamic Modules was, while powerful for those already invested in an OSGi platform, not the most natural accommodations for those trying to migrate large code into the OSGi environment, SpringSource created SpringSource dm Server. SpringSource dm Server is a robust solution. There are several editions available. The community edition is licensed under the GPL 3.0. You may download the source code and build it yourself. SpringSource dm Server provides tooling via Eclipse to help design solutions designed for dm Server.

SpringSource dm Server's many advances focus on delivering a solution, and not just a framework, for delivering OSGi–based enterprise applications. The lack of support for core enterprise features stems from OSGi's suitability for any of a number of target environments, including embedded devices. While you are able to use OSGi–friendly HTTP servlet containers to deploy web applications, it's been up to you to build that solution. Imagine piecing together a proper Java EE server, component by component! Thus, SpringSource dm Server provides value above and beyond a regular OSGi solution because it's already well integrated.

SpringSource dm Server provides a number of features geared toward minimizing the hassle of deploying large applications in an OSGi environment. It reduces the number of redundant JARs on a server through the use of a shared library repository, where JARs shared among many other artifacts may be stored. Significantly, this reduces the need to redeploy bundles, because they are automatically loaded from this repository. Large enterprise packages tend to be composed of a tapestry of dependencies, each of which depends on any permutation of other dependencies. OSGi–enabling all of these interwoven dependencies via the granular use of the `Import-Package` header would be tedious. Spring dm Server provides the ability to wholesale import an entire library and all packages therein to expedite the process. Additionally, SpringSource dm Server can effect an even more flexible isolation of services in an OSGi environment, preventing collisions caused by deployment of the same service with the same name without a need to use a service attribute or other discriminator.

SpringSource dm Server also allows you to bend the rules where necessary. For example, consider the application of an aspect using Spring's AOP. This might require weaving of classes, which in the case of a pointcut that matches classes deployed across multiple bundles, would prove cumbersome. SpringSource dm Server can intervene on Spring's behalf, propagating such changes across multiple bundles where necessary.

SpringSource dm Server works with four types of deployment formats. The first is a *bundle*, which we've discussed, and that works as you'd expect. The second is a *native Java EE* `.war` file. This is revolutionary because it provides support for out-of-the-box deployment of legacy `.war`–based applications. However, this format should be viewed as an intermediary step, as it loses out on many of the advantages of OSGi. Hybrid approaches are supported; a *shared-library* `.war` lets you deploy a `.war` whose dependencies are satisfied by the shared library. The server supports an enhanced format called a web module, which is an enhanced shared-library `.war`. The format removes the need for XML configuration to describe your web application to the container, relying entirely on the OSGi manifest. It, like a shared-library `.WAR`, can use Spring to inject OSGi services. The final format is called a *platform archive*. A platform archive is the ultimate form of an application. It provides the ability to group bundles together and provides application isolation. Application isolation is critical because it allows you to solve the issue of reconciliation of two services whose interfaces collide. You can use a `.PAR` to isolate services within the deployment unit.

SpringSource dm Server provides the robustness needed to commoditize enterprise application development in an OSGi environment, and definitely deserves a look. For a *really* good reference, specifically on SpringSource dm Server, I (Josh Long) would humbly recommend you investigate my co-author's in-depth treatment of the subject, *Pro SpringSource dm Server*, by Gary Mak and Daniel Rubio (Apress, 2009).

24-8. SpringSource's Tooling

Problem

You want to begin with SpringSource dm Server but need a way to rapidly turnaround development.

Solution

Use the SpringSource dm Server tooling available as part of SpringSource Tool Suite (STS).

How it Works

One of the best parts about dealing with OSGi, and in particular SpringSource's implementation, is that the tooling is prolific and refined. SpringSource has provided solid tooling for Eclipse, called dm Server Tools, which facilitate executing applications directly in a development environment. These tools—part of the broader SpringSource Tool Suite—are available as either a plug-in or as a stand-alone environment.

The path of least resistance, especially if you're just starting or if you plan on doing a lot of Spring development, is to download the stand-alone installation and use it, as it contains built-in support for Spring applications. We prefer the first approach, as interfacing with OSGi rarely requires more than a few minutes and rarely distracts from primary Java application development. We'll explore both approaches in this recipe.

We'll walk through installing the SpringSource Tool Suite plug-ins into an existing installation and not the individual dm Server Tools or Spring IDE. Both of these products are folded into SpringSource Tool Suite, and SpringSource Tool Suite was just recently made available for free.

Assuming you have a compatible build of Eclipse (the Eclipse Java EE developer's package is a solid start on top of which to install the tooling because it contains WTP and a lot of other useful tooling). The simplest installation mechanism is to point the update manager inside of Eclipse to the SpringSource Eclipse update site. To do this, choose Software Updates from Eclipse's Help menu and then open the Available Software tab. You can add the SpringSource update site(s) by clicking the Add Site button, and enter the following URLs (one at a time, assuming Eclipse 3.5 Galileo):

- http://www.springsource.com/update/e3.5
- http://dist.springsource.com/release/TOOLS/update/dependencies/e3.5

Once you enter both URLs, the Eclipse update screen will present you with two SpringSource Update Site for Eclipse 3.4 options. By choosing the top-level box, all SpringSource-related Eclipse plug-ins will be selected for download, including the dm Server Tools plug-in. Next, click the Install button to begin the installation. The next screen will prompt you to confirm your selection. Ensure that the dm Server Tools for dm Server 2.x.x is selected. Then proceed. Be aware that the installation may take quite a while, because it'll download a copy of SpringSource tc Server (the enhanced Tomcat Server) as well as dm Server and all the required Spring IDE tooling.

Summary

In this chapter, you got an introduction to OSGi, the specification as well as the Equinox platform implementation, which guarantees that certain resources are made available to plug-ins. OSGi, a module system that can be layered on top of the JVM, is important for its simplicity and powerful problem-solving abilities. You learned how to write simple raw OSGi clients and services. Remember that anything used by something else is called a service in OSGi. You then deployed the same client and service using Spring Dynamic Modules, a framework that sits on top of OSGi and is a powerful API for integration with OSGi. Spring dm Server is the OSGi-based Java server that minimizes the hassles of deploying large applications in an OSGi environment. You learned about a number of its capabilities and the four types of deployment formats with which it works. Finally, you learned how to install powerful tooling from SpringSource to support your Spring dm Server and OSGi applications.

This is the last chapter of this book. Congratulations on having learned so much about the Spring framework and surrounding projects! We hope you find this a valuable resource for years to come!

Index

� B

■ C

▓ D

M

CPSIA information can be obtained at www.ICGtesting.com
Printed in the USA
LVOW130249210911

247182LV00001B/3/P